W9-BMU-619

Fodor's

ESSENTIAL
USA

2nd Edition

Fodor's Travel Publications   New York, Toronto, London, Sydney, Auckland
www.fodors.com

Eugene Fodor:
The Spy Who Loved Travel

As Fodor's celebrates our 75th anniversary, we are honoring the colorful and adventurous life of Eugene Fodor, who revolutionized guidebook publishing in 1936 with his first book, *On the Continent, the Entertaining Travel Annual.*

Eugene Fodor's life seemed to leap off the pages of a great spy novel. Born in Hungary, he spoke six languages and graduated from the Sorbonne and the London School of Economics. During World War II he joined the Office of Strategic Services, the budding spy agency for the United States. He commanded the team that went behind enemy lines to liberate Prague, and recommended to Generals Eisenhower, Bradley, and Patton that Allied troops move to the capital city. After the war, Fodor worked as a spy in Austria, posing as a U.S. diplomat.

In 1949 Eugene Fodor—with the help of the CIA—established Fodor's Modern Guides. He was passionate about travel and wanted to bring his insider's knowledge of Europe to a new generation of sophisticated Americans who wanted to explore and seek out experiences beyond their borders. Among his innovations were annual updates, consulting local experts, and including cultural and historical perspectives and an emphasis on people—not just sites. As Fodor described it, "The main interest and enjoyment of foreign travel lies not only in 'the sites,' ... but in contact with people whose customs, habits, and general outlook are different from your own."

Eugene Fodor died in 1991, but his legacy, Fodor's Travel, continues. It is now one of the world's largest and most trusted brands in travel information, covering more than 600 destinations worldwide in guidebooks, on Fodors.com, and in ebooks and iPhone apps. Technology and the accessibility of travel may be changing, but Eugene Fodor's unique storytelling skills and reporting style are behind every word of today's Fodor's guides.

Our editors and writers continue to embrace Eugene Fodor's vision of building personal relationships through travel. We invite you to join the Fodor's community at fodors.com/community and share your experiences with like-minded travelers. Tell us when we're right. Tell us when we're wrong. And share fantastic travel secrets that aren't yet in Fodor's. Together, we will continue to deepen our understanding of our world.

Happy 75th Anniversary, Fodor's! Here's to many more.

Tim Jarrell, Publisher

FODOR'S ESSENTIAL USA
Editors: Matthew Lombardi, Eric Wechter

Production Editor: Carrie Parker
Maps & Illustrations: Mark Stroud, David Lindroth, *cartographers;* Bob Blake, Rebecca Baer, *map editors;* William Wu, *information graphics*
Design: Fabrizio La Rocca, *creative director;* Guido Caroti, Siobhan O'Hare, *art directors;* Tina Malaney, Nora Rosansky, Chie Ushio, Jessica Walsh, Ann McBride, *designers;* Melanie Marin, *senior picture editor*
Cover Photo: (Statue of Liberty; Monument Valley, Arizona; and Washington Monument): Digital Vision/MediaBakery. (Pumpkin Pie): Polka Dot/MediaBakery. (Trumpet): Frank-Peter Funke/Shutterstock. (Surfer): Manfred EpicStock/Shutterstock. (Las Vegas cowboy): Corbis. (Antique car): Manfred Steinbach/Shutterstock.
Production Manager: Angela L. McLean

2nd Edition

ISBN 978-0-307-48058-3

ISSN 1941-0190

SPECIAL SALES
This book is available at special discounts for bulk purchases for sales promotions or premiums. Special editions, including personalized covers, excerpts of existing books, and corporate imprints, can be created in large quantities for special needs. For more information, write to Special Markets/Premium Sales, 1745 Broadway, MD 6-2, New York, NY 10019, or e-mail specialmarkets@randomhouse.com.

AN IMPORTANT TIP & AN INVITATION
Although all prices, opening times, and other details in this book are based on information supplied to us at press time, changes occur all the time in the travel world, and Fodor's cannot accept responsibility for facts that become outdated or for inadvertent errors or omissions. So **always confirm information when it matters,** especially if you're making a detour to visit a specific place. Your experiences—positive and negative—matter to us. If we have missed or misstated something, **please write to us.** Share your opinion instantly through our online feedback center at fodors.com/contact-us.

PRINTED IN CHINA

10 9 8 7 6 5 4 3 2 1

CONTENTS

CONTENTS

ABOUT THIS BOOK

Our Ratings

Sometimes you find terrific travel experiences and sometimes they just find you. But usually the burden is on you to select the right combination of experiences. That's where our ratings come in.

As travelers we've all discovered a place so wonderful that its worthiness is obvious. And sometimes that place is so experiential that superlatives don't do it justice: you just have to be there to know. These sights, properties, and experiences get our highest rating, **Fodor's Choice**, indicated by orange stars throughout this book.

Black stars highlight sights and properties we deem **Highly Recommended**, places that our writers, editors, and readers praise again and again for consistency and excellence.

By default, there's another category: any place we include in this book is by definition worth your time, unless we say otherwise. And we will.

Disagree with any of our choices? Care to nominate a place or suggest that we rate one more highly? Visit our feedback center at www.fodors.com/feedback.

Budget Well

Hotel and restaurant price categories from ¢ to $$$$ are defined in the opening pages of each chapter. For attractions, we always give standard adult admission fees; reductions are usually available for children, students, and senior citizens. Want to pay with plastic? **AE, D, DC, MC, V** after restaurant and hotel listings indicate wheter American Express, Discover, Diners Club, MasterCard, and Visa are accepted.

Restaurants

Unless we state otherwise, restaurants are open for lunch and dinner daily. We mention dress only when there's a specific requirement and reservations only when they're essential or not accepted—it's always best to book ahead.

Hotels

Hotels have private bath, phone, TV, and air-conditioning and operate on the European Plan (aka EP, meaning without meals), unless we specify that they use the Continental Plan (CP, with a Continental breakfast), Breakfast Plan (BP, with a full breakfast), or Modified American Plan (MAP, with breakfast and dinner), or are all-inclusive (AI, including all meals and most activities). We always list facilities but not whether you'll be charged an extra fee to use them, so when pricing accommodations, find out what's included.

Listings	
★	Fodor's Choice
★	Highly recommended
⊠	Physical address
↔	Directions or Map coordinates
⬧	Mailing address
☎	Telephone
🖶	Fax
⊕	On the Web
✎	E-mail
🖅	Admission fee
☉	Open/closed times
Ⓜ	Metro stations
▭	Credit cards
Hotels & Restaurants	
🏨	Hotel
🛏	Number of rooms
⚐	Facilities
⦿	Meal plans
✕	Restaurant
⚑	Reservations
⋔	Dress code
⤫	Smoking
⊕☐	BYOB
Outdoors	
🏌	Golf
⛺	Camping
Other	
☾	Family-friendly
⇨	See also
⊠	Branch address
☞	Take note

Experience
the USA

WHAT'S WHERE

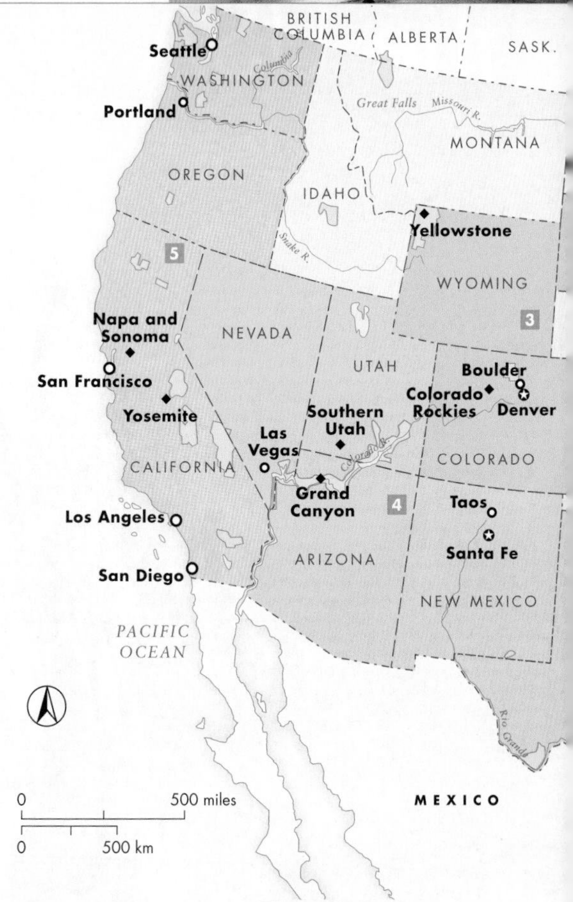

1 New England and the Mid-Atlantic. In the northeast region of the U.S. you get four of the country's most historic and intensely urban cities—**Boston, New York, Philadelphia,** and **Washington**—each of which has enough cultural attractions to merit a trip on its own. When the city dwellers want to unwind, they often head to **Cape Cod** and the **Maine Coast,** where lighthouses and lobster boats lend the coastline a Down East charm.

2 The South. The territory below the Mason-Dixon Line is bound together by centuries-old cultural ties, but there are scores of different experiences to be had when traveling here, from the old-school gentility of **Charleston** to the over-the-top theme parks of **Orlando** to the trendy, Spanish-accented culture of **Miami.** Farther west, the streets of **Nashville** and **New Orleans** ring with music.

3 The Midwest and the Rockies. America's heartland consists of vast prairies and a spectacular mountain range. **Chicago,** the Midwest's great metropolis, mixes big-city sophistication with a plain-spoken sensibility. A chain of lakes and every chain store imaginable converge in **Minneapolis.** The **Colorado Rockies** are a spectacular

outdoor destination in any season. **Mt. Rushmore** is home to an iconic American monument, while **Yellowstone National Park** holds a remarkable collection of geological wonders.

4 The Southwest. The rugged desert terrain that dominates this part of the country is one of the main reasons for paying it a visit. Whether it's the cavernous **Grand Canyon,** the rock formations that stud **Southern Utah,** or the open spaces of **Texas Hill**

Map

BRITISH COLUMBIA | ALBERTA | SASK.

Seattle○
WASHINGTON
Portland○
OREGON
IDAHO
Great Falls   Missouri R.
MONTANA
Yellowstone◆
WYOMING
Napa and Sonoma◆
NEVADA
UTAH
Boulder○
Colorado◆
Southern Utah◆
Colorado Rockies   Denver○
San Francisco◆
Yosemite◆
Las Vegas○
CALIFORNIA
COLORADO
Grand Canyon◆
Taos○
Los Angeles○
ARIZONA
Santa Fe○
San Diego○
NEW MEXICO
PACIFIC OCEAN
0   500 miles
0   500 km
MEXICO

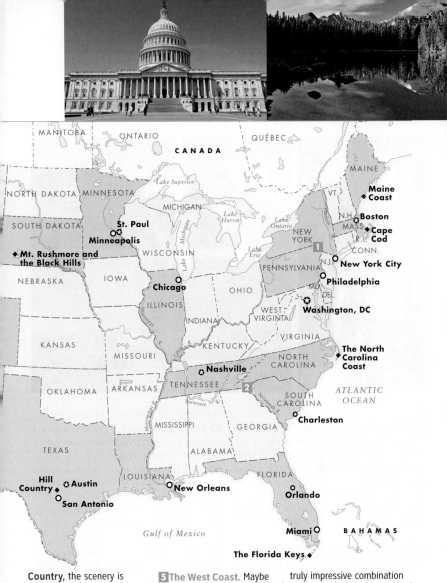

MANITOBA • ONTARIO • QUÉBEC
CANADA

Lake Superior
MAINE

NORTH DAKOTA • MINNESOTA
MICHIGAN
Maine Coast

SOUTH DAKOTA
St. Paul
Minneapolis
WISCONSIN
Lake Michigan
Lake Huron
Lake Ontario
VT
N.H. Boston
MASS. Cape Cod
R.I. CONN.

♦ Mt. Rushmore and the Black Hills
NEW YORK

NEBRASKA
IOWA
Chicago
ILLINOIS
OHIO
PENNSYLVANIA
N.J. New York City
MD. Philadelphia
DEL.
Washington, DC

INDIANA
WEST VIRGINIA

KANSAS
MISSOURI
KENTUCKY
VIRGINIA

Nashville
TENNESSEE
NORTH CAROLINA
The North Carolina Coast

OKLAHOMA
ARKANSAS
Tennessee R.
SOUTH CAROLINA
ATLANTIC OCEAN

MISSISSIPPI
GEORGIA
Charleston

TEXAS
ALABAMA

Hill Country ♦ Austin
LOUISIANA
New Orleans
FLORIDA

San Antonio
Orlando

Gulf of Mexico
Miami
BAHAMAS

The Florida Keys ♦

Country, the scenery is awesome. **Santa Fe** and **Taos** provide high art at high altitude, and for something completely different, there's nothing quite like the glitzy excesses of **Las Vegas.**

5 The West Coast. Maybe it's the mild weather, maybe the gorgeous shoreline—whatever the reason, the entire Pacific Coast has a reputation for being laid-back. The cities, from star-struck **Los Angeles** to foggy **San Francisco** to crunchy **Seattle,** all have a

truly impressive combination of natural and man-made attractions. Among the abundant parklands **Yosemite** is a particular standout. And **Napa and Somona Valleys** are home to not only America's most esteemed vineyards, but some of its best restaurants as well.

TOP ALL-AMERICAN LANDMARKS

The Freedom Trail, Boston

(A) This path through central Boston provides a chance literally to walk in the footsteps of America's forefathers. It leads past locations where much of the drama that would bring about the American Revolution unfolded, from Faneuil Hall to the Old North Church to the site of the Boston Massacre. (⇨ *Chapter 2.*)

The Statue of Liberty, New York

(B) Presented to the United States in 1886 as a gift from France, Lady Liberty is a near-universal symbol of freedom and democracy, standing 152 feet high atop an 89-foot pedestal on Liberty Island. You can get a sense of the thrill millions of immigrants must have experienced as you approach it on the ferry from Battery Park and see the statue grow from a vaguely defined figure on the horizon into a towering, stately colossus. (⇨ *Chapter 4.*)

The National Mall, Washington DC

(C) Washington's Mall is surrounded by a collection of great American landmarks, with the Capitol at one end, the Washington Monument at the other, and the Lincoln Memorial and Vietnam Memorial (among many others) near at hand. There are also nearly a dozen museums bordering the Mall. (⇨ *Chapter 6.*)

Independence Hall, Philadelphia

(D) In this building the Declaration of Independence was signed, George Washington was appointed commander in chief of the Continental Army, and the Constitution was ratified. In other words, there's no other structure in the United States that's loaded with more historical significance. The Hall is part of Independence National Historical Park, where you'll also find the Liberty Bell and several museums. (⇨ *Chapter 5.*)

Fort Sumter, Charleston, South Carolina

(E) The first shots of the Civil War were fired on this fort on a man-made island in Charleston's harbor. The 34-hour battle that ensued would result in defeat for the Union and turn Fort Sumter into a symbol of Southern resistance. Today the National Park Service oversees it, with rangers giving interpretive talks and conducting guided tours. (⇨ *Chapter 8.*)

Mount Rushmore, South Dakota

(F) In the midst of South Dakota's Black Hills, 60-foot-high likenesses of Presidents George Washington, Thomas Jefferson, Abraham Lincoln, and Theodore Roosevelt are carved into a massive granite cliff; the result is America's most famous memorial. From June through mid-September, the majestic faces are dramatically illuminated at night. (⇨ *Chapter 17.*)

The Alamo, San Antonio

(G) This one-time Franciscan mission stands as a monument to the 189 Texan volunteers who fought and died here during a 13-day siege in 1836 by Mexican general Antonio López de Santa Anna. The Texans lost the battle, but they ultimately won their bid for independence with "Remember the Alamo" as their rallying cry. (⇨ *Chapter 19.*)

The Golden Gate Bridge, San Francisco

(H) The suspension bridge connecting San Francisco with Marin County, completed in 1937, is a triumph in just about every way. With its 2-mi span and 750-foot towers, it's both beautiful and durable— it was built to withstand winds of more than 100 mph and was undamaged by the 1989 Loma Prieta quake. The bridge's walkway provides unparalleled views of the Bay Area. (⇨ *Chapter 27.*)

TOP NATURAL WONDERS

Acadia National Park, Maine

(A) Acadia doesn't have quite the jaw-dropping grandeur of the national parks of the West, but it holds many of the greatest pleasures to be experienced on a visit to the Maine coast: expansive views from the top of Cadillac Mountain, miles of paths for hiking and biking, a craggy coastline with an iconic lighthouse, inland ponds perfect for swimming, and remote outer islands. (⇨ *Chapter 1.*)

Cape Hatteras National Seashore, North Carolina's Outer Banks

(B) The barrier islands along the coast of North Carolina are one of the best places in America for a classic laid-back beach vacation, with miles of pristine sand, great surfing, and unparalleled shelling. The protected status of Cape Hatteras National Seashore keeps the influences of commercial development in check. (⇨ *Chapter 7.*)

John Pennekamp Coral Reef State Park, Florida Keys

(C) The pleasures here are found out on the water, and under it. Offshore you'll find Florida's best diving and snorkeling, through coral reefs, sea-grass beds, and mangrove swamps. The adjacent Florida Keys National Marine Sanctuary contains 40 species of coral and nearly 600 varieties of fish (⇨ *Chapter 11.*)

Trail Ridge Road, Rocky Mountain National Park, Colorado

(D) The highest continuous paved highway in North America provides views around each bend—of moraines and glaciers and craggy hills framing emerald meadows carpeted with columbine and Indian paintbrush—that are truly awesome. Numerous turnouts give you the opportunity to stop and take in the lush valleys and glacier-etched granite peaks. (⇨ *Chapter 16.*)

Yellowstone National Park, Wyoming

(E) America's first national park is still its most spectacular. The concentration of geological phenomena—geysers, mudpots, fumaroles, hot springs—is unequaled anywhere else in the world, and the abundant wildlife and the gorgeous terrain make it a nature-lover's paradise. Even in the height of the summer season, a well-planned hike can leave you alone with the great outdoors. (⇨ *Chapter 18.*)

The Grand Canyon, Arizona

(F) When it comes to the Grand Canyon, there are statistics, and there are sensations. While the numbers are impressive—the canyon measures in at an average width of 10 mi, length of 277 mi, and depth of a mile—they don't truly prepare you for that first impression. Seeing the canyon for the first time is an astounding experience. (⇨ *Chapter 21.*)

Delicate Arch, Arches National Park, Utah

(G) The red-rock landscape of Arches National Park feels like another world, with rocks balanced precariously on pedestals and some 2,500 sandstone arches framing the sky. The most famous, Delicate Arch, stands as tall as a four-story building and has become Utah's state icon, depicted on license plates and postage stamps. (⇨ *Chapter 23.*)

Yosemite Falls, Yosemite National Park, California

(H) The highest waterfall in North America (the fifth-highest in the world) is arguably the highlight of Yosemite, but it has lots of competition: Half Dome, El Capitan, Bridalveil Fall, Sentinel Dome, and the Merced River are all musts for a visit to the park. (⇨ *Chapter 26.*)

TOP NEIGHBORHOODS

Greenwich Village, New York

(A) It's no longer a haven for folk singers and artists (real-estate prices are now among the highest of any New York neighborhood), but you can still sense a touch of bohemian ambience amid the Village's restaurants, boutiques, and low-rise residential streets. It's not hard to imagine turning a corner and bumping into Freewheelin' Bob Dylan. (⇨ *Chapter 4.*)

Georgetown, Washington, D.C.

(B) Long before the District of Columbia was formed, Washington's oldest and wealthiest neighborhood was a separate city with a harbor full of ships and warehouses filled with tobacco. Today Georgetown retains its own unique identity while being one of Washington's main areas for restaurants, bars, nightclubs, and boutiques. (⇨ *Chapter 6.*)

Downtown Historic District, Charleston, South Carolina

(C) Wandering through Charleston's Historic District, you would swear it's a movie set. Steeples of more than 180 churches punctuate the low skyline, and horse-drawn carriages pass centuries-old mansions. Happily, after three centuries of epidemics, fires, and hurricanes Charleston has endured to become one of the South's best-preserved cities. (⇨ *Chapter 8.*)

South Beach, Miami Beach

(D) The hub of Miami Beach is South Beach, and its main drag is the lively Ocean Drive, which is lined with vintage art deco hotels that are worth exploring even if you're staying somewhere else. In South Beach life unfolds 24 hours a day: beautiful people pose in hotel lounges and sidewalk cafés, tanned cyclists zoom past palm trees, and visitors flock to see the action. (⇨ *Chapter 10.*)

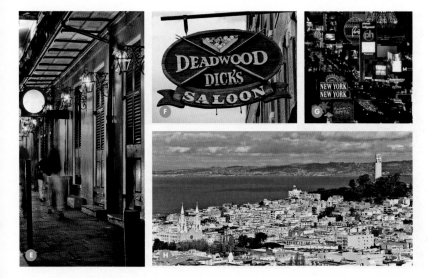

The French Quarter, New Orleans

(E) Since Hurricane Katrina, the French Quarter has resumed its role as a major center for entertainment in New Orleans. Music pours from the doorways of bars as freely as the drinks flow within them; on an ordinary evening a stroll through the Quarter is a moving concert, where the strains of traditional jazz, blues, classic rock and roll, and electronic dance beats all commingle. (⇨ *Chapter 13.*)

Downtown Deadwood, South Dakota

(F) For a step back into the Wild West, there's no place like Deadwood. Nearly $300 million has been dedicated to restoring this once infamous gold-mining boomtown, which has earned recognition as a National Historic Landmark. Small gaming halls, good restaurants, and hotels occupy virtually every storefront on Main Street, just as they did back in the city's late-19th-century heyday. (⇨ *Chapter 17.*)

The Strip, Las Vegas

(G) The Vegas Strip is a place unique unto itself, part lounge act, part amusement park ride, part glitzy hotel, part world-class restaurant—and oh yes, they gamble here, too. It's a monument to self-indulgence that would satisfy a Roman emperor, but could only be found in America. (⇨ *Chapter 22.*)

North Beach, San Francisco

(H) Beyond the aromas of cappuccino and focaccia, the café tables spilling onto the sidewalk, and the convivial air, North Beach is alive with the spirit of the Beat-niks, those revolutionary artists who electrified San Francisco and shocked the country in the 1950s and '60s. The rhythm of Beat poetry, inspired by Jack Kerouac, Allen Ginsberg, and Lawrence Ferlinghetti, still pulses in San Francisco's traditional Italian neighborhood. (⇨ *Chapter 27.*)

TOP THEME PARKS AND URBAN DIVERSIONS

Disney World, Orlando

(A) When it comes to amusement parks, there's Disney World and then there's everything else. Between the Magic Kingdom, Epcot, and Disney's Hollywood Studios, the only hardship here is choosing from among the overabundance of things to do. And while Disney takes dead aim at everyone's inner child, it provides plenty of adult-oriented attractions as well, including golf courses, luxe hotels, and fine dining. (⇨ *Chapter 9.*)

The Grand Ole Opry, Nashville

(B) The longest-running radio show in the United States, currently performed in the Grand Ole Opry House, has been broadcasting country music from Nashville since 1925. You may see superstars, legends, and up-and-coming stars on the Opry's stage. The auditorium seats about 4,400 people in deep wooden pews, and there's not a bad seat in the house. (⇨ *Chapter 12.*)

The Mall of America, Minneapolis

(C) Shopping malls are an American institution, so it's fitting that one named the Mall of America is the grandest, most over-the-top of them all. With 40 million visitors annually, it's the busiest mall in the world, and all those people aren't coming just to shop—along with more than 500 stores, the mall includes a theme park and an aquarium. (⇨ *Chapter 15.*)

Wrigley Field, Chicago

(D) When it comes to baseball, there's no place like home—and no place that's homier than Chicago's Wrigley Field. For going on a century fans have been coming to the "Friendly Confines" to root for their Cubbies through thick and through thin (mainly thin). An afternoon here gives new meaning to the old adage, "It's not whether you win or lose, it's how you play the game." (⇨ *Chapter 14.*)

Balboa Park, San Diego

(E) Overlooking downtown and the Pacific Ocean, 1,200-acre Balboa Park is the cultural heart of San Diego. Originally developed in 1889, it's a lush setting of cultivated and wild gardens in which you'll find most of the city's museums, art galleries, the Old Globe Theatre, and the world-famous San Diego Zoo. (⇨ *Chapter 24.*)

Paramount Pictures, Los Angeles

(F) For a classic L.A. experience, visit this studio, which dates from the 1920s and was home to some of Hollywood's most luminous stars, including Rudolph Valentino, Mae West, Mary Pickford, and Lucille Ball. (The lot still produces major movies and TV shows.) You can take a studio tour (reservations required) led by friendly guides who walk and trolley you around the back lots. (⇨ *Chapter 25.*)

Pike Place Market, Seattle

(G) It's most famous for its exuberant fishmongers, but Pike Place Market is about more than just flying seafood. Vendors sell produce, flowers, meats, coffee, tea, and countless other goods in a century-old marketplace that cascades down a bluff over Puget Sound. Across the street you can get your coffee fix at the original Starbucks. (⇨ *Chapter 30.*)

Washington Park, Portland

(H) Situated in the hills above downtown Portland, Washington Park is one of America's great urban parklands. Facilities range from the International Rose Test Garden (with more than 400 varieties of roses and gorgeous views of the city) to the Japanese Garden (deemed the most authentic outside Japan) to the Oregon Zoo. (⇨ *Chapter 29.*)

10 TIPS FOR GREAT ROAD TRIPS

Road-trippers come in all shapes and sizes, from college kids to families to retirees, but they all hit the road with a similar goal in mind—as the old Simon and Garfunkel song goes, "they've all come to look for America."

If you want to widen your horizons, see the country's sights, get a feel for the wide-open spaces, and meet all sorts of people along the way, there's no better way than to travel by car. The following tips will help you get the most out of your journey.

Estimate Your Expenses

There's no getting around it—fuel these days is a major expense. Thanks to the Internet, you can figure out roughly how big a bite gas will take out of your budget by using a fuel-cost calculator such as the one you'll find at ⊕ *www. fuelcostcalculator.aaa.com*. Add in what you expect to pay for food and accommodations, and see if the total is a price you can live with. (If you last traveled by car back in the days of cheap gas, you may be in for a case of sticker shock.)

A long-distance road trip isn't the quickest or easiest way to get from point A to point B, and it may no longer be the cheapest either. But it's a unique experience, and if you're committed to hitting the open road, you're ready to proceed to the next tip.

Get Your Car Road-Trip Ready

The great fear of any road trip is that your car will fail you. If you're going on a multiple-day journey with lots of time behind the wheel, visit your mechanic before you go and have him (or her) give the vehicle a once-over.

And remember the basics you can handle yourself: check the oil level, tire pressure, and tire wear—including the spare.

Replacing worn wipers can seem like a stroke of genius if you find yourself traveling on a rainy day.

Make Sure You Have Roadside Assistance

If despite your precautions you do encounter problems on the road, you'll want to have help at your beck and call. For drivers of older cars, it's worth the peace of mind to join an auto club (the biggest being the ubiquitous, and reliable, AAA, though there are some alternatives).

If you have a newer car, check to see whether your manufacturer provides free roadside assistance (often provided for the first five years you own the car), in which case an auto club membership isn't a necessity. Either way, be sure you have a toll-free number of your assistance provider at hand in case the need arises.

Bring the Electronics

It almost goes without saying that you should and will be traveling with a cell phone. (Don't forget the charger cord.) GPS isn't mandatory, but it's an undeniable asset—though you may get tired of that soulless voice telling you what to do.

Almost as valuable is a converter that allows you to play an iPod through the car's radio. As the miles and the hours roll by, you'll appreciate being able to control the soundtrack for your trip. The countryside can look a lot different depending on whether you're listening to Beethoven or Springsteen.

Also Bring Good Maps

GPS or no GPS, maps are invaluable for getting the lay of the land and taking scenic detours. At some point, too, there's a good chance you're just not going to trust what that GPS voice is telling you. Maps can quell your suspicions or confirm them.

Think of Your Car as a Suitcase

When you're driving there's little advantage to consolidating your belongings in a few suitcases the way you would when you fly. Make sure you have luggage suitable for overnight stops and unloading what you'll need at your final destination (if you have one), but don't overlook the advantages your car provides for carrying gear loosely. A raincoat tossed into a shopping bag might sit in the backseat the whole trip, serving only as an improvised pillow, or it might be a lifesaver if you're stuck in a thunderstorm.

Plan Your Detours Well

It's a commonly held belief that in order to get the most out of your trip you need to get off the interstate and explore the backroads. There's more than a little truth to this dictum, but if you're too casual about it, simply pulling off when the impulse grabs you, your greatest discovery is likely to be, "This is what the middle of nowhere looks like."

Do some research and make your detours with a destination in mind. You'll still have the chance to stumble across something unexpected along the way, and you're much less likely to wind up feeling you've wasted your time.

Go against the Flow

One of the pleasures of being on vacation is that you aren't tied to your set workaday schedule. Use this flexibility to your advantage when planning your route. Try to avoid passing by major cities during rush hour—there are few things more frustrating than getting stuck in a traffic jam of commuters that you could have avoided simply by lingering another hour or so in, say, a national park earlier in the day.

When traveling to and from major vacation destinations such as the Florida Keys or the Maine Coast, plan your arrival and departure to go against the flow of weekenders who clog the roads. You'll be rewarded for using your freedom wisely.

Read the Weather Report

Your flexibility also allows you to plan according to the weather. Check the extended forecast for each stop along the way before you depart. As much as circumstances allow, aim to see beautiful outdoor sights when the sun is shining. No view is a good view when it's shrouded in fog.

Come wintertime, weather can be a more serious issue. A snowstorm can bring travel to a standstill; the wisest choice may be not to hit the road at all.

Take a Different Route Home

If you're making a round trip, you can double your pleasure by taking different routes coming and going. On a cross-country drive plan a southern route one way and a northern route the other. If you're traveling along a coast, take the coastal road out and travel inland on the way back.

One of the two routes you choose will probably be what motivated you to take a road trip in the first place (driving the Pacific Coast Highway, for instance), but the second route could lead to you discovering places and experiences you'd never imagined.

THREE CLASSIC ROAD TRIPS

U.S. Route 1

The northernmost part of what's now U.S. Route 1 dates back to at least 1636—when it took four days to make the 100-mi journey from Philadelphia to New York City. Today, this 2,425 mi circuit links Fort Kent, Maine, to Key West, Florida, traveling through a good chunk of America's history.

The road takes travelers though colonial New England, on to New York City, Philadelphia, and Washington, D.C., then onto the U.S.'s oldest city (St. Augustine, Florida) and the thoroughly modern multicultural Miami, ending in ironically iconic Key West. Route 1 has some spectacular scenery (even the Great Dismal Swamp in southeastern Virginia/northeastern North Carolina is startlingly charming)—but it isn't always pretty, passing through plenty of urban blight and moldering towns that time forgot. That said, it's an endlessly fascinating highway—every bit of it has a story to tell.

Route 66

The Mother Road is America's most romanticized classic highway. One of the greatest joys of this 2,000-plus-mi journey from Chicago to Santa Monica, California, is the '50s time-warp you'll experience via the many kitschy roadside attractions, old diners, and motels that crop up in the middle of nowhere (often marked by elaborate neon signs)—all part of the "get your kicks on Route 66" nostalgia that is inseparably part of this road's ethos.

Only scattered segments of the old highway remain, but the remnants epitomize the classic American road trip. One of the longest surviving stretches starts in Arcadia, Oklahoma, just northeast of Oklahoma City (while you're here, look for the round red barn, a terrific little Route 66 museum and gift shop) and ends in Stroud, Oklahoma. The drive in New Mexico between Gallup and Grants across the Zuni and Navajo Nation Indian reservations (on what's now Highway 53) is also wonderful. Other high points include the Grand Canyon; the Cahokia Mounds in Collinsville, Illinois; and the Gateway Arch in St. Louis, Missouri.

Route 66 is not shown on modern maps. Before you set off on your journey, visit ⊕ *www.national66.com* to download meticulous turn-by-turn directions for the entire route.

The Pacific Coast Highway

One of the country's most scenic drives, this two-lane highway runs about 1,500 mi from the northwest tip of the United States at Olympic National Park almost to the Mexican border. It's a feast for the senses, hugging gorgeous stretches of the coast and passing by (and through) forests, farmland, California wine country, and spiffy little seaside towns.

A few caveats: The highway can get crowded—especially during the summer months—and drivers are often so amazed by the views that they forget to keep their eyes on the road. Drive carefully.

PCH highlights include redwood forests of Northern California; Big Sur (California); the views on the road between Florence and Lincoln City (Oregon) and from the scenic outlook at Cape Perpetua (just south of Yachats in Oregon); Hearst Castle in San Simeon (California); and Point Lobos State Wildlife Reserve (just south of Carmel, California).

The Pacific Coast Highway is easy to follow; it's marked on maps as Route 1 in California and Route 101 farther north.

FAVORITE REGIONAL FOODS

Members of the Fodors.com community made the following nominations for their favorite American regional foods. (Member comments follow a few entries.) The list is far from comprehensive, but it's a starting point for contemplating the good eats that await you on your travels.

New England and the Mid-Atlantic

Bagels (New York): "Not the fake Wonder Bread bagels—but real bagels that are chewy and almost tough." (nytraveler)

Blueberry pie (Maine)

Cheese steaks (Philadelphia)

Clam chowder (New England)

Corn chowder (Maryland)

Crab cakes (Maryland)

Fried clams (Massachusetts)

Half-smokes (Washington, D.C.)

Indian pudding (New England)

Knishes (New York)

Lobster rolls (New England)

Maple syrup (New England)

Pastrami (New York)

Shoo-fly pie (Pennsylvania)

The South

Barbecue (North Carolina)

Beignets (Louisiana)

Boiled peanuts (South Carolina)

Boudin (Louisiana)

Country ham (Kentucky)

Cuban sandwiches (Miami)

Étouffée (Louisiana)

Fried green tomatoes (The Deep South)

Mufaletta (Louisiana)

Red beans and rice (Louisiana)

Ropa vieja (South Florida)

Shrimp and grits (Charleston, S.C.)

The Midwest and the Rockies

Chili four-way (Cincinnati)

Deep-dish pizza (Chicago)

Hot dogs (Chicago)

Huckleberries (Montana and Wyoming)

Runza sandwiches (Nebraska): "Bread stuffed with ground beef and cabbage." (Musicfan)

Toasted ravioli (St. Louis)

Walleye pike (Minnesota)

Wild rice soup (Minnesota)

The Southwest

Barbecue (Texas)

Chicken-fried steak (Texas): "One of the few things I miss about no longer living in Texas." (PaulRabe)

Fry sauce (Southern Utah)

Gulf shrimp (Texas)

Hatch chile (New Mexico): "Posole (a stew with dried hominy) wouldn't be the same without it." (ElendilPickle)

Indian fry bread (Arizona)

Sopapillas (New Mexico)

Sonoran enchiladas (Arizona)

The West Coast

Apples (Central Washington)

Artichokes (Central California)

Carne asada burrito (San Diego)

Cioppino (San Francisco)

Dungeness crab (Northern California)

Fish/produce (Washington): "In thinking about the food I grew up with I remember the ingredients more than any singular dish—crab, trout, salmon, clams and oysters, berries, apples, etc., all served simply and with coffee or espresso." (POlson)

Fish tacos (San Diego)

Sourdough bread (San Francisco)

PLANNING A TRIP TO THE GREAT OUTDOORS

Everyone's Top 10

Packing lists for any trip vary according to the individual, but here are 10 essential things to bring if you're planning a vacation to a national park or another outdoor destination.

1. Binoculars. Many parks are a bird- (and animal)-watcher's dream. A pair of binos will help you spot feathered friends as well as larger creatures. Binoculars are sold according to power, or how much the objects you're viewing are magnified (i.e., 7x, 10x, 12x) and the diameter of objective lens, which is the one on the fat end of the binoculars (the bigger the objective lens, the more light that gets in and the sharper your image should be). 10x is a good choice for magnification, field of view, and steadiness. If the magnification is higher, the field of view is smaller, and your hand movements will prevent you from seeing well, unless you use a tripod.

2. Clothes that layer. Particularly in the West, days can be warm while nights turn chilly. The weather also can change quickly during the day, with things going from warm and sunny to windy and wet in a matter of minutes. This means you need to pack with both warm and cold (as well as wet and dry) weather in mind. The easiest ploy is to dress in layers. Experts suggest synthetics such as polyester (used in Coolmax and other "wicking" fabrics that draw moisture away from your skin, and fleece, which is an insulator) and lightweight merino wool. Look for socks in wicking wool or polyester. Don't forget a waterproof poncho or jacket.

3. Long pants and long-sleeved shirts. It's wise to minimize exposed skin when hiking, especially in higher altitudes and areas with poison ivy and/or ticks.

4. Sturdy shoes or hiking boots. If you plan to do a lot of backcountry hiking, then also consider ankle support, which helps on unpaved trails. Be sure to break in your boots before the trip.

5. Insect repellent. If you're hiking or camping in an area with lots of mosquitoes, a good bug spray can help keep your trip from being a swatting marathon. A repellent also helps deter ticks. Most experts recommend repellents with DEET (N,N-diethyl-meta-toluamide); the higher the level of DEET, the longer the product will be effective. Just be sure to use a separate sunscreen, not a single product with both ingredients (this is because you're supposed to reapply sunscreen every few hours, but doing so with DEET could deliver a dangerous dose of the chemical).

6. Skin moisturizer, sunscreen, and lip balm. You're likely to be outside for longer than you're used to at home, and possibly in higher altitudes and drier climates—all of which can leave your skin and lips parched, making you more vulnerable to sun- and windburn. Sunscreen should provide both UVA and UVB protection, with an SPF of at least 15; look for a lotion marked "sweatproof" or "sport."

7. Sunglasses and hat. Higher elevation means more ultraviolet radiation. Look for sunglasses that provide 100% UV protection.

8. Journal and camera. When your jaw drops at the glorious vistas and your head clears from all the fresh air, taking a picture may be your first instinct, but you also may find some thoughts of inspiration longing to be penned. Consider a journal that is weatherproof (sporting-goods stores often sell them). Journal entries may even help you later when it

comes time to identify and write captions for your photographs.

9. Snacks and water. Wilderness areas by their nature are remote, and some are very lacking in services. Bring plenty of healthy snacks with you, as well as water. When hiking in hot weather, experts recommend ½ to 1 quart of water (or another fluid) per person, per hour, to prevent potentially dangerous dehydration. High elevation can increase your chances of dehydration, as well. Even if you're not hiking, have some food in the car for long drives through the park, where facilities might be scarce.

10. First-aid kit. A solid kit should contain a first-aid manual, aspirin (or ibuprofen), razor blades, tweezers, a needle, scissors, adhesive bandages, butterfly bandages, sterile gauze pads, one-inch wide adhesive tape, an elastic bandage, antibacterial ointment, antiseptic cream, antihistamines, calamine lotion, and moleskin for blisters.

Hiking Items

For vacations on which you'll be going on hiking trips longer than an hour or two, consider investing in the following:

a compass and map (⇨ *Maps box*)

a daypack with enough room for everybody's essentials

energy bars (they may not be five-star dining, but they do give you energy and keep your kids—and you—from being cranky)

a hiking stick or poles, especially if you have bad knees

a water filter to treat water in the backcountry

bear bells if you're in bear country

MAPS

If you plan to do a lot of hiking or mountaineering, especially in the backcountry, invest in detailed maps and a compass. Topographical maps are sold in well-equipped outdoor stores (REI and Cabela's, for example). Maps in different scales are available from the U.S. Geological Survey. To order, go to ⊕ *www.usgs.gov/pubprod* or call ☎ *303/202–4700* or *888/275–8747*; you'll need to first request the free index and catalog, from which you can find and order the specific maps you need.

Camping Gear

Planning on saving money and roughing it on your vacation? In addition to a working tent (check the zipper before you go!) and tent pegs, sleeping bags and pillows, and, of course, the ingredients for s'mores (graham crackers, chocolate bars, and marshmallows), here are some things veteran campers recommend be among your gear:

camping chairs (folding or collapsible)

camp stove

cooking utensils and plates, cups, etc.

duct tape (great for covering tears)

flashlight or lantern

matches

paper towels, napkins

a multipurpose knife

a rope (for laundry or to help tie things down; pack clothespins, too)

a sleeping pad or air mattress (optional, but using one under your sleeping bag can make a big difference in a good night's sleep; another option is a cot)

a tarp (will help keep the bottom of your tent—and subsequently you!—dry)

New England and
the Mid-Atlantic Coast

WHAT'S WHERE

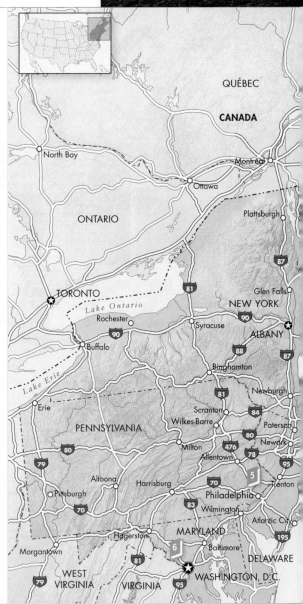

The following numbers refer to chapters in the book.

1 The Maine Coast. Much of the appeal of the Maine Coast lies in its geographical contrasts, from its long stretches of swimming beaches in the south to the cliff-edged, rugged rocky coasts in the north. Along the way you'll find towns with the freshest seafood, picturesque lighthouses, creative artisans, and folks who are down-to-earth.

2 Boston. History permeates everything here, from the scholarly institutions and dining venuesto the sports teams and cultural attractions. It's a city that thrives on change but strives to preserve its roots. Visitors are often awed by the dense concentration of sites. Locals, however, take them in stride. Their hometown is a living city, not a living history museum, and as such, it continues to evolve.

3 Cape Cod. Nearly everyone comes here for the seaside, yet the crimson cranberry bogs, forests of birch and beech, freshwater ponds, and marshlands that grace the Cape's interior are just as magnificent. Local history is fascinating, whale-watching is exhilarating, cycling trails lace the landscape, and you can dine on simple fresh seafood

inventive cuisine, or most anything in between.

4 New York City. NYC is the fiercely multicultural capitol of finance, fashion, and entertainment; boasts 19,000 restaurants and at least twice that many shops; has a lively theater district, arts, and music scene; and is home to more than a dozen world-class museums. Whatever you want, it's here. Prepare to be dazzled.

5 Philadelphia. As the birthplace of the country, the history of the U.S. is certainly celebrated here, from the Valley Forge Historical Park to the newly built Independence Mall. But there's also a more modern twist to Philadelphia culture—a stunning array of shops, restaurants, theaters, cafés, and galleries that can keep visitors busy for days.

6 Washington D.C. A city of vistas, D.C. is a marriage of geometry and art that isn't dominated by skyscrapers. The result: The world's first planned capital is also one of its most beautiful. And political persuasions aside, D.C. is a must-do family vacation. No place in America offers parents more teachable moments per square mile.

NEW ENGLAND–MID-ATLANTIC COAST TOP ATTRACTIONS

Acadia National Park

(A) Hosting more than 2 million visitors annually, this jewel of the Maine coast was the first national park to be established east of the Mississippi River. Take a drive around Mt. Desert Island's 20-mi Park Loop Road to acquaint yourself with the area and indulge in spectacular views of the mountains and the sea. Head to the top of Cadillac Mountain for amazing 360-degree views, or bike the scenic 45-mi carriage-road system, inspecting each of the 17 stone bridges along the way.

Statue of Liberty

(B) Presented to the United States in 1886 as a gift from France, Lady Liberty is a near-universal symbol of freedom and democracy, standing 152 feet high atop an 89-foot pedestal on Liberty Island. You can get a taste of the thrill millions of immigrants must have experienced as you approach Liberty Island on the ferry from Battery Park. The statue's crown

was closed to visitors for almost eight years following the September 11 attacks, but reopened on July 4, 2009.

Empire State Building

(C) From the 86th-floor observatory, which towers 1,050 feet above the city, you can see up to 80 mi away on a clear day. The views at night are equally stunning, with the glittering city lights French architect Le Corbusier once called "a Milky Way come down to earth." If you're afraid of heights, gazing at the building from afar will still deliver a dose of dazzle—especially after dark, when it's illuminated by colored lights that correspond to different holidays and events.

Independence Hall

(D) America's most historic building was constructed in 1732–56 as the Pennsylvania State House. What happened here between 1775 and 1787 changed the course of American history—and the name of the building to Independence

Hall. In the hall's Assembly Room, George Washington was appointed commander in chief of the Continental Army, the Declaration of Independence was signed, and later the Constitution of the United States was adopted.

Harvard University
(E) Massachusetts reportedly has the world's highest concentration of colleges and universities. None, however, is more famous than Harvard, a Cambridge landmark since 1636. To get a taste of the ivory tower without paying tuition, take a student-led campus tour. The complimentary hour-long walks are offered regularly; the university Web site has details (⊕ *www.harvard.edu*).

Cape Cod National Seashore
(F) Comprising 40 mi of sandy beaches and 44,000 acres of a landscape that has been the muse of countless painters and photographers, the Cape Cod National Seashore is the best of what New England has to offer, the perfect place for explorers and strollers looking for an untouched stretch of coastline. An exhaustive amount of programs—from guided bird walks to surf rescue demonstrations to snorkeling in Wellfleet's kettle ponds—take place year-round; most are free.

The Capitol
(G) Home of the Senate and the House of Representatives, the marble Capitol is an architectural marvel filled with frescoes and statues. Tours now begin at the new Capitol Visitor Center. A tour of the interior is impressive, but nothing beats attending a live debate on the House or Senate floor. The Capitol grounds are also stunning.

Smithsonian Museums
(H) Mostly flanking the National Mall in Washington D.C., these illustrious galleries hold everything from Kermit the Frog to the *Spirit of St. Louis* and the Hope Diamond to Rodin's *Burghers of Calais*.

TOP EXPERIENCES

Finding Your Muse(um)

Manhattan could be called Museumpalooza—within just one 30-block area there are nine world-class institutions, and, within that general vicinity there are a dozen or so merely excellent ones.

If New York City held no other museum than the colossal **Metropolitan Museum of Art,** you could still occupy yourself for days roaming its labyrinthine corridors. Thinking of exploring the **Smithsonian** museums in Washington D.C.? Well, there's 13 of them, all free, each one immense and engrossing. For just a superficial exploration, you'd better set aside two weeks. And even if you wanted to focus on the highlights of Boston's spectacular **Museum of Fine Arts, Museum of Science,** and **Isabella Stewart Gardner Museum,** you'd need more than a week.

Fact is, no single vacation can adequately cover the breadth of museums found in Washington, Boston, or New York. But the point isn't to see them all—most long-time residents don't even make such an attempt. Just decide which aspect of human achievement most inspires you, or which wonder of nature awes you, or what pop-culture icon amuses you, and schedule a day or two for museum exploration.

Plan ahead to find out about free admission hours or tour options. You may discover your inner cryptologist at the **International Spy Museum.** You can trace the history of broadcasting at the **Paley Center for Media,** or get acquainted with 2,000 of your favorite sea creatures at the **New England Aquarium.** Pick something, anything, that you're mildly, or wildly, fascinated by and chances are there's a museum for that.

Standing in the Shadows of Giants

It's been said that "democracy is messy," but there's no denying that some beautiful statues come of it. The historical figures who've struggled to create a nation that strives to be the land of the free are commemorated with some of the most spectacular monuments in the world.

At the **Lincoln Memorial** if you breathe deeply while reading the Gettysburg Address, carved high in the marble walls, you can almost feel a thickness in the air—as if the weight of the words from this great speech are filling your lungs. Stand beneath the colossal **Statue of Liberty** and you'll feel both dwarfed by her immensity and uplifted by her glory.

You've seen the images countless times— Lady Liberty, the **Washington Monument,** the **Iwo Jima Memorial**—but there's no denying the *feeling*—the reverence—that you experience when you physically stand in the presence of these great tributes. Some, like the **Vietnam Veteran's Memorial** or the **National World War II Memorial,** are indeed solemn reminders that democracy is messy; others are testaments to hope and inspiration. A trip to Manhattan's Ellis Island or a tour of the great monuments on the Mall in D.C. is an unforgettable experience.

Seeing History

With 10 of the 13 original colonies along this stretch of coast, there's simply no place else in the nation with as many opportunities to celebrate America's past.

Philadelphia has a nearly inexhaustible supply of historic touchstones. **Independence Mall** has **Independence Hall,** the **Liberty Bell,** and the **National Constitution Center,** all within a two-block radius. Right around the corner is the **Franklin Court,** built where Ben Franklin's house once stood. In the

same immediate area, you can find the **First Bank of Pennsylvania,** as well as **Christ Church,** the **Betsy Ross House,** and **Elfreth's Alley,** the oldest continually occupied residential street in the U.S.

Spend one day in Boston and you can physically travel to dozens of spots where life-and-country-altering moments took place. Stand inside **Faneuil Hall Marketplace** for a palpable sense of life in 18th-century America. From here, walk along the **Freedom Trail** past most of the city's most entertaining historical highlights, and up to the **Bunker Hill Monument.** Stroll through the oldest public park in the U.S. and over to the **Old South Meeting House,** where the first rumblings of the Boston Tea Party were heard in 1773.

In Washington D.C, it's hard to walk down a block without passing something of note, and the density increases the closer you move toward **Capitol Hill**. The city is also home to the nation's attic, the **Smithsonian** and dozens of other top-notch cultural institutions, including the **National Archives,** home to the *actual* Declaration of Independence, Constitution, and Bill of Rights.

Maine has arguably the richest maritime history of any of the New England States. The state's shipbuilding heritage goes back more than 200 years. The **Maine Maritime Museum** was built around the remnants of a 19th century shipyard, and the **Maine Lighthouse Museum** celebrates the lighted towers that have protected sailors from the craggy coast since the 18th century. Visit just about any marina, and you can see the entire spectrum of boats that have made Maine famous, from graceful Friendship sloops to simple lobster boasts to grand tall-masted Windjammers.

Catching a Broadway Show

Even if you're just a legend in your own mind, there's nothing quite like making your own grand entrance at a show on the Great White Way. As you find your way to your seat, the anticipation starts to rise; you sit, the houselights dim, and the orchestra strikes up the first notes of the overture, filling the theater with excitement. There is no other experience like it, and no visit to the New York—at least your first or second visit—is really complete if you haven't seen a Broadway show (or three). So stow away your ticket stub, take one last glance at your *Playbill,* shut off your cell phone, and prepare to be transported.

Peeping Leaves

Tourist season in most of New England is concentrated in the late spring and summer, but a resurgence happens in September and October, especially in the northern states, when leaf peepers from all corners descend by the car- and bus-load to see the leaves turn red, yellow, orange, and all shades in between. Foliage season can be fragile and unpredictable—temperature, winds, latitude, and rain all influence when the leaves turn and how long they remain on the trees—but that makes the season even more precious. Don't discount the beauty of fallen leaves; watch them glisten in fall rains or float in the winds of approaching winter.

GREAT ITINERARIES

HIGHLIGHTS OF THE MAINE COAST

Day 1: The Yorks

Start your trip in York Village with a leisurely stroll through the seven buildings of the Old York Historical Society, getting a glimpse of 18th-century life in this gentrified town. Spend time wandering among the shops or walking the nature trails and beaches around York Harbor. There are several grand lodging options here, most with views of the harbor. If you prefer a livelier pace, continue on to York Beach, a haven for families with plenty of entertainment venues.

Days 2 and 3: Ogunquit

For well over a century, Ogunquit has been a favorite vacation spot for those looking to combine the natural beauty of the ocean with a sophisticated environment. Take a morning walk along the Marginal Way to see the waves crashing on the rocks. In Perkins Cove, have lunch, stroll the shopping areas, or sign on with a lobster-boat cruise to learn about the industry that supplies more than 90% of the world's lobster market. See the extraordinary collection at the Ogunquit Museum of American Art, take in a performance at one of the several theater venues, or just spend time on the beach.

Day 4: The Kennebunks

Head north to the Kennebunks, allowing at least two hours to wander through the shops and historic homes of Dock Square in Kennebunkport. This is an ideal place to rent a bike and amble around the back streets, head out on Ocean Avenue to view the Bush estate, or ride to one of the several beaches to relax awhile.

Days 5 and 6: Portland

You can easily spend several days in Maine's largest city, exploring its historic neighborhoods, shopping and eating in the Old Port, or visiting one of several excellent museums. A brief side trip to Cape Elizabeth takes you to Portland Head Light, Maine's first lighthouse. It's on the grounds of Fort Williams Park and is an excellent place to enjoy a picnic. Be sure to wander the ample grounds. There are also excellent walking trails (and views) at nearby Two Lights State Park. If you want to take a boat tour while in Portland, get a ticket for Casco Bay Lines and see some of the islands that dot the bay.

Day 7: Bath to Camden

Head north from Portland to Bath, Maine's shipbuilding capital, and tour the Maine Maritime Museum or have lunch on the waterfront. Shop at boutiques and antiques shops, or view the plentitude of beautiful homes. Continue on U.S. 1 north through the towns of Wiscasset and Damariscotta, where you may find yourself pulling over frequently for outdoor flea markets or intriguing antiques shops.

Days 8 and 9: Camden

Camden is the quintessential seaside town: hundreds of boats bobbing in the harbor, immaculately kept antique homes, streets lined with boutiques, and restaurants serving lobster at every turn. The hills of nearby Mt. Battie offer good hiking and spots to picnic and view the surrounding area. Camden is one of the hubs for the beloved and historic windjammer fleet—there is no better way to see the area than from the deck of one of these graceful beauties. If you're an art lover, save some time for Rockland's Farnsworth Art Museum and the Wyeth Center.

Days 10 and 11: Mount Desert Island/Acadia National Park

From Camden, continue north along U.S. 1, letting your interests dictate where you stop. Once you arrive on Mount Desert Island, you can stay in Bar Harbor, the busiest village in the area, or in the quieter Southwest Harbor area; either way, the splendor of the mountains and the sea surround you. Several days are easily spent exploring Acadia National Park, boating or kayaking in the surrounding waters, and simply enjoying the stunning panorama.

BOSTON IN 4 DAYS

Day 1: Hit the Trail

About 3 million visitors walk the Freedom Trail every year—and there's a good reason why: Taken together, the route's 16 designated sites offer a crash course in colonial history. That makes the trail a must, so you might as well tackle it sooner rather than later. Linger wherever you like, leaving ample time for lunch amid magicians and mimes in Faneuil Hall Marketplace. Next, make tracks for the North End, where you'll find Old North Church and Paul Revere's former home

(Boston's oldest house, it was constructed almost 100 years prior to his arrival). After wandering the neighborhood's narrow Italian-tinged streets, fortify yourself with a gelato and keep going across the Charlestown Bridge. You can see the USS *Constitution* and climb the Bunker Hill Monument (a breathtaking site in more ways than one) before catching the MBTA water shuttle back to Downtown.

Day 2: Head for the Hill

Named for the light that topped it in the 1800s, Beacon Hill originally stood a bit taller until earth was scraped off its peak and used as landfill not far away. What remains—namely gas street lamps, shady trees, brick sidewalks, and stately Brahmin brownstones—evokes old Boston. When soaking up the ambience, don't forget to take in some of Beacon Hill's "official" attractions. After all, major sites from Boston's various theme trails, including the Massachusetts State House, Boston Athenaeum, African Meeting House, and Granary Burying Ground, are here. Afterward, stroll over to the Common and the Public Garden. (Both promise greenery and great people-watching.) If shopping is more your bag, cruise for antiques along Charles Street, the thoroughfare that separates them. In the evening, feast on affordable chow mein in Chinatown or go upscale at an über-trendy restaurant in the Theater District.

Day 3: Get an Overview

From the Back Bay you can cover a lot of Boston's other attractions in a single day. Start at the top (literally) by seeing 360-degree views from the Prudential Center's Skywalk Observatory. Once you understand the lay of the land, just plot a route based on your interests. Architecture aficionados can hit the ground running at the neoclassical Public Library and Romanesque Trinity Church. Shoppers, conversely, can opt for the stores of Newbury Street and Copley Place (a high-end mall anchored by Neiman Marcus). Farther west in the Fens, other choices await. Art connoisseurs might view the collection at the sprawling Museum of Fine Arts or the more manageably sized Isabella Stewart Gardner Museum. Quirky, carnival-like Fenway Park beckons baseball fans to the other side of the Fens. Depending on your taste—and the availability of tickets—cap the day with a Symphony Hall concert or a Red Sox game.

Day 4: On the Waterfront

Having spent so much time focusing on the old, why not devote a day to something new in the burgeoning Seaport District? Begin at the Institute of Contemporary Art (ICA) on Fan Pier. Boston's first new art museum in almost a century boasts a bold cantilevered design that makes the most of its waterside location. It makes the most of its art collection, too, by offering special programs that appeal even to little tykes and hard-to-please teens. Of course, keeping kids engaged may prove difficult given that the Children's Museum is close by. Check out its innovative exhibits or continue on to that old waterfront favorite, the New England Aquarium. Highlights include the Giant Ocean Tank, hands-on tidal pools, an engaging sea-lion show, and scores of happy-footed penguins. Outside the facility you can sign up for a harbor cruise, whale-watching trip, or ferry ride to the Boston Harbor Islands.

CAPE COD IN ONE WEEK: CLASSIC BEACHES AND BUSTLING VILLAGES

Day 1: Falmouth

Begin by crossing the Bourne Bridge and taking Route 28A south through some lovely little towns until you reach Falmouth, an excellent base for exploring the Upper Cape. Here you can stroll around the village green, look into some of the historic houses, and stop at the Waquoit Bay National Estuarine Research Reserve for a walk along the estuary and barrier beach. Take some time to check out the village of Woods Hole, the center for international marine research, and the year-round ferry port for Martha's Vineyard. A small aquarium in town has regional sea-life exhibits, and there are several shops and museums. If you have any extra time, spend it north of here in the lovely old town of Sandwich.

Days 2 and 3: Hyannis

The crowded Mid Cape is a center of activity, and its hub is Hyannis. Here you can take a cruise around the harbor or go on a deep-sea fishing trip. There are shops and restaurants along Main Street and plenty of kid-worthy amusements.

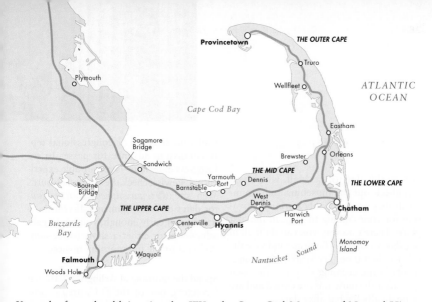

Kennedy fans shouldn't miss the JFK Museum. End the day with a concert at the Cape Cod Melody Tent. Spend your second day exploring the northern reaches of the Mid Cape with a drive along scenic Route 6A, which passes through the charming, slow-paced villages of Barnstable, Yarmouth Port, and Dennis. There are beaches and salt marshes, museums, antiques shops and galleries, and old graveyards along this route. Yarmouth Port's Bass Hole Boardwalk makes for a particularly beautiful stroll. In Dennis there are historic houses to tour, and the Cape Museum of Fine Arts merits a stop. End the day by climbing 30-foot Scargo Tower to watch the sun set.

Days 4 and 5: Chatham

Chatham, with its handsome Main Street, is a perfect base for strolling, shopping, and dining. You can watch glassblowing at the Chatham Glass Company, visit the Atwood House and Railroad museums, and drive over to take in the view from Chatham Light. Spend your second day detouring up to Brewster to check out the eclectic mix of antiques shops, museums, freshwater ponds for swimming and fishing, and miles of biking and hiking trails through Nickerson State Park. Don't miss

the Cape Cod Museum of Natural History. On the way north from Chatham, take the less-commercial end of Route 28 to Orleans, driving past sailboat-speckled views of Pleasant Bay. On the way up toward Provincetown, stop in Eastham at the National Seashore's Salt Pond Visitor Center.

Days 6 and 7: Provincetown

Bustling Provincetown has a lot to see and do. Catch a whale-watch excursion and take a trolley tour in town or bike through the National Seashore. Climb the Pilgrim Monument for a spectacular view of the area. Visit the museums and shops and art galleries, or spend the afternoon on one of the beautiful beaches. To escape the crowds, spend a day driving south through sleepy but scenic Truro and then park your car in Wellfleet's historic downtown, where you'll find a bounty of intriguing shops and galleries. Continue a bit south to historic Marconi Station, which was the landing point for the transatlantic telegraph early in the 20th century. It's also worth walking the short but stunning White Cedar Swamp Trail.

THREE DAYS IN D.C.

Day 1

Devote this day to the Mall, where you can check out the museums and monuments that were probably a prime motivation for your coming to D.C. in the first place. There's no way you can do it all in one day, so just play favorites and save the rest for next time. Try visiting the monuments in the evening: they remain open long after the museums are closed and are dramatically lighted after dark.

Keep in mind that the National Museum of Natural History is the most visited museum in the country, while the National Air and Space Museum, the National Gallery of Art, and the Museum of American History aren't too far behind; plan for crowds almost anytime you visit.

Cafés and cafeterias within the museums are your best option for lunch. Two excellent picks are the Cascade Café at the National Gallery of Art and the Mitsitam Café at the National Museum of the American Indian, where they serve creative dishes inspired by native cultures.

If the weather is fine, consider a walk from the Washington Monument to the Lincoln Memorial and around the Tidal Basin, where you can see the Jefferson Memorial and the FDR Memorial. It's a healthy walk, however, so don't attempt it if you are already weary with museum fatigue.

Day 2

Make this your day on Capitol Hill, where you'll have the option of visiting the Capitol, the U.S. Botanic Gardens, the Library of Congress, the Supreme Court, and the Folger Shakespeare Library. Call your senators or congressional representative in advance for passes to see Congress in session—a memorable experience. Likewise, check the Supreme Court's Web site (⊕ *www.supremecourtus.gov*) for dates of oral arguments. If you show up at court early enough, you might gain admission for either a short (three-minute) visit or the full morning session.

Day 3

Spend the morning at Arlington National Cemetery, one of the D.C. area's most moving experiences. While you're there, don't miss the changing of the guard at the Tomb of the Unknowns, which takes place every hour or half hour, depending on the time of year. A short detour north of the cemetery brings you to the Marine Corps War Memorial, a giant bronze rendering of one of the most famous images in U.S. military history.

After your quiet, contemplative morning, head across town to spend the afternoon in the neighborhoods of Adams Morgan and Dupont Circle, both of which have unusual shops, restaurants, and clubs. Lunch at one of Adams Morgan's Ethiopian, El Salvadoran, or Mexican restaurants, and take in the Dupont Circle art scene—there's an assortment of offbeat galleries, as well as the renowned Phillips Collection.

SIGHTSEEING NEW YORK CITY

Taking a guided tour in New York is a good idea, even if you prefer flying solo. For one thing, it will help you get your bearings in this city; for another, it's a great way to investigate out-of-the-way areas, or learn about a particular facet of the city's history, inhabitants, or architecture.

Boat Tours

In good weather a **Circle Line Cruise** (⊠ *Pier 83 at W. 42nd St., Midtown West* ☎ *212/563–3200* ⊕ *www.circleline42. com*) around Manhattan Island is one of the best ways to get oriented in the city. The three-hour, 35-mi circumnavigation gives a good sense of where things are. The cruises run at least once daily; the cost is $34 per person (there's also a shorter "semi-Circle" option available for $30).

Looking for a more historical experience? The **Shearwater** (⊠ *North Cove Marina, Lower Manhattan* ☎ *212/619–0885* ⊕ *www.shearwatersailing.com*) an 82-foot yacht dating from the 1920s, sails from the North Cove Marina at the World Financial Center and makes daily 90-minute public sails and Sunday brunch sails from mid-April through mid-October. Shearwater also offers two-hour sunset sails in June, July, and August. Reservations are advised, though they can only be made a maximum of two weeks in advance for sunset sails. Fares start at $45.

Walking Tours

The wisecracking PhD candidates of **Big Onion Walking Tours** (☎ *212/439–1090* ⊕ *www.bigonion.com*) lead themed tours such as "Irish New York" and "Jewish Lower East Side," as well as famous multiethnic eating tours and guided walks through every neighborhood from Harlem to the Financial District and Brooklyn. Tours run daily and cost $15; there's an additional $5 fee for the eating tours.

The **Municipal Art Society** (☎ *212/935–3960, 212/439–1049 recorded information* ⊕ *www.mas.org*) conducts a series of walking tours, which emphasize the architecture and history of particular neighborhoods. The cost is $15 per person. MAS also runs two weekly tours: Downtown Manhattan on Tuesday, and Grand Central Station on Wednesday. Both weekly tours begin at 12:30, and there's a $10 suggested donation.

New York City Cultural Walking Tours (☎ *212/979–2388* ⊕ *www.nycwalk.com*) have covered such topics as buildings' gargoyles and the Millionaire's Mile of 5th Avenue. Two-hour public tours run on some Sundays from March to December, and are $15 per person (no reservations needed); private tours can be scheduled throughout the week at $60 per hour (most tours run about three hours).

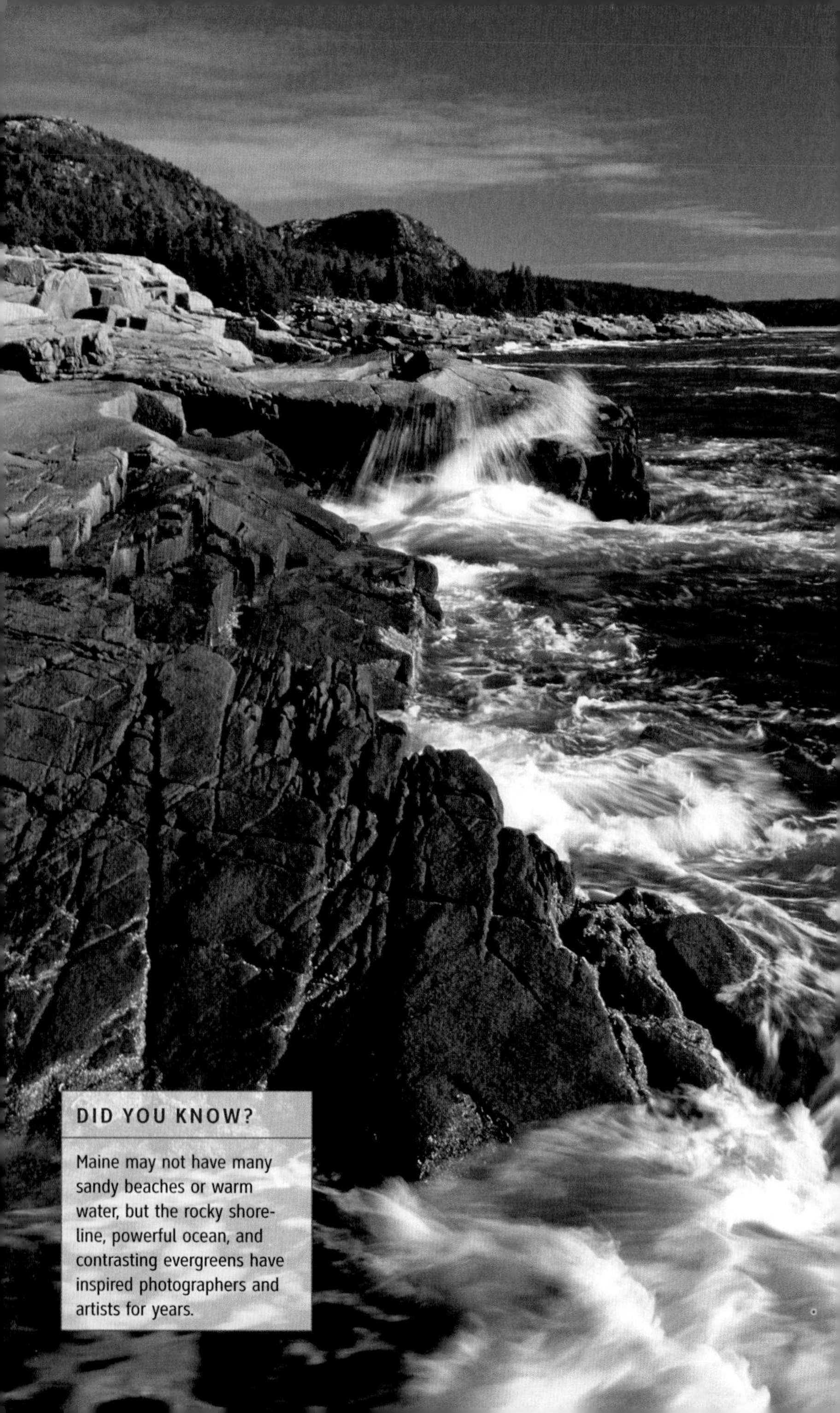

DID YOU KNOW?

Maine may not have many
sandy beaches or warm
water, but the rocky shoreline, powerful ocean, and
contrasting evergreens have
inspired photographers and
artists for years.

1

The Maine Coast

WORD OF MOUTH

"Rent bikes in Bar Harbor and plan your route to include popovers at [Acadia National Park's] Jordan Pond. It's a beautiful ride."

—cindyj

WELCOME TO THE MAINE COAST

TOP REASONS TO GO

★ **Perfection on a Bun:** It's not a Maine vacation without sampling the "lobster roll," lobster with a touch of mayo nestled in a buttery grilled hot-dog bun.

★ **Boating:** The coastline of Maine was made for boaters. Whether it's your own boat, a friend's, or a charter, make sure you get out on the water.

★ **Wild Maine Blueberries:** They may be tiny, but the wild blueberries pack a flavorful punch in season (late July to early September).

★ **Cadillac Mountain:** Drive the winding 3½-mi road to the 1,530-foot summit in Acadia National Park for the sunrise.

★ **Perfect Souvenir:** Buy a watercolor, hand-painted pottery, or handcrafted jewelry—artists and craftspeople abound.

1 The Southern Coast. Stretching north from Kittery to just outside Portland, this is Maine's most-visited region. The towns along the shore and miles of sandy expanses cater to summer visitors. Old Orchard Beach and York Beach feature Coney Island–like amusements, while Kittery, the Yorks, and the Kennebunks are more low-key getaways.

GETTING ORIENTED

Maine has a staggering 3,500 mi of coastline—if you were to stretch out its sandy shores and zigzagging, meandering waterways, you'd be out to California and on your way home again. Its reach is vast: Way Downeast the town of Eastport is the first place to feel the warming rays of sunrise. U.S. 1 is the main route along the shore, from Kittery all the way on up to the border of Canada at Ft. Kent. Local roads branching off from U.S. 1 will take you along all the crags and turns of the jagged shoreline.

2 Portland. Maine's largest and most cosmopolitan city, Portland balances its historic role as a working harbor with its newer identity as a center of sophisticated arts and shopping and innovative restaurants.

3 The Mid-Coast Region. North of Portland, from Brunswick to Monhegan Island, the craggy coastline winds its way around pastoral peninsulas. Its villages boast maritime museums, antiques shops, and beautiful architecture.

4 Penobscot Bay. This region combines lively coastal towns with dramatic natural scenery. Camden is one of Maine's most picture-perfect towns, with its pointed church steeples, antique homes, and historic windjammer fleet.

5 Acadia National Park and Mount Desert Island. Millions come to enjoy Acadia National Park's stunning peaks and vistas of the island's mountains. Bar Harbor is more of a visitor's haven, while Southwest Harbor and Bass Harbor offer quieter retreats.

As you drive across the border into Maine, a sign announces: "The way life should be." Romantics luxuriate in the feeling of a down comforter on a yellow pine bed or in the sensation of the wind and salt spray on their faces while cruising in a historic windjammer. Families love the unspoiled beaches and safe inlets dotting the shoreline. Hikers are revived while roaming the trails of Acadia National Park, and adventure seekers kayak along the coast.

The Maine Coast is several places in one. Portland may be Maine's largest metropolitan area, but its attitude is decidedly more big town than small city. South of Portland, Ogunquit, Kennebunkport, Old Orchard Beach, and other resort towns predominate along a reasonably smooth shoreline. North of Portland and Casco Bay secondary roads turn south off U.S. 1 onto so many oddly chiseled peninsulas that it's possible to drive for days without retracing your route. Slow down to explore the museums, galleries, and shops in the larger towns and the antiques and curio shops and harborside lobster shacks in the smaller fishing villages. Freeport is an entity unto itself, a place where numerous name-brand outlets and specialty stores have sprung up around the retail outpost of famous outfitter L.L. Bean. And no description of the coast would be complete without mention of popular Acadia National Park, with its majestic mountains that are often shrouded in mist.

If you come to Maine seeking an untouched fishing village with locals gathered around a potbellied stove in the general store, you'll likely come away disappointed; that innocent age has passed in all but the most remote spots. Tourism has supplanted fishing, logging, and potato farming as Maine's number-one industry, and most areas are well equipped to receive the annual onslaught of visitors. But whether you are stepping outside a cabin for a walk in the woods or watching a boat rock at its anchor, you can sense the wilderness nearby, even on the edges of the most urbanized spots.

PLANNING

WHEN TO GO

Maine's dramatic coastline and pure natural beauty can be enjoyed year-round, but note that many smaller museums and attractions are open only for high season—from Memorial Day to mid-October—as are many of the waterside attractions and eateries.

Summer begins in earnest on July 4, and many smaller inns and hotels from Kittery on up to the Bar Harbor region fill up early on weekends. Fall, with its fiery foliage, is when many inns and hotels are booked months in advance. After Halloween hotel rates drop significantly until ski season begins around Thanksgiving. Along the coast, bed-and-breakfasts that remain open will often rent rooms at far lower prices than in summer.

GETTING HERE AND AROUND

Maine has two major international airports, Portland International Jetport and Bangor International Airport, to get you to or close to your coastal destination. Manchester-Boston Regional Airport in New Hampshire is about 45 minutes away from the southern end of the Maine coastline. Boston's Logan Airport is the only truly international airport in the region; it's about 90 minutes south of the Maine border.

Amtrak offers regional service from Boston to Portland via its Downeaster line that originates at Boston's North Station and makes four stops in Maine: Wells, Saco, Old Orchard Beach (seasonal), and finally Portland. Greyhound and Concord Trailways also offer bus service from Boston to many towns along the Maine coast.

All that said, once you are here the best way to experience the winding back roads of the craggy Maine coast is in a car. There are miles and miles of roads far from the larger towns that no bus services go to, and you won't want to miss discovering your own favorite ocean vista while on a scenic drive.

ABOUT THE RESTAURANTS

Many breakfast spots along the coast open as early as 6 AM to serve the going-to-work crowd. Lunch generally runs 11–2:30; dinner is usually served 5–9. Only in the larger cities will you find full dinners being offered much later than 9, although you can usually find a bar or bistro serving a limited menu late into the evening.

Many restaurants in Maine are closed Monday, though this isn't true in resort areas in high season. However, resort-town eateries often shut down completely in the off-season. Unless otherwise noted, restaurants in this guide are open daily for lunch and dinner.

Credit cards are accepted for meals throughout Maine, even in some of the most modest establishments.

The one signature dinner on the Maine Coast is, of course, the lobster dinner. It generally includes boiled lobster, a clam or seafood chowder, corn on the cob, and coleslaw or perhaps a salad. Lobster prices vary from day to day, but generally a full lobster dinner should cost around $25; without all the add-ons, about $18.

OUTDOOR ACTIVITIES

No visit to the Maine Coast is complete without some outdoor activity—be it generated by two wheels, two feet, two paddles, or pulling a bag full of clubs.

Bicycling: The Bicycle Coalition of Maine (☎ 207/623-4511 ⊕ www.bikemaine.org) and **Explore Maine by Bike** (☎ 207/624-3300 ⊕ www.exploremaine.org/bike) are both excellent sources for trail maps and other riding information, including where to rent bikes.

Hiking: Exploring the Maine coast on foot is a quick way to acclimate to the relaxed pace of life here. **Healthy Maine Walks** (⊕ www.healthymainewalks.com) has comprehensive listings for quick jaunts as well as more involved hikes.

Kayaking: Nothing gets you literally off the beaten path like plying the salt waters in a graceful sea kayak. **Members of the Maine Association of Sea Kayaking Guides and Instructors** (⊕ www.maineseakayakguides.com) offer instructional classes and guided tours, plan trips, and rent equipment. More seasoned paddlers can get maps of Maine's famous sea trails system at the **Maine Island Trail Association** (☎ 207/761-8225 ⊕ www.mita.org).

ABOUT THE HOTELS

Beachfront and roadside motels and historic-home B&Bs make up the majority of accommodation options along the Maine Coast. There are a few large luxury resorts, such as the Samoset Resort in Rockport or the Bar Harbor Inn in Bar Harbor, but most accommodations are simple and relatively inexpensive. Many properties close during the off-season—mid-October until mid-May; some that stay open drop their rates dramatically. There is a 7% state hospitality tax on all room rates.

Hotel reviews have been condensed for this book. Please go to Fodors.com for full reviews of each property.

WHAT IT COSTS					
	¢	$	$$	$$$	$$$$
Restaurants	under $8	$8–$12	$13–$20	$21–$28	over $28
Hotels	under $80	$80–$120	$121–$170	$171–$220	over $220

Restaurant prices are per person for a main course at dinner. Hotel prices are for a standard double room during peak season and not including tax or gratuities. Some inns add a 15% service charge.

THE SOUTHERN COAST

Maine's southernmost coastal towns—Kittery, the Yorks, Ogunquit, the Kennebunks, and the Old Orchard Beach area—reveal a few of the stunning faces of the state's coast, from the miles and miles of inviting sandy beaches to the beautifully kept historic towns and carnival-like attractions. North of Kittery, long stretches of hard-packed white-sand beach are closely packed with beach cottages, motels, and oceanfront restaurants. The summer colonies of York Beach and Wells brim with crowds and ticky-tacky shorefront overdevelopment, but nearby quiet wildlife refuges and land reserves promise an easy escape. York evokes yesteryear sentiment with its acclaimed historic district, while upscale Ogunquit tantalizes visitors with its array of shops and a cliffside walk.

More than any other region south of Portland, Kennebunkport provides the complete Maine Coast experience: classic townscapes with white-clapboard houses, manicured lawns and gardens; rocky shorelines punctuated by sandy beaches; quaint downtown districts; harbors with lobster boats bobbing alongside yachts; rustic fried-clam and lobster shacks; and well-appointed dining rooms.

THE YORKS, OGUNQUIT, AND WELLS

One of the first permanently settled areas in Maine, colonial **York Village** enjoyed great wealth and success from fishing and lumber. The actual village is quite small, housing the post office, town hall, a few shops, and a stretch of antique homes.

York Harbor is busy with boats of all kinds, while the harbor beach is a good stretch of sand for swimming. More formal and subdued than York Beach, the area retains a somewhat more exclusive air.

York Beach has a long history of entertaining summer visitors. Just as they did back in the late 19th century, visitors today come here to eat ice cream, enjoy carnival-like novelties, and indulge in the sun and sea air.

A resort village in the 1880s, stylish **Ogunquit** gained fame as an artists' colony. Today it has become a mini Provincetown, with a gay population that swells in summer. Take the dramatic cliff-side walk on the Marginal Way to tidy and picturesque Perkins Cove.

Look beyond the commercialism of U.S. 1 in **Wells**—this family-oriented beach community has 7 mi of shoreline, along with nature preserves where you can explore salt marshes and tidal pools. **Crescent Beach, Wells Beach, and Drakes Island Beach** are favorites for beach-going.

WHERE TO EAT AND STAY

$$$$
ECLECTIC
Ogunquit
Fodor's Choice
★

✕ **Arrows.** Elegant simplicity is the hallmark of this restaurant in an 18th-century farmhouse 2 mi up a back road. You'll likely find delicacies such as cream-poached rabbit leg on the daily-changing menu—much of what appears depends on what is ready for harvest in the restaurant's abundant garden. The appetizers of roasted quail with fried noodles and of escargots with summer herb-butter are also beautifully executed. Try the "Indulgence Menu," a 10-course tasting menu prepared "at the whim of the chef," for $135. Guests are encouraged to dress up; no jeans or shorts. ⊠ *41 Berwick Rd.* ☎ *207/361–1100* ⊕ *www.arrowsrestaurant.com* ⌂ *Reservations essential* ☰ *MC, V* ☾ *Closed Mon. and Jan.–mid-Apr. No lunch.*

$$$–$$$$
AMERICAN
York Beach
Fodor'sChoice
★

✕ **Blue Sky on York Beach.** This wide-open and inviting restaurant adds a keen sense of swanky sophistication to this casual beach town. A massive stone fireplace anchors the great room of high ceilings, exposed ductwork, and warm wood floors; unusual hanging light fixtures attract the eye and cast a gentle glow. The menu, executed by well-known chef and owner Lydia Shire, takes regional New England fare to new heights. Memorable choices include the lamb pizza appetizer and the lobster stew; the deep-fried short ribs are painfully delicious, as is the charcoaled duck breast with sugar pumpkin. In good weather, sit out on the large deck with views of the town below. Sunday jazz brunch is also a winner here. ⊠ *2 Beach St., York Beach* ☎ *207/363–0050* ⊕ *www. blueskyonyorkbeach.com* ⌂ *Reservations essential* ☰ *AE, D, MC, V* ☾ *No weekday lunch Nov.–May.*

$$$–$$$$
YORK HARBOR
Fodor'sChoice
★

▦ **Chapman Cottage.** The luxuriant bedspreads, fresh flowers, antiques, and beautiful rugs only hint at the indulgence found at his impeccably restored inn. **Pros:** beautifully restored historic lodging; luxury appointments; attention to detail. **Cons:** no water views; most rooms on upper floors. ⊠ *370 York St.* ☎ *207/363–2059 or 877/363–2059* ⊕ *www. chapmancottagebandb.com* ⇆ *4 rooms, 2 suites* ⌂ *In-room: a/c, no phone, Wi-Fi. In-hotel: no kids under 12* ☰ *MC, V* ⑪ *BP.*

$$–$$$$
WELLS
Fodor'sChoice
★

▦ **Haven by the Sea.** Once the summer mission of St. Martha's Church in Kennebunkport, this exquisite inn has retained many of the original details from its former life as a seaside church. **Pros:** unusual structure with elegant appointments; nightly happy hour; walk to beach. **Cons:** not an in-town location. ⊠ *59 Church St.* ☎ *207/646–4194* ⊕ *www. havenbythesea.com* ⇆ *7 rooms, 2 suites* ⌂ *In-room: a/c, no phones, Wi-Fi. In-hotel: no kids under 12* ☰ *MC, V* ⑪ *BP.*

BEACHES

★
OGUNQUIT

Perkins Cove. This neck of land, connected to the mainland by Oarweed Road and a pedestrian drawbridge, has a jumble of sea-beaten fish houses. These have largely been transformed by the tide of tourism to shops and restaurants. Stroll out along **Marginal Way,** a mile-long footpath between Ogunquit and Perkins Cove that hugs the shore of a rocky promontory known as Israel's Head. Benches allow you to appreciate the open sea vistas, flowering bushes, and million-dollar homes.

THE KENNEBUNKS

Kennebunk is a classic small New England town with an inviting shopping district, steepled churches, and fine examples of 18th- and 19th-century brick and clapboard homes, there are also plenty of natural spaces for outdoor pursuits.

Kennebunk is divided between two villages; the upper one extends around the Mousam River on Route 9, while the lower one is several miles down Route 35, just shy of Kennebunkport proper. To get to the grand and gentle beaches of Kennebunk, go straight on Beach Avenue from the intersection of routes 9 and 35 in the lower village.

Kennebunkport has been a resort area since the 19th century. The presidential Bush family is often in residence in their immense home, which sits dramatically out on Walker's Point. The amount of wealth here is as tangible as the sharp sea breezes and the sounds of seagulls overhead. The area focused around the water and Dock Square in Kennebunkport is where you can find the most activity; winding alleys disclose shops and restaurants geared to the tourist trade, right in the midst of a hardworking harbor.

WHERE TO STAY

$$$$
KENNEBUNKPORT
Fodor's Choice
★

Captain Lord Mansion. Of all the mansions in Kennebunkport's historic district that have been converted to inns, the 1812 Captain Lord Mansion is the stateliest and most sumptuously appointed. **Pros:** elegant and luxurious historic lodging; in-town location; beautiful landscaped grounds. **Cons:** expensive; not a beachfront location. ⊠ *6 Pleasant St., Kennebunkport* ☎ *207/967–3141 or 800/522–3141* ⊕ *www.captainlord. com* ⬦ *19 rooms, 1 suite* ⬦ *In-room: a/c, Wi-Fi. In-hotel: bicycles, Internet terminal, spa, no kids under 12* ☐ *AE, D, MC, V* ⦿ *BP.*

$$$–$$$$
KENNEBUNKPORT
Fodor's Choice
★

The Colony. You can't miss this place—it's grand, white, and incredibly large, set majestically atop a rise overlooking the ocean. **Pros:** lodging in the tradition of grand old hotels; many ocean views; plenty of activities and entertainment for all ages. **Cons:** not intimate; rooms with ocean views come at steep prices. ⊠ *Ocean Ave.* ☎ *207/967–3331 or 800/552–2363* ⊕ *www.thecolonyhotel.com/maine* ⬦ *125 rooms* ⬦ *In-room: no a/c (some), no TV (some), Wi-Fi. In-hotel: restaurant, room service, bar, pool, beachfront, bicycles, some pets allowed* ☐ *AE, MC, V* ⦿ *Closed Nov.–mid-May* ⦿ *BP.*

PORTLAND

Maine's largest city is considered small by national standards—its population is just 64,000—but its character, spirit, and appeal make it feel much larger. Sheltered by the nearby Casco Bay islands and blessed with a deep port, Portland was a significant settlement right from its start in the early 17th century. Settlers thrived on fishing and lumbering, repeatedly building up the area while the British, French, and Native Americans continually sacked it. Many considered the region a somewhat dangerous frontier, but its potential for prosperity was so apparent that settlers came anyway to tap its rich natural resources.

Portland's first home was built on the peninsula now known as Munjoy Hill in 1632. The British burned the city in 1775, when residents refused to surrender arms, but it was rebuilt and became a major trading center. Much of Portland was destroyed again in the Great Fire on July 4, 1866, when a boy threw a celebratory firecracker into a pile of wood shavings; 1,500 buildings burned to the ground.

Today, there is an excellent restaurant scene and a great art museum, and the waterfront is a lively area to walk around in. Portland and its environs are well worth at least a day or two of exploration.

Portland's busy harbor is full of working boats, pleasure craft, and ferries headed to the Casco Bay Islands.

EXPLORING

THE OLD PORT

A major international port and a working harbor since the early 17th century, the Old Port bridges the gap between the city's historic commercial activities and those of today. It is home to fishing boats docked alongside whale-watching charters, luxury yachts, cruise ships, and oil tankers from around the globe. Commercial Street parallels the water, and is lined with brick buildings and warehouses that were built following the Great Fire of 1866. In the 19th century candle makers and sail stitchers plied their trades here; today specialty shops, art galleries, and restaurants have taken up residence.

As with much of the city, it's best to park your car and explore the Old Port on foot. Allow a couple of hours to wander at leisure on Market, Exchange, Middle, and Fore streets. The city is very pedestrian-friendly. Maine state law requires vehicles to stop for walkers in crosswalks.

THE WEST END

A leisurely walk through Portland's West End, beginning at the top of the Arts District, offers a real treat to historic architecture buffs. The neighborhood, on the National Register of Historic Places, reveals an extraordinary display of architectural splendor, from High Victorian Gothic to lush Italianate, Queen Anne, and Colonial Revival.

A good place to start is at the head of the Western Promenade, which has parking, benches, and a nice view. Pass by the Western Cemetery—inside is the ancestral plot of famous poet Henry Wadsworth Longfellow—and just beyond is the parking area.

CASCO BAY ISLANDS

The 140 islands of Casco Bay range from uninhabited ledges visible only at low tide to populous and year-round Peaks Island, a suburb of Portland. The brightly painted ferries of Casco Bay Lines are the islands' lifeline. There is frequent service to the most populated ones, including Peaks, Long, Little Diamond, and Great Diamond.

There are few restaurants, inns, or organized attractions other than the natural beauty of the islands themselves. Meandering about by bike or on foot is a good way to explore on a day trip.

CAPE ELIZABETH TO PROUTS NECK

Fodor's Choice
★

Portland Head Light. Familiar to many from photographs and the Edward Hopper painting *Portland Head-Light* (1927), this lighthouse was commissioned by George Washington in 1790. The towering white stone structure stands over the keeper's quarters, a white home with a blazing red roof, now the Museum at Portland Head Light. The lighthouse is in 90-acre Fort Williams Park, a sprawling green space with walking paths, picnic facilities, a beach and—you guessed it—a cool old fort. *Museum* ⊠ *1000 Shore Rd., Cape Elizabeth* ☎ *207/799–2661* ⊕ *www. portlandheadlight.com* 🖾 *$2* ⊙ *Memorial Day–mid-Oct., daily 10–4; Apr., May, Nov., and Dec., weekends 10–4.*

FREEPORT

17 mi northeast of Portland; 10 mi southwest of Brunswick.

Those who flock straight to L.L. Bean and see nothing else of Freeport are missing out. Beyond the shops are bucolic nature preserves with miles of walking trails and plenty of places for leisurely ambling; charming backstreets are lined with historic buildings and old clapboard houses. It's true, many who come to the area do so simply to shop—L.L. Bean is the store that put Freeport on the map, and plenty of outlets and some specialty stores have settled here.

WHERE TO EAT AND STAY

$$$
AMERICAN
Fodor's Choice
★

✕ **Five Fifty-Five.** Classic dishes are cleverly updated at this cozy Congress Street spot. The lobster mac and cheese boasts artisanal cheeses, hand-rolled pasta, and shaved black truffle. The menu changes seasonally (and sometimes daily) to reflect ingredients available within a 30-mi radius, but the seared local diver scallops, served in a buttery carrot-vanilla emulsion, are an exquisite mainstay. The space, which features exposed brick and copper accents, is a former 19th-century firehouse. ⊠ *555 Congress St.* ☎ *207/761–0555* ⊕ *fivefifty-five.com* ☐ *AE, MC, V* ⊙ *No lunch Mon.–Sat.*

$$
SEAFOOD
★

✕ **Gilbert's Chowder House.** This is the real deal, classic Maine, fuss-free and presented on a paper plate. Clam rakes and nautical charts hang from the walls of this unpretentious waterfront diner. The flavors are from the depths of the North Atlantic, prepared and presented simply: fish, clam, corn, and seafood chowders; fried shrimp; haddock; clam strips; and extraordinary clam cakes. A chalkboard of daily specials often features Alaskan king crab legs and various entrée and chowder combinations. Don't miss out on the lobster roll—a toasted hot-dog bun bursting with claw and tail meat lightly dressed with mayo but otherwise unadulterated. ⊠ *92 Commercial St.* ☎ *207/871–5636* ⊕ *www. gilbertschowderhouse.com* ▭ *D, MC, V.*

$$$–$$$$ 🖼 **Pomegranate Inn.** The common spaces behind the classic facade of this
Fodor'sChoice handsome inn have surprising combinations like bright, faux marble
★ walls, a painted checkerboard floor, and a leopard-print runner; most of the guest rooms are hand painted with splashy florals or polka dots. **Pros:** heaven for art lovers; close to Western Promenade. **Cons:** not within easy walking distance of Old Port. ⊠ *49 Neal St.* ☎ *207/772–1006 or 800/356–0408* ⊕ *www.pomegranateinn.com* 🛏 *8 rooms* ⌂ *In-room: a/c, no phone, Wi-Fi. In-hotel: Wi-Fi hotspot, no kids.*

NIGHTLIFE AND THE ARTS

Portland's nightlife scene is largely centered around the bustling Old Port and a few smaller, artsy spots on Congress Street. There's a great emphasis on local, live music and pubs serving award-winning local microbrews. Several hip wine bars have cropped up, serving appetizers along with a full array of specialty wines and whimsical cocktails. Art galleries and studios have spread throughout the city, infusing with new life many abandoned yet beautiful old buildings and shops. Many are concentrated along the Congress Street downtown corridor; others are hidden amid the boutiques and restaurants of the Old Port and the East End. The First Friday Art Walk (⊕ *www.firstfridayartwalk.com*), a self-guided, free tour of galleries, museums, and alternative art venues happens on the first Friday of each month.

SHOPPING

DOWNTOWN PORTLAND
Exchange Street is great for arts and crafts and boutique browsing, while Commercial Street caters to the souvenir hound—gift shops are packed with nautical items, and lobster and moose emblems are emblazoned on everything from T-shirts to shot glasses.

FREEPORT
Fodor'sChoice Founded in 1912 as a mail-order merchandiser of products for hunters,
★ guides, and anglers, **L. L. Bean** (⊠ *95 Main St. [U.S. 1]* ☎ *877/755–2326* ⊕ *www.llbean.com*) attracts more than 3 million shoppers a year to its giant store (open 24 hours a day) in the heart of Freeport's shopping district. You can still find the original hunting boots, along with cotton and wool sweaters, outerwear, camping and ski equipment, comforters, and hundreds of other things for the home, car, boat, and campsite. For items related to specific activities and the home, as well as discounted merchandise (available at the L.L. Bean Outlet), the company has several specialty stores. **L. L. Bean Outlet** (⊠ *One Freeport Village Station [Depot St.]* ☎ *207/552–7772*).

SPORTS AND THE OUTDOORS

When the weather's good, everyone in Portland heads outside. There are also many green spaces nearby Portland, including Fort Williams Park, home to Portland Head Light; Crescent Beach State Park; and Two Lights State Park. All offer biking and walking trails, picnic facilities, and water access. In Freeport is Wolfe's Neck Woods State Park, where you can take a guided nature walk and see nesting ospreys.

BOATING

Various Portland-based skippers offer whale-, dolphin-, and seal-watching cruises; excursions to lighthouses and islands; and fishing and lobstering trips. Board the ferry to see the nearby islands. Self-navigators can rent kayaks or canoes.

Casco Bay Lines (⊠ *Maine State Pier, 56 Commercial St.* ☎ *207/774–7871* ⊕ *www.cascobaylines.com*) provides narrated cruises and transportation to the Casco Bay islands. **Odyssey Whale Watch** (⊠ *Long Wharf, 170 Commercial St.* ☎ *207/775–0727* ⊕ *www.odysseywhalewatch. com*) leads whale-watching and deep-sea–fishing trips. For tours of the harbor and Casco Bay, including a trip to Eagle Island and an up-close look at several lighthouses, try **Portland Discovery Land & Sea Tours** (⊠ *Long Wharf, 170 Commercial St.* ☎ *207/774–0808* ⊕ *www. portlanddiscovery.com*).

THE MID-COAST REGION

Lighthouses dot the headlands of Maine's Mid-Coast region, where thousands of miles of coastline wait to be explored. Defined by chiseled peninsulas stretching south from U.S. 1, this area has everything from the sandy beaches and sandbars of Popham Beach to the jutting cliffs of Monhegan Island.

Along U.S. 1 charming towns, each unique, have an array of attractions. Brunswick, while a bigger, commercial city, has rows of historic wood and clapboard homes and is home to Bowdoin College. Bath is known for its maritime heritage. Wiscasset has arguably the best antiques shopping in the state. On its waterfront you can choose from a variety of seafood shacks competing for the best lobster rolls. Damariscotta, too, is worth a stop for its lively main street and good seafood restaurants.

South along the peninsulas the scenery opens to glorious vistas of working harbors and marinas. It's here you find the authentic lobster pounds where you can watch your catch come in off the traps. Boothbay Harbor is the quaintest town in the Mid-Coast; it's one of three towns where you can take a ferry to Monhegan Island, which seems to be inhabited exclusively by painters at their easels, depicting the cliffs and weathered homes with colorful gardens.

BATH

Bath has been a shipbuilding center since 1607. The result of its prosperity can be seen in its handsome mix of Federal, Greek Revival, and Italianate homes along Front, Centre, and Washington streets. An easily overlooked site is the town's City Hall. The bell in its tower was cast by Paul Revere in 1805.

The venerable Bath Iron Works completed its first passenger ship in 1890. During World War II BIW—as it's locally known—launched a new ship every 17 days. It is still building today, turning out destroyers for the U.S. Navy. ■TIP→ It's a good idea to avoid U.S. 1 on weekdays from 3:15 pm to 4:30 pm, when a major shift change takes place. You can tour BIW through the Maine Maritime Museum.

EXPLORING

Fodor'sChoice
★

Maine Maritime Museum. No trip to Bath is complete without a visit to this cluster of buildings that once made up the historic Percy & Small Shipyard. Plan on half a day at the museum, which examines the world of shipbuilding and is the only way to tour the Bath Iron Works. In summer, boat tours (a particular favorite is the lighthouse tour) cruise the scenic Kennebec River. A number of impressive ships, including the 142-foot Grand Banks fishing schooner *Sherman Zwicker,* are on display in summer. Inside the main museum building exhibits use ship models, paintings, photographs, and historical artifacts to tell the maritime history of the region. From May to November hour-long tours of the shipyard show how these massive wooden ships were built. You can watch boatbuilders wield their tools in the boat shop. A separate historic building houses a fascinating lobstering exhibit. It's worth coming here just to watch the 18-minute video on lobstering written and narrated by E. B. White. A gift shop and bookstore are on the premises, and you can grab a bite to eat in the café or bring a picnic to eat on the grounds. ⊠ 243 Washington St. ☎ 207/442–0961 ⊕ www.mainemaritimemuseum.org ☜ $12 ⊙ Daily 9:30–5.

WHERE TO STAY

$$$–$$$$
Fodor'sChoice
★

Sebasco Harbor Resort. This destination family resort spread across 550 acres at the foot of the Phippsburg Peninsula has an exceptional range of accommodations and services. **Pros:** ocean location; excellent food and service; kids' activities. **Cons:** pricey for large families. ⊠ 29 Kenyon Rd., off Rte. 217, Sebasco Estates ☎ 207/389–1161 or 800/225–3819 ⊕ www.sebasco.com ⇆ 110 rooms, 22 cottages ⚭ In-room: a/c (some), Wi-Fi. In-hotel: 2 restaurants, bar, golf course, tennis courts, pool, gym, bicycles, children's programs (ages 3–15), spa, Wi-Fi hotspot ⊟ AE, D, MC, V ⊙ Closed mid-Oct.–mid-May ⧩ MAP.

WISCASSET

10 mi north of Bath; 46 mi northeast of Portland.

Settled in 1663, Wiscasset sits on the banks of the Sheepscot River. It bills itself "Maine's Prettiest Village," and it's easy to see why: It has graceful churches, old cemeteries, and elegant sea captains' homes, many converted into antiques shops or galleries. Pack a picnic and take it down to the dock, where you can watch the fishing boats or grab a lobster roll from Red's Eats or the lobster shack nearby. U.S. 1 becomes Main Street, and traffic often slows to a crawl. You can walk to all galleries, shops, restaurants, and other attractions. ■ TIP→ You'll likely have success if you try to park on Water Street rather than Main.

PENOBSCOT BAY

Few could deny that Penobscot Bay is one of Maine's most dramatically beautiful regions. Its 1,000-mi-long coastline is made up of massive boulders, wild and often undeveloped shore, a sprinkling of colorful towns, and views of the sea and shore that are a photographer's dream.

The second-largest estuary in New England, Penobscot Bay stretches 37 mi from Port Clyde in the south to Stonington, the little fishing village at the tip of Deer Isle, in the north. It covers an estimated 1,070 square mi and is home to hundreds of islands.

In the 1800s, during the days of the great tall ships (or Down Easters, as they were often called), more wooden ships were built along Penobscot Bay than in any other place in the United States. This golden age of billowing sails and wooden sailing ships came to an end with the development of the steam engine. However, as you will see when traveling the coast, the tall ships have not disappeared—they have simply been revived as recreational boats, known as windjammers. Today, once again, there are more tall ships along Penobscot Bay than anywhere else in the country.

ROCKLAND

4 mi northeast of Thomaston; 14 mi northeast of Tenants Harbor.

Though once merely a place to pass through on the way to tonier ports like Camden, Rockland now gets attention on its own, thanks to a trio of attractions: the renowned Farnsworth Museum, the increasingly popular summer Lobster Festival, and the lively North Atlantic Blues Festival. Specialty shops and galleries line the main street, and the town is still a large fishing port and the commercial hub of this coastal area.

Rockland Harbor is the berth of more windjammer ships than any other port in the United States. The best place in Rockland to view these beautiful vessels as they sail in and out of the harbor is the mile-long granite breakwater, which bisects the outer portion of Rockland Harbor. To get there, go north on U.S. 1, turn right on Waldo Avenue, and right again on Samoset Road, then follow to its end.

EXPLORING

Fodor's Choice ★ **Farnsworth Art Museum.** This is one of the most important small museums in the country. The **Wyeth Center** is devoted to Maine-related works of the famous Wyeth family: N. C. Wyeth, an accomplished illustrator whose works were featured in many turn-of-the-20th-century books; his late son Andrew, one of the best-known painters in the country; and Andrew's son James, also an accomplished painter, who lives on nearby Monhegan Island. You may see works by Fitz Henry Lane, George Bellows, Frank W. Benson, Edward Hopper, Louise Nevelson, and Fairfield Porter; exhibits change seasonally. Works by living Maine artists are shown in the **Jamien Morehouse Wing.** The

Farnsworth Homestead, a handsome circa-1852 Greek Revival dwelling that is part of the museum, retains its original lavish Victorian furnishings. In nearby Cushing the museum also operates the **Olsen House** (⊠ *384 Hathorne Point Rd., Cushing*), which is depicted in Andrew Wyeth's famous painting *Christina's World.* ⊠ *16 Museum St., Rockland* ☎ *207/596–6457* ⊕ *www.farnsworthmuseum.org* ⊠ *$12* ☉ *Mid-May–Oct., daily 10–5; Nov.–mid-May, Wed.–Sun. 10–5.*

WHERE TO EAT

$$$$
MEDITERRANEAN
Fodor'sChoice
★

✕ **Primo.** Owner-chef Melissa Kelley and her world-class gourmet restaurant in a restored Victorian home have won many awards and been written about favorably in *Vanity Fair, Town and Country,* and *Food and Wine.* The cuisine combines fresh Maine ingredients with Mediterranean influences. The menu, which changes daily, may include local monkfish medallions with a peeky toe crab and risotto cake or a grilled Moulard duck breast. Pastry chef and co-owner Price Kushner creates unusual and delectable desserts, such as cannoli Siciliana, featuring crushed pistachios and amarena cherries. ⊠ *2 S. Main St., Rockland* ☎ *207/596–0770* ⊕ *www.primorestaurant.com* ⊟ *AE, D, MC, V* ☉ *Open Wed.–Sun. No lunch. Closed mid-Jan.–mid-Apr.*

CAMDEN

2 mi north of Rockport.

More than any other town along Penobscot Bay, Camden is the perfect picture postcard of a Maine coastal village, and is one of the most popular destinations on the Maine Coast.

Camden is famous not only for its geography, but also for its large fleet of windjammers, with their romantic histories and great billowing sails. The excursions, whether for an afternoon or a week, are best from June through September.

The town's compact size makes it perfect for exploring on foot: shops, restaurants, and galleries line Main Street, as well as side streets and alleys around the harbor. Camden's residential area is quite charming and filled with many historic homes; the Chamber of Commerce, at the Public Landing, can provide you with a walking map.

WHERE TO EAT AND STAY

$$$$
FRENCH-
AMERICAN
Fodor'sChoice
★

✕ **Natalie's.** This restaurant may be the most sought-after dining spot in town, at the Camden Harbour Inn. The creation of Dutch owners Raymond Brunyanszki and Oscar Verest, the restaurant is fine dining with a French-American flair, and offers a variety of prix-fixe menus, such as "The Menu Saisonnier," which showcases fresh, seasonal ingredients, and the "Homard Grand Cru," a cascade of lobster dishes (lobster gazpacho, lobster with squid ink, lobster with fiddleheads, lobster with beef cheek and foie-gras ravioli); there's also an à la carte menu. In the lounge enjoy a predinner cocktail in front of the big fireplace. ⊠ *83 Bay View St.* ☎ *207/236–7008* ⊕ *www.camdenharbourinn.com* ⊟ *AE, D, MC, V.*

The view from Camden Hills is a great way to see Penobscot Bay and the town of Camden.

$$$–$$$$ **Norumbega Inn.** This is the most photographed piece of real estate in
Fodor'sChoice   the state of Maine, and once you see it, you'll understand why. **Pros:**
★   beautiful views; close to town. **Cons:** many stairs to climb ⊠ *63 High
St. (U.S. 1)* ☎ *207/236–4646 or 877/363–4646* ⊕ *www.norumbegainn.
com* ⇌ *12 rooms* ⚴ *In-room: a/c, DVD (some), Wi-Fi. In-hotel: con-
cierge service* ⊟ *AE, MC, V* ⓘ *BP.*

BELFAST

10 mi north of Lincolnville; 46 mi northeast of Augusta.

Belfast has a full variety of charms: a beautiful waterfront; an old and
interesting main street climbing up from the harbor; a delightful array
of B&Bs, restaurants, and shops; and a friendly population. The down-
town even has old-fashioned streetlamps, which set the streets aglow at
night. If you like looking at old houses, many of which go all the way
back to the American Revolution and are in the Federal and Colonial
styles, just drive up and down some of the side streets.

WHERE TO STAY

$–$$$ **Penobscot Bay Inn & Restaurant.** This lovely accommodation is on 5
Fodor'sChoice   meadowed acres overlooking Penobscot Bay. **Pros:** you don't have to go
★   out for dinner. **Cons:** no special views from the restaurant; a drive from
Belfast's colorful downtown. ⊠ *192 Northport Ave.* ☎ *207/338–5715
or 800/335–2370* ⊕ *www.penobscotbayinn.com* ⇌ *19 rooms* ⚴ *In-
room: a/c, refrigerator (some). In-hotel: restaurant, bar* ⊟ *AE, D, MC,
V* ⓘ *BP.*

ACADIA NATIONAL PARK AND MOUNT DESERT ISLAND

With some of the most dramatic and varied scenery on the Maine Coast and home to Maine's only national park, Mount Desert Island (pronounced "Mount Dessert" by locals) is Maine's most popular tourist destination, attracting more than 2 million visitors a year. Much of the approximately 12-by-9-mi island belongs to Acadia National Park. The rocky coastline rises starkly from the ocean, appreciable along the scenic drives. Trails for hikers of all skill levels lead to the rounded tops of the mountains, providing views of Frenchman and Blue Hill bays and beyond. Ponds and lakes beckon you to swim, fish, or boat. Ferries and charter boats provide a different perspective on the island and a chance to explore the outer islands, all of which are part of Maine but not necessarily of Mount Desert. A network of old carriage roads lets you explore Acadia's wooded interior, filled with birds and a great variety of wildlife.

The island's major tourist destination is Bar Harbor, which has plenty of accommodations, restaurants, and shops. Less congested are the smaller communities of Northeast Harbor, Southwest Harbor, and Bass Harbor. Mount Desert Island is a place with three personalities: the hustling, bustling tourist mecca of Bar Harbor; the "quiet side" of the island composed of the little villages; and the vast natural expanse that is Acadia National Park.

ESSENTIALS

Visitor Information Bar Harbor Chamber of Commerce (✉ 1201 Bar Harbor Rd., Bar Harbor ☎ 207/288–5103 ⊕ www.barharborinfo.com). **Mount Desert Chamber of Commerce** (✉ 18 Harbor Rd., Northeast Harbor ☎ 207/276–5040 ⊕ www.mountdesertchamber.org). **Mount Desert Island Chambers and Acadia National Park Information Center** (✉ Rte. 3, Thompson Island ☎ 207/288–3411 ⊕ www.acadiachamber.com).

BAR HARBOR

160 mi northeast of Portland; 22 mi southeast of Ellsworth.

A resort town since the 19th century, Bar Harbor is the artistic, culinary, and social center of Mount Desert Island. It also serves visitors to Acadia National Park with inns, motels, and restaurants. Around the turn of the last century the island was known as the summer haven of the very rich because of its cool breezes. The wealthy built lavish mansions throughout the island, many of which were destroyed in a great fire that devastated the island in 1947, but many of those that survived have been converted into businesses. Shops are clustered along Main, Mount Desert, and Cottage streets. Take a stroll down West Street, a National Historic District, where you can see some fine old houses.

WHERE TO EAT AND STAY

$$$–$$$$
SEAFOOD
Fodor'sChoice
★

✕ **Burning Tree.** One of the top restaurants in Maine, this easy-to-miss gem is on Route 3 between Bar Harbor and Otter Creek. The ever-changing menu emphasizes freshly caught seafood, and seven species of fish are offered every day, all from the Gulf of Maine. Entrées include

pan-sautéed monkfish, oven-poached cod, and gray sole. There are always two or three vegetarian options and an emphasis on organic produce (much of it from the owners' garden). ☒ *69 Otter Creek Dr. (Rte. 3), Otter Creek* ☎ *207/288–9331* ⊟ *DC, MC, V* ⊘ *Closed Tues. and mid-Oct.–mid-June.*

$$$–$$$$
Fodor's Choice
★

🏠 **Bar Harbor Inn & Spa.** Originally established in the late 1800s as a men's social club, this waterfront inn has rooms spread out over three buildings on well-landscaped grounds. **Pros:** seems to meet every need; right at the harbor. **Cons:** not as close to Acadia National Park as some Bar Harbor properties. ☒ *Newport Dr.* ☎ *207/288–3351 or 800/248–3351* ⊕ *www.barharborinn.com* ⟿ *138 rooms, 15 suites* ♿ *In-room: a/c, safe (some), refrigerator, DVD (some), Wi-Fi. In-hotel: 2 restaurants, pool, gym, spa, Wi-Fi hotspot* ⊟ *AE, D, MC, V* ⊘ *Closed late Nov.–late Mar.* ⏐◯⏐ *CP.*

ACADIA NATIONAL PARK

4 mi northwest of Bar Harbor.

Fodor's Choice
★

With more than 30,000 acres of protected forests, beaches, mountains, and coastline, Acadia National Park holds some of the most spectacular scenery on the eastern seaboard: a jagged coastline of surf-pounded granite and an interior graced by sculpted mountains, quiet ponds, and lush deciduous forests. Cadillac Mountain (named after a Native American, not the car), the highest point of land on the East Coast, dominates the park. Although it's rugged, the park also has graceful stone bridges, horse-drawn carriages, and the Jordan Pond House restaurant (famous for its popovers).

The 27-mi Park Loop Road provides an excellent introduction, but to truly appreciate the park you must get off the main road and experience it by walking, biking, sea kayaking, or taking a carriage ride. A small part of the park is on Isle au Haut, more than 10 mi away out in the ocean.

PARK ESSENTIALS

A user fee is required to get in the park from May through October; the park is open year-round (watch for closed roads in winter). The fee is $10 (May–late June and October), $20 (late June–Sept) per vehicle for a seven-consecutive-day pass, or inquire about a National Pass. See ⊕ *www.nps.gov* for details.

Visitor center hours are 8–4:30 April 15–June, September, and October, and until 6 in July and August.

PARK CONTACT INFORMATION
Acadia National Park (⌂ *Acadia National Park, Box 177, Bar Harbor 04609* ☎ *207/288–3338* ⊕ *www.nps.gov/acad*).

Boston

WORD OF MOUTH

"The Freedom Trail is very interesting if you are a history buff . . . There are guided tours—some done in period character . . . I love the New England Aquarium on the harbor. The Aquarium, the historic sights of the Freedom Trail, the architecture, the harbor are all part of what make Boston unique."

—ktmc

WELCOME TO BOSTON

TOP REASONS TO GO

★ **The Freedom Trail.** Walk along Paul Revere's fated path for a glimpse of living American history.

★ **Posh purchases.** Strap on some stilettos and join the quest for fashionable finds on Newbury Street, Boston's answer to Manhattan's 5th Avenue.

★ **Red-Sox nation.** Boston's baseball team is the one thing that will bring the entire city to its feet—or its knees. Few baseball fans, Red Sox faithful or not, can deny the mystique of one of the game's most hallowed grounds—Fenway Park.

★ **Painted glory.** Gaze at paintings, listen to concerts, and stare down statuary at the beautiful Isabella Stewart Gardner Museum. While away hours upon hours at the Museum of Fine Arts, contemplating the works of French masters Edouard Manet, Camille Passarro, and Pierre-Auguste Renoir; and American painters such as Mary Cassatt, Childe Hassam, John Singer Sargent, and Edward Hopper.

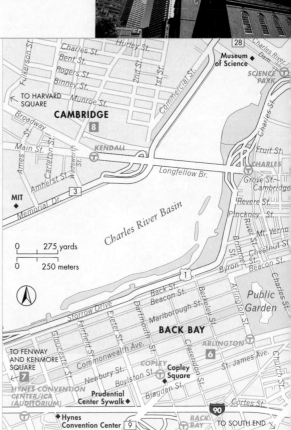

1 Beacon Hill and Boston Common. Beacon Hill is a wonderful place to walk. Below Beacon Hill lies Boston Common, a popular hangout since 1634.

2 Old West End. Big draws in the Old West End are the Museum of Science and TD Garden, home of Boston's pro hockey and basketball teams.

3 Government Center and the North End. Architecture buffs focus on Government Center, but most make a beeline for Faneuil Hall. The North End is crammed with American history, but Italian immigrants have also left their mark here since the 19th century.

4 Charlestown. Charlestown's top sight is the towering USS *Constitution*.

5 Downtown. Explore historic sights like the Old South Meeting House and Old State House. Families

2

GETTING ORIENTED

Boston comes together in a seemingly endless array of narrow and twisting one-way streets that radiate away from Boston Harbor in the east. As you travel north, Downtown gives way to Government Center, and then to the bustling streets of the Italian-flavored North End. Head generally southwest from here and you'll encounter the Old West End—home of the "Gah-den"—and Beacon Hill. The Back Bay's grid of streets runs southwest from the base of Beacon Hill, and to the south of the Back Bay is the eclectic and historic South End. Head west from here and you'll encounter the retail wonderland of Prudential Center, and then the Fenway, home to many of Boston's art museums, and, of course, the city's beloved Red Sox. The Charles River is a natural dividing line between Boston and its northern neighborhoods and suburbs, including Charlestown and the cities of Cambridge and Somerville. The Four Point Channel separates South Boston and the Dorchester neighborhood from the city proper.

are drawn in by the Aquarium and Children's Museum, and playgoers flock to the Theater District.

6 The Back Bay and South End. The chic Back Bay boasts the city's most impressive skyscrapers. There's a dense concentration of high-end stores on and around Newbury Street. The South End has enough style to win the "hippest hood" award.

7 The Fenway. Fenway Park, the Museum of Fine Arts, and Isabella Stewart Gardner Museum, as well as academic institutions like Boston University, Northeastern University, and Harvard Medical School are here.

8 Cambridge. A separate city across the Charles River, Cambridge is where you'll find Harvard and M.I.T., and a number of cafés, bookstores, and funky shops.

There's history and culture around every bend in Boston—skyscrapers nestle next to historic hotels, while modern marketplaces line the antique cobblestone streets. But to Bostonians, living in a city that blends yesterday and today is just another day in their beloved Beantown.

And though you might be tempted, it's difficult to fit a stereotype to this city because of Boston's many layers. The deepest is the historical one, the place where musket-bearing revolutionaries vowed to hang together or hang separately. The next tier, a dense spread of Brahmin fortune and fortitude, might be labeled the Hub. It was this elite caste of Boston society, descended from wealthy English Protestants who first settled the state, that funded and patronized the city's universities and cultural institutions, gaining Boston the label "the Athens of America" and felt only pride in the slogan "Banned in Boston." Over that layer lies Beantown, home to the Red Sox faithful and the raucous Bruins fans who crowded the old Boston "*Gah*-den"; this is the city whose ethnic loyalties account for its many distinct neighborhoods. Crowning these layers are the students who converge on the area's universities and colleges every fall, infuriating some but pleasing many with their infusion of high spirits and money from home.

With such a complex identity, it's no surprise that Boston, despite its relatively small size, offers visitors a diverse set of experiences. History buffs—and just about everyone else—will spend a day or more following the thick red line of the Freedom Trail and tracing Revolutionary history through town. Shopaholics can join the quest for fashionable finds on Newbury Street, while sports fiends gravitate toward Fenway Park for a tour (or if very lucky a game) of the beloved Boston Red Sox's home. The Museum of Fine Art's expansive catalog of French Impressionists and American painters, the Isabella Stewart Gardner Museum's palazzo of painting masters, and the Institute of Contemporary Art's modern works satisfy any artistic taste.

PLANNING

2

WHEN TO GO

Weather-wise, late spring and fall are the optimal times to come. Aside from mild temperatures, the former offers blooming gardens throughout the city and the latter sees the surrounding countryside ablaze with brilliantly colored foliage. At both times, however, you should expect hordes of visitors.

Students must be factored into the mix as well. More than 250,000 of them flood into the area each September and then pull out again in May and June. So hotels and restaurants fill up especially fast on move-in, move-out, and graduation weekends.

The good news is that this is a four-season destination. Along with the most reliable sunshine, summer brings sailboats to Boston Harbor, concerts to the Esplanade, and café tables to sidewalks. Summer is also prime for a classic shore vacation, but advance planning is imperative.

Even winter has its pleasures. Boston gets a holiday glow, thanks to the thousands of lights strung around the Common, Public Garden, and Commonwealth Avenue Mall. During the post-Christmas lull temperatures fall, but lodging prices do, too.

GETTING HERE AND AROUND

Air Travel: Flying to Boston takes about 1 hour from New York, 1½ hours from Washington, D.C., 2¼ hours from Chicago, 3¾ hours from Dallas, 5½ hours from Los Angeles, 7½ hours from London, and 21–22 hours from Sydney (including connection time). Delta, US Airways, and jetBlue have many daily shuttle flights from New York and Washington.

Boston's major airport, **Logan International Airport** (BOS ⊠ *I–90 east to Ted Williams Tunnel* ☎ *800/235–6426* ⊕ *www.massport.com/logan* ⓣ *Airport*), is across the harbor from Downtown, about 2 mi outside the city center, and can be easily reached by taxi, water taxi, or bus/subway via MBTA's Silver or Blue lines). A free airport shuttle runs between the terminals and airport hotels.

■TIP➔ The Boston Convention and Visitor Bureau's Web site ⊕ *www.bostonusa.com* has direct links to 19 airlines that service the city. You can book flights here, too.

Car Travel: In a place where roads often evolved from cow paths and colonial lanes, driving is no simple task. A surfeit of one-way streets makes for circuitous routing. Inconsistent signage and aggressive local drivers only add to the confusion. Nevertheless, having your own car is helpful (especially if you're taking side trips), and conditions are better now that the Big Dig is done. Just keep a detailed map handy.

If you would rather leave the driving to someone else, cabs are available 24/7. They wait outside major hotels, or line up near hot spots like Harvard Square, South Station, Faneuil Hall, Long Wharf, and the Theater District. You can call a cab or hail one on the street. Rides within the city cost $2.60 for the first 1/7 mi and 40¢ for each 1/7 mi thereafter (tolls, where applicable, are extra).

Public Transit. The "T," as the subway system is affectionately nick-named, is the cornerstone of a far-reaching public transit network that also includes aboveground trains, buses, and ferries. Its five color-coded lines will put you within a block of almost anywhere. Subways operate from about 5:30 am to 12:30 pm, as do buses, which crisscross the city and suburbia.

A standard adult subway fare is $1.70 with a CharlieCard or $2 with a ticket or cash. For buses it's $1.25 with a CharlieCard or $1.50 with a ticket or cash (more if you are using an Inner or Outer Express bus). Commuter rail and ferry fares vary by route. For details on schedules, routes, and rates, contact the **MBTA** (☎ *617/222–3200 or 800/392–6100* ⊕ *www.mbta.com*).

CharliePass and the CharlieCard: Retro music fans recall the 1959 Kingston Trio hit about a fellow named Charlie, who, unable to pay his fare, "never returned" from Boston's subway system. Charlie lives on as the mascot of the MBTA's somewhat confusing ticketing scheme. There are two stored-value options: a plastic CharlieCard or paper Charlie-Ticket, both of which are reusable and reloadable with cash or credit or debit cards. At a station, obtain a CharlieCard from an attendant or a CharlieTicket from a machine. CharlieCards make for cheaper trips, but can't yet be used on commuter rail, commuter boats, or Inner Harbor ferries. Most visitors' best deal will be the unlimited one-day ($9) or one-week ($15) LinkPass rather than either Charlie-named option.

EXPLORING BOSTON

"America's Walking City," with all its historic nooks and scenic crannies, is best explored on foot. But when hoofing it around town seems too arduous, there are alternatives. The best form of transportation within Boston or Cambridge/Somerville is the MBTA system, or the T, as it's known locally. Five subway lines—which are actually composed of underground trains, above-ground trolleys/light rail, and buses—run through the entire city and to the outlying suburbs. A series of buses fills in the gaps, and you can ride the T to every major point of interest in the city. A car is only necessary for getting out of town.

BEACON HILL AND BOSTON COMMON

Past and present home of the old-money elite, contender for the "Most Beautiful" award among the city's neighborhoods, and hallowed address for many literary lights, Beacon Hill is Boston at its most Bostonian. The redbrick elegance of its narrow streets sends you back to the 19th century just as surely as if you had stumbled into a time machine. But Beacon Hill residents would never make the social faux pas of being out of date. The neighborhood is home to hip boutiques and trendy restaurants, frequented by young, affluent professionals rather than D.A.R. matrons.

A good place to begin an exploration of Beacon Hill is at the **Boston Common Visitor Information Center** (⊠ *147 Tremont St.* ☎ *888/733–2678*

For a dramatic entrance, pull up to Rowes Wharf in a water shuttle from Logan airport.

⊕ *www.bostonusa.com* ⊙ *Mon.–Sat. 8:30–5, Sun. 10–6* Ⓣ *Park St.*),
where you can buy a map or a complete guide to the Freedom Trail.

WHAT TO SEE

Ⓒ
Fodor's Choice
★

Boston Common. Nothing is more central to Boston than the Common, the oldest public park in the United States. Dating from 1634, Boston Common started as 50 acres where the freemen of Boston could graze their cattle. (Cows were banned in 1830.) Latin names are affixed to many of the Common's trees; it was once expected that proper Boston schoolchildren be able to translate them.

On Tremont Street near Boylston stands the 1888 **Boston Massacre Memorial**; the sculpted hand of one of the victims has a distinct shine from years of sightseers' caresses. The Common's highest ground, near the park's Parkman Bandstand, was once called Flagstaff Hill. It's now surmounted by the **Soldiers and Sailors Monument,** honoring Civil War troops.

On the Beacon Street side of the Common sits the splendidly restored **Robert Gould Shaw 54th Regiment Memorial,** executed in deep-relief bronze by Augustus Saint-Gaudens in 1897. It commemorates the 54th Massachusetts Regiment, the first Civil War unit made up of free blacks, led by the young Brahmin Robert Gould Shaw. He and half of his troops died in an assault on South Carolina's Fort Wagner. The monument—first intended to depict only Shaw until his abolitionist family demanded it honor his regiment as well—figures in works by the poets John Berryman and Robert Lowell. This magnificent memorial makes a fitting first stop on the **Black Heritage Trail.** The **Central Burying Ground** may seem an odd feature for a public park, but remember that

Following the Freedom Trail

More than a route of historic sites, the Freedom Trail is a 2½-mi walk into history, bringing to life the events that exploded on the world during the Revolution. Its 16 way stations allow you to reach out and touch the very wellsprings of U.S. civilization. (And for those with a pinch of Yankee frugality, only three of the sites charge admission.) Follow the route marked on your maps, and keep an eye on the sidewalk for the red stripe that marks the trail.

It takes a full day to complete the entire route comfortably. The trail lacks the multimedia bells and whistles that are quickly becoming the norm at historic attractions, but on the Freedom Trail, history speaks for itself.

Begin at Boston Common. Get your bearings at the Visitor Information Center on Tremont Street, then head for the **State House,** Boston's finest piece of Federalist architecture. Several blocks away is the **Park Street Church,** whose 217-foot steeple is considered by many to be the most beautiful in all of New England.

Reposing in the church's shadows is the **Granary Burying Ground,** final resting place of Samuel Adams, John Hancock, and Paul Revere. A short stroll to Downtown brings you to **King's Chapel,** built in 1754 and a hotbed of Anglicanism during the colonial period. Follow the trail past the statue of Benjamin Franklin to the **Old Corner Bookstore** site, where Hawthorne, Emerson, and Longfellow were published. Nearby is the **Old South Meeting House,** where pretempest arguments, heard in 1773, led to the Boston Tea Party. Overlooking the site of the Boston Massacre is the earliest-known public building

Faneuil Hall

in Boston, the **Old State House,** a Georgian beauty.

Cross the plaza to **Faneuil Hall** and explore its upstairs Assembly Room, where Samuel Adams fired the indignation of Bostonians during those times that tried men's souls. Find your way back to the red stripe and follow it into the North End.

Stepping into the **Paul Revere House** takes you back 200 years—here are the hero's own saddlebags, a toddy warmer, and a pine cradle made from a molasses cask. Nearby Paul Revere Mall is a tranquil rest spot. Next to the Paul Revere House is one of the city's oldest brick buildings, the **Pierce-Hichborn House.**

Next, tackle a place guaranteed to trigger a wave of patriotism: **Old North Church** of "One if by land, two if by sea" fame—sorry, the 154 creaking stairs leading to the belfry are out-of-bounds for visitors. Then head toward **Copp's Hill Burying Ground,** cross the bridge over the Charles, and check out that revered icon the **USS** *Constitution,* "Old Ironsides."

The photo finish? A climb to the top of the **Bunker Hill Monument** for the incomparable vistas. Finally, head for the nearby Charlestown water shuttle, which goes directly to the downtown area, and congratulate yourself: you've just completed a unique crash course in American history.

in 1756, when the land was set aside, this was a lonely corner of the Common. It's the final resting place of Tories and Patriots alike, as well as many British casualties of the Battle of Bunker Hill. The Burying Ground is open daily 9–5. ✉ *Boylston St. near Tremont, Beacon Hill* Ⓣ *Park St.* ✉ *Bounded by Beacon, Charles, Tremont, and Park Sts., Beacon Hill* Ⓣ *Park St.*

☺ **Museum of African American History.** Ever since runaway slave Crispus
Fodor's Choice Attucks became one of the famous victims of the Boston Massacre
★ of 1770, the African American community of Boston has played an important part in the city's history. Throughout the 19th century, abolition was the cause célèbre for Boston's intellectual elite, and during that time, blacks came to thrive in neighborhoods throughout the city. The Museum of African American History was established in 1964 to promote this history. The umbrella organization includes a trio of historic sites: the Abiel Smith School, the first public school in the nation built specifically for black children; the African Meeting House, where in 1832 the New England Anti-Slavery Society was formed under the leadership of William Lloyd Garrison; and the African Meeting House on the island of Nantucket, off the coast of Cape Cod. Park Service personnel continue to lead tours of the **Black Heritage Trail**, starting from the Shaw Memorial. The museum is the site of activities, including lectures, children's storytelling, and concerts focusing on black composers. ✉ *46 Joy St., Beacon Hill* ☎ *617/725–0022* ⊕ *www.afroammuseum.org* 💰 *$5* ☽ *Mon.–Sat. 10–4* Ⓣ *Charles/MGH.*

THE OLD WEST END

Just a few decades ago the Old West End—separated from Beacon Hill by Cambridge Street—resembled a typical medieval city: thoroughfares that twisted and turned, maddening one-way lanes, and streets that were a veritable hive of people. Then, progress—or what passes for progress—all but eliminated the thriving Irish, Italian, Jewish, and Greek communities to make room for a mammoth project of urban renewal, designed in the 1960s by I.M. Pei.

WHAT TO SEE

Leonard P. Zakim Bunker Hill Bridge. The crown jewel of the "Big Dig" construction project, the 1,432-foot-long Zakim Bridge, designed by Swiss bridge architect Christian Menn, is one of the widest cable-stayed hybrid bridges ever built, and the first to use an asymmetrical design. The towers evoke the Bunker Hill Monument, and the distinctive fan shape of the cables gives the bridge a modern flair. The bridge was named after Lenny Zakim, a local civil-rights activist who headed the New England Region of the Anti-Defamation League and died of cancer in 1999, and the Battle of Bunker Hill, a defining moment in U.S. history. One of the best spots to view the bridge is from the Charlestown waterfront across the river. The best viewing is at night, when the illuminated bridge glows blue. ⊕ *www.leonardpzakimbunkerhillbridge.org.*

☺ **Museum of Science.** With 15-foot lightning bolts in the Theater of Elec-
Fodor's Choice tricity and a 20-foot-long Tyrannosaurus rex model, this is just the
★ place to ignite any child's scientific curiosity. Occupying a compound

of buildings north of Massachusetts General Hospital, the museum sits astride the Charles River Dam. More than 550 exhibits cover astronomy, astrophysics, anthropology, medical progress, computers, the organic and inorganic earth sciences, and much more. The emphasis is on hands-on education. ⊠ *Science Park at Charles River Dam, Old West End* ☎ *617/723–2500* ⊕ *www.mos.org* ⌲ *$20* ☉ *July 5–Labor Day, Sat.–Thurs. 9–7, Fri. 9–9; after Labor Day–July 4, Sat.–Thurs. 9–5, Fri. 9–9* Ⓣ *Science Park.*

GOVERNMENT CENTER

Government Center is a section of town Bostonians love to hate. Not only does it house what they can't fight—City Hall—but it also contains some of the bleakest architecture since the advent of poured concrete. But though the stark, treeless plain surrounding City Hall has been roundly jeered for its user-unfriendly aura, the expanse is enlivened by feisty political rallies, free summer concerts, and the occasional festival. On the corner of Tremont and Court streets the landmark Steaming Kettle, a gilded kettle cast in 1873 that once boiled around the clock, lightens the mood a bit. (It now marks a Starbucks.) More historic buildings are just a little farther on: 18th-century Faneuil Hall and the frenzied Quincy Market.

WHAT TO SEE

★ **Faneuil Hall.** The single building facing Congress Street is the real Faneuil Hall, though locals often give that name to all five buildings in this shopping complex. Bostonians pronounce it *Fan-*yoo'uhl or *Fan-*yuhl. It was erected in 1742, the gift of wealthy merchant Peter Faneuil, who wanted the hall to serve as both a place for town meetings and a public market. It burned in 1761 and was immediately reconstructed according to its original design. In 1763 the political leader James Otis helped inaugurate the era that culminated in American independence when he dedicated the rebuilt hall to the cause of liberty.

Inside Faneuil Hall are dozens of paintings of famous Americans, including the mural *Webster's Reply to Hayne,* Gilbert Stuart's portrait of Washington at Dorchester Heights. Park rangers give informational talks about the history and importance of Faneuil Hall on the hour and half-tour. The rangers are a good resource, as interpretive plaques are few. On the building's top floors are the headquarters and museum of the Ancient & Honorable Artillery Company of Massachusetts. Founded in 1638, it's the oldest militia in the Western Hemisphere, and the third oldest in the world, after the Swiss Guard and the Honorable Artillery Company of London. Its status is now strictly ceremonial, but it's justly proud of the arms, uniforms, and other artifacts on display. Admission is free. The museum is open weekdays 9 to 3:30. ☎ *617/227–1638* ⊠ *Faneuil Hall Sq., Government Center* ☎ *617/523–1300* ⊕ *www.cityofboston.gov/freedomtrail/faneuilhall. asp* ⌲ *Free* ☉ *Great Hall daily 9–5; informational talks every ½ hr. Shops Mon.–Sat. 10 am–9 pm, Sun. noon–6 pm* Ⓣ *Government Center, Aquarium, State.*

Fodor's Choice
★

Holocaust Memorial. At night its six 50-foot-high glass-and-steel towers glow like ghosts. During the day the monument seems at odds with the 18th-century streetscape of Blackstone Square behind it. Shoe-horned into the north end of Union Park, the Holocaust Memorial is the work of Stanley Saitowitz, whose design was selected through an international competition; the finished memorial was dedicated in 1995. Recollections by Holocaust survivors are set into the glass-and-granite walls; the upper levels of the towers are etched with 6 million numbers in random sequence, symbolizing the Jewish victims of the Nazi horror. Manufactured steam from grates in the granite base makes for a particularly haunting scene after dark. ⊠ *Union St. near Hanover St., Government Center.*

CHARLESTOWN

Boston started here. Charlestown was a thriving settlement a year before colonials headed across the Charles River at William Blaxton's invitation to found the city proper. Today the district's attractions include two of the most visible—and vertical—monuments in Boston: the Bunker Hill Monument, which commemorates the grisly battle that became a symbol of patriotic resistance against the British, and the USS *Constitution,* whose masts continue to tower over the waterfront where she was built more than 200 years ago.

WHAT TO SEE

Fodor's Choice
★

Bunker Hill Monument. Three misunderstandings surround this famous monument. First, the Battle of Bunker Hill was actually fought on Breed's Hill, which is where the monument sits today. Second, although the battle is generally considered a colonial success, the Americans lost. It was a Pyrrhic victory for the British Redcoats, who sacrificed nearly half of their 2,200 men; American casualties numbered 400–600. And third: the famous war cry "Don't fire until you see the whites of their eyes" may never have been uttered by American Colonel William Prescott or General Israel Putnam, but if either one did shout it, he was quoting an old Prussian command made necessary by the notorious inaccuracy of the musket. No matter. The Americans did employ a deadly delayed-action strategy on June 17, 1775, and conclusively proved themselves worthy fighters, capable of defeating the forces of the British Empire.

In 1823 the committee formed to construct a monument on the site of the battle chose the form of an Egyptian obelisk. Architect Solomon Willard designed a 221-foot-tall granite obelisk, a tremendous feat of engineering for its day. Daniel Webster's stirring words at the ceremony commemorating the laying of its cornerstone have gone down in history: "Let it rise! Let it rise, till it meets the sun in his coming. Let the earliest light of the morning gild it, and parting day linger and play upon its summit."

The monument's zenith is reached by a flight of 294 steps. There's no elevator, but the views from the observatory are worth the effort of the arduous climb. A statue of Colonel Prescott stands guard at the base. In the Bunker Hill Museum across the street, artifacts and exhibits tell the story of the battle, while a detailed diorama shows the action in miniature. ☎ *617/242–5641* ⊕ *www.nps.gov/bost/historyculture/bhm. htm.* ⚑ *Free* ⊙ *Museum daily 9–5, monument daily 9–4:30* Ⓣ *Community College.*

⟳ **USS Constitution.** Better known as "Old Ironsides," the USS *Constitution* rides proudly at anchor in her berth at the Charlestown Navy Yard. The oldest commissioned ship in the U.S. fleet is a battlewagon of the old school, of the days of "wooden ships and iron men"—when she and her crew of 200 succeeded at the perilous task of asserting the sovereignty of an improbable new nation. Every July 4 and on certain other occasions she's towed out for a turnabout in Boston Harbor, the very place her keel was laid in 1797.

Fodor'sChoice
★

The venerable craft has narrowly escaped the scrap heap several times in her long history. She was launched on October 21, 1797, as part of the nation's fledgling navy. Her hull was made of live oak, the toughest wood grown in North America; her bottom was sheathed in copper, provided by Paul Revere at a nominal cost. Her principal service was during Thomas Jefferson's campaign against the Barbary pirates, off the coast of North Africa, and in the War of 1812. In 42 engagements her record was 42–0.

The men and women who look after the *Constitution,* regular navy personnel, maintain a 24-hour watch. Sailors show visitors around the ship, guiding them to her top, or spar, deck, and the gun deck below. Another treat when visiting the ship is the spectacular view of Boston across Boston Harbor. ⊠ *Charlestown Navy Yard, 55 Constitution Rd., Charlestown* ☎ *617/242–7511* ⊕ *www.history.navy.mil/ USSconstitution/index.html* ⚑ *Free* ⊙ *Apr. 1–Oct., Tues.–Sun. 10–6; Nov.–Mar. 31, Thurs.–Sun. 10–4; last tour at 3:30* Ⓣ *North Station.*

DOWNTOWN

Boston's commercial and financial districts—the area commonly called Downtown—are concentrated in a maze of streets that seem to have been laid out with little logic; they are, after all, only village lanes that happen to be lined with modern 40-story office towers. Just as the Great Fire of 1872 swept the old Financial District clear, the Downtown construction in more-recent times has obliterated many of the buildings where 19th-century Boston businessmen sat in front of their rolltop desks. Yet many historic sites remain tucked among the skyscrapers; a number of them have been linked together to make up a fascinating section of the Freedom Trail.

WHAT TO SEE

⟳ **Children's Museum.** Most children have so much fun here that they don't realize they're actually learning something. Creative hands-on exhibits demonstrate scientific laws, cultural diversity, and problem solving. After completing a massive 23,000 square-foot expansion in 2007, the museum has updated a lot of its old exhibitions and added new ones. Some of the most popular stops are also the simplest, like the bubble-making machinery and the two-story climbing maze. At the Japanese House you're invited to take off your shoes and step inside a two-story

Fodor'sChoice
★

The *U.S.S. Constitution* is the oldest commissioned warship afloat in the world.

silk merchant's home from Kyoto. The "Boston Black" exhibit stimulates dialogue about ethnicity and community while children play in a Cape Verdean restaurant and the African Queen Beauty Salon. In the toddler PlaySpace, children under three can run free in a safe environment. There's also a full schedule of special exhibits, festivals, and performances. ⊠ *300 Congress St., Downtown* ☎ *617/426–6500* ⊕ *www.bostonkids.org* ✉ *$12, Fri. 5–9 $1* ⊙ *Sat.–Thurs. 10–5, Fri. 10–9* Ⓣ *South Station.*

New England Aquarium. This aquarium challenges you to really imagine life under and around the sea. Seals bark outside the West Wing, its glass-and-steel exterior constructed to mimic fish scales. Inside the main facility you can see penguins, sea otters, sharks, and other exotic sea creatures—more than 2,000 species in all. In the semi-enclosed outdoor space of the New Balance Foundation Marine Mammal Center visitors enjoy the antics of northern fur seals while gazing at a stunning view of Boston Harbor. Some of the aquarium's 2,000 sea creatures make their home in the four-story, 200,000-gallon ocean-reef tank, one of the largest of its kind in the world. Ramps winding around the tank lead to the top level and allow you to view the inhabitants from many vantage points. Don't miss the five-times-a-day feedings; each lasts nearly an hour and takes divers 24 feet into the tank. ⊠ *Central Wharf between Central and Milk Sts., 1 Central Wharf, Downtown* ☎ *617/973–5200* ⊕ *www.neaq.org* ✉ *$21.95, IMAX $9.95* ⊙ *July–early Sept., Sun.–Thurs. 9–6, Fri. and Sat. 9–7; early Sept.–June, weekdays 9–5, weekends 9–6* Ⓣ *Aquarium, State.*

Fodor's Choice ★

Old State House. This colonial-era landmark has one of the most recognizable facades in Boston, with its State Street gable adorned by a brightly gilded lion and unicorn, symbols of British imperial power. The original figures were pulled down in 1776. For proof that bygones are bygones, consider not only the restoration of the sculptures in 1880 but also that Queen Elizabeth II was greeted by cheering crowds on July 4, 1976, when she stood on the Old State House balcony (from which the Declaration of Independence was first read in public in Boston and which overlooks the site of the Boston Massacre). Immediately outside the Old State House, at 15 State Street, is a **visitor center** run by the National Park Service; it offers free brochures and has restrooms. ⊠ *206 Washington St., at State St., Downtown* ☎ *617/720–1713* ⊕ *www.bostonhistory.org* 🎫 *$7.50* ◷ *Sept.–Dec. and Feb.–June, daily 9–5; Jan., daily 9–4; July and Aug., daily 9–6* Ⓣ *State.*

THE BACK BAY AND THE SOUTH END

In the folklore of American neighborhoods, the Back Bay stands with New York's Park Avenue and San Francisco's Nob Hill as a symbol of propriety and high social standing. Before the 1850s it really was a bay, a tidal flat that formed the south bank of a distended Charles River. The filling in of land along the isthmus that joined Boston to the mainland (the Neck) began in 1850, and resulted in the creation of the South End. To the north a narrow causeway called the Mill Dam (later Beacon Street) was built in 1814 to separate the Back Bay from the Charles. By the late 1800s Bostonians had filled in the shallows to as far as the marshland known as the Fenway, and the original 783-acre peninsula had been expanded by about 450 acres. Thus the waters of Back Bay became the neighborhood of Back Bay.

The nearby South End lost many residents to the Back Bay in the late 19th century, but in the late 1970s, middle-class professionals began snapping up town houses at bargain prices and restoring them. Solidly back in fashion now, the South End's redbrick row houses in various states of refurbished splendor now house a mix of ethnic groups, the city's largest gay community, and some excellent shops.

WHAT TO SEE

Back Bay Mansions. If you like nothing better than to imagine how the other half lives, you'll suffer no shortage of old homes to sigh over in Boston's Back Bay. Most, unfortunately, are off-limits to visitors, but there's no law against gawking from the outside. Stroll Commonwealth, Beacon and Marlborough streets for the best views.

ⓒ **Boston Public Garden.** Although the Boston Public Garden is often lumped
Fodor's Choice together with Boston Common, the two are separate entities with different histories and purposes and a distinct boundary between them at
★ Charles Street. The Common has been public land since Boston was founded in 1630, whereas the Public Garden belongs to a newer Boston, occupying what had been salt marshes on the edge of the Common. By 1837 the tract was covered with an abundance of ornamental plantings donated by a group of private citizens. The area was defined in 1856

by the building of Arlington Street, and in 1860 the architect George Meacham was commissioned to plan the park.

The central feature of the Public Garden is its irregularly shaped pond, intended to appear, from any vantage point along its banks, much larger than its nearly 4 acres. Near the Swan Boat dock is what has been described as the world's smallest suspension bridge, designed in 1867 to cross the pond at its narrowest point.

The Public Garden is America's oldest botanical garden, and has the finest formal plantings in central Boston. The beds along the main walkways are replanted for spring and summer. The tulips during the first two weeks of May are especially colorful, and there's a sampling of native and European tree species.

The dominant work among the park's statuary is Thomas Ball's equestrian **George Washington** (1869), which faces the head of Commonwealth Avenue at the Arlington Street gate. This is Washington in a triumphant pose as liberator, surveying a scene that, from where he stood with his cannons at Dorchester Heights, would have included an immense stretch of blue water. Several dozen yards to the north of Washington (to the right if you're facing Commonwealth Avenue) is the granite-and-red-marble **Ether Monument,** donated in 1866 by Thomas Lee to commemorate the advent of anesthesia 20 years earlier at nearby Massachusetts General Hospital.

The park contains a special delight for the young at heart; follow the pathway between the pond and the park entrance at Charles and Beacon streets to the *Make Way for Ducklings* bronze sculptures, a tribute to the 1941 classic children's story by Robert McCloskey. The pond has been famous since 1877 for its foot-pedal-powered (by a captain) **Swan Boats,** which make leisurely cruises during warm months. For the modest price of a few boat rides you can amuse children here for an hour or more. ⊠ *Bounded by Arlington, Boylston, Charles, and Beacon Sts., Back Bay* 🖀 *617/522–1966* ⊕ *www.swanboats.com* 🚢 *Swan Boats $2.75* ⊙ *Swan Boats mid-Apr.–June 20, daily 10–4; June 21–Labor Day, daily 10–5; day after Labor Day–mid-Sept., weekdays noon–4, weekends 10–4* Ⓣ *Arlington.*

★ **Boston Public Library.** This venerable institution is a handsome temple to literature and a valuable research library. The Renaissance Revival building was opened in 1895; a 1972 addition emulates the mass and proportion of the original, though not its extraordinary detail; this skylighted annex houses the library's circulating collections. **Bates Hall** is one of Boston's most sumptuous interior spaces. This is the main reference reading room, 218 feet long with a barrel-arch ceiling 50 feet high. ⊠ *700 Boylston St., at Copley Sq., Back Bay* 🖀 *617/536–5400* ⊕ *www.bpl.org* ⊙ *Mon.–Thurs. 9–9, Fri. and Sat. 9–5; Oct.–May, also Sun. 1–5. Free guided art and architecture tours Mon. at 2:30, Tues. and Thurs. at 6, Fri. and Sat. at 11, Sun. (Oct.–May) at 2* Ⓣ *Copley.*

Rutland Square. Reflecting a time when the South End was the most prestigious Boston address, this slice of a park is framed by lovely Italianate bowfront houses. ⊠ *Rutland Sq. between Columbus Ave. and Tremont St.*

Union Park. Cast-iron fences, Victorian-era town houses, and a grassy area all add up to one of Boston's most charming mini-escapes. ⊠ *Union Park St. between Shawmut Ave. and Tremont St.*

THE FENWAY

The marshland known as the Back Bay Fens gave this section of Boston its name, but two quirky institutions give it its character: Fenway Park, which in 2004 saw the triumphant reversal of an 86-year drought for Boston's beloved Red Sox, and the Isabella Stewart Gardner Museum, the legacy of a high-living Brahmin who attended a concert at Symphony Hall in 1912 wearing a headband that read, "Oh, You Red Sox." Not far from the Gardner is another major cultural magnet: the Museum of Fine Arts. Kenmore Square, a favorite haunt for Boston University students, adds a bit of funky flavor to the mix.

WHAT TO SEE

Fodor's Choice ★ **Fenway Park.** For 86 years, the Boston Red Sox suffered a World Series dry spell, a streak of bad luck that fans attributed to the "Curse of the Bambino," which, stories have it, struck the team in 1920 when they sold Babe Ruth (the "Bambino") to the New York Yankees. All that changed in 2004, when a maverick squad broke the curse in a thrilling seven-game series against the team's nemesis in the Series semifinals. This win against the Yankees was followed by a four-game sweep of St. Louis in the finals. Boston, and its citizens' ingrained sense of pessimism, hasn't been the same since. The repeat World Series win in 2007 has just cemented Bostonians' sense that the universe is finally working correctly and made Red Sox caps the residents' semiofficial uniform. ⊠ *4 Yawkey Way, between Van Ness and Lansdowne Sts., The Fenway* ☎ *877/733–7699 box office, 617/226–6666 tours* ⊕ *www.redsox.com* 🎫 *Tours $12* ⊙ *Tours Mon.–Sat. 9–4, Sun. 9–3; on game days, last tour is 3 hrs before game time* Ⓣ *Kenmore.*

Fodor's Choice ★ **Isabella Stewart Gardner Museum.** A spirited young society woman, Isabella Stewart had come in 1860 from New York—where ladies were more commonly seen and heard than in Boston—to marry John Lowell Gardner, one of Boston's leading citizens. "Mrs. Jack" promptly set about becoming the most un-Bostonian of the Proper Bostonians. She decided to build the Venetian palazzo to hold her collected arts in an isolated corner of Boston's newest neighborhood. Her will stipulated that the building remain exactly as she left it—paintings, furniture, and the smallest object in a hall cabinet—and that is as it has remained. Today, it's probably America's most idiosyncratic treasure house. ⊠ *280 The Fenway, The Fenway* ☎ *617/566–1401, 617/566–1088 café* ⊕ *www. gardnermuseum.org* 🎫 *$12* ⊙ *Museum Tues.–Sun. 11–5, open some holidays; café Tues.–Fri. 11:30–4, weekends 11–4* Ⓣ *Museum.*

Fodor's Choice ★ **Museum of Fine Arts.** Count on staying a while if you have any hope of seeing what's here. Eclecticism and thoroughness, often an incompatible pair, have coexisted agreeably at the MFA since its earliest days. From Renaissance and baroque masters to impressionist marvels to African masks to sublime samples of Native American pottery and contemporary crafts, the collections are happily shorn of both cultural

The legendary Fenway Park, one of baseball's most historic ballfields.

snobbery and shortsighted trendiness. ✉ *465 Huntington Ave., The Fenway* ☏ *617/267–9300* ⊕ *www.mfa.org* ✉ *$17; by donation Wed. 4–9:45* ⊘ *Sat.–Tues. 10–4:45, Wed.–Fri. 10–9:45. 1-hr tours daily; call for scheduled times* Ⓣ *Museum.*

CAMBRIDGE

The city of Cambridge takes a lot of hits, most of them thrown across the Charles River by jealous Bostonians. But Boston's Left Bank—an überliberal academic enclave—is a must-visit if you're spending more than a day or two in the Boston area.

The city is punctuated at one end by the funky tech-noids of MIT and at the other by the grand academic fortress that is Harvard University. Civic life connects the two camps into an urban stew of 100,000 residents who represent nearly every nationality in the world, work at every kind of job from tenured professor to taxi driver, and are passionate about living on this side of the river.

WHAT TO SEE

Ⓒ **Harvard Square.** An afternoon in the square is people-watching raised Fodor'sChoice to a high art; the parade of quirkiness never quits. You'll hear earnest ★ conversations in dozens of foreign languages; see every kind of youthful uniform from Goth to impeccable prep; wander by street musicians playing Andean flutes, singing opera, and doing excellent Stevie Wonder or Edith Piaf imitations; and lean in on a tense outdoor game of pickup chess between a street-tough kid and an older gent wearing a beard and a beret, while you slurp a cappuccino or an ice-cream cone (the two major food groups here).

Harvard Square is where Mass Ave., coming from Boston, turns and widens into a triangle broad enough to accommodate a brick peninsula (above the T station). Harvard Yard, with its lecture halls, residential houses, libraries, and museums, is one long border of the square; the other three are comprised of clusters of banks and a wide variety of restaurants and shops.

Across Garden Street, through an ornamental arch, is **Cambridge Common,** decreed a public pasture in 1631. It's said that under a large tree that once stood in this meadow George Washington took command of the Continental Army on July 3, 1775. A stone memorial now marks the site of the "Washington Elm." Also on the Common is the Irish Famine Memorial by Derry artist Maurice Herron, unveiled in 1997 to coincide with the 150th anniversary of "Black '47," the deadliest year of the potato famine. It depicts a desperate Irish mother sending her child off to America. At the center of the Common a large memorial commemorates the Union soldiers and sailors who lost their lives in the Civil War. On the far side of the Common (on Waterhouse Street between Garden Street and Massachusetts Avenue) is a fantastic park. ⊕ *www.harvardsquare.com* Ⓣ *Harvard.*

★ **Harvard University.** The tree-studded, shady, and redbrick expanse of **Harvard Yard**—the very center of Harvard University—has weathered the footsteps of Harvard students for more than 300 years. In 1636 the Great and General Court of the Massachusetts Bay Colony voted funds to establish the colony's first college, and a year later chose Cambridge as the site. Named in 1639 for John Harvard, a young Charlestown clergyman who died in 1638 and left the college his entire library and half his estate, Harvard remained the only college in the New World until 1693, by which time it was firmly established as a respected center of learning. Local wags refer to Harvard as WGU—World's Greatest University—and it's certainly the oldest and most famous American university. It boasts numerous schools or "faculties," including the Faculty of Arts and Sciences, the Medical School, the Law School, the Business School, and the John F. Kennedy School of Government.

Many of Harvard's cultural and scholarly facilities are important sights in themselves, including the **Harvard Museum of Natural History,** the **Peabody Museum of Archaeology & Ethnology,** and the **Widener Library.** Be aware that most campus buildings, other than museums and concert halls, are off-limits to the general public.

Harvard University Events & Information Center. Harvard University Events & Information Center, run by students, includes a small library, a video-viewing area, computer terminals, and an exhibit space. It also distributes maps of the university area and has free student-led tours of Harvard Yard. The tour doesn't include visits to museums, and it doesn't take you into campus buildings, but it provides a fine orientation. The information center is open year-round (except during spring recess and other semester breaks), Monday through Saturday 9–5. Tours are offered September–May, weekdays at 10 and 2 and Saturday at 2 (except during university breaks). From the end of June through August, guides offer four tours Monday–Saturday at 10, 11:15, 2, and 3:15. Groups of 20 or more can schedule their tours ahead. ⊠ *Holyoke Center, 1350 Massachusetts Ave.* ☎ *617/495–1573* ⊕ *www.harvard. edu* ⊠ *Bounded by Massachusetts Ave. and Mt. Auburn, Holyoke, and Dunster Sts.* ☎ *617/495–1000* ⊕ *www.harvard.edu* Ⓣ *Harvard.*

WHERE TO EAT

In a city synonymous with tradition, Boston chefs have spent recent years rewriting culinary history. The stuffy, wood-paneled formality is gone; the endless renditions of chowdah, lobster, and cod have retired; and the assumption that true foodies better hop the next Amtrak to New York is also—thankfully—a thing of the past.

In their place, a crop of young chefs have ascended, opening small, upscale neighborhood spots that use local New England ingredients to delicious effect. Traditional eats can still be found (Durgin Park remains the best place to get baked beans), but many diners now gravitate toward innovative food in understated environs. Whether you're looking for casual French, down-home Southern cooking, some of the best sushi in the country, or Vietnamese banh mi sandwiches, Boston restaurants are ready to deliver.

WHAT IT COSTS

	¢	$	$$	$$$	$$$$
Restaurants	under $10	$10–$17	$18–$24	$25–$35	over $35

Price per person for a median main course or equivalent combination of smaller dishes.

BEACON HILL

$$–$$$
SEAFOOD
☺

✕ **Legal Sea Foods.** What began as a tiny restaurant upstairs over a Cambridge fish market has grown to important regional status, with more than 30 East Coast locations, plus a handful of national ones. The hallmark is the freshest possible seafood, whether you have it wood-grilled, in New England chowder, or doused with an Asia-inspired sauce. The smoked-bluefish pâté is delectable, and the clam chowder is so good it has become a menu staple at presidential inaugurations. This location has private dining inside its beautiful, bottle-lined wine cellar. ⊠ *26 Park Sq., Theater District* ☎ *617/426–4444* ⊕ *www.legalseafoods.com* ▭ *AE, D, DC, MC, V* Ⓣ *Arlington.*

$$$$
CONTINENTAL
Fodor's Choice
★

✕ **No. 9 Park.** The stellar cuisine at Chef Barbara Lynch's first restaurant continues to draw plenty of well-deserved attention from its place in the shadow of the State House's golden dome. Settle into the plush but unpretentious dining room and indulge in pumpkin risotto with rare lamb or the memorably rich prune-stuffed gnocchi drizzled with bits of foie gras, the latter of which is always offered even if you don't see it on the menu. The wine list bobs and weaves into new territory, but is always well chosen, and the savvy bartenders are of the classic ilk, so you'll find plenty of classics and very few cloying, dessertlike sips here. ⊠ *9 Park St., Beacon Hill* ☎ *617/742–9991* ⊕ *www.no9park.com* ⊟ *AE, D, DC, MC, V* Ⓣ *Park St.*

GOVERNMENT CENTER

$$ ✕ **Durgin Park Market Dining Room.** You should be hungry enough to cope
AMERICAN with enormous portions, yet not so hungry you can't tolerate a long
wait (or sharing a table with others). Durgin Park was serving its same
hearty New England fare (Indian pudding, baked beans, corned beef
and cabbage, and a prime rib that hangs over the edge of the plate) back
when Faneuil Hall was a working market instead of a tourist attraction.
The service is as brusque as it was when fishmongers and boat captains
dined here, but that's just part of its charm. ⊠ *340 Faneuil Hall Market
Pl., North Market Bldg.* ☎ *617/227–2038* ⊕ *www.arkrestaurants.com/
durgin_park.html* ⊟ *AE, D, DC, MC, V* Ⓣ *Government Center.*

DOWNTOWN

$$$$ ✕ **O Ya.** Despite its side-street location and hidden door, O Ya isn't
JAPANESE exactly a secret: dining critics from the *New York Times, Bon Appe-*
Fodor's Choice *tit,* and *Food & Wine* have all named this tiny, improvisational sushi
★ spot among the best in the country. Chef Tim Cushman's nigiri menu
features squid-ink bubbles, homemade potato chips—even foie gras.
Other dishes offer a nod to New England, such as the braised pork
with Boston baked beans and grilled lobster with a light shiso tempura.
Cushman's wife Nancy oversees an extensive sake list that includes spar-
kling and aged varieties. ⊠ *9 East St., Leather District* ☎ *617/654–9900*
⊕ *www.oyarestaurantboston.com* ⊟ *AE, MC, V* ☾ *Closed Sun. and
Mon. No lunch* Ⓣ *South Station.*

BACK BAY AND SOUTH END

$–$$ ✕ **B&G Oysters, Ltd.** Chef Barbara Lynch (of No. 9 Park, the Butcher
SEAFOOD Shop, and Sportello fame) has made yet another fabulous mark on
Fodor's Choice Boston with a style-conscious seafood restaurant that updates New
★ England's traditional bounty with flair. Designed to imitate the inside
of an oyster shell, the iridescent bar glows with silvery, candlelit tiles
and a sophisticated crowd. They're in for the lobster roll, no doubt—
an expensive proposition at $27, but worth every cent for its decadent
chunks of meat in a perfectly textured dressing. If you're sans reservation, be prepared to wait: the line for a seat can be epic. ⊠ *550 Tremont
St., South End* ☎ *617/423–0550* ⊕ *www.bandgoysters.com* ⟐ *Reservations essential* ⊟ *AE, D, DC, MC, V* Ⓣ *Back Bay/South End.*

$$$$ ✕ **Clio.** Years ago, when Ken Oringer opened his snazzy leopard skin–
FRENCH lined hot spot in the tasteful boutique Eliot Hotel, the hordes were
Fodor's Choice fighting over reservations. Things have quieted down since then, but
★ the food hasn't. Luxury offerings including foie gras, Maine lobster, and
Kobe sirloin share menu space with fail-safe crispy chicken and Scottish
salmon. A magnet for romantics and foodies alike, the place contin-
ues to serve some of the city's most decadent and well-crafted meals.
⊠ *Eliot Hotel, 370 Commonwealth Ave., Back Bay* ☎ *617/536–7200*
⊕ *www.cliorestaurant.com* ⟐ *Reservations essential* ⊟ *AE, D, MC, V*
☾ *No lunch* Ⓣ *Hynes.*

2

$$$$
FRENCH
Fodor's Choice
★

✕ **L'Espalier.** Chef-owner Frank McClelland's dishes—from caviar and roasted foie gras to venison with escargots de Bourgogne—are as elegant and sublime. In the evening, three-course prix-fixe and seasonal degustation menus tempt discriminating diners. A budget-minded, Power lunch as well as à la carte options are available weekday afternoons. Finger sandwiches and sublime sweets are served for weekend tea. ✉ *774 Boylston St., Back Bay* ☎ *617/262–3023* ⊕ *www.lespalier. com* 🍴 *Reservations essential* ▭ *AE, D, DC, MC, V* ⊙ *Closed Sun. No lunch weekends* Ⓣ *Copley.*

NORTH END

$
ITALIAN
Fodor's Choice
★

✕ **Antico Forno.** Many of the menu choices here come from the eponymous wood-burning brick oven, which turns out surprisingly delicate pizzas simply topped with tomato and fresh buffalo mozzarella. But though its pizzas receive top billing, Antico excels at a variety of Italian country dishes. Don't overlook the hearty baked dishes and handmade pastas; the specialty, gnocchi, is rich and creamy but light. The terracotta–walled room is cramped and noisy, but also homey and comfortable—which means that your meal will resemble a raucous dinner with an adopted Italian family. ✉ *93 Salem St., North End* ☎ *617/723–6733* ⊕ *www.anticofornoboston.com* ▭ *AE, D, MC, V* Ⓣ *Haymarket.*

$
SEAFOOD

✕ **Daily Catch.** You've just got to love this place—for the noise, the intimacy, the complete absence of pretense, and, above all, the food. Shoulder-crowdingly small and always brightly lighted, the storefront restaurant, a local staple for more than 30 years, specializes in calamari dishes, black-squid-ink pastas, and linguine with clam sauce. There's something about a big skillet of linguine and calamari that would seem less perfect if served on fine white china. ✉ *323 Hanover St., North End* ☎ *617/523–8567* ⊕ *www.dailycatch.com* 🍴 *Reservations not accepted* ▭ *No credit cards* Ⓣ *Haymarket.*

KENMORE SQUARE

$$
AMERICAN
Fodor's Choice
★

✕ **Eastern Standard Kitchen and Drinks.** A vivid red awning beckons patrons of this spacious brasserie-style restaurant. The bar area and red banquettes are filled most nights with Boston's power players (members of the Red Sox management are known to stop in), thirtysomethings, and students from the nearby universities all noshing on raw-bar specialties and comfort dishes such as lamb-sausage rigatoni, rib eye, and burgers. It's a Sunday-brunch hot spot, especially on game days (the Big Green Monster is a very short walk away). The cocktail list is one of the best in town, filled with old classics and new concoctions. A covered, heated patio offers alfresco dining much of the year. ✉ *528 Commonwealth Ave., Kenmore Sq.* ☎ *617/532–9100* ⊕ *www.easternstandardboston. com* ▭ *AE, D, MC, V* Ⓣ *Kenmore.*

WHERE TO STAY

At one time, great lodging was scarce in Boston. If you were a persnickety blueblood in town to visit relatives, you checked into the Charles or the old Ritz on Newbury. If you were a parent in town to see your kid graduate from one of the city's many universities, you suffered through a stay at a run-down chain. And if you were a young couple in town for a little romance, well, you could just forget it. A dearth of suitable rooms practically defined us. Oh, how things have changed.

About five years ago Boston finally got wise to modernization, and a rush of new construction took the local hotel scene by storm. Sleek, boutique accommodations began inviting guests to Cambridge and Downtown, areas once relegated to alumni and business traveler sets. New, mega-luxury lodgings infiltrated posh Back Bay, while high-end, hipster-friendly spots are drawing visitors to up-and-coming 'hoods.

Speaking of revamped, it seems that nearly every hotel in town just got a face-lift. From spruced up decor (good-bye, grandma's bedspread; hello, puffy white duvets) to hopping restaurant-bars to new spas and fitness centers, Boston's lodgings are feeling the competitive heat and acting accordingly. You don't just get a room anymore—you get an experience.

Of course, as in any industry, the recession hit a plethora of new and old properties hard. While business is picking up, many lodgings have slashed their rates—and introduced stellar weekend deals—so don't be afraid to aim four-star if you think you can only afford three.

Hotel reviews have been condensed for this book. Please go to Fodors. com for full reviews of each property.

WHAT IT COSTS FOR HOTELS

	¢	$	$$	$$$	$$$$
Hotels	under $100	$100–$199	$200–$299	$300–$399	over $400

Prices are for two people in a standard double room in high season, excluding 14.45% tax and service charges.

DOWNTOWN

$$$$
Fodor'sChoice
★

Boston Harbor Hotel at Rowes Wharf. Boston has plenty of iconic landmarks, but none are as synonymous with über-hospitality as the Boston Harbor Hotel's 80-foot-tall outdoor archway and rotunda. **Pros:** high-quality Meritage and Sea Grille restaurants; easy walk to Faneuil Hall; water shuttle to Logan Airport. **Cons:** pricey; the spa gets booked up early; less convenient to the Back Bay and South End. ⊠ *70 Rowes Wharf, Downtown/Waterfront* ☎ *617/439–7000 or 800/752–7077* ⊕ *www.bhh.com* ✍ *204 rooms, 26 suites* ⏃ *In-room: safe, Wi-Fi. In-hotel: restaurant, bar, pool, gym, spa, parking, some pets allowed* ⁑❘○❘ *No meals* Ⓣ *Aquarium, South Station.*

$$$$
Fodor'sChoice
★

Nine Zero. Nine Zero knows that hotel rooms can get a little lonely, and that's why the Downtown spot instated its "guppy love" program; yes, that's right, you get a pet fish on loan. **Pros:** pet-friendly; kid-friendly; lobby wine-tasting every evening (from 5 to 6); Mario Russo bath products. **Cons:** smallish rooms; high parking fees. ⊠ *90 Tremont St., Downtown* ☎ *617/772–5800 or 866/906–9090* ⊟ *617/772–5810* ⊕ *www.ninezero.com* ✍ *185 rooms, 5 suites* ⏃ *In-room: safe, Internet. In-hotel: restaurant, bar, gym, children's programs, parking (paid), some pets allowed* ⁑❘○❘ *No meals* Ⓣ *Park St., Government Center.*

$$$ ⌨ **Onyx Hotel.** Sexy, supper-club atmosphere oozes from this five-year-old contemporary Kimpton Group hotel a block from North Station, making it a favorite of hipsters and hoopsters alike. **Pros:** good location for catching a sporting event or concert at the Garden; near North Station commuter rail and T stop; near several inexpensive restaurants and bars. **Cons:** smallish rooms and bathrooms; small gym; neighborhood can get noisy at night. ⊠ *155 Portland St., Downtown* ☎ *617/557–9955 or 866/660–6699* ⊕ *www.onyxhotel.com* ⟿ *110 rooms, 2 suites* ⟁ *In-room: safe, Wi-Fi. In-hotel: restaurant, bar, gym, parking, some pets allowed* ⦿ *No meals* Ⓣ *North Station.*

$$ ⌨ **Renaissance Boston Waterfront Hotel.** Set along the working wharves of Boston Harbor, near the must-visit Institute of Contemporary Art, the Renaissance plays to a watery theme. **Pros:** sleek new lobby Capiz Bar and Lounge; close to the Silver Line (airport transportation) and convention center. **Cons:** some guest-room harbor views are more industrial than scenic; hordes of conventioneers; far from major city attractions. ⊠ *606 Congress St., Downtown/Seaport District* ☎ *617/338–4111 or 888/796–4664* ⊕ *www.renaissanceboston.com* ⟿ *450 rooms, 21 suites* ⟁ *In-room: safe, Wi-Fi. In-hotel: restaurant, bar, pool, gym, spa, children's programs, parking* ⦿ *No meals* Ⓣ *World Trade Center.*

BACK BAY AND SOUTH END

$$
Fodor'sChoice
★
⌨ **Charlesmark Hotel.** Hipsters and romantics who'd rather spend their cash on a great meal than a hotel bill have put this skinny little place on the map. **Pros:** fantastic price for the location; free Wi-Fi and water bottles. **Cons:** hot-air heating system is noisy; not much storage space; rooms at the front of the house can be noisy. ⊠ *655 Boylston St., Back Bay* ☎ *617/247–1212* ⊕ *www.thecharlesmarkhotel.com* ⟿ *40 rooms* ⟁ *In-room: Wi-Fi. In-hotel: bar* ⦿ *Breakfast* Ⓣ *Copley.*

$$$$
Fodor'sChoice
★
⌨ **Eliot Hotel.** One of the city's best small hotels expertly merges the old blue-blood Boston aesthetic with modern flair (See: zebra-print rugs mingling with crystal chandeliers), and everyone from well-heeled Sox fans to traveling CEOs to tony college parents has noticed. **Pros:** super location; top-notch restaurants; pet-friendly; beautiful rooms. **Cons:** very expensive; some complain of elevator noise. ⊠ *370 Commonwealth Ave., Back Bay* ☎ *617/267–1607 or 800/443–5468* ⊕ *www.eliothotel.com* ⟿ *16 rooms, 79 suites* ⟁ *In-room: Wi-Fi. In-hotel: restaurant, bar, parking, some pets allowed* ⦿ *No meals* Ⓣ *Hynes.*

$$$$
☾
Fodor'sChoice
★
⌨ **Fairmont Copley Plaza.** Past guests at the Fairmont, including one Judy Garland, felt at home in the decadent, unabashedly romantic hotel, and present guests feel much the same way, thanks to the meticulous preservation of the 1912 stallwart. **Pros:** very elegant; famous cozy bar. **Cons:** tiny bathrooms with scratchy towels; charge for Internet access (no charge on Fairmont Gold level); small fitness center. ⊠ *138 St. James Ave., Back Bay* ☎ *617/267–5300 or 866/540–4417* ⊕ *www.fairmont.com/copleyplaza* ⟿ *366 rooms, 17 suites* ⟁ *In-room: safe, Wi-Fi. In-hotel: restaurant, bar, gym, parking, some pets allowed* ⦿ *No meals* Ⓣ *Copley, Back Bay/South End.*

Shoppers take a break at a Newbury Street café.

KENMORE SQUARE

$$$
☺
Fodor'sChoice
★

🛏 **Hotel Commonwealth.** Luxury and service without pretense makes the hip spot a solid choice. **Pros:** free Wi-Fi; down bedding; perfect locale for Red Sox fans; happening bar scene at Eastern Standard. **Cons:** area is mobbed during Sox games; small gym. ✉ *500 Commonwealth Ave., Kenmore Square* 🕾 *617/933–5000 or 866/784–4000* ⊕ *www. hotelcommonwealth.com* 🖙 *149 rooms, 1 suite* ⚒ *In-room: safe, Wi-Fi. In-hotel: restaurant, bar, gym, children's programs, parking, some pets allowed* ⦿ *No meals* Ⓣ *Kenmore.*

SHOPPING

Shopping in Boston is a lot like the city itself: a mix of classic and cutting-edge, the high-end and the handmade, and international and local sensibilities. Though many Bostonians think too many chain stores have begun to clog their distinctive avenues, there remains a strong network of idiosyncratic gift stores, handicrafts shops, galleries, and a growing number of savvy, independent fashion boutiques. For the well-heeled, there are also plenty of glossy international designer shops.

There's no state sales tax on clothing. However, there's a 5% luxury tax on clothes priced higher than $175 per item; the tax is levied on the amount in excess of $175.

MAJOR SHOPPING DISTRICTS

Boston's shops and department stores are concentrated in the area bounded by Quincy Market, the Back Bay, and Downtown. There are plenty of bargains in the Downtown Crossing area. The South End's gentrification creates its own kind of consumerist milieus, from houseware shops to avant-garde art galleries. In Cambridge you can find lots of shopping around Harvard and Central squares, with independent boutiques migrating west along Massachusetts Avenue (or Mass Ave., as the locals and almost everyone else calls it) toward Porter Square and beyond.

BOSTON Pretty **Charles Street** is crammed beginning to end with top-notch antiques stores such as Judith Dowling Asian Art, Eugene Galleries, and Devonia, as well as a handful of independently owned fashion boutiques whose prices reflect their high Beacon Hill rents. River Street, parallel to Charles Street, is also an excellent source for antiques. Both are easy walks from the Charles Street T stop on the Red Line.

Copley Place (⊠ *100 Huntington Ave., Back Bay* ☎ *617/369–5000* Ⓣ *Copley*), an indoor shopping mall in the Back Bay, includes such high-end shops as Christian Dior, Louis Vuitton, and Gucci, anchored by the pricey but dependable Neiman Marcus and the flashy, overpriced Barneys. A skywalk connects Copley Place to the **Prudential Center** (⊠ *800 Boylston St., Back Bay* ☎ *800/746–7778* Ⓣ *Hynes*). The Pru, as it's often called, contains moderately priced chain stores such as Ann Taylor and the Body Shop.

Downtown Crossing (⊠ *Washington St. from Amory St. to about Milk St., Downtown* Ⓣ *Downtown Crossing, Park St.*) is a pedestrian mall with a Macy's, H&M, and TJ Maxx. Millennium Place, a 1.8-million-square-foot complex with a Ritz-Carlton Hotel, condos, a massive sports club, a 19-screen Loews Cineplex, and the brand new W Hotel turned this once seedy hangout into a happening spot.

Faneuil Hall Marketplace (⊠ *Bounded by Congress St., Atlantic Ave., the Waterfront, and Government Center, Downtown* ☎ *617/523–1300* Ⓣ *Government Center*) is a huge complex that's also hugely popular, even though most of its independent shops have given way to Banana Republic, Crate & Barrel, and other chains. The place has plenty of history, one of the area's great à la carte casual dining experiences (Quincy Market), and carnival-like trappings: pushcarts sell everything from silver jewelry to Peruvian sweaters, and buskers perform crowd-pleasing feats such as break dancing.

★ **Newbury Street** (Ⓣ *Arlington, Copley, Hynes*) is Boston's version of New York's 5th Avenue. The entire street is a shoppers' paradise, from high-end names such as Brooks Brothers to tiny specialty shops such as the Fish and Bone. Upscale clothing stores, up-to-the-minute art galleries, and dazzling jewelers line the street near the Public Garden. As you head toward Mass Ave., Newbury gets funkier and the cacophony builds, with skateboarders zipping through traffic and garbage-pail drummers burning licks outside the hip boutiques. The big-name stores run from Arlington Street to the Prudential Center. Parallel to Newbury Street is **Boylston Street**, where a few standouts, such as Shreve, Crump & Low, are scattered among the other chains and restaurants.

South End ([T] *Back Bay/South End*) merchants are benefiting from the ongoing gentrification that has brought high real-estate prices and trendy restaurants to the area. Explore the chic home-furnishings and gift shops that line Tremont Street, starting at Berkeley Street. The MBTA's Silver Line bus runs through the South End.

CAMBRIDGE **Central Square** (⊠ *East of Harvard Sq.* [T] *Central*) has an eclectic mix of furniture stores, used-record shops, ethnic restaurants, and small, hip performance venues.

Harvard Square ([T] *Harvard*) takes up just a few blocks but holds more than 150 stores selling clothes, books, records, furnishings, and specialty items.

A handful of chains and independent boutiques are clustered on **Brattle St.** (⊠ *Behind Harvard Sq.* [T] *Harvard*).

Porter Square (⊠ *West on Mass Ave. from Harvard Sq.* [T] *Porter*) has distinctive clothing stores, as well as crafts shops, coffee shops, natural-food stores, restaurants, and bars with live music.

SPECIALTY STORES

CLOTHING **Bobby from Boston.** For years this hidden gem was kept on the down
Fodor'sChoice low—but the word's out. Owner Bobby Garnett's been in the vintage
★ game for decades, and his one-of-a-kind finds are unmatched. The two-room space is mostly menswear, but there are plenty of finds for females, too. ⊠ *19 Thayer St., South End* ☎ *617/423–9299* ۞ *Tues.– Sun. noon–6. Closed Mon.*

SNEAKERS **Concepts.** Sneaker collectors love having what other people can't find.
Fodor'sChoice At Concepts, fanatics will line up around the block when a limited-
★ edition shoe debuts. Their store features exclusives by Nike, Jordan, Clarks, Adidas, and more. ⊠ *37 Brattle St., Cambridge* ☎ *617/868– 2001* ⊕ *cncpts.com* ۞ *Daily 10–7.*

BOOKS **Harvard Book Store.** The intellectual community is well served here, with
Fodor'sChoice a slew of new titles upstairs and used and remaindered books down-
★ stairs. The collection's diversity has made the store a favored destination for academics. ⊠ *1256 Massachusetts Ave., Cambridge* ☎ *617/661– 1515* [T] *Harvard*.

CLOTHING **Louis Boston.** Impeccably tailored designs, subtly updated classics, and
Fodor'sChoice the latest Italian styles highlight a wide selection of imported clothing
★ and accessories. Visiting celebrities might be trolling the racks along with you as jazz spills out into the street from the adjoining Restaurant L. ⊠ *60 Northern Ave., South Boston* ☎ *617/262–6100* ۞ *Mon.–Wed. 11–6, Thurs.–Sat. 11–7, Sun. 11:30–5* [T] *South Station*.

CLOTHING **Shake the Tree.** This one-stop shop has an eclectic array of contemporary
Fodor'sChoice clothing, bags, jewelry, gifts, and home items. ⊠ *67 Salem St., North*
★ *End* ☎ *617/742–0484* ⊕ *shakethetreeboston.com* ۞ *Mon. 11–6, Tues. and Wed. 11–7, Thurs. and Fri. 11–8, Sat. 10–8, Sun. noon–5.*

Cape Cod

WORD OF MOUTH

"The essence of Cape Cod is to relax, see the beaches, do some outdoor activities: bike, walk, see scenery, eat, perhaps visit some little artist galleries (the galleries are little, not the artists)."

—gail

WELCOME TO CAPE COD

TOP REASONS TO GO

★ **The Beaches:** The golden shore of Cape Cod National Seashore, the sheltered sands of Dennis and Barnstable, and the frothy surf of the islands' southern shores are enchanting.

★ **Country Inns:** You'll find dozens of rambling, historic B&Bs with glorious water views and museum-quality antiques.

★ **The Great Outdoors:** Numerous outfitters offer whale-watching and deep-sea-fishing charters, several parks and preserves contain hiking paths through gardens and woodlands, and bike paths lace the entire peninsula and the islands.

★ **The Arts and Crafts:** Creative spirits have long been drawn to the region, and you can browse their creations at countless galleries, many of them concentrated in Provincetown, Wellfleet, and on the islands.

★ **The Food:** The Cape abounds with romantic, upscale eateries serving innovative seafood and regional American fare.

1 The Upper Cape. This area has much to recommend it, starting with its proximity to the Massachusetts mainland. Cape Cod's oldest towns are here, plus there are fine beaches and fascinating little museums. Falmouth, the region's commercial center, has a tidy downtown with brick storefronts housing local businesses. Many old seafarer's homes line the streets, adding a sense of history.

2 The Mid Cape. The Mid Cape has a bit of a Jekyll-and-Hyde complex. Route 6A is home to sophisticated colonial-era hamlets lined with antiques shops, smart taverns, and romantic bed-and-breakfasts, whereas Route 28 is crammed with motels and miniature golf courses. In the midst of it all sits Hyannis, the Cape's unofficial capital.

3 The Lower Cape. Casual clam shacks, lovely lighthouses, funky art galleries—the things we typically associate with the Cape are found here in abundance. The region's most stellar attractions, though, may be the natural ones: Monomoy National Wildlife Refuge, Nickerson State Park, and the start of the Cape Cod National Seashore. The beaches in Brewster and Orleans are treasured for long walks at low tide.

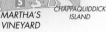

4 The Outer Cape. The narrow "forearm" of the Cape—less than 2 mi wide in some places—is famous for sand dunes, crashing surf, and scrubby pines. There's a sense of wild abandon here. The same can be said for Provincetown (the peninsula's "fist"). Frenetic and fun-loving, it's a leading gay getaway.

5 Martha's Vineyard. The Vineyard lies 5 mi off the Cape's southwest tip. The Down-Island towns are the most popular and most populated. But much of what makes this island special is found in its rural Up-Island reaches where dirt roads lead past crystalline ponds, cranberry bogs, and conservation lands.

6 Nantucket. Meaning "Far Away Island" in the Wampanoag tongue, Nantucket is some 25 mi south of Hyannis. Ferries dock in pretty Nantucket Town, where tourism services are concentrated. The rest of the island is mostly residential (trophy houses abound), and nearly all roads terminate in tiny beach communities.

GETTING ORIENTED

3

Henry David Thoreau, who famously traveled the sparsely populated mid-19th-century Cape Cod, likened the peninsula to "a bare and bended arm." Indeed—looking at a map the outline is obvious, and many people hold their own arm aloft and point to various places from shoulder to fist when asked for directions. There are three main roads that travel, more or less, the entire Cape: U.S. Highway 6, Route 28, and Route 6A, a designated historic road also called the Old King's Highway. Most visitors stick to these main byways, though the back roads can save time and aggravation in summer. The Cape is surrounded by water, though it's not a true island. Several bodies of water define the peninsula's land and seascapes: Just off the mainland to the southeast are the gentler, warmer waters of Buzzards Bay, Vineyard Sound, and Nantucket Sound. Cape Cod Bay extends north to the tip of Provincetown, where it meets the Atlantic Ocean.

Even if you haven't visited Cape Cod, you can likely imagine "sand dunes and salty air, quaint little villages here and there." As the 1950s Patti Page song promises, "you're sure to fall in love with old Cape Cod."

Cape Codders are fiercely protective of the environment. Despite some occasionally rampant development, planners have been careful to preserve nature and encourage responsible, eco-conscious building. Nearly 30% of the Cape's 412 square mi is protected from development, and another 35% has not yet been developed (on Nantucket and Martha's Vineyard, the percentages of protected land are far higher). Opportunities for sports and recreation abound, as the region is rife with biking and hiking trails, serene beaches, and waterways for boating and fishing. One somewhat controversial potential development has been a large-scale "wind farm" in Nantucket Sound, comprising some 130 turbines, each about 260 feet tall and several miles offshore.

Many don't realize that the Pilgrims landed here first: In November 1620, the lost and travel-weary sailors dropped anchor in what is now Provincetown Harbor and spent five weeks here, scouring the area for food and possible settlement. Were it not for the aid of the resident Native Americans, the strangers would have barely survived. Even so, they set sail again for fairer lands, ending up across Cape Cod Bay in Plymouth.

Virtually every period style of residential American architecture is well represented on Cape Cod, including, of course, the Cape-style house. These low, one-and-a-half-story domiciles with clapboard or shingle (more traditionally the latter in these parts) siding and gable roofs have been a fixture throughout Cape Cod since the late 17th century. You'll also find grand Georgian and Federal mansions, as well as handsome Greek Revival, Italianate, and Second Empire houses that date to Victorian times. Many of the most prominent residences were built for ship captains and sea merchants. In recent decades, the region has seen an influx of angular, glassy, contemporary homes, many with soaring windows and skylights and massive wraparound porches that take advantage of their enviable sea views.

PLANNING

WHEN TO GO

The Cape and islands teem with activity during high season: roughly Memorial Day to Labor Day or, in many cases, until Columbus Day. If you're dreaming of a classic shore vacation with lazy days at the beach, clambakes, and band concerts on the village green, this is prime time.

Needless to say, everyone knows it—which translates into daunting crowds and high costs. The good news is that the region is increasingly becoming a year-round destination. In fact, fall has begun to rival summer in popularity, at least on weekends through late October, when the weather is temperate and the scenery remarkable. A growing number of restaurants, shops, and hotels are remaining open in winter, too, making the area desirable even during the coldest months. On the islands and more far-flung sections of the Cape, though, many continue to close down January through March.

PLANNING YOUR TIME

The region can be enjoyed for a few days or a few weeks, depending on the nature of your trip. As the towns are all quite distinct on Cape Cod, it's best to cater your trip based on your interests: an outdoors enthusiast would want to head to the National Seashore region; those who prefer shopping and amusements would do better in the Mid-Cape area. As one Fodors.com forum member noted, the Cape is generally "not something to see . . . instead, people go to spend a few days or weeks, relax, go to the beach . . . that sort of thing." A full-day trip to Nantucket to wander the historic downtown is manageable; several days is best to appreciate Martha's Vineyard's diversity.

GETTING HERE

Air Travel. The major air gateways are Boston's Logan International Airport (BOS) and Providence's T. F. Green International Airport (PVD). Smaller municipal airports are located in Barnstable (HYA), Martha's Vineyard (MVY), Nantucket (ACK), and Provincetown (PVC).

Bus Travel. The Cape is served by the rather misleadingly named **Plymouth & Brockton Street Railway Company** (☎ 508/746–0378 ⊕ www.p-b. com). The line offers convenient connections from Logan International Airport and other mainland locales.

Car Travel. Cape Cod is easily reached from Boston via Route 3 and from Providence via I–195. Once you cross Cape Cod Canal, you can follow U.S. 6 all the way to the tip of the Cape. Without any traffic, it takes about an hour to 90 minutes to reach the Upper Cape (the portion nearest to mainland Massachusetts) from either Boston or Providence. Because delays getting onto and off Cape Cod are common throughout summer, allow an extra 30 to 60 minutes' travel time when driving in peak periods.

Ferry Travel. Bay State Cruise Company (☎ 617/748–1428 or 877/783–3779 ⊕ www.baystatecruisecompany.com) operates high-speed ferries between Boston and Provincetown from late spring to mid-October. **Boston Harbor Cruises** (☎ 617/227–4321 or 877/733–9425 ⊕ www. bostonharborcruises.com) is a good option for speedy trips between

Boston and Provincetown. **Capt. John Boats** (📞 *508/747–2400 or 800/242–2469* ⊕ *www.provincetownferry.com*) runs between Plymouth and Provincetown. **New England Fast Ferry** (📞 *866/683–3779* ⊕ *www.nefastferry.com*) shuttles passengers between New Bedford and Martha's Vineyard. **Vineyard Fast Ferry** (📞 *401/295–4040* ⊕ *www. vineyardfastferry.com*) runs between North Kingstown, Rhode Island, and Martha's Vineyard.

GETTING AROUND

Boat Travel. Freedom Cruise Line (📞 *508/432–8999* ⊕ *www.nantucketislandferry.com*) travels between Harwich Port and Nantucket.**Hy-Line** (📞 *508/778–2600 or 800/492–8082* ⊕ *www.hy-linecruises.com*) goes from Hyannis to Martha's Vineyard and Nantucket. **Island Queen** (📞 *508/548–4800* ⊕ *www.islandqueen.com*) connects Falmouth and Martha's Vineyard. The **Steamship Authority** (📞 *508/477–8600* ⊕ *www. steamshipauthority.com*) sails from Woods Hole to Martha's Vineyard, and from Hyannis to Nantucket.

Bus Travel. Cape Cod Regional Transit Authority (📞 *800/352–7155* ⊕ *www. capecodtransit.org*) provides service throughout the Cape. **Martha's Vineyard Transit Authority** (📞 *508/693–9940* ⊕ *www.vineyardtransit.com*) is a great way to get around Martha's Vineyard. **Nantucket Regional Transit Authority** (📞 *508/228–7025* ⊕ *www.shuttlenantucket.com*) circles Nantucket.

Car Travel. Unless you are planning to focus your attention on a single community, you'll probably need a car. Be aware that taking a vehicle onto Nantucket and Martha's Vineyard ferries is an expensive proposition (another option is renting upon arrival on either island).

EXPLORING CAPE COD

Continually shaped by ocean currents, this windswept land of sandy beaches and dunes has compelling natural beauty. Everyone comes for the seaside, yet the crimson cranberry bogs, forests of birch and beech, freshwater ponds, and marshlands that grace the interior are just as splendid. Local history is fascinating; whale-watching provides an exhilarating experience of the natural world; cycling trails lace the landscape; shops purvey everything from antiques to pure kitsch; and you can dine on simple fresh seafood, creative contemporary cuisine, or most anything in between.

Separated from the Massachusetts mainland by the 17.5-mi Cape Cod canal—at 480 feet, the world's widest sea-level canal—and linked to it by two heavily trafficked bridges, the Cape is likened in shape to an outstretched arm bent at the elbow, its Provincetown fist turned back toward the mainland.

Each of the Cape's 15 towns is broken up into villages, which is where things can get complicated. The town of Barnstable, for example, consists of Barnstable, West Barnstable, Cotuit, Marston Mills, Osterville, Centerville, and Hyannis. The terms Upper Cape and Lower Cape can also be confusing. Upper Cape—think upper arm, as in the shape of the Cape—refers to the towns of Bourne, Falmouth, Mashpee, and

Sandwich. Mid Cape includes Barnstable, Yarmouth, and Dennis. Brewster, Harwich, Chatham, Orleans, Eastham, Wellfleet, Truro, and Provincetown make up the Lower Cape.

THE UPPER CAPE

The Upper Cape has none of the briny, otherworldly breeziness of the Outer Cape and little of the resort feel of Lower Cape cousins like Chatham. The reason is solidly geographical: The Upper Cape's proximity to the mainland yields slightly less-brutal winters than elsewhere on the Cape and, consequently, a substantial year-round population; the region's beaches are intimate; and more of its attractions—freshwater ponds, conservation areas, and small museums—are inland.

If you're collecting superlatives, the Upper Cape is fertile. Sandwich is the oldest town on the Cape, Bourne was the Pilgrims' first Cape Cod settlement and an important trading area, and the first Native American reservation in the United States was established in Mashpee, which still has a large Wampanoag population and a tribal-council governing body.

Bourne. A quiet, year-round community, Bourne is the first town you reach on the Upper Cape. With cyclists exploring the Cape Cod Canal Bike Trail and anglers trolling in the waters of Buzzards Bay, Bourne is a diamond in the rough for outdoor enthusiasts.

Sandwich. With its streets lined with old homes, Sandwich is a glimpse into the Upper Cape's past. Don't miss the Sandwich Glass Museum, the restored 17th-century Grist Mill, and the 100-acre Heritage Museums and Gardens, featuring the J.K. Lilly III Automobile Collection.

Falmouth. This classic New England town, where sophisticated shopping and dining meet the best of beach and biking opportunities, includes the scientific enclave of Woods Hole, a lovely seaside village and embarkation point for ferries to Martha's Vineyard.

Mashpee. Home of the Native American Wampanoag Nation, Mashpee hosts a powwow every July. It draws discerning shoppers to Mashpee Commons and South Cape Village and avid golfers to top-tier courses like Willowbend and New Seabury.

WHAT TO SEE

Fodor's Choice
★

Heritage Museums and Gardens. These 100 beautifully landscaped acres overlooking the upper end of Shawme Pond are one of the region's top draws. Paths crisscross the grounds, which include gardens planted with hostas, heather, herbs, and fruit trees. Rhododendrons are in full glory from mid-May through mid-June, and daylilies reach their peak from mid-July through early August. In 1967, pharmaceuticals magnate Josiah K. Lilly III purchased the estate and turned it into a nonprofit museum. A highlight is the Shaker Round Barn, which showcases classic and historic cars—including a 1919 Pierce-Arrow, a 1915 Milburn Light Electric, and a 1911 Stanley Steamer, and a 1930 yellow-and-green Duesenberg built for movie star Gary Cooper. The history museum houses a semipermanent exhibit called "A Bird in the Hand," as well as seasonal exhibitions. The art museum has an extraordinary collection of New England folk art, including paintings, weather vanes,

Nantucket baskets, and scrimshaw. Both adults and children can enjoy riding on a Coney Island–style carousel dating from the early 20th century. Other features include Hidden Hollow, an outdoor activity center for families with children.

A shuttle bus—equipped with a wheelchair lift and space to stow baby strollers—transports visitors on certain days. In summer, concerts are held in the gardens, often on Wednesday or Saturday evening or Sunday afternoon. The center of the complex is about ¾ mi on foot from the in-town end of Shawme Pond. ⊠ *67 Grove St., Sandwich Center* ☎ *508/888–3300* ⊕ *www.heritagemuseumsandgardens.org* ⊠ *$12* ⊙ *Apr.–Nov., daily 10–5.*

THE MID CAPE

The Mid Cape includes the towns of Barnstable, Yarmouth, and Dennis, each divided into smaller townships and villages. Route 6A winds along the north shore through tree-shaded scenic towns and village centers, and Route 28 dips south through some of the more overdeveloped parts of the Cape. Generally speaking, if you want to avoid malls, heavy traffic, and cheesy motels, stay away from Route 28 from Falmouth to Chatham.

Barnstable, Hyannis, and Environs. Like a houseful of independently minded siblings, villages within Barnstable are widely different. The dignified village of Barnstable sits along historic Route 6A. West Barnstable, Cotuit, Osterville, Hyannis Port, Cummaquid, and Wianno are filled with art galleries and fine shops. Hyannis thrives on endless amusements.

Yarmouth. Along Route 6A and branching off onto many quiet lanes leading to the bay, Yarmouth Port is all grand architecture, fine art, and antiques. The sister towns of West Yarmouth and South Yarmouth are on the south side, right in the midst of the animated offerings along Route 28.

Dennis. Like Yarmouth, Dennis has multiple personalities. Dennis Village and East Dennis are quiet and historic, while Dennisport, West Dennis, and South Dennis have their share of lively entertainments.

WHAT TO SEE

John F. Kennedy Hyannis Museum. In Main Street's Old Town Hall, this museum explores JFK's Cape years (1934–63) through enlarged and annotated photographs culled from the archives of the JFK Library near Boston, as well as a seven-minute video narrated by Walter Cronkite. Also on-site is the **Cape Cod Baseball League Hall of Fame and Museum,** housed in several rooms in the basement of the JFK museum (which is appropriately referred to as "The Dugout"). Plaques of Hall of Famers, autographed items from former players who went on to play professional ball, and other Cape League memorabilia are on view; several films about the league and baseball itself are played continuously. ⊠ *397 Main St.* ☎ *508/790–3077* ⊕ *www.jfkhyannismuseum.org* ⊠ *$5; $8 for joint admission with baseball museum* ⊙ *Mid-Apr.–Memorial*

Much of the fragile landscape of the outer Cape is held together by its dune formations and the vegetation that grows within them.

Day, Mon.–Sat. 10–4, Sun. noon–4; Memorial Day–Oct., Mon.–Sat. 9–5, Sun. noon–5; Nov. and Dec., Thurs.–Sat. 10–4, Sun. noon–4.

THE LOWER CAPE

The towns of Harwich, Chatham, Brewster, Orleans, and Eastham make up the Lower Cape. Of these, only Brewster and Orleans touch Route 6A. Harwich, Chatham, and Orleans span Route 28—but have no fear. Although it's known for traffic, Route 28's congestion eases as the road winds toward the Lower Cape. Eastham sits along U.S. 6, which is the fastest way to get to all the towns—but if you're concerned about the journey as well as the destination, it's worthwhile to amble along Route 28 or 6A. Along the way, picturesque harbors, scenic side roads, and the towns' main streets, antiques stores, romantic inns, and colonial homes dot the landscape. Follow Route 28 into Chatham and make your way to the Chatham Lighthouse for breathtaking views of Nantucket Sound.

Brewster. Here you'll find an incredible number of beautifully preserved historic homes. Brewster beaches are famous for the expanse of sand revealed at low tide, as well as the striking sunsets. Visitors love the small-town feel, complete with plenty of unique shopping in specialty stores (no chains here) and antiques shops.

Harwich. Harwich has two personalities. The peaceful and more rural half is in Harwich, which has much history to share in its old cemeteries and museums. The fun-loving side with plenty of attractions to keep the kids happy is in Harwich Port, on Nantucket Sound.

Chatham. With a long Main Street filled with shops and restaurants, downtown Chatham is best explored on foot. You'll see grand houses at every turn, all meticulously kept with impressive gardens. Head to Chatham Light to see the untamed ocean, or ride a bike along back roads to see calm harbors.

Orleans. The commercial center of the lower Cape, Orleans retains its small-town feel. Rock Harbor, on Cape Cod Bay, is perfect for sunset watching. Nauset Beach is a major draw. Don't miss the lovely village of East Orleans, where you can launch a boat on Pleasant Bay.

Eastham. The Cape Cod National Seashore has a large visitor center here, as well as two beaches that make Eastham a popular spot. There is no distinct downtown, but the best attractions are its abundance of nature areas and beaches.

WHAT TO SEE

⊙ **Cape Cod Museum of Natural History.** A short drive west from the heart
Fodor's Choice of Brewster, this spacious museum and its pristine grounds include a
★ shop, a natural-history library, and exhibits such as a working beehive and a pond- and sea-life room with live specimens. Walking trails wind through 80 acres of forest, marshland, and ponds, all rich in birds and other wildlife. The exhibit hall upstairs has a wall display of aerial photographs documenting the process by which the famous Chatham sandbar was split in two. In summer there are guided field walks, nature programs, and art classes for preschoolers through ninth graders. ⊠ *869 Rte. 6A, West Brewster* ☎ *508/896–3867* ⊕ *www.ccmnh.org* ⊠ *$8* ⊙ *Oct.–Dec., Feb. and Mar., Wed.–Sun. noon–4; Apr. and May, Wed.–Sun. 10–4; June–Sept., daily 9:30–4.*

★ **Chatham Light.** The view from this lighthouse—of the harbor, the sandbars, and the ocean beyond—justifies the crowds. The lighthouse is especially dramatic on a foggy night, as the beacon's light pierces the mist. Coin-operated telescopes allow a close look at the famous "Chatham Break," the result of a fierce 1987 nor'easter that blasted a channel through a barrier beach just off the coast. The U.S. Coast Guard auxiliary, which supervises the lighthouse, offers free tours April through October on most Wednesdays. The lighthouse is also open on three special occasions during the year: Seafest, an annual tribute to the maritime industry held in mid-October; mid-May's Cape Cod Maritime Week; and June's Cape Heritage Week; otherwise, this working lighthouse is off-limits. There is free but limited parking in front of the lighthouse facing the beach: the 30-minute time limit is closely monitored. ⊠ *Main St. near Bridge St., West Chatham.*

THE OUTER CAPE

Making your way around narrow Outer Cape, you really have one key option for getting around: driving along U.S. 6. There are some less congested but slower and indirect roads between the area's two least-developed communities, Wellfleet and Truro. In Wellfleet, many businesses and attractions are strung along U.S. 6, but there's also a compact downtown with art galleries, cafés, and boutiques that's ideal for strolling. Truro has just the tiniest commercial district, and its few

DID YOU KNOW?

With 40 miles of beach along the National Seashore, lifeguards are on duty only at certain sections. Coast Guard Beach is one area that also has practical facilities, making it popular with families.

Artists and birders flock to the protected wildlife sancturaries on the Cape.

attractions are best reached by car, as they're somewhat far apart. In Provincetown, on the other hand, a car—especially in summer—can actually be a hindrance. This is a walkable town with two main thoroughfares, Commercial and Bradford streets. You could easily spend a full day or two just walking around downtown and checking out the dozens and dozens of shops, galleries, and restaurants. Provincetown also has some excellent beaches, which are a short drive or bike ride from downtown.

Wellfleet and South Wellfleet. Spread out along U.S. 6, Wellfleet has a densely clustered downtown of shops, galleries, and restaurants. Wellfleet is known for its stunning beaches, both bayside and on the ocean, and its lively arts culture. South Wellfleet, extending from the Eastham border, is a mostly residential area with no commercial hub.

Truro and North Truro. Lacking an obvious downtown area, Truro's appeal lies in its dramatic shoreline, immense dunes, and great natural beauty. There's less commercialism here than in other Outer Cape towns, though plenty of giant homes can be found off the main roads, many overlooking Cape Cod Bay. North Truro blends into Provincetown's outermost reaches.

Provincetown. Provincetown's main street is where the action is. You'll find drag shows, dance clubs, outdoor dining, and pure frivolity. But plenty of peace can be had in the town's outer reaches. Head out to the Provincelands for hiking and biking, or the beach for some sun and sand.

WHAT TO SEE

Fodor's Choice ★ **Provincetown Art Association and Museum.** Founded in 1914 to collect and show the works of artists with Provincetown connections, this facility has a 1,650-piece permanent collection, displayed in changing exhibits that mix up-and-comers with established 20th-century figures, including Milton Avery, Philip Evergood, William Gropper, Charles Hawthorne, Robert Motherwell, Claes Oldenburg, Man Ray, John Singer Sargent, Andy Warhol, and Agnes Weinrich. A stunning, contemporary wing has greatly expanded the exhibit space. The museum store carries books of local interest, including works by or about area artists and authors, as well as posters, crafts, cards, and gift items. Art classes (one day and longer) offer the opportunity to study under such talents as Hilda Neily, Franny Golden, and Doug Ritter. ⊠ *460 Commercial St., East End* ☎ *508/487–1750* ⊕ *www.paam.org* 🔁 *$7* ☉ *Late May–Sept., Mon.–Thurs. 11–8, Fri. 11–10, weekends 11–5; Oct.–late May, Thurs.–Sun. noon–5.*

MARTHA'S VINEYARD

From Memorial Day through Labor Day, Martha's Vineyard quickens into a vibrant, star-studded place. Edgartown floods with people who come to wander narrow streets flanked with elegant boutiques, stately whaling captains' homes, and charming inns. The busy main port, Vineyard Haven, welcomes day-trippers fresh off ferries and private yachts to browse in its own array of shops. Oak Bluffs, where pizza and ice-cream emporiums reign supreme, attracts diverse crowds with its boardwalk-town air and nightspots that cater to high-spirited, carefree youth.

Martha's Vineyard is far less developed than Cape Cod—thanks to a few local conservation organizations—yet more cosmopolitan than neighboring Nantucket. Summer regulars have included a host of celebrities over the years, among them the Obama family, William Styron, Art Buchwald, Walter Cronkite, Beverly Sills, Patricia Neal, Spike Lee, and Diane Sawyer. Former president Bill Clinton and his wife, Senator Hillary Clinton, are frequent visitors. Concerts, theater, dance performances, and lecture series draw top talent to the island; a county agricultural fair, weekly farmers' markets, and miles of walking trails provide earthier pleasures.

The island is roughly triangular, with maximum distances of about 20 mi east to west and 10 mi north to south. The west end of the Vineyard, known as Up-Island—from the nautical expression of going "up" in degrees of longitude as you sail west—is more rural and wild than the eastern Down-Island end, comprising Vineyard Haven, Oak Bluffs, and Edgartown.

Vineyard Haven. One of the island's busiest towns, Vineyard Haven sees ferry traffic all year long. A fairly compact downtown area keeps most shopping and dining options within easy reach.

Oak Bluffs. Once a Methodist campground, Oak Bluffs is a little less refined than the other towns. It has a vibrant vacation vibe, with lots of nightlife, dining, and shopping.

Edgartown. Dominated by the impeccably kept homes of 19th-century sea captains, Edgartown has a sense of sophistication. There's great history here, and several museums tell the story.

Chappaquiddick Island. Take the tiny ferry from Edgartown to explore Chappaquiddick Island's vast nature preserves. It's a favorite place for bird-watchers and anglers.

West Tisbury. There's beautiful farm country out this way, and the 1859 Grange Hall is still the center of action. During the warmer months, don't miss the bountiful West Tisbury Farmers' Market.

Chilmark. The beaches here, best reached by bike, are spectacular. Quiet Chilmark is mostly residential, lacking any large downtown center.

Menemsha. An active fishing harbor, Menemsha is known for its splendid sunsets. There are a few shops and galleries, and a couple of excellent take-out spots for the freshest of seafood.

Aquinnah. Known until recently as Gay Head, Aquinnah is famous for its grand and dramatic red clay cliffs, as well as the resident lighthouse.

WHAT TO SEE

Fodor'sChoice **Aquinnah Cliffs.** A National Historic Landmark, the spectacular Aquin-
★   nah Cliffs are part of the Wampanoag Reservation land. These dramatically striated walls of red clay are the island's major attraction, as
evidenced by the tour bus–filled parking lot. Native American crafts and
food shops line the short approach to the overlook, from which you
can see the Elizabeth Islands to the northeast across Vineyard Sound
and Noman's Land Island—a wildlife preserve—3 mi off the Vineyard's
southern coast. On-site is the **Aquinnah Lighthouse** (⊠ *Lighthouse Rd.*
☎ *508/645–2211* ⌂ *$5* ☾ *Fri.–Sun. evenings at sunset*), stationed pre-
cariously atop the rapidly eroding cliffs.

★ **Oak Bluffs Campground.** This 34-acre warren of streets is tightly packed
with more than 300 gaily painted Carpenter Gothic Victorian cottages
with wedding-cake trim. As you wander through this fairy-tale setting,
imagine it on a balmy summer evening, lighted by the warm glow of
paper lanterns hung from every cottage porch. This describes the scene
on Illumination Night at the end of the Camp Meeting season—which
is attended these days by some fourth- and fifth-generation cottagers.
Attendees mark the occasion as they have for more than a century,
with lights, song, and open houses for families and friends. The 90-
minute tours are conducted at 10 am on Tuesday and Thursday in July
and August. ⊠ *Off Circuit Ave.* ☎ *508/693–0525* ⊕ *www.mvcma.org/*
⌂ *Tour $10.*

NANTUCKET

Essentially Nantucket is *all* beach—a boomerang-shape sand spit con-
sisting of detritus left by a glacier that receded millennia ago. Off Cape
Cod, some 30 mi out to sea, the island measures 3½ by 14 mi at its
widest points while encompassing—such are the miracles of inlets and
bays—about 80 mi of sandy shoreline, all of it open, as a matter of local
pride, to absolutely everyone.

The island has only one town, which also goes by the name of Nantucket. The only other community of note is tiny Siasconset, a cluster of shingled seaside manses and lovingly restored fishing shacks 8 mi west of town. A 3-mi main road directly south of town leads to Surfside Beach, among the island's most popular. Nantucket's small but busy airport is located east of Surfside.

Nantucket Town. As the ferry terminal—from Hyannis and, seasonally, Martha's Vineyard—Nantucket Town is the hub of all activity and the starting point for most visits. At the height of summer, the narrow cobblestone streets are in a constant state of near-gridlock. Town itself is easily walkable, and bikes are available for exploring.

Siasconset and Wauwinet. An allee of green lawns leads to the exclusive summer community of Siasconset (or 'Sconset, as locals say). Tucked away on either side of the village center are warrens of tiny, rose-covered cottages, some of them centuries old. About 5 mi northwest is the even tinier community of Wauwinet, with the country's second-oldest yacht club.

WHAT TO SEE

Fodor's Choice
★

Whaling Museum. With exhibits that include a fully rigged whaleboat and a skeleton of a 46-foot sperm whale, this museum—a complex that includes a restored 1846 spermaceti candle factory—is a must-see attraction that offers a crash course in the island's colorful history. Items on display include harpoons and other whale-hunting implements; portraits of whaling captains and their wives (a few of whom went whaling as well); the South Seas curiosities they brought home; a large collection of sailors' crafts, a full-size tryworks once used to process whale oil; and the original 16-foot-high 1850 lens from Sankaty Head Lighthouse. The Children's Discovery Room provides interactive-learning opportunities. Be sure to climb—or take the elevator—up to the observation deck for a view of the harbor. ✉ *13–15 Broad St.* ☎ *508/228–1894* 🖥 *$15, $20 combination pass includes Hadwen House and Oldest House* ☉ *Mid-Feb.–mid-Apr., weekends 11–4; mid-Apr.–mid-May and mid-Oct.–mid-Dec., Thurs.–Mon. 11–4; May–mid-Oct., daily 10–5. Closed mid-Dec.–mid-Feb.*

WHERE TO EAT

Cape Cod kitchens have long been closely associated with seafood—the waters off the Cape and the Islands yield a bounty of lobsters, clams, scallops, and myriad fish that make their way onto local menus. In addition to the region's strong Portuguese influence, globally inspired and contemporary fare commonly flavor restaurant offerings. Also gaining in popularity is the use of locally—and often organically—raised produce, meat, and dairy.

Note that ordering an expensive lobster dinner may push your meal into a higher price category than this guide's price range shows for the restaurant.

You can indulge in fresh local seafood and clambakes at seat-your-self shanties for a lower price than at their fine-dining counterparts.

Often, the tackier the decor (plastic fish on the walls), the better the seafood. These laid-back local haunts usually operate a fish market on the premises.

WHAT IT COSTS					
	¢	$	$$	$$$	$$$$
Restaurants	under $8	$8–$14	$15–$24	$25–$32	over $32

Prices are per person, for a main course at dinner.

HYANNIS

$$$
ECLECTIC
Fodor'sChoice
★

✕ **Naked Oyster.** In a favored location on Main Street, this restaurant is known, not surprisingly, for its oysters. With its own oyster farm in nearby Barnstable, the kitchen—and diners—benefit from near-daily deliveries of the succulent bivalves. Well over 1,000 oysters are eaten here on an average summer weekend. You'll always find close to two dozen raw and "dressed" oyster dishes (such as barbecue oysters on the half shell with bleu cheese, caramelized onions, and bacon) plus a nice range of salads and appetizers. The oyster stew is also out of this world. Exposed brick walls inside and a few street-side tables outside make dining a pleasure. ✉ *410 Main St.* ☎ *508/778–6500* ⊕ *www.nakedoyster. com* ▤ *AE, D, MC, V.*

DENNIS VILLAGE

$$$
AMERICAN
Fodor'sChoice
★

✕ **Red Pheasant.** This is one of the Cape's best cozy country restaurants, with a consistently good kitchen where creative American food is prepared with elaborate sauces and herb combinations. For instance, organic chicken is served with an intense preserved-lemon and fresh thyme sauce, and exquisitely grilled veal chops come with a dense red wine–and–portobello mushroom sauce. In fall, look for the specialty game dishes, including venison and quail. Try to reserve a table in the more intimate Garden Room. The expansive wine list is excellent. A nice Sunday brunch is served from mid-October to June. "Don't miss the opportunity to try this place," says Fodors.com reader ciaotebaldi. ✉ *905 Rte. 6A* ☎ *508/385–2133* ⊕ *www.redpheasantinn.com* ⌲ *Reservations essential* ▤ *AE, D, MC, V* ☉ *No lunch.*

BREWSTER

$$$$
FRENCH
Fodor'sChoice
★

✕ **Chillingsworth.** One of the crown jewels of Cape restaurants, Chillingsworth combines formal presentation with an excellent French menu and a diverse wine cellar to create a memorable dining experience. Super-rich risotto, roast lobster, and grilled Angus sirloin are favorites. Dinner in the main dining rooms is prix-fixe and includes seven courses—appetizer, soup, salad, sorbet, entrée, "amusements," and dessert, plus coffee or tea. Less-expensive à la carte options for lunch, dinner, and Sunday brunch are served in the more casual, patio-style Bistro. There are also a few guest rooms here for overnighting. ✉ *2449 Rte. 6A, East Brewster* ☎ *508/896–3640* ⊕ *www.chillingsworth.com* ▤ *AE, DC, MC, V* ☉ *Closed Thanksgiving–mid-May.*

3

HARWICH PORT

$$$
AMERICAN
Fodor's Choice
★

✕ **Cape Sea Grille.** Sitting primly inside a dashing Gothic Victorian house on a side street off hectic Route 28, this gem with distant sea views cultivates a refined ambience with fresh flowers, white linens, and a vibrant, welcoming atmosphere. Chef-owner Douglas Ramler relies on the freshest ingredients. Specialties from the seasonally changing menu may include pan-seared lobster with pancetta, potatoes, grilled asparagus, and a Calvados-saffron reduction, or grilled Atlantic halibut with smoked bacon, fennel, and basil tart. In spring and fall, try the very popular three-course dinner for $25. There's also a generous wine, martini, and drink list. ✉ *31 Sea St., Harwich Port* ☎ *508/432–4745* ⊕ *capeseagrille.com* ▭ *AE, D, MC, V* ⊙ *Closed Mon.–Wed. Columbus Day–early Dec. and mid-Dec.–early Apr. No lunch.*

PROVINCETOWN

$$$
AMERICAN
Fodor's Choice
★

✕ **The Mews.** This perennial favorite with magnificent harbor views focuses on seafood and grilled meats with a cross-cultural flair. Some popular entrées include roasted vegetable and polenta lasagna with a tomato-olive sauce, and Vietnamese shaking beef wok sautéed with scallions and red onions and a lime–black pepper dipping sauce. A piano bar upstairs serves lunch (weekdays in summer) and dinner from a light, less-expensive café menu. The view of the bay from the bar is nearly perfect, and the gentle lighting makes this a romantic spot to have a drink. The restaurant claims its vodka bar is New England's largest, with some 285 varieties. ✉ *429 Commercial St., East End* ☎ *508/487–1500* ⊕ *www.mews.com* ▭ *AE, D, DC, MC, V* ⊙ *Closed Jan. No lunch weekdays off-season or Sat. mid-Oct.–late May.*

MARTHA'S VINEYARD

$$$$
AMERICAN
Fodor's Choice
★

✕ **Detente.** A dark, intimate wine bar and restaurant with hardwood floors and rich banquette seating, Detente serves more than a dozen wines by the glass as well as numerous half bottles. Even if you're not much of an oenophile, it's worth a trip just for the innovative food, much of it from local farms and seafood purveyors. Try the complex starter of ahi-tuna tartare with toasted pine nuts, vanilla-pear puree, and arugula salad, followed by such choice entrées as roasted venison loin with thyme spaetzle, sautéed Swiss chard, blue cheese, and roasted figs; or lemon-honey–basted halibut with potato au gratin, truffled leek puree, roasted artichokes, and oven-dried tomatoes. ✉ *Nevin Sq., off Water St.* ☎ *508/627–8810* ⊕ *www.detentewinebar.com* ▭ *AE, MC, V* ⊙ *Closed Tues. No lunch.*

$$$$
AMERICAN
Fodor's Choice
★

✕ **Sweet Life Café.** Housed in a charming Victorian house, this island favorite's warm tones, low lighting, and handsome antique furniture will make you feel like you've entered someone's home—but the cooking is more sophisticated than home-style. Dishes on the menu are prepared in inventive ways (and change often with the seasons); sautéed halibut is served with sweet-pea risotto, pine nuts, and a marjoram beurre blanc, while the white gazpacho is filled with steamed clams, toasted almonds, sliced red grapes, and paprika oil. The desserts are superb; try the warm chocolate fondant with toasted-almond ice cream. There's outdoor dining by candlelight in a shrub-enclosed garden. ⊠ *63 Upper Circuit Ave., at far end of town* ☎ *508/696–0200* ⊕ *www.sweetlifemv.com* ⌲ *Reservations essential* ⊟ *AE, D, MC, V* ⊙ *Closed Jan.–Mar.*

NANTUCKET

$$$ ✕ **Straight Wharf.** This loftlike restaurant with a harborside deck has enjoyed legendary status since the mid-'70s, when chef Marion Morash used to get a helping hand from culinary buddy Julia Child. The young couple now in command—Gabriel Frasca and Amanda Lydon—were fast-rising stars on the Boston restaurant scene, but their approach here is the antithesis of flashy. If anything, they have lent this venerable institution a more-barefoot air, appropriate to the place and season: Hurricane lamps lend a soft glow to well-spaced tables lined with butcher paper, and dish towels serve as napkins. Intense champions of local crops and catches, the chefs concoct stellar dishes like island creek oysters with Meyer lemon granita, and line-caught halibut with garlic-chive spaetzle. Their style could be synopsized as simplicity that sings. For a lower-priced preview, explore the menu at the adjoining bar. ⊠ *6 Harbor Sq.* ☎ *508/228–4499* ⊟ *AE, MC, V* ⊙ *Closed mid-Oct.–mid-May.*

NEW AMERICAN
Fodor'sChoice
★

WHERE TO STAY

Dozens of heritage buildings now welcome overnight guests, so you can bed down in a former sea captain's home or a converted church. Scores of rental homes and condominiums are available for long-term stays. Several large resorts encompass numerous amenities—swimming, golf, restaurants, children's programs—all on one property, but often lack the intimate charm and serenity of the smaller establishments. Large chain hotels exist in very small numbers in the region; the vast majority of lodging properties are locally owned. You'll want to make reservations for inns well in advance during peak summer periods. Smoking is prohibited in all Massachusetts hotels. For more information on the state-park camping areas on Cape Cod contact the Massachusetts Department of Conservation and Recreation (☎ *617/626–1250* ⊕ *www. mass.gov/dcr/forparks.htm*).

Hotel reviews have been condensed for this book. Please go to Fodors. com for full reviews of each property.

WHAT IT COSTS				
¢	$	$$	$$$	$$$$
Hotels	under $75	$75–$150	$151–$225	$226–$325	over $325

Prices are for two people in a standard double room in high season, excluding 12.45% tax and service charges.

SANDWICH

$$$ 🖵 **Belfry Inne & Bistro.** This one-of-a-kind inn comprises a 1901 former church, an ornate wood-frame 1882 Victorian, and an 1827 Federal-style house clustered on a main campus. **Pros:** great in-town location; bright, beautiful, and spacious rooms. **Cons:** some steep stairs.

Fodor'sChoice
★

⊠ *8 Jarves St., Sandwich Center* ☎ *508/888–8550 or 800/844–4542*
⊕ *www.belfryinn.com* 🛏 *20 rooms* ♿ *In-room: a/c, Wi-Fi (some). In-hotel: 2 restaurants, bar* ═ *AE, D, DC, MC, V* ⏽❶*BP.*

FALMOUTH

$$$$

Fodor's Choice

★

🏨 **Inn on the Sound.** At this understated but stylish inn, perched on a bluff overlooking Vineyard Sound, the living room and most of the guest rooms face the water. **ros:** grand water views, elegant setting. **Cons:** not an in-town location. ⊠ *313 Grand Ave., Falmouth Heights* ☎ *508/457–9666 or 800/564–9668* ⊕ *www.innonthesound.com* 🛏 *10 rooms* ♿ *In-room: a/c, Wi-Fi. In-hotel: beachfront, no kids under 10* ═ *MC, V* ⏽❶*BP.*

DENNIS VILLAGE

$–$$

Fodor's Choice

★

🏨 **Isaiah Hall B&B Inn.** Lilacs and pink roses trail along the white-picket fence outside this 1857 Greek Revival farmhouse on a quiet residential road near the bay. **Pros:** beautiful grounds; near beaches and attractions. **Cons:** some very steep steps; some rooms are on the small side. ⊠ *152 Whig St., Box 1007, Dennis Village* ☎ *508/385–9928* ⊕ *www. isaiahhallinn.com* 🛏 *10 rooms, 2 suites* ♿ *In-room: DVD, Wi-Fi. In-hotel: no kids under 7* ═ *AE, D, MC, V* ⏽❶*BP.*

HARWICH

$$$$

Fodor's Choice

★

🏨 **Wequassett Inn Resort & Golf Club.** Set on 22 acres of shaded landscape partially surrounded by Pleasant Bay, the Wequassett is an informally upscale resort. **ros:** waterfront setting; activities and programs for all ages; babysitting services. **Cons:** rates are very steep; not an in-town location. ⊠ *2173 Orleans Rd. (Rte. 28)* ☎ *508/432–5400 or 800/225–7125* ⊕ *www.wequassett.com* 🛏 *115 rooms, 7 suites* ♿ *In-room: a/c. In-hotel: 3 restaurants, room service, bar, tennis courts, pool, gym, water sports, children's programs (ages 4–12)* ═ *AE, D, DC, MC, V* ☉ *Closed Nov.–Mar.* ❶*FAP.*

CHATHAM

$$$–$$$$

Fodor's Choice

★

🏨 **Chatham Gables Inn.** New owners Brian Dougherty and Nick Robert embarked on a full-scale renovation to reveal the simple beauty of this 1839 former sea captain's home. **Pros:** exquisite historic lodging, 10-minute walk to town and beach, exceptional service. **Cons:** not a waterfront location, not for those traveling with small children. ⊠ *364 Old Harbor Rd.* ☎ *508/945–5859* ⊕ *www.chathamgablesinn.com* 🛏 *7 rooms* ♿ *In-room: a/c, no phone, DVD (on request), Wi-Fi. In-hotel: Wi-Fi hotspot, no kids under 10* ═ *D, DC, MC, V* ⏽❶*BP.*

SOUTH ORLEANS

$$$$

Fodor's Choice

★

🏨 **A Little Inn on Pleasant Bay.** This gorgeously decorated inn occupies a 1798 building on a bluff beside a cranberry bog. **ros:** great water views; abundant buffet breakfast; spacious, modern baths. **Cons:** not an in-town location. ⊠ *654 S. Orleans Rd., South Orleans* ☎ *508/255–0780 or 888/332–3351* ⊕ *www.alittleinnonpleasantbay.com* 🛏 *9 rooms* ♿ *In-room: a/c, no phone, no TV, Wi-Fi. In-hotel: no kids under 10* ═ *AE, MC, V* ⏽❶*CP* ☉ *Closed mid-Oct.–Apr.*

EASTHAM

$$$-$$$$
Fodor'sChoice
★

🏨 **Whalewalk Inn & Spa.** This 1830 whaling master's home is on 3 land-scaped acres; wide-board pine floors, fireplaces, and 19th-century country antiques provide historical appeal. **ros:** beautiful grounds; elegantly appointed rooms; decadent spa treatments. **Cons:** no water views or beachfront. ✉ *220 Bridge Rd.* ☎ *508/255–0617 or 800/440–1281* ⊕ *www.whalewalkinn.com* ⇥ *11 rooms, 6 suites △ In-room: kitchen (some), no phone, refrigerator (some), DVD, Wi-Fi. In-hotel: pool, gym, spa, no kids under 12* ⊟ *D, MC, V* ۞ *Closed Jan.–Mar.* ⊠| *BP.*

PROVINCETOWN

$$$-$$$$
Fodor'sChoice
★

🏨 **Crowne Pointe Historic Inn and Spa.** Created meticulously from six different buildings, this inn has not left a single detail unattended. **Pros:** great on-site amenities, posh and luxurious room decor, professional and well-trained staff. **Cons:** among the highest rates in town, significant minimum-stay requirements in summer, contemporary vibe. ✉ *82 Bradford St., Downtown Center* ☎ *508/487–6767 or 877/276–9631* ⊕ *www.crownepointe.com* ⇥ *37 rooms, 3 suites △ In-room: a/c, kitchen (some), refrigerator, DVD, Wi-Fi. In-hotel: pool, spa, laundry service, Wi-Fi hotspot, no kids under 16, some pets allowed (fee), parking (free)* ⊟ *AE, D, MC, V* ⊠| *BP.*

MARTHA'S VINEYARD

$$$$
Fodor'sChoice
★

🏨 **Hob Knob.** This 19th-century Gothic Revival boutique hotel blends the amenities and service of a luxury property with the ambience and charm of a small B&B. **ros:** spacious rooms; afternoon tea; removed from crowds. **Cons:** steep rates; not overlooking harbor. ✉ *128 Main St.* ☎ *508/627–9510 or 800/696–2723* ⊕ *www.hobknob.com* ⇥ *16 rooms, 1 suite △ In-room: a/c, refrigerator, DVD, Wi-Fi. In-hotel: gym, spa, bicycles, no kids under 7* ⊟ *AE, MC, V* ⊠| *BP.*

$$$$
Fodor'sChoice
★

🏨 **Winnetu Oceanside Resort.** A departure from most properties on the island, the contemporary Winnetu—styled after the grand multistory resorts of the Gilded Age— has successfully struck a fine balance in that it both encourages families and provides a contemporary seaside-resort experience for couples. **ros:** outstanding staff; tons of activities; fantastic restaurant. **Cons:** pricey; not an in-town location; lots of kids in summer. ✉ *31 Dunes Rd.* ☎ *866/335–1133 or 508/310–1733* ⊕ *www. winnetu.com* ⇥ *52 suites, 65 homes △ In-room: a/c, kitchen, DVD, Wi-Fi (some). In-hotel: 2 restaurants, room service, tennis courts, pools, gym, spa, children's programs (ages 3–12), laundry facilities, Wi-Fi hotspot* ⊟ *MC, V* ۞ *Closed late Oct.–mid-Apr.*

NANTUCKET

$$$-$$$$
Fodor'sChoice
★

🏨 **The Summer House.** Perched on a bluff overlooking 'Sconset Beach, this cluster of rose-covered cottages—cobbled from salvage in the 1840s—epitomizes Nantucket's enduring allure. **Pros:** romantic setting; excellent restaurants; pool on the beach. **Cons:** cottages can be snug; sounds of restaurant revelry. ✉ *17 Ocean Ave.,Siasconset* ☎ *508/257–4577* ⊕ *www.thesummerhouse.com* ⇥ *10 rooms △ In-room: a/c, Wi-Fi. In-hotel: 2 restaurants, bars, pool, beachfront* ⊟ *AE, MC, V* ۞ *Closed Nov.–late Apr.* ⊠| *CP.*

OUTDOOR ACTIVITIES

BEACHES

Cape Cod National Seashore. The region's most expansive national treasure, Cape Cod National Seashore was established in 1961 by President John F. Kennedy, for whom Cape Cod was home and haven. The 27,000-acre park, extending from Chatham to Provincetown, protects 30 mi of superb beaches; great rolling dunes; swamps, marshes, and wetlands; and pitch-pine and scrub-oak forest. Self-guided nature trails, as well as biking and horse trails, lace through these landscapes. Hiking trails lead to a red-maple swamp, **Nauset Marsh,** and to **Salt Pond,** in which breeding shellfish are suspended from floating "nurseries." Their offspring will later be used to seed the flats. Also in the seashore is the Buttonbush Trail, a nature path for people with vision impairments. A hike or bike ride to Coast Guard Beach leads to a turnout looking out over marsh and sea. A section of the cliff here was washed away in 1990, revealing the remains of a prehistoric dwelling.

The first visitor center of the Cape Cod National Seashore (the other is in Provincetown), **Salt Pond Visitor Center** offers guided walks, boat tours, demonstrations, and lectures from mid-April through Thanksgiving, as well as evening beach walks, campfire talks, and other programs in summer. The center includes a museum with displays on whaling and the old saltworks, as well as early Cape Cod artifacts including scrimshaw, the journal that Mrs. Penniman kept while on a whaling voyage with her husband, and some of the Pennimans' possessions, such as their tea service and the captain's top hat. An air-conditioned auditorium shows films on geology, sea rescues, whaling, Henry David Thoreau, and Guglielmo Marconi. ⊠ *Doane Rd. off U.S. 6* ☎ *508/255–3421* ⊕ *www.nps.gov/caco* ⊠ *Free* ☉ *Daily 9–4:30 (hrs extended slightly in summer).*

BICYCLING

Fodor's Choice The **Cape Cod Rail Trail** (☎ *508/896–3491* ⊕ *www.mass.gov/dcr/parks/southeast/ccrt.htm*) offers a scenic ride from South Dennis to South Wellfleet over terrain that is easy-to-moderate in difficulty and generally quite flat. Given the good conditions, Rail Trailers who feel the need for speed can cover its 25-mi length in about two hours. Yet most go at a more leisurely pace, lingering en route at salt marshes, woodlands, cranberry bogs, beaches, ponds, and Nickerson State Park (which maintains the trail and has its own bike path).

Of course, it isn't mandatory to tackle the trail in its entirety. Simply do a segment, perhaps starting in the middle near Nickerson State Park, then looping to one end and back. To return to your starting point by public transportation, the easiest way is to set off from Dennis, ride to Orleans, and catch the bike-rack-equipped H20 Line bus back. The Cape Cod Regional Transit Authority has schedules.

The Rail Trail begins at a parking lot off busy Route 134 south of U.S. 6, near Theophilus Smith Road in South Dennis, and ends in South Wellfleet, with a spur leading westward through Harwich to Chatham. Free maps are available at the Dennis Chamber of Commerce and other locations. In addition to distances, these mark amenities such as strategically placed parking lots and restrooms.

Fodor'sChoice ★ The wonderful **Shining Sea Bikeway** is an 11-mi paved bike path through four of Falmouth's villages, running from Woods Hole to North Falmouth. It follows the shore of Buzzards Bay, providing water views and dips into oak and pine woods; a detour onto Church Street takes you to Nobska Light. A brochure is available at the trailheads. If you're going to Martha's Vineyard with your bike, you can park your car in one of Falmouth's Steamship Authority lots and ride the Shining Sea Bikeway to the ferry. The free shuttle buses between the Falmouth lots and the Woods Hole ferry docks also have bike carriers.

NATURE PRESERVES

Fodor'sChoice ★ **Monomoy National Wildlife Refuge.** This 2,500-acre preserve includes the Monomoy Islands, a fragile 9-mi-long barrier-beach area south of Chatham. Monomoy's North and South islands were created when a storm divided the former Monomoy Island in 1978. A haven for bird-watchers, the refuge is an important stop along the North Atlantic Flyway for migratory waterfowl and shorebirds—peak migration times are May and late July. It also provides nesting and resting grounds for 285 species, including gulls—great black-backed, herring, and laughing—and several tern species. White-tailed deer wander the islands, and harbor and gray seals frequent the shores in winter. The only structure on the islands is the **South Monomoy Lighthouse,** built in 1849.

Monomoy is a quiet, peaceful place of sand and beach grass, tidal flats, dunes, marshes, freshwater ponds, thickets of bayberry and beach plum, and a few pines. Because the refuge harbors several endangered species, activities are limited. Certain areas are fenced off to protect nesting areas of terns and the threatened piping plover. In season, the *Rip Ryder* (☎ *508/945–5450* ⊕ *www.monomoyislandferry.com*) leads for bird- or seal-watching tours. **Monomoy Island Excursions** (☎ *508/430–7772* ⊕ *www.monomoyislandexcursions.com*) offers seal and seabird tours and boat trips out around Monomoy Island on a 43-foot high-speed catamaran. **Outermost Adventures** (☎ *508/945–5858* ⊕ *www. outermostharbor.com*) provides water-taxi services to Monomoy Island and offers fishing, birding, and seal-watching cruises.

Fodor'sChoice ★ **Mytoi.** The Trustees of Reservations' 14-acre preserve is a serene, beautifully tended, Japanese-inspired garden with a creek-fed pool spanned by a bridge and rimmed with Japanese maples, azaleas, bamboo, and irises. A boardwalk runs through part of the grounds, where you're apt to see box turtles and hear the sounds of songbirds. There are few more-enchanting spots on the island. ⊠ *Dike Rd.2 mi from intersection with Chappaquiddick Rd.* ☎ *508/627–7689* ⊠ *Free* ☉ *Daily sunrise–sunset.*

New York City

WORD OF MOUTH

"Hightlights of our stay were walking across Brooklyn Bridge, Top of the Rock, the great museums trio: Met, MOMA and Natural History, good meals, good Broadway shows.and mainly being in such a unique and extraordinary city. I like the way New Yorkers are, always in a rush but kind and helpful."

—Graziella5b

WELCOME TO NEW YORK CITY

TOP REASONS TO GO

★ **Experiencing the energy:** Nothing matches the rush of being a part of this huge, high-speed, open 24/7, creative madhouse.

★ **Art, music, theater:** Old, new, utterly outré, or classic, it's all here. The city's museums, galleries, and performance venues are home to things you've always wanted to experience in person—and things you probably never knew existed.

★ **Food glorious food:** New York is a buffet of world cuisine, making it an essential pilgrimage for foodies, and a delight to anyone who enjoys good eats.

★ **People-watching:** This is always a pleasure in NYC. You'll probably spot a few celebrities, but observing the locals and our many visitors is just as much fun. Grab a chair at a café, a bench at a park, or a space on the sidewalk, and enjoy watching the world dash by.

★ **The shopping:** Your credit card will probably melt from overuse, but hey, you only live once.

1 **Lower Manhattan.** The long and short of it is: Lower Manhattan includes the skyscrapers of Wall Street and the Ground Zero Memorial, the ramshackle tenements of Chinatown, the pulsating creative energy of NoLita and TrBeCa and the glamour of SoHo.

2 **The Village, Chelsea, and Union Square Area.** These adjacent neighborhoods teem with artists, writers, and other creative types—at least those who can afford the rent. Come nightfall, the area draws revelers from all over the city.

3 **Midtown.** Midtown is where New York does business; on the East Side commuters swarm into Grand Central; on the West Side they teem up the canyon that is 6th Avenue. For visitors, the lights and glamour of Broadway and Times Square dazzle.

4 **Uptown.** Manhattan's old-school residential zones, the Upper East and Upper West sides, hide some of the city's best culture, too. Museum Mile, the Natural History Museum, and Lincoln Center all call the area above 59th Street home. And don't forget Central Park!

GETTING ORIENTED

The map of Manhattan is, for the most part, easy to follow: north of 14th Street, streets are laid out in a numbered grid pattern. Numbered streets run east and west (crosstown), and broad avenues, most of them also numbered, run north (uptown) and south (downtown). The main exception is Broadway, which runs the entire length of Manhattan on a diagonal. Below 14th Street, street patterns get chaotic. In the West Village, West 4th Street intersects West 11th Street, and Greenwich Street runs roughly parallel to Greenwich Avenuecould. There's an East Broadway and a West Broadway, both of which run north–south, and neither of which is an extension of Broadway, leaving even locals scratching their heads.

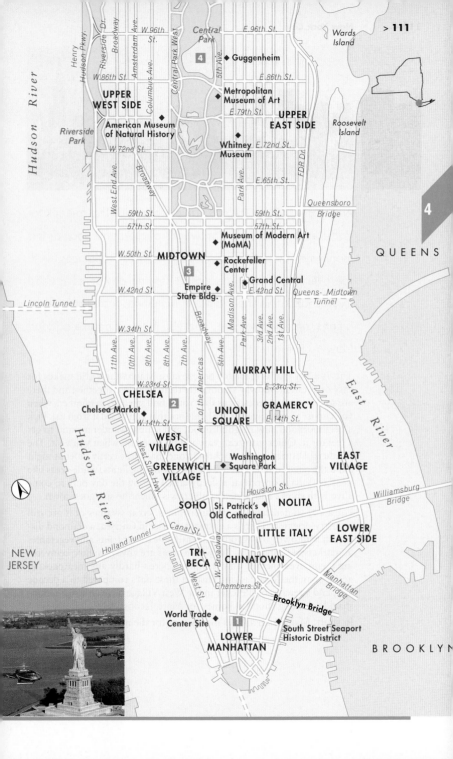

Hudson River

Henry Hudson Pkwy.

Riverside Dr.

Riverside Park

Broadway

Amsterdam Ave.

Columbus Ave.

W. 96th St.

Central Park West

W. 86th St.

UPPER WEST SIDE

American Museum
of Natural History

W. 72nd St.

West End Ave.

Broadway

Central Park

Wards Island

4

5th Ave.

◆ Guggenheim

E. 96th St.

E. 86th St.

◆ Metropolitan Museum of Art

E. 79th St.

UPPER EAST SIDE

Roosevelt Island

◆ Whitney Museum

E. 72nd St.

E. 65th St.

FDR Dr.

Queensboro Bridge

4

QUEENS

59th St.

57th St.

W. 50th St.

MIDTOWN

3

W. 42nd St.

Park Ave.

59th St.

57th St.

◆ Museum of Modern Art (MoMA)

◆ Rockefeller Center

◆ Grand Central

Empire
State Bldg.

E. 42nd St.

Queens-Midtown Tunnel

Lincoln Tunnel

W. 34th St.

11th Ave.

10th Ave.

9th Ave.

8th Ave.

7th Ave.

Broadway

Ave. of the Americas

5th Ave.

Madison Ave.

Park Ave.

3rd Ave.

2nd Ave.

1st Ave.

MURRAY HILL

W. 23rd St.

CHELSEA

2

Chelsea Market ◆

W. 14th St.

WEST VILLAGE

GREENWICH VILLAGE

UNION SQUARE

E. 23rd St.

GRAMERCY

E. 14th St.

◆ Washington Square Park

EAST VILLAGE

East River

West Side Hwy.

Hudson River

Houston St.

Williamsburg Bridge

SOHO

St. Patrick's
Old Cathedral ◆

NOLITA

Canal St.

Holland Tunnel

TRI-BECA

W. Broadway

CHINATOWN

LITTLE ITALY

LOWER EAST SIDE

Chambers St.

Manhattan Bridge

Brooklyn Bridge

NEW JERSEY

World Trade
Center Site ◆

West St.

1

LOWER MANHATTAN

◆ South Street Seaport
Historic District

BROOKLYN

New York, New York, is a quick-change artist, famous for transforming overnight—so what's packed and popular this month may be gone by the time you arrive. It's impossible to see everything, regardless of its staying power, so instead try to soak in the sheer amount of culture, restaurants, exhibitions, and people here, and you'll be acting like a jaded New Yorker in no time.

This is a city that is made for pedestrians: Manhattan's grid makes for easy orientation, subway stations are relatively close together, and there are so many other pedestrians that you'll find strength in numbers when you choose to cross against the light (not that you heard it from us). Pick a neighborhood, any neighborhood, and simply wander around to get a feel for it. Quick visits can vary wildly based on when you visit. The Financial District is a go-go 9-to-5 zone that turns eerily quiet at night amid the huge commercial towers and twinkling lights, while areas like the East Village operate at a sleepy crawl during the day only to come alive with shows and frenetic pub crawls when the sun goes down.

For a city so dedicated to the finer things, great swathes of it are still industry-oriented. There's a garment district in Chelsea, a diamond district in Midtown, and wholly unidentifiable exotic fruits and vegetables at markets in Chinatown. But whole areas are always in flux, reinventing themselves anew in an eye blink. There's hardly any meatpacking going on in the Meatpacking District these days compared to a decade ago, and stretches of Bleecker in the West Village have gone from ramshackle clothing shops to homes for Marc Jacobs and Ralph Lauren.

In short, Manhattan always makes way for the new.

PLANNING

WHEN TO GO

New York City weather, like its people, is a study in extremes. Much of winter brings bone-chilling winds and an occasional traffic-snarling snowfall, but you're just as likely to experience mild afternoons sandwiched by cool temperatures.

In late spring and early summer, streets fill with parades and sidewalk concerts, and Central Park has free performances. Late August temperatures sometimes claw skyward, giving many subway stations the feel and bouquet of dingy saunas (no wonder the Hamptons are so crowded). This is why September brings palpable excitement, with stunning yellow-and-bronze foliage complementing the dawn of a new cultural season. Between October and May museums mount major exhibitions, most Broadway shows open, and formal opera, ballet, and concert seasons begin.

GETTING HERE AND AROUND

AIR TRAVEL

The major air gateways to New York City are LaGuardia Airport (LGA) and JFK International Airport (JFK) in the borough of Queens, and Newark Liberty International Airport (EWR) in New Jersey. Cab fares are generally higher to and from Newark. The AirTrain link between Newark Airport and New Jersey Transit makes the journey in less than 15 minutes; then you must transfer to a NJ Transit train to Pennsylvania Station in Manhattan.

Car services can be a great deal, because the driver will often meet you on the concourse or in the baggage-claim area and help you with your luggage. The flat rates and tolls are often comparable to taxi fares, but some car services will charge for parking and waiting time at the airport. To eliminate these expenses, other car services require that you telephone their dispatcher when you land, so they can send the next available car to pick you up.

Outside the baggage-claim area at each of New York's major airports are taxi stands where a uniformed dispatcher helps passengers find taxis. Cabs are not permitted to pick up fares anywhere else in the arrivals area, so if you want a taxi, take your place in line. Shuttle services generally pick up passengers from a designated spot along the curb.

New York Airport Service runs buses between JFK and LaGuardia airports, and buses from those airports to Grand Central Terminal, Port Authority Bus Terminal, Penn Station, Bryant Park, and hotels between 31st and 60th streets in Manhattan. Fares cost between $12 and $15 one-way and $21 to $27 round-trip. Buses operate from 6:05 am to 11 pm from the airport; between 5 am and 10 pm going to the airport.

SuperShuttle vans travel to and from Manhattan to JFK, LaGuardia, and Newark. These blue vans will stop at your home, office, or hotel. There are courtesy phones at the airports. For travel to the airport, the company recommends that you make your request 24 hours in advance. Fares range from $13 to $22 per person.

CAR TRAVEL

If you plan to drive into Manhattan, try to avoid the morning and evening rush hours and lunch hour. The deterioration of the bridges to Manhattan, especially those spanning the East River, means that repairs will be ongoing for the next few years. Listen to traffic reports on the radio before you set off, and don't be surprised if a bridge is partially closed or entirely blocked with traffic.

Driving within Manhattan can be a nightmare of gridlocked streets, obnoxious drivers and bicyclists, and seemingly suicidal jaywalkers. Narrow and one-way streets are common, particularly downtown, and can make driving even more difficult. The most congested streets of the city lie between 14th and 59th streets and 3rd and 8th avenues.

SUBWAY AND BUS TRAVEL

The days when New York's subways were dangerous are long gone. Now the city's network of underground trains is the most efficient way to get around. (City buses are equally cheap, but can take forever to navigate through traffic, especially crosstown.) The subway is by no means flawless: Good luck understanding loudspeaker announcements on all but the newest trains; the floors are sticky; stations are sweltering in summer; and platforms are grimy year-round. In other words, it's quite obvious that the subway is more than 100 years old. Still, for now $2.50 gets you to almost any neighborhood in Manhattan or the outer boroughs, and lines that service the most popular destinations are generally clean, with maps and signs that clearly state where you're going. It gets crowded during rush hours, when you'll likely find that all the subway car seats are taken—and have to join your fellow riders in the particular New York sport of "strap-hanging."

TAXI TRAVEL

If you've got a long way to go and would rather be comfortable than thrifty, hail one of the ubiquitous yellow cabs that troll New York's streets around the clock. A December 2006 hike in taxi fares means that a 20-minute ride can now set you back more than $15. But you'll get to look at the scenery as you go and talk to the driver (who might be from as far away as Bangladesh or Ukraine). Avoid trying to hail a cab between 4 and 4:30 pm, unless you want to do a lot of futile streetside arm waving; it's when the drivers change shifts.

ESSENTIALS

Airport Information JFK International Airport (☎ 718/244-4444 ⊕ www.jfkairport.com). **LaGuardia Airport** (☎ 718/533-3400 ⊕ www.laguardiaairport.com). **Newark Liberty International Airport** (☎ 973/961-6000 or 888/397-4636 ⊕ www.newarkairport.com).

Airport Shuttle Service New York Airport Service (☎ 718/875-8200 ⊕ www.nyairportservice.com). **SuperShuttle** (☎ 800/258-3826 ⊕ www.supershuttle.com).

Schedule and Route Information Metropolitan Transit Authority (MTA) Travel Information Line (☎ 718/330-1234, 718/596-8585 travelers with disabilities ⊕ www.mta.info).

VISITOR INFORMATION
NYC & Company Convention & Visitors Bureau (✉ 810 7th Ave., between W. 52nd and W. 53rd Sts., 3rd fl., Midtown West ☎ 212/484–1222 ⊕ www.nycgo.com).

EXPLORING NEW YORK CITY

Made up of five boroughs, New York City packs a staggering range of sights and activities into 322 square mi. You'll probably want to focus most of your visit in Manhattan, a compact island of attractions. To experience the most from the city, you need to think like a New Yorker: Explore the city with your eyes open to everything around you; every city block offers new and unexpected sights.

Without a doubt, the best way to explore New York is on foot. No matter what neighborhood you're headed to, you'll get a better sense of it by wandering around; you can check out the architecture, pop into cool-looking shops and cafés, and observe the walk-and-talk of the locals.

LOWER MANHATTAN

Lower Manhattan is a microcosm of Manhattan and the city itself. Near the island's southern tip, the financial service industry holds sway. You'll see men and women in business attire rushing to work at a brokerage or to argue a case at the courthouse. From here visitors can catch the ferries to Staten Island, Ellis Island, and the Statue of Liberty, as well as pay their respects at Ground Zero. The South Street Seaport remains popular with kids. Farther north are Chinatown, which is almost always bustling with activity (and enterprise, if you need a knockoff handbag), and the few remaining blocks of Little Italy. These two areas are great bets for cheap eats—just pick your favorite kind of noodle. Glamorous types have staked a claim in TriBeCa, NoLita, and SoHo; swan through here to visit expensive designer clothing stores, walk the iconic streets, and see if it's possible to spot a celebrity.

WHAT TO SEE

Fodor'sChoice **Brooklyn Bridge.** "A drive-through cathedral" is how the critic James
★   Wolcott describes one of New York's noblest and most recognized landmarks, which spans the East River and connects Manhattan to Brooklyn. A walk across the bridge's promenade—a boardwalk elevated above the roadway and shared by pedestrians, in-line skaters, and bicyclists—takes about 40 minutes from the heart of Brooklyn Heights to Manhattan's civic center. Ⓜ 4, 5, 6 to Brooklyn Bridge/City Hall; J, M, Z to Chambers St.; A, C to High St.–Brooklyn Bridge.

Ground Zero. Although the World Trade Center grounds remain largely a construction site, people continue to visit and reflect on the tragedy of September 11, 2001, and the heroic acts of rescue workers and average New Yorkers who fiercely united the city in the aftermath. Dubbed Ground Zero, the fenced-in 16-acre work site that emerged from the rubble has come to symbolize the personal and historical impact of the attack.

A mix of old and new: Lower Manhattan's bright lights combine with the seaport's historic ships.

A steel "viewing wall" now encircles the site, bound on the north and south by Vesey and Liberty streets, and on the east and west by Church and West streets. Along the east wall are panels that detail the history of Lower Manhattan and the WTC site before, during, and after September 11. There are also panels bearing the names of those who perished on 9/11/01 and during the 1993 World Trade Center attack.

After years of delays, the process of filling the massive void at Ground Zero is well under way. "Reflecting Absence," the World Trade Center memorial designed by Michael Arad and Peter Walker, will be set in an oak-filled plaza. Water will cascade down into two subterranean reflecting pools outlining the twin towers' original footprints, and then tumble down into smaller square holes at the center of each pool. A museum and visitor center will be built below the plaza surface.

The memorial plaza will be bordered by four distinct new skyscrapers: the 1,776-foot Freedom Tower, and Towers 2, 3, 4, all designed by famous architects. The site will also include a performing arts center designed by Frank Gehry. An estimated date for the completion of the Freedom Tower is 2013, with other buildings following.

The corner of Vesey and Church streets is a good starting point for viewing Ground Zero; walk clockwise around the site. The main viewing area is on Liberty Street, but you'll have a better view from the two pedestrian bridges to the World Financial Center as well as in the WFC itself. ⊠ *Between Trinity and West Sts. and Vesey and Liberty Sts., Lower Manhattan* ☎ *212/267–2047 for the preview site* Ⓜ *1, R to Rector St.; 2, 3, 4, 5, A, C, J, M, Z to Fulton St./Broadway-Nassau; E to World Trade Center/Church St.* ⊕ *www.national911memorial.org.*

Fodor'sChoice **South Street Seaport Historic District.** Had this charming cobblestone cor-
★ ner of the city not been declared a historic district in 1977, we have no
doubt that you'd be glancing indifferently at yet more hyperdeveloped
skyscrapers in this spot rather than at the city's largest concentration
of early-19th-century commercial buildings.

If you've been to either Boston's Quincy Market or Baltimore's Har-
borplace, you may feel a flash of déjà vu—the same company leased,
restored, and adapted the existing buildings, preserving the commercial
feel of centuries past. The result blends a quasi-authentic historic district
with a homogeneous shopping mall.

At the intersection of Fulton and Water streets, the gateway to the
seaport, is the *Titanic* **Memorial,** a small white lighthouse that commemorates the sinking of the RMS *Titanic* in 1912. On the south side
of Fulton is the seaport's architectural centerpiece, **Schermerhorn Row,**
a redbrick terrace of Georgian- and Federal-style warehouses and count-
inghouses built from 1811 to 1812.

Also at 12 Fulton Street is the main lobby of the **South Street Seaport
Museum** (☎ 212/748–8786 ⊕ *www.seany.org* ⊗ *Apr.–Dec., Tues.–Sun.
10–6; Jan.–Mar., Thurs.–Sun. 10–5; only Schermerhorn Row Galleries open Mon.; ships open noon–4, weather permitting*), which hosts
walking tours, hands-on exhibits, and fantastic creative programs for
children, all with a nautical theme. You can purchase tickets ($15) at
either 12 Fulton Street or Pier 16 Visitors Center.

Cross South Street, once known as the Street of Ships, under an elevated
stretch of the FDR Drive to **Pier 16,** where historic ships are docked,
including the *Pioneer,* a 102-foot schooner built in 1885; the *Peking,*
the second-largest sailing bark in existence; the iron-hulled *Wavertree*;
and the lightship *Ambrose.* The Pier 16 ticket booth provides information and sells tickets to the museum, ships, tours, and exhibits. Pier 16
is the departure point for various seasonal cruises.

To the north is **Pier 17,** a multilevel dockside shopping mall with
national chain retailers such as Express and Victoria's Secret, among
others. Weathered-wood decks at the rear of the pier make a splendid spot from which to contemplate the river, with views as far north
as Midtown Manhattan and as far south as the Verrazano–Narrows
Bridge. ⊠ *South Street Seaport, Lower Manhattan* ☎ *212/732–7678
events and shopping information* ⊕ *www.southstreetseaport.com*
🎟 *Free; $5 to ships, galleries, walking tours, Maritime Crafts Center,
films, and other seaport events* Ⓜ *2, 3, 4, 5, A, C, J, M, Z to Fulton St./
Broadway-Nassau.*

Fodor'sChoice **Statue of Liberty.** For millions of immigrants the first glimpse of America
★ was the Statue of Liberty. You get a taste of the thrill they must have
experienced as you approach Liberty Island on the ferry from Battery
Park and witness the statue grow from a vaguely defined figure on the
horizon into a towering, stately colossus. (You're likely to share the
boat ride with people from all over the world, which lends an additional
dimension to the trip. The statue may be purely a tourist attraction, but
the tourists it attracts are a wonderfully diverse group.)

DID YOU KNOW?

Liberty Enlightening the World, as the Statue of Liberty is officially named, was given by France to the United States in 1886 to mark the U.S.'s centennial.

Liberty Enlightening the World, as the statue is officially named, was presented to the United States in 1886 as a gift from France. The 152-foot-tall figure was sculpted by Frederic-Auguste Bartholdi and erected around an iron skeleton engineered by Gustav Eiffel. It stands atop an 89-foot pedestal designed by Richard Morris Hunt, with Emma Lazarus's sonnet "The New Colossus" ("Give me your tired, your poor, your huddled masses.") inscribed on a bronze plaque at the base. Over the course of time the statue has become precisely what its creators dreamed it would be: the single most powerful symbol of American ideals, and, as such, one of the world's great monumental sculptures.

Inside, highlights include the original flame (which was replaced because of water damage), full-scale replicas of Lady Liberty's face and one of her feet, Bartholdi's alternative designs for the statue, and a model of Eiffel's intricate framework.

You're allowed access to the museum only as part of one of the free tours of the promenade (which surrounds the base of the pedestal) or the observatory (at the pedestal's top). The tours are limited to 3,000 participants a day; to guarantee a place, particularly on the observatory tour, you should order tickets ahead of time—they can be reserved up to 180 days in advance, by phone or over the Internet. The narrow, double-helix stairs leading to the statue's crown closed after 9/11, but access reopened on July 4, 2009. Approximately 240 people are allowed to visit the crown each day; tickets are available online. If you can't get tickets to the crown, you get a good look at the statue's inner structure on the observatory tour.

From the observatory itself there are fine views of the harbor and an up-close (but totally uncompromising) glimpse up Lady Liberty's dress. If you're on one of the tours, you'll go through a security check more thorough than any airport screening, and you'll have to deposit any bags in a locker. Liberty Island has a pleasant outdoor café for refueling. The only disappointment is the gift shop, which sells trinkets little better than those available from street vendors. ⊠ *Liberty Island* ☎ *212/363–3200, 877/523–9849 ticket reservations* ⊕ *www.statuecruises.com* 🎫 *Free; ferry $12 round-trip; crown tickets $3* ☉ *Daily 9:30–5; extended hrs in summer (current hrs available at* ⊕ *www.nps.gov/stli/planyourvisit/hours.htm).*

Fodor's Choice ★ **St. Patrick's Old Cathedral.** If you've watched *The Godfather,* you've peeked inside St. Patrick's Old Cathedral—the interior shots of the infamous baptism scene were filmed here. The unadorned exterior of the cathedral gives no hint of the splendors within, including an 1868 Henry Erben pipe organ. The enormous marble altar surrounded by hand-carved niches (reredos) house an extraordinary collection of sacred statuary and other Gothic exuberance. ⊠ *263 Mulberry St., corner of Mott and Prince Sts., Little Italy* ☎ *212/226–8075* ☉ *Hrs may vary, usually open 8 am–5 pm; Masses weekdays 9 and 12:10, Sat. 9, 12:10, and 5:30, Sun. 9:15, 10:15 (Chinese), 11:30 (Spanish), 12:45, and 7 pm* Ⓜ *R to Prince St.; 6 to Bleecker St.*

THE VILLAGE, CHELSEA, AND THE UNION SQUARE AREA

The Villages, East and West, Chelsea, and Union Square comprise what New Yorkers call "downtown." More than geographic shorthand, it stands for a lot of things at once: creative folks on their way up, creative folks who've settled in, and everyone else who likes to be in the orbit of the first two groups.

The East Village has followed the tradition of the West; what was once a scruffy but pretty (and cheap) area to live in is now packed with restaurants, bars, and expensive shops. There's still a punk ethos, but you have to visit the fringes to the far east (or far south, into the Lower East Side) to find them.

Greenwich Village and, to a lesser extent, the Meatpacking District and Chelsea, have streets that are some of the most picturesque in the city, with pricey real estate to match. Union Square is the hub of the downtown scene, even if it's more corporate than anarchist these days.

WHAT TO SEE

Chelsea Market. In the former Nabisco plant, where the first Oreos were baked in 1912, nearly two-dozen food wholesalers flank what is possibly the city's longest interior walkway in a single building—from 9th to 10th avenues. You can snack your way from one end to the other, nibbling Fat Witch brownies, Ronnybrook farmer's cheese, Amy's Bread sourdough, or just watch the bread being made as it perfumes the halls. ⊠ *75 9th Ave., between W. 15th and W. 16th Sts., Chelsea* ☎ *212/243–6005* ⊕ *www.chelseamarket.com* ⊗ *Mon.–Sat. 7–10, Sun. 8–8* Ⓜ *A, C, E, L to 14th St.*

Fodor's Choice ★

Empire State Building. The city's tallest building, whose pencil-slim silhouette is recognizable virtually worldwide as an art deco monument to progress, a symbol of New York City, and a star in some great romantic scenes, on- and off-screen. Its cinematic résumé—the building has appeared in more than 200 movies—means that it remains a fixture of popular imagination, and many visitors come to relive favorite movie scenes.

Fodor's Choice ★

Built in 1931 at the peak of the skyscraper craze, this 103-story limestone giant opened after a mere 13 months of construction. The framework rose at an astonishing rate of 4½ stories per week, making the Empire State Building the fastest-rising skyscraper ever built. Many floors were left completely unfinished so tenants could have them custom designed.

■ TIP➜ **Thanks to advance ticketing on the Internet ($2 extra), you can speed your way to the observatory on the 86th floor.** The 86th-floor observatory (1,050 feet high) is outdoors and spans the building's circumference. This is the deck to visit to truly see the city. If it rains, you can view the city between the clouds and watch the rain travel sideways around the building from the shelter of the enclosed walkway. The advantage of paying the extra $15 to go to the indoor 102nd floor is that this observatory affords an easy and less-crowded circular walk-around from which to view the city. It also feels more removed and quieter. Express tickets can be purchased for front-of-the-line admission for an extra $45.

Even if you skip the view from up top, be sure to step into the lobby and take in the ceilings, beautifully restored in 2009. The gilded gears and sweeping art deco lines are a romantic tribute to the Machine Age and part of the original vision for the building, lost, painted over, and covered with a drop ceiling until now.

Although some parents blanch when they discover both how much it costs and how it lurches, the second-floor **NY SKYRIDE** (☎ 212/279– 9777 or 888/759–7433 ⊕ www.nyskyride.com ☎ $36; $47 combo with observatory [discounts are available on their Web site] ⊗ Daily 8–10) is a favorite of the 7- and 8-year-old set. The ride presents a movie, motion, and sights, rolled up into New York's only aerial virtual-tour simulator. ⊠ 350 5th Ave., at E. 34th St., Murray Hill ☎ 212/736–3100 or 877/692–8439 ⊕ www.esbnyc.com ☎ $20 ⊗ Daily 8 am–2 am; last elevator up leaves at 1:15 am Ⓜ B, D, F, N, Q, R, M to 34th St./Herald Sq.; 6 to 33rd St.

4

⟳ **Washington Square Park.** NYU students, street musicians, skateboarders,
Fodor's Choice jugglers, chess players, and those just watching the grand opera of it all
★ generate a maelstrom of activity in this physical and spiritual heart of the Village. The newly restored 9½-acre park had inauspicious beginnings as a cemetery, principally for yellow fever victims—an estimated 10,000–22,000 bodies lie below.

At one time, plans to renovate the park called for the removal of the bodies; however, local resistance prevented this from happening. In the early 1800s the park was a parade ground and the site of public executions; bodies dangled from a conspicuous Hanging Elm that still stands at the northwest corner of the square. Today that gruesome past is all but forgotten, as playgrounds attract parents with tots in tow, dogs go leash-free inside the popular dog runs, and everyone else seems drawn toward the large central fountain.

The triumphal European-style **Washington Memorial Arch** stands at the square's north end, marking the start of 5th Avenue. In 1889 Stanford White designed a wood-and-papier-mâché arch, originally situated a half block north, to commemorate the 100th anniversary of George Washington's presidential inauguration. The arch was reproduced in Tuckahoe marble in 1892, and the statues—*Washington as General Accompanied by Fame and Valor* on the left, and *Washington as Statesman Accompanied by Wisdom and Justice* on the right—were added in 1916 and 1918, respectively. ⊠ 5th Ave. between Waverly Pl. and 4th St., Greenwich Village Ⓜ A, B, C, D, E, F, M to W. 4th St.

MIDTOWN

Midtown may not be as accessible to the visitor as other New York City neighborhoods, but it still has plenty to offer. On the East Side, there are scores of iconic buildings: the beaux arts Grand Central Terminal, the jazzy art deco of the Chrysler Building and Rockefeller Center, and the cool glass exterior of the United Nations.

In the 50s you'll find swanky shops like Bergdorf Goodman, Bloomingdales, and Saks. Over on the West Side things aren't quite as swank, but they are full of life. Here you'll find the lights, glitter, and glamour of Times Square and the marquees of Broadway's theaters. What's shocking is how far the area has come; it wasn't so long ago that it was strip clubs and adult shops. To the north the hub of commerce that is Columbus Circle lures locals and visitors to high-end eateries and shops.

WHAT TO SEE

Fodor's Choice
★
Grand Central Terminal. Grand Central is not only the world's largest (76 acres) and the nation's busiest (500,000 commuters and subway riders use it daily) railway station, but also one of the world's greatest public spaces A massive four-year renovation completed in October 1998 restored the 1913 landmark to its original splendor—and then some.

You can best admire Grand Central's exquisite beaux arts architecture from its ornate south face on East 42nd Street, modeled after a Roman triumphal arch. Crowning the facade's Corinthian columns and 75-foot-high arched windows, a graceful clock keeps time for hurried commuters. In the central window stands an 1869 bronze statue of Cornelius Vanderbilt, who built the station to house his railroad empire.

Step inside past the glimmering chandeliers of the waiting room to the majestic **Main Concourse,** 200 feet long, 120 feet wide, and 120 feet (roughly 12 stories) high, modeled after a Roman bath. Overhead, a twinkling, fiber-optic celestial map of the constellations covers the robin's egg–blue ceiling. During rush hours you'll be swept into the tides and eddies of human traffic, which swirl around the central information kiosk, a popular meeting place. For a real taste of the station's early years, head beyond the western staircase to the **Campbell Apartment,** a clubby cocktail lounge housed in the restored private offices and salon of 1920s tycoon John W. Campbell.

Despite its grandeur, Grand Central still functions primarily as a railroad station. Underground, more than 60 ingeniously integrated railroad tracks lead trains upstate and to Connecticut via Metro-North Commuter Rail. The subway connects here as well. The **Municipal Art Society** (⊠ *457 Madison Ave., between 50th and 51st Sts., Midtown East* ☎ *212/935–3960* ⊕ *www.mas.org*) leads architectural tours of the terminal that begin here on Wednesday at 12:30. Reservations are not required, and a $10 donation is suggested. Meet at the information booth, Main Concourse. *Main entrance* ⊠ *E. 42nd St. at Park Ave. S, Midtown East* ☎ *212/935–3960* ⊕ *www.grandcentralterminal.com* Ⓜ *4, 5, 6, 7, S to 42nd St./Grand Central.*

Fodor's Choice
★
Museum of Modern Art (MoMA). Novices and reluctant art enthusiasts are often awestruck by the masterpieces before them here, including Monet's *Water Lilies,* Picasso's *Les Demoiselles d'Avignon,* and van Gogh's *Starry Night.* In 2004 the museum's $425 million face-lift by Yoshio Taniguchi increased exhibition space by nearly 50%, including space to accommodate large-scale contemporary installations. The museum continues to collect: Most recently it obtained important works by Martin Kippenberger, David Wojnarowicz, Jasper Johns, Kara Walker, and Neo Rauch. One of the top research facilities in modern and contemporary art is housed inside the museum's eight-story "Education and Research" building.

Beneath its bright lights, Times Square has been transformed from a seedy strip into a tourist-friendly zone.

In addition to the artwork, one of MoMA's main draws is the building itself. A maze of glass walkways permits art viewing from many angles. The 110-foot atrium entrance (accessed from the museum's lobby on either 53rd or 54th Street) leads to the movie theaters and the main-floor restaurant, Modern, with Alsatian-inspired cuisine.

A favorite resting spot is the Abby Aldrich Rockefeller Sculpture Garden. Designed by Philip Johnson, it features Barnett Newman's *Broken Obelisk* (1962–69). The glass wall lets visitors look directly into the surrounding galleries from the garden. Contemporary art (1970 to the present) from the museum's seven curatorial departments shares the second floor of the six-story building, and the skylighted top floor showcases an impressive lineup of changing exhibits. ■TIP➔ **Entrance between 4 and 8 pm on Friday is free, but come expecting to wait in line.** ⊠ *11 W. 53rd St., between 5th and 6th Aves., Midtown East* ☎ *212/708–9400* ⊕ *www.moma.org* 🖃 *$20* ⊙ *Sat.–Mon., Wed., and Thurs. 10:30–5:30, Fri. 10:30–8. Closed Tues.* Ⓜ *E, M to 5th Ave./53rd St.; B, D, F, M to 47th–50th Sts./Rockefeller Center*

Fodor'sChoice
★
Top of the Rock. Rockefeller Center's multifloor observation deck, first opened in 1933 and closed in the early 1980s, reopened in 2005 to be embraced by visitors and locals alike. Arriving just before sunset affords a view of the city that morphs before your eyes into a dazzling wash of colors, with a bird's-eye view of the tops of the Empire State Building, the Citicorp Building, and the Chrysler Building, and sweeping views northward to Central Park and south to the Statue of Liberty.

Transparent elevators lift you to the 67th-floor interior viewing area, then an escalator leads to the outdoor deck on the 69th floor for sightseeing through nonreflective glass safety panels. Then, take another elevator or stairs to the 70th floor for a 360-degree outdoor panorama of New York City on a deck that is only 20 feet wide and nearly 200 feet long. Reserved-time ticketing eliminates long lines. ■ TIP➔ Local consensus is that the views from the Top of the Rock are better than those from the Empire State Building, in part because the Empire State is part of the skyline here. ⊠ *Entrance on 50th St., between 5th and 6th Aves., Midtown West* ☎ *877/692–7625 or 212/698–2000* ⊕ *www.topoftherocknyc.com* ⊠ *$20* ☉ *Daily 8–midnight; last elevator at 11 pm* Ⓜ *B, D, F, M to 47th–50th Sts./Rockefeller Center.*

UPTOWN

The Upper East and Upper West Sides are two peas in a pod separated by the majesty of Central Park. For locals, they offer some impressive housing, with old-school apartments on Park Avenue all the way into the 90s, claimed by families looking to expand. As such, the areas are quite family-friendly.

On the Upper East Side the Museum Mile includes the irreplaceable Metropolitan Museum of Art, the Guggenheim, and the Whitney. On the Upper West Side, as far as kids go it's hard to top the appeal of the dinosaur skeletons at the Museum of Natural History. Opera lovers should be sure to have a visit to the Metropolitan Opera, while general culture hounds should inquire as to what's playing at Lincoln Center.

WHAT TO SEE

Fodor'sChoice
★
American Museum of Natural History. The largest natural history museum in the world is also one of the most impressive sights in New York. Four city blocks make up its 45 exhibition halls, which hold more than 32 million artifacts and wonders from the land, the sea, and outer space. With all those wonders, you won't be able to see everything on a single visit, but you can easily hit the highlights in half a day. The **Rose Center for Earth and Space** should not be missed. ⊠ *Central Park W. at W. 79 St., Upper West Side* ☎ *212/769–5200* ⊕ *www.amnh.org* ⊠ *$20 suggested donation, includes admission to Rose Center for Earth and Space* ☉ *Daily 10–5:45. Rose Center until 8:45 on Fri* Ⓜ *B, C to 81st St.–Museum of Natural History.*

Fodor'sChoice
★
Central Park. The park's creators had a simple goal: Design a place where city dwellers can go to forget the city. And while the town eventually grew far taller than the trees planted to hide it, this goal never falters. A combination escape hatch and exercise yard, Central Park is an urbanized Eden that offers residents and visitors alike a bite of the apple. We can't imagine how insufferably stressed New York City would be without it. ⊕ *www.centralparknyc.org.*

Fodor'sChoice
★
The Metropolitan Museum of Art. If the city held no other museum than the colossal Metropolitan Museum of Art, you could still occupy yourself for days roaming its labyrinthine corridors. Because the Metropolitan has something approaching 3 million works on display over its more than 2 million square feet of exhibition space, you're going to have to make some hard choices. Looking at everything here could take a week. ⊠ *5th Ave. at 82nd St., Upper East Side* ☎ *212/535–7710*

The skyline with some of the park's 26,000 trees.

⊕ *www.metmuseum.org* ✉ *$20 suggested donation* ⊙ *Tues.–Thurs. and Sun. 9:30–5:30, Fri. and Sat. 9:30–9* Ⓜ *4, 5, 6 to 86th St.*

Solomon R. Guggenheim Museum. Frank Lloyd Wright's landmark museum building is visited as much for its famous architecture as for its superlative art. Opened in 1959, shortly after Wright's death, the Guggenheim is acclaimed as one of the greatest buildings of the 20th century. After a three-year restoration project completed at the end of October 2008, the Guggenheim building is once again a glorious vision. The museum has strong holdings of Wassily Kandinsky, Paul Klee, Marc Chagall, Pablo Picasso, and Robert Mapplethorpe. ■TIP→ The museum is pay-what-you-wish on Saturday from 5:45 to 7:45. Lines can be long, so go early. The last tickets are handed out at 7:15. ✉ *1071 5th Ave., between E. 88th and E. 89th Sts., Upper East Side* ☎ *212/423–3500* ⊕ *www.guggenheim. org* ✉ *$18* ⊙ *Sun.–Wed. 10–5:45, Fri. 10–5:45, Sat. 10–7:45. Closed Thurs.* Ⓜ *4, 5, 6 to 86th St.*

Whitney Museum of American Art. With its bold collection of 20th- and 21st-centuy and contemporary American art, this museum presents an eclectic mix drawn from its permanent collection of more than 18,000 works. The museum was originally a gallery in the studio of sculptor and collector Gertrude Vanderbilt Whitney, whose talent and taste were accompanied by the money of two wealthy families. In 1930, after the Met turned down Whitney's offer to donate her collection of 20th-century American art, she established an independent museum in Greenwich Village. Now uptown, the minimalist gray-granite building opened in 1966, and was designed by Marcel Breuer and Hamilton Smith.

Although the collection on display constantly changes, notable pieces often on view include Hopper's *Early Sunday Morning* (1930), Bellows's *Dempsey and Firpo* (1924), Alexander Calder's beloved *Circus,* and several of Georgia O'Keeffe's dazzling flower paintings. ✉ *945 Madison Ave., at E. 75th St., Upper East Side* ☎ *800/whitney* ⊕ *www. whitney.org* ▨ *$18* ⊙ *Wed., Thurs., and weekends 11–6, Fri. 1–9* Ⓜ *6 to 77th St.*

WHERE TO EAT

Ready to take a bite out of New York? Hope you've come hungry. In a city where creativity is expressed in many ways, the food scene takes center stage, with literally thousands of ways to get an authentic taste of what Gotham is all about. Whether they're lining up at street stands, gobbling down legendary deli and diner grub, or chasing a coveted reservation at the latest celebrity-chef venue, New Yorkers are a demanding, yet appreciative audience.

Amid newfound economic realities, there's been a revived appreciation for value, meaning you can tap into wallet-friendly choices at every end of the spectrum. At many restaurants you'll also notice an almost religious reverence for seasonal cuisine. Ready, set, eat. Rest assured, this city will do its part to satisfy your appetite.

WHAT IT COSTS AT DINNER				
	¢	$	$$	$$$	$$$$
Restaurants	under $10	$10–$17	$18–$24	$25–$35	over $35

Price per person for a median main course or equivalent combination of smaller dishes. Note: If a restaurant offers only prix-fixe (set-price) meals, it has been given the price category that reflects the full prix-fixe price.

LOWER MANHATTAN

$$
ITALIAN
Fodor'sChoice
★

✕**Emporio.** Emporio is a chic, welcoming hangout with warmth to spare. The brick-lined front room is a gathering spot for happy hour at the bar, featuring an appetizing selection of free small bites like frittata, white-bean salad, and ham-and-spinach *tramezzini* (finger sandwiches). The centerpiece of the large, skylit back room—great for small and large parties alike—is a wood-fired oven which turns out crisp, thin-crusted pizzas topped with staples like prosciutto, buffalo mozzarella, and arugula. Try house-made pastas like chewy garganelli with pork sausage and house-made ragu, entrées like whole roasted branzino with grilled lemon, then finish with piping-hot dessert calzone filled with ricotta, Nutella, and hazelnuts, or a delicate panna cotta with poached plums. ✉ *231 Mott St., between Prince and Spring Sts. NoLita* ☎ *212/966–1234* ⊕ *www.auroraristorante.com/emporio* ▭ *AE, D, DC, MC, V* Ⓜ *B, D, F, M, A, C, E to W. 4th St., 6 to Bleecker St.*

$$
NEW AMERICAN
Fodor'sChoice
★

✕**Hundred Acres.** The owners of Cookshop and Five Points have set up digs on MacDougal Street. Don't count on a big menu: The daily choices are limited to seven main dishes and one special entrée. The Rhode Island squid with fennel is particularly delicious. For the mains, try the black grouper with peas and garlic sausage or the flap steak with broccoli rabe. The classic burger made from pasture-raised beef, topped with Vermont cheddar and served with fries and Vidalia onion mayonnaise, should not be missed. ⊠ *38 MacDougal St., between Houston and Prince Sts., Soho* ☎ *212/475–7500* ⊕ *hundredacresnyc.com* ▭ *AE, DC, MC, V* Ⓜ *1 to Houston; C, E to Spring St., N, R to Prince St.*

¢ ✕ **Nha Trang.** You can get a great meal for under $10 at this low-atmosphere Vietnamese restaurant in Chinatown. Start with crispy spring rolls, sweet-and-sour seafood soup, or shrimp grilled on sugarcane. For a follow-up, don't miss the thin pork chops, which are marinated in a sweet vinegary sauce and grilled until charred. If the line is long, which it usually is, even with a second location around the corner at 148 Centre Street, you may be asked to sit at a table with strangers. ⊠ *87 Baxter St., between Bayard and Canal Sts., Chinatown* ☎ *212/233–5948* ▭ *No credit cards* Ⓜ *6, J, M, N, Q, R, Z to Canal St.*

VIETNAMESE
Fodor's Choice
★

THE VILLAGE, CHELSEA, AND UNION SQUARE AREA

$$$ ✕ **Aldea.** Bouley alumnus George Mendes has opened a restaurant that uses his Portuguese heritage as inspiration and takes it to new heights. Although there are no bad seats in the sleekly appointed bi-level space decorated with touches of wood, glass, and blue accents, watching Mendes work in his spotless tiled kitchen from one of the seats at the chef's counter in the back is undeniably exciting. *Petiscos* (small bites) like Kumamoto oysters and a farm-fresh egg with bacalao exhibit sophisticated cooking techniques and flavors presented in highly addictive packages. On the $85 five-course chef's tasting menu, the sea urchin on a crispy toast flat is a standout, as is the duck confit with chorizo and shatteringly crunchy duck-skin cracklings. ⊠ *31 W. 17th St., between 5th and 6th Aves., Flatiron District* ☎ *212/675–7223* ⊕ *www. aldearestaurant.com* ⌲ *Reservations essential* ▭ *AE, MC, V* ☉ *Closed Sun. No lunch Sat.* Ⓜ *N, R, Q, 4, 5, 6 to 14th St./Union Square; F, M to 14th St. and 6th Ave.*

MEDITERRANEAN
Fodor's Choice
★

$$$ ✕ **A Voce.** Executive chef Missy Robbins has a passion for Italian cuisine, and it shows. For five years prior to joining A Voce, she was the executive chef at Chicago's Spiaggia. Her menu is inspired, and represents regional dishes from all over Italy. The pasta is prepared fresh every day, and Robbins's fish and meat dishes are exceptional. The attentive staff also helps to make the dining experience here a real pleasure. A Voce's atmosphere is warm, and the 90-seat dining room has a retro Italian feel to it—walnut floors, pale green leather-top tables, and Eames chairs. There's also additional seating on the patio when weather permits. ⊠ *41 Madison Ave., between 25th and 26th Sts., Flatiron District* ☎ *212/545–8555* ⊕ *www.avocerestaurant.com* ▭ *AE, MC, V* Ⓜ *N, R to 23rd St.*

ITALIAN
Fodor's Choice
★

$ ✕ **Baoguette.** Vietnamese *Banh Mi* have taken New York by storm in the past couple of years, and Baoguette, a chainlet from restaurateur Michael Huynh, is a great place to try these spicy, multilayered baguette sandwiches. This is the flagship decorated with raffia walls and large photos of Vietnamese street scenes, and though there a few tables, the majority of customers get take-out sandwiches. Try the namesake sandwich, layered with savory pâté, flavorful pulled pork, and aromatic herbs, or the addictive Sloppy Bao, a sweet and savory sloppy joe with

VIETNAMESE
Fodor's Choice
★

At lower Manhattan's casual, eclectic restaurants it's not unusual to find waiters in classic French bistro attire serving diners in trucker caps.

curried beef, mango, and lemongrass. ✉ *37 St. Marks Pl., between 2nd and 3rd Aves., East Village* ☎ *212/380–1487* ⊕ *www.baoguettecafe. com* ⚘ *Reservations not accepted* ⊟ *No credit cards* Ⓜ *R to 8th St./ NYU; 6 to Astor Pl./4th Ave.*

$$
GASTROPUB
Fodor'sChoice
★

✕ **DBGB Kitchen & Bar.** The latest addition to Daniel Boulud's New York City restaurant fleet, DBGB forgoes the white tablecloths, formal service, and steep prices found at the famed chef's fancier digs, and instead pays homage to the grittier, younger feel of its Lower East Side location. (The name is a wink to CBGB.) The menu features 13 different varieties of sausages, decadently sinful burgers, and classic entrées like steak-frites, and lemon and rosemary roasted chicken. The $24 three-course, lunch prix-fixe is quite a steal. ✉ *299 Bowery, between Houston and 1st St., Lower East Side* ☎ *212/933–5300* ⊕ *www.danielnyc.com* ⚘ *Reservations essential* ⊟ *AE, D, DC, MC, V* ☺ *No lunch Mon.* Ⓜ *F to 2nd Ave.*

$$$$
NEW AMERICAN
Fodor'sChoice
★

✕ **Eleven Madison Park.** Under Swiss-born chef Daniel Humm, who was lured from San Francisco's Campton Place by restaurateur Danny Meyer, this art nouveau jewel overlooking Madison Park has become one of the city's most consistently exciting places to dine. EMP is now prix-fixe only; diners choose four or five courses, tell servers what they like and don't like—though the restaurant may independently research that fact—and go from there. It's brilliant, unexpected continental fare. ✉ *11 Madison Ave., at 24th St., Flatiron District* ☎ *212/889–0905* ⊕ *www.elevenmadisonpark.com* ⚘ *Reservations essential* ⊟ *AE, D, DC, MC, V* ☺ *Closed Sun. No lunch weekends* Ⓜ *N, R, 6 to 23rd St.*

$ ✕**Fatty Crab.** This rustic Malaysian cantina showcases the exciting cuisine of chef Zak Pelaccio, who spent years cooking at famous French restaurants before escaping to Southeast Asia for a year, where he fell in love with the flavors of the region. Start with the addictive pickled watermelon and crispy pork salad, an improbable combination that's both refreshing and decadent. The can't-miss signature dish is chili crab—cracked Dungeness crab in a pool of rich, spicy chili sauce, served with bread for dipping. It's messy for sure, but worth rolling up your sleeves for. Friday and Saturday the kitchen is open until 2 am. ✉ *643 Hudson St., between Gansevoort and Horatio Sts., West Village* ☎ *212/352–3590* ⊕ *www.fattycrab.com* ⌕ *Reservations not accepted for parties of 6 or fewer* ▭ *AE, D, MC, V* Ⓜ *A, C, E to 14th St.; L to 8th Ave.*

MALAYSIAN
Fodor'sChoice
★

$ ✕**Katz's Delicatessen.** Everything and nothing has changed at Katz's since it first opened in 1888, when the neighborhood was dominated by Jewish immigrants. The rows of Formica tables, the long self-service counter, and such signs as "Send a salami to your boy in the army" are all completely authentic. What's different are the area's demographics, but all types still flock here for succulent hand-carved corned beef and pastrami sandwiches, soul-warming soups, juicy hot dogs, and crisp half-sour pickles. ✉ *205 E. Houston St., at Ludlow St., Lower East Side* ☎ *212/254–2246* ⊕ *www.katzdeli.com* ▭ *AE, MC, V* Ⓜ *F to 2nd Ave.*

DELI
Fodor'sChoice
★

$$$$ ✕**Momofuku Ko.** A seasonal tasting menu full of clever combinations and esoteric ingredients explains the deafening buzz for James Beard Award–winning chef David Chang's latest venture. Ko's small, intimate space is sparsely furnished with a counter of blond wood and only a dozen stools. Diners get to see Ko's chefs in action as they prepare all manner of inventive dishes, including a signature preparation of frozen foie-gras torchon grated over lychee fruits and white-wine gelee. Reservations can only be made online, no more than seven days ahead, and are extremely difficult to get. Log on at 10 am (credit-card number needed just to get in the system), when new reservations are available, and keep hitting reload. ✉ *163 1st Ave., at E. 10th St., East Village* ☎ *212/228–0031 or 212/475–7899* ⊕ *www.momofuku.com* ⌕ *Reservations essential* ▭ *AE, MC, V* ⊘ *No lunch* Ⓜ *L to 1st Ave.; 6 to Astor Pl.*

ASIAN
Fodor'sChoice
★

¢ ✕**Shake Shack.** Though the newer, uptown location of Danny Meyer's patties 'n shakes joint is bigger by far, this is where it all began. Here in Madison Square Park there's no indoor seating—just snaking outdoor lines. Fresh steer burgers are ground daily, and a single will run you from $3.75 to $4.75, depending on what you want on it. The Shake Shack also offers beef and bird (chicken) hot dogs, french fries and fries drizzled with Shack-made cheddar and American cheese sauce, and a variety of delicious frozen custard desserts, and—of course—shakes! ✉ *Madison Square Park near Madison Ave. and E. 23rd St., Flatiron District* ☎ *212/889–6600* ⊕ *www.shakeshack.com* ▭ *AE, D, MC, V* Ⓜ *N, R, 6 to 23rd St.*

BURGER
Fodor'sChoice
★

MIDTOWN

$$$$ ✕**Adour Alain Ducasse.** Master chef Alain Ducasse adds to his growing empire with the upscale and elegant Adour, located in the equally sophisticated St. Regis Hotel. Celebratory couples of all ages gravitate to the Left and Right Bank rooms, while a mix of tourists, shoppers,

MODERN FRENCH
Fodor'sChoice
★

4

and businessmen settle on plush burgundy chairs and banquettes in the regal but relaxed main dining room. Beautifully baked baguettes and fragrant olive and sourdough rolls are flown in, parbaked, from Paris, and finished downstairs. Sommeliers help decipher an international wine list (displayed on interactive computer screens at the bar) with bottles that range from $35 to $19,000. ⊠ *2 E. 55th St., near 5th Ave., Midtown East* ☎ *212/710–2277* ⊕ *www.adour-stregis.com* ⚎ *Reservations essential* ⊟ *AE, D, DC, MC, V* ⊙ *No lunch* Ⓜ *E, M to 5th Ave./53rd St.; F to 57th St.*

¢ ✕ **Burger Joint.** What's a college burger bar, done up in particle board

BURGER and rec-room decor straight out of a *Happy Days* episode, doing hidden

Fodor'sChoice inside of a five-star Midtown hotel? This tongue-in-cheek lunch spot,

★ hidden behind a heavy red velvet curtain in the Parker Meridien hotel, does such boisterous midweek business that lines often snake through the lobby. Stepping behind the curtain, you can find baseball cap–wearing grease-spattered cooks dispensing paper-wrapped cheeseburgers and crisp thin fries. ⊠ *118 W. 57th St., between 6th and 7th Aves., Midtown West* ☎ *212/245–5000* ⊕ *www.parkermeridien.com* ⊟ *No credit cards* Ⓜ *F, N, Q, R to 57th St.*

$$$$ ✕ **L'Atelier de Joël Robuchon.** The New York branch of Joël Robuchon's

FRENCH superluxurious tapas bar, inside the Four Seasons Hotel, features essen-

Fodor'sChoice tially the same food (with a more natural-hue decor) as the Paris origi-

★ nal. And that, it turns out, is a very good thing. The perfectionist chef has installed a longtime protégé to uphold the standards that can make a Robuchon meal a life-changing experience. Skip the regular-size appetizers and entrées. Instead, secure a seat at the pear-wood counter and cobble together your own small-plate feast. But be warned: Robuchon's little bites come at a steep price. ⊠ *57 E. 57th St., between Madison and Park Aves., Midtown East* ☎ *212/350–6658* ⊕ *www.fourseasons.com/ newyorkfs/dining.html* ⚎ *Reservations essential* ⊟ *AE, MC, V* ⊙ *No lunch* Ⓜ *4, 5, 6 to 59th St.*

UPTOWN

$$ ✕ **Bar Boulud.** Acclaimed French chef Daniel Boulud, known for upscale

FRENCH New York City eateries Daniel and Café Boulud, shows diners his more

Fodor'sChoice casual side with this lively contemporary bistro and wine bar. The menu

★ emphasizes charcuterie, including terrines and pâtés designed by Parisian charcutier Gilles Verot, who relocated just to work with Boulud, as well as traditional French bistro dishes like steak frites and *poulet rôti à l'ail* (roast chicken with garlic mashed potatoes). The 500-bottle wine list is heavy on wines from Burgundy and the Rhône Valley. ⊠ *1900 Broadway, between 63rd and 64th Sts., Upper West Side* ☎ *212/595– 0303* ⊕ *www.barboulud.com* ⊟ *AE, DC, MC, V* Ⓜ *1 to 66th St./Lincoln Center; 1, A, C, B, D to 59th St./Columbus Circle.*

$$$$ ✕ **Daniel.** Celebrity-chef Daniel Boulud has created one of the most

FRENCH elegant dining experiences in Manhattan today, in an expansive space

Fodor'sChoice that recently underwent a multimillion-dollar renovation. The prix-

★ fixe–only menu (there are à la carte selections in the elegant lounge and bar) is predominantly French. Don't forget the decadent desserts and overflowing cheese trolley. A three-course vegetarian menu is also available. ⊠ *60 E. 65th St., between Madison and Park Aves., Upper*

East Side ☎ *212/288–0033* ⊕ *www.danielnyc.com/daniel* ⌕ *Reservations essential. Jacket required* ▤ *AE, DC, MC, V* ⊙ *Closed Sun. No lunch* Ⓜ *6 to 68th St./Hunter College.*

$$$$ ✕ **Marea.** Carefully sourced, meticulously prepared fish and seafood

ITALIAN take center stage at this glossy, well-pedigreed restaurant. Large pic-

Fodor's Choice ture windows in the dining room offer expansive views of Central

★ Park South, and silver-dipped shells on pedestals decorate the dining room. No expense is spared in importing the very best of the ocean's bounty, though you'd be remiss, if you skipped the pastas that made chef Michael White famous at the East Side's Convivio. They're served here in lusty iterations like rich fusilli with octopus and bone marrow and spaghetti with sea urchin. Service is flawless, and even the dishware—scalloped china embossed with the restaurant's name, tiny shell-shaped espresso cups—is special. ⊠ *240 Central Park S, between Broadway and 7th Ave., Midtown West* ☎ *212/582–5100* ⊕ *www.marea-nyc.com* ⌕ *Reservations essential* ▤ *AE, MC, V* Ⓜ *A, B, C, D, 1 to Columbus Circle.*

WHERE TO STAY

It's a buyer's market for hotels here in New York. But does that mean that New York is cheap? Not exactly. Deals are plentiful—if you're not set on specific properties. That said, if you want to stay in a specific place and the rate seems reasonable, book it—it's just as likely to go up, especially during peak seasons (spring and fall).

And how to choose? Well, the first thing to consider is location. Many New York City visitors insist on staying in the hectic Midtown area, but other neighborhoods are often just as convenient. Less-touristy areas, such as Gramercy, the Lower East Side, the Upper West Side—even Brooklyn—offer a far more realistic sense of New York life.

Also consider timing: The least expensive months to book rooms in the city are January and February. If you're flexible on dates, ask the reservationist if there's a cheaper time to stay during your preferred traveling month—that way you can avoid peak dates, like Fashion Week and the New York Marathon. And be sure to ask about possible weekend packages that could include a third night free. The Financial District in particular can be a discount gold mine on the weekend.

Hotel reviews have been condensed for this book. Please go to Fodors. com for full reviews of each property.

WHAT IT COSTS				
¢	$	$$	$$$	$$$$
Hotels	under $150	$150–$299	$300–$449	$450–$600	over $600

Prices are for a standard double room, excluding 14.75% city and state taxes.

LOWER MANHATTAN

$ 🛏 **Ace Hotel.** Step inside the Ace hotel, and any notion of what a hotel
Fodor'sChoice could and should be is left at the door; the eastern outpost of a West
★ Coast hotel chain provides the style and luxury you'd expect to find at
five-star hotel, minus the pretension and price. **Pros:** in-house restaurant,
the Breslin, means you won't have to travel far for trendy dining;
lobby java shop is by the excellent Stumptown Coffee Roasters. **Cons:**
caters to a young crowd; may be too sceney for some. ⊠ *20 W. 29th
St. at Broadway, Flatiron District* ☎ *212/679–2222* ⊕ *www.acehotel.
com* ⌁ *251 rooms, 11 suites* ⌂ *In-room: a/c, safe, refrigerator (some),
Wi-Fi. In-hotel: restaurant, room service, bars, gym, laundry service,
Wi-Fi hotspot, parking (paid), some pets allowed* ⊟ *AE, MC, V* Ⓜ *N,
R to 28th St.; 1 to 28th St.*

$$$ 🛏 **Crosby Street Hotel.** Here in SoHo's heart sits the Crosby Street Hotel,
Fodor'sChoice which in late 2009 became the first branch of the U.K.'s Firmdale Hotels
★ to open in the United States. Hotel design in New York is often a man's
world of leather and dark colors; here the pieces, all handpicked by
co-owner Kit Kemp, are colorful, light, and whimsical. **Pros:** unique
design; big, bright rooms; great bar. **Cons:** breakfast not included;
small gym. ⊠ *79 Crosby St., between Prince and Spring Sts., SoHo*
☎ *212/226–6400* ⊕ *www.firmdale.com* ⌁ *86 rooms* ⌂ *In-room: a/c,
safe (some), DVD, Wi-Fi. In-hotel: restaurant, room service, bar, gym,
laundry service, Wi-Fi, some pets allowed* ⊟ *AE, D, MC, V* Ⓜ *6 to
Spring St., R to Prince St.*

THE VILLAGE, CHELSEA, AND UNION SQUARE AREA

$ 🛏 **The Standard.** André Balazs's architectural statement on the West
Fodor'sChoice Side, the Standard is New York's buzziest hotel. **Pros:** beautiful building;
★ beautiful people; impressive restaurant space. **Cons:** noisy at
night; tight rooms; sceney. ⊠ *848 Washington St., between W. 13th
and Little W. 12th Sts., Meatpacking District* ☎ *212/645–4646* ⊕ *www.
standardhotels.com* ⌁ *337 rooms* ⌂ *In-room: a/c, Internet, Wi-Fi. In-
hotel: 2 restaurants, room service, bars, gym, spa, Wi-Fi hotspot* ⊟ *AE,
MC, V* Ⓜ *A, C, E, L to 14th St. and 8th Ave.*

$$ 🛏 **Thompson LES.** The Thompson LES is a stylish addition to the neigh-
Fodor'sChoice borhood, the smoked-glass tower contrasting with the Hotel on Riving-
★ ton's wide-open views. Rooms are stark black-and-white affairs, with
low platform beds whose headboards are lightboxes displaying works
by the photographer Lee Friedlander. **Pros:** great amenities; in the heart
of downtown; great views from suites. **Cons:** snobby staff; rooms stylish
but dark. ⊠ *190 Allen St., between Houston and Stanton Sts., Lower
East Side* ☎ *212/460–5300* ⊕ *www.thompsonhotels.com* ⌁ *131 rooms*
⌂ *In-room: a/c, safe, refrigerator, Wi-Fi. In-hotel: restaurant, room service, bars, pool, laundry service, Wi-Fi hotspot* ⊟ *AE, MC, V* Ⓜ *F, J,
M, Z to Delancey/Essex Sts.*

MIDTOWN

$$ 🛏 **Library Hotel.** Bookishly handsome, this stately landmark brownstone,
Fodor'sChoice built in 1900, is inspired by the New York Public Library a block away.
★ **Pros:** fun rooftop bar; playful book themes; stylish rooms. **Cons:** roof-
top often reserved for events; more books in rooms themselves would

be nice. ⊠ *299 Madison Ave., at E. 41st St., Midtown East* ☎ *212/983–4500 or 877/793–7323* ⊕ *www.libraryhotel.com* ↪ *60 rooms* ☖ *In-room: a/c, safe, refrigerator, DVD, Internet, Wi-Fi. In-hotel: restaurant, room service, bar, laundry service, parking (paid)* ☰ *AE, DC, MC, V* ⦿| *CP* Ⓜ *4, 5, 6, 7, S to 42nd St./Grand Central.*

$$$$ 　 ⛶ **Mandarin Oriental.** The Mandarin brings some Asian style to a rather
Fodor's Choice 　 staid corner of New York. Its cavernous lobby sizzles with energy
★ 　 from the 35th floor of the Time Warner Center. **Cons:** Trump hotel blocks portion of park views; expensive; mall-like surroundings. ⊠ *80 Columbus Circle, at 60th St., Midtown West* ☎ *212/805–8800* ⊕ *www. mandarinoriental.com* ↪ *203 rooms, 46 suites* ☖ *In-room: a/c, refrigerator, DVD, Internet, Wi-Fi. In-hotel: restaurant, room service, bar, pool, gym, spa, laundry service* ☰ *AE, D, DC, MC, V* Ⓜ *A, B, C, D, 1 to 59th St./Columbus Circle.*

$$$$ 　 ⛶ **The Peninsula.** Stepping through the Peninsula's beaux arts facade onto
Fodor's Choice 　 the grand staircase overhung with a monumental chandelier, you know
★ 　 you're in for a glitzy treat. **Pros:** brilliant service; fabulous rooms, with the best lighting of all city hotels (good angles, easy to use); unforgettable rooftop bar. **Cons:** expensive. ⊠ *700 5th Ave., at 55th St., Midtown East* ☎ *212/956–2888 or 800/262–9467* ⊕ *newyork.peninsula. com* ↪ *185 rooms, 54 suites* ☖ *In-room: a/c, safe, refrigerator, Internet, Wi-Fi. In-hotel: restaurant, room service, bars, pool, gym, spa, laundry service, parking (paid), some pets allowed* ☰ *AE, D, DC, MC, V* Ⓜ *E, M to 5th Ave.*

$$$$ 　 ⛶ **Plaza Hotel.** Eloise's adopted home on the corner of Central Park, the
Fodor's Choice 　 Plaza is back in the hotel game after a $400 million renovation. **Cons:**
★ 　 rooms aren't that big for the money; Oak Room restaurant is pricey. ⊠ *768 5th Ave., at Central Park S, Midtown West* ☎ *212/759–3000* ⊕ *www.theplaza.com* ↪ *282 rooms, 102 suites* ☖ *In-room: a/c, safe, DVD, Wi-Fi. In-hotel: 2 restaurants, room service, bar, gym, spa, laundry service, Wi-Fi hotspot* ☰ *AE, D, DC, MC, V* Ⓜ *N, R to 59th St.*

$$$$ 　 ⛶ **Ritz-Carlton New York, Central Park.** It's all about the park views here.
☾ 　 Service aside, the competition among properties near the Park's south
Fodor's Choice 　 side is fierce, and while the Ritz isn't the foremost of the bunch, it does
★ 　 offer some nice perks. **Pros:** great concierge; personalized service; stellar location; views. **Cons:** pricey; limited common areas. ⊠ *50 Central Park S, at 6th Ave., Midtown West* ☎ *212/308–9100 or 800/241–3333* ⊕ *www.ritzcarlton.com* ↪ *259 rooms, 47 suites* ☖ *In-room: a/c, safe, DVD (some), Internet, Wi-Fi. In-hotel: restaurant, room service, bar, gym, spa, laundry service, parking (paid), some pets allowed* ☰ *AE, D, DC, MC, V* Ⓜ *F, M to 57th St.*

$$$$ 　 ⛶ **The St. Regis.** Even without the hive of activity in its unparalleled pub-
Fodor's Choice 　 lic spaces, this 5th Avenue beaux arts landmark would rank near the top
★ 　 of any best-of list. **Pros:** rooms combine true luxury with helpful technology; easy-access butler service; superb in-house dining; prestigious location. **Cons:** expensive; too serious for families seeking fun. ⊠ *2 E. 55th St., at 5th Ave., Midtown East* ☎ *212/753–4500 or 877/787–3447* ⊕ *www.stregis.com* ↪ *164 rooms, 65 suites* ☖ *In-room: a/c, safe, refrigerator, DVD, Internet. In-hotel: restaurant, room service, gym, laundry service, parking (paid)* ☰ *AE, D, DC, MC, V* Ⓜ *E, M to 5th Ave.*

THE ARTS

New York has somewhere between 200 and 250 legitimate theaters (meaning those with theatrical performances, not movies or strip shows), and many more ad hoc venues—parks, churches, lofts, galleries, rooftops, even parking lots. The city is also a revolving door of special events: summer jazz, one-act-play marathons, film festivals, and music and dance celebrations from the classical to the avant-garde, to name just a few.

TICKETS 101

What do tickets sell for, anyway? Not counting the limited "premium seat" category (or discount deals), the top ticket price for Broadway musicals is now hovering at $130; the low end for musicals is in the $75 range. Nonmusical comedies and dramas start at about $60 and top out at about $120. Off-Broadway show tickets average $35–$80, while off-off-Broadway shows can run as low as $10–$15. Tickets to an opera start at about $25 for nosebleed seats and can soar close to $400 for prime locations. Classical music concerts go for $25 to $100 or more, depending on the venue. Dance performances are usually in the $15 to $60 range, but expect seats for the ballet in choice spots to cost more.

Scoring tickets is fairly easy, especially if you have some flexibility. But if timing or cost is critical, the only way to ensure you'll get the seats you want is to make your purchase in advance—and that might be months ahead for a hit show. In general, tickets for Saturday evenings and for weekend matinees are the toughest to secure.

For opera, classical music, and dance performances, go to the box office or order tickets through the venue's Web site. For smaller performing-arts companies, and especially for off-Broadway shows, try **Ticket Central** (✉ 416 W. 42nd St., between 9th and 10th Aves., Midtown West ☎ 212/279–4200 ⊕ www.ticketcentral.com ☉ Daily noon–8 pm Ⓜ A, C, E to 42nd St.), which is right in the center of Theater Row; service charges are nominal here. **SmartTix** (☎ 212/868–4444 ⊕ www.smarttix. com) is relatively new, but a completely reliable resource for (usually) smaller performing-arts companies, including dance and music; their service charges are nominal as well. Inside the Times Square Information Center is the **Broadway Concierge & Ticket Center** (✉ 1560 Broadway, between W. 46th and W. 47th Sts., Midtown West ☎ 888/broadway ⊕ www.livebroadway.com ☉ Ticket hrs: Mon.–Sat. 9–7, Sun. 10–6 Ⓜ 1, 2, 3, 7, N, Q, R, S to 42nd St./Times Sq.; N, R to 49th St.), where you can purchase full- and premium-price tickets for most Broadway (and some Off-Broadway) shows.

Sure bets for Broadway (and some other big-hall events) are the box office or either **Telecharge** (☎ 212/239–6200, 800/432–7250 outside NYC ⊕ www.telecharge.com) or **Ticketmaster** (☎ 212/307–4100, 866/448–7849 automated service, 212/220–0500 premium tickets ⊕ www.ticketmaster.com). Virtually all larger shows are listed with one service or the other, but never both; specifying "premium" will help you get elusive—and expensive (upwards of $200–$300)—seats. A broker or your hotel concierge should be able to procure last-minute tickets, but prices may even exceed "premium" rates. Be prepared to pay steep add-on fees (per ticket *and* per order) for all ticketing services.

■TIP→ The advantage of going to the box office is twofold: There are no add-on service fees, and a ticket seller can personally advise you about sight lines—and knee room—for the seat location you are considering. Broadway box offices do not usually have direct phone lines; their walk-in hours are generally 10 am until curtain.

BROADWAY (AND OFF) AT A DISCOUNT

The cheapest—though chanciest—ticket opportunities are found at participating theater box offices on the day of the performance. These "Rush" tickets, usually about $25, may be distributed by lottery and are usually for front-row (possibly neck-craning) seats. Check the comprehensive planner on ⊕ *www.nytix.com* or go to the box office of the show you are interested in to discover whether they have such an offer and how to pursue it. Obstructed-view seats or those in the very rear balcony are sometimes available for advance purchase; the price point on these is usually in the $35–$40 range.

But for advanced discount purchases, the best seating is likely available by using a discount "code"—procure these 20%- to 50%-off codes online. (You will need to register on each Web site.) The excellent no-subscription-required ⊕ *www.broadwaybox.com* site is comprehensive, and posts all discount codes currently available for Broadway shows. As with all discount codes offered through online subscriber services—**TheaterMania** (⊕ *www.theatermania.com*), **Playbill** (⊕ *www.playbill.com*), and **Best of Off Broadway** (⊕ *bestofoffbroadway.com*) among them—to avoid service charges, you must bring a printout of the offer to the box office, and make your purchase there.

For seats at 25%–50% off the usual price, go to one of the **TKTS booths** (✉ *Duffy Sq. at W. 47th St. and Broadway, Midtown West* Ⓜ *1, 2, 3, 7, N, Q, R, S, W to 42nd St./Times Sq.; N, R, W to 49th St.; 1 to 50th St.* ✉ *South St. Seaport at Front and John Sts., Lower Manhattan* Ⓜ *2, 3, 4, 5, A, C, E, J, M, Z to Fulton St./Broadway-Nassau* ✉ *Downtown Brooklyn, at the Myrtle St. Promenade and Jay St., Brooklyn* Ⓜ *A, C, F to Jay St.-Borough Hall; R, 2, 3, 4, 5 to Court St.–Borough Hall* ⊕ *www.tdf.org*). Although they do tack on a $4 per ticket service charge, and not all shows are predictably available, the broad choices and ease of selection—and of course, the solid discount—make TKTS the go-to source for the flexible theatergoer.

At the snazzily updated Duffy Square location (look for the bright red glass staircase), there is a separate *play only* window to further simplify—and speed—things. Duffy hours are Monday–Saturday 3–8 (for evening performances); for Wednesday and Saturday matinees 10–2; for Sunday matinees 11–3; Sunday evening shows, from 3 until a half hour before curtain.

Seaport hours are Monday–Saturday 11–6, Sunday 11–4. Brooklyn hours are weekdays 11–6. With the exception of matinees at the Seaport and Brooklyn locations (they sell these for next-day performances only), all shows offered are for that same day. Credit cards, cash, or traveler's checks are accepted *at all locations*. ■TIP→ Their Web site lists what was available at the booths in the previous week to give you an idea of what shows you'll find; and for all current shows it notes whether they are "frequently," "occasionally," "rarely," or "never" available at their booths.

NIGHTLIFE

The nightlife scene still resides largely downtown—in dives in the East Village and Lower East Side, classic jazz joints in the West Village, and the Meatpacking District's and Chelsea's see-and-be-seen clubs. Still, Midtown, especially around Hell's Kitchen, has developed quite the vibrant scene, too, and plenty of preppy hangouts dot the Upper East and Upper West sides.

For those of you trying to give NYC its "Fun City" rep back, *Paper* magazine has a good list of the roving parties. You can check their online nightlife guide, *PM* (NYC), via their Web site ⊕ *www.papermag. com*. Another streetwise mag, *The L Magazine* (⊕ *www.thelmagazine. com*), lists what's happening day by day at many of the city's lounges and clubs, as well as dance and comedy performances. The *New York Times* has listings of cabaret and jazz shows, most comprehensively in their Friday and Sunday Arts section. Bear in mind that a venue's life span is often measured in months, not years. Phone ahead to make sure your target hasn't closed or turned into a polka hall (although, you never know—that could be fun, too).

SHOPPING

New York shopping is a nonstop eye-opener, from the pristine couture houses flanking Madison Avenue to quirkier shops downtown. No matter which threshold you cross, shopping here promises to be an event. For every bursting department store there's an echoing, minimalist boutique; for every familiar national brand there's a secret local favorite.

Even for most New Yorkers, window-shopping is unavoidable. Residents can't help passing tempting displays while running to the office or dashing out for coffee. The must-hit shopping neighborhoods concentrate their temptations, sometimes with boutiques in nearly every address on a block, so you can easily spend a couple of hours just browsing.

SOHO

Jaded locals call this neighborhood a touristy outdoor mall. True, you'll see plenty of familiar company names, and several common, less expensive chains, but you can still hit a few clothing and housewares boutiques you won't find elsewhere in this country. The hottest shopping area runs west from Broadway over to 6th Avenue, between West Houston and Grand streets. Don't overlook a couple of streets east of Broadway: Crosby and Lafayette each have a handful of intriguing shops.

NOLITA

Like SoHo, NoLita (shorthand for "North of Little Italy) has gone from a locals-only, understated area to a crowded weekend magnet, as much about people-watching as it is about shopping. Still, unlike those of

A shop window in Soho.

its SoHo neighbor, these stores remain largely one-of-a-kind. Running along the parallel north–south spines of Elizabeth, Mott, and Mulberry streets, between East Houston and Kenmare streets, NoLita's boutiques tend to be small and, as real estate dictates, somewhat pricey.

5TH AVENUE AND 57TH STREET

Fifth Avenue from Rockefeller Center to Central Park South pogos between landmark department stores, glossy international designer boutiques, and casual national chains. What they all have in common: massive flagship spaces.

The intersection of 5th Avenue with 57th Street distills this mix of old and new, exclusive and accessible. From these corners you'll see blue-chip New York classics (jeweler Tiffany & Co., the Bergdorf Goodman department stores), luxury giants (Gucci and the glass box of Louis Vuitton), a high-tech wonderland (another glass box for Apple), and show-off digs for informal brands (NikeTown, Abercrombie & Fitch). Capping this shopping stretch at East 58th Street is the colossal, exceptional toy store FAO Schwarz. If large-scale doesn't do it for you, you're better off heading downtown.

MADISON AVENUE

If you're craving a couture fix, cab it straight to Madison Avenue between East 57th and East 79th streets. Here the greatest Italian, French, and American fashion houses form a platinum-card corridor for ladies who lunch.

Most occupy large, glass-facade spaces, but there are some exceptions, from intimate boutiques in old brownstones to the imposing turn-of-the-20th-century mansion now home to Ralph Lauren. Barneys, a full-fledged if very select department store, fits right in with the avenue's recherché roll call. But Madison isn't just a fashion funnel. A couple of marvelous booksellers and several outstanding antiques dealers and art galleries share this address as well.

THE MEATPACKING DISTRICT

For nearly a century, this industrial western edge of downtown Manhattan was defined by slaughterhouses and meatpacking plants, blood-splattered cobblestoned streets, and men lugging carcasses into warehouses way before dawn.

But in the late 1990s the area between West 14th Street, Gansevoort Street, Hudson Street, and 11th Avenue speedily transformed into another kind of meat market. Many of the old warehouses now house ultrachic shops, nightclubs, and restaurants packed with angular fashionistas. Despite the influx of a few chains—albeit stylish ones like Scoop—eclectic boutiques keep popping up.

LOWER EAST SIDE

Once home to multitudes of Jewish immigrants from Russia and Eastern Europe, the Lower East Side has traditionally been New Yorkers' bargain beat. The center of it all is Orchard Street, where vendors still holler, "Lady, have I got a deal for you!"

Here tiny, no-nonsense clothing stores and scrappy stalls hang on to the past, while funky local designers gradually claim more turf. Ludlow Street, one block east of Orchard, has become the main drag for twentysomethings with attitude, its boutiques wedged in between bars and low-key restaurants. For the full scope of this area, prowl from Allen to Essex streets, south of East Houston Street down to Broome Street.

WEST VILLAGE

It's easy to feel like a local, not a tourist, while shopping in the West Village. Unlike 5th Avenue or SoHo, the pace is slower, the streets relatively quiet, and the scale small. This is the place to come for unusual finds rather than global-brand goods (well, if you don't count Marc Jacobs).

Bleecker Street is a particularly good place to indulge all sorts of shopping appetites. Foodies love the blocks between 6th and 7th avenues for the specialty purveyors like Murray's Cheese (254 Bleecker St.). Fashion foragers prowl the stretch between West 10th Street and 8th Avenue, while Hudson Street and Greenwich Avenue are also prime boutique-browsing territory. Christopher Street, true to its connection with the lesbian and gay community, has a handful of rainbow-flag stops.

Philadelphia

WORD OF MOUTH

"Don't miss the Rodin and Art Museums and the Mutter and the U of PA Museum, the Italian and Reading Terminal Markets, Le Bec Fin, and the Fountain and some great street food, the Waterworks and Kelly Drive, the Parkway, City Hall, all the colonial stops, walking around Rittenhouse Square near your hotel . . . phew, I'm running out of breath here and I've just begun!"

—Amy

WELCOME TO PHILADELPHIA

TOP REASONS TO GO

★ **American icons:** The Country was born here, and Independence Hall and the Liberty Bell still stand as monuments to our founding fathers.

★ **Philadelphia Museum of Art:** The PMA is perhaps best known for having Rocky leap up its steps, but there's an amazing permanent collection inside.

★ **Going green:** One of the largest municipal parks in the world, Fairmount Park offers acre after rolling acre of pristine beauty.

★ **More than just cheesesteaks:** Known for rolls filled with meat and cheese, Philly actually has an incredible assortment of excellent cuisine.

KEY

⊢⊣ Airport Train

··· Broad St. Subway

-- Market-Frankford Subway

Ⓜ Metro Stops

NORTHERN LIBERTIES

OLD CITY

African American Museum

Betsy Ross House ◆

Market East Station

Independence National Historical Park [1]

Filbert St.

8TH AND MARKET

Liberty Bell ◆ **HISTORIC AREA**

Independence Hall

Independence Square

Washington Square

TO PENN'S LANDING →

Powell House ◆

Physick ◆ House

SOCIETY HILL

SOUTH PHILADELPHIA AND QUEEN VILLAGE

0	1/4 mile
0	400 meters

---

1 **Historic Area and Old City.** "America's most historic square mile" was the setting for the nation's march to independence. *Highlights are* Independence Hall and the Liberty Bell. Old City, north of the Historic Area, has with its own historic monuments.

2 **Society Hill and Penn's Landing.** Well-preserved Society Hill is lined with centuries-old cobblestone streets. Once home to sailing ships, Penn's Landing has become a 37-acre riverside park.

3 **Center City.** This is Philly's business district, anchored by skyscrapers and City Hall. The Pennsylvania Academy of Fine Arts and Reading Terminal are also here.

4 **Rittenhouse Square.** The prettiest of Philadelphia's public squares, Rittenhouse is the heart of upper-crust Philly. You'll find here the Curtis Institute of Music and the Rosenbach Museum and Library.

5 **Benjamin Franklin Parkway.** From City Hall the parkway stretches northwest to a Greco-Roman temple on a hill—the Philadelphia Museum of Art. Along the way are many of the city's finest cultural institutions.

6 **Fairmount Park.** The largest landscaped city park in the world, Fairmount offers a wide range of activities, including the Philadelphia Zoo.

GETTING ORIENTED

Today you can find Philadelphia's compact 5-square-mi downtown (William Penn's original city) between the Delaware and the Schuylkill (pronounced *skoo*-kull) rivers. Thanks to Penn's grid system of streets—laid out in 1681—the downtown area is a breeze to navigate. The traditional heart of the city is Broad and Market streets (Penn's Center Square), where City Hall now stands. Market Street divides the city north and south; 130 South 15th Street, for example, is in the second block south of Market Street. North–south streets are numbered, starting with Front (1st) Street, at the Delaware River, and increasing to the west. Broad Street is the equivalent of 14th Street. The diagonal Benjamin Franklin Parkway breaks the rigid grid pattern by leading from City Hall out of Center City into Fairmount Park, which straddles the Schuylkill River and Wissahickon Creek for 10 mi.

"On the whole, I'd rather be in Philadelphia." W.C. Fields may have been joking when he wrote his epitaph, but if he were here today, he would eat his words. They no longer roll up the sidewalks at night in Philadelphia. A construction boom, a restaurant renaissance, and cultural revival have helped transform the city. For more than 15 years there has been an optimistic mood, aggressive civic leadership, and national recognition of what the locals have long known: Philadelphia is a vibrant place to live—a city with an impressive past and a fascinating future.

Philadelphia is a place of contrasts: Grace Kelly and Rocky Balboa; Zahav—the ambitious modern Israeli restaurant that receives consistent raves from national foodie mags—and the humble stalls of Reading Terminal Market; Independence Hall and the Italian Market; 18th-century national icons with 21st-century–style skyscrapers soaring above them. The world-renowned Philadelphia Orchestra performs in a stunning concert hall—the focal point of efforts to transform Broad Street into a multicultural Avenue of the Arts. Along the same street, 25,000 Mummers dressed in outrageous sequins and feathers historically have plucked their banjos and strutted their stuff to the strains of "Oh, Dem Golden Slippers" on New Year's Day. City residents include descendants of the staid Quaker Founding Fathers, the self-possessed socialites of the Main Line (remember Katharine Hepburn and Cary Grant in *The Philadelphia Story*?), and the unrestrained sports fans, who are as vocal as they are loyal.

PLANNING

WHEN TO GO

Any time is right to enjoy the area's attractions, and a variety of popular annual events take place throughout the year. To avoid the largest crowds and be assured that all seasonal attractions are open, visit in May and June or September and October. If you don't mind waiting in longer lines to see popular attractions, visit around July 4, when the city comes alive with fireworks, parades, and festivals. The top draw is the **Welcome America!** festival, whose climax on the Benjamin Franklin Parkway usually boasts a blockbuster musician or two. There are special activities in the Historic Area all summer long. Concert and theater seasons run from October through the beginning of June—but the World Champion Phillies play from summer through the fall. You may find some better lodging deals—and a beautiful snowfall—in winter, if you don't mind bundling up. In spring the city's cherry blossoms bloom, rivaling those of Washington, D.C.'s Tidal Basin.

Like other northeastern American cities, Philadelphia can be hot and humid in summer and cold in winter (winter snowfall averages 21 inches).

GETTING HERE AND AROUND

AIR TRAVEL

The major gateway to Philadelphia is Philadelphia International Airport (PHL), 8 mi from downtown in the southwest part of the city. Renovations in the past few years have made the terminals more appealing; shops and more eating options are welcome additions. For $7 you can take the SEPTA Regional Rail R1 line directly into Center City from each of the four main airport terminals.

Airport Information Philadelphia International Airport (*PHL* ✉ *8000 Essington Ave., off I–95* ☎ *215/937–6937 or 800/745–4283* ⊕ *www.phl.org*).

Allow at least a half-hour, more during rush hour, for the 8-mi trip between the airport and Center City. By car the airport is accessible via I–95 south or I–76 east.

Taxis at the airport are plentiful but expensive—a flat fee of $28.50 plus tip—or, if you're heading to a location south of South Street, you can ask to use the meter for a slightly reduced fare. Follow the signs in the airport and wait in line for a taxi. Limousine service and shuttle buses are also available. Shuttle buses cost $10 and up per person, and will make most requested stops downtown as well as in the suburbs. You can make shuttle arrangements at the centralized ground transportation counter in the baggage claim areas.

The Southeastern Pennsylvania Transportation Authority (SEPTA) runs the Airport Rail line R1, which leaves the airport every 30 minutes from 5:09 am to 12:09 am. The trip to Center City takes about 20 minutes and costs $7. Trains serve the 30th Street, Suburban (Center City), Market East, and University City stations.

Limousines Carey Limousine Philadelphia (☎ *610/595–2800*). **London Limousine & Town Car Service** (☎ *215/745–8519* ⊕ *www.londonlimousine.net*).

Shuttles **Priority Shuttle** (☎ 215/632–2885 ⊕ www.priorityshuttle.com).
Suvana Philadelphia Airport Shuttle (☎ 267/390–4122 ⊕ www.suvana.com/
philadelphia-airport-shuttle.html).

Train **Airport Information Desk** (☎ 800/745–4283). **SEPTA** (☎ 215/580–7800
⊕ www.septa.org).

CAR TRAVEL

Getting to and around Philadelphia by car can be difficult—at rush hour
it can be a nightmare. Laid out in a grid pattern by its founder William
Penn, you would think that Center City would be relatively easy to
navigate by car. Despite its regularity, many streets are one-way, and
the main thoroughfares are often congested with traffic. Furthermore,
parking can be tough. A spot at a parking meter, if you're lucky enough
to find one, costs $1 to $2 per hour. Parking garages are plentiful but
can charge up to $1.50 per 15 minutes and up to $20 or more per day.
Police officers are vigilant about ticketing. Your best bet is to walk and
to supplement walking with public transportation and taxis as needed.

PUBLIC TRANSPORTATION

Philadelphia's **SEPTA buses** provide good coverage of Old City and the
Historic Area, Center City, and farther west to University City. A bus
ride costs $2 in cash with exact change. Find fares, maps, and schedules
at the Independence Visitor Center and online at ⊕ www.septa.org.
From May through October purple **Phlash trolleys** follow a Center City
route to 27 downtown sights; you can buy a hop-on, hop-off all-day
pass for $5 (or $10 for a family) at the Independence Visitor Center or
when you board the trolley.

The **SEPTA subway** trains come regularly, but the underground stations
are rather dank, and the two lines are limited. One runs east–west along
Market Street, the other north–south along Broad Street, and stations
are few and far between.

TAXI TRAVEL

If you're tired of pounding the pavement, taxis are plentiful in Center City, especially along Broad, Market, Walnut, and Chestnut streets
and near any major hotels and train stations. They're hailed streetside.
Fares rise according to distance—$2.70 plus 23¢ for each one-tenth of
a mile—and you can now pay using credit cards. The standard tip for
cabdrivers is about 15% of the fare.

VISITOR INFORMATION

Philadelphia Convention and Visitors Bureau (✉ 1700 Market St., Suite 3000
☎ 215/636–3300 or 215/636–3327 ⊕ www.philadelphiausa.travel).

EXPLORING PHILADELPHIA

Philadelphia is a city of superlatives: the world's largest municipal park;
the best collection of public art in the United States; the widest variety
of urban architecture in America; and according to some experts, the
greatest concentration of institutions of higher learning in the country.

Although Philadelphia is the sixth-largest city in the nation (nearly 1.5
million people live in the city, 6.2 million in the metropolitan area), it

maintains a small-town feel. It's a cosmopolitan, exciting, but not over-whelming, city, a town that's easy to explore on foot yet big enough to keep surprising even those most familiar with it.

THE HISTORIC AREA

Fodor'sChoice
★

Any visit to Philadelphia, whether you have one day or several, should begin in the city area that comprises **Independence National Historical Park.** Philadelphia was the birthplace of the United States, the home of the country's first government, and nowhere is the spirit of those miraculous early days—the boldness of conceiving a brand-new nation—more pal-pable than along the cobbled streets of the city's most historic district.

In the late 1940s, before civic-minded citizens banded together to save the area and before the National Park Service stepped in, the Indepen-dence Hall neighborhood was crowded with factories and run-down warehouses. Then the city, state, and federal government took interest. Some buildings were restored, and others were reconstructed on their original sites; several attractions were built for the 1976 bicentennial celebration. In recent years a flurry of construction has again trans-formed the area, with several notable buildings—including an expanded visitor center, a more attractive home for the Liberty Bell, the National Constitution Center, the National Museum of American Jewish His-tory, and the President's House: Freedom and Slavery in Making a New Nation. Today the park covers 42 acres and holds close to 40 buildings. Urban renewal in Independence Mall plaza and in Washington Square East (Society Hill) have ensured that Independence Hall will never again keep unsightly company. The city's most historic area is now also one of its loveliest.

WHAT TO SEE

★ **Independence Hall.** The birthplace of the United States, this redbrick building with its clock tower and steeple is one of the nation's greatest icons. America's most historic building was constructed in 1732–56 as the Pennsylvania State House. What happened here between 1775 and 1787 changed the course of American history—and the name of the building to Independence Hall. The delegates to the Second Continental Congress met in the hall's Assembly Room in May 1776, united in anger over the blood that had been shed when British troops fired on citizens in Concord, Massachusetts. In this same room George Washington was appointed commander in chief of the Continental Army, Thomas Jefferson's eloquent Declaration of Independence was signed, and later the Constitution of the United States was adopted.

In the **East Wing**—attached to Independence Hall by a short colon-nade—you can embark on free tours that start every 15 to 20 minutes and last 35 minutes. Admission is first-come, first-served; you may have to wait in line. The **West Wing** of Independence Hall contains an exhibit of the National Historical Park's collection of our nation's founding documents: the final draft of the Constitution, a working copy of the Articles of Confederation, and the first printing of the Declaration of Independence.

Independence Hall, arguably the most important building in American history.

■ TIP➔ From March through December and on major holidays, free, timed tickets from the visitor center are required for entry. Tickets also can be reserved by calling ☎ 877/444–6777 or by logging on to ⊕ *www. recreation.gov.* ✉ *500 Chestnut St., between 5th and 6th Sts., Historic Area* ☎ *215/965–2305* ⊕ *www.nps.gov/inde* ✉ *Free* ⊘ *Daily 9–5.*

★ **Liberty Bell.** The bell fulfilled the biblical words of its inscription when it rang to "proclaim liberty throughout all the land unto all the inhabitants thereof," beckoning Philadelphians to the State House yard to hear the first reading of the Declaration of Independence. Ordered in 1751 and originally cast in England, the bell cracked during testing and was recast in Philadelphia by Pass and Stow two years later. To keep it from falling into British hands during the Revolution—they would have melted it down for ammunition—the bell was spirited away by horse and wagon to Allentown, 60 mi to the north. The bell is the subject of much legend; one story says it cracked when tolled at the funeral of Chief Justice John Marshall in 1835. Actually, the bell cracked slowly over a period of years. It was repaired but cracked again in 1846 and was then forever silenced. It was called the State House Bell until the 1830s, when a group of abolitionists adopted it as a symbol of freedom and renamed it the Liberty Bell.

After more than 200 years inside Independence Hall, the bell was moved to a glass-enclosed pavilion for the 1976 bicentennial, which for many seemed an incongruous setting for such a historic object. In mid-2003 the bell once again moved to another glass-enclosed pavilion with red-brick accents. This time, great care was taken to improve access to the bell and the view of its former home at Independence Hall, which is seen against the backdrop of the sky—rather than 20th-century buildings. The Liberty Bell complex houses a bell chamber, an interpretive exhibit area with historic displays and memorabilia, and a covered area for waiting in line. ⊠ *6th and Chestnut Sts., Historic Area* ☎ *215/965–2305* ⊕ *www.nps.gov/inde/liberty-bell-center.htm* ⊠ *Free* ◷ *Daily 9–5.*

OLD CITY

In colonial days the rich folks in residential Society Hill whispered of those who lived "north of Market," for this area, between Front and 5th streets and Chestnut and Vine streets, was the city's commercial district for industry and wholesale distributors, filled with wharves and warehouses and taverns. It also held the modest homes of craftsmen and artisans. Old City (as it became known some 40 years ago, to distinguish it from the national park area around Independence Hall) is aptly named: it's one of the city's oldest and most historic neighborhoods, home to Elfreth's Alley; the Betsy Ross House; and Christ Church, where George Washington and John Adams came (across the tracks!) to worship at services. There's evidence of the Quaker presence here, too, in the Arch Street Meeting House.

Today Old City is one of Philadelphia's trendiest neighborhoods, a local version of New York's SoHo. Many cast-iron building facades remain, though the old warehouses, with telltale names such as the Sugar Refinery and the Hoopskirt Factory, now house well-lighted loft apartments popular with artists and architects. There are small theaters—the Painted Bride, the Arden Theatre Company—and numerous art galleries and boutiques. The Old City Arts Association hosts a festive, popular event the first Friday of each month—known, appropriately enough, as First Friday—when the galleries throw open their doors during evening hours.

WHAT TO SEE

★ **African American Museum in Philadelphia.** The centerpiece of this museum is "Audacious Freedom: African Americans in Philadelphia 1776–1876," a permanent exhibit that uses video and touch-screen monitors to tell the stories of such pioneers as Frances Ellens Watkins Harper, a conductor on the Underground Railroad and suffragist, Thomas Morris Chester, a journalist and lawyer who was the first black to argue a case before the U.S. Supreme Court, and Elizabeth Taylor Greenfield, a renowned singer who performed for Queen Victoria. ⊠ *701 Arch St., Old City* ☎ *215/574–0380* ⊕ *www.aampmuseum.org* ⊠ *$10* ◷ *Tues.– Sat. 10–5, Sun. noon–5.*

☕ **Betsy Ross House.** It's easy to find this little brick house with the gabled ★ roof: just look for the 13-star flag displayed from its second-floor window. Whether Betsy Ross, also known as Elizabeth Griscom Ross Ashbourn Claypoole (1752–1836)—who worked in her family's flag-making and upholstery business—actually lived here and whether she really made the first Stars and Stripes is debatable. Nonetheless, the house, built about 1760, is a splendid example of a Colonial Philadelphia home and is fun to visit. You may have to wait in line, as this is one of the city's most popular attractions. The house, with its winding narrow stairs, is not accessible to people with disabilities. ✉ *239 Arch St., Old City* ☎ *215/686–1252* ⊕ *www.betsyrosshouse.org* 🖃 *$3; $2 charge for audio tour* ⊙ *Memorial Day–Labor Day, daily 10–5; Labor Day–Memorial Day, Tues.–Sun. 10–5.*

★ **Elfreth's Alley.** The alley, the oldest continuously occupied residential street in America, dates to 1702. Much of Colonial Philadelphia resembled this area, with its cobblestone streets and narrow two- or three-story brick houses. These were modest row homes, most built for rent, and lived in by craftsmen, such as cabinetmakers, silversmiths, and pewterers, and their families. They also housed captains and others who made their living in the city's busy shipping industry. The earliest houses (two stories) have pent eaves; taller houses, built after the Revolution, show the influence of the Federal style. The Elfreth's Alley Museum includes two homes that have been restored by the Elfreth's Alley Association. ✉ *Front and 2nd Sts. between Arch and Race Sts., Old City* ☎ *215/574–0560* ⊕ *www.elfrethsalley.org* 🖃 *Alley free; museum $5* ⊙ *Mar.–Oct., Mon.–Sat. 10–5, Sun. noon–5; Nov.–Feb., Thurs.–Sat. 10–5, Sun. noon–5.*

SOCIETY HILL

During the 18th century Society Hill was Philadelphia's showplace. A carefully preserved district, it remains the city's most photogenic neighborhood, filled with hidden courtyards, delightful decorative touches such as chimney pots and brass door knockers, wrought-iron foot scrapers, and other remnants from the days of horse-drawn carriages and muddy, unpaved streets.

A trove of Colonial- and Federal-style brick row houses, churches, and narrow streets, Society Hill stretches from the Delaware River to 8th Street, south of Independence National Historical Park. Those homes built before 1750 in the Colonial style generally have 2½ stories and a dormer window jutting out of a steep roof. The less heavy, more graceful houses built after the Revolution were often in the Federal style, popularized in England during the 1790s.

Today many Colonial homes in this area have been lovingly restored by modern pioneers who moved into the area nearly 50 years ago and rescued Society Hill from becoming a slum. Inspired urban renewal efforts have transformed vast empty factory spaces into airy lofts; new town houses were carefully designed to blend in with the old. As a result, Society Hill is not just a showcase for historic churches and mansions, but a living, breathing neighborhood.

WHAT TO SEE

★ **Physick House.** Built in 1786, this is one of two remaining freestanding houses from this era in Society Hill (you will see plenty of the famous Philadelphia row houses here). It's also one of the most beautiful homes in America, with elegantly restored interiors and some of the finest Federal and Empire furniture in Philadelphia. The house's most famous owner was Philip Syng Physick, the "Father of American Surgery" and a leading physician in the days before anesthesia. The garden planted on three sides of the house is filled with plants common during the

19th century. ⊠ *321 S. 4th St., Society Hill* ☎ *215/925–7866* ⊕ *www.philalandmarks.org* ✉ *$5* ☉ *Thurs.–Sat., noon–4, Sun. 1–4; guided tours on hr, last tour at 3.*

★ **Powel House.** The 1765 brick Georgian house purchased by Samuel Powel in 1769 remains one of the most elegant homes in Philadelphia. Powel—the "Patriot Mayor"—was the last mayor of Philadelphia under the Crown and the first in the new republic. The lavish home, a former wreck saved from demolition in 1930, is furnished with important pieces of 18th-century Philadelphia furniture. ⊠ *244 S. 3rd St., Society Hill* ☎ *215/627–0364* ⊕ *www.philalandmarks.org* ✉ *$5* ☉ *Thurs.–Sat. noon–4, Sun. 1–4; guided tours on hr, last tour at 3.*

PENN'S LANDING

The spot where William Penn stepped ashore in 1682 is the hub of a 37-acre riverfront park that stretches from Market Street south to Lombard Street. Walk along the waterfront, and you can see scores of pleasure boats moored at the marina and cargo ships chugging up and down the Delaware River. Philadelphia's harbor, which includes docking facilities in New Jersey and Delaware, is one of the world's largest freshwater ports. Attractions at Penn's Landing include historic vessels like the world's largest four-masted tall ship, the *Moshulu*, which doubles as a restaurant. The waterfront is also the scene of the annual Memorial Day Jam on the River and July 4 fireworks, as well as jazz and big band concerts, ethnic festivals, and children's events.

WHAT TO SEE

☺ **Independence Seaport Museum.** Philadelphia's maritime museum houses
★ many nautical artifacts, figureheads, and ship models, as well as interactive exhibits that convey just what the Delaware and Schuylkill rivers have meant to the city's fortunes over the years. You can climb in the gray, cold wooden bunks used in steerage, unload cargo from giant container ships with a miniature crane, weld and rivet a ship's hull, or even hop in a scull and row along the Schuylkill. Enter the museum by passing under the three-story replica of the Benjamin Franklin Bridge. ⊠ *211 S. Columbus Blvd., at Walnut St., Penn's Landing* ☎ *215/925–5439* ⊕ *www.phillyseaport.org* ✉ *$12, includes admission to USS Becuna and USS Olympia; pay what you wish Sun. 10–noon* ☉ *Daily 10–5.*

CENTER CITY

For a grand introduction to the heart of the downtown area, climb the few steps to the plaza in front of the Municipal Services Building at 15th Street and John F. Kennedy Boulevard. You'll be standing alongside a 10-foot-tall bronze statue of the late Frank L. Rizzo waving to the people. Rizzo, nicknamed the "Big Bambino," was the city's police commissioner, two-term mayor (in the 1970s), and a five-time mayoral candidate. He shaped the political scene just as the structures that surround you—City Hall, the Philadelphia Saving Fund Society Building, the Art Museum, the skyscrapers at Liberty Place, Oldenburg's *Clothespin*, and more—shape its architectural landscape.

The story behind this skyline begins with Philadelphia's historic City Hall, which reaches to 40 stories and was the tallest structure in the metropolis until 1987. No law prohibited taller buildings, but the tradition sprang from a gentleman's agreement not to build higher. Once the barrier was broken (after much debate), Market Street west of City Hall became a district of high-rise office buildings, and the area became a symbol of the city's ongoing transformation from a dying industrial town to a center for service industries. Here, too, are a number of museums, the excellent Reading Terminal Market and the convention center, and Chinatown.

WHAT TO SEE

★ **City Hall.** Topped by a 37-foot bronze statue of William Penn, City Hall was Philadelphia's tallest building until 1987; you can study the trappings of government and also get a panoramic view of the city here. With 642 rooms, it's the largest city hall in the country and the tallest masonry-bearing building in the world: no steel structure supports it. Designed by architect John McArthur Jr., the building took 30 years to build (1871–1900) and cost taxpayers more than $23 million. Placed about the facade are hundreds of statues by Alexander Milne Calder, who also designed the statue of William Penn at the top. Calder's 27-ton cast-iron statue of Penn is the largest single piece of sculpture on any building in the world.

Many of the magnificent interiors—splendidly decorated with mahogany paneling, gold-leaf ceilings, and marble pillars—are patterned after the Second Empire salons of part of the Louvre in Paris. To top off your visit, take the elevator from the seventh floor up the tower to the observation deck at the foot of William Penn's statue for a 30-mi view of the city and surroundings. The elevator holds only four people per trip and runs every 15 minutes; the least-crowded time is early morning. The 90-minute building tour, including a trip up the tower, steps off weekdays at 12:30. The tour office is in Room 121. ⊠ *Broad and Market Sts., Center City* ☎ *215/686–2840 tour information* ⊕ *www.philadelphiacityhall.org* ✉ *$10 for tour and tower visit; $5 for tower only* ☉ *Tower: weekdays 9:30–4:15; 2–3 pm reserved for tour participants.*

★ **Masonic Temple.** The temple is one of the city's architectural jewels, but it remains a hidden treasure even to many Philadelphians. Historically, Freemasons were skilled stoneworkers of the Middle Ages who relied on secret signs and passwords. Their worldwide fraternal order—the Free and Accepted Masons—included men in the building trades, plus many honorary members; the secret society prospered in Philadelphia during colonial times. Brother James Windrim designed this elaborate temple as a home for the Grand Lodge of Free and Accepted Masons of Pennsylvania. The temple's ornate interior consists of seven lavishly decorated lodge halls. The temple also houses an interesting museum of Masonic items, including Benjamin Franklin's printing of the first book on Freemasonry published in America and George Washington's Masonic apron. ⊠ *1 N. Broad St., Center City East/Avenue of the Arts* ☎ *215/988–1917* ⊕ *www.pagrandlodge.org/tour/onsite.html* ✉ *$3* *for library and museum only, $8 for tour* ⊙ *45-min tours Sept.–June, Tues.–Fri. 10, 11, 2, and 3, Sat. 10, 11, and noon.*

★ **Pennsylvania Academy of the Fine Arts.** This High Victorian Gothic structure is a work of art in itself. Designed in 1876 by the noted, and sometimes eccentric, Philadelphia architects Frank Furness and George Hewitt, the multicolor stone-and-brick exterior is an extravagant blend of columns, friezes, and Richardsonian Romanesque and Moorish flourishes. The interior is just as lush, with rich hues of red, yellow, and blue and an impressive staircase. The nation's first art school and museum (founded in 1805) displays a fine collection that ranges from the Peale family, Gilbert Stuart, Benjamin West, and Winslow Homer to Andrew Wyeth and Red Grooms. Supplementing the permanent collection are constantly changing exhibitions of sculptures, paintings, and mixed-media artwork in the adjacent Samuel M. V. Hamilton Building. ⊠ *118–128 N. Broad St., at Cherry St., Center City West/Avenue of the Arts* ☎ *215/972–7600* ⊕ *www.pafa.org* 🎟 *$10* ⊙ *Tues.–Sat. 10–5, Sun. 11–5.*

Fodor's Choice ★ **Reading Terminal Market.** The market is nothing short of a historic treasure, and a food heaven to Philadelphians and visitors alike. One floor beneath the former Reading Railroad's 1891 train shed, the sprawling market has more than 75 food stalls and other shops, selling items from hooked rugs and handmade jewelry to South American and African crafts. Here, amid the local color, you can sample Bassett's ice cream, Philadelphia's best; down a cheesesteak, a hoagie, a bowl of snapper soup, or a soft pretzel; or nibble Greek, Mexican, Thai, and Indian specialties. From Wednesday through Saturday the Amish from Lancaster County cart in their goodies, including Lebanon bologna, shoofly pie, and scrapple. ⊠ *12th and Arch Sts., Center City East/Market East* ☎ *215/922–2317* ⊕ *www.readingterminalmarket.org* ⊙ *Mon.–Sat. 8–6, Sun. 9–5.*

RITTENHOUSE SQUARE AND AVENUE OF THE ARTS SOUTH

Rittenhouse Square, at 18th and Walnut streets, has long been one of the city's swankiest addresses. The square's entrances, plaza, pool, and fountains were designed in 1913 by Paul Cret, one of the people responsible for the Benjamin Franklin Parkway. The first house facing the square was erected in 1840, soon to be followed by other grand mansions. Almost all the private homes are now gone, replaced by hotels, apartments, and cultural institutions, and elegant restaurants and stylish cafés dot the neighborhood. The area south and west of the square is still largely residential and lovely, with cupolas and balconies, hitching posts, and stained-glass windows. On Delancey Place, blocks alternate narrow and wide. The wide blocks had the homes of the wealthy, and the smaller ones held dwellings for servants or horses (today these carriage houses are prized real estate).

Four blocks east of the square is the Avenue of the Arts, also known as Broad Street. "Let us entertain you" could be the theme of the ambitious cultural development project that has transformed North and South Broad Street from a commercial thoroughfare to a performing arts district. Dramatic performance spaces have been built, old landmarks have been refurbished, and South Broad Street has been spruced up with landscaping, cast-iron lighting fixtures, special architectural lighting of key buildings, and decorative sidewalk paving.

WHAT TO SEE

Fodor's Choice ★ **Rittenhouse Square.** Once grazing ground for cows and sheep, Philadelphia's most elegant square is reminiscent of a Parisian park. One of William Penn's original five city squares, the park was named in 1825 to honor David Rittenhouse, 18th-century astronomer, clock maker, and the first director of the United States Mint. Until 1950 town houses bordered the square, but they have now been replaced on three sides by swank apartment buildings and hotels. Some great houses remain, including the former residence of Henry P. McIlhenny on the southwest corner. The term "Rittenhouse Row" describes the greater Rittenhouse Square area, bordered by Pine, Market, 21st, and Broad streets. ✉ *Walnut St. between 18th and 19th Sts., Rittenhouse Square.*

★ **Rosenbach Museum and Library.** This 1863 three-floor town house and an adjoining building are filled with Persian rugs and 18th-century British, French, and American antiques, but the real treasures are the artworks, books, and manuscripts here. Amassed by Philadelphia collectors Philip H. and A. S. W. Rosenbach, the collection includes paintings by Canaletto, Sully, and Lawrence; drawings by Daumier, Fragonard, and Blake; book illustrations ranging from medieval illuminations to the works of Maurice Sendak, author of *Where the Wild Things Are*; the only known copy of the first issue of Benjamin Franklin's *Poor Richard's Almanack*; and the library's most famous treasure, the original manuscript of James Joyce's *Ulysses.* ✉ *2010 Delancey Pl., Rittenhouse Square* ☎ *215/732–1600* 🌐 *www.rosenbach.org* 🎟 *$10* 🕓 *Tues. and Fri. noon–5, Wed. and Thurs. noon–8, weekends noon–6; guided tours on the hr.*

THE BENJAMIN FRANKLIN PARKWAY

Alive with colorful flowers, flags, and fountains, the Benjamin Franklin Parkway stretches northwest from John F. Kennedy Plaza to the Kelly (East) and West River drives. This 250-foot-wide boulevard is crowned by the Philadelphia Museum of Art. French architects Jacques Greber and Paul Cret designed the parkway in the 1920s. Today a distinguished assemblage of museums, institutions, hotels, and apartment buildings line the street, competing with each other in grandeur. Here you can find the Free Library of Philadelphia and the Family Court, housed in buildings whose designs are copied from the palaces on Paris's Place de la Concorde.

WHAT TO SEE

★ **The Franklin Institute.** Founded more than 175 years ago to honor Benjamin Franklin, this science museum is as clever as its namesake, thanks to an abundance of dazzling hands-on exhibits. To make the best use of your time, study the floor plan before exploring. You can sit in the cockpit of a T-33 jet trainer, trace the route of a corpuscle through the world's largest artificial heart (15,000 times life size), and ride to

The Philadelphia Museum of Art sits perched above the city's waterworks.

nowhere on a 350-ton Baldwin steam locomotive. You'll also be able to explore **Sir Isaac's Loft,** which combines lessons in art and science, delve into the mechanics of more than two-dozen mechanical devices in **Amazing Machine,** and see Franklin's famous lightning rod. One don't-miss: the 30-foot-tall statue of Franklin. ⊠ *20th St. and Benjamin Franklin Pkwy., Logan Circle* ☎ *215/448–1200* ⊕ *www.fi.edu* 🖃 *$15.50–$23* ⊙ *Daily 9:30–5.*

Fodor's Choice ★   **Philadelphia Museum of Art.** The city's premier cultural attraction is one of the country's leading museums. One of the greatest treasures of the museum is the building itself. Constructed in 1928 of Minnesota dolomite, it's modeled after ancient Greek temples but on a grander scale. The museum was designed by Julian Francis Abele, the first African-American to graduate from the University of Pennsylvania School of Architecture. You can enter the museum from the front or the rear; choose the front and you can run up the 99 steps made famous in the movie *Rocky.*

Once inside, you'll see the grand staircase and Saint-Gaudens's statue *Diana;* she formerly graced New York's old Madison Square Garden. The museum has several outstanding permanent collections: the John G. Johnson Collection covers Western art from the Renaissance to the 19th century; the Arensberg and A. E. Gallatin collections contain modern and contemporary works by artists such as Duchamp, Brancusi, Braque, Matisse, and Picasso.

Perhaps the most spectacular objects in the museum are entire structures and great rooms moved lock, stock, and barrel from around the world: a 12th-century French cloister, a 16th-century Indian temple hall, a

16th-century Japanese Buddhist temple, a 17th-century Chinese palace hall, and a Japanese ceremonial teahouse. The Ruth and Raymond G. Perelman Building, across the street in the former Reliance Standard Life Insurance Building, is home to the museum's permanent collection of photography, costume, and contemporary design.

Friday evenings feature live jazz and world music performances in the Great Hall. The museum has a fine restaurant and a surprisingly good cafeteria. ⊠ *26th St. and Benjamin Franklin Pkwy., Fairmount* ☎ *215/763–8100* ⊕ *www.philamuseum.org* 🖂 *$16, 1st Sun. of month pay what you wish* ☉ *Tues.–Sun. 10–5, Fri. 10–8:45.*

★ **Rodin Museum.** This jewel of a museum holds the biggest collection outside France of the work of sculptor Auguste Rodin (1840–1917). You'll pass through a courtyard to reach Rodin's *Gates of Hell*—a 21-foot-high sculpture with more than 100 human and animal figures. In the exhibition hall the sculptor's masterworks are made even more striking by the use of light and shadow. ⊠ *22nd St. and Benjamin Franklin Pkwy., Fairmount* ☎ *215/763–8100* ⊕ *www.rodinmuseum.org* 🖂 *$5 donation suggested* ☉ *Tues.–Sun. 10–5.*

FAIRMOUNT PARK

Stretching from the edge of downtown to the city's northwest corner, Fairmount Park is the largest landscaped city park in the world. With more than 8,500 acres and 2 million trees (someone claims to have counted), the park winds along the banks of the Schuylkill River—which divides it into west and east sections—and through parts of the city. Quite a few city dwellers consider the park their backyard. On weekends the 4-mi stretch along Kelly Drive is crowded with joggers, young families, hand-holding senior citizens, collegiate crew teams sculling on the river, and budding artists trying to capture the sylvan magic just as Thomas Eakins once did.

Fairmount Park encompasses natural areas—woodlands, meadows, rolling hills, two scenic waterways, and a forested 5½-mi gorge. It also contains tennis courts, ball fields, playgrounds, trails, exercise courses, several celebrated cultural institutions, and some historic Early American country houses that are operated by the Philadelphia Museum of Art and open to visitors. Philadelphia has more works of outdoor art than any other city in North America, and more than 200 of these works—including statues by Frederic Remington, Jacques Lipchitz, and Auguste Rodin—are scattered throughout Fairmount Park. Some sections of the park that border depressed urban neighborhoods are neglected; it's better maintained along the Schuylkill.

WHERE TO EAT

Over the last decade or so Philadelphia has evolved into a bona fide dining destination, one that boasts every type of culinary experience, from authentic ethnic cuisine to chef-owned storefront bistros to high-profile four-star dining rooms. And there's no indication the surge is slowing.

You can trace the current explosion back to the 1970s and '80s, when a flurry of restaurant openings snuffed out the dark ages and heralded the beginning of a protracted dining renaissance. Soon, neighborhood by neighborhood, lights turned on and kitchens fired up. The march of the restaurants followed the march of development, from Old City to Northern Liberties and beyond.

The formation of dining pockets is the newest chapter in the Philadelphia dining story. Some of the culinary landmarks on Walnut Street's Restaurant Row have closed, but tens of restaurants opened during the same period. Some fill the fine-dining void left by the departing marquee restaurants, but most are more casual, ambitious spots grouped in less centrally located neighborhoods.

WHAT IT COSTS

	¢	$	$$	$$$	$$$$
Restaurants	under $10	$10–$14	$15–$19	$20–$24	over $24

Price per person for a median main course or equivalent combination of smaller dishes.

HISTORIC AREA AND OLD CITY

$$$
SPANISH
Fodor'sChoice
★

✕**Amada.** Since his debut with Amada in 2005, chef-restaurateur Jose Garces has opened three more restaurants in the city, all of them instant and enduring hits. The young Ecuadorian-American chef has taken Philadelphia by storm, and it was at Amada where he set the stage for his modus operandi of elevating authentic regional cuisine with choice ingredients and a modern touch. On offer are more than 60 tapas, each one worth trying, especially the white-bean stew with escarole and chorizo, and the flatbread topped with fig jam, Spanish blue cheese, and shredded duck. Ingredients—including glorious cheeses—are sourced from northern Spain. The large, festive front room can skew loud; for a quieter meal, ask for a table in the second dining room, beyond the open kitchen. ⊠ *217–19 Chestnut St., Old City* ☎ *215/625–2450* ⊕ *www.amadarestaurant.com* ⌣ *Reservations essential* ▤ *AE, D, MC, V* ⊙ *No lunch Sun.*

$$
ITALIAN

✕**La Locanda del Ghiottone.** Literally "the place of the gluttons," the small L-shaped dining room gets loud and crowded as patrons arrive and waiters shout orders from tableside into the open kitchen. It's all part of the charm. The server will forbid you from putting cheese on fish (a house rule), then he'll ask sweetly after your mother. This is homey food, comfort food—tender gnocchi, platters of pasta brimming with fresh seafood, and osso buco, to name a few of the amply proportioned dishes. ⊠ *130 N. 3rd St., Old City* ☎ *215/829–1465* ⌣ *Reservations essential* ▤ *No credit cards* ⌯ *BYOB* ⊙ *Closed Mon. No lunch.*

$$$
MEDITERRANEAN
Fodor'sChoice
★

✕**Zahav.** Chef Michael Solomonov has brought great buzz to several restaurant locations in Philadelphia. With his latest entry, steeped in the milk and honey and hummus and lamb of his native Israel—as well as the cultures that have left a mark on that Promised Land—he's done it again. Taking advantage of its dramatic perch above one of the city's oldest streets, the stripped-down Zahav relies on architectural features such as picture windows and soaring ceilings to create spectacle. The open kitchen, on view behind leaded glass, is the true stage. There a small staff mixes and matches a melting pot of flavors for a modern Israeli menu whose highlights include house-baked *laffa* (flatbread), kebabs of impossibly tender chicken cooked over hot coals and served with sumac onions and Israeli couscous, and addictive florets of fried cauliflower served with a lemon- and dill-spiked *lebneh* (yogurt cheese). Cap off your meal with truly innovative cocktails and desserts like pistachio baklava. ⊠ *237 St. James Pl., Old City* ☎ *215/625–8800* ⊕ *www. zahavrestaurant.com* ⊟ *AE, D, MC, V* ⊗ *No lunch.*

SOCIETY HILL AND SOUTH STREET

$$$ ╳ **Bistrot La Minette.** The cheery atmosphere inside the long, narrow bis-
FRENCH tro and in the outside courtyard illuminated by candles and twinkling strings of lights exudes warmth and attention to detail, from the flea-market knickknacks picked out by Chef Peter Woolsey and his French wife in Burgundy to the ceramic pitchers of house wine delivered to your table. Woolsey studied at the Cordon Bleu, fell in love with French food, culture, and his wife, a Frenchwoman, and came back to his native Philadelphia to share the bistro experience with his countrymen. The place has quickly become a neighborhood favorite, with regulars swearing by some standouts including the Alsatian-style Flammenkuchen appetizer of caramelized onions, bacon lardoons, and crème fraiche on flatbread; the perfectly simple lemon sole in white-wine butter sauce; and the light and airy beignets that speak to Woolsey's extensive training as a pastry chef. ⊠ *623 S. 6th St., South Street* ☎ *215/925–8000* ⊕ *www.bistrolaminette.com* ⊟ *AE, D, MC, V* ⊗ *No lunch.*

SOUTH PHILADELPHIA

$$$$ ╳ **James.** Chef Jim Burke repeatedly wins "best chef" accolades from
ITALIAN local and national magazines for his contemporary takes on Northern
Fodor'sChoice Italian fare—favorites are the hand-cut tagliatelle with a duck ragu
★ seasoned with shavings of Valrhona chocolate and orange peel; and a slow-roasted Four Story Hill Farm poularde that's the perfect antidote to a chilly evening. He cooks, and his wife Kristina does everything else in the sleek and chic little restaurant, including setting an effusive tone that comes out in the servers' enthusiastic descriptions of the kitchen's offerings. ⊠ *824 S. 8th St., Bella Vista* ☎ *215/629–4980* ⊕ *www. jameson8th.com* ⊟ *AE, D, MC, V* ⊗ *Closed Mon.*

CENTER CITY EAST

$$$ ╳ **Lolita.** In a town where liquor licenses are few and far between, lots of
MEXICAN restaurants are BYOB (bring your own bottle). Lolita's twist is BYOT, or bring your own tequila. They'll use it to blend a pitcher of some exotic-sounding margarita—try fresh strawberry puree and purple basil. The food—nouveau Mexican prepared with locally sourced ingredients—is pretty good, too. Lolita, one of the first in Philly's recent wave of ambitious Mexi-fusion restaurants, has a loyal following. ⊠ *106 S. 13th St., Center City East* ☎ *215/546–7100* ⊕ *www.lolitabyob.com* ⊟ *No credit cards* ⊞ *BYOB* ⊗ *No lunch.*

¢ ╳ **Reading Terminal Market.** When the Reading Company opened its train
ECLECTIC shed in 1892, it was the only one in the country with a market tucked
★ away in its cellar. The trains are long gone, but the food remains. And

The grill at Jim's Steaks, one of Philadelphia's many cheesesteak emporiums.

while disagreeing over the best cheesesteak is a popular pastime in Philly, pretty much everyone can agree on pancakes at the Dutch Eating Place, the roast pork sandwich at Dinic's, cupcakes at the Flying Monkey, and double chocolate-chip cookies at Famous 4th Street. Get here early to beat the lunch rush. Hours are 8–6 Monday–Saturday and 9–4 Sunday. Seventy-five-minute tours every Wednesday and Saturday at 10 highlight the market's history and offerings (call ☎ 215/545–8007 to make a reservation). ■TIP→ The Amish shops, which sell pastries, fresh cheeses, honey and jams, and more, are only open Wednesday through Saturday. ⊠ 12th and Arch Sts., Center City East ☎ 215/922–2317 ⊕ www. readingterminalmarket.org.

$$
AMERICAN
★
✕ **Tria.** Tria's brown interior and minimalist signage give off a wallflower vibe, but the tables packed with chic urbanites grazing lightly belie its inner beauty. The knowledgeable staff is serious about the restaurant's focus—the "fermentation trio" of wine, cheese, and beer—but not in a snobby way. They'll casually toss off suggestions for a cheese plate that's a phenomenal medley of textures and flavors. Then they'll recommend a zippy white wine or tasty pale ale that sets it off perfectly. ⊠ 1137 Spruce St., Center City East ☎ 215/629–9200 ⊕ www.triacafe. com ⊟ AE, MC, V ⊗ No lunch weekdays.

CENTER CITY WEST

$–$$
ECLECTIC
✕ **Continental Mid-town.** You're not sure what decade you're in once you enter the vast, retro playground that shares a name with the Old City martini lounge, also from blockbuster restaurateur Stephen Starr. Line up for a spot on the popular rooftop lounge or sit inside, in a swinging wicker basket chair, a sunken banquette, or a baby-blue vinyl

booth. The global tapas menu includes shoestring fries drizzled with Chinese mustard, a gargantuan crispy calamari salad, and a cheesesteak egg roll. Of the retro cocktails, the most popular is the Tang-rimmed Buzz Aldrin. ⊠ *1801 Chestnut St., Center City West* ☎ *215/567–1800* ⊕ *www.continentalmidtown.com* ⊟ *AE, MC, V.*

RITTENHOUSE SQUARE

$$$

FRENCH

Fodor's Choice

★

✕**PARC.** Restaurateur Stephen Starr's fondness for themes (a giant golden Buddha in his pan-Asian restaurant, Buddakan, and a mid-country, mid-century feel at the comfort food eatery Jones) has reached perfection in this vast but meticulous stage set placed on Philadelphia's most desirable corner. Brass rails, silvered mirrors, claret-hued banquettes, and oak wainscoting reclaimed from now-shuttered Parisian restaurants, imbue patina—while small touches like newspapers on wooden poles create extra realism. Similarly, standard menu items (roasted chicken, trout amandine) hold their own, but the little things—desserts and salads, fresh-baked goods (including house-made macaroons), and excellent onion soup—stand out. Ask for an indoor-outdoor table overlooking the park: You'll get generous views and the pleasant din of the 150 diners behind you without the deafening buzz that is the restaurant's one true downside. ⊠ *227 S. 18th St., Rittenhouse Square* ☎ *215/545–2262* ⊕ *www.parc-restaurant.com* ⊟ *AE, MC, V.*

5

WHERE TO STAY

From historic digs with four-poster beds to grand hotels serving room-service foie gras, Philadelphia has lodgings for every style of travel. Thanks to the Pennsylvania Convention Center and a hotel-building boom in the late 1990s, some mid-price chains have moved into town or have spruced up their accommodations. If you have greater expectations, you need look no further than the city's handful of swank hotels, each with its own gracious character.

Budget, moderate, and luxury properties are spread throughout the downtown area. The Historic Area, on the east side of downtown, centers on Independence Hall and extends to the Delaware River, and is a good base for sightseeing. Old City and Society Hill lodgings are also convenient for serious sightseeing; Society Hill is the quietest of the three areas. For business-oriented trips, Center City encompasses the heart of the downtown business district, centered on Broad and Market streets, and Rittenhouse Square hotels are also nearby.

If you prefer to keep your distance from the tourist throngs, check out the Benjamin Franklin Parkway–Museum Area along the parkway from 16th Street to the Philadelphia Museum of Art. There are also a couple of hotels in University City—just across the Schuylkill River in West Philadelphia and close to the University of Pennsylvania and Drexel University—a 5- to 10-minute drive or taxi ride from Center City.

Hotel reviews have been condensed for this book. Please go to Fodors. com for full reviews of each property.

WHAT IT COSTS					
	¢	$	$$	$$$	$$$$
Hotels	under $100	$100–$150	$151–$200	$201–$250	over $250

Prices are for a standard double room in high season.

OLD CITY

$$
Fodor'sChoice
★
Penn's View Inn. This cosmopolitan little hotel in a refurbished 19th-century commercial building on the fringe of Old City has its own brand of urban charm. **Pros:** good service; generous continental breakfast including waffles; romantic atmosphere. **Cons:** gym is tiny; rooms facing I–95 can be noisy. ⊠ *14 N. Front St., Old City* ☎ *215/922–7600 or 800/331–7634* ⊕ *www.pennsviewhotel.com* 🛏 *51 rooms, 2 suites* ⚒ *In-room: Internet, Wi-Fi. In-hotel: restaurant, room service, bar, gym, Wi-Fi, parking (paid), no-smoking rooms* ⊟ *AE, D, DC, MC, V* ⎡◯⎤ *CP.*

CENTER CITY WEST

$$
Fodor'sChoice
★
Hotel Palomar. Philadelphia's first Kimpton hotel is stylish down to its leopard-spotted bathrobes and zebra-striped Frette linens. **Pros:** close to best shopping areas; pet-friendly; in-room spa services. **Cons:** fee for Wi-Fi; some small rooms; valet parking only. ⊠ *117 S. 17th St.,Center City West* ☎ *215/563–5006 or 877/725–1778* ⊕ *www.hotelpalomarphiladelphia.com* 🛏 *213 rooms, 17 suites* ⚒ *In-room: safe, Internet, Wi-Fi. In-hotel: restaurant, room service, bar, fitness center, laundry service, Internet terminal, Wi-Fi, parking (paid), some pets allowed* ⊟ *AE, D, DC, MC.*

$$$$
☾
Fodor'sChoice
★
Westin Philadelphia. If luxurious accommodations and plenty of shopping are your top priorities, you're not going to beat the Westin. **Pros:** close to best shopping areas; excellent beds; comfortable furniture; quiet. **Cons:** pricey parking; $4.95 fee for Internet. ⊠ *99 S. 17th St., at Liberty Pl., Center City West* ☎ *215/563–1600 or 800/937–8461* ⊕ *www.westin.com/philadelphia* 🛏 *293 rooms, 19 suites* ⚒ *In-room: safe, Internet, Wi-Fi. In-hotel: restaurant, room service, bar, gym, laundry service, Internet terminal, Wi-Fi, parking (paid), some pets allowed* ⊟ *AE, D, DC, MC, V.*

CENTER CITY EAST

$–$$
Alexander Inn. The nicely refurbished rooms at this small hotel have an art deco feel. **Pros:** great location between Rittenhouse Square and historic district; quiet yet near lively nightlife; away from touristy spots; great service; Web specials on room rate. **Cons:** older building; no laundry facilities or services; bar downstairs can get noisy; tiny gym. ⊠ *12th and Spruce Sts., Center City East* ☎ *215/923–3535 or 877/253–9466* ⊕ *www.alexanderinn.com* 🛏 *48 rooms* ⚒ *In-room: safe, Wi-Fi. In-hotel: gym, Internet terminal, Wi-Fi, parking (paid)* ⊟ *AE, D, DC, MC, V* ⎡◯⎤ *CP.*

RITTENHOUSE SQUARE

$$$–$$$$
Fodor'sChoice
★
Rittenhouse 1715. On a small street near Rittenhouse Square, this refined, European-style mansion offers the luxury of a large hotel in an intimate space on the fourth floor. **Pros:** quiet option for downtown;

romantic. **Cons:** quiet. ✉ *1715 Rittenhouse Square St., Rittenhouse Square* ☎ *215/546–6500 or 877/791–6500* ⊕ *www.rittenhouse1715. com* ⇆ *23 rooms, 4 suites* ⚄ *In-room: safe, Wi-Fi. In-hotel: laundry service, Internet terminal, Wi-Fi* ▭ *AE, D, DC, MC, V* ⫿◯⫿ *CP.*

BENJAMIN FRANKLIN PARKWAY

$$$$ **⫿⫿ Four Seasons.** On the outskirts of the finance district, this landmark
ⓒ is within walking distance of the Philadelphia Museum of Art and
Fodor'sChoice the department stores along Walnut Street. Furnishings are in a for-
★ mal traditional style. **Pros:** excellent service; comfy beds; good pool.
Cons: be sure to dress up for the on-site restaurant and bar; rooms are
smaller than those of some of its luxury competitors; $12 fee for Wi-Fi.
✉ *1 Logan Circle, Benjamin Franklin Parkway* ☎ *215/963–1500 or
800/332–3442* ⊕ *www.fourseasons.com/philadelphia* ⇆ *364 rooms,
102 suites* ⚄ *In-room: safe, refrigerator, DVD, Internet, Wi-Fi. In-hotel:
3 restaurants, room service, bar, indoor pool, gym, spa, laundry service,
Internet terminal, Wi-Fi, parking (paid), some pets allowed* ▭ *AE, D,
DC, MC, V.*

NIGHTLIFE

Generally speaking, you can break down Philly's central nightlife hubs
into four distinct areas: South Street offers teens and young twentysomethings block after block of bars, tattoo parlors, and erotica shops;
Old City is very popular with out-of-towners and party people, with a
mix of both low- and higher-end clubs, bars, and restaurants, and, like
South Street, is swarmed on weekends; Northern Liberties is a boho
oasis, with artists, hipsters, and the edgily affluent mingling in the burgeoning bar scene there; and, finally, Rittenhouse Square offers high-end
libations and refreshment for the well-heeled, or for those wanting to
pretend for a night. Outside of Center City, University City has all the
standard (and not so standard) college-appropriate bars and clubs; East
Passyunk is an up-and-coming neighborhood, replete with an assortment of fine restaurants, hipster bars, and old-school South Philly Italian joints; and Manayunk is one of the spots of choice for those recently
graduated from college or working their first professional jobs.

For current information, check the entertainment pages of the *Philadelphia Inquirer,* the free alt-weekly *City Paper* or *Philadelphia Weekly,* the
Philadelphia Gay News (PGN), and *Philadelphia* magazine.

SHOPPING

Shopaholics love the City of Brotherly (and Sisterly) Love for its
style—funky artwork and highbrow housewares, fine jewels, and haute
couture.

Indeed, Philadelphia has spawned some influential fashion retailers. The
Urban Outfitters chain was born in a storefront in West Philadelphia.
Its sophisticated sister, Anthropologie, also has its roots in Philadelphia.
Lagos, the popular high-end jewelry line, was founded here, and all
items are still produced locally. High-fashion boutiques Joan Shepp,

Knit Wit, and Plage Tahiti, all in the Rittenhouse Square area, are well regarded by locals for designer clothing and accessories.

There are plenty of independent shops and boutiques, too. In Northern Liberties the Piazza at Schmidt's is a giant mixed-use development inspired by Rome's Piazza Navona, which houses 100,000 square feet of retail space bursting with creative entrepreneurs. Also worth a trip is the Third Street Corridor in Old City, home to well-curated clothing and home-design shops that often feature local talent.

SOUTH PHILADELPHIA

South Philadelphia is made up of a few smaller neighborhoods, including Society Hill, South Street, Queen Village (home to Fabric Row), and the Italian Market, and the shopping here is as varied as these nabes. South Street's streetwear shops and hippie holdovers give way to indie boutiques and thrift shops in the satellite streets. The quirky Italian Market's specialty stores are a home cook's dream. A few excellent independent bookshops survive throughout South Philly.

CENTER CITY EAST

Center City East (meaning the blocks east of Broad Street) has a lot of great shopping up Pine Street (Antique Row) near Washington Square and also a few blocks west, along the fun, colorful, bustling 13th Street corridor, also called Midtown Village. Antique Row has some holdovers that are traditional antiques shops, but some quirky housewares and gift shops make their home there, too. Street parking is possible by Antique Row, but is harder to find near 13th Street. Nearby Macy's has a parking garage, but your best bet is to cab it, walk, or take the bus.

CENTER CITY WEST AND RITTENHOUSE SQUARE

You'll find many upscale chains in Center City West, especially along Walnut Street between Broad and 18th streets, including Kenneth Cole, Banana Republic, Burberry, and Barneys Co-Op. Plenty of other chains, including Express and J. Crew, hold court at the Shops at Liberty Place. There is more local flavor off the beaten path, down numbered streets and smaller streets around Rittenhouse Square such as Sansom and Rittenhouse Square streets. Parking is tough in this area, and you'll pay a pretty penny for a meter or a lot. You'll have more fun and see much more if you walk these lively streets and let yourself get a little lost.

Washington, D.C.

WORD OF MOUTH

"I wish all Americans could go [to D.C.] at least once. It really makes you feel such a sense of pride and patriotism as you visit these wonderful symbols of our history and liberty."

—texasjo

WELCOME TO WASHINGTON, D.C.

TOP REASONS TO GO

★ **Shopping in Georgetown:** Stroll the cobblestone streets and dip into shops and boutiques offering cutting-edge fashion and priceless antiques.

★ **The Smithsonian:** Spend days discovering everything from dinosaur bones to interplanetary rockets in the Smithsonian's 13 museums, all free.

★ **Washington's Halls of Power:** At the White House, the Capitol, and the Supreme Court, it's fascinating to watch the wheels of government turning.

★ **The View from the Washington Monument:** A ride up the elevator rewards you with a view in every direction of this marble- and monument-laden city.

★ **Cross the Potomac:** Visit the final resting place for the some 340,000 members of the armed services at Arlington National Cemetery. A visit here can be both sobering and moving.

1 The Mall. This expanse of green is at the heart of D.C., stretching from the Capitol to the Washington Monument.

2 The Monuments. D.C.'s most famous monuments are concentrated west of the Mall and along the Tidal Basin.

3 The White House Area. The president's residence is a must-see for many visitors. There's also some great architecture surrounding Lafayette Square.

4 Capitol Hill. The Capitol, the Supreme Court, and the Library of Congress dominate this area.

GETTING ORIENTED

The city is divided into the four quadrants of a compass (NW, NE, SE, SW), with the U.S. Capitol at the center. Because the Capitol doesn't sit in the exact center of the city (the Washington Monument does), Northwest is the largest quadrant.

If someone tells you to meet them at 6th and G, ask them to specify the quadrant, because there are actually four different 6th and G intersections (one per quadrant). Within each quadrant, numbered streets run north–south, and lettered streets run east–west (the letter J was omitted to avoid confusion with the letter I). The streets form a fairly simple grid—for instance, 900 G Street NW is the intersection of 9th and G streets in the NW quadrant of the city.

5 Downtown. The Federal Triangle and Penn Quarter attract visitors to Ford's Theatre, the International Spy Museum, and the National Portrait Gallery.

6 Georgetown. The capital's wealthiest neighborhood is great for strolling, shopping, and partying.

7 Dupont Circle and Upper Northwest. Dupont Circle, with its fashionable restaurants and shops, is home to the most visible segment of the gay community. Woodley Park is where you'll find the National Zoo.

The Byzantine workings of the federal government, the sound bite–ready oratory of the well-groomed politicians, and the murky foreign policy pronouncements issued from Capitol Hill cause many Americans to cast a skeptical eye on anything that happens "inside the Beltway."

Washingtonians take it in stride—all in a day's work. Besides, such ribbing is a small price to pay for living in a city with charms that extend far beyond the bureaucratic. World-class museums and art galleries (nearly all of them free), tree-shaded and flower-filled parks and gardens, bars and restaurants that benefit from a large immigrant community and droves of young people, and nightlife that seems to get better with every passing year are as much a part of Washington as floor debates or filibusters.

The city that calls to mind politicking, back-scratching, and delicate diplomatic maneuvering is itself the result of a compromise. The deal was struck when Virginia's Thomas Jefferson agreed that the federal government would assume the war debts of the colonies if Alexander Hamilton and other Northern legislators would agree to locate the capital on the banks of the Potomac, near George Washington's estate at Mount Vernon. Soon after, in 1791, Pierre-Charles L'Enfant, a French engineer who had fought in the Revolution, designed a city with a "vast esplanade" now known as the "Mall," wide diagonal boulevards crossing a grid of streets, and a focal triangle formed by the Capitol, the president's house, and a statue where the Washington monument now sits. Although L'Enfant's plans seem grand now, for almost a century this city was little more than a sparsely populated swamp with empty dirt avenues.

PLANNING

WHEN TO GO

Washington has two delightful seasons: spring and autumn. In spring the city's ornamental fruit trees are budding, and its many gardens are in bloom. By autumn most of the summer crowds have left and you can enjoy the sights in peace. Summer can be uncomfortably hot and humid. Winter weather is mild by East Coast standards, but a handful of modest snowstorms each year bring this southern city to a standstill.

GETTING HERE AND AROUND
AIR TRAVEL

The major gateways to D.C. are Ronald Reagan Washington National Airport in Virginia, 4 mi south of downtown Washington; Dulles International Airport, 26 mi west of Washington, D.C.; and Baltimore/Washington International-Thurgood Marshall (BWI) Airport in Maryland, about 30 mi to the northeast. By taxi, expect to pay $10–$15 to get from National to downtown, $50–$60 from Dulles, and $90 from BWI.

The Metro subway ride downtown from Ronald Reagan Washington National Airport takes about 20 minutes and costs about $1.85, depending on the time of day and your final destination.

Washington Flyer links Dulles International Airport and the West Falls Church Metro station. The 20-minute ride is $10 one-way and $18 round-trip for adults, free for children under six. Buses run every half hour from 5:45 am to 10:15 pm. Fares may be paid with cash or credit card. The Washington Metropolitan Area Transit Authority (WMATA) operates express bus service between Dulles and several stops in Downtown D.C., including the L'Enfant Plaza Metro station. Bus 5A, which costs $3.10, runs every hour between 5:30 am and 11:30 pm. Exact fare is required.

Amtrak and Maryland Rail Commuter Service (MARC) trains run between BWI and Washington, D.C.'s Union Station from around 6 am to 10 pm. The cost of the 30-minute ride is $9–$44 on Amtrak and $6 on MARC, which runs only on weekdays. A free shuttle bus transports passengers between airline terminals and the train station. Washington Metropolitan Area Transit Authority (WMATA) operates express bus service (Bus B30) between BWI and the Greenbelt Metro station. Buses run between 6 am and 10 pm. The fare is $3.10.

National, Dulles, and BWI airports are served by SuperShuttle. The approximately 20-minute ride from Reagan National to downtown averages $14; the roughly 45-minute ride from Dulles runs $29; the ride from BWI, which takes about 60 minutes, averages $37.

BUS TRAVEL

The D.C. Circulator offers $1 rides to cultural and entertainment destinations along three routes within the city's central core. The north–south route runs from the D.C. Convention Center at 6th Street and Massachusetts NW, to the Southwest Waterfront, at 6th Street and Maine Avenue. The east–west route runs from Union Station at Columbus Plaza NW, to Georgetown, at M Street and Wisconsin Avenue NW. A third loop, operating on weekends only from 10 am to 6 pm, circles the National Mall and includes stops at the National Gallery of Art and the Smithsonian.

The red, white, and blue WMATA buses ($1.35, $3.10 on express buses) crisscross the city and the nearby suburbs. Buses require exact change in bills, coins, or both. You can eliminate the exact-change hassle by purchasing a seven-day bus Metrobus pass for $11, or better yet, the rechargeable SmarTrip card at the Metro Center sales office, open weekdays from 7:30 am to 6:30 pm.

CAR TRAVEL

A car is often a drawback in Washington, D.C. Traffic is horrendous, especially at rush hour, and driving is often confusing, with many lanes and some entire streets changing direction suddenly during rush hour. Interstate 95 skirts D.C. as part of the Beltway (also known as I–495 in parts), the six- to eight-lane highway that encircles the city.

Parking here is an adventure; the police are quick to tow away or immobilize with a boot any vehicle parked illegally. Private parking lots downtown often charge around $5 an hour and $25 a day.

METRO TRAVEL

The Metro, which opened in 1976, is one of the country's cleanest, most efficient, and safest subway systems. It begins operation at 5 am on weekdays and 7 am on weekends. The Metro closes on weekdays at midnight and weekends at 3 am. Lighted displays at the platforms show estimated arrival and departure times of trains, as well as the number of cars available. Eating, drinking, smoking, and littering in stations and on the trains are strictly prohibited.

The Metro's base fare is $1.65; the actual price you pay depends on the time of day and the distance traveled. Up to two children under age five ride free with a paying passenger. Buy your ticket at the Farecard machines, some of which accept credit cards.

TAXI TRAVEL

You can hail a taxi on the street just about anywhere in the city, though they tend to congregate around major hotels. There are a number of different cab companies in the city, and as a result D.C. cabs do not have a uniform appearance (unlike New York's yellow cabs, for example). And you may find yourself in a taxi that's older and a bit run-down. Drivers are allowed to pick up more than one fare at a time.

TRAIN TRAVEL

More than 80 trains a day arrive at Washington, D.C.'s Union Station. Amtrak's regular service runs from D.C. to New York in 3¼–3¾ hours and from D.C. to Boston in 7¾–8 hours. Acela, Amtrak's high-speed service, travels from D.C. to New York in 2¾–3 hours and from D.C. to Boston in 6½ hours.

TOURS

Old Town Trolley Tours ($32), orange-and-green motorized trolleys, take in the main downtown sights and also head into Georgetown and the upper Northwest in a speedy two hours if you ride straight through. However, you can hop on and off as many times as you like. Tourmobile buses, authorized by the National Park Service, operate in a similar fashion, making 25 stops at historic sites between the Capitol and Arlington National Cemetery. Tickets, available at kiosks at Union Station and Arlington National Cemetery, are $25 for adults.

ESSENTIALS

Air Contacts Baltimore/Washington International-Thurgood Marshall Airport (*BWI* ☏ *410/859–7100* ⊕ *www.bwiairport.com*). **Dulles International Airport** (*IAD* ☏ *703/572–2700* ⊕ *www.metwashairports.com/Dulles*). **Ronald Reagan Washington National Airport** (*DCA* ☏ *703/417–8000* ⊕ *www.metwashairports.com/National*).

Metro Contacts Washington Metropolitan Area Transit Authority (*WMATA* ☏ *202/637–7000 or 202/638–3780 TTY, 202/962–1195 lost and found* ⊕ *www.wmata.com*).

Taxis and Shuttle Contacts DC Taxicab Commission (☏ *202/645–6018* ⊕ *www.dctaxi.dc.gov*). **SuperShuttle** (☏ *800/258–3826 or 202/296–6662* ⊕ *www.supershuttle.com*). **Washington Flyer** (☏ *888/927–4359* ⊕ *www.washfly.com*).

Tour Contacts Old Town Trolley Tours (☏ *202/832–9800* ⊕ *www.historictours.com*). **Tourmobile** (☏ *202/554–5100 or 888/868–7707* ⊕ *www.tourmobile.com*).

Train Contacts Amtrak (☏ *800/872–7245* ⊕ *www.amtrak.com*). **Union Station** (✉ *50 Massachusetts Ave. NE* ☏ *202/371–9441* ⊕ *www.unionstationdc.com*).

Visitor Information DC Visitor Information Center (✉ *1300 Pennsylvania Ave. NW, White House Area* ☏ *866/324–7386 or 202/289–8317* ⊕ *www.dcchamber.org*).

DISCOUNTS AND DEALS

It's actually hard to spend money on activities in D.C. All the Smithsonian museums and national memorials are free, as are many other museums and attractions. Summertime is heaven for budget travelers, when free outdoor concerts and festivals occur every week.

PLANNING YOUR TIME

If you have a day or less in D.C., your sightseeing strategy is simple: take the Metro to the Smithsonian stop and explore the area around the Mall. Allow four or five hours to tour the monuments. This includes time to relax on a park bench and to grab a snack from a vendor or one of the snack bars east of the Washington Monument and near the Lincoln Memorial.

EXPLORING WASHINGTON, D.C.

Washington's centerpiece is the National Mall, a mile-long stretch of grass that reaches from the Capitol past the bulk of the Smithsonian's grand museums to the Washington Monument. The White House, due north of the Washington Monument, and the other major monuments, to the southwest, are not far away. In recent years Downtown, north of Pennsylvania from the Capitol to the White House, has become the city's nerve center, quickly gentrifying with new bars, restaurants, world-class theaters, and a renovated Smithsonian Museum of American Art and National Portrait Gallery. The tree-shaded streets of Georgetown, up Pennsylvania Avenue from the White House, are lined with million-dollar row houses and the city's best upscale shopping.

The America by Air gallery of the National Air and Space Museum.

THE MALL

The Mall is the heart of almost every visitor's trip to Washington. The front yard for nearly a dozen free museums, a picnicking park, a jogging path, and an outdoor stage for festivals, movies, musical performances, and fireworks, America's town green is the closest thing the capital has to a theme park.

WHAT TO SEE

National Air and Space Museum. This is the country's second most-visited museum, attracting 9 million people annually to the world's largest collection of historic aircraft and spacecraft. Its 23 galleries tell the story of aviation from the earliest human attempts at flight to supersonic jets and spacecraft. Look up to see the world's most famous aircraft: hovering above are the *Wright 1903 Flyer,* which Wilbur Wright piloted over the sands of Kitty Hawk, North Carolina; Charles Lindbergh's *Spirit of St. Louis;* the X-1 rocket plane in which Chuck Yeager broke the sound barrier; and the Lockheed Vega that Amelia Earhart piloted in 1932. Immerse yourself in space by taking in an IMAX film or a planetarium presentation. The movies—some in 3-D—employ swooping aerial scenes that make you feel as if you've left the ground and fascinating high-definition footage taken in deep space. ■ TIP→ To make sure you get in, buy IMAX theater and planetarium tickets up to two weeks in advance. ⊠ *Independence Ave. and 6th St. SW, The Mall* ☎ *202/357–1729, 202/357–1686 movie information, 202/357–1729 TDD* ⊕ *www. nasm.si.edu* ☞ *Free, IMAX $10, planetarium $8.50* ☉ *Daily 10–5:30* Ⓜ *Smithsonian.*

Fodor's Choice ★

⟳ **National Gallery of Art, East Building.** Architect I.M. Pei designed this dramatic structure, incorporating two interlocking spaces shaped like triangles. Despite its severe angularity, Pei's building is inviting. Inside, the sunlit atrium is dominated by a colorful 76-foot long Alexander Calder mobile. Masterpieces from every famous name in 20th-century art—Pablo Picasso, Jackson Pollock, Piet Mondrian, Roy Lichtenstein, Joan Miró, Georgia O'Keeffe, and dozens of others—fill the galleries. An underground concourse lined with gift shops, a café, and a cafeteria links to the West Building. ⊠ *Constitution Ave. between 3rd and 4th Sts. NW, The Mall* ☎ *202/737–4215, 202/842–6176 TDD* ⊕ *www.nga. gov* ⊒ *Free* ☉ *Mon.–Sat. 10–5, Sun. 11–6* Ⓜ *Archives/Navy Memorial.*

★ **National Gallery of Art, West Building.** The two buildings of the National Gallery hold one of the world's foremost collections of paintings, sculptures, and graphics. The rotunda, with 24 marble columns surrounding a fountain topped with a statue of Mercury, sets the stage for the masterpieces on display in more than 100 galleries. ■TIP→ **There are many free docent-led tours every day, and a recorded tour of highlights is available for a $5 rental fee on the main floor adjacent to the rotunda.** The permanent collection includes *Ginevra de' Benci*, the only painting by Leonardo da Vinci on display in the Western Hemisphere; *The Adoration of the Magi* by Fra Angelico and Filippo Lippi; *Daniel in the Lions' Den* by Peter Paul Rubens; a self-portrait by Rembrandt; Salvador Dalí's *Last Supper,* and works by impressionists such as Edgar Degas, Claude Monet, Auguste Renoir, and Mary Cassatt. ⊠ *4th St. and Constitution Ave. NW, The Mall* ☎ *202/737–4215, 202/842–6176 TDD* ⊕ *www.nga. gov* ⊒ *Free* ☉ *Mon.–Sat. 10–5, Sun. 11–6* Ⓜ *Archives/Navy Memorial.*

★ **National Museum of American History.** The 3 million artifacts in the country's largest history museum explore America's cultural, political, and scientific past, with holdings as diverse and iconic as Abraham Lincoln's top hat, Thomas Edison's lightbulbs, and Judy Garland's ruby slippers from *The Wizard of Oz.* The museum's nickname, "America's attic," is apt: its 20 exhibition galleries are crammed with unexpected items and stories from every nook and cranny of American history. ⊠ *Constitution Ave. and 14th St. NW, The Mall* ☎ *202/633–1000, 202/633–5285 TDD* ⊕ *www.americanhistory.si.edu* ⊒ *Free* ☉ *Daily 10–5:30* Ⓜ *Smithsonian or Federal Triangle.*

★ **United States Holocaust Memorial Museum.** A permanent exhibition tells the stories of the millions killed by the Nazis between 1933 and 1945, and it doesn't pull any punches. Upon arrival, you are issued an "identity card" that details the life of a holocaust victim. The museum recounts the Holocaust through documentary films, video- and audio-taped oral histories, and a collection that includes items such as a freight car like those used to transport Jews from Warsaw to the Treblinka death camp and the Star of David patches that Jews were made to wear. Timed-entry passes (distributed on a first-come, first-served basis at the 14th Street entrance starting at 10 or available in advance through the museum's Web site) are necessary for the permanent exhibition. ■TIP→ **Allow extra time to enter the building in spring and summer, when long lines can form.** ⊠ *100 Raoul Wallenberg Pl. SW, enter from Raoul Wallenberg Pl.*

6

or 14th St. SW, The Mall ☎ 202/488–0400, 800/400–9373 for tickets ⊕ www.ushmm.org ⊠ Free ⊗ Daily 10–5:30 Ⓜ Smithsonian.

MONUMENTS AND MEMORIALS

Washington is a city of monuments. In the middle of traffic circles, on tiny slivers of park, and at street corners and intersections, statues, plaques, and simple blocks of marble honor the generals, politicians, poets, and statesmen who helped shape the nation. The monuments dedicated to the most famous Americans are west of the Mall on ground reclaimed from the marshy flats of the Potomac. This is also the location of Washington's greatest single display of cherry trees, gifts from Japan.

WHAT TO SEE

Fodor's Choice
★
Arlington National Cemetery. More than 340,000 American war dead, as well as many notable Americans (among them Presidents William Howard Taft and John F. Kennedy, General John Pershing, and Admiral Robert E. Peary), are interred in these 612 acres across the Potomac River from Washington, established as the nation's cemetery in 1864. While you're here, there's a good chance you might hear the clear, doleful sound of a trumpet playing taps or the sharp reports of a gun salute. There are an average of 27 funerals held daily (it's projected that the cemetery will be filled in 2020). Although not the largest cemetery in the country, Arlington is certainly the best-known, a place where you can trace America's history through the aftermath of its battles.

To get here, you can take the Metro, travel on a Tourmobile bus, or walk across Arlington Memorial Bridge (southwest of the Lincoln Memorial). If you're driving, there's a large paid-parking lot at the skylighted visitor center on Memorial Drive. Stop at the center for a free brochure with a detailed map of the cemetery. If you're looking for a specific grave, the staff can consult microfilm records and give you directions. You should know the deceased's full name and, if possible, branch of service and year of death.

Tourmobile's 40-minute tours of the cemetery leave every 15–25 minutes from just outside the visitor center. Stops at the Kennedy graves, the Tomb of the Unknowns, and Arlington House. Touring the cemetery on foot means a fair bit of hiking, but it can give you a closer look at the thousands of graves spread over these rolling Virginia hills. ⊠ *West end of Memorial Bridge, Arlington, VA* ☎ *703/607–8000* ⊕ *www. arlingtoncemetery.org* ⊠ *Free, parking $1.75 per hr, Tourmobile $7.50* ⊗ *Apr.–Sept., daily 8–7; Oct.–Mar., daily 8–5* Ⓜ *Arlington Cemetery.*

☼ **Franklin Delano Roosevelt Memorial.** This 7½-acre memorial to the 32nd president employs waterfalls and reflection pools, four outdoor gallery rooms—one for each of Roosevelt's terms as president—and 10 bronze sculptures. The granite megaliths that connect the galleries are engraved with some of Roosevelt's most famous quotes. This was the first D.C. memorial purposely designed to be wheelchair accessible, and the first to honor a First Lady, Eleanor Roosevelt. ⊠ *West side of Tidal Basin* ☎ *202/426–6841* ⊕ *www.nps.gov/fdrm* ⊠ *Free* ⊗ *24 hrs; staffed daily 8 am–midnight* Ⓜ *Smithsonian.*

Fodor's Choice **Jefferson Memorial.** The monument honoring the third president of the
★ United States was modeled by John Russell Pope after a style that Jefferson had used himself when he designed the University of Virginia. In the 1930s Congress decided that Jefferson deserved a monument positioned as prominently as those in honor of Washington and Lincoln, so workers scooped and moved tons of river bottom to create dry land on this spot directly south of the White House. Dedicated in 1943, it houses a statue of Jefferson, and its walls are lined with inscriptions based on the Declaration of Independence and his other writings. ⊠ *Tidal Basin, south bank* ☎ *202/426–6841* ⊕ *www.nps.gov/thje* ☑ *Free* ☉ *Daily 8 am–midnight* Ⓜ *Smithsonian.*

★ **Korean War Veterans Memorial.** This memorial to the 1.5 million United States men and women who served in the Korean War (1950–53) highlights the high cost of freedom. Nearly 37,000 Americans were killed on the Korean peninsula, 8,000 were missing in action, and more than 103,000 were wounded. Nineteen oversize stainless-steel soldiers toil through a rugged triangular terrain toward an American flag; look beneath the helmets to see their weary faces. ⊠ *West end of Mall at Daniel French Dr. and Independence Ave.* ☎ *202/426–6841* ⊕ *www. nps.gov/kwvm* ☑ *Free* ☉ *24 hrs; staffed daily 8 am–midnight* Ⓜ *Foggy Bottom.*

★ **Lincoln Memorial.** Henry Bacon chose a Greek Doric style for this white Colorado-marble temple to Lincoln because he felt that a great defender of democracy should be memorialized in the style found in the birthplace of democracy. Although detractors thought it inappropriate that the humble president be honored with what amounts to a modified but grandiose Greek temple, this memorial has become one of the nation's most recognizable icons. Its powerful symbolism makes it a popular gathering place: In its shadow Americans marched for integrated schools in 1958, rallied for an end to the Vietnam War in 1967, and laid wreaths in a ceremony honoring the Iranian hostages in 1979. It may be best known, though, as the site of Martin Luther King Jr.'s "I Have a Dream" speech. ■TIP→ The best time to see the memorial itself is at night, when spotlights illuminate the facade. ⊠ *West end of Mall* ☎ *202/426–6841* ⊕ *www.nps.gov/linc* ☑ *Free* ☉ *24 hrs; staffed daily 8 am–midnight* Ⓜ *Foggy Bottom.*

★ **Martin Luther King Jr. National Memorial.** Located strategically between the Lincoln and Jefferson memorials and adjacent to the FDR Memorial, the crescent-shape King Memorial sits on a 4-acre site on the curved bank of the Tidal Basin. Visitors enter through a center walkway cut out of a huge boulder, the Mountain of Despair. From the Mountain, the Stone of Hope is visible. The symbolism of the mountain and stone are explained by King's words: "With this faith, we will be able to hew out of the mountain of despair a stone of hope." At this writing the memorial was set to open in summer of 2011, but there may be delays. ⊠ *401 F St. NW* ☎ *202/737–5420 or 888/484–3373* ⊕ *www.mlkmemorial.org* ☑ *Free* ☉ *24 hrs; staffed daily 8 am–midnight* Ⓜ *Smithsonian.*

★ **National World War II Memorial.** This somber monument honors the 16 million Americans who served in the armed forces, the more than

400,000 who died, and all who supported the war effort at home. An imposing circle of 56 granite pillars, each bearing a bronze wreath, represents the U.S. states and territories of 1941–45. Four bronze eagles, a bronze garland, and two 43-foot-tall arches inscribed with "Atlantic" and "Pacific" surround the large circular plaza. ⊠ *17th St. at east side of Washington Monument* ☏ *202/426–6841* ⊕ *www.wwiimemorial. com* ⊠ *Free* ⊙ *24 hrs* Ⓜ *Smithsonian.*

Fodor's Choice **Vietnam Veterans Memorial.** "The Wall," as it's commonly called, is one ★ of the most-visited sites in Washington. The names of more than 58,000 Americans who died in the Vietnam War are etched on its black granite panels, creating a somber, dignified, and powerful memorial. It was conceived by Jan Scruggs, a former infantry corporal who served in Vietnam, and designed by Maya Lin, then a 21-year-old architecture student at Yale. The names of more than 58,000 Americans are etched on the memorial's black granite panels, which reflect the sky, the trees, and the faces of those looking for the names of friends or relatives who died in the war. ⊠ *Constitution Gardens, 23rd St. and Constitution Ave. NW* ☏ *202/426–6841* ⊕ *www.nps.gov/vive* ⊠ *Free* ⊙ *24 hrs; staffed daily 8 am–midnight* Ⓜ *Foggy Bottom.*

☼ **Washington Monument.** At the western end of the Mall, the 555-foot, 5-inch Washington Monument, the world's tallest masonry structure, punctuates the capital like a huge exclamation point. The cornerstone was laid in 1848, but building stopped in 1854 for 20 years, in part because members of the anti-Catholic Know-Nothing party stole and destroyed a block donated by Pope Pius IX. During this period herds of cattle grazed on the grounds of the half-finished monument. A clearly visible ring about a third of the way up the obelisk testifies to this unfortunate stage of the monument's history: the stone used for the second phase of construction came from a different stratum. ■ TIP➔ A limited number of timed-entrance tickets are available each morning at the kiosk on 15th Street. Tickets are also available online. ⊠ *Constitution Ave. and 15th St. NW* ☏ *202/426–6841, 877/444–6777 for advance tickets* ⊕ *www.nps.gov/wamo, www.recreation.gov for advance tickets* ⊠ *Free; $1.50 service fee per advance ticket* ⊙ *Daily 9–5* Ⓜ *Smithsonian.*

THE WHITE HOUSE AREA

In a world full of recognizable images, few are better known than the whitewashed, 132-room mansion at 1600 Pennsylvania Avenue. The residence of perhaps the single most powerful person on the planet, the White House has an awesome majesty, having been the home of every U.S. president but George Washington.

WHAT TO SEE

Lafayette Square. With such an important resident across the street, the National Capital Region's National Park Service gardeners lavish extra attention on this square's trees and flower beds. During the construction of the White House, workers' huts and a brick kiln were set up, and soon residences began popping up around the square, including the Blair House, which is now used by heads of state visiting Washington. Soldiers camped in the square during the War of 1812 and the Civil War,

A statue of Andrew Jackson during the Battle of New Orleans presides over Lafayette Square.

turning it both times into a muddy pit. Today protesters set their placards up in Lafayette Square. ⊠ *Bounded by Pennsylvania Ave., Madison Pl., H St., and Jackson Pl., White House Area* Ⓜ *McPherson Sq.*

 White House. Irishman James Hoban's plan, based on the Georgian ★ design of Leinster Hall in Dublin and of other Irish country houses, was selected in a 1792 contest. The building has undergone many structural changes since then. Major renovations occurred after the British burned the House in 1814, and a piano almost broke through the second-story floor during President Truman's Administration because of the House's deteriorating condition. Truman had the entire structure gutted and restored, adding a second-story porch to the south portico.

■ TIP➔ To see the White House you need to contact your representative or senator. To visit in spring or summer, you should make your request about six months in advance. The self-guided tour includes several rooms on the ground floor and, on the State Floor, the large white-and-gold **East Room,** the site of presidential social events. In 1814 Dolley Madison saved the room's full-length portrait of George Washington from torch-carrying British soldiers by cutting it from its frame, rolling it up, and spiriting it out of the White House. The **State Dining Room,** second in size only to the East Room, is dominated by G. P. A. Healy's portrait of Abraham Lincoln, painted after the president's death. ⊠ *1600 Pennsylvania Ave. NW* ☎ *202/208–1631, 202/456–7041 24-hr info line* ⊕ *www.whitehouse.gov* ✉ *Free; reservations required* ◷ *Tours Tues.– Sat. 7:30–12:30* Ⓜ *Federal Triangle, Metro Center, or McPherson Sq.*

CAPITOL HILL

The people who live and work on "the Hill" do so in the shadow of the edifice that lends the neighborhood its name: the gleaming white Capitol. More than just the center of government, however, the Hill also includes charming residential blocks lined with Victorian row houses and a fine assortment of restaurants, bars, and shops.

WHAT TO SEE

Capitol. Tours start under the center of the **Rotunda's** dome, at the center of which is Constantino Brumidi's 1865 fresco, *Apotheosis of Washington.* South of the Rotunda is **Statuary Hall,** once the legislative chamber of the House of Representatives. The room has an architectural quirk that maddened early legislators: a slight whisper uttered on one side of the hall can be heard on the other. To the north, on the Senate side, is the chamber once used by the Supreme Court, and, above it, the splendid Old Senate Chamber, both of which have been restored.

Fodor's Choice ★

The **Capitol Visitor Center,** a $600-million subterranean education and information area beneath the east lawn of the Capitol, opened in December 2008. You can now register for tickets online or get them directly from the Center where tours will start. Free gallery passes to watch the House or Senate in session can be obtained only from your representative's or senator's office. ⊠ *East end of Mall, Capitol Hill* ☎ *202/226–8000* ⊕ *www.visitthecapitol.gov* ⊠ *Free* ☉ *Tours 8:30–4:30* Ⓜ *Capitol S or Union Station.*

Supreme Court Building. It wasn't until 1935 that the Supreme Court got its own building: a white-marble temple with twin rows of Corinthian columns designed by Cass Gilbert. Before then the justices had been moved around to various rooms in the Capitol; for a while they even met in a tavern. The Supreme Court convenes on the first Monday in October and remains in session until it has heard all of its cases and handed down all of its decisions (usually the end of June). On Monday through Wednesday of two weeks in each month, the justices hear oral arguments in the velvet-swathed court chamber. Visitors who want to listen can choose to wait in either of two lines. One, the "three- to five-minute" line, shuttles you through, giving you a quick impression of the court at work. If you choose the other, and you'd like to stay for the whole show, it's best to be in line by 8:30 am. ⊠ *One 1st St. NE, Capitol Hill* ☎ *202/479–3000* ⊕ *www.supremecourtus.gov* ⊠ *Free* ☉ *Weekdays 9–4:30; court in session Oct.–June* Ⓜ *Union Station or Capitol S.*

DOWNTOWN

In recent years developers have rediscovered the "East End," which had been a hole in the city since riots rocked the capital in 1968 after the assassination of Martin Luther King Jr. Buildings are now being torn down, built up, and remodeled at an amazing pace. **Penn Quarter,** the neighborhood immediately surrounding the once down-at-the-heels stretch of Pennsylvania Avenue, has blossomed into one of the hottest addresses in town for nightlife and culture.

WHAT TO SEE

○ **Ford's Theatre.** On the night of April 14, 1865, during a performance of *Our American Cousin,* John Wilkes Booth entered the state box at this successful music hall and shot Abraham Lincoln in the back of the head. The Ford's Theatre Society launched a two-year, $40-million campaign to transform the theater and its basement museum of Lincoln artifacts into a block-long, Lincoln-centered cultural campus commemorating the president. Opened in early 2009, it includes the renovated theater, the expanded museum, and the historically restored home of William Peterson, where Lincoln died. ⊠ *Ford's Theatre, 511 10th St. NW Petersen House, 516 10th St. NW, East End* ☎ *202/426–6924* ⊕ *www. fordstheatre.org* ✉ *Free* ◉ *Daily 9–5* Ⓜ *Metro Center or Gallery Pl.*

○ **International Spy Museum.** It's believed that there are more spies in Washington than in any other city in the world, making it a fitting home for this museum, which displays the world's largest collection of spy artifacts. There's a mix of flash and fun, with toys used by actual operatives as well as James Bond's Aston Martin and tales of celebrity spies like singer Josephine Baker, chef Julia Child, and actress Marlene Dietrich. "Operation Spy," a one-hour "immersive experience" works like a live-action game, dropping you in the middle of a high-stakes foreign intelligence mission. Advance tickets are recommended, particularly in spring and summer. ⊠ *800 F St. NW, East End* ☎ *202/393–7798* ⊕ *www.spymuseum.org* ✉ *$18; Operation Spy $14; combination admission $30* ◉ *Apr.–Oct., daily 9–8; Nov.–Mar., daily 10–6* Ⓜ *Gallery Pl./Chinatown.*

○ **National Archives.** The National Archives are at once monument, museum, and the nation's memory. Headquartered in a grand marble edifice on Constitution Avenue, the agency is charged with preserving and archiving the most historically important U.S. government records. Its 8 billion paper records and 4 billion electronic records date back to 1775. The star attractions are the Declaration of Independence, Constitution, and Bill of Rights. These are housed in the Archives' cathedral-like rotunda, each on a marble platform, encased in bulletproof glass, and floating in pressurized helium, which protects the irreplaceable documents. Reservations are recommended. ⊠ *Constitution Ave. between 7th and 9th Sts., The Mall* ☎ *202/501–5000, 202/501–5205 tours* ⊕ *www.nara.gov* ✉ *Free* ◉ *Mar. 15–Labor Day, daily 10–7; Labor Day–Mar. 14, daily 10–5:30; tours weekdays at 10:15 and 1:15* Ⓜ *Archives/Navy Memorial.*

National Portrait Gallery. Devoted to the intersection of art, biography, and history, this collection houses nearly 20,000 images of men and women who have shaped U.S. history. The gallery has the only complete collection of presidential portraits outside the White House, starting with Gilbert Stuart's iconic "Lansdowne" portrait of George Washington. Interesting perspectives include the plaster cast of Abraham Lincoln's head and hands; and Shepard Fairey's red, white, and blue portrait of President Barack Obama. From a moving bronze sculpture of Martin Luther King Jr. to Andy Warhol's Marilyn Monroe prints, to Madonna's 1985 *Time* magazine cover, the third-floor gallery offers a vibrant and colorful tour of the people who shaped today's culture.

✉ *8th and F Sts. NW, East End* ☎ *202/633–8300, 202/357–1729 TDD* ⊕ *www.npg.si.edu* ✇ *Free* ☉ *Daily 11:30–7* Ⓜ *Gallery Pl./Chinatown.*

Newseum. This landmark $450 million glass-and-silver structure is on Pennsylvania Avenue, set smack between the White House and the Capitol: a fitting location for a museum devoted to the First Amendment and the essential role of a free press in maintaining democracy. The 90-foot-high media-saturated atrium is overlooked by a giant breaking-news screen and a news helicopter suspended overhead. From there 14 galleries display 500 years of the history of news, including exhibits on the First Amendment, global news, and the way radio, television, and especially the Internet have transformed how we find out about the world. ✉ *555 Pennsylvania Ave. NW, East End* ☎ *888/639–7386* ⊕ *www.newseum.org* ✇ *$20* ☉ *Daily 9–5* Ⓜ *Archives/Navy Memorial.*

GEORGETOWN

Long before the District of Columbia was formed, Washington's oldest and wealthiest neighborhood was a separate city with a harbor full of ships and warehouses filled with tobacco. Washington has filled in around Georgetown over the years, but the former tobacco port retains an air of aloofness. This is one of Washington's main areas for restaurants, bars, nightclubs, and boutiques.

WHAT TO SEE

☺ **C&O Canal.** When it opened in 1850, this waterway's 74 locks linked Georgetown with Cumberland, Maryland, 184 mi to the northwest, and kept Georgetown open to shipping after its harbor had filled with silt. Lumber, coal, iron, wheat, and flour moved up and down the canal, but it was never as successful as its planners had hoped. Today the canal is part of the National Park system; walkers follow the towpath once used by mules, while canoeists paddle the canal's calm waters. You can glide into history aboard a mule-drawn canal boat ride. The National Park Service provides the hour-long rides from about mid-April through late October; tickets cost $7, and are available across the canal, next to the Foundry Building. ✉ *Canal Visitor Center, 1057 Thomas Jefferson St. NW, Georgetown* ☎ *202/653–5190* ⊕ *www.nps.gov/choh.*

Dumbarton Oaks. One of the loveliest places for a stroll in Washington is Dumbarton Oaks, the acres of enchanting gardens adjoining Dumbarton House in Georgetown. Planned by noted landscape architect Beatrix Farrand, the gardens incorporate elements of traditional English, Italian, and French styles such as a formal rose garden, an English country garden, and an orangery (circa 1810). You enter the gardens at 31st and R streets. In 1944 one of the most important events of the 20th century took place at **Dumbarton House,** when representatives of the United States, Great Britain, China, and the Soviet Union met in the music room to lay the groundwork for the United Nations. Today you'll find world-renowned collections of Byzantine and pre-Columbian art. ✉ *1703 32nd St. NW, Georgetown* ☎ *202/339–6401 or 202/339–6400* ⊕ *www.doaks.org* ✇ *Museum free; gardens $8, free Nov.–Mar.* ☉ *Museum: Tues.–Sun. 2–5; gardens: Apr.–Oct., Tues.–Sun. 2–6, Nov.–Mar., Tues.–Sun. 2–5.*

DUPONT CIRCLE AND UPPER NORTHWEST

The main thoroughfares of Connecticut, New Hampshire, and Massachusetts avenues all intersect at Dupont Circle, with a small, handsome park and a splashing fountain in the center. Upscale restaurants, offbeat shops, coffeehouses, art galleries, and specialty bookstores give the neighborhood a distinctive, cosmopolitan air. To the north is Woodley Park, where you'll find the National Zoo.

WHAT TO SEE

☾ **National Zoo.** While recent attention has focused on giant pandas Tian
★ Tian and Mei Xiang, the Smithsonian's free zoological park is full of red pandas, clouded leopards, and Japanese giant salamanders, as well as the traditional lions, tigers, and bears. The zoo makes for a picturesque stroll on warm days, but be prepared for crowds on sunny weekends. Carved out of Rock Creek Park, the zoo is a series of rolling, wooded hills that complement the many innovative compounds showing animals in their native settings. Elephant Trails is one of the newest additions to the park. This sprawling habitat gives the Asian elephants plenty of room to spread out. The zoo is known for its successful breeding programs, and everything from massive gorillas to tiny kiwis have been born on the premises. Locals often participate in naming them. ⊠ *3001 Connecticut Ave. NW, Woodley Park* ☎ *202/673–4800 or 202/673–4717* ⊕ *www. si.edu/natzoo* ☒ *Free, parking $10* ☾ *Apr.–Oct., daily 10–6; Nov.–Mar., daily 10–4:30.* Ⓜ *Cleveland Park or Woodley Park/Zoo.*

WHERE TO EAT

Dupont Circle is dense with restaurants and cafés, many with outdoor seating. On Georgetown's main drags, Wisconsin Avenue and M Street, white-tablecloth establishments coexist easily with hole-in-the-wall joints. Chinatown, centered on G and H streets NW between 6th and 8th, hosts Chinese, Burmese, Thai, and other Asian restaurants. Capitol Hill has a number of bars that cater to congressional types who need to fortify themselves with food and drink after a day spent running the country, and Union Station houses a large food court offering quick bites that range from barbecue to sushi.

WHAT IT COSTS					
	¢	$	$$	$$$	$$$$
Restaurants	under $10	$10–$17	$18–$25	$26–$35	over $35

Prices are per person for a main course at dinner.

CAPITOL HILL

¢ ✕ **Jimmy T's Place.** This D.C. institution is tucked in the first floor of an
AMERICAN old row house only five blocks from the Capitol. Sassy waiters, talk-
☾ ative regulars, and this small diner's two boisterous owners, who run the grill, pack the place daily. Soak in the local culture or read the paper as you enjoy favorites such as grits, bacon, omelets, or the homey eggs Benedict, made with a toasted English muffin, a huge piece of ham,

and lots of hollandaise sauce. The anything-goes atmosphere makes it a great place for kids. Breakfast is served all day. ✉ *501 E. Capitol St. SE, Capitol Hill* ☎ *202/546–3646* ▭ *No credit cards* ⏲ *Closed Mon. and Tues. No dinner* Ⓜ *Eastern Market.*

$$ SEAFOOD ✕ **Johnny's Half Shell.** The Southern-tinged mid-Atlantic fare—pristine Kumamoto oysters, flavorful seafood stews, fried oyster po'boys, and a stellar pickled-onion-and-blue-cheese-topped hot dog—is as good as it gets. And a new pastry chef is turning out a worthy coconut cake. Not surprisingly, the crowd is heavy on politicos drawn as much by the buzz and big-band tunes. Members of Congress can also be found downing a quick Gruyère-cheese omelet during breakfast on weekdays. ✉ *400 N. Capitol St. NW, Capitol Hill* ☎ *202/737–0400* 🌐 *www.johnnyshalfshell.net* ▭ *AE, MC, V* ⏲ *Closed Sun.* Ⓜ *Union Station.*

CHINATOWN

$$–$$$ INDIAN ✕ **Rasika.** This trendy Indian restaurant pairs an adventurous wine list with spicy fare in a supersleek setting. The chef, London export Vikram Sunderam (from Bombay Brasserie), comes from a town where curries never get short shrift. He has prepared a menu of traditional delights, like a fiery chicken green masala, alongside newer, more inspired ones, like lamb miniburgers, tiny crab cakes with Indian spices, and fried spinach leaves with sweet yogurt sauce. Libations at the bar are concocted with as much creativity as the food. Muted shades of cream, apple-green, and cinnabar and dangling crystals evoke the subcontinent but in a stylish, modern way. ✉ *633 D St. NW, Chinatown* ☎ *202/637–1222* 🌐 *www.rasikarestaurant.com* ▭ *AE, D, DC, MC, V* ⏲ *Closed Sun. No lunch weekends* Ⓜ *Archives/Navy Memorial.*

¢–$ MIDDLE EASTERN ✕ **Zaytinya.** This sophisticated urban dining room with soaring ceilings is a local favorite for meeting friends or dining with a group. Zaytinya, which means "olive oil" in Turkish, devotes practically its entire menu to Turkish, Greek, and Lebanese small plates, known as mezes. To get the full experience, make a meal of three or four of these, such as the popular braised lamb with eggplant puree and cheese, or the locally made goat cheese wrapped in grape leaves with tomato marmalade. **■ TIP→ So many options make this a great choice for vegetarians and meat lovers alike.** Reservations for times after 6:30 are not accepted; come prepared to wait on Friday and Saturday nights. Belly dancers perform on Wednesday nights. ✉ *701 9th St. NW, Downtown* ☎ *202/638–0800* 🌐 *www.zaytinya.com* ▭ *AE, DC, MC, V* Ⓜ *Gallery Pl./Chinatown.*

DOWNTOWN

$$–$$$ AMERICAN ✕ **Ceiba.** At this very popular Latin restaurant you'll probably want to start with a mojito or a pisco sour cocktail, then taste the smoked-swordfish carpaccio or Jamaican crab fritters. This is a menu meant for grazing, but the main courses, like rib eye with chimichurri sauce and *feijoada* (stew of beans and meat) made from pork shanks, still satisfy. Also stellar are desserts such as Mexican vanilla-bean cheesecake with guava jelly, and cinnamon-dusted churros to dip in Mexican hot chocolate. Island-theme murals, angular cream banquettes, an open kitchen, and vaulted ceilings set the scene. ✉ *701 14th St. NW, Downtown*

6

☏ *202/393–3983* ⊕ *www.ceibarestaurant.com* ▭ *AE, D, DC, MC, V*
☺ *Closed Sun. No lunch Sat.* Ⓜ *Metro Center.*

$$–$$$
FRENCH
Fodor'sChoice
★

✕ **Central Michel Richard.** French powerhouse chef Michel Richard has
set up camp Downtown with this semicasual bistro offering up Franco-
American spin-offs like fried chicken, leek-and-mussel chowder, and a
ginger-flecked tuna burger. Rows of hams hang in a glass case. Light
fixtures are subtly stamped with the word "Central." A jazzy portrait of
Richard (think Andy Warhol) stares down from one wall. The mood is
playful and low-key; cocktails and champagne flow. And there are even
a few carryovers from Richard's more formal Citronelle in Georgetown
like "Le Kit Kat," the chef's take on a Kit Kat bar. ✉ *1001 Pennsylvania
Ave. NW, Downtown* ☏ *202/626–0015* ⊕ *www.centralmichelrichard.
com* ⌖ *Reservations essential* ▭ *AE, D, MC, V* ☺ *No lunch weekends*
Ⓜ *Metro Center.*

$–$$
SOUTHERN

✕ **Georgia Brown's.** An elegant New South eatery and a favorite hangout of local politicians, Georgia Brown's serves shrimp Carolina-style
(head intact, with steaming grits on the side); thick, rich crab soup;
and such specials as grilled salmon and slow-cooked green beans with
bacon. Fried green tomatoes are filled with herb cream cheese, and a
pecan pie is made with bourbon and imported Belgian dark chocolate.
■ TIP➔ The Sunday "jazz brunch" adds live music and a decadent chocolate fondue fountain to the mix. The airy, curving dining room has white
honeycomb windows and unusual ceiling ornaments of bronze ribbons.
✉ *950 15th St. NW, Downtown* ☏ *202/393–4499* ⊕ *www.gbrowns.
com* ⌖ *Reservations essential* ▭ *AE, D, DC, MC, V* ☺ *No lunch Sat.*
Ⓜ *McPherson Sq.*

¢
JAPANESE

✕ **Teaism.** This informal teahouse stocks more than 50 teas (black, white,
and green) imported from India, Japan, and Africa, but it also serves
healthful and delicious Japanese, Indian, and Thai food as well as tea-
friendly sweets like ginger scones, plum muffins, and salty oat cookies.
You can mix small dishes—tandoori kebabs, tea-cured salmon, Indian
flat breads—to create meals or snacks. There's also a juicy ostrich burger
or *ochazuke,* green tea poured over seasoned rice. The smaller Connecticut Avenue branch (enter around the corner, on H Street; closed
on weekends), tucked neatly on a corner adjacent to Lafayette Park
and the White House, is a perfect spot to grab lunch after touring the
nation's power center. ✉ *400 8th St. NW, Downtown* ☏ *202/638–7740*
⊕ *www.teaism.com* ▭ *D, MC, V* Ⓜ *Archives/Navy Memorial* ✉ *800
Connecticut Ave. NW, Downtown* ☏ *202/835–2233* Ⓜ *Farragut W.*

DUPONT CIRCLE

$$–$$$
AMERICAN
Fodor'sChoice
★

✕ **Nora.** Chef and founder Nora Pouillon helped pioneer the sustain-
able-food revolution with the first certified organic restaurant in the
country, and her seasonal, sustainable ingredients are out of this world.
Settle into the sophisticated and attractive quilt-decorated dining room
and start with the mushroom, leek, and Brie tart or a locally grown
salad. Entrées such as pepper-crusted steak and roasted salmon with
parsnips emphasize the well-balanced, earthy ingredients. ✉ *2132
Florida Ave. NW, Dupont Circle* ☏ *202/462–5143* ⊕ *www.noras.com*
⌖ *Reservations essential* ▭ *AE, D, MC, V* ☺ *Closed Sun. No lunch*
Ⓜ *Dupont Circle.*

$ ✗**Pizzeria Paradiso.** A trompe-l'oeil ceiling adds space and light to a
ITALIAN simple interior at the ever-popular Dupont Circle Pizzeria Paradiso.
Ⓒ The restaurant sticks to crowd-pleasing basics: pizzas, panini, sal-
ads, and desserts. Although the standard pizza is satisfying, you can
enliven it with fresh buffalo mozzarella or unusual toppings such as
potatoes, capers, and mussels. Wines are well chosen and well priced.
The intensely flavored gelato is a house specialty. ⊠ *2003 P St. NW,
Dupont Circle* ☎ *202/223–1245* ⊕ *www.eatyourpizza.com* ⊟ *DC, MC,
V* Ⓜ *Dupont Circle.*

GEORGETOWN

$$$$ ✗**Citronelle.** See all the action in the glass-front kitchen at chef Michel
FRENCH Richard's flagship California-French restaurant. Appetizers might
Fodor's Choice include foie gras with lentils prepared three ways, and main courses
★ run to lobster medallions with lemongrass, saddle of lamb crusted with
herbs, and breast of squab. Desserts are luscious: a crunchy napoleon
with filament-like pastry and the very special "chocolate bar," Richard's
dense, rich take on a Snickers candy bar. A chef's table in the kitchen
gives you a ringside seat (reserve at least a month ahead). The fixed-
price menu costs $155, or $230 with wine pairings. The bar menu has
morsels such as mushroom "cigars" and Serrano ham. ⊠ *Latham Hotel,
3000 M St. NW, Georgetown* ☎ *202/625–2150* ⊕ *www.citronelledc.
com* ⌆ *Reservations essential; Jacket required* ⊟ *AE, D, DC, MC, V*
⊘ *No lunch.*

$–$$ ✗**Sushi-Ko.** At one of the city's best Japanese restaurants, daily specials
JAPANESE are always innovative: sesame oil–seasoned trout layered with crisp
wonton crackers, and a sushi special might be salmon topped with a
touch of mango sauce and a sprig of dill. You won't find the restaurant's
delicious ginger, mango, or green-tea ice cream at the local Baskin-
Robbins. ⊠ *2309 Wisconsin Ave. NW, Georgetown* ☎ *202/333–4187*
⌆ *Reservations essential* ⊟ *AE, D, MC, V* ⊘ *No lunch Sat.–Mon.*

WHERE TO STAY

Forced to cater to all stripes, from lobbyists with expense accounts to
tourists in town for the free museums, from bigwigs seeking attention
to those flying under the radar, Washington's rooms suit everyone. The
high-end and business-class hotels are located mainly near the halls of
power, whether in Georgetown row houses, near the White House, or
on Capitol Hill. Downtown, quickly becoming the city's nerve center,
also has its fair share.

*Hotel reviews have been condensed for this book. Please go to Fodors.
com for full reviews of each property.*

WHAT IT COSTS					
	¢	$	$$	$$$	$$$$
Hotels	under $125	$126–$210	$211–$295	$296–$399	over $400

Prices are for a standard double room in high season, excluding 14.5% room tax.

CAPITOL HILL

$$$$
Fodor's Choice
★

Hotel George. This hotel burst onto the scene in 1998, introducing the city to the concept of contemporary boutique lodging. **Pros:** close to Union Station; popular restaurant; updated fitness center. **Cons:** small closets; some reports of street noise; ultramodern feel not everyone's cup of tea. ✉ *15 E St. NW, Capitol Hill* ☎ *202/347–4200 or 800/576–8331* ⊕ *www.hotelgeorge.com* 🛏 *139 rooms, 1 suite* ♿ *In-room: safe, DVD, Internet, Wi-Fi. In-hotel: restaurant, room service, bar, gym, laundry service, Wi-Fi hotspot, parking (paid) some pets allowed* ⊟ *AE, D, DC, MC, V* Ⓜ *Union Station.*

DOWNTOWN

$$$$
Renaissance Mayflower Hotel. The magnificent block-long lobby of this grande dame hotel (opened in 1925) is a destination in itself, with its series of antique crystal chandeliers and gilded columns. **Pros:** historic building; near dozens of restaurants; a few steps from Metro. **Cons:** rooms vary greatly in size; no pool. ✉ *1127 Connecticut Ave. NW, Downtown* ☎ *202/347–3000 or 800/228–7697* ⊕ *www.marriott.com* 🛏 *657 rooms, 74 suites* ♿ *In-room: Internet. In-hotel: restaurant, room service, bar, gym, laundry service, Wi-Fi hotspot, parking (paid)* ⊟ *AE, D, DC, MC, V* Ⓜ *Farragut N.*

$$$$
Fodor's Choice
★

St. Regis Washington, D.C. Don't forget to admire the hand-painted ceiling in the newly restored lobby of the St. Regis, a 1926 landmark hotel that reopened in 2008 after an extensive 16-month restoration. **Pros:** close to White House; historic property; exceptional service. **Cons:** no pool; most rooms don't have great views; very expensive. ✉ *923 16th St. NW, Downtown* ☎ *202/638–2626* ⊕ *www.stregis.com/washington* 🛏 *175 rooms, 25 suites* ♿ *In-room: safe, refrigerator (some), DVD, Internet, Wi-Fi. In-hotel: restaurant, room service, bar, gym, laundry service, spa, Wi-Fi hotspot, parking (paid), some pets allowed* ⊟ *AE, D, DC, MC, V* Ⓜ *Farragut North.*

$
☾

Washington Doubletree Hotel. Just off Scott Circle, the Doubletree offers spacious, recently renovated guest rooms that have comfortable beds, well-equipped workstations, clock radios with MP3 players, and coffeemakers. **Pros:** child-friendly; good location; new fitness center. **Cons:** no pool; limited street parking. ✉ *1515 Rhode Island Ave. NW, Downtown* ☎ *202/232–7000 or 800/222–8733* ⊕ *www.washington.doubletree.com* 🛏 *181 rooms, 39 suites* ♿ *In-room: safe, refrigerator, Internet. In-hotel: restaurant, gym, Wi-Fi hotspot, parking (paid)* ⊟ *AE, D, DC, MC, V* Ⓜ *Dupont Circle.*

DUPONT CIRCLE

$$$
Fodor's Choice
★

Hotel Rouge. This postmodern hotel bathed in red succeeds at bringing Florida's South Beach club scene to D.C. guest rooms. **Pros:** great lounge scene; gay-friendly vibe; good location. **Cons:** no pool; the scene is not for everybody. ✉ *1315 16th St. NW, Dupont Circle* ☎ *202/232–8000 or 800/738–1202* ⊕ *www.rougehotel.com* 🛏 *137 rooms* ♿ *In-room: safe, kitchen (some), refrigerator (some), DVD. In-hotel: room service, bar, gym, Wi-Fi hotspot, parking (paid), some pets allowed* ⊟ *AE, D, DC, MC, V* Ⓜ *Dupont Circle.*

¢–$ **Hotel Tabard Inn.** Three Victorian town houses were consolidated to form the Tabard, one of the oldest hotels in D.C. **Pros:** affordable choice; lots of character; Sunday-night jazz in the hotel lounge. **Cons:** some shared bathrooms; limited privacy, steps to climb. ☒ *1739 N St. NW, Dupont Circle* ☎ *202/785–1277* ⊕ *www.tabardinn.com* ⇆ *40 rooms, 25 with bath* ⚿ *In-room: no TV (some), Wi-Fi. In-hotel: restaurant, bar, laundry facilities, Wi-Fi hotspot, some pets allowed* ▭ *AE, D, DC, MC, V* ⏍ *Continental breakfast* Ⓜ *Dupont Circle.*

$–$$ **The Inn at Dupont Circle South.** This is the inn where everybody knows your name; innkeeper Carolyn Torralba jokes that her guests are "her babies," and the personal attention shows—there are many repeat customers here. **Pros:** personable innkeeper; across from Metro; children welcome; airport shuttle. **Cons:** creaking floors; steps to climb; not all rooms have private baths. ☒ *1312 19th St. NW, Dupont Circle* ☎ *202/467–6777 or 866/467–2100* ⊕ *thedupontcollection.com* ⇆ *8 rooms, 3 with shared bath* ⚿ *In-room: safe, refrigerator, Wi-Fi. In-hotel: laundry facilities, Wi-Fi hotspot, parking (paid)* ▭ *AE, MC, V* ⏍ *Full breakfast* Ⓜ *Dupont Circle.*

GEORGETOWN

$$–$$$ **Embassy Suites Washington, D.C.** Plants cascade over balconies beneath a skylight in this modern hotel's atrium, which is filled with classical columns, plaster lions, wrought-iron lanterns, waterfalls, and tall palms. **Pros:** family-friendly; all suites; pool to keep the little ones—and sweaty tourists—happy. **Cons:** not a lot of character; museums not in walking distance. ☒ *1250 22nd St. NW, West End* ☎ *202/857–3388 or 800/362–2779* ⊕ *www.embassysuites.com* ⇆ *318 suites* ⚿ *In-room: refrigerator, Wi-Fi. In-hotel: restaurant, room service, bar, pool, gym, laundry service, parking (paid)* ▭ *AE, D, DC, MC, V* ⏍ *Full breakfast* Ⓜ *Foggy Bottom/GWU or Dupont Circle.*

$$$$ **Four Seasons Hotel.** After a whopping $40 million renovation, the Four Seasons has reasserted its role as Washington's leading hotel. Impeccable service and a wealth of amenities have long made this a favorite with celebrities, hotel connoisseurs, and families. **Pros:** edge of Georgetown makes for a fabulous location; lap-of-luxury feel; impeccable service. **Cons:** expensive; challenging street parking; far from Metro. ☒ *2800 Pennsylvania Ave. NW, Georgetown* ☎ *202/342–0444 or 800/332–3442* ⊕ *www.fourseasons.com/washington* ⇆ *160 rooms, 51 suites* ⚿ *In-room: safe, Internet, Wi-Fi. In-hotel: restaurant, room service, bar, children's programs, pool, gym, parking (paid), some pets allowed* ▭ *AE, D, DC, MC, V* Ⓜ *Foggy Bottom.*

Fodor's Choice ★

$ **Georgetown Inn.** Reminiscent of a gentleman's club, this Federal-style hotel seems like something from the 1700s. **Pros:** shoppers love the location; good price for the neighborhood; some nice views. **Cons:** a hike to Metro; congested area. ☒ *1310 Wisconsin Ave. NW, Georgetown* ☎ *202/333–8900 or 888/587–2388* ⊕ *www.georgetowncollection.com* ⇆ *86 rooms, 10 suites* ⚿ *In-room: Wi-Fi. In-hotel: restaurant, room service, bar, gym, Wi-Fi hotspot, parking (paid)* ▭ *AE, D, DC, MC, V* Ⓜ *Foggy Bottom.*

$ **George Washington University Inn.** This boutique hotel is in a quiet neighborhood a few blocks from the Kennedy Center, the State Department,

The coming of the cherry blosoms in spring is an annual cause for celebration in Washington.

and George Washington University. **Pros:** good price; close to Metro. **Cons:** not many amenities; far from museums. ⊠ *824 New Hampshire Ave. NW, Foggy Bottom* ☏ *202/337–6620 or 800/426–4455* ⊕ *www. gwuinn.com* ⤳ *64 rooms, 31 suites* ♿ *In-room: safe, kitchen (some), refrigerator, Wi-Fi. In-hotel: restaurant, bar, laundry facilities, laundry service, parking (paid)* ⊟ *AE, DC, MC, V* Ⓜ *Foggy Bottom/GWU.*

NIGHTLIFE AND THE ARTS

From buttoned-down political appointees to laid-back folks who were born here, Washingtonians have plenty of options when they head out for the night. Most bars are clustered in several key areas. Penn Quarter, near the Verizon Center, is quickly becoming one of the hottest spots in town. Georgetown has dozens of bars, nightclubs, and restaurants at the intersection of Wisconsin and M streets. The stretch of Pennsylvania Avenue between 2nd and 4th streets SE has a half-dozen Capitol Hill bars.

LIVE MUSIC

Fodor's Choice ★ **Black Cat.** Come here to see the latest local bands as well as indie stars such as Neko Case, Modest Mouse, and Clinic. Dave Grohl, lead singer of the Foo Fighters and formerly of Nirvana, owns a stake in the club. The post-punk crowd whiles away the time in the Red Room, a side bar with pool tables, an eclectic jukebox, and no cover charge. The club is also home to Food for Thought, a vegetarian café. ⊠ *1811 14th St. NW, U Street corridor* ☏ *202/667–7960* ⊕ *www.blackcatdc.com* Ⓜ *U Street/Cardozo.*

PERFORMANCE VENUES

Fodor's Choice **John F. Kennedy Center for the Performing Arts.** On the bank of the Potomac
★ River, the gem of the D.C. arts scene is home to the National Symphony
Orchestra, the Washington Ballet, and the Washington National Opera.
The best out-of-town acts perform at one of three performance spaces—
the Concert Hall, the Opera House, or the Eisenhower Theater. Eclectic
performers can be found at the Center's smaller venues, including the
Terrace Theater, showcasing chamber groups and experimental works;
the Theater Lab, home to cabaret-style performances like the audience-
participation hit Sheer Madness; the KC Jazz Club; and a 320-seat family theater. But that's not all. On the Millennium Stage in the center's
Grand Foyer you can catch free performances almost any day at 6 pm.
■TIP→ On performance days a free shuttle bus runs between the Center
and the Foggy Bottom/GWU Metro stop. ⊠ *New Hampshire Ave. at Rock
Creek Pkwy. NW, Foggy Bottom* ☎ *202/467–4600 or 800/444–1324*
⊕ *www.kennedy-center.org* Ⓜ *Foggy Bottom/GWU.*

THEATER

Shakespeare Theatre. This acclaimed troupe, known as one of the world's
three great Shakespearean companies, crafts fantastically staged and
acted performances of works by Shakespeare and his contemporaries.
The stage provides a 21st-century, state-of-the-art, mid-size venue for
an outstanding variety of performances, from Shakespeare's *Julius Caesar* to the hilarious *Abridged History of America.* ⊠ *450 7th St. NW,
Downtown* ☎ *202/547–1122* ⊕ *www.shakespearedc.org* Ⓜ *Gallery Pl./
Chinatown or Archives/Navy Memorial.*

Fodor's Choice **Woolly Mammoth.** Unusual avant-garde shows with edgy staging and solid
★ acting have earned Woolly Mammoth top reviews and favorable compar-
isons to Chicago's Steppenwolf. The troupe's talent is accentuated by its
modern 265-seat theater in Penn Quarter near the Verizon Center. ⊠ *641
D St. NW, Downtown* ☎ *202/393–3939* ⊕ *www.woollymammoth.net*
Ⓜ *Gallery Pl./Chinatown or Archives/Navy Memorial.*

SHOPPING

African masks; kitchenware as objets d'art; bargains on Christian Dior,
Hugo Boss, and Burberry; paisley scarves from India; American and
European antiques; books of every description; handicrafts from almost
two dozen Native American tribes; busts of U.S. presidents; textiles by
the armful; fine leather goods—all this and more can be found in the
nation's capital.

CAPITOL HILL

Eastern Market. Vibrantly colored produce and flowers; freshly caught
fish; fragrant cheeses; and tempting sweets are sold by independent vendors at Eastern Market, which first opened its doors in 1873. On weekends a flea market and an arts-and-crafts market add to the fun. ⊠ *7th
St. and North Carolina Ave. SE, Capitol Hill* ⊕ *www.easternmarketdc.
com* ☉ *Closed Mon.* Ⓜ *Eastern Market.*

DUPONT CIRCLE

Betsy Fisher. Catering to women of all ages and sizes in search of contemporary and trendy styles, this store stocks one-of-a-kind accessories, clothes, shoes, and jewelry by well-known designers like Diane Von Furstenberg. A small selection of up-and-coming designers is also available. ⊠ *1224 Connecticut Ave. NW, Dupont Circle* ☎ *202/785–1975* ⊕ *www.betsyfisher.com* Ⓜ *Dupont Circle.*

Fodor'sChoice
★ **Hemphill Fine Arts.** This spacious gem of a contemporary gallery shows established artists in all mediums, such as Jacob Kainen and William Christenberry, as well as emerging ones like Colby Caldwell. ⊠ *1515 14th St. NW, 3rd fl., Logan Circle* ☎ *202/234–5601* ⊕ *www. hemphillfinearts.com* ☉ *Closed Sun. and Mon.* Ⓜ *Dupont Circle.*

★ **Kid's Closet.** If filling a little one's closet is on your list, stop here for high-quality contemporary infant and children's clothing and toys. Open since 1982, the shop carries sizes 0–7 for boys and 0–16 for girls. ⊠ *1226 Connecticut Ave. NW, Dupont Circle* ☎ *202/429–9247* ⊕ *www.kidsclosetdc.com* ☉ *Closed Sun.* Ⓜ *Dupont Circle.*

★ **Kramerbooks & Afterwords.** One of Washington's best-loved independents, this cozy shop has a choice selection of fiction and nonfiction. Open 24 hours on Friday and Saturday, it's a convenient meeting place. Kramerbooks shares space with a café that has late-night dining and live music from Wednesday to Saturday. ■ TIP→ **There's a computer with free Internet access available in the bar.** ⊠ *1517 Connecticut Ave. NW, Dupont Circle* ☎ *202/387–1400* ⊕ *www.kramers.com* Ⓜ *Dupont Circle.*

GEORGETOWN

Fodor'sChoice
★ **Blue Mercury.** Hard-to-find skin-care lines—Laura Mercier, Trish McEvoy, are just two—are what set this homegrown, now national, chain apart. The retail space up front sells soaps, lotions, perfumes, cosmetics, and skin- and hair-care products. Behind the glass door is the "skin gym," where you can treat yourself to facials, waxing, massage, and oxygen treatments. ⊠ *3059 M St. NW, Georgetown* ☎ *202/965–1300* ⊕ *www.bluemercury.com* Ⓜ *Foggy Bottom/GWU* ⊠ *1619 Connecticut Ave. NW, Dupont Circle* ☎ *202/462–1300* Ⓜ *Dupont Circle.*

★ **Sassanova.** There are high-end shoes in this girly shop for every occasion—be it a walk on the beach or through a boardroom. Brands carried include Lulu Guinness, Emma Hope, and Sigerson Morrison. Jewelry, bags, and shoes for kids round out the selection. ⊠ *1641 Wisconsin Ave. NW, Georgetown* ☎ *202/471–4400* ⊕ *www.sassanova.com.*

The South

WHAT'S WHERE

The following numbers refer to chapters in the book.

7 **North Carolina's Outer Banks.** Nothing in the region compares with the Outer Banks. This thin band of barrier islands with wind-twisted oaks and gnarled pines has some of the East Coast's best beaches.

8 **Charleston, South Carolina.** Charleston anchors the Lowcountry in high style. The harbor town's past, dating to 1670, is evident in cobblestone streets, antebellum mansions and plantations, and Gullah accents. It also hosts the renowned Spoleto performing arts festival.

9 **Orlando and Theme Parks.** Orlando has enough sites, shops, and restaurants to make it a destination in its own right. Walt Disney World is the granddaddy of attractions. It's four theme parks in one—Magic Kingdom, Animal Kingdom, Epcot, and Hollywood Studios. At Universal Orlando, the movies are brought to life at Universal Studios while Islands of Adventure delivers gravity-defying rides and special-effects surprises. Marine mammals perform in SeaWorld's meticulously choreographed shows, and thrill seekers find their adrenaline rush on coasters.

10 Miami and Miami Beach. Greater Miami is hot—and we're not just talking about the weather. Art deco buildings and balmy beaches set the scene. Vacations here are as much about lifestyle as locale, so prepare for power shopping, club hopping, and decadent dining.

11 Florida Keys. This slender necklace of landfalls, strung together by a 110-mi highway, marks the southern edge of the continental United States. It's nirvana for anglers, divers, literature lovers, and Jimmy Buffett wannabes.

12 Nashville. Tennessee's state capital is also the country-music capital of the world. Music City, U.S.A, as Nashville is known, sits in the heart of Tennessee's rolling hills, and is home to powerhouse music publishers on Music Row, aspiring singers and songwriters, raucous honky tonks where music pours out onto the sidewalk, and the venerable Grand Ole Opry.

13 New Orleans. This colorful southern Louisiana city is filled to the brim with music, food, drink, and fun. The calendar is packed with festivals celebrating everything from jazz to gumbo to Tennessee Williams, but spontaneous parties can pop up at any time, for *any* reason—people even dance in the street after funerals here.

THE SOUTH
TOP ATTRACTIONS

Walt Disney World, Orlando

(A) Like one of Snow White's dwarfs, Orlando was sleepy until Uncle Walt arrived 40 years ago. Today the city is booming—and so is Walt Disney World, which has grown into a 47-square-mi complex with four separate parks, scores of hotels, and satellite attractions like Blizzard Beach and Downtown Disney. Thanks to innovative rides and dazzling animatronics, these feature prominently in every child's holiday fantasy. Adults, however, don't have to channel their inner eight-year-old to have fun, because Walt Disney World also has grown-up amenities including championship golf courses, sublime hotels and spas, and fine restaurants that rank among North America's best.

South Beach, Miami

(B) You can't miss the distinctive forms, vibrant colors, and extravagant flourishes of SoBe's architectural gems. The world's largest concentration of art deco edifices is right here; and the Art Deco District, with more than 800 buildings, has earned a spot on the National Register of Historic Places. The 'hood also has enough beautiful people to qualify for the Register of Hippest Places. The glitterati, along with assorted vacationing hedonists, are drawn by über-trendy shops and a surfeit of celeb-studded clubs. Divine eateries are the icing—umm, better make that the ganache—on South Beach's proverbial cake.

Cape Hatteras National Seashore, North Carolina

(C) The mighty Atlantic Ocean meeting a 70-mi ribbon of sand composes one of America's most beautiful beaches. Find

some of the country's best fishing, surfing, and seaside strolling, not to mention maritime history. Three lighthouses mark the coast, including the Cape Hatteras Lighthouse, the nation's tallest brick beacon, and Ocracoke Lighthouse, the second-oldest operating U.S. lighthouse.

Battery Park, Charleston, South Carolina

(D) This promenade affords lovely Charleston Harbor views, the city's most beautiful historic mansions, White Point Gardens' massive oaks, and views of Fort Sumter, where the Civil War's first shot was fired. Along the way you'll also see the Civil War prison Castle Pinckney, the Revolutionary War's Fort Moultrie, and the World War II aircraft carrier *USS Yorktown*.

The French Quarter, New Orleans

(E) Few other American cities have preserved as much of their bricks-and-mortar history as New Orleans. With some buildings dating back to the late 18th century, the French Quarter's stately Jackson Square, delicate wrought-iron balconies, and leafy courtyards reflect centuries of French, Spanish, and Caribbean influences. Walking amid the Quarter's historic buildings, you'll meet buskers and revelers, artists and ghosts. It's one of the most intriguing neighborhoods in the country.

John Pennekamp Coral Reef State Park, Florida Keys

(F) The Keys' aquarium-clear waters are populated by 40 species of coral and more than 600 of fish, which means divers and snorkelers can spot purple sea fans, blue tangs, yellow-tailed snappers, and more. Locals debate the premier place for viewing them, but John Pennekamp Coral Reef State Park is high on everyone's list. Underwater outings organized by park concessionaires let you put your best flipper forward.

TOP EXPERIENCES

Falling with Style

Love high-speed launches and stomach-churning multiple inversions? Immersive simulator rides that take you over cliffs or inside a cartoon? In Orlando, there are more ways to fly, fall, plunge, and plummet than any other destination in the U.S. Eat light, strap on your seat belt, and prepare for liftoff!

Roller Coasters. Coaster fans can't get enough of the Incredible Hulk at Islands of Adventure, Manta at SeaWorld, and Rock 'n' Roller Coaster at Disney's Hollywood Studios. There's also Expedition Everest at Animal Kingdom, Space Mountain at Magic Kingdom, Hollywood Rip Ride Rockit at Universal Studios, and SheiKra at Busch Gardens.

Simulators. Soarin' at Epcot gives you the sensation of hang gliding over California. Wild Arctic at SeaWorld takes you on a virtual helicopter ride above polar ice caps. The Simpsons Ride at Universal Studios is a cartoonish romp, and the Amazing Adventures of Spider Man uses 3-D technology and special effects to the max for high-voltage thrills. At DisneyQuest and WonderWorks you can "build," then ride, your own simulated roller coaster. Pretend you're an astronaut at Kennedy Space Center's Shuttle Launch Experience.

Wet Rides. Hot Florida days and wet thrill rides go together like burgers and fries. Cool off at Journey to Atlantis at SeaWorld; Popeye and Bluto's Bilge-Rat Barges and Dudley Do-Right's Ripsaw Falls at Islands of Adventure; Splash Mountain at the Magic Kingdom; and Kali River Rapids at Animal Kingdom.

Waterslides. Wedgie alert: get your bikini in a bunch on Humunga Kowabunga speed slide at Typhoon Lagoon, Summit Plummet at Blizzard Beach, Bomb Bay at Wet 'n Wild, and Dolphin Plunge at Aquatica.

Facing the Music

Nashville is known as Music City U.S.A., and venues—for country, of course, but rock, blues, jazz, and classical as well—dot the city. At the south end of downtown, you can't walk a block without hearing the familiar chords of a country song pouring out the doors of Broadway's honky tonks or from the lone guitars of sidewalk musicians. The Country Music Hall of Fame and the Ryman Auditorium, the "Mother Church of Country Music," are just a short walk away. Nearby Music Row, home to record labels and music publishers, beckons aspiring singers and songwriters.

In New Orleans, prepare to be blown away by the amount of good local music on tap, any night and in just about any neighborhood. While some of the city's most noteworthy musicians—from Louis Armstrong to Harry Connick Jr. and Marsalis brothers Wynton and Branford—sought fame and fortune elsewhere, quite a few elder statesmen (and women) who have spent their careers in New Orleans. Jazz gets most of the attention, but scratch around the city's club scene and you can find much more: rhythm and blues, funk, roots rock, zydeco, and even a little country. Clubs tend to be intimate and informal, and crowds are lively.

Getting Festive

Pick a weekend; chances are, there's a festival happening in or near New Orleans. Carnival, several days of pageantry, debauchery, and just plain silliness that culminate on Mardi Gras day, is the Big One. The New Orleans Jazz and Heritage Festival, in late April and early May, runs a close second. If you want to avoid big

crowds, there are countless smaller festivals like the Tennessee Williams Literary Festival, the French Quarter Festival, and celebrations dedicated to everything from tomatoes and gumbo to the lowly mirliton, or chayote.

Getting Out on the Water

Spanish explorer Ponce de León didn't find the Fountain of Youth when he swung through Florida in 1513. But if he'd lingered longer, he could have located 7,800 lakes, 1,700 rivers and creeks, and an estimated 350 springs. Over the centuries these have attracted American Indians, immigrants, opportunists, and, of course, countless outdoor adventurers. Boaters come for inland waterways and a 1,200-mi coast, and anglers are lured by 700 species of fish. (Florida claims 700 world-record catches, too, so concocting elaborate fish tales may not be necessary.) Snorkelers and divers curious to see what lies beneath can get face time with the marine life that thrives on the world's third-largest coral reef or bone up on maritime history in underwater archaeological preserves. Back on dry land, all those beaches are pretty impressive, too.

The blue ribbons of rivers, creeks, and streams do more than decorate the green landscape of the Carolinas. They're among the region's most popular destinations for outdoor enthusiasts. Jet Skis and pontoon boats can be found on the glass-smooth lakes, and canoes and kayaks are great for exploring mysterious swamps hung with Spanish moss. Anglers won't be disappointed, either. Children here don't just learn how to fish; they set crab traps with chicken necks and maneuver nets to bring home a mess of shrimp.

Aiming to escape the crowds? Set course for Cape Lookout National Seashore.

Accessible only by boat, its barrier islands are isolated enough to make Gilligan feel at home. One of North Carolina's most photogenic lighthouses (a diamond-patterned beauty) stands here, and the islands are otherwise undeveloped, so you relax in the shelter of dunes, not the shadow of high-rises.

Taking it Slow

If you don't need a vacation so much as an escape, head for one of the quieter locales in the South. Great for recharging your batteries, these places are not served by hourly direct flights and may have spotty cell phone service.

North Carolina's Outer Banks. If you're looking for a chill beach vacation, you've found the right place. Spread out your towel, close your eyes, and listen to the waves. Instant Nirvana.

The Florida Keys. Key West feels like the end of the world, and it's one of a handful of domestic destinations that actually feels like foreign locales. As you drive here from Miami, you'll pass over beautiful stretches of water and tiny spits of sand—and you'll be able to feel your blood pressure drop with each passing mile.

GREAT ITINERARIES

THE FLORIDA KEYS

Three Days

Spend your first morning diving or snorkeling at John Pennekamp Coral Reef State Park in **Key Largo**. If you aren't certified, sign up for a resort course and you'll be exploring the reefs by the afternoon. Dinner at a bay-side restaurant will give you your first look at a fabulous Keys sunset. On Day two get an early start to savor the breathtaking views on the two-hour drive to Key West. Along the way make a stop at the natural-history museum that's part of Crane Point Museum, Nature Center and Historic Site in **Marathon**. Another worthwhile detour is Bahia Honda Key State Park on **Bahia Honda Key,** where you can stretch your legs on a forest trail or snorkel on an offshore reef. Once you arrive in **Key West**, watch the sunset at one of the island's restaurants. The next morning, stroll Duval Street, visit a museum or two, or take a trolley tour of Old Town.

MIAMI

Three Days

Grab your lotion and head to the ocean, more specifically **Ocean Drive** on **South Beach**, and catch some rays while relaxing on the warm sands. Afterward, take a guided or self-guided tour of the **Art Deco District** to see what all the fuss is about, drop in at the News Café for breakfast anytime (or a snack), great coffee, and an outstanding selection of international magazines. Keep the evening free to socialize at Ocean Drive cafés or have a special dinner at one of the many Latin-European–fusion restaurants. The following day drive through **Little Havana** to witness the heartbeat of Miami's Cuban culture (stop for a high-octane Cuban coffee at Versaille's outside-counter window) on your way south to Coconut Grove's Vizcaya. Wrap up the evening a few blocks away in downtown **Coconut Grove,** enjoying its laid-back party mood and many nightspots. On the last day head over to **Coral Gables** to take in the eye-popping display of 1920s Mediterranean-revival architecture in the neighborhoods surrounding the city center and the majestic **Biltmore Hotel**; then take a dip in the fantastic thematic **Venetian Pool.** Early evening, stroll and shop Coral Gable's Miracle Mile—contrary to its name it's just a half mile, but every bit is packed with upscale shops, art galleries, and interesting restaurants.

DISNEY'S MAGIC KINGDOM WITH YOUNG KIDS

The Magic Kingdom is alive with thrilling distractions for young children, so let them take the lead now and then. Toddlers may want to jump from their strollers and dance along to the Barbershop Quartet on Main Street. Children who love good stories will be drawn to the Fairy Tale Garden for Story Time with Belle. These may be the most magical moments of your visit.

Stop and Smell the Roses

Head down Main Street, U.S.A. and, if you're lucky, the park's **Dapper Dans barbershop quartet** will be harmonizing sweet tunes and tossing out one-liners from a small alcove along the street. Small children are jazzed by the music and colorful costumes of these talented singers.

As you continue on toward the park's hub, veer right for the first **Kodak PictureSpot** on the Disney guide map. Take time out to snap one of the prettiest shots in

the park: of the kids by the rose garden amid Mickey and Minnie topiaries and with Cinderella Castle in the background. This photo is an ideal family keepsake and perfect for a holiday card.

Fantasyland is dead ahead, and after you've soared on **Dumbo the Flying Elephant** and nabbed a Fastpass for The Many Adventures of Winnie the Pooh, find a bench in the **Fairytale Garden** in the castle's shadow along Tomorrowland's border. Kids love to listen to (some even get to participate in) **Storytime with Belle**, a reenactment of scenes from *Beauty and the Beast*.

Put the Zip in Your Doo-Dah

If your timing is right and Mickey's Toontown Fair hasn't yet closed for the Fantasyland expansion—walk this way. Sure, little ones love the **Barnstormer** kiddie coaster, but they truly can't resist the free-play fun at **Toon Park** and on Donald's (leaky) Boat.

Board the **Walt Disney World Railroad** at Toontown Fair, Main Street, U.S.A., or Frontierland. While in Frontierland, too-short-to-ride kids can burn energy in the cavelike play area beneath **Splash Mountain** while parents take turns riding. And the short raft trip to **Tom Sawyer Island** is worth it for boys and tomboys who like exploring caves and forts. Not far from the Country Bear Jamboree, sure shots can take aim at Western-style targets in the often-missed **Frontierland Shooting Gallery**—at $1 per 35 shots, it's a blast for any aspiring sheriff.

Become the Character

Girls will get the makeover of a lifetime ($50–$190) at **Bibbidi Bobbidi Boutique** in Cinderella Castle. Hair, nails, makeup—even a sprinkling of pixie dust—it's all here. At the **Pirate's League**,

in Adventureland by Pirates of the Caribbean, a scurvy sea-dog makeover ($50–$125 including photos) lets the inner buccaneer emerge.

But the best-buy makeover (and fastest, too) is in Town Square, where the **Harmony Barber Shop** will transform your crowning glory with colored gel at $5 a pop. Of course, neither Mickey nor Goofy cares whether your hair is aglitter or your eye patch is on straight. Be sure not to miss a scheduled Character Meet and Greet (see *Times Guide*) so the little rascals get all the hugs, autographs, photos, and magical memories they deserve.

DISNEY'S MAGIC KINGDOM WITH OLDER KIDS

The kids are older, and they're interested in thrills, not magic. Or there aren't any kids in tow, and this is your golden opportunity to enjoy "me" time. Seize the day! The Magic Kingdom is a whole new experience without small children. Maximize the big adventures, take time to dine and shop, and discover your own brand of magic along the way.

Classic Thrills

As you pass beneath the train station and into Town Square, you're entering the Happiest Place on Earth, and it's time to grab the golden ring. If thrill riding tops your list, work that cardio for a power walk northwest from the park hub through Liberty Square to Frontierland, where you can grab your Fastpass to **Splash Mountain**, then go next door to ride the bumpy, scenic, runaway train at **Big Thunder Mountain Railroad**.

For many, just to see the Johnny Depp–look-alike Audio-Animatronic Captain

Jack Sparrow, is reason enough to ride the **Pirates of the Caribbean** in Adventureland, a short stroll from Splash Mountain. Cut back through the park hub and straight to **Space Mountain** in Tomorrowland for your other big-deal Fastpass. While you wait, sip an iced cappuccino or smoothie from **Auntie Gravity's Galactic Goodies** and immerse yourself in the futuristic scene reminiscent of *The Jetsons*.

Play, Dine, Shop

The interactive **Buzz Lightyear's Space Ranger Spin** is addictive for competitive types, who will probably want to ride more than once for a chance to raise their space ranger profile. (This attraction is also one of the best ways to spend time while waiting for your Space Mountain Fastpass to mature—just sayin'.)

Chill out afterward at **Tony's Town Square Restaurant,** a great, full-service, late-lunch spot where you can feast on pasta. Burn the calories shopping on Main Street for a make-your-own Mouse Ears souvenir from the **Chapeau** or a customized watch from **Uptown Jewelers.**

At **Crystal Arts** you could buy a fluted glass bowl then mosey to the rear of the glass shop to see an Arribas Brothers glassblower craft a piece using 2,100°F furnaces, a heated rod, and lots of talent. It takes about 20 minutes for the glassblower to shape a piece of glass and explain each step along the way.

Catch the Spirit(s)

You can skip the 3 pm parade crowds, and join 999 grim-grinning ghouls at the **Haunted Mansion** in Liberty Square. Afterward, stroll several paces to the Hall of Presidents, featuring President Barack Obama, and catch the patriotic spirit. Just around the corner in Fantasyland, don your goofy 3-D glasses for **Mickey's**

PhilharMagic, starring the largest cast of Disney animated stars performing in a single show. Cap the evening with the nighttime **SpectroMagic** parade—it'll dissolve any cynicism left in your psyche. When the lights go down and the **Wishes** fireworks paint the sky, you'll be glad you stayed for the fairy-tale ending.

OUTER BANKS, NORTH CAROLINA

Three Days

The Cape Hatteras National Seashore is a 33-mi-long, narrow ribbon of sand dotted with seven, close-set villages on a single road, making it an easy seaside tour with plenty of interesting stops along the way. Get an early start during the traffic-heavy summer season and on holiday weekends. Spring and fall are better times to go, but check off-season hours at attractions and businesses before you set off.

Starting far north, Corolla is home to the red brick, Currituck Beach Lighthouse on landscaped grounds that also host the historic Whalehead Club, a former luxury home and hunting lodge built between 1922 and 1925. Moving south, Amercia's first powered flight took place at Wright Brothers National Memorial, which includes a replica of the brothers' famous aircraft. Another beacon, the 1872 Bodie Island Lighthouse, sits at the head of Cape Hatteras National Seashore. On the way to the next tower, the famous black-and-white striped Cape Hatteras Lighthouse, America's tallest at 12 stories high, you'll pass the 5,800 acre Pea Island National Wildlife refuge, where 365 bird species have been spotted. See how precursors to today's Coast Guard rescued stranded sailors at the 1911 Chicamacomico Life-saving Station. Hatteras Island ends at

the NC Ferry Division landing, where vehicle ferries take off every 30 minutes for Ocracoke Island, a little village with a dozen miles of unspoiled beach and the 1823 Ocracoke Lighthouse.

Getting Here: You can fly into airports at Norfolk, Virginia (two hours away), Raleigh-Durham, North Carolina (five hours away), or New Bern, North Carolina (four hours away). You'll need a car to maneuver the Outer Banks. U.S. 17 and U.S. 64 both lead to the Outer Banks.

CHARLESTON, SOUTH CAROLINA

Three Days

Charleston is one of the most charming—and thoroughly Southern—cities in the Southeast. Historic buildings line the streets. There are more than 2,000 in the downtown area alone. Some restored homes, such as the Nathaniel Russell House, are open to the public, and give the best firsthand view of life in the South in the early 1800s. After getting a close-up view of the city, head to the Battery for picturesque views of the striking mansions and the busy port. Then travel farther away to visit Boone Hall Plantation and Garden for a look at plantation life—from the mansion to the slave cabins. Charlestonians love the arts as much as history. Museums and art galleries fill the city—and it hosts the annual Spoleto Festival USA performing arts spectacle for more than two weeks in May and June.

Getting Here: The 3½-hour drive from Charlotte to Charleston is a direct route. Take I–77 South, and then merge onto I–26 East outside Columbia, South Carolina.

NEW ORLEANS HIGHLIGHTS

Day 1: The French Quarter

Start by getting to know the city's most famous neighborhood. Sure, it's a cliché, but the café au lait and beignets at Café du Monde are a good place to begin, followed by a stroll around Jackson Square and St. Louis Cathedral. Cross the seawall and take in the views of the Mississippi River from Woldenberg Riverfront Park. Wander along North Peters Street to the shops and market stalls in the French Market, followed by a stroll around the mostly residential Lower Quarter and Faubourg Marigny. After lunch, explore the antiques stores and art galleries on Royal and Chartres streets, winding it all up with a cocktail in a shady courtyard; try Napoleon House, an atmospheric bar and café that makes a mean Pimm's Cup, or the French Quarter mainstay Pat O'Brien's. Save Bourbon Street for after dinner at one of the Quarter's esteemed restaurants; like anything that's lived hard and been around as long, it's much more attractive in low light.

Day 2: Uptown and the Garden District

The St. Charles Avenue streetcar rumbles past some of the South's most-prized real estate; take a seat in one of the antique wooden seats, raise a window, and admire the scenery on the way to leafy Audubon Park. Follow the paved footpath to the Audubon Zoo, keeping an eye out for the zoo's white tigers, a pair of albino brothers named Rex and Zulu. Board an inbound Magazine Street bus near the zoo entrance and take it a couple of blocks past Louisiana Avenue, where a number of restaurants, some with sidewalk tables, are clustered. Continue on Magazine to

Washington Avenue and head left through the Garden District. Prytania Street, just past Lafayette Cemetery No. 1 (Anne Rice fans, take note), is a good axis from which you can explore the neighborhood's elegant side streets. Catch a downtown-bound streetcar on St. Charles, or wrap up the afternoon shopping and dining on Magazine Street.

Day 3: Art, History, and Culture

Dedicate one day to a deeper exploration of the city's cultural attractions. Art lovers shouldn't miss the Warehouse District, where a pair of fine museums—the Ogden Museum of Southern Art and the Contemporary Arts Center—anchors a vibrant strip of contemporary art galleries, most of which feature local artists. History buffs will want to check out the National World War II Museum, also in the Warehouse District, and the Historical Collection of New Orleans in the French Quarter, which hosts changing exhibits in a beautifully restored town home. New Orleans music aficionados can browse the bins at the Louisiana Music Factory, which has a wide selection of CDs—and occasional in-store performances—by Louisiana musicians.

NASHVILLE

Explore the Capital of Country

For country music devotees, no destination looms larger than Nashville, Tennessee. Any proper pilgrimage here begins downtown at the **Country Music Hall of Fame and Museum**: a $37 million complex with state-of-the-art exhibits and cases containing outrageous outfits, gold records, and vintage instruments. It also hosts live performances and serves as the starting point for tours to **RCA Studio B**, the oldest recording studio on **Music Row**.

■ TIP→ When strolling—or boot scootin'—to the latter, remember to look down at the stars lining Music Mile's Walk of Fame.

If Music Row is the nerve center of the country-and-western industry, historic **Ryman Auditorium** (just north of the Hall of Fame) is its heart. Fervent fans understandably approach the 2,000-seat venue with reverence. Built as a gospel tabernacle in 1892, it was home to the Grand Ole Opry from 1942 to 1974 and is still known as the "Mother Church of Country Music." Aspire to stardom yourself? Along with an up-close look at memorabilia, auditorium tours provide on-stage photo ops. You can even cut souvenir CDs in the Ryman Recording Booth.

Of course, no one can come to Nashville without visiting its *numero uno* attraction: the Grand Ole Opry's current site, about 10 mi northeast of town. **Opryland** offers its own tours and exhibits, but it's the legendary live shows that really pull in crowds, staged Friday and Saturday nights year-round with an additional show Tuesday nights from March to December. After applauding the Opry's established acts, be sure to check out up-and-comers in local haunts like the **Bluebird Café** and **Station Inn**.

North Carolina's Outer Banks

WORD OF MOUTH

"The Outer Banks is not really a beach resort type atmosphere with lots of restaurants and bars everywhere. Most people are happy just getting local seafood and grilling it up on the deck vs. going out . . . [T]here's 100 miles of beach and dunes . . . so you can easily find a spot on the beach even in midsummer with nobody in sight." —weimarer

WELCOME TO NORTH CAROLINA'S OUTER BANKS

TOP REASONS TO GO

★ **Water, water everywhere:** Surfers delight in Cape Hatteras's formidable waves. Beach strollers love Ocracoke's remote, unspoiled shore.

★ **Lighting the darkness:** North Carolina's seven lighthouses each has its own personality.

★ **Roanoke Island's Lost Colony:** In a mystery for the ages, 117 settlers disappeared without a trace. Their story is presented both in historical context and dramatic entertainment in Manteo.

★ **Fresh seafood:** You can get fresh seafood of every variety fixed in practically every method—fried, grilled, stuffed, blackened, or raw.

1 **The Northern Beaches, Nags Head, and Roanoke Island.** Long stretches of wild beach are intermingled with small, lively towns on this ribbon of sand. The north end is a tourist mecca of shops, resorts, restaurants, beach cottages, and historic sites. Quieter villages and open, undeveloped beach mark the south end where travelers often hear nothing but surf and shorebirds. With just one two-lane road stretching the length of the Outer Banks, locals speak of mile markers instead of street numbers.

2 **Cape Hatteras National Seashore.** With challenging waves, myriad fish, and the impressive Cape Hatteras lighthouse anchoring the east end, this wide-open beach is a surfer's playground, an angler's dream, and a history buff's treasure.

GETTING ORIENTED

You could pick a destination and stick to it, but touring the entire Outer Banks is doable in a few days, especially in spring and fall when traffic is lighter. A vehicle is essential for navigating the coast here, as little public transportation is available. State-operated vehicle ferries and smaller private ferries run between islands and provide an enjoyable, relaxing tour. Boat touring is another option. Dozens of marinas line the shore, and the intracoastal waterway runs the length of the North Carolina coast.

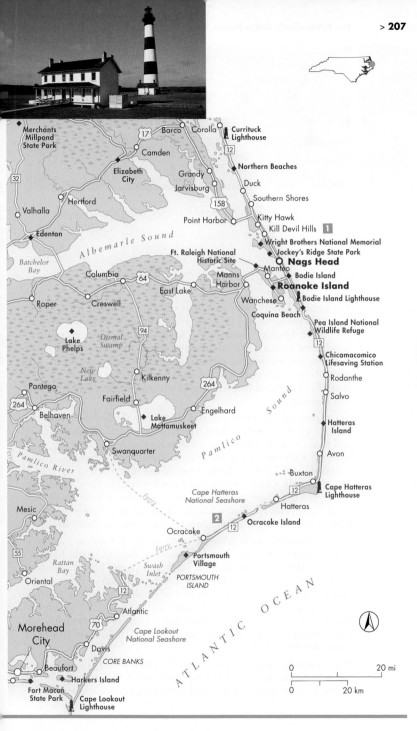

Merchants Millpond State Park

Barco
Corolla
Currituck Lighthouse

17
Camden

32
Elizabeth City
Grandy
Jarvisburg

12
Northern Beaches
Duck
Southern Shores

158
Hertford
Point Harbor
Kitty Hawk
Kill Devil Hills 1

Valhalla

Edenton

Albemarle Sound
Wright Brothers National Memorial
Jockey's Ridge State Park

Ft. Raleigh National Historic Site
Manteo
Nags Head

Batchelor Bay
Columbia
64
Manns Harbor
Roanoke Island
Bodie Island

Roper
East Lake
Wanchese
Bodie Island Lighthouse

Creswell
Coquina Beach

94
Pea Island National Wildlife Refuge

Lake Phelps
Dismal Swamp
12
Chicamacomico Lifesaving Station

Pantego
New Lake
Kilkenny
Rodanthe

264
Fairfield
264
Salvo

Belhaven
Lake Mattamuskeet
Engelhard
Pamlico
Sound
Hatteras Island

Swanquarter
Pamlico River
Avon

Mesic
Cape Hatteras National Seashore
Buxton

55
Ocracoke
12
Ocracoke Island
Cape Hatteras Lighthouse

Rattan Bay
Swash Inlet
Portsmouth Village
Hatteras

Oriental
12
PORTSMOUTH ISLAND

Atlantic
ATLANTIC OCEAN

Morehead City
70
Cape Lookout National Seashore

Davis
CORE BANKS

Beaufort

Fort Macon State Park
Harkers Island
Cape Lookout Lighthouse

0 ___ 20 mi
0 ___ 20 km

7

North Carolina's Outer Banks stretch from the Virginia state line south to Cape Lookout. Think of the OBX (shorthand used on popular bumper stickers) as a series of stepping stones in the Atlantic Ocean.

Throughout history, the treacherous waters surrounding these islands have been the nemesis of shipping, gaining them the nickname "Graveyard of the Atlantic." A network of lighthouses and lifesaving stations, which grew around the need to protect seagoing craft, attracts curious travelers, just as the many submerged wrecks attract scuba divers. The islands' coves and inlets, which sheltered pirates—the notorious Blackbeard lived and died here—now give refuge to anglers, bird-watchers, and sunbathers.

The region is divided into four coastal sections: the Northern Beaches, beginning with Corolla, followed by Roanoke Island, Hatteras Island, and then Ocracoke Island. For many years the Outer Banks remained isolated, with only a few hardy commercial fishing families. Today the islands are linked by bridges and ferries, and much of the area is included in the Cape Hatteras and Cape Lookout national seashores. The largest towns are also the most colorfully named: Kitty Hawk, Kill Devil Hills, Nags Head, and Manteo. Vacation rentals here are omnipresent—thousands of weekly rental cottages line the Outer Banks.

You can travel the region from the south end by taking a car ferry from Cedar Island to Ocracoke Island, then another from Ocracoke Island to Hatteras Island. Starting from the north, driving the 120-mi stretch of Route 12 from Corolla to Ocracoke can be managed in a day, but be sure to start early in the morning and allow plenty of time in summer for delays due to heavy traffic, for ferry waiting times, and for exploring the undeveloped beaches, historic lighthouses, and interesting beach communities along the way. Mile markers (MM) indicate addresses all along the Outer Banks.

Sudden squalls frequently blow up on the Outer Banks in summer, and the Atlantic hurricane season runs from June 1 to November 30. Be aware that during major storms and hurricanes, evacuations are mandatory and roads and bridges become clogged with traffic following the blue-and-white evacuation-route signs.

PLANNING

GETTING HERE AND AROUND

AIR TRAVEL

The closest large, commercial airports to the Outer Banks are Raleigh-Durham, a 5-hour drive, and Norfolk International in Virginia, a 1½-hour drive. Coastal Carolina Regional Airport in New Bern has connector flights, charter service, and car rentals available. Wilmington International Airport serves the Cape Fear Coast.

Barrier Island Aviation provides charter service between the Dare County Regional Airport and major cities along the East Coast. US Airways Express and Delta ASA fly into Coastal Carolina Regional Airport in New Bern. US Airways, Delta, and Allegiant serve Wilmington International Airport.

Air Contacts Barrier Island Aviation (✉ *407 Airport Rd., Manteo* ☏ *252/473–4247* ⊕ *www.barrierislandaviation.com*). **Coastal Carolina Regional Airport** (✉ *200 Terminal Dr., New Bern* ☏ *252/638–8591* ⊕ *www.newbernairport.com*). **Dare County Regional Airport** (✉ *410 Airport Rd., Manteo* ☏ *252/475–5570* ⊕ *www.co.dare.nc.us/airport*). **Norfolk International** (✉ *2200 Norview Ave.* ☏ *757/857–3351* ⊕ *www.norfolkairport.com*). **Wilmington International Airport** (✉ *1740 Airport Blvd.* ☏ *910/341–4125* ⊕ *www.flyilm.com*).

CAR TRAVEL

On the one hand, navigation in the Outer Banks is a snap because there's only one road—Route 12. On the other, traffic can make that single road two lanes of pure frustration on a rainy midsummer day when everyone is looking for something besides sunbathing. Low-lying areas of the highway are also prone to flooding.

ABOUT THE RESTAURANTS

Raw bars serve oysters and clams on the half shell; some seafood houses sell each day's local catch, be it tuna, wahoo, mahi, mackerel, shrimp, or blue crabs. This is, after all, the coast, though highly trained chefs are settling in the region and increasingly diversifying menus. Expect up to hour-long waits, sometimes longer, at many restaurants during summer and festival periods. Many places don't accept reservations. Restaurant hours are frequently reduced in winter.

ABOUT THE HOTELS

Hundreds of rental properties are available. Small beach cottages can be had, but increasingly so-called sand castles—large multistory homes—suit large groups. Motels and hotels clustered all along the Outer Banks are still the more affordable way to go.

Hotel reviews have been condensed for this book. Please go to Fodors. com for full reviews of each property.

WHAT IT COSTS					
	¢	$	$$	$$$	$$$$
Restaurants	under $10	$10–$14	$15–$19	$20–$24	over $24
Hotels	under $100	$100–$150	$151–$200	$201–$250	over $250

Restaurant prices are for a main course at dinner. Hotel prices are for two people in a standard double room in high season.

VISITOR INFORMATION

Contacts **National Park Service's Group Headquarters** (⊠ *1401 National Park Dr., Manteo* ☎ *252/473–2111* ⊕ *www.nps.gov/caha*).

NORTHERN BEACHES

Corolla: 91 mi south of Norfolk, VA, via U.S. 17, U.S. 158, and Rte. 12; 230 mi east of Raleigh via U.S. 64, U.S. 17, and Rte. 12. Duck: 16 mi south of Corolla. Kitty Hawk: 19 mi south of Corolla; 7 mi south of Duck.

The small northern beach settlements of Corolla and Duck are largely seasonal, residential enclaves full of summer rental condominiums. Drive slowly in Corolla: here freely wandering wild horses always have the right of way. Upscale Duck has lots of restaurants and shops. Kitty Hawk, with a few thousand permanent residents, has fewer rental accommodations. Given these communities' contiguous nature and similar looks, the uninitiated may not realize when they've crossed from Kitty Hawk into Kill Devil Hills. The towns' respective roles in the drama of the first powered flight occasionally create some confusion as well. When arriving at the Outer Banks, the Wright brothers first stayed in the then-remote fishing village of Kitty Hawk, but their flight took place some 4 mi south on Kill Devil Hill, a gargantuan sand dune where today the Wright Brothers National Memorial stands.

GETTING HERE AND AROUND

Most people drive to the northern beaches via U.S. 17, 64, and 264, which all link to the local U.S. 158 and Route 12. Some commercial and charter flights are available from nearby airports. Plan your time wisely, as heavy traffic can lead to long travel delays in summer. Marked paths and wide shoulders accommodate bikers and walkers along some roads. Guided tours are available, too. Still, a car is essential for getting around on your own time.

ESSENTIALS

Visitor Information **Aycock Brown Welcome Center** (⊠ *5230 N. Croatan Hwy., mile marker 1, Kitty Hawk* ☎ *877/629–4386*).

EXPLORING

Currituck Beach Lighthouse. The northernmost lighthouse on the Outer Banks, the Currituck Lighthouse was completed in 1875 and was built from about 1 million bricks, which remained unpainted. Except in high winds or thunderstorms, you can climb 214 steps to the top. ⊠ *1101 Corolla Village Rd., Rte. 12, north of Whalehead club sign, Corolla* ☎ *252/453–4939* ⊕ *www.currituckbeachlight.com* ☜ *$7 cash or check only* ⊗ *Easter–Thanksgiving, daily 9–5, hrs extended 9–8 Thurs. in summer.*

⟳ **Wright Brothers National Memorial.** A 60-foot granite monument that
★ resembles the tail of an airplane stands as a tribute to Wilbur and Orville Wright. The two bicycle mechanics from Ohio took to the air here on December 17, 1903. You can see a replica of the *Flyer* and stand on the spot where it made four takeoffs and landings, their longest flight a distance of 852 feet. Exhibits and an informative talk by a National Park Service ranger bring the event to life. The Wrights had to bring in the unassembled airplane by boat, along with all their food and supplies for building a camp. They made four trips to the site beginning in 1900. The First Flight is commemorated annually. ⊠ *1000 N. Croatan Hwy., off U.S. 158 at mile marker 7.5, 5 mi south of Kitty Hawk, Kill Devil Hills* ☎ *252/441–7430* ⊕ *www.nps.gov/wrbr* ☜ *$4* ⊗ *Sept.–May, daily 9–5; June–Aug., daily 9–6.*

WHERE TO EAT AND STAY

$$$–$$$$ ✕ **Blue Point Bar & Grill.** This upscale spot with an enclosed porch overlook-
SEAFOOD ing Currituck Sound is busy and boldly colorful—with a red, black, and
★ chrome interior. The menu mixes Southern style with local seafood, includ-
ing the ever-popular she-crab soup, a thick and rich concoction made with cream, sherry, herbs, Old Bay seasoning, and, of course, crab roe. Lunch is served Tuesday–Sunday. ⊠ *1240 Duck Rd., Duck* ☎ *252/261–8090* ⊕ *www.thebluepoint.com* ⊟ *AE, MC, V* ⊗ *No lunch Mon.*

¢–$ ✕ **Outer Banks Brewing Station.** Cooper accents, lots of wood, and fun,
AMERICAN retro touches characterize this huge white building, modeled after a
⟳ turn-of-the-19th-century lifesaving station. Beer rules here—five are on tap, including lemongrass wheat, which won a 2009 World Beer Cup silver medal—but kids are welcome and there are even a playground and pirate ship to explore outside. Rare, sesame-seed-crusted, local tuna tops a garden salad. Pan-fried pork chops are served with old-fashioned macaroni and cheese drizzled with truffle oil. Pizza, sand-wiches, plenty of bar munchies, and steamed and fried seafood are served, too. ⊠ *600 S. Croatan Hwy., U.S. 158, mile marker 8.5, Kill Devil Hills* ☎ *252/449–2739* ⊕ *www.obbrewing.com* ⚞ *Reservations not accepted* ⊟ *AE, D, MC, V.*

$$$–$$$$ ⌑ **Advice 5¢.** Although the name is lighthearted, Advice 5¢ is serious
★ about guest care. A roof with varied pitches and eaves tops this con-temporary, steely blue-gray beach house with white trim and multipane windows rising from the dunes. **Pros:** quiet and secluded but walking distance to commercial area. **Cons:** no ocean view; no pets allowed; no kids under age 16. ⊠ *111 Scarborough La., Duck* ☎ *252/255–1050 or 800/238–4235* ⊕ *www.advice5.com* ⟆ *4 rooms* ⟁ *In-room: no phone, Wi-Fi. In-hotel: restaurant, tennis courts, pool, no kids under 16* ⊟ *MC, V* ⊗ *Closed mid-Nov.–mid-Mar.* ⫟⃝ *BP.*

At Jockey's Ridge State Park you can hike to the top of the tallest natural sand dune in the Eastern United States.

NAGS HEAD

9 mi south of Kitty Hawk.

It's widely accepted that Nags Head got its name because pirates once tied lanterns around the necks of their horses to lure merchant ships onto the shoals hoping to wreck the vessels and profit from their cargo. Dubious citizenry aside, Nags Head was established in the 1830s and has become a North Carolina tourist haven.

The town—one of the largest on the Outer Banks, yet still with a population of only about 3,000 people—lies between the Atlantic Ocean and Pamlico Sound, along and between U.S. 158 ("the bypass") and Route 12 ("the beach road" or Virginia Dare Trail). Both roads are congested in the high season, and the entire area is commercialized.

Nags Head has 11 mi of beach with 41 public access points from Route 12, some with paved parking and some with restrooms and showers. ■ TIP→ It's easy to overlook the flagpoles stationed along many area beaches; but if there's a red flag flying from one of them, it means the water is too rough even for wading. These are not a suggestion—ignoring them can mean hefty fines.

GETTING HERE AND AROUND

From the east, arrive by car on U.S. 64 or from the north on U.S. 17 and U.S. 158. Although many people cycle and walk on designated paths, most exploring requires a car.

ESSENTIALS

Visitor Information Whalebone Welcome Center (⊠ *2 N.C. 12 Hwy., mile marker 17, Nags Head* ☎ *877/441–6644*).

EXPLORING

⟳ **Jockey's Ridge State Park** has 420 acres that encompass the tallest sand dune on the East Coast (about 80 to 100 feet). Walk along the 360-foot boardwalk from the visitor center to the edge of the dune. The climb to the top is a challenge; nevertheless, it's a popular spot for hang gliding, kite flying, and sand boarding. You can also explore an estuary, a museum, and a self-guide trail through the park. In summer, join the free Sunset on the Ridge program: Watch the sun disappear while you sit on the dunes and learn about their local legends and history. Covered footwear is a wise choice here, as the loose sand gets quite hot in the summer months. ⊠ *300 W. Carolista Dr., mile marker 12* ☎ *252/441–7132* ⊕ *www.jockeysridgestatepark.com* 🖃 *Free* ☉ *June–Aug., daily 8 am–9 pm; Mar., Apr., May, Sept., and Oct., daily 8–8; Nov.–Feb., daily 8–6.*

WHERE TO EAT

$$$–$$$$
SEAFOOD
⟳
★
✕ **Basnight's Lone Cedar Café.** Hearts were broken when this restaurant, owned by powerful North Carolina Senator Marc Basnight and family, burned in 2007, but the rebuilt contemporary setting with simple pine tables and a huge glass-walled wine rack in the main dining room is sleeker and larger than the original. Big windows all around allow everyone a chance to see the osprey mother and chicks nesting on a waterfront piling outside. North Carolina produce and seafood star here, and an extensive herb garden provides fresh seasoning. ⊠ *Nags Head–Manteo Causeway, 7623 S. Virginia Dare Trail* ☎ *252/441–5405* ⊕ *www.lonecedarcafe.com* ⌲ *Reservations not accepted* ☰ *D, MC, V* ☉ *Closed Jan. No lunch Mon.–Sat.*

$$$$
SEAFOOD
Fodor's Choice
★
✕ **Owens' Restaurant.** This family-owned restaurant, in business since 1946, is housed in a replica of a lifesaving station like those found on the Outer Banks in the early 19th century. The classic clapboard building has pine paneling and is filled with maritime artifacts. Stick with fresh-off-the-boat local seafood or prime beef; the kitchen staff excels at both. In summer, arrive early and expect to wait. The brass-and-glass Station Keeper's Lounge has entertainment Thursday, Friday, and Saturday nights in summer. ⊠ *U.S. 158, mile marker 16.5, 7114 S. Virginia Dare Trail* ☎ *252/441–7309* ⊕ *www.owensrestaurant.com* ⌲ *Reservations not accepted* ☰ *AE, D, MC, V* ☉ *Closed Jan. and Feb. No lunch.*

$–$$
SEAFOOD
⟳
✕ **Sam & Omie's.** This no-nonsense niche is named after two fishermen who were father and son. Opened in 1937, it's one of the oldest restaurants on the Outer Banks. Fishing illustrations hang on the walls, and country music plays in the background. It's open daily 7 to 10, serving every imaginable kind of seafood, and then some. Try the fine marinated tuna steak, Cajun tuna bites, or frothy crab-and-asparagus soup. Locals love breakfast here. ■TIP➜ Die-hard fans claim that Sam & Omie's serves the best oysters on the beach. ⊠ *U.S. 158, mile marker*

7

16.5, 7228 Virginia Dare Trail ☎ *252/441–7366* ⊕ *www.samandomies. net* ⚐ *Reservations not accepted* ▭ *D, MC, V* ☉ *Closed Dec.–Feb.*

WHERE TO STAY

$$$–$$$$
Fodor's Choice
★

⊞ **First Colony Inn.** Stand on the verandas that encircle this old, three-story, cedar-shingle inn and admire the ocean views. Two rooms have wet bars and kitchenettes; others have four-poster or canopy beds, handcrafted armoires, and English antiques. **Pros:** homey accommodations feel like grandma's house; some in-room hot tubs; microwaves in rooms. **Cons:** on a busy highway; you'll have to cross a road to get to the beach. ⊠ *6715 S. Croatan Hwy., U.S. 158, mile marker 16* ☎ *252/441–2343 or 800/368–9390* ⊕ *www.firstcolonyinn.com* ⤶ *26 rooms* ⚐ *In-room: kitchen (some), refrigerator, Wi-Fi. In-hotel: restaurant, pool* ▭ *AE, D, MC, V* ▯⦿*BP.*

BEACHES

Coquina Beach. In the Cape Hatteras National Seashore but just a few miles south of Nags Head, Coquina is considered by locals to be the loveliest beach in the Outer Banks. The wide-beam ribs of the shipwreck *Laura Barnes* rest in the dunes here. Driven onto the Outer Banks by a nor'easter in 1921, she ran aground north of this location; the entire crew survived. The wreck was moved to Coquina Beach in 1973 and displayed behind ropes, but subsequent hurricanes have scattered the remains and covered them with sand, making it difficult to discern. **Best for:** families, fishing, long walks, sunbathing, swimming. **Amenities:** parking in lots, showers, toilets. ⊠ *Off Rte. 12, mile marker 26, 8 mi south of U.S. 158.*

ROANOKE ISLAND

10 mi southwest of Nags Head.

On a hot July day in 1587, 117 men, women, and children left their boat and set foot on Roanoke Island to form the first permanent English settlement in the New World. Three years later, when a fleet with supplies from England landed, the settlers had disappeared without a trace, leaving a mystery that continues to baffle historians. Much of the 12-mi-long island, which lies between the Outer Banks and the mainland, remains wild. Of the island's two towns, Wanchese is the fishing village, and Manteo is tourist-oriented, with sights related to the island's history, as well as an aquarium.

GETTING HERE AND AROUND

From the east, drive to the island on U.S. 64; from the Outer Banks, follow U.S. 158 to U.S. 64. Although Manteo's main drag and downtown waterfront have sidewalks, a car is useful for visiting the town's various sites. Charter flights are available at Dare County Regional Airport.

ESSENTIALS

Visitor Information Outer Banks Welcome Center on Roanoke Island (⊠ *1 Visitors Center Circle, Manteo* ☎ *877/629–4386*).

At Roanoke Island Festival Park, you can help costumed 16th-century "sailors" set the sails and swab the decks of the *Elizabeth II*.

EXPLORING

Fort Raleigh National Historic Site. Fort Raleigh is a restoration of the original 1585 earthworks that mark the beginning of English-colonial history in America. ■TIP→ Be sure to see the orientation film before taking a guided tour of the fort. A nature trail through the 513-acre grounds leads to an outlook over Albemarle Sound. Native American and Civil War history is also preserved here. ***The Lost Colony*** (⊠ *1409 National Park Dr., off U.S. 64, 3 mi north of downtown Manteo* ☎ *252/473–2127 office, 252/473–3414 or 800/488–5012 box office* ⊕ *www.thelostcolony.org* 🎟 *$12–$24* ☉ *Sept.–May, daily 9–5; June–Aug., daily 9–6*), Pulitzer Prize–winner Paul Green's drama, was written in 1937 to mark the 350th birthday of Virginia Dare, the first English child born in the New World. Except from 1942 to 1947, it has played every summer since in Fort Raleigh National Historic Site's Waterside Theatre. It reenacts the story of the first colonists, who settled here in 1587 and mysteriously vanished. ⊠ *1401 National Park Dr., Manteo* ☎ *252/473–5772* ⊕ *www.nps.gov/fora* 🎟 *Free*.

North Carolina Aquarium at Roanoke Island. The aquarium occupies 68,000 square feet of space overlooking Croatan Sound. There are touch tanks, but *The Graveyard of the Atlantic* is the centerpiece exhibit. It's a 285,000-gallon ocean tank containing the re-created remains of the USS *Monitor*, sunk off Hatteras Island. The aquarium hosts a slew of activities and field trips, from feeding fish to learning about medicinal aquatic plants to kids' workshops. ⊠ *374 Airport Rd., off U.S. 64, 3 mi northeast of Manteo* ☎ *252/473–3493, 800/832–3474 for aquarium,*

252/473–3494 for educational programs ⊕ *www.ncaquariums.com* 🖾 *$8* ⊙ *Daily 9–5.*

Ⓒ **Roanoke Island Festival Park.** This history, educational, and cultural-arts attraction sits on the waterfront in Manteo. Costumed interpreters conduct tours of the 69-foot ship, *Elizabeth II,* a representation of a 16th-century vessel. The 25-acre state park also has an interactive museum representing 400 years of Outer Banks history and a gift shop, a re-created 16th-century settlement site, a Native America exhibit, and a fossil pit. ⊠ *Waterfront off Budleigh St., 1 Festival Park, Manteo* ☎ *252/475–1500, 252/475–1506 for event hotline* ⊕ *www. roanokeisland.com* 🖾 *$8* ⊙ *Mar.–Dec., daily 9–5.*

WHERE TO EAT AND STAY

$$–$$$
AMERICAN
★
✕**Full Moon Café and Grille.** Located in a renovated gas station, this wonderfully cheerful bistro has large front windows and lots of patio seating. The herbed hummus with toasted pita is fantastic, as are the fat crab cakes and baked crab-dip appetizer. Other choices include salads, veggie wraps, Cuban-style enchiladas, burgers of all kinds, and innovative and hearty sandwiches. Light eaters beware: even the Waldorf salad comes with a million pecans and apples; expect lots of cheese on any dish that includes it. ■TIP➜ The café also serves specialty cocktails, maintains a thoughtfully selected wine list, and offers North Carolina beers. ⊠ *207 Queen Elizabeth Ave., Manteo* ☎ *252/473–6666* ⊕ *www. thefullmooncafe.com* ▭ *AE, D, MC, V.*

¢
AMERICAN
✕**Magnolia Grille.** Freddy and Pam Ortega, cheerful New York transplants, run the immensely popular restaurant on Manteo's downtown waterfront. The place is hopping, even at breakfast; lunch gets the overflow from nearby Festival Park. ■TIP➜ If it's too busy, get takeout and savor your sandwich by the waterfront. You can choose from char-grilled chili cheeseburgers, hot dogs, quesadillas, salads, shrimp and grits, assorted sandwiches, hearty chicken dishes, and shellfish from the steam bar. Some dishes are intended—and others can be modified—for vegetarians. ⊠ *408 Queen Elizabeth Ave., Manteo* ☎ *252/475–9877* ▭ *AE, D, MC, V* ⊙ *No dinner Sun. and Mon.*

$$$–$$$$
Ⓒ
★
🏨**Tranquil House Inn.** This charming 19th-century-style inn sits waterfront, a few steps from shops, restaurants, and Roanoke Island Festival Park. The individually decorated rooms have classic, clean lines and muted colors; some have comfy sitting areas. **Pros:** easy walking distance from shops and restaurants; complimentary evening wine reception; children up to age 18 stay free in their parents' rooms. **Cons:** located on a busy commercial waterfront; small, cramped lobby; no smoking except on the porch. ⊠ *405 Queen Elizabeth Ave., Box 2045, Manteo* ☎ *252/473–1404 or 800/458–7069* ⊕ *www.1587.com* ⇆ *25 rooms* ⚃ *In-room: a/c, Wi-Fi. In-hotel: restaurant, bicycles* ▭ *AE, D, MC, V* ⦿*BP.*

Cape Hatteras Lighthouse, erected in 1870, is the tallest brick lighthouse in the United States.

CAPE HATTERAS NATIONAL SEASHORE

Longtime visitors to the Outer Banks have seen how development changes these once unspoiled barrier islands, so it's nice to know that the 70-mi stretch of the Cape Hatteras National Seashore will remain protected. Its pristine beaches, set aside as the first national seashore in 1953, stretch from the southern outskirts of Nags Head to Ocracoke Inlet, encompassing three narrow islands: Bodie, Hatteras, and Ocracoke.

These waters provide some of the East Coast's best fishing and surfing, and they're ideal for other sports such as windsurfing, diving, and boating. Parking is allowed only in designated areas. Fishing piers are in Rodanthe and Avon.

With 300 mi of coastline, there are plenty of beaches that don't have lifeguards on duty. ■TIP→ To identify beaches with trained staff, contact the Ocean Rescue in the town, or if you're in a national park, the Park Service.

HATTERAS ISLAND

15 mi south of Nags Head.

The Herbert C. Bonner Bridge arches for 3 mi over Oregon Inlet and carries traffic to Hatteras Island, a 42-mi-long curved ribbon of sand jutting out into the Atlantic Ocean. At its most distant point (Cape Hatteras), Hatteras is 25 mi from the mainland. About 85% of the island belongs to Cape Hatteras National Seashore, and the remainder is privately owned in seven small, quaint villages strung along Route 12, the island's fragile lifeline to points north. Among its nicknames, Hatteras is known as the blue marlin (or billfish) capital of the world. The fishing's so great here because the Continental Shelf is 40 mi offshore, and its current, combined with the nearby Gulf Stream and Deep West Boundary Current, create an unparalleled fish habitat.

GETTING HERE AND AROUND

From the north, reach Hatteras Island via U.S. 158. From the east, take U.S. 64 to U.S. 158. South of the Outer Banks, U.S. 70 leads to Route 12 and requires a couple of ferry rides. Some commercial and charter flights are available from nearby airports.

ESSENTIALS

Visitor Information **Hatteras Welcome Center** (⊠ *57190 Kohler Rd., Hatteras Village* ☎ *252/986–2203* ⊕ *www.outerbanks.org*).

EXPLORING

ⓒ ★ **Cape Hatteras Lighthouse.** The Cape Hatteras Lighthouse, authorized by Congress in 1794 to help prevent shipwrecks, was the first lighthouse built in the region. The original structure was lost to erosion and Civil War damage; this 1870 replacement is, at 210 feet, the tallest brick lighthouse in the United States. Endangered by the sea, in 1999 the lighthouse was actually raised and rolled some 2,900 feet inland to its present location. A visitor center is located near the base of the lighthouse. In summer the principal keeper's quarters are open for viewing, and you can climb the lighthouse's 248 steps (12 stories) to the viewing balcony. ■TIP➔ **Children under 42 inches tall aren't allowed in the lighthouse.** Offshore lay the remains of the USS *Monitor,* a Confederate ironclad ship that sank in 1862. ⊠ *Lighthouse Rd., off Rte. 12, 30 mi south of Rodanthe, Buxton* ☎ *252/995–4474* ⊕ *www.nps.gov/caha* 🎟 *Visitor center and keeper's quarters free, lighthouse tower $7* �é *Visitor center and keeper's quarters: daily 9–5. Lighthouse tower: mid-Apr.–Memorial Day and Labor Day–mid-Oct., daily 9–4:30; Memorial Day–Labor Day, daily 9–5.*

WHERE TO EAT AND STAY

$–$$

AMERICAN

✕ **The Captain's Table.** South of the entrance for the Cape Hatteras Lighthouse, this place is popular for its well-prepared food and homey manner. Stuffed shrimp, whole fried flounder, homemade chicken salad, burgers, and assorted sandwiches are among the offerings. In addition to seafood, the menu has pork barbecue, chicken, and beef. ⊠ *Hwy. 12, mile marker 61, Buxton* ☎ *252/995–5988* ▭ *MC, V* �é *Closed Dec.– early Apr.*

$–$$

🛏 **Sea Gull Motel.** The 1950s-era, family-operated Sea Gull offers beachside rooms in a two-story building as well as adjacent cottage properties, each of which sleeps up to six, rent ($$$$) by the week during high season. **Pros:** quiet setting; oceanfront pool; family-friendly; microwaves in room. **Cons:** remote location; no breakfast; no Wi-Fi. ⊠ *56883 N.C. Hwy. 12, between mile marker 70 and 71, Hatteras Village* ☎ *252/986–2550* ⊕ *www.seagullhatteras.com* ⤴ *15 rooms, 1 suite, 2 cottages* ⌕ *In-room: kitchen (some), refrigerator, Internet. In-hotel: pool, beachfront* ▭ *D, MC, V.*

OCRACOKE ISLAND

Ocracoke Village: 15 mi southwest of Hatteras Village.

Fewer than 1,000 people live on this, the last inhabited island in the Outer Banks, which can be reached only by water or air. The village is in the widest part of the island, around a harbor called Silver Lake. Canals run through the smaller residential area of Oyster Creek.

Centuries ago, however, Ocracoke was the stomping ground of Edward Teach, the pirate known as Blackbeard. A major treasure cache from 1718 is still rumored to be hidden somewhere on the island. Fort Ocracoke was a short-lived Confederate stronghold that was abandoned in August 1861 and blown up by Union forces a month later.

GETTING HERE AND AROUND

The only way to reach Ocracoke Island is by ferry or private boat. State car ferries land at either end of the island and depart as late as 8:30 pm to Cedar Island and midnight to Hatteras Island. Only one road, Route 12, traverses the island. Quiet streets shoot off to the left and right at the south end. Lots of cyclists come to Ocracoke, and many inns have bikes guests may use, but be careful when biking Route 12 from one end of the island to the other in summer; traffic can be heavy, and the designated bike path doesn't travel the highway's entire 13-mi length.

ESSENTIALS

Visitor Information National Park Service Visitor Center (✉ *Rte. 12, Ocracoke Island* ☎ *252/928–4531).*

EXPLORING

Ocracoke Pony Pen. From the observation platform, you can look out at the descendants of the Banker Ponies that roamed wild before the island came under the jurisdiction of Cape Hatteras National Seashore. The Park Service took over management of the ponies in 1960 and has helped maintain the population of about 30 animals; the wild herd once numbered nearly 500. All the animals you see today were born in captivity and are kept on a 180-acre range. Legends abound about the arrival of the island's ponies. Some believe they made their way to the island after the abandonment of Roanoke's Lost Colony. Others believe they were left by early Spanish explorers or swam to shore following the sinking of the *Black Squall,* a ship carrying circus performers. ✉ *Rte. 12, 6 mi southwest of Hatteras-Ocracoke ferry landing.*

WHERE TO EAT AND STAY

$$–$$$ ✕ **Back Porch Restaurant.** Seafood is the star here, whether it's crab beig-
SEAFOOD   nets or sautéed sea scallops with lime-cilantro butter. But there are notable beef, chicken, and vegetarian dishes, including pecan-crusted chicken breast in bourbon sauce and fettuccine with spinach in smoky tequila cream. You have the choice of enjoying your meal indoors or on a screened porch. The wine bar has a respectable wine list. ✉ *110 Back Rd., Ocracoke* ☎ *252/928–6401* ▭ *MC, V* ☽ *No lunch.*

$$–$$$ ✕ **Howard's Pub.** The atmosphere is boisterous and friendly at this res-
AMERICAN taurant, which is open every day of the year for lunch and dinner. Don't miss the fresh-cut fries, fine burgers, or the grilled fresh catch. Best of all are appetizers like conch fritters or creamy shrimp and crab dip paired

with any of the 25 beers on tap or 200 bottled beers from around the world. Check out the many license plates, college banners, and beer towels adorning the walls, or strike up a conversation with whoever is sitting next to you in the large, friendly dining room or on the screened porch. ⊠ *1175 Irvin Garrish Hwy., Ocracoke Village* ☎ *252/928–4441* ⊕ *www.howardspub.com* ⚒ *Reservations not accepted* ▭ *D, MC, V.*

$$–$$$ ⊡ **The Island Inn Villas.** The white-clapboard Island Inn that is on the National Register of Historic Places was built as a private lodge back in 1901; the old inn really shows its age, but rooms in the modern villas across the street are clean, spacious and great for families or groups of friends. **Cons:** no breakfast; no restaurant; lobby may be cluttered and messy. ⊠ *25 Lighthouse Rd., off Rte. 12, Box 9* ☎ *252/928–4351 or 877/456–3466* ⊕ *www.ocracokeislandinn.com* ⤴ *12 villas* ⚐ *In-room: a/c, kitchen, Wi-Fi. In-hotel: pool, laundry facilities* ▭ *AE, MC, V.*

BEACHES

☺ **Ocracoke Island Beaches.** The 16 mi of undeveloped shoreline here were
★ named America's best beach in 2007 by Dr. Beach (Stephen P. Leatherman, director of the Laboratory for Coastal Research at Florida International University). These beaches are among the least populated and most beautiful on the Cape Hatteras National Seashore, and is amazing. Four public-access areas are close to the main beach road, Route 12, and easy to spot; just look for large brown and white wooden signs. **Amenities:** camping facilities, free parking, toilets. ⊠ *Rte. 12.*

CAPE LOOKOUT NATIONAL SEASHORE

Southwest of Ocracoke Island via Cedar Island.

Extending for 55 mi from Portsmouth Island to Shackleford Banks, Cape Lookout National Seashore includes 28,400 acres of uninhabited land and marsh. The remote, sandy islands are linked to the mainland by private ferries. Loggerhead sea turtles, which have been placed on the federal list of threatened and endangered species, nest here. To the south, wild ponies roam Shackleford Banks. Four-wheel-drive vehicles are allowed on the beach, and primitive camping is allowed. There are primitive cabins (with and without electricity, no linens or utensils) with bunk beds. Private ferry service is available from Harkers Island to the Cape Lookout Lighthouse area, from Davis to Shingle Point, from Atlantic to an area north of Drum Inlet, and from Ocracoke Village to Portsmouth Village.

GETTING HERE AND AROUND

The park's various islands are accessible by boat only. A list of authorized ferry services can be found at the park's Web site: ⊕ *www.nps. gov/calo/planyourvisit/ferry.htm.*

ESSENTIALS

Visitor Information Cape Lookout Visitor Center (⊠ *131 Charles St., Harkers Island* ☎ *252/728–2250 for visitor center, 252/728–0942 or 252/728–0958 for cabins* ⊕ *www.nps.gov/calo* ⤴ *Park free, ferry ride $10–$30 or $75–$300 for vehicles* ☉ *Visitor center daily 9–5*) is on Harkers Island at the end of U.S. 70 East near a private ferry terminal.

Charleston, South Carolina

WORD OF MOUTH

"We went to the Aquarium and walked a short distance to catch a boat to Fort Sumter (a must-see). We started with a tour of the city in a small shuttle-type bus with a great guide. Fun to wander through, the City Market was a good place to buy your Sweet-grass Basket."

—Giovanna

WELCOME TO CHARLESTON, SOUTH CAROLINA

TOP REASONS TO GO

★ **Dining out:** Charleston has become a culinary destination, with talented chefs who offer innovative twists on the city's traditional Lowcountry cuisine.

★ **Seeing art:** The city is home to more than 100 galleries, so you'll never run out of places to see remarkable art.

★ **Spoleto Festival USA:** If you're lucky enough to visit in late May and early June, you'll find a city under a cultural siege: Spoleto's flood of indoor and outdoor performances (opera, music, dance, and theater) is impossible to miss and almost as difficult not to enjoy.

★ **The Battery:** The views from the point—both natural and man-made—are the loveliest in the city. Look west to see the harbor; to the east you'll find elegant Charleston mansions.

★ **Historic homes:** Step back in time in Charleston's preserved 19th-century houses like the Nathaniel Russell House.

Fort Sumter
National
Monument

1 **North of Broad.** The main part of the Historic District, where you'll find the lion's share of the Historic District's homes, B&Bs, and restaurants, is the most densely packed area of the city and will be of the greatest interest to tourists. King Street, Charleston's main shopping artery, is also here.

2 **The Battery and South of Broad.** The southern part of the Historic District is heavily residential, but it still has a few important sights and even some B&Bs, though fewer restaurants and shops than North of Broad.

GETTING ORIENTED

The heart of the city is on a peninsula, sometimes just called "downtown" by the nearly 60,000 residents who populate the area. Walking Charleston's peninsula is the best way to get to know the city.

8

Cooper River

0   1/4 mi
0   400 meters

Wandering through the city's Historic District, you would swear it's a movie set. Steeples of more than 180 churches punctuate the low skyline, and horse-drawn carriages pass centuries-old mansions. Happily, after three centuries of epidemics, fires, and hurricanes, Charleston has endured to become one of the South's best-preserved cities.

Home to Fort Sumter, where the Civil War began, Charleston is also famed for its elegant houses. These handsome mansions are showcases for the "Charleston style," a look that's reminiscent of the West Indies, and for good reason. Before coming to the Carolinas in the late 17th century, many early British colonists had first settled on Barbados and other Caribbean islands. In that warm, humid climate they learned to build homes with high ceilings and broad "piazzas" (porches) at each level to catch the sea breezes.

Through the hard times that followed the Civil War and an array of natural disasters, many of Charleston's earliest public and private buildings remained standing. Thanks to a rigorous preservation movement and strict architectural guidelines, the city's new structures blend in with the old.

Day in and out, diners feast at upscale Southern restaurants, shoppers browse museum-quality paintings and antiques, and lovers of the outdoors explore outlying beaches, parks, and marshes. But as cosmopolitan as the city has become, it's still the South, and just beyond the city limits are farm stands cooking up boiled peanuts, the state's official snack.

PLANNING

WHEN TO GO

There really is no bad time to visit Charleston. Spring and fall are high season, when the temperatures are best and hotel rates and occupancy are at their highest. Art shows, craft fairs, and music festivals (including the famous Spoleto USA festival) take place in summer. During the high season it's important to make your reservations as far in advance as possible for both hotels and restaurants.

GETTING HERE AND AROUND

AIR TRAVEL

Charleston International Airport is about 12 mi west of downtown. Charleston Executive Airport on John's Island is used by private (noncommercial) aircraft as is Mount Pleasant Regional Airport.

Airport Ground Transportation arranges shuttles, which cost $12 per person to downtown. You can be picked up by the same service when returning to the airport by making advance reservations with the driver.

Airport Information Charleston Executive Airport (✉ 2742 Fort Trenholm Rd., John's Island ☎ 843/559-2401). **Charleston International Airport** (✉ 5500 International Blvd., North Charleston ☎ 843/767-1100). **Mount Pleasant Regional Airport** (✉ 700 Faison Rd., Mount Pleasant ☎ 843/884-8837).

Airport Transfers Airport Ground Transportation (☎ 843/767-1100).

CAR TRAVEL

You'll need a car in Charleston if you plan on visiting destinations outside the city's Historic District, or if you plan to take trips to Walterboro, Edisto Island, Beaufort, or Hilton Head.

Interstate 26 traverses the state from northwest to southeast and terminates at Charleston. U.S. 17, the coastal road, also passes through Charleston. Interstate 526, also called the Mark Clark Expressway, runs primarily east–west, connecting the West Ashley area, North Charleston, Daniel Island, and Mount Pleasant.

VISITOR INFORMATION

Charleston Visitor Center (✉ 375 Meeting St., Upper King ⬦ 423 King St., 29403 ☎ 843/853-8000 or 800/868-8118 ⊕ www.charlestoncvb.com or www. explorecharleston.com). **Historic Charleston Foundation** (⬦ Box 1120, 29402 ☎ 843/723-1623 ⊕ www.historiccharleston.org). **Preservation Society of Charleston** (⬦ Box 521, 29402 ☎ 843/722-4630 ⊕ www.preservationsociety.org).

TOURS

CARRIAGE TOURS

Carriage tours are a great way to see Charleston. The going rate is $20 for an adult. Carolina Polo & Carriage Company, Old South Carriage Company (drivers wear mock Confederate uniforms), and Palmetto Carriage Works run horse- and mule-drawn carriage tours of the Historic District. Each tour, which follows one of four routes, lasts about one hour. Most carriages queue up at North Market and Anson streets. Charleston Carriage and Polo picks up passengers at the Doubletree Guest Suites Historic Charleston on Church Street. Palmetto offers free parking at their big red barn and has combo tickets for harbor tours.

Carriage Tour Contacts Charleston Carriage & Polo Company (☎ 843/577-6767 ⊕ www.cpcc.com). **Old South Carriage Company** (☎ 843/723-9712 ⊕ www.oldsouthcarriagetours.com). **Palmetto Carriage Works** (☎ 843/723-8145).

WALKING TOURS

Walking tours on various topics—horticulture, slavery, or women's history—are given by Charleston Strolls and the Original Charleston Walks. Bulldog Tours has walks that explore the city's supernatural side. Listen to the infamous tales of lost souls with Ghosts of Charleston, which travel to historic graveyards. They have expanded their offerings to include a sunset cruise and a culinary tour. They explore culinary strongholds where you can watch food artisans at work, while sampling and shopping along the way.

Pat Conroy Tours follow the pages of *South of Broad*, the novel from this famous South Carolina author. Mary Coy, a fourth-generation Charlestonian, bring the history and architecture of Charleston to life on her two-hour Charleston 101 Tour.

Walking Tour Contacts Bulldog Tours (✉ 40 N. Market St., Market area ☎ 843/568–3315 ⊕ www.bulldogtours.com). **Charleston 101 Tours** (✉ Tours start at Powder Magazine on Cumberland St., one block from City Market, Market area ☎ 843/556–4753 ⊕ www.charleston101tours.com ☑ $16). **Charleston Strolls** (✉ Charleston Pl., 130 Market St., Market area ☎ 843/766–2080 ⊕ www.charlestonstrolls.com). **Ghosts of Charleston** (✉ 184 E. Bay St., French Quarter ☎ 843/723–1670 or 800/723–1670). **Original Charleston Walks** (✉ 58½ Broad St., South of Broad ☎ 843/577–3800 or 800/729–3420). **Pat Conroy Tours** (✉ 115 Meeting St., Mills House Hotel, Market area ☎ 843/722–7033).

EXPLORING CHARLESTON

Everyone starts their tour of Charlestown in downtown's famous Historic District. Roughly bounded by Lockwood Boulevard on the Ashley River to the west, Calhoun Street to the north, East Bay Street on the Cooper River to the east, and the Battery to the south, this fairly compact area of 800 acres contains nearly 2,000 historic homes and buildings. The peninsula is divided up into several neighborhoods, starting from the south and moving north, including the Battery, South of Broad, Lower King Street, and Upper King Street ending near the "Crosstown," where U.S. 17 connects downtown to Mount Pleasant and West Ashley.

Beyond downtown, the Ashley River hugs the west side of the peninsula; the region on the far shore is called West Ashley. The Cooper River runs along the east side of the peninsula, with Mount Pleasant on the opposite side, with Charleston Harbor in between. Lastly, there are outlying sea islands with many beaches to choose from—James Island with its Folly Beach, John's Island, Kiawah and Seabrook islands, Isle of Palms, and Sullivan's Island—with their own appealing attractions. Everything that entails crossing the bridges is best explored by car or bus.

NORTH OF BROAD

During the early 1800s, large tracts of available land made the area North of Broad ideal for suburban plantations. A century later the peninsula had been built out, and today the resulting area is a vibrant mix of residential neighborhoods and commercial clusters, with parks scattered throughout. The district is comprised of three primary neighborhoods:

To experience Charleston in high style, opt for a carriage ride around the historic district.

Upper King, the Market area, and the College of Charleston. Though there are a number of majestic homes and pre-Revolutionary buildings in this area, the main draw is the rich variety of stores, museums, restaurants, and historic churches.

WHAT TO SEE

Charleston Museum. While housed in a modern-day brick complex, this institution was founded in 1773 and is the country's oldest city museum. To the delight of fans of *Antiques Roadshow,* the collection is especially strong in South Carolina decorative arts, from silver to snuff boxes. Kids love the permanent Civil War exhibition and have an interactive good old time on the second floor in galleries devoted to archaeology and natural history (don't miss the giant polar bear). ■TIP→Combination tickets that give you admission to the Joseph Manigault House and the Heyward-Washington House are a bargain at $22. ✉ *360 Meeting St., Upper King* ☎ *843/722–2996* ⊕ *www.charlestonmuseum.org* ⛛ *$10* ⏱ *Mon.–Sat. 9–5, Sun. 1–5.*

Children's Museum of the Lowcountry. Hands-on interactive environments at this top-notch museum will keep kids ages 3 to 10 occupied for hours. They can climb around a replica of a local shrimp boat, play in exhibits that show how water evaporates, and wander through the inner workings of a medieval castle. ✉ *25 Ann St., Upper King* ☎ *843/853–8962* ⊕ *www.explorecml.org* ⛛ *$7* ⏱ *Tues.–Sat. 9–5, Sun. 1–5.*

Fort Sumter National Monument. Set on a man-made island in Charleston's harbor, this is the hallowed spot where the Civil War began. On April 12, 1861, the first shot of the war was fired at the fort from Fort Johnson (now defunct) across the way. After a 34-hour battle, Union forces

Take the ferry to Fort Sumter National Monument to see where the first shots of the Civil War were fired.

surrendered and Confederate troops occupied Sumter, which became a symbol of Southern resistance. Today, the National Park Service oversees it, and rangers give interpretive talks and conduct guided tours. To reach the fort, you have to take a ferry; boats depart from Liberty Square Visitor Center, downtown, and from Patriot's Point in Mount Pleasant. There are six crossings daily between mid-March and mid-August. The schedule is abbreviated the rest of the year, so call ahead for details. The **Fort Sumter Liberty Square Visitor Center** (⊠ *340 Concord St., Upper King* ☎ *843/577–0242* ☏ *Free* ⊙ *Daily 8:30–5.*), next to the South Carolina Aquarium, contains exhibits on the Civil War. This is a departure point for ferries headed to Sullivan's Island, where Fort Sumter itself is located. ⊠ *1214 Middle St., Sullivan's Island, Charleston Harbor* ☎ *843/577–0242 or 843/883–3123* ⊕ *www.nps.gov/fosu* ☏ *Fort free; ferry $16* ⊙ *Mid-Mar.–early Sept., daily 10–5:30; early Sept.–mid-Mar., daily 10–4; 11:30–4 Jan. and Feb.*

Fodor's Choice ★ **Joseph Manigault House.** Considered by many to be the finest example of Federal-style architecture in the South, this 1803 home was built for rich rice-planting family of Huguenot heritage. Having toured Europe as a gentleman architect, Gabriel Manigault returned to design this house for his brother Joseph as the city's first essay in neoclassicism. The house glows in red brick and is adorned with a two-story piazza balcony. Inside, marvels await: a fantastic "flying" staircase in the central hall; a gigantic Venetian window; elegant plasterwork and mantels; notable Charleston-made furniture; and a bevy of French, English, and American antiques. ⊠ *350 Meeting St., Upper King* ☎ *843/722–2996* ⊕ *www.charlestonmuseum.org* ☏ *$10* ⊙ *Mon.–Sat. 10–5, Sun. 1–5.*

★ **Old Slave Mart Museum.** This is likely the only building still in existence that was used for slave auctioning, a practice that ended in 1863. It is part of a complex called Ryan's Mart, which contains the slave jail, the kitchen, and the morgue. It is now a museum that recounts the history of Charleston's role in the slave trade, an unpleasant story but one that is vital to understand. ⊠ *6 Chalmers St., Market area* ☎ *843/958–6467* ⊕ *www.charlestoncity.info* ⌾ *$7* ⊙ *Mon.–Sat. 9–5.*

Fodor'sChoice ★ **St. Philip's (Episcopal) Church.** The namesake of Church Street, this graceful late-Georgian building is the second one to rise on its site: the congregation's first building burned down in 1835 and was rebuilt in 1838. During the Civil War, the steeple was a target for shelling; a shell that exploded in the churchyard during services one Sunday didn't deter the minister from finishing his sermon. ⊠ *146 Church St., Market area* ☎ *843/722–7734* ⊕ *www.stphilipschurchsc.org* ⊙ *Church weekdays 9–11 and 1–4; cemetery daily 9–4.*

☾ ★ **South Carolina Aquarium.** The 38,000-gallon Great Ocean Tank houses the tallest aquarium window in North America. Exhibits include more than 5,000 creatures representing more than 350 species. You travel through the five major regions of the Southeast Appalachian Watershed: the Blue Ridge Mountains, the Piedmont, the Coastal Plain, the Coast, and the Atlantic Ocean. The 4-D theater combines 3-D imagery (with special effects like wind gusts and splashes of water), synchronized to favorite family films. ⊠ *100 Aquarium Wharf, Upper King* ☎ *843/720–1990 or 800/722–6455* ⊕ *www.scaquarium.org* ⌾ *$17.95* ⊙ *Apr.–Aug., daily 9–5; Sept.–Mar., daily 9–4.*

SOUTH OF BROAD

The heavily residential area South of Broad Street and west of the Battery brims with beautiful private homes, many of which have plaques bearing brief descriptions of the property's history. Mind your manners, but feel free to peek through iron gates and fences at the verdant displays in elaborate gardens.

WHAT TO SEE

Fodor'sChoice ★ **Battery.** Located at the southernmost point of Charleston's peninsula, this harbor-front park offers great views. Westward you can see Charleston Harbor and Fort Sumter; eastward, from the intersection of Water Street and East Battery, the vista takes in the city's most photographed mansions. Walk south along East Battery to White Point Gardens, where the street curves and becomes Murray Boulevard. Where pirates once hung from the gallows here, strollers now take in the serene setting from Charleston benches (small wood-slat benches with cast-iron sides). ⊠ *East Bay St. and Murray Blvd., South of Broad.*

Fodor'sChoice ★ **Nathaniel Russell House.** One of the nation's finest examples of Adam-style architecture, the Nathaniel Russell House was built in 1808. Russell came to Charleston at age 27 from his native Bristol, Rhode Island, and became one of the city's leading merchants and Federalist fathers in post-Revolutionary times. The ornate interior is distinguished by its Romney portraits, lavish period furnishings, and the famous "free-flying" staircase that spirals up three stories with no visible support. The extensive formal garden is worth a leisurely stroll. ⊠ *51 Meeting St., South of Broad* ☎ *843/724–8481* ⊕ *www.historiccharleston.org* ⌑ *$10; $16 with admission to Aiken-Rhett House* ⊗ *Mon.–Sat. 10–5, Sun. 2–5.*

WHERE TO EAT

Charleston, which is blessed with a bevy of Southern-inflected selections, from barbecue parlors to fish shacks, to traditional white-tablecloth restaurants. The attention to Southern foods has increased in recent years, largely because of improved exposure (thanks, Paula Deen!) and regional emphases. Charleston, to its credit, rests at distinguished crossroads, benefiting from established stock and newer flourishes, such as the nationally recognized Charleston Wine & Food Festival.

PRICES

Fine dining in Charleston can be expensive. One option to keep costs down might be to try several of the small plates that many establishments offer. To save money, drive over the bridges or go to the islands, including James and Johns islands.

WHAT IT COSTS				
	¢	$	$$	$$$	$$$$
Restaurants	under $10	$10–$14	$15–$19	$20–$24	over $24

Restaurant prices are for a main course at dinner, not including taxes (7.5% on food, 8.5% tax on liquor).

$$ ✕ **Basil.** The corner restaurant situated in the heart of downtown enjoys
ASIAN   the best reputation for Thai food in the city. Dinner hours generate
        extended waits times—no reservations allowed—as patrons angle for an
        outdoor or window table. Here, from the exposed, glassed-in kitchen,
        emerge popular specialties: the Tom Aban Talay, a hot-and-sour mixed
        seafood soup; the red curry duck, a boneless half-bird, deep-fried; and
        the tilapia with shrimp and ginger sauce. ⊠ *460 King St., Upper King*
        ☎ *843/724–3490* ⊕ *www.eatatbasil.com* ⊟ *AE, D, DC, MC, V* ⊗ *No
        lunch weekends.*

$$$$ ✕ **Charleston Grill.** Chef Michelle Weaver has succeeded her former boss,
SOUTHERN   the estimable Bob Waggoner, but the Grill's groundbreaking New South
Fodor'sChoice cuisine carries on. The restaurant continues to provide what many think
   ★   of as the city's highest gastronomic experience, with dinner served in
              a dining room highlighted by pale wood floors, flowing drapes, and
              elegant Queen Anne chairs. The menu is in four quadrants: simple, lush
              (foie gras and other delicacies), cosmopolitan, and Southern. A nightly
              tasting menu offers a way to sample it all. ⊠ *Charleston Place Hotel,
              224 King St., Market area* ☎ *843/577–4522* ⊕ *www.charlestongrill.com*
              ⌑ *Reservations essential* ⊟ *AE, D, DC, MC, V* ⊗ *No lunch.*

$$$ ✕ **FIG.** Acronyms are popular here; this name, for instance, stands for
SOUTHERN   Food Is Good. Chef Michael Lata's mantra is KIS, a reminder for him to
Fodor'sChoice keep it simple. Spend an evening here for fresh-off-the-farm ingredients
   ★   cooked with unfussy, flavorful finesse. The menu changes frequently,
              but the family-style vegetables might be as simple as young beets in

sherry vinegar placed in a plain white bowl. His dishes do get more complex: there's the pureed cauliflower soup with pancetta, incredible veal sweetbreads with smoked bacon and escarole, and grouper with a perfect golden crust accompanied by braised artichokes. The bar scene is lively. ⊠ *232 Meeting St., Market area* ☎ *843/805–5900* ⊕ *www. eatatfig.com* ⊟ *AE, D, DC, MC, V* ⊘ *No lunch.*

$
SOUTHERN
✕**Hominy Grill.** The wooden barber poles from the last century still frame the door of this small, homespun café. Chalkboard specials are often the way to go here, whether you are visiting for breakfast, lunch, or dinner. Chef Robert Stehling is a Carolina boy who lived in New York; that dichotomy shows in his "uptown" comfort food. Here, you can have the perfect soft-shell-crab sandwich with homemade fries, but leave room for the tangy buttermilk pie or the chocolate peanut butter pie. ⊠ *207 Rutledge Ave., Canonboro* ☎ *843/937–0930* ⊕ *www. hominygrill.com* ⊟ *AE, MC, V* ⊘ *No dinner Sun.*

$$
FRENCH
✕**La Fourchette.** French owner Perig Goulet moves agilely through the petite dining room of this unpretentious bistro. With back-to-back chairs making things cozy (and noisy), this place could be in Paris. Perig boasts of his country pâté, from a recipe handed down from his *grand-mère*. Other favorites include duck salad, scallops sautéed in cognac, and shrimp in a leek sauce. ⊠ *432 King St., Upper King* ☎ *843/722–6261* ⊕ *www.lafourchettecharleston.com* ⊟ *AE, MC, V* ⊘ *Closed Sun. No lunch Aug.–Mar.*

$$$$
AMERICAN
Fodor's Choice
★
✕**McCrady's.** Young chef Sean Brock has come of age, turning McCrady's into a superb culinary venture. Passionate about his profession, he spends his nights coming up with innovative pairings. He favors meat on the rare side for some tastes. For your appetizer, try the scallop and pork belly with kimchee puree and yuzu; follow with a main course such as the trio of lamb with almond polenta, green garlic, and locally grown carrots. The bar area has a centuries-old tavern feel and is frequented by well-heeled downtown residents. ⊠ *2 Unity Alley, Market area* ☎ *843/577–0025* ⊕ *www.mccradysrestaurant.com* ⊰ *Reservations essential* ⊟ *AE, MC, V* ⊘ *No lunch.*

8

WHERE TO STAY

Charleston is a city known for its lovingly restored mansions that have been converted into atmospheric bed-and-breakfasts, as well as deluxe inns, all found in the residential blocks of the Historic District. Upscale, world-class hotels as well as unique, boutique hotels that provide a one-of-a-kind experience are in the heart of downtown. Chain hotels line the busy, car-trafficked areas (like Meeting Street). In addition, there are chain properties in the nearby areas of West Ashley, Mount Pleasant, and North Charleston.

PRICES

Charleston's downtown lodgings have three seasons: high season (March to May and September to November); mid-season (June to August); and low season (late November to February). Prices drop significantly during the short low season, except during holidays and special events. High season is summer at the island resorts. Remember to factor in the cost of downtown parking; *if* a hotel offers free parking that is a huge plus. In the areas "over the bridges," parking is generally free.

Hotel reviews have been condensed for this book. Please go to Fodors. com for full reviews of each property.

WHAT IT COSTS					
	¢	$	$$	$$$	$$$$
Hotels	under $100	$100–$150	$151–$200	$201–$250	over $250

Prices are for two people in a standard double room in high season, not including 12.5% tax.

$$ 🛏 **Francis Marion Hotel.** Wrought-iron railings, crown moldings, and decorative plasterwork speak of the elegance of 1924, when the Francis Marion was the largest hotel in the Carolinas. **Pros:** architecturally and historically significant building; some of the best city views. **Cons:** rooms are small, as is closet space; located on a busy intersection. ⊠ *387 King St., Upper King* 🕿 *843/722–0600 or 877/756–2121* ⊕ *www.francismarioncharleston.com* ⤳ *217 rooms, 16 suites* ♢ *In-room: a/c, DVD, Wi-Fi. In-hotel: restaurant, room service, gym, spa, laundry service, parking (paid)* ⊟ *AE, D, DC, MC, V* ¶◎¶ *EP.*

$$$–$$$$ 🛏 **HarbourView Inn.** Ask for a room facing the harbor, and you can gaze out onto the kid-friendly fountain and 8 acres of Waterfront Park. **Pros:** Continental breakfast can be delivered to room; service is notable; only hotel on the harbor and Waterfront Park. **Cons:** rooms are off long, modern halls; rooms are not particularly spacious. ⊠ *2 Vendue Range, Market area* 🕿 *843/853–8439 or 888/853–8439* ⊕ *www. harbourviewcharleston.com* ⤳ *52 rooms* ♢ *In-room: a/c, safe, refrigerator, DVD, Wi-Fi. In-hotel: room service, dry cleaning, Internet terminal, Wi-Fi hotspot, parking (paid)* ⊟ *AE, D, DC, MC, V* ¶◎¶ *BP.*

$$$$ 🛏 **Market Pavilion Hotel.** The melee of one of the busiest corners in the
Fodor's Choice city vanishes as soon as the uniformed bellman opens the lobby door
★ to dark, wood-paneled walls, antique furniture, and chandeliers hung from high ceilings. **Pros:** opulent furnishings; architecturally impressive; conveniently located. **Cons:** the building was constructed to withstand hurricane-force winds, which can limit cell-phone reception; those preferring understated decor may find the interior over the top. ⊠ *225 E. Bay St., Market area* 🕿 *843/723–0500 or 877/440–2250* ⊕ *www. marketpavilion.com* ⤳ *61 rooms, 9 suites* ♢ *In-room: a/c, safe, refrigerator (some), DVD (some), Wi-Fi, Internet. In-hotel: 2 restaurants, room service, bars, pool, gym, spa, laundry service, Internet terminal, Wi-Fi hotspot* ⊟ *AE, D, DC, MC, V* ¶◎¶ *EP.*

$$$–$$$$ 🛏 **Mills House.** A favorite local landmark, from where several historic tours depart, the Mills House is the reconstruction of an 1853 hotel where Robert E. Lee once waved from the wrought-iron balcony. **Pros:** convenient to business district, Historic District, and art galleries; a popular Sunday brunch spot; excellent concierge desk. **Cons:** rooms are small, which is typical of hotels of this time period; it's on a very busy street. ⊠ *115 Meeting St., Market area* 🕿 *843/577–2400 or*

King Street is the perfect place to go antiquing in Charleston.

800/874–9600 ⊕ *www.millshouse.com* ↯ *199 rooms, 16 suites* ⌂ *In-room: a/c, refrigerator (some), Wi-Fi. In-hotel: restaurant, room service, bar, pool, gym, laundry service, Wi-Fi hotspot, parking (paid)* ⊟ *AE, D, DC, MC, V* ▯◯▮*EP.*

$–$$ ▦ **Old Village Post House.** This white wooden building anchoring Mount Pleasant's Historic District on the Cooper River is a cozy inn, an excellent restaurant, and a neighborly tavern. **Pros:** prices are as affordable as some chain motels; set on the "Main Street" of the most picturesque and walkable neighborhood in Mount Pleasant. **Cons:** some minor old building woes including creaky wood floors; not a traditional hotel, so service can be quirky. ⊠ *101 Pitt St., Mount Pleasant* ☎ *843/388–8935* ⊕ *www.oldvillageposthouse.com* ↯ *6 rooms* ⌂ *In-room: a/c, Wi-Fi. In-hotel: restaurant, bar, laundry service, Wi-Fi hotspot, parking (free)* ⊟ *AE, D, DC, MC, V* ▯◯▮*BP.*

$$$$ ▦ **Wentworth Mansion.** Guests admire the Second Empire antiques and
Fodor'sChoice   reproductions, the rich fabrics, inset wood paneling, and original
★   stained-glass windows in this, the most grand inn in town. **Pros:** luxurious bedding; new carpet and furnishings lend a fresh look. **Cons:** Second Empire style can strike some people as foreboding; has characteristics of an old building, including creaking staircases; location deems pedicab, bike, or car advisable to reach tourist areas. ⊠ *149 Wentworth St., College of Charleston Campus* ☎ *843/853–1886 or 888/466–1886* ⊕ *www.wentworthmansion.com* ↯ *21 rooms* ⌂ *In-room: a/c, safe, refrigerator, DVD, Wi-Fi. In-hotel: restaurant, room service, bar, spa, laundry service, Wi-Fi hotspot, parking (free), some pets allowed* ⊟ *AE, D, DC, MC, V* ▯◯▮*BP.*

THE ARTS

For 17 glorious days in late May and early June, Charleston gets a dose of culture from the **Spoleto Festival USA** (☎ 843/722–2764 ⊕ *www.spoletousa.org*). This internationally acclaimed performing-arts festival features a mix of distinguished artists and emerging talent from around the world. Performances take place in magical settings, such as beneath a canopy of ancient oaks or inside a centuries-old cathedral.

SHOPPING

One-of-a-kind, locally owned boutiques make up an important part of the Charleston shopping experience. Charleston has more than 25 fine-art galleries; local Lowcountry art, which includes both traditional landscapes of the region as well as more contemporary takes, is well represented.

The Market area is a cluster of shops and restaurants centered around the **City Market** (⊠ *E. Bay and Market Sts., Market area*). Sweetgrass basket weavers work here, and you can buy the resulting wares, although these artisan-crafts have become expensive. There are T-shirts and souvenir stores here as well as upscale boutiques. In the covered, open-air market, vendors have stalls with everything from jewelry to dresses and purses.

Fodor's Choice ★ **King Street** is Charleston's main street and the major shopping corridor downtown. The latest lines of demarcation dividing the street into districts: Lower King (from Broad to Market streets) is the Antiques District, as it is lined with high-end antiques dealers; Middle King (from Market to Calhoun streets) is now called the Fashion District and is a mix of national chains like Banana Republic and Pottery Barn, alternative shops, and locally owned landmark stores and boutiques; Upper King (from Calhoun Street to Spring Street) has been dubbed the Design District. This up-and-coming area has become known for its furniture and interior design stores selling home fashion. Check out the events and stores on ⊕ *www.kingstreetantiquedistrict.com*, ⊕ *www.kingstreetfashiondistrict.com*, and ⊕ *www.kingstreetdesigndistrict.com*.

Orlando, Disney, and Theme Parks

WORD OF MOUTH

"One thing the majority of the parents [visiting Disney World] say they are glad they did was to pack a day's worth of clothes (shirt, pants, socks, shoes, accessories) in a zip lock bag for each day. No hunting for things in the morning when you are trying to get out the door. If the [kids] are old enough, just hand them their bag."
—Connie

WELCOME TO ORLANDO, DISNEY, AND THEME PARKS

TOP REASONS TO GO

★ **Magic and Fantasy:** Unleash your inner child in the glow of Cinderella Castle at WDW's Magic Kingdom. Fireworks transform the night skies—and you—at this park and at Epcot. And, over at Universal's Islands of Adventure we have just two words: Harry Potter.

★ **The Planet and Beyond:** Visit Epcot's 11 countries, complete with perfect replicas of foreign monuments, unique crafts, and traditional cuisine.

★ **Amazing Animals:** Safari through Africa in Disney's Animal Kingdom, get splashed by Shamu at SeaWorld and kiss a dolphin at Discovery Cove.

1 Walt Disney World Resort. The granddaddy of vacation destinations, Disney welcomes you to four theme parks: Magic Kingdom, Animal Kingdom, Epcot, and Hollywood Studios. The 40-square-mi resort also delivers Blizzard Beach and Typhoon Lagoon water parks and the lively Downtown Disney area full of restaurants, shops, and entertainment diversions like the House of Blues and Cirque du Soleil. What else? Only a 220-acre sports complex, 34 hotels, lodges, and campsites, full-service spas, golf courses, dinner shows, a wedding pavilion, and plenty of other things that are the stuff of dreams.

2 Universal Orlando Resort. The area's big-thrill destination brings movies to life at Universal Studios

GETTING ORIENTED

Thanks to Disney World, Orlando is the gateway for many visitors to central Florida. The city sits about two hours east of Tampa (home to yet another theme park, Busch Gardens) and an hour southwest of Kennedy Space Center. Edging Orlando to the south is Kissimmee, with home-grown attractions like Gatorland. Looking for more laid-back local flavor? You'll find it 20 mi northeast of Orlando in the charming Winter Park suburb.

9

and delivers gravity-defying rides and special-effects surprises at Islands of Adventure. Nearby Wet 'n Wild is full of watery rides and adventures. Three on-site Universal resorts, including a Hard Rock Hotel, offer themed accommodations, and 12 partner hotels pick up the slack. CityWalk is the nightlife hub for themed restaurants, bars, movies, and clubs.

3 SeaWorld Orlando.
Marine life takes the stage at SeaWorld Orlando, where killer whales and other marine mammals perform in meticulously choreographed shows, and thrill seekers find their adrenaline rush on coaster and simulator attractions. Sister park Discovery Cove is a daylong, swim-with-the-dolphins beach escape.

There's magic in Orlando . . . and we don't just mean the NBA team. The city and its environs teem with magical experiences, both natural and Imagineered. With endless joys and excitements for people of all ages, it's no wonder that more than 50 million people visit every year.

The most obvious source of Orlando's magic is Disney World. And with four theme parks, two water parks, 20 or so themed hotels, shopping districts, and countless dining options, you could spend a lengthy vacation entirely on Disney property and still not see it all.

Universal Studios and Islands of Adventure offer their own thrills, including the new Wizarding World of Harry Potter. There's also Sea-World, Discovery Cove—where you can have the truly magical experience of swimming with the dolphins—and Busch Gardens Tampa. To take a break from the theme parks, you can visit Winter Park's Charles Hosmer Morse Museum for what may well be the world's largest collection of Tiffany glass and other art treasures; go hiking, swimming, or canoeing in Wekiwa Springs State Park; or head to Space Coast.

You could also just take it easy. Even in the midst of a whirlwind theme-park tour, you can laze by the pool, indulge in a spa treatment, play a round of golf, or leisurely shop an afternoon away.

The key to an ideal Orlando vacation is planning. Figure out well in advance who's going, what everyone wants to do on this trip, and what you'll save for the next. If your stay will center on theme parks, decide which parks to visit on which days, buy your ticket and hotel package, and make meal reservations—all long before leaving home.

When you're actually in Orlando, though, try to be flexible. Your plans form the backbone of your trip and you want it to be strong, but things will come up—moods will change, plans will alter. That's OK. For the most part, it's not difficult to change segments of your itinerary once you're on the ground. Planning is key to enjoying Orlando and all it offers, but so is taking a deep breath, allowing for the occasional detour, and going with the flow of your vacation.

PLANNING

WHEN TO GO

There's no down time at Orlando's theme parks. Crowds thin in January, after New Year's, and stay reasonable until around President's Day. From that point through Labor Day, though, crowds are either heavy (as in mid-February through early June and again in late August) or very heavy. Things lighten up after Labor Day, but grow busy again around Columbus Day. After that comes another light patch until right around Thanksgiving, which is huge in the parks. There's a slight lull in early December, right between Thanksgiving and Christmas vacations.

GETTING HERE AND AROUND

All the major and most discount airlines fly into **Orlando International Airport** (*MCO* ☎ *407/825–2001* ⊕ *www.orlandoairports.net*).

If you're spending your entire vacation on Disney property, you can use its fleet of buses, trams, boats, and monorail trains exclusively. If you're staying outside the Disney resort—or want to visit a non-Disney attraction—you'll need to use cabs, shuttles (your hotel may have a free one), and/or rental cars. Some hotels also offer shuttles to and from Universal and SeaWorld, which don't have transit systems.

CABS, SHUTTLES, AND PUBLIC TRANSPORTATION

Many non-Disney hotels offer free airport shuttles. If yours doesn't, cab fare from the airport to the Disney area runs $55–$75. Try **Star Taxi** (☎ *407/857–9999*) or **Yellow Cab Co.** (☎ *407/422–2222*). **Town & Country Transportation** (☎ *407/828–3035*) charges $75 one-way for a town car.

The **Mears Transportation Group** (☎ *407/423–5566* ⊕ *www. mearstransportation.com*) offers shuttle and charter services throughout the Orlando area.

The **I-Ride Trolley** (☎ *407/248–9590* ⊕ *www.iridetrolley.com*) serves most attractions in the I-Drive area (including SeaWorld). It won't get you to Disney or Universal. The **LYNX** (☎ *407/841–5969* ⊕ *www.golynx.com*) bus system provides service throughout Orlando.

CAR RENTAL

Rates vary seasonally and can begin as low as $30 a day/$149 a week for an economy car (excluding 6.5% rental car tax). If you're staying on Disney property but want to rent a car for a day, you might get a better daily rate if you reserve for two or more days, then return the car early. (Just be sure there aren't any penalties for this.)

■TIP➔ Gas stations on Disney property have some of the best prices in metro Orlando.

DISNEY PACKAGE

Magic Your Way Vacations. These packages bundle hotel, parks admission, and an array of add-on options—dining plans, airfare, Park Hopper passes, spa treatments—that make it easy to customize your trip. They can also offer good value for money. Just do your homework so you'll know that, if you *aren't* interested in seeing Cirque du Soleil, it's best not to splurge on the Platinum Plan, which includes tickets to this show.

You'll also be sure to determine how many park meals and snacks you'll truly need before investing in a dining plan.

UNIVERSAL PACKAGE

Vacation Package. Universal offers its own plans and ever-changing roster of deals to help you maximize value. (When starting your research, check out the "Hot Deals" section of the Web site.) Basic packages include hotel and park admission, but can be expanded to include airfare; dining; rental cars; show tickets; spa treatments; admission to SeaWorld, Wet'n Wild, Aquatica, Busch Gardens, and Discovery Cove; and a VIP treatment that lets you skip many theme-park lines. Note, though, that this last perk is free to guests at Universal hotels.

PARKS TICKETS

Per-day, per-person, at-the-gate admissions range from roughly $40–$50 at Wet 'n Wild to about $70–$85 at Universal, Disney, and Sea-World. Discovery Cove runs between $189 without a dolphin swim to $299 with it, though prices vary seasonally.

DISNEY

Magic Your Way: With this plan, the more days you stay, the greater your per-day savings. For instance, a one-day ticket costs $82 for anyone age 10 and up, whereas a five-day ticket costs $237 (or just under $48 per day). There are also add-ons:

Park Hopper: This lets you move from park to park within a single day and adds $54 to the price of a ticket, no matter how many days your ticket covers. The flexibility is fantastic—you can spend the day at Animal Kingdom, for example, then hit Magic Kingdom for fireworks.

Water Parks Fun and More: With this $54-per-ticket add-on, you get admission to Typhoon Lagoon, Blizzard Beach, and other Disney attractions.

No Expiration: This add-on (prices vary) lets you use your ticket for more than one trip to Disney (e.g., use five days of a seven-day Magic Your Way ticket on one visit and two days on another).

UNIVERSAL, SEAWORLD, BUSCH GARDENS TAMPA

Universal Parks: A one-day Park to Park ticket is $112 (ages 10 and up); a seven-day version is nearly $175 (a better per-day value at about $25 a day). Add the Express PLUS (prices vary) option to skirt ride lines; CityWalk Party Pass (roughly $12) for one-night venue access; CityWalk Party Pass and Movie ($15) for a free movie; and Length-of-Stay Wet'n Wild pass (about $48).

Orlando FlexTicket: This gives you up to 14 consecutive days' unlimited entry to (but not parking at) Universal and SeaWorld parks and select CityWalk venues. It costs nearly $260 (ages 10 and up). The Flex Ticket Plus (nearly $300) includes admission to Busch Gardens and free shuttle service between it and various Orlando locations.

DID YOU KNOW?

The quintessential Disney icon, the Cinderella Castle, was inspired by the palace built by the mad Bavarian king Ludwig II at Neuschwanstein. At 180 feet, it's 100 feet taller than Disneyland's Sleeping Beauty Castle.

Toy Story Midway Mania is a 3D target-shooting adventure-ride.

THE PARKS

THE MAGIC KINGDOM

The Magic Kingdom is the heart and soul of the Walt Disney World empire. It was the first Disney outpost in Florida when it opened in 1971, and it's the park that launched Disney's presence in France, Japan, and Hong Kong.

For a landmark that wields such worldwide influence, the 142-acre Magic Kingdom may seem small—indeed, Epcot is more than double the size of the Magic Kingdom, and Animal Kingdom is almost triple the size when including the park's expansive animal habitats. But looks can be deceiving. Packed into seven different "lands" are nearly 50 major crowd pleasers and that's not counting all the ancillary attractions: shops, eateries, live entertainment, character meet-and-greet spots, fireworks shows, and parades. Many rides are geared to the young, but the Magic Kingdom is anything but a kiddie park. The degree of detail, the greater vision, the surprisingly witty spiel of the guides, and the tongue-in-cheek signs that crop up in the oddest places—"Prince" and "Princess" restrooms in Fantasyland, for instance—all contribute to a delightful sense of discovery.

VISITING TIPS

Try to come toward the end of the week, because most families hit the Magic Kingdom early in a visit.

Ride a star attraction during a parade; lines ease considerably. (But be careful not to get stuck on the wrong side of the parade route when it starts, or you may never get across.)

At City Hall, near the park's Town Square entrance, pick up a guide map and a *Times Guide,* which lists showtimes, character-greeting times, and hours for attractions and restaurants.

Book character meals early. Main Street, U.S.A.'s **Crystal Palace Buffet** has breakfast, lunch, and dinner with Winnie the Pooh, Tigger, and friends. All three meals at the **Fairy Tale Dining** experience in Cinderella Castle are extremely popular—so much so that you should reserve your spot six months out. At a **Wonderland Tea Party** weekday afternoons in the Grand Floridian Resort, kids can interact with Alice and help decorate (and eat) cupcakes.

TOP ATTRACTIONS

FOR AGES 7 AND UP

Big Thunder Mountain Railroad. An Old West–themed, classic coaster that's not too scary; it's just a really good, bumpy, swervy thrill.

Buzz Lightyear's Space Ranger Spin. A shoot-'em-up ride where space ranger wannabes compete for the highest score.

Haunted Mansion. With its razzle-dazzle special effects, this classic is always a frightful hoot.

Mickey's PhilharMagic. The only 3-D film experience at Disney that features the main Disney characters and movie theme songs.

Space Mountain. The Magic Kingdom's scariest ride, recently renovated, zips you along the tracks in near-total darkness except for the stars.

Splash Mountain. A long, tame boat ride ends in a 52½-foot flume drop into a very wet briar patch.

FOR AGES 6 AND UNDER

Dumbo the Flying Elephant. The elephant ears get them every time. A fancy new Dumbo ride will open in the park's expanded Fantasyland by 2013.

9

Goofy's Barnstormer. WDW's starter coaster for kids who may be tall enough to go on Big Thunder Mountain and Space Mountain but who aren't sure they can handle it.

The Magic Carpets of Aladdin. On this must-do for preschoolers you can make your carpet go up and down to avoid water spurts as mischievous camels spit at you.

The Many Adventures of Winnie the Pooh. Hang onto your honey pot as you get whisked along on a windy-day adventure with Pooh, Tigger, Eeyore, and friends.

Pirates of the Caribbean. Don't miss this waltz through pirate country, especially if you're a fan of the movies.

EPCOT

Nowhere but at Epcot can you explore and experience the native food, entertainment, culture, and arts and crafts of countries in Europe, Asia, North Africa, and the Americas. What's more, employees at the World Showcase pavilions actually hail from the countries the pavilions represent.

Epcot, or "Experimental Prototype Community of Tomorrow," was the original inspiration for Walt Disney World. Walt envisioned a future in which nations coexisted in peace and harmony, reaping the miraculous harvest of technological achievement. The Epcot of today is both more and less than his original dream. Less, because the World Showcase presents views of its countries that are, as an Epcot guide once put it, "as Americans perceive them"—highly idealized. But this is a minor quibble in the face of the major achievement: Epcot is that rare paradox—a successful educational theme park that excels at entertainment, too.

VISITING TIPS

Epcot is so vast and varied you really need two days to explore. With just one day, you'll have to be highly selective.

Go early in the week, when others are at Magic Kingdom.

If you like a good festival, visit during the International Flower & Garden Festival (early to mid-March through May) or the International Food & Wine Festival (late September through mid-November).

TOP ATTRACTIONS

The American Adventure. Many adults and older children love this patriotic look at American history; who can resist the Audio-Animatronics hosts, Ben Franklin and Mark Twain?

IllumiNations. This amazing musical laser-fountains-and-fireworks show is Disney nighttime entertainment at its best.

Mission: SPACE. Blast off on a simulated ride to Mars, if you can handle the turbulence.

Soarin'. Everyone's hands-down favorite: Feel the sweet breeze as you "hang glide" over California landscapes.

Test Track. Your car revs up to 60 mph on a hairpin turn in this wild ride on a General Motors proving ground.

DISNEY'S HOLLYWOOD STUDIOS

Disney's Hollywood Studios were designed to be a trip back to Tinseltown's Golden Age, when Hedda Hopper, not tabloids, spread celebrity gossip and when the girl off the bus from Ohio could be the next Judy Garland.

The result is a theme park that blends movie-production capabilities and high-tech wonders with breathtaking rides and nostalgia. The park's old-time Hollywood ambience begins with a rosy-hued view of the moviemaking business presented in a dreamy stage set from the 1930s and '40s, amid sleek Art Moderne buildings in pastel colors, funky diners, kitschy decorations, and sculptured gardens populated by roving actors playing, well, roving actors. There are also casting directors, gossip columnists, and other colorful characters.

Thanks to a rich library of film scores, the park is permeated with music, all familiar, all evoking the magic of the movies, and all constantly streaming from the camouflaged loudspeakers at a volume just right for humming along. The park icon, a 122-foot-high Sorcerer Mickey

Hat that serves as a gift shop and Disney pin-trading station, towers over Hollywood Boulevard.

VISITING TIPS

Visit early in the week, when most people are at Magic Kingdom and Animal Kingdom.

Check the Tip Board periodically for attractions with short wait times to visit between Fastpass appointments.

Be at the Fantasmic! amphitheater at least an hour before showtime if you didn't book the dinner package.

Need a burst of energy? On-the-run hunger pangs? Grab a slice at Pizza Planet Arcade at **Streets of America**. Alternatively, **Hollywood Scoops Ice Cream** on Sunset is the place to be on a hot day.

If you're planning on a fast-food lunch, eat before 11 am or after 2:30 pm. There are quick-bite spots all over the park and several stands along Sunset. Get a burger (meat or veggie) or chicken strips at **Rosie's All-American Cafe,** a slice of pizza from **Catalina Eddie's,** or a hunk of smoked bird at **Toluca Legs Turkey Co.**

TOP ATTRACTIONS

FOR AGES
8 AND UP

The American Idol Experience. If you don't get chosen to test your pipes, you can vote for your favorite Idol wannabe.

Indiana Jones Epic Stunt Spectacular! The show's Indy double and supporting cast reenact *Raiders of the Lost Ark* scenes with panache.

The Magic of Disney Animation. Take a behind-the-scenes look at the making of Disney films.

Rock 'n' Roller Coaster Starring Aerosmith. Blast off to rockin' tunes on a high-speed, hard-core coaster.

Toy Story Midway Mania! 3-D glasses? Check. Spring-action shooter? Check. Ride and shoot your way through with Buzz, Woody, and others.

Twilight Zone Tower of Terror. The TV classic theming of this free-fall "elevator" screamer is meticulous.

FOR AGES 7
AND UNDER

Block Party Bash. It's a high-energy, interactive parade where you can play along with the toys from *Toy Story* or shout it out with Mike and Sully of *Monsters, Inc.*

Honey I Shrunk the Kids Movie Set Adventure. Youngsters love to romp among the giant blades of grass and bugs at this imaginative playground.

MuppetVision 3-D. Children (and most adults) shriek with laughter during this 3-D movie involving Kermit, Miss Piggy, and other lovable Muppets.

Playhouse Disney—Live on Stage! The preschool crowd can't get enough of the characters here from Disney Channel shows like "Mickey Mouse Clubhouse" and "Little Einsteins."

9

ANIMAL KINGDOM

Disney's Animal Kingdom explores the stories of all animals—real, imaginary, and extinct. Enter through the Oasis, where you hear exotic background music and find yourself surrounded by gentle waterfalls and gardens alive with exotic birds, reptiles, and mammals.

At 403 acres and several times the size of the Magic Kingdom, Animal Kingdom is the largest in area of all Disney theme parks. Animal habitats take up much of that acreage. Creatures here thrive in careful re-creations of landscapes from Asia and Africa. Throughout the park, you'll also learn about conservation in a low-key way.

Amid all the nature are thrill rides, a 3-D show (housed in the "root system" of the iconic Tree of Life), two first-rate musicals, and character meet and greets. Cast members are as likely to hail from Kenya or South Africa as they are from Kentucky or South Carolina. It's all part of the charm.

VISITING TIPS

Try to visit during the week. Pedestrian areas are compact, and the park can feel uncomfortably packed on weekends.

Plan on a full day here. That way, while exploring Africa's Pangani Forest Exploration Trail, say, you can spend 10 minutes (rather than just two) watching vigilant meerkats stand sentry or tracking a mama gorilla as she cares for her infant.

Arrive a half hour before the park opens as much to see the wild animals at their friskiest (morning is a good time to do the safari ride) as to get a jump on the crowds.

For updates on line lengths, check the Tip Board, just after crossing the bridge into Discovery Island.

Good places to rendezvous include the outdoor seating area of Tusker House restaurant in Africa, in front of DinoLand U.S.A.'s Boneyard, and at the entrance to Festival of the Lion King at Camp Minnie-Mickey.

TOP ATTRACTIONS

AFRICA **Kilimanjaro Safaris.** You're guaranteed to see dozens of wild animals, including giraffes, zebras, hippos, rhinos, and elephants, living in authentic, re-created African habitats. If you're lucky, the lions and cheetahs will be stirring, too.

ASIA **Expedition Everest.** The Animal Kingdom's cleverly themed roller coaster is a spine-tingling trip into the snowy Himalayas to find the abominable snowman. It's best reserved for brave riders 7 and up.

CAMP MINNIE-MICKEY **Festival of the Lion King.** Singers and dancers dressed in fantastic costumes representing many wild animals perform uplifting dance and acrobatics numbers and interact with children in the audience.

DINOLAND, U.S.A. **DINOSAUR.** Extremely lifelike giant dinosaurs jump out as your vehicle swoops and dips. We recommend it for fearless kids 8 and up.

Finding Nemo—The Musical. Don't miss a performance of this outstanding musical starring the most charming, colorful characters ever to swim their way into your heart.

DISCOVERY ISLAND **Tree of Life—It's Tough to Be a Bug!** This clever and very funny 3-D movie starring Flik from the Disney film *A Bug's Life* is full of surprises, including "shocking" special effects. Some kids under 7 are scared of the loud noises.

DISNEY WATER PARKS

There's something about a water park that brings out the kid in us, and there's no denying that these are two of the world's best. What sets them apart? It's the same thing that differentiates all Disney parks—the detailed themes.

Whether you're cast away on a balmy island at Typhoon Lagoon or washed up on a ski resort–turned–seaside playground at Blizzard Beach, the landscaping and clever architecture will add to the fun of flume and raft rides, wave pools, and splash areas. Another plus: The vegetation has matured enough to create shade. The Disney water parks give you that lost-in-paradise feeling on top of all those high-speed wedgie-inducing waterslides. They're so popular that crowds often reach overflow capacity in summer.

Your children may like them so much that they'll clamor to visit more than once. If you're going to Disney for five days or more between April and October, add the Water Park Fun & More option to your Magic Your Way ticket. Of course, check the weather to make sure the temperatures are to your liking for running around in a swimsuit.

WHAT TO EXPECT

Most people agree that kids under 7 and older adults prefer Typhoon Lagoon. Bigger kids and teens like Blizzard Beach better because it has more slides and big-deal rides. Indeed, devoted waterslide enthusiasts generally prefer Blizzard Beach to other water parks.

BLIZZARD BEACH Disney Imagineers have gone all out here to create the paradox of a ski resort in the midst of a tropical lagoon. Lots of verbal puns and sight gags play with the snow-in-Florida motif. The centerpiece is Mt. Gushmore, with its 120-foot-high Summit Plummet. Attractions have names like Teamboat Springs, a white-water raft ride. Themed speed slides include Toboggan Racer, Slush Gusher, and Snow Stormers. Between Mt. Gushmore's base and its summit, swim-skiers can also ride a chairlift converted from ski-resort to beach-resort use—with multihued umbrellas and snow skis on their undersides.

TYPHOON LAGOON You can speed down waterslides with names like Crush 'N' Gusher and Humunga Kowabunga or bump through rapids and falls at Mt. Mayday. You can also bob along in 5-foot waves in a surf pool the size of two football fields, or, for a mellow break, float in inner tubes along the 2,100-foot Castaway Creek. Go snorkeling in Shark Reef, rubberneck as fellow human cannonballs are ejected from the Storm Slides, or hunker down in a hammock or lounge chair and read a book. Ketchakiddie Creek for young children replicates adult rides on a smaller scale. It's Disney's version of a day at the beach—complete with friendly Disney lifeguards.

9

VISITING TIPS

In summer, come first thing in the morning (early birds can ride several times before the lines get long), late in the afternoon when park hours run later, or when the weather clears after a thundershower (rainstorms drive away crowds). Afternoons are also good in cooler weather, as the water is a bit warmer. To make a whole day of it, avoid weekends, when locals and visitors pack in.

Women and girls should wear one-piece swimsuits unless they want to find their tops somewhere around their ears at the bottom of the waterslide.

Invest in sunscreen and water shoes. Plan to slather sunscreen on several times throughout the day. An inexpensive pair of water shoes will save tootsies from hot sand and walkways and from grimy restroom floors.

Arrive 30 minutes before opening so you can park, buy tickets, rent towels, and snag inner tubes before the crowds descend, and, trust us, it gets very crowded.

UNIVERSAL STUDIOS

Universal Studios appeals primarily to those who like loud, fast, high-energy attractions—generally teens and adults. Covering 444 acres, it's a rambling montage of sets, shops, soundstages housing themed attractions, reproductions of New York and San Francisco, and some genuine moviemaking paraphernalia.

On a map, the park appears neatly divided into six areas positioned around a huge lagoon. There's Production Central, which covers the entire left side of the Plaza of the Stars; New York, with street performances at 70 Delancey; the bicoastal San Francisco/Amity; futuristic World Expo; Woody Woodpecker's KidZone; and Hollywood.

What's tricky is that—since it's designed like a series of movie sets—there's no straightforward way to tackle the park. You'll probably make some detours and do some backtracking. To save time and shoe leather, ask theme-park hosts for itinerary suggestions and time-saving tips.

TOURING TIPS

Upon entering, avoid the temptation to go left toward the towering soundstages, looping the park clockwise. Head right—bypassing shops, restaurants, and some crowds—to primary attractions like the Simpsons Ride and Men In Black.

Good rendezvous points include the Lucy Tribute near the entrance, Mel's Drive-In, and Beetlejuice's Graveyard Revue.

TOP ATTRACTIONS

FOR AGES 7 AND UP **Hollywood Rip Ride Rockit.** On this coaster, added in 2009, you select the sound track.

Men In Black: Alien Attack. The "world's first ride-through video game" gives you a chance to plug away at an endless swarm of aliens.

Revenge of the Mummy. It's a jarring, rocketing indoor coaster that takes you past scary mummies and billowing balls of fire (really).

Shrek 4-D. The 3-D film with sensory effects picks up where the original film left off—and adds some creepy extras in the process.

The Simpsons Ride. It puts you in the heart of Springfield on a wild-and-crazy virtual-reality experience.

Terminator 2 3-D. This explosive stage show features robots, 3-D effects, and sensations that all add extra punch to the classic film series.

Twister . . . Ride It Out. OK. It's just a special-effects show—but what special effects! You experience a tornado without having to head to the root cellar.

Universal Horror Make-Up Show. This sometimes gross, often raunchy, but always entertaining demonstration merges the best of stand-up comedy with creepy effects.

FOR AGES 6 AND UNDER **A Day in the Park with Barney.** Small children love the big purple dinosaur and the chance to sing along.

Animal Actors on Location! It's a perfect family show starring a menagerie of animals whose unusually high IQs are surpassed only by their cuteness and cuddle-ability.

Curious George Goes to Town. The celebrated simian visits the Man with the Yellow Hat in a small-scale water park.

ISLANDS OF ADVENTURE

When Islands of Adventure (IOA) opened in 1999 it took attractions to a new level—a practice that continues with the Wizarding World of Harry Potter, opened in 2010. From Marvel Super Hero Island and Toon Lagoon to Seuss Landing and the Lost Continent, most attractions are impressive—some even out-Disney Disney.

You pass through the turnstiles and into the Port of Entry plaza, a bazaar that brings together bits and pieces of architecture, landscaping, music, and wares from many lands—Dutch windmills, Indonesian pedicabs, African masks. Egyptian figurines adorn the massive archway inscribed with the notice "The adventure begins." From here, themed islands—arranged around a large lagoon—are connected by walkways that make navigation easy.

When you've done the full circuit, you'll recall the fantastic range of sights, sounds, and experiences and realize there can be truth in advertising. This park really *is* an adventure.

TOURING TIPS

Invest in a Universal Express Plus Pass for the right to head to the front of the line and see the park without a sense of urgency.

Ask hosts about their favorite experiences—and their suggestions for saving time.

If the park's open late, split the day in half. See part of it in the morning, head off-site to a restaurant for lunch, then head to your hotel for a swim or a nap (or both). Return in the cooler, less crowded evening.

Take time to explore little-used sidewalks and quiet alcoves and other sanctuaries that help counter the manic energy of IOA.

TOP ATTRACTIONS

FOR AGES
7 AND UP

Amazing Adventures of Spider-Man. Get ready to fight bad guys and marvel at the engineering and technological wizardry on this dazzling attraction.

Dudley Do-Right's Ripsaw Falls. Even if its namesake is a mystery to anyone born after the 1960s, everyone loves the super splashdown at the end of this log-flume ride dedicated to the exploits of the animated Canadian Mountie.

Eighth Voyage of Sindbad. Jumping, diving, punching—is it another Tom Cruise action film? No, it's a cool, live stunt show with a love story to boot.

Harry Potter and the Forbidden Journey. This ride truly brings J.K. Rowling's books to life on an adventure through Hogwarts and beyond with Harry, Hermione, and Ron.

Incredible Hulk Coaster. This super-scary coaster blasts you skyward before sending you on no less than seven inversions. It will be hard to walk straight after this one.

FOR AGES 6
AND UNDER

The Cat in the Hat. It's like entering a Dr. Seuss book: all you have to do is sit on a moving couch and see what it's like when the Cat in the Hat drops by to babysit.

Flight of the Hippogriff. Some of the younger Hogswarts "students" will enjoy this low-key coaster in Harry Potter's world.

Popeye and Bluto's Bilge-Rat Barges. This tumultuous (but safe) raft ride lets younger kids experience a big-deal ride that's not too scary—just wild and wet.

SEAWORLD AND DISCOVERY COVE

There's a whole lot more to SeaWorld than being splashed by Shamu. You can see manatees face-to-snout, learn to love an eel, and be spat at by a walrus. The park celebrates mammals, birds, fish, and reptiles that live in and near the ocean. It also tosses in roller coaster and water flume thrills. SeaWorld's performance venues, attractions, and activities surround a 17-acre lagoon, and the artful landscaping, curving paths, and concealing greenery sometimes lead to wrong turns. But armed with a map that lists showtimes, it's easy to plan an approach that lets you move fluidly from one show and attraction to the next and still have time for rest stops and meal breaks.

If you want to swim with dolphins, head to Discovery Cove. The daily cap on crowds makes it seem as if you have the park to yourself. Navigating the grounds is simple; signs point to swimming areas, cabanas, or the free-flight aviary—aflutter with exotic birds and accessible via a walkway or (even better) by swimming beneath a waterfall.

VISITING TIPS

Before investing in front-of-the-line Quick Queue passes at SeaWorld, remember that there are only a handful of big-deal rides, and space is seldom a problem at shows.

Wet and mild: Explore the peaceful, tropical beauty of the Snorkeling Pools in Discovery Cove.

If you bring your own food, remove all straws and lids before you arrive—they can harm fish and birds.

Arrive at least 30 minutes early for the Shamu show, which generally fills to capacity. Prepare to get wet in the "splash zone" down front.

At Discovery Cove, make the aviary one of your first stops, since the 250-plus birds within will be more active in the morning. Check-in starts at 8 am.

TOP ATTRACTIONS

SEAWORLD

Believe. The park's flagship attraction and mascot are irresistible. In a show four years in the making, you'll see several Shamus performing graceful aquabatics that are guaranteed to thrill.

Clyde and Seamore Take Pirate Island. Head for Sea Lion & Otter Stadium to watch this slapstick comedy routine starring an adorable team of water mammals and their trainers.

Journey to Atlantis. Although it seems a little dated, the Splash Mountain–esque ride still provides thrills—especially on its last, steep, wet drop.

Kraken. It takes you on a high-speed chase with a dragon. But who's chasing whom? Fast and furious.

Manta. SeaWorld likes to claim that this is two attractions in one: while waiting in line, you walk past 10 supercool aquariums filled with rays and fish. But the big thrill is the amazingly fast coaster at the front of the line.

Pets Ahoy. Anyone who has ever loved a pet, or wanted one, has to see the talented cats, dogs, birds, and pig in this cute and clever show.

DISCOVERY COVE **Private Cabanas.** Granted, admission to Discovery Cove isn't cheap, but if you can pony up a little more (about $175) you'll enjoy complete privacy, personalized service, and a well-stocked mini-refrigerator in these tropical waterfront sanctuaries.

Snorkeling Pools. The snorkeling pools may well be Discovery Cove's most underhyped attractions. It's a real thrill to float lazily and silently amid tropical fish, to swim beneath a waterfall into an elaborate aviary, and to dive down a few feet to peer at sharks and barracuda through the porthole of a wrecked ship. There's also on-site snorkeling instruction for novices.

Swim with Dolphins. The big draw is Dolphin Lagoon, where you can frolic with dolphins under careful supervision. For the exhilarating finale, catch hold of a dolphin's fin for your ride to shore.

WHERE TO EAT

You'll find the all-American-standby burger-and-fries combo everywhere in Orlando, yet the ambitious chefs behind Orlando's theme-park and independent restaurants provide loads of better options—much better. Locally sourced foods, creative preparations, and clever international influences are all the rage here, giving even die-hard foodies surprisingly satisfying meals. Theme-park complexes have some of the best restaurants in town, although you may opt for a car rental to seek out the local treasures.

Reservations are strongly recommended throughout Orlando. ■ TIP➔ **Make reservations for Disney restaurants and character meals at both Universal and Disney at least 90 (and up to 180) days out.** And be sure to ask about the cancellation policy—at a handful of Disney restaurants, for instance, you may be charged penalties if you don't give 24- to 48-hours' notice.

MEAL PLANS

Disney Magic Your Way Dining Plan allows you one table-service meal, one counter-service meal, and one snack per day of your trip at more than 100 theme-park and resort restaurants. For more money, you can upgrade the plan to include more; to save, you can downgrade to a counter-service-only plan.

Adding the plan to a vacation package costs about $42 per adult, per day, and less than $12 per child age 3–9, per day. This includes taxes but not gratuities. Used wisely, this plan is a steal; but Disney makes out like a bandit when you don't use all the meals on your plan, so absolutely do so. Plan ahead, and use "extra" meals to your advantage by swapping two table-service meals for a Disney dinner show, say, or an evening at a high-end restaurant like California Grill.

Universal Meal Deal is a daylong, all-you-can-eat offer at walk-up eateries inside Universal Studios and Islands of Adventure. Daily prices are $25 and $13 (both parks), and $21 and $11 (one park) for ages 10 and over and kids under 10, respectively. All-you-can-drink soft drinks are $9 daily for all who purchase a meal deal. A valid unlimited Meal Deal ticket lets you purchase a $6 add-on ticket good for one entrée at participating CityWalk restaurants.

WHAT IT COSTS					
	¢	$	$$	$$$	$$$$
Restaurants	under $8	$8–$14	$15–$21	$22–$30	over $30

Prices are per person for a median main course, at dinner, excluding tip and tax of 6.5 %.

RESTAURANTS

The following is a (very) select list of some of our favorite Orlando restaurants inside and outside the theme parks.

DISNEY WORLD AND DISNEY RESORTS

$$
AMERICAN
Hollywood
Studios
Fodor'sChoice
★

✕ **50's Prime Time Café**. Who says you can't go home again? If you grew up in middle America in the 1950s, just step inside. While *I Love Lucy* and *The Donna Reed Show* clips play on a television screen, you can feast on meat loaf, pot roast, or fried chicken, all served on a Formica tabletop. At $15, the meat loaf is one of the best inexpensive dinners in any local theme park. Enjoy it with a malted-milk shake or root-beer float (or a bottle of wine). The place offers some fancier dishes, such as olive oil–poached salmon, which are good but out of character with the diner theme. If you're not feeling totally wholesome, go for Dad's Electric Lemonade (rum, vodka, blue curaçao, sweet-and-sour mix, and Sprite), which is worth every bit of the $10.25 price tag. Just like Mother, the menu admonishes, "Don't put your elbows on the table!" ⊠ *Hollywood Blvd.* ☎ *407/939–3463* ▤ *AE, D, DC, MC, V.*

$$$$
AFRICAN
Animal Kingdom
Lodge
Fodor'sChoice
★

✕ **Boma—Flavors of Africa**. Boma takes Western-style ingredients and prepares them with an African twist—then invites guests to walk through an African marketplace–style dining room to help themselves at the extraordinary buffet. The dozen or so serving stations have entrées such as roasted pork, chicken, beef, and fish served with tamarind and other robust sauces; intriguing salads; and some of the best hummus this side of the Atlantic. Don't pass up the soups, as the hearty chicken corn porridge is excellent. The zebra dome dessert is chocolate mousse covered with white chocolate and striped with dark chocolate. All meals are prix fixe, and prices change seasonally. The South African wine list is outstanding. ⊠ *Disney's Animal Kingdom Lodge* ☎ *407/939–3463* ⌖ *Reservations essential* ▤ *AE, D, DC, MC, V* ☉ *No lunch.*

$$$$
AMERICAN
Magic Kingdom

✕ **Cinderella's Royal Table**. Cinderella and other Disney princesses appear at every Fairy Tale Dining meal at this eatery in the castle's old mead hall; you should book reservations up to 180 days in advance to be sure to see them. The breakfast offers all-you-can-eat options such as scrambled eggs, sausages, bacon, French toast, and beverages. The Fairytale Lunch, a prix-fixe table-service meal, includes entrées like pan-seared salmon with herbed rice and pasta pomodoro. The prix-fixe dinner features selections such as roast lamb chops with herb pesto and roast prime rib of beef with cabernet sauce. When you arrive at

9

the Cinderella Castle, a photographer snaps a shot of your group in the lobby. A package of photographs will be delivered to your table during your meal. ⊠ *Cinderella Castle* ☎ *407/939–3463* ⌕ *Reservations essential* ▤ *AE, D, DC, MC, V.*

¢–$
FAST FOOD
Animal Kingdom

✗ **Flame Tree Barbecue.** This counter-service eatery is one of the relatively undiscovered gems of Disney's culinary offerings. There's nothing fancy here, but you can dig into ribs, barbecued chicken, and pulled pork and barbecued beef sandwiches with several sauce choices. For something with a lower calorie count, try the smoked turkey served in a multigrain bun, or a great barbecued chicken and crisp green salad with vinaigrette dressing. The outdoor tables, set beneath intricately carved wood pavilions, make great spots for a picnic, and they're not usually crowded. ⊠ *Discovery Island* ▤ *AE, D, DC, MC, V.*

$$$$
AFRICAN
Animal Kingdom
Lodge
Fodor's Choice
★

✗ **Jiko.** The name of this restaurant means "the cooking place" in Swahili, and it is certainly that. The dining area surrounds two big, wood-burning ovens and a grill area where you can watch cooks in North African–style caps working on your meal. The menu here is more African-inspired than purely African, but does include authentic entrées like Swahili curry shrimp from an East African recipe and short ribs with a Kenyan coffee-barbecue sauce. The menu changes periodically, but typically includes entrées such as maize-crusted wreckfish with tomato-butter sauce, and chicken with goat-cheese potatoes, preserved lemon, and harissa. The restaurant offers more than 65 wines by the glass, including a large selection of African vintages. And if you want to have a private party (for up to 40 people), the wine room decorated with African sculptures is the place to have it. ⊠ *Disney's Animal Kingdom Lodge* ☎ *407/939–3463* ⌕ *Reservations essential* ▤ *AE, D, DC, MC, V* ☾ *No lunch.*

$$$
FRENCH
Epcot
Fodor's Choice
★

✗ **Les Chefs de France.** What some consider the best restaurant at Disney was created by three of France's most famous chefs: Paul Bocuse, Gaston Lenôtre, and Roger Vergé. Classic escargots, a good starter, are prepared in a casserole with garlic butter; you might follow up with roasted breast of duck and leg confit, or grilled beef tenderloin with black pepper sauce. Make sure you finish with crepes *au chocolat.* The nearby Boulangerie Pâtisserie offers tarts, croissants, éclairs, napoleons, and more, to go. ⊠ *France Pavilion* ☎ *407/939–3463* ▤ *AE, D, DC, MC, V.*

UNIVERSAL ORLANDO AREA

$$$$
CREOLE
City Walk
Fodor's Choice
★

✗ **Emeril's.** The popular eatery is a culinary shrine to Emeril Lagasse, the famous Food Network chef who occasionally makes an appearance. And while the interior of the restaurant with its modernistic interior of 30-foot ceilings, blond woods, a second-story wine loft, and lots of galvanized steel looks nothing like the Old French Quarter, the hardwood floors and linen tablecloths create an environment befitting the stellar nature of the cuisine. Entrées may include andouille-crusted red snapper with toasted pecans and crispy shoestring potatoes; bone-in rib eye with Emeril's Worcestershire sauce; chili-glazed rotisserie duck with wild-mushroom bread pudding; and double-cut pork chops with caramelized sweet potatoes. And Emeril knows your 9-year-old is not a New York food critic, so there are kids' offerings like cheese tortellini. Reservations are usually essential, but there's a chance of getting a walk-in seating if you show up for lunch (11:30 am) or early for dinner (5 pm). ✉ *6000 Universal Blvd.* ☎ *407/224–2424* ⊕ *www.emerils.com* ⌕ *Reservations essential* ▤ *AE, D, MC, V.*

$$
ECLECTIC
Islands of
Adventure

✕ **Mythos.** The name is Greek, but the dishes are eclectic. The menu, which changes frequently, usually includes mainstays like pistachio-crusted roast pork tenderloin and cedar-plank salmon with citrus butter. The building itself is enough to grab your attention. It looks like a giant rock formation from the outside and a huge cave (albeit one with plush upholstered seating) from the inside. Mythos also has a waterfront view of the big lagoon in the center of the theme park. (When it's not peak season, Mythos is only open for lunch.) ✉ *6000 Universal Blvd., Lost Continent* ☎ *407/224–4534* ▤ *AE, D, MC, V.*

ORLANDO METRO AREA AND CENTRAL ORLANDO

$$
AMERICAN
Celebration

✕ **Celebration Town Tavern.** This New England–cuisine eatery, operated by a family with Yankee roots, has a double personality. The interior is a brass, glass, and dark-wood-paneling kind of place, while the outside patio has table seating plus the Paddy O' Bar. The food ranges from landlubber treats like baby back ribs, prime rib, and gargantuan burgers to exquisite seafood including Ipswich clams and 2-pound lobsters, plus, on occasion, a salute to the Sunshine State with its Florida stone crabs in season. While the place has a clearly ultra-affluent demeanor, there are plenty of menu choices right out of a working-class Boston bar—meatball hoagies, Philly cheesesteak sandwiches, and Buffalo-style chicken wings. For dessert there's great—what else?—Boston cream pie. ✉ *721 Front St.* ☎ *407/566–2526* ⊕ *www.thecelebrationtowntavern. com* ▤ *AE, D, MC, V.*

$$$$
AMERICAN
Orlando Metro
Area
Fodor's Choice
★

✕ **Norman's.** Celebrity-chef Norman Van Aken brings impressive credentials to the restaurant that bears his name, as you might expect from the headline eatery in the first and only Ritz-Carlton in Orlando. Van Aken's culinary roots go back to the Florida Keys, where he's credited with creating "Floribbean" cuisine, a blend that is part Key West and part Caribbean—although he now weaves in flavors from all continents. The Orlando operation is a formal, sleek restaurant with marble floors, starched tablecloths, waiters in black-tie, and a creative, if expensive, menu. The offerings change frequently, and are offered à la carte and in four-, five-, and seven-course tasting menus. In addition to ceviches tossed table-side, classics from Norman's include yucca-stuffed crispy shrimp with sour-orange sauce, pan-cooked yellowtail with citrus butter, and grilled pork "Havana" with "21st-century" mole and smoky plantain crema. ✉ *Ritz-Carlton Grande Lakes, 4000 Central Florida Pkwy.* ☎ *407/393–4333* ⊕ *www.normans.com* ▤ *AE, D, DC, MC, V* ☾ *No lunch.*

$$$$
ITALIAN
Orlando Metro
Area
Fodor's Choice
★

✕ **Primo.** James Beard Award winner Melissa Kelly cloned her Italian-organic Maine restaurant in an upscale Orlando hotel and brought her farm-to-table sensibilities with her. Here the daily dinner menu pays tribute to Sicily's lighter foods with produce grown in a hotel garden. Homemade cavatelli is tossed with wild mushrooms and spinach and topped with shaved truffles. Duck breast is glazed with chestnut honey and paired with house-made pancetta, apple compote, roasted turnips, and braised red cabbage. Desserts are just as special, with the likes of

9

Meyer lemon–scented crème brûlée and a bowl of hot zeppole tossed in organic cinnamon and sugar. ⊠ *JW Marriott Orlando, Grande Lakes, 4040 Central Florida Pkwy., South Orlando* ☎ *407/393–4444* ⊕ *www.primorestaurant.com* ⚑ *Reservations essential* ▭ *AE, D, DC, MC, V* ☾ *No lunch.*

$$ ✕ **Seasons 52**. Parts of the menu change every week at this innovative restaurant, which serves different foods at different times of year, depending on what's in season. Meals here tend to be healthful yet hearty and very flavorful. You might have the grilled rack of lamb with Dijon sauce, pork tenderloin with polenta, or salmon cooked on a cedar plank and accompanied by grilled vegetables. An impressive wine list with dozens of selections by the glass complements the long and colorful menu. Another health-conscious concept adopted at Seasons 52 is the "mini indulgence" dessert: classics like chocolate cake, butterscotch pudding, and rocky-road ice cream served in portions designed not to bust your daily calorie budget. Although the cuisine is haute, the prices are modest—not bad for a snazzy, urbane, dark-wood-walled bistro and wine bar. It has live music nightly to boot. ⊠ *7700 Sand Lake Rd., I–4 Exit 75A* ☎ *407/354–5212* ⊠ *463 E. Altamonte Dr., I–4 Exit 92, Altamonte Springs* ☎ *407/767–1252* ⊕ *www.seasons52.com* ▭ *AE, D, DC, MC, V.*

AMERICAN
Sand Lake Road
Fodor's Choice
★

WINTER PARK

$$$ ✕ **Luma on Park**. Although Luma on Park is a 21st-century place, serving what it calls "progressive American cuisine," it's also very much in line with Winter Park's 19th-century past. The chic contemporary setting includes terrazzo floors accented by plush carpets and seating areas in alcoves that create a cozy feel. A high point is the wine cellar, which holds 80 varieties of fine wine, all available by the half glass, glass, and bottle. The farm-to-table menu changes daily and always includes pastas and salumi prepared from scratch. On recent visits standouts included two appetizers: roasted turnip-pear soup with Aleppo-pepper oil, and lacinato kale ravioli with toasted-garlic brodo. Notable entrées include Faroe Island ocean trout with quinoa, maitake mushrooms and tangerine broth, and Niman Ranch pork schnitzel with sage–brown-butter grits and honey-glazed cranberries. The restaurant offers a three-course, prix-fixe dinner Sunday through Tuesday for $35 per person, $45 with wine pairings. ⊠ *250 S. Park Ave.* ☎ *407/599–4111* ⊕ *www.lumaonpark.com* ⚑ *Reservations essential* ▭ *AE, MC, V.*

AMERICAN
Fodor's Choice
★

WHERE TO STAY

About 50 million visitors come to the Orlando area each year, making it the most popular tourism destination on the planet. More upscale hotels are opening, as visitors demand more luxurious surroundings. But no matter what your budget, lodging comes in such a wide range of prices, themes, color schemes, brands, meal plans, and guest-room amenities, that visitors will have no problem finding something that fits. Area resorts offer characters in costume performing for the kids, water parks, and massive indoor amusements, like the Gaylord Palms, which offers re-creations of the Everglades, old St. Augustine, and Key

West under a gargantuan glass roof, giving visitors the illusion of having visited more of Florida than they expected.

The area around the expanded Orange County Convention Center is going more upscale as the center draws savvy conventioneers who bring their families along to visit the theme parks. Despite tough economic times, several big resorts opened their doors, and many of the new and existing hotels are joining the trend in green lodging that is expanding in the area. But the number of hotel rooms means you can still find relative bargains throughout the Orlando area, even on Disney property, by researching your trip well and shopping wisely.

■TIP→ **No matter where you decide to stay, you should book months in advance (at least six months for hotels at Disney).**

HOTELS ON DISNEY AND UNIVERSAL PROPERTY

If you're interested solely in attractions at Disney or Universal, in-park hotels are best. They offer such convenient transportation options that you probably won't need a rental car—a huge cost savings.

Walt Disney World's massive campus is tied together by a dizzying array of complimentary monorails, buses, and water taxis. All will easily get you anywhere on the property you want to go. Universal provides complimentary shuttles and water taxis between its two theme parks and on-site hotels, though the hotels and parks are also within walking distance of one another.

Universal and Disney's on-site hotels also offer many perks—some designed to save money, some designed to save time. These perks don't necessarily extend to non-Disney-owned hotels on Disney property, so ask for those specifics before booking.

HOTELS OFF THEME-PARK PROPERTY

If you plan to visit several parks or go sightseeing elsewhere in Central Florida, consider off-site hotels. Those closest to Disney are clustered in a few principal areas: along I-Drive; in the U.S. 192 area and Kissimmee; and in the Downtown Disney–Lake Buena Vista Area, just off Interstate 4 Exit 68. Nearly every hotel in these areas provides frequent (sometimes free) transportation to and from Disney or even Universal. In addition, there are some noteworthy and money-saving, if far-flung, options in the greater Orlando area. One suburban caveat: traffic on Interstate 4 in Orlando experiences typical freeway gridlock during morning (7–9 am) and evening (4–6 pm) rush hours.

■TIP→ **Anyone can visit Disney hotels. To save money and still have on-site resort experiences, stay at a moderately priced hotel off-site and then plan to have lunch and visit the animals at the Animal Kingdom Lodge, say, or reserve lunch or high tea and rent a boat at the Grand Floridian.**

PRICES AND PRICE CHART

In the Orlando area there's an inverse relationship between temperature and room rates. The hot and humid weather in late summer and fall brings low prices and possibly hurricanes. Conversely, the balmy days of late February, March, and April attract lots of visitors; hotel owners charge accordingly. One note about hurricane season—it officially begins in June, but a hurricane in Florida before August is a rarity. Rates are often low from early January to mid-February, from late April to mid-June, and from mid-August to the third week in November.

Always call several places—availability and special deals can drive room rates at a $$$$ hotel down into the $$ range—and don't forget to ask whether you're eligible for a discount. You can always save by preparing a few meals in a room, suite, or villa with a kitchenette or kitchen. Web sites will often offer a better room rate, so compare the prices offered on the Web and through the hotel's local or toll-free number (if one is available). Always ask about special packages or corporate rates.

Hotel reviews have been condensed for this book. Please go to Fodors. com for full reviews of each property.

WHAT IT COSTS					
	¢	$	$$	$$$	$$$$
Hotels	Under $100	$100–$174	$175–$249	$250–$350	over $350

Price categories reflect the range between the least and most expensive standard double rooms in nonholiday high season, based on the European Plan (with no meals) unless otherwise noted. County and resort taxes (10%–12%) are extra.

HOTELS AND ACCOMMODATIONS

The following is a (very) select list of some of our favorite places to stay in Orlando inside and outside the theme parks.

MAGIC KINGDOM, ANIMAL KINGDOM, AND EPCOT RESORT AREAS

$
ANIMAL KINGDOM
☺
Fodor$Choice
★

All-Star Sports, All-Star Music, and All-Star Movies Resorts. Stay here if you want the quintessential Disney-with-your-kids experience, or if you're a couple that feels all that pitter-pattering of little feet is a reasonable tradeoff for a good deal on a room. **Pros:** unbeatable price for a Disney property. **Cons:** no kids' clubs or programs, possibly because this is on the bottom tier of Disney hotels in terms of room rates; distances between rooms and on-site amenities can seem vast. ☎ 407/939–5000 Sports, 407/939–6000 Music, 407/939–7000 Movies ✈ 1,700 rooms, 215 family suites at Music; 1,920 rooms at Movies and Sports ☽ In-room: safe, Internet. In-hotel: room service, bars, pools, laundry facilities, laundry service, Internet terminal ▭ AE, D, DC, MC, V.

$$$–$$$$
ANIMAL KINGDOM
Fodor$Choice
★

Animal Kingdom Lodge. Giraffes, zebras, and other wildlife roam three 11-acre savannas separated by the encircling arms of this grand hotel, designed to resemble a "kraal" or animal enclosure in Africa. **Pros:** extraordinary wildlife and cultural experiences; excellent on-site restaurants, Jiko, Boma, and Sanaa. **Cons:** shuttle to parks other than Animal Kingdom can take more than an hour; guided savanna tours available only to guests on the concierge level, where the least expensive room is $100 a night higher than the least expensive rooms in other parts of the hotel. ☎ 407/934–7639 ✈ 972 rooms, 499 suites or villas ☽ In-room: safe, Internet. In-hotel: 3 restaurants, bar, pools, gym, spa, children's programs (ages 4–12), laundry facilities, laundry service, Wi-Fi hotspot ▭ AE, D, DC, MC, V.

WHERE SHOULD WE STAY?

	VIBE	PROS	CONS
Disney	Thousands of rooms at every price; convenient to Disney parks; free transportation all over WDW complex.	Perks like early park entry, and Magical Express, which lets you circumvent airport bag checks.	Without a rental car, you likely won't leave Disney. On-site buses, while free, can take a big bite of time out of your entertainment day.
Universal	On-site hotels offer luxury and convenience. There are less expensive options just outside the gates.	Central to Disney, Universal, SeaWorld, malls, and I–4; free water taxis to parks from on-site hotels.	On-site hotels are pricey; expect heavy rush-hour traffic during drives to and from other parks.
I-Drive	A hotel, convention-center, and activities bonanza. A trolley runs from one end to the other.	Outlet malls provide bargains galore; diners enjoy world-class restaurants; it's central to parks; many hotels offer free shuttles.	Transportation can be pricey, in cash and in time, as traffic is often heavy. Crime is up, especially after dark, though area hotels and businesses have increased security.
Kissimmee	It's replete with mom 'n' pop motels and restaurants and places to buy saltwater taffy.	It's just outside Disney, very close to the Magic Kingdom. Lots of Old Florida charm.	Some motels here are a little seedy. Petty crime in which tourists are victims is rare—but not unheard-of.
Lake Buena Vista	Many hotel and restaurant chains here. Adjacent to WDW, which is where almost every guest in your hotel is headed.	Really close to WDW; plenty of dining and shopping options; easy access to I–4.	Heavy peak-hour traffic. As in all neighborhoods near Disney, a gallon of gas will cost 10%–15% more than elsewhere.
Central Orlando	Parts of town have the modern high-rises you'd expect. Other areas have oak-tree-lined brick streets winding among small, cypress-ringed lakes.	Lots of locally owned restaurants and some quaint B&Bs. City buses serve the parks. There's good access to I–4.	You'll need to rent a car. And you will be part of the traffic headed to WDW. Expect the 25-mi drive to take at least 45 minutes.
Orlando International Airport	Mostly business and flight-crew hotels and car-rental outlets.	Great if you have an early flight or just want to shop in a mall. There's even a Hyatt on-site.	Watching planes, buses, taxis, and cars arrive and depart is all the entertainment you'll get in.

$$
EPCOT
Fodor's Choice
★

🏨 **Coronado Springs Resort.** Because of its 95,000-square-foot convention center and the adjacent 60,000-square-foot ballroom, and moderate price, this is Disney's most popular convention hotel. **Pros:** great pool with a play area–arcade for kids and a bar for adults; lots of outdoor activities. **Cons:** some accommodations are a half-mile from the restaurants; standard rooms are on the small side; kids may find the subdued atmosphere boring. ☎ *407/939–1000* ⟿ *1,917 rooms* ⚭ *In-room: safe,*

Internet. In-hotel: 2 restaurants, room service, bar, pools, gym, spa, bicycles, laundry service, Wi-Fi hotspot ☰ *AE, D, DC, MC, V.*

$$$$ ▧ **Grand Floridian Resort & Spa**. Disney's flagship resort, with everything Fodor'sChoice from its best-appointed guest rooms to the high-quality hotel amenities, ★ such as a dock from which you can rent a boat or take the ferry across the adjoining lake. **Pros:** on the monorail route; Victoria & Albert's, the only AAA, five-diamond restaurant in Central Florida, is located here; if you're a couple with no kids, this can be among the least noisy of the on-property Disney hotels. **Cons:** some say it's not ritzy enough to match the room rates; conference center and convention clientele lend to the stuffiness. ☏ *407/824–3000* ⤳ *867 rooms, 90 suites* ⚿ *In-room: safe, Internet. In-hotel: 6 restaurants, bars, room service, tennis courts, pools, gym, spa, beachfront, children's programs (ages 4–12), laundry facilities, laundry service, Wi-Fi hotspot* ☰ *AE, D, DC, MC, V.*

OTHER ON-SITE HOTELS

¢–$ ▧ **Best Western Lake Buena Vista Resort**. A near-total face-lift during 2010 Fodor'sChoice gave this Best Western resort, just minutes away from Downtown Dis- ★ ney, a real boost. **Pros:** free Wi-Fi and parking, not to mention the price, makes this one of the best bargains on Hotel Row; close to Down- town Disney. **Cons:** inconvenient to Universal and downtown Orlando. ✉ *2000 Hotel Plaza Blvd., Lake Buena Vista* ☏ *407/828–2424 or 800/937–8376* ⊕ *www.lakebuenavistaresorthotel.com* ⤳ *325 rooms* ⚿ *In-room: Wi-Fi. In-hotel: 3 restaurants, room service, pools, gym, laundry facilities, laundry service, Wi-Fi hotspot* ☰ *AE, D, DC, MC, V.*

$$–$$$ ▧ **Walt Disney World Dolphin**. Outside, a pair of 56-foot-tall sea crea- tures bookend this 25-story glass pyramid designed by world-renowned architect Michael Graves. **Pros:** access to all facilities at the Walt Disney World Swan; easy walk or boat ride to BoardWalk and Epcot; good on- site restaurants. **Cons:** self-parking is $11 a day; a $10 a day "resort fee" covers Wi-Fi and Internet access, use of health club, and local phone calls; room-charge privileges stop at the front door, and don't extend to the Disney parks. ✉ *1500 Epcot Resorts Blvd., Lake Buena Vista* ☏ *407/934–4000 or 800/227–1500* ⊕ *www.swandolphin.com* ⤳ *1,509 rooms, 112 suites* ⚿ *In-room: safe, Internet. In-hotel: 9 restaurants, room service, bars, tennis courts, pools, gym, spa, beachfront, children's programs (ages 4–12), Wi-Fi hotspot* ☰ *AE, D, DC, MC, V.*

UNIVERSAL ORLANDO AREA

¢–$ ▧ **Doubletree Hotel at the Entrance to Universal Orlando**. This conveniently located hotel is a hotbed of business-trippers and pleasure-seekers thanks to a location right at the Universal Orlando entrance. **Pros:** within walking distance of Universal and area shops and restaurants; free shuttle to Universal. **Cons:** on a fast-lane tourist strip; need a rental car to reach Disney, I-Drive, or downtown Orlando; daily fee for Wi-Fi in room. ✉ *5780 Major Blvd., I–4 Exit 75B* ☏ *407/351–1000* ⊕ *www. doubltreeorlando.com* ⤳ *742 rooms, 15 suites* ⚿ *In-room: safe, Wi-Fi. In-hotel: restaurant, room service, pool, gym, laundry facilities, laundry service, Wi-Fi hotspot* ☰ *AE, D, DC, MC.*

$$$ ▧ **Portofino Bay Hotel**. The charm and romance of Portofino, Italy, are Fodor'sChoice conjured up at this lovely luxury resort by Loews. **Pros:** Italian villa ★ atmosphere; large spa; short walk or ferry ride to CityWalk, Universal

Studios, and Islands of Adventure; preferential treatment at Universal rides; you can charge meals and services (and use the pools) at the Hard Rock and the Royal Pacific Resort. **Cons:** rooms and meals are noticeably expensive; daily fee for in-room high-speed Internet or Wi-Fi, as well as for access to the fitness center. ✉ *5601 Universal Blvd., Universal Orlando* ☎ *407/503–1000 or 800/232–7827* ⊕ *www.universalorlando. com* ⇨ *699 rooms, 51 suites* ⚭ *In-room: safe, Internet, Wi-Fi. In-hotel: 3 restaurants, room service, bar, pools, gym, spa, children's programs (ages 4–14), laundry service, Wi-Fi hotspot, some pets allowed* ▤ *AE, D, DC, MC, V.*

ORLANDO METRO AREA

$$$–$$$$

Fodor'sChoice

★

Ritz-Carlton Orlando Grande Lakes. Orlando's first and only Ritz is a particularly extravagant link in the luxury chain; service is exemplary, from the fully attended porte-cochere entrance to the 18-hole golf course and 40-room spa. **Pros:** truly luxurious; impeccable service; great spa; golf course; shares amenities with Marriott. **Cons:** pricey; need a rental car to reach Disney and area shops and restaurants; $15.95 daily fee for Wi-Fi. ✉ *4012 Central Florida Pkwy., Orlando* ☎ *407/206–2400 or 800/576–5760* ⊕ *www.grandelakes.com* ⇨ *584 rooms, 64 suites* ⚭ *In-room: Wi-Fi. In-hotel: 6 restaurants, room service, bars, golf course, pool, gym, spa, children's programs (ages 5–12), laundry service, Wi-Fi hotspot* ▤ *AE, D, DC, MC, V.*

$

Wyndham Orlando Resort. Two-story villas, palm trees, turquoise pools, and romantic lagoons evoke a Caribbean getaway. **Pros:** convenient to Universal, SeaWorld, I-Drive, and outlet malls. **Cons:** $10 daily Internet fee; no free shuttle to Disney, which is about 30 minutes away. ✉ *8001 International Dr., I-Drive area, Orlando* ☎ *407/351–2420 or 800/996–3426* ⊕ *www.wyndham.com* ⇨ *1,052 rooms* ⚭ *In-room: safe, refrigerator, Internet. In-hotel: 3 restaurants, room service, pools, gym, spa, laundry service, Wi-Fi hotspot, some pets allowed* ▤ *AE, D, DC, MC, V.*

CELEBRATION AND LAKE BUENA VISTA

$–$$

CELEBRATION

Fodor'sChoice

★

Mona Lisa Suite Hotel. Much like a European boutique hotel in style, the Mona Lisa is very human in scale, and crisply minimalist in decor. **Pros:** free shuttle to downtown Celebration and all the theme parks; golf privileges at Celebration Golf; spa privileges at Celebration Day Spa; concierge service. **Cons:** busy U.S. 192 is close by; $12-a-day resort fee; if you want to go anywhere besides Celebration and the parks, you'll need a car. ✉ *225 Celebration Pl., Celebration* ☎ *866/404–6662 or 407/964–7000* ⊕ *www.monalisasuitehotel.com* ⇨ *240 suites: 93 1-bedroom, 147 2-bedroom* ⚭ *In-room: safe, kitchen, Wi-Fi. In-hotel: 2 restaurants, room service, bar, pool, Wi-Fi hotspot, parking (paid)* ▤ *AE, D, DC, MC, V.*

$$–$$$

☾

LAKE BUENA

VISTA

Fodor'sChoice

★

Nickelodeon Resort. The Nickelodeon theme extends everywhere, from the suites, where separate kids' rooms have bunk beds and SpongeBob wall murals, to the two giant water-park pools. **Pros:** extremely kid-friendly; free Disney, Universal Orlando, and SeaWorld shuttles; massive discounts (up to 50% off standard rates) for active-duty military; you can save about $20 on a room a night with memberships like

AAA and AARP; mini-golf course. **Cons:** not within walking distance of Disney or Downtown Disney; may be too frenetic for folks without kids. ✉ *14500 Continental Gateway, Orlando* ☎ *407/387–5437 or 866/462–6425* ⊕ *www.nickhotels.com* ➫ *777 suites* ⚬ *In-room: safe, kitchen (some), refrigerator, Internet. In-hotel: 7 restaurants, room service, pools, gym, children's programs (ages 4–12), laundry facilities, laundry service, Wi-Fi hotspot* ═ *AE, D, DC, MC, V.*

$$$–$$$$
LAKE BUENA
VISTA
Fodor'sChoice
★

▦ **Waldorf Astoria Orlando.** The Waldorf Orlando echoes the famed New York Waldorf with imagination and flair, from the clock under the dome in the center of the circular lobby to tiny, black-and-white accent tiles on the floors of the guest rooms. **Pros:** a lavish and luxurious hotel, spa, and golf resort, next to Disney. **Cons:** if you can bear to leave the cabana you'll need a car to see anything else in the area. ✉ *14200 Bonnet Creek Resort La., Orlando* ☎ *407/597–5500* ⊕ *www. waldorfastoriaorlando.com* ➫ *328 rooms, 169 suites* ⚬ *In-room: safe, Internet. In-hotel: 5 restaurants, room service, bars, golf course, pool, gym, spa, children's programs (ages 4–12), laundry service, Wi-Fi hotspot* ═ *AE, D, DC, MC, V.*

Miami and
Miami Beach

WORD OF MOUTH

"South beach is perfect.plenty of shopping, beautiful beach.great
restaurants, lots of fun."

—flep

WELCOME TO MIAMI AND MIAMI BEACH

TOP REASONS TO GO

★ **The Beach:** Miami Beach has been rated as one of the 10 best in the world. White sand, warm water, and bronzed bodies everywhere provide just the right mix of relaxation and people-gazing.

★ **Dining delights:** Miami's eclectic residents have transformed the city into a museum of epicurean wonders, ranging from Cuban and Argentine fare to fusion haute cuisine.

★ **Wee-hour parties:** A 24-hour liquor license means clubs stay open until 5 am, and after-parties go until noon the following day.

★ **Picture-perfect people:** Miami is a watering hole for the vain and beauti-ful of South America, Europe, and the Northeast. Watch them—or join them—as they strut their stuff on Lincoln Road, chow down in style at the Forge, and flaunt their tans on the white beds of the Shore Club hotel.

★ **Art deco district:** Candy colors and neon as far as the eye can see will put a lift in your step.

1 Downtown Miami. Weave through the glass-and-steel labyrinth of new condo construction to catch a Miami Heat game at the American Airlines Arena or a ballet at the spaceship-like Adrienne Arsht Center for the Performing Arts. To the far north is Little Haiti. To the southwest is Little Havana.

2 South Beach. People-watch from sidewalk cafés along Ocean Drive, lounge poolside at posh Collins Avenue hotels, and party 'til dawn at the nation's hottest clubs.

3 Coral Gables. Dine and shop on family-friendly Miracle Mile, and take a driving tour of the Mediterranean-style mansions in the surrounding neighborhoods.

4 Coconut Grove. Catch dinner and a movie and listen to live music at Coco Walk, or cruise the bohemian shops and locals' bars in this hip neighborhood.

5 Key Biscayne. Pristine parks and tranquillity make this upscale enclave a total antithesis to the South Beach party.

GETTING ORIENTED

Long considered the gateway to Latin America, Miami is as close to Cuba and the Caribbean as you can get within the United States. The 36-square-mi city is located at the southern tip of the Florida peninsula, bordered on the east by Biscayne Bay. Over the bay lies a series of barrier islands, the largest being a thin 18-square-mi strip called Miami Beach. To the east of Miami Beach is the Atlantic Ocean. To the south are the Florida Keys.

10

Think of Miami as a teenager: a young beauty with growing pains, cocky yet confused, quick to embrace the latest fads, exasperating yet lovable. This analogy may help you understand how best to tackle this imperfect paradise.

As cities go, Miami and Miami Beach really are young. Just a little more than 100 years ago, Miami was mosquito-infested swampland, with an Indian trading post on the Miami River. Then hotel builder Henry Flagler brought his railroad to the outpost known as Fort Dallas. Other visionaries—Carl Fisher, Julia Tuttle, William Brickell, and John Sewell, among others—set out to tame the unruly wilderness. Hotels were erected, bridges were built, the port was dredged, and electricity arrived. The narrow strip of mangrove coast was transformed into Miami Beach—and the tourists started to come.

Greater Miami is many destinations in one. At its best it offers an unparalleled multicultural experience: melodic Latin and Caribbean tongues, international cuisines and cultural events, and an unmistakable joie de vivre—all against a beautiful beach backdrop. In Little Havana the air is tantalizing with the perfume of strong Cuban coffee. In Coconut Grove, Caribbean steel drums ring out during the Miami/Bahamas Goombay Festival. Anytime in colorful Miami Beach restless crowds wait for entry to the hottest new clubs.

Miami, on the mainland, is South Florida's commercial hub. Miami Beach, on 17 islands in Biscayne Bay, is sometimes considered America's Riviera, luring refugees from winter with its warm sunshine; sandy beaches; graceful, shady palms; and tireless nightlife. The natives know well that there's more to Greater Miami than the bustle of South Beach and its Art Deco district. In addition to well-known places such as Coconut Grove and Bayside, the less reported spots—like the Museum of Contemporary Art in North Miami, the burgeoning Design District in Miami, and the mangrove swamps of Matheson Hammock Park in Coral Gables—are great insider destinations.

PLANNING

WHEN TO GO

Miami and Miami Beach are year-round destinations. Most visitors come October through April, when the weather is close to perfect; hotels, restaurants, and attractions are busiest; and each weekend holds a festival or event. "Season" kicks off in December with Art Basel Miami Beach, and hotel rates don't come down until after the college kids have left from spring break.

It's hot and steamy from May through September, but nighttime temperatures are usually pleasant. Also, summer is a good time for the budget traveler. Many hotels lower their rates considerably, and many restaurants offer discounts—especially during **Miami Spice** in August, when slews of top restaurants offer special tasting menus at a steep discount (sometimes Spice runs for two months, check ⊕ *www.iLoveMiamiSpice. com* for details).

GETTING HERE AND AROUND

AIR TRAVEL

Miami is serviced by Miami International Airport (MIA) near downtown and Fort Lauderdale-Hollywood International Airport (FLL) 18 mi north. Many discount carriers, like Spirit Airlines, Southwest Airlines, and AirTran fly into FLL, making it a smart bargain if you are renting a car. Otherwise, look for flights to MIA on American Airlines, Delta, and Continental. MIA is undergoing extensive renovations that are expected to conclude in the summer of 2011; delays and long walks to gates are a common occurrence.

CAR TRAVEL

Interstate 95 is the major expressway connecting South Florida with points north; State Road 836 is the major east–west expressway and connects to Florida's Turnpike, State Road 826, and Interstate 95. Seven causeways link Miami and Miami Beach, Interstate 195 and Interstate 395 offering the most convenient routes; the Rickenbacker Causeway extends to Key Biscayne from Interstate 95 and U.S. 1. **Remember U.S. 1 (aka Biscayne Boulevard)**—you'll hear it often in directions. It starts in Key West, hugs South Florida's coastline, and heads north straight through to Maine. You'll need a car to visit many attractions.

10

PUBLIC TRANSIT

Some sights are accessible via the public transportation system, run by the **Metro-Dade Transit Agency** (☎ *305/770–3131* ⊕ *www.miamidade. gov/transit*), which maintains 800 Metrobuses on 90 routes; the 22-mi Metrorail elevated rapid-transit system; and Metromover, an elevated light-rail system that serves the downtown Miami area.

Passengers can purchase an EASY Card or an EASY Ticket at all Metrorail stations, Miami International Airport, and select sales outlets throughout the County. The EASY Card, which can be reloaded and used up to three years, can be loaded with a monthly, weekly, or daily pass, or with monetary value of up to $150. The EASY Ticket, which can be reloaded and used up to 60 days, can be loaded with a weekly or daily pass or with monetary value of up to $40. Riders need a loaded EASY Card or EASY Ticket to ride the Metrorail system.

Stops for the **Metrobus** are marked with blue-and-green signs that have route information. Regular bus fare is $2 (exact change only); bus-to-bus transfers are free when using an EASY Card or EASY Ticket. Fare for express buses is $2.35. Transfers from Metrobus to Metrorail are 50¢ when using an EASY Card or EASY Ticket.

The elevated **Metrorail** trains run from downtown Miami north to Hialeah and neighboring cities, and south along U.S. 1 to Dadeland in the Kendall area. The system operates daily 5 am–midnight and the fare is $2. **Metromover,** which resembles an airport shuttle, serves the downtown Miami area, links major hotels, office buildings, and shopping areas. There is no fee to ride.

Tri-Rail (☎ 800/874–7245 ⊕ *www.tri-rail.com*), South Florida's commuter-train system, offers shuttle service to and from MIA from 3797 N.W. 21st Street. Tri-Rail stops at 18 stations along a 72-mi route. Prices range from $2.50 to $11.55 for a round-trip ticket.

VISITOR INFORMATION

For additional information about Miami and Miami Beach, contact the city's visitors bureaus: **Greater Miami Convention & Visitors Bureau** (⊠ *701 Brickell Ave., Suite 2700, Miami* ☎ *305/539–3000, 800/933–8448 in U.S.* ⊕ *www.miamiandbeaches.com*). **Miami Beach Chamber of Commerce & Visitors Center** (⊠ *1920 Meridian Ave., Miami Beach* ☎ *305/674–1300 or 800/666–4519* ⊕ *www.miamibeachchamber.com*)

EXPLORING MIAMI AND MIAMI BEACH

If you had arrived here 40 years ago with a guidebook in hand, chances are you'd be thumbing through listings looking for alligator wrestlers and you-pick strawberry fields or citrus groves. Things have changed. While Disney sidetracked families in Orlando, Miami was developing a unique culture and attitude that's equal parts beach town/big business, Latino/Caribbean meets European/American—all of which fuels a great art and food scene, as well as an exuberant nightlife and myriad festivals.

DOWNTOWN MIAMI

Downtown Miami dazzles from a distance. The skyline is fluid, thanks to the sheer number of sparkling glass high-rises between Biscayne Boulevard and the Miami River. Business is the key to downtown Miami's daytime bustle. Traffic congestion from the high-rise offices and expensive parking tend to keep the locals away, unless they're bringing out-of-town guests to touristy Bayside Marketplace. But change is in the air—the influx of condos and offices is bringing in shops and restaurants, most notably Mary Brickell Village, which serves as a culinary oasis for the starved business district. Thanks to the free Metromover, which runs inner and outer loops through downtown and to nearby neighborhoods to the south and north, this is an excellent tour to take by rail.

☺ ★ **Miami-Dade Cultural Center.** Containing three cultural resources, this fortress-like 3-acre complex is a downtown focal point. The **Miami Art Museum** (☎ *305/375–3000* ⊕ *www.miamiartmuseum.org* ☎ *$8, free for families every 2nd Sat.* ☉ *Tues.–Fri. 10–5, weekends noon–5*) is waiting to move into its new 120,000-square-foot home in Museum Park, which is to be completed in 2013. Meanwhile, the museum presents major touring exhibitions of work by international artists, with an emphasis on art since 1945. Every second Saturday entrance is free for families. Discover a treasure trove of colorful stories about the region's history at **HistoryMiami** (☎ *305/375–1492* ⊕ *www.historymiami.org* ☎ *$8 museum, $10 combo ticket art and history museums* ☉ *Tues.– Fri. 10–5, weekends noon–5*). Exhibits celebrate Miami's multicultural heritage, including an old Miami streetcar, and unique items chronicling the migration of Cubans to Miami. The **Main Public Library** (☎ *305/375–2665* ⊕ *www.mdpls.org* ☎ *Free* ☉ *Mon.–Wed., Fri., and Sat. 9–6, Thurs. 9–9, Sun. 1–5*) contains nearly 4 million holdings and a Florida Department that includes rare books, documents, and photographs recording Miami history. It also has art exhibits in the auditorium and in the second-floor lobby. ⊠ *101 W. Flagler St., between N.W. 1st and 2nd Aves., Downtown.*

★ **Wynwood Art District.** Just north of downtown Miami, the up-and-coming Wynwood Art District is peppered with galleries, art studios, and private collections accessible to the public. Visit during Wynwood's monthly gallery walk on the second Saturday evening of each month when studios and galleries are all open at the same time. Make sure a visit includes a stop at the **Margulies Collection at the Warehouse** (⊠ *591 N.W. 27th St., between NW 5th and 6th Aves., Downtown* ☎ *305/576–1051* ⊕ *www.margulieswarehouse.com*). Martin Margulies's collection of vintage and contemporary photography, videos, sculpture, painting, and installation art in a 45,000-square-foot space makes for eye-popping viewing. Entrance fee is a $10 donation, which goes to a local homeless shelter for women and children. It's open October to April, Wednesday to Saturday 11–4. Fans of edgy art will appreciate the **Rubell Family Collection** (⊠ *95 N.W. 29th St., between N. Miami Ave. and N.W. 1st Ave., Downtown* ☎ *305/573–6090* ⊕ *www. rfc.museum*). Mera and Don Rubell have accumulated work by artists from the 1970s to the present, including Jeff Koons, Cindy Sherman, Damien Hirst, and Keith Haring. Admission is $10, and the gallery is open Tuesday to Saturday 10–6.

LITTLE HAVANA

First settled en masse by Cubans in the early 1960s, after that country's Communist revolution, Little Havana is a predominantly working-class area and the core of Miami's Hispanic community. Spanish is the language that predominates, but don't be surprised if the cadence is less Cuban and more Salvadoran or Nicaraguan: the neighborhood is now home to people from all Latin American countries. Make sure to try the thimble-size cups of liquid energy (aka *café cubano*) that are passed

Playing dominoes is a favorite pastime at Maximo Gomez Park in Little Havana.

through the open windows of coffee shops. Small galleries showcasing modern art jostle up next to mom-and-pop food shops and high-end Cuban clothes and crafts. At Domino Park (officially Maximo Gomez Park), guayabera-clad seniors bask in the sun and play dominoes, while at corner bodegas and coffee shops (particularly Versailles) regulars share neighborhood gossip and political opinions.

MIAMI BEACH

The hub of Miami Beach is South Beach, with its energetic Ocean Drive. Here, life unfolds 24 hours a day. Beautiful people pose in hotel lounges and sidewalk cafés, tanned cyclists zoom past palm trees, and visitors flock to see the action. On Lincoln Road, café crowds spill onto the sidewalks, weekend markets draw all kinds of visitors and their dogs, and thanks to a few late-night lounges the scene is just as alive at night.

Quieter areas to the north on Collins Avenue are Surfside (from 88th to 96th streets), fashionable Bal Harbour (beginning at 96th Street), and Sunny Isles (between 157th and 197th streets). If you're interested in these areas and you're flying in, the Fort Lauderdale airport might be a better choice.

WHAT TO SEE

★ **Holocaust Memorial.** A bronze sculpture depicts refugees clinging to a giant bronze arm that reaches out of the ground and 42 feet into the air. Enter the surrounding courtyard to see a memorial wall and hear the music that seems to give voice to the 6 million Jews who died at the hands of the Nazis. It's easy to understand why Kenneth

Treister's dramatic memorial is in Miami Beach: the city's community of Holocaust survivors was once the second largest in the country. ✉ *1933–1945 Meridian Ave., at Dade Blvd.* ☎ *305/538–1663* ⊕ *www. holocaustmmb.org* ✉ *Free (donations welcome)* ⊙ *Daily 9–6.*

☼ **Lincoln Road Mall.** A playful 1990s redesign spruced up this open-air
Fodor's Choice pedestrian mall, adding a grove of 20 towering date palms, five linear
★ pools, and colorful broken-tile mosaics to the once-futuristic 1950s vision of Fontainebleau designer Morris Lapidus. Some of the shops are owner-operated boutiques with a delightful variety of clothing, furnishings, jewelry, and decorative design. Others are the typical chain stores of American malls. Remnants of tired old Lincoln Road—beauty supply and discount electronics stores on the Collins end of the strip—somehow fit nicely into the mix. The new Lincoln Road is fun, lively, and friendly for people old, young, gay, and straight—and their dogs. Folks skate, scoot, bike, or jog here. The best times to hit the road are during Sunday morning farmers' markets and on weekend evenings, when cafés bustle, art galleries open shows, street performers make the sidewalk their stage, and stores stay open late. ✉ *Lincoln Rd., between Collins Ave. and Alton Rd.*

CORAL GABLES

You can easily spot Coral Gables from the window of a Miami-bound jetliner—just look for the massive orange tower of the Biltmore Hotel rising from a lush green carpet of trees concealing the city's gracious homes. The canopy is as much a part of this planned city as its distinctive architecture, all attributed to the vision of George E. Merrick nearly 100 years ago.

The story of this city began in 1911, when Merrick inherited 1,600 acres of citrus and avocado groves from his father. Through judicious investment he nearly doubled the tract to 3,000 acres by 1921. Merrick dreamed of building an American Venice here, complete with canals and homes. Working from this vision, he began designing a city based on centuries-old prototypes from Mediterranean countries. Unfortunately for Merrick, the devastating no-name hurricane of 1926, followed by the Great Depression, prevented him from fulfilling many of his plans. He died at 54, an employee of the post office. Today Coral Gables has a population of about 43,000. In its bustling downtown, more than 150 multinational companies maintain headquarters or regional offices, and the University of Miami campus in the southern part of the Gables brings a youthful vibrancy to the area. A southern branch of the city extends down the shore of Biscayne Bay through neighborhoods threaded with canals. The gorgeous Fairchild Tropical Botanic Garden and beachfront Matheson Hammock Park dominate this part of the Gables.

WHAT TO SEE

☼ **Fairchild Tropical Botanic Garden.** With 83 acres of lakes, sunken gardens,
Fodor's Choice a 560-foot vine pergola, orchids, bellflowers, coral trees, bougainvillea,
★ rare palms, and flowering trees, Fairchild is the largest tropical botanical garden in the continental United States. The tram tour highlights

the best of South Florida's flora; then you can set off exploring on your own. A 2-acre rain-forest exhibit showcases tropical plants from around the world complete with a waterfall and stream. The conservatory, Windows to the Tropics, is home to rare tropical plants, including the Titan Arum (*Amorphophallus titanum*), a fast-growing variety that attracted thousands of visitors when it bloomed in 1998. (It was only the sixth documented bloom in this country in the 20th century.) The Keys Coastal Habitat, created in a marsh and mangrove area in 1995 with assistance from the Tropical Audubon Society, provides food and shelter to resident and migratory birds. Spicing up Fairchild's calendar are plant sales, afternoon teas, and genuinely special events year-round, such as outdoor art exhibitions and the International Mango Festival the second weekend in July. The excellent bookstore–gift shop carries books on gardening and horticulture, and the Garden Café serves sandwiches and, seasonally, smoothies made from the garden's own crop of tropical fruits. ⊠ *10901 Old Cutler Rd., Coral Gables* ☎ *305/667–1651* ⊕ *www.fairchildgarden.org* ⌦ *$25* ⊙ *Daily 9:30–4:30.*

Fodor's Choice ★

Venetian Pool. Sculpted from a rock quarry in 1923 and fed by artesian wells, this 825,000-gallon municipal pool completed a major face-lift in 2010. It remains quite popular because of its themed architecture— a fantasy version of a waterfront Italian village—created by Denman Fink. The pool has earned a place on the National Register of Historic Places and showcases a nice collection of vintage photos depicting 1920s beauty pageants and swank soirees held long ago. Paul Whiteman played here, Johnny Weissmuller and Esther Williams swam here, and you should, too (but no kids under 3). A snack bar, lockers, and showers make this must-see user-friendly as well. ⊠ *2701 De Soto Blvd., Coral Gables* ☎ *305/460–5306* ⊕ *www.gablesrecreation.com* ⌦ *$11 adults, free parking across De Soto Blvd.* ⊙ *June–Aug., weekdays 11–7:30, weekends 10–4:30; Sept., Oct., Apr., and May, Tues.–Fri. 11–5:30, weekends 10–4:30; Nov.–Mar., Tues.–Sun. 10–4:30.*

COCONUT GROVE

10

Eclectic and intriguing, Miami's Coconut Grove can be considered the tropical equivalent of New York's Greenwich Village. A haven for writers and artists, the neighborhood has never quite outgrown its image as a small village. During the day it's business as usual in Coconut Grove, much as in any other Miami neighborhood. But in the evening, especially on weekends, it seems as if someone flips a switch and the streets come alive. Locals and tourists jam into small boutiques, sidewalk cafés, and stores lodged in two massive retail-entertainment complexes. For blocks in every direction, students, honeymooning couples, families, and prosperous retirees flow in and out of a mix of galleries, restaurants, bars, bookstores, comedy clubs, and theaters. With this weekly influx of traffic, parking can pose a problem. There's a well-lighted city garage at 3315 Rice Street, or look for police to direct you to parking lots where you'll pay $5–$10 for an evening's slot. If you're staying in the Grove, leave the car behind, and your night will get off to an easier start.

Nighttime is the right time to see Coconut Grove, but in the day you can take a casual drive around the neighborhood to see its diverse architecture. Posh estates mingle with rustic cottages, modest frame homes, and stark modern dwellings, often on the same block. If you're into horticulture, you'll be impressed by the Garden of Eden–like foliage that seems to grow everywhere without care.

WHAT TO SEE

Fodor's Choice ★ **Vizcaya Museum and Gardens.** Of the 10,000 people living in Miami between 1912 and 1916, about 1,000 of them were gainfully employed by Chicago industrialist James Deering to build this European-inspired residence. Once comprising 180 acres, this national historic landmark now occupies a 50-acre tract that includes a native hammock and more than 10 acres of formal gardens with fountains overlooking Biscayne Bay. The house, open to the public, contains 70 rooms, 34 of which are filled with paintings, sculpture, antique furniture, and other fine and decorative arts. The collection spans 2,000 years and represents the Renaissance, baroque, rococo, and neoclassical periods. So unusual and impressive is Vizcaya that visitors have included many major heads of state. Guided and audio tours are available. Moonlight tours, offered from January through April on evenings that are nearest the full moon, provide a magical look at the gardens. Check Web site for dates. ✉ *3251 S. Miami Ave.* ☎ *305/250–9133* ⊕ *www.vizcayamuseum.org* 💲 *$15* 🕐 *Sun. and Mon. 9:30–4:30.*

KEY BISCAYNE AND VIRGINIA KEY

Once upon a time, these barrier islands were an outpost for fishermen and sailors, pirates and salvagers, soldiers and settlers. The 95-foot Cape Florida Lighthouse stood tall during Seminole Indian battles and hurricanes. Coconut plantations covered two-thirds of Key Biscayne, and there were plans as far back as the 1800s to develop the picturesque island as a resort for the wealthy. Fortunately, the state and county governments set much of the land aside for parks, and both keys are now home to top-ranked beaches and golf, tennis, softball, and picnicking facilities. The long and winding bike paths that run through the islands are favorites for in-line skaters and cyclists. Incorporated in 1991, the village of Key Biscayne is a hospitable community of about 10,500; Virginia Key remains undeveloped at the moment, making these two playground islands especially family-friendly.

WHERE TO EAT

Miami's restaurant scene has exploded in the last few years, with dozens of great new restaurants springing up left and right. The melting pot of residents and visitors has brought an array of sophisticated, tasty cuisine. Little Havana is still king for Cuban fare, while Miami Beach is swept up in a trend of fusion cuisine, which combines Asian, French, American, and Latin cuisine with sumptuous—and pricey—results. Downtown Miami and the Design District especially are home to some of the city's best spots, and they're all new. Since Miami dining is a part of the trendy nightlife scene, most dinners don't start until 8 or 9 pm, and may go well into the night. Hot spots fill up quickly, so come before 7 or make reservations. Attire is usually casual-chic, but patrons like to dress to impress. Prices tend to stay high in hot spots like Lincoln Road; but if you venture off the beaten path, you can find delicious food for reasonable prices. When you get your bill, check whether a gratuity is already included; most restaurants add between 15% and 18% (ostensibly for the convenience of, and protection from, the many Latin American and European tourists who are used to this practice in their homelands), but supplement it depending on your opinion of the service.

WHAT IT COSTS

	¢	$	$$	$$$	$$$$
Restaurants	under $10	$10–$15	$15–$20	$20–$30	over $30

Price per person for a median main course or equivalent combination of smaller dishes.

CORAL GABLES

$$$$
CARIBBEAN

✕ **Ortanique on the Mile.** Cascading ortaniques, a Jamaican hybrid orange, are hand-painted on columns in this warm, welcoming yellow dining room. Food is vibrant in taste and color, as delicious as it is beautiful. Though there is no denying that the strong, full flavors are imbued with island breezes, chef-partner Cindy Hutson's personal cuisine goes beyond Caribbean refinements. The menu centers on fish, since Hutson has a special way with it, and the Caribbean bouillabaisse is not to be missed. ⊠ *278 Miracle Mile* ☎ *305/446–7710* ⊕ *www. cindyhutsoncuisine.com* ▭ *AE, DC, MC, V* ⊙ *No lunch weekends.*

¢
CUBAN
Fodor'sChoice
★

✕ **Palacio de los Jugos.** This joint is one of the easiest and truest ways to see Miami's local Latin life in action. It's also one of the best fruit-shake shacks you'll ever come across (ask for a juice of—"*jugo de*"— mamey, melón, or guanabana, a sweet-tart equatorial fruit, and you can't go wrong). Besides the rows and rows of fresh tropical fruits and vegetables, and the shakes you can make with any of them, this boisterous indoor-outdoor market has numerous food counters where you can get just about any Cuban food—tamales, rice and beans, a *pan con lechón* (roast pork on Cuban bread), fried pork rinds, or a coconut split before you and served with a straw. Order your food at a counter and eat it along with local families at rows of outdoor picnic-style tables next to the parking lot. It's disorganized, chaotic, and not for those cutting calories, but it's delicious and undeniably the real thing. ⊠ *5721 W. Flagler St.* ☎ *305/264–8662* ⊕ *www.elpalaciodelosjugosonline.com* ▭ *No credit cards.*

MIAMI

DESIGN DISTRICT

$$
ITALIAN
Fodor'sChoice
★

✕ **Joey's.** This joyfully good and merrily buzzing new place is literally the only restaurant in Wynwood, an emerging neighborhood to the south of the Design District. But this new restaurant already has that rarest of blessings—the sizzling vibe of a thriving neighborhood restaurant that everyone seems to adore. Its contagious charm begins with the

10

service: informal, but focused, very professional, and attentive. Then comes the food: Veneto native chef Ivo Mazzon does homage to fresh ingredients prepared simply and perfectly. A full line of original flatbread pizzas contend for tops in Miami. The *dolce e piccante* has figs, Gorgonzola, honey, and hot pepper; it's unexpectedly sweet at first bite, and at bite 10 you'll be swearing it's the best you've ever had. ⊠ *2506 N.W. 2 Ave., Design District* ☎ *305/438–0488* ⊕ *www.joeyswynwood. com* ⊟ *AE, D, MC, V.*

$$$
AMERICAN
Fodor'sChoice
★

✕ **Michael's Genuine Food & Drink.** This indoor-outdoor bistro in Miami's Design District relies on fresh ingredients and a hip but unpretentious vibe to lure diners. Beautifully arranged combinations like sweet-and-spicy pork belly with kimchi explode with unlikely but satisfying flavor. Owner and chef Michael Schwartz, famous for South Beach's popular Nemo restaurant, aims for sophisticated American cuisine with an emphasis on local and organic ingredients. He gets it right. Portions are divided into small, medium, large and extra large plates, and the smaller plates are more inventive, so you can order several and explore. Reserve two weeks in advance for weekend tables; also, consider brunch. ⊠ *130 N.E. 40th St., Design District* ☎ *305/573–5550* ⊕ *www.michaelsgenuine.com* ⊟ *AE, MC, V* ⊗ *No lunch weekends.*

$$$
MEDITERRANEAN
Fodor'sChoice
★

✕ **Michy's.** Miami's homegrown star chef Michelle Bernstein made a huge splash with the shabby-chic decor and self-named restaurant on the north end of Miami's Design District. Bernstein serves exquisite French- and Mediterranean-influenced seafood dishes at over-the-causeway (read: non-tourist-trap) prices. Plates come in half portions and full portions, which makes the restaurant even more of a deal. Can't-miss entrées include the blue cheese and *jamón serrano* (serrano ham) *croquetas*, the beef short rib, and the steak frites au poivre. ⊠ *6927 Biscayne Blvd., Design District* ☎ *305/759–2001* ⊕ *www.michysmiami. com* ⊟ *AE, D, DC, MC, V* ⊗ *Closed Mon. No lunch.*

$$
SPANISH
Fodor'sChoice
★

✕ **Sra. Martinez.** For a good time with food, dial up Sra. Martinez. Michelle Bernstein's second restaurant (her first, Michy's, is a must-visit for Miami foodies) opened in December 2008; the name is a sly take on her name—her husband is David Martinez—which is good, because something as artful as this new restaurant deserves a signature. Bernstein anchors her menu at Sra. Martinez in Spanish cuisine, a brilliant jumping-off point for her wildly successful experiments in flavor, texture, and plate composition. The cuisine is modern, colorful and, above all, fun. Cocktail lovers will be delighted by the inventive, high-quality selections like the Jalisco Mule, a sly (and spicy) take on the traditional Moscow Mule, made with tequila and ginger beer, and laced with chili syrup. It's no wonder this restaurant has already become one of the best and most exciting in the city. ⊠ *4000 N.E. 2 Ave., Design District* ☎ *305/573–5474* ⊕ *www.sramartinez.com* ⊟ *AE, D, DC, MC, V* ⊗ *No lunch Mon.–Sat.*

DOWNTOWN MIAMI

$$$$
ECLECTIC
Fodor'sChoice
★

✕ **Azul.** From chef Clay Conley's exotically rendered Asian-Mediterranean cuisine to the thoughtful service staff who graciously anticipate your broader dining needs, Azul has sumptuously conquered the devil in the details. Does your sleeveless blouse leave you too cold to properly appreciate the Moroccan lamb and seared red snapper? Forgot your reading glasses and can't decipher the hanger steak with foie-gras sauce? Request a pair from the host. A risotto with Alba white truffles is typical of the way Azul will reach across the globe for the finest ingredients. The Moroccan-inspired Colorado lamb with eggplant and harissa is a perennial favorite. There is a lot of new competition for dining attention in town, but Azul is still at the pinnacle of its game. ⊠ *Mandarin Oriental Hotel, 500 Brickell Key Dr., Downtown Miami* ☎ *305/913–8358* ✍ *Reservations essential* ⊟ *AE, MC, V* ☉ *Closed Sun. No lunch.*

LITTLE HAVANA

$

CUBAN

Fodor's Choice

★

✕ **Versailles.** *¡Bienvenido a Miami!* To the area's Cuban population, Miami without Versailles is like rice without black beans. The storied eatery, where old émigrés opine daily about all things Cuban, is a stop on every political candidate's campaign trail, and it should be a stop for you as well. Order a heaping platter of *lechon asado* (roasted pork loin), *ropa vieja* (shredded beef), or *picadillo* (spicy ground beef), all served with rice, beans, and fried plantains. Battle the oncoming food coma with a cup of the city's strongest cafecito, which comes in the tiniest of cups but packs a lot of punch. Versailles operates a bakery next door as well—take some pastelitos home. ⊠ *3555 S.W. 8th St., between S.W. 35th and S.W. 36th Aves., Little Havana* ☎ *305/444–0240* ⊟ *AE, D, DC, MC, V.*

MIAMI BEACH

$$$

ITALIAN

Fodor's Choice

★

✕ **Timó.** Located in a glorified strip mall 5 mi north of South Beach, Timo (Italian for "thyme") is worth the trip from anywhere in South Florida. It's a kind of locals' secret that it's the best food in South Florida. The handsome bistro, co-owned by chef Tim Andriola and Rodrigo Martinez (former general manager and wine director at Norman's), has dark-wood walls, Chicago brick, and a stone-encased wood-burning stove. Andriola has an affinity for robust Mediterranean flavors: inexpensive, artisanal pizzas; homemade pastas and a four-course tasting menu available with or without a wine pairing. Every bite of every dish attests to the care given, and the service is terrific. ⊠ *17624 Collins Ave., Sunny Isles* ☎ *305/936–1008* ⊕ *www.timorestaurant.com* ⊟ *AE, DC, MC, V* ☉ *No lunch weekends.*

SOUTH BEACH

$

AMERICAN

Fodor's Choice

★

✕ **Big Pink.** The decor in this innovative, super-popular diner may remind you of a roller-skating rink—everything is pink Lucite, stainless steel, and campy (think sports lockers as decorative touches)—and the menu is 3 feet tall, complete with a table of contents. Food is solidly all-American, with dozens of tasty sandwiches, pizzas, turkey or beef burgers, and side dishes, each and every one composed with gourmet flair. Big Pink also makes a great spot for brunch. ⊠ *157 Collins Ave., South Beach* ⊕ *www.mylesrestaurantgroup.com* ☎ *305/531–0888* ⊟ *AE, MC, V.*

10

WHERE TO STAY

Room rates in Miami tend to swing wildly. In high season, which is January through May, expect to pay at least $150 per night. In summer, however, prices can be as much as 50% lower than the dizzying winter rates. You can also find great values between Easter and Memorial Day, which is actually a delightful time in Miami.

Business travelers tend to stay in downtown Miami, while most tourists stay on Miami Beach, as close as possible to the water. If money isn't an object, stay in one of the glamorous hotels lining Collins Avenue between 15th and 21st streets. Otherwise, stay on the quiet beaches farther north, or in one of the small boutique hotels on Ocean Drive, Collins, or Washington avenues between 10th and 15th streets. Two important considerations that affect price are balcony and view. If you're willing to have a room without an ocean view, you can sometimes get a price much lower than the standard rate. Many hotels are aggressive with specials and change their rates hour to hour, so it's worth calling around.

Hotel reviews have been condensed for this book. Please go to Fodors. com for full reviews of each property.

WHAT IT COSTS					
	¢	$	$$	$$$	$$$$
Hotels	under $150	$150–$200	$200–$300	$300–$400	over $400

Prices for hotels are for two people in a standard double room in high season, excluding 12.5% city and resort taxes.

CORAL GABLES

$$$
Fodor'sChoice
★

Biltmore Hotel. Built in 1926, this landmark hotel has had several incarnations over the years—including a stint as a hospital during World War II—and has changed hands more than a few times. Through it all, this grandest of grandes dames remains an opulent reminder of yesteryear. **Pros:** historic property; possibly best pool in the Miami area; great tennis and golf. **Cons:** far from Miami Beach. ⊠ *1200 Anastasia Ave.* ☎ *305/445–1926 or 800/727–1926* ⊕ *www.biltmorehotel.com* ⮎ *241 rooms, 39 suites* ⚑ *In-room: a/c, Wi-Fi. In-hotel: 4 restaurants, room service, bars, golf course, tennis courts, pool, gym, spa, Wi-Fi hotspot, parking (paid)* ⊟ *AE, D, DC, MC, V.*

KEY BISCAYNE

$$$$
Fodor'sChoice
★

Ritz-Carlton, Key Biscayne. There is probably no other place in Miami where slowness is lifted to a fine art. On Key Biscayne there are no pressures, there's no nightlife (outside of the hotel's great live Latin music weekends), and the dining choices are essentially limited to the hotel (which has four dining options, including the languorous, Havana-style Rumbar). In this kind of setting, it's natural to appreciate the Ritz brand of pampering. **ros:** private beach; quiet, luxurious family retreat. **Cons:** it will be too quiet if you're looking for a party—so you have to drive to Miami for nightlife. ⊠ *455 Grand Bay Dr.* ☎ *305/365–4500 or 800/241–3333* ⊕ *www.ritzcarlton.com/keybiscayne* ⮎ *364 rooms,*

38 suites △ In-room: a/c, safe, DVD (some), Internet, Wi-Fi. In-hotel: 4 restaurants, room service, bars, tennis courts, pools, gym, spa, beachfront, water sports, bicycles, laundry service, Internet terminal, Wi-Fi hotspot, parking (paid), some pets allowed ⊟ AE, D, DC, MC, V.

DOWNTOWN MIAMI

$$$$
Fodor'sChoice
★

Four Seasons Hotel Miami. Stepping off busy Brickell Avenue into this hotel, you see a soothing water wall trickling down from above. Inside, a cavernous lobby is barely big enough to hold the enormous sculptures—part of the hotel's collection of local and Latin American artists. **Pros:** sensational service; amazing gym and pool deck. **Cons:** no balconies. ⊠ *1435 Brickell Ave., Downtown Miami* ☎ *305/358–3535 or 800/819–5053* ⊕ *www.fourseasons.com/miami* ⤳ *182 rooms, 39 suites △ In-room: a/c, safe. In-hotel: restaurant, bars, pools, gym, spa, Internet terminal, Wi-Fi hotspot, parking (paid)* ⊟ *AE, D, DC, MC, V.*

FISHER AND BELLE ISLANDS

$$$$
Fodor'sChoice
★

Fisher Island Hotel & Resort. Want to explore Fisher Island? Assuming you don't have a private yacht, there are three ways to gain access to the island just off South Beach: you can either become a club member (initiation fee alone: $25,000), be one of the 750 equity members who have vacation places here (starting price: $8 million), or book a night at the club hotel (basic villa: $900 a night). **Pros:** great private beaches; exclusive surroundings; varied dining choices. **Cons:** ferry rides take time. ⊠ *1 Fisher Island Dr., Fisher Island/Miami Beach* ☎ *305/535–6000 or 800/537–3708* ⊕ *www.fisherisland.com* ⤳ *4 junior suites, 50 condo units, 6 villas, 3 cottages △ In-room: a/c, safe, refrigerator, DVD, Wi-Fi. In-hotel: 7 restaurants, golf course, tennis courts, pools, gym, spa, beachfront, water sports, children's programs (ages 4–12), laundry service, Internet terminal, Wi-Fi hotspot, parking (free), some pets allowed* ⊟ *AE, D, DC, MC, V.*

MID-BEACH

¢–$
Fodor'sChoice
★

Circa 39 Hotel. This stylish budget boutique hotel pays attention to every detail and gets them all right. **Pros:** affordable; chic; intimate; beach chairs provided. **Cons:** not on the beach side of Collins Avenue. ⊠ *3900 Collins Ave., Mid-Beach* ☎ *305/538–4900* ⊕ *www.circa39.com* ⤳ *100 rooms △ In-room: a/c, safe, kitchen, refrigerator, Wi-Fi. In-hotel: restaurant, bar, pool, gym, parking (paid), some pets allowed* ⊟ *AE, D, DC, MC, V* ⑷ *CP.*

$$$
Fodor'sChoice
★

Fontainebleau. Look out, South Beach—Mid-Beach is back. When this classic property reopened in late 2008 it became Miami's biggest hotel—twice the size of the Loews, with more than 1,500 rooms; it became, indeed, the fruit of the most ambitious and expensive hotel-renovation project in the history of Greater Miami. **Pros:** historic design mixed with all-new facilities; fabulous pools. **Cons:** away from the South Beach pedestrian scene; too big to be intimate. ⊠ *4441 Collins Ave., Miami Beach* ☎ *305/538–2000 or 800/548–8886* ⊕ *www.fontainebleau.com* ⤳ *1,504 rooms △ In-room: a/c, safe, kitchen (some), refrigerator, DVD (some), Wi-Fi. In-hotel: 11 restaurants, bars, pools, gym, spa, water sports, laundry service, Internet terminal, Wi-Fi hotspot, parking (paid)* ⊟ *AE, D, DC, MC, V.*

10

SUNNY ISLES

$$$$
Fodor'sChoice
★

⊡ Acqualina Resort & Spa on the Beach. When it opened in 2006, this hotel raised the bar for luxury in Miami, and it stands as one of the city's best hotels. **ros:** in-room check-in; luxury amenities; huge spa. **Cons:** guests have to pay an extra $40 to use the steam room or sauna. ⊠ *17875 Collins Ave., Sunny Isles* ☎ *305/918–8000* ⊕ *www.acqualinaresort.com* ⤴ *54 rooms, 43 suites* ♨ *In-room: a/c, safe, refrigerator, Wi-Fi. In-hotel: 3 restaurants, room service, bars, pools, gym, spa, beachfront, water sports, children's programs (ages 5–12), laundry service, Internet terminal, Wi-Fi hotspot, parking (paid)* ▭ *AE, D, DC, MC, V.*

¢
Fodor'sChoice
★

⊡ Travelodge Monaco Beach Resort. The last of a dying breed, the Travelodge Monaco is a true find. Peek inside the courtyard and you'll see older men and women playing shuffleboard. **Pros:** steps to great beach; wholly unpretentious; bottom-dollar cost. **Cons:** older rooms; not service-oriented. ⊠ *17501 Collins Ave., Sunny Isles* ☎ *305/932–2100 or 800/227–9006* ⊕ *www.monacomiamibeachresort.com* ⤴ *110 rooms* ♨ *In-room: Wi-Fi, safe, kitchen (some), refrigerator. In-hotel: restaurant, pool, beachfront, Wi-Fi hotspot, parking (paid)* ▭ *AE, D, DC, MC, V.*

SOUTH BEACH

$$$$
Fodor'sChoice
★

⊡ Delano. The decor of this grand hotel is inspired by Lewis Carroll's Alice in Wonderland, and as you make your way from the sparse, busy, spacious lobby past cascading white curtains and through rooms dotted with strange, whimsical furniture pieces, you will feel like you are indeed falling down a rabbit hole. **Pros:** electrifying design; lounging among the beautiful and famous. **Cons:** crowded; scene-y; small rooms; expensive. ⊠ *1685 Collins Ave., Miami Beach* ☎ *305/672–2000 or 800/555–5001* ⊕ *www.delano-hotel.com* ⤴ *194 rooms, 24 suites* ♨ *In-room: a/c, safe, Wi-Fi. In-hotel: 2 restaurants, room service, bars, pool, gym, spa, beachfront, laundry service, Wi-Fi hotspot, parking (paid)* ▭ *AE, D, DC, MC, V.*

$$
Fodor'sChoice
★

⊡ National Hotel. This luxurious, beautiful hotel serves as a bastion of calm in the sea of white-on-white mod decor and raucous reveling usually reserved for the beachfront masterpieces lining Collins Avenue between 15th and 20th streets. **Pros:** stunning pool; perfect location. **Cons:** tower rooms aren't impressive; neighboring hotels can be noisy on the weekends. ⊠ *1677 Collins Ave., South Beach* ☎ *305/532–2311 or 800/327–8370* ⊕ *www.nationalhotel.com* ⤴ *143 rooms, 9 suites* ♨ *In-room: a/c, safe, DVD, Internet, Wi-Fi. In-hotel: 2 restaurants, room service, bars, pools, gym, beachfront, laundry service, Internet terminal, Wi-Fi hotspot, parking (paid), some pets allowed* ▭ *AE, DC, MC, V.*

$$$$
Fodor'sChoice
★

⊡ The Tides. The Tides is the best boutique hotel in Miami, and the classiest of the Ocean Drive art deco hotels. The exceptionally tactful personalized service makes every guest feel like a celebrity, and the hotel looks like no other in the city. **Pros:** superior service; great beach location; ocean views from all suites plus the terrace restaurant. **Cons:** tiny elevators. ⊠ *1220 Ocean Dr., South Beach* ☎ *305/604–5070 or 866/438–4337* ⊕ *www.thetideshotel.com* ⤴ *45 suites* ♨ *In-room:*

For locals, the beach scene is often incorporated into daily life, from getting exercise to walking the dog.

a/c, safe, Internet, Wi-Fi. In-hotel: restaurant, pool, gym, beachfront, laundry service, Wi-Fi hotspot, parking (paid) ⊟ *AE, D, DC, MC, V.*

$ ⊡ **Townhouse**. Though sandwiched between the Setai and the Shore ★ Club—two of the coolest hotels on the planet—the Townhouse doesn't try to act all dolled up: it's comfortable being the shabby-chic, light-hearted, relaxed, no-frills, fun hotel on South Beach. **Pros:** a great budget buy for the style-hungry. **Cons:** no pool; small rooms not designed for long stays. ⊠ *150 20th St., east of Collins Ave., South Beach* ☎ *305/534–3800 or 877/534–3800* ⊕ *www.townhousehotel.com* ➥ *69 rooms, 2 suites* ⅏ *In-room: a/c, safe, Internet, Wi-Fi. In-hotel: restaurant, room service, bar, bicycles, laundry service, Wi-Fi hotspot, parking (paid)* ⊟ *AE, D, DC, MC, V* ⍐ *CP.*

BEACHES

MIAMI BEACH

NORTH MIAMI BEACH

Oleta River State Park. Tucked away in North Miami Beach is a ready-made family getaway. Nature lovers will find it easy to embrace the 1,128 acres of subtropical beauty along Biscayne Bay. Swim in the calm bay waters and bicycle, canoe, kayak, and bask among egrets, manatees, bald eagles, and fiddler crabs. Dozens of picnic tables, along with 10 covered pavilions, dot the stunning natural habitat, which has recently been restored with red mangroves to revitalize the ecosystem and draw endangered birds, like the roseate spoonbill. There's a playground for tots, a mangrove island accessible only by boat, 15 mi of mountain-bike trails, a half-mile exercise track, concessions, and outdoor showers.

If you want to continue the nature adventure into the evening, then reserve an overnight stay in primitive (but still air-conditioned) cabins, which run $62.15 per night. For cabin reservations go to ⊕ *www. reserveamerica.com* or call ☎ *800/326–3521.* ⊠ *3400 NE 163rd St., North Miami Beach* ☎ *305/919–1846* ⊕ *www.floridastateparks.org/ oletariver* 🎫 *$2 per person on foot or bike; $4 for single-occupant vehicle; $6 per vehicle up to 8 people; $2 each additional. Free entrance if renting a cabin* ☉ *Daily 8–sunset.*

SOUTH BEACH
Fodor's Choice
★

The 10-block stretch of white sandy beach hugging the turquoise waters along **Ocean Drive**—from 5th to 15th streets—is one of the most popular in America, known for drawing unabashedly modelesque sunbathers and posers. The beaches crowd quickly on the weekends with a blend of European tourists, young hipsters, and sun-drenched locals offering Latin flavor. Separating the sand from the traffic of Ocean Drive is palm-fringed Lummus Park, with its volleyball nets and chickee huts (huts made of palmetto thatch over a cypress frame) for shade. The beach at 12th Street is popular with gays, a section often marked with rainbow flags. Locals hang out on 3rd Street beach, where they watch fit Brazilians play foot volley, a variation of volleyball that uses everything but the hands. Because much of South Beach leans toward skimpy sunning—women are often in G-strings and casually topless—many families prefer the tamer sections of Mid- and North Beach. Metered parking spots next to the ocean are a rare find. Instead, opt for a public garage a few blocks away and enjoy the people-watching as you walk to find your perfect spot on the sand. ⊠ *Ocean Dr., between 1st and 22nd Sts., Miami Beach* ☎ *305/673–7714.*

KEY BISCAYNE AND VIRGINIA KEY

Fodor's Choice
★

Bill Baggs Cape Florida State Park. The picturesque drive down to the southern tip of Key Biscayne is only a hint of the natural beauty you will find when exploring this 410-acre park. For swimmers, the beach here is frequently ranked among the top 10 in North America by the University of Maryland's esteemed sandman, Dr. Beach. Families often picnic here, choosing the shade under any of the 19 shelters. For active wanderers, explore the nature trails, try your hand at the fishing piers, or take a breezy bike ride along paths that offer breathtaking views of the bay and Miami's skyline. History buffs can enjoy guided tours of the Cape Florida Lighthouse, South Florida's oldest structure. ⊠ *1200 S. Crandon Blvd., Key Biscayne* ☎ *305/361–5811 or 305/361–8779* 🎫 *$2 per person on foot, bike, or bus; $8 per vehicle with 2 to 8 people* ☉ *Daily 8–sunset, lighthouse tours Thurs.–Mon. 10 and 1.*

☾
★

Crandon Park North Beach. The 3-mi sliver of beach paradise is dotted with palm trees to provide a respite from the steamy sun, until it's time to take a dip in the clear-blue waters. On weekends, be prepared for a long hike from your car to the beach. There are bathrooms, outdoor showers, plenty of picnic tables, and concession stands. The family-friendly park offers abundant options for kids who find it challenging to simply sit and build sand castles. There are marine-theme play sculptures, a dolphin-shaped spray fountain, an old-fashioned outdoor roller rink, and a restored carousel (it's open weekends and major holidays 10–5, until 6 in summer, and you get three rides for $2). ⊠ *6747*

Crandon Blvd., Key Biscayne ☎ *305/361–5421* ✉ *$5 per vehicle week-days, $6 weekends* ⏱ *Daily 8–sunset.*

SHOPPING

Miami teems with sophisticated shopping malls and the bustling avenues of commercial neighborhoods. But this is also a city of tiny boutiques tucked away on side streets—such as South Miami's Red, Bird, and Sunset roads intersection—and outdoor markets touting unusual and delicious wares. Stroll through Spanish-speaking neighborhoods where shops sell clothing, cigars, and other goods from all over Latin America. At an open-air flea-market stall, score an antique glass shaped like a palm tree and fill it with some fresh Jamaican ginger beer from the table next door. Or stop by your hotel gift shop and snap up an alligator magnet for your refrigerator, an ashtray made of seashells, or a bag of gumballs shaped like Florida oranges. Who can resist?

MALLS

People fly to Miami from all over the world just to shop, and the malls are high on their list of spending spots. Stop off at one or two of these climate-controlled temples to consumerism, many of which double as mega-entertainment centers, and you'll understand what makes Miami such a vibrant shopping destination.

Fodor's Choice ★ **Bal Harbour Shops**. Local and international shoppers flock to this swank collection of 100 high-end shops, boutiques, and department stores, which include such names as Christian Dior, Gucci, Hermès, Salvatore Ferragamo, Tiffany & Co., and Valentino. Many European designers open their first North American signature store at this outdoor, pedestrian-friendly mall, and many American designers open their first boutique outside of New York here. Restaurants and cafés, in tropical garden settings, overflow with style-conscious diners. People-watching at outdoor café Carpaccio is the best in town. ✉ *9700 Collins Ave., Bal Harbour* ☎ *305/866–0311* ⊕ *www.balharbourshops.com.*

Fodor's Choice ★ **Village of Merrick Park**. At this Mediterranean-style shopping and dining venue Neiman Marcus and Nordstrom anchor 115 specialty shops. Designers such as Etro, Tiffany & Co., Burberry, Carolina Herrera, and Gucci fulfill most high-fashion needs, and Brazilian contemporary-furniture designer Artefacto provides a taste of the haute-decor shopping options. International food venues like C'est Bon and a day spa, Elemis, offer further indulgences. ✉ *358 San Lorenzo Ave., Coral Gables* ☎ *305/529–0200* ⊕ *www.villageofmerrickpark.com.*

SHOPPING DISTRICTS

If you're over the climate-controlled slickness of shopping malls and can't face one more food-court "meal," you've got choices in Miami. Head out into the sunshine and shop the city streets, where you'll find big-name retailers and local boutiques alike. Take a break at a sidewalk

10

café to power up on some Cuban coffee or fresh-squeezed OJ and enjoy the tropical breezes.

DOWNTOWN MIAMI

★ Miami is synonymous with good design, and this visitor-friendly shopping district is an unprecedented melding of public space and the exclusive world of design. Covering a few city blocks around N.E. 2nd Avenue and N.E. 40th Street, the **Miami Design District** (⊕ *www. miamidesigndistrict.net*) contains more than 200 showrooms and galleries, including Kartell, Poliform, and Luminaire. This trendy neighborhood is also a hip place to dine. Unlike most showrooms, which are typically the beat of decorators alone, the Miami Design District's showrooms are open to the public and occupy windowed, street-level spaces. Bring your quarters, as all of the parking is on the street and metered.

MIAMI BEACH

★ Give your plastic a workout in South Beach shopping at the many high-profile tenants on this densely packed two-block stretch of **Collins Avenue between 5th and 10th streets.** Think Club Monaco, M.A.C, Kenneth Cole, Barney's Co-Op, and A/X Armani Exchange. Sprinkled among the upscale vendors are hair salons, spas, cafés, and such familiar stores as the Gap, Urban Outfitters, and Banana Republic. Be sure to head over one street east and west to catch the shopping on Ocean Drive and Washington Avenue.

Fodor's Choice The eight-block-long pedestrian **Lincoln Road Mall** is the trendiest place
★ on Miami Beach. Home to more than 150 shops, 20-plus art galleries, about 50 restaurants and cafés, and the renovated Colony Theatre, Lincoln Road, between Alton Road and Collins Avenue, is like the larger, more sophisticated cousin of Ocean Drive. The see-and-be-seen theme is furthered by outdoor seating at every restaurant, where well-heeled patrons lounge and discuss the people (and pet) parade passing by. An 18-screen movie theater anchors the west end of the street, which is where most of the worthwhile shops are; the far east end is mostly discount and electronics shops. Sure, there's a Pottery Barn, a Gap, and a Williams-Sonoma, but the emphasis is on emporiums with unique personalities.

DOWNTOWN CORAL GABLES

Lined with trees and busy with strolling shoppers, **Miracle Mile** is the centerpiece of the downtown Coral Gables shopping district (⊕ *www. shopcoralgables.com*), which is home to men's and women's boutiques, jewelry and home-furnishings stores, and a host of exclusive couturiers and bridal shops. Running from Douglas Road to LeJeune Road and Aragon Avenue to Giralda Avenue, more than 70 first-rate restaurants offer everything from French to Indian cuisine, and art galleries and the Actors' Playhouse, as well as the Coral Gables Museum and the Coral Gables Art Cinema, give the area a cultural flair.

The Florida Keys

WORD OF MOUTH

"The keys are definitely a get out on the water type place instead of a driving up and down US 1 kind of place. Bars and restaurants open early and close early. Get out over the water. That is where the most amazing things in the keys are."

—GoTravel

WELCOME TO THE FLORIDA KEYS

TOP REASONS TO GO

★ **John Pennekamp Coral Reef State Park:** A perfect introduction to the Florida Keys, this nature reserve offers snorkeling, diving, camping, and kayaking. An underwater highlight is the massive Christ of the Deep statue.

★ **Under the sea:** Whether you scuba, snorkel, or ride a glass-bottom boat, don't miss gazing at the coral reef and its colorful denizens.

★ **Sunset at Mallory Square:** Sure it's touristy, but at least once you've got to witness the circuslike atmosphere of this nightly event.

★ **Duval crawl:** Shop, eat, drink, repeat. Key West's Duval Street and the nearby streets make a good day's worth of window-shopping and people-watching.

★ **Get on the water:** From angling for trophy-size fish to zipping out to the Dry Tortugas, a boat trip is in your future. It's really the whole point of the Keys.

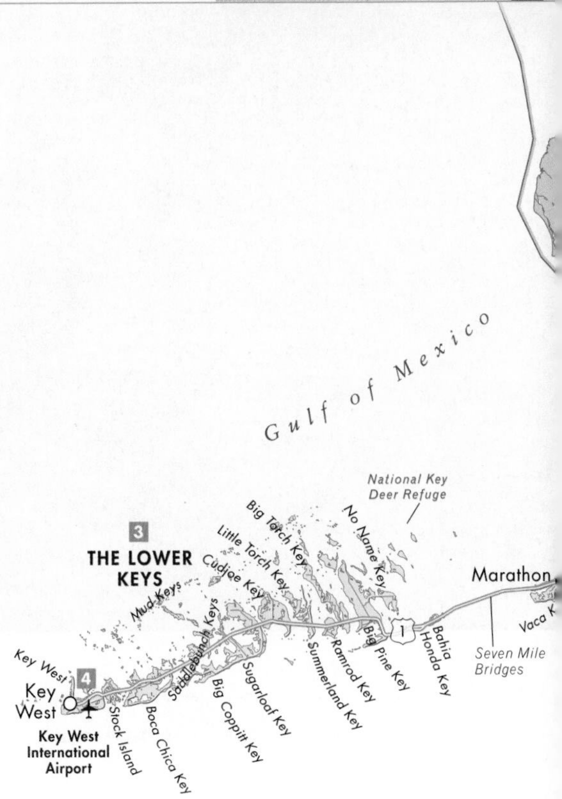

Gulf of Mexico

National Key Deer Refuge

3 THE LOWER KEYS

Big Torch Key
Little Torch Key
Cudjoe Key
Mud Keys
Saddlebunch Keys
No Name Key
Big Pine Key
Bahia Honda Key

Marathon

Vaca K

Seven Mile Bridges

1

Ramrod Key
Summerland Key
Sugarloaf Key
Big Coppitt Key

Key West
4
Key West
Stock Island
Boca Chica Key

Key West International Airport

1 Key Largo and the Upper Keys. The northernmost island in the chain introduces the watery world that is the Florida Keys. Here you'll find funky clubs, fine resorts, great seafood restaurants, and diving to die for. They stretch from Key Largo to the Long Key Channel (mile marker 106–65).

2 The Middle Keys. Centered around the town of Marathon, the Middle Keys hold most of the chain's historic and natural attractions outside of Key West. They go from Conch (pronounced *konk*) Key to the south side of the Seven Mile Bridge (mile marker 65–40).

Homestead
TO MIAMI
905A
Card Sound Bridge
1
905
Barnes Sound

Everglades National Park
9336

Straits of Florida

CAPE SABLE

Flamingo

Key Largo

THE UPPER KEYS 1
Key Largo
Tavernier
John Pennekamp Coral Reef State Park
Windley Key
Plantation Key

Florida Bay

Islamorada
Upper Matecumbe Key

THE MIDDLE KEYS
Layton
Lower Matecumbe Key
Craig Key

2
Marathon Airport
Long Key
Conch Key
Duck Key
Grassy Key
Flat Deer Key

A T L A N T I C   O C E A N

```
0          10 mi
0          10 km
```

GETTING ORIENTED

The Florida Keys are the dribble of islands off the peninsula's southern tip. From Miami International Airport, Key Largo is a 56-mi drive along the Overseas Highway. The rest of the Keys fall in succession for the 106 mi between Key Largo and Key West. At their north end, the Florida Keys front Florida Bay, which separates it from Everglades National Park. The Middle and Lower Keys front the Gulf of Mexico; the Atlantic Ocean borders the length of the chain on its eastern shores.

3 The Lower Keys. Pressure drops another notch in this laid-back part of the region, where wildlife and the fishing lifestyle peak. The Lower Keys go from Little Duck Key south through Big Coppitt Key (mile marker 40–9).

4 Key West. The ultimate in Florida Keys craziness, party town Key West isn't the place for those seeking a quiet retreat. It encompasses mile marker 9-0.

Being a Conch is a condition of the heart, and foreclosure on the soul. Many throughout the Florida Keys wear that label proudly, yet there's anything but a shared lifestyle here.

To the south, Key West has a Mardi Gras mood with Fantasy Festivals, Hemingway look-alike contests, and the occasional threat to secede from the Union. It's an island whose melting-pot character allows crusty natives to mingle (more or less peacefully) with eccentrics and escape artists. Although life elsewhere in the island chain isn't quite as offbeat, it's nearly as diverse. Flowering jungles, shimmering seas, and mangrove-lined islands are also, conversely, overburdened. Key Largo, nearest the mainland, is becoming more congested as it evolves into a bedroom community and weekend hideaway for residents of Miami and Fort Lauderdale.

A river of tourist traffic gushes along the Overseas Highway, the 110-mi artery linking the inhabited islands. The expansion of U.S. 1 to the mainland to four lanes by 2012 will further open the floodgates to increased traffic, population, and tourism. Despite the crawling weekend and high-season traffic, visitors find the utmost pleasure in cruising down the Overseas Highway. In most places the ocean and gulf are less than 4 mi apart. Try to get off the highway: rent a boat, anchor, fish, swim, or simply revel in the scenery. In the Atlantic, dive spectacular coral reefs or pursue grouper, blue marlin, dolphinfish, and other catches. Along Florida Bay's coastline, paddle to secluded islands and bays or seek out the bonefish, snapper, snook, and tarpon.

PLANNING

WHEN TO GO

High season in the Keys falls between Christmas and Easter. November to mid-December crowds are thinner, the weather is wonderful, and hotels and shops drastically reduce their prices. Summer, which is hot and humid, is becoming a second high season, especially among Floridians, families, recreational lobster divers, and European travelers. If you plan to attend the wild Fantasy Fest in October, book your room at least six months in advance. Accommodations are also scarce during the first weekend in August, the start of lobster season.

Winter is typically 10°F warmer than on the mainland; summer is usually a few degrees cooler. The Keys also get substantially less rain than the mainland. Most rainfalls are quick downpours on summer afternoons, except in June through October, when tropical storms can dump rain for several days. Winter cold fronts occasionally drag overnight temperatures down to the low 50s.

GETTING HERE AND AROUND

In 2009 **Key West International Airport (EYW)** (☎ 305/296–5439 ⊕ *www.keywestinternationalairport.com*) completed its four-year renovation, which includes a beach where travelers can catch their last blast of rays after clearing security. Many visitors to the region fly into Miami International Airport (MIA) and drive to the Keys.

By car, from MIA follow signs to Coral Gables and Key West, which puts you on LeJeune Road, then Route 836 west. Take the Homestead Extension of Florida's Turnpike south (toll road), which ends at Florida City and connects to the Overseas Highway (U.S. 1, currently under construction, so expect delays). Tolls from the airport run approximately $3. The alternative from Florida City is Card Sound Road (Route 905A), which has a bridge toll of $1. Turn right on Route 905, which rejoins the Overseas Highway 31 mi south of Florida City.

Getting lost in the Keys is almost impossible once you understand the address system. **Many addresses are simply given as a mile marker (MM) number.** The markers are small, green, rectangular signs along the side of the Overseas Highway (U.S. 1). They begin with MM 126, 1 mi south of Florida City, and end with MM 0 in Key West. **The abbreviation BS stands for the bay side of Overseas Highway, OS for ocean side.** South of Marathon, residents may refer to the bay side as the gulf side.

Greyhound's (☎ 800/231–2222 ⊕ *www.greyhound.com*) Keys Shuttle has multiple daily departures from MIA.

The Keys are full of marinas that welcome transient boaters, but there aren't enough slips for all the boats heading to these waters. Make reservations far in advance, and ask about channel and dockage depth—many marinas are quite shallow.

ABOUT THE RESTAURANTS

Seafood rules in the Keys' mostly casual restaurants. Things get more exotic in Key West. Restaurants serve cuisine that reflects the proximity of the Bahamas and the Caribbean. Florida spiny lobster is local and fresh August to March, and stone crabs mid-October to mid-May. Sampling conch, be it in a fritter or in ceviche, is a must. Authentic key lime pie consists of yellow custard in a graham-cracker crust.

ABOUT THE HOTELS

Throughout the Keys, the types of accommodations vary from '50s-style motels to cozy inns to luxurious lodges. Key West's lodging includes historic cottages, restored conch houses, and large resorts. Some larger properties throughout the Keys charge a mandatory daily resort fee of $15 or more, which can cover equipment rental, fitness-center use, and other services, plus expect another 12.5% (or more) sales/resort tax. Some guesthouses and inns do not welcome children, and many do not permit smoking.

Hotel reviews have been condensed for this book. Please go to Fodors. com for full reviews of each property.

WHAT IT COSTS					
	¢	$	$$	$$$	$$$$
Restaurants	under $10	$10–$15	$15–$20	$20–$30	over $30
Hotels	under $80	$80–$100	$100–$140	$140–$220	over $220

Restaurant prices are per person for a main course at dinner. Hotel prices are for a standard double room, excluding 12.5% sales tax (or more) in sales and resort taxes.

KEY LARGO, ISLAMORADA, AND THE UPPER KEYS

The first of the Upper Keys reachable by car, 30-mi-long Key Largo is also the largest island in the chain. Key Largo—named Cayo Largo ("Long Key") by the Spanish—makes a great introduction to the region.

If you've never tried diving, dozens of companies will be more than happy to show you the ropes. Nobody comes to Key Largo without visiting John Pennekamp Coral Reef State Park. It borders Key Largo National Marine Sanctuary, which encompasses about 190 square mi of coral reefs, sea-grass beds, and mangrove estuaries.

Fishing is the other big draw, and world records are broken regularly. Plenty of charter operations can help you find the big ones. Restaurants will cook your catch.

Key Largo offers all the conveniences of a major resort town, with most businesses lined up along the four-lane Overseas Highway (U.S. 1). Cars whiz past at all hours—something to remember when you're booking a room. Most lodgings are on the highway, so you'll want to be as far back as possible.

To the south, Islamorada (*eye*-la-mor-*ah*-da) is one of the world's top fishing destinations. You can get boats and equipment from the plethora of marinas along this 20-mi stretch of the Overseas Highway. Islamorada is one of the more affluent resort areas of the Keys. Sophisticated resorts and restaurants meet the needs of those in search of luxury, but there's also plenty for those looking for something more casual and affordable. Art galleries and boutiques make Islamorada's shopping scene the best in the Upper Keys, but if you're shopping for groceries, head to Marathon or Key Largo.

EXPLORING

John Pennekamp Coral Reef State Park. This state park is on everyone's list for close access to the best diving and snorkeling sites in Florida. The 78 square mi of coral reefs, sea-grass beds, and mangrove swamps lie adjacent to the Florida Keys National Marine Sanctuary, which contains 40 of the 52 species of coral in the Atlantic Reef System and nearly 600 varieties of fish. Concessionaires rent kayaks, powerboats,

Fodor's Choice
★

and snorkeling and diving equipment. You can also sign up for snorkeling and diving trips ($30 and $60, respectively) and glass-bottom-boat rides to the reef ($24). One of the most popular excursions is the snorkeling trip to see the 2-ton *Christ of the Deep*. The park also has short nature trails, two man-made beaches, picnic shelters, a snack bar, and a campground. ⊠ *102601 Overseas Hwy., (mile marker 102.5 OS)* ☎ *305/451–1202 for park, 305/451–6300 for excursions* ⊕ *www.pennekamppark.com* ⊡ *$4.50 for 1 person, $9 for 2 people, 50¢ each additional person* ☉ *Daily 8–sunset.*

ℭ **Robbie's Marina.** Huge prehistoric-looking, silver-sided tarpon congre-
★ gate around the docks here. Pay $4 to feed them sardines or $1 just to watch. Grab a bite to eat, do a little open-air shopping, or charter a boat in this Old Keys–style complex. ⊠ *77522 Overseas Hwy. (mile marker 77.5 BS), Lower Matecumbe Key* ☎ *305/664–9814 or 877/664–8498* ⊕ *www.robbies.com* ⊡ *Dock access $1* ☉ *Daily 8–5.*

SPORTS AND THE OUTDOORS

CANOEING AND KAYAKING

Paddle for a few hours, a whole day, or even several days on your own or with a guide. The **Florida Keys Overseas Paddling Trail** runs from Key Largo to Key West. You can paddle the entire distance, 110 mi on the Atlantic side, which takes 9–10 days. The trail also runs the chain's length on the bay side, which is a longer route.

SCUBA DIVING AND SNORKELING

Much of what makes the Upper Keys a singular dive destination is variety. Places like Molasses Reef, which begins 3 feet below the surface and descends to 55 feet, have something for everyone from novice snorkelers to experienced divers. The *Spiegel Grove,* a 510-foot vessel, lies in 130 feet of water, but its upper regions are only 60 feet below the surface. Expect to pay about $80 for a two-tank, two-site-dive trip with tanks and weights, or $35–$40 for a two-site snorkel outing. Get big discounts by booking multiple trips.

WHERE TO EAT

$$$ ✕**The Fish House.** Restaurants not on the water have to produce the
SEAFOOD highest-quality food to survive in the Keys. That's how the Fish House
★ has succeeded since the 1980s—so much so that it built the Fish House Encore next door to accommodate fans. The pan-sautéed grouper is just one of many headliners in this nautical eatery. Other top choices include mahimahi and yellowtail snapper that can be broiled, blackened, jerked, or fried, and shrimp, lobster, and stone crab. For a sweet ending, try the homemade key lime pie. ⊠ *102401 Overseas Hwy. (mile marker 102.4 OS)* ☎ *305/451–4665* ⊕ *www.fishhouse.com* ⊟ *AE, D, MC, V* ☉ *Closed Sept.*

$$$ ✕**Morada Bay Beach Café.** This bay-front restaurant wins high marks for
ECLECTIC its surprisingly stellar cuisine, tables planted in the sand, and romantic
ℭ tiki torches. Entrées feature alluring combinations like banana curry
★ lobster, and wahoo (a meaty local fish) with carrot-ginger puree. A tapas

menu caters to smaller appetites: grouper ceviche, conch fritters, tuna rolls, and the like. Lunch adds interesting sandwiches to the mix. Sit in a dining room outfitted with surfboards, or outdoors on a beach, where the sunset puts on a mighty show and kids play in the sand. There's nightly live music and a monthly full-moon party. ⊠ *81600 Overseas Hwy. (mile marker 81 BS), Upper Matecumbe Key (Islamorada)* ☎ *305/664–0604* ⊕ *www.moradabay-restaurant.com* ⊟ *AE, D, MC, V.*

WHERE TO STAY

$$$ 🖼 **Largo Lodge.** When you drive under the dense canopy of foliage at
★ the entrance to Largo Lodge you'll feel like you've escaped Highway 1's bustle. Vintage 1950s cottages are tucked amid 3 acres of palm trees, sea grapes, and orchids. **Pros:** lush grounds; great sunset views; affordable rates; boat docking. **Cons:** no pool; some traffic noise outdoors. ⊠ *101740 Overseas Hwy. (mile marker 101.7 BS)* ☎ *305/451–0424 or 800/468–4378* ⊕ *www.largolodge.com* 🛏 *2 rooms, 6 cottages* ⚐ *In-room: no phone, a/c, kitchen (some), refrigerator, Wi-Fi. In-hotel: beachfront, Wi-Fi hotspot, no kids under 14* ⊟ *MC, V.*

$$$$ 🖼 **The Moorings Village.** This tropical retreat is everything you imagine
Fodor's Choice when you think of the Keys—from hammocks swaying between towering trees to sugar-white sand (arguably the Keys' best resort beach)
★ lapped by aqua-green waves. **Pros:** romantic setting; good dining options with room-charging privileges; beautiful beach. **Cons:** minimum-night stays; no room service; extra fee for housekeeping; daily resort fee for activities. ⊠ *123 Beach Rd. (mile marker 81.6 OS), Upper Matecumbe Key (Islamorada)* ☎ *305/664–4708* ⊕ *www.themooringsvillage.com* 🛏 *18 cottages and houses* ⚐ *In-room: a/c, kitchen, Wi-Fi. In-hotel: tennis court, pool, gym, spa, beachfront, water sports, laundry facilities, Wi-Fi hotspot* ⊟ *AE, D, MC, V.*

THE MIDDLE KEYS

Most of the activity in the Middle Keys centers around the town of Marathon—the region's third-largest, with a number of good dining options. Fishing and diving are the main attractions, and beaches and natural areas provide stress-free diversion.

The Middle Keys also boast the region's two longest bridges: Long Key Viaduct and Seven Mile Bridge, both historic landmarks.

EXPLORING

🕙 **Crane Point Museum, Nature Center, and Historic Site.** Crane Point—part
★ of a 63-acre tract that contains the last-known undisturbed thatch-palm hammock—includes the **Museum of Natural History of the Florida Keys,** which has displays about local wildlife, seashells, and marine life. For kids there's is a replica of a 17th-century galleon and pirate dress-up room, plus the re-created **Cracker House** filled with insects, sea-turtle exhibits, and children's activities. On the 1-mi loop trail, visit the **Wild Bird Center** and the remnants of a Bahamian village, site

of the restored **George Adderly House.** It is the oldest surviving example of Bahamian tabby (a concretelike material created from sand and sea-shells) construction outside of Key West. From November to Easter docent-led tours are available. ⊠ *5550 Overseas Hwy. (mile marker 50.5 BS)* ☎ *305/743–9100* ⊕ *www.cranepoint.net* ☑ *$12* ☉ *Mon.–Sat. 9–5, Sun. noon–5; call to arrange trail tours.*

SPORTS AND THE OUTDOORS

BOATING

Brave the Atlantic waves and reefs or explore the backcountry islands on the gulf side. If you don't have a lot of boating and chart-reading experience, it's a good idea to tap into local knowledge on a charter.

FISHING

For recreational anglers, the fishing is superb in both bay and ocean. Marathon West Hump, one good spot, has depths ranging from 500 to more than 1,000 feet. Locals fish from a half-dozen bridges, including Long Key Bridge, the Old Seven Mile Bridge, and both ends of Tom's Harbor. Barracuda, bonefish, and tarpon all frequent local waters. Party boats and private charters are available.

SCUBA DIVING AND SNORKELING

Local dive operations take you to Sombrero Reef and Lighthouse, the most popular down-under destination in these parts. For a shallow dive and some lobster-nabbing, try Coffins Patch, off Key Colony Beach. A number of wrecks such as *Thunderbolt* serve as artificial reefs. Many operations out of this area will also take you to Looe Key Reef.

WHERE TO EAT

$$ ✕ **Keys Fisheries Market & Marina.** From the parking lot, this commercial
SEAFOOD warehouse flanked by fishing boats and lobster traps barely hints at the
★   restaurant inside. Order at the window outside, pick up your food, then dine at one of the waterfront picnic tables outfitted with rolls of paper towels. Fresh seafood and a token hamburger and chicken sandwich comprise the menu. A huge lobster Reuben ($14.95) served on thick slices of toast is signature. Other delights include the shrimpburger, very rich whiskey-peppercorn snapper, and the Keys Kombo (broiled or grilled lobster, shrimp, scallops, and mahimahi for $29). There's also sushi and an ice-cream station. Kids like feeding the fish while they wait. ⊠ *3390 Gulfview Ave. (turn west on 35th St.), end of 35th St. (mile marker 49 BS)* ☎ *305/743–4353 or 866/743–4353* ⊕ *www. keysfisheries.com* ☐ *MC, V.*

WHERE TO STAY

$$$$ ▦ **Tranquility Bay.** The 87 two- and three-bedroom town houses have
★   gingerbread trim, white-picket fences, and open-floor-plan interiors dec-orated in trendy cottage style. **Pros:** secluded setting; gorgeous design; lovely crescent beach. **Cons:** a bit sterile; no real Keys atmosphere; cramped building layout. ⊠ *2600 Overseas Hwy. (mile marker 48.5 BS)*

☎ *305/289–0888 or 866/643–5397* ⊕ *www.tranquilitybay.com* ⇌ *45 2-bedroom suites, 41 3-bedroom suites* ⚐ *In-room: a/c, kitchen, refrigerator, DVD, Wi-Fi. In-hotel: 2 restaurants, bars, pools, gym, beachfront, diving, water sports, Internet terminal, Wi-Fi hotspot* ☰ *AE, D, MC, V.*

THE LOWER KEYS

Beginning at Bahia Honda Key, the islands become smaller, more clustered, and more numerous. Here you're likely to see more birds and mangroves than other tourists, and more refuges and campgrounds than museums and hotels. Freshwater pools support alligators, snakes, deer, rabbits, raccoons, and migratory ducks. Nature was generous with her beauty in the Lower Keys, which have both Looe Key Reef, arguably the Keys' most beautiful tract of coral, and Bahia Honda State Park, considered one of the best beaches in the world for its fine-sand dunes, clear warm waters, and panoramic vistas. Big Pine Key is fishing headquarters for a laid-back community that swells with retirees in the winter. South of it, the dribble of islands can flash by in a blink of an eye if you don't take the time to stop at a roadside eatery or check out tours and charters at the little marinas.

BAHIA HONDA KEY

Mile marker 38 and 36.

Bahia Honda Key is devoted to its eponymous state park, which keeps it in a pristine state. Besides the park's outdoor activities, it offers an up-close look at the original railroad bridge.

EXPLORING

Fodor'sChoice **Bahia Honda State Park.** Most first-time visitors to the Keys are dismayed
★ by the lack of beaches—but then they discover Bahia Honda Key. The 524-acre park here sprawls across both sides of the highway, giving it 2½ mi of fabulous sandy coastline. For snorkelers, there's underwater life (soft coral, queen conchs, little fish) just a few hundred feet offshore. Although swimming, kayaking, fishing, and boating are the main reasons to visit, you shouldn't miss biking along the 2½ mi of flat roads or walking the ¼-mi Silver Palm Trail, with rare West Indian plants. There are rental cabins, a campground, snack bar, gift shop, 19-slip marina, nature center, and facilities for renting kayaks and arranging snorkeling tours. Get a panoramic view of the island from what's left of the railroad—the Bahia Honda Bridge. ⊠ *36850 Overseas Hwy. (mile marker 37 OS)* ☎ *305/872-2353* ⊕ *www.floridastateparks.org/ bahiahonda* ⚐ *$4.50 for 1 person, $9 for 2 people, 50¢ per additional person* ⊙ *Daily 8–sunset.*

BIG PINE KEY

Welcome to the Keys' most natural holdout, where wildlife refuges protect rare and endangered animals. Here you have left behind the commercialism of the Upper Keys for an authentic backcountry atmosphere.

EXPLORING

Blue Hole. A quarry left over from railroad days, the Blue Hole is the largest body of fresh water in the Keys. From the observation platform, you might see the resident alligator, turtles, and other wildlife. There are two well-marked trails: the Jack Watson Nature Trail (.6 mi) and the Fred Mannillo Nature Trail, wheelchair-accessible. ⊠ *Visitor Center–Headquarters, Big Pine Shopping Center (mile marker 30.5 BS), 179 Key Deer Blvd.* ☎ *305/872–2239* ⊕ *www.fws.gov/nationalkeydeer* ☞ *Free* ☾ *Daily sunrise–sunset; headquarters weekdays 8–5.*</R>

★ **National Key Deer Refuge.** This 84,351-acre refuge was established in 1957 to protect the dwindling population of the Key deer, which stands about 30 inches at the shoulders and is a subspecies of the Virginia white-tailed deer. They once roamed the Lower and Middle Keys, but hunting, destruction of their habitat, and a growing human population caused their numbers to decline to 27 by 1957. The deer have made a comeback, increasing their numbers to approximately 750. The best place to see Key deer in the refuge is at the end of Key Deer Boulevard and on No Name Key, a sparsely populated island just east of Big Pine Key. Mornings and evenings are the best time to spot them. Feeding them is against the law. The refuge also has 21 other listed endangered and threatened species of plants and animals, including five found nowhere else.

KAYAKING

There's nothing like the vast expanse of pristine waters and mangrove islands preserved by three national refuges from here to Key West. The mazelike terrain can be confusing, so it's wise to hire a guide at least the first time out.

WHERE TO STAY

$ ▦ **Big Pine Key Fishing Lodge.** Here you get a happy mix of tent campers
★ (who have fabulous waterfront real estate), RVers, and motel-dwellers. Rooms have tile floors and wicker furniture. **Pros:** local fishing crowd; nice pool; great price. **Cons:** RV park is too close to motel; deer often get into campers' food. ⊠ *33000 Overseas Hwy. (mile marker 33 OS)* ☎ *305/872–2351* ☞ *16 rooms; 158 campsites, 97 with full hookups, 61 without hookups* ♿ *In-room: a/c (some), no phone, kitchen (some), refrigerator. In-hotel: pool, laundry facilities, Internet terminal, Wi-Fi hotspot* ⊟ *D, MC, V.*

KEY WEST

Situated 150 mi from Miami, 90 mi from Havana, and an immeasurable distance from sanity, this end-of-the-line community has never been like anyplace else. Even after it was connected to the rest of the country— by the railroad in 1912 and by the highway in 1938—it maintained a strong sense of detachment.

Key West reflects a diverse population: Conchs (natives, many of whom trace their ancestry to the Bahamas), freshwater Conchs (longtime residents who migrated from somewhere else), Hispanics (primarily Cuban immigrants), recent refugees from the urban sprawl of mainland

Florida, military personnel, a sizeable gay population, and an assortment of vagabonds, drifters, and dropouts in search of refuge.

Although the rest of the Keys are known for outdoor activities, Key West has something of a city feel. As a tourist destination, it has a lot to sell—an average temperature of 79°F, 19th-century architecture, and a laid-back lifestyle. Duval Street is lined with garish signs for T-shirt shops and tour-company offices, and fills, especially when cruise ships are in, with day-trippers and the oddball lot of locals.

GETTING HERE AND AROUND

Between mile markers 4 and 0, Key West is the one place in the Keys where you could do without a car, especially if you plan on staying around Old Town. Trolleys, buses, bikes, scooters, and feet are suitable alternatives. To explore the beaches, New Town, and Stock Island, you might need a car.

Old Town Key West is the only place in the Keys where parking is a problem. Public parking lots charge by the hour or day; most hotels and B&Bs provide parking. If you arrive early, you can sometimes find a spot on side streets off Duval and Whitehead, where you can park for free—just be sure they're not marked for residential parking only. Your best bet is to bike or take the trolley around town if you don't want to walk. You can disembark and reboard at will.

EXPLORING

OLD TOWN

The heart of Key West, the historic Old Town area runs from White Street to the waterfront. Beginning in 1822, wharves, warehouses, chandleries, ship-repair facilities, and the U.S. Custom House sprang up around the deep harbor to accommodate the navy's ships and other sailing vessels. Wreckers, merchants, and sea captains built lavish houses near the bustling waterfront. A remarkable number of these fine Victorian structures have been restored to their original grandeur, and now serve as homes, guesthouses, shops, restaurants, and museums. These, along with the dwellings of famous writers, artists, and politicians who've come to Key West over the past 175 years, are among the area's approximately 3,000 historic structures. Old Town also has the city's finest restaurants and hotels, lively street life, and popular nightspots.

★ **Ernest Hemingway Home and Museum.** Amusing anecdotes spice up the guided tours of Ernest Hemingway's home, built in 1801 by the town's most successful wrecker. While living here between 1931 and 1942, Hemingway wrote about 70% of his life's work, including classics like *For Whom the Bell Tolls.* Few of his belongings remain aside from some books, but photographs help visualize his day-to-day life. Tours begin every 15 minutes and take 25–30 minutes; then you're free to explore on your own. ⊠ *907 Whitehead St.* ☎ *305/294–1136* ⊕ *www. hemingwayhome.com* ⛶ *$12* ☉ *Daily 9–5.*

Fodor's Choice **Key West Museum of Art & History in the Custom House.** The imposing red-★ brick-and–terra-cotta Richardsonian Romanesque–style building was built in 1891 and reopened as a museum and art gallery in 1999 after a $9 million restoration. Galleries have long-term and changing exhibits about local and national artists and Key West history. ⊠ *281 Front St.* ☎ *305/295–6616* ⊕ *www.kwahs.com* ⊡ *$10* ⊙ *Daily 9:30–4:30.*

The Southernmost Point. Possibly the most photographed site in Key West, this is a must-see for many visitors. Who wouldn't want a picture taken next to the big striped buoy that marks the spot? Signs around it tell Key West history. ⊠ *Whitehead and South Sts.* ☎ *No phone.*

NEW TOWN

The Overseas Highway splits as it enters Key West. The southern fork runs along the shore as South Roosevelt Boulevard (Route A1A), skirting Key West International Airport and New Town, the area east of White Street.

★ **Fort East Martello Museum & Gardens.** This redbrick Civil War fort never saw action. Today it serves as a historical museum, with exhibits including relics of the USS *Maine,* cigar factory and shipwrecking, and the citadel tower you can climb to the top. ⊠ *3501 S. Roosevelt Blvd.* ☎ *305/296–3913* ⊕ *www.kwahs.com* ⊡ *$6* ⊙ *Weekdays 10–4, weekends 9:30–4:30.*

SPORTS AND THE OUTDOORS

Unlike the rest of the region, Key West isn't known for outdoor pursuits. But everyone should devote at least half a day to relaxing on a boat tour, heading out on a fishing expedition, or pursuing some other adventure at sea. The ultimate excursion is a boat trip to Dry Tortugas National Park for snorkeling and exploring Fort Jefferson.

BEACH

★ **Fort Zachary Taylor Historic State Park.** Besides its 19th-century fort, the park boasts Key West's best and safest beach. There's an adjoining picnic area with barbecue grills and shade trees, a snack bar, and rental equipment. ⊠ *Box 6565; end of Southard St., through Truman Annex* ☎ *305/292–6713* ⊕ *www.floridastateparks.org/forttaylor* ⊡ *$4.50 for 1 person, $7 for 2 people, 50¢ per additional person ($2.50 for pedestrians and cyclists)* ⊙ *Daily 8–sunset, tours noon and 2.*

WHERE TO EAT

$$–$$$ ✕ **Ambrosia.** Ask any savvy local where to get the best sushi on the
JAPANESE   island, and you'll undoubtedly be pointed to this tiny wood-and-tatami-paneled dining room in a resort near the beach. Grab a seat at the sushi bar and watch owner and head sushi chef Masa prepare an impressive array of super-fresh sashimi delicacies. The Ambrosia special ($35) lets you sample five kinds of sashimi, seven pieces of sushi, and sushi rolls. There's an assortment of lightly fried tempura and teriyaki dishes and a killer bento box at lunch. ⊠ *Santa Maria Resort, 1401 Simonton St.* ☎ *305/293–0304* ⊕ *www.keywestambrosia.com* ⊟ *AE, D, MC, V* ⊙ *No lunch weekends. Closed 2 wks after Labor Day.*

$$$ ✕ **Blue Heaven.** The outdoor dining area here is often referred to as "the
CARIBBEAN   quintessential Keys experience." Nightly specials include black-bean
★   soup, Provençal sea scallops, and sautéed yellowtail snapper in citrus

Sunset Key cottages are right on the water's edge, far away from the action of Old Town.

beurre blanc. Desserts and breads are baked on the premises; the banana bread, pineapple pancakes, and lobster Benedict with key lime hollandaise are hits during "breakfast with the roosters," the restaurant's signature meal. ⊠ *729 Thomas St.* ☎ *305/296–8666* ⊕ *www.blueheavenkw. com* ♙ *Reservations not accepted* ⊟ *AE, D, MC, V* ☾ *Closed after Labor Day for 6 wks.*

$ ✕ **B.O.'s Fish Wagon.** What started out as a fish house on wheels appears
SEAFOOD to have broken down on the corner of Caroline and William Streets,
★ and is today the cornerstone for one of Key West's junkyard-chic dining institutions. Step up to the wood-plank counter window and order the specialty: a grouper sandwich fried or grilled and topped with key lime sauce. Other choices include fish nuggets, hot dogs, and shrimp or soft-shell-crab sandwiches. Grab some paper towels off one of the rolls hanging around and busy yourself reading graffiti, license plates, and irreverent signs. It's a must-do Key West experience. ⊠ *801 Caroline St.* ☎ *305/294–9272* ⊟ *No credit cards.*

$$$ ✕ **Café Marquesa.** Chef Susan Ferry presents seven or more inspired
CONTINENTAL entrées on her nightly changing menu; carefully executed dishes can
Fodor's Choice include yellowtail snapper with pear; ricotta pasta purses with caponata
★ and red pepper coulis; and Australian rack of lamb with goat-cheese crust and port-fig sauce. Enjoy a fine selection of wines and custom martinis in a setting that's equally relaxed and elegant. ⊠ *600 Fleming St.* ☎ *305/292–1244* ⊕ *www.marquesa.com* ⊟ *AE, DC, MC, V* ☾ *No lunch.*

$$$$ ✕ **Louie's Backyard.** Once you get over sticker shock on the seasonally
ECLECTIC changing menu (appetizers cost around $9–$18; entrées can hover
★ around the $37 mark), settle in on the outside deck with its killer ocean view and enjoy dishes like seared coriander scallops with tangerine

sauce and grilled fillet with wild mushrooms and tomato bordelaise. The Upper Deck serves more affordable tapas, such as flaming ouzo shrimp and Gruyère and duck confit pizza. The restaurant also opens for lunch and serves cocktails on the water until the wee hours. ⊠ *700 Waddell Ave.* ☎ *305/294–1061* ⊕ *www.louiesbackyard.com* ⌘ *Reservations essential* ⊟ *MC, V* ⊗ *Closed Labor Day–mid-Sept., Upper Deck closed Sun. and Mon.*

WHERE TO STAY

$$$–$$$$ 🏨 **Azul Key West.** The ultramodern—nearly minimalistic—redo of this classic circa-1903 Queen Anne mansion is a break from the sensory overload of Key West's other abundant Victorian guesthouses. **Pros:** lovely building; marble-floored baths; luxurious linens. **Cons:** on a busy street. ⊠ *907 Truman Ave.* ☎ *305/296–5152 or 888/253–2985* ⊕ *www. azulhotels.us* ↪ *10 rooms, 1 suite* ⌂ *In-room: Wi-Fi. In-hotel: pool, Wi-Fi hotspot, no kids under 21* ⊟ *AE, D, MC, V* ⊙⊣ *CP.*

$$$$
☺
★ 🏨 **Casa Marina Resort.** Set on a private beach, this 1920s gem has a richly appointed lobby with beamed ceilings, polished pine floor, and original art. **ros:** area's nicest resort beach; historic setting; away from the crowds. **Cons:** long walk to Old Town. ⊠ *1500 Reynolds St.* ☎ *305/296–3535 or 866/397–6342* ⊕ *www.casamarinaresort.com* ↪ *311 rooms, 68 suites* ⌂ *In-room: safe, Wi-Fi, a/c. In-hotel: restaurant, room service, bars, tennis courts, pools, gym, beachfront, diving, water sports, bicycles, children's programs (ages 4–12), laundry service, Internet terminal, Wi-Fi hotspot* ⊟ *AE, D, DC, MC, V.*

$$$$
★ 🏨 **Simonton Court.** A small world all of its own, this lodging makes you feel deliciously sequestered from Key West's crasser side, but close enough to get there on foot. **Pros:** lots of privacy; well-appointed accommodations; friendly staff. **Cons:** minimum stays required in high season. ⊠ *320 Simonton St.* ☎ *305/294–6386 or 800/944–2687* ⊕ *www. simontoncourt.com* ↪ *17 rooms, 6 suites, 6 cottages* ⌂ *In-room: safe, kitchen (some), refrigerator, Wi-Fi. In-hotel: pools, no kids under 18, Wi-Fi hotspot* ⊟ *D, DC, MC, V* ⊙⊣ *CP.*

$$$$
Fodor'sChoice
★ ✕ **Sunset Key.** This private island retreat feels completely cut off from the world, yet you're just minutes away from the action; board a 10-minute launch to 27-acre Sunset Key, where you'll find sandy beaches, swaying palms, flowering gardens, and a delicious sense of privacy. **Pros:** peace and quiet; roomy verandas; free 24-hour shuttle. **Cons:** luxury doesn't come cheap. ⊠ *245 Front St.* ☎ *305/292–5300 or 888/477– 7786* ⊕ *westinsunsetkeycottages.com* ↪ *39 cottages* ⌂ *In-room: safe, kitchen, DVD, Internet, Wi-Fi. In-hotel: restaurant, room service, bars, tennis courts, pool, gym, spa, beachfront, laundry service, Internet terminal, Wi-Fi hotspot* ⊟ *AE, D, DC, MC, V* ⊙⊣ *CP.*

NIGHTLIFE

Rest up: Much of what happens in Key West does so after dark. Open your mind and have a stroll. Scruffy street performers strum next to dogs in sunglasses. Brawls tumble out the doors of Sloppy Joe's. Drag queens strut across stages in Joan Rivers garb. And margaritas flow like a Jimmy Buffett tune.

Nashville

WORD OF MOUTH

"Country Music Hall of Fame & Museum . . . even if you think you don't like country music, there is a lot of pop culture in it, and I can't believe the average person 40+ wouldn't find something of interest. It's also very well done, quite interactive.and apparently they have good food. Do the Studio B tour if you can . . . well worth it!"

—musicfan

WELCOME TO NASHVILLE

TOP REASONS TO GO

★ **Music:** Nashville, aka Music City, U.S.A., is the capital of country music, with both small clubs and the spectacle of the Grand Ole Opry. And country isn't the only game in town: Nashville has everything from rock clubs to an impressive symphony hall.

★ **Antebellum mansions:** Tour the Hermitage, home and final resting place of President Andrew Jackson, and the Belle Meade Plantation, dubbed "The Queen of Tennessee Plantations."

★ **Museums:** The Country Music Hall of Fame is a must-see, and just a few blocks away the Frist Center for the Visual Arts is a first-class museum located in the city's old art deco post office.

1 Downtown. In Nashville's city center you'll find a concentration of cultural attractions, including the Country Music Hall of Fame, as well as the state capitol. You can hang out at Riverfront Park and adjacent Ft. Nashborough, overlooking the Cumberland River.

2 Greater Nashville. The East Nashville area has a dual personality: It has a well-restored 19th-century residential section, and it's the site of many of the small music clubs where up-and-coming performers hone their craft. A short drive north of the State Capitol is Germantown, a tight cluster of streets lined with old redbrick buildings recently reclaimed by young families and urban professionals. The Gulch, site of a former rail yard just southwest of downtown, now hosts some of Nashville's most talked-about eateries.

0 ___ 1/4 miles
0 ___ 400 meters

Harrison St.
10th Ave. N
Ja me
Gay St.
11th Ave. N
Charlotte Ave.
10th Ave.
Church St.
16th Ave. N.
12th Ave. N.
Broadway
70
Music Cir. E.
Division St.
Music Sq. E.
18th Ave. S.
Music Sq. W.
◆ **Historic RCA Studio B**
2 TO BELLE MEADE, CHEEKWOOD BOTANICAL GARDEN

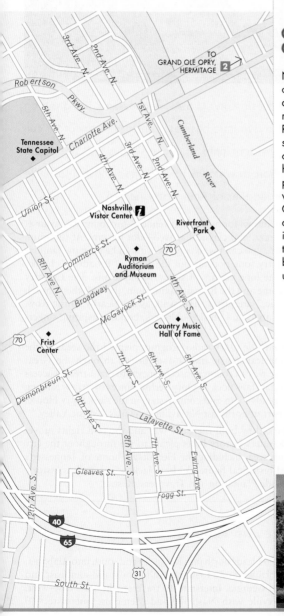

GETTING ORIENTED

Nashville sits in the heart of Tennessee's rolling hills, and is home to powerhouse music publishers on Music Row, struggling singers and songwriters with dreams of making it big, raucous honky tonks where music pours out onto the sidewalk, and the venerable Grand Ole Opry, which continues to pack devotees into its pew-lined auditorium for performances by country legends and up-and-coming stars.

Heralded as Music City, U.S.A., Tennessee's fast-growing capital city is a dynamic business center with a vibrant cultural life. A consistent influx of new residents and significant new construction downtown have helped move Nashville into the major leagues of American cities.

Nashville is best known for music, and venues—for country, of course, but rock, blues, jazz, and classical as well—dot the city. At the south end of downtown, you can't walk a block without hearing the familiar chords of a country song pouring out the doors of Broadway's honky tonks or from the lone guitars of sidewalk musicians. The Country Music Hall of Fame and the Ryman Auditorium, the "Mother Church of Country Music," are just a short walk away. Nearby Music Row, home to record labels and music publishers, beckons aspiring singers and songwriters.

Nashville's *Grand Ole Opry* radio program planted the seeds of the town as an American music mecca and thrived through the Great Depression all the way to country's ascendancy into mainstream success in the 1990s. Today, fans flock to Opry performances by artists ranging from country legends to up-and-coming stars in the sleek Opry House, in an outlying part of northeast Nashville known as "Music Valley."

With a past marked by both the Civil War and the civil rights movement, Nashville offers history buffs plenty to see throughout the city and surrounding area, including the Hermitage, home of Tennessee's most celebrated historical figure, Andrew Jackson, as well as historic homes Belle Meade Plantation and Travellers' Rest.

PLANNING

GETTING HERE AND AROUND
CAR TRAVEL
From Nashville I–65 leads north into Kentucky and south into Alabama, and I–24 leads northwest into Kentucky and Illinois and southeast into Chattanooga and Georgia. Interstate 40 traverses the state east–west, connecting Knoxville with Nashville and Memphis. Interstate 440

The Country Music Hall of Fame is housed in a block-long building with architectural elements evoking a piano, a Cadillac fin, and a radio tower.

connects I–40, I–65, and I–24, and helps circumvent clogged major arteries during Nashville's rush hour.

BUS TRAVEL

Metropolitan Transit Authority (MTA) buses serve the entire county; the fare is $1.60 (exact change). There are also free "Music City Circuit" buses that serve downtown and the Gulch—check the MTA web site for details on routes.

Bus Contacts Metropolitan Transit Authority (☎ 615/862–5950 ⊕ www. nashvillemta.org).

VISITOR INFORMATION

Nashville Visitor Center (✉ 150 4th Ave. N, Suite G-250, Downtown ☎ 800/657–6910 ⊕ www.visitmusiccity.com).

EXPLORING NASHVILLE

DOWNTOWN

Downtown Nashville has much to offer in the way of history, music, entertainment, dining, and specialty shopping. It's fairly easy to get around downtown by foot, although most hotels are clustered at the north end while many attractions—including the Country Music Hall of Fame and Broadway's famous honky tonks—lie at the south end, at the bottom of a hill. The Cumberland River horizontally bisects Nashville's downtown. Numbered avenues, running north–south, are

The Frist Center for the Visual Arts is located in what was once Nashville's downtown post office.

west of and parallel to the river; numbered streets are east of the river but also parallel to it.

WHAT TO SEE

★ **Country Music Hall of Fame and Museum.** This tribute to country music's finest, among them Hank Williams Sr., Loretta Lynn, Patsy Cline, and Johnny Cash, reopened in 2001 in a new $37 million facility just south of the Bridgestone Arena. A block long, with an exterior that evokes a piano, a Cadillac fin, and a radio tower, the museum contains plaques honoring country greats, a two-story wall with every gold and platinum country record ever made, a theater that screens a digital film on the industry, and daily live entertainment, not to mention Elvis Presley's solid-gold 1960 Cadillac limo. ■TIP→ **Buses depart regularly from the museum for tours of Historic RCA Studio B.** ⊠ *222 5th Ave. S, at Demonbreun St., Downtown* ☎ *615/416–2001* ⊕ *www. countrymusichalloffame.com* ⊠ *$19.99* ⊙ *Mar.–Dec., daily 9–5; Jan. and Feb., Wed.–Mon. 9–5.*

☾ **Frist Center for the Visual Arts.** This art gallery boasts 24,000 feet of
★ exhibit space and hosts first-class exhibitions of paintings, sculpture, and other visual art. The historic building, with its original art deco exterior, was formerly Nashville's downtown post office. In its current incarnation, the building houses art galleries, a children's discovery gallery, a 250-seat auditorium, a gift shop, a café, art workshops, and an art resource center. ⊠ *919 Broadway, Downtown* ☎ *615/244–3340* ⊕ *www.fristcenter.org* ⊠ *$15* ⊙ *Mon.–Wed. 10–5:30, Thurs. and Fri. 10–9, Sat. 10–5:30, Sun. 1–5:30.*

Historic RCA Studio B. In the first big Nashville hit factory, where Chet Atkins helped create the "Nashville sound," visitors can step through the same spaces where stars including Elvis, Roy Orbison, Dolly Parton, and the Everly Brothers laid down some of their greatest hits. Audio and video displays tell the history of the studio. Tickets are sold in conjunction with the Country Music Hall of Fame and Museum and shuttle buses from the Hall of Fame run here. ⊠ *1611 Roy Acuff Pl., Music Row* ☎ *615/416–2001* ⊕ *www.countrymusichalloffame.com* ⌦ *$12.99* ☉ *Daily 10:30–2:30.*

★ **Ryman Auditorium and Museum.** The Ryman's pew-filled auditorium, known as the "Mother Church of Country Music," was home to the Grand Ole Opry from 1943 to 1974 and is listed on the National Register of Historic Places. The former Union Gospel Tabernacle has acoustics that are said to rival Carnegie Hall's and seats more than 2,000 for live performances of classical, jazz, pop, gospel, and, of course, country. The Opry stages its popular live country show at the Ryman from November through January. Self-guided tours include photo-ops on the legendary stage and the museum, with its photographs and memorabilia of past performances. Backstage tours are also available. ⊠ *116 5th Ave. N, Downtown* ☎ *615/889–3060 tickets* ⊕ *www.ryman.com* ⌦ *Tours $13, backstage tour $17* ☉ *Daily 9–4; call for show schedules and ticket prices.*

Tennessee State Capitol. The state capitol is largely the same as when it was completed in 1859. It was designed by noted Philadelphia architect William Strickland (1788–1854), who was so impressed with his Greek revival creation that he requested—and received—entombment behind one of the building's walls. On the grounds you'll also find the graves of the 11th U.S. president, James K. Polk, and his wife. ⊠ *600 Charlotte Ave., between 6th and 7th Aves., Downtown* ☎ *615/741–1621* ⌦ *Free* ☉ *Tours weekdays on the hr 9–11 and 1–3.*

Yazoo Brewing Company and Taproom. Nashville's best-known local brewery started as a one-man operation in the early 2000s, when Linus Hall used to haul kegs of his homebrew to local restaurants in the back of his pickup. Now Hall's beers, named after his hometown of Yazoo, Mississippi, are distributed in major cities throughout the Southeast and have brought a loyal local following to the brewery's taproom. There you'll find trademark blends like Dos Perros (a Mexican-style beer) and Yazoo Pale Ale along with experimental kegs (Hop Project #36, anyone?) by the glass. Tours of the brewery are available on Saturday, once an hour from 2:30 to 6:30. ⊠ *910 Division St., The Gulch* ☎ *615/891–4649* ⊕ *www.yazoobrew.com* ⌦ *Tours $6* ☉ *Thurs. and Fri. 4–8, Sat. 2–8.*

GREATER NASHVILLE

To get a more complete feeling for the city, you'll want to explore the area beyond downtown, which includes historic plantations, museums covering everything from history to science, and some great places for kids, including the Nashville Zoo—not to mention the Grand Ole Opry, in "Music Valley," in northeast Nashville, which features the massive Gaylord Opryland Resort and Convention Center, with nearly 3,000 hotel rooms, numerous restaurants, and boat rides on an indoor artificial river.

WHAT TO SEE

★ **Belle Meade Plantation.** Known as the "Queen of Tennessee Plantations," this stunning Greek revival house is recognizable by the Civil War bullet holes that riddle its columns. Guides in period costumes lead you through the mansion, which is furnished in the antebellum style and is the centerpiece of a 3,300-acre estate that was one of the nation's first and finest Thoroughbred breeding farms. It was also the site of the famous Iroquois Steeplechase, the oldest amateur steeplechase in America, a society event now run each May in nearby Percy Warner Park. A Victorian carriage museum with an impressive collection continues the equine theme. A two-story visitor center is modeled after a traditional Southern paddock. The last tour of the day starts at 4, and the excellent restaurant here is called Belle. ⊠ *5025 Harding Pike, Belle Meade* ☎ *615/356–0501* ⊕ *www.bellemeadeplantation.com* 🎟 *$16* ☉ *Mon.– Sat. 9–5, Sun. 11–5.*

★ **Cheekwood Botanical Garden and Museum of Art.** Thirty acres of gardens showcase annuals, perennials, and seasonal wildflowers, and a carefully restored neo-Georgian mansion holds the museum. The permanent exhibition shows American art to 1945, while the Temporary Contemporary gallery presents local and national artists. A collection of Fabergé pieces—including three Imperial Easter eggs—from the Matilda Geddings Gray Foundation is also on display. ⊠ *1200 Forrest Park Dr., Belle Meade* ☎ *615/356–8000* ⊕ *www.cheekwood.org* 🎟 *$10* ☉ *Tues.– Sat. 9:30–4:30, Sun. 11–4:30.*

★ **Grand Ole Opry.** The longest running radio show in the United States, currently performed in the Grand Ole Opry House, has been broadcasting country music from Nashville since 1925. You may see superstars, legends, and up-and-coming stars on the Opry's stage. The auditorium seats about 4,400 people in deep wooden pews, and there's not a bad seat in the house. Performances (Broadcast live on WSM AM 650) are every Tuesday (7, March–mid-December only), Friday (7), and Saturday (7 and 9:30). Buy tickets ($28.50–$55) well in advance, particularly during CMA Music Festival week in June. The Opry also has a winter run at the Ryman Auditorium in downtown Nashville from November through January. ⊠ *2804 Opryland Dr., Music Valley* ☎ *615/871–6779, 800/733–6779 ticket information* ⊕ *www.opry.com.*

★ **The Hermitage.** The life and times of Andrew Jackson, known as "Old Hickory," are reflected with great care at this house and museum. Jackson built the mansion on 1,120 acres for his wife, Rachel, for whose honor he fought and won a duel. Both are buried in the family graveyard. The Andrew Jackson Center, a 28,000-square-foot museum, visitor center, and education center, contains many Jackson artifacts. By the 1840s, more than 140 African-American slaves lived and worked on the Hermitage Plantation, and archaeological digs have uncovered the remains of many slave dwellings—yard cabins, Alfred's Cabin, and field quarters. Mansion tours are led by costumed guides, while tours of the grounds are self-guided. Wagon tours are offered April through

A vista at Cheekwood Botanical Garden and Art Museum.

October. A museum store and dining options are on the grounds. The Hermitage is 12 mi east of Nashville; take I–40E to the Old Hickory Boulevard exit. ✉ *4580 Rachel's La., Hermitage* ☎ *615/889–2941* ⊕ *www.thehermitage.com* 🎟 *$14* ⊙ *Apr. 1–Oct. 15, daily 8:30–5; Oct. 16–Mar. 31, daily 9–4:30, closed 3rd wk in Jan.*

★ **Parthenon.** An exact copy of the Athenian original, Nashville's Parthenon was constructed for Tennessee's 1897 centennial exposition. Across the street from Vanderbilt University's campus, in Centennial Park, it's a magnificent sight, perched on a gentle green slope beside a duck pond. Inside are the 63-piece Cowan Collection of American art, traveling exhibits, and the 42-foot *Athena Parthenos*, the tallest indoor sculpture in the Western world. ✉ *West End and 25th Aves., West End/Vanderbilt* ☎ *615/862–8431* ⊕ *www.nashville.gov/parthenon* 🎟 *$6* ⊙ *Sept.–May, Tues.–Sat. 9–4:30; June and Aug., Tues.–Sat. 9–4:30, Sun. 12:30–4:30.*

Travellers' Rest. Following the fortunes of pioneer landowner and judge John Overton—the law partner, mentor, campaign manager, and life-long friend of Andrew Jackson, whose own home is nearby—this clap-board home metamorphosed from a four-room cottage built in 1799 to a 12-room mansion with Federal-influenced and Greek revival additions upon its completion in 1865. Each portion of the interior has been restored and decorated according to the time when it was built. The grounds contain a restored smokehouse, weaving house, and formal gardens. Travellers' Rest is off I–65 S at the Harding Place exit—look for signs. ✉ *636 Farrell Pkwy., Oak Mills* ☎ *615/832–8197* ⊕ *www. travellersrestplantation.org* 🎟 *$10 for guided house tour; $2 for self-guided grounds-only tour* ⊙ *Tues.–Sat. 10–4, Sun. 1–4.*

WHERE TO EAT

Nashville's dining scene has gone upscale. It's now possible to find inventive menus and creative combinations of ingredients in restaurants in revitalized neighborhoods like the Gulch and East Nashville, both a short hop from downtown. Many restaurants are also clustered in the neighborhoods around Vanderbilt University: Midtown, Elliston Place, and Hillsboro Village.

Despite Nashville's culinary revolution, diners are still often casually dressed and enjoy lingering over meals. Those craving old Southern favorites like catfish, barbecue, and the ever-popular, no-frills "meat and three" can find plenty of options alongside the city's trendier eateries.

WHAT IT COSTS					
	¢	$	$$	$$$	$$$$
Restaurants	under $7	$7–$11	$12–$16	$17–$22	over $22

Restaurant prices are for a main course at dinner.

DOWNTOWN

¢

SOUTHERN

★

✕ **Arnold's Country Kitchen.** Grab a tray and join the workaday lunchtime crowd at Formica tables tucking into Southern feasts inside this archetypal meat-and-three diner. A cheerful staff dishes out heaping helpings of carved ham, pork brisket, fried chicken, meat loaf, and other comfort foods from stainless-steel steam tables. Sides include turnip greens cooked with bacon and creamy coleslaw. A full slate of pies including peach, strawberry, and chocolate tempts already full diners. Arnold's is only open for lunch, but you may not need dinner if you chow down here! ⊠ *605 8th Ave. S, 8th Avenue South* ☎ *615/256–4455* ▭ *MC, V* ⊙ *No dinner. Closed weekends.*

$$$$

AMERICAN

★

✕ **Capitol Grille and Oak Bar.** This charming restaurant in downtown's historic Hermitage Hotel serves cuisine with a regional flair, including seafood and Black Angus beef, and is consistently ranked as one of Nashville's top restaurants. As a testament to its opulence, a 14-ounce, 21-day-dry-aged strip loin goes for $65. Breakfast, lunch, and dinner are served, as well as brunch on Sunday. Don't miss the men's bathroom—this art deco masterpiece of black and green leaded-glass tiles has served as the set of more than a few music videos and is so famous that women are allowed to take a peek inside. ⊠ *231 6th Ave. N, Downtown* ☎ *615/345–7116* ⊕ *www.thehermitagehotel.com* ⌂ *Reservations essential* ▭ *AE, D, DC, MC, V.*

$$$

AMERICAN

✕ **Whiskey Kitchen.** This former warehouse in the Gulch, one of Nashville's most happening entertainment districts, serves high-quality pub food—think juicy burgers, wood-fired pizzas, and spicy wings—with slick urban style and a touch of local flavor. Specialties include Tennessee whiskey yam fries and southern sliders served on tender buttermilk biscuits. Whiskey aficionados will appreciate the more than 60 varieties on offer. Come watch the game on one of the many flat-screen TVs, or stop by on a Friday or Saturday night for a pitcher of whiskey sours ($19.50) and see Nashville's twenty- and thirtysomethings on parade.

A late-night menu is available from 11 to 1. ⊠ *118 12th Ave. S., Downtown* ☎ *615/254–3029* ⊕ *www.whiskeykitchen.com* ▬ *AE, MC, V.*

AROUND VANDERBILT UNIVERSITY

¢–$

SOUTHERN

Fodor's Choice

★

✕ **Pancake Pantry.** This Nashville institution is the place to go for breakfast. It's a favorite haunt of celebrities like Garth Brooks and Alan Jackson and also popular with local politicos. Breakfast is the specialty, with more than 20 kinds of pancakes and homemade syrups. The menu also has soups and sandwiches for lunch. ■ TIP→ Get there by 8:15 weekdays to avoid lines, but be prepared to wait on weekends. ⊠ *1796 21st Ave. S, Hillsboro Village* ☎ *615/383–9333* ◿ *Reservations not accepted* ▬ *AE, D, DC, MC, V* ⊗ *No dinner.*

$$$–$$$$

AMERICAN

Fodor's Choice

★

✕ **Sunset Grill.** Seafood, pastas, steaks, and vegetarian specials highlight the menu of this restaurant that displays the work of local artist Paul Harmon. A good entrée choice is voodoo pasta, with andouille sausage, chicken, and shrimp tossed in a spicy black pepper sauce—this local favorite has been on the menu since the restaurant opened 20 years ago. Sublime homemade sorbet is a good finish to your meal, and the restaurant serves 70 wines by the glass. A special late-night menu is available from 10 pm to midnight Monday through Thursday, and 10 pm to 1:30 am Friday and Saturday. ⊠ *2001 Belcourt Ave., Hillsboro Village* ☎ *615/386–3663 or 866/496–3663* ⊕ *www.sunsetgrill.com* ▬ *AE, D, MC, V* ⊗ *No lunch Sat.–Mon.*

EAST NASHVILLE

$$$–$$$$

FRENCH

★

✕ **Margot Café and Bar.** The worn brick exterior shoehorned onto an East Nashville street belies the wizardry that goes on in the kitchen. With the emphasis on French and Italian flavors, the changing menu may include braised mackerel with roasted red pepper sauce, hanger steak with fingerling potatoes, and grilled cobia with preserved lemon and caper pesto. ⊠ *1017 Woodland St., East Nashville* ☎ *615/227–4668* ⊕ *www.margotcafe.com* ▬ *D, MC, V* ⊗ *No lunch. Closed Mon. Brunch only on Sun.*

GREATER NASHVILLE

$$$

ITALIAN

★

✕ **City House.** The ever-changing Italian-influenced menu at this Germantown outpost has been luring discerning diners since they dished up their first plate of house-made sausage in 2007. Sit at the chef's bar to get an up-close-and-personal look at chef Tandy Wilson and his crew as they cook up creative pasta dishes, wood-fired pizzas, and their trademark Carolina Trout cooked with breadcrumbs, peanuts, raisins, lemons, and parsley. Be sure to peruse the inventive cocktail list. For an even more memorable experience, stop by for "Sunday Supper," a no-menu night where your meal is chosen by the chef. ⊠ *1222 4th Ave. N, Germantown* ☎ *615/736–5838* ⊕ *www.cityhousenashville.com* ▬ *AE, MC, V* ⊗ *No lunch. Closed Tues.*

WHERE TO STAY

Nashville has an impressive selection of accommodations in all price categories and at all levels of luxury. Some establishments increase rates slightly during the peak summer travel season, especially CMA Music

Festival week in mid-June, and some downtown luxury hotels offer lower rates on weekends, when the legislators and business travelers have gone home. For a good selection of B&Bs throughout Nashville, check out ⊕ *www.bedandbreakfast.com/nashville-tennessee.html.*

Hotel reviews have been condensed for this book. Please go to Fodors. com for full reviews of each property.

WHAT IT COSTS				
¢	$	$$	$$$	$$$$
Hotels	under $70	$70–$110	$111–$160	$161–$220	over $220

Prices are for two people in a standard double room in high season, not including tax.

DOWNTOWN

$$-$$$
★
🔲 **Doubletree Hotel Nashville.** Newly remodeled in late 2008, this hotel is just a short hike to the State Capitol, Ryman Auditorium, and the Country Music Hall of Fame. Rooms are fitted out with large plasma-screen televisions and coffeemakers with gourmet coffee. **Pros:** executive floor, complimentary Internet in rooms. **Cons:** no airport shuttle. ⊠ *315 4th Ave. N, Downtown* 🕾 *615/244–8200* ⊕ *www.doubletree. com* ⤹ *331 rooms, 6 suites* ♿ *In-room: Internet. In-hotel: 2 restaurants, room service, bar, pool, gym, laundry service, Wi-Fi, parking (paid)* ⊟ *AE, D, MC, V.*

$$$-$$$$
★
🔲 **Hampton Inn & Suites Downtown Nashville.** This hotel, opened in 2007 in the rapidly developing area south of downtown, is just a stone's throw from the Country Music Hall of Fame. **Pros:** short walk to museums and honky tonks; good value for downtown; complimentary breakfast. **Cons:** no airport shuttle; no restaurant. ⊠ *310 4th Ave. S, Downtown* 🕾 *615/277–5000* ⊕ *www.hamptoninn.com* ⤹ *100 rooms, 54 suites* ♿ *In-room: refrigerator, Wi-Fi. In-hotel: pool, gym, laundry services, Wi-Fi, parking (paid)* ⊟ *AE, D, MC, V* ⫶○⫶ *CP.*

$$$$
Fodor's Choice
★
🔲 **The Hermitage Hotel.** Nashville's grandest hotel, the Hermitage is a downtown institution where everything is luxurious, from the large rooms to the plush robes to the marble bathrooms. **Pros:** sumptuous rooms; 24-hour fitness center and room service; a short walk to the Tennessee State Capitol and other downtown attractions. **Cons:** no pool; parking is not free. ⊠ *231 6th Ave. N, Downtown* 🕾 *615/244–3121 or 888/888–9414* ⊕ *www.thehermitagehotel.com* ⤹ *112 rooms, 10 suites* ♿ *In-room: refrigerator (some), DVD, Wi-Fi. In-hotel: restaurant, room service, bar, gym, spa, laundry service, Wi-Fi, parking (paid), some pets allowed* ⊟ *AE, D, DC, MC, V.*

$$$-$$$$
★
🔲 **Hilton Nashville Downtown.** An all-suites hotel in the center of Nashville's new cultural heart, the Hilton is within walking distance of the Bridgestone Arena, Schermerhorn Symphony Center, the Country Music Hall of Fame, the Ryman Auditorium, the downtown convention center, and Broadway's honky tonks. The soaring lobby is bright and airy. **Pros:** comfortable rooms; close to many downtown attractions. **Cons:** concierge could be a little more knowledgeable; main entrance is a bit crowded with a notable walk to check-in desk; limited public Wi-Fi. ⊠ *121 4th Ave. S, Downtown* 🕾 *615/620–1000* ⊕ *www.nashvillehilton.*

Country music stars light up the stage every week at the Grand Ole Opry.

com ⇥ *330 suites* & *In-room: refrigerator, Wi-Fi. In-hotel: 4 restaurants, room service, bars, indoor pool, fitness center, parking (paid)* ▭ *AE, D, DC, MC, V.*

GREATER NASHVILLE

$$$–$$$$ ⊞ **Gaylord Opryland Resort and Convention Center.** This massive hotel,
★ dining, and entertainment complex adjacent to the Grand Ole Opry
has three 3-acre glass-walled conservatories filled with 10,000 tropi-
cal plants and a skylit indoor area with water features and a half-acre
lake. **Pros:** no shortage of activities; conveniently located for Opry per-
formances. **Cons:** a little overwhelming—more a destination in and of
itself rather than a convenient spot from which to see the city. ✉ *2800
Opryland Dr., Music Valley* ☎ *615/889–1000* ⊕ *www.gaylordhotels.
com/gaylord-opryland* ⇥ *2,881 rooms, 165 suites* & *In-room: refrigera-
tor, Wi-Fi. In-hotel: 7 restaurants, room service, bars, golf course, pools,
fitness center, spa, laundry service, parking (paid)* ▭ *AE, D, MC, V.*

NIGHTLIFE

Musicians throughout Nashville will tell you it all starts with a song,
which is good news for fans of live music: Nashville is absolutely clut-
tered with music venues, spread throughout the city's neighborhoods.
Plenty of other entertainment options are available as well. To get an
idea of what's going on in town, check out weekly newspapers *All the
Rage* or *Nashville Scene*, available for free throughout downtown and
in many hotels. Both have extensive music and nightlife listings. You
can also check with the Nashville Visitor Center.

The scene on Broadway, with its strip of honky tonks and souvenir and record shops, perhaps best captures the stripped-down essence of country music: friendly and welcoming, yet a little wild and not averse to getting down in the gutter.

Robert's Western World (✉ *416 Broadway, Downtown* ☎ *615/244–9552*) was originally a clothing store; cowboy boots adorn the walls, but today country music is what makes it famous. For many years local legends BR5-49 (named after a long-running bit on *Hee Haw*) were the popular house band. Perhaps the most famous honky tonk on Broadway is **Tootsie's Orchid Lounge** (✉ *422 Broadway, Downtown* ☎ *615/726–0463*), where the music pours out the front door and onto the street.

Fodor's Choice ★ The **Grand Ole Opry** (✉ *2802 Opryland Dr., Music Valley* ☎ *615/889– 6611, 800/733–6779 ticket information* ⊕ *www.opry.com*) has drawn country fans since 1925. You never know who will turn up on the Opry's down-home stage. Show times are Friday at 7, Saturday at 7 and 9:30 (Saturday late shows are select dates only), and Tuesday at 7 (March–December only for Tuesday shows).

For a change of pace, check out some of Nashville's smaller music clubs.

At the famous **Bluebird Cafe** (✉ *4104 Hillsboro Rd., Green Hills* ☎ *615/ 383–1461* ⊕ *www.bluebirdcafe.com*), in a strip mall among gas stations and fast-food joints in an outlying neighborhood (look for the red neon lights), singers and songwriters try out their latest material as well as some old favorites. There's no stage—musicians sit in the middle of the intimate space, within elbow room of the tables. A strict no-talking rule gives guests the chance to hear fully the tales of heartache and, occasionally, happiness, pouring out of guitars and microphones. The kitchen turns out yummy snacks, and there's a full bar. Calling ahead for reservations is recommended.

New Orleans

WORD OF MOUTH

"Go to Commander's [Palace] for Sunday Jazz Brunch. Ask for a table in the Garden Room overlooking the patio. Go to Antoine's or Brennan's in the FQ. I prefer Brennan's. Splurge at Galatoire's or Emeril's, which is in the CBD."

—Littleman

WELCOME TO NEW ORLEANS

TOP REASONS TO GO

★ **Mardi Gras:** The quintessential party in America's party town.

★ **French Quarter Strolls:** Walking amid the city's historic buildings, you'll meet buskers and drunks, artists and ghosts. It's one of the most intriguing neighborhoods in the country.

★ **All That Jazz:** Entire chapters of America's musical history were written here—and you can still see some of the country's best artists perform here in incredibly intimate settings.

★ **Soul Food:** Eating in New Orleans is a way of life. Food shapes the celebrations that are the backbone of the city. New Orleans has many unique styles of cooking. There's Creole, Cajun, and southern comfort food, as well as ethnic eats and countless fusion cuisines.

1 The French Quarter. The geographic and cultural heart of the city since the early 1700s, the Quarter is a vibrant commercial and residential mélange of wrought-iron balconies, beckoning courtyards, antiques shops—and, of course, tawdry Bourbon Street.

2 Faubourg Marigny and Bywater. The Marigny, New Orleans's first suburb, has nightclubs, cafés, and some lovingly restored Creole cottages; grittier Bywater, despite gentrification, retains its working-class credentials while accommodating a burgeoning arts scene.

3 Tremé. The cradle of jazz and second-line parades fell into decline when much of it was razed to make room for a freeway and public "improvements" like Armstrong Park. But a trip to the tiny Backstreet Cultural Museum conjures memories of the historically African-American neighborhood's heyday.

4 CBD and Warehouse District. Most of the city's newer hotels are clustered here, near Canal Street or the sprawling Morial Convention Center. There also are classy museums, fine restaurants, a bustling

casino, and the city's most adventurous art galleries.

5 The Garden District. Stunning early-19th-century mansions make this a great neighborhood for walking, followed by an afternoon browsing the shops and cafés along bustling Magazine Street.

Rue Bourbon
Bourbon

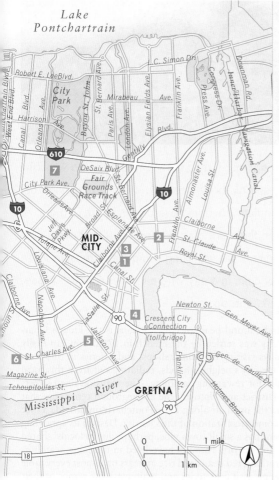

Lake
Pontchartrain

Robert E. Lee Blvd.

City
Park

Mirabeau   Ave.

Harrison

610

7

DeSaix Blvd.

City Park Ave.

Fair
Grounds
Race Track

10

10

MID-
CITY

3
1

Claiborne   Ave.

St. Claude   Ave.

Royal St.

2

Canal St.

Newton St.   Gen. Meyer Ave.

90   4   Crescent City
Connection
(toll bridge)

5   Jackson Ave.

6   St. Charles Ave.

Magazine St.

Tchoupitoulas St.

Mississippi   River   GRETNA

90

18

0   1 mile
0   1 km

GETTING ORIENTED

13

The city occupies an 8-mi stretch between the Mississippi River and Lake Pontchartrain, covering roughly 365 square mi of flat, swamp-drained land. The heart of the city, downtown, includes the famous old area called the Vieux Carré (Old Square), or the French Quarter; the historic African-American district of Tremé; the Central Business District (CBD); and the Warehouse District. Across the river from downtown is an extension of New Orleans known as the Westbank, which includes the neighborhood of Algiers Point. Downriver from the French Quarter are the Faubourg Marigny and the Bywater districts. And Canal Street divides the French Quarter from the "American Sector," as it was designated in the early days following the Louisiana Purchase.

6 Uptown. Audubon Park and the campuses of Tulane and Loyola universities anchor oak-shaded Uptown; hop on the St. Charles streetcar to survey it in period style.

7 Bayou St. John and Mid-City. Rambling City Park and the New Orleans Museum of Art are the main draws here, but there are also some good, inexpensive restaurants and lively bars.

8 Metairie and the Lakefront. The south shore of Lake Pontchartrain is a good place for a bike ride or picnic; suburban Metairie hosts the Metairie Cemetery and Longue Vue House and Gardens.

Sometime during your visit to New Orleans, find a wrought-iron balcony, an oak-shaded courtyard, or a columned front porch and sit quietly, favorite beverage in hand, at 6 am. At this hour, when the moist air sits heavy on the streets, New Orleans is a city of mesmerizing tranquility. Treasure those rare minutes of calm in a city where there is so much to see, hear, eat, drink, and do.

The spiritual and cultural heart of New Orleans is the French Quarter, where the city was settled by the French in 1718. You can easily spend several days visiting museums, shops, and eateries in this area. Yet the rest of the city's neighborhoods, radiating out from this focal point, also make for rewarding rambling. The mansion-lined streets of the Garden District and Uptown, the aboveground cemeteries that dot the city, and the open air along Lake Pontchartrain provide a nice balance to the commercialization of the Quarter. Despite its sprawling size, New Orleans has a small-town vibe, perhaps due to locals' shared cultural habits and history. Families have lived in the same neighborhoods for generations; red beans and rice appears on almost every table on Monday; people visit cemeteries and whitewash the tombs of their departed on All Saints' Day; and from the smartest office to the most down-home local bar, New Orleanians are ready to celebrate anything at the drop of a hat.

PLANNING

WHEN TO GO

May through September is hot and humid—double-100 days (100F and nearly 100% humidity) aren't uncommon. These long, hot summers may explain why things are less hurried down here. If you visit during sticky July and August, you'll find lower hotel prices, but some restaurants are closed for the summer.

June through November there are heavy rains and occasional hurricanes. These conditions occur mainly with quick changes in temperature that accompany cold fronts in the fall. Although winters are mild compared with those in northern climes, the high humidity can put a chill in the air December through February. Nevertheless, the holiday season is a great time to visit, with few conventions in town, a beautifully bedecked French Quarter, and "Papa Noel" discounted rates at many hotels. Perhaps the best time to visit the city is early spring. Days are pleasant, except for seasonal cloudbursts, and nights are cool.

New Orleans is nothing if not festive, and festivals play an important role in the city's cultural and entertainment calendars. Some of the more significant events include the Mardi Gras celebrations and the Jazz & Heritage Festival, which runs from late April to early May. Smaller festivals held throughout the year may not be quite as showy as Fat Tuesday, but they often give visitors a better understanding of New Orleans.

13

GETTING HERE

AIR TRAVEL

Most major and a few regional airlines serve **Louis Armstrong International Airport** (☎ *504/464–0831*) in Kenner, 15 mi east of downtown New Orleans. A taxi from the airport to the French Quarter costs a flat rate of $28 for two people; for more than two passengers the fixed rate is $12 per person. Shared-ride shuttles to hotels are available for about $15 per person. If you're traveling light and have a lot of extra time, you can take Jefferson Transit's airport bus, which runs between the main terminal entrance and the Central Business District (CBD). Fare is $1.60.

CAR TRAVEL

Interstate 10 runs from Florida to California and passes directly through the city (from up north, take I–55). To get to the CBD (Central Business District), exit at Poydras Street near the Louisiana Superdome. For the French Quarter, look for the Orleans Avenue/Vieux Carré exit.

TRAIN TRAVEL

Three Amtrak lines serve New Orleans: the *City of New Orleans* from Chicago; the *Sunset Limited* service between New Orleans and Los Angeles; and the *Crescent*, which connects New Orleans and New York by way of Atlanta. For tickets and schedules, call ☎ *800/872–7245* or visit ⊕ *www.amtrak.com.*

GETTING AROUND

On public transportation: Streetcars are a great way to see the city. The St. Charles line runs from Canal Street to the intersection of Claiborne and Carrollton avenues; along the way it passes the Garden District, Audubon Park, and Tulane and Loyola universities. The Riverfront line skirts the French Quarter along the Mississippi, from Esplanade Avenue to the Ernest N. Morial Convention Center. Some Canal line streetcars make a straight shot from the Quarter to the cemeteries at City Park Avenue; others take a spur at Carrollton Avenue that goes to City Park and the New Orleans Museum of Art.

At present, bus travel in New Orleans is a pretty depressing experience, but a few lines are of use. The Magazine bus runs the length of shopping mecca Magazine Street, from Canal and Camp streets to the Audubon Zoo entrance at the far edge of Audubon Park. The Esplanade bus serves City Park, and drops Jazz Fest passengers off a few blocks from the Fair Grounds.

Fares for streetcars and buses are $1.25 ($1.50 for express lines); Visi-Tour visitors' passes have one-day unlimited rides for $5 and a three-day unlimited pass for $12. For route maps, timetables, and more information, visit ⊕ *www.norta.com.*

By car: If you don't plan to drive outside the city limits, you probably won't need a car—you'll save money traveling by streetcar, cab, and on foot. If you do decide to drive, keep in mind that some streets are in ragged condition, traffic lights routinely malfunction, and parking in the Quarter is tight (and parking regulations vigorously enforced).

By taxi: Taxis are often the most convenient way to move around, and drivers are used to short trips, so don't hesitate to grab a cab if you're leery about walking late at night. Locals recommend United Cabs, Yellow Checker, and Veterans. Don't get into an unlicensed/unmarked "gypsy" cab. Rates are $1.60 per mi or 20¢ for every 40 seconds of waiting, plus a base of $2.50; each additional passenger is $1.

SAFETY

Much of the post-Katrina media coverage has focused on New Orleans's escalating crime rate. Sadly, this isn't just sensationalism, there's a growing homelessness problem, the murder rate is among the highest in the nation, and armed robberies occur all too frequently. These grim statistics should not dissuade you from visiting, but you need to exercise caution if you venture outside the well-touristed and highly trafficked areas—especially at night.

After an April 20, 2010, explosion, the Deepwater Horizon oil rig leaked huge quantities of oil into the Gulf of Mexico near Louisiana. New Orleans is approximately 100 mi inland from affected areas, and at the time of this writing there are no negative impacts for visitors. **A word about seafood:** Health, environmental, and fisheries agencies continue to monitor coastal and nearby inland areas daily, testing seafood, soils, and drinking water for safety. At the time of this writing, only 11% of Louisiana's costal fishing remains shut down from a peak of 37%.

For updates, visit the Louisiana Tourism Office (⊕ *www.louisianatravel.com/oil-spill-response*), the Louisiana Department of Wildlife and Fisheries (⊕ *www.wlf.louisiana.gov*), or the Louisiana Department of Environmental Quality (⊕ *www.deq.louisiana.gov*).

EXPLORING NEW ORLEANS

To experience this fun-filled city, you can begin with the usual tourist attractions, but you must go beyond them. Linger in a corner grocery store, sip a cold drink in a local joint, or chat with a stoop-sitter. New Orleanians, for all their gripes and grumbling, love their city. They treasure custom and tradition, take in stride the semitropical climate, and face life with a laid-back attitude and an undying sense of hope and faith that sometimes seems fatalistic to outsiders.

THE FRENCH QUARTER

On an ordinary evening, a stroll through the French Quarter is also a moving concert, where the strains of traditional jazz, blues, classic rock and roll, and electronic dance beats all commingle. During the day, the Quarter offers several different faces to its visitors. The streets running parallel to the river all carry distinct personas: Decatur Street is a strip of tourist shops and hotels uptown from Jackson Square; downtown from the square, it becomes an alternative hangout for leather-clad regulars drawn to shadowy bars, vintage clothing resellers, and novelty shops. Chartres Street is a relatively calm stretch of inviting shops and eateries. Royal Street is the address of sophisticated antiques shops and many of the Quarter's finest homes. Bourbon Street claims the sex shops, extravagant cocktails, and music clubs filmmakers love to feature. Dauphine and Burgundy streets are more residential, with just a few local restaurants and bars.

WHAT TO SEE

Bourbon Street. Crude and crass, New Orleans's most famous entertainment strip isn't to everyone's taste, but you have to see it at least once—preferably under the nighttime neon lights. Tawdry strip clubs and souvenir shops scream for attention, but look closer and you'll find local jazz musicians showing off their chops, elegant restaurants, and faded bars where luminaries like Mark Twain and Tennessee Williams imbibed.

Hermann-Grima House. One of the largest and best-preserved examples of American architecture in the Quarter, this Georgian-style house has the only restored private stable and the only working 1830s Creole kitchen in the Quarter. American architect William Brand built the house in 1831. Cooking demonstrations on the open hearth are held here all day Thursday from October through May. ✉ *820 St. Louis St., French Quarter* ☎ *504/525–5661* 🎫 *$10, combination ticket with the Gallier House $18* ◷ *Tours Mon., Tues., Thurs., Fri. 10, 11, noon, 1, 2, Sat. noon, 1, 2, 3.*

Fodor's Choice ★

Jackson Square. Flanked by St. Louis Cathedral, the antebellum Pontalba apartment buildings, and the Mississippi River, postcard-pretty Jackson Square has been the hub of New Orleans life since the city's colonial start. Artists, musicians, and fortune-tellers congregate on the plaza surrounding the square, but the manicured park itself is a peaceful oasis.

FAUBOURG MARIGNY AND BYWATER

Although you won't find the head-swiveling density of sights here that you will in the French Quarter, a tour through the Faubourg Marigny (pronounced FOE-berg MARE-uh-Nee) and especially the Bywater gives you a feel for New Orleans as it lives day to day, in a colorful, overgrown, slightly sleepy cityscape reminiscent of island communities and tinged with a sense of elegant decay. With architectural styles ranging from classic Creole cottage to Victorian mansion, the Marigny is a residential extension of the Quarter. The streets are more peaceful and the residents more bohemian. **Frenchmen Street**, the Marigny's main

strip, is lined with music clubs, coffee shops, and restaurants; music lovers spill into the streets on most weekend nights. Many of the streets intersect at odd angles; look for street names in inlaid tiles at corners. The **Bywater**, a crumbling yet beautiful old neighborhood, is a haven to those musicians and artists who find the Marigny too expensive and crowded. The **New Orleans Center for Creative Arts** (NOCCA) occupies a beautiful campus of renovated warehouses at its edge. The Mississippi runs the length of its boundary. The bars and coffee shops scattered around this neighborhood combine elements of its working-class roots and more recent hipster influx.

TREMÉ

Across Rampart Street from the French Quarter, the neighborhood of Tremé (pronounced truh-MAY) claims to be the oldest African-American neighborhood in the country. Once the site of the Claude Tremé plantation, it became home to many free people of color during the late 18th and early 19th centuries. Although most of the neighborhood did not see significant flooding from Katrina. and the residents continue to restore its brightly colored historic homes. Never a highly touristed area, the Tremé now offers an even more quiet and reflective experience (unless, of course, you happen upon a second-line parade!). ■ TIP➔ **Like many New Orleans neighborhoods beyond the French Quarter, the Tremé has had problems with crime. Visit this area during the day, and enjoy having its rich, small museums to yourself.**

CBD AND WAREHOUSE DISTRICT

Bordered by the river, St. Charles Avenue, Poydras Street, and the Interstate 10 expressway and filled with former factories and cotton warehouses, the Warehouse District began its renaissance when the city hosted the World's Fair here in 1984. Old abandoned buildings were renovated to host the fair and its events, setting the scene for future development, including the structures that now make up the New Orleans Morial Convention Center and a number of hotels, restaurants, bars, and music clubs. The Warehouse District is one of the hottest residential and arts-and-nightlife areas of the city, dotted with modern renovations of historic buildings, upscale loft residences, excellent eateries, and a number of bars and music clubs.

The Central Business District (CBD) covers the ground between Canal Street and Poydras Avenue, with some spillover into the Warehouse District's official territory. The neighborhood includes many iconic buildings, including the Louisiana Superdome, the World Trade Center, and Harrah's Casino. There are also beautiful old government and office buildings, particularly around central Lafayette Square. Canal Street is the CBD's main artery and the official dividing line between the business district and the French Quarter.

WHAT TO SEE

Fodor'sChoice
★

Blaine Kern's Mardi Gras World at Kern Studios. Mardi Gras World's entertainment complex moved from Algiers Point to join Blaine Kern Studios and new private-event venues on the east bank of New Orleans in early 2009. Located just upriver of the New Orleans Convention Center, the massive 400,000-square-foot complex brings the fun of its West Bank predecessor closer to the city center with an enhanced guided tour through a maze of video presentations, decorative sculptures, and favorite megafloats from Mardi Gras parades such as Bacchus, Rex, and Endymion. If you're not here for the real thing, Mardi Gras World is a fun (and family-friendly) backstage look at the history and artistry of Carnival. Admission includes cake and coffee. ✉ *1380 Port of New Orleans Pl., Warehouse* ☎ *504/361–7821 or 800/362–8213* ⊕ *www. mardigrasworld.com* ✉ *$18* ☉ *Daily 9:30–5.*

Fodor'sChoice
★

National World War II Museum. Exhibits take visitors from the Normandy invasion to the sands of Pacific Islands and the Home Front. The brainchild of historian and writer Dr. Stephen Ambrose, who taught for many years at the University of New Orleans, this moving examination of World War II covers far more ground than D-Day. The seminal moments are re-created through propaganda posters and radio clips from the period; biographical sketches of the military personnel involved; a number of short documentary films; and collections of weapons, personal items, and other artifacts from the war. One spotlighted exhibit, in a large, open portion near the entrance, is a replica of the Higgins boat troop landing craft, which were manufactured in New Orleans and shaped the D-Day attack on Normandy. In 2009 the museum unveiled the first phase of its $300 million expansion, which will eventually quadruple the size of the facility. Across the street from the current facility, there's a 4-D theater experience produced by Tom Hanks and a canteen featuring the food of celebrity chef John Besh. This is the first of six new pavilions proposed for the expanded campus, due to be completed in 2015. Check the Web site for updates on the expansion and a list of current movies, lectures, events, and programs. ✉ *925 Magazine St. (main entrance on Andrew Higgins Dr.), Warehouse* ☎ *504/527–6012* ⊕ *www.nationalww2museum.org* ✉ *$14* ☉ *Daily 9–5.*

GARDEN DISTRICT

With its beautifully landscaped gardens surrounding elegant antebellum homes, the Garden District lives up to its name. Although its homes aren't open to the public, outside of occasional special-event tours, enjoying the sights from outside the cast-iron fences is well worth the visit.

Originally the Livaudais Plantation, the Garden District was laid out in the late 1820s and remained part of the city of Lafayette until incorporated into New Orleans in 1852. The neighborhood attracted "new-moneyed" Americans who constructed grand houses with large English-style gardens featuring lush azaleas, magnolias, and camellias. Magazine Street, lined with antiques shops, boutiques, restaurants, and cafés, serves as a southern border to the Garden District. St. Charles Avenue forms the northern border.

UPTOWN

Lying west of the Garden District, Uptown is the residential area on both sides of St. Charles Avenue along the streetcar route, upriver from Louisiana Avenue. It includes many mansions as sumptuous as those in the Garden District, as well as Loyola and Tulane universities and a large urban park named for John James Audubon. Traveling along the avenue from downtown to uptown provides something of a historical narrative: the city's development unfolded upriver, and the houses grow more modern the farther uptown you go.

WHAT TO SEE

Fodor's Choice
★
The St. Charles Avenue streetcar, which runs down the length of the avenue, from Canal Street to the Carrollton Riverbend, provides a wonderful way to take in the neighborhood. In the early 1900s streetcars were the most prominent mode of public transit and ran on many streets. Today, they operate along the riverfront, Canal Street, St. Charles Avenue, and Carrollton Avenue. ■TIP→ Avoid rush hours—from 7 to 9 and 3 to 6—or you may have to stand still much of the way and will not be able to enjoy the scenery.

Another main artery, Magazine Street, traverses the Uptown area with miles of antiques and home decor shops, boutiques, galleries, restaurants, and cafés. The Magazine Street bus can take you up and down the length of the street, which culminates at Audubon Park, a lush stretch of green that encompasses a track, fields, zoo, and golf course.

BAYOU ST. JOHN AND MID-CITY

Above the French Quarter and below the lakefront, neither Uptown nor quite downtown, Mid-City is an amorphous yet proud territory, which includes the massive, lush City Park. It is a neighborhood of tremendous ethnic and economic diversity. Here you'll find great restaurants, cultural landmarks such as Rock and Bowl, restored former plantation homes, and crumbling inner-city neighborhoods. Actual sights are few and far between in Mid-City, and the neighborhood suffered heavily from flooding during Hurricane Katrina, but the area is recovering. The neighborhood around Bayou St. John near City Park is still one of the more picturesque in town and is fruitful for walks.

METAIRIE AND THE LAKEFRONT

The historic **Longue Vue House and Gardens,** tucked along what seems like a country road, and the New Orleans Country Club are in the center of a particularly attractive, suburban area. Carving out several acres in the middle of Old Metairie, the elaborate tombs of the Lake Lawn Metairie Cemetery, the city's largest, are visible from the Interstate 10 Expressway. Outside of old Metairie, however, the area has a more modern, suburban feel. The newer sections of Metairie extend to the lakefront, much of which was heavily damaged by Hurricane Katrina. Although renovation and rebuilding continue in various degrees in many pockets, some houses and buildings remain empty and untended, with high floodwater lines still marking their exteriors. Still, a stroll, drive, or picnic along Lakeshore Drive on a sunny day is a pleasant way to take in **Lake Pontchartrain.**

WHERE TO EAT

13

New Orleans is known as much for its sensory expression as it is for its joie de vivre, and nowhere is this more evident than in the stellar cuisine offered at local restaurants. Traditional Louisiana dishes, such as jambalaya, red beans and rice, gumbo, and étouffée are readily available, but the delectable surprise of dining in New Orleans is the diversity of dishes and cuisines that are available, not to mention the culinary ingenuity on display.

Old or new, the menus at New Orleans's restaurants reflect three centuries of multiple cultures constantly contributing to the always-simmering culinary gumbo pot. What influences can you expect to taste? The list is long, but it's easy to find dashes of Spanish, French, Italian, German, African, Caribbean, and Croatian flavor—and increasingly, Asian and Latin influences.

WHAT IT COSTS					
	¢	$	$$	$$$	$$$$
Restaurants	under $9	$9–$16	$17–$25	$26–$35	over $35

Restaurant prices are for a main course at dinner, excluding sales tax of 9.5%.

FRENCH QUARTER

$ ✕ **Acme Oyster and Seafood Restaurant.** A rough-edge classic in every way,
SEAFOOD this no-nonsense eatery at the entrance to the French Quarter is a prime
☺ source for cool and salty raw oysters on the half shell; shrimp, oyster, and roast-beef po'boys; and tender, expertly seasoned red beans and rice. Table service, once confined to the main dining room out front, is now provided in the rear room as well. Expect lengthy lines outside, often a half-block long (trust us though, it's worth it). Crowds lighten in the late afternoon. ⊠ *724 Iberville St., French Quarter* ☎ *504/522–5973* ⊕ *www.acmeoyster.com* ⟳ *Reservations not accepted* ▭ *AE, D, DC, MC, V.*

$$$ ✕ **Arnaud's.** This grande dame of classic Creole restaurants still sparkles.
CREOLE In the main dining room, ornate etched glass reflects light from charm-
Fodor'sChoice ing old chandeliers while the late founder, Arnaud Cazenave, gazes from
★ an oil portrait. The adjoining jazz bistro offers the same food but is a more casual and music-filled dining experience. The ambitious menu includes classic dishes as well as more contemporary ones. Always reliable are Shrimp Arnaud—cold shrimp in a superb rémoulade—and Oysters Bienville, Petit Filet Lafitte, and praline crepes. Jackets are requested in the main dining room. Be sure to visit the Mardi Gras museum upstairs. ⊠ *813 Bienville St., French Quarter* ☎ *504/523–5433*

Any visit to New Orleans must include a generous sampling of traditional Louisiana dishes.

⊕ *www.arnauds.com* ⇗ *Reservations essential* ▭ *AE, D, DC, MC, V* ⊗ *No lunch Sat.*

¢ ✕ **Café du Monde**. No trip to New Orleans is complete without a cup
CAFÉ of chicory-laced café au lait and addictive sugar-dusted beignets in this
venerable Creole institution. The tables under the green-and-white-
striped awning are jammed at every hour with locals and tourists feast-
ing on powdery doughnuts and views of Jackson Square. ■ **TIP→** **If
there's a line for table service, head around back to the takeout window
and get your coffee and beignets to go. Enjoy them overlooking the river
right next door, or in Jackson Square.** ⊠ *800 Decatur St., French Quarter*
☎ *504/525–4544* ⊕ *www.cafedumonde.com* ▭ *No credit cards.*

$ ✕ **Central Grocery**. This old-fashioned Italian grocery store produces
CAFÉ authentic muffulettas, one of the gastronomic gifts of the city's Italian
immigrants. Good enough to challenge the po'boy as the local sandwich
champ, it's made by filling round loaves of seeded bread with ham,
salami, mozzarella, and a salad of marinated green olives. Sandwiches,
about 10 inches in diameter, are sold in wholes and halves. ■ **TIP→** **The
muffulettas are huge! Unless you're starving, you'll do fine with a half.** You
can eat your muffuletta at a counter, or get it to go and dine on a bench
on Jackson Square or the Moon Walk along the Mississippi riverfront.
The Grocery closes at 5:30 pm. ⊠ *923 Decatur St., French Quarter*
☎ *504/523–1620* ▭ *D, MC, V* ⊗ *No dinner.*

$$$ ✕ **Galatoire's**. Galatoire's has always epitomized the old-style French-
CREOLE Creole bistro. Many of the recipes date to 1905. Fried oysters and bacon
Fodor'sChoice en brochette are worth every calorie, and the brick-red rémoulade sauce
★ sets a high standard. Other winners include veal chops in béarnaise
sauce, and seafood-stuffed eggplant. The setting downstairs is a single,

narrow dining room lighted with glistening brass chandeliers; bentwood chairs and white tablecloths add to its timelessness. You may reserve a table in the renovated upstairs rooms, though the action is on the first floor, where partying regulars inhibit conversation but add good people-watching entertainment value. Friday lunch starts early and continues well into early evening. A jacket is required. ✉ *209 Bourbon St., French Quarter* ☎ *504/525–2021* ⊕ *www.galatoires.com* 🖃 *AE, D, DC, MC, V* ☽ *Closed Mon.*

13

$$$
CAJUN
✕ **K-Paul's Louisiana Kitchen.** In this comfortable French Quarter café of glossy wooden floors and exposed brick, chef Paul Prudhomme started the blackening craze and added "Cajun" to America's culinary vocabulary. Two decades later, thousands still consider a visit to New Orleans partly wasted without a visit to K-Paul's for his inventive gumbos, fried crawfish tails, blackened tuna, roast duck with rice dressing, and sweet potato–pecan pie. Prices are steep, but servings are generous. And although you can make reservations these days, it's still tradition to line up along Chartres Street before the doors open. ✉ *416 Chartres St., French Quarter* ☎ *504/524–7394* ⊕ *www.kpauls.com* ⌲ *Reservations essential* 🖃 *AE, D, DC, MC, V* ☽ *Closed Sun. No lunch Mon.–Wed.*

$$$
ECLECTIC
Fodor's Choice
★
✕ **Stella!** Chef Scott Boswell has evolved into one of the city's most innovative and daring culinarians. Try the shrimp and chanterelle or lobster mushroom risotto. The porcini-crusted rack of Australian lamb and lamb rib eye is strictly upscale comfort food, the perfect prelude to chocolate cake with hot buttered pink lemonade. Stella! now sits comfortably among New Orleans's best fine-dining restaurants. ✉ *1032 Chartres St., French Quarter* ☎ *504/587–0091* ⊕ *www.restaurantstella. com* 🖃 *AE, D, DC, MC, V* ☽ *No lunch.*

CBD AND WAREHOUSE DISTRICT

$$$
SOUTHERN
Fodor's Choice
★
✕ **August.** If the Gilded Age is long gone, someone forgot to tell the folks at August, whose main dining room shimmers with masses of chandelier prisms, thick brocade fabrics, and glossy woods. Service is anything but stuffy, however, and chef John Besh's modern technique adorns every plate. Nothing is mundane here: Handmade gnocchi with blue crab and winter truffle shares menu space with slow-cooked pork belly and butter-poached main lobster with black truffles. Expect the unexpected—like slow-roasted Kobe beef short ribs with Jerusalem artichokes. The sommelier is happy to confer with you on the surprisingly affordable wine list. ✉ *301 Tchoupitoulas St., CBD* ☎ *504/299–9777* ⊕ *www.restaurantaugust.com* ⌲ *Reservations essential* 🖃 *AE, MC, V* ☽ *No lunch Sat.–Thurs.*

$$
CAJUN
✕ **Cochon.** Chef-owned restaurants are common in New Orleans, but this one builds on the owner's family heritage. Chef Donald Link prepares Cajun dishes he learned to cook at his grandfather's knee. The interior may be a bit too rustic and noisy for some patrons, but the food will make up for it. Try the fried boudin with pickled peppers—trust us on this one. Then move on to black-eyed pea and pork gumbo, and a hearty Louisiana cochon (pork) with turnips, cracklings, and cabbage. If you want to experience true regional cuisine, this is the place. Check out Cochono Butcher around the corner for sandwiches, snacks, and house-cured meats. ✉ *930 Tchoupitoulas St., Warehouse*

☎ 504/588–2123 ⊕ *www.cochonrestaurant.com* ☜ *Reservations not accepted* ☰ *AE, MC, V.*

$$$
AMERICAN

✕ **Emeril's.** Celebrity-chef Emeril Lagasse's urban-chic flagship restaurant is always jammed. A wood ceiling in a basket-weave pattern muffles much of the clatter and chatter. The ambitious menu gives equal emphasis to Creole and modern American cooking—try the barbecue shrimp here for one of the darkest, richest versions of the local specialty. Desserts, such as the renowned banana cream pie, verge on the gargantuan. Service is meticulous, and the wine list's depth and range should soothe even the most persnickety imbiber. ⊠ *800 Tchoupitoulas St., Warehouse* ☎ *504/528–9393* ⊕ *www.emerils.com* ☜ *Reservations essential* ☰ *AE, D, DC, MC, V* ☺ *No lunch weekends.*

$$$
CREOLE
Fodor'sChoice
★

✕ **Commander's Palace.** No restaurant captures New Orleans's gastronomic heritage and celebratory spirit as well as this one, long considered the grande dame of New Orleans's fine dining. The recent renovation has added new life, especially upstairs, where the Garden Room's glass walls have marvelous views of the giant oak trees on the patio below; other rooms promote conviviality with their bright pastels. The menu's classics include sugarcane-grilled pork tenderloin; a spicy and meaty turtle soup; terrific bourbon-lacquered Mississippi quail; and a wonderful griddle-seared gulf fish. Among the over-the-top desserts is the bread-pudding soufflé. Weekend brunches are a New Orleans tradition. Jackets are preferred at dinner. ⊠ *1403 Washington Ave., Garden District* ☎ *504/899–8221* ⊕ *www.commanderspalace.com* ☜ *Reservations essential* ☰ *AE, D, DC, MC, V.*

WHERE TO STAY

Deciding where to stay in New Orleans has everything to do with what you want from your visit. To be in the center of the action and to experience the city's rich culture, a French Quarter accommodation is your best choice. For a quieter, more serene experience in close proximity to major attractions, head to comfortable properties Uptown, in the Garden District, and in surrounding areas like the Faubourg Marigny. Business travelers will find the elegant, well-appointed Central Business District (CBD) hotels convenient and comfortable. And if you appreciate the contemporary-chic ambience of historic warehouses and commercial buildings that have been refashioned into elegant hotels, head to the Warehouse District, where massive spaces with exposed-brick walls add distinctive atmosphere to both moderately priced and upscale hotels.

If you are visiting for the first time, book a hotel that is centrally located downtown and within walking distance of major attractions. Many hotels are located near the city's streetcar lines, which run the entire length of the city. If you plan to visit the city more than once, try to create a different lodging experience each time. For your next visit, perhaps choose a romantic getaway in an outlying guesthouse, where old-world charm and atmosphere are so proudly preserved.

Hotel reviews have been condensed for this book. Please go to Fodors. com for full reviews of each property.

WHERE TO STAY

NEIGHBORHOOD	VIBE	PROS	CONS
French Quarter	The tourist-focused main event is action packed, yet charming. Lodging runs the gamut from small inns to luxury hotels.	Lots of visitor attractions and nationally acclaimed restaurants. Everything is within walking distance of your hotel.	Crowded, high-traffic area. If you're sound sensitive, request a room that does not face a main street.
Faubourg Marigny	More neighborhoody than the adjacent French Quarter, stay here if you want to be close to the action but not in the middle of it. Many nice bed-and-breakfast options.	Balanced residential/commercial community. Close to French Quarter nightlife, but a more peaceful alternative.	Can be confusing to navigate for newcomers. Don't forget your map!
CBD and Warehouse District	The Warehouse District is also known as New Orleans's arts district. It's a great area for visitors who prefer accommodations in luxurious high-rise hotels or smaller boutique properties.	Good retail and restaurants, and some of the best galleries and museums in the city. Within walking distance of the French Quarter.	Crowded. Street vendors can be annoying.
Garden District/Uptown	Residential, upscale, and fashionable, this neighborhood is a slower-paced alternative to staying downtown.	Beautiful and right on the historic St. Charles Ave. streetcar line. Traffic here is not as heavy as downtown.	Far from the French Quarter and tourist attractions; must drive or take public transportation.
Mid-City	This is primarily an urban/residential area, with few lodging options.	Many local businesses and mid-price restaurants. Home to City Park, the largest urban park in the country.	Not easy for tourists to navigate—far from tourist attractions. Will need car, and public transportation is not convenient.

13

WHAT IT COSTS

	¢	$	$$	$$$	$$$$
Hotels	under $100	$100–$149	$150–$199	$200–$275	over $275

Prices are for two people in a standard double room in high season, excluding 13% city and state taxes.

FRENCH QUARTER

$$ **Hotel Maison de Ville.** Delightfully secluded amid the hustle and bustle

Fodor's Choice of the French Quarter, this property oozes refined elegance and romance.

★ **Pros:** unique rooms; personal and consistently above-average service. **Cons:** tough to get a reservation. ⊠ *727 Toulouse St., French Quarter* ☎ *504/561–5858 or 800/634–1600* ⊕ *www.maisondeville.com* ⤳ *14 rooms, 2 suites, 7 cottages* ⌂ *In-room: Wi-Fi. In-hotel: pool, parking (paid), no kids under 12* ☰ *AE, D, DC, MC, V* ⧖ *CP.*

$$$$ 🖼 **Hotel Monteleone.** The grande dame of French Quarter hotels—with
Fodor'sChoice its ornate baroque facade, liveried doormen, and shimmering lobby
★ chandeliers—was built in 1886 and renovated in 2004. **Pros:** ideal
central location offering access to French Quarter and downtown
locations; civilized, old New Orleans feel; recently renovated. **Cons:**
while the Hunt Room Grill is nice, the hotel's more casual restaurant
offers mediocre food and poor service. ⊠ *214 Royal St., French Quarter* 🕾 *504/523–3341 or 800/535–9595* ⊕ *www.hotelmonteleone.com*
🛏 *600 rooms, 55 suites* ♿ *In-room: Wi-Fi. In-hotel: 2 restaurants, bar,*
pool, gym, spa, Wi-Fi hotspot ═ *AE, D, DC, MC, V.*

$ 🖼 **Melrose Mansion.** Down pillows and fine-milled soaps; a full breakfast
Fodor'sChoice served poolside, in a formal dining room, or in your room; and rooms
★ filled with 19th-century Louisiana antiques are among the attractions
of this handsome 1884 Victorian mansion. **Pros:** pure luxury; very private; lots of pampering. **Cons:** unreasonable refund policy on reservations—and full room charges must be paid in advance. ⊠ *937 Esplanade*
Ave., French Quarter 🕾 *504/944–2255* ⊕ *www.melrosemansion.com*
🛏 *8 rooms, 4 suites* ♿ *In-room: Wi-Fi. In-hotel: bar, pool* ═ *AE, D,*
MC, V ⧍○⧌ *BP.*

$$$$ 🖼 **Soniat House.** This singularly handsome property comprises three
Fodor'sChoice meticulously restored town houses built in the 1830s. **Pros:** sheer
★ refined elegance; incomparable privacy; expert service; afternoon wine
service that is as civilized as it gets. **Cons:** the breakfast is delicious, but
portions and menu options are limited. ⊠ *1133 Chartres St., French*
Quarter 🕾 *504/522–0570 or 800/544–8808* ⊕ *www.soniathouse.com*
🛏 *20 rooms, 13 suites* ♿ *In-room: Wi-Fi. In-hotel: parking (paid)*
═ *AE, MC, V.*

CBD AND WAREHOUSE DISTRICT

$$$ 🖼 **Loews New Orleans Hotel.** A refashioned bank building in the heart of
Fodor'sChoice downtown is home to this plush 21st-century hotel. **Pros:** well managed;
★ accessible to everything that counts downtown; reliable service and
product. **Cons:** located in one of the most high-traffic downtown areas.
⊠ *300 Poydras St., CBD* 🕾 *504/595–5310 or 800/235–6397* ⊕ *www.*
loewshotels.com 🛏 *273 rooms, 12 suites* ♿ *In-room: Wi-Fi. In-hotel:*
restaurant, bar, pool, gym, spa, laundry service ═ *AE, D, DC, MC, V.*

$$$ 🖼 **Windsor Court Hotel.** Exquisite, gracious, elegant, eminently civilized—
Fodor'sChoice these words are frequently used to describe Windsor Court, but all fail
★ to capture the wonderful essence of this hotel. **Pros:** old-world elegance;
superior service. **Cons:**. lobby is on the 11th floor; only two elevators
from ground level to lobby. ⊠ *300 Gravier St., CBD* 🕾 *504/523–6000*
or 800/262–2662 ⊕ *www.windsorcourthotel.com* 🛏 *58 rooms, 266*
suites, 1 penthouse ♿ *In-room: Wi-Fi. In-hotel: 2 restaurants, bar, pool,*
gym, laundry service, parking (paid) ═ *AE, D, DC, MC, V.*

GARDEN DISTRICT

$$ 🖼 **Grand Victorian Bed & Breakfast.** Each lavishly appointed room in this
Fodor'sChoice grand Victorian evokes old Louisiana with period pieces and distinc-
★ tive private baths. **Pros:** true elegance; rooms are exquisitely appointed;
possibly the best bed-and-breakfast value in the area. **Cons:** located
on a high-traffic street. ⊠ *2727 St. Charles Ave., Garden District*

☎ *504/895–1104 or 800/977–0008* ⊕ *www.gvbb.com* ⤴ *8 rooms* ♿ *In-room: Wi-Fi. In-hotel: restaurant* ▭ *AE, D, MC, V.*

NIGHTLIFE

People come here to eat, listen to live music, and party; and the city still delivers on all three counts. No American town places such a premium on pleasure as New Orleans. From swank hotel lounges to sweaty dance clubs, refined jazz clubs and raucous Bourbon Street bars, this city is serious about frivolity—and famous for it. Partying is more than an occasional indulgence in this city—it's a lifestyle.

Although Bourbon Street, with its bright lights and beers-to-go, is usually one of the first stops for visitors, it's not truly representative of the city. The real soul of New Orleans nightlife lies in the out-of-the-way clubs, the impromptu street parties, and the music that wafts from rustic dives.

AROUND TOWN

The **French Quarter** and the **Faubourg Marigny** are the easiest places to hear music. Dozens of quality bands play nightly at clubs that are within walking distance of one another, and the myriad dining options make it convenient to spend a whole evening here. Frenchmen Street in the Marigny is currently the hottest music strip in town. Locals also flock to this area for the food and the street life. Much of Frenchmen's activity is within a three-block area. You can roam the streets, pub crawl, or simply people-watch outside on the sidewalk—a popular activity on weekend nights and during peak festival seasons. Some clubs along this strip charge a $5–$10 cover for music, but many charge none at all. Snug Harbor, the premiere modern-jazz venue in town, is pricier, with shows usually costing $10–$20, but a seat is always guaranteed.

Uptown is rich in clubs, although they are far less concentrated, tucked instead down various residential and commercial streets. A minor hub has formed around the Riverbend area, far uptown where St. Charles Avenue and Carrollton Avenue intersect. Cooter Brown's, right at the levee, is a good stop for imported beers and local grub, served all night. Some blocks away, near Carrollton and Oak streets, the Maple Leaf hosts live music every night of the week. Around the corner you will find Carrollton Station, which has bands on the weekends, although walking the few short blocks is not a good idea. Another hub is Magazine Street in the lower Garden District, where you can sit at an outdoor table at the Bulldog or drink on the balcony at the Balcony Bar. Although driving the two minutes from one spot to the next might seem silly, for safety's sake it's best to call a taxi at night.

The **Warehouse District** harbors a number of good bars and clubs, some of them in renovated 19th-century warehouses that harken back to the city's cotton exporting heyday. The enormous New Orleans Convention Center runs along the edge of this district, and many spots are often filled with dazed conventioneers. The Central Business District (CBD) is mostly quiet at night, but closer to the edge of Canal Street and the French Quarter are some terrific nightspots, like the Sazerac Bar in the

At Jazz Festival it's often the anonymous bluesman or obscure brass band who make the greatest impression on you.

newly renovated Roosevelt Hotel or the swanky dance club and lounge Ampersand in the converted Whitney Bank building.

Perhaps the edgiest local scene is in the **Bywater** District, home to a dozen low-key bars, straight, gay, and mixed. The corner of Royal and Franklin streets forms something of a hub, with a smattering of bars catering to a varied crowd. At the far end of the Bywater, you can be sure to find one of the hippest events of the week when Kermit Ruffins plays Vaughan's every Thursday. On Sunday a miniparty takes place in the courtyard of the wine retail shop, Bacchanal.

Mid-City, the area near City Park and Bayou St. John, is chock-full of neighborhood joints. There are some hidden treasures, from unique wine and cocktail bars like Clever Wine Bar in the renovated American Can Company building overlooking the bayou, to the ever-popular Rock 'n' Bowl, moved down the street to a new location in 2009. Venues are fairly spread out, so a car or taxi is necessary.

MUSIC VENUES

First-time visitors to New Orleans are often bowled over by the amount of both musical talent the city contains and the opportunities to witness it live—in clubs, coffee shops, at festivals, even on the street. French Quarter and Faubourg Marigny jazz clubs usually get going around 8 pm, with sets going late into the night. Some clubs present music in the afternoon as well, usually on weekends. If you're heading out to a nightclub in other parts of town, it's advisable to call ahead or double-check the event listing in one of the city's periodicals. The opening sets at neighborhood bars and rock clubs usually don't start until 10 pm or later, and the listed time is rarely when the band actually begins.

★ **Preservation Hall**. The jazz tradition that flowered in the 1920s is

FRENCH QUARTER   enshrined in this cultural landmark by a cadre of distinguished New Orleans musicians, most of whom were schooled by an ever-dwindling group of elder statesmen. There is limited seating on benches—many patrons end up squatting on the floor or standing in back—and no beverages are served or allowed. Nonetheless, the legions of satisfied customers regard an evening here as an essential New Orleans experience. Cover charge is $10, but can run a bit higher for special appearances. Call ahead for performance times; sometimes the show ends before you even begin pre-partying. ⊠ *726 St. Peter St., French Quarter* ☎ *504/522–2841 or 504/523–8939.*

Fodor'sChoice   **Maple Leaf**. Wonderfully atmospheric, with pressed-tin walls and a lush

★   tropical patio, the Maple Leaf is of the city's best venues for blues, New

UPTOWN   Orleans–style R&B, funk, zydeco, and jazz. On Sunday, the bar hosts the South's longest-running poetry reading. It's a long haul from the French Quarter, but worth the trip, especially if combined with a visit to one of the restaurants clustered near this commercial stretch of Oak Street. ⊠ *8316 Oak St., Uptown* ☎ *504/866–9359.*

★ **Tipitina's**. A bust of legendary New Orleans pianist Professor Longhair

UPTOWN   greets visitors at the door of this Uptown landmark, which takes its name from one of his most popular songs. As the concert posters pinned to the walls attest, Tip's hosts a wide variety of touring bands and local acts. The long-running Sunday-afternoon Cajun dance still packs the floor. ⊠ *501 Napoleon Ave., Uptown* ☎ *504/895–8477.*

SHOPPING

Shopping in New Orleans is like opening a treasure chest in which everything you want is at your fingertips, from rare antiques to novelty T-shirts, artwork, jewelry, and packaged foods that represent the city's flavors and culture.

New Orleanians have a deep love and devotion for the Crescent City and the varied ethnic components that make it up. For shoppers, this translates into merchandise that reflects that pride, including jewelry and clothing bearing city icons such as the fleur-de-lis—a French symbol associated with the city since its early days—Mardi Gras masks, tributes to its world-class food and culture, and unique and often humorous statements about Hurricane Katrina and its effects on New Orleans, political issues, and local personalities. New Orleanians also strongly support local entrepreneurs, which means shoppers can find many unique works by Crescent City artists and items produced in the city.

Make sure you take home some of the city's local artwork, including the posters designed for Mardi Gras and the New Orleans Jazz & Heritage Festival (which often become collector's items). The special sounds of New Orleans—Dixieland and contemporary jazz, rhythm and blues, Cajun, and zydeco—are available in music stores like Louisiana Music Factory and Peaches Records, and at live-music venues such as Preservation Hall, Snug Harbor, and House of Blues. Bookstores stock a plethora of local cookbooks, photography, history, and local literature and lore. Clothing stores focus on items that wear well in the subtropical heat, with styles ranging from the latest runway fashions, European designer wear, and vintage items, as well as styles from local designers.

WHAT'S WHERE

The main shopping areas in the city are the French Quarter, with narrow, picturesque streets lined with specialty, gift, fashion, and antiques shops and art galleries; the Central Business District (CBD), populated mostly with specialty and department stores; the Warehouse District, best known for contemporary-arts galleries and cultural museums; Magazine Street, home to antiques shops, art galleries, home-furnishings stores, dining venues, fashion boutiques, and specialty shops; and the Riverbend/Maple Street area, which offers clothing, jewelry, and bookstores, as well as some specialty shops.

The shops that line the French Quarter's streets are filled with an array of clothing, jewelry, novelties, works of art, and antique furniture and accessories. If your energy lags, plenty of cafés, coffee shops, candy shops, and bistros will provide a boost.

CBD AND WAREHOUSE DISTRICT

This area between the French Quarter and the Magazine Street shopping district is filled with boutique hotels, upscale malls, locally owned and national chain department stores, and (in the Warehouse District) museums and art galleries displaying a variety of artworks and crafts from local, regional, and nationally known artists. Julia Street in particular is a cornucopia of small art galleries, many of them artist-owned.

MAGAZINE STREET

Magazine Street has become a favorite shopping area for locals and university students as well as visitors, who are charmed by the historic area. Many of the stores are in shotgun houses and cottages that once served as residences. The 6-mi-long street that curves from Canal Street to Carrollton Avenue is one of the oldest and most diverse shopping districts in the city—second only to the French Quarter.

City buses provide transportation to and along Magazine Street, and streetcars travel along St. Charles Avenue, which runs parallel to Magazine Street. The **Magazine Street Merchants Association** (☎ 866/679–4764 or 504/342–4435 ⊕ www.magazinestreet.com) publishes a free brochure with maps and store descriptions; it's available in hotels and stores, or you can request one from the association's Web site. **Macon Riddle** (☎ 504/899–3027 ⊕ www.neworleansantiquing.com) shares her expertise in antiques and collectibles in half- or full-day shopping expeditions tailored to her clients' needs.

MAPLE STREET/RIVERBEND

Shops and restaurants here are housed in turn-of-the-20th-century cottages, but most of the wares are contemporary and modern. On Maple Street, the shops run about six blocks, from Carrollton Avenue to Cherokee Street, and in the Riverbend they dot the streets behind a shopping center on Carrollton Avenue. St. Charles Avenue streetcars provide an easy way to get to the area.

MARDI GRAS

Mardi Gras (French for "Fat Tuesday") is the final day of Carnival, an entire Christian holiday season that begins on the Twelfth Night of Christmas (January 6) and comes crashing to a halt on Ash Wednesday, the first day of Lent. Though Mardi Gras is technically merely one day within the season, the term is used interchangeably with Carnival, especially as the season builds toward the big day. Carnival claims elaborately developed traditions of food, drink, and music, as well as a blend of public celebration (the parades) and more-exclusive festivities, which take the form of elaborate private balls.

On Mardi Gras day, many New Orleanians don costumes, face paint, and masks, and then take to the streets for the last hurrah before Lent. It's an official city holiday, with just about everyone but the police and bartenders taking the day off. People roam the streets, drink Bloody Marys for breakfast and switch to beer in the afternoon, and admire one another's finery. The Zulu, Rex, and the "trucks" parades roll Uptown to downtown with large floats carrying riders who throw plastic beads and trinkets to onlookers. They call it America's largest street party, and that seems about right. Don't be smug: if you visit, you'll catch the fervor. Be prepared to drape layers of beads around your neck, sip from a plastic "go-cup" as you dance in the streets, and have a grand old time.

JAZZ AND HERITAGE FESTIVAL

Don't let the four-letter word at the center of its name intimidate you. This is no stuffy, high-toned event for music scholars; Jazz Fest, as it's known to locals, is a sprawling, rollicking celebration of Louisiana music, food, and culture held the last weekend in April and the first weekend in May. It takes place at the city's historic Fair Grounds Race Course, which reverberates with the sounds of rock, Cajun, zydeco, gospel, rhythm and blues, hip-hop, folk, world music, country, Latin, and, yes, traditional and modern jazz. Throw in world-class arts and crafts, exhibitions and lectures, and an astounding range of Louisiana-made food—reason enough alone for many Jazz Fest fans to make the trek—and you've got a festival worthy of America's premiere party town. Over the years, Jazz Fest lineups have come to include internationally known performers—Simon and Garfunkel, Pearl Jam, Lionel Richie, and the Allman Brothers topped the bill in 2010—but at its heart the festival is about the hundreds of Louisiana musicians who live, work, and cut their chops in the Crescent City.

The Midwest
and the Rockies

WHAT'S WHERE

The following numbers refer to chapters in the book.

14 Chicago. Chicagoans are a proud lot; they don't take the Second City title lightly. Many residents unabashedly consider this the best city in America, and they point to the cutting-edge architecture, legendary blues, lavish shopping, and scrumptious dining as proof. If that's not enough they'll wax poetic about the world-class museums, lake views, glorious parks, deep-dish pizza, and piled-high hot dogs. And don't even get them started about their complicated relationship with Bulls, Bears, Sox, or Cubs.

15 Minneapolis and St. Paul. Minnesotans haven't let the cold stop them from creating a hot destination for arts fans, outdoors enthusiasts and the shopping crowd. In the summer, locals revel in the warm weather by flooding outdoor restaurants and cafés, while in the winter, they play outside during St. Paul's famous "Winter Carnival."

16 Denver, Boulder, and the Colorado Rockies. Colorado is famous as one big playground, from snowcapped ski resorts to biking and hiking trails to white-water rivers and hot springs. Denver and Boulder are the state's best bases for exploration, or with plenty

of magnificent dining options and cultural attractions, they make intriguing destinations in their own right.

17 Mount Rushmore and the South Dakota Black Hills. A few hundred miles east of the Rockies sit the Black Hills, an ancient mountain range that crosses the Wyoming–South Dakota border. Western legends such as Deadwood Dick and the Sundance Kid once roamed its canyons and prairies; today you can see their legacy in Deadwood, site of one of the country's largest ongoing historic preservation projects. The biggest draw is Mount Rushmore National Memorial, with its unblinking granite faces of four iconic presidents.

18 Yellowstone National Park. Best known for its gushing geysers and flowing hot springs, Yellowstone National Park—the oldest national park in the world—is a wonderland of hydrothermal activity. It has more than 2.2 million acres of wilderness on more than 1,100 mi of trails.

THE MIDWEST AND THE ROCKIES TOP ATTRACTIONS

Deadwood, South Dakota

(A) This famous Wild West town, once the epicenter of America's last gold rush, is still filled with brick-paved streets and Victorian buildings.

Presidential Trail, Mount Rushmore National Memorial, South Dakota

(B) The Presidential Trail is an easy walk and a great way to get a close view of Mount Rushmore. You'll walk along a boardwalk that brings you right beneath the impossibly massive carvings—awe-inspiring from any angle, they're a particularly astounding sight from the base of the mountain.

Crazy Horse Memorial, South Dakota

(C) When completed, this mountain monument to Native American leaders will be the largest sculpture in the world; until then, you can watch the carving in progress—perhaps including a few dynamite blasts.

Millennium Park, Chicago

(D) Make a beeline for Frank Gehry's, where an incredible sound system allows audiences to enjoy concert-hall sound in the great outdoors. The Bean, formally known as *Cloud Gate*, is a luminous polished-steel sculpture that plays tricks with the reflection of Chicago's skyline. In warmer months children of all ages can't resist a splash in the Crown Fountain, twin 50-foot towers that project close-up video images of Chicagoans "spitting" jets of water.

Art Institute of Chicago

(E) This Chicago cultural gem has the country's best collection of impressionist and postimpressionist art, as well as the brand-new Renzo Piano–designed modern wing. It's also a great place to see all those paintings you've only seen on postcards, like *American Gothic* and *Nighthawks*.

Willis (Sears) Tower Skydeck, Chicago

(F) Take the ear-popping ride to the 103rd-floor observatory, where on a clear day you can see as far as Michigan, Wisconsin, and Indiana. At the top, interactive exhibits feature notable Chicagoans. Kids love Knee-High Chicago, a 4-foot-high exhibit that has cutouts of Chicago sports, history, and cultural icons at a child's eye-level. Fearless folks can step out onto the Ledge, twin glass boxes extending 4.3 feet from the Skydeck and suspended a dizzying 1,353 feet above the city. Security is very tight, so figure in a little extra time for your visit to the Skydeck.

Rocky Mountain National Park, Colorado

(G) Estes Park is the gateway town to Rocky Mountain National Park, full of lush forests, high-alpine lakes, snow-capped peaks, wildflower-covered meadows, and 355 mi of trails. Abundant wildlife like black bear, elk, and bighorn sheep, and even more abundant crowds are drawn to this year-round paradise.

Larimer Square, Denver, Colorado

(H) Specialty stores, superior people-watching, and some of Denver's top restaurants and nightlife bring tourists and locals alike to the city's oldest street.

Old Faithful, Yellowstone National Park

(I) Currently erupting approximately every 94 minutes, Yellowstone's most frequently erupting big geyser—although not its largest or most regular—reaches heights of 100 to 180 feet, averaging 130 feet. Witnessing this geothermal event up close never gets old.

TOP EXPERIENCES

Getting the Blues in Chicago

Explore jumping North Side clubs, like Kingston Mines, or South Side venues like the Checkerboard or Lee's Unleaded Blues (where greats like Muddy Waters and buddy Guy first hone their talent) for the sound Chicago gave birth to—the scintillating electric blues. If you're visiting in June (book well in advance if you are), don't miss the Chicago Blues Festival, which packs in fans from all over the country.

Staying at the Old Faithful Inn

The lobby of Old Faithful Inn in Yellowstone may be as jaw-dropping as the park that, literally, created it. It's 76 feet high with four levels of balconies supported by gnarled branches from a tangle of trees that reach the ceiling. Built in 1904 by the Northern Pacific Railroad and the Yellowstone Park Association, the stunning inn is a one-time architectural achievement—the raw materials were assembled by cutting down trees, gathering wood, and quarrying rock inside the park, which is now illegal. The 1904-era rooms have thick wood timber walls and ceilings. Rooms with a shared bath can start at $99, and rooms with bathrooms in either the Old House or the "modern" wings (built in 1913 and 1927) are $200-plus. The park's most famous geyser, Old Faithful, is less than 100 yards from the inn. Approximate times for the geyser's eruptions are posted in the lobby.

Visiting Yellowstone in the Winter

To have a spectacularly different Yellowstone experience than most of the park's visitors, come in winter. Rocky outcroppings are smoothed over. Waterfalls are transformed into jagged sheets of ice. The best reason for a visit to Yellowstone between December and March is the opportunity to experience the park without the crowds. The first thing that strikes you during this season is the quiet. The gargantuan snowpack—as many as 200 inches annually at low elevation—seems to muffle the sounds of bison foraging in the geyser basins and of hot springs simmering. Yet even in the depths of a deep freeze, the park is never totally still: the mudpots bubble, geysers shoot skyward, and wind rustles the snow-covered pine trees. Above these sounds, the cry of a hawk, the yip of a coyote, or even on rare occasions the howl of a wolf may pierce the air.

Animals in Yellowstone head *down* when the thermometer falls. Herbivores like elk and bison head to the warmer, less snowy valleys to find vegetation; predators like wolves and cougars follow them. As a result, you're more likely to see these animals in the frontcountry in winter. The snow also makes it easier to pick out animal tracks.

Driving the Trail Ridge Road

Rocky Mountain National Park's Trail Ridge Road is the country's highest continuously paved road, with a maximum elevation of 12,183 feet. Connecting the park's east and west entrances, the road crosses the Continental Divide at Milner Pass and can take up to two months to clear of snow for its Memorial Day opening. The entire 48-mi drive can be done in a couple hours, but allow more time to stop and gaze out from the many turnouts. You'll behold one breathtaking vista after another—glaciers, lush meadows covered in columbine and Indian paintbrush, rocky cliffs and outcroppings. The road passes through three ecosystems—montane, subalpine, and arctic tundra—and climbs 4,300 feet.

Seeing What's on Tap in Colorado

Although fancy cocktails and wine continue to make headway against beer elsewhere in the country, Colorado is still the land of microbrews. Pool tables, multiple televisions for sports viewing, and live music make the brewpub an essential part of the weekend scene in most major cities and towns. Many of the best Denver brewpubs are in LoDo, or lower downtown. These offer tasting flights much like wineries, served with food that runs the gamut from pub grub to upscale. Many microbreweries also have tasting rooms open to the public, where growlers (half-gallon glass jugs) of fresh beer can be purchased for takeout, perfect for picnics and tailgate parties. A few to try:

Boulder Beer Company, Boulder. Colorado's first microbrewery offers a British-style ale, amber, pale, golden, and India pale ales and a stout, to name a few—and has a pub attached that offers a solid roster of grub.

New Belgium Brewing Company, Fort Collins. Fat Tire Amber Ale resonates with Coloradans because of its mountain-biking history, and is this microbrewery's most popular beer. It's readily available around the state, but a visit to the 100% wind-powered brewery is the best way to check it out.

Wynkoop Brewing Co. Denver. You can see part of the brewing operation through large glass windows at this popular brewpub in LoDo. The Railyard Ale is one of the signature beers, but the spicy chili beer is a local favorite.

Taking in Mount Rushmore's Majesty

For a truly inspiring start to your day, have breakfast with the presidents at Mount Rushmore National Memorial. The colossal carving is best viewed in morning light, followed by a leisurely stroll up the Avenue of Flags where the Grand View Terrace affords a commanding view of the granite visages of Washington, Jefferson, Lincoln, and Theodore Roosevelt. If you're not an early riser, check out Mount Rushmore's nightly program with a ranger talk, film and the enhanced lighting of the memorial, which ranks as the National Park Service's most popular interpretive program.

Ogling Architecture in Chicago and the Twin Cities

Every great city has great buildings, but Chicago *is* its great buildings. Everything Chicagoans do is framed by some of the most remarkable architecture anywhere. From the sky-scraping of its tall towers to the horizontal sweep of its Prairie School designs, Chicago's built environment is second to none. Daniel Burnham, Mies van der Rohe, H.H. Richardson, Skidmore, Owings & Merrill, and, of course, Frank Lloyd Wright all made their marks on the reborn metropolis. The Chicago Architecture Foundation offers excellent walking, bus, and boat tours throughout the city—be sure to take one.

The Twin Cities offers several architectural must-sees, both modern and historical. St. Paul is marked by Romanesque sandstone mansions and the iconic Cathedral of St. Paul, while Minneapolis is thoroughly modern with a smattering of the historic preserved. The architectural biggies of Minneapolis have received national coverage, bringing a sense of pride to the locals. To cover your bases, check out the IDS Center, Walker Art Center, Guthrie Theater, Minneapolis Central Library and Weisman Art Museum.

GREAT ITINERARIES

CONNECTING THE DOTS IN COLORFUL COLORADO

Arriving in Denver

Denver is filled with folks who stopped to visit and never left. After a few days in the Mile High City and surrounding metro area it's easy to see why: Colorado's capital has much to recommend it, including a thriving cultural scene, restaurants representing every ethnicity, plenty of sunshine, outdoor options galore, and snowcapped peaks for visual variety.

The Old West still holds sway in visitors' imaginations, and there are plenty of throwback trappings to check out, but the reality is that Denver is a modern metropolis that offers cosmopolitan amenities and state-of-the-art amusements.

Logistics: There are myriad well-marked ground transportation options near baggage claim at the sprawling Denver International Airport (DEN). Head to the taxi stand to pay about $55 to get downtown, or visit the RTD desk for bus schedules (SkyRide operates multiple routes starting at $8 one-way). Several independent companies operate shuttles from desks within the airport for about $19 one-way, and many hotels have complimentary shuttles for their guests.

All of the major car-rental companies operate at DEN. The rental-car counters that you see in the main terminal are there merely to point you toward the shuttles that take you to the car-rental center. Depending on time of day and traffic, it will take 30 minutes to an hour to reach downtown Denver and another 30 minutes for Boulder and the foothills.

Days 1–2: Denver and Boulder

OPTION 1: METRO DENVER

After you've settled into your hotel, head downtown, or if you're already staying there—always a good option to truly explore the city—make your way to Lower Downtown, or LoDo. The historic district is home to many of the city's famous brewpubs, art galleries, and Coors Field, as well as popular restaurants and some of the area's oldest architecture.

Hop on the free MallRide, the shuttle bus run by RTD, to head up the 16th Street Mall, a pedestrian-friendly, shopping-oriented strip that runs through the center of downtown. From there you can walk to Larimer Square for more shopping and restaurants, as well as the Denver Art Museum, the Colorado History Museum, the Colorado State Capitol, the Molly Brown House, and the U.S. Mint.

Logistics: Vending machines at each station for TheRide, Denver's light-rail, show destinations and calculate your fare ($1.50–$2.75 depending on the number of zones crossed). The machines accept bills of $20 or less and any coin except pennies. Children under age 5 ride free when accompanied by a fare-paying adult. RTD buses also provide an excellent way to get around; schedules are posted inside shelters and are available at Civic Center Station at the south end of the 16th Street Mall and Market Street Station toward the north end. Fares are $1.50 one-way.

OPTION 2: BOULDER

Boulder takes its fair share of ribbing for being a Birkenstock-wearing, tofu-eating, latter-day hippie kind of town, but the truth is that it is one healthy, wealthy area, exceedingly popular and rapidly heading toward overdevelopment. For now, though, it's still a groovy place to

visit. Stroll along the Pearl Street Mall and sample the excellent restaurants and shops, catching one of the dozens of street performers; or head just outside the city to tour Celestial Seasonings, the tea manufacturer; or to Chautauqua Park to hike in the shadow of the dramatic Flatiron Mountains. In winter, Eldora Mountain Resort is a 21-mi jaunt up a steep, switchback-laden road with no lift lines as payoff. The University of Colorado campus here means there is a high hip quotient in much of the nightlife.

Logistics: You can take an RTD bus to Boulder from Denver, but it's just as easy to drive up U.S. 36, and if you're going to go beyond the Pearl Street Mall, it's nice to have a car once you're there. Parking, though, can be quite tight.

Days 3–7: The Rockies
ESTES PARK, ROCKY MOUNTAIN NATIONAL PARK, AND GRAND LAKE

Rocky Mountain National Park (RMNP) is a year-round marvel, a park for every season: summer's hiking, fall's elk-mating ritual, winter's snowcapped peaks, and spring's wildflowers. Estes Park is the gateway to RMNP but a worthwhile destination itself, a small town swelling to a large one with the tourists who flock to its Western-theme shops and art galleries. The alpine-surrounded Grand Lake is a rustic charmer, a mecca for the sports person, and an idyllic locale for a family vacation.

Logistics: Estes Park is a hop-skip from Denver and Boulder, about 65 mi northwest of Denver via Interstate 25 and then CO–66 and U.S. 36. To get to RMNP, simply take U.S. 34 or U.S. 36 into the park. Grand Lake is on the other side of RMNP via U.S. 34, or from Denver, it's 100 mi by taking Interstate 70 to U.S. 40

over Berthoud Pass through Winter Park, Fraser, and Granby, and then turning onto U.S. 34 to Grand Lake. It can be a bit more challenging in winter.

YELLOWSTONE IN ONE DAY

If you plan to spend just one full day in the park, your best approach would be to concentrate on one or two of the park's major areas, such as the two biggest attractions: the famous Old Faithful geyser and the Grand Canyon of the Yellowstone. En route between these attractions, you can see geothermal activity and most likely some wildlife.

Plan on at least two hours for Old Faithful, one of the most iconic landmarks in America. Eruptions are approximately 90 minutes apart, though they can be as close as 60 minutes apart. Before and after an eruption you can explore the surrounding geyser basin and Old Faithful Inn. To the north of Old Faithful, make Grand Prismatic Spring your can't-miss geothermal stop; farther north, near Madison, veer off the road to the west to do the short Firehole Canyon Drive to see the Firehole River cut a small canyon and waterfall (Firehole Falls).

If you're arriving from the east, start with sunrise at **Lake Butte, Fishing Bridge, and the wildlife-rich Hayden Valley** as you cross the park counterclockwise to **Old Faithful**. To try and see wolves or bears, call ahead and ask when/if rangers will be stationed at roadside turnouts with spotting scopes. Alternatively, hike any trail in the park at least 2 mi—and remember that you're entering the domain of wild and sometimes dangerous animals, so be alert and don't hike alone.

If you're entering through the North or Northeast entrance, begin at dawn looking for wolves and other animals in Lamar Valley, then head to **Tower-Roosevelt** and take a horseback ride into the surrounding forest. After your ride, continue west to **Mammoth Hot Springs,** where you can hike the **Lower Terrace Interpretive Trail** past Liberty Cap and other strange, brightly colored limestone formations. If you drive 1½ mi south of the visitor center you will reach the **Upper Terrace Drive,** for close-ups of hot springs. In the late afternoon, drive south, keeping an eye out for wildlife as you go—you're almost certain to see elk, buffalo, and possibly even a bear. Alternatively, from Tower-Roosevelt you can head south to go through **Canyon Village** to see the north or south rim of the **Grand Canyon of the Yellowstone** and its waterfalls, and then head west through Norris and Madison.

When you reach **Old Faithful,** you can place the famous geyser into context by walking the 1½-mi **Geyser Hill Loop.** Watch the next eruption from the deck of the **Old Faithful Inn.**

DAKOTAS' BLACK HILLS DRIVING TOUR: HOT SPRINGS TO DEADWOOD

Wind Cave National Park

DAY 1

Start in Hot Springs, the southern gateway to Wind Cave National Park. Here you can see historic sandstone buildings and an active dig site where the remains of fossilized full-sized mammoths have been discovered. The mammoths fell into a sinkhole, became trapped, died, and have been preserved for thousands of years. They remain in situ. After viewing the 52

THE PLAN

DISTANCE: 120 mi

TIME: 5–7 days

BREAKS: Overnight in Hot Springs or Custer, SD; Custer State Park, SD; Keystone, SD; Rapid City, SD; Deadwood, SD.

mammoths unearthed to date at ❶**Mammoth Site,** take a dip into ❷**Evans Plunge**—the world's largest natural warm-water indoor swimming pool, holding 1 million gallons. (You can also enjoy waterslides, swinging rings, hot tubs, arcades, and a full-service health club here.) After lunch, drive 6 mi north on U.S. 385 to ❸**Wind Cave National Park.** The park has 28,000 acres of wildlife habitat above ground and the world's fourth-longest cave below. Take an afternoon cave tour and a short drive through the park. Overnight at nearby Custer State Park or stay in one of the Custer Resort Lodges—or possibly stay in one of the B&Bs around Hot Springs or Custer.

Custer State Park

DAY 2

Spend today at ❹**Custer State Park,** just 5 mi east of Custer on U.S. 16A. The 110-square-mi park has exceptional drives, lots of wildlife, and fingerlike granite spires rising from the forest floor. Relax on a hayride and enjoy a chuck wagon supper, or take a Jeep tour into the buffalo herds. Overnight in one of four enchanting mountain lodges.

Jewel Cave National Monument and Crazy Horse Memorial

DAY 3

Today, venture down U.S. 16 to ❺**Jewel Cave National Monument,** where you can see the beautiful nailhead and dogtooth

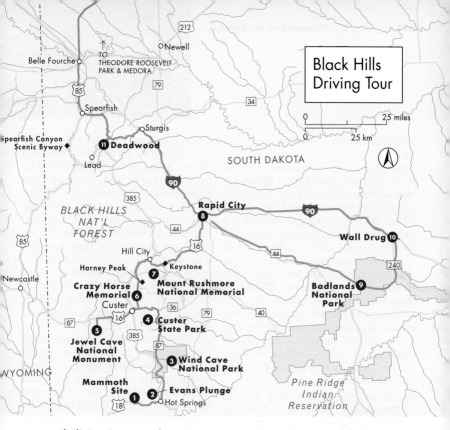

**Black Hills
Driving Tour**

spar crystals lining its more than 100 mi of passageways. As you head from Custer State Park to Jewel Cave National Monument, you pass through the friendly community of Custer on U.S. 385. It's surrounded by some of the Black Hills' most striking scenery—picture towering rock formations spearing out of ponderosa pine forests. If you have extra time, explore Cathedral Spires, Harney Peak, and Needles Highway (Highway 87).

After visiting Jewel Cave, head back to Custer and take U.S. 16/385 toward the former gold and tin mining town of Hill City. Along the way you'll hit ❻**Crazy Horse Memorial**, the colossal mountain carving of the legendary Lakota leader. The memorial's complex includes the Indian Museum of North America, which displays beautiful bead- and quill-work from many of the continent's native

nations. Overnight at one of the hotels in and around Keystone, such as the K Bar S Lodge, or stay at a hotel in Hill City.

Mount Rushmore National Memorial
DAY 4

This morning, travel just 3 mi from Keystone (10 from Hill City) on Route 244 (the Gutzon Borglum Memorial Highway) to ❼**Mount Rushmore National Memorial**, where you can view the huge, carved renderings of presidents Washington, Jefferson, Roosevelt, and Lincoln. Afterward, head northwest for 17 mi on U.S. 16 to ❽**Rapid City**, western South Dakota's largest city and the eastern gateway to the Black Hills. Overnight here and enjoy visiting the many museums and touring the sites. Great family spots include Reptile Gardens, Bear Country, the Journey Museum, Storybook Island, and Dinosaur Hill.

Badlands National Park
DAY 5

Begin your day early and drive 55 mi on Route 44 to the North Unit of ❾**Badlands National Park.** Badlands Loop Road wiggles through this moonlike landscape for 32 mi. When you've had enough of this 380-square-mi geologic wonderland, head back to the hills. Exit onto Route 240 at the northeast entrance to catch I–90. For a fun excursion, take a little detour east to Wall for its world-famous ❿**Wall Drug Store.** Founded on the premise that free ice water would attract road-weary travelers, the huge emporium carries all manner of Westernalia—including 6,000 pairs of cowboy boots. Enjoy lunch at the Western Art Gallery Restaurant or the picnic area out back.

Spend this afternoon and tonight in ⓫**Deadwood,** reached via U.S. 14 and 14A. This Old West mining town has 80 gaming halls, including Old Style Saloon No. 10, which bills itself as "the only museum in the world with a bar." Upstairs, at the Deadwood Social Club, you can discover outstanding food at reasonable prices and the best wine selection in the state. To view rare artifacts from the town's colorful past, such as items that once belonged to Wild Bill Hickok, visit Adams Memorial Museum. Overnight in Deadwood's Franklin Hotel (built in 1903), where past guests have included Theodore Roosevelt, Babe Ruth, John Wayne, and country duo Big & Rich.

SIGHTSEEING CHICAGO

Two Hours in Town

If you've only got a bit of time, go to a museum. Although you could spend days in any of the city's major museums, two hours will give you a quick taste of Chicago's cultural riches. Take a brisk walk around the **Art Institute** to see Grant Wood's *American Gothic,* Edward Hopper's *Nighthawks,* and one of the finest Impressionist collections in the country. Or check out the major dinosaur collection or the gorgeous Native American regalia at the **Field Museum.** Take a close look at the sharks at the **Shedd Aquarium.** If the weather's nice, stroll along the lakefront outside the **Adler Planetarium**—you'll see one of the nicest skyline views in the city. Wander down State Street, the Magnificent Mile, or around Millennium Park. If you're hungry, indulge in one of Chicago's three famous culinary treats—deep-dish pizza (head to **Pizzeria Due** to avoid the lines at **Giordano's, Gino's,** and **Pizzeria Uno**); garden-style hot dogs; or Italian beef sandwiches. After dark? Hear some music at a local club. Catch some blues at **Blues Chicago** to get a taste of authentic Chicago.

■ TIP→ Remember that many of the smaller museums are closed Monday.

Sightseeing in the Loop

State Street, that Great Street, is home to the old **Marshall Field's,** which has been reborn as Macy's; Louis Sullivan's ornate iron entrance to the **Sullivan Center** (once the home to Carson Pirie Scott) a nascent theater district; as well as great people-watching. Start at Harold Washington Library at Van Buren Street and State Street and walk north, venturing a block east to the beautiful **Chicago Cultural Center** when you hit Randolph Street. Grab lunch at the Museum of Contemporary Art's serene Wolfgang Puck café, **Puck's at the MCA,** and then spend a couple of hours with in-your-face art. Go for steak at Morton's or the Palm before a night of Chicago theater. Broadway touring shows

are on Randolph Street at the Ford Center for the Performing Arts Oriental Theatre or the Cadillac Palace, or head elsewhere downtown for excellent local theater—the Goodman, Steppenwolf, Lookingglass, and Chicago Shakespeare will each give you a night to remember.

Get Outdoors

Begin with a long walk (or run) along the lakefront, or rent a bike or in-line skates and watch the waves on wheels. Then catch an El train north to **Wrigley Field** for Cubs baseball; grab a dog at the seventh-inning stretch, and sing your heart out to "Take Me Out to the Ball Game." Afterward, soak up a little beer and atmosphere on the patio at one of the local sports bars. Finish up with an outdoor concert in **Grant or Millennium parks.**

Family Time

Start at **Navy Pier**—or heck, spend all day there. The **Chicago Children's Museum** is a main attraction, but there's also an IMAX theater, a Ferris wheel, a swing ride, a fun house, a stained-glass museum, and, in summer, Chicago-themed miniature golf in Pier Park. If the crowds at the Pier get to be too much, walk to **Millennium Park,** where kids of all ages can ice-skate in winter and play in the fountain in summer, and where giant digital portraits of Chicagoans spit streams of water to help cool you off. Whatever the weather, make sure to get your picture taken in the mirrored center of the Bean—the sculpture that's formally known as *Cloud Gate.* At night in summertime, take a stroll by Buckingham Fountain, where the dancing sprays jump to music and are illuminated by computer-controlled colored lights, or take a turn on the dance floor during Chicago's nightly SummerDance celebration.

■ TIP→ Fireworks explode near Navy Pier every Wednesday at 9:30 pm and Saturday night at 10:15 pm Memorial Day through Labor Day.

Cityscapes

Start at the top. Hit the heights of the **John Hancock Center** or the **Willis (Sears) Tower Skydeck** for a grand view of the city and the lake. Then take a walking tour of downtown with a well-informed docent from the **Chicago Architecture Foundation.** In the afternoon, wander north to the **Michigan Avenue Bridge,** where you can take an informative boat tour of the Chicago River. Enjoy the architecture as you float by, resting your weary feet.

Shop Chicago

Grab your bankroll and stroll the **Magnificent Mile** in search of great buys and souvenirs. Walking north from around the Michigan Avenue Bridge, window-shop your way along the many upscale stores. Hang a left on **Oak Street** for the most elite boutiques. **Accent Chicago** (⊠ *875 N. Michigan Ave.*) is where serious souvenir hunters spent their cash. Dedicated shoppers will want to detour a little farther south to **State Street** in the Loop for a walk through the landmark Marshall Field's building, now Macy's. For a culture buzz, check out the **Museum of Contemporary Art** (closed Monday). After making a tough restaurant choice (prime rib at Smith & Wolensky's or Lawry's? or deep-dish pizza at Giordano's?), consider a nightcap at the **Signature Room** at the 95th-floor bar on top of the John Hancock Center—the city will be spread beneath your feet.

Chicago

WORD OF MOUTH

"Chicago gets my vote for the most interesting-looking city in the U.S. The architecture is amazing, seemingly everywhere in town. Maybe it has just been the areas I've roamed around, but each block was absolutely filled with buildings that you just wanted to linger at and let your eyes enjoy the meal."

—rizzuto

WELCOME TO CHICAGO

TOP REASONS TO GO

★ **Lake Michigan.** "Cooler by the lake" is an oft-used weather term wisely adapted by local marketing types to describe how everything is just a little bit nicer in the environs of the city's stunning lakefront.

★ **The Magnificent Mile.** Four lavish malls and more than 460 stores along the stretch of Michigan Avenue that runs from the Chicago River to Oak Street makes the Mag Mile one of the best shopping strips in the world.

★ **Wrigley Field.** It doesn't matter if the Cubs are winning (and let's be honest, they're probably not), a trip to the "Friendly Confines" is a history lesson, sociological study, and all-around perfect way to spend a summer afternoon in Chicago.

★ **Summer in the City.** Locals like to say that if Chicago summers—filled with legendary street fairs, sidewalk café dining, and frolicking on the lakefront—lasted all year long, the whole world would want to move here.

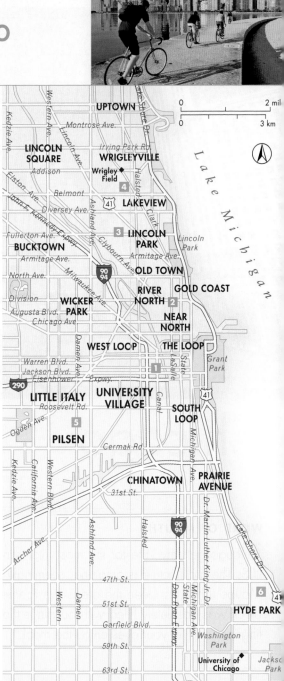

1 The Loop, West Loop, and South Loop. Bounded by looping El tracks between Lake and Van Buren streets and Wells Street and Wabash Avenue, the city's business center pulses with latte-toting professionals scurrying between high-rise architectural landmarks. Restaurants and galleries dominate the West Loop, and the once-desolate South Loop now teems with college students and condo conversions.

2 Near North and River North. Shoppers stroll the Magnificent Mile between the John Hancock Center and the Chicago River (to the north and south), passing landmarks such as the Water Tower and Tribune Tower. Just north, stately mansions dominate the Gold Coast. Anchored by the Merchandise Mart, River North juxtaposes tourist traps with a thriving gallery scene.

3 Lincoln Park. Beyond the 1,200-acre park and the zoo, Lincoln Park boasts cafés and high-end boutiques.

4 Lakeview. Baseball fans pilgrimage to Wrigley Field, home of the Chicago Cubs. Just south of the ballpark on Clark Street you'll find memorabilia shops and sports bars; or head a block east to Halsted Street, site of gay enclave Boystown.

5 Pilsen, Little Italy, and Chinatown. Mexican restaurants, Mom-and-Pop shops, and Spanish signage line 18th Street, the heart of Pilsen. Gone are many of the Near West Side's Italian groceries and shops, but you can still get a mean veal marsala on Taylor Street. Bypass the tacky souvenirs in Chinatown and head straight for the restaurants, teahouses, and bakeries.

6 Hyde Park. This South Side neighborhood's main draw is the University of Chicago. You might overhear a Nobel Prize–winning physicist matching wits with a prominent economist in a bar or noodle shop on 55th Street or in a 57th Street bookstore. Visitors preferring sensory pleasures over intellectual pursuits should stroll Promontory Point for breathtaking lake and skyline views.

GETTING ORIENTED

Chicago is famously known as a city of neighborhoods. The Loop is Chicago's epicenter of business, finance, and government. Neighborhoods surrounding the Loop include River North (an area populated by art galleries and high-end boutiques), Streeterville (bordered by Lake Michigan and Navy Pier), and West Loop and South Loop, both up-and-coming areas with trendy residential areas and hip dining and shopping options. Chicago streets generally follow a grid pattern, running north–south or east–west and radiating from a center point at State and Madison streets in the Loop. East and west street numbers go up as you move away from State Street; north and south street numbers rise as you move away from Madison Street. Each block is represented by a hundred number (so the 12th block north of Madison will be the 1200 block).

14

The Windy City, the Second City, the City of Big Shoulders, My Kind of Town, Hog Butcher Capital to the World . . . Chicago might as well be called the City of Nicknames. This plethora of monikers proves that Chicago has something for everyone—it's a proud, down-to-earth, Midwestern city that easily rivals the global greats when it comes to culture and sophistication.

Chicago's charm is indisputable—the impeccably clean streets, the alluring mix of lush parks, Lake Michigan, and slick skyscrapers. But it's got a gritty side, too—you're never far from the sound of a screeching El train, and plenty of factories and blue collar bars dot the stunning architectural landscape. This is a city of contrasts: Some of the most rabid sports fans in the country coexist with culture vultures who spend their free time gallery hopping or attending the opera. You can sample an international array of street food or sit down to a multicourse meal at some of the country's best restaurants; check out edgy, groundbreaking theater or productions bound for Broadway; and shop for the toniest brands or scour ethnic enclaves for killer bargains.

PLANNING

WHEN TO GO

June, September, and October are mild and sunny. November through March the temperature ranges from crisp to frigid, April and May can fluctuate between cold/soggy and bright/warm, and July and August can either be perfect or serve up the dreaded combo of high heat and high humidity. That said, the only thing certain about Chicago's weather, according to locals, is that it can change in an instant.

GETTING HERE AND AROUND

Chicago has an excellent network of buses as well as trains, which are collectively called the El (for "elevated," which many of them are). The combination should bring you within ¼ mi of any place you'd like to go. Those with city smarts will find it safe to take any train, any time.

Others may want to take extra caution after 11 pm. Buses are almost always safe; there are several express buses running from downtown to destinations like the Museum of Science and Industry.

As of this writing, the fare for the bus is $2 and the train is $2.25 and a transfer is 25¢ with a Transit Card; if you're paying cash, all rides are $2.25. Travelers may want to get a Visitor Pass at their hotel, airport CTA stations, or any visitor center. These passes allow unlimited rides for a small fee and are worth it as long as you take three trips a day.

For directions to specific places via public transportation, for public transportation maps, and for places to buy Transit Cards, see ⊕ *www. transitchicago.com.*

If you drive downtown, park in one of the giant city-owned parking lots underneath Millennium Park or by the Museum Campus, which charge a flat fee. Private lots usually cost double.

14

AIR TRAVEL

The major gateway to Chicago is **O'Hare International Airport** (ORD). As one of the world's busiest airports, all major airlines pass through O'Hare. The sprawling structure is 19 mi from downtown, in the far northwest corner of the city. It can take anywhere from 30 to 90 minutes to travel between downtown and O'Hare, based on time of day, weather conditions, and construction on the Kennedy Expressway (Interstate 90). The Blue Line El train offers a reliable 40-minute trip between the Loop and O'Hare.

Airport Information Midway Airport (☎ 773/838–0600 ⊕ www.chicago-mdw. com or www.flychicago.com). **O'Hare International Airport** (☎ 773/686–2200 or 800/832–6352 ⊕ www.ohare.com or www.flychicago.com).

CAR TRAVEL

There are several main arteries that lead directly to Chicago: I–90, which runs from Seattle to Boston, runs right through downtown Chicago, where it partners up with I–94, another east–west interstate that runs from Michigan to Montana, to form the Kennedy Expressway. I–55 starts in Louisiana and ends in Chicago, where the portion of the freeway is known as the Stevenson Expressway.

Having a car in Chicago can be more of a liability than an asset. Traffic is often heavy, on-street parking can be nearly impossible to find, parking lots are expensive, and congestion—especially during rush hours—can create frustrating delays. Plus, there's seemingly never-ending construction on the major roads and highways. (Local joke: Chicago only has two seasons: winter and construction.) Cars are best used only for trips to the outlying suburbs and areas not easily accessible by public transportation.

TAXI TRAVEL

You can hail a cab on just about any busy street in Chicago; hotel doormen will get one for you as well. Cabs aren't all yellow anymore, and, in some cases, may be minivans. Chicago taxis are metered, with fares beginning at $2.25 upon entering the cab and $1.80 for each additional mile, plus a $1 fuel surcharge. There's also a charge of $1 for the first

additional passenger and 50 cents
for each additional passenger after
that.

MONEY-SAVING TIP
If you plan to hit several major
attractions, consider a **Chicago
City Pass** at participating locations
or online (⊕ *www.citypass.com/
chicago*). It will save you a combined total of about $65 on admis-
sion to these major attractions:
the Shedd Aquarium, the Field
Museum, the Adler Planetarium,
the Museum of Science and Indus-

FINDING FACTS

For information about the city's
architectural treasures, contact the **Chicago Architecture
Foundation** (☎ *312/922-8687
or 312/922-3432* ⊕ *www.
architecture.org*) or the **Chicago Convention and Tour-
ism Bureau** (☎ *312/567-8500*
⊕ *www.choosechicago.com/
architecture.html*).

try, and either the John Hancock Observatory or the Willis (Sears)
Tower Skydeck.

EXPLORING CHICAGO

THE LOOP

Noisy and mesmerizing, the Loop is a living architectural museum that
sidles alongside shimmering Lake Michigan. Gleaming modern towers
vie for space with 19th-century buildings while striking sculptures by
Picasso, Miró, and Chagall watch over plazas alive with music and
farmers' markets in summer.

Internationally known landmarks like the Willis (formerly Sears) Tower,
Millennium Park, and Buckingham Fountain blanket the Loop landscape, and visitors and locals gush over the masterpieces at the Art Institute and the merchandise at State Street's stores. LaSalle Street, home
of the thriving financial district, earned the moniker the Canyon (and
the feel of one) because of the large buildings that flank either end of
the relatively narrow street. The Loop oozes with Midwest friendliness,
charm, and culture—it has a world-class symphony, first-class theater,
fine restaurants, and a swinging nightlife.

For an especially good meal, head to the West Loop. What was once
Skid Row and meatpacking warehouses is now a vibrant community
with trendy restaurants. Greektown, a five-block stretch of Halsted
Street, serves up authentic saganaki. A thriving art scene has emerged
around Fulton Market. And yes, Harpo Studios, where Oprah Winfrey's
show is produced (until it ends in September 2011), is here.

The South Loop's claim to fame is the Museum Campus—The Field
Museum, Shedd Aquarium, and Adler Planetarium. Jutting out into
the lake, it affords amazing skyline views. To the north, giant gargoyles (supposedly owls signifying wisdom) loom atop the Harold
Washington Library. East on Congress at Michigan Avenue is the
Romanesque Revival–style Auditorium Building designed by architects Sullivan and Adler.

Pose with one of the two bronze lions at the entrance of the Art Institute.

WHAT TO SEE

The Art Institute of Chicago. With its flanking lions and marble lobby, the Michigan Avenue main building was once part of the World's Columbian Exposition; it opened as The Art Institute on December 8, 1893. Come for the sterling collection of Impressionists (an entire room is dedicated to Monet) and Old Masters; linger over the extraordinary and comprehensive photography collection; take in a number of fine American works; and discover paintings, drawings, sculpture, and design spanning the ancient to the contemporary world. Don't leave without exploring the Renzo Piano-designed Modern Wing: 264,000 square feet of the finest in 20th- and 21st-century art. The outdoor third-floor Nichols Bridgeway, connecting the Art Institute to Millennium Park, offers stunning views of the skyline and Lake Michigan. ⊠ *111 S. Michigan Ave., South Loop* ☎ *312/443–3600* ⊕ *www.artic.edu/aic* ⌸ *$18* ⊙ *Mon.–Wed. 10:30–5, Thurs. and Fri. 10:30–8, weekends 10–5.*

Field Museum. More than 6 *acres* of exhibits fill this gigantic world-class museum, which explores cultures and environments from around the world. Interactive exhibits examine such topics as the secrets of Egyptian mummies, the people of Africa and the Pacific Northwest, and the living creatures in the soil. Originally funded by Chicago retailer Marshall Field, the museum was founded in 1893 to hold material gathered for the World's Columbian Exposition; its current neoclassical home opened in 1921. ⊠ *South Loop* ☎ *312/922–9410* ⊕ *www.fieldmuseum. org* ⌸ *$15; 3-D theater and some exhibits cost extra; All-Access Pass, $29; free basic admission 2nd Mon. of the month* ⊙ *Daily 9–5; last admission at 4.*

DID YOU KNOW?

Much to locals' chagrin, the Sears Tower was rechristened the Willis Tower after its new tenant, Willis Group holdings, a London-based insurance broker, in the summer of 2009. It joins Marshall Field's (Macy's) and Comiskey Park (Cellular Field) as major Chicago institutions to be renamed.

Grant Park & Buckingham Fountain. Bordered by Lake Michigan to the east, a spectacular skyline to the west, and the Museum Campus to the south, Grant Park serves as the city's front yard and unofficial gathering place. This pristine open space is decked out with walking paths, a stand of stately elm trees, and formal rose gardens, where Loop dwellers and 9-to-5-ers take refuge from the concrete and steel. The park also hosts many of the city's largest outdoor events, including the annual Taste of Chicago, a vast picnic featuring foods from more than 70 restaurants. The event precedes a fireworks show around July Fourth. The centerpiece of Grant Park is the gorgeous, tiered **Buckingham Fountain** (⊠ *Between Columbus and Lake Shore Drs. east of Congress Plaza*), which has intricate designs of pink-marble seashells, water-spouting fish, and bronze sculptures of sea horses. Built in 1927, it was patterned after a fountain at Versailles but is about twice the size of its model. See it in all its glory between May 1 and October 1, when it's elaborately illuminated at night and sprays colorfully lighted waters. ⊠ *South Loop* ☎ *312/742–7529.*

Millennium Park. The showstopper here is Frank Gehry's stunning **Jay Pritzker Pavilion,** with dramatic 40-foot ribbons of stainless steel wrapping the music stage. The sound system, suspended by a trellis that spans the great lawn, provides concert-hall sound during the city's many outside concerts. When the mercury rises, kids love splashing in the jets of water shooting out from **Crown Fountain.** Spanish sculptor Jaume Plensa's whimsical work features close-up images of Chicagoans on 50-foot-high glass blocks. When a face purses its lips to "spit," water shoots out an opening lined up with the mouth. The gleaming polished steel **Cloud Gate** sculpture, otherwise known as "the Bean," awaits your delighted *ooohs* and *aaahs*. Located between Washington and Madison streets, its curved reflective surface provides a fun-house mirror view of Chicago's storied skyline. In summer the carefully manicured plantings in the **Lurie Garden** bloom; in winter the **McCormick Tribune Ice Rink** is open for public skating. ⊠ *Bounded by Michigan Ave., Columbus Dr., Randolph Dr., and Monroe St., Loop* ⊕ *www.millenniumpark.org* ⊠ *Free* ⊙ *Daily 6 am–11 pm.*

Fodor's Choice ★

Willis Tower. In Chicago, size matters. This soaring 110-story skyscraper, designed by Skidmore, Owings & Merrill in 1974, was originally named the Sears Tower and was the world's tallest building until 1996. The Petronas Towers in Kuala Lumpur, Malaysia, claimed the title, but it transferred hands again in 2004 to Taipei 101 in Taiwan. Today, Dubai's Burj Khalifa owns the bragging rights. Still, nothing quite beats Willis Tower's 103rd-floor **Skydeck** and the Ledge. Suspended 4.3 feet out from the building, this glass box offers thrills along with views; on a clear day, a whopping four states, Illinois, Michigan, Wisconsin, and Indiana, are visible. ■ TIP→ Check the visibility ratings at the security desk before you decide to ride up and take in the view. ⊠ *233 S. Wacker Dr.; for Skydeck, enter on Jackson Blvd. between Wacker Dr. and Franklin St., Loop* ☎ *312/875–9696* ⊕ *www.the-skydeck.com* ⊠ *$15.95* ⊙ *Apr.–Sept., daily 9 am–10 pm; Oct.–Mar., daily 10–8.*

Fodor's Choice ★

14

NEAR NORTH AND THE RIVER NORTH

With art galleries, the famous Magnificent Mile, the Gold Coast, and upscale dining options, River North and Near North hold some of the city's greatest attractions. Navy Pier and the Children's Museum are great family-friendly stops, and serious shoppers will have a chance to seriously exercise their credit cards on Michigan Avenue's Magnificent Mile.

At the beginning of the Mag Mile, check the architecture of the Tribune Tower. Then browse the shops on Michigan Avenue as well as the upscale boutiques on Oak and the many other side streets. The John Hancock Center offers one of the best sky-high views of the city. Instead of shelling out bucks at the observatory, get a drink at its Signature Lounge for about the same price; the view comes free.

The Gold Coast hugs the lakeshore north of the famous shopping district. Potter Palmer (the developer of State Street and the Palmer House Hotel) transformed the area when he built a mansion here, and his social-climbing friends followed his lead. The less-fortunate residents thought the new arrivals must have pockets lined with gold.

To the east of the Mag Mile on Grand Avenue, Navy Pier stretches ½ mi into Lake Michigan. Packed with restaurants, souvenir stalls, and other folks out for a stroll, this perpetually busy wonderland is adored by kids and visitors alike.

WHAT TO SEE

RIVER NORTH

Fodor's Choice ★

John Hancock Center. Designed by the same team that designed the Willis (formerly Sears) Tower (Skidmore, Owings & Merrill), this multiuse skyscraper is distinguished by its tapering shape and the enormous X braces, which help stabilize its 100 stories. Soon after it went up in 1970, it earned the nickname "Big John." No wonder: at 1,127 feet (1,502 feet counting the antennae at the top), 2.8 million square feet, and 46,000 tons of steel, there's nothing little about it. Packed with retail space, parking, offices, a restaurant, and residences, it has been likened to a city within a city. Impressive from any angle, it offers mind-boggling views from a 94th-floor observatory (as with the Willis Tower, you can see to four states on clear days). For anyone afflicted with vertigo, a sensible option is a seat in the bar of the 95th-floor Signature Room. The tab will be steep, but you'll be steady on your feet—maybe. ⊠ 875 N. Michigan Ave., Near North ☎ 888/175–8439 ⊕ www.hancockobservatory.com ⌐ Observatory $15; Total Tower Experience, $21 ⊙ Daily 9 am–11 pm; last ticket sold at 10:30 pm.

Fodor's Choice ★

Museum of Contemporary Art. A group of art patrons who felt the great Art Institute was unresponsive to modern work founded the MCA in 1967, and it has remained a renegade art museum ever since. It doesn't have any permanent exhibits; even the works from its collection are constantly rotating. This gives it a feeling of freshness, but it also makes it impossible to predict what will be on display at any time. Special exhibits are devoted mostly to original shows you can't see anywhere else. ⊠ 220 E. Chicago Ave., Near North ☎ 312/280–2660 ⊕ www.

mcachicago.org ✉ *Suggested admission $12, free Tues.* ☉ *Tues. 10 am–8 pm, Wed.–Sun. 10 am–5 pm.*

NEAR NORTH

Navy Pier. No matter the season, Navy Pier is a fun place to spend a few hours. Constructed in 1916 as a commercial-shipping pier, it was renamed in honor of the Navy in 1927 (the Army got Soldier Field). The once-deserted pier is now home to the Chicago Children's Museum, a carousel, a 15-story Ferris wheel, and an ice-skating rink; Crystal Gardens, one of the country's largest indoor botanical parks; an IMAX theater; an outdoor beer garden; and shopping promenades loaded with Chicago souvenirs, restaurants, and bars. ✉ *600 E. Grand Ave., Near North* ☎ *312/595–7437* ⊕ *www.navypier.com.*

14

LINCOLN PARK, BUCKTOWN, AND WICKER PARK

In 1864, Lincoln Park—the *park,* which extends from North Avenue to Foster Avenue—became the city's first public playground. Its zoo is legendary. The area adjacent to it, bordered by Armitage Avenue, Diversey Parkway, the lake, and the Chicago River, took the same name. Today, Lincoln Park epitomizes all the things that people love to hate about yuppified urban areas: stratospheric housing prices, teeny boutiques with big-attitude salespeople, and plenty of fancy-schmancy coffee shops, wine bars, and cafés. That said, it's also got some of the prettiest residential streets in the city, that gorgeous park, a great nature museum, a thriving arts scene, and the famous Steppenwolf Theatre.

Old Town, bordered by Division Street, Armitage Avenue, Clark Street, and Larrabee Street, began in the 1850s as a modest German working-class neighborhood. Now its diverse population resides in some of the oldest—and most expensive—real estate in Chicago. Its most renowned tenants are the comedy clubs Second City and Zanies.

Bucktown, which surrounds Milwaukee Avenue north of North Avenue, got its name from the goats kept by the area's original Polish and German immigrants. Wicker Park, the area south of North Avenue to Division Street, is now inhabited by creative types, young families, thirtysomething professionals, and university students. Cutting-edge galleries, coffeehouses, nightclubs, and funky shops line its streets—a far cry from the Mag Mile.

WHAT TO SEE

Fodor'sChoice ★ **Chicago History Museum.** The museum went through a major rehaul in late 2006 when it changed its name from the Chicago Historical Society in honor of its 150th birthday. The new permanent sights include a Costume and Textile Gallery and the exhibit "Chicago: Crossroads of America," which demystifies historic tragedies like the Great Chicago Fire and Haymarket Affair. ✉ *1601 N. Clark St., Lincoln Park* ☎ *312/642–4600* ⊕ *www.chicagohistory.org* ✉ *$14, Mon. free* ☉ *Mon.–Sat. 9:30–4:30, Sun. noon–5.*

Fodor'sChoice ★ **Lincoln Park Zoo.** At this urban zoo you can face off with lions (separated by a window, of course) outside the Lion House; or watch about two dozen gorillas go ape in the sprawling, state-of-the-art Regenstein Center for African Apes.

Animals both slithery (pythons) and cuddly (koalas) reside in the glass-dome Regenstein Small Mammal and Reptile House; if you're looking for the big guys (elephants, giraffes, black rhinos), they're in the large-mammal house. For youngsters, there are the children's zoo, the Farm-in-the-Zoo (farm animals and a learning center with films and demonstrations), the Conservation Station (which has hands-on activities), and the LPZoo Children's Train Ride. Be sure to leave time for a ride (or two) on the Endangered Species Carousel, featuring a menagerie of 48 rare and endangered animals. ⊠ *2200 N. Cannon Dr., Lincoln Park* ☏ *312/742-2000* ⊕ *www.lpzoo.com* ☎ *Free* ☉ *Apr.–late May, daily 10–5; late May–early Sept., weekdays 10–5, weekends 10–6:30; early Sept.–Oct., daily 10–5; Nov.–Mar., daily 10–4:30.*

LAKEVIEW

Lakeview got its name from the 1850s-built Hotel Lake View. By 1889 Chicago took the town for its own. Today it is a massive neighborhood made up of small enclaves, each with its own distinct personality. There's Wrigley Field surrounded by the beer-swilling, Cubby-blue-'til-we-die sports-bar fanaticism of Wrigleyville; the gay bars, shops, and clubs along Halsted Street in Boystown; and an air of urban chic along Southport Avenue, where young families stroll amid the trendy boutiques and ice-cream shops.

ⓒ
Fodor'sChoice
★

Wrigley Field. The venerable, ivy-covered home of the Chicago Cubs is the nation's second-oldest major league ballpark. The first major league game was played there on April 23, 1914. Today, the original scoreboard is still used. Score-by-innings and players' numbers are done manually as well as strikes, outs, hits, and errors. Find the die-hard fans in the bleachers, while the more gentrified prefer to watch the games from the box seats at the first and third baselines. If you look up along Sheffield Avenue on the east side of the ballpark you can see the rooftop patios where baseball fans pay high prices to cheer for the home team. Ticketless fans sit in lawn chairs on Sheffield during the games, waiting for foul balls to fly their way. ⊠ *Addison and Sheffield, Wrigleyville, Lakeview* ☏ *773/404–2827* ⊕ *www.mlb.com/chc/ballpark/index.jsp* ☎ *$25 for tours.*

PILSEN, LITTLE ITALY, AND CHINATOWN

A jumble of ethnic neighborhoods stretches west of the Loop and from the south branch of the Chicago River to the Eisenhower Expressway (I–290). Once home to myriad 20th-century immigrants, the area is now dominated by Pilsen's Mexican community, Little Italy, and the University of Illinois's Medical District and Circle Campus.

Formerly an enclave of Bohemian and Czechoslovakian immigrants, Pilsen has an arts community with galleries and dramatic, colorful murals that showcase Mexican history, culture, and religion. It's bounded on the east by 800 West Halsted Street, on the west by 2400 West Western Avenue, on the north by 16th Street, and on the south by the Chicago River.

North of Pilsen is Little Italy, which, despite the encroachment by the University of Illinois at Chicago (UIC), still contains plenty of yummy Italian restaurants, bakeries, groceries, and sandwich shops. Extending west to 1600 West Ashland and south to 1200 South Roosevelt, Little Italy blends into University Village at its northeast corner. The village, UIC's booming residential area, lies west of Roosevelt Road and centers on Halsted Street, spanning south to 14th Street.

In the 1870s, the Prairie Avenue Historic District was Chicago's first Gold Coast. Prominent Chicagoans, including George Pullman and Marshall Field, had homes in the area two blocks east of Michigan Avenue, between 18th and 22nd streets. It's close to Chinatown, where Wentworth and Archer avenues are chockablock with restaurants and shops that might just make you forget you're in the Midwest.

14

WHAT TO SEE

PILSEN

18th Street. Pilsen's main commercial strip is loaded with tempting restaurants, bakeries, and Mexican grocery stores. East on 18th Street past the "bienvenidos a pilsen" sign is **Nuevo León**, a brightly painted family restaurant that has been an anchor in the neighborhood since the Gutiérrez family set up shop in 1962. ⊠ *18th St., Pilsen.*

Fodor's Choice
★

National Museum of Mexican Art. Formerly the Mexican Fine Arts Museum Center, this is the largest Latino museum in the country, half art museum, half cultural exploration center. After the big downtown museums, this is the one you shouldn't miss. Galleries house impressive collections of contemporary, traditional, and meso-American art from both sides of the border, as well as vivid exhibits that trace immigration woes and political fights. Every fall the giant Day of the Dead exhibit stuns Chicagoans with its altars from artists across the country. ⊠ *1852 W. 19th St., Pilsen* ☎ *312/738–1503* ⊕ *www.nationalmuseumofmexicanart.org* ⊠ *Free* ⊗ *Tues.–Sun. 10–5.*

LITTLE ITALY

Taylor Street. In the mid-19th century, when Italians started to migrate to Chicago, about one-third of them settled mostly in and around Taylor Street, a 12-block stretch between Ashland and University of Illinois Chicago. It is best known for its Italian restaurants, though Thai food, tacos, and other ethnic food options are starting to fill the street as well. ⊠ *Taylor St., Little Italy.*

CHINATOWN

Chinatown Gate. South of the Prairie Avenue district, this Chinese microcosm sits in the shadows of modern skyscrapers and 21st-century American life. The neighborhood is anchored by the Chinatown Gate and the enormous green-and-red pagoda towers of the **Pui Tak Center,** a church-based community center in the former On Leong Tong Building. Most visitors to Chinatown only come to eat, stock up on almond cookies, or scout out the gift and furniture shops for bargains on Wentworth Street. But Chinatown is more than just dim sum and chop suey. Ghosts of the Old World haunt the streets bordered by 24th Place, Archer, Cermak/22nd Street, Princeton, and Wentworth. At grocery stores that the locals frequent, walls are lined with huge bags of rice. Live fish and crabs fill the vats, while unidentifiable canned items and dried things bulge from the shelves. ⊠ *Chinatown.*

HYDE PARK

Hyde Park is something of a trek from downtown Chicago, but it's worth the extra effort. Today the neighborhood is considered a vibrant, eclectic part of the city. The community is rich in academic and cultural life, and it is also considered one of the country's most successfully integrated neighborhoods, which is reflected in everything from the people you'll meet on the street to the diverse cuisine available.

Best known as the home of the University of Chicago, the neighborhood only began to see significant growth in the late 19th century, when the university opened in 1892 and the World's Columbian Exposition attracted an international influx a year later. The exposition spawned the Midway Plaisance and numerous Classical Revival buildings, including the behemoth Museum of Science and Industry. The Midway Plaisance still runs along the southern edge of the University of Chicago's original campus.

A number of architecturally riveting buildings are here, including two by Frank Lloyd Wright, the Robie House and Heller House. There are also a thriving theater scene and several art and history museums.

WHAT TO SEE

☽ **Museum of Science and Industry.** The beloved MSI is one of the most-visited sites in Chicago, and for good reason. The sprawling open space has 2,000 exhibits on three floors, with new exhibits being added constantly. The museum's high-tech interior is hidden by the Classical Revival exterior; it was designed in 1892 by D.H. Burnham & Company as a temporary structure to house the Palace of Fine Arts for the World's Columbian Exposition. It and the Art Institute are the fair's only surviving buildings. On a nice day, take a walk behind the museum to the beautifully landscaped Jackson Park and its peaceful Osaka Garden, a Japanese-style garden with a waterfall. ⊠ *5700 S. Lake Shore Dr., Hyde Park* ☏ *773/684–1414* ⊕ *www.msichicago.org* ☏ *$15, museum and Omnimax admission $23, parking $16* ⊙ *Memorial Day–Labor Day, Mon.–Sat. 9:30–5:30, Sun. 11–5:30; Labor Day–Memorial Day, Mon.–Sat. 9:30–4, Sun. 11–4.*

Fodor's Choice ★

WHERE TO EAT

Sure, this city has great architecture, museums, and sports venues. But at its heart, Chicago really is a food town. This is evident in the priority that good eating takes, no matter the occasion. Rain or shine, locals wait in a line that snakes around the corner for dolled-up dogs at Hot Doug's. They reserve part of their paychecks to dine at inventive Alinea. And they love to talk about their most recent meal—just ask.

So it's no wonder that outdoor festivals are often centered on food, from Taste of Chicago in summer, which packs the grounds at Grant Park, to smaller celebrations, like the German-American fest in Lincoln Square, a mini-Oktoberfest, in fall.

Although the city has always had options on the extreme ends of the spectrum—from the hole-in-the wall Italian beef sandwich shops to the special-occasion spots, it's now easier to find eateries in the middle that serve seasonal menus with a farm-to-table mantra. For the budget conscious, it's also a great time to dine: Some talented chefs aren't bothering to wait for a liquor license, opening BYOB spots turning out polished fare instead (just try Urban Belly on the Far North Side).

WHAT IT COSTS					
	¢	$	$$	$$$	$$$$
Restaurants	under $10	$10–$18	$19–$27	$28–$36	over $36

Prices are per person for a typical main course or equivalent combination of smaller dishes, excluding tax. Note: If a restaurant offers only prix-fixe (set-price) meals, it has been given the price category that reflects the full prix-fixe price.

THE LOOP

$$$
NEW AMERICAN
Fodor'sChoice
★

✕ **Blackbird.** Being cramped next to your neighbor has never been as fun as it is at this hot spot run by foodie chef Paul Kahan. Celebs pepper the sleek see-and-be-seen crowd who come for the creative dishes. While the menu changes constantly, you'll always find choices that highlight seasonal ingredients, such as rack of lamb with leeks and *spigarello* (wild broccoli) in spring, or grilled sturgeon with mustard spaetzle in winter. It all plays out against a minimalist backdrop of white walls, blue-gray banquettes, and aluminum chairs. Reservations aren't required, but they might as well be; the dining room is typically booked solid on Saturday night. ⊠ *619 W. Randolph St., West Loop* ☎ *312/715–0708* ⊕ *www.blackbirdrestaurant.com* ⩙ *Reservations essential* ═ *AE, D, MC, V* ☽ *Closed Sun. No lunch Sat.*

¢
AMERICAN

✕ **Epic Burger.** After walking through exhibits at the Art Institute, follow the local college crowd to this order-at-the-counter eatery. While the ambience is kitschy (think bright orange walls and televisions broadcasting cartoons), the food is, as owner David Friedman describes it, "more mindful." Friedman sources fresh, natural beef for Epic's burgers, which are shaped by hand, cooked to order, and served atop fresh buns on non-petroleum-based plates. In addition, burger add-ons include Wisconsin cheese, nitrate-free bacon, and an organic fried egg. There's also a second location in Old Town. ⊠ *517 S. State St., South Loop* ☎ *312/913–1373* ⊠ *1000 W. North Ave., Old Town* ☎ *312/440–9700* ⊕ *www.epicburger.com* ═ *AE, MC, V.*

NEAR NORTH AND RIVER NORTH

$
ITALIAN

✕ **Pizzeria Uno.** Chicago deep-dish pizza got its start here in 1943, and both local and out-of-town fans continue to pack in for filling pies. Housed in a Victorian brownstone, Uno offers a slice of old Chicago in dim paneled rooms with reproduction light fixtures. Spin-off Due down the street handles the overflow. Plan on two thick, cheesy slices or less as a full meal. This is no quick-to-your-table pie, so do order salads and be prepared to entertain the kids during the inevitable wait. ⊠ *29 E. Ohio St., River North* ☎ *312/321–1000* ⊕ *www.unos.com* ═ *AE, MC, V.*

14

$ ✕**Xoco.** By opening a third restaurant next door to perennial favorites
MEXICAN Frontera Grill and Topolobampo, celeb chef Rick Bayless has taken
control of this River North block. With Xoco, he's giving the city the
ultimate place for *tortas* (Mexican sandwiches) filled with spiced-up
fare such as *cochinita pibil* (suckling pig with pickled red onions, black
beans, and searing habanero salsa) and *caldos,* generous bowls of pozole
and other Latin-inspired soups served after 3 pm. First timers shouldn't
pass up the hot chocolate (available at breakfast, lunch, and dinner)
made from cacao beans that are roasted and ground on the premises;
a steaming cup is as rich as a chocolate bar and best consumed with a
plate of hot churros. Enter around the corner on Illinois Street and join
the (often long) line; orders are taken at the counter. ✉ *449 N. Clark St.,
River North* ☎ *312/334–3688* ⊕ *www.rickbayless.com* ⌖ *Reservations
not accepted* ▭ *AE, D, DC, MC, V* ⊗ *Closed Sun. and Mon.*

LINCOLN PARK

$$$$ ✕**Alinea.** Believe the hype and book well in advance. Chicago's most
CONTEMPORARY exciting restaurant demands an adventurous spirit and a serious com-
Fodor'sChoice mitment of time and money. If you have four hours and $225 to spare,
★ the more-than-20-course tasting menu is the best way to experience
chef Grant Achatz's stunning cutting-edge food. The gastronomic roller
coaster (there's also a less-pricey 12-course version for $150) takes you
on a journey through intriguing aromas, visuals, flavors, and textures.
The menu changes frequently, but you might find green beans perched
on a pillow that emits nutmeg-scented air, sweetbreads served with
burnt bread and toasted hay, and Earl Grey paired with caramelized
white chocolate. Though some dishes—they range in size from one to
four bites—may look like science projects, there's nothing gimmicky
about the endless procession of bold and elegant tastes. ✉ *1723 N.
Halsted St., Lincoln Park* ☎ *312/867–0110* ⊕ *www.alinea-restaurant.
com* ⌖ *Reservations essential* ▭ *AE, D, DC, MC, V* ⊗ *Closed Mon.
and Tues. No lunch.*

$$$ ✕**Boka.** If you're doing Steppenwolf pretheater dinner on North Halsted
NEW AMERICAN Street, this unpretentious, though upscale spot gets foodies' stamp of
Fodor'sChoice approval, particularly with Charlie Trotter alumnus Giuseppe Tentori
★ in the kitchen. A seasonally driven menu constantly changes, offering
creative fare such as squid with spicy pineapple, chamomile-dusted
quail with caramelized fennel, and venison with brussels sprouts, wild
rice, dates, juniper berries, and a chestnut cake. The slick lounge and
outdoor patio both serve food, drawing a following independent of
curtain time. ✉ *1729 N. Halsted St., Lincoln Park* ☎ *312/337–6070*
⊕ *www.bokachicago.com* ▭ *AE, MC, V* ⊗ *No lunch.*

$$ ✕**The Bristol.** While Bucktown isn't wanting for dining options, this
AMERICAN self-proclaimed "eatery and bar" sets itself apart by focusing intently
Fodor'sChoice on the food. TRU alumnus chef Chris Pandel sources local produce
★ and features meat from sustainably raised animals. As a consequence,
it isn't rare to find braised goat on the frequently changing menu. He
also offers playful takes on more familiar fare, turning out popular
small plates such as chicken wings stuffed with chorizo, baked-to-order
monkey bread, and the raviolo, a plate-size stuffed pasta filled with
ricotta and egg yolk. Arrive early; seating in the boisterous dining room

is first come, first served. Or wait in the lounge upstairs for a spot to free up. ⊠ *2152 N. Damen Ave., Bucktown* ☎ *773/862–5555* ⊕ *www. thebristolchicago.com* ▭ *AE, MC, V* ⊙ *No lunch Mon.–Sat.*

$$$
AMERICAN
Fodor'sChoice
★

✕ **North Pond.** A former Arts and Crafts–style warming house for ice-skaters at Lincoln Park's North Pond, this gem in the woods fittingly champions an uncluttered culinary style. Talented chef Bruce Sherman emphasizes organic ingredients, wild-caught fish, and artisanal farm products. Menus change seasonally, but order the Midwestern favorite walleye pike if available. Like the food, the wine list seeks out boutique producers. The food remains top-notch at lunch, but the scene, dense with strollers and high chairs, is far less serene than dinner service. ⊠ *2610 N. Cannon Dr., Lincoln Park* ☎ *773/477–5845* ⊕ *www. northpondrestaurant.com* ▭ *AE, D, DC, MC, V* ⊙ *Closed Mon. and Tues. Jan.–Apr. No lunch Oct.–May.*

PILSEN AND LITTLE ITALY

$
AMERICAN

✕ **Honky Tonk Barbeque.** The twang of country meets the tang of sauce at this Pilsen spot known for (literally) award-winning barbecue. In 2008, owner Willie Wagner placed third in the pork-shoulder category at the prestigious Memphis in May barbecue cooking contest. Although there's plenty of meat—from ribs and brisket to whole-smoked chicken—on the menu, try the tender pulled pork first with a dab of regular or spicy sauce. As for the address, it's easy to spot: Look for the flames painted alongside the entrance. ⊠ *1213 W 18th St., Pilsen* ☎ *312/226–7427* ⊕ *www.honkytonkbbqchicago.com* ⌕ *Reservations not accepted* ▭ *AE, MC, V* ⊙ *Closed Mon. No lunch Tues.–Sat.*

¢
AMERICAN

✕ **Sweet Maple Cafe.** On a Sunday morning, this breakfast-all-day spot is easy to find on Taylor Street: just look for the line out the door. In fact, expect a line on most days as customers ranging from students to police officers and politicians wait for a table in anticipation of warm, buttery biscuits and a side of generous hospitality. Laurene Hynson's menu has something for everyone: buttermilk pancakes and hefty omelets for those who prefer American classics as well as dishes such as the Dias and Noches Scramble, eggs cooked with grilled chicken and jalapenos and served with a side of freshly made salsa. For non–breakfast eaters, well-executed salads and soups are available after 11:30 on weekdays. *1339 W. Taylor St., Little Italy* ☎ *312/243–8908* ⊕ *sweetmaplecafe.com* ⌕ *Reservations not accepted* ▭ *AE, MC, V* ⊙ *No dinner.*

NORTH SIDE AND FAR NORTH SIDE

¢
HOT DOGS
☺
Fodor'sChoice
★

✕ **Hot Doug's.** Don't tell the zealots who have made Hot Doug's famous that these are *just* hot dogs—these "encased meats" go beyond your standard Vienna wiener. The gourmet purveyor wraps buns around chipotle chicken sausage, smoked crawfish and pork sausage with spicy remoulade, lamb sausage with raita, and even antelope sausage on occasion. Make the trek on a Friday or Saturday, when the indulgent (and locally infamous) duck-fat fries are available. The clientele is a curious mix of hungry hard hats and serious foodies, neither of which care about the lack of frills or inevitable long line. ⊠ *3324 N. California Ave., Far North Side* ☎ *773/279–9550* ⊕ *www.hotdougs.com* ▭ *No credit cards* ⊙ *Closed Sun. No dinner.*

14

$	✕**Urban Belly**. It's easy to strike up a conversation with local foodies at
ASIAN	this favorite casual BYOB Asian street-food spot. And there's a lot to
Fodor's Choice	discuss: should you go for a bowl of udon noodles swimming in a chili-
★	lime broth or the pho-spiced duck dumplings and "phat rice" (fried rice
with diced pork belly and short rib)? Either way, it's hard to go wrong
with anything chef Bill Kim (formerly of Le Lan) creates in his tiny
kitchen. But come early: Despite the restaurant's out-of-the-way location in the residential Avondale neighborhood, seating at the four long
communal tables is first-come, first-served, and spots fill up quickly.
⊠ *3053 N. California Ave., Far North Side* ☎ *773/583–0500* ⊕ *www.
urbanbellychicago.com* ⊟ *AE, D, MC, V* ☉ *Closed Mon.*

WHERE TO STAY

Chicago hotel rates are as temperamental as the city's climate. And just
as snow in April and 70° weather in November are not uncommon,
it is widely accepted that a hotel's room rates may drop $50 to $100
overnight—and rise again the next day. It all depends on the season and
what's happening around town.

Even so, it's wise to shop around. Focus on a neighborhood of interest,
such as the Michigan Avenue area, also called Near North, and you'll
find budget chains like Embassy Suites and luxury properties like the
Four Seasons Hotel Chicago within a few blocks of each other.

On the lower end, expect well-maintained yet boxy and sparsely decorated rooms. The good news is that free Wi-Fi is now a feature of most
budget-friendly hotels, like the Best Western and Holiday Inn chains,
or local outfits like the Essex Inn.

Top-tier hotels have no problem filling their rooms: in some cases, this
has little to do with amenities. Instead, their vibrant bar scenes are the
draw, as is the case at the W Chicago Lakeshore, W Chicago–City Center, the Wit, and the James Hotel. Rooms at these hot spots usually don't
go for under $250, but the "it" factor is huge, with attractive crowds
queuing at the bar and lounging in the restaurants.

*Hotel reviews have been condensed for this book. Please go to Fodors.
com for full reviews of each property.*

WHAT IT COSTS				
¢	$	$$	$$$	$$$$
Hotels	under $150	$150–$219	$220–$319	$320–$420	over $420

Prices exclude service charges and Chicago's 15.4% room tax.

THE LOOP, WEST LOOP, AND SOUTH LOOP

$	🔲 **Essex Inn**. Along with being a five-minute walk from the Museum
☺	Campus, this family-friendly hotel offers package deals with popular
Fodor's Choice	attractions such as the Shedd Aquarium, Art Institute, Field Museum,
★	and Willis (Sears) Tower. **Pros:** good value; pool complete with a life-
guard. **Cons:** rooms can be drafty during winter months; staff can
be slow to address complaints. ⊠ *800 S. Michigan Ave., South Loop*

WHERE SHOULD I STAY?

	Neighborhood Vibe	Pros	Cons
The Loop	Mostly historic hotels of architectural interest in an area trolled by business-people on weekdays and shoppers on weekends. The scene has become increasingly hip over the years.	Accessible public transportation and abundant cabs; packed with business types during the day; the area has recently blossomed into a worthy nighttime destination.	El train noise; construction common; streets can sometimes be bare in late evening. It draws an older, more established crowd.
West Loop and South Loop	Mixed residential and business neighborhoods that are gentrifying, although empty buildings and storefronts are common. This area has seen a lot of new life in the last couple of years.	Hotels are cheaper; streets are quieter; Museum Campus and McCormick Place are within easy reach; family-friendly; appealing to hipster set with many new lounges and restaurants.	Long walks to public transportation; minimal shopping; quiet at night with many darkened streets. If you're looking for entertainment, it might require a quick drive or a long walk.
Near North	The pulse of the city, on and around North Michigan Avenue, has ritzy high-rise hotels and plenty of shopping and restaurants. As you go farther north, streets become residential.	Many lodging options, including some of the city's most luxurious hotels. Lively streets abuzz until late night; safe. The shopping couldn't be better for those with deep pockets.	Some hotels on the pricey side; crowded sidewalks; popular tourist destination. And don't expect to find many bargains here.
River North	Lots of chains, from hotels to restaurants to shops, patronized mostly by travelers. Though this is a tourist haven, the area has become home to many art galleries and antiques stores.	Affordable lodging; easy access to public transportation; attractions nearby are family-friendly, especially during the day; high concentration of nightclubs.	Area might be too touristy for some. This is Chicago's home for chain restaurants; parking is a drag.
Lincoln Park	Small, boutique hotels tucked on quiet, tree-lined streets with many independent shops and restaurants. Pedestrian-friendly area; you don't need a car to find a restaurant, bar, or bank.	Low crime; great paths for walks; lots of parkland. From hot dogs to sushi, this place has it all; eclectic collection of shops and restaurants, ranging from superaffordable to the ultrapricey.	Limited hotel selection; long walks to El train. Parking is almost impossible in some spots, and garages don't come cheap; very young and trendy crowd.
Lakeview and Far North Side	Especially lively around Wrigley Field, where both Chicagoans and travelers congregate in summertime; the area's lodging is midsize boutique hotels and B&Bs.	Low crime; moderately priced hotels; shopping and dining options at all price ranges, including many vintage-clothing boutiques; a plethora of sports-themed bars.	Congested traffic; panhandlers common, especially around El stations and Wrigley Field. Parking is nightmarish when the Cubs are playing in town.

14

☎ *312/939–2800 or 800/621–6909* ⊕ *www.essexinn.com* ⟿ *254 rooms* ⬠ *In-room: a/c, refrigerator, Wi-Fi. In-hotel: restaurant, room service, pool, gym, laundry service, Internet terminal, parking (paid)* ▤ *AE, D, DC, MC, V* ⵊ◯⎮ *EP.*

$$$ ⌗ **Hotel Burnham.** Making creative use of a city landmark, this hotel
Fodor's Choice is housed in the famed 13-story Reliance Building, which D.H. Burn-
★   ham & Company built in 1895. **Pros:** property has a storied past; beautifully restored building; good location. **Cons:** small guest rooms may make it difficult to sprawl out. ⊠ *1 W. Washington St., The Loop* ☎ *312/782–1111 or 877/294–9712* ⊕ *www.burnhamhotel.com* ⟿ *103 rooms, 19 suites* ⬠ *In-room: a/c, safe, refrigerator, Wi-Fi. In-hotel: restaurant, room service, bar, gym, laundry service, Wi-Fi hotspot, parking (paid), some pets allowed* ▤ *AE, D, DC, MC, V* ⵊ◯⎮ *EP.*

$$$ ⌗ **Renaissance Blackstone.** Ask about this hotel's storied past; both presi-
Fodor's Choice dents and mob bosses have stayed here, and a complete renovation has
★   restored this once-faded building to its original splendor. **Pros:** new owners spared no expense in this beautifully redone space; exceptional service **Cons:** decor can be a bit too ornate for some. ⊠ *636 S. Michigan Ave., South Loop* ☎ *312/447–0955* ⊕ *www.theblackstonehotel.com* ⟿ *328 rooms, 4 suites* ⬠ *In-room: a/c, safe, refrigerator, Internet, Wi-Fi. In-hotel: restaurant, room service, bars, gym, laundry service, Internet terminal, Wi-Fi hotspot, parking (paid)* ▤ *AE, D, DC, MC, V* ⵊ◯⎮ *EP.*

NEAR NORTH AND RIVER NORTH

$$ ⌗ **Hotel Sax Chicago.** Visitors to Chicago would be hard-pressed to find
Fodor's Choice a more chic or tech-savvy place than the Hotel Sax. **Pros:** no need
★   to leave the hotel for nightlife, thanks to the Crimson Lounge; the House of Blues is right next door. **Cons:** rooms and hallways can be too dim. ⊠ *333 N. Dearborn St., River North* ☎ *312/245–0333* ⊕ *www.hotelsaxchicago.com* ⟿ *328 rooms, 26 suites* ⬠ *In-room: a/c, safe, Internet, Wi-Fi (paid). In-hotel: 6 restaurants, room service, bars, gym, laundry service, Internet terminal, Wi-Fi hotspot, parking (paid)* ▤ *AE, D, DC, MC, V* ⵊ◯⎮ *EP.*

$$ ⌗ **The James Hotel.** If you don't get the hint from the bustling bar
Fodor's Choice scene spilling into the lobby or the antique-suitcases art piece near the
★   elevator, the James further announces its hipster pedigree when you enter your room and are greeted by preprogrammed alt-rock on the iPod-ready stereo system perched on the bar. **Pros:** new and sleek with rich colors; not your typical, cookie-cutter chain. **Cons:** tiny elevators; awkward room layout. ⊠ *55 E. Ontario St., at Rush St., Near North* ☎ *312/337–1000* ⊕ *www.jameshotels.com* ⟿ *243 rooms, 54 suites* ⬠ *In-room: a/c, safe, refrigerator, Wi-Fi. In-hotel: restaurant, room service, bar, gym, spa, laundry service, Wi-Fi hotspot, parking (paid), pets allowed* ▤ *AE, D, DC, MC, V* ⵊ◯⎮ *EP.*

$$$$ ⌗ **Peninsula Chicago.** Committed to keeping its guests well fed and well
Fodor's Choice rested, the Peninsula is home to one of the city's most creative restau-
★   rants (Avenues), a lavish and popular afternoon tea, and on weekends the lobby lounge features an overflowing chocolate buffet. **Pros:** top-notch bath products; separate shower and bath. **Cons:** in-house dining options are not the best for families with children. ⊠ *108 E. Superior St., Near North* ☎ *312/337–2888 or 866/288–8889* ⊕ *www.peninsula.*

com ⌁ *256 rooms, 83 suites* ⌂ *In-room: a/c, safe, refrigerator, Internet, Wi-Fi. In-hotel: 4 restaurants, room service, bar, pool, gym, spa, laundry service, parking (paid), some pets allowed* ⊟ *AE, D, DC, MC, V* ⦶*EP.*

$$ ⌘ **Ritz-Carlton Chicago.** Perched over Water Tower Place, Michigan Avenue's best-known shopping mall, the Ritz-Carlton specializes in showering guests with attention. **Pros:** guests feel pampered; great stay for families with small children. **Cons:** some guests complain of slow room service. ⊠ *160 E. Pearson St., Near North* ☎ *312/266–1000, 800/621–6906 outside Illinois* ⊕ *www.fourseasons.com/chicagorc* ⌁ *344 rooms, 91 suites* ⌂ *In-room: a/c, safe, refrigerator, DVD (some), Wi-Fi. In-hotel: restaurant, room service, bar, pool, gym, spa, laundry service, Internet terminal, Wi-Fi hotspot, parking (paid), some pets allowed* ⊟ *AE, D, DC, MC, V* ⦶*EP.*

Fodor'sChoice
★

$$ ⌘ **W Chicago Lakeshore.** This sleek, high-energy hotel is the only one in Chicago directly overlooking Lake Michigan. **Pros:** cool, hip vibe; guest rooms feel like swank lounges. **Cons:** service not commensurate with the price. ⊠ *644 N. Lake Shore Dr., Near North* ☎ *312/943–9200 or 877/946–8357* ⊕ *www.whotels.com/lakeshore* ⌁ *498 rooms, 27 suites* ⌂ *In-room: a/c, safe, DVD, Internet, Wi-Fi. In-hotel: restaurant, room service, bar, pool, gym, spa, laundry service, Wi-Fi hotspot, parking (paid), some pets allowed* ⊟ *AE, D, DC, MC, V* ⦶*EP.*

Fodor'sChoice
★

14

NIGHTLIFE

Chicago's entertainment varies from loud and loose to sophisticated and sedate. You'll find classic Chicago corner bars in most neighborhoods, along with trendier alternatives like wine bars and lounges. The strains of blues and jazz provide much of the backbeat to the city's groove, and an alternative country scene is flourishing. As far as dancing is concerned, take your pick from cavernous clubs to smaller spots with DJs spinning dance tunes; there's everything from hip-hop to swing. Wicker Park/Bucktown and River North have the hottest nightlife, but prime spots are spread throughout the city.

Shows usually begin at 9 pm; cover charges generally range from $3 to $20, depending on the day of the week (Friday and Saturday nights are the most expensive). Most bars stay open until 2 am Friday night and 3 am Saturday, except for a few after-hours spots and some larger dance clubs, which are often open until 4 am Friday night and 5 am Saturday. Some bars are not open seven days a week, so call before you go.

MUSIC CLUBS

BLUES

Fodor'sChoice
★

Buddy Guy's Legends (⊠ *754 S. Wabash Ave., South Loop* ☎ *312/427–0333*) serves up Louisiana-style barbecue along with the blues. The big club has good sound, good sight lines, and pool tables if you get restless in between sets. Look for local blues acts during the week and larger-scale touring acts on weekends. Don't miss Grammy Award–winning blues performer/owner Buddy Guy in January, when he

Bluesman Jimmy Burns singing at Buddy Guy's Legends.

performs a monthlong home stand of shows (tickets go on sale one month in advance).

FOLK AND ETHNIC

★ **Old Town School of Folk Music** (⊠ *4544 N. Lincoln Ave., Far Northwest Side* ☎ *773/728–6000*), Chicago's first and oldest folk-music school, has served as folk central in the city since it opened in 1957. This welcoming spot in Lincoln Square hosts outstanding performances by national and local acts in an intimate-feeling 420-seat concert hall boasting excellent acoustics. If you can, book a table seat next to the stage.

JAZZ

★ **Green Mill** (⊠ *4802 N. Broadway, Far North Side* ☎ *773/878–5552*), a Chicago institution off the beaten track in not-so-trendy Uptown, has been around since 1907. Deep leather banquettes and ornate wood paneling line the walls, and a photo of Al Capone occupies a place of honor on the piano behind the bar. The jazz entertainment is both excellent and contemporary—the club launched the careers of Kurt Elling and Patricia Barber—and the Uptown Poetry Slam, a competitive poetry reading, takes center stage on Sunday.

PIANO BAR

Fodor'sChoice **Pump Room** (⊠ *Omni Ambassador East Hotel, 1301 N. State Pkwy.,*
★ *Near North* ☎ *312/266–0360*) shows off its storied past with photos of celebrities covering the walls. The bar at this restaurant has live piano music and a small dance floor that calls out for dancing cheek to cheek, especially on weekends.

ROCK

The owners of **Lincoln Hall** (✉ *2424 N. Lincoln Ave., Lincoln Park* ☎ *773/525–2501*) transformed a former movie theater into an intimate concert space with great sight lines, an excellent sound system, and a wraparound balcony with seating. There's a separate bar and dining area up front for preshow dining.

★ **Metro** (✉ *3730 N. Clark St., Lakeview* ☎ *773/549–0203*) brings in progressive, nationally known artists and the cream of the local crop. A former movie palace, it's an excellent place to see live bands, whether you're moshing on the main floor or above the fray in the balcony. In the basement is **Smart Bar,** a late-night dance club that starts hopping after midnight.

14

COMEDY AND IMPROV CLUBS

Chicago was the birthplace of the improvisational comedy form some 50-odd years ago, and the city remains the country's primary breeding ground for this challenging art form. Performers, usually working in an ensemble, ask the audience for a suggestion, then launch into short, long, silly, serious, or surreal scenes loosely related to that original audience input. Most comedy clubs have a cover charge ($5 to $20); many have a two-drink minimum on top of that.

Fodor's Choice **Second City** (✉ *1616 N. Wells St., Near North* ☎ *312/337–3992*), an institution since 1959, has served as a launching pad for some of the hottest comedians around. Alumni include Dan Aykroyd and the late John Belushi. It's the anchor of Chicago improv. The revues on the company's main stage and in its smaller e.t.c. space next door are actually sketch comedy shows, but the scripts in these pre-rehearsed scenes have been developed through improvisation and there's usually a little time set aside in each show for the performers to demonstrate their quick wit. Most nights there is a free improv set after the late show, featuring cast members and invited guests (sometimes famous, sometimes not, never announced in advance).

SHOPPING

A potent concentration of famous retailers around Michigan Avenue and neighborhoods bursting with one-of-a-kind shops combine to make Chicago a shopper's city.

THE LOOP

The Loop's main thoroughfare State Street has had its share of ups and downs. After serving as Chicago's retail corridor for much of the 20th century, the street lost its stature; by the 1980s, few stores remained. Today "that great street" is once again on the ascent, with a number of discount retailers like Old Navy, New York & Company, and Filene's Basement dotted in between the two remaining department stores, Macy's (formerly Marshall Field's) and Sears. The recent opening of Block 37 injected fresh excitement into the area. The glass-enclosed mall features major retail chains like Anthropologie, Zara, and Sephora alongside local independent shops. One block east, Wabash Street's "Jewelers Row" is home to a series of high-rises and street-level shops hawking serious bling.

THE NEAR NORTH AND THE RIVER NORTH

North of the Chicago River you'll find two distinct shopping enclaves: River North, home to galleries and home furnishings stores, and the tony Gold Coast, with its high-end boutiques.

Cozying up against the famous shopping stretch of Michigan Avenue known as the Magnificent Mile is the Gold Coast, an area that's as moneyed as it sounds. The streets teem with luxury hotels, upscale restaurants, and snazzy boutiques, mainly concentrated on Oak and Rush streets. There's also a huge new Barneys New York on East Oak Street just off Rush. Between the Gold Coast and the Chicago River, River North represents a mix of home furnishings stores, art galleries, and, oddly, touristy megarestaurants—including Ed Debevic's, Rainforest Café, and a humongous flagship McDonald's.

THE MAGNIFICENT MILE

We've got news for shopaholics who consider the Midwest flyover country: If you haven't shopped Chicago's Magnificent Mile, you simply haven't shopped. With more than 450 stores along the stretch of Michigan Avenue that runs from the Chicago River to Oak Street, the Mag Mile is one of the best shopping strips the world over. (Many also consider swanky Oak Street part of the Mag Mile, though neighboring streets technically are not.) Chanel, Hermes, and Gucci are just a few of the legendary fashion houses with fabulous boutiques here. Other notables like Anne Fontaine, Kate Spade, and Prada also have Mag Mile outposts, recognizing the everybody-who's-anybody importance of the address. Shoppers with down-to-earth budgets will find there's plenty on the Mag Mile as well, with national chains making an extra effort at their multilevel megastores here.

LINCOLN PARK, BUCKTOWN, AND WICKER PARK

Lincoln Park was an established shopping destination way back when rents were low and the vibe still gritty in Bucktown/Wicker Park. Start your visit on Armitage Avenue, where you'll find boutiques selling everything from of-the-moment clothing and shoes to bath products and goods for pampered pooches. Around the corner on Halsted Street, independent shops are dotted in among big-name clothing stores. Hit North and Clybourn avenues for housewares from the flagship Crate&Barrel, Restoration Hardware, and other chains. Today the ever-more-gentrified neighborhoods of Bucktown and Wicker Park are clogged with hip clothing stores, trendy restaurants, and galleries, mostly centered on the intersection of North, Damen, and Milwaukee avenues and along Division Street.

Minneapolis and St. Paul

WITH THE MALL OF AMERICA

WORD OF MOUTH

"The entire downtown Minneapolis is connected via SkyWays, so you never have to go outside. If you visit after Thanksgiving the animated Christmas show might be going on in the Macy's auditorium on the main mall. Vikings and Timberwolf games are within the walking area of downtown Minneapolis. No transportation needed."

—TC

WELCOME TO MINNEAPOLIS AND ST. PAUL

TOP REASONS TO GO

★ **Theater:** The Guthrie is one of three theaters in the U.S. to attract London's Royal Shakespeare Company. The Hennepin Avenue Theatre District brings Broadway to Minneapolis, or try one of the many experimental theaters.

★ **Architecture:** Between the world-class architects who have added their modern designs and the old art deco preserved in the historic landmarks, architecture lovers will have a full itinerary.

★ **Mall of America:** The largest enclosed mall in the nation.

★ **Sports:** Spend an evening at the new Minnesota Twins baseball stadium. Add in the Vikings, Timberwolves, and Wild, and there's bound to be a game while you're in town.

★ **Chain of Lakes:** Rent a canoe at Lake Calhoun. Enjoy an outdoor concert at Lake Harriet, or head out to Lake Minnetonka for the ultimate boating experience.

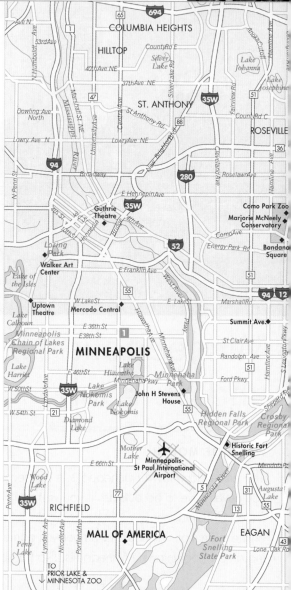

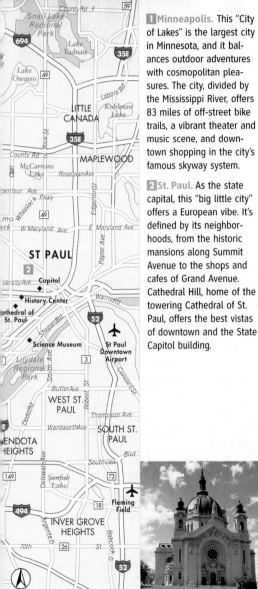

1 Minneapolis. This "City of Lakes" is the largest city in Minnesota, and it balances outdoor adventures with cosmopolitan pleasures. The city, divided by the Mississippi River, offers 83 miles of off-street bike trails, a vibrant theater and music scene, and downtown shopping in the city's famous skyway system.

2 St. Paul. As the state capital, this "big little city" offers a European vibe. It's defined by its neighborhoods, from the historic mansions along Summit Avenue to the shops and cafes of Grand Avenue. Cathedral Hill, home of the towering Cathedral of St. Paul, offers the best vistas of downtown and the State Capitol building.

GETTING ORIENTED

The Mississippi River crosses through Minneapolis before it heads east to St. Paul: The two cities' downtowns are about 10 miles apart. Downtown Minneapolis is nestled on the Mississippi's western bank in the geographic center of the city. Right across the river is Northeast Minneapolis, an up-and-coming dining and shopping destination built on the patch of land on which the city was founded. The popular Uptown neighborhood lies to the southwest of downtown, and east of the "Chain of Lakes." Head east to St. Paul, Minnesota's state capital. Summit Avenue, a divided parkway dotted with historic mansions, bisects the city and runs 5 mi from west to east before ending near the Cathedral of St. Paul and the State Capitol. Grand Avenue, a commercial thoroughfare of restaurants and shops, runs parallel to Summit, one block to its south.

15

Minnesotans may be too nice to claim the Twin Cities as the "Minne-Apple," rivaling New York City, but there's a reason the name stuck. The Cities offer an extensive repertoire of cultural events, putting it on par with other major destinations around the U.S. In fact Minneapolis has more theater seats per capita than any other U.S. city, only beat by the true Big Apple.

Recent years have ushered in a cultural rebirth for the Twin Cities. Swiss architects Jacques Herzog and Pierre de Meuron created a bold aluminum addition to the acclaimed modern-art Walker Art Center. Minneapolis opened a new central library downtown, a light-filled space designed by Cesar Pelli, and the venerable Guthrie Theater relocated to a dramatic structure on the Mississippi River by renowned French architect Jean Nouvel. Not to be left out of the action, the Minneapolis Institute of Arts expanded with a Michael Graves–designed new wing.

There's also been a sports renaissance, with two shining new stadiums adding to the Minneapolis skyline. The University of Minnesota's TCF Bank football stadium opened to rave reviews in 2009 and hosts Big 10 Football games on fall Saturdays. The Minnesota Twins opened their Target Field ballpark in 2010. The stadium rests on the edge of downtown, and left-field seats have spectacular views of the downtown skyline on summer nights.

Whether you're looking for highbrow sophistication or a quiet picnic on the Chain of Lakes, the Twin Cities has something for everyone. The range of possible choices for what to see and do at any given moment is expansive, and limited only by your time and interests.

PLANNING

WHEN TO GO
Summer showcases all the best that the Twin Cities has to offer— local farmers' markets, flowers in full bloom, water activities on the nearly 10,000 lakes in the surrounding area, outdoor dining and music

options, festivals . . . you get the idea. Too bad summer is also one of the briefest seasons. Fall brings beautiful foliage—take a scenic drive to capture the changing colors of the season. If you must come in winter, the miles-long enclosed skyway system in both downtowns will allow you to park, go to lunch, shop, and see a show, all while never setting a foot out in the blistery cold. For those brave enough for the challenge, several winter events, including downtown's Holidazzle Parade and St. Paul's Winter Carnival, almost make the cold weather bearable.

SUMMER FESTIVALS

Summer brims with endless local festivals, but the most celebrated are the Minnesota State Fair (⊕ *www.mnstatefair.org*) and the Uptown Art Fair (⊕ *www.uptownminneapolis.com/art-fair*). Both events take place in August. The Uptown Art Fair in Minneapolis draws more than 400 exhibitors with art ranging from jewelry to pottery to abstract sculptures. Prices tend to lean toward the serious art set, but there are still some affordable bargains to be found. The Minnesota State Fair heralds the end of the summer for many Minnesotans. Running at the end of August through Labor Day, it's something that cannot be adequately explained, just an experience to behold. Some highlights include foods of all kind on a stick and/or deep-fried, several animal barns, blue-ribbon winners for baking, art exhibits, and national music acts.

GETTING HERE AND AROUND

407 mi northwest of Chicago via I–94; 336 mi northwest of Milwaukee, WI, via I–94; 243 mi north of Des Moines, IA, via I–35; 240 mi southeast of Fargo, ND, via I–94.

AIR TRAVEL AND TRANSFERS

The **Minneapolis/St. Paul International Airport** (MSP ⊕ *www.mspairport. com*) is close to the Cities and offers many direct flights to and from major destinations. The airport serves as a hub for Delta Air Lines. The light rail runs from the airport into downtown Minneapolis as well as to the Mall of America.

BUS/LIGHT RAIL/TRAIN TRAVEL

Public buses canvas the Cities day and night. The light rail provides convenient service every 10 to 15 minutes from Target Field, home of the Minnesota Twins, through downtown to the airport and the Mall of America. One-way fare for both buses and light rail is $1.75 (non–rush hour), and a one-day pass is available at $6 for unlimited rides. Transfers can be used to go between the buses and light-rail trains. The Northstar Commuter Rail Line provides limited service to the northwestern suburbs, and fares depend on how far you travel. Go to ⊕ *www.metrotransit.org* for more information.

CAR TRAVEL

Interstate 94 runs from Michigan through North Dakota, passing through Chicago, Milwaukee, and the Twin Cities. For downtown St. Paul, exit at 5th Street. For downtown Minneapolis, exit at 11th Street. Be warned, the highways are not a fun place to be during rush hour, especially I–94.

Getting around the Twin Cities is easiest with a car, which will allow you the farthest reach of activities. Avoid rush hour for optimal driving conditions (and four-wheel drive is a blessing in the winter snow). Both downtowns have ample parking garages and metered parking, but keep alert for the one-way streets. Note that the popular Nicollet Mall, downtown Minneapolis's shopping and eating hub, is open only to buses and cabs, and the I–94 Lyndale/Hennepin exit to Uptown can also be tricky.

TAXI TRAVEL

Taxis are popular in downtown areas and less numerous elsewhere in the Cities. You can hail a cab after major sporting, theater, and music events, or head toward one of the many downtown hotels that have cab stands. Always be prepared to call one just in case. Reliable companies include Yellow Cab and Red & White Taxi. Cabs have a minimum of $5 per ride.

Contacts Yellow Cab (☎ 612/824–4000). **Red & White Taxi** (☎ 612/871–1600).

15

ABOUT THE RESTAURANTS

The Twin Cities dining scene has blossomed in the last decade, and its restaurants are starting to bring home the hardware to show for it: The James Beard Awards honored local chefs in 2009 (Tim McKee, La Belle Vie) and 2010 (Alex Roberts, Restaurant Alma) with the Best Chef-Midwest award, and a slew of other local chefs were in the running. Restaurants are also buying into the local, organic trend, embracing the notion that it's not only better for the environment, but it tastes better, too. The region's best restaurants are not only notable for the great food, but for what they lack: pretentiousness. Jeans and a sweater are usually sufficient at Minneapolis favorites such as 112 Eatery, and the service lives up to the region's Minnesota Nice reputation—creating an entire industry of approachable fancy food for lifelong foodies and novices alike. The growing immigrant population has introduced ethnic food to the Twin Cities' cuisine; head to 17-block Eat Street (⊠ *Nicollet Ave. from Grant to 29 St.*) for the best slice of authenticity.

ABOUT THE HOTELS

The Twin Cities hotel scene has been defined by a new crop of boutique hotels that have flooded the Minneapolis market in recent years: Many of them opened in refurbished historic buildings in the months prior to the 2008 Republican National Convention. These hotels bring a whole new level of hip to the downtown scene. There are trendy hotel bars that attract locals in the know and a whole spate of luxury amenities for everybody from business travelers to couples in town for a romantic weekend. Try the new W Minneapolis, which houses the legendary Manny's Steakhouse, for a weekend of pampering in the heart of downtown's business and shopping district.

But families shouldn't despair: The Radisson Hotel near the Mall of America is attached to an enormous indoor water park and offers amenities to keep the adults happy, too.

Hotel reviews have been condensed for this book. Please go to Fodors. com for full reviews of each property.

	¢	$	$$	$$$	$$$$
WHAT IT COSTS					
Restaurants	under $8	$8–$12	$13–$18	$19–$25	over $25
Hotels	under $80	$80–$120	$121–$170	$171–$230	over $230

Restaurant prices are for a main course at dinner. Hotel prices are for two people in a standard double room in high season, excluding service charges.

VISITOR INFORMATION

Meet Minneapolis (☎ 612/767–8000 ⊕ www.minneapolis.org).

St. Paul RiverCentre Convention and Visitors Authority (☎ 800/627–6101 ⊕ www.stpaulcvb.org).

EXPLORING MINNEAPOLIS AND ST. PAUL

Locals know that the each neighborhood defines the character of the Twin Cities. From downtown Minneapolis, head southwest to the hopping Uptown neighborhood, where you can stroll or bike around the scenic Chain of Lakes before shopping at a variety of local boutiques or eating at some of Minneapolis's trendiest restaurants. Northeast Minneapolis, which sits across the river from downtown, was built by immigrants, and it is now the artistic heart of the city, with a plethora of art galleries, bars, and restaurants.

In St. Paul, drive the 5 mi down the famous Summit Avenue between Cretin Avenue and the iconic Cathedral of St. Paul to look at the city's historic mansions (including the Governor's Mansion at 1006 Summit Avenue). Grand Avenue, which runs parallel to Summit, offers urban shopping and dining that locals love.

Interested in learning more about the mighty Mississippi River and the two towns linked by it? Start with Historic Fort Snelling, a living-history park with 1820s fort life reenactments. Also check out the Minnesota History Center in St. Paul. The kid-friendly center houses Minnesota-related exhibits in addition to a research library and museum store. The **Mill City Museum** (⊠ 704 S. 2nd St. ☎ 612/341–7555 ⊕ www.millcitymuseum.org) provides a good overview of the proud past of a productive milling town.

MINNEAPOLIS

The mirrored, 51-story **IDS Center** (⊠ 80 S. 8th St., Downtown, Minneapolis) is the tallest building in Minneapolis, and contains **Crystal Court,** a focal point of the skyway system, with shops, restaurants, and offices. The building—the crossroads of downtown activity—is one of the more handsome structures in the city, and on clear days can be seen for miles around the greater Minneapolis area.

☾ **Nicollet Mall,** a mile-long pedestrian shopping strip, runs from Washing-
★ ton Avenue S to Grant Street E, with an extensive system of skyways connecting its many shops. It's home to the new Cesar Pelli–designed

Minneapolis Central Library
(⊠ *300 Nicollet Mall, Downtown, Minneapolis* ☎ *952/847–8000* ⊘ *Tues., Thurs. 10–8, Mon., Wed., Fri., Sat. 10–6, Sun. noon–5).* The modern, light-filled structure houses a significant children's collection, a teen library center, and a coffee shop.

Target Field. Come watch hometown hero Joe Mauer in action at the Minnesota Twins' brand new open-air baseball stadium. The whole city's buzzing about Target Field, a compact ballpark right in the heart of Minneapolis. The open construction of the stadium allows you to keep an eye on the field even as you head to the concession windows, which feature local favorites such as North Shore Creamery, Mill City Grill, and Grain Belt beer. Make sure to try Tony O's Cuban

15

Sandwich, named after Twins great Tony Oliva. ESPN recently dubbed the new complex the best stadium in North America for fans. ■TIP➜ Sit along the third base line for a great view of the field and the city skyline. ⊠ *1 Twins Way, Downtown, Minneapolis* ☎ *800/338-9467* ⊕ *www. twinsbaseball.com* ⊠ *Prices vary.*

Fodor'sChoice
★
Uptown (⊠ *Centered at intersection of Lake St. and Hennepin Ave., Minneapolis* ⊕ *www.uptownminneapolis.com*)is a funky enclave of unique shops, restaurants, and bars. The one-room **Uptown Theatre** (⊠ *2906 Hennepin Ave.* ☎ *612/825–6006*) is the place to catch independent and foreign-language films. Nearby, **Lake Calhoun** is often packed with jogging and biking locals, or people just looking for a quiet spot to read or enjoy a spectacular sunset.

Fodor'sChoice
★
The **Walker Art Center** has an outstanding collection of 20th- and 21st-century American and European sculpture, prints, and photography, as well as traveling exhibits and national and international acts. Adjacent to the Walker is the **Minneapolis Sculpture Garden** (⊠ *Free*), the nation's largest outdoor urban sculpture garden. The **Irene Hixon Whitney Footbridge,** designed by sculptor Siah Armajani, connects the arts complex to Loring Park across I–94. The footbridge provides a clear view of the 250-foot dome of the **Basilica of St. Mary** (⊠ *88 N. 17th St.*). The exterior was completed in 1914, when the basilica celebrated its first Mass. It became the first designated basilica in the U.S. in 1926. ⊠ *1750 Hennepin Ave., Loring Park, Minneapolis* ☎ *612/375-7600* ⊕ *www.walkerart. org* ⊠ *$10, free Thurs. evenings and 1st Sat. of month* ⊘ *Tues., Wed., Sat., Sun. 11–5, Thurs. and Fri. 11–9; closed Mon.*

From atop Summit Hill the magnificent Cathedral of St. Paul illuminates the night sky.

ST. PAUL

Fodor's Choice
★

The **Cathedral of St. Paul** (⊠ *239 Selby Ave., Cathedral Hill, St. Paul* ☎ *651/228–1766*), a classic Renaissance-style domed church in the style of St. Peter's in Rome, lies ¼ mi southwest of the capitol. Inside are beautiful stained-glass windows, statutes, paintings, and other works of art, as well as a small historical museum on the lower level.

Interactive exhibits at the **Minnesota History Center** show the story of the state from the perspectives of Native Americans, explorers, and settlers. Traveling exhibits in recent years have focused on broader history issues, such as the history of chocolate and George Washington. A research library and museum store are on-site. ⊠ *345 Kellogg Blvd. W., St. Paul* ☎ *651/259–3000 or 800/657–3773* ⊕ *www.minnesotahistorycenter.org* 🖃 *$10, free Tues. evening.* ⊗ *Closed Mon.*

Minnesota Zoo. About 20 mi from downtown St. Paul in Apple Valley, this zoo is the largest in Minnesota. See bears, sea otters, and wild boars in an elaborate exhibit called Russia's Grizzly Coast, or see the dolphins or even touch sharks at the zoo's Discovery Bay. ⊠ *1300 Zoo Blvd., Apple Valley* ☎ *952/431–9200* ⊕ *www.mnzoo.org* 🖃 *$16* ⊗ *Hrs change seasonally.*

The **Science Museum of Minnesota** (⊠ *120 W. Kellogg Blvd., Downtown* ☎ *651/221–9444* ⊕ *www.smm.org* 🖃 *$11, films extra* ⊗ *Hrs change seasonally. Closed Mon. in fall*) has exhibits on archaeology, technology, and biology and many hands-on exhibits for kids. In the **McKnight Omnitheater** 70mm films are projected overhead on a massive dome screen.

★ St. Paul's **Summit Avenue,** which runs 4½ mi from the cathedral to the Mississippi River, has the nation's longest stretch of intact residential Victorian architecture. F. Scott Fitzgerald was living at 599 Summit in 1919 when he wrote *This Side of Paradise.*

WHERE TO EAT

MINNEAPOLIS

$–$$$$ ✕ **112 Eatery.** This small urban bistro, which serves upscale comfort
AMERICAN food, is one of *the* restaurants in Minneapolis. The pan-fried gnocchi side is big enough to share, but fights might ensue over the last scrumptious pieces. For a main course, try the tagliatelle pasta with fois-gras meatballs, and don't miss the *tres leches* (three milks) cake for dessert—it's splendid. Try to get a seat at one of two first-come, first-served bars, or enjoy the cozy leather booths with friends. The joint's open late. ✉ *112 N. 3rd St., Minneapolis* ☎ *612/343–7696* 🚍 *AE, D, MC, V* ☾ *No lunch.*

$$$ ✕ **Chino Latino.** Street food from hot zones around the equator is how
ECLECTIC this restaurant describes its unique cuisine, served family-style. It's the
Fodor'sChoice place to see and be seen in Uptown—it's for the hip, young crowd
★ with lots of money to spend. There's also a sushi bar and imaginative drink list, including the Chinopolitan, a cosmo garnished with dry ice. Don't forget your hearing aid, because this place is a scene all week long, especially during happy hour. ✉ *2916 Hennepin Ave. S, Minneapolis* ☎ *612/824–7878* ⌆ *Reservations essential* 🚍 *AE, D, DC, MC, V* ☾ *No lunch.*

$$$–$$$$ ✕ **La Belle Vie.** A must-stop for serious foodies, La Belle Vie's elegant
FRENCH atmosphere and unparalleled service perennially send it to the top of
Fodor'sChoice the Twin Cities' best dining lists (it's also garnered national recognition—Chef Tim McKee won the 2009 James Beard Award for Best Chef-
★ Midwest). The restaurant offers a five- or eight-course tasting menu as well as many à la carte choices. For special occasions, eat in the formal dining rooms, or try the hip lounge for a more laid-back experience. ✉ *510 Groveland Ave., Minneapolis* ☎ *612/874–6440* ⌆ *Reservations essential* 🚍 *AE, D, DC, MC, V.*

$$$$ ✕ **Origami.** In-the-know locals head
JAPANESE to this serene Warehouse District destination for Japanese classics and fresh sushi. The exposed-brick interior shimmers with lilac lights and flickering candles, and a sidewalk patio is open in summer. Make sure to try the maguro tartare appetizer. ✉ *30 N. 1st St., Minneapolis* ☎ *612/333–8430* ⊕ *www.origamirestaurant.com* 🚍 *AE, D, MC, V* ☾ *No lunch weekends.*

> ### CITY OF LAKES
>
> Nicknamed the City of Lakes, three of Minneapolis's 22 make up the Chain of Lakes, encircled by a 13 mile biking and walking path. Rent a canoe at Lake Calhoun or enjoy an outdoor concert at Lake Harriet Bandshell. No trip to the lakes is complete without a stop at **Sebastian Joe's** (✉ *4321 Upton Ave S* ⊕ *www.sebastianjoesicecream.com* ☎ *612/926–7916*) for the *best* Oreo ice cream.

15

$$$–$$$$
CONTEMPORARY
Fodor'sChoice
★

✕**Restaurant Alma.** This contemporary eatery near the University of Minnesota campus is firmly nestled at the top of the list for best dining in the Twin Cities. Chef Alex Roberts won the 2010 James Beard Award for Best Chef-Midwest. Candles and track lighting make the restaurant feel cozy despite exposed ceilings and an industrial design. Order the three-course tasting menu that changes seasonally, or select from à la carte options. ✉ *528 University Ave. S.E., Minneapolis* 🕾 *612/379–4909* ⊕ *www.restaurantalma.com* ⚑ *Reservations essential* 🚍 *AE, D, MC, V.*

$$$
CONTEMPORARY

✕**Spoonriver.** Nestled next to the imposing Guthrie Theater, this restaurant serves local, organic cuisine to theatergoers and natural foods enthusiasts alike. Try the wild mushroom and pistachio terrine appetizer before heading to a show, or stop by afterward for a drink from the restaurant's extensive cocktail menu. Looking for a daytime picnic? Grab food from the deli case for a picnic in nearby Gold Medal Park. ✉ *750 S. 2nd St., Mill District, Minneapolis* 🕾 *612/436–2236* ⊕ *www.spoonriver.com* ⚑ *Reservations essential* 🚍 *D, MC, V* ☾ *Closed Mon.*

$$$$
FRENCH

✕**Vincent A Restaurant.** This romantic French bistro on Nicollet Mall serves sophisticated French cuisine. A local favorite is the Vincent Burger, made of ground beef, braised short ribs, and smoked gouda: it's also served at Twins baseball games at nearby Target Field. ✉ *1100 Nicollet Mall, Minneapolis* 🕾 *612/630–1189* ⊕ *www.vincentarestaurant.com* ⚑ *Reservations essential* 🚍 *AE, D, DC, MC, V* ☾ *No lunch weekends.*

ST. PAUL

$$$
FRENCH

✕**Meritage.** A classic New York–style French brassierie, Meritage is a hot summer destination in St. Paul, particularly for its scenic terrace dining. In the heart of the downtown business area, this restaurant has received rave reviews since it opened in 2008. Go for lunch while in town for business or catch dinner there before a show at the nearby Ordway Center for Performing Arts. ✉ *410 St. Peter St., Downtown, St. Paul* 🕾 *651/222–5670* ⊕ *www.meritage-stpaul.com* ⚑ *Reservations essential* 🚍 *AE, D, MC, V* ☾ *Closed Mon.*

¢–$
AMERICAN
☺

✕**Mickey's Diner.** On the National Register of Historic Places, this quintessential 1930s diner is accented with lots of chrome and vinyl. Sit at the lunch counter or in one of the few tiny booths to enjoy stick-to-your-ribs fare; breakfast is the most popular meal of the day. ✉ *36 W. 7th St., at St. Peter St., Downtown, St. Paul* 🕾 *651/222–5633* 🚍 *D, MC, V.*

$$–$$$$
ITALIAN

✕**Pazzaluna.** A floor-to-ceiling mural of the face of Botticelli's Venus overlooks this artfully designed trattoria, which manages to be busy and tranquil at once. Pazzaluna stakes its reputation on innovative dishes such as the *fritto misto* (fried calamari and vegetable strips) but brings panache to standards like handmade fettuccine in a Bolognese meat sauce. ✉ *360 St. Peter St., Downtown, St. Paul* 🕾 *651/223–7000* ⊕ *www.pazzaluna.com* 🚍 *AE, D, DC, MC, V.*

$$$$
CONTINENTAL
★

✕**W.A. Frost and Company.** In this romantic Victorian house each dining room has a fireplace, Oriental rugs, and marble-topped tables. Country French and Mediterranean flavors dominate the cuisine. The huge patio, lush with plants, is popular in the summer, and there's a bar and lounge for more casual first-come, first-served dining. The menu changes seasonally. ✉ *374 Selby Ave., St. Paul* ☎ *651/224–5715* ⊕ *www.wafrost. com* ⌥ *Reservations essential* ⊟ *AE, D, DC, MC, V.*

WHERE TO STAY

MINNEAPOLIS

$$–$$$$ **The Grand Hotel Minneapolis.** This boutique hotel in the heart of the
★ Business District offers traditional rooms with crown molding, an on-site spa, and complimentary access to a 58,000-square-foot gym. **Pros:** the gym is routinely chosen as one of the best hotel gyms in America; location is great for business travelers, part of downtown skyway system **Cons:** not great for kids. ✉ *615 2nd Ave. S, Minneapolis* ☎ *612/288–8888* ⊕ *www.grandhotelminneapolis.com* ⤳ *140 rooms, 19 suites* ⌂ *In-room: Wi-Fi. In-hotel: restaurant, bar, pool, spa, gym, laundry service* ⊟ *AE, D, DC, MC, V.*

$ **Hotel Ivy.** A quiet haven for business travelers, this luxury hotel is slightly off the beaten path in downtown Minneapolis. **Pros:** the staff is friendly and eager to please; within a few blocks of downtown's shopping and dining destinations **Cons:** no pool; not great for families. ✉ *201 S. 11th St., Downtown* ☎ *612/746–4600* ⊕ *www.lc.com/ minneapolis* ⤳ *136 rooms* ⌂ *In-room: a/c, Wi-Fi. In-hotel: restaurant, bar, gym, spa, dry-cleaning services, some pets allowed* ⊟ *AE, D, DC, MC, V* ⫶ *CP.*

$$$–$$$$ **Le Méridien Chambers.** Eclectic art from the private collection of hotel owner Ralph Burnet adorns the gleaming white walls of this ultrahip and trendy boutique hotel in the downtown Theatre District. **Pros:** an on-site art gallery; located in the center of the Theater District. **Cons:** hotel gym is small; not kid-friendly. ✉ *901 Hennepin Ave., Minneapolis* ☎ *612/767–6900* ⊕ *www.lemeridienchambers.com* ⤳ *60 rooms* ⌂ *In-room: a/c, refrigerator, Wi-Fi. In-hotel: restaurant, room service, bars, gym, laundry service* ⊟ *AE, D, MC, V.*

$$$–$$$$ **The Marquette.** This boutique hotel in downtown Minneapolis is part of the IDS Center complex, an early 1970s glass-front skyscraper designed by Philip Johnson. **Pros:** at the center of the action; it's on the skyway system. **Cons:** the upscale hotel doesn't have a spa; not kid-friendly. ✉ *710 Marquette Ave., Downtown, Minneapolis* ☎ *612/333–4545 or 800/328–4782* ⊕ *www.marquettehotel.com* ⤳ *281 rooms, 12 suites* ⌂ *In-room: Wi-Fi. In-hotel: restaurant, bar, gym, laundry service, some pets allowed* ⊟ *AE, D, DC, MC, V.*

$ **Radisson Bloomington/Water Park of America.** Designed to look like a luxurious Minnesota cabin in the woods, this hotel is attached to a 75,000-square-foot indoor waterpark, billed as the largest in the nation. **Pros:** the water park includes 10-story-high water slides, a surfing simulator, a wave pool, a lazy river, and more; hourly shuttle service to the airport and Mall of America. **Cons:** far from downtown nightlife, shopping, and dining destinations. ✉ *1700 E. American Blvd., Bloomington* ☎ *952/854–8700* ⊕ *www.radisson.com/bloomingtonbymoa* ⤳ *405 rooms* ⌂ *In-room: a/c, Wi-Fi. In-hotel: restaurant, bar, gym, spa, water*

15

sports, laundry service, children's programs, parking, some pets allowed ▭ *AE, D, MC, V* ⍩ *CP.*

$ 🛏 **W Minneapolis.** The definition of hip, this hotel is for those who like being at the center of the action. **Pros:** hotel restaurant Manny's Steakhouse is outstanding; guests get complimentary access to the Foshay Tower observation deck on the 30th floor; there's free car service if you're traveling within five miles. **Cons:** if you don't like pink, this place is not for you. ✉ *821 Marquette Ave., Downtown* ☎ *612/215–3700* ⊕ *www.whotels.com/minneapolis* ⌀ *229 rooms* ⚲ *In-room: a/c, Wi-Fi. In-hotel: restaurant, bar, gym, some pets allowed* ▭ *AE, D, MC, V.*

ST. PAUL

$$$ 🛏 **Saint Paul Hotel.** This 12-story, marble-pillared 1910 landmark on
★   Rice Park has been a stopover for presidents, heads of state, and celebrities. **Pros:** great service; gym has views of the river; the hotel restaurant is a local classic. **Cons:** no pool; not kid-friendly. ✉ *350 Market St., St. Paul* ☎ *651/292–9292 or 800/292–9292* ⊕ *www.stpaulhotel.com* ⌀ *255 rooms* ⚲ *In-room: a/c, Internet. In-hotel: 2 restaurants, bar, laundry service* ▭ *AE, D, DC, MC, V.*

NIGHTLIFE

Music venues and neighborhood bars are the number-one and -two draws in the Twin Cities nightlife scene, with big downtown dance clubs taking a distinctive third place. The Twin Cities music scene is vibrant: The area draws national acts and gave plenty of musicians their start (Prince, the Replacements, Bob Dylan, and Atmosphere, to name a few). If nightclubs are your thing, head to 1st Avenue North in downtown Minneapolis, where the clubs populate the old warehouses that give the city's Warehouse District its name. Downtown's Hennepin Avenue Theater District offers Broadway shows. Hipsters and trendsetting young professionals populate the bars of Uptown, a popular neighborhood a few miles southwest of downtown. For a more laid-back atmosphere, or for several top-notch karaoke bars, head to Northeast Minneapolis, across the Mississippi from downtown.

In recent years St. Paul's nightlife has blossomed with several new restaurants and bars around Mears' Park, a small neighborhood park near downtown St. Paul.

For restaurants (including a Hard Rock Cafe), bars and clubs, and a movie theater under one roof, check out **Block E** on Hennepin Avenue in downtown Minneapolis. The **Shout House** (✉ *650 Hennepin Ave.* ☎ *612/337–6700*) dueling piano bar is always packed. The big Warehouse District clubs are right down the street.

★   The **Dakota Jazz Club and Restaurant** (✉ *1010 Nicollet Mall, Downtown, Minneapolis* ☎ *612/332–1010* ⊕ *www.dakotacooks.com*) is one of the best jazz bars in the Midwest, with some of the Twin Cities' finest performers.

★ The intimate **Fine Line Music Café** (✉ *318 1st Ave. N, Downtown, Minneapolis* ☏ *612/338–8100* ⊕ *www.finelinemusic.com*) gets you up close and personal to locally and nationally known rock musicians.

Fodor's Choice ★ The iconic **First Avenue & Seventh Street Entry** (✉ *701 1st Ave. N, Downtown, Minneapolis* ☏ *612/332–1775* ⊕ *www.first-avenue.com*) is where locals go to hear top rock groups and to get their groove on. This place appeals to everybody from college kids coming to see their favorite jam band to baby boomers who have been regulars since the place opened in 1970. Saturday night's Too Much Love dance party is one of the best in the city. Prince played as a regular at the club in the '80s, and it was featured in his movie *Purple Rain*.

Fodor's Choice ★ The **Guthrie Theater** (✉ *818 S. 2nd St., Downtown, Minneapolis* ☏ *877/447–8243* ⊕ *www.guthrietheater.org*) has a repertory company praised for its balance of classic and avant-garde productions.

Nye's Polonaise Room (✉ *112 E. Hennepin Ave., Northeast, Minneapolis* ☏ *612/379–2021* ⊕ *www.nyespolonaise.com*) was named the Best Bar in America by *Esquire*, and it's certainly a place you won't want to miss: the dining room is a piano bar at night, and the attached Polka Lounge features the World's Most Dangerous Polka Band, as well as a lot of drunk people—college students and boomers alike—trying to polka. The Polish food is amazing, too.

15

Trendy bars and fun restaurants scattered around **Uptown's** main intersection at Lake Street and Hennepin Avenue are always rocking with nightlife debauchery. Try especially hot spots the **Independent** (✉ *Calhoun Square, 3001 Hennepin Ave.* ☏ *612/378–1905*) and **Chino Latino** (✉ *2916 Hennepin Ave.* ☏ *612/824–7878*), and the rooftop at **Stella's Fish Bar** (✉ *1400 West Lake St.* ☏ *612/824–8862*).

SHOPPING

The Mall of America is ground zero for shoppers visiting the Twin Cities. Located in Bloomington, several miles from Minneapolis's southern border, the "Megamall" has more than 500 stores, an aquarium, and an indoor amusement park. If you can, visit during the week, when the mall is not overrun with people. On Friday and Saturday evenings children under 16 are not admitted without adults. Come here for your big department stores, standard chain retailers, and Minnesota souvenirs. The best part about shopping in Minnesota? There's no tax on clothes.

To experience more local flavor, venture beyond the mall to some of the Cities' best neighborhood shopping districts. Unique local shops and trendy national stores such as Apple and North Face dot Hennepin Avenue in Minneapolis' Uptown area, southwest of the city's downtown. Spend an afternoon strolling down Grand Avenue in St. Paul, which is home to several one-of-a-kind shops, particularly on the strip between Dale Street and Lexington Avenue. Still looking for more? Consider the neighborhoods of Highland Park and St. Anthony Park in St. Paul and the Warehouse District and North Loop in Minneapolis.

In the posh suburb of Edina you'll find the Galleria, a shopping mall with luxury favorites such as Tiffany & Co., Louis Vuitton, and BCBG Max Azria.

Downtown Minneapolis's Nicollet Mall is actually a street rather than a mall, but the thoroughfare at the center of the business district is lined with department stores, shops, and restaurants. It's also a main access point to the city's skyway system, where you can get lost for hours looking for everything from cute shoes to an ATM.

If you crave the mall experience without the crowds of the Mall of America, try some of the region's smaller malls, such as Rosedale (⊠ *10 Rosedale Center, Roseville*) located 15 minutes north of downtown Minneapolis, or Southdale (⊠ *10 Southdale Center, Edina*), which was the nation's first indoor mall, located 10 minutes south of downtown Minneapolis.

Gaviidae Common (⊠ *655 Nicollet Mall, Downtown, Minneapolis*), has three levels of upscale shops, including Neiman Marcus and Saks Fifth Avenue's discount outlet Off Fifth. Cater-corner is **Macy's**, the city's largest department store.

↻ Appropriately nicknamed the Megamall, the **Mall of America** (⊠ *24th Ave. S and Killebrew Dr., Bloomington* ☎ *952/883–8800* ⊕ *www. mallofamerica.com*) brings in more than 40 million guests annually, and it is so big that seven baseball stadiums could fit inside it. The mall has more than 500 stores, an aquarium, movie theater, amusement park, and even a wedding chapel.

Fodor's Choice
★

★ Visit more than 40 (mostly) one-of-a-kind, hip urban shops in **Uptown** (⊠ *Lake St. and Hennepin Ave., Uptown, Minneapolis*), with a smaller shopping center on Calhoun Square.

Galleria. Shop luxury brands in a serene, small mall 10 minutes south of downtown Minneapolis. More than 60 stores and restaurants cater to serious shoppers. ⊠ *3510 Galleria, Edina* ☎ *952/925–4321* ⊕ *www. galleriaedina.com* ☉ *Weekdays 10–9, Sat. 10–8, Sun. 11–5.*

Victoria Crossing (⊠ *870 Grand Ave., St. Paul*) is a collection of small shops and specialty stores among the 200-plus stores on the 2½-mi-long **Grand Avenue**. Be sure to stop by **Cafe Latté** (⊠ *850 Grand Ave.* ☎ *651/224–5687*) to refuel with the legendary desserts. Down the road is **Just Truffles** (⊠ *1363 Grand Ave.* ☎ *651/690–0075*), an artisanal chocolatier that concocted a special truffle for Luciano Pavarotti.

Denver, Boulder, and the Colorado Rockies

WORD OF MOUTH

"There are lots of high-end brand name hotels in [Denver], but I suggest The Brown Palace for a real Denver treat, like no other city. Just be sure to get a room in the original building, not across the street. Get a suite if you can afford it."

—PeaceOut

WELCOME TO DENVER, BOULDER, AND THE COLORADO ROCKIES

TOP REASONS TO GO

★ **LoDo, Larimer Square, and the 16th Street Mall:** These three connected, walkable areas of downtown Denver can be seen in a day, but are home to a lifetime's worth of history, shops dining, and people-watching.

★ **Microbrews:** Colorado is rich with beer history, and the Denver metro area has one of the highest concentration of microbreweries and brewpubs in the country.

★ **Pearl Street:** Boulder's hip, happening hub is packed with shops, restaurants, galleries, and more, with an inviting vibe and entertainment courtesy of traveling buskers.

★ **Rocky Mountain National Park:** Peer out over dozens of lakes, gaze up at majestic mountain peaks, and look around at pine-scented woods that are perfect for whiling away an afternoon. Trek to the summit of Longs Peak or go rock climbing on Lumpy Ridge. Spot elk and bighorn sheep; there are more than 2,000 and 800 of them, respectively.

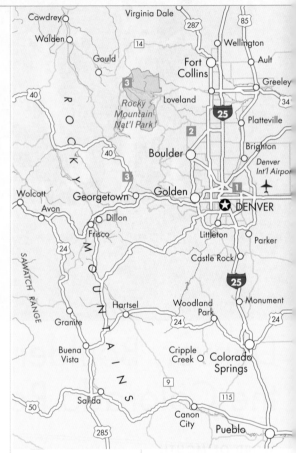

1 Denver. Colorado's capital and largest city, Denver is unmatched in its combination of urban pleasures and easy access to outdoor recreation.

2 Boulder. College town Boulder balances high-tech with bohemia. Estes Park abuts Rocky Mountain National Park's eastern entrance, while Grand Lake is its quieter western gateway.

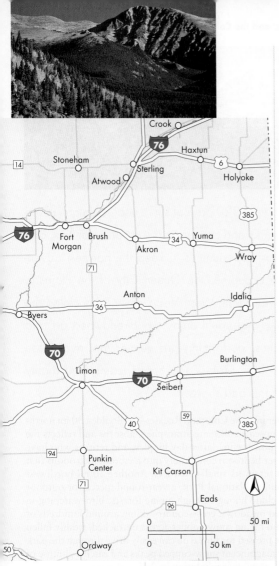

3 The Colorado Rockies. Scenic highway I–70 ascends into the foothills through historic towns Idaho Springs and Georgetown. The wilderness and alpine tundra at Rocky Mountain National Park welcome wildlife and outdoor enthusiasts year-round.

GETTING ORIENTED

Denver's downtown is laid out at a 45-degree angle to the rest of the metro area, which is visibly lined along its western edge by the Front Range. Interstate 25 bisects Denver north to south, and Interstate 70 runs east to west. I–70 stitches together Denver, Golden, Idaho Springs, and Georgetown before crossing the Continental Divide through the Eisenhower Tunnel. Outside of Denver, Boulder, northwest via U.S. 36, and Fort Collins, due north along I–25, are the two biggest and most prominent cities of the region. To the west are the proud, independent mountain hamlets of Lyons, Nederland, Ward, and Jamestown. Beyond the high peaks are broad valleys dotted with unpretentious ranching communities, and right in the middle of it all is the area's crown jewel, Rocky Mountain National Park, with its two gateways, Grand Lake and Estes Park.

16

With an average of 320 days of sun a year, a unique blend of Old West quirks and contemporary urban amenities, and enough outdoor opportunities to keep the hardiest adventurer endlessly occupied, the Queen City of the Plains is truly the gateway to the West. Visit Denver, also called the Mile High City, and you'll enjoy world-renowned art and science museums, performing arts venues that rival those on the coasts, three professional sports teams, and highly lauded restaurants and shops.

Or venture farther into the Colorado Rockies—to Boulder, 30 mi northwest, where the upscale collegiate atmosphere absorbs and reflects the energy from the power elite, latter-day hippies, and retirees who have swelled this former bedroom community into a vibrant metropolis that still manages to retain its small-town feel. Another 30 mi northwest sits Rocky Mountain National Park, a year-round mecca for outdoor activities that include hiking through alpine forests, bird-watching in wildflower-dotted meadows, cross-country skiing around hundreds of miles of trails, and racing snowmobiles across untracked, freshly fallen powder. If you're pressed for time, you can easily drive through the park to experience its magnificent snow-capped peaks and catch a glimpse of the many species of wildlife inhabiting its 265,770 acres.

When you visit the Colorado Rockies, you should be prepared for an altitude adjustment—and perhaps an attitude one as well. The dress code in Denver and the surrounding metro area is what locals like to call "Rocky Mountain formal"—your suit jacket won't be required, even in the fanciest of restaurants. Jeans, cowboy boots, and a laid-back mind-set are always in fashion. It's part of what makes Colorado's Rocky Mountain welcome such a warm one.

PLANNING

WHEN TO GO

Many locals claim that the best seasons in Colorado are the spring and fall "mud seasons," when the tourists are gone and the trails are empty. In spring the Front Range mountains are carpeted with fresh new growth, while late September brings the shimmering gold of turning aspens. The interstate is well maintained. It's rare, but atop the mountain passes and at the Eisenhower Tunnel it's possible to see a bit of snow during the summer. Ski resorts are packed from roughly October to April, and Denver itself often bears the traffic. Visiting Boulder and the Front Range is pleasurable in any season. Wintertime in the urban corridor is generally mild, but the mountainous regions can be cold and snowy. Snowfall along the Front Range is highest in spring, particularly March, making for excellent skiing but unpredictable driving and potentially lengthy delays. Spring is capricious—75°F one day and a blizzard the next—and June can be hot or cool (or both). July through September is high summer with 90-plus–degree days at lower elevations. In the higher mountains summer temperatures are generally 15–20 degrees cooler than in the urban corridor.

GETTING HERE AND AROUND

Denver is 70 mi north of Colorado Springs via I–25; 383 mi north of Santa Fe via I–25; 565 mi east of Salt Lake City via I–15 and I–70; 612 mi west of Kansas City via I–70; and 915 mi southwest of Minneapolis via I–35 and I–70

AIR TRAVEL AND TRANSFERS

Denver International Airport (DEN) (⊠ 8500 Peña Blvd., Denver ☎ 800/247–2336 or 303/342–2000 ⊕ www.flydenver.com), known to locals as DIA, 23 mi northeast of downtown Denver, is the primary airport serving north central Colorado. Denver Airport's **Ground Transportation Information Center** (☎ 303/342–4059 ⊕ www.flydenver.com/gt/index.axp) assists visitors with car rentals, door-to-door shuttles, public transportation, wheelchair services, charter buses, and limousine services. Boulder is approximately 45 mi (45 minutes–1 hour) from DIA; Granby approximately 110 mi (a little more than 2 hours); Fort Collins approximately 80 mi (1¼–1½ hours); and Estes Park approximately 80 mi (about 2 hours).

Estes Park Shuttle (☎ 970/586–5151 ⊕ www.estesparkshuttle.com ⚠ Reservations essential) serves Estes Park and Rocky Mountain National Park from Denver, DIA, and Boulder. **Super Shuttle** (☎ 303/370–1300 ⊕ www.supershuttle.com) serves Denver and Boulder. Between the airport and downtown Denver, Super Shuttle makes door-to-door trips. The region's public bus service, **Regional Transportation District/ SkyRide** (☎ 303/299–6000 for route and schedule information ⊕ www.rtd-denver.com), runs SkyRide to and from the airport; the trip takes 50 minutes, and the fare is $8–$12 each way.

BUS TRAVEL

Denver has one of the best city bus systems in the country. In downtown Denver free shuttle-bus service operates about every 10 minutes until 1:35 am, running the length of the 16th Street Mall (which bisects downtown) and stopping at one-block intervals. The region's public bus

16

service, **RTD** (☎ *303/299–6000 or 800/366–7433* ⊕ *www.rtd-denver. com*), is comprehensive, with routes throughout the metropolitan area. The service also links Denver to outlying towns such as Boulder, Longmont, and Nederland. You can buy bus tokens at grocery stores or pay with exact change on the bus. Fares vary according to time and zone. Within the city limits, buses cost $2.

CAR TRAVEL

Interstate 25, the most direct route from Denver to Fort Collins, is the north–south artery that connects the cities in the urban corridor along the Front Range. From Denver, U.S. 36 runs through Boulder, Lyons, and Estes Park to Rocky Mountain National Park. The direct route from Denver to Grand County is I–70 west to U.S. 40 (Empire exit) and to U.S. 34. If you're driving directly to Fort Collins or Estes Park and Rocky Mountain National Park from DIA, take the E–470 tollway to Interstate 25. U.S. 36 between Boulder and Estes Park is heavily traveled, but highways 119, 72, and 7 have much less traffic and are exceptionally scenic, but also curvy and gravel in some portions.

Although it is often severely overcrowded on weekends and holidays, I–70 is still the quickest and most direct route from Denver to the High Rockies. It slices through the state, separating it into northern and southern halves. In late fall, winter, and early spring, it's a good idea to have all-weather or snow tires and bring a shovel along. Road reports and signage on the highways will indicate whether chains or four-wheel-drive vehicles are required.

The most convenient place to rent a car is at Denver International Airport. You can save money if you rent from the other offices of major car companies, but you'll have to take a shuttle or taxi to the city locations.

Car Travel Contacts **AAA Colorado** (☎ *303/753–8800*). **Colorado Department of Transportation CDOT Road Information** (☎ *303/639–1111 or 877/315–7623* ⊕ *www.coloradodot.info*). **Colorado State Patrol** (☎ *303/239–4501, *277 from cell phone*). **Rocky Mountain National Park Road Information** (☎ *970/586–1333*).

TRAIN TRAVEL

Amtrak (☎ *800/872–7245 or 303/534–2812* ⊕ *www.amtrak.com*) provides passenger rail service to and within north central Colorado. The Chicago–San Francisco *California Zephyr* stops in downtown Denver, in Winter Park/Fraser, and in Granby, once each day in both directions.

ABOUT THE RESTAURANTS

Thanks to the influx of people from around the world, you have plenty of options here. Restaurants in north central Colorado run the gamut—you'll find simple diners with tasty, homey basics and elegant establishments with wine lists featuring hundreds of vintages. Increasingly, eateries are featuring organic and sustainable ingredients, and several serve exclusively organic meals and locally produced foods. Some restaurants take reservations, but many, particularly those in the middle price range, seat on a first-come, first-served basis.

As befits a multiethnic crossroads, Denver lays out a dizzying range of eateries. Head for LoDo, 32nd Avenue in the Highland District, or south of the city for the more inventive kitchens. Try Federal Street for cheap ethnic eats—especially Mexican and Vietnamese—and expect more authentic takes on classic Italian, French, and Asian cuisines than the city has offered in the past.

ABOUT THE HOTELS

Bed-and-breakfasts and small inns in north central Colorado include old-fashioned cottages, rustic lodges, and modern, sleek establishments. Ever-popular guest ranches and spas are places to escape and be pampered after having fun outdoors. In the high-country resorts of Estes Park and Grand Lake and in towns nearby, the elevation keeps the climate cool, which means that there are very few air-conditioned accommodations. The region is also full of chain motels and hotels, often at the access points to cities.

Denver's lodging choices include the stately Brown Palace, bed-and-breakfasts, and business hotels. Unless you're planning a quick escape to the mountains, consider staying in or around downtown, where most of the city's attractions are within walking distance. Many of the hotels cater to business travelers, and slash their rates in half on Friday and Saturday.

Hotel reviews have been condensed for this book. Please go to Fodors. com for full reviews of each property.

16

WHAT IT COSTS					
	¢	$	$$	$$$	$$$$
Restaurants	under $8	$8–$12	$13–$18	$19–$25	over $25
Hotels	under $80	$80–$120	$121–$170	$171–$230	over $230

Restaurant prices are for a main course at dinner, excluding 5.75%–8.46% tax. Hotel prices are for two people in a standard double room in high season, excluding service charges and 5.75%–10.25% tax.

DENVER

You can tell from its skyline alone that Denver is a major metropolis, with a Major League Baseball stadium at one end of downtown and the State Capitol building at the other. But look to the west to see where Denver distinguishes itself in the majestic Rocky Mountains, snow-peaked and breathtakingly huge, looming in the distance. This combination of urban sprawl and proximity to nature is what gives the city and surrounding region its character and sets it apart as a destination.

Many Denverites are unabashed nature lovers who can also enjoy the outdoors within the city limits, walking along the park-lined river paths downtown. For Denverites, preserving the environment and the city's rich mining and ranching heritage are of equally vital importance to the quality of life. LoDo buzzes with jazz clubs, restaurants, and art galleries housed in carefully restored century-old buildings. The culturally diverse populace avidly supports the Denver Art Museum, the Denver Museum of Nature & Science, the Colorado History Museum, and the Museo de las Americas. The Denver Performing Arts Complex is the nation's second-largest theatrical venue, bested in capacity only by New York's Lincoln Center. An excellent public transportation system, including a popular, growing light-rail system and 400 mi of bike paths, makes getting around easy.

EXPLORING

DOWNTOWN

★ **16th Street Mall.** Outdoor cafés and tempting shops line this pedestrians-only 12-block thoroughfare, shaded by red-oak and locust trees. The Mall's businesses run the entire socioeconomic range. There are popular meeting spots for business types at places like the Irish pub Katie Mullen's in the Sheraton Hotel; great people-watching from the sidewalk patio at the Paramount Cafe, around the corner from the Paramount Theatre; and plenty of fast-food chains. You can find Denver's best people-watching here. ■TIP➔ Catch one of the free shuttle buses here that run the length of downtown. Pay attention when you're wandering across the street, as the walking area and bus lanes are the same color and are hard to distinguish. ⊠ *From Broadway to Wynkoop St., LoDo.*

↻ **Denver Art Museum.** Unique displays of Asian, pre-Columbian, Spanish
Fodor's Choice   Colonial, and Native American art are the hallmarks of this model
★   of museum design. Among the museum's regular holdings are John DeAndrea's sexy, soothing, life-size polyvinyl painting *Linda* (1983); Claude Monet's dreamy flowerscape *Le Bassin des Nympheas* (1904); and Charles Deas's red-cowboy-on-horseback *Long Jakes, The Rocky Mountain Man* (1844). The works are thoughtfully lighted, though dazzling mountain views through hallway windows sometimes steal your attention. Imaginative hands-on exhibits, game- and puzzle-filled Family Backpacks, and video corners appeal to children. With the 2007 opening of the Daniel Libeskind–designed Frederic C. Hamilton building, the museum doubled in size. To the east of the museum is an outdoor plaza—you'll know it by the huge orange metal sculpture—that leads to the Denver Public Library next door. ⊠ *100 W. 14th Ave. Pkwy., Civic Center* ☎ *720/865–5000* ⊕ *www.denverartmuseum.org* 🎫 *$13* ☉ *Tues.–Thurs., Sat. 10–5, Fri. 10–10, Sun. noon–5.*

Fodor's Choice   **Larimer Square.** Larimer Square is on the oldest street in the city, immor-
★   talized by Jack Kerouac in his seminal book *On the Road.* It was saved from the wrecker's ball by a determined preservationist in the 1960s, when the city went demolition-crazy in its eagerness to present a more youthful image. Much has changed since Kerouac's wanderings; Larimer Square's rough edges have been cleaned up in favor of upscale retail and chic restaurants. The Square has become a serious late-night party district thanks to spillover from the expanded LoDo neighborhood and Rockies fans flowing out from the baseball stadium. ⊠ *Larimer and 15th Sts., LoDo* ☎ *303/685–8143* ⊕ *www.larimersquare.com.*

LoDo. Officially the Lower Downtown Historic District, the 25-plus square-block area that was the site of the original 1858 settlement of Denver City, is nicknamed LoDo. It's home to art galleries, chic shops, nightclubs, and restaurants ranging from Denver's most upscale to its

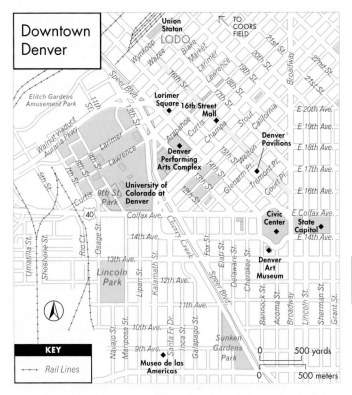

Downtown
Denver

Union
Station

TO
COORS
FIELD

LODO

Wynkoop

Wazee

Blake

Market

Larimer

Lawrence

21st St.

22nd St.

20th St.

19th St.

18th St.

17th St.

Broadway

21st St.

Speer Blvd.

16th St.

Larimer Square

16th Street Mall

11th St.

13th St.

Elitch Gardens
Amusement Park

Walnut Viaduct

Auraria Pkwy.

Larimer

Lawrence

Arapahoe

Curtis

Champa

Stout

California

Denver
Pavilions

E. 20th Ave.

E. 19th Ave.

E. 18th Ave.

E. 17th Ave.

E. 16th Ave.

8th St.

9th St.

5th St.

7th St.

Denver
Performing
Arts Complex

15th St. Walton

14th St.

13th St.

12th St.

Glenarm Pl.

Tremont Pl.

Court Pl.

40

Curtis

9th St.
Park

University of
Colorado at
Denver

Colfax Ave.

E. Colfax Ave.

Civic
Center

State
Capitol

Umatilla St.

Rio Ct.

Osage St.

Shoshone St.

14th Ave.

Cherry Creek

Fox St.

Elati St.

Delaware St.

Cherokee St.

E. 14th Ave.

Denver
Art
Museum

16

13th Ave.

Lincoln
Park

Lipan St.

Kalamath St.

12th Ave.

Speer Blvd.

Bannock St.

Acoma St.

Broadway

Lincoln St.

Sherman St.

Grant St.

11th Ave.

Navajo St.

Mariposa St.

10th Ave.

Santa Fe Dr.

Inca St.

Galapago St.

Sunken
Gardens
Park

0   500 yards

KEY

9th Ave.

Museo de las
Americas

0   500 meters

Rail Lines

most down-home. This part of town was once the city's thriving retail
center, then it fell into disuse and slid into slums. Since the early 1990s
LoDo has metamorphosed into the city's cultural center, thanks to its
resident avant-garde artists, retailers, and loft dwellers who have taken
over the old warehouses and red bricks. The handsome **Coors Field**
(⊠ *Blake and 20th Sts., LoDo*), home of baseball's Colorado Rockies,
has further galvanized the area. Its old-fashioned brick and grillwork
facade was designed to blend in with the surrounding Victorian warehouses. As with cuddly Wrigley Field, on the north side of Chicago,
Coors Field has engendered a nightlife scene of sports bars, restaurants,
and dance clubs. ⊠ *From Larimer St. to South Platte River, between
14th and 22nd Sts., LoDo* ⊕ *www.lodo.org.*

CENTRAL PLATTE VALLEY

Less than a mile west of downtown is the booming Central Platte Valley.
Once the cluttered heart of Denver's railroad system, it's now overflowing with attractions. The imposing glass facade of the NFL Broncos'
Invesco Field at Mile High, the stately Pepsi Center sports arena, the
Downtown Aquarium, and the flagship REI outdoors store are but four
more crowd-pleasers to add to the growing list in Denver. New restaurants, a couple of coffeehouses, and a few small, locally owned shops,
including some that sell sporting goods and a wine boutique, make it
appealing to wander around.

☺ **Downtown Aquarium.** On the north side of the South Platte across from
★ Elitch Gardens, this is the only million-gallon aquarium between Chicago and the West Coast. It has four sections that show aquatic life in all its forms, from the seas to the river's headwaters in the Colorado mountains. The 250-seat Aquarium Restaurant surrounds a 150,000-gallon tank filled with sharks and fish. Other highlights include an expanded stingray touch pool, a gold-panning area, animatronic creatures, and an interactive shipwreck. The aquarium also has a lounge with a weeknight happy hour. ⊠ *700 Water St., off Exit 211 of I–25, Jefferson Park* ☎ *303/561–4450* ⊕ *www.downtownaquariumdenver.com* ⊠ *$15.99; discount after 6 pm with dining receipt* ☉ *Sun.–Thurs. 10–9, Fri. and Sat. 10–9:30.*

☺ **Elitch Gardens.** This elaborate and thrilling park was a Denver family
★ tradition long before its 1995 relocation from northwest Denver to its current home on the outskirts of downtown. The park's highlights include hair-raising roller coasters and thrill rides; for younger kids and squeamish parents there are also plenty of gentler attractions hosted by characters such as Bob the Builder. Twister II, an update of the classic, wooden Mister Twister, is from the original Elitch Gardens, as is a 100-foot-high Ferris wheel that provides sensational views of downtown. A 10-acre water-adventure park is included in the standard entry fee. You can spend a whole day at either the water park or the main park. Locker and stroller rentals are available; discounted tickets are available online. ⊠ *I–25 and Speer Blvd., Auraria* ☎ *303/595–4386* ⊕ *www.elitchgardens.com* ⊠ *$40.99 unlimited-ride pass* ☉ *June–Aug., daily; Apr., May, Sept., and Oct., Fri.–Sun.; hrs vary so call ahead.*

CITY PARK AND ENVIRONS

☺ **Denver Museum of Nature & Science.** Founded in 1900, the museum has
Fodor'sChoice amassed more than 775,000 objects, making it the largest natural history museum in the western United States. It houses a rich combination of traditional collections—dinosaur remains, animal dioramas, a mineralogy display, an Egyptology wing—and intriguing hands-on exhibits. In the Hall of Life you can test your health and fitness on a variety of contraptions and receive a personalized health profile. The Prehistoric Journey exhibit covers the seven stages of earth's development. The massive complex also includes an IMAX movie theater and a planetarium whose Space Odyssey exhibit simulates a trip to Mars. An impressive eating-and-relaxation area has a full-window panoramic view of the Rocky Mountains. ⊠ *2001 Colorado Blvd., City Park* ☎ *303/322–7009 or 800/925–2250* ⊕ *www.dmns.org* ⊠ *Museum $11, IMAX $7; $18 for combined pass (IMAX or planetarium)* ☉ *Daily 9–5, IMAX showtimes vary.*

WHERE TO EAT

$$$ ✗**Fruition.** Well-crafted, elegant comfort food made from seasonal ingre-
NEW AMERICAN dients is served in compelling combinations, like grilled pork chops with
Central Denver yellow corn spoonbread and pan-roasted ostrich loin with black-fig salad. A nightly offering of two courses of delightful dishes includes many vegetarian options, but many diners choose to make a meal from

Denver is often called the Queen City of the Plains.

the amazing appetizer roster. The two small but nicely spaced dining rooms are gently lighted for a warm-toned atmosphere that fades into the background, allowing the evening to focus on the food and the expertly chosen and fairly priced wine list. ⊠ *1313 E. 6th Ave., Central Denver* ☎ *303/831–1962* ⊕ *www.fruitionrestaurant.com* ⊟ *AE, D, MC, V* ⊗ *No lunch.*

$
MEXICAN
North Denver
☺

✕ **Jack-n-Grill.** The friendly family that runs this small, pepper-decorated place moved to Denver from New Mexico, and they brought their love of chilies with them. The green chilie is fire-breathing spicy, and the red is a smoky, complex brew. The best item, though, is the plate of chicken or beef *vaquero* tacos, slathered with a sticky-sweet barbecue sauce and served on buttery tortillas. Get it with a bowl of freshly roasted corn off the cob. Lunch is always packed, so arrive early, and don't be afraid to tackle a gigantic breakfast burrito, either. There's a mean margarita and there are cervesas, too. ⊠ *2424 Federal Blvd., North Denver* ☎ *303/964–9544* ⊕ *www.jackngrill.com* ⚑ *Reservations essential* ⊟ *MC, V.*

$$$
MEXICAN
Highland
Fodor's Choice
★

✕ **LoLa Mexican Seafood.** This casual seafood eatery brings in a young, hip clientele, and provides a spectacular view of the city skyline from most of the sunny dining room, the bar, and the patio. Tableside guacamole, more than 90 tequilas, superior margaritas, and a clever, glass-lined bar area are just a few of the reasons the lovely LoLa remains a locals' hangout. The food is modern Mexican, with fresh seafood in *escabeche* (marinated, poached fish), *ceviche* (lime-cooked fish), and salads, as well as smoked rib eye and chicken *frito* (fried chicken). A Mexican-style brunch is served Saturday and Sunday. ⊠ *1575 Boulder*

St., Highland 📞 720/570–8686 ⊕ *www.loladenver.com* ⚖ *Reservations essential* 🟰 *AE, DC, MC, V* ⊘ *No lunch.*

$$$$
NEW AMERICAN
Central Denver
Fodor'sChoice
★

✕ **Mizuna.** Chef-owner Frank Bonanno knows how to transform butter and cream into comforting masterpieces at this cozy eatery with warm colors and intimate seating. His menu is reminiscent of California's French Laundry, with quirky dishes such as "liver and onions" (foie gras and a sweet-onion tart), and his Italian heritage has given him the ability to work wonders with red sauce, such as in his inimitable ragout. Be sure to try the elaborately conceived desserts, and expect to be served by the most professional staff, trained by Jacqueline Bonanno, in town. ⊠ *225 E. 7th Ave., Central Denver* 📞 *303/832–4778* ⊕ *www. mizunadenver.com* ⚖ *Reservations essential* 🟰 *AE, MC, V* ⊘ *Closed Sun. and Mon. No lunch.*

$$$$
MEDITERRANEAN
Downtown
Fodor'sChoice
★

✕ **Restaurant Kevin Taylor.** Elegant doesn't do justice to this restaurant's dining room, a classy, soothing space done in tones of gold and hunter green. Exclusive upholstery, flatware, and dishes add to the upscale attitude, as does the formal service style and a top-shelf wine list. The contemporary menu has an updated Mediterranean bent underscored by French techniques, with such classics as Kobe rib eye sharing space with Colorado bison and lamb confit. The tasting menu, geared to theatergoers heading to the Denver Performing Arts Complex a block away, provides a rare chance to try chef Taylor's eclectic creations, and the stone-lined wine cellar makes for intimate private dining. ⊠ *1106 14th St., Downtown* 📞 *303/820–2600* ⊕ *www.ktrg.net* ⚖ *Reservations essential* 🟰 *AE, DC, MC, V* ⊘ *Closed Sun. No lunch.*

$
DINER
Downtown
☾

✕ **Sam's No. 3.** Greek immigrant Sam Armatas opened his first eatery in Denver in 1927, and his three sons use the same recipes Pop did in their updated version of his all-American diner, from the famous red and green chilies to the Coney Island–style hot dogs and the creamy rice pudding. The room is a combination of retro diner and a fancy Denny's, and the bar is crowded with theatergoers and hipsters after dark. Good luck choosing: the menu is 10 pages long, with Greek and Mexican favorites as well as diner classics. The chunky mashed potatoes rule, and breakfast, which is served all day, comes fast. ⊠ *1500 Curtis St., Downtown* 📞 *303/534–1927* ⊕ *www.samsno3.com* ⚖ *Reservations not accepted* 🟰 *AE, D, DC, MC, V.*

WHERE TO STAY

$$$$
DOWNTOWN
Fodor'sChoice
★

🏨 **Brown Palace.** This grande dame of Colorado lodging has hosted public figures from President Eisenhower to the Beatles since it first opened its doors in 1892. **Pros:** sleeping here feels like being part of history; exceptional service; spacious and comfortable rooms. **Cons:** one of the most expensive hotels in Denver; parking costs extra. ⊠ *321 17th St., Downtown* 📞 *303/297–3111 or 800/321–2599* ⊕ *www.brownpalace. com* 🛏 *205 rooms, 36 suites* ⚴ *In-room: refrigerator (some), Internet. In-hotel: 4 restaurants, room service, bars, gym, spa, concierge, laundry service, public Wi-Fi, parking (paid)* 🟰 *AE, D, DC, MC, V.*

$$$–$$$$
DOWNTOWN
★

🏨 **Hotel Monaco.** Celebrities and business travelers check into this hip property, which occupies the historic 1917 Railway Exchange Building and the 1937 Art Moderne Title Building, for the modern perks and Art

Deco–meets–classic French style. **Pros:** one of the pet-friendliest hotels in town; welcoming complimentary wine hour; central location. **Cons:** may be too pet-friendly; pricier than nearby options. ✉ *1717 Champa St., Downtown* ☎ *303/296–1717 or 800/990–1303* ⊕ *www.monaco-denver.com* ⤴ *157 rooms, 32 suites* ⚃ *In-room: refrigerator, Internet, Wi-Fi. In-hotel: restaurant, room service, bar, gym, spa, concierge, laundry service, public Internet, parking (paid), some pets allowed* ▭ *AE, D, DC, MC, V.*

$$$–$$$$
DOWNTOWN
★

🏨 **Hotel Teatro.** With 12-foot ceilings, the earth-tone rooms at the Teatro are sleek and stylish, featuring Frette linens, the latest technology, and spacious bathrooms with soaking tubs and rain forest showers, as well as televisions. **Pros:** great location for theater and other downtown pursuits; excellent restaurants; lovely rooms and hotel spaces. **Cons:** noisy and chaotic area; costly parking; some rooms are tiny. ✉ *1100 14th St., Downtown* ☎ *303/228–1100 or 888/727–1200* ⊕ *www.hotelteatro. com* ⤴ *110 rooms, 7 suites* ⚃ *In-room: Internet, Wi-Fi. In-hotel: 2 restaurants, room service, bar, gym, concierge, laundry service, parking (paid)* ▭ *AE, D, DC, MC, V.*

$$–$$$
LODO
Fodor's Choice
★

🏨 **Oxford Hotel.** During the Victorian era this hotel was an elegant fixture on the Denver landscape, and civilized touches like complimentary shoe shines, afternoon sherry, and morning coffee remain. **Pros:** prime LoDo location, gorgeous historic setting, great restaurants on-site and nearby. **Cons:** noisy ballpark crowds in-season turn LoDo area into a big party. ✉ *1600 17th St., LoDo* ☎ *303/628–5400 or 800/228–5838* ⊕ *www.theoxfordhotel.com* ⤴ *71 rooms, 9 suites* ⚃ *In-room: Internet, Wi-Fi. In-hotel: restaurant, room service, bars, gym, spa, public Wi-Fi, parking (paid)* ▭ *AE, D, DC, MC, V.*

16

SHOPPING

The **Denver Pavilions** (✉ *16th St. Mall between Tremont and Welton Sts., LoDo* ☎ *303/260–6000* ⊕ *www.denverpavilions.com*) is downtown Denver's youngest and hippest shopping and entertainment complex, a three-story, open-air structure that houses national chain stores like Barnes & Noble, Niketown, Forever 21 and Banana Republic. There are also restaurants, including Denver's Hard Rock Cafe, and a 15-screen movie theater, the UA Denver Pavilions. Don't expect distinctive local flavor, but it's a practical complement to Larimer Square a few blocks away.

Historic **Larimer Square** (✉ *14th and Larimer Sts., LoDo* ⊕ *www. larimersquare.com*) houses distinctive shops and restaurants. Some of the square's retail highlights are Dog Savvy, a boutique devoted to pets complete with spa treatments; Cry Baby Ranch, which specializes in all things Western and cowboy-nostalgic; and John Atencio Designer Jewelry. **Tabor Center** (✉ *16th St. Mall, LoDo* ⊕ *www.taborcenter.com*) is a light-filled atrium whose 20 specialty shops and restaurants include the ESPN Zone–theme restaurant and the Shirt Broker. **Writer Square** (✉ *1512 Larimer St., LoDo*) is in the midst of a multimillion-dollar remodel and features shops and restaurants.

SPORTING GOODS

★ **REI.** Denver's REI flagship store, one of three such shops in the country, is yet another testament to the city's adventurous spirit. The store's 94,000 square feet are packed with all stripes of outdoors gear and some special extras: a climbing wall, a mountain-bike track, a white-water chute, and a "cold room" for gauging the protection provided by coats and sleeping bags. There's also a Starbucks inside. Behind the store is the Platte River Greenway, a park path and water area that's accessible to dogs, kids, and kayakers. ⊠ *1416 Platte St., Jefferson Park* ☎ *303/756–3100* ⊕ *www.rei.com.*

SPORTS AND THE OUTDOORS

BASEBALL

The Colorado Rockies, Denver's National League baseball team, play April–October in **Coors Field** (⊠ *2001 Blake St., LoDo* ☎ *303/292–0200 or 800/388–7625* ⊕ *www.coloradorockies.com*). Because of high altitude and thin air, the park is among the hardest in the major leagues for pitchers—and the Rockies have had a tough time preserving young arms. But each year they manage to finish on a high enough note to bring the fans back into the stands the next season.

BASKETBALL

The Denver Nuggets of the National Basketball Association have been the ugly duckling in Denver's professional-sports scene for years. However, they continue to raise expectations with top-draft picks and exciting young players. From November to April the Nuggets play at the **Pepsi Center** (⊠ *1000 Chopper Circle, Auraria* ☎ *303/405–8555* ⊕ *www. nba.com/nuggets*)☎ *303/405–1100.* The 19,000-seat arena, which opened in 1999, is also the primary spot in town for large musical acts such as Bruce Springsteen and Miley Cyrus.

BICYCLING AND JOGGING

The **Denver Parks Department** (☎ *720/913–0696* ⊕ *www.denvergov.org/ parks*) has suggestions for bicycling and jogging paths throughout the metropolitan area's 250 parks, including the popular Cherry Creek and Chatfield Reservoir State Recreation areas. With more than 400 mi of off-road paths in and around the city, cyclists can move easily between urban and rural settings.

FOOTBALL

The National Football League's Denver Broncos play September–December at **Invesco Field at Mile High** (⊠ *1701 Bryant St., Exit 210B off I–25, Sun Valley* ☎ *720/258–3000* ⊕ *www.denverbroncos.com*). Every game eventually sells out, despite the Broncos' tepid success in the post–John Elway world, but tickets can be found if you plan ahead.

HIKING

Fodor's Choice
★
Fifteen miles southwest of Denver, **Red Rocks Park and Amphitheatre** is a breathtaking, 70-million-year-old wonderland of vaulting oxblood-and-cinnamon-color sandstone spires. The outdoor music stage is in a natural 9,000-seat amphitheater (with perfect acoustics, as only nature could have designed). Just want a look? The 5-mi scenic drive offers

a glorious glimpse of the 868 acres of sandstone, and there are picnic and parking areas along the way for photos and a rest. The Trading Post loop hiking trail, at 6,280 feet, is 1.4 mi long and quite narrow with drop-offs and steep grades. The trail closes one-half hour before sunset. The park is open from 5 am to 11 pm daily. ✉ *17598 W. Alameda Pkwy., Morrison, I–70 west to Exit 259, turn left to park entrance* ⊕ *www.redrocksonline.com.*

BOULDER

No place in Colorado better epitomizes the state's outdoor mania than Boulder, where sunny weather keeps locals busy through all seasons. There are nearly as many bicycles as cars in this uncommonly beautiful and beautifully uncommon city, and Boulder has more than 1,500 mi of trails for hiking, walking, jogging, and bicycling.

Boulder is also a brainy place. The University of Colorado at Boulder and Naropa University are located here. In addition, Boulder is home to more than a dozen national laboratories, including the National Center for Atmospheric Research (NCAR) and the National Oceanic and Atmospheric Administration (NOAA).

16

EXPLORING

The late-19th- and early-20th-century commercial structures of the **Downtown Boulder Historic District** once housed mercantile stores and saloons. The period architecture—including Queen Anne, Italianate, and Romanesque styles in stone or brick—has been preserved, but stores inside cater to modern tastes, with fair-trade coffees and Tibetan prayer flags. The area is bounded by the south side of Spruce Street between 10th and 16th streets, Pearl Street between 9th and 16th streets, and the north side of Walnut Street between Broadway and 9th Street.

Pearl Street, between 8th and 20th streets in the downtown area, is the city's hub, an eclectic collection of boutiques, consignment shops, bookstores, art galleries, cafés, bars, and restaurants. A four-block pedestrian mall was set aside in 1976, between 11th and 15th streets.

South of downtown is the **University of Colorado at Boulder.** Red sandstone buildings with tile roofs (built in the "Rural Italian" architectural style that Charles Z. Klauder created in the early 1920s) complement the campus's green lawns and small ponds.

A favorite student hangout is the funky neighborhood known as **the Hill,** just across Broadway from the CU campus (✉ *13th St. between Pennsylvania St. and College Ave.*), which is home to eateries, music and dance venues, record shops, bars, coffeehouses, and hip boutiques.

The **Boulder Museum of Contemporary Art** hosts local and national contemporary art exhibits, performance art, dance, experimental film, and poetry readings. From May to September, when the farmers' market takes place in front of the museum, hours are extended until 8 pm on Wednesday. ✉ *1750 13th St.* ☎ *303/443–2122* ⊕ *bmoca.org* 💲 *$5* ⊙ *Tues.–Fri. 11–5, Sat. 9–4, Sun. noon–3.*

PARKS AND GREENBELTS

★ For the prettiest views of town, follow Baseline Rd. west from Broadway to **Chautauqua Park** (✉ *900 Baseline Rd.*), site of the Colorado Music Festival and a favorite picnic spot for locals on weekends. Continue farther up Flagstaff Mountain to Panorama and Realization points, where people jog, bike, and climb.

★ **Eldorado Canyon State Park,** with its steep walls and pine forests, offers outdoor activities for thrill-seekers and observers. Kayakers get adrenaline rushes on the rapids of South Boulder Creek, while rock climbers scale the canyon's granite walls. Picnickers can choose from 42 spots, and anglers' catches average 8 inches. Bird-watchers and artists find plenty of inspiration, and hikers have 12 mi of trails to wander. The **Streamside Trail** is a mostly level, 1-mi round-trip that parallels South Boulder Creek 0.5 mi to West Ridge; 300 feet of the trail is wheelchair accessible. For the best views of the canyon and the Front Range plains, head up **Rattlesnake Gulch Trail.** The round-trip 3-mi switchback trail ends at an overlook 800 feet higher in elevation than the trailhead, where you can see the high Rockies of the Continental Divide. **Eldorado Canyon Trail** is open to horseback riding. ✉ *9 Kneale Rd. Drive south on Broadway (Hwy. 93) 3 mi to Eldorado Canyon Dr. (Rte. 170). The paved road ends at the village of Eldorado Springs. Drive through town to park entrance Eldorado Springs* ☎ *303/494–3943* 🌐 *www.parks.state.co.us/Parks/eldoradocanyon* 🎟 *$7 (May 1–Sept. 30), $6 (Oct. 1–Apr. 30) per vehicle.*

WHERE TO EAT

$–$$ CAFÉ Fodor's Choice ★ ✕ **Boulder Dushanbe Teahouse.** Unique to Colorado, this teahouse was a gift from Boulder's sister city Dushanbe, Tajikistan, and opened in 1998. Tajik artisans decorated the building in a traditional style that includes ceramic Islamic art and a carved, painted ceiling. The menu presents a culinary cross section of the world; your meal could include such dishes as Basque-style steak, Tajik shish kebab, or Tabrizi *kufteh* (Persian meatballs with dried fruits, nuts, and herbs in a tomato sauce). Relax during high tea at 3 pm (reservations required) with one of more than 80 varieties of tea. Creekside patio tables have views of Central Park. Brunch is served on weekends. ✉ *1770 13th St.* ☎ *303/442–4993* 🌐 *www.boulderteahouse.com* 💳 *AE, D, MC, V.*

$$$–$$$$ ITALIAN ✕ **Frasca Food and Wine.** In the Friuli region of Italy the *frasca* (tree branch) is a historic marker for a neighborhood eatery where you'll be warmly welcomed and well fed. At this Frasca, you can start with *salumi*, a platter of northern Italian cured meats such as *prosciutto daniele, speck,* and *salumeria biellese coppa,* then dig into sliced Quebec veal loin salad, house-made *tagliatelle*, or butter-roasted Atlantic halibut. The menu is based on locally and naturally raised foods, while the extensive wine list focuses on Italian regional wines. On Monday nights, try the four-course tasting menu for $45. ✉ *1738 Pearl St.* ☎ *303/442–6966* 🌐 *www.frascafoodandwine.com* ✍ *Reservations essential* 💳 *AE, D, MC, V* ⏲ *Closed Sun. No lunch.*

$$$ ✕ **The Kitchen.** This unique "community bistro" offers an elegant yet
AMERICAN relaxed dinner with great service, and includes a casual wine and beer
Fodor'sChoice lounge on its second floor. Locals come in for "shared plates" during
★ Community Hour (3 to 5:30 weekdays), a boardinghouse-like experi-
ence that provides the same great food and drinks at reduced prices.
Exceptional entrées like the rainbow trout and the Colorado lamb spot-
light free-range meats and organic and seasonal local produce. Don't
forget dessert: pot au chocolat and a glass of muscatel or the sticky
toffee pudding with vanilla ice cream and a cup of robust coffee are
heavenly. The combination of chic bistro and big-city hot spot can be
a bit loud. ⊠ *1039 Pearl St.* ☎ *303/544–5973* ⊕ *www.thekitchencafe.
com* ⌣ *Reservations essential* ▭ *AE, D, MC, V.*

WHERE TO STAY

$ ⊡ **Foot of the Mountain Motel.** With its distinctive knotty-pine siding,
bright red doors, and colorful flower boxes, this motel is near the
mouth of Boulder Canyon and the Boulder Creek Path. **Pros:** excel-
lent value for the area; quiet neighborhood; close to recreation. **Cons:**
no-frills accommodations; no on-site restaurant. ⊠ *200 Arapahoe Ave.*
☎ *303/442–5688 or 866/773–5489* ⊕ *www.footofthemountainmotel.
com* ↩ *18 rooms, 2 suites* ♿ *In-room: no a/c, refrigerator. In-hotel:
parking (free), some pets allowed* ▭ *D, MC, V.*

$$$ ⊡ **Hotel Boulderado.** The gracious lobby of this elegant 1909 beauty
Fodor'sChoice has a soaring stained-glass ceiling, and the mezzanine beckons with
★ romantic nooks galore. **Pros:** well-maintained historic building; downtown location; excellent restaurants. **Cons:** on busy and noisy streets;
large, busy hotel. ⊠ *2115 13th St.* ☎ *303/442–4344 or 800/433–4344*
⊕ *www.boulderado.com* ↩ *135 rooms, 25 suites* ♿ *In-room: Wi-Fi,
refrigerator. In-hotel: 3 restaurants, bars, public Wi-Fi* ▭ *AE, D, DC,
MC, V* ⦿| *EP.*

$$$$ ⊡ **St. Julien Hotel & Spa.** Unwind in the indulgent luxury of this classy
yet casual hotel. **Pros:** convenient downtown location; close to outdoor
activities and mountains. **Cons:** large hotel; quite busy. ⊠ *900 Walnut
St.* ☎ *720/406–9696 or 877/303–0900* ⊕ *www.stjulien.com* ↩ *201
rooms, 6 suites* ♿ *In-room: a/c, safe, Wi-Fi. In-hotel: 2 restaurants,
room service, bar, pool, gym, spa, parking (paid)* ▭ *AE, D, DC, MC, V.*

SPORTS AND THE OUTDOORS

The **City of Boulder Open Space & Mountain Parks** administers most of the
150 mi of trails in and close to Boulder. Most trails are open to dogs,
provided they are leashed or under voice control and registered with the
city's Voice and Sight Dog Tag Program. There are 34 trailheads in and
around Boulder. Most are free, but a few require a $3 parking permit
for all non-resident vehicles. You can purchase a daily pass either at
self-serve kiosks in the mountain parks or at the OSMP office. ⊠ *66 S.
Cherryvale Rd.* ☎ *303/441–3440* ⊕ *www.osmp.org* ☉ *Weekdays 8–5.*

IN BOULDER For a relaxing amble, take the **Boulder Creek Path,** which winds from west
of Boulder through downtown and past the university to the eastern
part of the city—there are multiple places to access the trail. Within the

16

The Colorado Rockies provide some of the most dramatic mountain scenery in the Midwest.

eastern city limits are ponds, gaggles of Canada geese, and prairie-dog colonies. You'll have great views of the mountains as you walk back toward downtown.

Even a short walk up the grassy slope between **Chautauqua Park** and the base of the mountains brings out hikers and their dogs to take in some sun. On sunny summer mornings the dining hall at Chautauqua Park fills with hungry people ready to tuck into a hearty breakfast. To reach the parking lot, take Baseline Road west from Broadway. The park is on the left just past the intersection with 9th Street.

★ Locals love the **Chautauqua Trail** (✉ *Trailhead: 900 Baseline Rd., Main parking lot*), a 1.6-mi round-trip loop, for its great views of the city and occasional peeks at the rock climbers on the Flatirons. From the trailhead, go up the Chautauqua Trail 0.6 mi to the Bluebell/Baird trail. Go left 0.4 mi and then left again onto the Mesa Trail, which takes you the 0.6 mi back to the parking area. The trail is a long slope at the beginning, but once you're in the trees you won't gain much more elevation. Allow a couple of hours for a leisurely walk on this easy hike. The 4-mi round-trip **Royal Arch Trail** (✉ *Trailhead: 900 Baseline Rd., Main parking lot*) leads to Boulder's own rock arch. The Royal Arch is definitely worth the steep hike, as are the views of the foothills and cities of the Front Range. The trail spurs off the Chautauqua Trail loop and follows along the base of the Flatirons. You'll climb 1,270 feet in 2 mi. Go under the arch to the precipice for the views. If you turn around, the arch frames a couple of Flatirons for a good photo.

IN THE
MOUNTAINS

Two popular trails on the edge of town get you into the mountains quickly. The parking areas are across the street from each other and fill fast, so it's best to go early in the morning or later in the afternoon. Carry a picnic on the **Red Rocks Loop** (⊠ *Trailhead: Mapleton Ave., 1 mi west of Broadway on left*) and enjoy the mountain and city views. The Red Rocks Trail goes to the right from the parking lot and takes you through wildflowers and grassy meadows on the way up to the rock outcropping. The 0.5-mi round-trip trek takes about 20 minutes and gains 340 feet. If you have time for the full 2.3-mi loop, allow about an hour. You'll gain most of the 600 feet in elevation change on the way back. The **Sanitas Valley Loop** (⊠ *Trailhead: Mapleton Ave., 1 mi west of Broadway on left*), known locally as Mount Sanitas, is an easy 3.5-mi hike that provides constant mountain scenery in Sunshine Canyon as you climb 540 feet going up the west flank of Mount Sanitas. From the trailhead, head onto the Mount Sanitas Trail, which becomes the East Ridge Trail as it wraps around the north side of the mountain. From here you can descend to the right on either the Sanitas Valley Trail back to the parking area or along the Dakota Ridge Trail if you want more city views. Be sure not to take the sharp left at the Dakota Ridge intersection, which leads straight downhill to town. Boulder will be on your left all the way back to the trailhead. Allow two hours.

★ **Flagstaff Mountain Open Space** offers hikers several different hikes. An easy walk along the **Boy Scout Trail** to May's Point offers glorious views of the city and Boulder Valley along the way and exceptional views of the Indian Peaks once you reach May's Point. The 1.5-mi round-trip trail starts at Sunrise Amphitheater, where it goes to the left into the spruce forest. After about 0.75 mi and only 140 feet elevation gain, head to the right at the fork in the trail. It's a short distance to May's Point. ⊠ *Trailhead: Drive west on Baseline Rd. to sharp curve to right that is Flagstaff Rd., then turn right at Summit Rd. The trail starts from parking area about 0.5 mi in.*

16

Green Mountain Loop, which begins in Boulder Mountain Park, rewards ambitious hikers with beautiful vistas of the Front Range and the Indian Peaks. The Gregory Canyon, Ranger, E. M. Greenman, and Saddle Rock trails create a 5.5-mi loop that takes three to four hours to hike. It's a 2,344-foot gain in elevation to Green Mountain's summit at 8,144 feet. Follow the Gregory Canyon Trail to the Ranger Trail, and go left. Stay to the right at the E. M. Greenman Trail. At the intersection with Green Mountain West Ridge Trail, turn left. Go on to the summit and descend along the E. M. Greenman and Saddle Rock trails after taking in the view. ⊠ *Trailhead (Gregory Canyon Trail): Drive west on Baseline Rd. to Flagstaff Rd., and then turn left immediately after curve. Parking area is at end of short road where trail starts.*

THE COLORADO ROCKIES

FOOTHILLS NEAR DENVER

If you want to head into the High Country for a few hours, take the MillerCoors tour in Golden, then head up to the Buffalo Bill Museum. If you want to climb even higher, take a walk around the lake in the center of Evergreen and visit some of the local shops in the tiny downtown area.

GOLDEN

15 mi west of Denver via I–70 or U.S. 6 (W. 6th Ave.).

Golden was once the territorial capital of Colorado. City residents have smarted ever since losing that distinction to Denver by "dubious" vote in 1867, but in 1994 then-Governor Roy Romer restored "ceremonial" territorial-capital status to Golden. Today it is one of Colorado's fastest-growing cities, boosted by the high-tech industry as well as MillerCoors Brewery and Colorado School of Mines. Locals love to kayak along Clear Creek as it runs through Golden; there's even a racecourse on the water.

WHAT TO SEE

★ Thousands of beer lovers make the pilgrimage to the venerable **MillerCoors Brewery** each year. Founded in 1873 by Adolph Coors, a 21-year-old German stowaway, today it's the largest single-site brewery in the world and part of MillerCoors. The free self-paced tour explains the malting, brewing, and packaging processes. Informal tastings are held at the end of the tour for those 21 and over in the lounge, where you can buy souvenirs in the gift shop. A free shuttle runs from the parking lot to the brewery. ⊠ *13th and Ford Sts.* ☎ *303/277–2337* ⊕ *www.millercoors.com* ☜ *Free* ☽ *Mon.–Sat. 10–4 and Sun. noon–4 in summer. After Labor Day Thurs.–Mon. 10–4 and Sun. noon–4* ☞ *Children under 18 must be accompanied by an adult.*

WHERE TO EAT

$–$$
AMERICAN
Fodor's Choice
★

✕**Woody's Wood Fired Pizza.** Woody's has a full menu, with pastas, chicken, calzones, and burgers, but it's more fun to choose the $9.99 all-you-can-eat pizza, soup, and salad bar. The choices on the pizza bar range from classic to It's Greek to Me and Margherita, and the salad is always fresh. Woody's is so popular that the choices are always just out of the oven. Don't be surprised if you have to join the throng of families and college students waiting outside for a table on a busy night. ⊠ *1305 Washington Ave.* ☎ *303/277–0443* ⊕ *www.woodysgolden.com* ☐ *AE, D, MC, V* ☽ *Daily 11 am–midnight.*

IDAHO SPRINGS

11 mi south of Central City via Central City Pkwy. and I–70; 33 mi west of Denver via I–70.

Colorado prospectors struck their first major vein of gold here on January 7, 1859. That year local mines dispatched half of all the gold used by the U.S. Mint—ore worth a whopping $2 million. Today the quaint town recalls its mining days, especially along portions of Colorado Boulevard, where pastel Victorians will transport you back to a century giddy with all that glitters.

WHAT TO SEE

Fodor's Choice
★

St. Mary's Glacier is a great place to enjoy a mountain hike and the outdoors for a few hours. From the exit, it's a beautiful 10-mi drive up to a forested hanging valley to the glacier trailhead. The glacier, technically a large snowfield compacted in a mountain saddle at the timberline, is thought to be the southernmost glacier in the United States. During drought years it all but vanishes; a wet winter creates a wonderful Ice Age playground throughout the following summer. Most visitors are content to make the steep 0.75-mi hike on a rock-strewn path up to the base of the glacier to admire the snowfield and sparkling sapphire lake. There are no facilities or parking, except for a rough pull-out area near the base of the trail, and you risk a ticket if you park on private property. Don't look for a St. Mary's Glacier sign on I–70; it's off the Fall River Road sign. ⊠ *I–70 Exit 238, west of Idaho Springs.*

Fodor's Choice
★

The incomparable **Mount Evans Scenic and Historic Byway**—the highest paved road in the United States—leads to the summit of 14,264-foot-high Mount Evans. This is one of only two Fourteeners in the United States that you can drive up (the other is her southern sister, Pikes Peak). More than 7,000 feet are climbed in 28 mi, and the road tops out at 14,134 feet, 130 feet shy of the summit, which is a ¼-mi stroll from the parking lot. The toll road winds past placid lakes and through stands of towering Douglas firs and bristlecone pines. This is one of the best places in the state to catch a glimpse of shaggy white mountain goats and regal bighorn sheep. Keep your eyes peeled for other animals, including deer, elk, and feather-footed ptarmigans. ⊠ *From Idaho Springs, State Rd. 103 leads south 14 mi to entrance to Hwy. 5, which is beginning of scenic byway. The U.S. Forest Service fee station is here on State Rd. 3* ☎ *303/567–3000* ⊕ *www.mountevans.com* 🏷 *$10($5 when last 5 mi are closed)* ☯ *The road is open only when road conditions are safe. Generally, the last 5 mi to summit, Memorial Day–Labor Day.*

16

BOULDER ENVIRONS

ESTES PARK
40 mi northwest of Boulder via U.S. 36 (28th St. in Boulder).

The scenery on the U.S. 36 approach to Estes Park gives little hint of the grandeur to come, but if ever there was a classic picture-postcard Rockies view, Estes Park has it. The town sits at an altitude of more than 7,500 feet, in front of a stunning backdrop of 14,255-foot Longs Peak and surrounding mountains. The town itself is very family-oriented, albeit somewhat kitschy, with lots of stores selling Western-themed trinkets. Many of the small businesses and hotels lining the roads are mom-and-pop outfits that have been passed down through several generations. Estes Park is also the most popular gateway to Rocky Mountain National Park (RMNP), which is just a few miles down the road.

GETTING HERE AND AROUND
To get to Estes Park from Boulder, take U.S. 36 north through Lyons and the town of Pinewood Springs (about 38 mi). You also can reach Estes Park via the incredibly scenic **Peak-to-Peak Scenic and Historic Byway.** To reach the byway from Boulder, take Highway 119 west to Nederland and turn right (north) onto Highway 72, or follow Sunshine Canyon Drive/Gold Hill Road into Ward, and pick up Highway 72 there.

Estes Park's main downtown area is walkable, which is good news on summer weekends, when traffic can be heavy (and parking can be challenging).

DID YOU KNOW?

A pine beetle epidemic that is affecting forests nation-wide has caused some of the Rocky Mountain National Park's trees to turn a reddish color and eventually die. The mitigation efforts of the park service are to remove hazard trees and protect "high value" trees near campgrounds, pic-nic areas, and visitor centers.

The National Park Service operates a free bus service in and around Estes Park and between Estes Park and Rocky Mountain National Park. Buses operate daily from early June to Labor Day, then on weekends only until the end of September.

WHERE TO STAY

$$$–$$$$ **Stanley Hotel.** Perched regally on a hill, with a commanding view
★ of the town, the Stanley is one of Colorado's great old hotels, impeccably maintained in its historic state since it opened in 1909, yet with all the modern conveniences. **Pros:** historic hotel; many rooms have been updated recently; good restaurant. **Cons:** some rooms are small and tight, building is old; no air-conditioning. ⊠ *333 Wonderview Ave.* ☎ *970/577–4000 or 800/976–1377* ⊕ *www.stanleyhotel.com* ⤸ *127 rooms, 11 suites* ♿ *In-room: no a/c, TV (some), Wi-Fi. In-hotel: restaurant, bar, pool, spa, public Wi-Fi, parking (free)* ▤ *AE, D, DC, MC, V.*

FORT COLLINS

The city sits on the cusp of the high plains of eastern Colorado, but is sheltered on the west by the lower foothills of the Rockies, giving residents plenty of nearby hiking and mountain-biking opportunities. By plugging a couple of gaps in the foothills with dams, the city created Horsetooth Reservoir, which you won't be able to see from town. To view the high mountains, you'll need to head up into **Lory State Park** or **Horsetooth Mountain Park**, which are just west of town. A walk through **Old Town Square** and the neighborhoods to its south and west demonstrates Fort Collins's focus on historic preservation.

There are plenty of shops and art galleries worth visiting in this relaxed university city. With the Budweiser brewery and six microbreweries—the most microbreweries per capita in the state—crafting ales, lagers, and stouts, it's the perfect location for the two-day **Colorado Brewers' Festival** every June.

ROCKY MOUNTAIN NATIONAL PARK

Fodor's Choice Rocky Mountain National Park's 416-square-mi wilderness of mead-
★ ows, mountains, and mirrorlike lakes lie just 65 mi from Denver. The park is nine times smaller than Yellowstone, yet it receives almost as many visitors—3 million a year.

Anyone who delights in alpine lakes, mountain peaks, and an abundance of wildlife—not to mention dizzying heights—should consider Rocky Mountain National Park. Here, a single hour's drive leads from a 7,800-foot elevation at park headquarters to the 12,183-foot apex of the twisting and turning Trail Ridge Road. More than 355 mi of hiking trails take you to the park's many treasures: meadows flushed with wildflowers, cool dense forests of lodgepole pine and Engelmann spruce, and the noticeable presence of wildlife, including elk and bighorn sheep.

ADMISSION FEES AND PERMITS

Entrance fees are $20 for a weekly pass, or $10 if you enter on bicycle, motorcycle, or foot. An annual pass costs $40.

SCENIC DRIVE

Trail Ridge Road. This is the park's star attraction and the highest continuous paved highway in the continental United States, topping out at 12,183 feet. The 48-mi road connects the park's gateways of Estes Park and Grand Lake. The views around each bend—of moraines and glaciers, and craggy hills framing emerald meadows carpeted with columbine and Indian paintbrush—are truly awesome. As it passes through three ecosystems—montane, subalpine, and arctic tundra—the road climbs 4,300 feet in elevation. **Many Parks Curve** affords views of the crest of the Continental Divide and of the **Alluvial Fan,** a huge gash a vicious flood created after an earthen dam broke in 1982. ■TIP→ Pick up a copy of the *Trail Ridge Road Guide,* available at visitor centers, for an overview of what you will be seeing as you drive the road. In normal traffic, it's a two-hour drive across the park, but it's best to give yourself three to four hours to allow for leisurely breaks at the overlooks. Note that the middle part of the road closes down again by mid-October, though you can still drive up about 10 mi from the west and 8 mi from the east. ✉ *Trail Ridge Rd. (U.S. 34)* ☉ *June–mid-Oct.*

SCENIC STOP

Bear Lake. Thanks to its picturesque location, easy accessibility, and the good hiking trails nearby, this small alpine lake below Flattop Mountain and Hallett Peak is one of the most popular destinations in the park. Free park shuttle buses can take you here. ✉ *Bear Lake Rd., 10 mi southwest of Beaver Meadows Visitor Center, off Hwy. 36.*

HIKING

Rocky Mountain National Park contains more than 355 mi of hiking trails, so theoretically you could wander the park for weeks. Most visitors explore just a small portion of these trails, so some of the park's most accessible and scenic paths can resemble a backcountry highway on busy summer days. The high-alpine terrain around Bear Lake is the park's most popular hiking area, and it's well worth exploring. However, for a truly remote experience, hike one of the trails in the far northern end of the park or in the Wild Basin area to the south. Keep in mind that trails at higher elevations may have some snow on them even in July. And because of afternoon thunderstorms on most summer afternoons, an early morning start is highly recommended; the last place you want to be when a storm approaches is on a peak or anywhere above the tree line.

Bear Lake to Emerald Lake. This scenic, caloric-burning hike begins at Bear Lake and takes you first on a moderately level, ½ mi journey to **Nymph Lake.** From here, the trail gets steeper, with a 425-foot elevation gain, as it winds around for 0.6 mi to **Dream Lake.** The last stretch is the most arduous part of the hike, an almost all-uphill 0.7-mi trek to lovely **Emerald Lake,** where you can perch on a boulder and enjoy the view. Round-trip, the hike is 3.6 mi, with an elevation gain of 605 feet. Allow two hours or more, depending on stops. ✉ *Trailhead at Bear Lake, off Bear Lake Rd.*

Mount Rushmore and the Black Hills

WORD OF MOUTH

"Early in the morning we headed to Mt. Rushmore, driving along the winding, scenic Iron Mountain Road in Custer State Park. I highly recommend this approach to the park. There are a couple tunnels which frame the monument as you drive from this direction."

—texasbookworm

WELCOME TO MOUNT RUSHMORE AND THE BLACK HILLS

TOP REASONS TO GO

★ **Wild and Wooly Deadwood:** The Wild West lives on in the town that was once the epicenter of America's last gold rush.

★ **The majesty of Mount Rushmore:** "America's Shrine to Democracy" is one of the nation's most enduring icons.

★ **Crazy Horse Memorial:** When completed, this monument to Native American leaders will be the largest sculpture in the world.

★ **Custer State Park:** For wildlife sightings and natural beauty, this is the place to go.

1 Deadwood. Made famous as an 1870s gold mining camp and the permanent resting place of Wild West legends such as Wild Bill Hickok and Calamity Jane, this northern Black Hills community is now a prime visitor destination, with gaming halls, brick streets, and historic trolleys.

2 Rapid City. Western South Dakota's largest town and commercial hub, Rapid City serves as a gateway to Mount Rushmore and the Black Hills, with the most dining and lodging options in a 250-mi radius.

3 Mount Rushmore. Located a half-hour southwest of Rapid City, Mount Rushmore is a must-see on any visit to the Black Hills. Along with the colossal heads of the presidents,

GETTING ORIENTED

The 2 million acres of the Black Hills are about evenly split between private property and the Black Hills National Forest. Fortunately for visitors, the national forest is one of the most developed in the United States. Roads are numerous and generally well maintained, and navigation is easy. Towns with services are plentiful (compared with the Wyoming plains to the west), so you needn't worry about how much gas you've got in your tank or where you'll find a place to stay at night. Rapid City, the largest community in the region, is the most popular base for exploring the Black Hills. The northern towns of Deadwood and Spearfish have almost as many services, with less traffic and fewer tourists.

17

there are museums and forest trails. The impressive night lighting ceremony is among the most popular programs put on by the National Park Service.

4 Crazy Horse Memorial. This mountain carving in progress, 5 mi north of Custer City, pays tribute to all North American Indian tribes. At its base there's an impressive Native American museum along with numerous galleries.

5 Custer State Park. At 110 square mi, this exceptional preserve is home to four mountain lodges, alpine lakes, gurgling streams, scenic drives, elk, deer, mountain lion, wild turkey, antelope, and the largest herd of American bison outside of Yellowstone National Park.

It's been called "an emerald isle in a sea of prairie." With alpine meadows, thick forests, and creek-carved canyons, the Black Hills region more closely resembles Big Horn and Yellowstone country than it does South Dakota's typical flat farmland.

The Black Hills rise up from the western South Dakota plains just over the Wyoming state line and about 150 mi east of the Big Horn range of the Rocky Mountains. They aren't as high—Harney Peak, their tallest summit, measures 7,242 feet—and they cover a territory only 50 mi wide and 120 mi long, but these ponderosa-covered mountains have a majesty all their own.

The region is anchored by Rapid City; with 65,491 residents, it's the largest city for 350 mi in any direction. Perhaps better known, however, are the region's 19th-century frontier towns, including Spearfish, Lead, and Deadwood. The Black Hills also can claim one of the highest concentrations of public parks, monuments, and memorials in the world. Among the more famous are Badlands National Park, Jewel Cave National Monument, and Mount Rushmore National Memorial, whose giant stone carvings of four U.S. presidents have retained their stern grandeur for nearly 70 years.

As in neighboring Wyoming and Montana, outdoor recreation reigns supreme in the Black Hills. Whatever your pleasure—hiking, mountain biking, rock climbing, horseback riding, fishing, boating, skiing, snowmobiling, cross-country skiing—you can do it here, before a backdrop of stunning countryside.

PLANNING

WHEN TO GO

Weather forecasters hate the Black Hills. Snow can fall in the upper elevations every month of the year, and temperatures in January occasionally register above 60°F. However, anomalies like these rarely last more than a day or two. For the most part, expect the thermometer to range between 80°F and 100°F in summer, and know that winter temperatures can plunge below 10°F. Most visitors come in the warmer months, June to September, which is an optimal time for outdoor activities. Thanks to an average annual snowfall of 150 inches, more winter-sports enthusiasts are beginning to discover the area's many skiing and snowmobiling opportunities. Nevertheless, the colder months are the least crowded in the Black Hills.

PLANNING YOUR TIME

Every small town in the Black Hills has something to offer—a fact that you may find surprising. With the highest concentration of parks, monuments, and memorials in the United States, the Black Hills and badlands are more than just a stopover on the way to and from the huge national parks of western Montana and Wyoming. You can see the highlights of southwestern South Dakota in 24 or 48 hours—but if you spend five days or more here, you will be amply rewarded.

You might consider a top-down approach, first exploring the Northern Hills around Deadwood, then moving on to Rapid City and nearby Mount Rushmore. When you've covered the central region, shift down to the southern hills and visit the Crazy Horse Memorial.

GETTING HERE AND AROUND

AIR TRAVEL

Although there are several landing strips and municipal airports in the Black Hills, the only airport with commercial service is in Rapid City. Rapid City Regional Airport, one of the fastest-growing airports in the United States, is 11 mi east of town on Highway 44.

Delta Air provides a connection to Rapid City from Salt Lake City, Northwest has service from Minneapolis, United flies from Denver and Chicago, Frontier also has flights from Denver, American Eagle flies to Dallas and Chicago, and Allegiant Air has weekly service from Las Vegas and Phoenix.

Airlines **Allegiant Air** (☎ 800/432–3810 ⊕ www.allegiantair.com).**American Eagle** (☎ 800/433–7300 ⊕ www.aa.com). **Delta Air** (☎ 800/221–1212 ⊕ www. delta.com). **Frontier Airlines** (☎ 800/432–1359 ⊕ www.frontierairlines.com). **United Airlines** (☎ 800/241–6522 ⊕ www.ual.com).

Airport Information **Rapid City Regional Airport** (✉ 4550 Terminal Rd., Rapid City ☎ 605/393–9924 ⊕ www.rapairport.org).

CAR TRAVEL

Unless you come to the Black Hills on an escorted package tour, a car is essential. I–90 cuts directly through South Dakota from west to east, connecting the northern towns of Spearfish, Sturgis, and Deadwood (which lies about 14 mi off the interstate) with Rapid City. From there the interstate turns straight east, passing Wall and Badlands National Park on its way to Sioux Falls.

Minor highways of importance include U.S. 385, which connects the interior of the Black Hills from south to north, and U.S. 16, which winds south of Rapid City toward the Mount Rushmore and Crazy Horse memorials. Within the Black Hills, seven highway tunnels have limited clearance; they are marked on state maps and in the state's tourism booklet.

17

Snowplows work hard to keep the roads clear in winter, but you may have trouble getting around immediately after a major snowstorm, especially in upper elevations.

Contact the South Dakota State Highway Patrol for information on road conditions.

Information South Dakota State Highway Patrol (☎ 511 ⊕ hp.state.sd.us).

ABOUT THE RESTAURANTS

Like neighboring Wyoming, the Black Hills are not known for culinary diversity, and no matter where you go in this part of the world, beef is king. Nevertheless, thanks to a growing population and increasing numbers of visitors, the area is beginning to see more dining options. Rapid City has an abundance of national chain restaurants as well as local eateries. Although dining in Deadwood's casinos usually involves an all-you-can-eat buffet, the tiny town also claims some of the best-ranked restaurants in South Dakota. Don't be afraid to try wild game dishes: buffalo, pheasant, and elk are relatively common ingredients in the Black Hills.

ABOUT THE HOTELS

New chain hotels with modern amenities are plentiful in the Black Hills, but when booking accommodations consider a stay at one of the area's historic properties. From grand brick downtown hotels to intimate Queen Anne homes converted to bed-and-breakfasts, historic lodgings are easy to locate.

Hotel reviews have been condensed for this book. Please go to Fodors. com for full reviews of each property.

WHAT IT COSTS				
	¢	$	$$	$$$	$$$$
Restaurants	under $8	$8–$12	$13–$20	$21–$30	over $30
Hotels	under $70	$70–$120	$121–$175	$176–$250	over $250

Restaurant prices are for a main course at dinner, excluding sales tax of 4%–7%. Hotel prices are for two people in a standard double room in high season, excluding service charges and 5%–10% tax.

VISITOR INFORMATION

Numerous publications, ranging from small booklets to thick magazines, provide information—and lots of advertising—to visitors headed to the Black Hills. You can pick up many of these at hotels and restaurants, usually for free.

Information Black Hills, Badlands and Lakes Association (✉ 1851 Discovery Circle, Rapid City ☎ 605/355–3600 ⊕ www.blackhillsbadlands.com).

DEADWOOD

Fodor'sChoice
★

42 mi northwest of Rapid City via I–90 and U.S. 14A.

Its brick-paved streets plied by old-time trolleys, illuminated by period lighting, and lined with original Victorian architecture, Deadwood

Downtown Deadwood embraces its Wild West past.

today owes much of its historical character to casinos. In 1989 South Dakota voters approved limited-stakes gaming for the town, on the condition that a portion of revenues be devoted to historic preservation. Since then nearly $300 million has been dedicated to restoring and preserving this once infamous gold-mining boomtown, which has earned recognition as a National Historic Landmark. Small gaming halls, good restaurants, and hotels occupy virtually every storefront on Main Street, just as they did back in Deadwood's late-19th-century heyday. You can walk in the footsteps of legendary lawman Wild Bill Hickok, cigar-smoking Poker Alice Tubbs, and the fabled Calamity Jane, who swore she could outdrink, outspit, and outswear any man—and usually did.

VISITOR INFORMATION
Deadwood Area Chamber of Commerce & Visitor Bureau (✉ *735 Main St., Deadwood* ☎ *605/578–1876 or 800/999–1876* ⊕ *www.deadwood.com*).

EXPLORING

A tour of the restored **Adams House** includes an explanation of the tragedies and triumphs of two of the community's founding families (the Franklins and the Adamses) who lived here. The 1892 Queen Anne–style mansion was closed in the mid-1930s and sat empty for more than 50 years, preserving the original furniture and decor that you see today. ✉ *22 Van Buren Ave.* ☎ *605/578–3724* ⊕ *www. adamsmuseumandhouse.org* ✉ *$8* ⊙ *May–Sept., daily 9–5; Oct.–Apr., Tues.–Sat. 10–4.*

The **Adams Museum,** between the massive stone-block post office and the old railroad depot, houses three floors of displays, including the first locomotive used in the area, photographs of the town's early days, and a reproduction of the largest gold nugget (7¾ troy ounces) ever discovered in the Black Hills. ✉ *54 Sherman St.* ☎ *605/578–1714* ⊕ *www. adamsmuseumandhouse.org* ☜ *Donations accepted* ☉ *May 1–Sept. 30, daily 9–5; Oct. 1–Apr. 30, Tues.–Sat. 10–4.*

Built in 1903, the imposing **Franklin Hotel** has housed many famous guests, including John Wayne, Teddy Roosevelt, and Babe Ruth. It still has its original banisters, ceilings, and fireplace. The street-level casino, card rooms, lobby and lounge have witnessed a multimillion-dollar restoration that returned the property to its original grandeur. The Franklin's veranda, above the white-columned hotel entrance, affords guests an ideal spot to enjoy a cocktail while overlooking historic Main Street. ✉ *700 Main St.* ☎ *605/578–2241* ⊕ *www.silveradofranklin.com* ☜ *Free* ☉ *Daily 24 hrs.*

Mount Moriah Cemetery, also known as Boot Hill, is the final resting place of Wild Bill Hickok, Calamity Jane, and other notable Deadwood residents. The aging landmark was revitalized by three-year, $3 million restoration project completed in 2003, including the addition of a visitor center that houses a leather Bible, a stained-glass window, and pulpit chairs from the first and second Methodist churches of Deadwood, which were destroyed in 1885 and 2003, respectively. From the top of the cemetery you'll have the best panoramic view of the town. ✉ *Top of Lincoln St.* ☎ *605/722–0837* ☜ *$1* ☉ *Memorial Day–Labor Day, daily 7 am–8 pm; Labor Day–end of Sept., daily 9–5.*

WHERE TO EAT

$$ ✕ **Deadwood Grille.** The grille and its companion watering hole, Oggie's
CONTINENTAL Sports Bar & Emporium—both part of the Deadwood Lodge—are
★ favored rest stops for locals drawn to the welcoming atmosphere of native stone and wood, the great food, the friendly staff, and the reasonable prices. The grille features coffee-rubbed filet mignon and a sampling of seafood on its expansive menu. Next door you can get a great burger at Oggie's, which also touts its homemade pizzas and meatloaf sandwiches. ✉ *100 Pine Crest* ☎ *605/584–4800 or 866/290–2403* ⊕ *www.deadwoodlodge.com* ☰ *AE, MC, V.*

$$ ✕ **Deadwood Social Club.** On the second floor of historic Saloon No. 10,
ITALIAN this warm restaurant surrounds you with wood and old-time photo-
Fodor's Choice graphs of Deadwood's past. Light jazz and blues play over the sound
★ system. The decor is Western, but the food is northern Italian, a combination that keeps patrons coming back. The menu stretches from wild-mushroom pasta-and-seafood nest with basil cream to chicken *piccata* (sautéed and served with a lemon and parsley sauce) and melt-in-your-mouth Black Angus rib eyes. The wine list had nearly 200 selections at last count. Reservations are a good idea. ✉ *657 Main St.* ☎ *605/578–1533* ☰ *AE, MC, V.*

WHERE TO STAY

$–$$$ The Lodge at Deadwood. The town's most popular upscale resort, this $47-million casino, hotel, and convention center commands a perch high above Deadwood with spectacular views. **Pros:** great location; all the virtues of a new facility; among the best dining in town. **Cons:** short on genuine Old West charm. ⊠ *100 Pine Crest La., U.S. Hwy. 85* ☎ *605/584–48001* ⊕ *www.deadwoodlodge.com* ⤳ *140 rooms, 14 suites* ♺ *In-room: refrigerators, Wi-Fi. In-hotel: restaurant, room service, bar, pool, gym, laundry facilities* ⊟ *AE, D, MC, V.*

$$$ Spearfish Canyon Lodge. About midway between Spearfish and Dead-
★   wood, near the bottom of Spearfish Canyon, this lodge-style hotel commands some of the best views in the Black Hills. **Pros:** scenery unmatched by any hotel in the area; a mile from one of the most breathtaking waterfalls in the region; on snowmobile trail that offers riders more than 300 mi of groomed trails. **Cons:** secluded—nearly 15 mi from the closest amenities; winding approach road can be dangerous during the winter months. ⊠ *10619 Roughlock Falls Rd., Lead* ☎ *877/975–6343 or 605/584–3435* 🖷 *605/584–3990* ⊕ *www.spfcanyon.com* ⤳ *54 rooms* ♺ *In-room: Internet. In-hotel: restaurant, room service, bar, laundry facilities* ⊟ *AE, D, MC, V.*

EN ROUTE   The easiest way to get from Deadwood to Rapid City and the central Black Hills is east through Boulder Canyon on U.S. 14A, which joins I–90 in Sturgis. However, it's worth looping north and taking the long way around on **Spearfish Canyon Scenic Byway,** a 20-mi route past 1,000-foot limestone cliffs and some of the most breathtaking scenery in the region. The canyon opens onto the small city of Spearfish, home to several restaurants, hotels, and Black Hills State University.

RAPID CITY

42 mi southeast of Deadwood via U.S. 14A and I–90.

The central Black Hills, one of the most developed and best-traveled parts of the region, is anchored by Rapid City (population 65,491). The largest population center in a 350-mi radius, it's the cultural, educational, medical, and economic hub of a vast region. Most of the numerous shops, hotels, and restaurants in the city cater specifically to tourists, including a steady flow of international visitors.

VISITOR INFORMATION
Rapid City Chamber of Commerce and Convention & Visitors Bureau
(⊠ *Civic Center, 444 N. Mt. Rushmore Rd., Box 747, Rapid City* ☎ *605/343–1744 or 800/487–3223* ⊕ *www.visitrapidcity.com*).

EXPLORING

★   The interactive exhibits at the **Journey Museum** explore the history of the Black Hills from the age of the dinosaurs to the days of the pioneers. The complex combines the collections of the **Sioux Indian Museum,** the **Minnilusa Pioneer Museum,** the **Museum of Geology,** the **State Archaeological Research Center,** and a private collection of Native

American artifacts into a sweeping pageant of the history and evolution of the Black Hills. A favorite among visitors is the tepee in the Sioux Indian Museum; you have to crouch down and peer inside to watch a holographic Lakota woman talk about the history and legends of her people. ⊠ *222 New York St.* ☎ *605/394–6923* ⊕ *www.journeymuseum. org* ⊠ *$7* ⊙ *Memorial Day–Labor Day, daily 9–6; Labor Day–Memorial Day, Mon.–Sat. 10–5, Sun. 1–5.*

WHERE TO EAT AND STAY

$$ ✕ **Botticelli Ristorante Italiano.** With a wide selection of delectable veal and
ITALIAN   chicken dishes as well as creamy pastas, this Italian eatery provides a
★   welcome respite from midwestern meat and potatoes. The artwork and traditional Italian music in the background give the place a European atmosphere. ⊠ *523 Main St.* ☎ *605/348–0089* ▭ *AE, MC, V.*

$$ ✕ **Enigma.** Rapid City's version of European fine dining, this restau-
AMERICAN   rant is warm and welcoming, and the food is a treat. Austrian-trained chefs create culinary sensations, complimented by soft candelight, marvelous martinis, a well-stocked wine cellar, and delectable desserts. ⊠ *Radisson Hotel, 445 Mt. Rushmore Rd.* ☎ *605/348–8300* ⊕ *www. enigmarestaurant.com* ▭ *AE, D, MC, V.*

$–$$ ⛨ **Radisson Hotel Rapid City/Mount Rushmore.** Murals of the surrounding landscape and a large Mount Rushmore mosaic in the marble floor distinguish the lobby of this nine-floor hotel in the heart of downtown Rapid City. **Pros:** centrally located downtown; Sleep Number beds; one of the premier fine-dining restaurants in the area; very clean rooms. **Cons:** rooms on the "bar side" can be noisy during busy nights; on-site parking can be crowded because of the popularity of its restaurant, Enigma. ⊠ *445 Mt. Rushmore Rd.* ☎ *605/348–8300* ⊟ *605/348–3833* ⊕ *www.radisson.com/rapidcitysd* ⇘ *176 rooms, 5 suites* ⚠ *In-room: refrigerators (some). In-hotel: pool, gym, Wi-Fi* ▭ *AE, D, MC, V.*

MOUNT RUSHMORE NATIONAL MEMORIAL

Fodor'sChoice   *24 mi southwest of Rapid City via U.S. 16 and U.S. 16A.*
★
At Mount Rushmore, one of the nation's most famous sights, 60-foot-high likenesses of Presidents George Washington, Thomas Jefferson, Abraham Lincoln, and Theodore Roosevelt grace a massive granite cliff, which, at an elevation of 5,725 feet, towers over the surrounding countryside and faces the sun most of the day. The memorial is equally spectacular at night in June through mid-September, when a special lighting ceremony dramatically illuminates the carving.

GETTING HERE AND AROUND

Access is well marked off U.S. 16. With its southeasterly exposure, Mount Rushmore is best viewed in the morning light. Early risers also get to have breakfast with the presidents while encountering fewer people than crowds that flock to the memorial later in the day, as well as to the night lighting ceremony, the busiest interpretive program in the national parks system.

EN ROUTE

The fastest way to get from Mount Rushmore to Crazy Horse Memorial and the southern Black Hills is along Highway 244 west and U.S. 16/U.S. 385 south. This route, like all of the drives in the Black Hills, is full of beautiful mountain views, but the **Peter Norbeck National Scenic Byway** is an even more stunning, though much longer, route. Take U.S. 16A south into Custer State Park, then drive north on Highway 87 through the Needles, towering granite spires that rise above the forest. A short drive off the highway reaches 7,242-foot Harney Peak, the highest point in North America east of the Rockies. Highway 87 finally brings you to U.S. 16/U.S. 385, where you head south to the Crazy Horse Memorial. Because the scenic byway is a challenging drive, and because you'll likely want to stop a few times to admire the scenery, plan on spending two to three hours on this drive.

WHERE TO EAT AND STAY

¢–$ ✕ **Buffalo Dining Room.** The only restaurant within the bounds of the
AMERICAN memorial affords commanding views of Mount Rushmore and the surrounding ponderosa pine forest, and exceptional food at a reasonable price. The menu includes New England pot roast, buffalo stew, and homemade rhubarb pie. It's open for breakfast, lunch, and dinner. ⊠ *Beginning of Ave. of Flags* ☎ *605/574–2515* ▱ *AE, D, MC, V* ⊘ *No dinner mid-Oct.–early Mar.*

$$$ ✕ **Creekside Dining.** Dine on very good American cuisine at this casual
AMERICAN Keystone restaurant with a patio view of Mount Rushmore. Chef Bear's finest dishes are the hearty platters of prime rib, buffalo, lamb, chicken, and fish. Desserts, which include bread pudding, crème brûlée, and peach cobbler, are also excellent. A kids' menu is available. ⊠ *610 U.S. 16A, Keystone* ☎ *605/666–4904* ▱ *MC, V* ⊘ *Closed Nov.–May.*

$–$$$ ▦ **Coyote Blues Village B&B.** This European-style lodge on 30 Black Hills
★ acres (12 mi north of Hill City) displays an unusual mix of antique furnishings and contemporary art. Swiss "no need for lunch" breakfasts include a variety of breads. Some rooms have a private deck with a hot tub. A creek runs through the property. **Pros:** probably the only touch of Europe in Black Hills; miles from highway with no neighbors; exceptional food. **Cons:** no walking distance to other restaurants. ⊠ *23165 Horseman's Ranch Rd., Rapid City* ☎ *605/574–4477 or 888/253–4477* 🖷 *605/574–2101* ⊕ *www.coyotebluesvillage.com* ⤳ *10 rooms* ⚐ *In-room: refrigerator. In-hotel: gym* ▱ *AE, D, MC, V.*

17

CRAZY HORSE MEMORIAL

Fodor'sChoice *15 mi southwest of Mount Rushmore National Memorial via Hwy.*
★ *244 and U.S. 16.*

Designed to be the world's largest sculpture (641 feet long by 563 feet high), this tribute to all North American tribes depicts Crazy Horse, the legendary Lakota leader who helped defeat General Custer at Little Bighorn, astride his steed. The work-in-progress is advancing quickly owing to major private contributions realized in 2010. Thus far, the warrior's head has been carved out of the mountain, and the head of his

America's Shrine of Democracy

Like most impressive undertakings, Mount Rushmore's path to realization was one of personalities and perseverance.

When Gutzon Borglum, a talented and patriotic sculptor, was invited to create a giant monument to Confederate soldiers in Georgia in 1915, he jumped at the chance. The son of Danish immigrants, Borglum was raised in California and trained in art in Paris, even studying under Auguste Rodin, who influenced his style. Georgia's Stone Mountain project was to be massive in scope—encompassing the rock face of an entire peak—and would give Borglum the opportunity to exercise his artistic vision on a grand scale.

But the relationship between the project backers and Borglum went sour, causing the sculptor to destroy his models and flee the state as a fugitive. Fortunately, state officials in South Dakota had a vision for another mountain memorial, and Borglum was eager to jump on board. His passion and flamboyant personality were well matched to the project, which involved carving legends of the Wild West on a gigantic scale. In time, Borglum persuaded local officials to think larger, and the idea of carving a monument to U.S. presidents on a mountainside was born.

Borglum began carving Mount Rushmore in 1927 with the help of some 400 assistants. In consultation with U.S. Senator Peter Norbeck and State Historian Doane Robinson, Borglum chose the four presidents to signify the birth, growth, preservation, and development of the nation. In 6½ years of carving over a 14-year period, the sculptor and his crew drilled and dynamited a masterpiece,

the largest work of art on Earth. Borglum died in March 1941, leaving his son, Lincoln, to complete the work only a few months later.

Follow the Presidential Trail through the forest to gain excellent views of the colossal sculpture, or stroll the Avenue of Flags for a different perspective. Also on-site are an impressive museum, an indoor theater where films are shown, an outdoor amphitheater for live performances, and concession facilities. The nightly ranger program and lighting of the memorial is reportedly the most popular interpretive program in the whole national parks system.

The **Mount Rushmore Information Center,** between the park entrance and the Avenue of Flags, has a small exhibit with photographs of the presidents' faces as they were being carved. There's also an information desk here, staffed by rangers who can answer questions about the memorial or the surrounding Black Hills. A nearly identical building across from the information center

houses restrooms, telephones, and soda machines. ✉ *Beginning of Ave. of Flags* ☎ *605/574–3198* ⊕ *www. nps.gov/moru* 🖳 *Free; parking $10* ⊙ *May–Sept., daily 8 am–10 pm; Oct.– Apr., daily 8–5.*

MOUNT RUSHMORE ATTRACTIONS

Avenue of Flags. Running from the entrance of the memorial to the museum and amphitheater at the base of the mountain, the avenue represents each state, commonwealth, district, and territory of the United States.

Lincoln Borglum Museum. This giant granite-and-glass structure underneath the viewing platform has permanent exhibits on the carving of the mountain, its history, and its significance. There also are temporary exhibits, a bookstore, and an orientation film. Admission is free, and it is open year-round.

Presidential Trail. This easy hike along a boardwalk and down some stairs leads to the very base of the mountain. Although the trail is thickly forested, you'll have more than ample opportunity to look straight up the noses of the four giant heads. The trail is open year-round, so long as snow and ice don't present a safety hazard.

Sculptor's Studio. Built in 1939 as Gutzon Borglum's on-site workshop, this building has displays of tools used by the mountain carvers, scale models of the memorial, and a model depicting the unfinished Hall of Records. This was actually the last of three studios; it was used during the latter stages of the mountain carving. The scale models on display are the ones used by the carvers, who took measurements, multiplied them by 12, and transferred them to the mountain in a sophisticated process of pointing and measuring. One inch on the model equaled one foot on the mountain. Admission is free. Open May–September.

17

horse is beginning to emerge; when work is under way, you can expect to witness frequent blasting. Self-taught sculptor Korczak Ziolkowski conceived this memorial to Native American heritage in 1948, and after his death in 1982 his family took on the project. The completion date is unknown, since activity is limited by weather and funding. Near the work site are a vast orientation center, the Indian Museum of North America, Ziolkowski's studio/home and workshop, indoor and outdoor sculpture galleries, and a restaurant. ⊠ *Ave. of the Chiefs* ☎ *605/673– 4681* 🖃 *Free* ⊙ *May–Sept., daily 8 am–9 pm; Oct.–Apr., daily 8–4:30.*

When Ziolkowski agreed to carve Crazy Horse at the invitation of a Lakota elder, he determined that he wouldn't stop with the mountain. He wanted an educational institution to sit at the base of the mountain, complete with a center showcasing examples of Native American culture and heritage. The construction in 1972 of the **Indian Museum of North America,** built from wood and stone blasted from the mountain, was the initial step in that direction. The permanent collection of paintings, clothing, photographs, and artifacts represents many of the continent's tribes. There is also a space for temporary exhibits that often showcase works by modern Native American artists. ☎ *605/673–4681* ⊕ *www.crazyhorse.org* 🖃 *$10 per adult or $24 per carload for more than 2 adults* ⊙ *May–Sept., daily 8 am–9 pm; Oct.–Apr., daily 8–4:30.*

CUSTER STATE PARK

Fodor'sChoice ★ *13 mi south of Mount Rushmore National Memorial via Hwy. 244 and U.S. 16.*

Down the road less traveled, in 71,000-acre Custer State Park, scenic backcountry is watered by crisp, clear trout streams. Elk, antelope, deer, mountain goats, bighorn sheep, mountain lions, wild turkeys, prairie dogs, and the second-largest publicly owned herd of bison in the world (after the one in Yellowstone National Park) walk the pristine land. Some of the most scenic drives in the country roll past fingerlike granite spires and panoramic views. Each year at the Buffalo Roundup and Arts Festival thousands of spectators watch the park's 1,500 bison thunder through the hills at the start of a Western-theme art and food expo. ⊠ *U.S. 16A, 4 mi east of Custer* ☎ *605/255–4515* ⊕ *www.sdgfp. info/parks/Regions/Custer* 🖃 *$10–28. Several options available, including 7-day passes for individuals and cars, as well as season passes for both* ⊙ *Year-round.*

Yellowstone National Park

WORD OF MOUTH

"Rarely do you find in one place the geological wonders and diversity Yellowstone has to offer. Add to that the diversity of the wildlife, and you've got almost the perfect picture of the totality of nature's collective handiwork in one location, and all in peaceful co-existence."

—dfr4848

WELCOME TO YELLOWSTONE

TOP REASONS TO GO

★ **Hot spots:** Thinner-than-normal crust depth and a huge magma chamber beneath the park explain Yellowstone's abundant geysers, steaming pools, hissing fumaroles, and bubbling mudpots.

★ **Bison:** They're just one of many species that roam freely here. Seemingly docile, the bison make your heart race if you catch them stampeding across Lamar Valley.

★ **Hiking:** Yellowstone has more than 1,000 mi of trails, along which you can summit a 10,000-foot peak, follow a trout-filled creek, or descend into the Grand Canyon of the Yellowstone.

★ **Yellowstone Lake:** Here you can fish, boat, kayak, stargaze, and bird-watch on black obsidian beaches—just don't stray too far into the frigid water.

★ **Canyon:** The Yellowstone River runs through the park, creating a deep yellow-color canyon with two impressive waterfalls.

1 Grant Village/West Thumb. Named for President Ulysses S. Grant, Grant Village is on the western edge of Yellowstone Lake.

2 Old Faithful area. Famous for its regularity and awesome power, Old Faithful erupts every 94 minutes or so. The most important geyser site in the world is a full-service area with inns, restaurants, campsites, cabins, a visitor center, and general stores.

3 Madison. Here the Madison River is formed by the joining of the Gibbon and Firehole rivers. Fly-fishermen will find healthy stocks of brown and rainbow trout and mountain whitefish.

4 Norris. The Norris area is the hottest and most changeable part of Yellowstone National Park. There are campsites here and a small information center.

5 Mammoth Hot Springs. This full-service fortlike area has an inn, restaurants, campsites, a visitor center, and general stores.

6 Tower-Roosevelt. This least-visited area of the park is the place to go for solitude, horseback riding, and animal sightings. There are a lodge, restaurant, and campsites here.

7 **Canyon area.** The Yellowstone River runs through here, and the yellow walls of the canyon plunge more than 1,500 feet. Two massive waterfalls highlight "downtown" Yellowstone, where cars, services, and natural beauty all converge.

8 **Lake area.** The largest body of water within the park, Yellowstone Lake is believed to have once been 200 feet higher than it presently is. This is a full-service area with a hotel, lodge, restaurants, campsites, cabins, and general stores.

GETTING ORIENTED

At more than 2.2 million acres, Yellowstone National Park is considered one of America's most scenic and diverse national parks. The park has five entrances, each with its own attractions: the south has the Lewis River canyon; the east Sylvan Pass; the west the Madison River valley; the north the beautiful Paradise Valley; and the northeast the spectacular Beartooth Pass.

18

MONTANA

Cooke City
Silver Gate
Northeast Entrance

Undine Falls
Blacktail Deer Plateau
Wraith Falls
Roosevelt Lodge
6 Tower-Roosevelt
Slough Creek
Pebble Creek
TO RED LODGE
212
Tower Fall
Lamar Valley
Specimen Ridge
Lamar Cache Creek

UPPER LOOP
Mount Washburn

Visitor Center

Canyon Village
4
7 Inspiration Point
Artist Point
Virginia Cascade
Yellowstone Falls
Grand Loop Road
Hayden Valley
Mud Volcano
Central Plateau

RANGE

Lake Yellowstone Hotel
Fishing Bridge
Visitor Center

LOWER LOOP
Lake Village
Bridge Bay

Avalanche Peak
Lake Butte
East Entrance
TO CODY
14 16 20

8 Yellowstone Lake
West Thumb
Sylvan Lake

Grant Village
Visitor Center
Continental

ABSAROKA

Lewis Lake
Heart Lake

Lewis Lake
Mount Sheridan
191 287 89
Lewis Falls

Divide

River

South Entrance

Flagg Ranch

0 — 20 miles
0 — 35 km

TO JACKSON
AND GRAND TETON
NATIONAL PARK

A trip to Yellowstone has been a rich part of the American experience for five generations now. Though it's remote, we come 3,000,000 strong year after year.

When we arrive, we gasp at the incomparable combination of natural beauty, rugged wilderness, majestic peaks, and abundant wildlife. Indescribable geysers, mudpots, fumaroles, and hot springs make this magma-filled pressure cooker of a park unlike any place else on earth. If you're not here for the geysers, chances are that you've come to spot some of the teeming wildlife, from grazing bison to cruising trumpeter swans.

PLANNING

WHEN TO GO

There are two major seasons in Yellowstone: summer (May–October), the only time when most of the park's roads are open to cars; and winter (mid-December–February), when over-snow travel (snowmobiles, snow coaches, and skis) takes a fraction of the number of visitors to a frigid, bucolic sanctuary. Except for services at park headquarters at Mammoth Hot Springs, the park closes from October to mid-December and from March to late April or early May.

You'll find big crowds from mid-July to mid-August. There are fewer people in the park and more visible wildlife the month or two before and after this peak season, but there are also fewer facilities open. There's also more rain, especially at lower elevations. Except for holiday weekends, there are few visitors in winter. Snow is possible year-round at high elevations.

GETTING HERE AND AROUND

Yellowstone National Park is served by airports in nearby communities, including Cody, Wyoming, one hour east; Jackson, Wyoming, one hour south; Bozeman, Montana, 90 minutes north; and West Yellowstone, Montana, just outside the park's west gate, which has only summer service. The best places to rent cars in the region are at airports in Cody, Jackson, Bozeman, and West Yellowstone. There is no commercial bus service to Yellowstone.

Yellowstone is well away from the interstates, so drivers make their way here on two-lane highways that are long on miles and scenery. From Interstate 80, take U.S. 191 north from Rock Springs; it's about 177 mi to Jackson, then another 60 mi north to Yellowstone. From Interstate 90, head south at Livingston, Montana, 80 mi to Gardiner and the park's North Entrance. From Bozeman, travel south 90 mi to West Yellowstone.

Yellowstone has five primary entrances. Many visitors arrive through the South Entrance, north of Grand Teton National Park and Jackson, Wyoming. Other entrances are the East Entrance, with a main point of origin in Cody, Wyoming; the West Entrance at West Yellowstone, Montana, and the North Entrance at Gardiner, Montana (the West and North entrances are the only two open in winter); and the Northeast Entrance at Cooke City, Montana, which can be reached from either Cody, Wyoming, via the Chief Joseph Scenic Highway, or from Red Lodge, Montana, over Beartooth Pass.

■ TIP➜ The best way to keep your bearings in Yellowstone is to remember that the major roads form a figure eight, known as the Grand Loop, which all entrance roads feed into. It doesn't matter at which point you begin, as you can hit most of the major sights if you follow the entire route.

Road work is likely every summer in some portion of the park—check the *Yellowstone Today* newspaper or ask a ranger. On holiday weekends road construction usually halts, so there are no construction delays for travelers. Remember, snow is possible any time of year in almost all areas of the park.

FLORA AND FAUNA

18

Eighty percent of Yellowstone is forest, and the great majority of it is lodgepole pine. Miles and miles of the "telephone pole" pines burned in the massive 1988 fire that burned more than 35% of the park. The fire's heat created the ideal condition for the lodgepole pine's serotinous cones to release their seeds—creating a stark juxtaposition between 20-year-old and 100-year-old trees.

Yellowstone's scenery astonishes any time of day, though the play of light and shadow makes the park most appealing in early morning and late afternoon. That's exactly when you should be looking for wildlife, as most are active around dawn and dusk, moving out of the forest in search of food and water. May and June are the best months for seeing baby bison, moose, and other young arrivals. Look for glacier lilies among the spring wildflowers and goldenrod amid the changing foliage of fall. Winter visitors see the park at its most magical, with steam billowing from geyser basins to wreath trees in ice, and elk foraging close to roads transformed into ski trails.

Bison, elk, and coyotes populate virtually all areas; elk and bison particularly like river valleys and the geyser basins. Moose like marshy areas along Yellowstone Lake and in the northeast corner of the park. Wolves are most common in the Lamar Valley and areas south of Mammoth; bears are most visible in the Pelican Valley–Fishing Bridge area, near Dunraven Pass, and near Mammoth. Watch for trumpeter swans

The Yellowstone River runs north through the park, feeding and draining Yellowstone Lake and carving out two spectacular falls.

along the Yellowstone River and for sandhill cranes near the Firehole River and in Madison Valley.

PARK ESSENTIALS

ACCESSIBILITY

Yellowstone has long been a National Park Service leader in providing for people with disabilities. Restrooms with sinks and flush toilets designed for those in wheelchairs are in all developed areas except Norris and West Thumb, where more rustic facilities are available. Accessible campsites and restrooms are at Bridge Bay, Canyon, Madison, Mammoth Hot Springs, and Grant Village campgrounds, while accessible campsites are found at both Lewis Lake and Slough Creek campgrounds. Ice Lake has an accessible backcountry campsite. An accessible fishing platform is about 3½ mi west of Madison at Mt. Haynes Overlook.

If you need a sign-language interpreter for NPS interpretive programs, arrange for it by calling ☎ *307/344–2251* three weeks in advance. For details, contact the accessibility coordinator at ☎ *307/344–2018*.

ADMISSION FEES

Entrance fees of $25 per car, $20 per motorcycle, and $12 per visitor (16 and older) arriving on a bus, motorcycle, or snowmobile provide visitors with access for seven days to both Yellowstone and Grand Teton. An annual pass to the two parks costs $50.

ADMISSION HOURS

Depending on the weather, Yellowstone is generally open late April to November and mid-December to early March. In winter only one road, going from the Northeast Entrance at Cooke City to the North Entrance at Gardiner, is open to wheeled vehicles; other roads are used by over-snow vehicles. The park is in the Mountain time zone.

SHOPS AND GROCERS

A dozen Yellowstone general stores are located throughout the park. The 1950s-inspired Canyon General Store, the 100-year-old "Hamilton's Store" at Old Faithful, and the Fishing Bridge store are three of the largest, combining architectural significance with a broad variety of groceries, books, apparel, outdoor needs, and soda-fountain-style food service.

Hours vary seasonally, but most stores are open 7:30 am to 9:30 pm from late May to September; all except Mammoth General Store close for the winter. All accept credit cards.

WIRELESS COMMUNICATION

Cell-phone coverage in the park is hit or miss, and generally confined to developed areas like Old Faithful, Canyon, Grant, and Mammoth. Lake and Roosevelt villages lack service. In general, don't count on it. Public telephones are near visitor centers and major park attractions. Wireless Internet access is available for a fee at Mammoth and Old Faithful. ■ TIP→ Try to use inside phones rather than outside ones, so your conversation doesn't distract you from being alert to wildlife that might approach you while you're on the phone.

PARK CONTACT INFORMATION

Yellowstone National Park ⌂ *Box 168, Mammoth, WY 82190-0168* ☎ *307/344–7381* ⊕ *www.nps.gov/yell.*

EXPLORING YELLOWSTONE

Along the park's main drive—the Grand Loop—are eight primary "communities," or developed areas. On the West Yellowstone map are five of those communities—Grant Village, Old Faithful, Madison, Norris, and Mammoth Hot Springs—with their respective sights, while the East Yellowstone map shows the remaining three—Tower-Roosevelt, Canyon, and Lake (for Yellowstone Lake area)—with their respective sights.

GRANT VILLAGE AND WEST THUMB

Along the western edge of Yellowstone Lake (called the West Thumb), Grant Village is the first community you encounter from the South Entrance. It has basic lodging and dining facilities.

SCENIC STOPS

☙ **West Thumb Geyser Basin.** The primary Yellowstone caldera was created by one volcanic eruption, while West Thumb came about as the result of another, later volcanic eruption. This unique geyser basin is the only place to see active geothermal features in Yellowstone Lake. Two boardwalk loops are offered; take the longer one to see features like Fishing Cone, where fishermen used to catch fish, pivot, and drop their fish straight into boiling water for cooking. This area is particularly popular for winter visitors, who take advantage of the nearby warming hut and a stroll around the geyser basin before continuing their trip via snow coach or snowmobile. ⊠ *Grand Loop Rd., 22 mi north of South Entrance, West Thumb.*

OLD FAITHFUL

★ The world's most famous geyser is the centerpiece of this area, which has extensive boardwalks through the Upper Geyser Basin and equally extensive visitor services, including several choices in lodging and dining. In winter you can dine and stay in this area and cross-country ski or snowshoe through the geyser basin.

HISTORICAL SITES

Fodor's Choice

★

Old Faithful Inn. It's hard to imagine how any work could be accomplished when snow and ice blanket the region, but this historic hotel was constructed over the course of a single winter in 1903. This massive log structure is an attraction in its own right. Even if you don't spend a night at the Old Faithful Inn, walk through or take the free 45-minute guided tour to admire its massive open-beam lobby and rock fireplace (where tours begin). There are antique writing desks on the second-floor balcony, and during evening hours a pianist plays there as well. You can watch Old Faithful geyser from two second-floor outdoor decks. ⊠ *Old Faithful Bypass Rd., Old Faithful* ☎ *307/344–7901* ⊙ *May–mid-Oct.; tours daily, times vary.*

SCENIC STOPS

Biscuit Basin. North of Old Faithful, this basin is also the trailhead for the Mystic Falls Trail. The namesake "biscuit" formations were reduced to crumbs when Sapphire Pool erupted after the 1959 Hebgen Lake earthquake. Now Sapphire is a calm, beautiful blue pool again, but that could change at any moment. ⊠ *3 mi north of Old Faithful on Grand Loop Rd., Old Faithful.*

Black Sand Basin. There are a dozen hot springs and geysers near the cloverleaf entrance from Grand Loop Road to Old Faithful. Emerald Pool is one of the prettiest. ⊠ *North of Old Faithful on Grand Loop Rd., Old Faithful*

Lower Geyser Basin. Shooting more than 150 feet in the air, the Great Fountain Geyser is the most spectacular sight in this basin. Less impressive but more regular is White Dome Geyser, which shoots from a 20-foot-tall cone. You'll also find pink mudpots and blue pools at the basin's Fountain Paint Pots. ⊠ *Midway between Old Faithful and Madison on Grand Loop Rd.*

Midway Geyser Basin. Called "Hell's Half Acre" by writer Rudyard Kipling, Midway Geyser Basin is a series of boardwalks winding their way to Excelsior Geyser, which deposits 4,000 gallons of water per minute into the Firehole River. Just above Excelsior is Yellowstone's largest hot spring, Grand Prismatic Spring. Measuring 370 feet in diameter, it's deep blue in color with yellow and orange rings formed by bacteria that give it the effect of a prism. ⊠ *Between Old Faithful and Madison on Grand Loop Rd.*

Fodor's Choice

★

Old Faithful. Almost every visitor includes the world's most famous geyser on his or her itinerary. Yellowstone's most predictable big geyser—although not its largest or most regular—sometimes reaches 180 feet,

Grand Prismatic Spring is the world's third-largest hot spring, at more than 370 feet across. Heat-loving microorganisms (bacteria and algae) tint the Grand Prismatic Spring with a rainbow of colors.

but it averages 130 feet. The mysterious plumbing of Yellowstone has lengthened Old Faithful's cycle somewhat in recent years, to every 94 minutes or so. To find out when Old Faithful is likely to erupt, check at the visitor center or at any of the lodging properties in the area. You can view the eruption from a bench just yards away, from inside the visitor center or lodge cafeteria, or the second-floor balcony of Old Faithful Inn. The 1-mi hike to Observation Point yields yet another view—from above—of the geyser and its surrounding basin. ⊠ *Southwest segment, Grand Loop Rd.*

Upper Geyser Basin. With Old Faithful as its central attraction, this mile-square basin contains about 140 different geysers—one-fifth of the known geysers in the world. It's an excellent place to spend a day or more exploring. Highlights include the deep blue Morning Glory Pool and stately Castle Geyser, which has the biggest cone in Yellowstone. You will find a complex system of boardwalks and trails—some of them used as bicycle trails—that take you to the basin's various attractions. The Geyser Hill complex is a 1.3-mi boardwalk close to Old Faithful where the geyser Giantess spouts just a few times each year, reaching 100 to 250 feet in the air in sporadic bursts that can continue for 12 to 43 hours. ⊠ *Old Faithful.*

VISITOR CENTER

Old Faithful Visitor Center. The park's LEED-certified visitor center is the best place to inquire about geyser eruption predictions. Interpretive exhibits explain Yellowstone's geothermal plumbing in layman's terms. In the separate children's exhibit a very cool transparent model geyser is routinely surrounded by rapt children and adults alike. ⊠ *Old Faithful*

Bypass Rd. ☎ *307/545–2750* ⊙ *Late May–late Sept., daily 8–7; late Dec.–early Mar., daily 9–6.*

MADISON

The area around the junction of the West Entrance Road and the Lower Loop is a good place to break as you travel through the park, because you will almost always see bison grazing along the Madison River and often elk as well. Limited visitor services are here, including no dining facilities.

VISITOR CENTER

Madison Information Center. In this National Historic Landmark the ranger shares the space with a Yellowstone Association bookstore. You may find spotting scopes set up for wildlife viewing out the rear window; if this is the case, look for eagles, swans, bison, elk, and more. Rangers provide basic hiking information and maps and issue permits for backcountry camping and fishing. Picnic tables, toilets, and an amphitheater for summer-evening ranger programs are shared with the nearby Madison campground. The park encourages Junior Rangers to start here. ⊠ *Grand Loop Rd. at West Entrance Rd.* ☎ *307/344–2821* ⊙ *Late May–late Sept., daily 9–6.*

NORRIS

The area at the western junction of the Upper and Lower Loops has the most active geyser basin in the park. The underground plumbing occasionally reaches such high temperatures—the ground itself has heated up in areas to nearly 200°F—that a portion of the basin is periodically closed for safety reasons. There are limited visitor services: two museums, a bookstore, and a picnic area. ■ **TIP→ Ask rangers at the Norris Geyser Basin Museum when different geysers are expected to erupt and to plan your walk accordingly.**

SCENIC STOPS

♻ **Norris Geyser Basin.** From the Norris Ranger Station, choose either Por-
★ celain Basin or Back Basin, or both. These volatile thermal features are constantly changing, although you can expect to find a variety of geysers and springs here at any time. In the Back Basin, Steamboat Geyser is the world's largest when it erupts fully (most recently in 2005), climbing 400 feet above the basin. More often, Steamboat growls and spits constantly, sending clouds of steam high above the basin. Kids will love the Puff 'n' Stuff Geyser and the mysterious cave-like Green Dragon Spring. The area is accessible via an extensive system of boardwalks, some of them suitable for people with disabilities. The famous Steamboat Geyser is here. ⊠ *Grand Loop Rd. at Norris.*

MAMMOTH HOT SPRINGS

This northern community in the park is known for its massive natural terraces, where mineral water flows continuously, building an ever-changing display. (Note, however, that water levels can fluctuate, so if it's late in a particularly dry summer, you won't see the terraces in all their glory.) Elk often graze here. In the early days of the park it was the site of Fort Yellowstone, and the brick buildings constructed during that era are still used for park administration.

SCENIC STOPS

☺ **Mammoth Hot Springs Terraces.** Multicolor travertine terraces formed by
★ slowly escaping hot mineral water mark this unusual geological formation. Highlights include the dormant, 37-foot Liberty Cap cone,
at the area's north end, and the bright and ornately terraced Minerva
Spring. Walking the boardwalks, you may spy elk, as they graze nearby.
■ TIP➜ There are lots of steps on the lower terrace boardwalks, so plan to
take your time there. ⊠ *Northwest corner of Grand Loop Rd.*

TOWER-ROOSEVELT

The northeast region of Yellowstone is the least-visited part of the park,
making it a great place to explore without running into as many people.
Packs of wolves may be spotted in the Lamar Valley.

SCENIC STOPS

☺ **Tower Fall.** This is one of the easiest waterfalls to see from the roadside
(follow signs to the lookout point); you can also view volcanic pinnacles here. Tower Creek plunges 132 feet at this waterfall to join the
Yellowstone River. A trail runs to the base of the falls, but it is closed
at this writing (and for the foreseeable future) because of erosion several hundred yards above the bottom of the canyon; thus, there is no
access to the base of Tower Fall from this trail at present. ⊠ *2 mi south
of Roosevelt on Grand Loop Rd.*

CANYON

The Yellowstone River winds its way through the heart of the park,
entering Yellowstone Lake then heading northward under Fishing
Bridge through Hayden Valley. When it cuts through the multicolored
Grand Canyon of the Yellowstone, it creates one of the most spectacular gorges in the world, enticing visitors with its steep canyon walls
and waterfalls. All types of visitors' services are here, as well as lots of
hiking opportunities.

SCENIC STOPS

Fodor's Choice **Grand Canyon of the Yellowstone.** This stunning canyon is 23 mi long, and
★ there is only one trail from rim to base, a strenuous six-hour hike called
Seven Mile Hole. A majority of park visitors clog the north and south
rims, where a number of viewpoints look out on the majestic Upper and
Lower Falls. Artist Point on the south rim is the most popular viewpoint
to see the 308-foot Lower Falls, with two different viewing levels, one of
which is wheelchair accessible. On the north rim, Lookout Point shows
off the red-and-ochre canyon walls, topped with emerald-green forest.
It's a feast of color. Also look for ospreys, which nest in the canyon's
spires and precarious trees. ⊠ *Canyon.*

Upper Falls View. Just above the canyon, a spur road off Grand Loop
Road south of Canyon Village gives you access to the west end of the
North Rim Trail and takes you down a fairly steep trail for a view of
Upper Falls from almost directly above. ⊠ *Off Grand Loop Rd., ¾ mi
south of Canyon.*

VISITOR CENTER

☺ **Canyon Visitor Center.** With a number of interactive exhibits for adults
★ and kids, the focus here is volcanoes and earthquakes, and a movie
examines the geo- and hydrothermal basis for the park. As at all visitor

18

centers, you can obtain park information, backcountry camping permits, etc. The adjacent bookstore has a great selection of guidebooks, trail maps, gifts, and hundreds of books on the park, its history, and the science surrounding it. ⊠ *Canyon Village* ☎ *307/242–2552* ☉ *Late May–late Sept., daily 8–8; early–mid-May, daily 9–5.*

LAKE AREA

In the park's southeastern segment, the area is permeated by the tranquillity of massive Yellowstone Lake. Near Fishing Bridge you might see grizzly bears hunting for spawning fish or swimming near the lake's outlet to the Yellowstone River. Visitor centers include Lake Yellowstone Hotel, Fishing Bridge RV Park (for hard-sided vehicles only), and Bridge Bay Campground, the park's largest, with 432 sites.

HISTORICAL SITES

★ **Lake Yellowstone Hotel.** Completed in 1891, this structure on the National Register of Historic Places is the oldest lodging in any national park. Casual daytime visitors can lounge in white wicker chairs in the sunroom and watch the waters of Yellowstone Lake through massive windows. Robert Reamer, the architect of the Old Faithful Inn, added its columned entrance in 1903 to enhance the original facade. ⊠ *Lake Village Rd., Lake Village* ☎ *307/344–7901* ☉ *Mid-May–early Oct.*

SCENIC STOPS

☉ **Mud Volcano.** Gasses hiss from parking-lot vents, underscoring the volatile nature of this area's geothermal features. The ¾-mi round-trip Mud Volcano Interpretive Trail loops gently around seething, sulfuric mudpots with names such as Black Dragon's Cauldron (which roars like a dragon) before making its way around Mud Volcano itself, a boiling pot of brown goo. ⊠ *10 mi south of Canyon; 4 mi north of Fishing Bridge on Grand Loop Rd., Fishing Bridge.*

☉ **Yellowstone Lake.** One of the world's largest alpine lakes, encompassing
Fodor'sChoice 132 square mi, Yellowstone Lake was formed when glaciers that once
★ covered the region melted into a caldera—a crater formed by a volcano. The lake has 141 mi of shoreline, about one-third of it followed by the East Entrance Road and Grand Loop Road, along which you will often see moose, elk, waterfowl, and other wildlife. In winter you can sometimes see otters and coyotes stepping gingerly onto the ice at the lake's edge. Many visitors head here for the excellent fishing—streams flowing into the lake give it an abundant supply of trout. ⊠ *Intersection of East Entrance Rd. and Grand Loop Rd., between Fishing Bridge and Grant Village.*

VISITOR CENTER

☉ **Fishing Bridge Visitor Center.** If you can't distinguish between a Clark's nuthatch and an ermine (note: one's a bird, the other a rodent), check out the extensive exhibits on park birds and other smaller wildlife at this historic stone-and-log building. Step out the back door to find yourself on one of the beautiful black obsidian beaches of Yellowstone Lake. An adjacent amphitheater features ranger presentations nightly in the summer. ⊠ *East Entrance Rd., 1 mi from Grand Loop Rd.* ☎ *307/242–2450* ☉ *Memorial Day–late Sept., daily 8–7.*

SCENIC DRIVES

Firehole Canyon Drive. The 2-mi narrow asphalt road twists through a deep canyon and passes the 40-foot Firehole Falls. In summer look for a sign marking a swimming hole. This is one of only two places in the park (Boiling River on the North Entrance Road is the other) where you can safely and legally swim in the park's thermally heated waters. Watch for osprey and other raptors. ⊠ *1 mi south of Madison junction off Grand Loop Rd.*

Hayden Valley on Grand Loop Road. Bison, bears, coyotes, wolves, and birds of prey all call Hayden Valley home almost year-round. Once part of Yellowstone Lake, the broad valley now features peaceful meadows, rolling hills, and the placid Yellowstone River. Multiple turnouts and picnic areas on the 16-mi drive offer views of the river and valley. Ask a ranger about "Grizzly Overlook," an unofficial site where wildlife watchers, including NPS rangers with spotting scopes for the public to use, congregate in the summer. It's three turnouts north of Mud Volcano—there's no sign, so look for the timber railings. ⊠ *Between Canyon and Fishing Bridge on Grand Loop Rd.*

Fodor's Choice ★ **Northeast Entrance Road and Lamar Valley.** The 29-mi road features the richest diversity of landscape of the five entrance roads. Just after you enter the park, you cut between 10,928-foot Abiathar Peak and the 10,404-foot Barronette Peak. You pass the extinct geothermal cone called Soda Butte, plus the two nicest campgrounds in the park, Pebble Creek and Slough Creek. Lamar Valley is home to hundreds of bison, while the rugged peaks and ridges adjacent to it host some of the park's famous wolf packs (reintroduced in 1995). The main wolf-watching activities in the park occur here during early-morning and late-evening hours year-round. ⊠ *From Northeast Entrance near Cooke City to junction with Grand Loop Rd. at Roosevelt Lodge.*

18

SPORTS AND THE OUTDOORS

BOATING

Motorized boats are allowed only on Lewis Lake and Yellowstone Lake. Kayaking or canoeing is allowed on all park lakes except Sylvan Lake, Eleanor Lake, Twin Lakes, and Beach Springs Lagoon; however, most lakes are inaccessible by car, so accessing the park's lakes requires long portages. Boating is not allowed on any park river, except for the Lewis River between Lewis Lake and Shoshone Lake, where nonmotorized boats are permitted.

You must purchase a seven-day, $5 permit for boats and floatables, or a $10 permit for motorized boats at Bridge Bay Ranger Station, South Entrance Ranger Station, Grant Village Backcountry Office, or Lewis Lake Ranger Station (at the campground). Nonmotorized permits are available at the Northeast entrance, West Yellowstone Information Center; backcountry offices at Mammoth, Old Faithful, and Canyon; Bechler Ranger Station; and locations where motorized permits are sold. Annual permits are also available for $20.

Boat permits issued in Grand Teton National Park are honored in Yellowstone, but owners must register their vessel in Yellowstone and obtain a no-charge Yellowstone validation sticker from a permit issuing station.

OUTFITTERS AND EXPEDITIONS

Watercraft, from rowboats to powerboats, are available for trips on Yellowstone Lake at **Bridge Bay Marina** (⊠ *Grand Loop Rd., 2 mi south of Lake Village, Lake area* ☎ *307/344–7311* 🖂 *$76–$96/hr for guided cruisers for fishing or sightseeing; $10/hr for rowboat; $47/ hr for small boat with outboard motor* ☉ *Late May–early Sept., daily 8:30–8:30*). You also can rent 22- and 34-foot cabin cruisers with a guide. Daily rentals must be returned by 7 pm. Run by Xanterra Parks & Resorts, **Yellowstone Lake Scenic Cruises** (⊠ *Bridge Bay Marina, Lake area* ☎ *307/344–7311* 🖂 *Cruises $14.25* ☉ *Late May–mid-Sept., daily 8:30 am–8:30 pm*) take visitors on one-hour cruises aboard the *Lake Queen II* throughout the day. The vessel makes its way from Bridge Bay to Stevenson Island and back. Reservations are strongly recommended.

FISHING

Anglers flock to Yellowstone beginning the Saturday of Memorial Day weekend, when fishing season begins. By the time the season ends in November, thousands have found a favorite spot along the park's rivers and streams. Native cutthroat trout are one of the prize catches, but four other varieties—brown, brook, lake, and rainbow—along with grayling and mountain whitefish, inhabit Yellowstone's waters. Popular sportfishing opportunities include the Gardner and Yellowstone rivers, as well as Soda Butte Creek, but the top fishing area is the Madison River, known to fly fishermen throughout the country.

Yellowstone fishing permits are required for anglers over age 16. Montana and Wyoming fishing permits are not valid in the park. Yellowstone fishing permits cost $15 for a three-day permit, $20 for a seven-day permit, or $35 for a season permit. Anglers ages 12 to 15 must have a (nonfee) permit or fish under direct supervision of an adult with a permit. Anglers younger than 12 don't need a permit but must be with an adult who knows the regulations. Permits are available at all ranger stations, visitor centers, and Yellowstone general stores.

HIKING

Fountain Paint Pots Nature Trail. Take the easy ½-mi loop boardwalk of Fountain Paint Pot Nature Trail to see fumaroles (steam vents), blue pools, pink mudpots, and mini-geysers in this thermal area. It's popular in both summer and winter because it's right next to Grand Loop Road. ⊠ *Trailhead at Lower Geyser Basin, between Old Faithful and Madison.*

MODERATE

Fodor's Choice ★

Mystic Falls Trail. From the Biscuit Basin boardwalk's west end, this trail gently climbs 1 mi through heavily burned forest to the lava-rock base of 70-foot Mystic Falls. An optional loop switchbacks up Madison Plateau to a lookout with the park's least-crowded view of Old Faithful, 3½ mi round-trip from Biscuit Basin in all. ⊠ *Trailhead 3 mi north of Old Faithful Village off Grand Loop Rd., Old Faithful.*

MAMMOTH HOT SPRINGS

MODERATE **Bunsen Peak Trail.** Past the entrance to Bunsen Peak Road, the moderately difficult trail is a 4-mi, three-hour round-trip that climbs 1,300 feet to Bunsen Peak for a panoramic view of Blacktail Plateau, Swan Lake Flats, the Gallatin Mountains, and the Yellowstone River valley. (Use a topographical map to find these landmarks.) ⊠ *Trailhead at Grand Loop Rd., 1½ mi south of Mammoth Hot Springs.*

TOWER-ROOSEVELT

MODERATE
Fodor's Choice
★
Slough Creek Trail. Starting at Slough Creek Campground, this trail climbs steeply along a historic wagon trail for the first 1½ mi before reaching expansive meadows and prime fishing spots, where moose are common and grizzlies occasionally wander. From this point the trail, now mostly level, meanders another 9½ mi to the park's northern boundary. Anglers absolutely rave about this trail. ⊠ *Trailhead 7 mi east of Tower-Roosevelt off Northeast Entrance Rd.*

CANYON

★ **North Rim Trail.** Offering great views of the Grand Canyon of the Yellowstone, the 3-mi North Rim Trail runs from Inspiration Point to Chittenden Bridge. You can wander along small sections of the trail or combine it with the South Rim Trail. Especially scenic is the 0.5-mi section of the North Rim Trail from the Brink of the Upper Falls parking area to Chittenden Bridge that hugs the rushing Yellowstone River as it approaches the canyon. This trail is paved and fully accessible between Lookout Point and Grand View. ⊠ *Trailhead 1 mi south of Canyon.*

LAKE

EASY
☾
★
Storm Point Trail. Well marked and mostly flat, this 1½-mi loop leaves the south side of the road for a perfect beginner's hike out to Yellowstone Lake. The trail passes moose habitat on its way to Yellowstone Lake's Storm Point, named for its frequent afternoon windstorms and crashing waves. Heading west along the shore, you're likely to hear the shrill chirping of yellow-bellied marmots and see ducks, pelicans, and trumpeter swans. You will pass several small beaches where kids can explore on warm summer mornings. ⊠ *Trailhead 3 mi east of Lake Junction on East Entrance Rd., Fishing Bridge.*

DIFFICULT
Fodor's Choice
★
Avalanche Peak Trail. On a busy day in summer, maybe six parties will fill out the trail register at the Avalanche Peak trailhead, so you won't have a lot of company on this hike. Starting across from a parking area on the East Entrance Road, the difficult 4-mi, four-hour round-trip climbs 2,150 feet to the peak's 10,566-foot summit, from which you'll see the rugged Absaroka Mountains running north and south. Look around the talus and tundra near the top of Avalanche Peak for alpine wildflowers and butterflies. Avoid bears and snow by hiking here June through August. ⊠ *Trailhead 2 mi east of Sylvan Lake on north side of East Entrance Rd., Fishing Bridge.*

HORSEBACK RIDING

Xanterra Parks & Resorts offers horseback rides of one and two hours in length at Mammoth, Tower-Roosevelt, and Canyon. Advance reservations are recommended. Guides (and horses) cater to beginning riders (they estimate 90% of riders have not been on a horse in at least

18

West Thumb Geyser Basin at sunset.

10 years), but let them know if you're an experienced rider and would like a more challenging pace or ride.

Private stock can be brought into the park. Horses are not allowed in front-country campgrounds but are permitted in certain backcountry campsites. For information on planning a backcountry trip with stock, call the Backcountry Office (☎ 307/344–2160).

OUTFIT-TER AND EXPEDITIONS ☾ One- and two-hour horseback trail rides run by **Xanterra Parks & Resorts** (☎ 307/344–7311 ⊕ www.yellowstonenationalparklodges.com ✉ $38–$58) leave from three sites in the park: Mammoth Hot Springs, Roosevelt Lodge, and Canyon Village. Children must be at least 8 years old and 48 inches tall; kids ages 8 to 11 must be accompanied by someone age 16 or older. In order not to spook horses or wildlife, guests are prohibited from bringing cameras or cell phones.

SKIING, SNOWSHOEING, AND SNOWMOBILING

Yellowstone can be the coldest place in the continental United States in winter, with temperatures of -30°F not uncommon. Still, winter-sports enthusiasts flock here when the park opens for its winter season the last week of December. Until early March the park's roads teem with over-snow vehicles like snowmobiles and snow coaches. Its trails bristle with cross-country skiers and snowshoers.

Snowmobiling is an exhilarating way to experience Yellowstone. It's also controversial: There's heated debate about the pollution and disruption to animal habitats. The number of riders per day is limited, and you must have a reservation, a guide, and a four-stroke engine (which is less polluting than the more common two-stroke variety). About a dozen companies have been authorized to lead snowmobile excursions into the park from the North, West, South, and East entrances. Prices vary, as do itineraries and inclusions—be sure to ask about insurance, guides, taxes, park entrance fees, clothing, helmets, and meals. Regulations are subject to change.

OUTFIT-
TERS AND
EXPEDITIONS
At Mammoth Hot Springs Hotel and Old Faithful Snow Lodge, **Xanterra Parks & Resorts** (☎ *307/344–7901* ⊕ *www.yellowstone-nationalparklodges.com*) rents skis, snowmobiles, and snowshoes. Ski rentals (including skis, poles, gloves, and gaiters) are $12 per half day, $18.50 per full day. Snowshoe rentals are $10 per half day, $15 per full day. Shuttle service is $15 from Snow Lodge or Mammoth. Group and private lessons are available. Skier shuttles run from Mammoth Hotel to Indian Creek and from Old Faithful Snow Lodge to Fairy Falls. Guided tours on snowmobiles start at $275/person. Guided snow-coach tours are available for $30 to $150. Both types of tours run from late December through early March. The **Yellowstone Association Institute** (☎ *307/344–2293* ⊕ *www.yellowstoneassociation.org*) offers everything from daylong cross-country skiing excursions to multiday Lodging and Learning trips geared around hiking, skiing, and snowshoeing treks. Expect to pay $200 to $500 for excursions; $500 to $1,000 or more for Lodging and Learning trips.

EDUCATIONAL OFFERINGS

CLASSES AND SEMINARS

Yellowstone Institute. Stay in a log cabin in Lamar Valley or at the new field campus near Mammoth while taking a course about the park's ecology, history, or wildlife. Search with a historian for the trail the Nez Perce Indians took in their flight a century ago from the U.S. Army, or get the perfect shot with tips from professional photographers. Facilities are fairly primitive—guests do their own cooking and camp during some of the courses—but prices are reasonable. Some programs are specifically designed for young people and families. ✉ *North Park Rd., between Tower-Roosevelt and Northeast Entrance* ☎ *307/344–2294* ⊕ *www.yellowstoneassociation.org/institute* ☉ *Year-round, programs vary with season.*

RANGER PROGRAMS

Yellowstone offers a busy schedule of guided hikes, talks, and campfire programs. For dates and times, check the park's *Yellowstone Today* newsletter, available at all entrances and visitor centers.

☺
★
Evening Programs. Gather around to hear tales about Yellowstone's fascinating history, with hour-long programs on topics ranging from the return of the bison to 19th-century photographers. Every major area hosts programs, but check visitor centers or campground bulletin boards for updates. Most programs begin at 9 or 9:30 pm, though there are earlier programs at Norris, Fishing Bridge, and Old Faithful. ☉ *June–Aug., nightly at 9 and 9:30.*

☺
Daytime Walks and Talks. Ranger-led programs run during both the winter and summer seasons. Ranger Adventure Hikes are more strenuous and must be reserved in advance (the number of participants is limited),

but anyone can join the regular ranger talks and ranger walks. Winter programs are held at West Yellowstone, Old Faithful, and Mammoth.

🐻 **Junior Ranger Program.** Children ages 5 to 12 are eligible to earn patches and become Junior Rangers. Pick up the Junior Ranger Newspaper at Madison, Canyon, or Old Faithful for $3 and start the fun, self-guided curriculum.

TOURS

Old Yellow Bus Tour. The historic 14-passenger yellow buses are originals built in 1937. Restored and reintroduced in 2007, the White Motors' vehicles are the most elegant way to learn about the park. More than a dozen itineraries range from one hour to all day, and likely include wildlife sightings, photo opportunities, and some of the park's favorite landmarks. Yellow buses depart from various locations, including the Grey Wolf Inn in West Yellowstone and Canyon Lodge in Canyon. ☎ 866/439–7375 ⊕ *www.yellowstonenationalparklodges.com* 🖃 *$39–$70* ⊙ *June–Sept.*

WHERE TO EAT

In Yellowstone it's always a good idea to pack a cooler—that way you can carry some snacks and lunch items for a picnic and not have to worry about making it to one of the developed areas of the park, where all restaurants and cafeterias are managed by two companies (Xanterra and Delaware North). Generally, you'll find burgers and sandwiches at cafeterias and full meals (as well as a kids' menu) at restaurants. There is a good selection of entrées, such as free-range beef and chicken, game meats like elk and trout, and organic vegetables. At the several delis and general stores you can purchase picnic items, snacks, sandwiches, and desserts like fudge and ice cream. Considering that you are in one of the country's most remote outposts, selection is above average—but expect to pay more. Reservations are often needed for dinner at the dining rooms June through September.

WHAT IT COSTS				
¢	$	$$	$$$	$$$$
Restaurants under $8	$8–$12	$13–$20	$21–$30	over $30

Restaurant prices are per person for a main course at dinner.

$ ✕ **Canyon Lodge Cafeteria.** This busy lunch spot serves such traditional
AMERICAN   and simple American fare as country-fried steak and hot turkey sandwiches. Grab a tray and get in line. It stays open for late diners and is open for early risers, too, with a full breakfast menu. ⊠ *Canyon Village* ☎ *307/344–7311* 🖃 *AE, D, DC, MC, V* ⊙ *Closed early Sept.–early June.*

$$–$$$ ✕ **Grant Village Dining Room.** The floor-to-ceiling windows of this lake-
AMERICAN   shore restaurant provide views of Yellowstone Lake through the thick stand of pines. The most contemporary of the park's restaurants, it makes you feel at home with pine-beam ceilings and cedar-shake walls. You'll find dishes ranging from pasta to wild salmon to bison meat loaf; in late

season you'll find a sandwich buffet on Sunday. ⊠ *About 2 mi south of West Thumb junction in Grant Village* ☎ *307/344–7311* ⌕ *Reservations essential* ▤ *AE, D, DC, MC, V* ⊘ *Closed early Oct.–late May.*

¢–$ ╳ **Lake Lodge Cafeteria.** One of the park's most inspiring views overlook-
AMERICAN   ing the lake does not make up for this casual eatery's dreary cafeteria
⊙   menu. Roast turkey breast, Stroganoff, and pot roast are typical fare. On
the plus side, portions are hearty. It also has a full breakfast menu. ⊠ *At
end of Lake Village Rd., about 1 mi south of Fishing Bridge junction*
☎ *307/344–7311* ▤ *AE, D, DC, MC, V* ⊘ *Closed mid-Sept.–early June.*

$$–$$$$ ╳ **Lake Yellowstone Hotel Dining Room.** Opened in 1893 and renovated by
AMERICAN   Robert Reamer beginning in 1903, this double-colonnaded dining room
Fodor's Choice   off the hotel lobby is the most elegant dining experience in the park.
★   Arrive early and enjoy a beverage in the airy Reamer Lounge. The din-
ner menu includes attractive starters like an artisanal cheese plate and
organic salads. Main courses feature elk, buffalo, steak, and at least one
imaginative pasta, vegetarian, and fish entrée. The wine list focuses on
wines from California, Oregon, and Washington—with prices as high
as $125 for a bottle of Mondavi Reserve Cabernet. Reservations are
not needed for breakfast or lunch, but are essential for dinner; you can
make them up to a year in advance with your hotel room reservations;
or 60 days in advance without a hotel reservation. ⊠ *Approximately
1 mi south of Fishing Bridge Junction at Lake Village Rd., Lake Vil-
lage* ☎ *307/344–7311* ⌕ *Reservations essential* ▤ *AE, D, DC, MC, V*
⊘ *Closed early Oct.–mid-May*

$$–$$$ ╳ **Mammoth Hot Springs Dining Room.** A wall of windows overlooks an
AMERICAN   expanse of green that was once a military parade and drill field at
Mammoth Hot Springs. The art deco–style restaurant, decorated in
shades of gray, green, and burgundy, has an airy feel with its bentwood
chairs. Montana beef, bison, and fish are featured, and there is always
at least one pasta and vegetarian dish. ⊠ *5 mi south of North Entrance
in village of Mammoth Hot Springs* ☎ *307/344–7311* ⌕ *Reservations
essential* ▤ *AE, D, DC, MC, V* ⊘ *Closed mid-Oct.–mid-Dec. and
mid-Mar.–mid-May.*

¢–$ ╳ **Mammoth Terrace Grill.** Although the exterior looks rather elegant, this
FAST FOOD   restaurant in Mammoth Hot Springs serves only fast food, ranging from
biscuits and gravy for breakfast to hamburgers and veggie burgers for
lunch and dinner. ⊠ *Mammoth Springs Hotel, Mammoth Hot Springs,
5 mi south of North Entrance* ☎ *307/344–7311* ▤ *AE, D, DC, MC, V*
⊘ *Closed late Sept.–mid-May.*

$$–$$$$ ╳ **Obsidian Dining Room.** From the wood-and-leather chairs etched with
STEAK   figures of park animals to the intricate lighting fixtures that resemble
Fodor's Choice   snowcapped trees, there's ample Western atmosphere at this smaller
★   dining room (capacity: 106 guests) inside the Old Faithful Snow Lodge.
Aside from Mammoth Hot Springs Dining Room, this is the only place
in the park where you can enjoy a full dinner in winter. The French
onion soup will warm you up on a chilly afternoon; among the main
courses, look for prime rib, elk, beef, or salmon. ⊠ *Old Faithful Snow
Lodge, south end of Old Faithful Village* ☎ *307/344–7311* ▤ *AE, D,
DC, MC, V* ⊘ *Closed mid-Oct.–mid-Dec. and mid-Mar.–early May.
No lunch.*

18

$$–$$$
AMERICAN
✕ **Old Faithful Inn Dining Room.** Just behind the lobby, the original dining room designed by Robert Reamer in 1903—and expanded by him in 1927—has lodgepole-pine walls and ceiling beams and a giant volcanic-rock fireplace graced with a contemporary painting of Old Faithful by the late Paco Young. Note the etched-glass panels featuring par-tying cartoon animals that separates the dining room from the Bear Pit Lounge. These are reproductions of oak panels commissioned by Reamer in 1933 to celebrate the end of Prohibition. A buffet offers quantity over quality: bison, chicken, shrimp, two salads, two soups, and a dessert. You're better off choosing from nearly a dozen entrées on the à la carte menu, including grilled salmon, baked chicken, prime rib, and bison rib eye. Expect at least one vegetarian entrée in addition to a choice of salads and soups. Save room for a signature dessert such as the Caldera, a chocolate truffle torte with a molten middle. The most extensive wine list in the park offers more than 50 (all American) choices, including sparkling and nonalcoholic varieties (from $20 to $70 per bottle). For breakfast, there's a buffet as well as individual entrées. ✉ *Take first left off Old Faithful Bypass Road for hotel park-ing lot; Old Faithful Village* 🕾 *307/344–7311* 🖄 *Reservations essential* 🚍 *AE, D, DC, MC, V* ⊗ *Closed late Oct.–early May.*

¢–$$
AMERICAN
🕲
✕ **Old Faithful Lodge Cafeteria.** As you navigate this noisy family-oriented eatery, remember that you came for the park, not the services. This caf-eteria serves kid-friendly fare such as pizza and hamburgers. Its redeem-ing feature is that it has some of the best views of Old Faithful, so you can watch it erupt while you eat. It is not open for breakfast, but the snack shop just outside is, offering a small selection of baked goods and cereal. ✉ *At end of Old Faithful Bypass Rd., less than 300 yards east of Old Faithful* 🕾 *307/344–7311* 🚍 *AE, D, DC, MC, V* ⊗ *Closed mid-Sept.–mid-May.*

$$–$$$
AMERICAN
🕲
✕ **Roosevelt Lodge Dining Room.** At this rustic log cabin in a pine forest the menu ranges from barbecued ribs and baked beans to hamburgers and fries. Don't miss the killer cornbread muffins. Arrive early and watch horses and stagecoaches come and go from the front porch. For a real Western adventure, call ahead to join the popular chuckwagon cookout ($55; reservations essential) that includes an hour-long trail ride or a stagecoach ride. ✉ *Tower-Roosevelt, immediately south of junction of Northeast Entrance Rd. and Grand Loop Rd.* 🕾 *307/344–7311* 🚍 *AE, D, DC, MC, V* ⊗ *Closed early Sept.–early June.*

WHERE TO STAY

When deciding on which community to stay overnight in at the park, first consider whether you want to camp or stay in a hotel, then take into account the length of your trip. If you're only going to spend a day or two in the park, choose one location in the area that is most important for you to visit.

If you've never been to the park before and you only have a day or two, you'll probably want to choose Old Faithful, so you're near Yellow-stone's most famous geyser. But if you're more interested in seeing the wildlife, you may want to choose the Canyon or Lake area, so you're near Hayden and Pelican valleys.

On the other hand, if you're going to spend five days to a week or more in the park, you'll benefit from splitting your time between two or more regions (such as Old Faithful and Canyon), so you aren't spending all of your time driving to the various communities.

ABOUT THE HOTELS

Park lodgings range from two of the National Park System's magnificent old hotels to simple cabins to bland modern motels. Make reservations at least a year in advance for July and August for all park lodgings. Old Faithful Snow Lodge and Mammoth Hot Springs Hotel are the only accommodations open in winter. Ask about the size of beds, bathrooms, thickness of walls, and room location when you book, especially in the older hotels, where accommodations vary and upgrades are ongoing. Telephones have been put in some rooms, but there are no TVs. All park lodging is no-smoking. There are no roll-away beds available.

Hotel reviews have been condensed for this book. Please go to Fodors. com for full reviews of each property.

ABOUT THE CAMPGROUNDS

Yellowstone has a dozen frontcountry campgrounds scattered around the park, in addition to more than 200 backcountry sites. Most campgrounds have flush toilets; some have coin-operated showers and laundry facilities. ■TIP➔ **Fishing Bridge RV Park is the only campground offering water, sewer, and electrical hookups, and it is for hard-sided vehicles only (no tents or tent-trailers are allowed).**

The seven small campgrounds operated by the National Park Service—Norris, Lewis Lake, Mammoth, Indian Creek, Tower Fall, Slough Creek, and Pebble Creek—are available on a first-come, first-served basis. Choice sites like those at Slough Creek fill up by 10 am each day in the summer. To get a site in a NPS campground, arrive in the morning, pick out your site, pay (cash only, no change available) at a drop box near the campground host (look for a sign near the entrance to the campground), and leave your receipt and an inexpensive item (empty cooler, water jug, etc.) at the campsite. NPS limits campers to 14 days maximum at any one location in the summer.

The campgrounds run by Xanterra Parks & Resorts—Bridge Bay, Canyon, Fishing Bridge, Grant Village, and Madison—accept bookings in advance, although you'll pay about a $5 premium over the National Park Service campsites. These campgrounds are in great settings, but they are large—more than 250 sites each—and can feel very crowded. Tents and RVs coexist, although Xanterra designates certain areas as "tent only." Larger groups can reserve space in Bridge Bay, Grant, and Madison from late May through September. To reserve, call ☎307/344–7311.

If you're prepared to carry your own water and other necessities, you could also consider a backcountry campsite. There are more than 300 backcountry sites in the park, located as little as 2 mi from parking lots and trailheads. Check availability and obtain the required (though

18

free) permit at any ranger station, visitor center, or backcountry office; you may also pay $20 to reserve one of these sites in advance (the reservations open on April 1 each year). Talk to the park's accessibility coordinator about ADA-accessible backcountry sites.

Hotel reviews have been condensed for this book. Please go to Fodors. com for full reviews of each property.

WHAT IT COSTS					
	¢	$	$$	$$$	$$$$
Hotels	under $70	$70–$100	$101–$150	$151–$200	over $200
Campgrounds	under $10	$10–$17	$18–$35	$36–$49	over $50

Hotel prices are per night for two people in a standard double room in high season, excluding taxes and service charges. Camping prices are for a standard (no hookups, pit toilets, fire grates, picnic tables) campsite per night.

CANYON

$–$$ **Canyon Cabins.** These unassuming pine-frame cabins with private bathrooms are mostly in clusters of four, six, and eight units. **Pros:** affordability; location; private baths. **Cons:** too much asphalt; too many neighbors; no central lodge for hanging out. ✉ *North Rim Dr. at Grand Loop Rd., Canyon Village* ☎ *307/344–7901* ⊕ *www. yellowstonenationalparklodges.com* ↗ *428 cabins* ♿ *In-room: no a/c, no phone, no TV* ☰ *AE, D, DC, MC, V* ☯ *Closed late Sept.–late May.*

CAMPING   ⚠ **Canyon.** A massive campground with 250-plus sites, the Canyon camp-
$$ ground accommodates everyone from hiker/biker tent campers to large
☯   RVs. The campground is accessible to Canyon's many short trails. **Pros:** a great base in the middle of the park; stores, laundry, ranger station are close by. **Cons:** tents and RVs may share close quarters; not a very quiet campground; highest elevation (and therefore coldest!) campground in the park. ✉ *North Rim Dr., ¼ mi east of Grand Loop Rd., Canyon Village* ☎ *307/344–7311* ⊕ *www.yellowstonenationalparklodges.com* ♿ *Flush toilets, drinking water, guest laundry, showers, bear boxes, fire pits, picnic tables, public telephone, ranger station* ⚠ *272 sites* ☰ *AE, D, DC, MC, V* ☯ *Early June–early Sept.*

GRANT VILLAGE

CAMPING   ⚠ **Grant Village.** The park's second-largest campground, Grant Village
$$ has some sites with great views of Yellowstone Lake. Some of the sites are wheelchair accessible. **Pros:** group sites available; ease of access to Grand Teton National Park. **Cons:** huge campground means lots of noise; a long way from Mammoth Hot Springs and the wildlife-rich Lamar Valley. ✉ *South Entrance Rd., 2 mi south of West Thumb* ☎ *307/344–7311* ⊕ *www.yellowstonenationalparklodges.com* ♿ *Flush toilets, dump station, drinking water, guest laundry, showers, bear boxes, picnic tables, public telephone, ranger station* ⚠ *425 sites* ☰ *AE, D, DC, MC, V* ☯ *Late June–late Sept.*

MADISON

CAMPING
$$

⚠**Madison.** The largest National Park Service–operated campground, where no advance reservations are accepted, Madison has eight loops and nearly 300 sites. The outermost loop backs up to the Madison River, but other sites feel a bit claustrophobic. You can't beat the location, though, halfway between the Old Faithful village and the West Entrance. **Pros:** location; rivers; nearby geysers. **Cons:** no store for last-minute purchases; it's a busy junction (for both cars and buffalo). *⊠ Grand Loop Rd., Madison ☎307/344–7311 ⊕www. yellowstonenationalparklodges.com ⚒ Flush toilets, dump station, drinking water, bear boxes, fire pits, picnic tables, public telephone, ranger station ⚠ 277 tent/RV sites ▤AE, D, DC, MC, V ⊗ Closed late Oct.–early May.*

MAMMOTH HOT SPRINGS

$–$$

🏨**Mammoth Hot Springs Hotel and Cabins.** Built in 1937, this hotel has a spacious art deco lobby and rooms that are a bit smaller than at the park's other two historic hotels. **Pros:** great rates for a historic property; terrific place to watch elk in fall; "green" heat comes from recycled cooking oil. **Cons:** those elk can create traffic jams; rooms can get hot during the day. *⊠ Mammoth Hot Springs ☎307/344–7901 ⊕www. yellowstonenationalparklodges.com ⤳97 rooms, 67 with bath; 2 suites; 115 cabins, 76 with bath ⚒ In-room: no a/c, no phones (some), no TV. In-hotel: restaurant, bar ▤AE, D, DC, MC, V ⊗ Closed mid-Oct.–late-Dec. and early Mar.–early May.*

NORRIS

CAMPING
$

⚠**Norris.** Straddling the Gibbon River, a few of the "walk-in" sites here are among the best in the park. Anglers come for the brook trout and grayling. **Pros:** a fisherman's dream; some sites are especially secluded. **Cons:** the secret is out—this campsite fills up quickly. *⊠ Grand Loop Rd., Norris ☎307/344–2177 ⚒ Flush toilets, drinking water, bear boxes, fire pits, picnic tables, ranger station ⚠ 116 tent/RV sites ▤No credit cards ⊗ Closed late Sept.–mid-May.*

18

OLD FAITHFUL AREA

$$$–$$$$

Fodor's Choice
★

🏨**Old Faithful Inn.** This National Historic Landmark has been a favorite of five generations of park visitors. The so-called Old House, originally built in 1904, is worth a visit regardless of whether you are staying the night. **Pros:** a one-of-a-kind property, Old House rooms are truly memorable. **Cons:** thin walls; waves of tourists in the lobby; shared baths make you recall college dorm days. *⊠ Old Faithful Village ⊹ Take first left off Bypass Rd. to hotel parking lot and miss busy geyser parking area, Old Faithful ☎307/344–7901 ⊕www. yellowstonenationalparklodges.com ⤳324 rooms, 246 with bath; 6 suites ⚒ In-room: no a/c, no phone (some), no TV. In-hotel: restaurant, bar ▤AE, D, DC, MC, V ⊗ Closed early Oct.–early May.*

¢–$$

🏨**Old Faithful Lodge Cabins.** Typical of cabins throughout the park, these 97 cabins sitting at the northeast end of the village are very basic—lacking most amenities (including bathrooms in about one-third of the cabins), views, or character. However, the location can't be beat—cabins are almost as close to the geyser as Old Faithful Inn. **Pros:** a stone's

The Old Faithful Inn, which has been designated a National Historic Landmark, is worth a visit regardless of whether you plan to stay the night.

throw from Old Faithful geyser, all area services are within walking distance. **Cons:** some cabins lack private bathrooms; pretty basic. ✉ *South end of Old Faithful Bypass Rd.* ☎ *307/344–7901* ⊕ *www. yellowstonenationalparklodges.com* ⇨ *96 cabins, 60 with bath* ⬧ *In-room: no a/c, no phone, no TV. In-hotel: restaurant* ▤ *AE, D, DC, MC, V* ⊗ *Closed late Sept.–mid-May.*

$$$ 🏠 **Old Faithful Snow Lodge.** Built in 1998, this massive structure brings back the grand tradition of park lodges by making good use of heavy timber beams and wrought-iron accents. **Pros:** the most modern hotel in the park; the lobby and adjacent breezeway are great for relaxing. **Cons:** pricey, but you're paying for location and some modern conveniences. ✉ *Far end of Old Faithful Bypass Rd., Old Faithful* ☎ *307/344–7901* ⊕ *www.yellowstonenationalparklodges.com* ⇨ *100 rooms* ⬧ *In-room: no a/c, no TV. In-hotel: restaurant, bicycles* ▤ *AE, D, DC, MC, V* ⊗ *Closed mid-Oct.–mid-Dec. and mid-Mar.–late Apr.*

TOWER-ROOSEVELT

¢–$$ 🏠 **Roosevelt Lodge Cabins.** Near the beautiful Lamar Valley in the park's northeast corner, some of these rustic cabins have bathrooms, but most do not (there is a bathhouse nearby). Roughrider cabins may have woodstoves as the only heating system. You can make arrangements here for horseback and stagecoach rides. **Pros:** closest cabins to Lamar Valley and its world-famous wildlife; authentic Western ranch feel; Roughrider cabins are the most inexpensive in the park. **Cons:** cabins are close together; many lack private bathrooms. ✉ *Tower-Roosevelt Junction on Grand Loop Rd., Tower-Roosevelt* ☎ *307/344–7901* ⊕ *www.yellowstonenationalparklodges.com* ⇨ *80 cabins, 14 with bath*

♿ *In-room: no a/c, no TV. In-hotel: restaurant* ▭ *AE, D, DC, MC, V* ☾ *Closed early Sept.–early June.*

$ ◬ **Slough Creek.** Down the most rewarding 2 mi of dirt road in the park,
★ Slough Creek is a gem. Nearly every site is adjacent to the creek, which is prized by anglers. **Pros:** one of the last campgrounds to close annually; lower elevation often means warmer temps. **Cons:** with fewer than three-dozen sites here, arrive early in summer. ⊠ *Northeast Entrance Rd., 10 mi east of Tower-Roosevelt Junction* ☎ *No phone* ♿ *Pit toilets, bear boxes, fire pits, picnic tables* ◬ *29 tent/RV sites* ▭ *No credit cards* ☾ *Closed late Oct.–late May.*

YELLOWSTONE LAKE AREA

$$$–$$$$ ⌂ **Lake Yellowstone Hotel.** Dating from 1891, the white-and-pastel-color
★ hotel has maintained an air of refinement. **Pros:** the best views of any park lodging. **Cons:** the most expensive property in the park; not particularly kid-friendly. ⊠ *Lake Village Rd., Lake Village, about 1 mi south of Fishing Bridge* ☎ *307/344–7901* ⊕ *www.yellowstonenationalparklodges. com* ⌦ *194 rooms* ♿ *In-room: no a/c, no TV. In-hotel: restaurant, bar* ▭ *AE, D, DC, MC, V* ☾ *Closed late Sept.–mid-May.*

¢–$$ ⌂ **Lake Lodge Cabins.** Just beyond the Lake Yellowstone Hotel lies one
☺ of the park's hidden treasures: Lake Lodge, built in 1920. **Pros:** the best front porch in Yellowstone; affordability; good for families. **Cons:** no frills of any kind; sound of dribbling basketballs in the employee gym can ruin the lobby atmosphere. ⊠ *Lake Village Rd., Lake Village, about 1 mi south of Fishing Bridge* ☎ *307/344–7901* ⊕ *www. yellowstonenationalparklodges.com* ⌦ *186 rooms, 100 with bath* ♿ *In-room: no a/c, no phones, no TV. In-hotel: restaurant, bar* ▭ *AE, D, DC, MC, V* ☾ *Closed mid-Sept.–early June.*

CAMPING ◬ **Bridge Bay.** The park's largest campground, Bridge Bay is adjacent
$$ to the park's major marina. **Pros:** the best spot for boaters **Cons:** far
★ from a wilderness camping experience. ⊠ *3 mi southwest of Lake Village on Grand Loop Rd., Bridge Bay* ☎ *307/344–7311* ⊕ *www. yellowstonenationalparklodges.com* ♿ *Flush toilets, dump station, drinking water, showers, bear boxes, fire pits, picnic tables, public telephone, ranger station* ◬ *432 tent/RV sites* ▭ *AE, D, DC, MC, V* ☾ *Closed mid-Sept.–late May.*

$$ ◬ **Fishing Bridge RV Park.** Fishing Bridge is the only facility in the park that caters exclusively to recreational vehicles; RV services like tank filling/emptying and plug-ins are available. **Pros:** Fishing Bridge general store has supplies and groceries. **Cons:** this is active bear country, so safeguard your food, children, and pets. ⊠ *East Entrance Rd. at Grand Loop Rd.* ☎ *307/344–7311* ⊕ *www.yellowstonenationalparklodges. com* ◬ *344 RV sites* ♿ *Flush toilets, full hookups, dump station, drinking water, guest laundry, showers, bear boxes, picnic tables, public telephone, ranger station* ▭ *AE, D, DC, MC, V* ☾ *Closed late Sept.–mid-May.*

18

The Southwest

WHAT'S WHERE

The following numbers refer to chapters in the book.

19 **San Antonio, Austin, and Hill Country.** Texas's capital is known for its buzzing arts scene, some of the best live music in the country, and its friendly, laid-back, liberal population. Tourist mecca San Antonio has the colorful and lively Riverwalk, the legendary Alamo, and a myriad of family-fun spots like SeaWorld and Six Flags Fiesta Texas. In between is Hill Country, the land of the open road and one of Texas's most scenic regions. Along its rolling hills you'll encounter outpost towns, popular lakes, several caves, and historic attractions.

20 **Santa Fe and Taos.** On a 7,000-foot-high plateau at the base of the Sangre de Cristo Mountains, Santa Fe is one of the most visited small cities in the United States, with an abundance of museums, one-of-a-kind cultural events, art galleries, and distinctive restaurants and shops. Taos, 65 mi away, is smaller, feistier, quirkier, tougher, and very independent. Rustic and comfortably unpretentious, the town contains a handful of upscale restaurants with cuisines and wine lists as innovative as what you might find in New York.

21 **The Grand Canyon.** One of nature's longest-running

works in progress, the canyon both exalts and humbles the human spirit. Whether you select the popular South Rim or the remote North Rim, don't just peer over the edge—take the plunge into the canyon on a mule train, on foot, or on a raft trip.

22 Las Vegas. Sure, you've heard that what happens in Vegas, stays in Vegas—and there's no shortage of opportunities for you to put the "sin" in Sin City. But when you're ready to jump off the bar and curb your gambling habit, you can find plenty of other indulgences to quicken your pulse, smooth the edges, or delight the senses: luxurious spas, fascinating museums, headline shows, thrilling coasters, sprawling pools, and lavish buffets—often under one roof!

23 Southern Utah. Zion and Bryce and Arches—oh, my! Southern Utah may not be over the rainbow, but this stunning region, full of hoodoos, buttes, spires, and other improbably spectacular geological formations, is a dreamland for outdoor enthusiasts. Capitol Reef and Canyonlands complete the quintuple of National Parks in this part of the state where finding your verb (hike, bike, jeep, raft, climb, explore, etc.) or finding your bliss is what it's all about.

THE SOUTHWEST TOP ATTRACTIONS

Canyon Road, Santa Fe, New Mexico

(A) Canyon Road is lined with galleries, shops, and restaurants housed in adobe compounds, with thick walls, and lush courtyard gardens. Santa Fe is filled with public art and nowhere is it more apparent than along Canyon Road. The architectural influence of Old Mexico and Spain, and the indigenous Pueblo cultures, makes this street as historic as it is artistic.

Taos Pueblo, Taos, New Mexico

(B) A United Nations World Heritage Site, Taos Pueblo has the largest collection of multistory pueblo dwellings in the United States. These mud-and-straw structures have sheltered Tiwa-speaking Native Americans for almost 1,000 years (about 100 Taos Native Americans still live here full-time, practicing traditional ways of life, while 2,000 others live nearby in conventional homes).

The Strip, Las Vegas, Nevada

(C) Ever since Steve Wynn plopped a spewing, fiery volcano in front of his Mirage hotel, the competition in Vegas for your attention has gone into the Stratosphere. Each megaresort along the Strip attempts to outdo the other with a decidedly more-is-more ethos that has produced, among other things, a 45-foot bronze lion, a one-third-size Eiffel Tower re-creation, and a beam of light from atop of a 350-foot glass pyramid, which can be seen from space. Put your feet on the ground, plant you tongue firmly in your cheek, and prepare to be dazzled by the colossal excesses of Las Vegas Boulevard.

Delicate Arch, Arches National Park, Utah

(D) The iconic image on the state license plate is the reward for a 3-mi round-trip hike through sagebrush, over slickrock, and around a couple of treacherous spots in Arches National Park. Bring water and

snacks, and even little ones can make it, so long as you're prepared to carry them occasionally. Want to see more? There are nearly 2,000 more arches across this wind-carved landscape.

Angels Landing Trail, Zion National Park, Utah

(E) One of the Zion's most popular hikes, Angels Landing also happens to be one of the most spectacular. Stop at Scout's Lookout for a breathtaking view. This isn't the trail to take, though, if you are afraid of heights.

Hoodoos, Bryce Canyon National Park, Utah

(F) Best seen at sunrise or sunset, catch Bryce Canyon National Park's incomparable natural rock formations before they disappear! Relax, you have millions of years, but the red-and-orange towers and spires erode slowly and steadily. Queen's Garden and Wall Street are two of the more accessible and prominent trails.

The Alamo, San Antonio, Texas

(G) All Texans know about this site that inspired the battle cry for Texas independence, and John Wayne helped cement this historic mission firmly in the minds of everyone else. The building is small, but significant for its role in the fight against Mexico. All the soldiers who fought to defend it lost their lives here.

The North Rim, Grand Canyon National Park, Arizona

(H) Far less visited than the South Rim, and about 1,000 feet higher, the North Rim of the Grand Canyon has thinner crowds and fewer facilities. Less accessible, but arguably more spectacular with seven incredible viewpoints in a remote setting, the North Rim is well worth the extra effort.

TOP EXPERIENCES

Stargazing

Away from the American Southwest's metropolitan areas, the night sky is clear and unpolluted by lights or smog. In December, in the desert, the Milky Way stretches like a chiffon scarf across the celestial sphere. Lie on your back on the hood of your car at night, allow your eyes time to adjust to the darkness, and you'll see more stars than you could possibly have imagined.

Myriad astronomy books and Web sites have star charts that you can use to explore the cosmos; *National Geographic* has a cool interactive version with images from the Hubble Space Telescope (⊕ *www.nationalgeographic.com/stars/ chart*). To search for planets, visit ⊕ *www. stardate.org* or ⊕ *www.space.com/nightsky* before your trip. Or better yet, take a closer look at one of the Southwest's many observatories.

Hiking the Grand Canyon

You could spend the rest of your life hiking the Grand Canyon and never cover all the trails. There are hiking and walking trails aplenty, for all levels of fitness. Bright Angel Trail is the most famous, but it's tough: with an elevation change of more than 5,000 feet, don't try to hike to the Colorado River and back in one day. Less strenuous is part of the 12-mi Rim Trail, a paved, generally horizontal walk. Other outstanding choices are the South Kaibab Trail and the Hermit Trail. Many short routes lead to epic viewpoints, like the Cape Royal and Roosevelt Point trails on the North Rim.

River Rafting the Grand Canyon

Viewing the Colorado River from an overlook is one thing, but looking up at the canyon from the middle of the river is quite another. The river is a fickle beast. It's a whitewater, white-knuckle thrill ride that rumbles and hisses through the canyon one moment, and it's a relaxing stretch of lazy currents the next. As you float down the tranquil sections and take in the grandiose rock formations, you may even spot a mountain goat or two. Multiday trips include camping on the shore.

Staying in a National Park Lodge

Railroad companies in the early 1900s laid track to lure wealthy Easterners westward, and then took it an inspired step further by building luxury hotels at the end of the line. The Atchison, Topeka, and Santa Fe Railway built the spectacular Arizona lodge El Tovar, and Union Pacific ponied up dough for lodges at Bryce, Zion, and the Grand Canyon. Today, the rails don't drive tourism to the national parks they way they used to, but the lodges still do. And you don't have to be fabulously wealthy to stay in one. What makes them great? Previous wilderness accommodations were built like city hotels, but park lodges were designed to make guests feel comfortable in accommodations that grew out of nature. Some were built more than 100 years ago, when rooms and beds were smaller. However, the difference in room size is more than offset by the breathtaking surroundings and huge amount of public space offered on the lodge properties.

El Tovar. Set atop the South Rim of the Grand Canyon, El Tovar so blends into the landscape, with its stone, wood, and earthy tones, that it looks almost like another tier of the multilayered, multihued canyon. With the elegance of a European villa and warm atmosphere of a rustic log cabin, it is arguably the most luxurious of the lodges.

Bryce Canyon Lodge. Bryce Canyon Lodge, set in a grove of ponderosa pines within walking distance of the rim, opened in 1925 with 70 guest rooms, three deluxe suites, one studio room, and 40 log cabins. The property was known for its sing-aways, where employees lined up in front of the lodge and sang a farewell to departing guests.

Two more supreme in-the-park lodge experiences are **Zion Park Lodge**, Zion National Park, and **Grand Canyon Lodge**, North Rim, Grand Canyon National Park.

Staying in a Las Vegas Resort

A beguiling aspect of the Las Vegas megaresorts is that for all their immensity, they do not dwarf the individual. Step inside these grand sensoriums and you begin to feel as expansive as your surroundings. Perhaps it's the slight scent of cocoa butter in the air or the heady aroma of Mario Batali's Italian barbecue. Maybe it's the agreeable chimes and intermittent cheers from the casino floor. These elements combine and delight as you wander the seemingly endless floor plan, and soon you don't feel overwhelmed by the epic expanse, you feel broadened by it. This is the alchemy of the Las Vegas allure. Vegas is an equation where you + more = more of you: more chances to explore aspects of your personality that may be confined by the routine of daily life. A (very) short list of our favorites include: Encore, the Bellagio, THEHotel at Mandalay Bay, and Aria at CityCenter.

Gallery-Hopping in Santa Fe

Santa Fe, while holding strong in its regional art identity, emerged in the late 1990s as a more international art scene. Native American and Hispanic arts groups now include the work of contemporary artists who have pressed beyond the bounds of tradition. Bold color and the oft-depicted New Mexico landscape are still evident, but you're just as likely to see mixed-media collages by a Chinese artist currently living in San Francisco. A few Santa Fe outlets, such as the Riva Yares Gallery and evo Gallery, are dedicated to representing artists with Latin American roots. And just as Santa Fe welcomed early modernist painters who responded to the open landscape and the artistic freedom it engendered, contemporary artists working with edgier media, such as conceptual, performance, and installation art, are finding welcoming venues in Santa Fe, specifically at SITE Santa Fe museum. There are nearly 200 galleries in greater Santa Fe to explore with the best of representational, nonobjective, Native American, Latin American, cutting-edge, photographic, and soulful works that defy categorization.

Strolling the River Walk, San Antonio

Strolling along San Antonio's River Walk, away from the car traffic above, brings serenity and a different perspective on the city. In addition to walking it day or night, you can dine alfresco at one of the dozens of restaurants along the walk, or take a cruise on the river. With the recent expansion of the River Walk you'll have even more options and have a way to be connected to almost all of San Antonio's main attractions.

GREAT ITINERARIES

CANYON COUNTRY DRIVING TOUR

Zion and Bryce Canyon

DAYS 1 AND 2

From Las Vegas, head up I–15, and take the Route 9 exit to **①Zion National Park.** Spend your afternoon in the park—if it's April to October, take the National Park Service bus down Zion Canyon Scenic Drive (in fact, when the bus is "in season," cars are not allowed in the canyon). Overnight in Springdale, the bustling town right next to the park. The Best Western Zion Park Inn is your best bet for getting a room in the high season. Its Switchback Grille is excellent and open for breakfast, lunch, and dinner.

Spend the next morning in Zion. For a nice hike, try the short and easy (read: family-friendly) Canyon Overlook Trail, where you can gaze at the massive rock formations, such as East and West Temples. It won't take very long, even if you linger with your camera, so follow it with a stroll along the Emerald Pools Trail in Zion Canyon itself, where you might come across tame wild turkeys and ravens looking for handouts.

Depart the area via Route 9, the **②Zion–Mount Carmel Highway.** You'll pass through a 1.1-mi-long tunnel that is so narrow, RVs and towed vehicles must pay for an escort through. When you emerge, you are in slickrock country, where huge, petrified sandstone dunes are etched by ancient waters. Stay on Route 9 for 23 mi and then turn north onto U.S. 89. After 42 mi, you will reach Route 12, where you should turn east and drive 14 mi to the entrance of **③Bryce Canyon National Park.** The overall trip from Zion to Bryce Canyon is about 90 minutes.

THE PLAN

DISTANCE: 1,000–1,200 mi

TIME: 10 days

BREAKS: Overnight in Springdale, Bryce, Torrey, and Moab, UT; Cortez, CO; Monument Valley or Tuba City, AZ; Tusayan or South Rim, AZ

Central to your tour of Bryce Canyon is the 18-mi main park road, from which numerous scenic turnouts reveal vistas of bright red-orange rock (we recommend starting with the view at Sunrise Point). You'll notice that the air is a little cooler here than it was at Zion, so get out and enjoy it. Trails most worth checking out include the Bristlecone Loop Trail and the Navajo Loop Trail, both of which you can easily fit into a day trip and will get you into the heart of the park with minimum effort. Listen for peregrine falcons deep in the side canyons, and keep an eye out for the species of prairie dog that only lives in these parts. Overnight in the park or at Ruby's Inn, near the junction of Routes 12 and 63.

Capitol Reef

DAY 3

Head out this morning on the spectacular **④Utah Scenic Byway–Route 12.** If the views don't take your breath away, the narrow, winding road with little margin for error will. Route 12 winds over and through **⑤Grand Staircase-Escalante National Monument.** The views from the narrow hogback are nothing short of incredible. About 14 mi past the town of Escalante on Route 12 you can stop at **⑥Calf Creek Recreation Area** to stretch your legs or make a 5½-mi round-trip hike to a gorgeous backcountry waterfall.

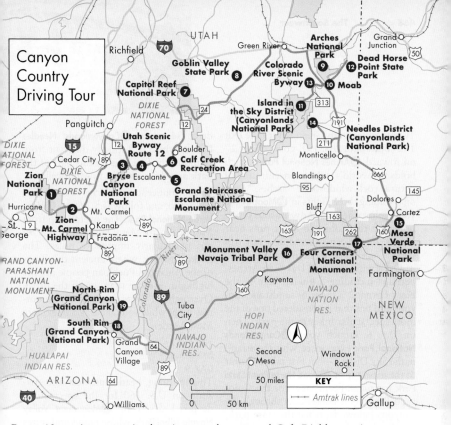

Canyon Country Driving Tour

Route 12 continues to gain elevation as you pass over Boulder Mountain.

At the intersection of Routes 12 and 24, turn east onto Route 24. You have traveled 112 mi from Bryce Canyon to reach ⓻Capitol Reef National Park. The crowds are smaller here than at other national parks in the state, and the scenery is stunning. Orchards in the small enclave of Fruita produce fruit—peaches, pears, and apples—in the late summer and early fall, and are close by ancient Indian rock art. If it's still daylight when you arrive, hike the 1-mi Hickman Bridge Trail if you want to explore a little, or stop in at the visitor center until 4:30 pm (later in the summer) and view pioneer and American Indian exhibits, talk with rangers about geography or geology, or watch a film. Nearby Torrey is your best bet for lodging, and be sure to eat at the seasonal Cafe Diablo, serving some of Utah's finest Southwest cuisine from late April to late October. Enjoy freshly brewed coffee and baked goods at Robber's Roost Books and Beverages while perusing a selection of regionally themed books, viewing local artisan jewelry, or even browsing the Internet.

Arches and Canyonlands

DAYS 4–6

Explore Capitol Reef more the next morning. When you leave, travel east and north for 75 mi on Route 24. If you want a break after about an hour, stop at the small ⓼Goblin Valley State Park, 12 mi west off Route 24. Youngsters love to run around the sandstone formations known as "goblins." Return to Route 24 and take it to I–70, turn east and continue your journey.

Twenty miles from Green River take exit 182 south onto U.S. 191, going about 27 mi toward ❾Arches National Park, which holds the world's largest concentration of natural rock windows or "arches." Plan on spending three nights in ❿Moab while you explore the area. Adventurous types, note that the Colorado River runs near Moab. If you can squeeze in a raft trip on this legendary Western waterway, do it. Otherwise, dedicate Day 5 to Arches, perhaps including a guided hike in the Fiery Furnace, a maze of sandstone canyons and fins that is considered one of the most scenic hikes in the park. Then on Day 6, launch your ⓫Canyonlands National Park experience with the Island in the Sky District—but first take a detour to the mesa top at ⓬Dead Horse Point State Park for magnificent views of the Colorado River as it goosenecks through the canyons below. To reach the state park, go 10 mi north of Moab on U.S. 191 to Route 313. Drive west for 15 mi, then turn right onto the unnamed road; continue for 6 mi to the Dead Horse fee station. To get from Dead Horse to Islands in the Sky, return to Route 313 and drive 7 mi past the Dead Horse turnoff to reach the park visitor center.

On your way back to Moab, enjoy the natural scenery on the ⓭Colorado River Scenic Byway (Route 128), which runs for about 44 mi along the river, or view manmade art by traveling down Route 279 (Potash Road), where ancient American Indian rock-art panels pop up after 4.8 mi from the U.S. 191 turnoff.

Mesa Verde
DAYS 7 AND 8
On Day 7, travel 42 mi south of Moab on U.S. 191. At this point, you have a choice to make. Either turn onto Route 211 and drive 34 mi to ⓮Canyonlands' Needles District, which is distinctly different from Island in the Sky, or skip this part of the park and drive straight to Monticello.

From Monticello, take U.S. 491 to Cortez, Colorado, and follow U.S. 160 to ⓯Mesa Verde National Park. The overall trip from Monticello to Mesa Verde is about 90 not particularly impressive miles. The park, however, where ancient dwellings of the Ancestral Puebloan people are the highlight, is more than worth the drive. Overnight in Cortez tonight and tomorrow night while you take Day 8 to explore Mesa Verde.

The Four Corners and Monument Valley
DAY 9
This morning, head southwest into Arizona on U.S. 160 for the spectacular, deep-red desert of ⓰Monument Valley Navajo Tribal Park, whose buttes and spires you will recognize from countless movie westerns and television commercials—if you want to do the 17-mi self-guided drive here, give yourself a couple of hours, or take a tram tour. Long before you get here, though, stop for a fun photoop at ⓱Four Corners National Monument, which straddles Colorado, New Mexico, Arizona, and Utah. Call it a night at Gouldings Lodge in Monument Valley, or in Tuba City. You'll want to get a good night's sleep and start early for your finale at **Grand Canyon National Park.**

The Grand Canyon
DAY 10
From Tuba City, you can reach the park via U.S. 89 and Route 64 for the South Rim, or Alternate 89 and Route 67 for the North rim. If you have only one day, do the ⓲South Rim. A good hike is the South Rim Trail, part of which is paved and

wheelchair accessible. You can overnight just outside the park in Tusayan or stay on the edge of the canyon in El Tovar (reserve far in advance).

To complete the loop, you can reach Zion National Park from the ⑲ **North Rim** by taking Alternate 89 north through the mountains. The road is winding and steep, but oh so beautiful. If you're heading back to Las Vegas from the South Rim take Route 64 south to Williams and then pick up I–40 West to U.S. 93 North.

TEXAS HILL COUNTRY DRIVING TOUR

The Hill Country is one of Texas's most scenic regions. It spans 23 counties and is filled with small towns, popular lakes, several caves, and historic attractions. The drive can be done in a few days or in a week, depending on how often you stop along the way. For the purpose of this itinerary, we've set it up as a four-day trip, with a full day in Fredericksburg and an afternoon in Austin. We've set it up from San Antonio, but you can jump in anywhere along the route.

Day 1: Cowboys and Art

Leaving from San Antonio, travel about 52 mi northwest to **Bandera**. It's known as the "Cowboy Capital of the World," both a reminder of its Wild West history and a symbol of its present-day Western theme–inspired tourism. The town is surrounded by numerous dude ranches that offer you a chance to take to the saddle for a few days of cowboy fun. Rodeos, country-Western music, and horse racing are also found in the area. If you want to get out and walk a bit, Hill Country State Natural Area is a good place to do

it. It has 5,300 acres of hills, creeks, and live oaks.

For lunch, stop in at the Full Moon Café, if you're after healthy fare, or at the O.S.T. Restaurant if you want that artery-busting, but oh-so-good chicken-fried steak.

In the afternoon, head north on Highway 173 for approximately 25 mi to **Kerrville**. Attractions in the area include the Y.O. Ranch, one of the most famous in the nation (you can call ahead for a tour ☎ *830/257–4440*), and the Museum of Western Art. If you want to stay overnight here, you can try the Y.O. or Guadalupe RV Resort (which has cabins with kitchens as well as campsites). Otherwise, take a brief detour west for 7 mi to **Ingram** to peruse the small cluster of art galleries and shops. (Note that most of the shops are closed on Monday.) When you're ready to call it a day, drive 32 mi (via Highway 16 from Kerrville) to Fredericksburg, the most popular city in the Hill Country.

Day 2: German Infusion

Welcome to Texas's enclave of German heritage. **Fredericksburg** is a longtime favorite with shoppers and bed-and-breakfast lovers. Downtown, the National Museum of the Pacific War honors Fredericksburg native Admiral Chester Nimitz, World War II commander-in-chief of the Pacific, and Wildseed Farms is the largest working wildflower farm in the United States. Or venture to nearby Enchanted Rock State Natural Area. This park contains the largest stone formation in the West; both easy and challenging climbs are available. In summer start early to avoid midday heat. For dinner, try German cuisine at a restaurant on Main Street.

Day 3: LBJ Day

On Day 3, head east on U.S. 290 for about 10 mi to **Stonewall**, the birth and burial place of Lyndon B. Johnson. At the Lyndon B. Johnson State Historical Park, you can catch a guided tour of the LBJ Ranch.

Approximately 10 mi east of Stonewall on U.S. 290 is **Johnson City**, named for LBJ's grandfather's nephew. The future president moved here from Stonewall when he was five years old. The Lyndon B. Johnson National Historic Park (different from the state one noted above) is here; it is the simply titled Boyhood Home of LBJ. Have lunch at the Silver K Café in Johnson City.

From Johnson City, head east on U.S. 290 for about 40 mi, then north on I–35 into **Austin**. The centerpiece of the city as well as the state government is the State Capitol. Guided tours of the statehouse, which stands taller than the national capitol, are offered daily. If you have time, visit the Governor's Mansion, just south of the capitol. It is filled with historic reminders of the many governors of the Lone Star State. You're taken past the main staircase, through the formal parlor, and finally into the dining room.

But if your time is limited, head just north of the capitol to learn more about LBJ at the University of Texas at Austin, the largest university in the nation. On its campus, the Lyndon Baines Johnson Library and Museum traces the history of Johnson's presidency through exhibits and films. On the eighth floor you can tour a model of the Oval Office as it looked during LBJ's administration. Spend the evening in Austin; if you love live music, be sure to visit Sixth Street while in town.

Day 4: The I–35 Strip

Approximately 40 mi south of Austin at Exit 206 off I–35 is **San Marcos**, a favorite with shoppers from around the state who come to browse its two massive outlet malls. Summer visitors find recreation along the banks of the San Marcos River. It's popular with snorkelers for its clear waters and is home to many fish (including some albino catfish) and various types of plant life.

When you've finished shopping, continue south to **Gruene** (pronounced Green), a former town and now technically a neighborhood in New Braunfels. From its founding in the 1870s, Gruene was a happening place with a swinging dance hall and busy cotton gin. But when the boll weevil arrived in Texas with the Great Depression on its heels, Gruene became a ghost town. Today that former ghost town is alive with small shops and restaurants as well as Texas's oldest dance hall, Gruene Hall—as lively today as it was in the late 1800s.

From Gruene, reach **New Braunfels** by returning to I–35 and continuing south, or by traveling south on Gruene Road. The self-proclaimed "Antique Capital of Texas" has numerous antiques shops, most in the downtown region. New Braunfels recalls its German heritage with many German festivals and even the name of its waterpark, Schlitterbahn (the largest in the state). Summer visitors will have the chance to canoe, raft, or inner-tube down the city's Guadalupe and Comal rivers. Outside of New Braunfels, you'll find cool conditions year-round in Natural Bridge Caverns.

From New Braunfels, take Highway 46 W for about 50 mi back to Bandera, or continue on I–35 back to San Antonio.

San Antonio, Austin, and Texas Hill Country

WORD OF MOUTH

"San Antonio has some really outstanding attractions and is good for at least three days. The Riverwalk is simply beautiful and very relaxing (especially a boat ride). San Antonio downtown has many neighborhoods which are pleasure just to stroll through. It is a very walkable city with sights and attractions at every corner"
—Echnaton

WELCOME TO SAN ANTONIO, AUSTIN, AND TEXAS HILL COUNTRY

TOP REASONS TO GO

★ **Peace Like a River Walk:** Savor its cypress-draped serenity on a dinner cruise aboard a river barge.

★ **Hispanic Culture:** From the Alameda Museum's Latino arts to Market Square, a Mexican sensibility saturates San Antonio.

★ **Great Live Music.** Austin's got the musicians and bands to suit your fancy—whether in an old-time dancehall, grimy hole-in-the-wall, or sleek, modern performance space.

★ **World-Class Food.** Austinites are passionate seekers of barbecue joints and Tex-Mex eateries, but also embrace a wide spectrum of world cuisines, for all tastes and budgets.

★ **Fredericksburg:** An afternoon on Main Street will likely net a collection of shopping bags, a hearty German meal, and a few samplings of German beer and Texas wine.

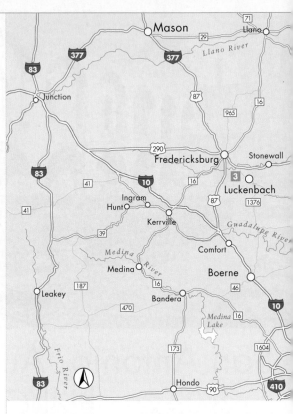

1 San Antonio. Remember the Alamo? The city's—and state's—famous landmark is here, though it sometimes gets lost amid the charm of the ever-popular River Walk, a shady pedestrian walkway along the San Antonio River that winds through town. Outside of town, Six Flags Fiesta Texas and SeaWorld San Antonio make a big splash with families and thrill seekers.

2 Austin. The state capital is home to the sprawling University of Texas campus and energetic 6th

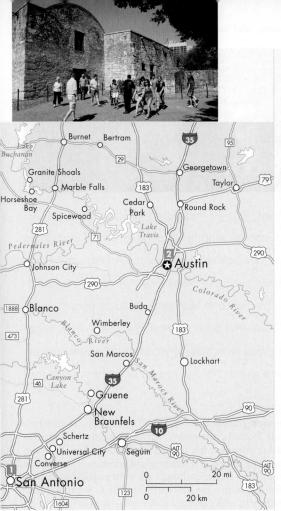

GETTING ORIENTED

Centrally located in Texas, you can access the Hill Country from I–35 or I–10, coming from the north and south or east and west, respectively. The area's gateway cities are Austin and San Antonio. Interstate 35 marks the Hill Country's eastern border, while San Antonio's State Loop 1604 forms the southern limit. The northern border is ambiguous, but generally includes everything south of Lake Buchanan and along State Highway 29. The western border is also open to interpretation, but is best followed along U.S. Highway 83 from Junction to Uvalde. Austin lies in Central Texas, about 163 mi southeast of the state's true center. On Austin's western border is the Hill Country, its eastern border the much flatter Blackland Prairie. Dallas is about 190 mi to the north, Houston 160 mi to the east.

19

Street—where music thumps into the wee hours of the night—and there are treasures like the Bob Bullock Texas State History Museum, a repository for exhibits about the Lone Star State's fascinating history.

3 The Hill Country. Dude ranches, lakes, wineries, German-flavored Fredericksburg, and lots of hills comprise Central Texas's Hill Country, west of Austin and north and northwest San Antonio. Scenic drives are popular here, and the best time of year to visit without a doubt is springtime, when the bluebonnets burst forth, coloring the landscape with their vibrant blue-violet hue.

The word "Texas" evokes images of wild prairies, ranches, and the Rio Grande winding through a desert populated with cacti and cowboy clones of John Wayne—or oil barons like J.R. Ewing living in plantation-style mansions in suburban Dallas. But the Lone Star State is much more than the sum of its Western and pop-culture stereotypes—it's a huge, diverse place filled with natural wonders, sophisticated cities, culinary treasures, historic towns, and vibrant arts and nightlife scenes.

Texas's number-one regional treasure, the Hill Country, is between two thriving, centrally located cities—artsy, left-wing Austin and internationally infused San Antonio. It's an area filled with rolling hills and placid lakes, charming towns, and independent wineries. The area has a dozen or more towns—Fredericksburg is the most popular with tourists—but its defining feature is the land itself. The Hill Country is etched with dramatic slopes of rocky terrain, wide-open vistas displaying an endless horizon of blue sky, and roads that seemingly go on forever. Graying cedar posts wrapped in rusty barbed wire meander about a rough-hewn landscape contrasted with rugged mesquite-plagued pastures and fields of vibrant wildflowers (especially colorful and fragrant come spring, when the famous bluebonnets blanket the hills). Majestic cypress trees shade idyllic spring-fed rivers, while sprawling-armed oak trees cool the sides of weather-worn ranch houses.

PLANNING

WHEN TO GO
There really isn't a bad time to visit the Austin, San Antonio, and Hill Country areas. However, if you are averse to heat, keep in mind that summer daily high temperatures average 90°–95° (some days above 100°), with high humidity to boot. Winters are mild, with days averaging 50°. October and April are prime months for a comfortable visit.

March and April are also peak season for viewing wildflowers, particularly the state's famed bluebonnets. Many seasonal events take place in spring or fall.

GETTING HERE AND AROUND

AIR TRAVEL

San Antonio International Airport (SAT) and Austin-Bergstrom International Airport (AUS) are the most direct and economical gateways to the Hill Country by air.

Airport Contacts Austin–Bergstrom International Airport (✉ *3600 Presidential Blvd., Austin* ☎ *512/530–2242* ⊕ *www.ci.austin.tx.us/austinairport*). **San Antonio International Airport** (✉ *9800 Airport Blvd., San Antonio* ☎ *210/207–3411* ⊕ *www.sanantonio.gov/aviation*).

Austin Airport Shuttle SuperShuttle (☎ *512/258–3826* ⊕ *www.supershuttle.net*).

San Antonio Airport Shuttle SATRANS (☎ *210/281–9900*).

CAR TRAVEL

SAN ANTONIO   Three interstate highways converge in San Antonio: I–35 links San Antonio with Dallas and Austin to the north and Laredo and the Mexican border to the south; I–10 connects San Antonio to Houston to the east and then veers northwest before heading to El Paso and the West Coast; and I–37 connects San Antonio to Corpus Christi on the Gulf of Mexico. In most cases, having a car in San Antonio is extremely helpful. As in most Texas cities, things are quite spread out. If, however, you're focusing on the River Walk and surrounding area, you should park at your hotel and sightsee on foot (or via the downtown streetcars ⊕ *www.viainfo.net/BusService/Streetcar.aspx*).

AUSTIN   The major entryway into Austin is I–35. Loop 1 (also known as MoPac) joins with I–35 on Austin's northern and southern outskirts. U.S. 183 runs at a slight north–south diagonal. East–west Highway 71 and U.S. 290 connect Austin and Houston.

Although the highways are clearly marked, many of them have been given other names as they pass through Austin. Keep in mind that U.S. 183 runs parallel to Research Boulevard for one stretch, Anderson Lane at another, and Ed Bluestein Boulevard at yet another, while Highway 71 is also known as Ben White Boulevard.

Downtown is laid out in a conventional grid of numerical streets. The majority of these are one-way streets: even-numbered streets generally run one way to the west, and odd-numbered streets generally run one way to the east.

HILL COUNTRY   This is the land of the open road. The best, and really the *only* way to access the Hill Country is by car. From San Antonio International Airport, take Highway 281 north for about 90 mi through Blanco, Johnson City, Marble Falls, and Burnet, or cut across on State Loop 1604 heading west to I–10 West and you'll go through Boerne, Comfort, and Kerrville, and can then easily make your way to Bandera and Medina, or Fredericksburg and Mason. From Austin-Bergstrom International Airport, take Highway 290 west to Highway 281 to get to most of the Hill Country towns.

19

ABOUT THE RESTAURANTS

SAN ANTONIO

San Antonio is big enough and has enough demanding conventioneers to support fine dining. But it still has a relaxed small-town feel that makes it easy to eat out almost anywhere without much fuss. Few restaurants require jackets; the dress code at most other nice restaurants pretty much stops at "no shorts, please." Reservations and long waits are rare except at a few high-end restaurants and at peak times on the River Walk. Essentially, San Antonio cuisine is about two things: Mexican-inspired flavors and meat. Mexican, Tex-Mex, Latin, and a variety of other fusion variations crowd this bi-cultural town.

AUSTIN AND HILL COUNTRY

Apart from tourist- and student-heavy 6th Street, Austin's restaurant scene is geared to local tastes, and is as diverse as it's celebrated music scene. Though Mexican, Tex-Mex, and barbecue are the default cuisines, everything from Brazilian to Pacific Rim fusion has made headway here, and there are strong vegetarian and natural-food followers. There are several fine barbecue options within the city limits, mostly simple places where your meat is sliced and placed unceremoniously on the plate with pickles, onions, and jalapeño slices. Fine dining is well represented in Austin, and upscale continental—especially Central European (the area was settled by Germans and Czechs)—and New American establishments offer traditional fare and inventive dishes with Southwestern touches.

The Hill Country is an extension of the great eating opportunities—the amazing Tex-Mex and barbecue—of San Antonio and Austin, with the addition of heavy German influences. Fredericksburg certainly corners the market for relatively authentic German fare, but Boerne, Comfort, New Braunfels, and everywhere in between serve decent schnitzel and wurst. Barbecue bests are spread all over. On the Hill Country backroads you're not going to get a whole lot of haute cuisine delivered by celebrity chefs, but you'd be surprised at some of the fine dining experiences you can have here. With the exception of a few live-music bars and venues, most restaurants and cafés are finished serving by 9 or 10.

ABOUT THE HOTELS

SAN ANTONIO

Many visitors choose to stay downtown to be close to the Alamo, River Walk, museums, and other attractions. Downtown almost everything is accessible on foot or via river taxi or trolley. The city has one shuttle service from the airport that serves all downtown hotels ($14 one-way, $24 round-trip). Several national chain hotels are concentrated along the River Walk and adjacent to the convention center. Historic hotels and several boutique hotels have opened up, promoting spa weekends and indulgent getaways.

Several full-service resorts about a 20- to 30-minute drive from downtown, most near SeaWorld and Six Flags, offer golf, tennis, on-site water parks, children's activities, and restaurants. Bed-and-breakfasts are concentrated in a few of the national historic districts. San Antonio is a major convention destination; peak seasons are generally spring and

Take a scenic stroll through San Antonio on the famed River Walk.

late fall. At the right time you can get some great deals for top-quality accommodations, but during special events (Fiesta week, major conventions, Spurs games) expect to pay top dollar and make reservations months in advance.

AUSTIN

Finding a place to stay in Austin isn't hard. Finding a place with personality is harder. Downtown, ample brand-name high-rises offer anonymous luxury, but despite Austin's history and capital status there are only a few stately, historic hotels. The I–35 corridor is a logjam of chain motels ranging from pleasant to horrid. In the tech-centered Northwest it's hard to drive any distance without passing an all-suites executive lodging.

Downtown, the Driskill is a *grande dame* that still shines. A couple of old motor courts on South Congress capture Austin's bohemian charms. There are also several well-run bed-and-breakfasts in historic homes. You'll especially need to plan ahead during a University of Texas home football game, the South by Southwest festival in March, the Austin City Limits festival in September, or legislative sessions (held in odd-numbered years). At slower times many hotels offer deep discounts. In general, only hotels near Austin–Bergstrom International Airport have free airport shuttles.

HILL COUNTRY

There are chain hotels sprinkled throughout the region, particularly in Fredericksburg and Marble Falls, but you're missing out on the local flavor if you don't try or (at least investigate) the many bed-and-breakfasts, guesthouses, ranches, and small resorts in the area. From historic and authentically restored guesthouses in Fredericksburg to the plush mini-resort luxury of Escondida Resort in Medina there's a lot from which to choose.

Bed-and-breakfasts and guesthouses are not the same thing. Reservation agencies such as the Gästehaus Schmidt, in Fredericksburg, or Boerne Reservations will help you determine what accommodations are right for you.

Hotel reviews have been condensed for this book. Please go to Fodors. com for full reviews of each property.

WHAT IT COSTS				
¢	$	$$	$$$	$$$$
Restaurants	under $8	$8–$12	$13–$20	$21–$30	over $30
Hotels	under $50	$50–$100	$101–$150	$151–$200	over $200

Hotel prices are per night for two people in a standard double room in high season, excluding taxes (16.75% for San Antonio; 15% for Austin; 8. 25%–13% in Hill Country) and service charges.

SAN ANTONIO

Wake up in the Alamo City with the scent of huevos rancheros in the air and the sound of mariachis and you know you're someplace special. The heart of the visitor area is the *Paseo del Rio*—the River Walk—winding through downtown below street level. Nestled among tall buildings and cypress trees, and protected from traffic noises, the River Walk attracts crowds to its high-rise and boutique hotels, specialty shops, and restaurants with alfresco dining. Meanwhile, families are drawn to the big theme parks on the northwestern edge of town, SeaWorld San Antonio and Six Flags Fiesta Texas. Given the city's proximity to Mexico, it's not surprising that the rich tapestry of San Antonio's heritage has a good deal of Hispanic culture woven into it. Visitors can browse in shops selling Mexican crafts and jewelry, dine on Tex-Mex food, and enjoy Spanish music and mariachi bands at Market Square. The city also reflects German, French, and African influences—truly a multicultural experience.

EXPLORING

Much of downtown San Antonio can be explored on foot or by way of the trolley system that runs frequently between points of interest. Depending on whom you ask, the number of neighborhoods in San Antonio varies. The San Antonio Convention & Visitors Bureau breaks the city into quadrants—Northside, Eastside, Southside, and Westside, with museums in the north, heritage sites on the east and west, and missions in the south.

DOWNTOWN AND THE RIVER WALK

Fodor's Choice
★

Alamo. At the heart of San Antonio, this one-time Franciscan mission stands as a repository of Texas history, a monument to the 189 Texan volunteers who fought and died here during a 13-day siege in 1836 by Mexican dictator General Antonio López de Santa Anna. The Texans lost, but the defeat inspired a later victory in Texas's bid for independence with the rallying cry "Remember the Alamo." Today the historic shrine and barracks contain the guns and other paraphernalia used by such military heroes as William Travis, James Bowie, and Davy Crockett, who all died defending the Alamo. You can step inside the small mission and tour on your own, and then listen to a 20-minute history talk (talks occur every 30 minutes during operating hours except at noon, 12:30, and 1). ⊠ *300 Alamo Plaza, Houston and Crockett, Downtown* ☎ *210/225–1391* ⊕ *www.thealamo.org* ✉ *Free* ☺ *Mon.–Sat. 9–5:30, Sun. 10–5:30 (it generally stays open until 7 Fri. and Sat. July and Aug.).*

Fodor's Choice
★

River Walk. The *Paseo del Rio* is the city's (and the state's) leading tourist attraction. Built a full story below street level, it comprises about 7 mi of scenic stone pathways lining both banks of the San Antonio River as it flows through downtown, connecting many of the city's tourist attractions. In some places the walk is peaceful and quiet; in others it is a mad conglomeration of restaurants, bars, hotels, shops, and strolling mariachi bands, all of which can also be seen from river taxis and charter boats. ⊠ *Access from many points downtown; it starts near Rivercenter Mall at 849 E. Commerce St.* ☎ *210/227–4262* ⊕ *www. thesanantonioriverwalk.com* ✉ *Free.*

KING WILLIAM AND MONTE VISTE HISTORIC DISTRICTS

In the late 19th century, leading German merchants settled the 25-block King William Historic District south of downtown. Today the area's Victorian mansions, set in a quiet, leafy neighborhood, are a pleasure to behold. Each December, on the first Saturday, you can tour several of the homes during the King William Home Tour. During Fiesta each April the area hosts a fair. For a map of the area and information on district events, contact the **King William Association** (⊠ *1032 S. Alamo St., San Antonio* ☎ *210/227–8786* ⊕ *www.kingwilliamassociation.org*).

ALAMO HEIGHTS AND BRACKENRIDGE PARK

The area north of downtown (but south of the airport) is known as Alamo Heights. This affluent residential neighborhood contains an abundance of cultural establishments, a top university, and the lush, locally loved (and much used) Brackenridge Park.

Fodor's Choice
★

Brackenridge Park. The 343-acre green space between U.S. 281 and Broadway Street makes an excellent setting for a picnic or a stroll, and also offers jogging trails, public art, athletic fields, a golf course, concessions, and rides on a carousel and miniature train. The park is much more than just an outdoorsy retreat. It's home to—or in the vicinity of—many noteworthy attractions: the San Antonio Zoo, the San Antonio Botanical Gardens, the Japanese Tea Gardens, McNay Art Museum, and the Witte Museum. Budget at least half a day here. ⊠ *3910 N. Saint Mary's St., Alamo Heights* ☎ *210/207–8480* ✉ *Free* ☺ *Daily 5 am–11 pm.*

19

SOUTHSIDE

The main attractions south of downtown are the historic missions.

★ Except for the Alamo, San Antonio's missions constitute **San Antonio Missions National Historical Park** (✉ *2202 Roosevelt Ave.* ☎ *210/932–1001 visitor center, 210/534–8833 headquarters* ⊕ *www.nps.gov/saan* ✍ *Free* ⊙ *Daily 9–5*). Established along the San Antonio River in the 18th century by Franciscan friars, the missions stand as reminders of Spain's most successful attempt to extend its New World dominion northward from Mexico. The missions were also centers of work, education, and trade. They represented the greatest concentration of Catholic missions in North America, and were the basis of the founding of San Antonio. Today the four missions are active parish churches, and each illustrates a different concept of mission life.

Start your tour at the stunning **Mission San José**, the "Queen of Missions." It's adjacent to the visitor's center, where a National Park Service ranger or docent illuminates the history of the missions. Here you can pick up a driving map of the Mission Trail that connects San José with the other missions. ✉ *6701 San José Dr.* ☎ *210/922–0543* ✍ *Free* ⊙ *Daily 9–5.*

Mission Concepción, the oldest unrestored stone church in the nation, is known for its colorful frescoes, or wall paintings. ✉ *807 Mission Rd., at Felisa St.* ☎ *210/534–1540* ✍ *Free* ⊙ *Daily 9–5.*

Mission San Juan, with its Romanesque arches, has a serene chapel. This mission once supplied all its own needs, from cloth to crops, and a trail behind the mission winds along the low river-bottom land and provides a look at the many indigenous plants formerly used by the mission. ✉ *9101 Graf Rd.* ☎ *210/534–0749* ✍ *Free* ⊙ *Daily 9–5.*

Mission Espada, the southernmost mission, was named for St. Francis of Assisi, founder of the monastic order of Franciscans (its full name is San Francisco de la Espada). The mission includes an Arab-inspired aqueduct that was part of the missions' famous *acequia* water management system. ✉ *10040 Espada Rd.* ☎ *210/627–2021* ✍ *Free* ⊙ *Daily 9–5.*

NORTH AND NORTHWEST

⊙ **Six Flags Fiesta Texas.** Set within 100-foot quarry walls, this amusement park features sectors highlighting Texas's rich diversity, from the state's Mexican and German culture to its rip-roarin' Western past. Eight take-it-to-the-max roller coasters are here, including Superman: Krypton Coaster (the Southwest's largest steel coaster) and the new Goliath, a suspended looping coaster that opened in spring 2008. The more than 40 other rides include a white-water-rapids flume and a tower drop. Rounding out the offerings are many excellent family-friendly musical shows. Concerts with big-name artists are also held periodically throughout the season. ✉ *17000 I–10 W, at jct. of Loop 410, Northwest* ☎ *210/697–5050* ⊕ *www.sixflags.com/fiestaTexas* ✍ *$54.99* ⊙ *Mar.–Dec., hrs vary.*

Fodor's Choice ★

⊙ **SeaWorld San Antonio.** Sprawled across 250 acres northwest of the city, this Texas-sized marine-themed amusement park (the world's largest such park) delights animal lovers with its whales, dolphins, sharks, and sea lions, as well as thrilling rides—including the Great White, Texas's

Fodor's Choice ★

19

first inverted steel coaster, and the Steel Eel, a "hypercoaster" reaching speeds of 65 mph. SeaWorld's newest coaster, Journey to Atlantis, has a water component and spins you backward. The park's newest attraction, Sesame Street Bay of Play, features children's rides and opportunities to meet favorite Sesame characters. Amid acres of manicured gardens, the huge park also offers marine shows and a water park with swimming pools and waterslides—a guaranteed hit with water-lovin' kids. Shamu, of course, is the most beloved animal in the park. His performance tank/arena has lots of water—5 million gallons of it, in fact (except when it's being splashed all over audience members who dare to sit too close). ⊠ *10500 Sea World Dr., Northwest* ☎ *800/700–7786* ⊕ *www.seaworld.com/sanantonio* ⊠ *$59.99* ⊗ *Mar.–Dec., hrs vary.*

WHERE TO EAT

$$–$$$$
AMERICAN
River Walk
Fodor's Choice
★

✕ **Biga on the Banks.** Like Texas, enthusiastic chef Bruce Auden's menu is big and eclectic, and the dining atmosphere manages to be both bigger than life and romantic. Dishes change daily to take advantage of the freshest food available, ranging from seared red grouper grits to 11-spice Axis venison chops. Don't skip out on dessert, which may be the best in town: the sticky toffee pudding is a must. This is one of the best spots for a leisurely dinner on the River Walk, if you can get a reservation. ⊠ *203 S. Saint Mary's St. (W. Market St.), River Walk* ☎ *210/225–0722* ⊕ *www.biga.com* ⌖ *Reservations essential* ⊟ *AE, D, MC, V* ⊗ *No lunch.*

¢–$$
BURGER
King William

✕ **Casbeers at the Church.** Since 1932, Casbeers has been serving up live music with their famous enchiladas and mammoth hamburgers. Now located in the old Alamo Methodist Church building, Casbeers remains a local institution, with Kinky Friedman among its many fans. In fact, there's a burger named after him. Come here for the rustic environs, some good music, and a slice of old San Antonio, but don't expect a culinary revelation. Beer and wine flow freely. ⊠ *1150 S. Alamo St., King William* ☎ *210/271–7791* ⊟ *AE, MC, V* ⊗ *Closed Sun. except for occasional "Sunday Brunches."*

$$$$
SOUTHWESTERN
Northwest
Fodor's Choice
★

✕ **Francesca's at Sunset.** As the name would suggest, stunning views of the evening sky are part of the draw at the Westin at La Cantera's showcase restaurant. But chef Ernie Estrada, a San Antonio native, also adds considerable local flair to a Southwestern menu originally crafted by world-renowned restaurateur Mike Miller. Those wanting a truly memorable dining experience can choose from powerful eclectic dishes ranging from fillet of antelope to spicy grilled duck to chili-rubbed buffalo rib eye. If you can nab a reservation, it's well worth the trip across town. ⊠ *Westin La Cantera Resort, 16641 La Cantera Pkwy., Northwest* ☎ *210/558–6500 Ext. 4803* ⌖ *Reservations essential* ⊟ *AE, D, DC, MC, V* ⊗ *No lunch.*

$$
TEX-MEX
Downtown
Fodor's Choice
★

✕ **Mi Tierra Café and Bakery.** In the heart of Market Square lies one of San Antonio's most venerable culinary landmarks. Opened in 1941 as a place for early-rising farmers to get breakfast, Mi Tierra is now 24-hour traditional Mexican restaurant, bakery, and bar. Its hallmark breakfasts are served all day, and the *chilaquiles famosas*—eggs scrambled with corn tortilla strips and topped with *ranchero* (mild tomato-based) sauce and cheese—are alone worth coming back for again and again. Truly memorable tacos, enchiladas, chalupas, and house specialties, all made from fresh ingredients, are served at lunch and dinner. The giant carved oak bar serves up aged tequilas, authentic margaritas, draft beer, and mixed drinks. The bakery has an enormous selection of *pan dulces* (Mexican pastries) and excellent coffee. ⊠ *218 Produce Row, Market Square* ☎ *210/225–1262* ⌘ *Reservations not accepted* ⊟ *AE, D, DC, MC, V.*

$$$ ✕**Ostra.** This is the high-energy, but romantic dining room at the
SEAFOOD Mokara Hotel. Executive Chef John Brand "fishes" for seafood from
River Walk around the world, producing exotic new dishes as well as tempting standards. Ostra also boasts an oyster bar, a great wine list, and terrace dining with spectacular views of the river. ⊠ *212 W. Crockett St., River Walk* ☎ *210/396–5800* ⊟ *AE, D, DC, MC, V.*

WHERE TO STAY

$$ ▦ **Drury Inn & Suites San Antonio Riverwalk.** One of the best values among
RIVER WALK River Walk hotels, the Drury Inn & Suites is in the landmark Petroleum Commerce Building on the riverfront. **Pros:** Great value for families and business travelers, premium location for sightseeing, free nightly cocktail reception. **Cons:** Solid traditional rooms and decor nothing to write home about. ⊠ *201 N. Saint Mary's St., River Walk* ☎ *210/212–5200* ⊕ *www.druryhotels.com* ⇥ *150 rooms, 38 suites* ⌂ *In-room: refrigerator, Internet, Wi-Fi. In-hotel: restaurant, bar, pool, gym, laundry facilities, laundry service, Wi-Fi hotspot, parking (paid), some pets allowed* ⊟ *AE, D, DC, MC, V* ⎮⎺⎥*BP.*

$$$$ ▦ **The Fairmount.** At the pinnacle of boutique luxury lodgings in San
DOWNTOWN Antonio, this historic hotel offers premium amenities such as flat-screen
Fodor's Choice TVs, canopy beds, verandas, and marble baths. **Pros:** Dripping with
★ character and charm. **Cons:** Expensive, and not exactly right in the thick of the River Walk/downtown action. ⊠ *401 S. Alamo St., Downtown* ☎ *210/224–8800 or 877/ 229–8808* ⊕ *www.thefairmounthotel-sanantonio.com* ⇥ *37 rooms 37 suites* ⌂ *In-room: refrigerator (some), Wi-Fi. In-hotel: restaurant, room service, gym, bar, laundry service, Wi-Fi hotspot, parking (paid), some pets allowed* ⊟ *AE, D, DC, MC, V.*

$$$$ ▦ **Hyatt Regency Hill Country Resort.** Step into relaxation at this sophisti-
NORTH/ cated yet homey country resort with lots of shade—a key feature when
NORTHWEST the mercury soars during a San Antonio summer. **Pros:** Great value for
⟲ an expansive resort; tons of activities to keep the kids busy; great gen-
Fodor's Choice eral store on-site. **Cons:** Quite a distance from the city's main downtown
★ and River Walk attractions. ⊠ *9800 Hyatt Resort Dr., North/Northwest* ☎ *210/647–1234* ⊕ *www.hillcountry.hyatt.com* ⇥ *428 rooms, 72 suites* ⌂ *In-room: safe, refrigerator, Internet, Wi-Fi. In-hotel: 7 restaurants, room service, bars, golf courses, tennis courts, pools, gym, spa, bicycles, children's programs (ages 3–12), laundry facilities, parking (free), Internet terminal, Wi-Fi hotspot* ⊟ *AE, D, DC, MC, V.*

$$$–$$$$ ▦ **Menger Hotel.** Since its 1859 opening, the Menger has lodged, among
DOWNTOWN others, Robert E. Lee, Ulysses S. Grant, Theodore Roosevelt, Oscar
★ Wilde, Sarah Bernhardt, Roy Rogers, and Dale Evans. **Pros:** Close to Alamo; good food. **Cons:** Rooms are more worn than at newer

19

properties. ✉*204 Alamo Plaza, Downtown* ☎*210/223–4361 or 800/345–9285* ⊕ *mengerhotel.com* ⚲*290 rooms, 26 suites* ⚹ *In-room: kitchen (some), Internet. In-hotel: restaurant, room service, bar, pool, gym, spa, laundry service, Wi-Fi hotspot, parking (paid), some pets allowed* ▤*AE, D, DC, MC, V.*

$$$$
KING WILLIAM
Fodor's Choice
★

▦ **Ogé House.** This gorgeous B&B sits on 1½ acres that back up to a quiet section of the river running through the King William Historic District. **Pros:** Exquisitely decorated; staff goes beyond the call of duty. **Cons:** Pricey; River Walk area not within easy walking distance. ✉*209 Washington St., King William Historic District* ☎*210/223–2353 or 800/242–2770* ⊕ *www.ogeinn.com* ⚲*10 rooms* ⚹ *In-room: refrigerator, DVD (some), Internet, Wi-Fi. In hotel: Internet terminal, Wi-Fi hotspot, parking (free), no kids under 16* ▤*AE, D, DC, MC, V* ▦◎*BP.*

$$$$
RIVER WALK
Fodor's Choice
★

▦ **Mokara Hotel & Spa.** Luxury accommodations and services are offered at this hotel in the historic 19th-century L. Frank Saddlery Building with an entrance facing the River Walk. **Pros:** Everything a five-star hotel professes to be; quiet River Walk location, excellent spa. **Cons:** Pricey; some extra charges for sundries, expensive parking. ✉*212 West Crockett St., River Walk* ☎*210/396–5800 or 866/605–1212* ⊕*www. mokarahotels.com* ⚲*96 rooms, 2 suites* ⚹ *In-room: safe, Wi-Fi. In-hotel: 2 restaurants, room service, bar, pool, gym, spa, laundry service, Wi-Fi hotspot, parking (paid), some pets allowed* ▤*AE, D, DC, MC, V.*

$$$$
NORTH/
NORTHWEST
★

▦ **Westin La Cantera.** Make a list of the things you'd look for in a luxury, full-service resort, and La Cantera has it. **Pros:** San Antonio's top resort hotel, lush common areas and rooms; virtually every amenity you could ask for. **Cons:** Removed from downtown and the River Walk; expensive. ✉*16641 La Cantera Pkwy., North/Northwest* ☎*210/558–6500* ⊕*www.westinlacantera.com* ⚲*445 rooms, 25 suites, 38 villas* ⚹ *In-room: safe, kitchen (some), Internet. In-hotel: 4 restaurants, room service, bars, golf courses, tennis courts, pools, gym, spa, children's programs (ages 3–17), laundry facilities, laundry service, Internet terminal, public Wi-Fi hotspot, parking (free)* ▤*AE, D, DC, MC, V.*

NIGHTLIFE AND ENTERTAINMENT

Much of San Antonio's nightlife is concentrated around the major tourist zones such as the River Walk area, and is aimed at pleasing the convention crowd with mainstream jazz and mariachi serenades. Jim Cullum's Jazz Band's Dixieland at the **Landing** (✉*Hyatt Regency, 123 Losoya St., Downtown* ☎*210/233–7266*) in the Hyatt Regency is a city institution. Another longtime River Walk favorite is the sing-alongs at **Durty Nellie's Pub** in the Hilton Palacio del Rio. Strolling troubadors troll River Walk eateries offering Mexican favorites for a tip. A younger tourist crowd fills venues such as **Dick's Last Resort** where you can grab a drink in the afternoon—provided you have a thick enough skin to withstand the intentionally surly staff. Don't miss the **Menger Bar** at the Menger Hotel, a fun place to go with friends for a drink or a great place to go to meet the locals. For a River Walk venue with a hipper atmosphere, try **Vbar** (✉*150 E. Houston St.* ☎*210/227–9700*) at the Hotel Valencia, one of the hottest places in town.

Farther afield, you can sip your drink while taking in a bird's-eye view of the city at **Bar 601** atop the Tower of the Americas in Hemisfair Park. **Sunset Station**, east of downtown, features four live-music stages, five dance floors, and three restaurants. Nightly music choices range from country and western to merengue, and the food runs the gamut from Aldaco's Mexican Cuisine to Ruth's Chris Steak House. The depot is open during the day, but the bands take the stage after dark.

SHOPPING

San Antonio is a wonderful place to buy Mexican imports, most of them inexpensive and many of high quality. A good number of shopping options are in the popular **River Walk** area. There you'll find plenty of restaurants and bars that make perfect pit stops as you stroll. Nearby, the shops and galleries at **La Villita** delight shoppers bent on discovering homemade treasures. Some of the shops in this block-long historic arts village along the San Antonio River are in adobe buildings dating from the 1820s. Stores are open daily from 10 to 6, with some staying open later. Mainstream shopping is also around the corner at **Rivercenter**, a fairly standard shopping mall right on the river, as well a ticket office and stop for the river-barge rides.

San Antonio's most unusual shopping area, **El Mercado** (⊠ *514 W. Commerce St.* ☎ *210/207–8600* ⊕ *www.marketsquaresa.com)*, is a Mexican market building that is part of Market Square. There are about 35 shops, including stores selling blankets, Mexican dresses, men's guayabera shirts, and strings of brightly painted papier-mâché vegetables.

SPORTS AND THE OUTDOORS

San Antonio has several fantastic parks—Crownridge Canyon, Eisenhower, McAllister, Stone Oak, and Walker Ranch among them. The city's star park, however, is picturesque **Brackenridge Park,** at Broadway and Funston, northeast of downtown in Alamo Heights. There are also a number of great golf courses in and around San Antonio. If you'd rather watch a game, the San Diego Padre's AA affiliate, the San Antonio Missions, play America's pastime in "the Wolf" (Nelson Wolff Municipal Stadium), the jewel of the Texas League. The city is also home to an AHL hockey team, the San Antonio Rampage.

The pride and joy of the Alamo City, the NBA's **San Antonio Spurs** (☎ *210/444–5000* ⊕ *www.spurs.com*) host games at the **AT&T Center** (⊠ *One AT&T Center Pkwy., Downtown* ☎ *210/444–5000* ⊕ *www. attcenter.com*) from October through April. Seats are available in every price range; a seat in the rafters can be had for as little as $10—or you can sit courtside for about $600.

19

AUSTIN

Austin is an open and welcoming place—where you're not only allowed but *expected* to be yourself. People tend to be laissez-faire, and may even be newcomers themselves. The city ranks high on many national best-places-to-live lists—where creativity and maverick thinking are valued. Such things weren't on the mind of Mirabeau B. Lamar, president-elect of the Texas Republic, when he set out to hunt buffalo in 1838 but returned home with a much greater catch: a site for the new republic's capital. Half a century later, the University of Texas at Austin was founded. Fed by the 1970s "outlaw country" movement popularized by Willie Nelson, Waylon Jennings, and others, the city bills itself as the "Live Music Capital of the World." Today Austin is further transforming as high-tech industries migrate to the area. There are a few vestiges of a small-town atmosphere, but Austin's days as a sleepy college town are long gone.

EXPLORING

Begin downtown, where the pink-granite **Texas State Capitol**, built in 1888, is the most visible manmade attraction. The Colorado River, which slices through Austin, was once an unpredictable waterway, but it's been tamed into a series of lakes, including two within the city limits. Twenty-two-mile-long Lake Austin, in the western part of the city, flows into Lady Bird Lake (formerly Town Lake), a narrow stretch of water that meanders for 5 mi through the center of downtown.

The sprawling **University of Texas**, one of the largest universities in the U.S., flanks the capitol's north end. Among other things, it is home to both the **Blanton Museum of Art** and the **Lyndon Baines Johnson Library and Museum**. UT's northwestern border is flanked by Guadalupe Street, which for these blocks is known as The Drag, a fun and funky student-centered commercial strip.

The downtown's Warehouse District and Second Street District, which run from west of Congress to roughly Nueces Street, and north from the lake to 6th Street, are where you'll find some of Austin's liveliest (and newest) restaurants, bistros, and pubs, along with hip boutiques and other shops.

In the late afternoon hours locals grab their sneakers and head to **Zilker Park**, just west and a bit south of downtown, for a jog or a leisurely walk. When the sun sets on summer days, everyone's attention turns to the lake's **Congress Avenue Bridge**, under which the country's largest urban colony of Mexican free-tailed bats hangs out (literally). The bats make their exodus after sunset to feed on insects in the surrounding Hill Country, putting on quite a show in the process.

■ TIP→ If it's your first time in Austin, your first stop should be the Austin Visitor Center (209 E. 6th St., between Brazos and San Jacinto) for brochures galore and friendly advice.

DOWNTOWN AND CAPITOL AREA

Ⓒ   **Bob Bullock Texas State History Museum.** Four blocks north of the capitol,
Fodor's Choice   the Bullock History Museum tells the "Story of Texas" with three floors
★   of interactive exhibits, special effects shows in the Texas Spirit Theater, and Austin's only IMAX(R) theater. Throughout the year you can explore the permanent exhibits with the sights, sounds, and even smells of Texas history. The Museum also has a café with indoor and outdoor

Built in 1910, the Congress Avenue Bridge is an Austin landmark.

seating and a Museum Store with unique Texas gifts. ⊠ *1800 N. Congress Ave.* ☎ *512/936–8746* ⊕ *www.thestoryoftexas.com* ✉ *Museum $9, IMAX $7* ☉ *Mon.–Sat. 9–6, Sun. noon–6; IMAX open evenings.*

Fodor's Choice **Texas State Capitol.** Built in 1888 of Texas pink granite, this impres-
★ sive structure is even taller than the U.S. Capitol (yes, everything *is* bigger in Texas). The building dominates downtown Austin. The surrounding grounds are nearly as striking. Stand in the center of the star on the ground floor under the rotunda and look up, up, up into the dome—it's a Texas rite of passage. Catch one of the free historical tours, offered 8:30–4:30. ⊠ *1100 Congress Ave., Downtown & Capitol Area* ☎ *512/463–0063.*

UNIVERSITY OF TEXAS

Envisioning Austin without the University of Texas is well-nigh impossible. The sprawling campus itself is home to both intimate charm (winding pathways past stone university buildings) and spectacle (the landmark UT Tower, the Blanton Museum of Art, the LBJ Library and Museum, and of course Darrell K. Royal–Texas Memorial Stadium, home of those Longhorns). Parking can be a problem anywhere on or around campus. ☎ *512/471–3434* ⊕ *www.utexas.edu.*

ELSEWHERE IN AUSTIN

★ **Austin Museum of Art–Laguna Gloria.** Set on a lush Lake Austin peninsula, this 1915 Mediterranean-style villa was once home to Clara Driscoll Sevier, who led the fight to save the Alamo from demolition in the early 20th century. In this lovely if relatively diminutive setting the museum showcases its expanding collection of 20th-century American paintings, sculpture, and photographs, and hosts outside exhibits and family-focused art programs. An art school shares the idyllic setting of this building, which is listed on the National Register of Historic Places. Staffers are extremely helpful and informative. ⊠ *3809 W. 35th St.* ☎ *512/458–8191* ⊕ *www.amoa.org* ☜ *$3 suggested donation* ☉ *Tues. and Wed. noon–4, Thurs.–Sun. 10–4 (villa); Mon.–Sat. 9–5, Sun. 10–5 (grounds).*

⟲ **Mount Bonnell.** Several miles northwest of Barton Creek Greenbelt stands Mount Bonnell. At 750 feet, the crag offers a sweeping panorama of Austin, the rolling hills to its west, and the Colorado River. You can't get much higher than this in the Austin area, and if the view itself doesn't convince you of that, the 100 steps to the top surely will. ⊠ *3800 Mount Bonnell Rd., off Scenic Dr.* ☎ *512/974–6700* ☜ *Free* ☉ *Daily 5 am–10 pm.*

WHERE TO EAT

$$$$
NEW AMERICAN
Downtown
Fodor'sChoice
★

✕ **Driskill Grill.** Dominated by shiny, dark paneling and etched glass, this would-be cattle barons' club inside the Driskill Hotel recalls the palatial restaurants of the 19th century (on a more intimate scale)—until you look at the menu. Executive Chef Jonathan Gelman takes tasteful liberties with the meat-and-potatoes format by integrating world-cuisine influences. Entrées include hot smoked Bandera quail, pistachio-crusted sea scallops, and pan-roasted duck breast. Nightly piano music adds to the charming ambience. ⊠ *604 Brazos St., Downtown & Capitol Area* ☎ *512/391–7162* ⊕ *www.driskillgrill.com* ☐ *AE, D, DC, MC, V.* ☉ *Closed Sun. and Mon.*

$–$$
ITALIAN
South Austin
Fodor'sChoice
★

✕ **Enoteca Vespaio.** Vespaio's kid sister has quickly harnessed the lion's share of popularity on South Congress. Known for its tantalizing antipasti counter filled with delectable charcuterie, pâtés, cheeses, and salads, this more casual café has an authentic trattoria feel complete with brightly colored Italian countryside tablecloths. Sink your fork into a bowl of plump gnocchi bathed in garlicky tomato-arrabiata sauce, or nibble on a slice of classic Margherita pizza studded with garden-fresh basil. Juicy hanger steak and crispy french fries (bistecca con patate fritte) leave you wanting more, but don't fill up on dinner; the dessert case is home to some phenomenal treats. Pastries for breakfast or lunch on the patio are alone worth the visit. ⊠ *1610 S. Congress, South Austin* ☎ *512/441–7672* ☐ *AE, D, MC, V* ☉ *Sun. brunch only 10–3.*

$$$–$$$$
NEW AMERICAN
North Austin
Fodor'sChoice
★

✕ **Jasper's.** Executives and upscale tourists alike are drawn to this handsome, 9,000-square-foot eatery for its "gourmet backyard cuisine"—that's how owner and celebrated chef Kent Rathbun describes his Texas-based chain. This branch is in the chi-chi Domain right across from Joe DiMaggio's. Seafood features prominently on the inventive menu, the star is Allen Brothers' dry-aged prime steak, served with a choice of six sauces. Entrées, from a tender grilled flatiron steak with portobello whipped potatoes to a Cajun grilled redfish sandwich, are attractively plated and well conceived. If you want to go upscale on a tight budget, try the pizza-size three-cheese focaccia with caramelized shallots and portobellos for $10. Servers are attentive, but not overly familiar. Decor is midtown Manhattan modern. ⊠ *The Domain* *shopping center, 11506 Century Oaks Terr., North Austin* ☎ *512/834–4111* ⊕ *www.jaspers-restaurant.com* ▭ *AE, DC, MC, V.*

¢–$ ✕ **Juan in a Million.** The not-so-secret weapon of this classic East Austin
MEXICAN breakfast spot is its owner and namesake, local legend Juan Meza, who
East Austin has run his modest eatery since 1981 and still greets every diner with a
bone-crushing handshake and a smile. Juan's strong community spirit
is catching, but the simple, filling, and reliably good fare will start your
day off right on its own. The Don Juan taco (a massive mound of eggs,
potato, bacon, and cheese) is the true East Austin breakfast of champi-
ons; *machacado con huevo* (shredded dried beef scrambled with eggs),
migas (eggs scrambled with torn corn tortillas, onions, chili peppers,
cheese, and spices), and huevos rancheros are also above average. A vari-
ety of inexpensive Tex-Mex and Mexican specialties are served at lunch.
⊠ *2300 E. Cesar Chavez St., East Austin* ☎ *512/472–3872* ⊕ *www.
juaninamillion.com* ⌲ *Reservations not accepted* ▭ *AE, D, MC, V.*

$$–$$$$ ✕ **Lamberts.** On an up-and-coming block near City Hall, Lamberts
NEW AMERICAN draws businessmen, Web types, trenchermen, and foodies for its "fancy
Second Street/ barbecue," aka stylish twists on Texas classics. You know this isn't
Warehouse your father's barbecue joint when you hear Belle & Sebastian on the
District speakers instead of LeAnn Rimes or Merle Haggard. Chimay beer is
Fodor'sChoice available *on draft,* and the Frito pie costs $10 and contains goat cheese.
★ Appetizers range from Asian-style crispy wild-boar ribs to broiled Gulf
oysters with apple-smoked bacon. Desserts, like lemon chess pie with
blueberry sauce, are tangy-sweet and satisfying. They even make a
decent cappuccino. Service is competent and cheerful. The restaurant
is housed in a historic two-story 1873 brick building; the front room
has whitewashed brick, green leatherette '60s banquettes, and a bar
serving top single-malt Scotches. The second floor has a bar with a few
tables and a stage where bands play the nights away. ⊠ *401 W. 2nd
St., Warehouse District* ☎ *512/494–1500* ⊕ *www.lambertsaustin.com*
▭ *AE, D, DC, MC, V.*

$$–$$$$ ✕ **Uchi.** You've heard the term "extreme sports"? Uchi is "extreme
JAPANESE sushi." Respectful of traditional sushi and sashimi methods—but not
South Austin limited by them—this standout sushi bar (a consistent critical and popu-
Fodor'sChoice lar favorite) starts with super-fresh ingredients. After that, anything
★ goes, including touches of the South or South of the Border: yellowtail
with ponzu sauce and sliced chilies, panku fried green tomatoes, or
baked tiger shrimp and crab served in avocado, Belgian endive, roasted
red grapes, and cilantro; unusual salsas enliven most any dish. You
can make a tapas-style meal from the cold and hot "tastings" menu. If
you sit at the sushi bar you can watch the enthusiastic kitchen staff at
work. Attentive, knowledgeable service seals the deal. ⊠ *801 S. Lamar
Blvd., South Austin* ☎ *512/916–4808* ⊕ *www.uchiaustin.com* ▭ *AE,
MC, V* ☽ *No lunch.*

19

WHERE TO STAY

$$$$ ▦ **Driskill Hotel.** Built in 1886 and impeccably restored, the Driskill is a
DOWNTOWN beautiful public space created when people relished mingling in grand
Fodor'sChoice settings. **ros:** Flawless restoration; historic; lots of personality. **Cons:**
★ No pool; immediate neighborhood is an unattractive city block. ⊠ *604*

Brazos St., Downtown & Capitol Area 🕾 *512/474–5911 or 800/252–9367* ⊕ *www.driskillhotel.com* 🛏 *176 rooms, 13 suites* 🖒 *In-room: safe, Internet, Wi-Fi. In-hotel: 2 restaurants, room service, bar, gym, laundry service, parking (free), some pets allowed* ☰ *AE, D, DC, MC, V.*

$$$$
DOWNTOWN
Fodor'sChoice
★

🖫 **Four Seasons.** You get what you pay for in superior service and amenities at this elegant hotel on beautifully manicured grounds overlooking Lady Bird Lake. **Pros:** Beautiful, with resort feel; central downtown location. **Cons:** Expensive, parking among priciest in town. ⊠ *98 San Jacinto Blvd., Downtown & Capitol Area* 🕾 *512/478–4500 or 800/332–3442* ⊕ *www.fourseasons.com* 🛏 *291 rooms* 🖒 *In-room: safe, DVD, Internet, Wi-Fi. In-hotel: 2 restaurants, room service, bar, pool, gym, spa, bicycles, laundry service, Wi-Fi hotspot, parking (paid), some pets allowed* ☰ *AE, DC, MC, V.*

$$–$$$
NORTH AUSTIN
★

🖫 **Habitat Suites Hotel.** Native flowering plants, organic vegetable gardens, and fruit-bearing trees surround this environmentally friendly all-suites lodging. **Pros:** Eco-conscious, attractive landscaping, hospitable staff. **Cons:** The nearby Highland Mall area can be quite noisy at times. ⊠ *500 E. Highland Mall Blvd., North Austin* 🕾 *512/467–6000 or 800/535–4663* ⊕ *www.habitatsuites.com* 🛏 *96 suites* 🖒 *In-room: Wi-Fi. In-hotel: pool, laundry facilities, laundry service, parking (free)* ☰ *AE, D, DC, MC, V* ⊺◯⏌ *CP.*

$$–$$$$
DOWNTOWN
Fodor'sChoice
★

🖫 **Mansion at Judges' Hill.** History and modern amenities come together in this exquisite boutique hotel near the southern edge of UT's main campus. **Pros:** Beautifully restored; historic; perfect for romantic getaways; attentive staff. **Cons:** Parking somewhat limited; no pool. ⊠ *1900 Rio Grande St., Downtown & Capitol Area* 🕾 *512/495–1800 or 800/311–1619* ⊕ *www.mansionatjudgeshill.com* 🛏 *48 rooms* 🖒 *In-room: Internet, Wi-Fi, DVD (some). In-hotel: restaurant, bar, Internet terminal, Wi-Fi hotspot, laundry service, parking (free), some pets allowed* ☰ *AE, D, DC, MC, V.*

ARTS AND ENTERTAINMENT

Even when Austin was a backwater burg it enjoyed a modicum of culture thanks to the University of Texas. The city's current culture vultures are still indebted to the construction-crazed university for its state-of-the-art concert halls like the Bass, which can accommodate grand symphonic, operatic, and theatrical performances. But in a town as creatively charged as Austin, the venues are virtually limitless, from hillsides in parks to the pavement of the Congress Avenue Bridge, and from dark, smoky clubs to Victorian Gothic cathedrals.

Numerous traveling and homegrown bands play nightly in the city's music venues, many of which are clustered around downtown's 6th Street, between Red River Street and Congress Avenue. While not as famous as Bourbon Street in New Orleans, 6th Street has an entertaining mix of comedy clubs, blues bars, electronica, and dance clubs. It's also the site of two "Old Pecan Street" outdoor fairs, held in May and September, with live bands, food vendors, and craftspeople.

College students are a large presence on 6th, but the Warehouse District around 4th Street and the newer 2nd Street District (which runs between

San Antonio Street and Congress Avenue for two blocks north of the river) cater to a more mature crowd looking for good food and great drinks. South Congress also has a lively scene, especially on the first Thursday of each month, when vendors set up booths with art, jewelry, and a variety of other creations all along the street. The shops stay open late, and bands perform live along the streets. (Warning: Parking during "First Thursdays" is a challenge. Expect to park many blocks back and walk.) To find out who's playing where, pick up the *Austin Chronicle* (a free alternative weekly). Most of the larger venues in Austin sell tickets through **Front Gate Tickets** (☎ *512/389–0315* ⊕ *www.fronttickets.com*). But **AusTix** (☎ *512/474–8497* ⊕ *www.austix.com*) is a good resource for theater as well as smaller dance and music performances. Meanwhile, **GetTix** (☎ *866/443–8849* ⊕ *www.gettix.net*) is a smaller purveyor of advance tickets in Austin, but sells for popular venues such as La Zona Rosa, Austin Music Hall, and Emo's.

NIGHTLIFE

To say Austin's night scene is dominated by live music is an understatement. In fact, it's hard to fully distinguish bar from club from live-music venue, as they tend to all blend together. Bands will play anywhere people will listen, and that's pretty much everywhere. Depending on where you are in town, activity tends to bubble up in two waves: the social and professional, happy hour faction and the music-loving nightlife crowd. If visiting Austin for a short time, check out some of the classic venues such as Antone's, the Continental Club, and Stubb's.

BARS/LIVE MUSIC

Antone's. This is a local musical institution that books legendary blues and funk acts. Guiding spirit Clifford Antone, a blues fan's blues fan, passed away in 2006, but his legacy lives on at the club he founded. ⊠ *213 W. 5th St., Downtown & Capitol Area (2nd St. & Warehouse District)* ☎ *512/320–8424* ⊕ *www.antones.net*.

Continental Club. Rustic, quirky, and no bigger than your parents' basement, this smoky, no-frills club is one of Austin's signature entertainment spaces. The club hosts a variety of live acts from rock to blues and country. Try to catch a performance by Heybale, a quintet of local pros that includes Redd Volkaert and Earl Poole Ball. ⊠ *1315 S. Congress Ave., South Austin* ☎ *512/441–2444* ⊕ *www.continentalclub.com/Austin.html*.

★ **Elephant Room.** Jazz fanatics hold court at the basement locale here, where serious jazz plays long into the night all week long. Named one of the top 10 jazz venues in the United States by the famed Wynton Marsalis, this long-standing Austin venue is what gives this town its Live Music Capital status. ⊠ *315 Congress Ave., Downtown & Capitol Area* ☎ *512/473–2279* ⊕ *www.elephantroom.com*.

Fodor'sChoice **Stubb's Bar-B-Que.** You know you're in Austin when the smell of smoky
★ barbecue wafts throughout the venue as a top-billed band prepares to take the outdoor stage. It's not heaven, it's Stubb's, a true Austin live-music icon. If you're in town long enough and want to revive your spiritual side, take in a session of the Sunday gospel hour, when a sizeable buffet brunch awaits along with a soulful performance of gospel

19

Austin has a live-music scene that electrifies the night.

music. ✉ *801 Red River, Downtown & Capitol Area* ☎ *512/480–8341* ⊕ *www.stubbsaustin.com.*

SHOPPING

For an authentic Austin shopping experience, browse the funky shops along revitalized **South Congress** (locally called "SoCo"), gaze at the hip downtown storefronts of the up-and-coming **2nd Street District,** and stroll among the high-end galleries, antiques, and home-furnishings emporia of the **West End.** You can trek to legions of book, computer, and music stores, then peruse the handicrafts of local artisans. Along the way, fuel up on organic foods and fresh-roasted coffee.

Out in Northwest Austin and Round Rock upscale shopping malls are popping up all over the place. The **Domain** in North Austin is an ambitious project of mixed-use retail, office, and residential space that's extending the affluent downtown vibe practically into the suburbs.

♻ Fodor's Choice ★ **Toy Joy.** This fantastic place is so much the ultimate toy store of your childhood fantasies that it's too good to save for actual children— don't be embarrassed to come in even if you don't have little ones of your own. It's *the* place to get Marie Antoinette, Shakespeare, and Einstein action figures, red rubber duckies with devil horns, repros of fave toys you played with as a kid, and floor-to-ceiling diversions for all ages, including science toys, metal robots, stuffed animals, hard-to-find candy, baubles and bangles, and more. ✉ *2900 Guadalupe St., University of Texas* ☎ *512/320–0090* ⊕ *www.toyjoy.com.*

AUSTIN MUSIC FESTIVALS

SEPTEMBER

Austin City Limits Music Festival. Austinites love any excuse to party outside, especially when music is involved. This unofficial farewell-to-summer shindig takes over Zilker Park for three days in early October. Fans come to hear 130 international, national, and local bands on eight stages. Performers have included the likes of Bob Dylan, Coldplay, Tom Petty, Bjork, the White Stripes, Sheryl Crow, Lucinda Williams, Steve Earle, and the Indigo Girls. ⊠ *2100 Barton Springs Rd., West Austin/Zilker Park* ☎ *512/389–0315* ⊕ *www.aclfestival. com* ✑ *$85–$185.*

MARCH

South by Southwest. The grand-daddy of all music fests arrives in early spring. Usually shortened to SXSW, this event's festivals and conferences combine to form a huge music, film, and interactive extravaganza. In addition to all the fans, SXSW brings a fleet of hundreds of hopeful musicians, producers, and record label execs to Austin to perform and network. It's such a take-over-the-city event that many Austin families evacuate town to some far-off spring break destination. Hotel rooms are scarce, restaurants and bars are packed, and everything from SXSW VIPs to plain, music-loving plebeians mix and mingle in expectation of finding "the next big thing." ■TIP→ First-time participants should know that it pays to be organized in terms of the bands you want to see, since SXSW happens all over town. ⊠ *Throughout Austin* ☎ *512/467–7979* ⊕ *www. sxsw.com* ✑ *$130–$175.*

★ **The University Co-Op.** The beating burnt-orange heart of Longhorn Nation is on display at the ultimate showcase of UT sports paraphernalia. You can find burnt-orange-and-Longhorn-logo'd everything at this three-level emporium. Founded in 1896 and modeled after a similar co-op at Harvard, UT's Co-Op claims to be the largest seller of used textbooks in the country. ⊠ *2246 Guadalupe St., University of Texas* ☎ *512/476–7211* ⊕ *www.universitycoop.com.*

Waterloo Records & Video. This large independent shop is an Austin institution that's been an integral part of the local music scene since 1982. Its outstanding selection, customer service, and free in-store concerts (including some pretty impressive names during SXSW week) mean it may be the only Austin record store you'll ever need. ⊠ *600A N. Lamar Blvd., Downtown* ☎ *512/474–2500* ⊕ *www.waterloorecords.com*

SPORTS AND THE OUTDOORS

With its lakes, abundant greenbelts and parks, and miles of hike-and-bike trails—not to mention year-round mild and mostly sunny weather (searingly hot summers and occasional gully washers aside)—Austin and its surroundings are made for outdoor enthusiasts and weekend athletes of all ages and abilities. Whether you live to run marathons, climb rocks, or just stroll through a wildflower garden, Austin's got you covered.

19

Although the city lacks major-league pro sports teams, fervor for UT's football Longhorns, a perennial collegiate top contender, fills the gap to such an extent that many Austinites avoid driving downtown on UT home game days, when thousands of faithful who "bleed orange" are visibly (and audibly) out and about.

✪ NATURAL AREAS AND PARKS

Austin has more than 200 parks within the city limits. Amenities in the parks range from playgrounds, swimming pools, and skate parks (the city's first was established at Maybel Davis District Park in south Austin) to artwork and historic sites, such as Umlauf Sculpture Garden at Zilker Park and Treaty Oak Square in northwest Austin.

✪ **Lady Bird Johnson Wildflower Center.** This 279-acre complex, founded in
★ 1982 by Lady Bird Johnson and actress Helen Hayes, has extensive plantings of native Texas wildflowers that bloom year-round (although spring is an especially attractive time). The grounds include a visitor center, nature trails, observation tower, elaborate stone terraces, and flower-filled meadows. ⊠ *4801 La Crosse Ave.* ☎ *512/232–0100* ⊕ *www.wildflower.org* 🔳 *$8* ⊙ *Tues.–Sat. 9–5:30, Sun. noon–5:30.*

✪ **Zilker Park.** Austin's everyday backyard park, the 355-acre site along the shores of Lady Bird Lake includes Barton Springs Pool, numerous gardens, a meditation trail, and a Swedish log cabin dating from the 1840s. Canoe rentals are available for the hour or day (⊕ *www.zilkerboats. com*). In March the park hosts a kite festival. During spring months concerts are held in the park's Beverly S. Sheffield Zilker Hillside Theater, a natural outdoor amphitheater beneath a grove of century-old pecan trees; in July and August musicals and plays take over. ⊠ *2201 Barton Springs Rd.* ☎ *512/974–6700 (Parks Dept.), 512/477–5335 (theater), 512/445–5582 (museum)* ⊕ *www.ci.austin.tx.us/zilker* 🔳 *Free (main park), parking $3 per vehicle* ⊙ *Daily dawn–dusk (park); Wed.–Fri. 10–4:30, weekends 1–4:30 (museum).*

TEXAS HILL COUNTRY

If Texas is indeed a state of mind, the Hill Country is the reason why. The region is etched with dramatic slopes of rocky terrain, wide vistas displaying an endless horizon of blue sky, and roads that go on forever. Creeks meander through mesquite-filled pastures; in spring blooming bluebonnets and other wildflowers transform the rough-hewn landscape. The Hill Country's defining feature is, of course, the hills. (The lovely lakes and rivers are a close second, though.) Limestone formations create perfect environments for many freshwater springs and extensive underground caverns. The area is a ranching hub and one of the nation's leading Angora goat and mohair-producing regions. The Hill Country is also a retreat for businesspeople from Austin and San Antonio, who trade designer suits and city sights for Levis and ranch life each weekend. Visitors are drawn here to splash in the lakes, explore the Texas Wine Trail, sample fruit at roadside farm stands, and become short-term cowpokes at local dude ranches.

EXPLORING

The Hill Country encompasses the region west and southwest of Austin and north of San Antonio. The distance between these two gateway cities is 60 mi.

WESTERN HILL COUNTRY

Bandera. Dust off your chaps, loosen your saddle cinch, and stay a while in Bandera, where mythic tales of the "cowboy way" are all true. Not only will you see beat-up boots, worn Wrangler jeans, and more than a few cowboy hats, you may even catch a glimpse of one of the local ranch hands riding his horse to the general store on Main Street. After all, this isn't considered the "Cowboy Capital of Texas" for nothing. Open rodeos take place twice weekly from Memorial Day through Labor Day, and you can't drive any direction outside of town without passing a dude ranch.

Comfort. At first glance, Comfort resembles a lot of quiet Hill Country towns. It has the standard Dairy Queen and a small main street with historic buildings and antiques shops. But a closer look reveals an interesting history. Originally settled in the 1840s by German "Freethinkers," many of the buildings on High Street, such as the **Comfort Common,** now a B&B, were constructed in the late 1800s by noted British architect Alfred Giles, and are listed on the National Register of Historic Places.

Fredericksburg. Once a secret weekend getaway for Texans in the know, Fredericksburg is now a destination hot spot featured in the likes of *Travel & Leisure,* and *National Geographic.* It's hard not to love the town where you can shop all day on Main Street and still not see everything, spend a day touring the Texas Wine Trail, or spend an afternoon hiking Enchanted Rock, and then unwind in one of 300 guesthouses and B&Bs. That is, of course, after you've savored a schnitzel and beer at a German restaurant. Fredericksburg wears its German heritage proudly. The city square is called Marketplatz, there's a "Willkommen" sign hanging from every shop door, and the main B&B booking organization is Gästehaus Schmidt. It's Oktoberfest year-round in this hot little town. Save time to visit the excellent **National Museum of the Pacific War**.

North of town the pink dome of **Enchanted Rock** protrudes from the earth, rising to 1,825 feet—the second-largest in the nation, after Georgia's Stone Mountain. Its bald vastness can be seen from miles away. Today the massive batholith is part of the 624-acre Enchanted Rock State Natural Area, and one of the most popular destinations in the Hill Country region. Perfect for day hikers, the rock also presents a number of facets to test the skills of technical rock climbers. Arrive early; park officials close the park to protect the resources once parking lots reach capacity. Amenities include restrooms, an interpretive center, and campgrounds (⇨ *Where to Stay*). ✉ *16710 RR 965* ☎ *830/ 685–3636* ⊕ *www.tpwd.state.tx.us* 🖙 *$6.*

Johnson City. Notable as the home of President Lyndon Baines Johnson—though he's not the town's namesake—Johnson City was actually founded in the late 1870s by James Polk Johnson, a second cousin to the former U.S. president. The main attraction here is the **LBJ Boyhood Home,** part of the nearby **Lyndon B. Johnson National Historical Park.** ✉ *100 Ladybird La., Johnson City* 🕾 *830/868–7128* ⊕ *www.nps.gov/ lyjo/* ✆ *Free* ⊙ *9–4:30.*

Luckenbach. Hardly a town at all, but more a cul-de-sac at the end of a country road, Luckenbach is an attitude. It's a place to which Texas songwriters and music lovers from Nacogdoches to El Paso dream of traveling to pay homage to Texas music legends. Aside from the general store, post office, rows of picnic tables, and ample parking for the many daily visitors, there's not much else here. The famous **Dance Hall** presents live music seven days a week.

Medina. If you like the remote feel of Bandera, head farther west on Highway 16 to Medina, a quiet treasure along its namesake river. Today Medina is known as the "Apple Capital of Texas," mainly thanks to **Love Creek Orchards,** where you can pick your own fruit or shop in the adjacent store. The **Old Timer** gas station at the junction of Ranch Road 337 is a good place to catch local gossip at an old picnic table.

Farther west toward Vanderpool on Ranch Road 337 and then north on Farm Road 187 is **Lost Maples State Park** (✉ *37221 FM Rd. 187* 🕾 *830/966–3413* ⊕ *www.tpwd.state.tx.us* ✆ *$6*). You'll find yourself on arguably one of the most breathtaking drives in the state. If you're here during the fall, you'll likely be joined by a few thousand leaf-peepers, trying to catch one of the few patches of Texas where the change in seasons creates vivid colors.

CENTRAL HILL COUNTRY

Gruene. Ask many Central Texans if they've ever two-stepped in this little town and you'll see a nostalgic gleam in their eye. Just north of New Braunfels, Gruene stands as a pristine portrait of Texas history, and is revered as a place of Texas legends. The entire town has been added to the National Register of Historic Places, and many of the buildings carry medallions from the Texas Historical Commission. Settled in the late 1840s by German farmer Ernst Gruene and his sons, the town gained most of its prosperity from the family's cotton business. Gruene's second son, Henry D. Gruene, built a Victorian-style home that is now the iconic **Gruene Mansion Inn.** A trip to Gruene isn't complete without a turn on the old hardwood floors of legendary **Gruene Hall** (✉ *1281 Gruene Rd., New Braunfels* 🕾 *830/606–1281* ⊕ *www. gruenehall.com* ✆ *Varies with show* ⊙ *Open daily. Call for showtimes*), known as the oldest continuously operating dance hall in the entire state. Many famous musicians owe their success to performances on this fabled stage, including Willie Nelson, Lyle Lovett, George Strait, Garth Brooks, Jerry Lee Lewis, and the Dixie Chicks.

Fodor'sChoice
★

At **Natural Bridge Caverns** guides lead an incredible journey on a half-mile of paved trails underground at the largest known cavern in Texas. It's a "live" cave with formations that still grow due to dripping and flowing water creating its "soda straws" and other delicate formations.(✉ *26495 Natural Bridge Caverns Rd., I–35 Exit 175 FM 3009* 🕾 *210/651–6101* ⊕ *www.naturalbridgecaverns.com* ✆ *$17.95*

☉ *Daily; call for hrs*). Next to the caverns you can go on a driving safari at the **Natural Bridge Wildlife Ranch.**

New Braunfels. New Braunfels was the first of the Adelsverein movement in the 1840s to secure land in Texas for German immigrants. The town was founded by Prince Carl of Solms-Braunfels, the Commissioner General of the Adelsverein. In 1845 he led hundreds of sea-weary German settlers recently docked in Galveston to a plot of land north of San Antonio on the banks of the Comal River. The settlement was named for his hometown in Germany, Braunfels (pronounced brawn-fells). The settlement endured a shaky beginning, but by 1850 was a thriving community and the fourth largest city in Texas. New Braunfels is a lively place, with visitors coming to tube down the Guadalupe River and splash around at **Schlitterbahn WaterPark Resort** (⊠ *381 E. Austin St., New Braunfels* ☎ *830/625–2351* ⊕ *www.schlitterbahn.com* ⊠ *49.98* ☉ *Late Apr.–mid-Sept.; call for hrs*) or to get a taste (literally) of the annual **Wurstfest** celebrating the town's German heritage in late October and early November.

San Marcos. The largest town between Austin and San Antonio on I–35, San Marcos is home to former President Lyndon B. Johnson's alma mater, **Texas State University,** the crystal-clear **Aquarena Springs** that feed the San Marcos River, and the **Southwestern Writers Collection** at the Alkek Library. For the most part it's a college town, but many visitors to San Marcos buzz right by downtown and hit the state's best outlet-mall shopping at the Prime Outlet and the Tanger Outlet malls.

Wimberley. The winding little roads, towering oak and cypress trees, and compact town square give Wimberley the feel of an English village. Established in 1848 with only a small trading post to its name, Wimberley's first industries were lumber and shingle making. The Blanco River and Cypress Creek, which run through the city, fueled the Wimberley Mill. The 1980s saw a revitalization in Wimberley as it evolved into a retirement and artists' community. Galleries and shops selling local artists' Hill Country creations, from paintings and sculptures to crafts, are found throughout Wimberley Village Square.

NORTHERN HILL COUNTRY

Lake Travis, one of the Highland Lakes (along with Lakes Buchanan, Inks, LBJ, and Marble Falls) fed by the Colorado River, is a refreshing playscape for the Austin area. When the sun sets on the lake, some of the most brilliant views are enjoyed from the decks of hillside restaurants, where spectators applaud the visual pyrotechnics.

Bustling **Marble Falls,** named for the natural falls formed by a shelf of limestone that runs diagonally across the Colorado River, has become a popular destination for a quick weekend getaway from Austin. Sparkling Lake Marble Falls is the primary summer attraction here, but also of interest are nearby **Quarry Mountain** (which furnished granite for the Texas State Capital) and the renowned golf courses of the **Horseshoe Bay Resort.** The town's 19th-century Main Street offers gift, home-decor, and apparel shops, as well as excellent restaurants. And if you happen to be in the area around the holidays, Marble Falls is noted for having some of the most amazing Christmas lights along the lake.

19

View fascinating, dripping cave formations at Natural Bridge Caverns.

WHERE TO EAT

$$$–$$$$
CONTEMPORARY
Fredricksburg
Fodor'sChoice
★

✕ **August E's.** This polished, contemporary spot is one of the rare places where you *can't* order schnitzel. Chef-owner Leu Savanh offers a constantly evolving seasonal menu. He also adds a subtle hint of his Thai background to such dishes as the New Zealand lamb with balsamic honey-glaze, and a cloudlike fillet of Hawaiian escolar pan-seared and served with a tempura-fried lobster tail, baby bok choy, and mascarpone whipped potatoes. August E's is the only place in town for sushi and sake. ⊠ *203 E. San Antonio* ☎ *830/997–1585* ▬ *AE, D, MC, V.*

¢–$$
AMERICAN
Marble Falls
★

✕ **The Blue Bonnet Café.** Don't even think about coming to Marble Falls without taking a seat at this small-town diner. There's a sign above the hostess stand reading "Eat some pie." We suggest you follow these directions. At least 10 different types of pie are made fresh daily. From mountainous meringue to creamy custards, the geniuses behind these sweet concoctions mean business. If you come between 3 and 5 pm you've made it for "Pie Happy Hour," when you can have a slice of pie and a cup of joe for $3! They also serve everything you'd find at an old-fashioned diner. ⊠ *211 Hwy. 281* ☎ *830/693–2344* ▬ *No credit cards.*

$–$$
AMERICAN
Gruene
Fodor'sChoice
★

✕ **Huisache Grille.** Hidden near the train tracks off San Antonio Street, the Huisache (pronounced wee-satch) is a must-stop. As it consistently delivers fantastic soups, salads, sandwiches, and main dishes, there's a lot to love about this place, and the beautiful historic 1920s building only adds to the experience. For lunch the ham and Gouda sandwich with sweet caramelized onions offers a nice adult version of a grilled cheese. Pecan-dusted pork chops soar with apple-brandy butter sauce. ⊠ *303 W. San Antonio St.* ☎ *830/620–9001* ▬ *AE, D, MC, V.*

Talking Texan

Texans use the word "y'all" a lot. You'll hear it in pretty much any type of conversation, and you'll likely incorporate it into your vocabulary before heading home. (It really is a useful word, and it sounds so nice—at least when Texans say it.) There are a few other sayings and pronunciations that are unique to the Lone Star State:

"He's all hat and no cattle": Used to describe someone who is all talk and no action.

"This ain't my first rodeo": I wasn't born yesterday.

"You can put your boots in the oven, but that don't make them biscuits":

Say what you want, but that doesn't make it true.

"We've howdied, but we ain't shook yet": We've made a brief acquaintance, but have not been formally introduced.

Burnet: "Burn-it"

Pedernales: "Pur-dah-nallis"

Guadalupe: "Gwaa-dah-loop" (when referring to the street (aka "the Drag") in Austin

Manchaca: "Man-shack"

San Felipe: "San Fill-a-pee"

WHERE TO STAY

Serving Fredericksburg for more than 20 years, the **Gästehaus Schmidt** (⌂ *231 W. Main St.* ☎ *866/427–8374 or 830/997–5612* ⊕ *www.fbglodging.com*) is the place to consult when seeking the perfect B&B or guesthouse. This booking operation manages more than a third of the 300-plus accommodations in the town, but it's also a great resource to turn to for local travel advice.

$$$$
MEDINA
Fodor'sChoice
★

⌨ **Escondida Resort.** A pristine, luxe Mexican-style villa this small resort and adjacent Spa at Escondida are the creation of property host Christy Carnes and Texas television personality Bob Philips. **Pros:** Beautiful surroundings and private accommodations; on-site chef; library and living rooms in main portion of the villa. Pet-friendly with advance notice. **Cons:** One-hour drive from San Antonio; two hours from Austin; palatial bathrooms lack large bathtubs. Cell service sometimes intermittent. ⌂ *23670 Hwy. 16 N, Medina* ☎ *888/589–7507 or 830/589–7507* ⊕ *www.escondidaresort.com* ↳ *10 rooms, 1 suite* ⌃ *In-room: kitchen (some), refrigerator, safe, DVD, Internet (some), Wi-Fi. In-hotel: pool, spa, gym, Wi-Fi hotspot, some pets allowed, parking (free), no kids under 21* ▭ *AE, D, MC, V* ⊪ *AP.*

$$–$$$
FREDRICKSBURG
★

⌨ **Hangar Hotel.** This fun (yet not overdone) hotel was built to look like a 1940s airplane hangar; stepping into the lobby is like entering an old black-and-white movie. **ros:** $10 discounts for military and seniors. **Cons:** Not many activity options on-site or nearby, and not an easy location to find. ⌂ *155 Airport Rd.* ☎ *830/997–9990* ⊕ *www.hangarhotel.com* ↳ *50 rooms* ⌃ *In-room: refrigerator, Wi-Fi. In-hotel: restaurant, bar, public Wi-Fi, no-smoking rooms, parking (free)* ▭ *AE, MC, V* ⊪ *CP.*

19

$$$$ ⛺ **Riven Rock Ranch.** The three ranch-style cottages and one late-1800s
COMFORT   farmhouse at Riven Rock have immaculate Texas-meets-French-coun-
Fodor'sChoice   tryside interiors, gas fireplaces, and beautiful views of the hills. **Pros:**
★   Immaculate property with beautifully designed accommodations; after-
noon refreshments are a nice bonus. **Cons:** Remote location makes visit-
ing area towns a longer journey; fairly expensive compared to other Hill
Country accommodations. ⊠ *390 Hermann Sons Rd.* ☎ *877/726–2490
or 830/995–4045* ⊕ *www.rivenrockranch.com* ⤴ *9 rooms* ⚒ *In-room:
Wi-Fi, DVD, kitchen. In-hotel: restaurant, pool, Wi-Fi hotspot* ⊟ *AE,
D, MC, V* ⧖ *BP.*

SHOPPING

Fredericksburg has become a shopping mecca for weekenders from all
over Texas.

You'll find shops selling a wide variety of wares including antiques,
designer fashions, rustic furniture and home accessories, gourmet foods,
and herbal soaps and lotions. Seriously, it can take an entire day just
to cover both sides of the town's expansive Main Street, including a
few stops for refreshment at some of Fredericksburg's enticing cafés
and bakeries.

In Wimberley it soon becomes clear that the **Wimberley Village Square**—
a virtual spider web at the intersection of RR 12 and a number of small
Wimberley streets—is the place for an afternoon of shopping. For that
last-minute gift for a friend's new baby or the kids back home, stop
in at **Blue Bacon Toys** (⊠ *14011 RR 12* ☎ *512/847–2150*), which offers
an extremely unusual assortment of children's toys. Take a detour to
Wimberley Glassworks, one of the art community's most impressive con-
tributors, to watch artisans blow and shape beautiful glass creations
⊠ *6469 RR 12* ☎ *512/393–3316 or 800/ 929–6686* ⊕ *www.wgw.com*
⊙ *Open daily.*

Santa Fe and Taos

WORD OF MOUTH

"As the sun dips in downtown Santa Fe, the warm fiery light and long shadows create living art that challenges even the wealth of wonderful, colorful creations that can be found in Santa Fe's plentiful and eclectic art galleries."

—PeteFoley, fodors.com member

WELCOME TO SANTA FE AND TAOS

TOP REASONS TO GO

★ **A culinary adventure.** Start with rellenos for breakfast and tapas for dinner. Enjoy strawberry habanero gelato or sip an Aztec Warrior Chocolate Elixir. Santa Fe is an exceptional dining town, the perfect place to push the frontiers of your palate.

★ **Market mashup.** Summer offers the phenomenal International Folk Art Market, the famed Indian Market, and the two-for-one weekend of Traditional Spanish Market and Contemporary Hispanic Market.

★ **Indigenous roots.** The Taos Pueblo and its inhabitants have lived in this region for centuries and continue to play a vital role in local art, culture, and civic life.

★ **Desert solitaire.** Few panoramas in the Southwest can compare with that of the 13,000-foot Sangre de Cristo Mountains soaring over the adobe homes of Taos, and beyond that, the endless high-desert mesa that extends for miles to the west.

1 Santa Fe. One of the most visited small cities in the United States, Santa Fe has an abundance of museums, one-of-a-kind cultural events, art galleries, and distinctive restaurants and shops.

2 Taos. Stellar museums and galleries, stunning views of the desert and Sangre de Cristo Mountains, and charming, cottonwood-shaded streets lined with adobe buildings are a few of this small town's attractions. Nearby Taos Pueblo and Taos Ski Valley are major draws.

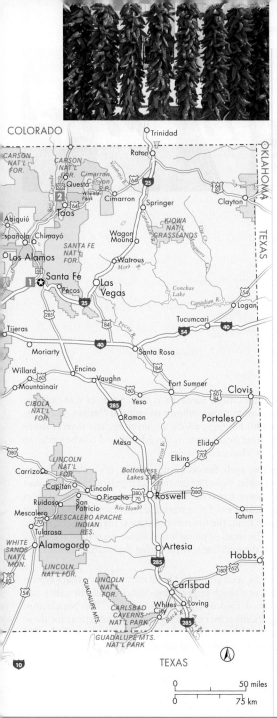

COLORADO

OKLAHOMA

TEXAS

Trinidad

Raton

CARSON NAT'L FOR.

CARSON NAT'L FOR.

Cimarron Canyon

Questa

Wheeler Park

Cimarron

Springer

Clayton

64

25

Abiquiú

Taos

Española Chimayó

Wagon Mound

KIOWA NAT'L GRASSLANDS

Los Alamos

SANTA FE NAT'L FOR.

Watrous

Santa Fe

Pecos

Las Vegas

Conchas Lake

25

Canadian R.

Logan

54

Tijeras

Pecos R.

285

84

Tucumcari

54

40

Moriarty

40

Santa Rosa

Willard

Encino

60

Vaughn

84

Fort Sumner

Clovis

Mountainair

60

Yeso

60

84

CIBOLA NAT'L FOR.

285

Ramon

Portales

Mesa

Elida

70

380

Elkins

LINCOLN NAT'L FOR.

Bottomless Lakes S.P.

Carrizozo

Capitán

Lincoln

Picacho

380

70

Roswell

380

Ruidoso

San Patricio

Rio Hondo

Mescalero

MESCALERO APACHE INDIAN RES.

70

Tatum

Tularosa

WHITE SANDS NAT'L MON.

Alamogordo

Artesia

Hobbs

LINCOLN NAT'L FOR.

285

180

62

Carlsbad

54

GUADALUPE MTS.

LINCOLN NAT'L FOR.

CARLSBAD CAVERNS NAT'L PARK

Whites City

Loving

285

GUADALUPE MTS. NAT'L PARK

10

TEXAS

0   50 miles
0   75 km

GETTING ORIENTED

Interstate 25 cuts just south of Santa Fe, which is 62 mi northeast of Albuquerque. U.S. 285/84 runs north–south through the city. The NM 599 bypass, also called the Santa Fe Relief Route, cuts around the west side of the city from Interstate 25's Exit 276, southwest of the city, to U.S. 285/84, north of the city; it's a great shortcut if you're heading from Albuquerque to Española, Abiquiu, Taos, or other points north of Santa Fe. It's difficult to reach Taos without a car, and you'll need one to reach those attractions outside the village center (the Rio Grande Gorge, Millicent Rogers Museum, and the area's best skiing and hiking), as well as to many accommodations and restaurants. The narrow, historic streets near the Plaza can be choked with traffic in the peak summer and winter seasons, especially on Friday and Sunday—ask locals about the several shortcuts for avoiding traffic jams, and try walking when exploring the blocks around the Plaza.

On a plateau at the base of the Sangre de Cristo Mountains—at an elevation of 7,000 feet—Santa Fe is brimming with reminders of nearly four centuries of Spanish and Mexican rule, and of the Pueblo cultures that have been here for hundreds more. The town's placid central Plaza, which dates from the early 17th century, has been the site of bullfights, gunfights, political rallies, promenades, and public markets over the years.

A one-of-a-kind destination, Santa Fe is fabled for its rows of chic art galleries, superb restaurants, vibrant tri-cultural (Native American, Hispanic, and Anglo) heritage, adobe architecture, and diverse shops selling everything from Southwestern furnishings and cowboy gear, to Tibetan textiles and Moroccan jewelry.

Taos casts a lingering spell. Set on a rolling mesa, it's a place of piercing light and spectacular views, where the desert palette changes almost hourly as the sun moves across the sky. Adobe buildings—some of them centuries old—lie nestled amid pine trees and scrub, some in the shadow of majestic Wheeler Peak, the town's (and state's) highest point, at just over 13,000 feet. The smell of piñon wood smoke rises from the valley from early autumn through late spring; during the warmer months, the air smells of fragrant sage.

Taos supports a retail, restaurant, and hotel infrastructure that's typical of what you'd find in a much larger town. Still, overall, the valley and soaring mountains of Taos enjoy relative isolation, low population-density, and magnificent scenery, making this an ideal retreat for those aiming to escape, slow down, and embrace a distinct regional blend of art, cuisine, outdoor recreation, and natural beauty.

PLANNING

WHEN TO GO

Santa Fe has four distinct seasons. June through August temperatures are high 80s to low 90s during the day, 50s at night, with afternoon rain showers—monsoons—cooling the air. Prices for accommodations are highest during this time. September and October bring beautiful weather and a marked reduction in crowds. Temperatures—and prices—drop significantly after Halloween. From December (except Holiday time) to March, which is ski season, prices are the lowest. Spring comes late at this elevation. April and May are blustery. Daily warm weather (70s and above) arrives in late May. ■TIP→ The high elevation here catches people unawares and altitude sickness can utterly ruin a day of fun. Drink water, drink more water, and then have a little more.

The summer high season in Taos brings warm days (80s) and cool nights (50s), as well as frequent afternoon thunderstorms. A packed arts and festival schedule in summer means hotels and B&Bs sometimes book well in advance, lodging rates are high, restaurants are jammed, and traffic anywhere near the Plaza can slow to a standstill. Spring and fall are stunning and favor mild days and cool nights, fewer visitors, and reasonable hotel prices. In winter, especially during big years for snowfall, skiers arrive en masse but tend to stay close to the slopes and only venture into town an occasional meal or shopping raid.

GETTING HERE AND AROUND

SANTA FE

Air Travel. Among the smallest state capitals in the country, Santa Fe has only a small airport (Albuquerque's is the nearest major one, about an hour away). Tiny Santa Fe Municipal Airport is served by one commercial airline, American Eagle, with daily flights to Dallas (DFW) and Los Angeles (LAX). The airport is 9 mi southwest of downtown.

Airport Contacts Albuquerque International Sunport (*ABQ* ☎ *505/244–7700* ⊕ *www.cabq.gov/airport*). **Santa Fe Municipal Airport** (*SAF* ✉ *Airport Rd. and NM 599* ☎ *505/473–4118*).

Bus Travel. The city's bus system, Santa Fe Trails, covers 10 major routes through town and is useful for getting from the Plaza to some of the outlying attractions. Individual rides cost $1, and a daily pass costs $2. Buses run about every 30 minutes on weekdays, every hour on weekends.

Bus Contacts Santa Fe Trails (☎ *505/955–2001* ⊕ *www.santafenm.gov*).

Car Travel. Santa Fe is served by several national rental car agencies, including Avis, Budget, and Hertz. Additional agencies with locations in Santa Fe include Advantage, Enterprise, Sears, and Thrifty.

Car Rental Contacts Advantage (☎ *505/983–9470* ⊕ *www.advantage.com*). **Enterprise** (☎ *505/473–3600* ⊕ *www.enterprise.com*). **Sears** (☎ *505/984–8038* ⊕ *www.sears.avis.com*). **Thrifty** (☎ *505/474–3365 or 800/367–2277* ⊕ *www. thrifty.com*).

Capital City Cab (☎ *505/438–0000*) controls all the cabs in Santa Fe. The taxis aren't metered; you pay a flat fee based on how far you're going,

20

usually $6–$10 within the downtown area. There are no cab stands; you must phone to arrange a ride.

Train Travel. The Rail Runner offers a scenic, efficient alternative to reaching Santa Fe from the airport in Albuquerque (a shuttle bus operates between Albuquerque's downtown train station and the airport).

Train Contact **New Mexico Rail Runner Express** (☎ 866/795-7245 ⊕ www. nmrailrunner.com).

TAOS

Air Travel. Albuquerque International Sunport (⇨ *above*), **about 130 mi away is** the nearest major airport to Taos. The small Santa Fe Municipal Airport (⇨ *above*), a 90-minute drive, also has daily service on American Airlines from Dallas and Los Angeles. Alternatively, as Taos is one of the gateway towns to New Mexico if coming from Colorado, some visitors fly into Denver (5-hour drive) or Colorado Springs (4 hours) as part of trip to both states.

Car Travel. Given the relatively reasonable rates for rental cars at Albuquerque's airport, a car is your most practical means both for reaching and getting around Taos. The main route from Santa Fe is via U.S. 285 north to NM 68 north, also known as the Low Road, which winds between the Rio Grande and red-rock cliffs before rising to a spectacular view of the plain and river gorge. You can also take the wooded High Road to Taos, which takes longer but offers a wonderfully scenic ride—many visitors come to Taos via the Low Road, which is more dramatic when driven south to north, and then return to Santa Fe via the High Road (⇨ *High Road to Taos below*), which has better views as you drive south.

Cottam Walker Ford and Enterprise are the two local car-rental agencies in Taos; rates typically start around $200 per week but vary greatly depending on the season.

Car Rental Contacts **Cottam Walker Ford** (✉ 1320 Paseo del Pueblo Sur ☎ 575/751-3200 ⊕ www.forddetaos.com). **Enterprise** (✉ 1354 Paseo del Pueblo Sur ☎ 575/758-5553 ⊕ www.enterprise.com).

Taxi Travel. Taxi service in Taos is sparse, but Faust's Transportation and Taos Shuttle both serve the area. Rates are $5 at pick up, $2.50 per each additional person, and $1 per mile.

Taxi Contacts **Faust's Transportation** (☎ 575/758-3410 or 888/231-2222 ⊕ www.newmexiconet.com/trans/faust/faust.html). Taos Shuttle (☎ 575/779-5641).

SANTA FE

Cosmopolitan visitors from around the world are consistently surprised by the city's rich and varied cultural offerings despite its relatively small size. Often referred to as the "City Different," Santa Fe became the first American city to be designated a UNESCO Creative City, acknowledging its place in the global community as a leader in art, crafts, design, and lifestyle.

The adobe-like architecture that dominates the skyline is part of what makes Santa Fe the "City Different."

EXPLORING

Five Santa Fe museums participate in the Museum of New Mexico pass (four state museums and the privately run Museum of Spanish Colonial Art) and it is by far the most economical way to visit them all. The four-day pass costs $20 and is sold at all five of the museums, which include the New Mexico History Museum/Palace of the Governors, Museum of Fine Arts, Museum of Indian Arts and Culture, Museum of International Folk Art, and Museum of Spanish Colonial Art.

THE PLAZA

Much of the history of Santa Fe, New Mexico, the Southwest, and even the West has some association with Santa Fe's central Plaza, which New Mexico governor Don Pedro de Peralta laid out in 1607. The Plaza was already well established by the time of the Pueblo revolt in 1680. Freight wagons unloaded here after completing their arduous journey across the Santa Fe Trail. The American flag was raised over the Plaza in 1846, during the Mexican War, which resulted in Mexico's loss of all its territories in the present southwestern United States. For a time the Plaza was a tree-shaded park with a white picket fence. In the 1890s it was an expanse of lawn where uniformed bands played in an ornate gazebo.

WHAT TO SEE

Fodor's Choice ★

The New Mexico History Museum. The new museum is the anchor of a campus that encompasses the **Palace of the Governors,** the **Museum of New Mexico Press,** the **Fray Angélico Chávez History Library,** and **Photo Archives** (an assemblage of more than 750,000 images dating from the 1850s). Behind the Palace on Lincoln Avenue, the museum thoroughly encompasses the early history of indigenous people, Spanish colonization, the Mexican Period, and travel and commerce on the legendary Santa Fe Trail. Opened in May 2009, the museum has permanent and changing exhibits, such as "Jewish Pioneers of New Mexico," which explores the vital role Jewish immigrants played during the late 19th and early 20th centuries in the state's civic, economic, and cultural development. With advance permission, students and researchers have access to the comprehensive Fray Angélico Chávez Library and its rare maps, manuscripts, and photographs (more than 120,000 prints and negatives). The Museum of New Mexico Press, which prints books, pamphlets, and cards on antique presses, also hosts bookbinding demonstrations, lectures, and slide shows. The Palace of the Governors is a humble one-story neo-Pueblo adobe on the north side of the Plaza, and is the oldest public building in the United States. Its rooms contain period furnishings and exhibits illustrating the building's many functions over the past four centuries. Built at the same time as the Plaza, circa 1610 (scholars debate the exact year), it was the seat of four regional governments—those of Spain, Mexico, the Confederacy, and the U.S. territory that preceded New Mexico's statehood, which was achieved in 1912. The building has served as the residence for 100 Spanish, Mexican, and American governors, including Governor Lew Wallace, who wrote his epic *Ben Hur* in its then drafty rooms.

Dozens of Native American vendors gather daily under the portal of the Palace of the Governors to display and sell pottery, jewelry, bread, and other goods. With few exceptions, the more than 500 artists and craftspeople registered to sell here are Pueblo or Navajo Indians. The merchandise for sale is required to meet strict standards: all items are handmade or hand-strung in Native American households; silver jewelry is either sterling (92.5% pure) or coin (90% pure) silver; all metal jewelry bears the maker's mark, which is registered with the Museum of New Mexico. Prices tend to reflect the high quality of the merchandise but are often significantly less that what you'd pay in a shop. Please remember not to take photographs without permission. There's an outstanding gift shop and bookstore with many high-quality, New Mexico–produced items. ⊠ *Palace Ave., north side of Plaza, Lincoln Ave., west of Palace* ☎ *505/476–5100* ⊕ *www.nmhistorymuseum.org* ▧ *$9, 4-day pass $20 (good at all 4 state museums and Museum of Spanish Colonial Art), free Fri. 5–8* ☉ *Tues.–Thurs. and weekends 10–5, Fri. 10–8 (also Mon. 10–5 June–early Sept.).*

CANYON ROAD

Once a trail used by indigenous people to access water and the lush forest in the foothills east of town, Canyon Road is now lined with upscale art galleries, shops, and restaurants. The road stretches for about 2 mi at a moderate incline toward the base of the mountains. Lower Canyon Road is where you'll find the galleries, shops, and restaurants. Upper Canyon Road (above East Alameda) is narrow and residential, with access to hiking and biking trails along the way, and the Randall Davey Audubon Center at the very top.

Most establishments are in authentic, old adobe homes with thick, undulating walls that appear to have been carved out of the earth.

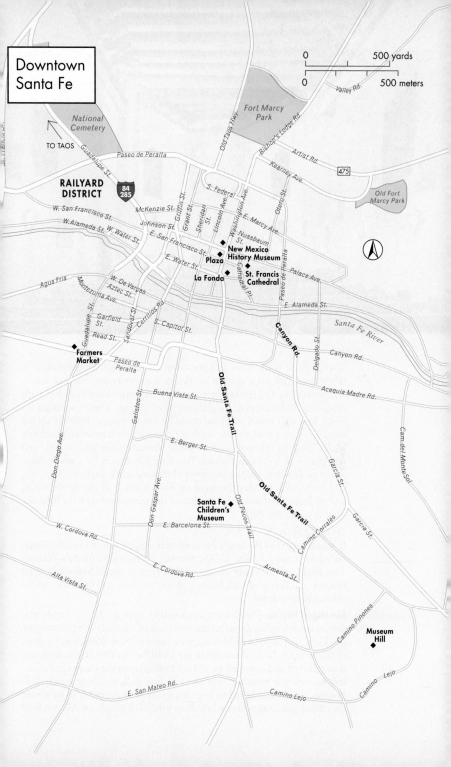

Visit Santa Fe's San Miguel Mission and enter the oldest church still in use in the United States.

Within those walls is art ranging from cutting-edge contemporary to traditional and even ancient works. Some artists are internationally renowned, like Fernando Botero, others' identities have been lost with time, like the weavers of magnificent Navajo rugs. There's so much art to see here that visual overload could hit before you get halfway up the road. Even on a cold day the walk is a pleasure, with massive, glistening icicles hanging off roofs and a silence shrouding the side streets, and few places as festive as Canyon Road on Christmas Eve, when thousands of farolitos (paper lanterns) illuminate walkways, walls, roofs, and even trees. In May the scent of lilacs wafts over the adobe walls, and in August red hollyhocks enhance the surreal color of the blue sky on a dry summer day.

OLD SANTA FE TRAIL

It was along the Old Santa Fe Trail that wagon trains from Missouri rolled into town in the 1800s, forever changing Santa Fe's destiny. This street, off the south corner of the Plaza, is one of Santa Fe's most historic and is dotted with houses, shops, markets and the state capitol several blocks down.

Fodor's Choice ★ **San Miguel Mission.** The oldest church still in use in the United States, this simple earth-hue adobe structure was built in the early 17th century by the Tlaxcalan Indians of Mexico, who came to New Mexico as servants of the Spanish. Badly damaged in the 1680 Pueblo Revolt, the structure was restored and enlarged in 1710. On display in the chapel are priceless statues and paintings and the San José Bell, weighing nearly 800 pounds, which is believed to have been cast in Spain in 1356. In winter the church sometimes closes before its official closing hour. Mass is held on Sunday at 5 pm. Next door in the back of the Territorial-style dormitories of the old St. Michael's High School, a **Visitor Information Center** can help you find your way around northern New Mexico. ✉ *401 Old Santa Fe Trail* ☎ *505/983–3974* 💲 *$1* ⊙ *Mon.–Sat. 9–4:30, Sun. 10–4.*

MUSEUM HILL

Fodor's Choice **Museum of Spanish Colonial Art.** This 5,000-square-foot adobe museum
★ occupies a classically Southwestern former home designed in 1930 by acclaimed regional architect John Gaw Meem. The Spanish Colonial Art Society formed in Santa Fe in 1925 to preserve traditional Spanish-colonial art and culture, and the museum, which sits next to the Museum of International Folk Art and the Museum of Indian Arts and Culture complex, displays the fruits of the society's labor—one of the most comprehensive collections of Spanish colonial art in the world. Objects here, dating from the 16th century to the present, include *retablos* (holy images painted on wood or tin), elaborate santos, tinwork, straw appliqué, furniture, ceramics, and ironwork. The contemporary collection of works by New Mexico Hispanic artists of the 20th century helps put all this history into regional context. ✉ *750 Camino Lejo* ☎ *505/982–2226* ⊕ *www.spanishcolonial.org* 💲 *$6, 4-day pass $20, good at all 4 state museums and the Museum of Spanish Colonial Art* ⊙ *Tues.–Sun. 10–5 (also Mon. 10–5 June–Sept.).*

RAILYARD DISTRICT

The most significant development in Santa Fe in recent years has taken place in the Railyard District, a neighborhood just south of the Plaza that was for years called the Guadalupe District. Comprising a few easily walked blocks, the district has been revitalized with a snazzy new park and outdoor performance space, a shopping complex, a new permanent indoor-outdoor home for the farmers' market, and several new restaurants and galleries.

This historic warehouse and rail district endured several decades of neglect after the demise of the train route through town. But rather than tearing the buildings down (this is a city where 200-year-old mud-brick buildings sell at a premium, after all), developers gradually converted the low-lying warehouses into artists' studios, antiques shops, bookstores, indie shops, and restaurants. The restored scenic train to Lamy and the Rail Runner commuter train to Albuquerque have put the rail tracks as well as the vintage Mission-style depot back into use.

20

A central feature of the district's redevelopment is the **Railyard Park**, at the corner of Cerrillos Road and Guadalupe Street, which was designed to highlight native plants and provide citizens with a lush, urban space. The adjoining buildings contain the vibrant **Santa Fe Farmers' Market**, the teen-oriented community art center **Warehouse21, SITE Santa Fe** museum, art galleries, shops, restaurants, and live-work spaces for artists. This dramatic development reveals the fascinating way Santa Feans have worked to meet the needs of an expanding city while paying strict attention to the city's historic relevance.

WHERE TO EAT

Eating out is a major pastime in Santa Fe and it's well worth coming here with a mind to join in on the fun. Restaurants with high-profile chefs stand beside low-key joints, many offering unique and intriguing variations on regional and international cuisine. You'll find restaurants full of locals and tourists alike all over the downtown and surrounding areas. Although Santa Fe does have some high-end restaurants where dinner for two can easily exceed $200, the city also has plenty of reasonably priced dining options. Waits for tables are very common during the busy summer season, so it's a good idea to call ahead even when reservations aren't accepted, if only to get a sense of the waiting time. Reservations for dinner at the better restaurants are a must in summer and on weekends the rest of the year.

WHAT IT COSTS					
	¢	$	$$	$$$	$$$$
Restaurants	under $10	$10–$17	$18–$24	$25–$30	over $30

Prices are per person, for a main course at dinner.

THE PLAZA

$$$
CONTEMPORARY
Fodor'sChoice
★

✕ **Cafe Pasqual's.** A perennial favorite, this cheerful cubbyhole dishes up Southwestern and Nuevo Latino specialties for breakfast, lunch, and dinner. Don't be discouraged by lines out front—it's worth the wait. The culinary muse behind it all is Katharine Kagel, who championed organic, local ingredients, and whose expert kitchen staff produces mouthwatering breakfast and lunch specialties like the breakfast relleno (a big, cheese-stuffed chili with eggs and a smoky tomato salsa served with beans and tortillas), huevos motuleños (eggs in a tangy tomatillo salsa with black beans and fried bananas), and the sublime grilled free-range chicken sandwich. Dinner is a more formal, though still friendly and easygoing, affair: char-grilled lamb with pomegranate-molasses glaze, steamed sugar-snap peas, and pan-seared potato cakes is a pleasure; the kicky starter of the Thai mint salad with chicken is a revelation. Mexican folk art, colorful tiles, and murals by Oaxacan artist Leovigildo Martinez create a festive atmosphere. Try the chummy communal table, or go late morning or after 1:30 pm to (hopefully) avoid the crush. ⊠ *121 Don Gaspar Ave.* ☎ *505/983–9340* ⊕ *www. pasquals.com* ⊟ *AE, MC, V* ⚄ *No reservations for breakfast and lunch.*

$$
SPANISH
Fodor'sChoice
★

✕ **La Boca.** This little restaurant, a clean, bright room within an old adobe building, earns rave reviews and become a local favorite for its intriguingly prepared Spanish food and excellent wine list. Chef James Campbell Caruso has created a menu just right for Santa Fe's eating style; a wide, changing array of delectable tapas and an edited selection of classic entrées, like the paella. The friendly, efficient staff is happy to advise on wine and food selections. The chef's tasting menu for $55 per person (additional $25 for wine or sherry pairings) is a fun way to experience Caruso's well-honed approach to his food. Desserts, like the rich chocolate pot-au-feu, are sumptuous. The room tends to be loud and can get stuffy during winter when the Dutch door and windows are closed, but crowds are friendly and you never know who you'll end up next to in this town of low-key luminaries and celebrities. Half-price tapas, during Tapas en la Tarde, from 3 to 5 during the week, make a perfect and economical late lunch. ✉ *72 W. Marcy St., The Plaza* ☎ *505/982–3433* ⊕ *www.labocasf.com* ▭ *AE, D, DC, MC, V* ☺ *No lunch Sun.*

$ ✗ **The Shed.** The lines at lunch attest to the status of this downtown New

NEW MEXICAN Mexican eatery. The rambling, low-doored, and atmospheric adobe

Fodor'sChoice dating from 1692 is decorated with folk art, and service is downright

★ neighborly. Even if you're a devoted green chili sauce fan, you must try the locally grown red chili the place is famous for; it is rich and perfectly spicy. Specialties include red-chili enchiladas, green-chili stew with potatoes and pork, comforting posole, and their charbroiled Shedburgers. The mushroom bisque is a surprising and delicious offering. Homemade desserts, like the mocha cake, are a yummy way to smooth out the spice. There's a full bar, too. ✉ *113½ E. Palace Ave.* ☎ *505/982–9030* ⊕ *www. sfshed.com* ▭ *AE, DC, MC, V* ☺ *Closed Sun.*

CANYON ROAD

$$$$ ✗ **Geronimo.** At this bastion of high cuisine, the complex dishes range

CONTEMPORARY from pan-roasted Kurobuta pork tenderloin with spicy soy apricot glaze

Fodor'sChoice and scallion black pepper risotto, to fiery sweet-chili-and-honey-grilled

★ Mexican sweet prawns with jasmine-almond rice cakes, frisée-and-red-onion salad, and *yuzu* (Japanese citrus fruit)-and-basil aioli. Chef Eric Di Stefano's peppery elk tenderloin remains a perennial favorite. Desserts are artful and rich and the Sunday brunch is well regarded. Located in the Borrego House, a massive-walled adobe dating from 1756, the intimate, white dining rooms have beamed ceilings, wood floors, fireplaces, and cushioned *bancos* (banquettes). The restaurant is renowned for both its cuisine and its highly refined service. In summer you can dine under the front portal; in winter the bar with fireplace is inviting. For a less formal experience, dine in the dark, seductive bar—the cocktails are excellent. ✉ *724 Canyon Rd.* ☎ *505/982–1500* ⊕ *www. geronimorestaurant.com* ▭ *AE, MC, V* ☺ *No lunch Mon.*

RAILYARD DISTRICT

¢ ✗ **Aztec Cafe.** If a cup of really tasty, locally roasted, noncorporate coffee

CAFÉ in a funky, creaky-wood-floored old adobe sounds like nirvana to you,

Fodor'sChoice then this is the place. Cozy, colorful rooms inside are lined with local

★ art (and artists), the staff is laid-back and friendly, and the shady patio outside is a busy meeting ground for locals. Food is homemade, healthy, and flavorful. The menu includes sandwiches such as the Martin-roast turkey, green apples, and Swiss cheese; fabulous, fluffy quiches; soups, breakfast burritos, and super-yummy homemade ice cream in the warm season. Brunch happens on the weekends. It's open until 7 (6 pm Sunday) in case you get late-afternoon munchies. There's free Wi-Fi and a public computer with Internet access, and beer and wine are available. ✉ *317 Aztec St., Railyard District* ☎ *505/820–0025* ⊕ *www.azteccafe. com* ⌕ *Reservations not accepted* ▭ *AE, MC, V.*

20

Santa Fe's restaurants and hotels are often housed in modern adobe structures.

WEST OF THE PLAZA

¢ ✕ Bumble Bee's Baja Grill. A bright, vibrantly colored restaurant with
MEXICAN closely spaced tables, piñatas, and ceiling fans wafting overhead,
Fodor's Choice Bumble Bee's (it's the nickname of the ebullient owner, Bob) delights
★ locals with its super-fresh Cal Mex–style food. If you like fish tacos, the
mahimahi ones with creamy, nondairy slaw are outstanding; try them
with a side of salad instead of beans and rice and *hijole*. What a meal!
Mammoth burritos with a wide range of fillings (including asparagus—yum!), roasted chicken with cilantro-lime rice, char-grilled trout
platters, and a wide variety of vegetarian options keep folks pouring
through the doors. You order at the counter, grab some chips and any
one of a number of freshly made salsas from the bar, and wait for your
number to come up. Beer, wine, and Mexican soft drinks are served.
Try a homemade Mexican chocolate brownie for dessert. There's live
jazz on Saturday night. ✉ *301 Jefferson St.* ☎ *505/820–2862* ⊕ *www.
bumblebeesbajagrill.com* ✉ *3701 Cerrillos Rd.* ☎ *505/988–3278*
⊟ *AE, D, MC, V.*

OLD LAS VEGAS HIGHWAY

¢ ✕ Bobcat Bite. It'll take you 15 easy minutes from downtown to drive
AMERICAN to this tiny roadhouse southeast of town—and it's worth it. Folks drive
Fodor's Choice a lot farther for Bobcat Bite's steaks and chops ($17) but come espe-
★ cially for one thing: the juiciest burgers in the area. Locals prefer them
topped with cheese and green chilies. Only early dinners are available
(and no dessert is served), as the place closes by 8 most nights; you'll
want to arrive early to get a seat. ✉ *Old Las Vegas Hwy., 4½ mi south
of Old Pecos Trail exit off I-25* ☎ *505/983–5319* ⊕ *www.bobcatbite.*

com & *Reservations not accepted* ▤ *No credit cards* ☉ *Closed Sun. and Mon. (also closed Tues. in winter).*

$
ECLECTIC
☾
Fodor's Choice
★

✕ **Harry's Roadhouse.** This busy, friendly, art-filled compound just southeast of town consists of several inviting rooms, from a diner-style space with counter seating to a cozier nook with a fireplace—there's also an enchanting courtyard out back with juniper trees and flower gardens. The varied menu of contemporary diner favorites, pizzas, New Mexican fare, and bountiful salads is supplemented by a long list of daily specials—which often include delicious ethnic dishes. Favorites include smoked-chicken quesadillas and grilled-salmon tacos with tomatillo salsa and black beans. Breakfast is fantastic. On weekends, if you're there early, you might just get a chance at one of owner–pastry chef Peyton's phenomenal cinnamon rolls. Desserts here are homey favorites, from the chocolate pudding to the blueberry cobbler. Many gluten-free and veggie options are available, and Harry's is also known for stellar margaritas. The owners are committed to recycling and sustainable business practices. ✉ *96-B Old Las Vegas Hwy., 1 mi east of Old Pecos Trail exit off I–25* ☏ *505/989–4629* ⊕ *www.harrysroadhousesantafe. com* ▤ *AE, D, MC, V.*

WHERE TO STAY

In Santa Fe you can ensconce yourself in quintessential Southwestern style or anonymous hotel-chain decor, depending on how much you want to spend—the city has costlier accommodations than anywhere in the Southwest. Cheaper options are available on Cerrillos (pronounced sir-*ee*-yos) Road, the rather unattractive business thoroughfare southwest of downtown. Quality varies greatly on Cerrillos, but some of the best-managed, most attractive properties are (from most to least expensive) the Holiday Inn, the Courtyard Marriott, and the Motel 6. You generally pay more as you get closer to the Plaza, but for many visitors it's worth it to be within walking distance of many attractions. Some of the best deals are offered by B&Bs—many of those near the Plaza offer much better values than the big, touristy hotels. Rates drop, often from 30% to 50%, from November to April (excluding Thanksgiving and Christmas).

Hotel reviews have been condensed for this book. Please go to Fodors. com for full reviews of each property.

WHAT IT COSTS				
	¢	$	$$	$$$	$$$$
Hotels	under $70	$70–$130	$131–$190	$191–$260	over $260

Prices are for two people in a standard double room in high season, excluding tax.

THE PLAZA

$$$
Fodor's Choice
★

☷ **Hacienda Nicholas.** It is rare to find classic Santa Fe accommodations—this actually *is* an old hacienda—blocks from the Plaza for reasonable prices: This is one such place. **Pros:** rates are significantly lower than one would expect for the level of service and amenities here; the

20

inn is one of the most eco-friendly in town. **Cons:** no hot tub or pool, though guests have privileges at El Gancho Health & Fitness Club 15 minutes away. ✉ *320 E. Marcy St., The Plaza* ☎ *505/986–1431 or 888/284–3170* ⊕ *www.haciendanicholas.com* ↩ *7 rooms* ⟂ *In-room: Wi-Fi. In-hotel: Wi-Fi hotspot* ⊟ *AE, D, MC, V.*

$$$$
Fodor's Choice
★
 ▦ **Inn of the Anasazi.** Unassuming from the outside, this first-rate boutique hotel is one of Santa Fe's finest, with superb architectural detail. **Pros:** staff is thorough, gracious, and highly professional. **Cons:** standard rooms tend to be small for the price; few rooms have balconies; no hot tub or pool. ✉ *113 Washington Ave.* ☎ *505/988–3030 or 800/688–8100* ⊕ *www.innoftheanasazi.com* ↩ *58 rooms* ⟂ *In-room: a/c, safe, Wi-Fi. In-hotel: restaurant, bar, parking (paid), some pets allowed* ⊟ *AE, D, DC, MC, V.*

EAST SIDE

$$$
Fodor's Choice
★
 ▦ **Inn on the Alameda.** Near the Plaza and Canyon Road is one of the Southwest's best small hotels. **Pros:** the solicitous staff is first-rate; excellent, expansive breakfast buffet with lots of extras. **Cons:** rooms closest to Alameda can be noisy; no pool. ✉ *303 E. Alameda St.* ☎ *505/984–2121 or 888/984–2121* ⊕ *www.innonthealameda.com* ↩ *59 rooms, 10 suites* ⟂ *In-room: a/c, refrigerator (some), Wi-Fi. In-hotel: bar, gym, laundry facilities, parking (free), some pets allowed* ⊟ *AE, D, DC, MC, V* ⊧⊙⊧ *CP.*

OLD SANTA FE TRAIL

$$$$
Fodor's Choice
★
 ▦ **Inn of the Five Graces.** There isn't another property in Santa Fe to compare to this sumptuous yet relaxed inn with an unmistakable East-meets-West feel. **Pros:** tucked into a quiet, ancient neighborhood; the Plaza is only minutes away; fantastic staff, attentive but not overbearing. **Cons:** rates are steep. ✉ *150 E. DeVargas St.* ☎ *505/992–0957 or 866/992–0957* ⊕ *www.fivegraces.com* ↩ *22 suites, 1 house* ⟂ *In-room: kitchen (some), refrigerator, Wi-Fi. In-hotel: parking (free), some pets allowed* ⊟ *AE, D, MC, V* ⊧⊙⊧ *BP.*

SOUTH SIDE

$
Fodor's Choice
★
 ▦ **El Rey Inn.** The kind of place where Lucy and Ricky might have stayed during one of their cross-country adventures, the El Rey was built in 1936 but has been brought gracefully into the 21st century, its rooms and bathrooms handsomely updated without losing any period charm. **Pros:** excellent price for a distinctive, charming property. **Cons:** rooms closest to Cerrillos can be noisy; some rooms are quite dark. ✉ *1862 Cerrillos Rd.* ☎ *505/982–1931 or 800/521–1349* ⊕ *www. elreyinnsantafe.com* ↩ *86 rooms* ⟂ *In-room: a/c, kitchen (some), Wi-Fi. In-hotel: pool, gym, laundry facilities, parking (free)* ⊟ *AE, DC, MC, V* ⊧⊙⊧ *CP.*

RAILYARD DISTRICT

$$
Fodor's Choice
★
 ▦ **Hotel Santa Fe.** The light, airy rooms and suites at this handsome Pueblo-style hotel are traditional Southwestern, with locally handmade furniture, wooden blinds, and Pueblo paintings; many have balconies. **Pros:** professional, helpful staff; lots of amenities. **Cons:** standard rooms are fairly small. ✉ *1501 Paseo de Peralta* ☎ *505/982–1200 or*

800/825–9876 ⊕ *www.hotelsantafe.com* ⤤ *40 rooms, 91 suites* ♿ *In-room: a/c, Wi-Fi. In-hotel: restaurant, bar, pool, laundry service, parking (free)* ⊟ *AE, D, DC, MC, V.*

NORTH OF THE PLAZA

$$$ ☷ **Ten Thousand Waves.** Devotees appreciate the authentic atmosphere

Fodor'sChoice of this Japanese-style health spa and small hotel above town. **Pros:**

★ artful furnishings; peaceful setting; warm service. **Cons:** a bit remote, especially considering lack of a restaurant. ⊠ *3451 Hyde Park Rd., 4 mi northeast of the Plaza* ✒ *Box 10200 87504* ☎ *505/982–9304* ⊕ *www.tenthousandwaves.com* ⤤ *12 cottages, 1 trailer* ♿ *In-room: no a/c, kitchen (some), refrigerator, no TV (some), Wi-Fi (some). In-hotel: spa, parking (free), some pets allowed* ⊟ *D, MC, V.*

SHOPPING

Shopping in Santa Fe consists mostly of one-of-a-kind independent stores. Canyon Road, packed with art galleries, is the perfect place to find unique gifts and collectibles. The downtown district, around the Plaza, has unusual gift shops, clothing, and shoe stores that range from theatrical to conventional, curio shops, and art galleries. The funky, revitalized Railyard District, less touristy than the Plaza, is on downtown's southwest perimeter and includes the Sanbusco Market Center and the Design Center, both hubs of unique and wonderful boutiques.

ART GALLERIES

The following are only a few of the nearly 200 galleries in greater Santa Fe—with the best of representational, nonobjective, Native American, Latin American, cutting-edge, photographic, and soulful works that defy categorization. The Santa Fe Convention and Visitors Bureau has a more extensive listing. *The Collectors Guide to Santa Fe, Taos, and Albuquerque* is a good resource available on the Web at ⊕ *www. collectorsguide.com.* Check the "Pasatiempo" pullout in the *Santa Fe New Mexican* on Friday for a preview of gallery openings.

Fodor'sChoice **Andrew Smith Gallery** (⊠ *122 Grant Ave., The Plaza* ☎ *505/984–1234*

★ ⊕ *www.andrewsmithgallery.com*) is a significant photo gallery dealing in works by Edward S. Curtis and other 19th-century chroniclers of the American West. Other major figures are Ansel Adams, Edward Weston, O. Winston Link, Henri Cartier-Bresson, Eliot Porter, Laura Gilpin, Dorothea Lange, Alfred Stieglitz, Annie Liebovitz, and regional artists like Barbara Van Cleve.

Bellas Artes (⊠ *653 Canyon Rd., Canyon Road* ☎ *505/983–2745* ⊕ *www.bellasartesgallery.com*), a sophisticated gallery and sculpture garden, has a captivating collection of ceramics, paintings, photography, and sculptural work, and represents internationally renowned artists like Judy Pfaff, Phoebe Adams, and Olga de Amaral. The vanguard modernist work of sculptor Ruth Duckworth is also well-represented.

Fodor'sChoice **Eight Modern** (⊠ *231 Delgado St., Canyon Road* ☎ *505/995–0231*

★ ⊕ *www.eightmodern.net*), in an unassuming building just off Canyon Road, showcases modern and contemporary painting, photography, and sculpture by established artists from around the world. Eight

20

Modern has staked a notable claim in Santa Fe's art world by bringing a number of internationally acclaimed artists here for the first time.

Fodor'sChoice ★ **evo Gallery** (⊠ *554 S. Guadalupe St., Railyard District* ☎ *505/982–4610* ⊕ *www.evogallery.org*) is another gallery that affirms Santa Fe's reputation as a leading center of contemporary art. Powerhouse artists like Jenny Holzer, Ed Ruscha, Donald Judd, Jasper Johns, and Agnes Martin, as well as emerging artists, are represented in this huge space in the Guadalupe District.

Fodor'sChoice ★ **Gerald Peters Gallery** (⊠ *1011 Paseo de Peralta* ☎ *505/954–5700* ⊕ *www.gpgallery.com*) is Santa Fe's leading gallery of American and European art from the 19th century to the present. It has works by Max Weber, Albert Bierstadt, the Taos Society, the New Mexico modernists, and Georgia O'Keeffe, as well as contemporary artists.

Fodor'sChoice ★ **James Kelly Contemporary** (⊠ *1601 Paseo de Peralta, Railyard District* ☎ *505/989–1601* ⊕ *www.jameskelly.com*) mounts sophisticated, high-caliber shows by international and regional artists, such as Johnnie Winona Ross, Nic Nicosia, Peter Sarkisian, Tom Joyce, and Sherrie Levine in a renovated warehouse directly across from SITE Santa Fe. James Kelly has been instrumental in transforming the Railyard District into Santa Fe's hub for contemporary art.

★ **Nedra Matteucci Galleries** (⊠ *1075 Paseo de Peralta, Canyon Road* ☎ *505/982–4631* ⊠ *555 Canyon Rd.* ⊕ *www.matteucci.com* ☎ *505/983–2731*) exhibits works by California regionalists, members of the early Taos and Santa Fe schools, and masters of American Impressionism and Modernism. Spanish colonial furniture, Indian antiquities, and a fantastic sculpture garden are other draws of this well-respected establishment. The old adobe building the gallery is in is a beautifully preserved example of Santa Fe–style architecture.

Santa Fe Art Institute (⊠ *1600 St. Michael's Dr., South of the Railyard District* ☎ *505/424–5050*), a nonprofit educational art organization that sponsors several artists in residence and presents workshops, exhibitions, and lectures, has a respected gallery whose exhibits change regularly. The institute is set inside a dramatic contemporary building designed by Mexican modernist architect Ricardo Legorreta. Past artists in residence have included Richard Diebenkorn, Larry Bell, Moon Zappa, Henriette Wyeth Hurd, and Judy Pfaff.

ⓒ **Fodor'sChoice** ★ **Shidoni Foundry and Galleries** (⊠ *B1508 Bishop's Lodge Rd., 5 mi north of Santa Fe, North of the Plaza, Tesuque* ☎ *505/988–8001* ⊕ *www.shidoni.com*) casts work for established and emerging artists from all over North America. On the grounds of an old chicken ranch, Shidoni has a rambling sculpture garden and a gallery. Self-guided foundry tours are permitted Saturday 9–5 and weekdays noon–1, but the sculpture garden is open daily during daylight hours; you can watch bronze pourings most Saturday afternoons. This is a dream of a place to expose your kids to large-scale art and enjoy a lovely and, in this area, rare expanse of green grass at the same time.

Beautiful, southwestern terra-cotta ceramics can be found in many Santa Fe galleries and markets.

CLOTHING AND ACCESSORIES

Many tourists arrive in clothing from mainstream department stores and leave bedecked in Western garb looking like they've stepped from a bygone era. If you simply cannot live without a getup Annie Oakley herself would envy, you will find shopping options beyond your wildest dreams. But take a look around at the striking and highly individualized styles of the locals and you'll see that Western gear is mixed with pieces from all over the globe to create what is the real Santa Fe style. There are few towns where you'll find more distinctive, sometimes downright eccentric, expressions of personal style on every age and every shape. Indians, cowboys, hipsters, students, artists, yogis, immigrants from all over the world, and world travelers all bring something to the style mix of this town and you'll find plenty of shops that will allow you to join in the fun.

Fodor's Choice ★ **Back at the Ranch** (⊠ 209 E. Marcy St., The Plaza ☎ 505/989–8110 or 888/962–6687) is the place for cowboy boots. The cozy space in an old, creaky-floored adobe is stocked with perhaps the finest handmade cowboy boots you will ever see—in every color, style, and embellishment imaginable. Other finds, like funky ranch-style furniture, 1950s blanket coats, jewelry, and belt buckles are also sold. The staff is top-notch and the boots are breathtaking.

Fodor's Choice ★ **Double Take at the Ranch** (⊠ 321 S. Guadalupe St., Railyard District ☎ 505/820–7775) ranks among the best consignment stores in the West, carrying elaborately embroidered vintage cowboy shirts, hundreds of pairs of boots, funky old prints, and amazing vintage Indian pawn and Mexican jewelry. The store adjoins its sister consignment store, also called Double Take, which carries a wide range of contemporary clothing and accessories for men and women; and Santa Fe Pottery, which carries the works of local artists.

Fodor's Choice ★ **O'Farrell Hats** (⊠ *111 E. San Francisco St., The Plaza* ☎ 505/989–9666 ⊕ *www.ofarrellhatco.com*) is the domain of America's foremost hat-making family. Founder Kevin O'Farrell passed away in 2006, but the legacy continues with his son Scott and the highly trained staff. This quirky shop custom crafts one-of-a-kind beaver-felt cowboy hats that make the ultimate Santa Fe keepsake. This level of quality comes at a cost, but devoted customers—who have included everyone from cattle ranchers to U.S. presidents—swear by O'Farrell's artful creations.

Fodor's Choice ★ For gear related to just about any outdoors activity you can think of, check out **Sangre de Cristo Mountain Works** (⊠ *328 S. Guadalupe St., Railyard District* ☎ 505/984–8221 ⊕ *www.sdcmountainworks. com*), a well-stocked shop that both sells and rents hiking, climbing, camping, trekking, snowshoeing, and skiing equipment. There's a great selection of clothing and shoes for men and women. The super-active, knowledgeable staff here can also advise you on the best venues for local recreation.

JEWELRY

Fodor's Choice ★ **Patina** (⊠ *131 W. Palace Ave., The Plaza* ☎ 505/986–3432 or 877/877–0827 ⊕ *www.patina-gallery.com*) presents outstanding contemporary jewelry, textiles, and sculptural objects of metal, clay, and wood, in a airy, museum-like space. With a staff whose courtesy is matched by knowledge of the genre, artists-owners Ivan and Allison Barnett have used their fresh curatorial aesthetic to create a showplace for more than 110 American and European artists they represent—many of whom are in permanent collections of museums such as MoMA.

MARKET

Fodor's Choice ★ Browse through the vast selection of local produce, meat, flowers, honey, and cheese—much of it organic—at the thriving **Santa Fe Farmers' Market** (⊠ *1607 Paseo de Peralta* ☎ 505/983–4098 ⊕ *www. santafefarmersmarket.com*). The market is now housed in its new, permanent building in the Railyard and it's open year-round. It's a great people-watching event, with entertainment for kids as well as a snack bar selling terrific breakfast burritos and other goodies. With the growing awareness of the importance and necessity of eating locally grown and organic food, this market offers living testimony to the fact that farming can be done successfully, even in a high-desert region like this one.

NATIVE AMERICAN ARTS AND CRAFTS

Fodor's Choice ★ The **Rainbow Man** (⊠ *107 E. Palace Ave., The Plaza* ☎ 505/982–8706 ⊕ *www.therainbowman.com*), established in 1945, does business in an old, rambling adobe complex, part of which dates from before the 1680 Pueblo Revolt. The shop carries early Navajo, Mexican, and Chimayó textiles, along with photographs by Edward S. Curtis, a breathtaking collection of vintage pawn and Mexican jewelry, Day of the Dead figures, Oaxacan folk animals, New Mexican folk art, kachinas, and contemporary jewelry from local artists. The friendly staff possesses an encyclopedic knowledge of the art here.

Fodor's Choice ★ **Robert Nichols Gallery** (⊠ *419 Canyon Rd., Canyon Road* ☎ *505/982–2145* ⊕ *www.robertnicholsgallery.com*) represents a remarkable group of Native American ceramics artists doing primarily nontraditional work. Diverse artists such as Glen Nipshank, whose organic, sensuous shapes would be right at home in MoMA, and Diego Romero, whose Cochiti-style vessels are detailed with graphic-novel-style characters and sharp social commentary, are right at home here. It is a treat to see cutting-edge work that is clearly informed by indigenous traditions.

Fodor's Choice ★ "Eclectic Modern Vintage" is **Shiprock Santa Fe**'s (⊠ *53 Old Santa Fe Trail, The Plaza* ☎ *505/982–8478* ⊕ *www.shiprocksantafe.com*) tagline, and it accurately sums up their incredible collection of pottery, textiles, painting, furniture, and sculpture. The gallery is notable for its dedication to showcasing exquisite vintage pieces alongside vanguard contemporary works.

SPORTS AND THE OUTDOORS

The Santa Fe National Forest is right in the city's backyard and includes the Dome Wilderness (5,200 acres in the volcanically formed Jémez Mountains) and the Pecos Wilderness (223,333 acres of high mountains, forests, and meadows at the southern end of the Rocky Mountain chain). The 12,500-foot Sangre de Cristo Mountains (the name translates as "blood of Christ," for the red glow they radiate at sunset) fringe the city's east side, constant and gentle reminders of the mystery and power of the natural world. To the south and west, sweeping high desert is punctuated by several less formidable mountain ranges. The dramatic shifts in elevation and topography around Santa Fe make for a wealth of outdoor activities. Head to the mountains for fishing, camping, and skiing; to the nearby Rio Grande for kayaking and rafting; and almost anywhere in the area for bird-watching, hiking, and biking.

For a one-stop shop for information about recreation on public lands, which include national and state parks, contact the **New Mexico Public Lands Information Center** (⊠ *301 Dinosaur Trail* ☎ *505/954–2002* ⊕ *www.publiclands.org*). It has maps, reference materials, licenses, permits—just about everything you need to plan an adventure in the New Mexican wilderness.

20

BICYCLING

You can pick up a map of bike trips—among them a 30-mi round-trip ride from downtown Santa Fe to Ski Santa Fe at the end of NM 475—from the New Mexico Public Lands Information Center, or at the bike shops listed below. One excellent place to mountain bike is the Dale Ball Trail Network, which is accessed from several points.

Fodor's Choice ★ **Mellow Velo** (⊠ *638 Old Santa Fe Trail, Lower Old Santa Fe Trail and South Capital* ☎ *505/995–8356* ⊕ *www.melovelo.com*) is a friendly, neighborhood bike shop offering group tours, privately guided rides, bicycle rentals ($35 per day—make reservations), and repairs. The helpful staff at this well-stocked shop offers a great way to spend a day—or seven!

HIKING

Hiking around Santa Fe can take you into high-altitude alpine country or into lunaresque high desert as you head south and west to lower elevations. For winter hiking, the gentler climates to the south are less likely to be snow packed, while the alpine areas will likely require snowshoes or cross-country skis. In summer, wildflowers bloom in the high country, and the temperature is generally at least 10 degrees cooler than in town. The mountain trails accessible at the base of the Ski Santa Fe area (end of NM 475) stay cool on even the hottest summer days. Weather can change with one gust of wind, so be prepared with extra clothing, rain gear, food, and lots of water. Keep in mind that the sun at 10,000 feet is very powerful, even with a hat and sunscreen. *See the Side Trips from Santa Fe section, below, for additional hiking areas near the city.*

For information about specific hiking areas, contact the New Mexico Public Lands Information Center. Any of the outdoor gear stores in town can also help with guides and recommendations. The **Sierra Club** (⊕ *www.riogrande.sierraclub.org*) organizes group hikes of all levels of difficulty; a schedule of hikes is posted on the Web site.

HORSEBACK RIDING

Bishop's Lodge (⊠ *1297 Bishop's Lodge Rd.* ☎ *505/983–6377*) provides rides and guides year-round. Call for reservations.

TAOS

Taos is small and resolutely rustic, but for the prosaic stretch of chain motels and strip malls that greet you as you approach from the south. Persevere to the central Plaza, and you'll find several highly walkable blocks of galleries, shops, restaurants, and art museums.

Whereas Santa Fe, Aspen, Scottsdale, and other gallery hubs in the West tend toward pricey work, much of it by artists living elsewhere, Taos remains very much an ardent hub of local arts and crafts production and sales. A half-dozen excellent museums here also document the town's esteemed artistic history.

EXPLORING

Easygoing Taoseños are a welcoming lot, and if you ever lose your orientation, you'll find locals happy to point you where you need to go. The Museum Association of Taos includes five properties: the Harwood Museum, Taos Art Museum, Millicent Rogers Museum, E. L. Blumenschein Home and Museum, and La Hacienda de los Martínez. Each of the museums charges $8 for admission, but you can buy a combination ticket—$25 for all five, valid for one year.

Fodor'sChoice **Harwood Museum.** The Pueblo Revival former home of Burritt Elihu
★ "Burt" Harwood, a dedicated painter who studied in France before moving to Taos in 1916, is adjacent to a museum dedicated to the works of local artists. Traditional Hispanic northern New Mexican artists, early art-colony painters, post–World War II modernists, and

Taos Pueblo is the largest collection of multistory Pueblo dwellings in the United States.

contemporary artists such as Larry Bell, Agnes Martin, Ken Price, and Earl Stroh are represented. Mabel Dodge Luhan, a major arts patron, bequeathed many of the 19th- and early-20th-century works in the Harwoods' collection, including *retablos* (painted wood representations of Catholic saints) and *bultos* (three-dimensional carvings of the saints). In the Hispanic Traditions Gallery upstairs are 19th-century tinwork, furniture, and sculpture. Downstairs, among early-20th-century art-colony holdings, look for E. Martin Hennings's *Chamisa in Bloom,* which captures the Taos landscape particularly beautifully. A tour of the ground-floor galleries shows that Taos painters of the era, notably Oscar Berninghaus, Ernest Blumenschein, Victor Higgins, Walter Ufer, Marsden Hartley, and John Marin, were fascinated by the land and the people linked to it. An octagonal gallery exhibits works by Agnes Martin. Martin's seven large canvas panels (each 5 feet square) are studies in white, their precise lines and blocks forming textured grids. Operated by the University of New Mexico since 1936, the Harwood is the second-oldest art museum in the state. ⊠ *238 Ledoux St.* ☎ *575/758–9826* ⊕ *www.harwoodmuseum.org* ✉ *$8, 5-museum Museum Association of Taos combination ticket $25* ⊘ *Tues.–Sat. 10–5, Sun. noon–5.*

Fodor'sChoice
★   **Millicent Rogers Museum.** More than 5,000 pieces of spectacular Native American and Hispanic art, many of them from the private collection of the late Standard Oil heiress Millicent Rogers, are on display here. Among the pieces are baskets, blankets, rugs, kachina dolls, carvings, paintings, rare religious artifacts, and, most significantly, jewelry (Rogers, a fashion icon in her day, was one of the first Americans to appreciate the turquoise-and-silver artistry of Native American jewelers). Other

important works include the pottery and ceramics of Maria Martinez and other potters from San Ildefonso Pueblo (23 mi north of Santa Fe). Docents conduct guided tours by appointment, and the museum hosts lectures, films, workshops, and demonstrations. The two-room gift shop has exceptional jewelry, rugs, books, and pottery. ⊠ *1504 Millicent Rogers Rd.; from Taos Plaza head north on Paseo del Pueblo Norte and left at sign for CR BA030 (Millicent Rogers Rd.)* 🕾 *575/758–2462* ⊕ *www.millicentrogers.com* 🖃 *$8, 5-museum Museum Association of Taos combination ticket $25* ☾ *Daily 10–5; closed Mon. in Nov.*

Fodor'sChoice
★
Taos Art Museum and Fechin House. The interior of this extraordinary adobe house, built between 1927 and 1933 by Russian émigré and artist Nicolai Fechin, is a marvel of carved Russian-style woodwork and furniture. Fechin constructed it to showcase his daringly colorful paintings. The house became host to the Taos Art Museum in 2003, with a collection of paintings from more than 50 Taos artists, including founders of the original Taos Society of Artists, among them Joseph Sharp, Ernest Blumenschein, Bert Phillips, E. I. Couse, and Oscar Berninghaus. ⊠ *227 Paseo del Pueblo Norte* 🕾 *575/758–2690* ⊕ *www.taosartmuseum.org* 🖃 *$8, 5-museum Museum Association of Taos combination ticket $25* ☾ *Tues.–Sun. 10–5.*

☼ Fodor'sChoice
★
Taos Pueblo. For nearly 1,000 years the mud-and-straw adobe walls of Taos Pueblo have sheltered Tiwa-speaking Native Americans. A United Nations World Heritage Site, this is the largest collection of multistory pueblo dwellings in the United States. The pueblo's main buildings, Hlauuma (north house) and Hlaukwima (south house), are separated by a creek. These structures are believed to be of a similar age, probably built between 1000 and 1450. The dwellings have common walls but no connecting doorways—the Tiwas gained access only from the top, via ladders that were retrieved after entering. Small buildings and corrals are scattered about.

The pueblo today appears much as it did when the first Spanish explorers arrived in New Mexico in 1540. The adobe walls glistening with mica caused the conquistadors to believe they had discovered one of the fabled Seven Cities of Gold. The outside surfaces are continuously maintained by replastering with thin layers of mud, and the interior walls are frequently coated with thin washes of white clay. Some walls are several feet thick in places. The roofs of each of the five-story structures are supported by large timbers, or vigas, hauled down from the mountain forests. Pine or aspen *latillas* (smaller pieces of wood) are placed side by side between the vigas; the entire roof is then packed with dirt.

Even after 400 years of Spanish and Anglo presence in Taos, inside the pueblo the traditional Native American way of life has endured. Tribal custom allows no electricity or running water in Hlauuma and Hlaukwima, where varying numbers (usually fewer than 150) of Taos Native Americans live full-time. About 1,900 others live in conventional homes on the pueblo's 95,000 acres. The crystal-clear Rio Pueblo de Taos, originating high above in the mountains at the sacred Blue Lake, is the primary source of water for drinking and irrigating. Bread is still baked in *hornos* (outdoor domed ovens). Artisans of the Taos Pueblo produce and sell (tax-free) traditionally handcrafted wares, such as mica-flecked pottery and silver jewelry. Great hunters, the Taos Native Americans are also known for their work with animal skins and their excellent moccasins, boots, and drums.

The pueblo **Church of San Geronimo,** or St. Jerome, the patron saint of Taos Pueblo, was completed in 1850 to replace the one destroyed by the U.S. Army in 1847 during the Mexican War. With its smooth symmetry, stepped portal, and twin bell towers, the church is a popular subject for photographers and artists (though the taking of photographs inside is discouraged).

The public is invited to certain ceremonial dances held throughout the year (a full list of these is posted on the Pueblo Web site): highlights include the Feast of Santa Cruz Foot Race and Corn Dance (May 3); Taos Pueblo Pow Wow (July 8–10); Feast of San Geronimo Sunset Dance (July 25 and 26, September 29 and 30); Vespers and Bonfire Procession (December 24); and Deer Dance or Matachines Dance (December 25). While you're at the pueblo, respect the "restricted area" signs that protect the privacy of residents and native religious sites; do not enter private homes or open any doors not clearly labeled as curio shops; do not photograph tribal members without asking permission; do not enter the cemetery grounds; and do not wade in the Rio Pueblo de Taos, which is considered sacred and is the community's sole source of drinking water. ⊠ *Head to right off Paseo del Pueblo Norte just past Best Western Kachina Lodge* ☎ *575/758–1028* ⊕ *www.taospueblo.com* ☞ *Tourist fees $10; guided tours; photography and video permits $6 per camera, cell phone (if you're using it to take pictures), or video-recording device; commercial photography, sketching, or painting only by prior permission from governor's office (575/758–1028); fees vary; apply at least 10 days in advance* ◷ *Daily 8–4:30, tours by appointment. Closed for funerals, religious ceremonies, and for 10-wk quiet time in late winter or early spring, and last part of Aug.; call ahead before visiting at these times.*

WHERE TO EAT

20

For a relatively small town many miles from any big city, Taos has a sophisticated and eclectic dining scene. It's as fine a destination for authentic New Mexican fare as any town its size in the state, but you'll also find several upscale spots serving creative fare utilizing mostly local ingredients, a smattering of excellent Asian and Middle Eastern spots, and several very good cafés and coffeehouses perfect for light but bountiful breakfast and lunch fare.

WHAT IT COSTS					
	¢	$	$$	$$$	$$$$
Restaurants	under $10	$10–$17	$18–$24	$25–$30	over $30

Prices are per person, for a main course at dinner.

$$$
GERMAN
Taos Pueblo
Fodor'sChoice
★

✕ **The Bavarian.** The restaurant inside the romantic, magically situated alpine lodge, which also offers Taos Ski Valley's most luxurious accommodations, serves outstanding contemporary Bavarian-inspired cuisine, such as baked artichokes and Gruyère, and braised pork loin with garlic-mashed potatoes and red cabbage. Lunch is more casual and less expensive, with burgers and salads available—in summer this is an excellent spot to fuel up before attempting an ambitious hike, as the restaurant is steps from the trailhead for Wheeler Peak and other popular mountains. There's an extensive wine list, plus a nice range of beers imported from Spaten Brewery in Munich. ✉ *100 Kachina Rd.* ✆ *Box 653, Taos Ski Valley 87525* ☎ *575/776–8020* ⊕ *www.thebavarian.net* ▭ *AE, MC, V* ✆ *Closed early Apr.–late May and mid-Oct.–late Nov.; closed Mon.–Wed. in summer.*

$$
ECLECTIC
Fodor'sChoice
★

✕ **Graham's Grille.** The folks who frequent this upscale bar and eatery tend to be hip and sophisticated—just like the artful, Southwestern-based but cross-cultural food served in this minimalist environment. Local, seasonal produce, cage-free chickens, and homemade stocks are key to the fresh flavors and creative combinations prepared by chef Leslie Fay, a long-time Taos restaurateur. Small plates worth sampling include mac-and-cheese with mild green chilies and hickory-smoked bacon, duck-breast flatbread with orange-*charmoula* sauce, and black bean soup with a touch of cumin. The buffalo-brisket sandwich is a winner at lunch. Main courses range from blue corn–crusted red trout with cilantro-lime butter to hearty tamale pies. Worthy desserts include a coconut cake with mango cream and a lemon-and-piñon pound cake with blueberry coulis. There's a memorable Sunday brunch. ✉ *106 Paseo del Pueblo Norte* ☎ *575/751–1350* ⊕ *www.thefayway.com/ dining* ▭ *AE, MC, V.*

$$$
AMERICAN

✕ **Lambert's of Taos.** Superb service and creative cuisine define this Taos landmark located 2½ blocks south of the Plaza. Among starters, don't miss the marinated roasted-beet salad with warm goat cheese and pumpkin seeds, sautéed lobster and shallots with a vanilla-champagne sauce, and corn-and-applewood-smoked-bacon chowder. Or have all three and call it a night. The signature entrées include pepper-crusted lamb with a red-wine demi-glace and roasted duck with an apricot-chipotle glaze. Memorable desserts are a warm-apple-and-almond crisp topped with white-chocolate ice cream and a dark-chocolate mousse with raspberry sauce. A small-plate bistro menu is available in the cozy bar or in the spacious dining rooms. The lengthy wine list includes some of California's finest vintages. The owners also operate the Old Blinking Light up near Arroyo Seco *(⇨ below).* ✉ *309 Paseo del Pueblo Sur* ☎ *575/758–1009* ⊕ *www.lambertsoftaos.com* ▭ *AE, DC, MC, V* ✆ *No lunch.*

$
ECLECTIC
Fodor'sChoice
★

✕ **Love Apple.** It's easy to drive by the small adobe former chapel that houses this delightful restaurant a short drive north of the Plaza, just beyond the driveway for Hacienda del Sol B&B. But slow down—you don't want to miss the culinary magic inside. Chef Andrea Meyer uses organic, mostly local ingredients in the preparation of simple yet sophisticated farm-to-table creations like homemade sweet-corn tamales with red-chili mole, a fried egg, and crème fraîche, and robustly seasoned posole stew with grilled lamb sausage, pancetta, caramelized onion, and radish-lime relish. The price is right, too—just remember it's cash-only. ✉ *803 Paseo del Pueblo Norte* ☎ *575/751–0050* ⊕ *www.theloveapple. net* ▤ *No credit cards* ◷ *Closed Mon. No lunch.*

$ ✕ **Rellenos Cafe.** Touted as the only organic New Mexican restaurant

NEW MEXICAN   in town, this casual eatery from by the talented team behind Antonio's and Sabor also offers wheat-free, gluten-free, and vegan menu options. Popular specialties include killer chiles rellenos topped with a brandy-cream sauce, grilled garlic shrimp, and seafood paella. Service is friendly—don't be put off by the bland exterior on a busy stretch of Paseo del Pueblo (there's a nice patio in back). The house drink, a fruity sangria, is served in gargantuan Mexican glasses. ✉ *135 Paseo del Pueblo Sur* ☎ *575/758–7001* ⌲ *Reservations not accepted* ▤ *MC, V* ◷ *Closed Sun.*

$$$ ✕ **Sabroso.** Reasonably priced, innovative cuisine and outstanding

MEDITERRANEAN   wines are served in this 150-year-old adobe hacienda, where you can

Taos Ski Valley   also relax in lounge chairs near the bar, or on a delightful patio sur-

Fodor's Choice   rounded by plum trees. The Mediterranean-influenced contemporary

★   menu changes regularly, but an evening's entrée might be pan-seared sea scallops, risotto cakes, and ratatouille, or rib-eye steak topped with a slice of Stilton cheese. There's live jazz and cabaret in the piano bar several nights a week. Order from the simpler bar menu if you're seeking something light—the antipasto plate and white-truffle-oil fries are both delicious. ✉ *470 NM 150, Taos Ski Valley Rd.* ☎ *575/776–3333* ⊕ *www.sabrosotaos.com* ▤ *AE, MC, V* ◷ *No lunch.*

$$$$ ✕ **Stakeout Grill and Bar.** On Outlaw Hill in the foothills of the Sangre

STEAK   de Cristo Mountains, this old adobe homestead has 100-mi-long views

Fodor's Choice   and sunsets that dazzle. The outdoor patio encircled by a piñon forest

★   has kiva fireplaces to warm you during cooler months. The decadent fare is well prepared, fully living up to the view it accompanies—try filet mignon with béarnaise sauce, buffalo rib eye with chipotle-cilantro butter, almond-crusted wild sockeye salmon with shaved fennel, or fall-off-the-bone braised Colorado lamb shank with orange and port-wine jus. Don't miss the tasty Kentucky bourbon pecan pie and crème brûlée with toasted coconut for dessert. ✉ *Stakeout Dr.; 8 mi south of Taos Plaza, east of NM 68, look for cowboy sign* ☎ *575/758–2042* ⊕ *www. stakeoutrestaurant.com* ▤ *AE, D, DC, MC, V* ◷ *No lunch.*

20

WHERE TO STAY

The hotels and motels along NM 68 (Paseo del Pueblo), most of them on the south side of town, suit every need and budget; rates vary little between big-name chains and smaller establishments—Comfort Suites is the best-maintained of the chains. Make advance reservations and expect higher rates during ski season (usually from late December to early April, and especially for lodgings on the north side of town, closer to the ski area) and in the summer. Skiers have many lodging choices, from in town to spots nestled beneath the slopes, although several of the hotels up at Taos Ski Valley have been converted to condos in recent years, diminishing the supply of overnight accommodations. Arroyo Seco is a good alternative if you can't find a room right up in the Ski

Valley. The area's many B&Bs offers some of the best values, when you factor in typically hearty full breakfasts, personal service, and often roomy casitas with private entrances.

Hotel reviews have been condensed for this book. Please go to Fodors. com for full reviews of each property.

WHAT IT COSTS					
	¢	$	$$	$$$	$$$$
Hotels	under $70	$70–$130	$131–$190	$191–$260	over $260

Prices are for two people in a standard double room in high season, excluding tax.

$$$$ **The Bavarian.** This luxurious, secluded re-creation of a Bavarian lodge has the only midmountain accommodations in the Taos Ski Valley. ⊠ *100 Kachina Rd.,Taos Ski Valley* ☎ *575/776–8020* ⊕ *www. thebavarian.net* ⤵ *4 suites* ⌂ *In-room: no a/c, kitchen, Wi-Fi. In-hotel: restaurant* ☰ *AE, MC, V* ☉ *Closed early Apr.–late May and mid-Oct.– late Nov.* ⦿ *BP.*

$ **Casa Europa.** The main part of this exquisite 18th-century adobe
Fodor'sChoice estate has been tastefully expanded to create an unforgettable B&B
★ with old-world romance. **Pros:** attentive service; memorable setting and sophisticated style; smallest rooms are very affordable. **Cons:** short drive to town. ⊠ *840 Upper Ranchitos Rd.* ☎ *575/758–9798* ⊕ *www. casaeuropanm.com* ⤵ *5 rooms, 2 suites* ⌂ *In-room: a/c, refrigerators, Wi-Fi. In-hotel: some pets allowed* ☰ *MC, V* ⦿ *BP.*

$$ **Casa Gallinas.** This peaceful compound of three stylishly appointed
Fodor'sChoice casitas is out in a rural area near the Hacienda de los Martinez
★ museum—a spot where you can hear the birds sing and enjoy relative isolation, but you're still just a five-minute drive from the restaurants and shopping on the Plaza. **Pros:** gorgeously furnishings; pastoral setting; significant discount for stays of a week or more. **Cons:** you're on your own for breakfast, but each unit has a kitchen; not within walking distance of town. ⊠ *613 Callejon* ☎ *575/758–2306* ⊕ *www. casagallina.net* ⤵ *3 casitas* ⌂ *In-room: no a/c kitchen, DVD, Wi-Fi* ☰ *No credit cards.*

$$ **Cottonwood Inn.** This rambling, two-story adobe house with 11 fire-
Fodor'sChoice places and such classic regional architectural details as *bancos, nichos,*
★ and high latilla-and-viga ceilings is right along the road to the ski valley, just a couple of miles south of Arroyo Seco's quaint village center. **Pros:** closer to Taos than most accommodations in Arroyo Seco; some of the largest and fanciest bathrooms of any B&Bs Taos; great views of mesa and mountains. **Cons:** not within walking distance of any restaurants. ⊠ *NM 230, just beyond junction with NM 150* ☎ *575/776–5826 or 800/324–7120* ⊕ *www.taos-cottonwood.com* ⤵ *8 rooms* ⌂ *In-room: no a/c, no phone, refrigerator, DVD, Wi-Fi. In-hotel: some pets allowed* ☰ *AE, MC, V.*

$$ **Hacienda del Sol.** Art patron Mabel Dodge Luhan bought this house
Fodor'sChoice about a mile north of the Plaza in the 1920s, and it became a guesthouse
★ for visiting notables; Frank Waters wrote *People of the Valley* here— other guests have included Willa Cather and D. H. Lawrence. **Pros:**

cozy public rooms; private setting; some excellent restaurants within walking distance. **Cons:** traffic noise; some rooms are less private than others. ⊠ *109 Mabel Dodge La.* ☎ *575/758–0287 or 866/333–4459* ⊕ *www.taoshaciendadelsol.com* ⇗ *11 rooms* ⚬ *In-room: a/c, refrigerator (some), no TV, Wi-Fi* ⊟ *AE, D, MC, V* ⏍*BP.*

$$ ⚏ **Historic Taos Inn.** A 10-minute walk north of Taos Plaza, this celebrated property is a local landmark, with some devotees having been regulars here for decades. **Pros:** a short walk from the Plaza; lushly furnished rooms, exudes character and history. **Cons:** noise from street traffic and the bar; some rooms are very small. ⊠ *125 Paseo del Pueblo Norte* ☎ *575/758–2233 or 888/518–8267* ⊕ *www.taosinn.com* ⇗ *40 rooms, 3 suites* ⚬ *In-room: a/c (some), Internet. In-hotel: restaurant, bar, Wi-Fi hotspot* ⊟ *AE, DC, MC, V.*

SHOPPING

Retail options on Taos Plaza consist mostly of T-shirt emporiums and souvenir shops that are easily bypassed, though a few stores carry quality Native American artifacts and jewelry. The more upscale galleries and boutiques are two short blocks north on Bent Street, including the John Dunn House Shops. Kit Carson Road (U.S. 64), has a mix of the old and the new. There's metered municipal parking downtown, though the traffic can be daunting. Some shops worth checking out are in St. Francis Plaza in Ranchos de Taos, 4 mi south of the Plaza near the San Francisco de Asís Church. Just north of Taos off NM 522 you can find Overland Ranch (including Overland Sheepskin Co.), which has gorgeous sheepskin and leather clothing, along with a few other shops and galleries (plus a restaurant), and an outdoor path winding through displays of wind sculptures. You'll find another notable cluster of galleries and shops, along with a few good restaurants, in the village of Arroyo Seco, a 15-minute drive north of Taos toward the ski valley.

ART GALLERIES

For at least a century, artists have been drawn to Taos's natural grandeur. The result is a vigorous art community with some 80 galleries, a lively market, and an estimated 1,000 residents producing art full- or part-time. Many artists explore themes of the Western landscape, Native Americans, and adobe architecture; others create abstract forms and mixed-media works that may or may not reflect the Southwest. Some local artists grew up in Taos, but many—Anglo, Hispanic, and Native Americans—are adopted Taoseños.

Farnsworth Gallery Taos (⊠ *133 Paseo del Pueblo Norte, Plaza and Vicinity* ☎ *575/758–0776* ⊕ *www.johnfarnsworth.com*) contains the work of artist John Farnsworth, best known for his finely detailed paintings of horses, and also includes colorful local landscapes, large-scale still-lifes, and scenes of Native American kiva dancers.

Inger Jirby Gallery (⊠ *207 Ledoux St., Plaza and Vicinity* ☎ *575/758–7333* ⊕ *www.jirby.com*) displays Jirby's whimsical, brightly colored landscape paintings. Be sure to stroll through the lovely sculpture garden.

J. D. Challenger Gallery (⊠ *221 Paseo del Pueblo Norte, Plaza and Vicinity* ☎ *575/751–6773 or 800/511–6773*) is the home base of

20

personable painter J. D. Challenger, who has become famous for his dramatically rendered portraits of Native Americans from tribes throughout North America.

Mission Gallery (⊠ *138 E. Kit Carson Rd., Plaza and Vicinity* ☎ *575/758–2861*) carries the works of early Taos artists, early New Mexico modernists, and important contemporary artists. The gallery is in the former home of painter Joseph H. Sharp.

Nichols Taos Fine Art Gallery (⊠ *403 Paseo del Pueblo Norte, Plaza and Vicinity* ☎ *575/758–2475*) has exhibits of oils, watercolors, pastels, charcoal, and pencils from artists representing many prestigious national art organizations.

Fodor's Choice
★
Robert L. Parsons Fine Art (⊠ *131 Bent St.* ☎ *575/751–0159 or 800/613–5091* ⊕ *www.parsonsart.com*) is one of the best sources of early Taos art colony paintings, antiques, and authentic antique Navajo blankets. Inside you'll find originals by such luminaries as Ernest Blumenschein, Bert Geer Phillips, Oscar Berninghaus, Joseph Bakos, and Nicolai Fechin.

Stray Arts Gallery (⊠ *120 Camino de la Placita, Plaza and Vicinity* ☎ *575/758–9780* ⊕ *www.strayhearts.org/stray_arts.php*) sells donated, bargain-priced art to raise funds for the Stray Hearts Animal Shelter. Of course, in a town like Taos, you can find works here by prominent artists (Ouray Meyers, Harriet Green, R. C. Gorman, and many others), making this something of an unexpected find as well as a great cause.

Total Arts Gallery (⊠ *122-A Kit Carson Rd., Plaza and Vicinity* ☎ *575/758–4667* ⊕ *www.totalartsgallery.com*) comprises several rooms displaying works by some of the area's most celebrated artists, including Barbara Zaring, David Hettinger, Doug Dawson, and Ken Elliott. Themes vary greatly from contemporary paintings and sculptures to more traditional landscapes and regional works.

Fodor's Choice
★
At **Two Graces Gallery** (⊠ *San Francisco Plaza South Side* ☎ *575/758–4639*) owner and artist Robert Cafazzo displays an astonishing assortment of traditional Indian pottery and kachinas, contemporary art by local artists, old postcards, and rare books on area artists.

SKIING

Fodor's Choice
★
With 72 runs—more than half of them for experts—and an average of more than 300 inches of annual snowfall, **Taos Ski Valley** ranks among the country's most respected—and challenging—resorts. The slopes, which cover a 2,600-foot vertical gain of lift-served terrain and another 600 feet of hike-in skiing, tend to be narrow and demanding (note the ridge chutes, Al's Run, Inferno), but 25% (e.g., Honeysuckle) are for intermediate skiers, and 24% (e.g., Bambi, Porcupine) for beginners. Taos Ski Valley is justly famous for its outstanding ski schools, one of the best in the country. If you're new to the sport, this is a terrific resort to give a try. ⊠ *Village of Taos Ski Valley* ☎ *575/776–2291* ⊕ *www.skitaos.org* 🎫 *Lift tickets $71* ☉ *Late Nov.–early Apr.*

The Enchanted Circle is a gorgeous 84-mi loop through the Carson National Forest.

SIDE TRIPS FROM SANTA FE AND TAOS

THE HIGH ROAD TO TAOS

Fodor's Choice ★ The main highway to Taos (NM 68) is a good, even scenic, route if you've got limited time, but by far the most spectacular route is what is known as the High Road. Towering peaks, lush hillsides, orchards, and meadows surround tiny, ancient Hispanic villages that are as picturesque as they are historically fascinating. The High Road follows U.S. 285/84 north to NM 503 (a right turn just past Pojoaque), to County Road 98 (a left toward Chimayó), to NM 76 northeast to NM 75 east, to NM 518 north. The drive takes you through the badlands of stark, weathered rock—where numerous westerns have been filmed—quickly into rolling foothills, lush canyons, and finally into pine forests. Although most of these insular, traditional Hispanic communities offer little in the way of shopping and dining, the region has become a haven for artists.

From Chimayó to Peñasco, you can find mostly low-key but often high-quality art galleries, many of them run out of the owners' homes. During the final two weekends in September each year, more than 100 artists show their work in the **High Road Art Tour** (☎ 866/343–5381 ⊕ *www.highroadnewmexico.com*); call or visit the Web site for a studio map.

Depending on when you make this drive, you're in for some of the state's most radiant scenery. In mid-April the orchards are in blossom;

summer turns the valleys into lush green oases; and in fall the smell of piñon adds to the sensual overload of golden leaves and red-chili ristras hanging from the houses. In winter the fields are covered with quilts of snow, and the lines of homes, fences, and trees stand out like bold pen-and-ink drawings against the sky. But the roads can be icy and treacherous—if in doubt, stick with the Low Road to Taos. If you decide to take the High Road just one way between Santa Fe and Taos, you might want to save it for the return journey—the scenery is even more stunning when traveling north to south.

THE ENCHANTED CIRCLE

Fodor's Choice ★ The Enchanted Circle, an 84-mi loop north from Taos and back, rings Wheeler Peak, New Mexico's highest mountain, and takes you through glorious panoramas of alpine valleys and the towering mountains of Carson National Forest. You can see all the major sights as an ambitious one-day side trip, or take a more leisurely tour and stay overnight.

From Taos, head north about 15 mi via U.S. 64 to NM 522, keeping your eye out for the sign on the right that points to the D. H. Lawrence Ranch and Memorial. You can visit the memorial, which is well-marked from the road, but the other buildings on the ranch are closed to the public. Continue north a short way to reach Red River Hatchery, and then go another 5 mi to the village of Questa. Here you have the option of continuing north on NM 522 and detouring for some hiking at Wild Rivers Recreation Area, or turning east from Questa on NM 38 and driving for about 12 mi to the unpretentious, family-friendly town of Red River, a noteworthy ski town in winter and an increasingly popular summer-recreation hub during the warmer months.

From here, continue 16 mi east along NM 38 and head over dramatic Bobcat Pass, which rises to just under 10,000 feet. You'll come to the sleepy, old-fashioned village of Eagle Nest, comprising a few shops and down-home restaurants and motels. From here, U.S. 64 joins with NM 38 and runs southeast about 15 mi to one of the state's fastest-growing communities, Angel Fire, an upscale ski resort that's popular for hiking, golfing, and mountain biking in summer. It's about a 25-mi drive west over 9,000-foot Palo Flechado Pass and down through winding Taos Canyon to return to Taos.

TIMING Leave early in the morning and plan to spend the entire day on this trip. Especially during ski season, which runs from late November to early April. In summer you may want to spend a night or more in Red River, which has a number of mostly rustic lodges and vacation rentals, or in Angel Fire, which is becoming increasingly respected as a year-round resort. Watch for snow and ice on the roads from late fall through early spring.

Grand Canyon National Park

WORD OF MOUTH

"My favorite thing to do at the South Rim is to walk along the rim from Bright Angel Trail to Hopi Point. The beauty of this is you have several places you can pick up the free shuttle. Walking from Mather Point to Bright Angel trailhead is another one to do, too. Great views and plenty of places to take photos!"

—utahtea

WELCOME TO GRAND CANYON NATIONAL PARK

TOP REASONS TO GO

★ **Its status:** This is one of those places where you really want to say, "Been there, done that!"

★ **Awesome vistas:** Painted Desert, sandstone canyon walls, pine and fir forests, mesas, plateaus, volcanic features, the Colorado River, streams, and waterfalls make for some jaw-dropping moments.

★ **Year-round adventure:** Outdoor junkies can bike, boat, camp, fish, hike, ride mules, white-water raft, watch birds and wildlife, cross-country ski, and snowshoe.

★ **Continuing education:** Adults and kids can have fun learning, thanks to free park-sponsored nature walks and interpretive programs.

★ **Sky-high and river-low experiences:** Experience the canyon via plane, train, and automobile, as well as helicopter, oar- or motor-boat, bike, mule, or on foot.

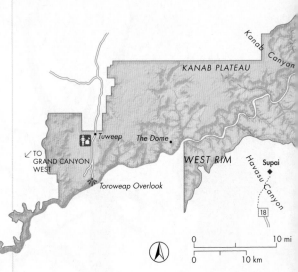

1 South Rim. The South Rim is where the action is: Grand Canyon Village's lodging, camping, eateries, stores, and museums, plus plenty of trailheads into the canyon. Visitor services and facilities are open and available daily, including holidays. Four free shuttle routes cover more than 35 stops, and visitors who'd rather relax than rough it can treat themselves to comfy hotel rooms and elegant restaurant meals (lodging and camping reservations are essential).

2 North Rim. Of the nearly 5 million people who visit the park annually, 90% enter at the South Rim, but many consider the North Rim even more gorgeous—and worth the extra effort. Open only from mid-May to about mid-October (or the first good snowfall), the North Rim has legitimate bragging rights: at more than 8,000 feet above sea level (1,000 feet higher than the South Rim), it has precious solitude and seven developed viewpoints. Rather than staring into the canyon's depths, you get a true sense of its expanse.

GETTING ORIENTED

Grand Canyon National Park is a superstar—biologically, historically, and recreationally. One of the world's best examples of arid-land erosion, the canyon provides a record of three of the four eras of geological time. Almost 2 billion years worth of Earth's history is written in the colored layers of rock stacked from the river bottom to the top of the plateau. In addition to its diverse fossil record, the park reveals long-ago traces of human adaptation to an unforgiving environment. It's also home to several major ecosystems, five of the world's seven life zones, three of North America's four desert types, and all kinds of rare, endemic, and protected plant and animal species.

When it comes to the Grand Canyon, there are statistics, and there are sensations. While the former are impressive—the canyon measures in at an average width of 10 mi, length of 277 river mi, and depth of 1 mi—they don't truly prepare you for that first impression. Seeing the canyon for the first time is an astounding experience—one that's hard to wrap your head around. In fact, it's more than an experience, it's an emotion, one that is only just beginning to be captured with the superlative "Grand."

Roughly 5 million visitors come to the park each year. They can access the canyon via two main points: the South Rim and the North Rim. The width from the North Rim to the South Rim varies from 600 feet to 18 mi, but traveling between rims by road requires a 215-mi drive. Hiking arduous trails from rim to rim is a steep and strenuous trek of at least 21 mi, but it's well worth the effort. You'll travel through five of North America's seven life zones. (To do this any other way, you'd have to journey from the Mexican desert to the Canadian woods.) In total, more than 600 mi of mostly very primitive trails traverse the canyon, with about 51 of those miles maintained. West of Grand Canyon National Park, the tribal lands of the Hualapai and the Havasupai lie along the so-called West Rim of the canyon.

PLANNING

WHEN TO GO

There's no bad time to visit the canyon, though the busiest times of year are summer and spring break. Visiting during these peak seasons, as well as holidays, requires patience and a tolerance for crowds. Note that weather changes on a whim in this exposed high-desert region. *The North Rim shuts down from mid-October through mid-May due to weather conditions and related road closures.*

PLANNING YOUR TIME

Plan ahead: mule rides require at least a six-month advance reservation, and longer for the busy season (most can be reserved up to 13 months in advance). Multiday rafting trips should be reserved at least a year in advance. For lodgings in the park, reservations are also essential; they're taken up to 13 months in advance. **Xanterra Parks & Resorts** (☎ 888/297–2757 ⊕ *www.grandcanyonlodges.com*) runs the South Rim park lodging as well as Phantom Ranch, deep inside the canyon. For North Rim reservations, contact **Grand Canyon Lodge** (☎ 877/386–4383 ⊕ *www.grandcanyonlodgenorth.com*).

Before you go, get the complimentary *Trip Planner,* updated regularly, from the **Grand Canyon National Park** (⊕ *www.nps.gov/grca*). Once you arrive, pick up the free detailed map and *The Guide,* a newspaper with a schedule of free programs.

The park is most crowded near the east and, especially, the south entrances and in Grand Canyon Village, as well as on the scenic drives, particularly the 23-mi Desert View Drive. ⇨ *See Tips for Avoiding Grand Canyon Crowds.*

GETTING HERE AND AROUND: SOUTH RIM

Air Travel: North Las Vegas Airport in Las Vegas is the primary air hub for charter flights to **Grand Canyon National Parks Airport** (*GCN* ☎ 928/638–2446).

Car Travel: The best route into the park from the east or south is from Flagstaff, Arizona. Take U.S. 180 northwest to the park's southern entrance and Grand Canyon Village. An excellent alternative if you'd rather forgo bringing a car to the South Rim is to take the Grand Canyon Railway from Williams. From the west on Interstate 40, the most direct route to the South Rim is on U.S. 180 and Highway 64.

Park Shuttle Travel: The South Rim is open to car traffic year-round, though access to Hermits Rest is limited to shuttle buses part of the year. There are four free shuttle routes: The **Hermits Rest Route** operates March through November, between Grand Canyon Village and Hermits Rest. The **Village Route** operates year-round in the village area near the Grand Canyon Visitor Center. The **Kaibab Trail Route** goes from the visitor center to Yaki Point, including a stop at the South Kaibab Trailhead. The **Tusayan Route** operates summer only and runs from Grand Canyon Visitor Center to the town Tusayan. ■TIP→ In summer, South Rim roads are congested, and it's easier, and sometimes required, to park your car and take the free shuttle. Running from one hour before sunrise until one hour after sunset, shuttles arrive every 15 to 30 minutes at 30 clearly marked stops.

Shuttle Travel: Xanterra (☎ 928/638–2822) offers 24-hour taxi service in Tusayan and the South Rim. **Arizona Shuttle** (☎ 928/226–8060 or 877/226–8060 ⊕ *www.arizonashuttle.com*) has service from Phoenix to Flagstaff and Grand Canyon Village. **Open Road Tours** (☎ 928/226–8060 or 877/226–8060 ⊕ *www.openroadtours.com*) will transport you from Flagstaff and Williams to Tusayan and Grand Canyon Village.

GETTING HERE AND AROUND: NORTH RIM

Park services on the more remote North Rim shut down in winter and following the first major snowfall (usually around mid-November); Highway 67 south of Jacob Lake is closed. The nearest airport to the North Rim is **St. George Municipal Airport** (☎ *435/634–5822* ⊕ *www.sgcity.org/airport*) in Utah, 164 mi north, with regular service provided by both Delta and United Airlines. From mid-May to mid-October, the **Trans Canyon Shuttle** (☎ *928/638–2820* ⊕ *www.trans-canyonshuttle.com*) travels daily between the South and North rims—the ride takes 4½ hours each way. One-way fare is $80, round-trip $150. Reservations are required.

ESSENTIALS
ADMISSION FEES AND PERMITS

A fee of $25 per vehicle or $12 per person for pedestrians and cyclists is good for one week's access at both rims.

The $50 Grand Canyon Pass gives unlimited access to the park for 12 months. The annual America the Beautiful **National Parks and Recreational Land Pass** (☎ *888/275–8747* ⊕ *store.usgs.gov/pass* 🖅 *$80)* provides unlimited access to all national parks and federal recreation areas for 12 months.

No permits are needed for day hikers; but **backcountry permits** (☎ *928/638–7875 or 928/638–2125* ⊕ *www.nps.gov/grc* 🖅 *$10, plus $5 per person per night*) are necessary for overnight hikers. Permits are limited, so make your reservation as far in advance as possible—they're taken up to four months ahead of arrival. **Camping** in the park is restricted to designated campgrounds (☎ *877/444–6777* ⊕ *www.recreation.gov*).

VISITOR CENTERS

Desert View Information Center. ⊠ *East entrance* ☎ *800/858–2808 or 928/638–7893* ☉ *Daily 9–5; hrs vary in winter.*

Grand Canyon Visitor Center. ⊠ *East side of Grand Canyon Village* ☎ *928/638–7888* ☉ *Daily 8–5, outdoor exhibits may be viewed anytime.*

North Rim Visitor Center. ⊠ *Near parking lot on Bright Angel Peninsula* ☎ *928/638–7864* ☉ *Mid-May–mid-Oct., daily 8–6.*

GRAND CANYON SOUTH RIM

Visitors to the canyon converge mostly on the South Rim, and mostly in summer. Grand Canyon Village is here, with most of the park's lodging and camping, trailheads, restaurants, stores, and museums, along with a nearby airport and railroad depot. Believe it or not, the average stay in the park is a mere half day or so; this is not advised! You need to spend several days to truly appreciate this marvelous place, but at the very least, give it a full day. Hike down into the canyon, or along the rim, to get away from the crowds and experience nature at its finest.

BEST GRAND CANYON VIEWS

21

The best time of day to see the canyon is before 10 am and after 4 pm, when the angle of the sun brings out the colors of the rock, and clouds and shadows add dimension. Colors deepen dramatically among the contrasting layers of the canyon walls just before and during sunrise and sunset.

Hopi Point is the top spot on the South Rim to watch the sunset; **Yaki** and **Pima** points also offer vivid views. For a grand sunrise, try **Mather** or **Yaki** points.

■TIP→ Arrive at least 30 minutes early for sunrise views and as much as 90 minutes for sunset views at these points. For another point of view, take a leisurely stroll along the Rim Trail and watch the color change along with the views. Timetables are listed in *The Guide* and are posted at park visitor centers.

SCENIC DRIVES

Desert View Drive. This heavily traveled 23-mi stretch of road follows the rim from the East entrance to the Grand Canyon Village. Starting from the less-congested entry near Desert View, road warriors can get their first glimpse of the canyon from the 70-foot-tall watchtower, the top of which provides the highest viewpoint on the South Rim. Eight overlooks, the remains of an Ancestral Puebloan dwelling at the Tusayan Ruin and Museum, and the secluded and lovely Buggeln picnic area make for great stops along the South Rim. The Kaibab Trail Route shuttle bus travels a short section of Desert View Drive and takes 30 minutes to ride round-trip without getting off at any of the three stops: South Kaibab Trailhead, Yaki Point, and Pipe Creek Vista.

Hermit Road. The Santa Fe Company built Hermit Road, formerly known as West Rim Drive, in 1912 as a scenic tour route. Nine overlooks dot this 7-mi stretch, each worth a visit. The road is filled with hairpin turns, so make sure you adhere to posted speed limits. A 1.5-mi Greenway trail offers easy access to cyclists looking to enjoy the original 1912 Hermit Rim Road. From March through November, Hermit Road is closed to private auto traffic because of congestion; during this period, a free shuttle bus carries visitors to all the overlooks. Riding the bus round-trip without getting off at any of the viewpoints takes 75 minutes; the return trip stops only at Pima, Mohave, and Powell points.

SCENIC STOPS

The Abyss. At an elevation of 6,720 feet, the Abyss is one of the most awesome stops on Hermit Road, revealing a sheer drop of 3,000 feet to the Tonto Platform, a wide terrace of Tapeats sandstone about two-thirds of the way down the canyon. From the Abyss you'll also see several isolated sandstone columns, the largest of which is called the Monument. ⊠ *About 5 mi west of Hermit Rd. Junction on Hermit Rd.*

 Desert View and Watchtower. From the top of the 70-foot stone-and-mortar watchtower, even the muted hues of the distant Painted Desert to the east and the Vermilion Cliffs rising from a high plateau near the Utah border are visible. In the chasm below, angling to the north toward Marble Canyon, an imposing stretch of the Colorado River reveals itself. Up several flights of stairs, the watchtower houses a glass-enclosed observatory with powerful telescopes. ⊠ *About 23 mi east of Grand Canyon Village on Desert View Dr.* ☎ *928/638–2736* ⊙ *Daily 8–8; hrs vary in winter.*

Grandview Point. At an elevation of 7,399 feet, the view from here is one of the finest in the canyon. To the northeast is a group of dominant buttes, including Krishna Shrine, Vishnu Temple, Rama Shrine, and Sheba Temple. A short stretch of the Colorado River is also visible. Directly below the point, and accessible by the steep and rugged Grandview Trail, is Horseshoe Mesa, where you can see remnants of Last Chance Copper Mine. ⊠ *About 12 mi east of Grand Canyon Village on Desert View Dr.*

★ **Hermits Rest.** This westernmost viewpoint and Hermit Trail, which descends from it, were named for "hermit" Louis Boucher, a 19th-century French-Canadian prospector who had a number of mining claims and a roughly built home down in the canyon. Views from here include Hermit Rapids and the towering cliffs of the Supai and Redwall formations. In the stone building at Hermits Rest you can buy curios and snacks, and sit in the same chair Theodore Roosevelt once sat in. ⊠ *About 8 mi west of Hermit Rd. Junction on Hermit Rd.*

★ **Hopi Point.** From this elevation of 6,800 feet, you can see a large section of the Colorado River; although it appears as a thin line, the river is nearly 350 feet wide below this overlook. The overlook extends farther into the canyon than any other point on Hermit Road. The unobstructed views make this a popular place to watch the sunset. Across the canyon to the north is Shiva Temple, which remained an unexplored section of the Kaibab Plateau until 1937. That year, Harold Anthony of the American Museum of Natural History led an expedition to the rock formation in the belief that it supported life that had been cut off from the rest of the canyon. Imagine the expedition members' surprise when they found an empty Kodak film box on top of the temple—it had been left behind by Emery Kolb, who felt slighted for not having been invited to partake of Anthony's tour. Directly below Hopi Point lies Dana Butte, named for a prominent 19th-century geologist. In 1919, an entrepreneur proposed connecting Hopi Point, Dana Butte, and the Tower of Set across the river with an aerial tramway, a technically feasible plan that fortunately has not been realized. ⊠ *About 4 mi west of Hermit Rd. Junction on Hermit Rd.*

Lipan Point. Here, at the canyon's widest point, you can get an astonishing visual profile of the gorge's geologic history, with a view of every eroded layer of the canyon—you can also observe one of the longest stretches of visible Colorado River. The spacious panorama stretches to the Vermilion Cliffs on the northeastern horizon and features a multitude of imaginatively named spires, buttes, and temples—intriguing rock formations named after their resemblance to ancient pyramids. You can also see Unkar Delta, where a creek joins the Colorado to form powerful rapids and a broad beach. Ancestral Puebloan farmers worked the Unkar Delta for hundreds of years, growing corn, beans, and melons. ⊠ *About 25 mi east of Grand Canyon Village on Desert View Dr.*

★ **Mather Point.** You'll likely get your first glimpse of the canyon from this viewpoint, one of the most impressive and accessible (and most crowded) on the South Rim. Named for the National Park Service's first director, Stephen Mather, this spot yields extraordinary views of the Grand Canyon, including deep into the inner gorge and numerous buttes: Wotans Throne, Brahma Temple, and Zoroaster Temple, among others. The Grand Canyon Lodge, on the North Rim, is almost directly north from Mather Point and only 10 mi away—yet you have to drive 215 mi to get from one spot to the other. ⊠ *Near Grand Canyon Visitor Center.*

Mohave Point. Some of the canyon's most magnificent stone spires and buttes visible from this lesser-known overlook include the Tower of Set; the Tower of Ra; and Isis, Osiris, and Horus temples. From here you can view the 5,401-foot Cheops Pyramid, a grayish rock formation behind Dana Butte, plus some of the strongest rapids on the Colorado River. The Granite and Salt Creek rapids are navigable, but not without plenty of effort. ⊠ *About 5 mi west of Hermit Rd. Junction on Hermit Rd.*

Trailview Overlook. Look down on a dramatic view of the Bright Angel and Plateau Point trails as they zigzag down the canyon. In the deep gorge to the north flows Bright Angel Creek, one of the region's few permanent tributary streams of the Colorado River. Toward the south is an unobstructed view of the distant San Francisco Peaks, as well as Bill Williams Mountain (on the horizon) and Red Butte (about 15 mi south of the canyon rim). ⊠ *About 2 mi west of Hermit Rd. Junction on Hermit Rd.*

Yaki Point. Stop here for an exceptional view of Wotan's Throne, a flat-top butte named by François Matthes, a U.S. Geological Survey scientist who developed the first topographical map of the Grand Canyon. The overlook juts out over the canyon, providing unobstructed views of inner-canyon rock formations, South Rim cliffs, and Clear Creek canyon. About a mile south of Yaki Point, you'll come to the trailhead for the South Kaibab Trail. The point is one of the best places on the South Rim to watch the sunset. ⊠ *2 mi east of Grand Canyon Village on Desert View Dr.*

Fodor's Choice ★ **Yavapai Point.** This is also one of the best locations on the South Rim to watch the sunset. Dominated by the Yavapai Observation Station, this point displays panoramic views of the mighty gorge through a wall of windows. Exhibits here include videos of the canyon floor and the Colorado River, a scaled diorama of the canyon with national park boundaries, fossils and rock fragments used to re-create the complex layers of the canyon walls, and a display on the natural forces used to carve the chasm. Rangers dig even deeper into Grand Canyon geology with free ranger programs. A guided afternoon nature walk completes the options. Check ahead for special events and walk and program schedules. There's also a bookstore. ⊠ *Adjacent to Grand Canyon Village* 🖾 *Free* ☉ *Daily 8–8; hrs vary in winter.*

Tips for Avoiding Grand Canyon Crowds

It's hard to commune with nature while you're searching for a parking place, dodging video cameras, and stepping away from strollers. However, this scenario is likely only during the peak summer months. One option is to bypass Grand Canyon National Park altogether and head to the West Rim of the canyon, tribal land of the Hualapai and Havasupai. If only the park itself will do, the following tips will help you to keep your distance and your cool.

TAKE ANOTHER ROUTE

Avoid road rage by choosing a different route to the South Rim, forego-ing the traditional highways 64 and U.S. 180 from Flagstaff. Take U.S. 89 north from Flagstaff instead, pass-ing near Sunset Crater and Wupatki national monuments. When you reach the junction with Highway 64, take a break at Cameron Trading Post (1 mi north of the junction)—or stay over-night. This is a good place to shop for Native American artifacts, souvenirs, and the usual postcards, dream-catch-ers, recordings, and T-shirts. There are also high-quality Navajo rugs, jewelry, and other authentic handicrafts, and you can sample Navajo tacos. U.S. 64 to the west takes you directly to the park's east entrance; the scenery along the Little Colorado River gorge en route is eye-popping. It's 23 mi from the east entrance to the visitor center at Grand Canyon Visitor Center.

SKIP THE SOUTH RIM

Although the North Rim is just 10 mi across from the South Rim, the trip to get there by car is a five-hour drive of 215 mi. At first it might not sound like the trip would be worth it, but the payoff is huge. Along the way, you will travel through some of the prettiest parts of the state and be granted even more stunning views than those on the more easily accessible South Rim. Those who make the North Rim trip often insist it has the canyon's most beautiful views and best hiking. To get to the North Rim from Flagstaff, take U.S. 89 north past Cameron, turn-ing left onto U.S. 89A at Bitter Springs. En route you'll pass the area known as Vermilion Cliffs. At Jacob Lake, take Highway 67 directly to the Grand Canyon North Rim. North Rim services are closed from mid-October through mid-May because of heavy snow, but in summer months and early fall, it's a wonderful way to beat the crowds at the South Rim.

RIDE THE RAILS

There is no need to deal with all of the other drivers racing to the South Rim. Sit back and relax in the comfy train cars of the **Grand Canyon Railway**. Live music and storytell-ing enliven the trip as you journey past the landscape through prairie, ranch, and national park land to the log-cabin train station in Grand Canyon Village. You won't see the Grand Canyon from the train, but you can walk or catch the shuttle at the restored, century-old Grand Canyon Depot. The vintage train departs from the Williams Depot every morning, and makes the 65-mi journey in 2¼ hours. You can do the round-trip in a single day; however, it's a more relax-ing and enjoyable strategy to stay for a night or two at the South Rim before returning to Williams. ⇨ *See Grand Canyon Railway Hotel in Where to Stay.* ☎ *800/843–8724* ⊕ *www. thetrain.com* ✉ *$70–$130 round-trip.*

SPORTS AND THE OUTDOORS

21

AIR TOURS

★ Flights by plane and helicopter over the canyon are offered by a number of companies, departing for the Grand Canyon Airport at the south end of Tusayan. Though the noise and disruption of so many aircraft buzzing the canyon is controversial, flightseeing remains a popular, if expensive, option. You'll have more visibility from a helicopter but they are louder and more expensive than the fixed-wing planes. Prices and lengths of tours vary, but you can expect to pay about $110–$125 per adult for short plane trips and approximately $160–$250 for brief helicopter tours (and about $400 for tours leaving from Vegas). These companies often have significant discounts in winter—check the company Web sites to find the best deals.

OUTFITTERS AND EXPEDITIONS **Air Grand Canyon** (✉ *Grand Canyon Airport, Tusayan* ☎ *928/638–2686 or 800/247–4726* ⊕ *www.airgrandcanyon.com*) runs 40- to 50-minute fixed-wing air tours over the North Rim, the Kaibab Plateau, and the Dragon Corridor, one of the cross canyons. Tours start at 9 am and run every hour on the hour. **Grand Canyon Airlines** (✉ *Grand Canyon Airport Tusayan* ☎ *928/638–2359 or 866/235–9422* ⊕ *www. grandcanyonairlines.com*) flies a fixed-wing on a 50-minute tour of the eastern edge of the Grand Canyon, the North Rim, and the Kaibab Plateau. All-day combination tours combine flightseeing with jeep tours and float trips on the Colorado River. The company also schedules helicopter tours that leave from Las Vegas. Get an up-close view of Grand Canyon geology and the Colorado River on 30- and 50-minute tours with **Grand Canyon Helicopters** (✉ *Grand Canyon Airport Tusayan* ☎ *928/638–2764 or 800/541–4537* ⊕ *www.grandcanyonhelicoptersaz. com/gch*). **Maverick Helicopters** (✉ *Grand Canyon Airport Tusayan* ☎ *928/638–2622 or 800/962–3869* ⊕ *www.maverickhelicopters.com*) offers 25- and 45-minute tours of the eastern Grand Canyon, the North Rim, and the Dragon Corridor. A landing tour option sets you down in the canyon for a short snack below the rim. **Papillon Grand Canyon Helicopters** (✉ *Grand Canyon Airport Tusayan* ☎ *928/638–2419 or 800/528–2418* ⊕ *www.papillon.com*) offers a variety of fixed-wing and helicopter tours, leaving both from Grand Canyon Airport and Vegas, of the canyon and combination tours with off-road jeep tours and smooth-water rafting trips.

HIKING

Although permits are not required for day hikes, you must have a backcountry permit for longer trips (⇨ *See Admission Fees and Permits at the start of this chapter*). Some of the more popular trails are listed in this chapter; more detailed information and maps can be obtained from the Backcountry Information Centers. Also, rangers can help design a trip to suit your abilities.

Remember that the canyon has significant elevation changes and, in summer, extreme temperature ranges, which can pose problems for people who aren't in good shape or who have heart or respiratory problems. Carry plenty of water and energy foods. The majority of each year's 400 search-and-rescue incidents result from hikers underestimating the size of the canyon, hiking beyond their abilities, or not packing sufficient food and water.

⚠ Under no circumstances should you attempt a day hike from the rim to the river and back. Remember that when it's 80°F on the South Rim, it's 110°F on the canyon floor. Allow two to four days if you want to hike rim to rim (it's easier to descend from the North Rim, as it is more than 1,000 feet higher than the South Rim). Hiking steep trails from rim to rim is a strenuous trek of at least 21 mi and should only be attempted by experienced canyon hikers.

EASY
Fodor's Choice
★

Rim Trail. The South Rim's most popular walking path is the 12-mi (one-way) Rim Trail, which runs along the edge of the canyon from Pipe Creek Vista (the first overlook on Desert View Drive) to Hermits Rest. This walk, which is paved to Maricopa Point and for the last 1.5 mi to Hermits Rest, visits several of the South Rim's historic landmarks. Allow anywhere from 15 minutes to a full day; the Rim Trail is an ideal day hike, as it varies only a few hundred feet in elevation from Mather Point (7,120 feet) to the trailhead at Hermits Rest (6,650 feet). The trail also can be accessed from several spots in Grand Canyon Village and from the major viewpoints along Hermit Road, which are serviced by shuttle buses during the busy summer months. ■ TIP➔ On the Rim Trail, water is only available in the Grand Canyon Village area and at Hermits Rest.

MODERATE
★

Bright Angel Trail. Well maintained, this is one of the most scenic hiking paths from the South Rim to the bottom of the canyon (9.6 mi each way). Rest houses are equipped with water at the 1.5- and 3-mi points from May through September and at Indian Garden (4 mi) year-round. Water is also available at Bright Angel Campground, 9.25 mi below the trailhead. Plateau Point, on a spur trail about 1.5 mi below Indian Garden, is as far as you should attempt to go on a day hike; plan on spending six to nine hours. Bright Angel Trail is the easiest of all the footpaths into the canyon, but because the climb out from the bottom is an ascent of 5,510 feet, the trip should be attempted only by those in good physical condition and should be avoided in midsummer due to extreme heat. The top of the trail can be icy in winter. Originally a bighorn sheep path and later used by the Havasupai, the trail was widened late in the 19th century for prospectors and is now used for both mule and foot traffic. ■ TIP➔ Hikers going downhill should yield to those going uphill. Also note that mule trains have the right-of-way—and sometimes leave unpleasant surprises in your path. ⊠ *Trailhead: Kolb Studio, Hermits Rd.*

DIFFICULT

Hermit Trail. Beginning on the South Rim just west of Hermits Rest (and 7 mi west of Grand Canyon Village), this steep, 9.7-mi (one-way) trail drops more than 5,000 feet to Hermit Creek, which usually flows year-round. It's a strenuous hike back up and is recommended for experienced long-distance hikers only; plan for six to nine hours. There's an abundance of lush growth and wildlife, including desert bighorn sheep, along this trail. The trail descends from the trailhead at 6,640 feet to the Colorado River at 2,300 feet. Day hikers should not go past Santa Maria Spring at 5,000 feet. For much of the year, no water is available along the way; ask a park ranger about the availability of water at Santa Maria Spring and Hermit Creek before you set out. All water from these sources should be treated before drinking. The route leads down to the Colorado River and has inspiring views of Hermit Gorge and the Redwall and Supai formations. Six miles from the trailhead are the ruins of Hermit Camp, which the Santa Fe Railroad ran as a tourist camp from 1911 until 1930. ⊠ *Trailhead: Hermits Rest, Hermits Rd.*

★ **South Kaibab Trail.** This trail starts near Yaki Point, 4 mi east of Grand Canyon Village and is accessible via the free shuttle bus. Because the route is so steep (and sometimes icy in winter)—descending from the trailhead at 7,260 feet down to 2,480 feet at the Colorado River—and has no water, many hikers return via the less-demanding Bright Angel Trail; allow four to six hours. During this 6.4-mi trek to the Colorado River, you're likely to encounter mule trains and riders (although mule rides are prohibited on the trail through at least 2011 while crews work on improving sections of the trail). At the river, the trail crosses a suspension bridge and runs on to Phantom Ranch. Along the trail there is no water and very little shade. There are no campgrounds, though there are portable toilets at Cedar Ridge (6,320 feet), 1.5 mi from the trailhead. Toilets and an emergency phone are also available at the Tipoff, 4.6 mi down the trail (3 mi past Cedar Ridge). The trail corkscrews down through some spectacular geology. Look for (but don't remove) fossils in the limestone when taking water breaks. ■TIP→ **Even though an immense network of trails winds through the Grand Canyon, the popular corridor trails (Bright Angel and South Kaibab) are recommended for hikers new to the region.** ⊠ *Trailhead: Yaki Point, Desert View Dr.*

MULE RIDES

★ Mule rides provide an intimate glimpse into the canyon for those who have the time, but not the stamina, to see the canyon on foot. ■TIP→ **Reservations are essential and are accepted up to 13 months in advance.**

These trips have been conducted since the early 1900s. A comforting fact as you ride the narrow trail: no one's ever been killed while riding a mule that fell off a cliff. (Nevertheless, the treks are not for the faint of heart or people in questionable health.)

OUTFITTERS **Xanterra Parks & Resorts Mule Rides.** These trips delve into the canyon from the South Rim to Phantom Ranch, or west along the canyon's edge to a famed viewpoint called the Abyss (the Plateau Point rides were discontinued in 2009). Riders must be at least 55 inches tall, weigh less than 200 pounds, and understand English. Children under 15 must be accompanied by an adult. Riders must be in fairly good physical condition, and pregnant women are advised not to take these trips. The three-hour ride to the Abyss costs $118.40 (snack included). An overnight with a stay at Phantom Ranch at the bottom of the canyon is $481.72 ($850.31 for two riders). Two nights at Phantom Ranch, an option available from November through March, will set you back $637.80 ($1,121.36 for two). Meals are included. Reservations, especially during the busy summer months, are a must, but you can check at the Bright Angel Transportation Desk to see if there's last-minute availability. ⌂ *6312 S. Fiddlers Green Circle, Suite 600, N. Greenwood Village, CO*

DID YOU KNOW?

Mule trips take riders on the Bright Angel and South Kaibab trails. Day trips go partway down the canyon and two-day trips include an overnight stay at Phantom Ranch on the canyon floor.

80111 ☎ 303/297–2757 or 888/297–2757 ⊕ www.grandcanyonlodges. com ☼ Phantom Ranch rides May–Sept., daily; Abyss rides mid-Mar.– Oct., twice daily; Nov.–mid-Mar., once daily ⚲ Reservations essential.

GRAND CANYON NORTH RIM

The North Rim stands 1,000 feet higher than the South Rim and has a more alpine climate, with twice as much annual precipitation. Here, in the deep forests of the Kaibab Plateau, the crowds are thinner, the facilities fewer, and the views even more spectacular. Due to snow, the North Rim is off-limits in winter. The park buildings and concessions are closed mid-October through mid-May. The road closes when the snow makes it impassable—usually by the end of November.

Lodgings are available but limited; the North Rim only offers one historic lodge and restaurant and a single campground. Dining options have opened up a little with the addition of the Grand Cookout, offered nightly with live entertainment under the stars. Your best bet may be to pack your camping gear and hiking boots and take several days to explore the lush Kaibab Forest. The canyon's highest, most dramatic rim views also can be enjoyed on two wheels (via primitive dirt access roads) and on four legs (courtesy of a trusty mule).

SCENIC DRIVE

★ **Highway 67**. Open mid-May to roughly mid-November (or the first big snowfall), the two-lane paved road climbs 1,400 feet in elevation as it passes through the Kaibab National Forest. Also called the "North Rim Parkway," this scenic route crosses the limestone-capped Kaibab Plateau—passing broad meadows, sun-dappled forests, and small lakes and springs—before abruptly falling away at the abyss of the Grand Canyon. Wildlife abounds in the thick ponderosa pine forests and lush mountain meadows. It's common to see deer, turkeys, and coyotes as you drive through this remote region. Point Imperial and Cape Royal can be reached by spurs off this scenic drive running from Jacob Lake to Bright Angel Point.

SCENIC STOPS

★ **Bright Angel Point**. The trail, which leads to one of the most awe-inspiring overlooks on either rim, starts on the grounds of the Grand Canyon Lodge and runs along the crest of a point of rocks that juts into the canyon for several hundred yards. The walk is only 0.5 mi round-trip, but it's an exciting trek accented by sheer drops on each side of the trail. In a few spots where the route is extremely narrow, metal railings ensure visitors' safety. The temptation to clamber out to precarious perches to have your picture taken could get you killed—every year several people die from falls at the Grand Canyon. ✉ *North Rim Dr.*

Cape Royal. A popular sunset destination, Cape Royal showcases the canyon's jagged landscape; you'll also get a glimpse of the Colorado River, framed by a natural stone arch called Angels Window. In autumn, the aspens turn a beautiful gold, adding even more color to an already magnificent scene of the forested surroundings. At Angels Window Overlook, **Cliff Springs Trail** starts its 1-mi route (round-trip) through a forested ravine. The trail terminates at Cliff Springs, where the forest opens to another impressive view of the canyon walls. ⊠ *Cape Royal Scenic Dr., 23 mi southeast of Grand Canyon Lodge.*

Point Imperial. At 8,803 feet, Point Imperial has the highest vista point at either rim; it offers magnificent views of both the canyon and the distant country: the Vermilion Cliffs to the north, the 10,000-foot Navajo Mountain to the northeast in Utah, the Painted Desert to the east, and the Little Colorado River canyon to the southeast. Other prominent points of interest include views of Mount Hayden, Saddle Mountain, and Marble Canyon. ⊠ *2.7 mi left off Cape Royal Scenic Dr. on Point Imperial Rd., 11 mi northeast of Grand Canyon Lodge.*

Fodor's Choice
★
Point Sublime. Talk about solitude. Here you can camp within feet of the canyon's edge. Sunrises and sunsets are spectacular. The winding road, through gorgeous high country, is only 17 mi, but it will take you at least two hours, one way. The road is intended only for vehicles with high-road clearance (pickups and four-wheel-drive vehicles). It is also necessary to be properly equipped for wilderness road travel. Check with a park ranger or at the information desk at Grand Canyon Lodge before taking this journey. You may camp here only with a permit from the Backcountry Information Center. ⊠ *North Rim Dr., Grand Canyon; about 20 mi west of North Rim Visitor Center.*

Roosevelt Point. Named after the president who gave the Grand Canyon its national monument status in 1908 (it was upgraded to national park status in 1919), this is the best place to see the confluence of the Little Colorado River and the Grand Canyon. The cliffs above the Colorado River south of the junction are known as the Palisades of the Desert. A short woodland loop trail leads to this eastern viewpoint. ⊠ *Cape Royal Rd., 18 mi east of Grand Canyon Lodge.*

SPORTS AND THE OUTDOORS

HIKING

EASY   **Cape Final Trail.** This 2-mi hike follows an old jeep trail through a ponderosa pine forest to the canyon overlook at Cape Final with panoramic views of the northern canyon, the Palisades of the Desert, and the impressive spectacle of Juno Temple. ⊠ *Trailhead: dirt parking lot 5 mi south of Roosevelt Point on Cape Royal Rd.*

☺   **Roosevelt Point Trail.** This easy 0.2-mi round-trip trail loops through the
★   forest to the scenic viewpoint. Allow 20 minutes for this short, secluded hike. ⊠ *Trailhead: Cape Royal Rd.*

☺   **Transept Trail.** This 3-mi (round-trip), 1½-hour trail begins at 8,255 feet near the Grand Canyon Lodge. Well maintained and well marked, it has little elevation change, sticking near the rim before reaching a dramatic view of a large stream through Bright Angel Canyon. The route leads to a side canyon called Transept Canyon, which geologist Clarence Dutton named in 1882, declaring it "far grander than Yosemite."

DID YOU KNOW?

The North Rim's isolated Toroweap overlook (also called Tuweep) is perched 3,000 feet above the canyon floor; a height equal to stacking the Sears Town and Empire State Building on top of each other.

Check the posted schedule to find a ranger talk along this trail; it's also a great place to view fall foliage. Flash floods can occur any time of the year, especially June through September when thunderstorms develop rapidly. ⚠ **Check forecasts before heading into the canyon and use caution when hiking in narrow canyons and drainage systems.** ⊠ *Trailhead: near Grand Canyon Lodge's east patio.*

MODERATE **Ken Patrick Trail.** This primitive trail travels 10 mi one way (allow six hours) from the trailhead at 8,250 feet to Point Imperial at 8,803 feet. It crosses drainages and occasionally detours around fallen trees. The end of the road brings the highest views from either rim. Note that there is no water along this trail. ⊠ *Trailhead: east side of North Kaibab trailhead parking lot.*

Uncle Jim Trail. This 5-mi, three-hour loop trail starts at 8,300 feet and winds south through the forest, past Roaring Springs and Bright Angel canyons. The highlight of this rim hike is Uncle Jim Point, which, at 8,244 feet, overlooks the upper sections of the North Kaibab Trail. ⊠ *Trailhead: North Kaibab Trail parking lot.*

★ **Widforss Trail.** Round-trip, Widforss Trail is 9.8 mi, with an elevation change of 200 feet. Allow five to seven hours for the hike, which starts at 8,080 feet and passes through shady forests of pine, spruce, fir, and aspen on its way to Widforss Point, at 7,900 feet. Here you'll have good views of five temples: Zoroaster, Brahma, and Deva to the southeast and Buddha and Manu to the southwest. You are likely to see wildflowers in summer, and this is a good trail for viewing fall foliage. It's named in honor of artist Gunnar M. Widforss, renowned for his paintings of national park landscapes. ⊠ *Trailhead: across from North Kaibab Trail parking lot.*

DIFFICULT **North Kaibab Trail.** At 8,241 feet, this trail, like the roads leading to the North Rim, is open only from May through late October or early November (depending on the weather). It is recommended for experienced hikers only, who should allow four days for the full hike. The long, steep path drops 5,840 feet over a distance of 14.5 mi to Phantom Ranch and the Colorado River, so the National Park Service suggests that day hikers not go farther than Roaring Springs (5,020 feet) before turning to hike back up out of the canyon. After about 7 mi, Cottonwood Campground (4,080 feet) has drinking water in summer, restrooms, shade trees, and a ranger. ■TIP→ **For a fee, a shuttle takes hikers to the North Kaibab trailhead twice daily from Grand Canyon Lodge.** ⊠ *Trailhead: 2 mi north of Grand Canyon Lodge.*

MULE RIDES

OUTFITTER **Canyon Trail Rides.** This company leads mule rides on the easier trails of
ℭ the North Rim. A one-hour ride (minimum age seven) runs $40. Half-day trips on the rim or into the canyon (minimum age 10) cost $75; full-day trips (minimum age 12) go for $165. Weight limits vary from 200 to 220 pounds. Available daily from May 15 to October 15, these excursions are popular, so make reservations far in advance. ⌂ *Box 128, Tropic, UT 84776* ☎ *435/679–8665* ⊕ *www.canyonrides.com/grand_canyon_rides.html.*

WHAT'S NEARBY

The northwest section of Arizona is geographically fascinating. In addition to the Grand Canyon, it's home to national forests, national monuments, and national recreation areas. Towns, however, are small and scattered. Many of them cater to visiting adventurers, and Native American reservations dot the map.

NEARBY TOWNS AND ATTRACTIONS

NEARBY TOWNS

Towns near the canyon's South Rim include the tiny town of Tusayan, just 1 mi south of the entrance station, and Williams, the "Gateway to the Grand Canyon," 58 mi south.

Tusayan has the basic amenities and an airport that serves as a starting point for airplane and helicopter tours of the canyon. The cozy mountain town of **Williams,** founded in 1882 when the railroad passed through, was once a rough-and-tumble joint, replete with saloons and bordellos. Today it reflects a much milder side of the Wild West, with 3,300 residents and more than 25 motels and hotels. Wander along main street—part of historic Route 66, but locally named, like the town, after trapper Bill Williams—and indulge in Route 66 nostalgia inside antiques shops or souvenir and T-shirt stores.

The communities closest to the North Rim—all of them tiny and with limited services—include Fredonia, 76 mi north; Marble Canyon, 80 mi northeast; Lees Ferry, 85 mi east; and Jacob Lake, 45 mi north.

Fredonia, a small community of about 1,050, approximately an hour's drive north of the Grand Canyon, is often referred to as the gateway to the North Rim; it's also relatively close to Zion and Bryce Canyon national parks in Utah. **Marble Canyon** marks the geographical beginning of the Grand Canyon at its northeastern tip. It's a good stopping point if you are driving U.S. 89 to the North Rim. En route from the South Rim to the North Rim is **Lees Ferry,** where most of the area's river rafts start their journey. The tiny town of **Jacob Lake,** nestled high in pine country at an elevation of 7,925 feet, was named after Mormon explorer Jacob Hamblin, also known as the "Buckskin Missionary." It has a hotel, café, campground, and lush mountain countryside.

ESSENTIALS

Visitor Information Kaibab National Forest, North District (⊠ *430 S. Main St., Fredonia* ☎ *928/643–7395* ⊕ *www.fs.fed.us/r3/kai*). **Kaibab National Forest, Tusayan Ranger District** (⊠ *Hwy. 64, Grand Canyon* ☎ *928/638–2443* ⊕ *www.fs.fed.us/r3/kai*). **Kaibab National Forest, Williams Ranger District** (⊠ *742 S. Clover Rd., Williams* ☎ *928/635–5600* ⊕ *www.fs.fed.us/r3/kai*). **Kaibab Plateau Visitor Center** (⊠ *Hwy. 89A/AZ 67, HC 64, Jacob Lake* ☎ *928/643–7298* ⊕ *www.fs.fed.us/r3/kai*). **Williams Visitor Center** (⊠ *200 W. Railroad Ave., at Grand Canyon Blvd., Williams* ☎ *928/635–1418 or 800/863–0546* ⊕ *www. williamschamber.com* ☉ *Spring, fall, and winter, daily 8–5; summer, daily 8–6:30*).

NEARBY ATTRACTION

★ **Vermilion Cliffs**. West from the town of Marble Canyon are these spectacular cliffs, more than 3,000 feet high in many places. Keep an eye out for condors; the giant endangered birds were reintroduced into the area in 1996. Reports suggest that the birds, once in captivity, are surviving well in the wilderness.

SCENIC DRIVES AND VISTAS

U.S. 89. The route north from Cameron Trading Post (Cameron, Arizona) on U.S. 89 offers a stunning view of the **Painted Desert** to the right. The desert, which covers thousands of square miles stretching to the south and east, is a vision of subtle, almost harsh beauty, with wind-swept plains and mesas, isolated buttes, and barren valleys in pastel patterns. About 30 mi north of Cameron Trading Post, the Painted Desert country gives way to sandstone cliffs that run for miles. Brilliantly hued and ranging in color from light pink to deep orange, the **Echo Cliffs** rise to more than 1,000 feet in many places. They are essentially devoid of vegetation, but in a few high places, thick patches of tall cottonwood and poplar trees, nurtured by springs and water seepage from the rock escarpment, manage to thrive.

U.S. 89A. At Bitter Springs, 60 mi north of Cameron, U.S. 89A branches off from U.S. 89, running north and providing views of **Marble Canyon,** the geographical beginning of the Grand Canyon. Like the Grand Canyon, Marble Canyon was formed by the Colorado River. Traversing a gorge nearly 500 feet deep is **Navajo Bridge,** a narrow steel span built in 1929 and listed on the National Register of Historic Places. Formerly used for car traffic, it now functions only as a pedestrian overpass.

WHERE TO EAT AND STAY

ABOUT THE RESTAURANTS

INSIDE THE PARK
Within the park, you can find everything from cafeteria food to casual café fare to creatively prepared, Western- and Southwestern-inspired American cuisine. There's even a coffeehouse with organic joe. Reservations are accepted (and recommended) only for dinner at El Tovar Dining Room; they can be made up to six months in advance with El Tovar room reservations, 30 days in advance without. You can also make dinner reservations at the Grand Canyon Lodge Dining Room on the North Rim—they're less essential here but still a good idea in summer. The dress code is casual across the board, but El Tovar is your best option if you're looking to dress up a bit and thumb through an extensive wine list. On the North Rim there's a restaurant, a cafeteria, and a chuck-wagon-style Grand Cookout experience. Drinking water and restrooms are not available at most picnic spots.

OUTSIDE THE PARK
Options outside the park generally range from mediocre to terrible—you didn't come all the way to the Grand Canyon for the food, did you? Our selections highlight your best options. Of towns near the park, Williams definitely has the leg up on culinary variety and quality, with Tusayan and Jacob Lake to the north mostly either fast food or merely

adequate sit-down restaurants. Near the park, even the priciest places welcome casual dress.

ABOUT THE HOTELS

INSIDE THE PARK The park's accommodations include three "historic rustic" facilities and four motel-style lodges, all of which have undergone significant upgrades over the past decade. Of the 922 rooms, cabins, and suites, only 203, all at the Grand Canyon Lodge, are at the North Rim. Outside El Tovar Hotel, the canyon's architectural highlight, accommodations are relatively basic but comfortable, and the most sought-after rooms have canyon views. Rates vary widely, but most rooms fall in the $150 to $190 range, though the most basic units at the South Rim go for just $90.

Reservations are a must, especially during the busy summer season. ■ TIP→ **If you want to get your first choice (especially Bright Angel Lodge or El Tovar), make reservations as far in advance as possible; they're taken up to 13 months ahead.** You might find a last-minute cancellation, but you shouldn't count on it. Although lodging at the South Rim will keep you close to the action, the frenetic activity and crowded facilities are off-putting to some. With short notice, the best time to find a room on the South Rim is in winter. And though the North Rim is less crowded than the South Rim, lodging is available only from mid-May through mid-October, though remember that rooms are limited.

OUTSIDE THE PARK Just south of the park's boundary, Tusayan's hotels are in a convenient location but without bargains, while Williams can provide price breaks on food and lodging, as well as a respite from the crowds. Extra amenities (e.g., swimming pools and gyms) are also more abundant. Reservations are always a good idea.

ABOUT THE CAMPGROUNDS

INSIDE THE PARK Within the national park, camping is permitted only in designated campsites. Some campgrounds charge nightly camping fees in addition to entrance fees, and some accept reservations up to five months in advance through ⊕ *www.recreation.gov*. Others are first-come, first-served. The South Rim has three campgrounds, one with RV hookups. The North Rim's single in-park campground does not offer hookups. All four campgrounds are near the rims and easily accessible. In-park camping in a spot other than a developed rim campground requires a permit from the Backcountry Information Center, which also serves as your reservation. Permits can be requested by mail or fax; applying well in advance is recommended. Call ☎ *928/638–7875* between 1 and 5 weekdays for information. Numerous backcountry campsites dot the canyon—be prepared for a considerable hike. The three established backcountry campgrounds require a trek of 4.6 to 16.6 mi.

OUTSIDE THE PARK Outside the park boundaries, two campgrounds, one with hookups, are within 7 mi of the South Rim, and two are within about 45 mi of the North Rim. Developed and undeveloped campsites are available, first-come, first-served, in the Kaibab National Forest. There is no camping on the West Rim, but you can pitch a tent on the beach near the Colorado River at the primitive campground on Diamond Creek Road.

Hikers heading to the falls in Havasu Canyon can stay at the primitive campground in Supai.

WHAT IT COSTS					
	¢	$	$$	$$$	$$$$
Restaurants	under $8	$8–$12	$13–$20	$21–$30	over $30
Hotels	under $70	$70–$120	$121–$175	$176–$250	over $250

Restaurant prices are per person for a main course at dinner. Hotel prices are for a standard double in high season, excluding taxes and service charges.

WHERE TO EAT

IN THE PARK: SOUTH RIM

$$$

STEAK

✕ **Arizona Room.** The canyon views from this casual Southwestern-style steak house are the best of any restaurant at the South Rim. Enjoy the view while you sip a signature prickly pear margarita. The menu includes such delicacies as chili-crusted pan-seared wild salmon, chipotle barbecue baby back ribs, pulled-pork-and-avocado quesadillas, and half-pound buffalo burgers with Gorgonzola aioli. For dessert, try the cheesecake with prickly-pear syrup paired with one of the house's specialty coffee drinks. Seating is first-come, first served, so arrive early to avoid the crowds. ⊠ *Bright Angel Lodge, Desert View Dr., Grand Canyon Village* ☎ *928/638–2631* ⊕ *www.grandcanyonlodges.com* ⚐ *Reservations not accepted* ☰ *AE, D, DC, MC, V* ☉ *Closed Jan. and Feb. No lunch Nov. and Dec.*

$

SOUTHWESTERN

✕ **Bright Angel Restaurant.** The draw here is casual, affordable, if uninspired dining. No-surprises dishes will fill your belly at breakfast, lunch, or dinner. Entrées include such basics as salads, steaks, lasagna, fajitas, and fish tacos. Or you can step it up a notch and order some of the same selections straight from the Arizona Room menu including prime rib, baby back ribs, and wild salmon. For dessert try the warm apple grunt cake topped with vanilla ice cream. Be prepared to wait for a table: the dining room bustles all day long. The plain decor is broken up with large-pane windows and original artwork. ⊠ *Bright Angel Lodge, Desert View Dr., Grand Canyon Village* ☎ *928/638–2631* ⊕ *www.grandcanyonlodges.com* ⚐ *Reservations not accepted* ☰ *AE, D, DC, MC, V.*

$$$

SOUTHWESTERN

Fodor'sChoice

★

✕ **El Tovar Dining Room.** No doubt about it—this is the best restaurant for miles. Modeled after a European hunting lodge, this rustic 19th-century dining room built of hand-hewn logs is worth a visit. The cuisine is modern Southwestern with an exotic flair. Start with the smoked salmon–and–goat cheese crostini or the acclaimed black bean soup. The dinner menu includes such hearty yet creative dishes as citrus-marmalade-glazed duck with roasted poblano black bean rice, grilled New York strip steak with buttermilk-cornmeal onion rings, and a wild salmon tostada topped with organic greens and tequila vinaigrette. The dining room also has an extensive wine list. ■TIP→ Dinner reservations can be made up to six months in advance with room reservations and 30 days in advance for all other visitors. If you can't get a

21

TOP PICNIC SPOTS

Bring your picnic basket and enjoy dining alfresco surrounded by some of the most beautiful backdrops in the country. Be sure to bring water, as it's unavailable at many of these spots, as are restrooms.

■ **Buggeln,** 15 mi east of Grand Canyon Village on Desert View Drive, has some secluded, shady spots.

■ **Cape Royal,** 23 mi south of the North Rim Visitor Center, is the most popular designated picnic area on the North Rim due to its panoramic views.

■ **Grandview Point** has, as the name implies, grand vistas; it is 12 mi east of the village on Desert View Drive.

■ **Point Imperial,** 11 mi northeast of the North Rim Visitor Center, has shade and some privacy.

dinner table, consider lunch or breakfast—the best in the region with dishes like polenta corncakes with prickly pear–pistachio butter, and blackened breakfast trout and eggs. ⊠ *El Tovar Hotel, Desert View Dr.* ⌂ *10 Albright Ave., Grand Canyon Village 86023* ☏ *303/297–2757, 888/297–2757 reservations only, 928/638–2631 Ext. 6432* ⊕ *www. grandcanyonlodges.com* ⌂ *Reservations essential* ⊟ *AE, D, DC, MC, V.*

IN THE PARK: NORTH RIM

¢ ✕ **Deli in the Pines.** Dining choices are very limited on the North Rim,
AMERICAN but this is your best bet for a meal on a budget. Selections include pizza, salads, deli sandwiches, hot dogs, homemade breakfast pastries, and soft-serve ice cream. Best of all, there is an outdoor seating area for dining alfresco. It's open for breakfast, lunch, and dinner. ⊠ *Grand Canyon Lodge, Bright Angel Point, North Rim* ☏ *928/638–2611 Ext. 766* ⊕ *www.grandcanyonforever.com* ⌂ *Reservations not accepted* ⊟ *AE, D, DC, MC, V* ☉ *Closed mid-Oct.–mid-May.*

$$$ ✕ **Grand Canyon Lodge Dining Room.** The historic lodge has a huge, high-
AMERICAN ceilinged dining room with spectacular views and decent food, though
★ the draw here is definitely the setting. You might find pork medallions, bison flank steak, and grilled ruby trout for dinner. The filling, simply prepared food here takes a flavorful turn with Southwestern spices and organic selections. It's also open for breakfast and lunch. A full-service bar and an impressive wine list add to the relaxed atmosphere of the only full-service, sit-down restaurant on the North Rim. Dinner reservations aren't required, but they're a good idea in summer and on spring and fall weekends. ⊠ *Grand Canyon Lodge, Bright Angel Point, North Rim* ☏ *928/638–2611 Ext. 760* ⊕ *www.grandcanyonforever.com* ⊟ *AE, D, DC, MC, V* ☉ *Closed mid-Oct.–mid-May.*

$$$$ ✕ **Grand Cookout.** Dine under the stars and enjoy live entertainment at
AMERICAN this chuck-wagon-style dining experience—a popular family-friendly
☺ choice among the North Rim's limited dining options. Fill up on Western favorites including barbecue beef brisket, roasted chicken, baked beans, and cowboy biscuits. The food is basic and tasty, but the real draw is the nightly performance of Western music and tall tales. Transportation from the Grand Canyon Lodge to the cookout

is included in the price. Be sure to call before 4 pm for dinner reservations. Advance reservations are taken up to seven days ahead at the Grand Canyon Lodge registration desk. ⊠ *Grand Canyon Lodge, North Rim* ☎ *928/638–2611* ⌂ *Reservations essential* ▤ *AE, D, DC, MC, V* ☾ *Closed mid-Oct.–mid-May.*

WHERE TO STAY

Hotel reviews have been condensed for this book. Please go to Fodors. com for full reviews of each property.

IN THE PARK: SOUTH RIM

$–$$
Bright Angel Lodge. Famed architect Mary Jane Colter designed this 1935 log-and-stone structure, which sits within a few yards of the canyon rim and blends superbly with the canyon walls. **Pros:** some rooms have canyon vistas; all are steps away from the rim; Internet kiosks and transportation desk for the mule ride check-in are in the lobby; good value for the amazing location. **Cons:** the popular lobby is always packed; parking is a bit of a hike. ⊠ *Desert View Dr., Grand Canyon Village* ⌂ *Box 699, Grand Canyon 86023* ☎ *888/297–2757 reservations only, 928/638–2631* ⊕ *www.grandcanyonlodges.com* ↩ *37 rooms, 18 with bath; 49 cabins* ⌂ *In-room: a/c (some), safe (some), refrigerator (some), Wi-Fi (some). In-hotel: 2 restaurants, bar* ▤ *AE, D, DC, MC, V.*

$$$–$$$$
Fodor's Choice
★
El Tovar Hotel. A registered National Historic Landmark, the "architectural crown jewel of the Grand Canyon" was built in 1905 of Oregon pine logs and native stone. **Pros:** historic lodging just steps from the South Rim; fabulous lounge with outdoor seating and canyon views; best in-park dining on-site. **Cons:** books up quickly. ⊠ *Desert View Dr., Grand Canyon Village* ⌂ *Box 699, Grand Canyon 86023* ☎ *888/297–2757 reservations only, 928/638–2631* ⊕ *www.grandcanyonlodges.com* ↩ *66 rooms, 12 suites* ⌂ *In-room: a/c, refrigerator, Wi-Fi. In-hotel: restaurant, room service, bar, Wi-Fi hotspot* ▤ *AE, D, DC, MC, V.*

$$
Kachina Lodge. On the rim halfway between El Tovar and Bright Angel Lodge, this motel-style lodge has many rooms with partial canyon views ($10 extra). **Pros:** partial canyon views in half the rooms; family-friendly; steps from the best restaurants in the park. **Cons:** check-in takes place at El Tovar Hotel; limited parking; pleasant but bland furnishings. ⊠ *Desert View Dr., Grand Canyon Village* ⌂ *Box 699, Grand Canyon 86023* ☎ *888/297–2757 reservations only, 928/638–2631* ⊕ *www.grandcanyonlodges.com* ↩ *49 rooms* ⌂ *In-room: no a/c, safe, refrigerator, Wi-Fi (some)* ▤ *AE, D, DC, MC, V.*

$$
Maswik Lodge. Only a short walking distance from the rim, Maswik Lodge is made up of a group of two story buildings, each with about a dozen rooms. **Pros:** quiet location; plenty of parking; family-friendly; may see elk and deer right from your window. **Cons:** rooms lack personality. ⊠ *Desert View Dr., Grand Canyon Village* ⌂ *Box 699, Grand Canyon 86023* ☎ *888/297–2757 reservations only, 928/638–2631* ⊕ *www.grandcanyonlodges.com* ↩ *250 rooms* ⌂ *In-room: a/c, safe, refrigerator, Wi-Fi (some). In-hotel: restaurant* ▤ *AE, D, DC, MC, V.*

$$ ⓣ **Thunderbird Lodge.** This motel with comfortable, simple rooms with the modern amenities you'd expect at a typical mid-price chain hotel is next to Bright Angel Lodge in Grand Canyon Village. **Pros:** partial canyon views in some rooms; family-friendly. **Cons:** rooms lack personality; check-in takes place at Bright Angel Lodge; limited parking. ⊠ *Desert View Dr., Grand Canyon Village* ⓓ *Box 699, Grand Canyon 86023* ☎ *888/297–2757 reservations only, 928/638–2631* ⊕ *www.grandcanyonlodges.com* ⤴ *55 rooms* ⚙ *In-room: a/c (some), safe, refrigerator, Wi-Fi (some)* ⊟ *AE, D, DC, MC, V.*

$–$$ ⓣ **Yavapai Lodge.** The largest motel-style lodge in the park is tucked in a piñon and juniper forest at the eastern end of Grand Canyon Village, near the RV park. **Pros:** transportation-activities desk on-site in the lobby; near Market Plaza in Grand Canyon Village; forested grounds. **Cons:** farthest in-park lodging from the rim. ⊠ *Grand Canyon Village* ⓓ *Box 699, Grand Canyon 86023* ☎ *888/297–2757 reservations only, 928/638–2961* ⊕ *www.grandcanyonlodges.com* ⤴ *358 rooms* ⚙ *In-room: a/c (some), refrigerator, Wi-Fi (some). In-hotel: restaurant, Internet terminal* ⊟ *AE, D, DC, MC, V* ⊙ *Closed Jan. and Feb.*

CAMP-
GROUNDS
AND RV PARKS

¢ ⚠ **Bright Angel Campground.** This campground is near Phantom Ranch on the South and North Kaibab trails, at the bottom of the canyon. There are toilet facilities and running water, but no showers. If you plan to eat at the Phantom Ranch Canteen, book your meals ahead of time. Reservations for all services, taken up to four months in advance, are a must. Reservations are taken weekdays from 1 pm to 5 pm (MT) A backcountry permit, which serves as your reservation, is required to stay here. **Pros:** incredible setting in bottom of canyon; close to Phantom Ranch. **Cons:** extremely remote; long hike from either rim. ⊠ *Intersection of South and North Kaibab trails, Grand Canyon* ⓓ *Backcountry Information Center, Box 129, Grand Canyon 86023* ☎ *928/638–7875* 🖷 *928/638–2125* ⤴ *30 tent sites, 2 group sites* ⚙ *Flush toilets, drinking water, picnic tables* ⚲ *Backcountry permit required* ⊙ *Open year-round.*

¢ ⚠ **Desert View Campground.** Popular for spectacular views of the canyon from the nearby watchtower, this campground fills up fast in summer. Fifty RV (without hookups) and tent sites are available on a first-come, first-served basis. **Pros:** right off the main road, steps from wonderful canyon views; farther from crowds and RVs than other South Rim campgrounds but only 2.5 mi from Canyon Village; the most inexpensive campground on the North Rim. **Cons:** no RV hookups; fills up fast. ⊠ *Desert View Dr., 23 mi east of Grand Canyon Village off Hwy. 64* ⓓ *Backcountry Information Center, Box 129, Grand Canyon 86023* ☎ *928/638–7875* ⤴ *50 campsites* ⚙ *Flush toilets, drinking water, grills, picnic tables* ⚲ *Reservations not accepted* ⊙ *May–mid-Oct.*

¢ ⚠ **Mather Campground.** Mather has RV and tent sites but no hookups.
★ No reservations are accepted from mid-November through February (when rates drop slightly), but the rest of the year, especially during the busy spring and summer seasons, they are a good idea, and can be made up to five months in advance. Ask at the campground entrance for same-day availability. **Pros:** walking distance to several South Rim restaurants and grocery store; open year-round; great for tent campers.

Cons: no hookups for RVs; in crowded part of South Rim; maximum vehicle length of 30 feet. ⊠ *Off Village Loop Dr., Grand Canyon Village* ☎ *877/444–6777* ⊕ *www.recreation.gov* ⤳ *308 sites for RVs and tents* ⚴ *Flush toilets, dump station, drinking water, guest laundry, showers, fire grates, picnic tables, public telephone* ☉ *Open year-round.*

IN THE PARK: NORTH RIM

$–$$

Fodor's Choice

★

🏨 **Grand Canyon Lodge.** This historic property, constructed mainly in the 1920s and '30s, is the premier lodging facility in the North Rim area. **Pros:** steps away from gorgeous North Rim views; close to several easy hiking trails. Guests may request a specific cabin but it cannot be guaranteed. **Cons:** as the only in-park North Rim lodging option, this lodge fills up fast; few amenities and no Internet access. ⊠ *Grand Canyon National Park, Hwy. 67, North Rim* ☎ *877/386–4383, 928/638–2611 May–Oct., 928/645–6865 Nov.–Apr.* ⊕ *www.grandcanyonforever.com* ⤳ *40 rooms, 178 cabins* ⚴ *In-room: no a/c, refrigerator (some), no TV. In-hotel: 3 restaurants, bar, bicycles, laundry facilities (at the campground)* ⊟ *AE, D, MC, V* ☉ *Closed mid-Oct.–mid-May.*

CAMPGROUND

¢

⚠ **North Rim Campground.** The only designated campground at the North Rim of Grand Canyon National Park sits 3 mi north of the rim, and has 83 RV and tent sites (no hookups). You can reserve a site up to five months in advance. Leashed pets are allowed at the campground. **Pros:** only camping at North Rim and mostly geared towards tents; attractive pine-shaded setting. **Cons:** no hookups for RVs; closed much of the year. ⊠ *Hwy. 67, North Rim* ☎ *877/444–6777* ⊕ *www.recreation. gov* ⤳ *83 campsites* ⚴ *Flush toilets, dump station, drinking water, guest laundry, showers, fire grates, picnic tables, general store* ⚐ *Reservations essential* ☉ *Mid-May–Sept., possibly later, weather permitting.*

OUTSIDE THE PARK: NORTH RIM

$–$$

🏨 **Jacob Lake Inn.** The bustling lodge at Jacob Lake Inn is a popular stop for those heading to the North Rim, 45 mi south. **Pros:** grocery store, coffee shop, and restaurant; quiet rooms. **Cons:** small bathroom in cabins; old-fashioned key locks. ⊠ *Hwy. 67/U.S. 89A, Fredonia* ☎ *928/643–7232* ⊕ *www.jacoblake.com* ⤳ *32 rooms, 26 cabins* ⚴ *In-room: no a/c (some), no phone (some), no TV (some) Wi-Fi (some). In-hotel: restaurant, some pets allowed* ⊟ *AE, D, MC, V.*

$

★

🏨 **Marble Canyon Lodge.** This Arizona Strip lodge popular with anglers and rafters opened in 1929 on the same day the Navajo Bridge was dedicated. **Pros:** convenience store and trading post; great fishing on the Colorado River. **Cons:** no-frills rustic lodging; more than 70 mi to the Grand Canyon North Rim. ⊠ *0.25 mi west of Navajo Bridge on U.S. 89A* ⌂ *Box 6001, Marble Canyon 86036* ☎ *928/355–2225 or 800/726–1789* ⊕ *www.marblecanyoncompany.com* ⤳ *46 rooms, 8 apartments* ⚴ *In-room: a/c, no phone, kitchen (some), Wi-Fi. In-hotel: restaurant, bar, laundry facilities, some pets allowed* ⊟ *AE, D, MC, V.*

Las Vegas

WORD OF MOUTH

"If you have your heart set on a particular Cirque show, book ahead. Even if you book ahead, you can still get a discount at the official Cirque site, which offers various discounts and packages."

—cherylli

WELCOME TO LAS VEGAS

TOP REASONS TO GO

★ **The Spectacle:** Las Vegas is a place you must see even if you've only rolled dice for a Yahtzee game.

★ **The Adrenaline:** The variety of gambling and entertainment, the level of stakes, the quality of dealers, the sheer numbers of players at the tables, and the overall energy radiating from the Strip and its environs makes Vegas a unique kind of rush.

★ **The People:** It's not just a people-watcher's paradise, Vegas provides a fantastic opportunity to interact. Belly up to a craps table and you'll see why.

★ **The Food:** The days of the $4.95 steak dinner are over; in their place are scores of world-class restaurants of all cuisines.

★ **The Smiles:** When people go to Las Vegas they come alive, because the city provides so many opportunities to become a slightly different person. You'll rarely get reminders of your daily routine, because t Vegas is like nowhere else you've ever been.

1 South Strip. Between fight nights at the MGM Grand and concerts at Mandalay Bay, the section of Strip between the sprawling City Center and the iconic "Welcome to Las Vegas" sign could be considered the entertainment hub of Vegas. Resorts in this area include the Tropicana, Monte Carlo, New York–New York, Excalibur, MGM Grand, and Luxor. Rooms on this side of town generally are within 15 minutes of the airport and are slightly more affordable than their Center and North Strip counterparts.

2 Center Strip. The heart of the Strip is home to iconic casinos such as Bellagio, the Mirage, and Caesars Palace, as well as the sprawling CityCenter. Room rates in the Center Strip tend to vary, with smaller resorts being the most affordable. Another draw is the shopping at Crystals (inside CityCenter), the Miracle Mile Shops (inside Planet Hollywood), and the Forum Shops (inside Caesars).

3 North Strip. The North Strip is defined by luxury. Wynn Las Vegas and the Encore have some of the swankiest rooms in town. At the Venetian and the Palazzo, standard rooms have a sunken living room. Clubs and restaurants here are some of the best in town. Perhaps the only downside: Prices are among the most expensive in town.

4 Downtown. Hotels are cheaper and favored for their strictly adult pleasures: dice and drinks. They exist in the old Vegas tradition, when guests were expected to spend most of their hours in the casinos, not their rooms; consequently, rooms range from scuzzy to semipleasant. Stay here if you want to spend less than $60 per night and enjoy lower table limits.

5 Paradise Road. Parallel to the Strip, a short drive or 15-minute walk east, is the mellower Paradise Road area, which includes the Convention Center. There's less traffic, and there's monorail service along one stretch. Hotel options include the Las Vegas Hilton, Hard Rock Hotel, Hooters, and the Platinum.

Nevada State Museum and Historical Society

TO SUN BUGGY FUN RENTALS; RICHARD PETTY DRIVING EXPERIENCE

Bonanza Rd.

Fremont Experience

95 Expressway

95

TO SOUTHERN NEVADA ZOOLOGICAL BOTANICAL PARK

Martin L King Blvd

15

Main Street Station
Plaza
Golden Gate
Golden Nugget

Four Queens

4

Neon Museum

DOWNTOWN

Alta Ave.

Charleston Blvd.

Rancho Dr.

Casino Center Blvd.

Main St.

Las Vegas Blvd.

Viva Las Vegas Wedding Chapel ◆

◆ Little White Wedding Chapel

604

Oakey Blvd.

Oakey Blvd.

Stratosphere ▽

◆ Chapel of the Flowers

Sahara Ave.

Sahara Ave.

Sahara

15

Circus Circus

Paradise Rd.

Las Vegas Hilton

Las Vegas Country Club

Vegas Indoor Skydiving
Haunted Vegas Tours

Las Vegas Convention Center

Guardian Angel Cathedral

Trump International Hotel & Tower

3

Encore

Fashion Show Dr.

Las Vegas Monorail

Desert Inn Rd.

Renaissance

Spring Mountain Rd.   **THE STRIP**

Wynn Las Vegas

Treasure Island

Palazzo

Sands Ave.

PARADISE ROAD

5

Mirage   Harrah's   **Venetian**

Flamingo Hotel

Bill's Gambling Hall

Westin Casuarina

Atomic Testing Museum

Rio

Caesars Palace

The Strip

Flamingo Rd.

2

Bellagio   Bally's

Flamingo Rd.

◆ Platinum Hotel

Vdara   Paris

Planet Hollywood

Hard Rock

Mandarin Oriental

City Center   Aria   Monte Carlo

◆Gameworks

Harmon Av.

University of Nevada at Las Vegas (UNLV)

New York–New York ◆

MGM Grand

Hooters   Tropicana Ave.

1

Excalibur

Tropicana

McCarran International Airport

TO PINBALL HALL OF FAME; THE GUN STORE

15

Luxor

Las Vegas Blvd.

Paradise Rd.

THEhotel

The Little Church of the West

Mandalay Bay

Four Seasons

0   1/2 mi

0   1/2 km

22

GETTING ORIENTED

Las Vegas is an easy city to navigate. The principal north–south artery is Las Vegas Boulevard (Interstate 15 runs roughly parallel to it, less than a mile to the west). A 4-mi stretch of Las Vegas Boulevard South is known as the Strip, where a majority of the city's hotels and casinos are clustered. Many major streets running east–west (Tropicana Avenue, Flamingo Road, Desert Inn Road, Sahara Avenue) are named for the casinos built at their intersections with the Strip. Highway 215 and Interstate 15 circumnavigate the city, and the Interstate 515 freeway connects Henderson to Las Vegas and then to Summerlin.

Washington, D.C., may be America's seat of power, but if you want its seat of promise, it just might reside in the land of glitz, glamour and silicone, where particular ATMs only dispense $100 bills and all-you-can-eat buffets challenge you to eat your weight in jumbo shrimp, Alaskan crab legs, and prime rib. And the promise takes many forms, 24/7. Whether you go for the volcanic excess and passionate consumerism of the Strip, the more humble (but still neon-bathed) downtown experience, or the grittier locals' joints, Las Vegas promises wealth, excitement, and a temporary sense of importance to all who visit.

For the millions who visit Las Vegas every year, the city offers an ever-increasing array of sights, sounds, and experiences to play on their unsatisfied needs. We desire travel to exotic locales, so we stay in a hotel modeled after one, like the Mirage or the Venetian. We want to experience adventure, so we play casino games: a good adrenaline proxy for physical risk. Just for a moment we want to own and consume finer things than we have, so we visit opulent restaurants and visit any of several concentrations of high-end shopping districts, looking to buy items that would be just beyond our reach back in the "real" world.

Beyond and to some degree within the spectacle, the people of Las Vegas are quintessentially American. It shines through in the out-of-staters who settled in Southern Nevada for a million different reasons over the years, who deal blackjack and drive cabs. But also evident is the melting pot; Las Vegas is the city on the hill for immigrants from all over the world. For visitors and many locals as well, Las Vegas knows what you want and doles it out in spades. It's both exotic and comfortably familiar at the same time. But the city goes beyond merely reflecting American tastes and ideals; it consumes, amplifies, and blasts them out at high volume.

PLANNING

22

WHEN TO GO

Summer highs hover around 100°F, but with no humidity and ever-present air-conditioning, you'll be comfortable as long as you have water on hand. With 300 days of sunshine a year, the chances of a rain-out are slim. On the other hand, nights can be chilly between late fall and early spring, so bring a sweater or windbreaker for evening strolls. Winter months are colder than many people expect with temperatures in the mid 40s to 60s during the day, and as low as the 30s at night.

Las Vegas doesn't have a high or low season by the standard definition, but you'll find it the least crowded between November and January. Hotels are at their fullest July through October. Specific events—New Year's Eve, spring break, major conventions, sporting events—draw big crowds, so plan accordingly.

GETTING HERE

AIR TRAVEL

The gateway to Las Vegas is **McCarran International Airport (LAS)** (☎ 702/261–5211 ⊕ *www.mccarran.com*), 5 mi south of the business district and immediately east of the southern end of the Strip. The airport, just a few minutes' drive from the Strip, is consistently rated among the most passenger-friendly airports in the United States.

GROUND TRANSPORTATION **By shuttle van:** This is the cheapest way from McCarran to your hotel. The service is shared with other riders, and costs $5 or $6 per person to the Strip, $7 to $8 to downtown, and $7 to $24 to outlying casinos. The vans wait for passengers outside the terminal in a marked area. Because the vans make numerous stops at different hotels, it's not the best means of transportation if you're in a hurry.

By taxi: The trip from the airport to most hotels on the south end of the Strip should cost $11 to $14, to the north end of the Strip should cost $14 to $25, and to downtown should cost $20 to $23. ■TIP→ Be sure to specify to your driver that you do not want to take Interstate 15 or the airport tunnel on your way to or from the airport. This is always the longer route distance-wise, which means it's the most expensive, but it can sometimes save you 5 to 10 minutes on the trip if traffic is heavy on the Strip. Drivers who take passengers through the airport tunnel without asking are committing an illegal practice known as "long-hauling."

CAR TRAVEL

Las Vegas is a drivable weekend destination for residents of Southern California and Arizona. Los Angelenos will take I–15 through Barstow. Phoenix residents don't have the luxury of a straight shot to Las Vegas. The best they can do is wind through the notoriously dangerous U.S. 93 that makes its way through Wikieup before meeting I–40.

If you're coming from farther away, you'd better plan on staying the night somewhere. For those approaching from the east on I–40, why not take a moment to contemplate your life at the South Rim of the Grand Canyon? Or if you're coming from the northwest down I–15, clear your head for a night at St. George, Utah, on the edge of the stunning Zion National Park.

The Luxor Sphinx and the giant, jade MGM Grand resort are among the colossal structures found on the South Strip.

GETTING AROUND

Las Vegas is a walking town—particularly the North, Center, and South Strip. You can find broad sidewalks, escalators, and moving walkways all over town. Pedestrian bridges over the Strip make it easy to cross the busy intersections. Be aware that distances can be deceiving. It may well seem like you're just next door to Caesar's Palace, but by the time you find your way out of your own hotel, walk along the busy sidewalks of the Strip, and travel the long moving sidewalks leading into Caesar's, you'll find 20 minutes have elapsed.

BUS TRAVEL

Public bus transportation's available on **Citizens Area Transit** (☎ *702/228–7433 or 800/228–3911* ⊕ *www.rtcsouthernnevada.com/transit/*), but is geared more to locals than visitors. Both CAT buses and trolleys ply the Strip but can take forever in traffic—the fare on both is $2.

The Deuce, the special double-decker CAT buses that ride the Strip 24/7, is geared more to the tourist. It's $3 (exact change required; $1 bills are accepted); 24-hour passes are Stops are located every quarter mile and are marked with signs or shelters; from transfer points, you can connect to other city buses that go all over town.

CAR TRAVEL

A car gives you easy access to all the casinos and attractions; lets you make excursions to Lake Mead, Hoover Dam, and elsewhere at your leisure; and gives you the chance to cruise the Strip and bask in its neon glow. If you plan to spend most of your time on the Strip, a car may not be worth the trouble, but otherwise, especially given the relatively high costs of taxis, renting or bringing a car is a good idea.

RENTAL CARS   All the airport's rental car companies are off-site at a central location known as **McCarran Airport Rent-a-Car Center** (☎ *702/261–6001*), about 2 mi from the main airport complex, and visitors must take shuttle buses from just outside the baggage claim to get there. The new facility reduces congestion in and around the airport, and offers visitors the opportunity to check bags for flights on some airlines without stepping foot in the main terminal. Still, the centralized location is so far from the airport that it can add anywhere from 15 to 20 minutes to your travel time, so be sure to leave yourself plenty of time to return the vehicle and catch your flight.

MONORAIL TRAVEL

The **Las Vegas Monorail Company** (☎ *702/699–8200* ⊕ *www.lvmonorail. com*) costs $5 for one ride, $12 for a one-day pass, and $28 for a three-day pass. It runs from the MGM Grand to Harrah's before making a jog out to the Convention Center and terminating at the Sahara. It's a fast way to get from one end of the Strip to another, especially on the weekends when even the Strip's back streets are full of traffic. The trains run 7 am–2 am weekdays; 7 am–3 am weekends.

TAXI TRAVEL

You can find cabs waiting at the airport and at every hotel in town. If you dine at a restaurant off the Strip, the restaurant will call a cab to take you home. ■ TIP→ Cabs aren't allowed to pick up passengers on the street, so you can't hail a cab New York–style. You have to wait in a hotel taxi line or call a cab company. Cabs aren't cheap ($3.30 initial fare plus $2.40 per mile) but can be very convenient and worthwhile, especially if you're splitting a fare (no more than five people allowed in a cab). You may save a few bucks renting a car, but you'll pay a price in aggravation.

Taxi Companies Checker (☎ *702/873–8012*). **Desert Cab** (☎ *702/386–4828*). **Henderson** (☎ *702/384–2322*). **Taxi Cab Authority** (☎ *702/668–4000* ⊕ *www.taxi.state.nv.us*). **Yellow/Star** (☎ *702/873–2000*). **Whittlesea** (☎ *702/384–6111*).

WHERE TO STAY AND PLAY

The world of Vegas-area casino hotels changes constantly. In the early 2000s, just about every resort was investing heavily in family-friendly accommodations and activities. Today, however, most places have refocused squarely on decadence and debauchery.

No property exemplifies this transition better than TI. Once known as Treasure Island, it dropped its pirate theme to embrace a more sensual motif—one with scantily clad dancers gyrating upon the very same pirate ships once used for family-friendly shows.

Some of these rebranded resorts have been more successful than others. A 2009 addition at the Hard Rock at the Mirage resulted in one of the most popular clubs (Vanity) and popular restaurants (Rare 120) on the entire Strip. Other newcomers like the Palazzo have established new benchmarks in amenities. When it opened in early 2008, the Palazzo welcomed the first new Barneys New York in 25 years. Encore, Steve Wynn's newest property, boasts some of the town's most spacious and richly appointed rooms and suites, as well as the hottest "party pool" in the Encore Beach Club. Then, of course, there's City Center, which cost $8.5 billion and boasts four separate hotels, a high-end shopping mall and one of the most remarkable collections of public art ever assembled.

Despite competition from these up-and-comers, the old standards still pack 'em in. Bellagio's rooms still carry cachet, and the Mirage—the hotel that started the megaresort trend 20 years ago—continues to sell out. At Wynn Las Vegas and the Venetian, two of the priciest properties on the Strip, guests rave about everything from comfy beds to exquisite restaurants and great shopping. At Caesars Palace the constantly evolving Qua Baths & Spa might be one of the tops in town. And for overall experience, the Four Seasons–Las Vegas, which occupies top floors of the tower at Mandalay Bay Resort & Casino, is still one of the best.

Hotel reviews have been condensed for this book. Please go to Fodors. com for full reviews of each property.

WHAT IT COSTS

	¢	$	$$	$$$	$$$$
Hotels	under $70	$70–$139	$140–$219	$220–$320	over $320

All prices are for a standard double room, excluding 10% tax.

ON THE STRIP

$$$–$$$$
★

Aria. Lauded across town as the "new kid on the block," Aria truly deserves the attention it receives. **Pros:** high-tech rooms; natural light; service. **Cons:** limited cellular service; weird shower set-up. ⊠ *3730 Las Vegas Blvd. S, Center Strip* ☎ *702/590–7757* ⊕ *www.arialasvegas. com* ⌨ *3,436 rooms, 568 suites* ⚷ *In-room: a/c, safe, Internet, Wi-Fi. In-hotel: 15 restaurants, room service, 8 bars, pools, gym, spa, laundry service, parking (free)* ▭ *AE, D, DC, MC, V.*

$$$$
Fodor's Choice
★

Bellagio. After more than 10 years, Bellagio remains a top getaway despite the considerable competition from upscale properties. It's impressive more for its refined elegance than for gimmicks. **Pros:** centrally located; posh suites; classy amenities. **Cons:** not kid-friendly; pricey; hoity-toity attitude among some guests. ⊠ *3600 Las Vegas Blvd. S, Center Strip* ☎ *702/693–7111 or 888/987–6667* ⊕ *www.bellagio.com* ⌨ *3,421 rooms, 512 suites* ⚷ *In-room: safe, DVD, Internet, refrigerator (some). In-hotel: 14 restaurants, room service, 8 bars, 5 pools, gym, spa, concierge, laundry service, parking (free)* ▭ *AE, D, DC, MC, V.*

$$$–$$$$
★

Caesars Palace. Caesars was one of the first properties in town to create rooms so lavish that guests might actually want to spend time in them; today the rooms are as sumptuous as any on the Strip. **Pros:** Arctic ice rooms at Qua; 650-square-foot rooms in new Octavius Tower; history. **Cons:** hard to navigate without a map; small casino; limited on-site parking. ⊠ *3570 Las Vegas Blvd. S, Center Strip* ☎ *702/731–7110 or 866/227–5938* ⊕ *www.caesarspalace.com* ⌨ *3,060 rooms, 289 suites* ⚷ *In-room: safe, Internet. In-hotel: 13 restaurants, room service, 6 bars, 7 pools, gym, spa, laundry service, parking (free)* ▭ *AE, D, DC, MC, V.*

DID YOU KNOW?

One of the best places to view the Bellagio's famous dancing fountains is from the Eiffel Tower's observation deck, directly across the street.

$$$$
Fodor's Choice
★

🏨 **Encore.** After building the Mirage, Bellagio, and Wynn Las Vegas, fabled Vegas hotelier Steve Wynn decided he needed to build one more megaresort—Encore, which sits just north of Wynn Las Vegas. **Pros:** huge suites; glorious pools; fun (but intimate) casino. **Cons:** cab-ride to other casinos; pricey. ✉ *3131 Las Vegas Blvd. S, North Strip* ☎ *702/770–7171 or 888/320–7125* ⊕ *www.encorelasvegas.com* 🛏 *2,034 suites* ⚬ *In-room: safe, Internet. In-hotel: 5 restaurants, room service, 7 bars, pools, gym, spa, concierge, laundry service, parking (free)* ▭ *AE, D, MC, V.*

$$$–$$$$
★

🏨 **Mandarin Oriental, Las Vegas.** As a brand, Mandarin Oriental prides itself on providing everything for the business traveler, and this property is no exception. **Pros:** efficiency; valet closet. **Cons:** small-ish rooms; almost overly formal. ✉ *3752 Las Vegas Blvd. S, Center Strip* ☎ *702/590–8888* ⊕ *www.mandarinoriental.com/lasvegas* 🛏 *335 rooms, 57 suites* ⚬ *In-room: a/c, safe, Internet, Wi-Fi. In-hotel: 4 restaurants, room service, 4 bars, pools, gym, spa, laundry service, parking (free)* ▭ *AE, D, DC, MC, V.*

$$–$$$
★

🏨 **Mandalay Bay.** This resort is actually three hotels in one—the namesake Mandalay Bay, THEhotel, and the Four Seasons-Las Vegas; Mandalay itself is decked out like a South Seas beach resort, complete with the scent of coconut oil drifting through the casino and pagodas rising out of the vast casino floor. **Pros:** coconut-scented rooms; Minus 5 bar; the Beach. **Cons:** difficult to navigate the multiple properties on-site; concerts can be loud. ✉ *3950 Las Vegas Blvd. S, South Strip* ☎ *702/632–7777 or 877/632–7800* ⊕ *www.mandalaybay.com* 🛏 *2,775 rooms, 436 suites* ⚬ *In-room: safe, DVD, Internet. In-hotel: 18 restaurants, room service, 9 bars, pools, gym, spa, beachfront, concierge, laundry service, parking (free)* ▭ *AE, D, DC, MC, V.*

$$–$$$

🏨 **MGM Grand.** The self-proclaimed "City of Entertainment" is loosely based on Oz, with a regal, bronze rendering of the roaring MGM lion mascot in front of its four emerald-green, fortresslike towers. **Pros:** something for everyone; great concerts and fights; fantastic restaurants. **Cons:** easy to get lost; schlep to parking. ✉ *3799 Las Vegas Blvd. S, South Strip* ☎ *702/891–7777 or 877/880–0880, 877/646–5638 Skylofts* ⊕ *www.mgmgrand.com* 🛏 *4,293 rooms, 751 suites* ⚬ *In-room: safe, Internet, Wi-Fi. In-hotel: 18 restaurants, room service, 9 bars, 5 pools, gym, spa, concierge, laundry service, parking (free)* ▭ *AE, D, DC, MC, V.*

$$–$$$

🏨 **Mirage.** In 1989, The Mirage rang in the modern era of Las Vegas, and thanks an end-to-end makeover, it's still as modern as the neighbors it spawned. **Pros:** classic Vegas; incredible views; one of the best pools in town. **Cons:** smoky casino; lack of stellar restaurants; Internet access spotty. ✉ *3400 Las Vegas Blvd. S, Center Strip* ☎ *702/791–7111 or 800/374–9000* ⊕ *www.mirage.com* 🛏 *2,763 rooms, 281 suites* ⚬ *In-room: safe, Internet. In-hotel: 14 restaurants, room service, 6 bars, 2 pools, gym, spa, laundry service, parking (free)* ▭ *AE, D, DC, MC, V.*

$$–$$$

🏨 **Planet Hollywood.** Everything at Planet Hollywood is designed to make ordinary people feel like stars, and the lodging accommodations are no exception. **Pros:** classic Hollywood vibe; incredible views; posh suites. **Cons:** service can be lax; in-room bath products are nothing special. ✉ *3667 Las Vegas Blvd. S, Center Strip* ☎ *702/785–5555 or*

866/517–3263 ⊕ *www.planethollywoodresort.com* ⇆ 2,486 rooms, 134 suites ⚿ In-room: safe, Internet. In-hotel: 8 restaurants, room service, 5 bars, pools, gym, spa, concierge, laundry service, parking (free) ▭ AE, D, DC, MC, V.

$$$–$$$$ ▧ **Venetian.** Some of the Strip's largest and plushest suites are found
Fodor$Choice at this elegant, gilded resort that's a hit with foodies, shoppers, and
★ high rollers alike. **Pros:** exquisite artwork; modern amenities; those remote-controlled curtains. **Cons:** sprawling property; unpredictable service; seemingly never-ending construction. ⊠ *3355 Las Vegas Blvd. S, North Strip* ☎ *702/414–1000 or 866/659–9643* ⊕ *www.venetian.com* ⇆ 4,027 suites ⚿ In-room: safe, Internet. In-hotel: 21 restaurants, room service, 6 bars, 3 pools, gym, spa, concierge, laundry service, executive floor, parking (free) ▭ AE, D, DC, MC, V.

OFF STRIP AND DOWNTOWN

$ ▧ **Golden Nugget Hotel & Casino.** Among its neighbors in what is known
DOWNTOWN as "Old Vegas," the Golden Nugget has the biggest and best pool, and certainly the best amenities. **Pros:** living Vegas history; poker room a favorite spot for pros to tune up before big tournaments. **Cons:** despite its charm, downtown Vegas can be sketchy. ⊠ *129 E. Fremont St., Downtown* ☎ *702/385–7111 or 800/846–5336* ⊕ *www.goldennugget. com* ⇆ 1,716 rooms, 99 suites ⚿ In-room: safe, Internet (some). In-hotel: 8 restaurants, room service, 5 bars, pool, gym, spa, concierge, laundry service, parking (free) ▭ AE, D, DC, MC, V.

$$$–$$$$ ▧ **Hard Rock Hotel & Casino.** No matter where you go in this rock-fixated
PARADISE ROAD resort, it's impossible to forget you're in the Hard Rock: even the hall carpeting's decorated with musical notes. **Pros:** party central; great restaurants (Rare 120 and Ago); lively casino. **Cons:** rowdy crowd; minuscule sports book. ⊠ *4455 Paradise Rd., Paradise Road* ☎ *702/693–5000 or 800/693–7625* ⊕ *www.hardrockhotel.com* ⇆ 1,056 rooms, 449 suites ⚿ In-room: safe, Wi-Fi. In-hotel: 8 restaurants, room service, 6 bars, pool, gym, spa, beachfront, concierge, laundry services, parking (free) ▭ AE, D, DC, MC, V.

$$$ ▧ **The Palms Las Vegas.** Standard rooms at the Palms are large, opulent,
FLAMINGO ROAD and modern, with some unusual amenities for Las Vegas, such as beds with ultrafirm mattresses, duvets, coffeemakers, and ample minibars. **Pros:** renowned, three-story spa; excellent coin games; low table-game minimums. **Cons:** debauched atmosphere not ideal for kids. ⊠ *4321 W. Flamingo Rd., West Side* ☎ *702/942–7777* ⊕ *www.palms.com* ⇆ 1,302 rooms, 306 suites ⚿ In-room: safe, Internet. In-hotel: 11 restaurants, room service, 9 bars, pool, gym, spa, concierge, laundry service, parking (free) ▭ AE, D, DC, MC, V.

$$$ ▧ **Red Rock Casino, Resort & Spa.** This swanky property looks out on the
SUMMERLIN ochre-red Spring Mountains, and sits a stone's throw from Red Rock National Conservation Area. **Pros:** movies; bowling; VIP section of sports book. **Cons:** waitress service in gaming areas can be slow; day-use fee in spa (about $20) is a bit steep. ⊠ *11011 W. Charleston Blvd., Summerlin* ☎ *702/797–7777 or 866/767–7773* ⊕ *www.redrocklasvegas. com* ⇆ 735 rooms, 81 suites ⚿ In-room: safe, Internet, Wi-Fi. In-hotel: 10 restaurants, room service, 5 bars, pool, spa, laundry service, concierge, parking (free), some pets allowed ▭ AE, D, DC, MC, V.

WHERE TO EAT

Casino-resort dining basically falls into one of three categories. In the top echelon are the several properties that now have a half-dozen or more bona fide star-status restaurants: Aria, Bellagio, Caesars, Encore, Mandalay Bay, MGM Grand, Venetian/Palazzo, and Wynn Las Vegas, plus the nearby Palms and Hard Rock properties. At the next level are those resorts with one or two stellar restaurants and a smaller range of worthwhile but not quite top-of-the-line options. On the Strip, these include Luxor, Mirage, Monte Carlo, New York–New York, Paris, Planet Hollywood, and TI. Off the Strip, you can add M Resort, the Rio All-Suite Hotel, Green Valley Ranch, the JW Marriott and Red Rock Resort to this mix. And then there's everybody else: casino-resorts with maybe a decent eatery or two but that simply aren't known for great food.

Outside of casino properties, Las Vegas has a number of marquee restaurants with increasing cachet among foodies from out of town—places like André's Las Vegas, Origin India Restaurant & Bar, ENVY Steakhouse, Rosemary's, Marché Bacchus, and Lotus of Siam. There's great food to be had off the beaten path in Las Vegas, and you'll pay a lot less in these areas, too.

WHAT IT COSTS					
	¢	$	$$	$$$	$$$$
Restaurants	under $10	$11–$20	$21–$30	$31–$40	over $40

Prices are per person for a median main course or equivalent combination of smaller dishes.

ON THE STRIP

$$$$
SEAFOOD
CityCenter

✕ **American Fish.** As the name suggests, Michael Mina's newest Vegas restaurant pays homage to fish of all shapes and sizes. The eatery is designed to look like a lodge, and diners can select fish entrées from a list that includes branzino, rainbow trout, diver scallops, and big-eye tuna (yes, there's a selection of meat, as well). All fish orders are prepared in one of four different cooking methods: salt-baking, wood-grilling, cast-iron griddling, and ocean-water poaching. Still, some of the menu's biggest treasures are in the appetizers section: fried geoduck clam, smoked salmon BLT, New Bedford mussels and chorizo, and Kobe beef and abalone shabu-shabu. Also pay attention to the side-dishes; the collard greens, ham hock, and maple syrup is addicting. ⊠ *Aria, 3730 Las Vegas Blvd. S, Center Strip* ☎ *702/590–8610* ⊕ *www.arialasvegas. com* ⌕ *Reservations essential* ☰ *AE, D, DC, MC, V* ⊗ *Closed Tues.*

$$$$
AMERICAN
Mandalay Bay

✕ **Aureole.** Celebrity-chef Charlie Palmer re-created his famed New York restaurant for Mandalay Bay. He and designer Adam Tihany added a few playful, Las Vegas–style twists: a four-story wine tower, for example, holds 10,000 bottles that are reached by "wine fairies," who are hoisted up and down via a system of electronically activated pulleys. Seasonal specialties on the three-course, fixed-price ($75) menu might include roasted guinea fowl with sautéed foie gras, ravioli, and natural juices, or roasted rack of venison with glazed chestnuts, parsnip-potato puree, and orange-rosemary sauce. For dessert, try innovative offerings like warm blue cheese-and-poached pear tart with port-wine vinaigrette or citrus tea–infused crème brûlée. ⊠ *Mandalay Bay Resort & Casino, 3950 Las Vegas Blvd. S, South Strip* ☎ *702/632–7401* ⊕ *www.aureolelv. com* ⚑ *Reservations essential* ☰ *AE, D, DC, MC, V* ⊘ *No lunch*.

$$$ ✕ **Bouchon.** Ask many chefs to name their idol, and more than a few will
FRENCH
Venetian
cite French Laundry chef Thomas Keller, who oversees this stunning, capacious French bistro and oyster bar in the Venezia Tower at the Venetian. Soaring Palladian windows, antique lighting, and painted tile lend a sophisticated take on French country design, but the service and overall quality don't always match up to the standards you'd expect. Bouchon's folded brown-paper menu opens to reveal classics like steak frites, mussels with white wine, and an extensive raw bar. Finish with profiteroles, a lemon tart, or crème caramel. Bouchon does turn out a memorable breakfast, where you might try bread pudding–style French toast or a smoked-salmon baguette. ⊠ *The Venetian, 3355 Las Vegas Blvd. S, North Strip* ☎ *702/414–6200* ⊕ *www.venetian.com* ☰ *AE, D, DC, MC, V.*

$$$ ✕ **KOI Las Vegas.** It's only fitting that KOI, a see-and-be-seen restaurant
ASIAN
Planet
Hollywood
Fodor's Choice
★
with locations in New York, Bangkok, and Los Angeles, has launched a third U.S. outpost at the renovated Planet Hollywood Resort & Casino in Las Vegas. The cavernous 220-seat eatery attracts A- and B-list celebrities who line up for sublime Asian-fusion fare that includes baked lobster roll with creamy sauce, yellowtail carpaccio with soy-citrus and truffle essence, and Kobe-beef filet mignon. The main dining room can get noisy, so ask for a table along the back wall. After dinner, hit the swanky lounge to order a cosmo or martini, then head for the open-air patio to enjoy the fountains at Bellagio across the street. ⊠ *Planet Hollywood Resort & Casino, 3667 Las Vegas Blvd. S, Center Strip* ☎ *702/454–4555* ⊕ *www.koirestaurant.com* ☰ *AE, D, DC, MC, V.*

$$$ ✕ **Mesa Grill.** Playful splashes of bright green, blue, red, and yellow
SOUTHWESTERN
Caesars Palace
offset the swanky curved banquettes and earth tones at Iron Chef and grill-meister Bobby Flay's first restaurant outside New York City. The menu's decidedly Southwestern, but with plenty of contemporary twists, with choices like a starter of barbecued duck with habanero chili–star anise sauce over blue-corn pancakes; and main dishes like mango-and-spice-encrusted tuna steak with green peppercorn and green chili sauce or ancho-chili honey-glazed salmon with spicy black-bean sauce and roasted jalapeño crema. Some tables have views of the casino sports book. There's an impressive weekend brunch. ⊠ *Caesars Palace, 3570 Las Vegas Blvd. S, Center Strip* ☎ *702/731–7731* ⊕ *www.mesagrill. com/lasvegas* ☰ *AE, D, DC, MC, V.*

$$$$ ✕ **Nobhill Tavern.** San Francisco cuisine is the star at Michael Mina's
AMERICAN
MGM Grand
Fodor's Choice
★
handsome, understated brasserie with clean lines and polished-wood floors. The restaurant's concept and image (it opened as simply "Nob-hill") was tweaked in 2008. Now known as Nobhill Tavern, the atmosphere's a bit more casual and the emphasis is on seasonal, globally inspired favorites such as caramelized-puree of celeriac soup with toasted walnuts; lobster potpie (containing a huge 2-pound Maine

lobster and baby vegetables in truffle cream), and bacon-wrapped scallops with lentil stew and baby carrots. There are no weak spots in Mina's repertoire. A selection of five flavors of mashed potatoes, such as lobster, curry, or basil, is included with dinner, and you can bet the sourdough bread's the real deal. ⊠ *MGM Grand Hotel & Casino, 3799 Las Vegas Blvd. S, South Strip* 🕾 *702/891–7337* ⊕ *www.michaelmina. net/mm_nobhill_lasvegas/* ⊟ *AE, D, DC, MC, V* ☺ *No lunch.*

$$$$
JAPANESE
Wynn
Fodor'sChoice
★

✕ **Okada.** At the helm in this kitchen is award–winning chef Masa Ishizawa, a standout in both Japanese and contemporary French cuisine. The attractively designed restaurant, like most of the others at Wynn, is set away from the din of the casino. There are sake and sushi bars (with some unusual cuts of fish, such as abalone and jackfish), as well as a teppanyaki grill that features items such as Chilean sea bass, Japanese Kobe beef sirloin, and Scottish salmon. A floating pagoda table has views of the lagoon, and many tables overlook the serene gardens. ⊠ *Wynn Las Vegas, 3131 Las Vegas Blvd. S, North Strip* 🕾 *702/248– 3463* ⊕ *www.wynnlasvegas.com* ⊟ *AE, D, DC, MC, V* ☺ *No lunch.*

$$$
AMERICAN
Forum Shops

✕ **Spago Las Vegas.** His fellow chefs raised eyebrows in wonder when Wolfgang Puck opened this branch of his famous Beverly Hills eatery in the culinary wasteland that was Las Vegas in 1992, but Spago Las Vegas has become a fixture in this ever-fickle city, and it remains consistently superb. The less expensive café, which overlooks the busy Forum Shops at Caesars, is great for people-watching; inside, the dinner-only dining room is more intimate. Both menus are classic Puck. In the café, sample pancetta-wrapped meat loaf or Thai-style chicken salad. Top picks in the dining room include dishes such as stir-fried Maine lobster with egg noodles and confit pork belly, and red wine-braised beef short ribs with roasted vegetables and homemade gnocchi. ⊠ *Forum Shops at Caesars, 3500 Las Vegas Blvd. S, Center Strip* 🕾 *702/369–6300* ⊕ *www.wolfgangpuck.com* ⊟ *AE, D, DC, MC, V.*

$$$$
STEAKHOUSE
Encore

🎦 **Switch Steak.** Dinner is theater at this one-of-a-kind steakhouse overlooking Encore's swanky pool complex. At least once an hour, the lights dim, music comes up and the walls and ceiling quite literally "switch" from one motif to another (hence the name). The effect is hokey at times; thankfully, the food holds its own. Sure, the place sells a variety of Nebraskan corn-fed beef steaks, but Chef Rene Lenger also has put together an eclectic menu of other options. Depending on the season, selections might include Chilean sea bass with olive oil-poached tomatoes or Jidori chicken with macerated golden raisins and pine nuts. One word of warning: on Friday and Saturday nights, patrons lining up for entry into Surrender next door can be obnoxiously loud. *Encore* ⊠ *3121 S. Las Vegas Blvd., North Strip* 🕾 *702/248–3463* ⊕ *www.wynnlasvegas. com/dining/switch-steak* ⌂ *Reservations essential.*

$$$$
FRENCH
CityCenter

✕ **Twist.** Located on the 23rd floor of the Mandarin Oriental, Las Vegas, this is the only place in the U.S. to experience food from internationally renowned Chef Pierre Gagnaire. The French chef pioneered the "fusion" movement in cooking, and every dish blends together flavor and texture in surprising ways. To wit: the appetizer of sea bream tartlette with mozzarella ice cream; or the entrée of beef sirloin with burgundy escargots sauce. Desserts are just as appealing—try the baba cake with limoncello and citrus gelée. The restaurant is sexy and sophisticated, with an expansive wine loft (reached by a glass staircase) and nearly 300 illuminated globelike spheres that float above the dining room like tiny moons. ⊠ *Mandarin Oriental, 3752 Las Vegas Blvd. S, Center Strip* ☎ *888/881–9367* ⊕ *www.mandarinoriental.com/lasvegas/dining/twist* ⌕ *Reservations essential* ▭ *AE, D, DC, MC, V* ⊗ *No lunch.*

22

OFF STRIP AND GREATER LAS VEGAS

$

JAPANESE

West Side

Fodor'sChoice

★

✕ **Ichiza.** Open daily until 3 am and jam-packed at all hours, this modest space is on the second floor of one of the many gaudy shopping centers in the city's burgeoning Little Asia section along Spring Mountain Road. Ichiza has developed a cult following for its sublimely delicious, authentic Japanese fare. Seating is at the bar, in a few booths, or at a pair of wooden communal tables. Look beyond the traditional menu of sushi and noodle bowls and instead study the hundreds of signs (written in both English and Japanese) pasted on the walls of this boisterous restaurant, each listing a daily special. Red snapper carpaccio, salmon-skin salad, skewered gingko nut, wasabi–green bean tempura, and stir-fried calamari with ginger butter are a few notables you're likely to see many nights—it's best to order with a sense of adventure. ⊠ *4355 Spring Mountain Rd. #205, West Side* ☎ *702/367–3151* ▭ *AE, D, MC, V* ⊗ *No lunch.*

$

THAI

East Side

Fodor'sChoice

★

✕ **Lotus of Siam.** Despite being in a dreary shopping center northeast of the Strip, this simple Thai restaurant has attained near-fanatical cult status, with some critics hailing it the best in North America. What's all the fuss? Consider the starter of marinated prawns, which are wrapped with bacon and rice-paper crepes, then deep-fried and served with a tangy sweet-and-sour sauce. For a main course, try either the charbroiled beef liver mixed with green onion and chili, or the chicken and vegetables with Issan-style red curry. Be warned—this is some of the spiciest food you'll ever try. But another of Lotus's surprises is the phenomenal wine list, on which you might find a vintage to cool your palate. ⊠ *953 E. Sahara Ave., East Side* ☎ *702/735–3033* ⊕ *www.saipinchutima.com* ▭ *AE, D, MC, V* ⊗ *No lunch weekends.*

$$$$

STEAKHOUSE

The Palms

✕ **N9NE Steakhouse.** There's a good chance you'll spot a young Hollywood type at this beef lover's hangout tucked in the corner of the Palms (Leonardo DiCaprio is such a fan he once had the kitchen reopen especially for him after arriving in town after hours). N9NE serves high-quality, innovatively prepared cuts of meat in a jaunty setting of dark-walnut and leather furniture. N9NE serves plenty of other superb entrées, including roasted Colorado lamb chops, sautéed sea scallops with grilled artichokes, and chicken rigatoni with pancetta. If you're feeling ritzy, spring for the "lobster to the nines" special: 1½ pounds of coldwater lobster tail with scampi butter and lemon (the cost, however, is astronomical). The pumpkin cheesecake with huckleberry sauce makes a sweet ending. ⊠ *The Palms, 4321 W. Flamingo Rd., West Side* ☎ *702/933–9900* ⊕ *www.n9negroup.com* ▭ *AE, D, MC, V* ⊗ *No lunch.*

$$$

STEAKHOUSE

Red Rock Casino

🏛 **T-Bones Chop House & Lounge.** Locals insist that high-priced Strip steakhouses have nothing on this modern and lively eatery inside Red Rock Hotel, Casino & Spa. The menu features oversized dry-aged prime steaks, signature bone-in meats and fresh fish flown in daily. There's also a 7,500-bottle wine loft. But the most happening part of the restaurant is the lounge, a spacious area with floor-to-ceiling windows that overlook the pool. Some of the more popular food items include pulled pork sliders and chili and cheese tater tots. Value in Vegas has never looked (or tasted) so good. ⊠ *Red Rock Hotel, Casino & Spa 11011 W. Charleston Blvd., Summerlin* ☎ *702/797–7576* ⊕ *www. redrocklasvegas.com/dining/tbones.php* ⊰ *Reservations essential.*

SHOWS

The star power that made the old "supper club" days glitter with names like Frank Sinatra and Dean Martin is making a latter-day comeback in showcases by veteran concert acts Barry Manilow and Cher. Nationally known performers such as Penn & Teller and Carrot Top have come to roost on the Strip alongside homegrown successes such as Lance Burton. *Jubilee!* hangs in there as a shimmering example of the "feather shows" that made an icon of the showgirl, while technologically advanced shows such as *Blue Man Group* and Cirque du Soleil's O have modernized the spectacle. Female impersonators, "dirty" dancers, comedians—all perpetuate the original style of razzle-dazzle entertainment that Las Vegas has popularized for the world.

In the not-so-olden days, shows were intended to draw patrons who would eventually wind up in the casino. Nowadays, the accounting's separate and it will cost you at least $93 to see Tom Jones and as much as $225 (before taxes and service charges) for Cher.

You can still find a few of the old names, such as Don Rickles or Tony Bennett, along with a new generation of resident headliners such as Frank Caliendo. The Cirque spectaculars also remain a Las Vegas trademark, presenting little or no language barrier to the city's large numbers of international tourists. Cirque du Soleil's Viva Elvis opened at Aria in early 2010 as the company's seventh resident Vegas title.

Fodor's Choice **Blue Man Group.** The first half of the program defines the troupe's quirky
★ comic aesthetic: three silent characters in utilitarian uniforms, their heads bald and gleaming from cobalt-blue greasepaint, prowl the stage committing twisted "science projects" that are alternately highbrow and juvenile. The early antics deliberately leave much of the stage in the dark, until it comes time to reveal gorgeous high-resolution video effects and the towering set with lighting designs by Pink Floyd tour collaborator Marc Brickman. And it's all scored to a live rock band with percussion instruments made from PVC pipe. ⊠ *The Venetian, 3355 Las Vegas Blvd. S, North Strip* ☎ *702/414–7469* ⊕ *www.blueman.com* ⊡ *$65–$149* ⊙ *Call for show times.*

Jubilee! This is the last place to experience the over-the-top vision of Vegas showman Donn Arden, who produced shows on the Strip from 1952 to 1994. A cast of 80 or more performs in a theater with 1,100 seats, but the show is stolen by the gargantuan sets and props, such as the sinking of the *Titanic* and Samson destroying the temple. It's the last bastion of showgirls parading about in a spectacle of feathers and bare breasts, even as recent attempts to freshen some of the

O, at the Bellagio, is one of Las Vegas's seven Cirque du Soleil shows.

segments middle out between retro nostalgia and a modern reinvention of the form. ⊠ *Bally's Las Vegas, 3645 Las Vegas Blvd. S, Center Strip* ☎ *702/967–4567* 🖃 *$53–$113* ☉ *Sat.–Thurs. 7:30 and 10:30 pm.*

LOVE. Meet the Beatles again, well sort of, in the most popular show on the Strip. Before he died, George Harrison convinced the surviving Beatles (and Yoko Ono) to license the group's music to Cirque du Soleil for its fifth Las Vegas production. Even if you keep your eyes closed, the remixed music by producer George Martin and his son Giles is revelatory on the state-of-the-art sound system, often like hearing the songs for the first time. Coming up with visuals to match was more of a challenge. Instead of merely scoring the usual acrobatics with the famous songs, Cirque created a theatrical environment to bring many of the musical characters to life in a fanciful version of Liverpool, telling the story of Beatlemania and the postwar generation without literally depicting the Fab Four. ⊠ *Mirage Las Vegas, 3400 Las Vegas Blvd. S, Center Strip* ☎ *702/792–7777* 🖃 *$119–$181* ☉ *Thurs.–Mon. 7 and 9:30 pm.*

Fodor's Choice ★ **O.** More than $70 million was spent on Cirque du Soleil's theater at Bellagio and it's the liquid stage that takes over as the real star of the show. It was money well spent: O marked its 10th anniversary in October 2008 and remains one of the best-attended titles on the Strip. The title is taken from the French word for water (*eau*), and water is everywhere—1.5 million gallons of it, 12 million pounds of it, contained by a "stage" that, thanks to hydraulic lifts, can change shape and turn into dry land in no time. The intense and nonstop action by the show's acrobats, aerial gymnasts, trapeze artists, synchronized swimmers, divers, and contortionists takes place above, within, and even on the surface of the water, making for a stylish spectacle that manages to have a vague theme about the wellspring of theater and imagination. ⊠ *Bellagio Las Vegas, 3600 Las Vegas Blvd. S, Center Strip* ☎ *702/693–7722* ☜ *$112–$179* ⊙ *Wed.–Sun. 7:30 and 10:30 pm.*

Viva Elvis. Cirque du Soleil brings an American icon back to the Strip in the company's seventh Las Vegas production. The theater is agreeably retro, with design touches inspired by Graceland. Director Vincent Paterson—who worked with Michael Jackson and Madonna—tries to add an American pop sensibility to the Canadian circus. Elvis's recorded voice is set against live band arrangements, which may rankle purists in their attempt to update his '50s-rock classics. Elvis is the only male voice heard in the show, but live female singers sometimes join him in "duets." ⊠ *Aria, 3730 Las Vegas Blvd., City Center* ☎ *702/531–2031* ⊕ *www. arialasvegas.com/viva-elvis* ☜ *$125–$209* ⊙ *Fri.–Tues. 7 and 9:30 pm.*

SHOWROOMS

RESIDENT HEADLINERS

Celine Dion. The Canadian superstar returns home to the 4,200-seat theater built in 2003 for the five-year run of "A New Day." She's signed on for another three-year hitch starting in March 2011, but this time trims the schedule to about 70 shows per year. A new approach drops the Cirque du Soleil–style ensemble cast in favor of a 31-piece orchestra and a connecting theme based on romantic Hollywood movies, allowing her to cover some standards along with her own titanic hits. ⊠ *Caesars Palace, 3570 Las Vegas Blvd. S, Center Strip* ☎ *702/731–7110* ☜ *$55–$250* ⊙ *Call for times. No shows Mon. and Thurs.*

Garth Brooks. Casino developer Steve Wynn lured Brooks, one of the biggest-selling acts in music history, out of an early retirement by buying him a private jet so he could commute from Oklahoma without missing his daughters' soccer games. So far, the five-year deal lets Wynn recoup on production costs: Brooks strolls out on a bare stage with an acoustic guitar and plays whatever comes to mind. His own hits are balanced with covers of the singers who inspired him, from Merle Haggard to Billy Joel. The results are entirely mesmerizing, a dramatic contrast to overproduced spectacles such as Cher. ■TIP➔ Brooks plays longer on Friday and Sunday, when there is only one show, than he does on two-show Saturday. ⊠ *Wynn Las Vegas, 3131 Las Vegas Blvd., Center Strip* ☎ *702/770–7469* ⊕ *https://boxoffice.wynnlasvegas.com* ⊙ *Call for times and tickets.*

★ **Penn & Teller.** Eccentric comic magicians Penn & Teller once seemed an unlikely fit for Las Vegas, but they now seem like part of the landscape after more than five years in a gorgeous 1,500-seat auditorium. Penn's verbal overkill and the duo's flair for the grotesque make them an acquired taste, but what once was a fringe act has become almost mainstream as the familiar duo age gracefully in Las Vegas. Their magic is unusual and genuinely baffling, and their comedy provocative and thoughtful, albeit blasphemous. ⊠ *Rio All-Suite Hotel & Casino, 3700 W. Flamingo Rd., West Side* ☎ *702/777–7776* ☜ *$75* ⊙ *Wed.–Sun. 9 pm.*

AFTER DARK

Despite the recent rocky economy, Las Vegas's nightlife remains relatively hot. Still fueled by the "What happens in Vegas, stays in Vegas" advertisements (read: "All your sins here get expunged completely as soon as you pay your bookie, loan shark, and/or credit card bill"), nightlife impresarios on the Strip keep dipping into their vast pockets in order to create over-the-top experiences where party-mad Visigoths—plus, well, you and me—can live out some wild fantasies. The number of high-profile nightclubs, trendy lounges, and sizzling strip bars continues to grow, each attempting to trump the other in order to attract not just high rollers, but A-list celebrities and the publicity that surrounds them.

BARS AND LOUNGES

★ **The Beatles Revolution Lounge.** Designed for synergy with Cirque du Soleil's Beatles-theme *Love* next door, the "Rev" wows tourists and locals alike with its private alcoves, hippie-outfitted servers, beanbag chairs, and eye-popping, ever-shifting psychedelic fractal wall projections. The low lighting and high volume deemphasize the "lounge" aspect of "ultralounge" here, but late at night, the inevitable Fab Four tunes give way to pumping dance music. Best of all are Monday's Cirque du Soleil "Family Nights," when the performers from all the Cirque shows citywide gather here to dance like the adrenaline fiends they are. ✉ *The Mirage, 3400 Las Vegas Blvd. S, Center Strip* ☎ *702/692–8383* ⊕ *thebeatlesrevolutionlounge.com.*

Fodor's Choice ★ **Blush.** Sophisticated and subtle, this is a fever-dream of an ultralounge. The interior's as glossy and gorgeous as the drop-dead clientele, diaphanous curtains billow around glass-legged divans, white paper lanterns sway over the onyx dance floor, and sequined servers approach with come-hither smiles—you get the point. When you factor in the outdoor garden and its proximity to Tryst (an ideal next stop from here), this is simply the best ultralounge we know. ✉ *Wynn Las Vegas, 3131 Las Vegas Blvd. S, North Strip* ☎ *702/770–3633* ⊕ *www.wynnlasvegas.com.*

Fodor's Choice ★ **Drai's.** All hail Victor Drai, classiest of Vegas nightlife sultans. Once the tables of his tony restaurant are cleared away, the wild scene inside this after-hours titan is closer to a dance club or a rave than to a lounge, even though its three modestly sized rooms are as gorgeous as any lounge in town. The vibe of decadence can reach an extraordinary pitch, but this, of course, is exactly how an after-hours club *should* be, right? Besides, you'll be hard-pressed to find a more beautiful insider crowd anywhere in city limits. ✉ *Bill's Gamblin' Hall & Saloon, 3595 Las Vegas Blvd. S, Center Strip* ☎ *702/737–0555* ⊕ *www.drais.net.*

★ **Lavo.** From the people who brought us the titanic Tao comes this restaurant-lounge-dance club with a vaguely—though attractive—Middle Eastern vibe. Although Lavo's advertising tagline reads, "Hookahs Not Included," it's actually all about the water pipes here, at least until you finish dinner and ascend past cisterns and ceramics to the top floor's dome-roofed dance floor, complete with go-go dancers, chandeliers, boa-clad servers, eccentrically shaped bars, and a bendy-trendy crowd.

✉ *The Palazzo, 3325 Las Vegas Blvd., North Strip* ☎ *702/791–1800* ⊕ *www.lavolv.com.*

★ **Tabú Ultra Lounge.** Here you'll find the high-tech touches of a big dance club, with square tables that double as "canvases" for projected images and "murals" of light that change depending on the perspective of the viewer. But the peach-color banquettes and mirrored columns lend it the coziness of a lounge. The fine deejays actually understand the music they play. Not exactly cutting-edge, but it's still worth a pop-in, especially for Rokbox (hip-hop–meets-rock Monday). Also, every third Thursday has a party called Soundbar, and every Sunday features the hip-hop fest, Slide. ✉ *MGM Grand, 3799 Las Vegas Blvd. S, South Strip* ☎ *702/891–7183* ⊕ *www.tabulv.com.*

DANCE CLUBS

★ **Bank.** "Status is everything!" goes the motto at this white-hot, new, megadance club, which has replaced that old favorite known as Light. One of the biggest celeb hangs in town, with Leo DiCaprio a special fan, Bank would probably even turn on that earlier Leonardo, namely Mr. da Vinci, thanks to its etched-glass walls pulsing with rainbow lights, tilted avant-garde chandeliers, entrance foyer lined floor to ceiling with illuminated Cristal bottles, and sunken dance floor ringed by VIP tables. The staff is every bit as classy and hot-looking as at other Vegas night-spots. The weekends are absolutely sizzling here, but other nights boast special parties, promo events, live performances, with Sunday being its especially good Industry Night. ✉ *Bellagio, 3600 Las Vegas Blvd. S, Center Strip* ☎ *702/693–8300* ⊕ *www.lightgroup.com.*

Fodor'sChoice ★ **PURE.** In addition to its supercool Tuesday-night party and alluring crowd, PURE has a secret weapon in its outdoor terrace—one complete with waterfalls, private cabanas, dance floor, and a view that places you right in the middle of the action on the Strip. Indoor types party in a cream-color main room or in the smaller Red Room, which is a special VIP area. ✉ *Caesars Palace, 3570 Las Vegas Blvd. S, Center Strip* ☎ *702/731–7873* ⊕ *www.purethenightclub.com.*

★ **Tao.** Nowhere else in Vegas furnishes you with the four Ds—dining, drinking, dancing, and drooling—in quite as alluring a mix as this multilevel (and multimillion-dollar) playground. The ground floor and mezzanine levels are exquisite enough (you almost tumble into rosewater baths before you're in the door), but once you get off the elevator at the top floor, where an army of dramatically lighted stone deities greets you, the party truly begins. Chinese antiques, crimson chandeliers, and a so-called Opium Room set the mood. It's still one of the two or three best dance clubs in Vegas, with one of the most popular theme parties with its Thursday locals' "Worship" night. ✉ *The Venetian, 3355 Las Vegas Blvd. S, North Strip* ☎ *702/388–8588* ⊕ *www.taolasvegas.com.*

Fodor'sChoice ★ **Tryst.** Nothing in town matches the beauty of Tryst's interior design, the quality of the music (sometime they even play rock!), the friendliness of the staff. Sure it lacks the spectacular aerial views of Ghostbar or Mix, but what other club has its own *waterfall* to gape at. And dig that eerie red lighting, the gorgeous stairway at the entrance, the ample outdoor space, and the cleverly curtained VIP section. If

The great music, friendly staff, ample outdoor space, and beautiful waterfall make Tryst one of the best dance clubs on the Strip.

you're in for the weekend, make sure you stick around for the Sunday-night extravaganza. ⊠ *The Wynn, 3131 Las Vegas Blvd. S, North Strip* ☎ *702/770–3375.*

Fodor's Choice **XS.** XS, a bigger, bouncier and more beautiful big sister to Tryst, fea-
★ tures multiple indoor bars; gorgeously subtle lighting; a chandelier that turns into a psychedelic, spinning, disco ball; light fixtures that turn into stripper poles; tireless go-go dancers; golden drapes; walls that feature equally golden body casts (the waitresses modeled for them); and a dance floor that opens out onto a large swimming pool. At the pool are 31 cabanas, another bar, and outdoor gaming, where the sexiest croupiers in town ply their trade. Still, if 40,000 square feet of pleasure isn't sufficient for you, you can always rent the private cream-and-crocodile-patterned booth. ⊠ *Encore, 3131 Las Vegas Blvd. S, North Strip* ☎ *702/770–5350.*

SHOPPING

It's the variety of options that has pushed Las Vegas near the ranks of New York City, London, and Rome. Most Strip hotels offer designer dresses, swimsuits, jewelry, and menswear; almost all have shops offering logo merchandise for the hotel or its latest show. Inside the casinos the gifts are elegant and exquisite. Outside, all the Elvis clocks and gambling-chip toilet seats you never wanted to see are available in the tacky gift shops. Beyond the Strip, Vegas shopping encompasses such extremes as a couture ball gown in a vintage store and, in a Western store, a fine pair of Tony Lamas boots left over from the town's cowboy days.

MALLS ON THE STRIP

Crystals. Imagine visiting a huge neighborhood shopping mall, except in the place of stores like Bebe, Express, and GAP, you'll find boutiques like Marni, Mikimoto, and Tom Ford. Now add premiere architecture to the equation and you have the new Crystals at CityCenter shopping venue. One of the most appreciated features of Crystals is the fact the 500,000-square-foot mall allows pedestrians entrance into boutiques from the Strip, a first for luxury retail on Las Vegas Boulevard. Boutiques such as Lanvin, Carolina Herrera, and Miu Miu speak to the great strides Las Vegas has made in giving Rodeo Drive and 5th Avenue a run for their money. Roberto Cavalli has a two-story boutique that sells everything Cavalli—even the pet line—and features a built-in catwalk. Louis Vuitton has opened one of its largest locations in North America with two levels that extend beyond just leather goods to include men and women's ready-to-wear, shoes, jewelry, textiles, ties, and more. ⊠ *3720 S. Las Vegas Blvd., Center Strip* ☎ *866/754–2489* ⊕ *www.crystalscitycenter.com.*

★ **Fashion Show.** It's impossible to miss this swanky, fashion-devoted mall due to one big element: The Cloud, a futuristic steel shade structure that looms high above the mall's entrance. Ads and footage of the mall's own fashion events are continuously projected onto the eye-catching architecture (think Times Square à la Las Vegas). The mall delivers on its name—fashion shows are staged in the Great Hall on an 80-foot-long catwalk that rises from the floor Friday–Sunday, every hour from noon–6 pm.

Not everything here is overpriced. Although you do find many of the same stores that are at the casino malls, such as Louis Vuitton, there's also a smattering of different fare: Sandwich, the European-based brand that distinguishes itself from the competition with comfort-focused, naturally made clothes; and the yoga-inspired store lululemon. Neiman Marcus, Saks Fifth Avenue, Macy's, Bloomingdale's Home, Nordstrom, and Dillard's serve as the department-store anchors. Fashion Show is next to the Trump Hotel Las Vegas. ⊠ *3200 Las Vegas Blvd. S, North Strip* ☎ *702/369–8382* ⊕ *www.thefashionshow.com.*

Fodor's Choice
★ **The Forum Shops at Caesars Palace.** The Forum Shops resemble an ancient Roman streetscape, with immense columns and arches, two central piazzas with fountains, and a cloud-filled ceiling with a sky that changes from sunrise to sunset over the course of three hours. The Festival Fountain (in the west wing of the mall) puts on its own show every hour on the hour daily starting at 10 am; the "Atlantis" show (in the east wing) plays out every hour on the half hour starting at 10:30 am.

If you can tear yourself away from the animatronic wizardry, you find designer shops and the old standbys. For fashionistas, there are all the hard-hitters: Christian Dior, Calvin Klein, Gucci, Fendi, Pucci, Louis Vuitton, Dolce & Gabbana, Marc Jacobs, and Balenciaga. Pick up your diamonds at Harry Winston, DeBeers, or Chopard, or go for a sparkling handbag at Judith Leiber. If your purse strings are a little tighter, there are always the ubiquitous Gap or Abercrombie stores. Cosmetics queens will keep themselves busy at the MAC Pro Store, one of only six in the country. The mall is open late (until 11 Sunday through Thursday, until midnight Friday and Saturday). ✉ *Caesars Palace, 3500 Las Vegas Blvd. S, Center Strip* ☎ *702/896–5599 Appian Way, 702/893–4800 Forum Shops* ⊕ *www.forumshops.com.*

Fodor's Choice ★ **Grand Canal Shoppes.** This is one of the most unforgettable shopping experiences on the Strip. Duck into shops like Dooney & Bourke, Burberry, Lior, or Paige Premium Denim as you amble under blue skies alongside a Vegas-ified Grand Canal. Eventually, all the quaint bridges and walkways lead you to St. Mark's Square, which is full of little gift-shop carts and street performers. If you're loaded down with bags, hail a gondola—it's one of the kitschiest experiences in any of the megamalls ($16 per person).

Two must-see stores are Il Prato, which sells unique Venetian collectibles, including masks, stationery sets, and pen-and-inkwell sets, and Ripa de Monti, which carries luminescent Venetian glass. The mall is open late (until 11 Sunday through Thursday, until midnight Friday and Saturday). ✉ *The Venetian, 3355 Las Vegas Blvd. S, North Strip* ☎ *702/733–1004* ⊕ *www.venetian.com.*

Fodor's Choice ★ **Miracle Mile Shops.** Miracle Mile balances its fashion designer boutiques with an even scale of modestly priced shops: there are Betsey Johnson, Herve Leger, Urban Outfitters, and Ben Sherman. Other quality shops to check out include H&M, True Religion, Bettie Page, Sephora, and ABC Stores—a Hawaiian outpost for aloha wear. Many of the 170 stores are at your local mall, but you still may discover a treasure here. ✉ *Planet Hollywood Resort & Casino, 3663 Las Vegas Blvd. S, Center Strip* ☎ *702/866–0703 or 888/800–8284* ⊕ *www.miraclemileshopslv.com.*

Fodor's Choice ★ **The Shoppes at The Palazzo.** This lavish mall stepped up Las Vegas's shopping game to truly certify the city as one of the premier shopping destinations in the world. Such powerhouse names in the fashion industry as Diane von Furstenberg, Catherine Malandrino, Michael Kors, Chloé, Bottega Veneta, and Tory Burch set up shop in Vegas for the first time with this early 2008 arrival. Shoe lovers will swoon over the Christian Louboutin and Jimmy Choo boutiques, and jewelry aficionados won't want to leave stores like Piaget and Van Cleef & Arpels. For the vintage aficionados, Annie Creamcheese is a treasure trove. The real attraction, though, comes in the form of the mall's anchor, Barneys New York. The reputable department store brings in up-and-coming, cutting-edge designers as well as established, exclusive ones like Balenciaga and Lanvin. ✉ *Palazzo, 3325 Las Vegas Blvd. S, North Strip* ☎ *702/607–7777* ⊕ *www.palazzolasvegas.com.*

★ **Town Square.** After hours spent at the craps table, head outdoors for some fresh air and spend some of those winnings. Opened in late 2007, this mall was constructed to resemble Main Street America with open-air shopping and dining. More than 150 shops including Juicy Couture, Michael Stars, a 27,000-square-foot H&M, Martin + Osa, Sephora, Apple, and Fruits & Passion will help you break the bank. And, if you're tired of shopping, there's also a children's area, an outdoor concert venue, and Rave Motion Pictures, a multiplex cinema. If it's pampering you're interested in, ElevenSpa Vegas, featuring the Ken Paves Salon,

St. Mark's Square, inside the Venetian's Grand Canal Shoppes, is full of gift-shop carts and street performers.

also calls Town Square home. Need to make a quick stop? Town Square Las Vegas offers curbside parking so you don't have to schlep all the way from the parking lot to your shopping destination. ⊠ *6605 Las Vegas Blvd. S, just south of Mandalay Bay, Airport* ☎ *702/269–5000* ⊕ *www.townsquarelasvegas.com.*

★ **Via Bellagio.** Steve Wynn spared no expense to create Bellagio, so be prepared to spare no expense shopping at its exclusive boutiques. Elegant stores such as Yves Saint Laurent, Prada, Chanel, Giorgio Armani, Gucci, Fred Leighton, and Tiffany & Co line a long passage. When you're ready to cool your heels, dine on the balcony at **Olives,** right in the promenade, to snag the best seat for watching the Fountains of Bellagio (otherwise known as the dancing waters). ⊠ *Bellagio, 3600 Las Vegas Blvd. S, Center Strip* ☎ *702/693–7111* ⊕ *www. bellagio.com/shopping.*

OUTLET MALLS

Las Vegas Outlet Center. Immerse yourself in one of the country's largest discount malls, which is, ironically, just a few miles from the Strip's most exclusive and expensive shopping. Anne Taylor Factory Store, Jones New York, Tommy Kids, and Calvin Klein are among the 130 stores selling pretty much everything at discount prices: clothing, jewelry, toys, shoes, beauty products, souvenirs, and more. The mall has two food courts and a full-size carousel. OFF 5th Saks Fifth Avenue occupies the majority of space at Las Vegas Outlet Center Annex, a small separate building on the south side. To get here, take Las Vegas Boulevard South

3 mi south from the Tropicana Avenue intersection. ⊠ *7400 Las Vegas Blvd. S, Airport* ☎ *702/896–5599* ⊕ *www.lasvegasoutletcenter.com.*

Fodor's Choice **Las Vegas Premium Outlets.** A 2007 renovation has brought the number
★ of stores up to 150, including rarely seen outlets of some heavy fashion hitters, such as Dolce & Gabbana, St. John Company Store, Brooks Brothers Factory Store, Catherine Malandrino, Diesel, Juicy Couture, Michael Kors, Ted Baker, M Missoni, Ed Hardy, and A/X Armani Exchange. Fashion jeweler David Yurman and coveted shoe designer Stuart Weitzman were also added. The upscale mix at this racetrack-shaped downtown outlet mall, which stands on the grounds of the old Union Pacific rail yards, also includes names you can find at your own mall, such as Nine West, Charlotte Russe, and Quiksilver, but with better discounts. The mall runs a $1 shuttle from the California Hotel, the Golden Nugget, and the Downtown Transportation Center, but if you want to drive, two parking garages allow easy access to the mall. ⊠ *875 S. Grand Central Pkwy., Downtown* ☎ *702/474–7500* ⊕ *www. premiumoutlets.com.*

SIDE TRIPS FROM LAS VEGAS

The vast majority of Nevada's population resides in Clark County and the nearby lakes, state parks, and geological wonders entertain even the most jaded city dwellers. Those pressed for time can take a short drive from Vegas to go skiing at Mt. Charleston, hiking in the Humboldt–Toiyabe National Forest, or rock climbing in Red Rock Canyon. Those with a little more time can explore the wonderland of nearby waterways, stunning rock formations, and laid-back ranching communities. Water enthusiasts head to Lakes Mead, Mohave, and Havasu. Nature lovers find prime wildlife watching along the Colorado River and in nature preserves in Lincoln County state parks. And those looking for the grandest spectacle in the region can take the longer drive to the Grand Canyon.

WHAT TO SEE

Fodor's Choice **Grand Canyon.** If you take only one side trip from Las Vegas, make it to
★ the Grand Canyon. There's nothing like standing on the rim and looking down and across at layers of distance, color, and shifting light. *(⇨ See Chapter 21 for more information.)*

★ **Hoover Dam.** In 1928 Congress authorized $175 million for construction of a dam on the Colorado River to control destructive floods, provide a steady water supply to seven Colorado River Basin states, and generate electricity. Considered one of the seven wonders of the industrial world, the art deco Hoover Dam is 726 feet high (the equivalent of a 70-story building) and 660 feet thick (more than the length of two football fields) at the base. Construction required 4.4 million cubic yards of concrete—enough to build a two-lane highway from San Francisco to New York. Originally referred to as Boulder Dam, the structure was later officially named Hoover Dam in recognition of President Herbert Hoover's role in the project. ⊠ *U.S. 93 east of Boulder City* ☎ *702/494–2517 or 866/730–9097* ⊕ *www.usbr.gov/lc/*

hooverdam ⌨ *Hoover Dam Tour $30, Powerplant Tour $11, parking $7, visitor center $8* ⊙ *Daily 9–5* ☞ *Security, road, and Hoover Dam crossing information: 888/248–1259.*

★ **Mt. Charleston.** In winter Las Vegans crowd the upper elevations of the Spring Mountains to throw snowballs, sled, cross-country ski, and even slide downhill at a little ski area. In summer they return to wander the high trails and escape the valley's 115°F heat (temperatures are at least 20°F cooler than in the city), and maybe even make the difficult hike to the range's high point. Easier trails lead to seasonal waterfalls or rare, dripping springs where dainty columbine and stunted aspens spill down ravines and hummingbirds zoom. Or they might lead onto high, dry ridges where ancient bristlecone trees have become twisted and burnished with age. ✛ Take U.S. 95 from Las Vegas. At the intersection of U.S. 95 and Route 157, turn left to Kyle Canyon. ⊠ *4701 N. Torrey Pines Dr., Las Vegas* ☎ *702/515–5400* ⊕ *www.fs.fed.us.*

★ **Red Rock Canyon National Conservation Area.** Red sandstone cliffs and dramatic desert landscapes await day-trippers and outdoors enthusiasts at Red Rock Canyon. Operated by the Bureau of Land Management (BLM), the 195,819-acre national conservation area features narrow canyons, fantastic rock formations, seasonal waterfalls, desert wildlife, and rock art sites. The elevated Red Rock Overlook provides a fabulous view of the cream and red sandstone cliffs. For a closer look at the stunning scenery, take the 13-mi, one-way scenic drive through the canyon. Other activities including hiking, mountain biking, rock climbing, canyoneering, picnicking, and wildlife watching. A developed campground, located 2 mi from the visitor center, has 71 campsites ($10 per night; $25 for group sites), pit toilets, and drinking water for visitors wanting to extend their stay. ✛ *The canyon is a half hour west of the Strip via Charleston Blvd.*

Southern Utah

WORD OF MOUTH

"Southern Utah is one giant piece of eye candy. From the time we first entered Utah near Lake Powell, the interesting scenery is pretty much non-stop all the way until we got to Rte 15 to return to Las Vegas 6 days later. This part of the trip from Capitol Reef was very scenic, as well."

—Governator

WELCOME TO SOUTHERN UTAH

TOP REASONS TO GO

★ **The Subway:** Formed by millennia of running water, this route in the Zion backcountry is attempted only by the sturdiest of canyoneers—who often must proceed through chest-deep water, holding their backpacks above their heads.

★ **Thor's Hammer:** The most fancifully named of Bryce's limestone hoodoos, this formation was shaped by years and years of erosion.

★ **Cathedral Valley:** Exploring the backcountry of Capitol Reef is a spiritual experience—silent, uncrowded, and beneath massive stone formations that are stained by the golden light of the setting sun.

★ **Island in the Sky:** From here you can take in all of sprawling Canyonlands, from deep river-carved gorges to mazelike canyons to tall rock formations.

★ **Delicate Arch:** The most famous arch in Arches graces one of Utah's license plates.

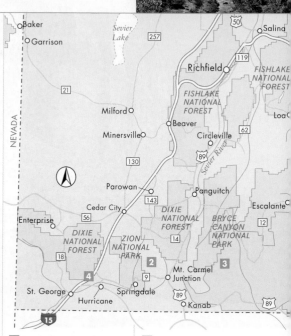

1 **Capitol Reef National Park.** Formed by cataclysmic forces that have pushed and compressed the earth, Capitol Reef National Park is an otherworldly landscape with oversize, unique sandstone formations, some layered with plant and animal fossils.

2 **Zion National Park.** With its sheer 2,000-foot cliffs and river-carved canyons Zion is a hiker's dream, and the roadways provide ample viewing opportunities.

3 **Bryce Canyon National Park.** The bizarrely shaped, bright red-orange rocks that are this park's signature formation are known as hoodoos. If you can hit the trails at sunrise or sunset, your reward will be amazing colors.

4 **Southwestern Utah.** You can play golf year-round in the booming retirement community of St. George,

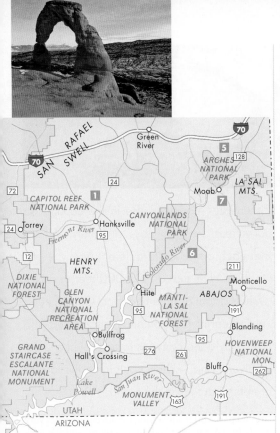

GETTING ORIENTED

Three interstates cover the main approaches to the state: I–15 connects Yellowstone (5 hours north of Salt Lake City), Utah's capital, Bryce, Zion, St. George, Las Vegas and, ultimately, Los Angeles; I–70 connects east–west travelers from Denver (via Moab and Canyon country); and I–80 delivers you from northern California and Reno across the Bonneville Salt Flats.

but the region's best attractions are not man-made. Venture onto trails, view an active dinosaur excavation site, or lose yourself in the mostly roadless, expansive Grand Staircase–Escalante National Monument.

5 Arches National Park. The largest collection of natural sandstone arches in the world—more than 2,000— are found here. Located near the town of Moab, the park is easy to visit, particularly because you can see many of its dramatic rock formations without even getting out of your car.

6 Canyonlands National Park. This is the place where you can hike, mountain bike, raft, or drive through some of the wildest, most untouched country in the United States. Dramatic scenery is plentiful here, with mushroomlike rock formations rising randomly out of the ground, twisting into spires, pinnacles, buttes, and mesas, as bald eagles and red-tail hawks float above.

7 Moab. Home to the world-famous Slick Rock mountain bike trail—and some of America's best river rafting—Moab is a countercultural retreat with quirky and original boutiques, restaurants, bars, and locals. The perfect base for Arches and Canyonlands National Parks.

Southern Utah is unique—nowhere else in the country do five national parks exist in such close proximity. What's fascinating is that each one is quite different from the others: Zion with its sheer cliffs that drop 2,000 feet or more; Bryce Canyon with its bright orange hoodoos; Capitol Reef, a 100-mi fold in the earth; Canyonlands, segmented into three distinct regions by deep canyons formed by the Colorado and Green Rivers; and Arches, containing the largest concentration of natural arches in the world.

Southern Utah's national parks offer something for adventurers of every ability level. Hiking is by far the most popular activity, and it's wise to consult with a ranger ahead of time to discuss trip length, level of difficulty, and the likelihood of flash flooding (not as much an issue at Bryce as at the lower elevation parks). Rafting is especially popular along the Green and Colorado rivers inside (and outside) Canyonlands.

Ancient Indian tribes made their homes in many of the canyons of Southern Utah. The Horseshoe Canyon section of Canyonlands has some especially wonderful examples of rock art, including the famed Great Gallery. You can occasionally spot granaries on some of the steep alcoves and cliffs, and you can also find evidence of the early pioneers who first settled (or tried to settle) these often arid lands. It's a lot to take in, and it's pretty much impossible to do all of them justice in one short trip. But that's OK, because Southern Utah is the kind of place that keeps drawing people back time and again for adventure and exploration.

PLANNING

WHEN TO GO

June, July, and August are especially hot in Arches, Canyonlands, and Capitol Reef, but this just means that many people don't stray far from their air-conditioned vehicles or tour buses (or go rafting to cool off). April, May, September, and even early October can be very comfortable times for exploring. It's less crowded during this time, perfect for mountain biking or hiking; campers delight in the warm, comfortable nights. In winter, December through March, you can find even fewer people. Bryce is at the highest elevation, and therefore the coldest. It's also the snowiest, which attracts snowshoers and cross-country skiers.

GETTING HERE AND AROUND

To enjoy Utah's pristine beauty you'll need a car, motorcycle, or RV. In summer winding mountain roads and long dry basins are either a boon (convertibles, motorcycles) or bane (some roads were clearly not built with RVs in mind). In winter, high elevations and serious storms make a sturdy car or SUV the best option. Storms occasionally shut down highway passes and/or resort access, so be flexible.

AIR TRAVEL

The major gateway to Utah is Salt Lake City International Airport. Flights to smaller, regional, or resort-town airports generally connect through Salt Lake City. A convenient gateway to southern Utah, particularly Zion and Bryce Canyon national parks, is McCarran International Airport in Las Vegas. More and more visitors to southern Utah (and the north rim of the Grand Canyon) are using St. George Municipal Airport, which has daily Delta and SkyWest flights to Salt Lake City and Los Angeles. There are limited services, but you can rent cars here and it's less than an hour to Zion National Park once you're on the road.

Airport Information McCarran International Airport (LAS) (☎ 702/261–5211 ⊕ www.mccarran.com). **Salt Lake City International Airport (SLC)** (☎ 801/575–2400 ⊕ www.slcairport.com). **St. George Municipal Airport (SGU)** (✉ 317 S. Donlee Dr. ☎ 435/634–5822 ⊕ www.sgcity.org/airport).

CAR TRAVEL

The automobile rules this expansive state, and it's the only way to connect the national parks with the services, hotels, and restaurants you'll need to enjoy your visit. I–15 is the main north–south thoroughfare, branching off to U.S. 6 toward Moab and to Arches and Canyonlands National Parks in the southeast, passing west of Capitol Reef National Park in the south–central region, and continuing all the way to the St. George area for Zion and Bryce National Parks in the southwest. Many visitors approach the southern Utah parks by way of I–70, which runs west from Denver through Grand Junction, Colorado, and Moab.

ABOUT THE RESTAURANTS

In the southwestern corner of the state, reflecting the pioneer heritage of the region, traditional and contemporary American cuisines are most common, followed closely by those with Mexican and Southwestern influences. St. George and Springdale have the greatest number and diversity of dining options. Don't presume a restaurant serves beer, much less wine or cocktails, especially in the smaller towns.

Moab area restaurants have pretty much anything you might be craving. The smaller towns in southeastern Utah don't have quite the culinary kaleidoscope and focus mostly on all-American, meat-centered meals. Most restaurants are family-friendly, and dress tends to be casual.

ABOUT THE HOTELS

Southwestern Utah is steeped in pioneer heritage, and you'll find many older homes that have been refurbished as bed-and-breakfasts. The area also has its share of older independent motels in some of the smaller towns. Most of the major hotel and motel chains have opened up at least one facility in the region. With the exception of Brian Head, the high season is summer, and logic dictates that the closer you want to be to a major attraction, the further in advance you have to make reservations. If you are willing to find a room upward of an hour from your destination, perhaps with fewer amenities, you may be surprised not only by same-day reservations in some cases, but also much lower room rates. The Utah Office of Tourism Web site is your single best bet for information on lodging and amenities in the southwestern part of the state.

Some of the best values in Moab are condominiums. Moab Lodging and Central Reservations, a very professional firm, handles reservations for these units and dozens of other motels, condos, and B&Bs in all price ranges in southeastern Utah.

Hotel reviews have been condensed for this book. Please go to Fodors. com for full reviews of each property.

WHAT IT COSTS					
	¢	$	$$	$$$	$$$$
Restaurants	under $8	$8–$12	$13–$20	$21–$30	over $30
Hotels	under $70	$70–$100	$101–$150	$151–$200	over $200
Camping	under $10	$10–$17	$18–$35	$36–$50	over $50

Restaurant prices are for a main course at dinner, excluding sales tax of 7½%–8½%. Hotel prices are for two people in a standard double room in high season, excluding service charges and 11%–12¼% tax. Camping prices are for a standard campsite per night.

CAPITOL REEF NATIONAL PARK

Capitol Reef National Park preserves the Waterpocket Fold, a 100-mi-long wrinkle in the earth's crust amidst a jumble of colorful cliffs, massive domes, soaring spires, and twisting canyons. You can walk the park's trails in relative solitude and enjoy the beauty without confronting crowds on the roads or paths. Look for signs of ancient Fremont Native Americans and Mormon settlers.

EXPLORING

WHAT TO SEE

Capitol Gorge. At the entrance to this gorge Scenic Drive becomes unpaved. The short drive to the end of the road leads to some interesting hiking trails to the water-holding "tanks" eroded into the sandstone. ⊠ *Scenic Dr., 9 mi south of visitor center.*

Capitol Reef Scenic Drive. This paved road starts at the visitor center and winds its way through the Fruita Historic District and colorful sandstone cliffs into Capitol Gorge; a side road, Grand Wash Road, provides access into the canyon. At Capitol Gorge, the route becomes unpaved, and road conditions may vary because of weather and amount of use. Check with the visitor center before entering Capitol Gorge. Capitol Reef Scenic Drive, called simply Scenic Drive by locals, is 9 mi long, with about the last quarter of it unpaved.

Chimney Rock. Even in a landscape of spires, cliffs, and knobs, this deep-red landform is unmistakable. ⊠ *Hwy. 24, about 3 mi west of visitor center.*

SCENIC DRIVES

Fodor'sChoice ★ **Utah Scenic Byway 12.** Named as one of only 20 All-American Roads in the United States by the National Scenic Byways Program, Highway 12 is not to be missed. The 32-mi stretch between Torrey and Boulder winds through alpine forests and passes vistas of some of America's most remote and wild landscape. It is not for the faint of heart or those afraid of narrow, winding mountain roads.

Utah Scenic Byway 24. For 62 mi between Loa and Hanksville, you'll cut right through Capitol Reef National Park. Colorful rock formations in all their hues of red, cream, pink, gold, and deep purple extend from one end of the route to the other. The vibrant rock finally gives way to lush green hills and the mountains west of Loa.

WHERE TO EAT AND STAY

There is not even a snack bar within Capitol Reef, but close by in Torrey you can find everything from high-end southwestern cuisine to a basic hamburger.

There are no lodging options within Capitol Reef, but you'll find clean and comfortable accommodations no matter what your budget in nearby Torrey and not far beyond in Bicknell and Loa. Reservations are recommended in summer.

Campgrounds in Capitol Reef fill up fast between Memorial Day and Labor Day, though that goes mainly for the super-convenient Fruita Campground and not the more remote backcountry sites. Most of the area's state parks have camping facilities, and the region's two national forests offer many wonderful sites.

$$$
SOUTHWESTERN
Torrey
Fodor'sChoice ★

✕ **Cafe Diablo.** This popular Torrey restaurant is one of the state's best. Innovative southwestern entrées include pecan chicken and usually some variation of tamales. The rattlesnake cakes, made with free-range desert rattler and served with ancho-rosemary aioli, are delicious and a steadfast menu item. ⊠ *599 W. Main St./Hwy. 24, Torrey*

🕾 *435/425–3070* ⊕ *www.cafediablo.net* ▤ *AE, D, MC, V* ◷ *Closed mid-Oct.–Apr. No lunch.*

$
ⓒ
Fodor'sChoice
★

$ ⚠ **Fruita Campground.** Near the orchards and the Fremont River, this shady campground is a great place to call home for a few days. The sites nearest the river or the orchards are the very best. Loop C is most appropriate for RVs, although the campground has no hookups. Sites are first-come, first-served, and in summer the campground fills up early in the day. **Pros:** central park location; cool and shady. **Cons:** fills quickly; 10-minute drive from Torrey. ⊠ *Scenic Dr., about 1 mi south of visitor center* 🕾 *435/425–3791* ⚠ *71 tent/RV sites* ⚴ *Flush toilets, drinking water, grills, picnic tables* ▤ *AE, D, MC, V.*

$$$–$$$$
Teasdale
Fodor'sChoice
★

$$$–$$$$ ⊡ **Lodge at Red River Ranch.** You'll swear you've walked into one of the great lodges of western legend when you enter the Red River Ranch. **Pros:** furnishings and artifacts so distinctive they could grace the pages of a design magazine. **Cons:** rooms are on the small side; in summer you may wish for air-conditioning. ⊠ *2900 W. Hwy. 24, Teasdale* 🕾 *435/425–3322 or 800/205–6343* ⊕ *www.redriverranch.com* ⟿ *15 rooms* ⚴ *In-room: a/c, Wi-Fi, no TV. In-hotel: restaurant* ▤ *DC, MC, V.*

SPORTS AND THE OUTDOORS

FOUR-WHEELING

You can explore Capitol Reef in a 4X4 on a number of exciting back-country routes. Road conditions can vary greatly. Spring and summer rains can leave the roads muddy, washed out, and impassable even to four-wheel-drive vehicles. Always check at the park visitor center for current conditions before you set out, and take water, supplies, and a cell phone with you.

Cathedral Valley Scenic Backway. The north end of Capitol Reef, along this backcountry road, is filled with towering monoliths and panoramic vistas. The area is remote and the road through it unpaved and including two water crossings, so do not enter without a high-clearance vehicle, some planning, and a cell phone (although reception is spotty). The drive through the valley is a 58-mi loop that you can begin at River Ford Road off Highway 24. Including stops, allow a half day for this drive. ■ TIP→ If your time is limited, you may want to tour only the Caineville Wash Road, which takes about two hours. At the visitor center you can check for road conditions and pick up a self-guided auto tour brochure for $2. ⊠ *River Ford Rd., 11.7 mi east of visitor center on Hwy. 24.*

HIKING

Many park trails in Capitol Reef include steep climbs, but there are a few easy-to-moderate hikes. A short drive from the visitor center takes you to a dozen trails, and a park ranger can advise you on combining trails or locating additional routes.

Guided hikes can be arranged with Hondoo Rivers & Trails.

★ **Capitol Gorge Trail and the Tanks.** Starting at the Pioneer Register, about a mile from the Capitol Gorge parking lot, is a trail that climbs to the Tanks, two holes in the sandstone, formed by erosion, that hold water after it rains. After a scramble up about 0.2 mi of steep trail with cliff drop-offs, you can look down into the Tanks and can also see a natural bridge below the lower tank. Including the walk to the Pioneer Register, allow an hour or two for this interesting little hike. ⊠ *Trailhead at end of Scenic Dr., 9 mi south of visitor center.*

Fodor's Choice ★ **Hickman Bridge Trail.** This trail leads to a natural bridge of Kayenta sandstone, which has a 135-foot opening carved by intermittent flash floods. Early on, the route climbs a set of steps along the Fremont River, and as the trail tops out onto a bench, you'll find a slight depression in the earth. This is what remains of an ancient Fremont pit house, a kind of home that was dug into the ground and covered with brush. The trail splits, leading along the right-hand branch to a strenuous uphill climb to the Rim Overlook and Navajo Knobs. Stay to your left to see the bridge, and you'll encounter a moderate up-and-down trail. As you continue up the wash on your way to the bridge, you'll notice a Fremont granary on the right side of the small canyon. Allow about 1½ hours to walk the 2-mi round-trip. ⊠ *Trailhead at Hwy. 24, 2 mi east of visitor center.*

23

ZION NATIONAL PARK

The walls of Zion Canyon soar more than 2,000 feet above the valley below. Erosion has left behind a collection of domes, fins, and blocky massifs bearing the names and likenesses of cathedrals and temples, prophets and angels.

Trails lead deep into side canyons and up narrow ledges to waterfalls, serene spring-fed pools, and shaded spots of solitude.

EXPLORING

WHAT TO SEE

★ **Court of the Patriarchs.** This trio of peaks bears the names of, from left to right, Abraham, Isaac, and Jacob. Hike the trail that leaves from the Court of the Patriarchs Viewpoint to get a much better view of the sandstone prophets. ⊠ *Zion Canyon Scenic Dr., 1½ mi north of Canyon Junction.*

Fodor's Choice ★ **The Narrows.** This sinuous 16-mi crack in the earth where the Virgin River flows over gravel and boulders is one of the most stunning gorges in the world. If you hike through it (⇨ *Hiking*), you'll find yourself surrounded—and sometimes, nearly closed in by—smooth walls stretching high into the heavens. You also will get wet, as the river still flows through here. ⊠ *Begins at Riverside Walk.*

WHERE TO EAT AND STAY

There is only one full-service restaurant in Zion National Park. The town of Springdale has the greatest number and diversity of dining options.

The Zion Canyon Lodge is rustic but comfortable. Nearby Springdale has many lodging options to choose from, from quaint smaller motels and bed-and-breakfasts, to upscale hotels with modern amenities and

View stunning vistas on Angel's Landing Trail, but take note that it's not for those with acrophobia.

riverside rooms. Look farther afield to Panguitch and Hurricane for particularly good and inexpensive options.

$–$$
AMERICAN

✕ **Red Rock Grill at Zion Lodge.** The menu won't have you doing back flips, but the solid American fare with a southwestern twang is serviceable. The restaurant is adorned with historic photos dating back to the early days of the lodge. You take in the scenery while you eat from the grill's comfortable patio. A good selection of steak, fish, and poultry is offered for dinner as well as decent vegetarian options and an expansive dessert menu. The lunch menu consists of simpler plates (burgers, sandwiches, salads, etc.); breakfast is also served. ⊠ *1 Zion Lodge, Springdale* ☎ *435/772–7760* ⊕ *www.zionlodge.com* ⌂ *Reservations essential* ⊟ *AE, D, DC, MC, V.*

$$$
★

⌸ **Zion Lodge.** Knotty pine woodwork and log and wicker furnishings accent the lobby, rooms are modern but not fancy, and the historic western-style cabins have gas-log fireplaces. **Pros:** guests can drive their cars all the way up to the lodge, even during shuttle-only season; beautifully re-created lodge; gets nice and dark at night. **Cons:** no in-room coffee; bring a flashlight to make your way to your cabin; staff seems overwhelmed at busiest times. ⊠ *1 Zion Lodge, Springdale* ☎ *888/297–2757* ⊕ *www.zionlodge.com* ⇗ *75 rooms, 6 suites, 40 cabins* ⌂ *In-room: Wi-Fi, no TV. In-hotel: restaurant, Internet terminal* ⊟ *AE, D, DC, MC, V.*

$–$$
★

⌂ **Watchman Campground.** This large campground on the Virgin River operates on a reservation system between April and October (⊕ *www. recreation.gov*), but you do not get to choose your own site. **Pros:** the only campground in the park open year-round; right by the south entrance. **Cons:** some campsites feel stacked on top of each other; the closest showers require a ride on the park shuttle. ⊠ *Access road off Zion Canyon Visitor Center parking lot* ☎ *877/444–6777 reservations* ⚘ *160 tent/RV sites, 91 with hookups* ⚏ *Flush toilets, partial hookups (electric), dump station, drinking water, fire grates, picnic tables* ▭ *AE, D, MC, V.*

SPORTS AND THE OUTDOORS

23

Hiking is the most popular activity at Zion, with a panoply of trails leading to extreme slot canyons, gorgeous overlooks, verdant meadows, and dripping springs. Some sections of the Virgin River are ideal for canoeing (inner tubes are not allowed). In the winter, hiking boots can be exchanged for snowshoes and cross-country skis, but check with a ranger to determine backcountry snow conditions.

HIKING

Fodor's Choice ★ **Angels Landing Trail.** This hike beneath the Great White Throne is one of the most challenging in the park. Leave your acrophobia at home as you work your way through Walter's Wiggles, a series of 21 switchbacks built out of sandstone blocks. From here you traverse sheer cliffs with chains bolted into the rock face to serve as handrails in some places. Allow 2½ hours round-trip if you stop at Scout's Lookout, and four hours if you keep going to the top. The trail is not appropriate for children. ⊠ *Trailhead at Zion Canyon Scenic Dr., about 4½ mi north of Canyon Junction.*

Fodor's Choice ★ **Canyon Overlook Trail.** Located near the parking area just east of Zion–Mount Carmel tunnel, this trail is moderately steep but only 1 mi round-trip; allow an hour to hike it. The overlook at trail's end gives you views of the West and East Temples, Towers of the Virgin, the Streaked Wall, and other Zion Canyon cliffs and peaks. The elevation change is 160 feet. ⊠ *Trailhead at Rte. 9, east of Zion–Mount Carmel Tunnel.*

Emerald Pools Trail. Two small waterfalls cascade (or drip, in dry weather) into algae-filled pools along this trail. The path leading to the lower pool is paved and appropriate for strollers and wheelchairs. The quarter-mile from lower pool to the middle pool gets rocky and steep but offers increasingly scenic views. A less crowded and exceptionally enjoyable return route follows the Kayenta Trail connecting on to the Grotto Trail. Allow 50 minutes round-trip to the lower pool and 2½ hours round-trip to the middle and upper pools. ⊠ *Trailhead at Zion Canyon Scenic Dr., about 3 mi north of Canyon Junction.*

BRYCE CANYON NATIONAL PARK

Bryce, known for its fanciful "hoodoos," is actually an amphitheater, not a canyon. The hoodoos took on their unusual shapes because the top layer of rock—"cap rock"—is harder than the layers below it. If erosion undercuts the soft rock beneath the cap too much, the hoodoo will tumble.

EXPLORING

WHAT TO SEE

★ **Natural Bridge.** This 85-foot arch formation is an essential Bryce photo-op. The rusty buttress, formed over millions of years by wind, water, and chemical erosion, contrasts sharply against the pine forest that peeks through from below. ⊠ *11 mi south of park entrance.*

★ **Sunrise Point.** Named for its stunning views at dawn, this overlook is the starting point for the Queen's Garden Trail and the Fairyland Loop Trail. You have to descend the Queen's Garden Trail to get a regal glimpse of **Queen Victoria,** a hoodoo that appears to sport a crown and glorious full skirt. The trail is popular and marked clearly, but moderately strenuous with 300 feet of elevation change. ⊠ *2 mi south of park entrance near Bryce Canyon Lodge.*

SCENIC DRIVE

Fodor'sChoice **Main Park Road.** Following miles of canyon rim, this thoroughfare gives
★ access to more than a dozen scenic overlooks. Allow two to three hours to travel the entire 36 mi round-trip. The road is open year-round, but may be closed temporarily after heavy snowfalls to allow for clearing. Major overlooks are rarely more than a few minutes' walk from the parking areas, and many let you see more than 100 mi on clear days. ■TIP➔ The park shuttle is an easy way to get around but if you must drive all overlooks lie east of the road—to keep things simple (and left turns to a minimum), you can proceed to the southern end of the park and stop at the overlooks on your northbound return. Trailers are not allowed beyond Sunset Campground. Day users may park trailers at the visitor center or other designated sites; check with park staff for parking options. RVs can drive throughout the park, but vehicles longer than 25 feet are not allowed at Paria View.

WHERE TO EAT AND STAY

$$$ 🖼 **Bryce Canyon Lodge.** A few feet from the amphitheater's rim and
Fodor'sChoice trailheads is this rugged and rustic stone-and-wood lodge. **Pros:** fine
★ Western-style lodging; friendly and attentive staff; bright orange hoo-doos only a short walk away. **Cons:** closed in the winter; few amenities; grounds are dark at night, so bring a flashlight to dinner! ⊠ *Hwy. 63, Bryce* 🖀 *435/834–8700 or 877/386–4383* ⊕ *www.brycecanyonforever. com/* ⟿ *70 rooms, 3 suites, 40 cabins* ⚹ *In-room: Wi-Fi, no a/c, no TV. In-hotel: restaurant* ⊟ *AE, D, DC, MC, V* ☺ *Closed Nov.–Mar.*

SPORTS AND THE OUTDOORS

To explore the park's hoodoos, set aside a half day to hike into the amphitheater. Note that no below-rim trails are paved. For trail maps, information, and ranger recommendations, stop at the visitor center. Bathrooms are located at most trailheads but not down in the amphitheater.

Hikers in Bryce are rewarded with vistas highlighting the park's colorful landscape.

Queen's Garden Trail. This hike is the easiest way down into the amphitheater. Three hundred feet of elevation change will lead you to a short tunnel, quirky hoodoos, and many like-minded hikers. Allow two hours total to hike the 1.5-mi trail plus the ½-mi rim-side path back to the parking area. ⊠ *Trailhead at Sunrise Point, 2 mi south of park entrance.*

SOUTHWESTERN UTAH

The land settlers tamed for planting cotton and fruit is now a playground for golfers, bikers, and hikers. Arts festivals and concerts take place under canyon walls. Ruins, petroglyphs, pioneer graffiti, and ghost towns beckon new explorers.

ST. GEORGE AND SPRINGDALE

50 mi southwest of Cedar City via I–15.

Brigham Young dispatched 309 LDS families in 1861 to found St. George. St. Georgians now number approximately 75,000, many of whom are retirees attracted by the hot, dry climate and the numerous golf courses. St. George is a popular destination for families, as well.

Springdale's growth has followed that of next-door neighbor Zion National Park, Utah's most popular park. Many businesses along Zion Park Boulevard, the main drag, double as shuttle stops for the bus system that carts tourists into the jaw-dropping sandstone confines of Zion Canyon, the town's main attraction.

EXPLORING

★ **Snow Canyon State Park.** Red Navajo sandstone mesas and formations are crowned with black lava rock, creating high-contrast vistas from either end of Snow Canyon. From the campground you can scramble up huge sandstone mounds and overlook the entire valley. ⊠ *1002 Snow Canyon Dr., Ivins 8 mi northwest of St. George* ☎ *435/628–2255* ⊕ *www. stateparks.utah.gov* ⊴ *$6* ⊙ *Daily 6 am to 10 pm.*

WHERE TO EAT AND STAY

¢–$ ✕ **Bear Paw Coffee Company.** The menu is full of American and European
AMERICAN flavors, but breakfast is the star of the show here (served all day, every
St. George day)—Belgian waffles, crepes, and French toast are standouts. ⊠ *75*
★ *N. Main St.* ☎ *435/634–0126* ⊕ *bearpawcafe.com* ▭ *AE, D, MC, V*
⊙ *No dinner* ✢ *C1.*

$$–$$$ ✕ **Bit & Spur Restaurant and Saloon.** This restaurant has been a legend in
SOUTHWESTERN Utah for almost 30 years. The house favorites menu lists traditional
Springdale Southwestern dishes like the *bistec asado* (chili-rubbed rib-eye steak).
Fodor'sChoice Housemade desserts include fruit crisp made with local fruit and a
★ brownie crème brulee. ■TIP→ This is the best place to hear live music
in southern Utah. ⊠ *1212 Zion Park Blvd.* ☎ *435/772–3498* ⊕ *www. bitandspur.com* ▭ *AE, D, MC, V* ⊙ *No lunch.*

$$–$$$ ▦ **Desert Pearl Inn.** Every room at this comfortable inn has vaulted ceil-
Springdale ings, thick carpets, cushy throw pillows, Roman shades, oversize win-
Fodor'sChoice dows, and sleeper sofas, as well as a large balcony or patio overlooking
★ either the Virgin River or the pool. **ros:** spacious, condolike rooms.
Cons: fills up early during high season. ⊠ *707 Zion Park Blvd., Box 407* ☎ *435/772–8888 or 888/828–0898* ⊕ *www.desertpearl.com* ⇗ *73 rooms, 4 suites* ⚬ *In-room: safe, kitchen, refrigerator, DVD, Internet, Wi-Fi. In-hotel: pool, laundry facilities, Internet* ▭ *AE, D, MC, V.*

$$$$ ▦ **Red Mountain Spa.** This active resort is designed for fitness and reju-
St. George venation. **ros:** down-to-earth spa experience, healthy food. **Cons:** some
Fodor'sChoice may not be ready for the wake-up-at-dawn-to-hit-the-gym ethos that
★ pervades the place—although it's pretty low-key. ⊠ *1275 E. Red Mountain Circle, Ivins, 7 mi northwest of St. George* ☎ *435/673–4905 or 877/246–4453* ⊕ *www.redmountainspa.com* ⇗ *82 rooms, 24 villa suites* ⚬ *In-room: safe, Internet. In-hotel: 2 restaurants, pools, gym, spa, water sports, bicycles, laundry facilities, Internet, some pets allowed, no kids under 12* ▭ *AE, D, MC, V* ⊙❙ *FAP* ✢ *A1.*

GRAND STAIRCASE–ESCALANTE NATIONAL MONUMENT

Encompassing 1.7 million acres in south-central Utah, the Grand Staircase–Escalante National Monument offers remote backcountry experiences that include waterfalls, Native American ruins and petroglyphs, and shoulder-width slot canyons. The small towns of Escalante and Boulder offer access, information, outfitters, lodging, and dining.

WHAT TO SEE

Fodor'sChoice Though the **Highway 12 Scenic Byway** starts at the intersection of U.S.
★ 89, west of Bryce Canyon National Park, the stretch that begins in Escalante is the most spectacular and scenic. Be sure to stop at the eye-

popping overlooks. Beware: the paved road is twisting and steep, and often shouldered by sheer drop-offs.

WHERE TO EAT

$$$ ✕ **Hell's Backbone Grill.** One of the best restaurants in southern Utah,
ECLECTIC this remote spot is worth the drive from any distance. The breakfast
Boulder and dinner menus are inspired by Native American, Western Range,
Fodor'sChoice Southwestern, and Mormon pioneer recipes. Chef-owners Jen Castle
★ and Blake Spalding use only fresh, organic foods that have a historical
connection to the area, so you might find various cuts of local beef or
chicken tumbleweed enchiladas on the menu, and salads might contain
strawberries, jicama, pine nuts, and dried corn. Their cookbook, *With
a Measure of Grace,* is a gem worth owning, too. ⊠ *20 N. Rte. 12, in
Boulder Mountain Lodge* ☎ *435/335–7464* ⊕ *www.hellsbackbonegrill.
com* ⊟ *AE, D, MC, V* ☉ *Closed Dec.–Feb. No lunch.*

23

ARCHES NATIONAL PARK

Throughout the red rock landscape of Arches National Park, balanced rocks teeter unthinkably on pedestals; sandstone arches—of which there are more than 2,500—frame the sky with peekaboo windows; and formations like the Three Penguins greet you at points throughout the 73,379-acre park.

EXPLORING

WHAT TO SEE

Fodor'sChoice **Delicate Arch.** The familiar symbol of Arches National Park, Delicate
★ Arch is tall enough to shelter a four-story building. You can drive a
couple of miles off the main road to view the arch from a distance, or
you can hike right up to it. The trail is a moderately strenuous 3-mi
round-trip hike. ⊠ *13 mi from park entrance, 2.2 mi off main road.*

★ **Landscape Arch.** This natural rock opening competes with Kolob Arch at
Zion for the title of largest geologic span in the world. Measuring 306
feet from base to base, it appears as a delicate ribbon of rock bending
over the horizon. You can reach it by walking a rolling, gravel 1.4-mi-
long trail. ⊠ *Devils Garden, 18 mi park entrance off main road.*

SCENIC DRIVE

Arches Main Park Road. The main park road and its two short spurs allow you to see much of the park from your car. The main road takes you through Courthouse Towers, where you can see Sheep Rock and the Three Gossips, then alongside the Great Wall, the Petrified Dunes and Balanced Rock. A drive to the Windows section takes you to attractions like Double Arch and you can see Skyline Arch along the roadside as you approach the campground. The road to Delicate Arch allows you hiking access to one of the park's main features. Allow about two hours to drive the 36-mi round-trip, more if you explore the spurs and their features and stop at viewpoints along the way.

Landscape Arch in Arches National Park is one of the largest geological spans in the world.

WHERE TO EAT AND STAY

There are no dining facilities in the park itself, but downtown Moab has plenty of supermarkets, bakeries, and delis. Enjoy your packed lunch at one of several picnic areas.

Though there is no lodging in the park itself, in the surrounding area, every type of lodging is available, from economy chain motels to B&Bs and high-end, high-adventure resorts.

The Devils Garden Campground in the park is wonderful, though it is often full and does not provide an RV dump station. Another favorite is the Dead Horse State Park Campground, which is particularly popular with RV campers.

CANYONLANDS NATIONAL PARK

Canyonlands' mushroomlike rock formations rise randomly out of the ground, twisting into all manner of shapes: pinnacles, spires, buttes, and mesas. The Green and Colorado rivers traverse the canyons, where the rich browns, verdant greens, and fresh yellows of the pinyon-juniper forests complement the deep reds, baby pinks, bright oranges, and milky whites of the rocks. The park's dirt roads appeal to mountain bikers, and the rising rapids of Cataract Canyon challenge rafters.

EXPLORING

WHAT TO SEE

★ **Grand View Point.** At the end of the main road of Island in the Sky, don't miss this 360-degree view that extends all the way to the San Juan Mountains in Colorado on a clear day. ✉ *Off main road, 12 mi from park entrance, Island in the Sky.*

★ **Mesa Arch.** You simply can't visit Island in the Sky without taking the quick ½-mi walk to Mesa Arch. The arch is above a cliff that drops 800 feet to the canyon bottom. Views through Washerwoman Arch and surrounding buttes, spires, and canyons make this a favorite photo opportunity. ✉ *Off main road, 6 mi from park entrance, Island in the Sky.*

SCENIC DRIVE

Island in the Sky Park Road. This 12-mi long road connects to a 5-mi side road to the Upheaval Dome area. You can enjoy many of the park's vistas by stopping at the overlooks—get out of your car for the best views. Once you get to the park, allow about two hours to explore.

23

WHERE TO EAT AND STAY

There are no dining facilities in the park itself. Needles Outpost, just outside the entrance to the Needles District, has a small grocery store for picnicking necessities. Restaurants in Blanding offer simple meals, and most do not serve alcohol.

There is no lodging inside Canyonlands. The towns of Blanding and Bluff offer basic motels, both family-owned and national chains.

At the Needles District, campers will enjoy fairly private campsites tucked against red rock walls and dotted with pinyon and juniper trees. At Island in the Sky, starry nights and spectacular vistas make the small campground an intimate treasure. Hookups are not available in either of the park's campgrounds; however, the sites are long enough to accommodate units up to 28 feet long. There are no RV dump stations in the park.

$ ★ **Squaw Flat Campground.** The sites at Squaw Flat are spread out in two different areas, giving each site almost unparalleled privacy. Each site has a rock wall at its back, and shade trees. The sites are filled on a first-come, first-served basis. **Pros:** close to great day hikes like Chesler Park; private; each site has some much-needed shade. **Cons:** fills up in spring and fall, so have a back-up plan; no hookups for RVs; toasty in summer. ✉ *About 5 mi from park entrance off main road, Needles* ☎ *435/719–2313* ⚠ *26 tent/RV sites* ♿ *Flush toilets, drinking water, fire pits, picnic tables* ▭ *No credit cards.*

SPORTS AND THE OUTDOORS

At Canyonlands, adrenaline junkies can rock climb, mountain bike treacherous terrain, tackle world-class white-water rapids, and drive 4X4 vehicles over steep cliffs along precipitous drops.

BICYCLING

White Rim Road. This 112-mi road around Island in the Sky traverses steep roads and ledges as well as long stretches that wind through the canyons. Permits are not required for day use, but if you're biking White Rim without an outfitter you'll need careful planning and backcountry reservations (make them as far in advance as possible through the reservation office ☎ 435/259–4351). Information about permits can be found at ⊕ *www.nps.gov/cany.* There's no water on this route. White Rim Road starts at the end of Shafer Trail. ⊕ *Off main park road about 1 mi from entrance, then about 11 mi on Shafer Trail; or off Potash Rd. (Rte. 279) at Jug Handle Arch turnoff about 18 mi from U.S. 191, then about 5 mi on Shafer Trail; Island in the Sky.*

FOUR-WHEELING

Nearly 200 mi of challenging backcountry roads lead to campsites, trailheads, and natural and cultural features in Canyonlands. All of the roads require high-clearance, four-wheel-drive vehicles, and many are inappropriate for inexperienced drivers. Double-check to see that your vehicle is in top-notch condition, for you definitely don't want to break down in the interior of the park: towing expenses can exceed $1,000. Overnight four-wheeling trips require a $30 permit, which you can reserve by contacting the Backcountry Reservations Office (☎ 435/259–4351). Watch out for cyclists on all roads. It's best to check at the visitor center for current road conditions before taking off into the backcountry. You must carry a washable, reusable toilet with you in the Maze District and carry out all waste.

HIKING

Many of the park's trails are long, rolling routes over slickrock and sand in landscapes dotted with juniper, pinyon, and sagebrush. Interconnecting trails in the Needles District provide excellent opportunities for weeklong backpacking excursions. The Maze trails are primarily accessed via four-wheel-drive vehicle. Horseshoe Canyon Trail takes a considerable amount of effort to reach, as it is more than 100 mi from Moab, 32 mi of which are a bumpy, and often sandy, dirt road.

MOAB

Don't let Moab's touristy exterior fool you. At its core, this is a frontier outpost, where people have been forced to create their own livelihoods for more than 100 years, first as farmers and ranchers in the late 1880s and then as miners during the uranium boom of the 1950s. After a massive downturn in the mining industry Moab eventually was able to rebuild itself with the dollars of sightseers, four-wheelers, bikers, and boaters.

EXPLORING

WHAT TO SEE

★ **Dead Horse Point State Park.** Overlooking a sweeping oxbow of the Colorado River, some 2,000 feet below, Dead Horse Point itself is a small peninsula connected to the main mesa by a narrow neck of land. As the story goes, cowboys used to drive wild horses onto the point and pen them there with a brush fence. Some were accidentally forgotten and left to perish. There's a visitor center (with interpretive programs April–October) and museum, as well as a 21-site campground with drinking water, electricity, and an overlook. ⊠ *32 mi west of Moab at end of Rte. 313* ☎ *435/259–2614, 800/322–3770 campground reservations* ⊕ *www.stateparks.utah.gov* ⊠ *$10 per vehicle* ☉ *Daily 6–10.*

SCENIC DRIVE

23

Fodor'sChoice **Colorado River Scenic Byway—Route 128.** This scenic drive starts 2 mi
★ north of Moab off U.S. 191 and runs along the Colorado River northeast to I–70. First passing through a high-walled corridor, the drive eventually passes the monoliths of Fisher Towers and Castle Rock, which you may recognize from various car commercials and old cowboy movies. Near the end of the 44-mi drive is the tiny town of Cisco. ⊠ *Rte. 128, from Moab to Cisco.*

WHERE TO EAT AND STAY

$$–$$$ ✕ **Buck's Grill House.** For a taste of the American West, try the thick and
SOUTHWESTERN tender steaks, buffalo meat loaf or elk stew served at this popular din-
Fodor'sChoice ner spot. A selection of Southwestern entrées, including duck tamales
★ and buffalo chorizo tacos, round out the menu. Vegetarian diners will find some tasty choices, too. A surprisingly good wine list will complement your meal. Outdoor patio dining with the trickle of a waterfall will end your day perfectly. For a more urbane experience, sit in Buck's new **Frontier Lounge**, a full bar within the restaurant that offers a city-like interior and a limited menu. ⊠ *1393 N. U.S. 191* ☎ *435/259–5201* ⊕ *www.bucksgrillhouse.com* ▤ *D, MC, V* ☉ *Closed Thanksgiving–mid-Feb. No lunch.*

$$$ ✕ **Desert Bistro.** Set in a beautifully restored ranch house dating to 1896,
SOUTHWESTERN the Desert Bistro specializes in casual fine dining with a southwestern flair. In the warmer months, dine on the front porch or garden patio under towering cottonwood trees as you sample marinated pork tenderloin with apple-chipotle sauce or a variety of game entrées including bison, smoked elk and antelope. The menu varies seasonally, and vegetarian options are available. You will savor every bite of the house-made desserts to complete a remarkable dining experience at this oasis in the desert. ⊠ *1266 N. Hwy. 191, Moab* ☎ *435/259–0756* ⊕ *www.desertbistro.com* ▤ *AE, D, MC, V* ☉ *Closed late-Dec.–Feb.*

$ ✕ **Moab Brewery.** This spacious place is one of the most comfortable
ECLECTIC spots to grab some pub grub and a beer brewed right on the spot. The best bets are the burgers and sandwiches—not to mention the nachos, which are huge and fabulous. ⊠ *686 S. Main* ☎ *435/259–6333* ⊕ *www.themoabbrewery.com* ▤ *AE, D, MC, V.*

$$$$ ▦ **Sorrel River Ranch.** The rooms at this lavish ranch are opulent, with
Fodor'sChoice a cowboy motif that permeates the private decks, picture windows,
★ and custom-made, bright wooden furniture. **Pros:** the most luxurious hotel in the Moab area by far; very attentive staff. **Cons:** half an hour from Moab; rooms are a fair walk from the parking area. ⊠ *Rte. 128, Box K, mile marker 17* ☎ *435/259–4642 or 877/359–2715* ⊕ *www.*

sorrelriver.com ⊅ *55 rooms* ♿ *In-room: kitchen, VCR (some), Wi-Fi. In-hotel: restaurant, room service, tennis court, pool, gym, spa, laundry facilities, laundry service, some pets allowed* ▭ *AE, D, MC, V* ⎯○⎯ *CP.*

$$$ ⊞ **Sunflower Hill Bed and Breakfast.** On a quiet neighborhood street, this turn-of-the-20th-century dwelling is operated by a family that ensures that their guests feel truly welcome. **ros:** central location; wonderful gardens. **Cons:** music is sometimes overwhelming in breakfast area; not a uniquely Southwestern experience. ⊠ *185 N. 300 East* ☎ *435/259–2974 or 800/662–2786* ⊕ *www.sunflowerhill.com* ⊅ *9 rooms, 3 suites* ♿ *In-room: no phone, DVD (some). In-hotel: pool, no elevator, laundry facilities, public Wi-Fi* ▭ *AE, D, MC, V* ⎯○⎯ *BP.*

$$ – $$$ ⬭ **Moab Valley RV Resort.** Just 2 mi from Arches National Park, this
Ⓒ campground is convenient for sightseeing, river rafting, and all types of
Fodor'sChoice area attractions and activities. On-site you can pitch some horseshoes,
★ perfect your putting, or soak in the hot tub. Kids and parents alike will enjoy the playgrounds, including a giant chess- and checkerboard. **Pros:** beautiful surroundings; most of the RV sites are shady and quaint. **Cons:** tent sites are downright unattractive; though the park is pretty central, it's too far from Arches or town to walk to either. ⊠ *1773 N. U.S. 191* ☎ *435/259–4469* ⊕ *www.moabvalleyrv.com* ⬭ *108 sites (62 with full hookups, 7 with water and electric only, 39 tent sites); 33 cabins* ♿ *Flush toilets, full hookups, dump station, drinking water, guest laundry, showers, grills, picnic tables, public telephone, general store, play area, swimming (pool), Wi-Fi* ▭ *AE, D, MC, V* ⊘ *Mar.–Oct.*

SPORTS AND THE OUTDOORS

Moab's towering cliffs and deep canyons can be intimidating and unreachable without the help of a guide. Fortunately, guide services are abundant in Moab, whether you are interested in a 4X4 expedition into the backcountry, a river-rafting trip, bicycle tours, rock-art tours, or a scenic air flight. It's always best to make reservations, but cancellations or unsold spots sometimes make it possible to jump on a tour with short notice.

HIKING

The Moab area has plenty of hiking trails for all fitness levels. For a great view of the Moab valley and surrounding red rock country, hike up the steep **Moab Rim Trail.** For something a little less taxing, hike the shady, cool path of **Negro Bill Canyon,** which is off Route 129. At the end of the trail you'll find giant Morning Glory Arch towering over a cool pool created by a natural spring. If you want to take a stroll through the heart of Moab, hop on the **Mill Creek Parkway,** which winds along the creek from one side of town to the other. It's paved and perfect for bicycles, strollers, or joggers. For a taste of slickrock hiking that feels like the backcountry but is easy to access, try the **Corona Arch Trail,** off Route 279. You'll be rewarded with two large arches hidden from view of the highway. The Moab Information Center carries a free hiking trail guide to these and other trails. Don't forget to explore the many trails in the nearby Arches and Canyonlands national parks.

MOUNTAIN BIKING

Fodor's Choice
★

Moab is known as the mountain-biking capital of the world, drawing riders of all ages off the pavement and onto rugged four-wheel-drive roads and trails. One of the many popular routes is the **Slickrock Trail,** a stunning area of steep Navajo Sandstone dunes a few miles east of Moab. ■ TIP→ Beginners should master the 2½-mi practice loop before attempting the longer, and very challenging, 10½-mi loop. More moderate rides can be found on the **Gemini Bridges** or **Monitor and Merrimac** trails, both off U.S. 191 north of Moab. **Klondike Bluffs**, just north of Moab, is an excellent ride for novices. The Moab Information Center carries a free biking trail guide. Mountain-bike rentals range from $40 for a good bike to $75 for a top-of-the-line workhorse. If you want to go on a guided ride, expect to pay between $120 to $135 per person for a half day and $155 to $190 for a full day, including the bike rental. You can save money by banding together with a larger group to keep the per-person rates down; even a party of two will save drastically over a single rider. Several companies offer shuttles to and from the trailheads.

RIVER EXPEDITIONS

Fodor's Choice
★

The easy-flowing stretch of the Colorado River northeast of Arches and very near Moab is the perfect place to take the family or to learn to kayak with the help of an outfitter. A day trip on this stretch of the river will take you about 15 mi. Outfitters offer full-, half-, or multiday adventures here.

White-water awaits more adventuresome rafters both upstream and down. Upriver, in narrow, winding Westwater Canyon near the Utah–Colorado border, the Colorado River cuts through the oldest exposed geologic layer on Earth. This section of the river is rocky and considered highly technical for rafters and kayakers. Most outfitters offer this trip as a one- to three-day getaway. A permit is required from the Bureau of Land Management (BLM) in Moab to run Westwater Canyon. Heart-stopping multiday trips through Cataract Canyon are for folks ready for a real adventure.

The West Coast

WHAT'S WHERE

The following numbers refer to chapters in the book.

24 San Diego. San Diego's historic Gaslamp Quarter and Mexican-theme Old Town have a human scale—but it's big-ticket animal attractions like SeaWorld and the San Diego Zoo that pull in planeloads of visitors.

25 Los Angeles. Go for the glitz of the entertainment industry, but stay for the rich cultural attributes and myriad communities of people from different cultures.

26 Yosemite. Yosemite National Park. The views immortalized by photographer Ansel Adams—of towering granite monoliths, verdant glacial valleys, and lofty waterfalls—are still camera-ready.

27 San Francisco. To see why so many have left their hearts here, you need to veer off the beaten path and into the city's neighborhoods—posh Pacific Heights, the Hispanic Mission, and gay-friendly Castro.

28 Napa and Sonoma. Napa and Sonoma counties retain their title as *the* California wine country, by virtue of award-winning vintages, luxe lodgings, and epicurean eats.

29 Portland. With its pedestrian-friendly downtown and super public transit, Portland is easy to explore. The city has become a magnet for fans of artisanal food, beer, and wine, and its leafy parks and miles of bike lanes make it a mecca for outdoors enthusiasts.

30 Seattle. Seattle is a sprawling city shaped by many beautiful bodies of water. On the west is Puget Sound; on the east is massive Lake Washington. The Emerald City sits in the middle, bisected by Highway I–5 and further divvied up by more lakes and canals.

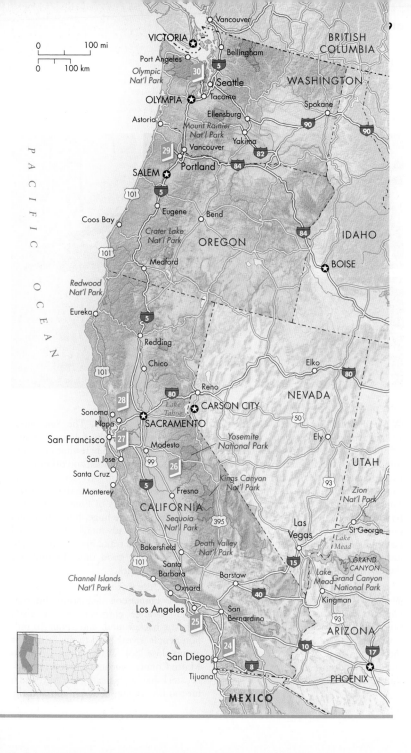

WEST COAST TOP ATTRACTIONS

Pike Place Market, Seattle

(A) The Pacific Northwest abounds with stellar farmers' markets, but creaky, colorful Pike Place Market—the oldest continuously operated public market in the United States—is the mother of them all: More than 250 businesses, including 70 eateries. Breathtaking views of Elliott Bay. A pedestrian-friendly central shopping arcade that buzzes to life each day beginning at 6:30 am. Strumming street musicians. Cobblestones, flying fish, and the very first Starbucks.

Washington Park, Portland

(B) Spend a day at Washington Park where you can absorb recreation and inspiration. Stroll through the International Rose Test Garden, the Japanese Garden, the Oregon Zoo, World Forestry Center and the Children's Museum all within a short distance of each other.

The San Diego Zoo

(C) One word: pandas. The San Diego Zoo has several of the roly-poly crowd pleasers. And yes, they're that cute. But the conservation-minded zoo offers much more, from Elephant Odyssey, the pachyderms' new $45-million habitat, to oh-so-close encounters of lions, tigers, and bears. Explore the huge, hilly attraction by foot, or take advantage of the guided bus tours, aerial tram, and seated shows. Also a roaring good time: Escondido's Wild Animal Park.

Golden Gate Bridge, San Francisco

(D) San Francisco's signature International Orange entryway is the city's majestic background, and about 10 million people a year head to the bridge for an up-close look. Walking the 1.7 mi to Marin County—inches from roaring traffic, steel shaking beneath your feet, and a far-too-low railing between you and the

water 200 feet below—is much more than a superlative photo op (though it's that, too).

Yosemite Falls, Yosemite National Park

(E) Waterfalls in the Yosemite Valley tumble from breathtaking heights, and none is more dramatic than the nearly 2,500 ft. Yosemite Falls. Stand near this mighty triple cascade and the water's roar sounds like a tornado. Don't forget to bring a rainproof jacket!

Grauman's Chinese Theatre and the Walk of Fame, Los Angeles

(F) An iconic metaphor for Hollywood, this elaborate Chinese-theme theater opened in 1927 with the premier of Cecil B. DeMille's *King of Kings*. That's when the tradition of stars imprinting their hands or feet into the cement began with an "accidental" footprint by Norma Talmadge. Among the more unique prints are

the nose of Jimmy Durante and hoofs of Trigger. The Walk of Fame runs a mile along Hollywood Boulevard, with the imprints of more than 1,600 stars.

Schramsberg Winery, Napa Valley

(G) One of the most entertaining tours in Napa is at sparkling wine producer Schramsberg, where a tour of their 19th-century cellars reveals millions of bottles stacked in ceiling-high piles. After you learn about how their bubblies are made using the laborious *méthode champenoise* process, and how their bottles are "riddled" (turned every few days) by hand, you can try generous samples of several during a seated tasting.

TOP EXPERIENCES

Coffeehouse-Crawling in Seattle

Sure, for kicks, it's worth stopping by the original branch of Starbucks, which is across the street from Pike Place Market. But as arguably the nation's coffeehouse capital, Seattle has far more interesting java joints to consider. Especially fertile (coffee) grounds for coffeehouse-hopping include the Capitol Hill, Queen Anne, Ballard, and Fremont neighborhoods—try Vivace, Caffe Vita, Fremont Coffee Company, or Caffe Fiore for stellar espresso.

Hitting the Beach in San Diego

California's coast has a great deal to boast about, but the state's southernmost region stands apart when it comes to sand, surf, and sea. Step onto the beach and smell the fresh salty air, feel the plush sand at your feet, hear waves breaking enticingly from the shore, and see the often breathtaking vistas. San Diego's sandstone bluffs offer spectacular views of the Pacific as a palette of blues and greens: there are distant indigo depths, emerald coves closer to shore, and finally, the mint-green swirls of the foamy surf. On land, the beach is silvery brown, etched with wisps of darker, charcoal-color sand and flecked with fool's gold. San Diego's beaches have a different vibe from their northern counterparts in neighboring Orange County and glitzy Los Angeles farther up the coast. San Diego is more laid-back and relaxed and less of a scene. Cyclists on cruiser bikes whiz by as surfers saunter toward the waves and sunbathers bronze under the sun, be it July or November.

Pedaling in Portland

Portland is probably the most bike-friendly city in the U.S. For many residents it's their sole mode of transportation, and for most it's their favorite form of recreation. Visitors are often astonished by the sheer number of cyclists on the roads and pathways. Bike lanes are well-marked, bike paths meander through parks and along the banks of the Willamette River, and street signs remind motorist to yield to cyclists at most intersections. Educators, advocates, riding groups, businesses, and the city government are working toward making Portland even more bike-friendly and safe. An intended 950-plus mi of bike paths are to be added over the next two decades. Despite the occasionally daunting hills and frequent wintertime rain, cycling is one of the best ways to see what Portland offers. Bike Paths on both the east and west sides of the Willamette River continue south of downtown, and you can easily make a several-mile loop by crossing bridges to get from one side to the other. Portland has more than 300 mi of bike lanes, paths, and boulevards, so get your bike and ride!

Driving the 1

One of the world's (yes world's) most scenic drives, California's State Route 1 (also known as Highway 1, the Pacific Coast Highway, or the PCH) stretches along the edge of the state for nearly 660 mi, from Southern California's Dana Point to its northern terminus near Leggett, about 40 mi north of Fort Bragg. As you travel south to north, the water's edge transitions from long, sandy beaches and low-lying bluffs to towering dunes, craggy cliffs, and ancient redwood groves. The ocean changes as well; the relatively tame and surfable swells lapping the Southern California shore give way to the frigid, powerful waves crashing against weather-beaten rocks in the north. Experience this journey at your own pace, stopping when and where you wish. Hike a beachside trail, dig your toes in the sand, and search for creatures in the tide pools. Buy

some artichokes and strawberries from a roadside farm stand. Talk to people along the way (you'll run into everyone from soul-searching meditators, farmers, and beatniks to city-slackers and working-class folks). Take lots of pictures, and don't rush—you could easily spend a lifetime discovering the secret spots along this route.

Hiking in Yosemite

Yosemite is the place where Nature puts on her grandest displays. The park is home to El Capitan (the world's largest exposed granite monolith, rising 3,593 feet above the glacier-carved valley floor) and Yosemite Falls (North America's tallest cascade). In Yosemite's signature stand of giant sequoias—the Mariposa Grove—even the trees are Bunyanesque. Everything is so astonishingly big and beautiful here that you may feel that unless you've got weeks to hike into the backcountry, you'll barely cover anything by foot. And while it's true that the 740,000-acre park has 800 mi of trails to explore, there are many that offer immediate scenic rewards or even away-from-crowd experiences. But don't take our word for it. Here's what Yosemite Park Ranger Scott Gediman has to say: "I really enjoy hiking in Yosemite; in my opinion there's no better way to see the park. My favorite is the classic hike up the Mist Trail to Vernal Fall. I've done it literally hundreds of times. If you can only take one hike in Yosemite, do this one, especially in spring and summer."

Wine-Tasting in Napa and Sonoma

The tantalizing pop of a cork. Roads unspooling through hypnotically even rows of vines. Sun glinting through a glass of sparkling wine or ruby-color cabernet. If these are your daydreams, you won't be disappointed when you get to Napa and Sonoma. The vineyard-blanketed hills, shady town squares, and ivy-draped wineries really *are* that captivating. Napa and Sonoma are outstanding destinations for both wine newcomers and serious wine buffs. Tasting rooms range from modest to swanky, offering everything from a casual conversation over a few sips of wine to in-depth tours of winemaking facilities and vineyards. And there's a tremendous variety of wines to taste. The one constant is a deep, shared pleasure in the experience of wine tasting. Wineries in Napa and Sonoma range from faux châteaux with vast gift shops to rustic converted barns where you might have to step over the vintner's dog in the doorway. Many are regularly open to the public, usually daily from around 10 to 5. Others require advance reservations to visit, and still others are closed to the public entirely. When in doubt, call ahead.

Riding a Cable Car in San Francisco

Sure locals rarely use the cable cars for commuting these days, so you'll likely be packed in with plenty of fellow sightseers. You may even be approaching cable-car fatigue after seeing its image on so many souvenirs. But if you fear the magic is gone, simply climb on board, and those jaded thoughts will dissolve. Grab the pole and gawk at the view as the car clanks down an insanely steep grade toward the bay. Listen to the humming cable, the clang of the bell, and the occasional quip from the gripman. It's an experience you shouldn't pass up, whether on your first trip or your 50th.

GREAT ITINERARIES

PACIFIC NORTHWEST DRIVING TOUR

North Cascades National Park

DAY 1

Start in ❶**Sedro-Woolley**, where you can pick up information about ❷**North Cascades National Park** at the park headquarters. From Sedro-Woolley it's a 45-minute drive on Route 20 to the park entrance. Take your first stroll through an old-growth forest from the visitor center in Newhalem, then devote the rest of the day to driving through the **Cascades** on Route 20, stopping at various overlooks. Exit the park and continue through the **Methow Valley**. Head south on Route 20, then Route 153, then U.S. 97, then I–82 (just over 300 mi total) to ❸**Yakima** to stay the night.

Mount Rainier National Park

DAYS 2 AND 3

On the morning of Day 2, take U.S. 12 west from Yakima 102 mi to Ohanapecosh, the southern entrance to ❹**Mount Rainier National Park.** When you arrive, take the 31-mi two-hour drive on Sunrise Road, which reveals the "back" (northeast) side of Rainier. A room at the **Paradise Inn** is your base for the next two nights. On Day 3, energetic hikers will want to tackle one of the four- to six-hour trails that lead up among the park's many peaks. Or try one of the ranger-led walks through wildflower meadows. Another option is to hike to Panorama Point near the foot of the **Muir Snowfield** for breathtaking views of the glaciers and high ridges of Rainier overhead. After dinner at the inn, watch the sunset's alpenglow on the peak from the back porch.

THE PLAN

DISTANCE: 1,450 mi

TIME: 10 days

BREAKS: Overnight in Yakima, Mount Rainier National Park, Port Angeles, and Olympic National Park, WA; and Florence, Crater Lake National Park, and Ashland, OR.

Mount St. Helens and the Olympic Foothills

DAY 4

Today, follow Routes 706 and 7 to U.S. 12 from Paradise, heading west to I–5. When you reach the interstate, drive south to Route 504 to spend the day visiting the ❺**Mount St. Helens National Volcanic Monument,** where you can see the destruction caused from the 1980 volcanic eruption. Return to I–5 the way you came in and head north to Olympia, where you should pick up U.S. 101 North. The highway winds through scenic Puget Sound countryside, skirting the Olympic foothills and periodically dipping down to the waterfront. Stop at ❻**Port Angeles,** 136 mi (three hours) from the junction of Route 504 and I–5, to have dinner and spend the night.

Olympic National Park

DAYS 5 AND 6

The next morning, launch into a full day at ❼**Olympic National Park.** Explore the **Hoh Rain Forest** and **Hurricane Ridge** before heading back to Port Angeles for the evening. Start Day 6 with a drive west on U.S. 101 to Forks and on to ❽**La Push** via Route 110, a total of about 45 mi. Here, an hour-long lunchtime stroll to **Second or Third Beach** will offer a taste of the wild Pacific coastline. Back on U.S. 101, head

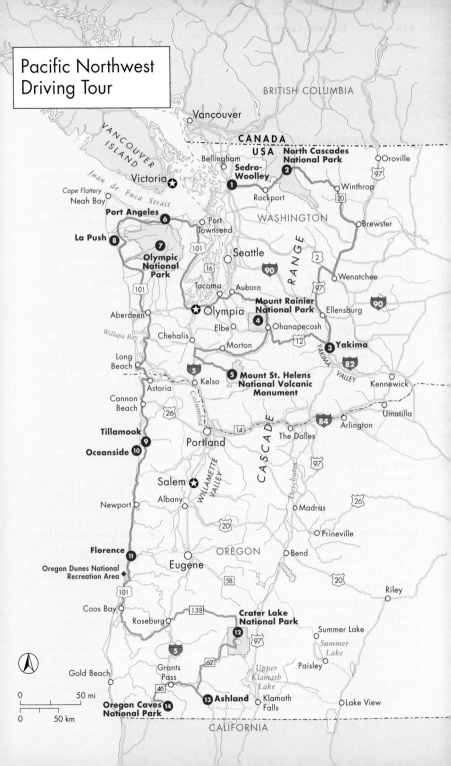

Pacific Northwest Driving Tour

south to **Lake Quinault,** which is about 98 mi from Lake Crescent. Check into the Lake Quinault Lodge, then drive up the river 6 mi to one of the rain-forest trails through the lush Quinault Valley.

The Pacific Coast

DAY 7

Leave Lake Quinault early on Day 7 for the long but scenic drive south on U.S. 101. Here the road winds through coastal spruce forests, periodically rising on headlands to offer Pacific Ocean panoramas. Once you're in Oregon, small seaside resort towns beckon with cafés, shops, and inns. In **9 Tillamook** (famous for its cheese), take a detour onto the Three Capes Loop, a stunning 35-mile byway off U.S. 101. Stop in **10 Oceanside** (on the loop) for lunch. Once you're back on U.S. 101, continue south. Your final stop is the charming village of **11 Florence,** 290 mi (six to eight hours) from Lake Quinault; spend the night.

Crater Lake National Park

DAYS 8 AND 9

From Florence, take U.S. 101 south to Reedsport, Routes 38 and 138 east to Sutherlin, I–5 south to Roseburg, and Route 138 east again to **12 Crater Lake National Park,** 180 mi total. Once inside the park, you can continue along Rim Drive for another half hour for excellent views of the lake. Overnight in the park or in Fort Klamath.

The following morning, take the lake boat tour and a hike through the surrounding forest. In the afternoon, head south on Route 62 to I–5, and on to **13 Ashland,** 83 mi (about two hours) from Crater Lake. Plan to stay the night in one of Ashland's many superb B&Bs. Have dinner and attend one of the **Oregon Shakespeare Festival** productions (mid-February through early November).

> **TIPS**
>
> ■ Pike Place Market and waterfront attractions are open daily all year.
>
> ■ The ride to the top of the Needle is not worth the charge if the day is overcast or rainy.
>
> ■ Remember that Pioneer Square's galleries may not be open on Monday. They do, however, have late hours on the first Thursday of every month.
>
> ■ When leaving the city for an all-day hiking trip, try to time things so that you're not hitting I–5 during evening rush hour. Unless you get a very early start—or don't leave until 9:30 am or 10 am—you probably won't be able to avoid sitting in some morning rush-hour traffic.

Oregon Caves National Monument

DAY 10

On Day 10, head back north on I–5 from Ashland to Grants Pass, then turn south on U.S. 199. At Cave Junction, 67 mi from Ashland, you can take a three-hour side trip to **14 Oregon Caves National Monument.** Guided tours of the unique marble caves last 90 minutes; in the summer the day's final tour is by candlelight, which will give you a sense of what it might have been like for early explorers.

SEATTLE HIGHLIGHTS

Though Seattle's not always the easiest city to navigate, it's small enough that you can see a great deal of it in a week. If you've only got a long weekend here, you can easily mix and match any of the

days in this itinerary. Before you explore, you'll need three things: comfortable walking shoes, layered clothing, and a flexible mind-set: it's easy and advisable to meander off-track.

Day 1: Pike Place Market and Downtown's Major Sights

Spend the first day seeing some of the major sights around Downtown. Get up early and stroll to Pike Place Market. Grab a latte or have a hearty breakfast at a café, then spend the morning wandering through the fish, fruit, flower, and crafts stalls. When you've had your fill, head a bit south to the Seattle Art Museum; take the steps down to the docks and visit the Seattle Aquarium; or stroll to Belltown to take in the views at the Olympic Sculpture Park. Stop for a simple lunch at El Puerco Lloron or Macrina Bakery. If you're not too tired, head to 1st Avenue in Belltown or to Downtown's Nordstrom and environs for some late-afternoon shopping. Have dinner and drinks in either Belltown or Downtown—both have terrific restaurants that will give you a first taste of that famous Pacific Northwest cuisine.

Day 2: Seattle Center or Pioneer Square

Take the two-minute monorail ride from Downtown's Westlake Center to the Seattle Center. Travel up the Space Needle for 360-degree city views. Then take in one of Seattle Center's many ground-level attractions: the Pacific Science Center, the Children's Museum, and the Experience Music Project/Science Fiction Museum. If you didn't visit it the day before, walk southwest down Broad Street to the Olympic Sculpture Park. From there, cab or take the bus to the International District. Visit the Uwajimaya superstore,

stroll the streets, and have dinner in one of the neighborhood's many restaurants.

If you can do without the Space Needle, skip Seattle Center and start your day in Pioneer Square. Tour a few galleries (most of which open late-morning), peek into some shops, and then head to nearby International District for more exploring—don't miss the Wing Luke Asian Museum. If you still want to see the Space Needle, you can go after dinner; the observation deck is open until 11 PM most nights.

Day 3: Stepping Off the Tourist Trail

Since you covered Downtown on Days 1 and 2, today you can sleep in a bit and explore the vastly differing residential neighborhoods. Visit Capitol Hill for great shopping, strolling, café culture, and people-watching. Or head north of the Lake Washington Ship Canal to Fremont and Ballard. Wherever you end up, you can start your day by having a leisurely breakfast or coffee fix at an independent coffee shop. To stretch your legs, make the rounds at Volunteer Park in Capitol Hill or follow the Burke-Gilman Trail from Fremont Center to Gasworks Park. Both the Woodland Park Zoo (slightly north of Fremont) and the Hiram M. Chittenden Locks ("Ballard" Locks) are captivating. In Capitol Hill or in the northern neighborhoods, you'll have no problem rounding out the day by ducking into shops and grabbing a great meal. If you're looking for late-night entertainment, you'll find plenty of nightlife options in both areas, too.

Day 4: Last Rays of Sun and Loose Ends

Spend at least half of your last day in Seattle outdoors exploring Discovery Park or in the University District to rent kayaks from Agua Verde Paddle Club for a trip around Portage Bay or into Lake Washington. Linger in your favorite neighborhood (you'll have one by now). Note that you can combine a park visit with kayaking if you head to the Washington Park Arboretum and Japanese Garden first. From there, it's a quick trip to the U-District.

SAN FRANCISCO SCENES

Work the Wharf

Fisherman's Wharf and the surrounding attractions may be touristy with a capital T, but there are some fun experiences to be had. With your prereserved ticket in hand (do this in advance, since tours frequently sell out), set out for Alcatraz. When the ferry docks back at Pier 33, head north along the waterfront to Pier 39. If you're on a kitschy-souvenir hunt, browse through the pier's overpriced stores. Otherwise, see if you can spot sea lions basking on floating platforms next to the pier. Take a step back in time to early-20th-century San Francisco at delightful Musée Mécanique, then grab an Irish coffee at the Buena Vista.

As tempting as it might be to dine on the water, most Fisherman's Wharf restaurants have less-than-spectacular food (Gary Danko is an exception). A better and cheaper option is to pick up some to-go Dungeness crab from one of the outdoor vendors and eat as you stroll along the waterfront. Or hop the Powell–Hyde or Powell–Mason cable-car line for better dining in Russian Hill and North Beach, respectively.

Golden Gate Park

Golden Gate Park is better than usual on Sunday, when its main arteries are closed to cars (a more limited closure occurs on Saturday from April to September). Start your day at the glorious Conservatory of Flowers (closed Monday). Be sure to take in the scenes ingeniously rendered in flowers out front. Pace the wooden bridges and stone pathways of the Japanese Tea Garden before hitting the San Francisco Botanical Garden at Strybing Arboretum. Next up: the striking, controversial de Young Museum (closed Monday) and the glorious reopened California Academy of Sciences. Make your way west, stopping at Stow Lake, where you can rent a boat and paddle near Strawberry Hill. Back on land, continue west toward Ocean Beach and the endless Pacific. Cap off your tour by kicking back with a pint to enjoy the sunset ocean view at the Beach Chalet.

Take It to the Bridge

Start with a stroll and a search for picnic supplies in the Marina, before heading to the gorgeous Palace of Fine Arts. If you're traveling with kids, be sure to visit the Exploratorium (closed Monday) next door. Don't miss its bizarre-but-cool Tactile Dome.

Continue west into the Presidio and make for Crissy Field, the marshland and sandy beach along the northern shore, for your picnic. With the Golden Gate Bridge view to inspire you, head onto or over the bridge itself. Be sure to wear comfortable shoes; the bridge is 1.7 mi across. Save this for a sunny day—and don't forget your jacket!

Bay Views and Real Estate Envy

Start at terraced Ina Coolbrith Park on Russian Hill for broad vistas of the bay. Ascend the Vallejo Steps and you're within easy reach of many of Russian Hill's hidden lanes. Explore famous Macondray Lane; then head around the corner to Leavenworth Street just north of Union Street and look left for the steps to equally lovely but virtually unknown Havens Place. Continue north to zigzag down crooked Lombard Street. If you still have some stamina, head west to Pacific Heights, where you can check out the Haas-Lilienthal House, a Queen Anne treasure, and scads of other Victorians. Want to snap a picture of that iconic row of "painted ladies" with the city's skyline in the background? You'll need to head to Alamo Square in the Western Addition (Hayes and Steiner streets). Finally, head back to Hyde Street for dinner at one of Russian Hill's trendy eateries.

SAN DIEGO IN A DAY

If you've only got 24 hours to spare, start at **Balboa Park,** the cultural heart of San Diego. Stick to El Prado, the main promenade, where you'll pass by peaceful gardens and soaring Spanish colonial revival architecture (Balboa Park's unforgettable look and feel date to the 1914 Panama-California Exposition). Unless you're a serious museum junkie, pick whichever of the park's many offerings most piques your interest—choices range from photography to folk art. If you're with the family, don't even think of skipping the **San Diego Zoo.** You'll want to spend the better part of your day there, but make an early start of it so you can head for one of San Diego's **beaches** while there's still daylight. Kick back under the late afternoon sun and linger for sunset. Or, wander around **Seaport Village** and the **Embarcadero** before grabbing a bite to eat in the **Gaslamp Quarter,** which pulses with nightlife until last call (around 1:40 am).

PORTLAND IN A DAY

Spend the morning exploring downtown. Visit the Portland Art Museum or the Oregon History Center, stop by the historic First Congregational Church and Pioneer Courthouse Square, and take a stroll along the Park Blocks or Waterfront Park. Eat lunch and do a little shopping along Northwest 23rd Avenue or at Powell's Books in the early afternoon, and be sure to get a look at the beautiful historic homes in Nob Hill. From there, drive up into the northwest hills by the Pittock Mansion, and finish off the afternoon at the Japanese Garden and the International Test Rose Garden in Washington Park. If you still have energy, head across the river for dinner on Hawthorne Boulevard; then drive up to Mt. Tabor Park for Portland's best sunset.

DID YOU KNOW?

Goldfish Point in La Jolla is named after the garibaldi damselfish, which resemble goldfish, found in these waters. The garibaldi is California's official marine fish.

San Diego

WORD OF MOUTH

"[In San Diego] the actual traffic downtown is much less difficult than trying to get to or from downtown from an outlying area. . . . The actual downtown area is quite small. Downtown (or Hillcrest, my favorite) is close to Balboa Park (and its Zoo), to the bay, to the ocean."

—d_claude_bear

WELCOME TO SAN DIEGO

TOP REASONS TO GO

★ **Beautiful beaches:** San Diego's shore shimmers with crystalline Pacific waters rolling up to some of the prettiest stretches of sand on the West Coast.

★ **Good eats:** Taking full advantage of the region's bountiful produce and seafood, San Diego's chefs surprise, dazzle, and delight diners with inventive California-colorful cuisine.

★ **History lessons:** The well-preserved and reconstructed historic sites in California's first European settlement help you imagine what the area was like when explorers first arrived.

★ **Stellar shopping:** Horton Plaza, the Gaslamp Quarter, Seaport Village, Coronado, Old Town, La Jolla . . . no matter where you go in San Diego, you'll find great places to do a little browsing.

★ **Urban oasis:** Balboa Park's 1,200 acres contain most of San Diego's museums and its world-famous zoo.

1 **Balboa Park.** San Diego's cultural heart is where you'll find most of the city's museums and its world-famous zoo.

2 **Downtown.** San Diego's downtown area is delightfully urban and accessible, filled with walkable A-list attractions like the Gaslamp Quarter, Horton Plaza, and the harbor.

3 **Coronado.** Home to the Hotel Del, this islandlike peninsula is a favorite celebrity haunt.

4 **Harbor and Shelter Islands & Point Loma.** Yachts and resorts, fast-food shacks and motels—plus gorgeous views of Coronado and the downtown skyline.

5 **Mission Bay.** Home to 27 mi of shoreline (and SeaWorld), this 4,600 acre aquatic park is San Diego's monument to sports and fitness.

6 **Old Town.** California's first permanent European settlement is now preserved as a state historic park.

7 **La Jolla.** This luxe, bluff-top enclave fittingly means "the jewel" in Spanish. Come here for fantastic upscale shopping and unspoiled stretches of the coast.

La Jolla Beach

Shell Beach

La Jolla Cove

Museum of Contemporary Art

Torrey Pines Rd.

Marine St. Beach

7 **LA JOLLA**

La Jolla Blvd.

Pacific Beach

Mission Blvd.

MISSION BAY

Mission Beach

OCEAN BEACH

Ocean Beach

Sunset Cliffs Blvd.

Catalina Blvd.

P A C I F I C   O C E A N

POINT LOMA

Cabrillo Memorial Dr.

Cabrillo ◆ National Monument

0 — 2 mi

0 — 2 km

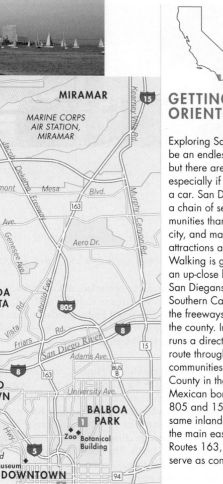

24

GETTING ORIENTED

Exploring San Diego may be an endless adventure, but there are limitations, especially if you don't have a car. San Diego is more a chain of separate communities than a cohesive city, and many of the major attractions are miles apart. Walking is good for getting an up-close look at how San Diegans live, but true Southern Californians use the freeways that crisscross the county. Interstate 5 runs a direct north–south route through the coastal communities from Orange County in the north to the Mexican border. Interstates 805 and 15 do much the same inland. Interstate 8 is the main east–west route. Routes 163, 52, and 94 serve as connectors.

San Diego is a big California city—second only to Los Angeles in population—with a small-town feel. It also covers a lot of territory, roughly 400 square mi of land and sea, stretching from its 70 mi of beaches, inland over a series of mesas and canyons, and ending in the arid Anza-Borrego Desert.

The San Diego area, the birthplace of California, was claimed for Spain by explorer Juan Rodríguez Cabrillo in 1542, and eventually came under Mexican rule. You'll find reminders of San Diego's Spanish and Mexican heritage throughout the region——in architecture and place-names, in distinctive Mexican cuisine, and in the historic buildings of Old Town.

In 1867 developer Alonzo Horton, who called the town's bay front "the prettiest place for a city I ever saw," began building a hotel, a plaza, and prefab homes on 960 downtown acres. The city's fate was sealed in 1908, when President Theodore Roosevelt's Great White Fleet sailed into the bay. The U.S. Navy, impressed by the city's excellent harbor and temperate climate, decided to build a destroyer base on San Diego Bay in the 1920s. The newly developed aircraft industry soon followed (Charles Lindbergh's plane *Spirit of St. Louis* was built here). The military operates many bases and installations throughout the county, which, added together, form the largest military base in the world.

PLANNING

GETTING HERE AND AROUND
AIR TRAVEL
The major airport is San Diego International Airport, called Lindbergh Field locally. Major airlines depart and arrive at Terminal 1 and Terminal 2; commuter flights with a 3000 sequence flight number depart from a third commuter terminal. A red shuttle bus provides free transportation between terminals.

Airport San Diego International Airport (☎ 619/400–2400 ⊕ www.san.org).

Airport Transfers **Access Shuttle** (☏ *619/282–1515* ⊕ *www.accessshuttle.net*).
Cloud 9 Shuttle/SuperShuttle (☏ *800/974–8885* ⊕ *www.cloud9shuttle.com*).

BUS AND TROLLEY TRAVEL

The Greyhound terminal is downtown at Broadway and 1st Avenue, a block from the Civic Center trolley station.

San Diego County is served by a coordinated, efficient network of bus and rail routes that include service to Oceanside in the north, the Mexican border at San Ysidro, and points east to the Anza-Borrego Desert. The bright-red trolleys of the San Diego Trolley light-rail system connect with San Diego Transit bus routes.

Bus and Trolley Contacts San Diego Metropolitan Transit System (MTS)
(☏ *619/238–0100 for bus, 619/595–4949 for trolley* ⊕ *www. sdmts.com*).

CAR TRAVEL

When traveling in the San Diego area it pays to consider the big picture to avoid getting lost. Water lies to the west of the city. To the east and north, mountains separate the urban areas from the desert. Parking is fairly easy, with pay lots and meters available at most sites, and free parking in Balboa Park and at most beaches.

TAXI TRAVEL

Taxi stands are at shopping centers and hotels; otherwise you must call and reserve a cab. If you're going someplace other than downtown, ask whether the company serves that area.

Taxi Companies Orange Cab (☏ *619/223–5555* ⊕ *www.orangecabsandiego. com*). **Silver Cabs** (☏ *619/280–5555* ⊕ *www.sandiegosilvercab.com*). **Yellow Cab** (☏ *619/444–4444* ⊕ *www.driveu.com*).

TRAIN TRAVEL

Amtrak serves downtown San Diego's Santa Fe Depot with daily trains to and from Los Angeles, Santa Barbara, and San Luis Obispo. Connecting service to points beyond is available in Los Angeles.

Coaster commuter trains, which run between Oceanside and San Diego Monday–Saturday, stop at the same stations as Amtrak, plus others.

Information Amtrak (☏ *800/872–7245* ⊕ *www.amtrak.com*). **Coaster** (☏ *760/966–6500* ⊕ *www.gonctd.com*).

VISITOR INFORMATION

City Contacts San Diego Convention & Visitors Bureau International Visitor Information Center (☏ *619/236–1212* ⊕ *www.sandiego.org*). **San Diego Visitor Information Center** (☏ *800/827–9188* ⊕ *www.infosandiego.com*).

San Diego County Contacts Coronado Visitor Center (☏ *619/437–8788* ⊕ *www.coronadovisitorcenter.com*). **Promote La Jolla, Inc.** (☏ *858/454–5718* ⊕ *www.lajollabythesea.com*).

EXPLORING SAN DIEGO

DOWNTOWN

Nearly written off in the 1970s, today downtown San Diego is a testament to conservation and urban renewal. The turnaround began with the revitalization of the Gaslamp Quarter Historic District and massive redevelopment that gave rise to the Horton Plaza shopping center and the San Diego Convention Center, as well as to elegant hotels, upscale condominium complexes, and trendy restaurants and cafés. Like many modern U.S. cities, downtown San Diego's story is as much about its rebirth as its history.

Although many consider downtown to be the 16½-block Gaslamp Quarter, it actually comprises eight neighborhoods, also including East Village, Little Italy, and Embarcadero. Considered the liveliest of the bunch, Gaslamp's 4th and 5th avenues are peppered with trendy nightclubs and chic restaurants. East Village is the city's largest downtown neighborhood, with its urban design of cafés, galleries, and sleek hotels. Sparking the rebirth of this former warehouse district was construction of the San Diego Padres' baseball stadium, PETCO Park. North of Broadway along India Street, the charming neighborhood of Little Italy is filled with lively and authentic cafés, gelato shops, and restaurants. Cutting a scenic swath along the harbor front, the Embarcadero connects today's downtown San Diego to its maritime roots. There are reasonably priced ($4–$7 per day) parking lots along Harbor Drive, Pacific Highway, and lower Broadway and Market Street. Most restaurants offer valet parking at night, but beware of fees of $15 and up.

WHAT TO SEE

Ⓢ **Maritime Museum.** A must for anyone with an interest in nautical history,
Fodor's Choice this collection of restored and replica ships affords a fascinating glimpse
★ of San Diego during its heyday as a commercial seaport. The museum's headquarters are the *Berkeley,* an 1898 ferryboat moored at the foot of Ash Street. The museum features Russian and U.S. submarines, as well as the oldest active iron sailing ship in the world, the *Star of India.* You can take to the water in the museum's other sailing ship, the *Californian,* designated the state's official tall ship. Weekend sails, typically from noon to 4, cost $42. ⊠ *1492 N. Harbor Dr.* ☎ *619/234–9153* ⊕ *www. sdmaritime.org* ⚓ *$14 includes entry to all ships except the Californian* ⊗ *9–8, until 9 pm Memorial Day–Labor Day.*

BALBOA PARK

Overlooking downtown and the Pacific Ocean, 1,200-acre Balboa Park is the cultural heart of San Diego. Ranked as one of the world's best parks by the Project for Public Spaces, it's also where you can find most of the city's museums, art galleries, the Tony Award–winning Old Globe Theatre, and the world-famous San Diego Zoo.

Thanks to the "Mother of Balboa Park," Kate Sessions, who suggested hiring a landscape architect in 1889, gardens both cultivated and wild

The lily pond outside the Botanical Building is a beautiful spot to take a break.

are an integral part of the park, featuring 350 species of trees. What Balboa Park would have looked like had she left it alone can be seen at Florida Canyon—an arid landscape of sagebrush, cactus, and a few small trees.

In addition, the captivating architecture of Balboa's buildings, fountains, and courtyards gives the park an enchanted feel. Historic buildings dating from San Diego's 1915 Panama–California International Exposition are strung along El Prado, which leads from 6th Avenue eastward over the Cabrillo Bridge, the park's official gateway.

East of Plaza de Panama, El Prado becomes a pedestrian mall and ends at a footbridge to the perfectly tended Rose Garden, which has more than 2,000 rosebushes. In the adjacent Desert Garden, trails wind around prickly cacti and soft green succulents from around the world. Palm Canyon, north of the Spreckels Organ Pavilion, has more than 50 varieties of palms along a shady bridge.

A visit here is worth peeling yourself away from the beaches for at least one day, as to overlook Balboa Park would be to miss out on the city's most cherished treasure.

WHAT TO SEE

Fodor's Choice ★ **Botanical Building.** The graceful redwood-lath structure, built for the 1915 Panama-California International Exposition, now houses more than 2,000 types of tropical and subtropical plants, plus changing seasonal flower displays. Ceiling-high tree ferns shade fragile orchids and feathery bamboo. There are benches beside miniature waterfalls for resting in the shade. The rectangular pond outside, filled with lotuses and water lilies that bloom in spring and fall, is popular with

The San Diego Zoo has more giant pandas than any other zoo in the United States.

photographers. ✉ *1550 El Prado, Balboa Park* ☎ *619/239–0512* ✉ *Free* ⊗ *Fri.–Wed. 10–4.*

🌙 ★ **San Diego Air and Space Museum.** This kid-friendly museum is filled with exhibits about aviation and aerospace pioneers, including examples of enemy planes from the world wars. The museum displays a growing number of space-age exhibits, including the actual Apollo 9 command module, and a collection of real and replicated aircraft fills the central courtyard. ✉ *2001 Pan American Plaza, Balboa Park* ☎ *619/234–8291* ⊕ *www.sandiegoairandspace.org* ✉ *$16.50, restoration tour $5 extra* ⊗ *Daily 10–4:30, until 5:30 Memorial Day–Labor Day.*

★ **San Diego Museum of Art.** Known primarily for its baroque and Renaissance paintings, including works by El Greco, Goya, Rubens, and van Ruisdael, San Diego's most comprehensive art museum also has strong holdings of South Asian art, Indian miniatures, and contemporary California paintings. An outdoor Sculpture Court and Garden exhibits both traditional and modern pieces. Free docent tours are offered throughout the day. ✉ *1450 El Prado, Balboa Park* ☎ *619/232–7931* ⊕ *www.sdmart.org* ✉ *$12* ⊗ *Tues.-Sat. 10–5, Sun. noon–5; Memorial Day–Labor Day until 9 Thurs.*

🌙 Fodor'sChoice ★ **San Diego Zoo.** Balboa Park's—and perhaps the city's—most famous attraction is its 100-acre zoo. Nearly 4,000 animals of some 800 diverse species roam in hospitable, expertly crafted habitats that replicate natural environments as closely as possible. Exploring the zoo fully requires the stamina of a healthy hiker, but open-air double-decker buses zip through three-quarters of the exhibits on a guided tour. The Skyfari Aerial Tram gives a good overview of the zoo's layout, and on clear days, panoramic views to the ocean. The zoo is at its best when you wander its paths, such as the mist-shrouded trails of **Tiger River,** the zoo's simulated Asian rain forest. Popular exhibits include the **Polar Bear Plunge,** where you can watch the featured animals take a chilly dive, and **Absolutely Apes,** where orangutans and siamangs climb, swing, and generally live almost as they would in the wild.

The San Diego Zoo houses the largest number of koalas outside Australia, and its walk-through **Koala Exhibit** gets you up close with these cute creatures. The zoo's star attraction remains the pandas, and especially the baby pandas, at the **Giant Panda Research Station,** the largest collection at any zoo in the U.S.

For more animal adventures, head to the San Diego Wild Animal Park, the zoo's 1,800-acre extension to the north at Escondido. ⊠ *2920 Zoo Dr., Balboa Park* ☎ *619/234–3153, 888/697–2632 Giant panda hotline* ⊕ *www.sandiegozoo.org* ✉ *$37 adult, $27 children (3–11) includes Skyfari and bus tour; 2-Visit Pass ($70 adult, $50 children age 3–11) grants 1 entry each to San Diego Zoo and San Diego Wild Animal Park or 2 entries to one park, within 1 year of purchase; zoo parking free* ▭ *AE, D, MC, V* ☺ *July–Sept., daily 9–9; Oct.–June, daily 9–dusk (hrs may extend during special events or holiday periods; call for more info); Children's Zoo and Skyfari ride generally close 1 hr earlier.*

★ **Spreckels Organ Pavilion.** The 2,400-bench-seat pavilion, dedicated in 1915 by sugar magnates John D. and Adolph B. Spreckels, holds the 4,518-pipe Spreckels Organ, the largest outdoor pipe organ in the world. You can hear this impressive instrument at one of the year-round, free, 2 pm Sunday concerts—a highlight of a visit to Balboa Park. On Monday evenings from mid-June to August, internationally renowned organists play evening concerts. ⊠ *2211 Pan American Rd., Balboa Park* ☎ *619/702–8138* ⊕ *www.sosorgan.com.*

CORONADO

Although it's actually an isthmus, easily reached from the mainland if you head north from Imperial Beach, Coronado has always seemed like an island, and is often referred to as such. As if freeze-framed in the 1950s, Coronado's quaint appeal is captured in its old-fashioned storefronts and well-manicured gardens. The streets of Coronado are wide, quiet, and friendly, and many of today's residents live in grand Victorian residences handed down for generations. Coronado's long relationship with the U.S. Navy and its desirable real estate have made it an enclave for military personnel; it's said to have more retired admirals per capita than anywhere else in the United States.

Coronado is accessible via the arching blue 2.2-mi-long San Diego–Coronado Bay Bridge, and the view of the harbor, downtown, and the island is breathtaking, day and night.

Alternatively, you can board the Coronado Ferry, operated by **San Diego Harbor Excursion** (☎ *619/234–4111, 800/442–7847 in CA* ⊕ *www.sdhe. com*), at the Broadway Pier on the Embarcadero in downtown San Diego; you'll arrive at the Ferry Landing Marketplace in Coronado.

Boats depart every hour on the hour from the Embarcadero and every hour on the half hour from Coronado; the fare is $3.75 each way.

WHAT TO SEE

Fodor's Choice
★

Hotel Del Coronado. One of San Diego's best-known sites, the hotel opened in 1888 and has been a National Historic Landmark since 1977. It has a colorful history, integrally connected with that of Coronado itself, making it worth a visit even if you don't stay here.

The Del's distinctive red-tile roofs and Victorian gingerbread architecture have served as a set for many movies, political meetings, and extravagant social happenings. It's speculated that the Duke of Windsor may have first met Wallis Simpson here, and the film *Some Like It Hot*—starring Marilyn Monroe, Jack Lemmon, and Tony Curtis—used the hotel as a backdrop. Tours of the Del are available Tuesday at 10:30 and Friday–Sunday at 2 for $15 per person. Reservations are required through the Coronado Visitor Center (☎ 619/437–8788). ⊠ *1500 Orange Ave.* ☎ *619/435–6611* ⊕ *www.hoteldel.com.*

HARBOR AND SHELTER ISLANDS AND POINT LOMA

The populated outcroppings that jut into the bay just west of downtown and the airport demonstrate the potential of human collaboration with nature. Point Loma, Mother Nature's contribution to San Diego's attractions, has always protected the center city from the Pacific's tides and waves. It's shared by military installations, funky motels and fast-food shacks, stately family homes, and private marinas packed with sailboats and yachts. Newer to the scene, Harbor and Shelter islands are landfill. Created out of sand dredged from the San Diego Bay in the second half of the past century, they've become tourist hubs—their high-rise hotels, seafood restaurants, and boat-rental centers looking as solid as those anywhere else in the city.

WHAT TO SEE

ⓒ
Fodor's Choice
★

Cabrillo National Monument. This 160-acre preserve marks the site of the first European visit to San Diego, made by 16th-century explorer Juan Rodríguez Cabrillo. Today the site, with its rugged cliffs and outstanding overlooks, is one of the most frequently visited of all the national monuments.

The **visitor center** presents films and lectures about Cabrillo's voyage, the sea-level tide pools, and migrating gray whales. **Interpretive stations** have been installed along the walkways that edge the cliffs. The moderately steep **Bayside Trail,** 2½-mi round-trip, winds through coastal sage scrub, curving under the cliff-top lookouts to the bay-front scenery. The climb back leads up to the **Old Point Loma Lighthouse.**

The western and southern cliffs are prime whale-watching territory. A sheltered **viewing station** has high-powered telescopes that help you focus on the whales' water spouts. More accessible sea creatures can be seen in the **tide pools** at the foot of the monument's western cliffs. ⊠ *1800 Cabrillo Memorial Dr., Point Loma* ☎ *619/557–5450* ⊕ *www.nps.gov/cabr* 🖰 *$5 per car, $3 per person entering on foot or by bicycle* ☉ *Park daily 9–5.*

MISSION BAY AND SEAWORLD

Mission Bay Park is San Diego's monument to sports and fitness. This 4,600-acre aquatic park has 27 mi of shoreline including 19 of sandy beach. Playgrounds and picnic areas abound on the beach and low grassy hills of the park. On weekday evenings joggers, bikers, and skaters take over. In the daytime, swimmers, water-skiers, anglers, and boaters—some in single-person kayaks, others in crowded powerboats—vie for space in the water. One Mission Bay caveat: swimmers should note signs warning about water pollution; on occasions when heavy rains or other events cause pollution, swimming is dangerous.

WHAT TO SEE

SeaWorld San Diego. One of the world's largest marine-life amusement parks, SeaWorld is spread over 189 tropically landscaped bayfront acres—and it seems to be expanding into every available square inch of space with new exhibits, shows, and activities. The majority of SeaWorld's exhibits are walk-through marine environments. Kids get a particular kick out of the **Shark Encounter,** a 57-foot clear acrylic tube that passes through the 280,000-gallon shark habitat. The hands-on **California Tide Pool** exhibit gives you a chance to get to know San Diego's indigenous marine life, while at **Forbidden Reef** you can feed bat rays and go nose-to-nose with creepy moray eels. SeaWorld's highlights are its large-arena entertainments. Starring Shamu the Killer Whale, **Believe** features synchronized whales and brings down the house. **Blue Horizons** brings dolphins, pilot whales, tropical birds, and aerialists together in a spectacular performance.

SeaWorld San Diego also offers two adventure rides, passengers on **Shipwreck Rapids** careen down a river in a raftlike inner tube, while **Journey To Atlantis** involves a heart-stopping 60-foot plunge to explore a lost, sunken city. ⊠ *500 SeaWorld Dr., near west end of I–8, Mission Bay* ☎ *800/257–4268* ⊕ *www.seaworld.com* ⊠ *$69 adults, $59 kids; parking $12 cars; 1-hr behind-the-scenes walking tours $13 extra* ⊟ *AE, D, MC, V* ☉ *Daily 10–dusk; extended hrs in summer.*

Fodor's Choice

24

OLD TOWN

San Diego's Spanish and Mexican roots are most evident in Old Town, the area north of downtown at Juan Street that was the site of the first European settlement in Southern California. Although Old Town was largely a 19th-century phenomenon, the pueblo's true beginnings were much earlier and on a hill overlooking it, where soldiers from New Spain established a military outpost in May 1769. Two months later Father Junípero Serra established the first of the California's missions, San Diego de Alcalá.

On San Diego Avenue, the district's main drag, art galleries and expensive gift shops are interspersed with tacky curio shops, restaurants, and open-air stands selling inexpensive Mexican pottery, jewelry, and blankets.

WHAT TO SEE

☺ **Old Town San Diego State Historic Park.** The six square blocks on the site
Fodor'sChoice of San Diego's original pueblo are the heart of Old Town. Most of the
★ 20 historic buildings preserved or re-created by the park cluster around
Old Town Plaza, a pleasant place to rest and watch passersby. The
noncommercial houses are open daily 10–5; none charges admission.
Free tours depart daily from the Robinson-Rose House at 11 and 2.

The **Robinson-Rose House** (☎ *619/220–5422*), on Wallace Street facing
Old Town Plaza, was the original commercial center of Old San Diego.
Built in 1853, it has been reconstructed and now serves as the park's
visitor center.

The **Casa de Estudillo** (⊠ *4001 Mason St., Old Town*), the largest and
most elaborate of the original adobe homes, was built on Mason Street
in 1827. The **San Diego Union Museum** (⊠ *Twigg St. and San Diego Ave.,
Old Town*) is in a New England–style, wood-frame house restored to
replicate the newspaper's offices of 1868.

Also worth exploring in the plaza area are the free **Cosmopolitan Hotel,
Seeley Stable, Wells Fargo History Museum, and the First San Diego
Courthouse.** Ask at the visitor center for locations.

LA JOLLA

La Jollans have long considered their village to be the Monte Carlo
of California. Its coastline curves into natural coves backed by verdant hillsides dotted with homes worth millions. Although La Jolla
is a neighborhood of the city of San Diego, it has its own postal code
and a coveted sense of class; the ultrarich from around the globe own
second homes here—the seaside zone between the neighborhood's bustling downtown and the cliffs above the Pacific has a distinctly European flavor—and old-monied residents maintain friendships with the
visiting film stars and royalty who frequent the area's exclusive luxury
hotels and private clubs. The town has a cosmopolitan air that makes
it a popular vacation resort.

Prospect Street and Girard Avenue, the village's main drags, are lined
with expensive shops and office buildings. Through the years the
shopping and dining district has spread to Pearl and other side streets.
Although there is metered parking on the streets, parking is otherwise
hard to find.

WHAT TO SEE

☺ **La Jolla Cove.** This shimmering blue inlet is what first attracted everyone
Fodor'sChoice to La Jolla, from Native Americans to the glitterati; it's the secret to
★ the village's enduring cachet. You'll find the cove beyond where Girard
Avenue dead-ends into Coast Boulevard, marked by towering palms
that line a promenade where people strolling in designer clothes are as
common as Frisbee throwers.

An underwater preserve at the north end of La Jolla Cove makes the
adjoining beach the most popular one in the area. The **Children's Pool,**
at the south end of the park, has a curving beach protected by a seawall from strong currents and waves. Since the pool and its beach have

become home to an ever-growing colony of Harbor seals, it cannot be used by swimmers. It is, however, the best place on the coast to view these engaging creatures. ⊹ *From Torrey Pines Road, turn right on Prospect, then right on Coast Blvd. The park is at bottom of hill* ☎ *619/235–1169* ⊕ *www.sandiego.gov/lifeguards/beaches/cove.shtml.*

FodorśChoice ★ **Museum of Contemporary Art, San Diego.** California artists figure prominently in the museum's permanent collection of post-1950s art, but the museum also includes examples of every major art movement since that time. Important pieces by artists from San Diego and Tijuana were acquired in the 1990s. The museum also gets major visiting shows. A second branch of the museum is located downtown in the old baggage building of the historic Santa Fe Depot, and features rotating large-scale installations that take advantage of the open and flexible gallery space. Museum admission is good for seven days at both locations. Free exhibit tours are offered weekends at 2. ⊠ *700 Prospect St.* ☎ *858/454–3541* ⊕ *www.mcasd.org* 🖂 *$10, free 3rd Thurs. of month 5–7* ☉ *Thurs.–Tues. 11–5, closed Wed.*

FodorśChoice ★ **Torrey Pines State Natural Reserve.** *Pinus torreyana,* the rarest native pine tree in the United States, enjoys a 1,700-acre sanctuary at the northern edge of La Jolla. About 6,000 of these unusual trees, some as tall as 60 feet, grow on the cliffs here. The reserve has several hiking trails leading to the cliffs, 300 feet above the ocean; trail maps are available at the park station. Cool down after your hike at Torrey Pines State Beach, just below the reserve. ⊠ *N. Torrey Pines Rd.* ⊹ *Exit off I–5 onto Carmel Valley Rd. going west, then turn left (south) on Old Hwy. 101* ☎ *858/755–8219* 🖂 *Parking $10* ☉ *Daily 8–dusk.*

WHERE TO EAT

San Diego's unbeatable weather combined with gorgeous ocean views and the abundance of locally grown produce make it a satisfying place to be a chef or a diner. Although most of the top restaurants offer seasonal California cuisine, San Diego also boasts excellent examples of ethnic cuisines available at all prices. Local specialties include fish tacos and spiny lobster. Meal prices in San Diego have caught up with those of other major metropolitan areas. Reservations are always a good idea; we mention them only when they're essential or not accepted.

WHAT IT COSTS					
	¢	$	$$	$$$	$$$$
Restaurants	under $10	$10–$18	$19–$27	$28–$35	over $35

Dining prices are for a main course at dinner, excluding 8.75% tax.

CORONADO

$$$$ AMERICAN ✕ **1500 Ocean.** The fine-dining restaurant at Hotel Del Coronado offers a memorable evening that showcases the best organic and naturally raised ingredients the region has to offer. Chef Brian Sinnott presents sublimely subtle dishes such as chilled king crab with compressed Asian

pear salad; wild prawns with kale, smoked bacon, and shelled beans; and Kurobuta pork tenderloin with creamy polenta. The interior, at once inviting and elegant, evokes a posh cabana, while the terrace offers ocean views. An excellent international wine list and equally clever desserts and artisanal cheeses complete the experience. ⊠ *Hotel Del Coronado, 1500 Orange Ave.* ☎ *619/522–8490* ⊟ *AE, D, DC, MC, V* ⊘ *No lunch. Closed Sun. and Mon.*

DOWNTOWN

$

FRENCH

Fodor'sChoice

★

✕ **Café Chloe.** The intersection of 9th and G is now the meeting point for San Diego's café society, thanks to the superchic and friendly Café Chloe. This pretty Parisian spot is frequented by the area's residents for breakfast, lunch, and dinner. Start the day with whole-wheat pancakes and sour-cherry sauce; lunch on smoked trout and apple salad or a casserole of macaroni, pancetta, and Gorgonzola; or enjoy chicken vol-au-vent or steak frites for dinner. Enjoy wines by the glass, imported teas, and coffee with desserts like lemon-curd tartlets or chocolate pot de crème. ⊠ *721 9th Ave., East Village* ☎ *619/232–3242* ⊟ *AE, MC, V.*

$$$$

MEXICAN

✕ **Candelas.** The scents and flavors of imaginative Mexican cuisine with a European flair permeate this handsome, romantic restaurant and nightspot. Candles glow everywhere around the small, comfortable dining room. There isn't a burrito or taco in sight. Fine openers such as cream of black bean soup, and salad of watercress with bacon and pistachios warm diners up for local lobster stuffed with mushrooms, jalapeño peppers, and aged tequila; or tequila-flamed jumbo prawns over creamy, seasoned goat cheese. The adjacent bar pours many elegant tequilas, offers entertainment, and has become a popular, often jam-packed nightspot. They also serve a Mexican-style breakfast on weekends. ⊠ *416 3rd Ave., Gaslamp Quarter* ☎ *619/702–4455* ⊟ *AE, D, DC, MC, V* ⊠❘ *Breakfast weekends only 8:30–2.*

LA JOLLA

$$$$

AMERICAN

Fodor'sChoice

★

✕ **George's California Modern.** Formerly George's at the Cove, an extensive makeover brought a new name and sleek updated look to this eternally popular restaurant overlooking La Jolla Cove. Hollywood types and other visiting celebrities can be spotted in the sleek main dining room with its wall of windows. Simpler, more casual preparations of fresh seafood, beef, and lamb reign on the new menu chef Trey Foshee enlivened with seasonal produce from local specialty growers. Give special consideration to succulent roasted chicken with escarole, local swordfish with prosciutto-wrapped gnocchi, and cider-glazed Niman Ranch pork chops. For less expensive dining and a sweeping view of the coast, try the rooftop Ocean Terrace. ⊠ *1250 Prospect St.* ☎ *858/454–4244* ♨ *Reservations essential* ⊟ *AE, D, DC, MC, V* ⊘ *No lunch in main restaurant, only Ocean Terrace.*

$$$

AMERICAN

Fodor'sChoice

★

✕ **Nine-Ten.** In the sleekly contemporary dining room of the elegant Grande Colonial Hotel, acclaimed Chef Jason Knibb serves satisfying seasonal fare at breakfast, lunch, and dinner. At night the perfectly executed menu may include tantalizing appetizers like lobster risotto or Maine scallops with cauliflower custard. The kitchen's creative flair comes through with dishes such as jerk pork belly with habeñero gelée, and *sous vide* salmon in an orange–olive oil emulsion. Delicious desserts include rosewater panna cotta with lychee-raspberry sorbet. ⊠ *910 Prospect St.* ☎ *858/964–5400* ═ *AE, D, DC, MC, V* ☾ *No dinner Sun. or Mon.*

WHERE TO STAY

Many hotels promote discounted weekend packages to fill rooms after convention and business customers leave town. Since the weather is great year-round, don't expect substantial discounts in winter. If an ocean view is important, request it when booking, but be aware that it will cost significantly more.

Hotel reviews have been condensed for this book. Please go to Fodors. com for full reviews of each property.

24

WHAT IT COSTS				
	¢	$	$$	$$$	$$$$
Hotels	under $100	$100–$199	$200–$299	$300–$400	over $400

Lodging prices are for a standard double room in high (summer) season, excluding 10.5% tax.

CORONADO

$$$

☺

Fodor'sChoice

★

Hotel Del Coronado. The Victorian-style "Hotel Del," situated along 28 oceanfront acres, is as much of a draw today as it was when it opened in 1888. The resort is always alive with activity, as guests and tourists marvel at the fanciful architecture and gorgeous ocean views. **Pros:** romantic; on the beach; hotel spa. **Cons:** some rooms are small; expensive dining; public areas are very busy. ⊠ *1500 Orange Ave.* ☎ *800/468–3533 or 619/435–6611* ⊕ *www.hoteldel.com* ↵ *757 rooms, 65 suites, 43 villas, 35 cottages* ⚅ *In-room: a/c, safe, Wi-Fi. In-hotel: 5 restaurants, room service, bars, pools, gym, spa, beachfront, water sports, bicycles, children's programs (ages 4–17), Internet terminal, laundry service, parking (paid)* ═ *AE, D, DC, MC, V.*

DOWNTOWN

$

Gaslamp Plaza Suites. On the National Register of Historic Places, this 10-story structure a block from Horton Plaza was built in 1913 as one of San Diego's first "skyscrapers." The public areas have old marble, brass, and mosaics. **Pros:** historic building; good location; well priced. **Cons:** books up early; smallish rooms. ⊠ *520 E St., Gaslamp Quarter* ☎ *619/232–9500 or 800/874–8770* ⊕ *www.gaslampplaza.com* ↵ *12 rooms, 52 suites* ⚅ *In-room: a/c, refrigerator, DVD, Wi-Fi. In-hotel: bar, laundry service, parking (paid)* ═ *AE, D, DC, MC, V* ◖ *CP.*

$$$

Fodor'sChoice

★

Hotel Solamar. For its first entry onto San Diego's hotel scene, the Kimpton boutique hotel chain renovated an old warehouse, hitting the right notes with striking high style. **Pros:** great restaurant; attentive service; upscale rooms. **Cons:** busy valet parking; bars are crowded on weekends. ⊠ *435 6th Ave., Gaslamp Quarter* ☎ *619/531–8740 or 877/230–0300* ⊕ *www.hotelsolamar.com* ↵ *217 rooms, 16 suites*

The Hotel Del Coronado is a classic old resort with fanciful architecture and gorgeous ocean views.

⌂ *In-room: a/c, safe, Wi-Fi. In-hotel: 2 restaurants, room service, bars, pools, gym, laundry service, Wi-Fi hotspot, parking (paid), some pets allowed* ▭ *AE, D, DC, MC, V.*

OLD TOWN AND VICINITY

$ 🖥 **Holiday Inn Express–Old Town.** Already an excellent value for Old Town, this cheerful property throws in such perks as a free breakfast buffet. Rooms have a European feel; a $1 million renovation in 2007 added new carpet, linens, and bathroom granite and fixtures. **Pros:** good location; hot continental breakfast. **Cons:** smallish rooms; few nightlife options. ✉ *3900 Old Town Ave.* ☎ *619/299–7400 or 800/465–4329* ⊕ *www.hioldtownhotel.com* ↘ *125 rooms, 2 suites* ⌂ *In-room: a/c, refrigerator, Internet. In-hotel: pool, laundry facilities, laundry service, Wi-Fi hotspot, parking (paid)* ▭ *AE, D, DC, MC, V* ⊺⊙⫯ *CP.*

LA JOLLA

$$$ 🖥 **Grande Colonial.** This white wedding cake–style hotel has ocean views
Fodor'sChoice and is in the heart of La Jolla village. **Pros:** near shopping; near beach;
★ superb restaurant. **Cons:** somewhat busy street. ✉ *910 Prospect St.* ☎ *858/454–2181 or 888/530–5766* ⊕ *www.thegrandecolonial.com* ↘ *52 rooms, 41 suites* ⌂ *In-room: a/c, safe, kitchen (some), Wi-Fi. In-hotel: restaurant, room service, bar, pool, laundry service, parking (paid)* ▭ *AE, D, DC, MC, V.*

$$$$ 🖥 **Lodge at Torrey Pines.** This beautiful Craftsman-style lodge sits on a
Fodor'sChoice bluff between La Jolla and Del Mar, and commands a coastal view.
★ The warm and understated rooms are spacious and furnished with antiques and reproduction turn-of-the-20th-century pieces. **Pros:** upscale rooms; good service; near golf. **Cons:** not centrally located;

expensive. ✉ *11480 N. Torrey Pines Rd.* ☎ *858/453–4420 or 800/995–4507* ⊕ *www.lodgetorreypines.com* ⤵ *164 rooms, 6 suites* ⚐ *In-room: a/c, safe, kitchen (some), Internet, Wi-Fi. In-hotel: 2 restaurants, bars, golf course, pool, gym, spa, Wi-Fi hotspot, laundry service, parking (paid)* ☰ *AE, D, DC, MC, V.*

MISSION BAY AND THE BEACHES

$$$

Fodor's Choice
★

Catamaran Resort Hotel. Exotic macaw parrots perch in the lush lobby of this appealing hotel on Mission Bay. Tiki torches light the way through grounds thick with tropical foliage to the six two-story buildings and the 14-story high-rise. **Pros:** recently upgraded rooms; spa; free cruises. **Cons:** not centrally located. ✉ *3999 Mission Blvd., Mission Beach* ☎ *858/488–1081 or 800/422–8386* ⊕ *www.catamaranresort. com* ⤵ *311 rooms, 50 suites* ⚐ *In-room: a/c, safe, kitchen (some), refrigerator (some), Internet, Wi-Fi. In-hotel: restaurant, room service, bar, pool, gym, spa, beachfront, bicycles, parking (paid)* ☰ *AE, D, DC, MC, V.*

$$

The Dana on Mission Bay. There's a modern chic feel to the earth-toned lobby of this beach hotel, making it feel you've arrived somewhere much more expensive. The resort's rooms all have sofa sleepers—great for families—and bay views. **Pros:** free parking; water views; two pools. **Cons:** slightly confusing layout; not centrally located. ✉ *1710 W. Mission Bay Dr., Mission Bay* ☎ *619/222–6440 or 800/445–3339* ⊕ *www. thedana.net* ⤵ *259 rooms, 12 suites* ⚐ *In-room: a/c, refrigerator, Wi-Fi. In-hotel: 2 restaurants, room service, bar, pools, bicycles, laundry service, Wi-Fi hotspot, parking (paid)* ☰ *AE, D, DC, MC, V.*

24

BEACHES

Water temperatures are generally chilly, ranging from 55°F to 65°F from October through June, and 65°F to 73°F from July through September. For a surf and weather report, call ☎ *619/221–8824.* Lifeguards are stationed at city beaches in the summertime, but coverage in winter is provided by roving patrols only. Smoking and alcoholic beverages are completely banned on city beaches. Fires are allowed only in fire rings or elevated barbecue grills. Finding a parking spot near the ocean can be hard in summer, but unmetered parking is at all San Diego city beaches. *Beaches are listed geographically, south to north.*

CORONADO

Coronado Beach. With the famous Hotel Del Coronado as a backdrop, ★ this stretch of sandy beach is one of San Diego County's largest and most picturesque. It's perfect for sunbathing, people-watching, or Frisbee. Exercisers include Navy SEAL teams, as well as the occasional Marine Recon unit, who do training runs on the beaches in and around Coronado. Parking can be difficult on the busiest days. There are plenty of restrooms and service facilities, as well as fire rings on the north end. ⊹ *From San Diego-Coronado bridge, turn left on Orange Ave. and follow signs, Coronado.*

MISSION BAY AND BEACHES

Mission Beach. San Diego's most popular beach draws huge crowds on hot summer days, but it's lively year-round. The 2-mi-long stretch extends from the north entrance of Mission Bay to Pacific Beach. A wide boardwalk paralleling the beach is popular with walkers, joggers, roller-skaters, bladers, and bicyclists. Surfers, swimmers, and volleyball players congregate at the south end. Toward its north end, near the Belmont Park roller coaster, the beach narrows and the water becomes rougher. For parking, you can try for a spot on the street, but your best bets are the two big lots at Belmont Park. ✦ *Exit I–5 at Grand Ave. and head west to Mission Blvd. Turn south and look for parking near roller coaster at West Mission Bay Dr., Mission Bay.*

LA JOLLA

Fodor's Choice

La Jolla Cove. This is one of the prettiest spots on the West Coast. A palm-lined park sits on top of cliffs formed by the incessant pounding of the waves. At low tide the tide pools and cliff caves are a destination for explorers. Divers, snorkelers, and kayakers can discover the underwater delights of the San Diego–La Jolla Underwater Park Ecological Reserve. ✦ *Follow Coast Blvd. north to signs, or take La Jolla Village Dr. exit from I–5, head west to Torrey Pines Rd., turn left, and drive downhill to Girard Ave. Turn right and follow signs, La Jolla.*

La Jolla Shores. This is one of San Diego's most popular beaches, with an incredible view of La Jolla peninsula, a wide sandy beach, an adjoining grassy park, and the gentlest waves in San Diego. In fact, several surf schools teach here and kayak rentals are nearby. A concrete boardwalk parallels the beach. Arrive early to get a parking spot in the lot at the foot of Calle Frescota. ✉ *8200 Camino del Oro* ✦ *From I–5 take La Jolla Village Dr. west and turn left onto La Jolla Shores Dr. Head west to Camino del Oro or Vallecitos St. Turn right, La Jolla.*

DEL MAR

Torrey Pines State Beach. One of San Diego's best beaches encompasses 2,000 acres of bluffs and bird-filled marshes. A network of meandering trails leads to the sandy shoreline below. The large parking lot is rarely full; there are bathrooms, showers, and lifeguards on patrol. Guided tours of the nature preserve here are offered on weekends. ✦ *Take Carmel Valley Rd. exit west from I–5, turn left on Rte. S21, Del Mar* ☎ *858/755–2063* ⊕ *www.torreypine.org* ⌷ *Parking $10.*

Los Angeles

WORD OF MOUTH

"One great thing about my trip to L.A. was all of the free guided tours I was able to take (El Pueblo de Los Angeles, Walt Disney Concert Hall, Central Library). There are so many great places to visit without spending a dime."

—yk

WELCOME TO LOS ANGELES

TOP REASONS TO GO

★ **Hollywood magic:** A massive chunk of the world's entertainment is developed, written, filmed, edited, distributed, and sold here; you'll hear people discussing "The Industry" wherever you go.

★ **The beach:** Getting some sand on the floor of your car is practically a requirement here, and the beach is an integral part of the SoCal lifestyle.

★ **Chic shopping:** From Beverly Hills' Rodeo Drive and Downtown's Fashion District to the funky boutiques of Los Feliz, Silver Lake, and Echo Park, L.A. is a shopper's paradise.

★ **Trendy restaurants:** Celebrity is big business here, so it's no accident that the concept of the celebrity chef is a key part of the city's dining scene.

★ **People-watching:** Celeb-spotting in Beverly Hills, trying to get past the velvet rope at hip clubs, hanging out on the Venice Boardwalk . . . there's always something (or someone) interesting to see.

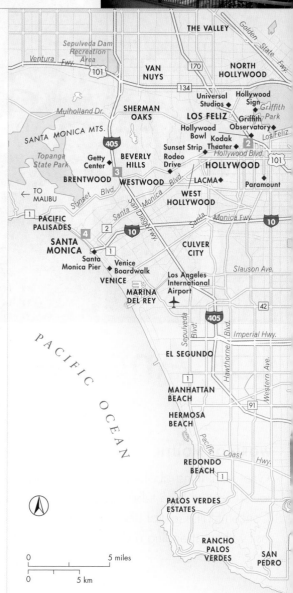

1 **Downtown Los Angeles.** Spectacular modern architecture, ethnic neighborhoods, and some of the city's key cultural institutions characterize this area.

2 **Hollywood and the Studios.** Glitzy and tarnished, good and bad, fun and sad—Hollywood is just like the entertainment business itself. There's the Walk of Fame, Grauman's Chinese Theatre, as well as the studios.

3 **The Westside and Beverly Hills.** Go for the extravagance, glitz, and glamour, but don't forget the Westside's cultural attractions—especially the dazzling Getty Center. West Hollywood's an area for urban indulgences—shopping, restaurants, nightspots—rather than sightseeing.

4 **Santa Monica, Venice, and Malibu.** These desirable beach communities move from ultrarich, ultracasual Malibu to Venice with its raffish mix of artists, beach punks, and yuppies, to liberal, Mediterranean-style Santa Monica in the middle.

5 **Pasadena and Environs.** Pasadena is a quiet area with outstanding Arts and Crafts homes, good dining, and a pair of exceptional museums.

GETTING ORIENTED

Looking at a map of sprawling Los Angeles, first-time visitors are sometimes overwhelmed. Where to begin? What to see first? And what about all those freeways? Here's some advice: Relax. Begin by setting your priorities—movie and television buffs should first head to Hollywood, Universal Studios, and a taping of a television show. Beach lovers and nature types might start out in Santa Monica or Venice or Malibu, or spend an afternoon in Griffith Park, one of the largest city parks in the country. Culture vultures should make a beeline for the twin Gettys (the center in Brentwood and the villa near Malibu), the Los Angeles County Museum of Art (LACMA), or the Norton Simon Museum. And urban explorers might begin with Downtown Los Angeles.

25

Los Angeles is as much a fantasy as it is a physical city. It's a mecca for face-lifts, film noir, shopping starlets, beach bodies, and mind-numbing traffic.

Contrary to popular myth, however, that doesn't mean you have to spend all your time in a car. In fact, getting out of your car is the only way to really get to know Los Angeles. You can tour on foot through the various entertainment-industry-centered, financial, beachfront, wealthy, and fringe neighborhoods and mini-cities that make up the vast L.A. area. But remember, no single locale—whether it's Malibu, Downtown, Beverly Hills, or Burbank—fully embodies Los Angeles. It's in the mix that you'll discover the city's character.

PLANNING

WHEN TO GO

Almost any time of the year is the right time to go to Los Angeles; the climate is mild and pleasant year-round. Winter brings crisp, sunny, unusually smogless days from about November to May (expect brief rains from December to April). Los Angeles summers, which are virtually rainless, can lead to air-quality alerts. Prices skyrocket and reservations are a must when tourism peaks from July through early October.

GETTING HERE AND AROUND

AIR TRAVEL

It's generally easier to navigate the secondary airports than to get through sprawling LAX, the city's major gateway. Bob Hope Airport in Burbank is closest to downtown L.A., and domestic flights to it can be cheaper than flights to LAX—it's definitely worth checking out.

Airports Bob Hope Airport (*BUR* 🖀 *818/840–8830* ⊕ *www.bobhopeairport.com*). **Los Angeles International Airport** (*LAX* 🖀 *310/646–5252* ⊕ *www.lawa.org*).

BUS TRAVEL

The Metropolitan Transit Authority DASH (Downtown Area Short Hop) minibuses cover six different circular routes in Hollywood, Mid-Wilshire, and the downtown area. The buses stop every two blocks or so. The Santa Monica Municipal Bus Line, also known as the Big Blue Bus, is a pleasant and inexpensive way to move around the Westside, where the MTA lines leave off. There's also an express bus to and from downtown L.A., and a shuttle bus, the Tide Shuttle, which runs between Main Street and the Third Street Promenade and stops at hotels along the way.

Bus Information DASH (☎ 213/626–4455 or 310/808–2273 ⊕ www. ladottransit.com/dash). **Metropolitan Transit Authority (MTA)** (☎ 213/626–4455 ⊕ www.mta.net). **Santa Monica Municipal Bus Line** (☎ 310/451–5444 ⊕ www.bigbluebus.com).

CAR TRAVEL

Be aware that a number of major streets have similar-sounding names (Beverly Drive and Beverly Boulevard, or numbered streets north to south Downtown and east to west in Hollywood, West Hollywood, and Beverly Hills) or exactly the same name (San Vicente Boulevard in West L.A., Brentwood, Santa Monica, and West Hollywood).

Most freeways are known by a name and a number; for example, the San Diego Freeway is I–405, the Hollywood Freeway is U.S. 101, the Ventura Freeway is a different stretch of U.S. 101, the Santa Monica Freeway is I–10, and the Harbor Freeway is I–110. Distance in miles doesn't mean much, depending on the time of day you're traveling: The short 10-mi distance between the San Fernando Valley and Downtown Los Angeles might take an hour to travel during rush hour but only 20 minutes at other times.

Information California Highway Patrol (☎ 800/427–7623 in California). **City of Los Angeles** (⊕ www.ci.la.ca.us ⊕ www.sigalert.com ⊕ trafficinfo.lacity.org).

Emergency Services Freeway Service Patrol (☎ 213/922–2957 general information).

Local Car Rental Agencies Beverly Hills Budget Car Rental (☎ 310/274–9173 or 800/227–7117 ⊕ www.budgetbeverlyhills.com). **Beverly Hills Rent-A-Car** (☎ 310/337–1400 or 800/479–5996 ⊕ www.bhrentacar.com). **Enterprise** (☎ 800/736–8222 ⊕ www.enterprise.com).

METRO RAIL TRAVEL

Metro Rail covers a limited area of L.A.'s vast expanse, but what there is, is helpful and frequent. The underground Red Line runs from Union Station downtown through Mid-Wilshire, Hollywood, and Universal City on its way to North Hollywood, stopping at the most popular tourist destinations along the way. The Web site is the best way to get info on Metro Rail.

Metro Rail Information Metropolitan Transit Authority (MTA) (☎ 800/266–6883 or 213/626–4455 ⊕ www.mta.net).

TAXI AND LIMOUSINE TRAVEL

Don't even try to hail a cab on the street in Los Angeles. Instead, phone one of the many taxi companies. The metered rate is $2.45 per mi, plus a $2.65 per-fare charge. Taxi rides from LAX have an additional $2.50 surcharge. If you open any L.A.–area yellow pages, the number of limo companies will astound you. Most charge by the hour, with a three-hour minimum.

25

Limo Companies **ABC Limousine & Sedan Service** (☎ *818/980–6000 or 888/753–7500*). **American Executive** (☎ *213/250–2121 or 800/927–2020*). **Black & White Transportation Services** (☎ *800/924–1624*).

Taxi Companies **Checker Cab** (☎ *800/300–5007*). **United Independent Taxi** (☎ *800/411–0303 or 800/822–8294*). **Yellow Cab/LA Taxi Co-Op** (☎ *800/200–1085 or 800/200–0011*).

TRAIN TRAVEL

Union Station in downtown Los Angeles is one of the great American railroad stations. As the city's rail hub, it's the place to catch an Amtrak train. Among Amtrak's Southern California routes are 13 daily trips to San Diego and seven to Santa Barbara.

Information **Amtrak** (☎ *800/872–7245* ⊕ *www.amtrak.com*). **Union Station** (✉ *800 N. Alameda St.* ☎ *213/683–6979*).

VISITOR INFORMATION

Contacts **Beverly Hills Conference and Visitors Bureau** (☎ *310/248–1000 or 800/345–2210* ⊕ *www.beverlyhillsbehere.com*). **California Office of Tourism** (☎ *916/444–4429 or 800/862–2543* ⊕ *www.visitcalifornia.com*). **Hollywood Chamber of Commerce Info Center** (☎ *323/469–8311* ⊕ *www. hollywoodchamber.net*). **L.A. Inc./The Convention and Visitors Bureau** (☎ *213/624–7300 or 800/228–2452* ⊕ *discoverlosangeles.com*).

EXPLORING LOS ANGELES

Star-struck . . . excessive . . . smoggy . . . superficial. . . . There's a modicum of truth to each of the adjectives regularly applied to L.A. But Angelenos—and most objective visitors—dismiss their prevalence as signs of envy from people who hail from places less blessed with fun and sun. Pop Culture, for instance, *does* permeate life in LaLaLand: A massive economy employing millions of Southern Californians is built around it.

However, this city also boasts high-brow appeal, having amassed an impressive array of world-class museums and arts venues. Moreover, it has burgeoning neighborhoods that bear little resemblance to those featured on *The Hills* or *Entourage*. America's second-largest city has more depth than paparazzi shutters can ever capture.

DOWNTOWN LOS ANGELES

Once the lively heart of Los Angeles, Downtown has been a glitz-free businessman's domain of high-rises for the past few decades. But if there's one thing Angelinos love, it's a makeover, and city planners are in the middle of a dramatic revitalization. Glance in every direction and you'll find construction crews building luxury lofts and retail space.

WHAT TO SEE

Fodor'sChoice   **Cathedral of Our Lady of the Angels.** Controversy surrounded Spanish
★   architect José Rafael Moneo's unconventional, costly, austere design for the seat of the Archdiocese of Los Angeles. But judging from the swarms of visitors and the standing-room-only holiday masses, the church has carved out a niche for itself in Downtown's daily life. Opened in 2002,

From Griffith Observatory there's a sweeping panorama of the city.

the ocher-concrete cathedral looms up by the Hollywood Freeway. Imposing bronze entry doors are decorated with multicultural icons and New World images of the Virgin Mary. The canyonlike interior of the church is spare, polished, and airy. Make sure to go underground to wander the bright, somewhat incongruous, mazelike white-marble corridors of the mausoleum. Free guided tours start at the entrance fountain at 1 on weekdays. ■ TIP→ The café in the plaza has become one of Downtown's favorite lunch spots. ⊠ *555 W. Temple St., Downtown* ☎ *213/680–5200* ⊕ *www.olacathedral.org* ✉ *Free, parking $4 every 20 min, $18 maximum* ☉ *Weekdays 6:30–6, Sat. 9–6, Sun. 7–6.*

★ **The Geffen Contemporary.** Originally opened in 1982 as a temporary exhibit hall while the **Museum of Contemporary Art (MOCA)** was under construction at California Plaza, this large flexible space, designed by architect Frank Gehry, charmed visitors with its antiestablishment character and lively exhibits. Thanks to its hit reception, it remains one of two satellite museums of the MOCA (the other is outside the Pacific Design Center in West Hollywood). Named the Geffen Contemporary, after receiving a $5 million gift from the David Geffen Foundation, this museum houses a sampling of MOCA's permanent collection and usually one or two offbeat exhibits that provoke grins from even the stuffiest museumgoer. Call before you visit, as the museum sometimes closes for installations. ⊠ *152 N. Central Ave., Downtown* ☎ *213/626–6222* ⊕ *www.moca-la.org* ✉ *$10, free with MOCA admission on same day and on Thurs.* ☉ *Mon. 5–8, Fri. 11–5, Thurs. 11–8, weekends 11–6.*

Fodor's Choice ★ **The Museum of Contemporary Art (MOCA).** The MOCA's permanent collection of American and European art from 1940 to the present divides itself between three spaces: this linear red-sandstone building at California Plaza, the **Geffen Contemporary**, in nearby Little Tokyo, and the satellite gallery at West Hollywood's **Pacific Design Center.** Likewise, its exhibitions are split between the established and the cutting-edge. Works by heavy hitters such as Mark Rothko, Franz Kline, Susan Rothenberg, Diane Arbus, and Robert Frank are part of the permanent collection that are rotated into exhibits at different times, while at least 20 themed shows are featured annually. The museum occasionally closes for exhibit installation. ⊠ *250 S. Grand Ave., Downtown* ☎ *213/626–6222* ⊕ *www.moca.org* ⊠ *$10, free on same day with Geffen Contemporary admission and on Thurs.* ☉ *Mon. and Fri. 11–5, Thurs. 11–8, weekends 11–6.*

☾ ★ **Olvera Street.** This busy pedestrian block tantalizes with piñatas, mariachis, and fragrant Mexican food. As the major draw of the oldest section of the city, known as **El Pueblo de Los Angeles,** Olvera Street has come to represent the rich Mexican heritage of L.A. Vendors sell puppets, leather goods, sandals, serapes (woolen shawls), and handicrafts from stalls that line the center of the narrow street. ■TIP→ To see Olvera Street at its quietest, visit late on a weekday afternoon, when long shadows heighten the romantic feeling of the passageway. For information, stop by the **Olvera Street Visitors Center** (⊠ *622 N. Main St., Downtown* ☎ *213/628–1274* ⊕ *www.olvera-street.com*) in the Sepulveda House, a Victorian built in 1887. Free hour-long walking tours leave here at 10, 11, and noon Tuesday–Saturday.

HOLLYWOOD AND THE STUDIOS

The Tinseltown mythology of Los Angeles was born in Hollywood. Daytime attractions can be found on foot around the recently relocated home of the Academy Awards at the Kodak Theatre, part of the Hollywood & Highland entertainment complex. The adjacent Grauman's Chinese Theatre delivers silver screen magic with its cinematic facade and ornate interiors from a bygone era. Walk the renowned Hollywood Walk of Stars to find your favorite celebrities' hand- and footprints. In summer, visit the crown jewel of Hollywood, the Hollywood Bowl, which features shows by the Los Angeles Philharmonic.

The San Fernando Valley gets a bad rap. There are even some Angelenos who swear, with a sneer, that they will never set foot in "the Valley." But despite all the snickering, it's where the majority of studios that have made Los Angeles famous are located.

WHAT TO SEE

★ **Grauman's Chinese Theatre.** A place that inspires the phrase "only in Hollywood," this fantasy of Chinese pagodas and temples has become a shrine to stardom. Although you have to buy a movie ticket to appreciate the interior trappings, the courtyard is open to the public, though weekend tours are also available. Here you can find those oh-so-famous cement hand- and footprints. The main theater itself is worth visiting, if only to see a film in the same seats as hundreds of celebrities who have attended big premieres here. You can also take a tour of the theaters and

Grauman's Chinese Theatre, an iconic L.A. movie palace.

VIP lounge. ✉ *6925 Hollywood Blvd., Hollywood* ☎ *323/461–3331, 323/463–9576 for tours* ⊕ *www.manntheatres.com.*

★ **Griffith Observatory.** High on a hillside overlooking the city, the Griffith Observatory is one of the most celebrated icons of Los Angeles, and now, after a massive expansion and cosmic makeover, its interior is as rich as its exterior, featuring sleek exhibits with dramatic lighting and graphics.

A lower level was dug deep into the hillside for the expansion. In true L.A. style, the Leonard Nimoy Event Horizon Theater presents guest speakers and shows on current topics and discoveries. The planetarium now features a new dome, laser digital projection system, theatrical lighting, and a stellar sound system. Shows are $7. The Café at the End of the Universe serves delicious food created by celebrity chef Wolfgang Puck of Spago. Come at sunset to watch the sky turn fiery shades of red and catch up on California geography as you see the city's outline silhouetted. You might recognize the observatory and grounds from such movies as *Rebel Without a Cause* and *The Rocketeer.* ✉ *2800 E. Observatory Rd., Griffith Park* ☎ *213/473–0800* ⊕ *www.griffithobservatory. org* ⊙ *Tues.–Fri. noon–10, weekends 10–10.*

★ **Hollywood & Highland.** Now an extremely busy tourist attraction (read: not a lot of locals), this hotel-retail-entertainment complex was a dramatic play to bring glitz, foot traffic, and commerce back to Hollywood. The design pays tribute to the city's film legacy with a grand staircase leading up to a pair of white stucco 33-foot-high elephants, a nod to the 1916 movie *Intolerance.* ■ TIP→ Pause at the entrance arch, Babylon Court, which frames the "Hollywood" sign in the hills above for a picture-perfect view. There are plenty of clothing stores and eateries—and you may find yourself ducking into these for a respite from the crowds and street artists. ✉ *Hollywood Blvd. and Highland Ave., Hollywood-* ⊕ *www.hollywoodandhighland.com* 🅿 *Parking $2 with validation* ⊙ *Mon.–Sat. 10–10, Sun. 10–7.*

Hollywood Bowl. Classic Hollywood doesn't get better than this. Summer-evening concerts have been a tradition since 1922 at this amphitheater cradled in the Hollywood Hills. The Bowl is the summer home of the Los Angeles Philharmonic, but the musical fare also includes pop and jazz. A new much larger shell arrived in 2004, improving the acoustics and allowing the occasional dance and theater performance on stage with the orchestra. Dollar tickets are available for some weeknight classical and jazz performances. Come early to picnic on the grounds.

Before the concert, or during the day, visit the **Hollywood Bowl Museum** (☎ *323/850–2058* ⊙ *Tues.–Fri. 10–5, Sat. by appointment*) for a time-capsule version of the Bowl's history. ✉ *2301 N. Highland Ave., Hollywood* ☎ *323/850–2000* ⊕ *www.hollywoodbowl.com, www. laphil.com* 🅰 *museum free* ⊙ *Grounds daily dawn–dusk, call or check online for performance schedule.*

★ **Hollywood Sign.** With letters 50 feet tall, Hollywood's trademark sign can be spotted from miles away. The sign, which originally read "Hollywoodland," was erected on Mt. Lee in the Hollywood Hills in 1923 to promote a real-estate development. A fence and surveillance equipment have since been installed to deter intruders. Use caution if driving up to the sign on residential streets, since many cars speed around the blind corners. ⊕ *www.hollywoodsign.org.*

★ **Hollywood Walk of Fame.** Along Hollywood Boulevard runs a trail of affirmations for entertainment-industry overachievers. On this mile-long stretch of sidewalk, inspired by the concrete handprints in front of Grauman's Chinese Theatre, the names are embossed in brass, each at the center of a pink star embedded in dark-gray terrazzo. More than 1,600 stars have been immortalized since the first batch was placed in 1960. To aid you in spotting celebrities you're looking for, stars are identified by one of five icons: a motion-picture camera, a radio microphone, a television set, a record, or a theatrical mask. Contact the **Hollywood Chamber of Commerce** (✉ *7018 Hollywood Blvd.* ☎ *323/469–8311* ⊕ *www.hollywoodchamber.net*) for celebrity star locations and information on future star installations.

Fodor's Choice

★ **Paramount Pictures.** With a history dating to the early 1920s, this studio was home to some of Hollywood's most luminous stars, including Rudolph Valentino, Mae West, Mary Pickford, and Lucille Ball, who filmed episodes of *I Love Lucy* here. The lot still churns out memorable movies and TV shows, including *Forrest Gump, Titanic,* and *Star Trek.* You can take a studio tour (reservations required) led by friendly guides who walk and trolley you around the back lots. You can also be part of an audience for a live TV taping. Tickets are free; call for listings and times. ✉ *5555 Melrose Ave., Hollywood* ☎ *323/956–1777* ⊕ *www. paramount.com* 🅰 *Tours $35.*

☾ **Universal Studios Hollywood.** Although most first-time Los Angeles visitors consider this to be a must-see stop, bear in mind there many other
★

Doheny Drive, one of the major thoroughfares through Beverly Hills.

attractions that define Hollywood without the steep prices and tourist traps found here. Despite the amusement park clichés, hard-core sightseeing and entertainment junkies will make this required visiting. ■TIP→ If you get here when the park opens, you'll likely save yourself from long waits in line—arriving early pays off. ⊠ *100 Universal City Plaza, Universal City* ☎ *818/622–3801* ⊕ *www.universalstudioshollywood. com* ⊇ *$74, parking $15 ($10 after 3)* ⊙ *Contact park for seasonal hrs.*

BEVERLY HILLS AND THE WESTSIDE

If you only have a day to see L.A., see Beverly Hills. Love it or hate it, it delivers on a dramatic, cinematic scale of wealth and excess. West Hollywood is not a place to see things (like museums or movie studios) as much as it is a place to do things—like go to a nightclub, eat at a world-famous restaurant, or attend an art gallery opening.

The three-block stretch of Wilshire Boulevard known as Museum Row, east of Fairfax Avenue, racks up five intriguing museums and a prehistoric tar pit to boot. Only a few blocks away are the historic Farmers Market and The Grove shopping mall, a great place to people-watch over breakfast. Wilshire Boulevard itself is something of a cultural monument—it begins its grand 16-mi sweep to the sea in Downtown Los Angeles.

WHAT TO SEE

Fodor's Choice
★

Farmers Market and The Grove. The saying "Meet me at 3rd and Fairfax" became a standard line for generations of Angelenos who ate, shopped, and spotted the stars who drifted over from the studios for a breath of unpretentious air. Once a humble shop for farmers selling produce out of their trucks. the market now includes 110 stalls and more than 20 counter-order restaurants. In 2002 a massive expansion called The Grove opened; this highly conceptualized outdoor mall has a pseudo-European facade, with cobblestones, marble mosaics, and pavilions. ⊠ *Farmers Market, 6333 W. 3rd St.; The Grove, 189 The Grove Dr., Fairfax District* ☎ *323/933–9211 Farmers Market, 323/900–8080 The Grove* ⊕ *www.farmersmarketla.com* ☉ *Farmers Market weekdays 9–9, Sat. 9–8, Sun. 10–7; The Grove Mon.–Thurs. 10–9, Fri. and Sat. 10–10, Sun. 11–8.*

☾ **The Getty Center.** With its curving walls and isolated hilltop perch, the
Fodor's Choice Getty Center resembles a pristine fortified city of its own. You may have
★ been lured up by the beautiful views of L.A. (on a clear day stretching all the way to the Pacific Ocean), but the architecture, uncommon gardens, and fascinating art collections will be more than enough to capture and hold your attention. If you want to start with a quick overview, pick up the brochure in the entrance hall that guides you to 15 highlights of the collection. There's also an audio tour ($5) with commentaries by art historians. ■TIP➔ On-site parking is subject to availability, and usually fills up by late afternoon on holidays and summer weekends, so try to come early in the day. You may also take public transportation (MTA Bus 561 or Santa Monica Big Blue Bus 14). ⊠ *1200 Getty Center Dr., Brentwood* ☎ *310/440–7300* ⊕ *www.getty.edu* ▨ *Free, parking $15* ☉ *Tues.–Fri 10–5:30, Sat. 10–9, Sun. 10–5:30.*

★ **La Brea Tar Pits.** Do your children have dinos on the brain? Show them where dinosaurs come from by taking them to the stickiest park in town. About 40,000 years ago, deposits of oil rose to the earth's surface, collected in shallow pools, and coagulated into asphalt. In the early 20th century, geologists discovered that all that goo contained the largest collection of Pleistocene, or Ice Age, fossils ever found at one location: more than 600 species of birds, mammals, plants, reptiles, and insects. Roughly 100 tons of fossil bones have been removed in excavations over the last seven decades, making this one of the world's most famous fossil sites. The nearby **Page Museum at La Brea Tar Pits** displays fossils from the tar pits. ⊠ *Hancock Park, Miracle Mile* ⊕ *www.tarpits.org* ▨ *$7, free on 1st Tues. of each month.*

Fodor's Choice **Los Angeles County Museum of Art (LACMA).** Serving as the focal point of the
★ museum district along Wilshire Boulevard, LACMA's vast, encyclopedic collection of more than 100,000 objects dating from ancient times to the present is widely considered one of the most comprehensive in the western United States. LACMA's abundant holdings in works by such leading Latin American artists as Diego Rivera and Frida Kahlo; prominent Southern California artists; collections of Islamic and European art; paintings by Henri Matisse, Rene Magritte, Paul Klee, and Wassily Kandinsky; art representing the ancient civilizations of Egypt, the Near East, Greece, and Rome; plus a vast costume and textiles collection. ⊠ *5905 Wilshire Blvd., Miracle Mile* ☎ *323/857–6000* ⊕ *www.lacma. org* ▨ *$15, free 2nd Tues. of month, after 5 policy: "pay what you wish"* ☉ *Mon., Tues., and Thurs. noon–8, Fri. noon–9, weekends 11–8.*

For over half a century the Sunset Strip has been a hub of Los Angeles nightlife.

Fodor's Choice ★ **Rodeo Drive.** The ultimate shopping indulgence—Rodeo Drive is one of Southern California's bona fide tourist attractions; here you can shop for five-digit jewelry or a $35 handbag. The arts of window-shopping and window displays play out among the retail elite: Tiffany & Co., Gucci, Jimmy Choo, Valentino, Harry Winston, Prada . . . you get the picture. Several nearby restaurants have patios where you can sip a drink while watching shoppers saunter by with shopping bags stuffed with superfluous delights. At the southern end of Rodeo Drive (at Wilshire Boulevard) is **Via Rodeo**, a curvy cobblestone street designed to resemble a European shopping area or a Universal Studio backlot—take your pick. ✉ *Beverly Hills.*

★ **Sunset Strip.** For 60 years Hollywood's night owls have headed for the 1¾-mi stretch of Sunset Boulevard between Crescent Heights Boulevard on the east and Doheny Drive on the west, known as the Sunset Strip.

Parking and traffic around the Strip can be tough on weekends—expect to pay around $10–$25 to park, which can take a bite out of your partying budget—but the time and money may be worth it if you plan to make the rounds.

SANTA MONICA, VENICE, AND MALIBU

Hugging Santa Monica Bay in an arch, the desirable communities of Malibu, Santa Monica, and Venice move from the ultrarich, ultracasual Malibu to the bohemian/seedy Venice. What they have in common, however, is cleaner air, mild temperatures, horrific traffic, and an

The boardwalk of Venice Beach is a congregating point for street performers and free spirits.

emphasis on the beach-focused lifestyle that many people consider the hallmark of Southern California.

WHAT TO SEE

Fodor's Choice ★ **Getty Villa Malibu.** Feeding off the cultures of ancient Rome, Greece, and Etruria, the remodeled Getty Villa opened in 2006 with much fanfare—and some controversy concerning the acquisition and rightful ownership of some of the Italian artifacts on display. The antiquities are astounding, but on a first visit even they take a backseat to their environment. This megamansion sits on some of the most valuable coastal property in the world. Modeled after an ancient Roman country home, the Getty Villa includes beautifully manicured gardens, reflecting pools, and statuary. ■ TIP➔ An advance timed entry ticket is required for admission. Tickets are free and may be ordered from the Web site or by phone. ✉ *17985 Pacific Coast Hwy., Pacific Palisades* ☎ *310/440–7300* ⊕ *www.getty.edu* ✆ *Free, reservations required. Parking $15, cash only* ☉ *Wed.–Mon. 10–5.*

Santa Monica Pier. Souvenir shops, a psychic adviser, arcades, eateries, and **Pacific Park** are all part of this truncated pier at the foot of Colorado Boulevard below Palisades Park. The pier's trademark 46-horse Looff Carousel, built in 1922, has appeared in several films, including *The Sting.* Free concerts are held on the pier in summer. ✉ *Colorado Ave. and ocean, Santa Monica* ☎ *310/458–8900* ⊕ *www.santamonicapier. org* ✆ *Rides $1* ☉ *Carousel May–Sept., Tues.–Fri. 11–9, weekends 10–9; Oct.–Apr., Thurs.–Sun., hrs vary.*

Fodor's Choice ★ **Venice Beach Oceanfront Walk.** This is often called a "boardwalk," which is a bit of a misnomer—it's really a five-block section of paved walkway—but this L.A. mainstay delivers year-round action. Bicyclists zip along and bikini-clad rollerbladers attract crowds as they put on impromptu demonstrations, vying for attention with magicians, fortune-tellers, a chain-saw juggler, and sand mermaids. At the adjacent Muscle Beach, bodybuilders pump iron at an outdoor gym. You can rent in-line skates, roller skates, and bicycles at the south end of the boardwalk.

PASADENA AND ENVIRONS

Although seemingly absorbed into the general Los Angeles sprawl, Pasadena is a separate and distinct city. Noted for its Tournament of Roses, seen around the world each New Year's Day, the city brims with noteworthy spots, from its gorgeous Craftsman homes to its exceptional museums, particularly the Norton Simon and the Huntington Library, Art Collections, and Botanical Gardens. Where else can you see a Chaucer manuscript and rare cacti in one place?

25

WHAT TO SEE

Fodor's Choice ★ **Huntington Library, Art Collections, and Botanical Gardens.** If you have time for only one stop in the Pasadena area, it should be the Huntington, built in the early 1900s as the home of railroad tycoon Henry E. Huntington. Henry and his wife Arabella (who was his aunt by marriage) voraciously collected rare books and manuscripts, botanical specimens, and 18th-century British art. The institution they established became one of the most extraordinary cultural complexes in the world. The library contains more than 700,000 books and 4 million manuscripts, including such treasures as a Gutenberg Bible and the Ellesmere manuscript of Chaucer's *Canterbury Tales*. Although the art collections are increasingly impressive here, don't resist being lured outside into the stunning Botanical Gardens. On the grounds is the charming **Rose Garden Tea Room**, where traditional afternoon tea is served. ✉ *1151 Oxford Rd., San Marino* ☎ *626/405–2100* ⊕ *www.huntington.org* 🖼 *$15 weekdays, $20 weekends, free 1st Thurs. of month* ⊗ *Tues.–Fri. noon–4:30, weekends 10:30–4:30.*

Fodor's Choice ★ **Norton Simon Museum.** Long familiar to television viewers of the New Year's Day Rose Parade, this low-profile brown building is more than just a background for the passing floats. It's one of the finest small museums anywhere, with an excellent collection that spans more than 2,000 years of Western and Asian art. Don't miss a living artwork outdoors: the garden, whose tranquil pond was inspired by Monet's gardens at Giverny. ✉ *411 W. Colorado Blvd., Pasadena* ☎ *626/449–6840* ⊕ *www.nortonsimon.org* 🖼 *$8* ⊗ *Wed., Thurs., and Sat.–Mon. noon–6, Fri. noon–9.*

WHERE TO EAT

Dining out in Los Angeles tends to be a casual affair, and even at some of the most expensive restaurants you're likely to see customers in jeans. Despite its veneer of decadence, L.A. is not a particularly late-night city for eating. (The reenergized Hollywood dining scene is emerging as a notable exception.) The peak dinner times are from 7 to 9, and most restaurants won't take reservations after 10 pm. Generally speaking, restaurants are closed either Sunday or Monday. Most places are open for lunch on weekdays.

WHAT IT COSTS					
	¢	$	$$	$$$	$$$$
Restaurants	under $10	$10–$17	$18–$24	$24–$35	over $35

Restaurant prices are per person for a main course or equivalent combination of smaller plates (e.g., tapas, sushi), excluding 9.75% sales tax.

DOWNTOWN

¢–$
AMERICAN
ۆ
Fodor'sChoice
★

✕ **Philippe the Original.** L.A.'s oldest restaurant (1908), Philippe claims the French dip sandwich originated here. You can get one made with beef, pork, ham, lamb, or turkey on a freshly baked roll; the house hot mustard is as famous as the sandwiches. Its reputation is earned by maintaining traditions, from sawdust on the floor to long communal tables where customers debate the Dodgers or local politics. The home cooking includes huge breakfasts, chili, pickled eggs, and an enormous pie selection. The best bargain: a cup of java for just 10¢ including tax. ⊠ *1001 N. Alameda St., Downtown* ☎ *213/628–3781* ⌂ *Reservations not accepted* ▭ *No credit cards.*

HOLLYWOOD

$$
ITALIAN
Fodor'sChoice
★

✕ **Cube Café & Marketplace.** Cheese, charcuterie, and pasta lovers take heed: this dark and cozy Italian restaurant will ruin you for all the others. With more than 85 varieties of cheese, an enviable salami selection, pasta made in-house, and a passionate and earnest staff, this former pasta company turned upscale café and gourmet market is one of L.A.'s more affordable culinary gems. Take a seat at the cheese bar and order the *Sleepless in Salumi* plate or the *When in Rome* and pair it with a glass of Italian wine. For dinner, order the antipasti of braised octopus, and then move onto the seasonally driven pasta dishes, like the wild-boar gnocchi, veal ravioli, or pumpkin-stuffed pasta. ⊠ *615 N. La Brea Blvd., Hollywood* ☎ *323/939–1148* ⌂ *Reservations recommended* ▭ *AE, D, DC, MC, V* ☯ *Mon.–Sat. 11 am–10:30 pm. Closed Sun.*

$$–$$$$
AMERICAN

✕ **Musso & Frank Grill.** Liver and onions, lamb chops, goulash, shrimp Louis salad, gruff waiters—you'll find all the old favorites here in Hollywood's oldest restaurant. A film-industry hangout since it opened in 1919, Musso & Frank still attracts the working studio set to its maroon faux-leather booths, along with tourists and locals nostalgic for Hollywood's golden era. Great breakfasts are served all day, but the kitchen's famous "flannel cakes" (pancakes) are served only until 3 pm. ⊠ *6667 Hollywood Blvd., Hollywood* ☎ *323/467–7788* ▭ *AE, DC, MC, V* ☯ *Closed Sun. and Mon.*

$$
ITALIAN
Fodor'sChoice
★

✕ **Pizzeria Mozza.** The more casual half of Nancy Silverton, Mario Batali, and Joseph Bastianich's Mozza partnership gives newfound eminence to the humble "pizza joint." With traditional Mediterranean items like white anchovies, lardo, squash blossoms, and Gorgonzola, Mozza's pies—thin-crusted delights with golden, blistered edges—are much more Campania than California, and virtually every one is a winner. Utterly simple salads sing with vibrant flavors, and daily specials include lasagna. ⊠ *641 N. Highland Ave., Hollywood* ☎ *323/297–0101* ⚱ *Reservations essential* ▭ *AE, MC, V.*

BEVERLY HILLS

$$$$
MODERN
Fodor'sChoice
★

✕ **Spago Beverly Hills.** Wolfgang Puck's famed flagship restaurant is justifiably a modern L.A. classic. The illustrious restaurant centers on a buzzing outdoor courtyard shaded by 100-year-old olive trees. The people-watching here is worth the price of admission, but the clientele is surprisingly inclusive, from the biggest Hollywood stars to midwestern tourists to foodies. The daily-changing menu might offer a four-cheese pizza topped with truffles, *côte de boeuf* with Armagnac-peppercorn sauce, and some traditional Austrian specialties. Acclaimed pastry chef Sherry Yard works magic with everything from an ethereal apricot soufflé to Austrian *Kaiserschmarrn* (crème fraîche pancakes with fruit). ⊠ *176 N. Cañon Dr., Beverly Hills* ☎ *310/385–0880* ⚱ *Reservations essential* ▭ *AE, D, DC, MC, V* ☉ *No lunch Sun.*

$$$$
JAPANESE
Fodor'sChoice
★

✕ **Urasawa.** Shortly after celebrated sushi chef Masa Takayama packed his knives for the Big Apple, his soft-spoken protégé Hiroyuki Urasawa settled into the master's former digs. The understated sushi bar has few precious seats, resulting in incredibly personalized service. At a minimum of $350 per person for a strictly *omakase* (chef's choice) meal, Urasawa remains the priciest restaurant in town, but the endless parade of masterfully crafted, exquisitely presented dishes renders few regrets. The maple sushi bar, sanded daily to a satin-like finish, is where most of the action happens. You might be served velvety bluefin toro paired with beluga caviar, slivers of foie gras to self-cook *shabu shabu* style, or egg custard layered with *uni* (sea urchin), glittering with gold leaf. This is also the place to come during *fugu* season, when the legendary, potentially deadly blowfish is artfully served to adventurous diners. ⊠ *2 Rodeo, 218 N. Rodeo Dr., Beverly Hills* ☎ *310/247–8939* ⚱ *Reservations essential* ▭ *AE, DC, MC, V* ☉ *Closed Sun. No lunch.*

WEST HOLLYWOOD

$$–$$$
MEDITERRANEAN
Fodor'sChoice
★

✕ **A.O.C.** Since it opened in 2002, this restaurant and wine bar has revolutionized dining in L.A., pioneering the small-plate format that has now swept the city. The space is dominated by a long, candle-laden bar serving more than 50 wines by the glass. There's also a charcuterie bar, an L.A. rarity. The tapaslike menu is perfectly calibrated for the wine list; you could pick duck confit, clams with sherry and garlic toast, an indulgent slab of pork *rillettes* (a sort of pâté), or just plunge into one of the city's best cheese selections. ⊠ *8022 W. 3rd St., south of West Hollywood* ☎ *323/653–6359* ⚱ *Reservations essential* ▭ *AE, DC, MC, V* ☉ *No lunch.*

SANTA MONICA

$$$$
FRENCH
Fodor'sChoice
★

✕ **Mélisse.** In a city where informality reigns, this is one of L.A.'s dressier—but not stuffy—restaurants. A crystal chandelier hangs in the dining room, above well-spaced tables topped with flowers and Limoges china. The garden room loosens up with a stone fountain and a retractable roof. Chef-owner Josiah Citrin enriches his modern French cooking

25

with seasonal California produce. Consider seared sweet corn agnolotti in brown butter–truffle froth, lobster bolognese, or duck confit. ⊠ *1104 Wilshire Blvd., Santa Monica* ☎ *310/395–0881* ⌕ *Reservations essential* ▭ *AE, D, DC, MC, V* ⊗ *Closed Sun. and Mon. No lunch.*

$$$–$$$$
ITALIAN
Fodor'sChoice
★

✕ **Valentino.** Renowned as one of the country's top Italian restaurants, Valentino has a truly awe-inspiring wine list. With nearly 2,800 labels consuming 130 pages, this restaurant is nothing short of heaven for serious oenophiles. In the 1970s, suave owner Piero Selvaggio introduced L.A. to his exquisite modern Italian cuisine, and he continues to impress guests with dishes like a timballo of wild mushrooms with rich Parmigiano-Reggiano–*saffron fonduta*, a memorable osso buco, and sautéed branzino with lemon emulsion. A recent addition is its more casual V-vin bar for wine tasting, crudo, and carpaccio. ⊠ *3115 Pico Blvd., Santa Monica* ☎ *310/829–4313* ⌕ *Reservations essential* ▭ *AE, DC, MC, V* ⊗ *Closed Sun. No lunch Sat. and Mon.–Thurs.*

WHERE TO STAY

When looking for a hotel, don't write off the pricier establishments immediately. Price categories are determined by "rack rates"—the list price of a hotel room, which is usually discounted. Specials abound, particularly Downtown on weekends. Many hotels have packages that include breakfast, theater tickets, spa services, or exotic rental cars. Pricing is very competitive, so always check out the hotel Web site in advance for current special offers. When making reservations, particularly last-minute ones, check the hotel's Web site for exclusive Internet specials or call the property directly.

Hotel reviews have been condensed for this book. Please go to Fodors. com for full reviews of each property.

WHAT IT COSTS					
	¢	$	$$	$$$	$$$$
Hotels	under $100	$100–$199	$200–$299	$300–$399	over $400

For hotels, taxes (10%–15.5%) are extra. In listings, we always name the facilities available, but we don't specify whether they cost extra. When pricing accommodations, always ask what's included.

DOWNTOWN

$$$
Fodor'sChoice
★

▦ **Hilton Checkers Los Angeles.** Opened as the Mayflower Hotel in 1927, Checkers retains much of its original character; its various-size rooms all have charming period details, although they also have contemporary luxuries like pillow-top mattresses, coffeemakers, 24-hour room service, and cordless phones. **Pros:** historic charm; business-friendly; rooftop pool and spa. **Cons:** no on-street parking; some rooms compact; urban setting. ⊠ *535 S. Grand Ave., Downtown* ☎ *213/624–0000 or 800/445–8667* ⊕ *www.hiltoncheckers.com* ⤴ *188 rooms, 5 suites* ⌂ *In-room: a/c, Internet, Wi-Fi. In-hotel: restaurant, room service, bar, pool, gym, spa, laundry service, Wi-Fi hotspot, parking (paid)* ▭ *AE, D, DC, MC, V.*

$$$ Millennium Biltmore Hotel. One of downtown L.A.'s true treasures, the gilded 1923 beaux arts masterpiece exudes ambience and history. These days, the Biltmore hosts business types drawn by its central downtown location, ample meeting spaces, and services such as a well-outfitted business center that stays open 24/7. **Pros:** historic character; famed filming location; club-level rooms have many hospitable extras. **Cons:** pricey valet parking; standard rooms are truly compact. ⊠ *506 S. Grand Ave., Downtown* ☎ *213/624–1011 or 866/866–8086* ⊕ *www.thebiltmore. com* ↩ *635 rooms, 48 suites* ♿ *In-room: a/c, Internet, Wi-Fi. In-hotel: 3 restaurants, room service, bar, pool, gym, laundry service, Internet terminal, Wi-Fi hotspot, parking (paid)* ⊟ *AE, D, DC, MC, V.*

$$ The Standard, Downtown L.A. Built in 1955 as Standard Oil's company's headquarters, the building was completely revamped under the sharp eye of owner André Balazs. The large guest rooms are practical and funky: all have sexy see-through showers, windows that actually open, and platform beds.**Pros:** on-site Rudy's barbershop for grooming; 24/7 coffee shop for dining; rooftop pool and lounge for fun. **Cons:** disruptive party scene weekends and holidays; street noise; hipper-than-thou scene in lounge. ⊠ *550 S. Flower St., Downtown* ☎ *213/892–8080* ⊕ *www.standardhotel.com* ↩ *171 rooms, 36 suites* ♿ *In-room: a/c, safe, refrigerator, DVD. In-hotel: restaurant, room service, 3 bars, pool, gym, laundry service, Internet terminal, Wi-Fi hotspot, parking (paid), some pets allowed* ⊟ *AE, D, DC, MC, V.*

BEVERLY HILLS

$$$$ Four Seasons Hotel, Los Angeles at Beverly Hills. High hedges and patio gardens make this hotel a secluded retreat that even the hum of traffic can't permeate. It's a favorite of Hollywood's elite, so don't be surprised by a well-known face poolside or in the Windows bar. **Pros:** expert concierge; deferential service; celebrity magnet. **Cons:** small gym; Hollywood scene in bar and restaurant means rarefied prices. ⊠ *300 S. Doheny Dr., Beverly Hills* ☎ *310/273–2222 or 800/332–3442* ⊕ *www. fourseasons.com/losangeles* ↩ *185 rooms, 100 suites* ♿ *In-room: a/c, safe, kitchen (some), refrigerator, DVD, Internet, Wi-Fi. In-hotel: 2 restaurants, room service, bar, pool, gym, spa, laundry service, Internet terminal, Wi-Fi hotspot, parking (paid), some pets allowed (fee)* ⊟ *AE, DC, MC, V.*

$$$$

Fodor'sChoice

★

Peninsula Beverly Hills. This French Rivera–style palace is a favorite of Hollywood bold-face names, but all kinds of visitors consistently describe their stay as near perfect—though expensive. **Pros:** central, walkable Beverly Hills location; stunning flowers; one of the best concierges in the city. **Cons:** serious bucks required to stay here. ⊠ *9882 S. Santa Monica Blvd., Beverly Hills* ☎ *310/551–2888 or 800/462–7899* ⊕ *www.beverlyhills.peninsula.com* ↩ *142 rooms, 36 suites, 16 villas* ♿ *In-room: a/c, safe, refrigerator, DVD, Internet, Wi-Fi. In-hotel: restaurants, room service, 3 bars, pool, gym, spa, laundry service, Internet terminal, Wi-Fi hotspot, parking (paid), some pets allowed* ⊟ *AE, D, DC, MC, V.*

$$$ SLS Hotel at Beverly Hills. Imagine dropping into Alice in Wonderland's rabbit hole: This is the colorful, textured, and tchotchke-filled lobby of the SLS from design maestro Philippe Starck. **Pros:** a vibrant

25

newcomer with lofty ambitions; excellent design and cuisine. **Cons:** standard rooms are compact, but you pay for the scene; pricey hotel dining. ⊠ *465 S. La Cienega Blvd., Beverly Hills* ☎ *310/247–0400* ⊕ *www. slshotels.com* ⇆ *236 rooms, 61 suites* ⟁ *In-room: a/c, safe, DVD, Internet, Wi-Fi. In-hotel: 3 restaurants, room service, bars, pool, gym, spa, laundry service, Internet terminal, Wi-Fi hotspot, parking (paid), some pets allowed* ▭ *AE, D, DC, MC, V.*

WEST HOLLYWOOD

$$ ▦ **The London West Hollywood.** Just off the Sunset Strip, cosmopolitan and chic in design, the London WeHo is a remake of 1984-built Bel Age. The large suites and rooftop pool with city-wide views remain, but all else has been spiffed and brightened up with luxury textures like ultrasuede-covered hallway walls, framed mirrors throughout, and glam touches like gold-lame leather couches. **Pros:** perfectly designed interiors; hillside and city views in generous-size suites all with balconies and steps from the Strip. **Cons:** too refined for kids to be comfortable; lower floors have mundane views. ⊠ *1020 N. San Vicente Blvd., West Hollywood* ☎ *310/854–1111 or 866/282–4560* ⊕ *www.thelondonwesthollywood. com* ⇆ *200 suites* ⟁ *In-room: a/c, safe, refrigerator, Internet, Wi-Fi. In-hotel: restaurant, room service, bars, pool, gym, laundry service, Internet terminal, Wi-Fi hotspot, parking (paid), some pets allowed* ▭ *AE, D, MC, V.*

SANTA MONICA

$$ ▦ **The Ambrose.** An air of tranquillity pervades the four-story Ambrose, which blends right into its mostly residential Santa Monica neighborhood. The decor incorporates many Asian accents, following the principles of feng shui. **Pros:** L.A.'s most eco-conscious hotel, with nontoxic housekeeping products and recycling bins in each room. **Cons:** quiet, residential area of Santa Monica; no restaurant on-site. ⊠ *1255 20th St., Santa Monica* ☎ *310/315–1555 or 877/262–7673* ⊕ *www. ambrosehotel.com* ⇆ *77 rooms* ⟁ *In-room: a/c, safe, refrigerator, DVD, Internet, Wi-Fi. In-hotel: room service, gym, bicycles, laundry service, Internet terminal, Wi-Fi hotspot, parking (free)* ▭ *AE, D, DC, MC, V* ⦿| *CP.*

VENICE

$

FodorśChoice
★

▦ **Hotel Erwin.** Formerly a Best Western, this now bona fide boutique hotel just off the Venice Beach boardwalk got a major face-lift before reopening in July 2009. The biggest addition: a rooftop bar and lounge, appropriately named High, that's even attracting locals. **Pros:** great location, great food; close to Santa Monica without hefty prices. **Cons:** some rooms face alley. ⊠ *1697 Pacific Ave., Venice* ☎ *310/452–1111 or 800/786–7789* ⊕ *www.hotelerwin.com* ⇆ *119 rooms* ⟁ *In-room: a/c, safe, kitchen (some), refrigerator, DVD, Internet, Wi-Fi. In-hotel: restaurant, room service, bar, gym, beachfront, bicycles, laundry service, Internet terminal, Wi-Fi, parking (paid), some pets allowed* ▭ *AE, MC, V.*

PASADENA

$$ ⚏ **The Langham Huntington, Pasadena.** An azalea-filled Japanese garden
☾ and the unusual Picture Bridge, with murals celebrating California's
Fodor'sChoice history, are just two of this grande dame's picturesque attributes. **Pros:**
★ great for a romantic escape; excellent restaurant; elegant landscap-
ing and tranquil garden. **Cons:** set in a suburban neighborhood far
from local shopping and dining. ⊠ *1401 S. Oak Knoll Ave., Pasadena*
☎ *626/568–3900* ⊕ *www.pasadena.langhamhotels.com* ⤸ *342 rooms,
38 suites* ♿ *In-room: a/c, safe, refrigerator, Internet, Wi-Fi. In-hotel: 2
restaurants, room service, bar, tennis courts, pool, gym, spa, bicycles,
laundry service, Internet terminal, Wi-Fi, parking (paid), some pets
allowed* ⊟ *AE, D, DC, MC, V.*

NIGHTLIFE

Although the ultimate in velvet-roped vampiness and glamour used to
be the Sunset Strip, in the past couple of years the glitz has definitely
shifted to Hollywood Boulevard and its surrounding streets. The lines
are as long as the skirts are short outside the Hollywood club du jour
(which changes so fast, it's often hard to keep track). But the Strip still
has plenty going for it, with comedy clubs, hard-rock spots, and res-
taurants. West Hollywood's Santa Monica Boulevard bustles with gay
and lesbian bars and clubs. For less conspicuous—and congested—alter-
natives, check out the events in downtown L.A.'s performance spaces
and galleries. Silver Lake and Echo Park are best for boho bars and
live music clubs.

Note that parking, especially after 7 pm, is at a premium in Hollywood.
In fact, it's restricted on virtually every side street along the "hot zone"
of West Hollywood (Sunset Boulevard from Fairfax to Doheny). Posted
signs indicate the restrictions, but these are naturally harder to notice
at night. Paying $7 to $20 for valet or lot parking is often the easiest
way to go.

For a thorough listing of local events, ⊕ *www.la.com* and *Los Ange-
les Magazine* are both good sources. The Calendar section of the *Los
Angeles Times* (⊕ *www.calendarlive.com*) also lists a wide survey of Los
Angeles arts events, especially on Thursday and Sunday, as do the more
alternative publications *LA Weekly* and *Citybeat Los Angeles* (both
free, and issued every Thursday). Call ahead to confirm that what you
want to see is ongoing.

BEACHES

Los Angeles County beaches (and state beaches operated by the county)
have lifeguards on duty year-round, with expanded forces during the
summer. Public parking is usually available, though fees can range any-
where from $8 to $20; in some areas it's possible to find free street and
highway parking. Both restrooms and beach access have been brought
up to the standards of the Americans with Disabilities Act. Generally,
the northernmost beaches are best for surfing, hiking, and fishing, and

The pier along Santa Monica beach is the site of arcades, restaurants, and a famous Ferris wheel.

the wider and sandier southern beaches are better for tanning and relaxing. ■TIP→ Almost all are great for swimming, but beware: Pollution in Santa Monica Bay sometimes approaches dangerous levels, particularly after storms. Call ahead for beach conditions (☎310/457–9701) or go to ⊕ *www.watchthewater.com* for specific beach updates. The following beaches are listed in north–south order:

Fodor'sChoice
★
Robert H. Meyer Memorial State Beach. Part of Malibu's most beautiful coastal area, this beach is made up of three minibeaches: El Pescador, La Piedra, and El Matador—all with the same spectacular view. "El Mat" has a series of caves, Piedra some nifty rock formations, and Pescador a secluded feel; but they're all picturesque and fairly private. ■TIP→ One warning: Watch the incoming tide and don't get trapped between those otherwise scenic boulders. ⊠ *32350, 32700, and 32900 Pacific Coast Hwy., Malibu* ☎ *818/880–0350* ☞ *Parking, 1 roving lifeguard unit, restrooms.*

★
Santa Monica State Beach. It's the first beach you'll hit after the Santa Monica Freeway (I–10) runs into the PCH, and it's one of L.A.'s best known. Wide and sandy, Santa Monica is *the* place for sunning and socializing: be prepared for a mob scene on summer weekends, when parking becomes an expensive ordeal. Swimming is fine (with the usual poststorm pollution caveat); for surfing, go elsewhere. For a memorable view, climb up the stairway over the PCH to Palisades Park, at the top of the bluffs. ⊠ *1642 Promenade, Pacific Coast Hwy. at California Incline, Santa Monica* ☎ *310/305–9503* ☞ *Parking, lifeguard (year-round), restrooms, showers.*

★ **Redondo Beach.** The Redondo Beach Pier marks the starting point of this wide, sandy, busy beach along a heavily developed shoreline community. Restaurants and shops flourish along the pier, excursion boats depart from launching ramps, and a reef formed by a sunken ship creates prime fishing and snorkeling conditions. A series of free rock and jazz concerts takes place at the pier every summer. ⊠ *Torrance Blvd. at Catalina Ave., Redondo Beach* ☎ *310/372–2166* ☞ *Parking, lifeguard (year-round), restrooms, food concessions, showers.*

SHOPPING

AROUND BEVERLY HILLS

N.Y. has 5th Avenue, but L.A. has famed **Rodeo Drive.** The triangle, between Santa Monica and Wilshire boulevards and Beverly Drive, is one of the city's biggest tourist attractions and is lined with shops featuring the biggest names in fashion. You'll see well-coifed and -heeled ladies toting multiple packages to their Mercedes and paparazzi staking out street corners. Steep price tags on designer labels make it a "just looking" experience for many residents and tourists alike, but salespeople are used to the ogling and window-shopping. In recent years more mid-range shops have opened up on the strip and surrounding blocks. ■TIP→ There are several well-marked, free (for two hours) parking lots around the core shopping area.

25

HOLLYWOOD

Local shops may be a mixed bag, but at least you can read the stars below your feet as you browse along Hollywood Boulevard. Lingerie and movie memorabilia stores predominate here, but there are numerous options in the retail-hotel-dining-entertainment complex Hollywood & Highland. Hollywood impersonators (Michael Jackson, Marilyn Monroe, and, er, Chewbacca) join break-dancers and other street entertainers in keeping tourists entertained on Hollywood Boulevard's sidewalks near the Kodak Theater, home to the Oscars. Along La Brea Avenue, you'll find plenty of trendy, quirky, and hip merchandise, from records to furniture and clothing.

LOS FELIZ, SILVER LAKE, AND ECHO PARK

There's a hipster rock-and-roll vibe to this area, which has grown in recent years to add just the slightest shine to its edge. Come for home-grown, funky galleries, vintage shops, and local designers' boutiques. Shopping areas are concentrated along Vermont Avenue and Hollywood Boulevard in Los Feliz; Sunset Boulevard in both Silver Lake (known as Sunset Junction) and Echo Park; and Echo Park Avenue in Echo Park. ■TIP→ Keep in mind that things are spread out enough to necessitate a couple of short car trips, and many shops in these neighborhoods don't open until noon but stay open later, so grab dinner or drinks at one of the area's über-cool spots after shopping.

WEST HOLLYWOOD AND MELROSE AVENUE

West Hollywood has everything from upscale art, design, and antiques stores to ladies-who-lunch clothing boutiques to megamusic stores and specialty book vendors. Melrose Avenue, for instance, is part bohemian-punk shopping district (from North Highland to Sweetzer) and part upscale art and design mecca (upper Melrose Avenue and Melrose Place). Discerning locals and celebs haunt the posh boutiques around Sunset Plaza (Sunset Boulevard at Sunset Plaza Drive), on Robertson Boulevard (between Beverly Boulevard and 3rd Street), and along upper Melrose Avenue.

The huge blue Pacific Design Center, on Melrose at San Vicente Boulevard, is the focal point for this neighborhood's art- and interior design–related stores. The Beverly–La Brea neighborhood also claims a number of trendy clothing stores. Perched between Beverly Hills and West Hollywood, 3rd Street (between La Cienega and Fairfax) is a magnet for small, friendly designer boutiques. The Fairfax District has the historic Farmers Market, at Fairfax Avenue and 3rd Street, and The Grove; and some excellent galleries around Museum Row at Fairfax Avenue and Wilshire Boulevard.

SANTA MONICA AND VENICE

The breezy beachside communities of Santa Monica and Venice are ideal for leisurely shopping. Scads of tourists (and some locals) gravitate to the Third Street Promenade, a popular pedestrians-only strolling–shopping area that is within walking range of the beach and historic Santa Monica Pier. The sleek, three-story Santa Monica Place, at the south end of the promenade, reopened in summer 2010 as an upscale shopping mall, and draws fashion-savvy locals and tourists alike. Main Street between Pico Boulevard and Rose Avenue offers upscale chain stores, cafés, and some original shops, while Montana Avenue is a great source for distinctive clothing boutiques and child-friendly shopping, especially between 7th and 17th streets. ■ TIP→ Parking in Santa Monica is next to impossible on Wednesday, when some streets are blocked off for the farmers' market, but there are several parking structures with free parking for an hour or two. In Venice, Abbot Kinney Boulevard is abuzz with mid-century furniture stores, art galleries and boutiques, and cafés.

Yosemite National Park

WORD OF MOUTH

"I tried cross-country skiing for the first time in Yosemite. An avid downhill skier, I quickly learned that cross-country is more physically demanding, slower going, but scenically spectacular. I chose to use the time to find the perfect shot of Half Dome."

—photo by Sarah Corley, Fodors.com member

WELCOME TO
YOSEMITE NATIONAL PARK

TOP REASONS TO GO

★ **Feel the earth move:** An easy stroll brings you to the base of Yosemite Falls, America's highest, where thundering springtime waters shake the ground.

★ **Tunnel to heaven:** Winding down into Yosemite Valley, Wawona Road passes through a mountainside and emerges before one of the park's most heart-stopping vistas.

★ **Touch the sky:** Watch clouds scudding across the bright blue dome that arches above the High Sierra's Tuolumne Meadows, a wide-open alpine valley ringed by 10,000-foot granite peaks.

★ **Walk away from it all:** Early or late in the day, leave the crowds behind and take a forest hike on one of Yosemite's 800 mi of trails.

★ **Powder your nose:** Winter's hush floats into Yosemite on snowflakes. Wade into a fluffy drift, lift your face to the sky, and listen to the trees.

1 **Yosemite Valley.** At an elevation of 4,000 feet, in the center of the park, beats Yosemite's heart. This is where you'll find the park's most famous sights and biggest crowds.

2 **Wawona and Mariposa Grove.** The park's southeastern tip holds Wawona, with its grand old hotel and pioneer history center, and the Mariposa Grove of Big Trees, filled with giant sequoias. These are closest to the South Entrance, 35 mi (a one-hour drive) south of Yosemite Village.

3 **Tuolumne Meadows.** The highlight of east-central Yosemite is this wildflower-strewn valley with hiking trails, nestled among sharp, rocky peaks. It's a two-hour drive northeast of Yosemite Valley along Tioga Road (closed mid-October–late May).

4 **Hetch Hetchy.** The most remote, least-visited part of Yosemite accessible by automobile, this glacial valley is dominated by a reservoir and veined with wilderness trails. It's near the park's western boundary, about a half-hour drive north of Big Oak Flat Entrance.

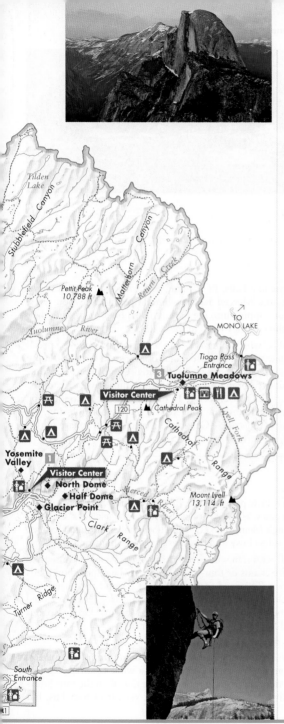

GETTING ORIENTED

Yosemite is so vast that you can think of it as five parks. Yosemite Valley, famous for waterfalls and cliffs, and Wawona, where the giant sequoias stand, are open all year. Hetch Hetchy, home of less-trodden backcountry trails, closes after the first big snow and reopens in May or June. The subalpine high country, Tuolumne Meadows, is open for summer hiking and camping; in winter it's accessible only via cross-country skis or snowshoes. Badger Pass Ski Area is open in winter only. Most visitors spend their time along the park's southwestern border, between Wawona and Big Oak Flat Entrance; a bit farther east in Yosemite Valley and Badger Pass Ski Area; and along the east–west corridor of Tioga Road, which spans the park north of Yosemite Valley and bisects Tuolumne Meadows.

26

By merely standing in Yosemite Valley and turning in a circle, you can see more natural wonders than you can anywhere else.

Half Dome, Yosemite Falls, El Capitan, Bridalveil Fall, the meadows, Sentinel Dome, the Merced River, white-flowering dogwood trees, maybe even bears ripping into the bark of fallen trees or sticking their snouts into beehives—they're all in the Valley.

In the mid-1800s, when tourists began arriving, the Valley's special geologic qualities, and the giant sequoias of Mariposa Grove 30 mi to the south, so impressed a group of influential Californians that they persuaded President Abraham Lincoln to grant those two areas to the state for protection. On October 1, 1890—thanks largely to lobbying efforts by naturalist John Muir and Robert Underwood Johnson, the editor of *Century Magazine*—Congress set aside 1,500 square mi for Yosemite National Park.

PLANNING

WHEN TO GO

During extremely busy periods—like July 4—you may experience delays at the entrance gates. ■TIP➜ For fewer crowds, visit midweek. Or come mid-April through Memorial Day or mid-September through October, when the park is less busy and the days are often sunny and clear.

Summer rainfall is rare. In winter, heavy snows occasionally cause road closures, and tire chains or four-wheel drive may be required on roads that remain open. The road to Glacier Point beyond the turnoff for Badger Pass is closed after the first major snowfall; Tioga Road is closed from late October through May or mid-June. Mariposa Grove Road is typically closed for a shorter period in winter.

GETTING HERE AND AROUND

Approximately 200 mi from San Francisco, 300 mi from Los Angeles, and 500 mi from Las Vegas, Yosemite takes a while to reach—and its sites and attractions merit substantially more time than the four hours rangers typically advise. Most people arrive via car or tour bus, but public transportation (courtesy of Amtrak and the regional YARTS bus system) is also an option.

Of the park's four entrances, Arch Rock is the closest to Yosemite Valley. The road that goes through it, Route 140 from Merced and Mariposa, snakes alongside the boulder-packed Merced River. Route 41, through Wawona, is the best route from Los Angeles. Route 120, through Crane Flat, is the most direct route from San Francisco. Tioga Road is the only way in from the east. It's the most scenic approach, but only open from early June through mid-October due to snow accumulation.

Once you're in the Valley, take advantage of the free shuttle buses, which make 21 stops and run every 10 minutes or so from 9 am to 6 pm year-round; a separate (and also free) summer-only shuttle runs to El Capitan. Also during the summer, you can pay to take the morning "hikers' bus" from Yosemite Valley to Tuolumne or to Glacier Point. Bus service from Wawona is geared toward people staying there who want to spend the day in Yosemite Valley. Free and frequent shuttles transport people between the Wawona Hotel and Mariposa Grove. During the snow season, buses run regularly between Yosemite Valley and Badger Pass Ski Area. For more information, visit ⊕ *www.nps.gov/ yose/planyourvisit/bus.htm* or call ☎ *209/372–1240*.

26

There are few gas stations within Yosemite (Crane Flat, Tuolumne Meadows, and Wawona; none in the Valley), so fuel up before you reach the park. From late fall until early spring the weather is unpredictable, and driving can be treacherous. You should carry chains. For road conditions, call ☎ *800/427–7623 or 209/372–0200* from within California or go to ⊕ *www.dot.ca.gov*.

PARK ESSENTIALS

ADMISSION FEES AND PERMITS

The admission fee, valid for seven days, is $20 per vehicle or $10 per individual.

If you plan to camp in the backcountry, you must have a wilderness permit. Availability of permits, which are free, depends upon trailhead quotas. It's best to make a reservation, especially if you will be visiting May through September. You can reserve two days to 24 weeks in advance by phone, mail, or fax (⌂ *Box 545, Yosemite, CA 95389* ☎ *209/372–0740* 🖷 *209/372–0739*); a $5 per person processing fee is charged when your reservations are confirmed. Requests must include your name, address, daytime phone, number of people in your party, trip date, alternative dates, starting and ending trailheads, and a brief itinerary. Without a reservation, you may still get a free permit on a first-come, first-served basis at wilderness permit offices at Big Oak Flat, Hetch Hetchy, Tuolumne, Wawona, the Wilderness Center (in Yosemite Village), and Yosemite Valley in summer; fall through spring, visit the Valley Visitor Center.

ADMISSION HOURS

The park is open 24/7 year-round. All entrances are open at all hours, except for Hetch Hetchy Entrance, which is open between dawn and dusk. Yosemite is in the Pacific Time Zone.

EMERGENCIES

In an emergency, call 911. You can also call the Yosemite Medical Clinic in Yosemite Village at 209/372–4637. The clinic provides 24-hour emergency care.

PARK CONTACT INFORMATION

Yosemite National Park ✆ *Information Office, Box 577, Yosemite National Park, CA 95389* ☎ *209/372–0200* ⊕ *www.nps.gov/yose.*

EXPLORING YOSEMITE NATIONAL PARK

HISTORIC SITES

Ahwahneechee Village. This cluster of re-created structures, accessed by a short loop trail, is a vision of Indian life here in the 1870s. One interpretive sign points out that Miwok referred to the 19th-century newcomers as "Yohemite" or "Yohometuk," which translates as "some of them are killers." ⊠ *Northside Dr., Yosemite Village* ⊡ *Free* ☉ *Daily sunrise–sunset.*

Pioneer Yosemite History Center. Some of Yosemite's first structures—those not occupied by American Indians, that is—were relocated here in the 1950s and 1960s. You can spend a pleasurable half-hour walking and reading the signs, perhaps springing for a self-guided-tour pamphlet (50¢) to enhance the history lesson. Wednesday through Sunday in the summer, costumed docents conduct free blacksmithing and "wet-plate" photography demonstrations, and for a small fee you can take a stagecoach ride. ⊠ *Rte. 41, Wawona* ☎ *209/375–9531 or 209/379–2646* ⊡ *Free* ☉ *Building interiors are open mid-June–Labor Day, daily 9–5.*

SCENIC STOPS

★ **El Capitan.** Rising 3,593 feet—more than 350 stories—above the Valley, El Capitan is the largest exposed-granite monolith in the world. Since 1958 people have been climbing its entire face, including the famous "nose." ⊠ *Off Northside Dr., about 4 mi west of Valley Visitor Center.*

Fodor'sChoice **Glacier Point.** If you lack the stamina to hike more than 3,200 feet up
★ to Glacier Point, you can drive or take a bus from the Valley for a bird's-eye view. You'll likely encounter a lot of day-trippers on the short, paved trail that leads to the main overlook. For details about the summer-only buses, call ☎ *209/372–1240.* ⊠ *Glacier Point Rd., 16 mi northeast of Rte. 41.*

★ **Half Dome.** Visitors flock to this remarkable granite formation that tops out at more than 4,700 feet above the Valley floor. You can hike to the top of Half Dome on an 8.5-mi (one way) trail, whose last 400 feet must be ascended while holding a steel cable. To see Half Dome reflected in the Merced River, view it from Sentinel Bridge just before sundown, or stay for sunset, when the sun floods it in a brilliant orange light.

Hetch Hetchy Reservoir. When Congress green-lighted the O'Shaughnessy Dam in 1913, pragmatism triumphed over the aesthetics. Some 2.4 million residents of the San Francisco Bay Area continue to get their water from this 117-billion-gallon reservoir, although spirited efforts are being made to restore the Hetch Hetchy Valley to its former glory.

Eight miles long, the reservoir is Yosemite's largest body of water, and can be seen from several trails. ⊠ *Hetch Hetchy Rd., about 15 mi north of Big Oak Flat Entrance Station.*

★ **Mariposa Grove of Big Trees.** Of Yosemite National Parks' three sequoia groves, Mariposa is by far the largest and easiest to walk around. Approximately 2,700 years old, Grizzly Giant, whose base measures 96 feet, is estimated to be the world's 25th largest tree in volume. Up the hill you'll find more sequoias, a small museum, and fewer people. Summer weekends are especially crowded here. Consider taking the free shuttle from Wawona. ⊠ *Rte. 41, 2 mi north of South Entrance Station.*

★ **Tuolumne Meadows.** The largest subalpine meadow in the Sierras (at 8,600 feet) is a popular way station for backpacking along the Pacific Crest and John Muir trails. The setting is not as dramatic as Yosemite Valley, 56 mi away, but the almost perfectly flat basin, about 2½ mi long, is intriguing, and in July it's resplendent with wildflowers. The most popular day hike is to the top of Lembert Dome, where you'll find awesome views of the basin below. Keep in mind that Tioga Road rarely opens before June, and usually closes by mid-October. ⊠ *Tioga Rd. (Rte. 120), about 8 mi west of Tioga Pass Entrance Station.*

WATERFALLS

Yosemite's waterfalls are at their most spectacular in May and June. By summer's end some falls, including the mighty Yosemite Falls, dry up. They begin flowing again in late fall, and in winter they're laced with ice. Even in drier months, the waterfalls are breathtaking. If you choose to hike any of the trails, be sure to wear shoes with no-slip soles; the rocks can be slick. Stay on trails at all times.

■TIP→ Visit the park during a full moon, and you can stroll in the evening without a flashlight and still make out the ribbons of falling water, as well as silhouettes of the giant granite monoliths.

Bridalveil Fall. The 620-foot, filmy waterfall is often diverted as much as 20 feet one way or the other by the breeze. It is the first marvelous view of Yosemite Valley you will see if you come via Route 41. ⊠ *Yosemite Valley, access from parking area off Wawona Rd.*

Nevada Fall. Climb Mist Trail from Happy Isles for a close-up view of this 594-foot cascading beauty, the first major fall as the Merced River plunges down from the high country toward the eastern end of Yosemite Valley. ⊠ *Yosemite Valley, access via Mist Trail from Nature Center at Happy Isles.*

Ribbon Fall. At 1,612 feet, this is the highest single fall in North America. It's also the first Valley waterfall to dry up in summer. Look west of El Capitan from the Valley floor for the best view of the fall from the base of Bridalveil Fall. ⊠ *Yosemite Valley, west of El Capitan Meadow.*

Vernal Fall. Fern-covered black rocks frame this 317-foot fall, and rainbows materialize at its base. ⊠ *Yosemite Valley, access via Mist Trail from Nature Center at Happy Isles.*

Fodor's Choice
★ **Yosemite Falls.** Actually three falls in one, they constitute the highest waterfall in North America and the fifth-highest in the world. The water from the top descends a total of 2,425 feet, and when the falls run hard,

you can hear them thunder across the Valley. When they dry up in late summer, the Valley seems naked without the tower of spray. ■TIP➡ If you hike the partially paved, mile-long loop trail to the base of the Lower Falls during the peak water flow in May, expect to get soaked. ⊠ *Yosemite Valley, access from Yosemite Lodge or trail parking area.*

VISITOR CENTERS

Le Conte Memorial Lodge. This small but striking National Historic Landmark is Yosemite's first permanent public information center. To find out about evening programs, check the kiosk out front, or visit ⊕ *www.sierraclub.org.* ⊠ *Southside Dr., about ½ mi west of Curry Village* ⊙ *Memorial Day–Labor Day, Wed.–Sun. 10–4.*

Valley Visitor Center. At this center you can learn about the formation of Yosemite Valley, its vegetation, animals, and human inhabitants. Don't leave without watching the superb *Spirit of Yosemite,* a 23-minute introductory film that runs every half-hour. ⊠ *Yosemite Village* ☎ *209/372–0299* ⊙ *Late May–early Sept., daily 9–6; early Sept.–late May, daily 9–5.*

SPORTS AND THE OUTDOORS

BICYCLING

One of the most enjoyable ways to tour Yosemite Valley is to ride a bike beneath its lofty granite monoliths. The eastern valley has 12 mi of paved, flat bicycle paths, with bike racks at convenient stopping points. For a greater challenge, you can ride on 196 mi of paved park roads—but bicycles are not allowed on hiking trails or in the backcountry. Kids under 18 must wear a helmet.

You can get **Yosemite bike rentals** (⊠ *Yosemite Lodge or Curry Village* ☎ *209/372–1208* ⊕ *www.yosemitepark.com* ▨ *$9.50/hr, $25.50/day* ⊙ *Apr.–Oct.*) from either Yosemite Lodge or Curry Village bike stands. Bikes with child trailers, baby-jogger strollers, and wheelchairs are available.

BIRD-WATCHING

Nearly 250 bird species have been spotted in the park, including the sage sparrow, pygmy owl, blue grouse, and mountain bluebird. Park rangers lead free bird-watching walks in Yosemite Valley one day a week in summer; check at a visitor center or information station for times and locations. Binoculars are sometimes available for loan.

The Yosemite Association sponsors one- to four-day **birding seminars** (☎ *209/379–2321* ⊕ *www.yosemite.org* ▨ *$82–$254* ⊙ *Apr.–Aug.*) for beginner and intermediate birders.

HIKING

The staff at the **Wilderness Center** (☎ *209/372–0740*), in Yosemite Village, provides free wilderness permits, which are required for overnight camping (advance reservations are available for $5 and are highly recommended for popular trailheads from May through September and on weekends). The staff provides maps and advice to hikers heading to the backcountry. From April through November, **Yosemite Mountaineering**

School and Guide Service (✉ *Yosemite Mountain Shop, Curry Village* ☎ *209/372–8344*) leads two-hour to full-day treks.

MODERATE

★ **Mist Trail.** Except for Lower Yosemite Falls, more visitors take this trail than any other in the park. The trek up and back from Vernal Fall is 3 mi. Add another 4 mi by continuing up to the 594-foot Nevada Fall, where the trail becomes quite steep and slippery in its final stages. The elevation gain to Vernal Fall is 1,000 feet; Nevada Fall is an additional 1,000 feet. ✉ *Trailhead at Happy Isles.*

★ **Panorama Trail.** Few hikes come with the visual punch of this 8½-mi trail. The star attraction is Half Dome, visible from many intriguing angles, but you also see three waterfalls and walk through a manzanita grove. Before you begin, look down on Yosemite Valley from Glacier Point. ✉ *Trailhead at Glacier Point.*

DIFFICULT

Fodor's Choice
★ **John Muir Trail to Half Dome.** Ardent trekkers can continue on from the top of Nevada Fall, off Mist Trail, to the top of Half Dome. Some hikers attempt this entire 10- to 12-hour, 16¾-mi round-trip trek from Happy Isles in one day, but, remember that the 4,800-foot elevation gain and 8,842-foot altitude can cause shortness of breath. Another option: Hike to a campground in Little Yosemite Valley near the top of Nevada Fall the first day, then climb to the top of Half Dome and hike out the next; getting your wilderness permit reservations at least a month in advance is recommended. Be sure to wear hiking boots and bring gloves. The last pitch up the back of Half Dome is very steep—the only way to climb this sheer rock face is to pull yourself up using steel cable handrails that are in place only from late spring to early fall. ✉ *Trailhead at Happy Isles.*

HORSEBACK RIDING

Reservations for guided trail rides must be made in advance at hotel tour desks or by phone. For overnight saddle trips, which use mules, check online at ⊕ *www.yosemitepark.com* and fill out a lottery application for the following year. Scenic trail rides range from two hours to a full day; six-day High Sierra saddle trips are also available.

Tuolumne Meadows Stables (✉ *Off Tioga Rd., 2 mi east of Tuolumne Meadows Visitor Center* ☎ *209/372–8427* ⊕ *www.yosemitepark.com*) runs two-, four-, and eight-hour trips, which cost $53, $69, and $96, respectively. High Sierra four- to six-day camping treks on mules begin at $625. Reservations are essential. **Wawona Stables** (✉ *Rte. 41, Wawona* ☎ *209/375–6502*) has two- and five-hour rides, starting at $53. Reservations are essential. You can tour the Valley and the base of the high country on two-hour and four-hour rides at **Yosemite Valley Stables** (✉ *At entrance to North Pines Campground, 100 yards northeast of Curry Village* ☎ *209/372–8348* ⊕ *www.yosemitepark.com*). Reservations are required for the $60 and $80 trips.

RAFTING

Rafting is permitted only on designated areas of the Middle and South forks of the Merced River. Check with the Valley Visitor Center for closures and other restrictions.

The per-person rental fee at **Curry Village raft stand** (⊠ *South side of Southside Dr., Curry Village* ☎ *209/372–8319* ⊕ *www.yosemitepark. com* ✉ *$20.50* ⊙ *Late May–July*) covers the four- to six-person raft, two paddles, and life jackets, plus a shuttle to the launch point on Sentinel Beach.

ROCK CLIMBING

Fodor's Choice
★

The one-day basic lesson at **Yosemite Mountaineering School and Guide Service** (⊠ *Yosemite Mountain Shop, Curry Village* ☎ *209/372–8344* ⊕ *www.yosemitepark.com* ✉ *$117–$300* ⊙ *Apr.–Nov.*) includes some bouldering and rappelling and three or four 60-foot climbs. Climbers must be at least 10 (kids under 12 must be accompanied by a parent or guardian) and in reasonably good physical condition. Intermediate and advanced classes include instruction in belays, self-rescue, summer snow climbing, and free climbing.

ICE-SKATING

Curry Village ice-skating rink. Winter visitors have skated at this outdoor rink for decades, taking in views of Half Dome and Glacier Point. ⊠ *South side of Southside Dr., Curry Village* ☎ *209/372–8319* ✉ *$8 per 2 hrs, $3 skate rental* ⊙ *Mid-Nov.–mid-Mar., afternoons and evenings daily, morning sessions weekends; noon–2:30 pm on weekends as well (hrs vary).*

SKIING AND SNOWSHOEING

Badger Pass Ski Area. California's first ski resort has five lifts and 10 downhill runs, as well as 90 mi of groomed cross-country trails. Free shuttle buses from Yosemite Valley operate during ski season (December through early April, weather permitting). Lift tickets are $38, downhill equipment rents for $24, and snowboard rental with boots is $35. The gentle slopes of Badger Pass make **Yosemite Ski School** (☎ *209/372–8430*) an ideal spot for children and beginners to learn downhill skiing or snowboarding for as little as $28 for a group lesson. The highlight of Yosemite's cross-country skiing center is a 21-mi loop from Badger Pass to Glacier Point. You can rent cross-country skis for $23 per day at the **Cross-Country Ski School** (☎ *209/372–8444*), which also rents snowshoes ($22 per day), telemarking equipment ($29), and skate-skis ($24). **Yosemite Mountaineering School** (⊠ *Badger Pass Ski Area* ☎ *209/372–8344* ⊕ *www.yosemitemountaineering.com*) conducts snowshoeing, cross-country skiing, telemarking, and skate-skiing classes starting at $30. ⊠ *Badger Pass Rd., off Glacier Point Rd., 18 mi from Yosemite Valley* ☎ *209/372–8430.*

26

EDUCATIONAL PROGRAMS

CLASSES AND SEMINARS

Art Classes. Professional artists conduct workshops in watercolor, etching, drawing, and other mediums. Bring your own materials or purchase the basics at the Art Activity Center, next to the Village Store. Call for scheduling. ⊠ *Art Activity Center, Yosemite Village* ☎ *209/372–1442* ⊕ *www.yosemitepark.com* ✉ *Free* ⊙ *Apr.–early Oct., Tues.–Sat., 10 am–2 pm.*

DID YOU KNOW?

Yosemite's granite formations provide sturdy ground for climbers of all skill levels. The sheer granite monolith El Capitan—simply "El Cap" to climbers—is the most famous, climbed even by Captain Kirk (if you believe the opening scene of *Star Trek V: The Final Frontier*), but climbers tackle rocks up in the mountains too.

Yosemite Outdoor Adventures. Naturalists, scientists, and park rangers lead educational outings on topics from woodpeckers and fire management to pastel painting. Most sessions take place spring through fall, but a few focus on winter phenomena. ⊠ *Various locations* ☎ *209/379–2321* ⊕ *www.yosemite.org* ⊠ *$82–$465.*

RANGER PROGRAMS

Junior Ranger Program. Children ages 3 to 13 can participate in the informal, self-guided Little Cub and Junior Ranger programs. A park activity handbook ($8) is available at the Valley Visitor Center or the Nature Center at Happy Isles. ⊠ *Valley Visitor Center or Nature Center at Happy Isles* ☎ *209/372–0299.*

Ranger-Led Programs. Rangers lead walks and hikes at different locations several times a day from spring through fall; the schedule is reduced in winter. In the evenings at Yosemite Lodge and Curry Village, rangers, slide shows, and documentary films provide unique perspectives on Yosemite. On summer weekends Camp Curry and Tuolumne Meadows Campground host sing-along campfire programs.

TOURS

★ **Ansel Adams Photo Walks.** Photography enthusiasts shouldn't miss these two-hour guided camera walks offered four mornings each week—Monday, Tuesday, Thursday, and Saturday—by professional photographers. Some are hosted by the Ansel Adams Gallery, others by Delaware North; meeting points vary. All are free, but participation is limited to 15 people. Reservations are essential. To reserve a spot, call up to three days in advance or visit the gallery. ☎ *209/372–4413 or 800/568–7398* ⊕ *www.anseladams.com* ⊠ *Free.*

DNC Parks and Resorts. The main concessionaire at Yosemite National Park, this organization operates guided tours and programs throughout the park, including the **Big Trees Tram Tour** of the Mariposa Grove of Big Trees, the **Glacier Point Tour,** the **Grand Tour** (both Mariposa Grove and Glacier Point), the **Moonlight Tour** of Yosemite Valley, the **Tuolumne Meadows Tour,** and the **Valley Floor Tour.** ☎ *209/372–1240* ⊕ *www.yosemitepark.com* ⊠ *Free.*

26

WHERE TO EAT

WHAT IT COSTS				
	¢	$	$$	$$$	$$$$
Restaurants	under $8	$8–$12	$13–$20	$21–$30	over $30

Restaurant prices are per person for a main course at dinner.

RESTAURANTS

$$$–$$$$

CONTINENTAL

Fodor'sChoice

★

✕**Ahwahnee Hotel Dining Room.** With floor-to-ceiling windows, a 34-foot-high ceiling with interlaced sugar-pine beams, and massive chandeliers, this dining room is one of the most beautiful in the state. Dinner is pricey here, and though many still applaud the experience, others report a recent dip in the service and the quality of the food. However, Sunday brunch ($49) receives high marks. Reservations are always advised, and for dinner, attire is "resort casual." ⊠ *Ahwahnee Hotel, Ahwahnee Rd., about ¾ mi east of Yosemite Valley Visitor Center, Yosemite Village* ☎ *209/372–1489* ⚓ *Reservations essential* ☰ *AE, DC, MC, V.*

$$–$$$ ✕ **Mountain Room.** Though the food is good, it's the view of Yosemite
AMERICAN   Falls through the dining room's wall of windows that's the main attrac-
★   tion. The chef uses local, organic ingredients, so you can be assured of fresh greens and veggies here. The Mountain Room Lounge, a few steps away, has a bar with about 10 beers on tap. ⊠ *Yosemite Lodge, Northside Dr. about ¾ mi west of visitor center, Yosemite Village* ☎ *209/372–1281* ☰ *AE, D, DC, MC, V* ☾ *No lunch.*

$$–$$$ ✕ **Tuolumne Meadows Lodge.** At the back of a small building, this restau-
AMERICAN   rant serves hearty American fare for breakfast and dinner. ⊠ *Tioga Rd. (Rte. 120)* ☎ *209/372–8413* ⚓ *Reservations essential* ☰ *AE, D, DC, MC, V* ☾ *Closed late Sept.–Memorial Day. No lunch.*

$$–$$$$ ✕ **Wawona Hotel Dining Room.** Watch deer graze on the meadow while
AMERICAN   dining in the candlelit dining room of the Wawona Hotel, which dates
★   from the late 1800s. The American-style cuisine favors fresh California ingredients and flavors; trout is a menu staple. ⊠ *Wawona Hotel, Rte. 41, Wawona* ☎ *209/375–1425* ⚓ *Reservations essential* ☰ *AE, D, DC, MC, V* ☾ *Closed Jan.–Mar.*

PICNIC AREAS

Considering the size of the park and the 3.5 million people who visit every year, it's surprising that Yosemite has so few formal picnic areas, though there's no shortage of smooth rocks to sit on to enjoy breathtaking views. The convenience stores sell picnic supplies, and prepackaged lunches are available. Those options come in handy at midday, when you'd prefer to spend precious hours in a spectacular setting rather than in a restaurant. These spots don't have drinking water; most have some type of toilet. Optimum spots include Cathedral Beach, Church Bowl, Swinging Bridge, and Yellow Pine.

WHERE TO STAY

■TIP➔ **Reserve your room or cabin in Yosemite as far in advance as possible.** You can make a reservation up to a year before your arrival (within minutes after the reservation office makes a date available, the Ahwahnee, Yosemite Lodge, and Wawona Hotel often sell out their weekends, holiday periods, and all days between May and September).

Hotel reviews have been condensed for this book. Please go to Fodors. com for full reviews of each property.

WHAT IT COSTS				
	¢	$	$$	$$$	$$$$
Hotels	under $50	$50–$100	$101–$150	$151–$200	over $200

Hotel prices are per night for two people in a standard double room in high season, excluding taxes and service charges.

$$$$

Fodor's Choice

★

The Ahwahnee. The guest rooms at this National Historic Landmark have American Indian design motifs and its public spaces are decorated with oriental rugs and elaborate woodwork. **Pros:** best lodge in Yosemite (if not California); concierge. **Cons:** expensive; some reports that service has slipped in recent years. ⊠ *1 Ahwahnee Rd., about ¾ mi east of Yosemite Valley Visitor Center, Yosemite Village* 1 *Ahwahnee Rd., Yosemite National Park 95389* 209/372–1407 *or 801/559–5000* *www.yosemitepark.com* *99 lodge rooms, 4 suites, 24 cottage rooms* *In-room: a/c, refrigerator, Wi-Fi. In-hotel: restaurant, room service, bar, pool, Wi-Fi* ☰ *AE, D, DC, MC, V.*

$–$$

Curry Village. Opened in 1899, Curry Village has modestly priced, standard motel rooms, cabins, and tent cabins, which are a step up from camping, with linens and blankets provided; some even have heat. **Pros:** comparatively economical; family-friendly. **Cons:** crowded; often noisy. ⊠ *South side of Southside Dr., Yosemite Valley* 801/559–5000 *www.yosemitepark.com* *18 rooms, 527 cabins* *In-room: no a/c, no phone, no TV. In-hotel: 3 restaurants, bar, pool, bicycles* ☰ *AE, D, DC, MC, V.*

$$–$$$

Wawona Hotel. This 1879 National Historic Landmark sits at Yosemite's southern end, a 15-minute drive from the Mariposa Grove of Big Trees. It's an old-fashioned New England–style estate, with pleasant, no-frills rooms decorated with period pieces. **Pros:** lovely; peaceful atmosphere; close to Mariposa Grove. **Cons:** few modern in-room amenities; half the rooms have no baths. ⊠ *Hwy. 41, Wawona* 801/559–5000 *www.yosemitepark.com* *104 rooms, 50 with bath* *In-room: no a/c, no phone, no TV. In-hotel: restaurant, bar, golf course, tennis court, pool* ☰ *AE, D, DC, MC, V* *Closed Jan. through Mar. and Nov. 28–Dec. 14.*

$–$$

White Wolf Lodge. Set in a subalpine meadow, White Wolf offers rustic accommodations in tent cabins. This is an excellent base camp for hiking the backcountry. Breakfast and dinner are served home-style in the snug main building. **Pros:** quiet; convenient for hikers; good restaurant. **Cons:** far from the Valley; not much to do here except hiking. ⊠ *Off Tioga Rd. (Rte. 120), 25 mi west of Tuolumne Meadows and 15 mi east of Crane Flat* 801/559–5000 *24 tent cabins, 4 cabins* *In-room: no a/c, no phone, no TV. In-hotel: restaurant* ☰ *AE, D, DC, MC, V* *Closed mid-Sept.–early June.*

$$$

Yosemite Lodge at the Falls. Though this lodge near Yosemite Falls dates from 1915, it looks like a 1960s motel-resort complex. Rooms have two double beds; larger rooms have dressing areas and patios or balconies, and a few have views of the falls. **Pros:** centrally located; clean rooms; many tours leave from out front. **Cons:** can feel impersonal; appearance is a little dated. ⊠ *Northside Dr. about ¾ mi west of visitor center, Yosemite Village* 559/252–4848 *www.yosemitepark.com* *245 rooms* *In-room: no a/c. In-hotel: restaurant, bar, pool, bicycles, Wi-Fi hotspot* ☰ *AE, D, DC, MC, V.*

CAMPING

The 464 campsites within Yosemite Valley are the park's most tightly spaced, and along with the 304-site campground at Tuolumne Meadows, the most difficult to secure on short notice.

26

The park's backcountry and the surrounding wilderness have some unforgettable campsites, but they can only be reached via long, often difficult hikes or horseback rides. Delaware North operates five High Sierra camps with comfortable, furnished tent cabins in the remote reaches of Yosemite; rates include breakfast and dinner service. The park concessionaire books the popular backcountry camps by lottery; applications are due by late November for the following summer season. Phone ☎ *801/559–4909* for more information, or check for current availability online ⊕ *www.yosemitepark.com* at the High Sierra Camps pages.

To camp in a High Sierra campground you must obtain a wilderness permit. Make reservations up to 24 weeks in advance by visiting the park's Web site (⊕ *www.nps.gov/yose/planyourvisit/backpacking.htm*) and checking availability. For a $5 nonrefundable fee you can make reservations by phone (☎ *209/372–0740*) or by mail (✉ *Box 545, Yosemite, CA 95389*); make checks payable to "Yosemite Association."

Reservations are required at most of Yosemite's campgrounds, especially in summer. You can reserve a site up to five months in advance; bookings made more than 21 days in advance require prepayment. Unless otherwise noted, book your site through the central **National Park Service Reservations Office** (✉ *Box 1600, Cumberland, MD 21502* ☎ *800/436–7275* ⊕ *www.recreation.gov* ▭ *D, MC, V* ⊙ *Daily 7–7.*

Delaware North Companies Parks and Resorts (✉ *6771 N. Palm Ave., Fresno, CA 93704* ☎ *801/559–5000* ⊕ *www.yosemitepark.com*), which handles most in-park reservations, takes reservations beginning one year plus one day in advance of your proposed stay. Or you can roll the dice by showing up and asking if there have been any cancellations.

San Francisco

WORD OF MOUTH

"The part I was really looking forward to was walking down [Telegraph Hill] and looking for parrots. I'd seen the movie The Wild Parrots of Telegraph Hill, and the neighborhood was one of the things that meant 'San Francisco' to me. The neighborhood itself was beautiful, and we did indeed see parrots."

—sunny16

WELCOME TO SAN FRANCISCO

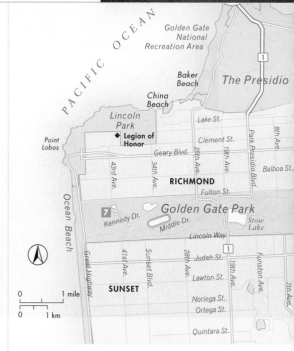

TOP REASONS TO GO

★ **The bay:** It's hard not to gasp as you catch sight of sunlight dancing on the water when you crest a hill, or watch the Golden Gate Bridge vanish and reemerge in the summer fog.

★ **The food:** San Franciscans are serious about what they eat, and with good reason. Home to some of the nation's best chefs, top restaurants, and finest local produce, it's hard not to eat well here.

★ **The shopping:** Shopaholics visiting the city will not be disappointed: San Francisco is packed with browsing destinations, everything from quirky boutiques to massive malls.

★ **The good life:** A laid-back atmosphere, beautiful surroundings, and oodles of cultural, culinary, and aesthetic pleasures . . . if you spend too much time here, you might not leave!

★ **The great outdoors:** From Golden Gate Park to sidewalk cafés in North Beach, San Franciscans relish their outdoor spaces.

1 Union Square and Chinatown. Union Square has hotels, public transportation, and shopping; walking through Chinatown is like visiting another country.

2 SoMa and Civic Center. SoMa is anchored by SFMOMA and Yerba Buena Gardens; the city's performing arts venues are in Civic Center.

3 Nob Hill and Russian Hill. Nob Hill is old-money San Francisco; Russian Hill's steep streets have excellent eateries and shopping.

4 North Beach. This small Italian neighborhood is a great place to enjoy an espresso.

5 On the Waterfront. Head here to visit the exquisitely restored Ferry Building, Fisherman's Wharf, Pier 39, and Ghirardelli Square.

6 The Marina and the Presidio. The Marina has trendy boutiques, restaurants, and cafés; the wooded Presidio offers great views of the Golden Gate Bridge.

7 Golden Gate Park and the Western Shoreline. San Francisco's 1,000-acre

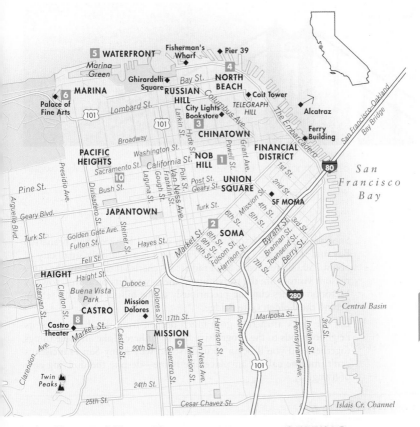

backyard has sports fields, windmills, museums, and gardens; the windswept Western Shoreline stretches for miles.

8 The Haight, the Castro, and Noe Valley. After you've seen the blockbuster sights, come to these neighborhoods to see where the city's heart beats.

9 The Mission. This Latino neighborhood has destination restaurants, bargain ethnic eateries, and a hip bar scene.

10 Pacific Heights and Japantown. Pacific Heights has some of the city's most opulent real estate; Japantown is packed with authentic Japanese shops and restaurants.

GETTING ORIENTED

San Francisco is a compact city, just 46½ square mi. Essentially a tightly packed cluster of extremely diverse neighborhoods, the city dearly rewards walking. The areas that most visitors cover are easy (and safe) to reach on foot, but many have steep—make that *steep*—hills.

27

San Francisco's charms are great and small. You won't want to miss Golden Gate Park, the Palace of Fine Arts, the Golden Gate Bridge, or a cable-car ride over Nob Hill.

Snuggling on a 46½-square-mi strip of land between San Francisco Bay and the Pacific Ocean, San Francisco is a relatively small city of about 750,000 residents. San Franciscans cherish their city for the same reasons visitors do: the proximity to the bay and its pleasures, rows of Victorian homes clinging precariously to the hillsides, the sun setting behind the Golden Gate Bridge.

But the city's attraction goes much deeper, from the diversity of its neighborhoods to the progressive free spirit here. Take all these things together, and you'll begin to understand why many San Franciscans can't imagine calling anyplace else home—despite the dizzying cost of living.

PLANNING

WHEN TO GO
The best time to visit San Francisco is September and October, when the city's summerlike weather brings outdoor concerts and festivals. Summers can be chilly, although the temperature rarely drops below 40°F, and anything warmer than 80°F is considered a heat wave. Be prepared for rain in winter, especially December and January.

GETTING HERE AND AROUND
AIR TRAVEL
The major gateway to San Francisco is San Francisco International Airport (SFO), 15 mi south of the city. Oakland International Airport (OAK) is just across the bay, but traffic on the Bay Bridge may lengthen travel times considerably.

Airports Oakland International Airport (*OAK* ☎ *510/563–3300* ⊕ *www. flyoakland.com*). **San Francisco International Airport** (*SFO* ☎ *800/435–9736* ⊕ *www.flysfo.com*).

Airport Transfers **American Airporter** (☎ *415/202–0733* ⊕ *www. americanairporter.com*). **BayPorter Express** (☎ *877/467–1800* ⊕ *www. bayporter.com*). **Caltrain** (☎ *800/660–4287* ⊕ *www.caltrain.com*).

BART TRAVEL

Bay Area Rapid Transit (BART) trains, which run until midnight, connect San Francisco with Oakland, Berkeley, and other East Bay cities. Within San Francisco, stations are limited to downtown, the Mission, and a couple of outlying neighborhoods.

Trains travel frequently from early morning until evening on weekdays. After 8 pm weekdays and on weekends there's often a 20-minute wait between trains on the same line. BART trains connect downtown San Francisco to San Francisco International Airport; a ride is $8.10.

Intracity San Francisco fares are $1.75; intercity fares are $2.90 to $6.35. BART bases its ticket prices on miles traveled and does not offer price breaks by zone.

Contact Bay Area Rapid Transit (*BART* ☎ *415/989–2278 or 650/992–2278* ⊕ *www.bart.gov*).

CABLE CAR TRAVEL

The fare (for one direction) is $5. You can buy tickets on board (exact change isn't necessary) or at the kiosks at the cable car turnarounds at Hyde and Beach streets and at Powell and Market streets.

The heavily traveled Powell–Mason and Powell–Hyde lines begin at Powell and Market streets near Union Square and terminate at Fisherman's Wharf; lines for these routes can be long, especially in summer. The California Street line runs east and west from Market and California streets to Van Ness Avenue; there is often no wait to board this route.

CAR TRAVEL

Driving in San Francisco can be a challenge because of the one-way streets, snarly traffic, and steep hills. The first two elements can be frustrating enough, but those hills are tough for unfamiliar drivers. ■ TIP→ Remember to curb your wheels when parking on hills—turn wheels away from the curb when facing uphill, toward the curb when facing downhill. You can get a ticket if you don't do this.

MUNI TRAVEL

The San Francisco Municipal Transportation Agency, or Muni, operates light-rail vehicles, the historic F-line streetcars along Fisherman's Wharf and Market Street, trolley buses, and the world-famous cable cars. Muni provides 24-hour service on select lines to all areas of the city.

On buses and streetcars the fare is $2. Exact change is required, and dollar bills are accepted in the fare boxes. For all Muni vehicles other than cable cars, 90-minute transfers are issued free upon request at the time the fare is paid. Cable cars cost $5 and include no transfers (⇨ *see Cable Car Travel, above*).

One-day ($13), three-day ($20), and seven-day ($26) Passports valid on the entire Muni system can be purchased at the cable-car ticket booth at Powell and Market streets and the visitor information center downstairs in Hallidie Plaza. The San Francisco CityPass, a discount ticket

27

DID YOU KNOW?

Cable cars have been running up and down the hills of San Francisco since 1873. For the first two days after they were introduced, rides were free because passengers were afraid to get on.

4
POWELL AND MARKET
HYDE & BEACH
FISHERMANS WHARF

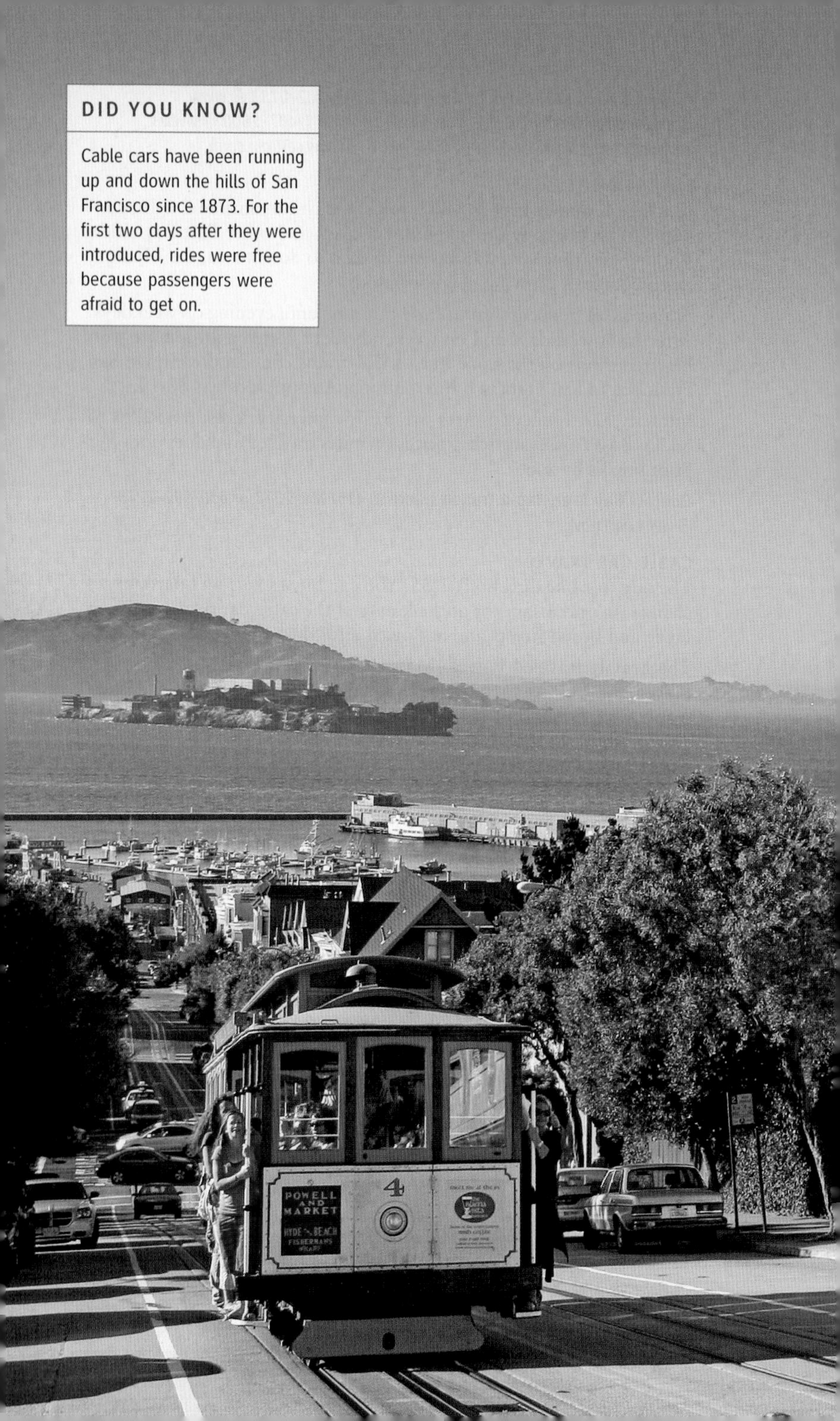

booklet to several major city attractions, also covers all Muni travel for seven consecutive days.

Bus Lines Golden Gate Transit (☎ 415/923–2000 ⊕ www.goldengate.org). **San Francisco Municipal Transportation Agency** (Muni ☎ 415/673–6864 ⊕ www.sfmta.com).

VISITOR INFORMATION

The San Francisco Convention and Visitors Bureau can mail you brochures, maps, and festivals and events listings. Once you're in town, you can stop by their info center near Union Square. If you're planning to hit big-ticket stops like the California Academy of Sciences and ride the cable cars, consider picking up a CityPass here (or at any of the attractions it covers). ■TIP→ The CityPass ($64, $39 ages 5–12), good for nine days including seven days of transit, will save you about 50%.

Contacts San Francisco Visitor Information Center (⌧ Hallidie Plaza, lower level, 900 Market St., Union Sq. ☎ 415/391–2000 or 415/283–0177 ⊕ www. onlyinsanfrancisco.com).

EXPLORING SAN FRANCISCO

UNION SQUARE AND CHINATOWN

The Union Square area bristles with big-city bravado, while just a stone's throw away is a place that feels like a city unto itself, Chinatown. The two areas share a strong commercial streak, although manifested very differently. In Union Square the crowds zigzag among international brands, trailing glossy shopping bags. A few blocks north people dash between small neighborhood stores, their arms draped with plastic totes filled with groceries or souvenirs.

WHAT TO SEE

Union Square. The heart of San Francisco's downtown since 1850, a 2½-acre square surrounded by department stores and the St. Francis Hotel, is about the only place you can sit for free in this part of town. Union Square's 2002 redesign added a café, an open-air stage, and a visitor information booth. And there's a familiar kaleidoscope of characters: office workers sunning and brown-bagging, street musicians, shoppers taking a rest, and a fair number of homeless people.

SOMA AND CIVIC CENTER

To a newcomer, SoMa (short for "south of Market") and Civic Center may look like cheek-by-jowl neighbors—they're divided by Market Street. To locals, though, these areas are firmly separate entities. SoMa is less a neighborhood than it is a sprawling area of wide, traffic-heavy boulevards lined with office high-rises and pricey live-work lofts. Across Market Street from the western edge of SoMa is Civic Center, with San Francisco's eye-catching, gold-domed City Hall.

WHAT TO SEE

Fodor'sChoice ★ **San Francisco Museum of Modern Art (SFMOMA).** With its brick facade and a striped central tower lopped at a lipstick-like angle, architect Mario Botta's SFMOMA building fairly screams "modern-art museum."

■ TIP→ Taking in all of SFMOMA's four exhibit floors can be overwhelming. Keep in mind that the museum's heavy hitters are on floors 2 and 3. Floor 2 gets the big-name traveling exhibits and collection highlights such as Matisse's *Woman with the Hat* and Diego Rivera's *The Flower Carrier.* Floor 3 showcases the photography of Ansel Adams and Alfred Stieglitz. The large-scale contemporary exhibits on floors 4 and 5 can usually be seen quickly (or skipped). Don't miss sculptor Jeff Koons' memorably creepy, life-size gilded porcelain *Michael Jackson and Bubbles,* on the fifth floor at the end of the Turret Bridge, a vertiginous catwalk dangling under the central tower. Caffè Museo provides a refuge for quite good, reasonably priced light meals. It's easy to drop a fortune at the museum's wonderful store ⊠ *151 3rd St., SoMa* ☎ *415/357–4000* ⊕ *www.sfmoma.org* ⊠ *$18, free 1st Tues. of month, ½ price Thurs. 6–9* ☉ *Labor Day–Memorial Day, Fri.–Tues. 11–5:45, Thurs. 11–8:45; Memorial Day–Labor Day, Fri.–Tues. 10–5:45, Thurs. 10–8:45.*

ⓒ ★ **Yerba Buena Gardens.** There's not much south of Market that encourages lingering outdoors, or indeed walking at all, with this notable exception. These two blocks encompass the **Center for the Arts, Metreon, Moscone Convention Center,** and the convention center's rooftop **Zeum,** but the gardens themselves are the everyday draw. Office workers escape to the green swath of the East Garden; the memorial to Martin Luther King Jr. is the focal point here. ■ TIP→ The gardens are liveliest during the week and especially during the **Yerba Buena Gardens Festival** (May–October ⊕ www.ybgf.org), when free performances run from Latin music to Balinese dance.

Atop the Moscone Convention Center perch a few lures for kids. The historic **Looff carousel** ($3 for two rides) twirls daily 11–6. South of the carousel is **Zeum** (☎ *415/820–3320* ⊕ *www.zeum.org*), a high-tech, interactive arts-and-technology center (adults, $10; kids 3–18, $8) where kids can make Claymation videos and work in a computer lab. Also part of the rooftop complex are gardens, an ice-skating rink, and a bowling alley. ⊠ *Bordered by 3rd, 4th, Mission, and Folsom Sts., SoMa* ☎ *No phone* ⊕ *www.yerbabuenagardens.org* ⊠ *Free* ☉ *Daily sunrise–10 pm.*

27

NOB HILL AND RUSSIAN HILL

In place of the quirky charm and cultural diversity that mark other San Francisco neighborhoods, Nob Hill exudes history and good breeding. Topped with some of the city's most elegant hotels, Gothic Grace Cathedral, and private blue-blood clubs, it's the pinnacle of privilege. One hill over, across Pacific Avenue, is another old-family bastion, Russian Hill. It may not be quite as wealthy as Nob Hill, but it's no slouch—and it's known for its jaw-dropping views.

View of North Beach and Coit Tower as seen from Lombard Street.

WHAT TO SEE

★ **Ina Coolbrith Park.** If you make it all the way up here, you may have the meditative setting and spectacular views all to yourself, or at least feel like you do. The park's terraces are carved from a hill so steep that it's difficult to see if anyone else is there or not. A California poet laureate, Oakland librarian, and niece of Mormon prophet Joseph Smith, Ina Coolbrith (1842–1928) entertained literary greats in her Macondray Lane home near the park. ⊠ *Vallejo St. between Mason and Taylor Sts., Russian Hill.*

Lombard Street. The block-long "Crookedest Street in the World" makes eight switchbacks down the east face of Russian Hill between Hyde and Leavenworth streets. Join the line of cars waiting to drive down the steep hill, or walk down the steps on either side of Lombard. You take in super views of North Beach and Coit Tower whether you walk or drive—though if you're the one behind the wheel, you'd better keep your eye on the road lest you become yet another of the many folks who ram the garden barriers. ■ TIP→ Thrill seekers of a different stripe may want to head two blocks south of Lombard to Filbert Street. At a gradient of 31.5%, the hair-raising descent between Hyde and Leavenworth streets is the city's steepest. ⊠ *Lombard St. between Hyde and Leavenworth Sts., Russian Hill.*

Fodor'sChoice **Macondray Lane.** San Francisco has no shortage of impressive, grand
★ homes, but it's the tiny fairy-tale lanes that make most folks want to move here, and Macondray Lane is the quintessential hidden garden. Enter under a lovely wooden trellis and proceed down a quiet, cobbled pedestrian lane lined with Edwardian cottages and flowering plants and

trees. A flight of steep wooden stairs at the end of the lane leads to Taylor Street—on the way down you can't miss the bay views. ⊠ *Between Jones and Taylor Sts., and Union and Green Sts., Russian Hill.*

NORTH BEACH

San Francisco novelist Herbert Gold calls North Beach "the longest-running, most glorious American bohemian operetta outside Greenwich Village." Indeed, to anyone who's spent some time in its eccentric old bars and cafés, North Beach evokes everything from the Barbary Coast days to the no-less-rowdy Beatnik era. With its outdoor café tables, throngs of tourists, and holiday vibe, this is probably the part of town Europeans are thinking of when they say San Francisco is the most European city in America.

WHAT TO SEE

★ **City Lights Bookstore.** Take a look at the exterior of the store: the replica of a revolutionary mural destroyed in Chiapas, Mexico, by military forces; the poetry in the windows; and the sign that says "Turn your sell [sic] phone off. Be here now." This place isn't just doling out best sellers. Designated a city landmark, the hangout of Beat-era writers—Allen Ginsberg and store founder Lawrence Ferlinghetti among them—remains a vital part of San Francisco's literary scene. ■ TIP➔ Be sure to check their calendar of literary events.

Ferlinghetti cemented City Lights' place in history by publishing Ginsberg's *Howl and Other Poems* in 1956. The small volume was ignored in the mainstream . . . until Ferlinghetti and the bookstore manager were arrested for corruption of youth and obscenity. In the landmark First Amendment trial that followed, the judge exonerated both, saying a work that has "redeeming social significance" can't be obscene. *Howl* went on to become a classic.

Embedded in the pavement of Kerouac Alley, next to City Lights, are quotes from Lawrence Ferlinghetti, Maya Angelou, Confucius, John Steinbeck, and, of course, the namesake himself. ⊠ *261 Columbus Ave., North Beach* ☎ *415/362–8193* ⊕ *www.citylights.com* ☉ *Daily 10 am–midnight.*

★ **Coit Tower.** This 210-foot tower is among San Francisco's most distinctive skyline sights.

You can ride the elevator to the top of the tower—the only thing you have to pay for here—to enjoy the view of the Bay Bridge and the Golden Gate Bridge; due north is Alcatraz Island. ■ TIP➔ The views from the base of the tower are also expansive—and free. Parking at Coit Tower is limited; save yourself some frustration and take the 39 bus all the way up to the tower's base or, if you're in good shape, hike up. ⇨ *For more details on the lovely stairway walk, see Telegraph Hill, below.* ⊠ *Telegraph Hill Blvd. at Greenwich St. or Lombard St., North Beach* ☎ *415/362–0808* 🎟 *Free; elevator to top $5* ☉ *Daily 10–6.*

Fodor's Choice **Telegraph Hill.** Hill residents have some of the best views in the city, as
★ well as the most difficult ascents to their aeries. The hill rises from the east end of Lombard Street to a height of 284 feet, and is capped by

27

Coit Tower (*see above*). If you brave the slope you'll be rewarded with a "secret treasure" SF moment. Filbert Street starts up the hill, then becomes the Filbert Steps. Cut between these and another flight, the Greenwich Steps, on up to the hilltop. As you climb, you can pass some of the city's oldest houses and be surrounded by beautiful, flowering private gardens. The hill's name comes from its status as the first Morse code signal station back in 1853. ⊠ *Bordered by Lombard, Filbert, Kearny, and Sansome Sts., North Beach.*

ON THE WATERFRONT

San Francisco's waterfront neighborhoods have fabulous views and utterly different personalities. Kitschy, overpriced Fisherman's Wharf struggles to maintain the last shreds of its existence as a working wharf, while Pier 39 is a full-fledged consumer circus. The Ferry Building draws well-heeled locals with its culinary pleasures. Between the Ferry Building and Pier 39, a former maritime no-man's land is beginning to fill in—especially near Pier 33, where the perpetually booked Alcatraz cruises depart.

WHAT TO SEE

Fodor'sChoice ★ **Alcatraz.** Thousands of visitors a day take the 15-minute ferry ride to "the Rock" to walk in the footsteps of Alcatraz's notorious criminals. Definitely take the splendid audio tour; gravelly voiced former inmates and hardened guards bring one of America's most notorious penal colonies to life. Allow at least three hours for the visit and boat rides combined, and buy tickets in advance, even in the off-season. ⊠ *Pier 33, Fisherman's Wharf* ☎ *415/981–7625* ⊕ *www.nps.gov/alca, www.parkconservancy.org/visit/alcatraz, www.alcatrazcruises.com* ⊡ *$26, including audio tour; $33 evening tour, including audio* ☉ *Ferry departs every 30–45 min Sept.–late May, daily 9:30–3:20, 4:20 for evening tour Thurs.–Mon. only; late May–Aug., daily 9–4, 5:55 and 6:45 for evening tour.*

Fodor'sChoice ★ **Ferry Building.** Renovated in 2003, the Ferry Building is the jewel of the Embarcadero. On the morning of April 18, 1906, the 230-foot tower's four clock faces, powered by the swinging of a 14-foot pendulum, stopped at 5:17—the moment the great earthquake struck—and stayed still for 12 months.

Today San Franciscans flock to the street-level Market Hall, stocking up on supplies from local favorites such as Acme Bread, Scharffen Berger Chocolate, and Cowgirl Creamery. Take your purchases around to the building's bay side, where benches face views of the Bay Bridge. Saturday mornings the plaza in front of the building buzzes with an upscale, celebrity-chef-studded farmers' market. Ferries sail from behind the building to Sausalito, Larkspur, Tiburon, and the East Bay. ⊠ *Embarcadero at foot of Market St., Embarcadero* ⊕ *www.ferrybuildingmarketplace.com.*

ⓒ **Fisherman's Wharf.** It may be one of the city's best-known attractions, but the wharf is a no-go zone for most locals, who shy away from the difficult parking, overpriced food, and cheesy shops at third-rate shopping centers like the Cannery at Del Monte Square. If you just can't resist a visit here, come early to avoid the crowds and get a sense of the wharf's functional role—it's not just an amusement park replica.

Most of the entertainment at the wharf is schlocky and overpriced, with one notable exception: the splendid **Musée Mécanique** (☎ 415/346–2000 ⊘ *Weekdays 10–7, weekends 10–8*), a time-warped arcade with antique mechanical contrivances, including peep shows and nickelodeons. Admission is free, but you'll need quarters to bring the machines to life. ⊠ *Jefferson St. between Leavenworth St. and Pier 39, Fisherman's Wharf.*

THE MARINA AND THE PRESIDIO

Yachts bob at their moorings, satisfied-looking folks jog along the Marina Green, and multimillion-dollar homes overlook the bay in this picturesque, if somewhat sterile, neighborhood. Does it all seem a bit too perfect? Well, it got this way after hundreds of homes collapsed in the 1989 Loma Prieta earthquake. Just west of this waterfront area is a more natural beauty: the Presidio. Once a military base, this inviting, sprawling park is mostly green space, with hills, woods, and the marshlands of Crissy Field.

WHAT TO SEE

☺ **Exploratorium.** Walking into this fascinating "museum of science, art, and ★ human perception" is like visiting a mad scientist's laboratory. Most of the exhibits are supersize, and you can play with everything. In the shadow room, a powerful flash freezes an image of your shadow on the wall. "Pushover" demonstrates cow-tipping, but for people: Stand on one foot and try to keep your balance while a friend swings a striped panel in front of you (trust us, you're going to fall).

More than 650 other exhibits focus on sea and insect life, computers, electricity, patterns and light, language, the weather, and much more. "Explainers" demonstrate cool scientific tools and procedures, like DNA sample-collection and cow-eye dissection. One surefire hit is the pitch-black Tactile Dome, where you crawl through a course of ladders, slides, and tunnels, relying solely on your sense of touch. ■ TIP→ Reservations are required for the Tactile Dome. You have to be at least seven years old, and the space is not for the claustrophobic. ⊠ *3601 Lyon St., at Marina Blvd., Marina* ☎ *415/561–0360 general information, 415/561–0362 Tactile Dome reservations* ⊕ *www.exploratorium. edu* ⊡ *$15, free 1st Wed. of month; Tactile Dome $5 extra* ⊘ *Tues.– Sun. 10–5.*

Fodor's Choice **Golden Gate Bridge.** The suspension bridge that connects San Francisco ★ with Marin County has long wowed sightseers with its simple but powerful art deco design. Completed in 1937, the 2-mi span and its 750-foot towers were built to withstand winds of more than 100 mph. It's also not a bad place to be in an earthquake: designed to sway up to 27.7 feet, the Golden Gate Bridge, unlike the Bay Bridge, was undamaged by the 1989 Loma Prieta quake. Though it's frequently gusty and misty—always bring a jacket, no matter what the weather—the bridge provides unparalleled views of the Bay Area. From the bridge's eastern-side walkway—the only side pedestrians are allowed on—you

27

can take in the San Francisco skyline and the bay islands, the wild hills of the Marin Headlands, the curving coast south to Land's End, and the Pacific Ocean. ■TIP➔ A vista point on the Marin side gives you a spectacular city panorama.

But there's a well-known, darker side to the bridge's story, too. The bridge is perhaps the world's most popular suicide platform, with an average of about 20 jumpers per year. (The first leaped just three months after the bridge's completion, and the official count was stopped in 1995 as the 1,000th jump approached.) Signs along the bridge read "There is hope. Make the call," referring the disconsolate to the special telephones on the bridge. ⊠ *Lincoln Blvd. near Doyle Dr. and Fort Point, Presidio* ☎ *415/921–5858* ⊕ *www.goldengatebridge.org* ☉ *Pedestrians Mar.–Oct., daily 5 am–9 pm; Nov.–Feb., daily 5 am–6 pm; hrs change with daylight saving time. Bicyclists daily 24 hrs.*

Fodor's Choice **Palace of Fine Arts.** At first glance this stunning, rosy rococo palace seems
★ to be from another world, and indeed, it's the sole survivor of the many tinted-plaster structures built for the 1915 Panama-Pacific International Exposition. Bernard Maybeck designed this faux–Roman classical beauty, which was reconstructed in concrete and reopened in 1967.

A victim of the elements, the Palace completed a piece-by-piece renovation in 2008. The massive columns (each topped with four "weeping maidens"), great rotunda, and swan-filled lagoon have been used in countless fashion layouts, films, and wedding photo shoots. ⊠ *Baker and Beach Sts., Marina* ☎ *415/561–0364 Palace history tours* ⊕ *www. exploratorium.edu/palace* ⊠ *Free* ☉ *Daily 24 hrs.*

★ **Presidio.** When San Franciscans want to spend a day in the woods, they head here. The Presidio has 1,400 acres of hills and majestic woods, two small beaches, and—the one thing Golden Gate Park doesn't have—stunning views of the bay, the Golden Gate Bridge, and Marin County. ■TIP➔ The best lookout points lie along Washington Boulevard, which meanders through the park.

Part of the **Golden Gate National Recreation Area,** the Presidio was a military post for more than 200 years.

Today the area is being transformed into a self-sustaining national park with a combination of public, commercial, and residential projects. Bay Area filmmaker George Lucas's **Letterman Digital Arts Center occupies** 23-acres along the Presidio's eastern edge; a new Walt Disney museum has opened, and a lodge at the Main Post is in the planning stages.

GOLDEN GATE PARK AND THE WESTERN SHORELINE

More than 1,000 acres, stretching from the Haight all the way to the windy Pacific coast, Golden Gate Park is a vast patchwork of woods, trails, lakes, lush gardens, sports facilities, museums—even a herd of buffalo. There's more natural beauty beyond the park's borders, along San Francisco's wild Western Shoreline.

In the Haight you'll still find remnants of the '60s counterculture that thrived there.

WHAT TO SEE

Fodor's Choice ★ **Legion of Honor.** You can't beat the location of this museum of European art—situated on cliffs overlooking the ocean, the Golden Gate Bridge, and the Marin Headlands. A pyramidal glass skylight in the entrance court illuminates the lower-level galleries, which exhibit prints and drawings, English and European porcelain, and ancient Assyrian, Greek, Roman, and Egyptian art. The 20-plus galleries on the upper level display the permanent collection of European art from the 14th century to the present day. Two galleries are dedicated to the work of Auguste Rodin, and an original cast of *The Thinker* welcomes you in the courtyard. ■TIP→ Admission to the Legion also counts as same-day admission to the de Young Museum. ⊠ *34th Ave. at Clement St., Outer Richmond* ☎ *415/750–3600* ⊕ *www.thinker.org* ☜ *$10, $2 off with Muni transfer, free 1st Tues. of month* ☉ *Tues.–Sun. 9:30–5:15.*

THE HAIGHT, THE CASTRO, AND NOE VALLEY

Once you've seen the blockbuster sights and you're getting curious about the neighborhoods where the city's soul resides, come out to these three areas. They wear their personalities large and proud, and all are perfect for just strolling around. You can move from the Haight's residue of 1960s counterculture to the Castro's connection to 1970s and '80s gay life to 1990s gentrification in Noe Valley. Although history thrust the Haight and the Castro onto the international stage, both are anything but stagnant—they're still dynamic areas well worth exploring. Noe Valley may lack the headlines, but a mellow morning walk here will make you feel like a local.

THE MISSION DISTRICT

The Mission has a number of distinct personalities: it's the Latino neighborhood, where working-class folks raise their families and where gangs occasionally clash; it's the hipster hood, where tattooed and pierced twenty- and thirtysomethings hold court in the coolest cafés and bars in town; it's a culinary epicenter, with the strongest concentration of destination restaurants and affordable ethnic cuisine; and it's the artists' quarter, where murals adorn literally blocks of walls. It's also the city's equivalent of the Sunshine State—this neighborhood's always the last to succumb to fog.

WHAT TO SEE

★ **Mission Dolores.** Tiny, adobe **Mission San Francisco de Asís is the city's** oldest standing structure. Completed in 1791, it's the sixth of the 21 California missions founded by Father Junípero Serra in the 18th and early 19th centuries. The chapel includes frescoes and a hand-painted wooden altar, a small museum covers the mission's founding and history, and the pretty little mission cemetery (made famous in Alfred Hitchcock's *Vertigo*) maintains the graves of mid-19th-century European immigrants and thousands of natives. ⊠ *Dolores and 16th Sts., Mission* ☎ *415/621–8203* ⊕ *www.missiondolores.org* ✉ *$5 donation, audio tour $7* ☉ *Nov.–Apr., daily 9–4; May–Oct., daily 9–4:30.*

PACIFIC HEIGHTS AND JAPANTOWN

Pacific Heights and Japantown are something of an odd couple: privileged, old-school San Francisco and the workaday commercial center of Japanese-American life in the city, stacked virtually on top of each other. The sprawling, extravagant mansions of Pacific Heights gradually give way to the more modest Victorians and unassuming housing tracts of Japantown. The most interesting spots in Japantown huddle in the Japan Center, the neighborhood's two-block centerpiece, and along Post Street.

WHERE TO EAT

San Francisco is a vital culinary crossroads, with nearly every ethnic cuisine represented. Although locals have long headed to the Mission District for Latin food, Chinatown for Asian food, and North Beach for Italian food, they also know that every part of the city offers dining experiences beyond the neighborhood tradition.

Some renowned restaurants are booked weeks or even months in advance. But you can get lucky at the last minute if you're flexible—and friendly. Most restaurants keep a few tables open for walk-ins and VIPs. Show up for dinner early (5:30 pm) or late (after 9 pm) and politely inquire about any last-minute vacancies or cancellations.

27

WHAT IT COSTS IN U.S. DOLLARS					
	¢	$	$$	$$$	$$$$
Restaurants	under $10	$10–$14	$15–$22	$23–$30	over $30

Prices are per person for a main course at dinner.

NORTH BEACH

$ ✕**L'Osteria del Forno.** Customers who pass through the door of this
ITALIAN modest storefront, with its sunny yellow walls and friendly waitstaff,
☺ feel as if they've stumbled into a homey trattoria in Italy. The kitchen
Fodor'sChoice produces small plates of simply cooked vegetables, a few pastas, a daily
★ special or two, a roast of the day, and thin-crust pizzas. Wine drink-
ers will find a good match for any dish they order on the all-Italian
list. ⊠ *519 Columbus Ave., North Beach* ☎ *415/982–1124* ▭ *No credit
cards* ☾ *Closed Tues.*

FISHERMAN'S WHARF AND MARINA

$$$ ✕**A16.** Marina residents—and, judging from the crowds, everybody
ITALIAN else—gravitate to this lively trattoria, named for the autostrada that
Fodor'sChoice winds through Italy's sunny south. The kitchen serves the food of
★ Naples and surrounding Campania, such as *burrata* (cream-filled moz-
zarella) with olive oil and crostini and crisp-crust pizzas, including a
classic Neapolitan Margherita (mozzarella, tomato, and basil). Among
the regularly changing mains are chicken meatballs with fennel and
salsa verde (green sauce) and rock cod, scallops, and clams in *acqua
pazza* (literally, "crazy water"). The long space includes an animated
bar scene near the door; ask for a table in the quieter alcove at the
far end. ⊠ *2355 Chestnut St., Marina* ☎ *415/771–2216* ▭ *AE, MC, V*
☾ *No lunch Sat.–Tues.*

$$$$ ✕**Gary Danko.** Be prepared to wait your turn for a table behind chef
NEW AMERICAN Gary Danko's legion of loyal fans; plan on reserving two months in
Fodor'sChoice advance. The cost of a meal ($66–$98) is pegged to the number of
★ courses, from three to five. The seasonal menu may include pancetta-
wrapped frogs' legs, shellfish with Thai red curry, and quail stuffed with
foie gras and pine nuts. A diet-destroying chocolate soufflé with two
sauces is usually among the desserts. The wine list is the size of a small-
town phone book, and the banquette-lined room, with beautiful wood
floors and stunning floral arrangements, is as memorable as the food.
⊠ *800 N. Point St., Fisherman's Wharf* ☎ *415/749–2060* ⌦ *Reserva-
tions essential* ▭ *D, DC, MC, V* ☾ *No lunch.*

¢ ✕**Mijita Cocina Mexicana.** Famed local chef Traci Des Jardins' casual
MEXICAN taquería and weekend brunch spot serves tacos with handmade corn
tortillas and fillings like *carnitas* (slow-cooked pork) and mahimahi,
a superb meatball soup, and Oaxacan chicken tamales. Kid-size bur-
ritos (beans and cheese) and quesadillas will keep your niños happy.
Seating is simple—wooden tables and benches—but a perfect perch for
watching gulls on the bay. Plan to eat dinner early; Mijita closes at 7
on weekdays, 8 on weekends. ⊠ *Ferry Bldg., Embarcadero at Market
St., Embarcadero* ☎ *415/399–0814* ▭ *AE, MC, V* ☾ *No dinner Sun.*

HAYES VALLEY

$$$$
NEW AMERICAN
Fodor'sChoice
★

✕ **Jardinière.** The epitome of a special-occasion restaurant, Jardinière takes its name from chef-owner Traci Des Jardins, and the sophisticated interior fills nightly with locals and out-of-towners alike. The equally sophisticated French-cum-Californian dining-room menu, served upstairs in the atrium, changes daily but regularly includes such high-priced adornments as caviar, foie gras, and truffles. Downstairs, the lounge menu, with smaller plates and smaller prices ($8 to $25), is ideal for when you want to eat light or tame your hunger before or after the nearby opera or symphony. ⊠ *300 Grove St., Hayes Valley* ☎ *415/861–5555* ⚐ *Reservations essential* ═ *AE, DC, MC, V* ☉ *No lunch.*

$
SEAFOOD
Fodor'sChoice
★

✕ **Swan Oyster Depot.** Half fish market and half diner, this small seafood operation, open since 1912, has no tables, only a narrow marble counter. Most people come in to buy perfectly fresh salmon, halibut, crabs, and other seafood to take home. Everyone else hops onto one of the rickety stools to enjoy a bowl of clam chowder—the only hot food served—a dozen oysters, half a cracked crab, or a big shrimp salad. Come early or late to avoid a long wait. ⊠ *1517 Polk St., Van Ness/Polk* ☎ *415/673–1101* ⚐ *Reservations not accepted* ═ *No credit cards* ☉ *Closed Sun. No dinner.*

$$$
MEDITERRANEAN
Fodor'sChoice
★

✕ **Zuni Café.** After one bite of chef Judy Rodgers's succulent brick-oven-roasted whole chicken with Tuscan bread salad, you'll understand why she's a national star. Food is served here on two floors; the rabbit warren of rooms on the second level includes a balcony overlooking the main dining room. The crowd reflects the makeup of the city: casual and dressy, young and old, hip and staid. At the long copper bar trays of briny-fresh oysters on the half shell are dispensed along with cocktails and wine. The southern French–Italian menu changes daily (though the signature chicken, prepared for two, is a fixture); desserts are simple and satisfying. The lunchtime burger on rosemary focaccia with shoestring potatoes is a favorite with locals. ⊠ *1658 Market St., Hayes Valley* ☎ *415/552–2522* ═ *AE, MC, V* ☉ *Closed Mon.*

27

THE HAIGHT AND THE MISSION

$$$
ITALIAN
Fodor'sChoice
★

✕ **Delfina.** The wild enthusiasm of Delfina patrons has made patience the critical virtue for anyone wanting a reservation here. The interior is comfortable, with a casual, friendly atmosphere. The daily-changing menu may include salt cod *mantecato* (whipped with olive oil) with fennel flatbread and grilled squid with warm white-bean salad. On warm nights, try for a table on the outdoor heated patio. The storefront next door is home to pint-size Pizzeria Delfina. ⊠ *3621 18th St., Mission* ☎ *415/552–4055* ⚐ *Reservations essential* ═ *MC, V* ☉ *No lunch.*

$
INDIAN

✕ **Dosa.** This temple of South Indian cuisine, done in cheerful tones of tangerine and turmeric, serves not only the large, thin savory pancake for which it is named, but also curries, uttapam (open-face pancakes), and various starters, breads, rice dishes, and chutneys. Queues for this Mission District spot convinced the owners to open a second branch on the corner of Fillmore and Post in Japantown. ⊠ *995 Valencia St., at 21st St., Mission* ☎ *415/642–3672* ═ *AE, D, MC, V* ☉ *No lunch.*

$$
AMERICAN

✕ **Nopa.** This casual space North of the Panhandle ("Nopa"), with its high ceilings, concrete floor, and long bar, suits the high-energy crowd that fills it every night. They come primarily for the rustic fare, like an irresistible flatbread topped with fennel sausage and chanterelles; smoky, crisp-skinned rotisserie chicken; and dark ginger cake with caramelized pears and cream. The lively spirit of the place sometimes means that raised voices are the only way to communicate. ⊠ *560 Divisadero St., Haight* ☎ *415/864–8643* ▭ *AE, MC, V* ⊗ *No lunch.*

EMBARCADERO

$$$$ ✕ **Boulevard.** Two of San Francisco's top restaurant celebrities—chef
AMERICAN   Nancy Oakes and designer Pat Kuleto—are responsible for this high-
Fodor's Choice   profile, high-priced eatery in the magnificent 1889 Audiffred Building,
★   a Parisian look-alike and one of the few downtown structures to survive the 1906 earthquake. Well-dressed locals and flush out-of-towners enjoy generous portions of seasonal dishes like roasted quail stuffed with sweetbreads and chanterelle bisque with pan-seared ricotta gnocchi. Save room (and calories) for one of the dynamite desserts, such as butterscotch-almond apple tart Tatin with cinnamon ice cream. ⊠ *1 Mission St., Embarcadero* ☎ *415/543–6084* ⌂ *Reservations essential* ▭ *AE, D, DC, MC, V* ⊗ *No lunch weekends.*

WHERE TO STAY

San Francisco is one of the country's best hotel towns, offering a rich selection of properties that satisfy most tastes and budgets.

San Francisco hotel prices, among the highest in the United States, may come as an unpleasant surprise. Weekend rates for double rooms in high season average about $132 a night citywide. Rates may vary according to room availability; always inquire about special rates and packages when making reservations; call the property directly, but also check its Web site and try Internet booking agencies.

Hotel reviews have been condensed for this book. Please go to Fodors. com for full reviews of each property.

WHAT IT COSTS IN U.S. DOLLARS					
	¢	$	$$	$$$	$$$$
Hotels	under $80	$80–$149	$150–$199	$200–$250	over $250

Prices are for a double room in high season, excluding 14% tax.

UNION SQUARE, SOMA, AND THE FINANCIAL DISTRICT

$ 📺 **Cornell Hotel de France.** Discovering this French family-operated hotel is like finding a bit of Paris near Union Square. **Pros:** special packages and discounts available upon request, a little bit of France in SF. **Cons:** several blocks from the center of things, surrounding area can be dodgy after dark. ⊠ *715 Bush St., Union Square* ☎ *415/421–3154 or 800/232–9698* ⊕ *www.cornellhotel.com* 🛏 *55 rooms* ⌂ *In-room: no a/c, safe, Wi-Fi. In-hotel: restaurant, Wi-Fi hotspot, parking (fee)* ⊗ *AE, D, DC, MC, V* ⎮⊙⎮ *BP.*

$$$$ 🔲 **Four Seasons Hotel San Francisco.** Occupying floors 5 through 17 of a
🕐 skyscraper, this luxurious hotel is sandwiched between multimillion-
Fodor'sChoice dollar condos, elite shops, and a premier sports-and-fitness complex.
★ Elegant rooms with contemporary artwork and fine linens have floor-
to-ceiling windows overlooking either Yerba Buena Gardens or historic
downtown. **Pros:** near museums, galleries, restaurants, and clubs; terrific fitness facilities. **Cons:** pricey. ⊠ *757 Market St., SoMa* ☎ *415/633–
3000, 800/332–3442, or 800/819–5053* ⊕ *www.fourseasons.com/
sanfrancisco* ⮌ *231 rooms, 46 suites* ⚭ *In-room: a/c, safe, DVD,
Internet, Wi-Fi. In-hotel: restaurant, room service, bar, pool, gym, spa,
laundry service, Internet terminal, parking (paid), some pets allowed*
⊟ *AE, D, DC, MC, V.*

$–$$ 🔲 **Hotel Beresford Arms.** Surrounded by fancy molding and 10-foot-tall
🕐 windows, the red-carpet lobby of this ornate brick Victorian explains
why the building is on the National Register of Historic Places. **Pros:**
moderately priced; suites with kitchenettes and Murphy beds are a
plus for families with kids. **Cons:** no a/c. ⊠ *701 Post St., Union Square*
☎ *415/673–2600 or 800/533–6533* ⊕ *www.beresford.com* ⮌ *83
rooms, 12 suites* ⚭ *In-room: no a/c, kitchen (some), refrigerator, Wi-Fi.
In-hotel: laundry service, Internet terminal, Wi-Fi hotspot, parking
(paid), some pets allowed* ⊟ *AE, D, DC, MC, V* ⏯*CP.*

NORTH BEACH

$$$$ 🔲 **Mandarin Oriental, San Francisco.** Spectacular panoramas from one of
Fodor'sChoice San Francisco's tallest buildings grace every room, and windows open
★ so you can hear that trademark "ding ding" of the cable cars some
40 floors below. **Pros:** spectacular "bridge-to-bridge" views; attentive
service. **Cons:** located in a business area that's quiet on weekends; restaurant is excellent but expensive (as is the hotel). ⊠ *222 Sansome
St., Financial District* ☎ *415/276–9600 or 800/622–0404* ⊕ *www.
mandarinoriental.com/sanfrancisco* ⮌ *151 rooms, 7 suites* ⚭ *In-room:
a/c, safe, DVD, Wi-Fi. In-hotel: restaurant, room service, bar, gym,
laundry service, Internet terminal, Wi-Fi hotspot, parking (paid), some
pets allowed* ⊟ *AE, D, DC, MC, V.*

¢ 🔲 **San Remo Hotel.** A few blocks from Fisherman's Wharf, this three-
Fodor'sChoice story 1906 Italianate Victorian—once home to longshoremen and
★ Beat poets—has a narrow stairway from the street leading to the front
desk and labyrinthine hallways. Rooms are small but charming, with
lace curtains, forest-green-painted wood floors, brass beds, and other
antique furnishings; the top floor is brighter. **Pros:** inexpensive. **Cons:**
some rooms are dark; no private bath; spartan amenities. ⊠ *2237
Mason St., North Beach* ☎ *415/776–8688 or 800/352–7366* ⊕ *www.
sanremohotel.com* ⮌ *64 rooms with shared baths, 1 suite* ⚭ *In-room:
no phone, no a/c, no TV, Wi-Fi. In-hotel: laundry facilities, Wi-Fi hotspot, parking (paid)* ⊟ *AE, D, MC, V.*

FISHERMAN'S WHARF

$$$–$$$$ 🔲 **Argonaut Hotel.** When the four-story Haslett Warehouse was a fruit-
🕐 and-vegetable canning complex in 1907, boats docked right up against
Fodor'sChoice the building. Today it's a hotel with nautical decor that reflects its unique
★ partnership with the San Francisco Maritime National Historical Park.

27

Rock music one day and salsa the next keeps a diverse crowd coming to El Rio.

Pros: bay views; near Hyde Street cable car; sofa beds; toys for the kids. **Cons:** cramped public areas; service can be hit or miss; location is a bit of a hike from other parts of town. ⊠ *495 Jefferson St., at Hyde St., Fisherman's Wharf* ☎ *415/563–0800 or 866/415–0704* ⊕ *www. argonauthotel.com* ➫ *239 rooms, 13 suites* ⅜ *In-room: a/c, safe, refrigerator, Internet, Wi-Fi. In-hotel: restaurant, room service, bar, gym, laundry service, Wi-Fi terminal, parking (paid), some pets allowed* ⊟ *AE, D, DC, MC, V.*

PACIFIC HEIGHTS

$$$–$$$$

Fodor's Choice

★

🏨 **Hotel Drisco.** Pretend you're a resident of one of the wealthiest and most beautiful residential neighborhoods in San Francisco at this understated, elegant 1903 Edwardian hotel. **Pros:** great service; comfortable rooms; quiet residential retreat. **Cons:** small rooms; far from downtown. ⊠ *2901 Pacific Ave., Pacific Heights* ☎ *415/346–2880 or 800/634–7277* ⊕ *www.hoteldrisco.com* ➫ *29 rooms, 19 suites* ⅜ *In-room: no a/c, safe, refrigerator, DVD. In-hotel: laundry service, Internet terminal* ⊟ *AE, D, DC, MC, V* ⦿⦿ *CP.*

$$–$$$

Fodor's Choice

★

🏨 **Queen Anne.** Built in the 1890s as a girls' finishing school, this Victorian mansion has a large comfortable parlor done up in red brocade, lace, and heirloom antiques. **Pros:** free weekday car service, character. **Cons:** far from downtown. ⊠ *1590 Sutter St., Pacific Heights* ☎ *415/441–2828 or 800/227–3970* ⊕ *www.queenanne.com* ➫ *41 rooms, 7 suites* ⅜ *In-room: Wi-Fi. In-hotel: laundry service, concierge, Wi-Fi hotspot, parking (fee)* ⊟ *AE, D, DC, MC, V* ⦿⦿ *CP.*

NIGHTLIFE

This small city packs the punch of a much larger metropolis after dark. Sophisticated, trendy, relaxed, quirky, and downright outrageous could all be used to describe San Francisco's diverse and vibrant collection of bars, clubs, and performance venues.

Entertainment information is printed in the pink Sunday "Datebook" section (⊕ *www.sfgate.com/datebook*) and the more calendar-based Thursday "96 Hours" section (⊕ *www.sfgate.com/96hours*) in the *San Francisco Chronicle.* Also consult the free alternative weeklies, notably the *SF Weekly* (⊕ *www.sfweekly.com*), which blurbs nightclubs and music, and the *San Francisco Bay Guardian* (⊕ *www.sfbg.com*), which lists neighborhood, avant-garde, and budget events. SF Station (⊕ *www. sfstation.com*; online only) has an up-to-date entertainment calendar.

BARS AND LOUNGES

Cliff House. With impressive, sweeping views of Ocean Beach, the Cliff House is our pick for oceanfront restaurant/bar. The best window seats are reserved for diners, but there's a small upstairs lounge where you can watch gulls sail high above the vast blue Pacific. Come before sunset. ✉ *1090 Point Lobos, at Great Hwy., Lincoln Park* ☎ *415/386–3330* ⊕ *www.cliffhouse.com.*

Hôtel Biron. Sharing an alleylike block with the backs of Market Street restaurants, this tiny, cavelike (in a good way) spot draws well-behaved twenty- to thirtysomethings who enjoy the cramped quarters, good range of wines and prices, off-the-beaten path location, soft lighting, and hip music. If it's too crowded, CAV is just around the corner. ✉ *45 Rose St., off Market St., Hayes Valley* ☎ *415/703–0403* ⊕ *www. hotelbiron.com.*

MUSIC

BooM BooM RooM. John Lee Hooker's old haunt has been an old-school blues haven for years, attracting top-notch acts from all around the country. ✉ *1601 Fillmore St., at Geary Blvd., Japantown* ☎ *415/673–8000* ⊕ *www.boomboomblues.com.*

Great American Music Hall. You can find top-drawer entertainment at this great, eclectic nightclub. Acts range from the best in blues, folk, and jazz to up-and-coming college-radio and American-roots artists to of-the-moment indie rock stars (OK Go, Mates of State) and the establishment (Cowboy Junkies). The colorful marble-pillared emporium, built in 1907 as a bordello, also serves pub grub most nights. ✉ *859 O'Farrell St., between Polk and Larkin Sts., Tenderloin* ☎ *415/885–0750* ⊕ *www.gamh.com.*

Yoshi's. The city's outpost of the legendary Oakland club that has pulled in some of the world's best jazz musicians—Pat Martino, Betty Carter, and Dizzy Gillespie, to name just a few—has terrific acoustics, a 9-foot Steinway grand piano (broken in by Chick Corea), and seating for 411; it's been hailed as "simply the best jazz club in the city." Yoshi's also serves Japanese food in an adjoining restaurant and at café tables in the club. Be advised, the club is in a tough neighborhood; take advan-

27

tage of the valet parking. ✉ *1330 Fillmore St., at Eddy St., Japantown* ☎ *415/655–5600* ⊕ *www.yoshis.com.*

THE ARTS

San Francisco's symphony, opera, and ballet all perform in the Civic Center area, also home to the 928-seat Herbst Theatre, which hosts many fine soloists and ensembles. **San Francisco Performances** (✉ *500 Sutter St., Suite 710* ☎ *415/398–6449* ⊕ *www.performances.org*) brings an eclectic array of top-flight global music and dance talents, such as the Los Angeles Guitar Quartet and Midori, to various venues.

City Box Office (✉ *180 Redwood St., Suite 100, off Van Ness Ave. between Golden Gate Ave. and McAllister St., Civic Center* ☎ *415/392–4400* ⊕ *www.cityboxoffice.com*), a charge-by-phone service, offers tickets for many performances and lectures. You can charge tickets for everything from jazz concerts to Giants games by phone or online through **Tickets.com** (☎ *800/955–5566* ⊕ *www.tickets.com*). Half-price, same-day tickets for many local and touring stage shows go on sale at the **TIX Bay Area** (✉ *Powell St. between Geary and Post Sts., Union Square* ☎ *415/433–7827* ⊕ *www.tixbayarea.com*) booth on Union Square.

MUSIC

San Francisco Symphony. One of America's top orchestras, the San Francisco Symphony performs from September through May, with additional summer performances of light classical music and show tunes. Music director Michael Tilson Thomas is known for his innovative programming of 20th-century American works; he and his orchestra often perform with soloists of the caliber of Andre Watts, Gil Shaham, and Renée Fleming. ✉ *Davies Symphony Hall, 201 Van Ness Ave., at Grove St., Civic Center* ☎ *415/864–6000* ⊕ *www.sfsymphony.org.*

☾ **Stern Grove Festival.** The nation's oldest continual free summer music festival hosts Sunday-afternoon performances of symphony, opera, jazz, pop music, and dance. The amphitheater is in a beautiful eucalyptus grove below street level, perfect for picnicking before the show. (Dress for cool weather.) ✉ *Sloat Blvd. at 19th Ave., Sunset* ☎ *415/252–6252* ⊕ *www.sterngrove.org.*

THEATER

American Conservatory Theater. One of the nation's leading regional theaters, ACT presents approximately eight plays, from classics to contemporary works, during its fall—spring season. ✉ *425 Geary St., Union Square* ☎ *415/749–2228* ⊕ *www.act-sf.org.*

Teatro ZinZanni. Contortionists, chanteuses, jugglers, illusionists, and circus performers ply the audience as you're served a surprisingly good five-course dinner in a fabulous antique Belgian traveling-dance-hall tent. Tickets are $117 to $195. Dress fancy. ✉ *Pier 29, Embarcadero at Battery St., Embarcadero* ☎ *415/438–2668* ⊕ *www.zinzanni.org.*

SHOPPING

THE CASTRO AND NOE VALLEY

The Castro, often called the gay capital of the world, is filled with men's clothing boutiques and home-accessories stores geared to the neighborhood's fairly wealthy demographic. Of course, there are plenty of places hawking kitsch, too, and if you're looking for something to shock your Aunt Martha back home, you've come to the right place. Just south of the Castro on 24th Street, largely residential Noe Valley is an enclave of fancy-food stores, bookshops, and specialty gift stores.

CHINATOWN

Chinatown's 24 blocks of shops, restaurants, and markets are a nonstop tide of activity. Dominating the exotic cityscape are the sights and smells of food: crates of bok choy, tanks of live crabs, cages of live partridges, and hanging whole chickens. Racks of Chinese silks, baskets, and carved figurines are displayed chockablock on the sidewalks, alongside fragrant herb shops where your bill might be tallied on an abacus. And if you need to knock off cheap souvenir shopping for the kids and office mates in your life, this is the place.

FISHERMAN'S WHARF

A constant throng of sightseers crowds Fisherman's Wharf, and with good reason: Pier 39, the Anchorage, Ghirardelli Square, and the Cannery are all here, each with shops and restaurants, as well as outdoor entertainment. Best of all are the Wharf's view of the bay and its proximity to cable-car lines, which can shuttle shoppers directly to Union Square. Many of the tourist-oriented shops border on tacky, peddling the requisite Golden Gate tees, taffy, and baskets of shells.

27

THE HAIGHT

Haight Street is a perennial attraction for visitors, if only to see the sign at Haight and Ashbury streets—the geographic center of the Flower Power movement during the 1960s, so it can be a bummer to find this famous intersection is now the turf for Gap and Ben & Jerry's. Don't be discouraged; it's still possible to find high-quality vintage clothing, funky shoes, and used records and CDs galore in this always-busy neighborhood.

HAYES VALLEY

A community park called Patricia's Green breaks up a crowd of cool shops just west of the Civic Center. Here you can find everything from hip housewares to art galleries to handcrafted jewelry. The density of unique stores—as well as the lack of chains anywhere in sight—makes it a favorite destination for many San Francisco shoppers.

JAPANTOWN

Unlike the ethnic enclaves of Chinatown, North Beach, and the Mission, the 5-acre **Japan Center** (⊠ *Bordered by Laguna, Fillmore, and Post Sts. and Geary Blvd.* ☏ *No phone*) is under one roof. The three-block complex includes a reasonably priced public garage and three buildings, where shops sell things like bonsai trees, antique kimonos, *tansu* (Japanese chests), and colorful glazed dinnerware and teapots.

THE MARINA DISTRICT

With the city's highest density of (mostly) nonchain stores, the Marina is an outstanding shopping nexus. Union Street and Chestnut Street in particular cater to the shopping whims of the grown-up sorority sisters and frat boys who live in the surrounding pastel Victorians.

THE MISSION

The aesthetic of the resident Pabst Blue Ribbon–downing hipsters and starving-artist types contributes to the affordability and individuality of shopping here. These night owls keep the city's best vintage-furniture shops, alternative bookstores, and, increasingly, small clothing boutiques afloat. Many of the city's best bakeries and cafés keep shoppers' blood-sugar levels up.

NORTH BEACH

Although it's sometimes compared to New York City's Greenwich Village, North Beach is only a fraction of the size, clustered tightly around Washington Square and Columbus Avenue. Most of its businesses are small eateries, cafés, and shops selling clothing, antiques, and vintage wares. Once the center of the Beat movement, North Beach still has a bohemian spirit that's especially apparent at the rambling City Lights Bookstore, where Beat poetry lives on.

PACIFIC HEIGHTS

The rest of the city likes to deprecate its wealthiest neighborhood, but no one has any qualms about weaving through the mansions to come to Fillmore and Sacramento streets to shop. With grocery and hardware stores sitting alongside local clothing ateliers and international designer outposts, these streets manage to mix small-town America with big-city glitz.

UNION SQUARE

Serious shoppers head straight to Union Square, San Francisco's main shopping area and the site of most of its department stores, including Macy's, Neiman Marcus, and Saks Fifth Avenue. Nearby are such platinum-card international boutiques as Cartier, Emporio Armani, Gucci, Hermès of Paris, Louis Vuitton, and Barneys CO-OP.

Besides the sheer scale of the mammoth **Westfield San Francisco Shopping Centre** (⊠ *865 Market St., between 4th and 5th Sts., Union Square* ☎ *415/495–5656*), anchored by Bloomingdale's and Nordstrom. The mall is notable for its gorgeous atriums and top-notch dining options (no typical food courts here—instead you'll find branches of a few top local restaurants).

Napa and Sonoma

WORD OF MOUTH

"I specifically wanted to visit Sonoma on this trip in order to compare to Napa. . . . Sonoma is quieter, more rural and spread out. Napa is a bit glitzier and the wineries seem more densely packed. . . . Both areas are a really nice experience though; the scenery was lovely with the rolling vineyards."

—Miramar

WELCOME TO
NAPA AND SONOMA

TOP REASONS TO GO

★ **Touring the Wineries:** Sure, the landscape is lovely and the food is delicious, but the main reason you're here is to sip your way through the region while exploring the diverse wineries.

★ **Biking:** Cycling is one of the best ways to see the Wine Country—the Russian River and Dry Creek valleys are particularly beautiful.

★ **Browsing the farmers' markets:** Almost every town in Napa and Sonoma has a seasonal farmers' market, each rounding up an amazing variety of local produce.

★ **Canoeing on the Russian River:** Trade in your car keys for a paddle and glide down the Russian River. May through October is the best time to be on the water.

★ **Cocktails at Cyrus:** At the bar of Healdsburg's well-loved restaurant, the bartenders mix superb, inventive drinks with house-made infused syrups and seasonal ingredients like local Meyer lemons.

1 Napa Valley. You'll find big names all around, from high-profile wineries to world-renowned chefs. Napa, the valley's oldest town, sweet-life St. Helena, and down-to-earth Calistoga all make good home bases here. (Calistoga has the extra draw of local thermal springs.) Yountville has become a culinary boomtown, while the tiny communities of Oakville and Rutherford are surrounded by major vintners like Robert Mondavi and Francis Ford Coppola. Rutherford in particular is the source for outstanding cabernet sauvignon.

2 Sonoma Valley. Historic attractions and an unpretentious attitude prevail here. The town of Sonoma, with its atmospheric central plaza, is rich with 19th-century buildings. Glen Ellen, meanwhile, has a special connection with author Jack London.

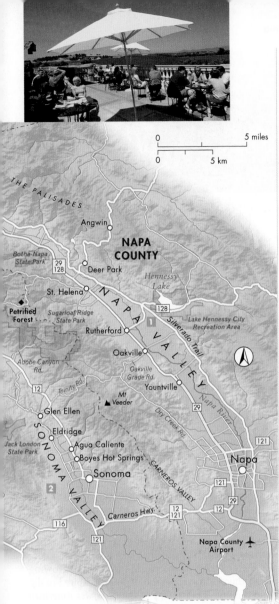

NAPA COUNTY

Bothe-Napa State Park
29 128
Deer Park
Hennessy Lake
St. Helena
Petrified Forest
Sugarloaf Ridge State Park
128
Lake Hennessy City Recreation Area
Adobe Canyon Rd.
Rutherford
Oakville
Oakville Grade Rd.
12
Trinity Rd.
Mt Veeder
Yountville
Dry Creek Rd.
29
Napa River
Glen Ellen
Eldridge
Jack London State Park
Agua Caliente
Boyes Hot Springs
121
Sonoma
Napa
121
2
CARNEROS VALLEY
121
29
116
Carneros Hwy.
12 121
12
121
Napa County Airport

THE PALISADES
Angwin
NAPA VALLEY
Silverado Trail
SONOMA VALLEY

0 ——— 5 miles
0 ——— 5 km

GETTING ORIENTED

The Napa and Sonoma valleys run roughly parallel, northwest to southeast, and are separated by the Mayacamas Mountains. Northwest of the Sonoma Valley are several more important viticultural areas in Sonoma County, including the Dry Creek, Alexander, and Russian River valleys. The Carneros region, which spans southern Sonoma and Napa counties, is just north of San Pablo Bay, and the closest of all these wine regions to San Francisco.

28

3 Elsewhere in Sonoma. The winding, rural roads here feel a world away from Napa's main drag. The lovely Russian River, Dry Creek, and Alexander valleys are all excellent places to seek out pinot noir, zinfandel, and chardonnay. The small town of Healdsburg gets lots of attention, thanks to its terrific restaurants, bed-and-breakfasts, and chic boutiques.

Life is lived well in the California Wine Country. Eating and, above all, drinking are cultivated as high arts. It's little wonder that so many visitors to San Francisco take a day or two—or five or six—to unwind in the Napa and Sonoma valleys. They join the locals in the tasting rooms, from serious wine collectors making their annual pilgrimages to wine newbies who don't know the difference between a merlot and mourvèdre but are eager to learn.

Great dining and wine go hand in hand, and the local viticulture has naturally encouraged a robust passion for food. Several outstanding chefs have taken root here, sealing the area's reputation as one of the best restaurant destinations in the country.

Napa and Sonoma counties are also rich in history. In the town of Sonoma, for example, you can explore buildings from California's Spanish and Mexican past. Some wineries have cellars or tasting rooms dating to the late 1800s, while the town of Calistoga is a flurry of Steamboat Gothic architecture, gussied up with the fretwork favored by late-19th-century spa goers.

Binding all these temptations together is the sheer scenic beauty of the place. Even the climate cooperates, as the hot summer days and cool evenings that make the area one of the world's best grape-growing regions make good weather for traveling, too. If you're inspired to dig further into the Wine Country, grab a copy of the *Compass American Guide: California Wine Country*.

PLANNING

WHEN TO GO

"Crush," the term used to indicate the season when grapes are picked and crushed, usually takes place in September or October. From September until November the entire Wine Country celebrates its bounty with street fairs and festivals.

In season (April through November), Napa Valley draws crowds of tourists, and traffic along Route 29 from St. Helena to Calistoga is often backed up on weekends. The Sonoma Valley, Santa Rosa, and Healdsburg are popular as well, though less crowded than Napa. In season and over holiday weekends it's best to book lodging, restaurant, and winery reservations at least a month in advance. Many wineries give tours at specified times and require appointments.

To avoid crowds, visit the Wine Country during the week and get an early start (most wineries open around 10). Summer is usually hot and dry, and autumn can be even hotter, so dress appropriately if you go during these times.

GETTING HERE AND AROUND

CAR TRAVEL

Five major roads cut through the Napa and Sonoma valleys. U.S. 101 and Routes 12 and 121 travel through Sonoma County. Route 29 heads north from Napa. The 25-mi Silverado Trail, which runs parallel to Route 29 north from Napa to Calistoga, is Napa Valley's more scenic, less-crowded alternative to Route 29.

■ TIP→ Remember, if you're wine-tasting, either select a designated driver or be careful of your wine intake. Also, keep in mind that you'll likely be sharing the road with cyclists; keep a close eye on the shoulder.

From San Francisco to Napa: Cross the Golden Gate Bridge, then go north on U.S. 101. Next go east on Route 37 toward Vallejo, then north on Route 121, also called the Carneros Highway. Turn left (north) when Route 121 runs into Route 29. This should take about 1½ hours when traffic is light.

From San Francisco to Sonoma: Cross the Golden Gate Bridge, then go north on U.S. 101, east on Route 37 toward Vallejo, and north on Route 121, aka the Carneros Highway. When you reach Route 12, take it north. If you're going to any of the Sonoma County destinations north of the valley, take U.S. 101 all the way north through Santa Rosa to Healds-burg. This should take about an hour, not counting substantial traffic.

TOURS

Full-day guided tours of the Wine Country generally include lunch and cost about $60–$100 per person. Reservations are usually required.

Gray Line (✉ *Pier 43½, Embarcadero, San Francisco* ☎ *415/434–8687 or 888/428–6937* ⊕ *www.grayline.com*) has a tour that covers both the southern Napa and Sonoma valleys in a single day, with a stop for lunch in Yountville. In addition to renting bikes by the day, **Wine Country Bikes** (✉ *61 Front St., Healdsburg* ☎ *707/473–0610* ⊕ *www. winecountrybikes.com*) organizes both one-day and multiday trips throughout Sonoma County.

ABOUT THE RESTAURANTS

Star chefs from around the world have come into the Wine Country's orbit, drawn by the area's phenomenal produce, artisanal foods, and wines. Although excellent meals can be found virtually everywhere in the region, the small town of Yountville has become a culinary center under the influence of chef Thomas Keller. If a table at Keller's famed

28

French Laundry is out of reach, keep in mind that he's also behind two more modest restaurants in town. And the buzzed-about restaurants in Sonoma County, including Cyrus and Farmhouse Inn, offer plenty of mouthwatering options. On the inexpensive end of the spectrum, delis and farmers markets sell superb picnic fare.

With few exceptions (which are noted in individual restaurant listings), dress is informal. Where reservations are indicated as essential, you may need to make them a week or more ahead. In summer and early fall you may need to book several weeks ahead.

ABOUT THE HOTELS

Napa and Sonoma's inns and hotels range from low-key to utterly luxurious and generally maintain high standards. Most of the bed-and-breakfasts are in historic Victorian and Spanish buildings, and the breakfast part of the equation often involves fresh local produce. The newer hotels tend to have a more modern, streamlined aesthetic.

All of this comes with a hefty price tag. Santa Rosa, the largest population center in the area, has the widest selection of moderately priced rooms. Try there if you've failed to reserve in advance or have a limited budget. In general, accommodations in the area often have lower rates on weeknights, and prices are about 20% lower in winter.

On weekends, two- or even three-night minimum stays are commonly required, especially at smaller inns and B&Bs. Many B&Bs book up long in advance of the summer and fall seasons, and many of them aren't suitable for children.

Hotel reviews have been condensed for this book. Please go to Fodors. com for full reviews of each property.

BED-AND-BREAKFAST ASSOCIATIONS

Bed & Breakfast Association of Sonoma Valley (☎ 800/969–4667 ⊕ www. sonomabb.com). **The Wine Country Inns of Sonoma County** (☎ 800/946–3268 ⊕ www.winecountryinns.com).

WHAT IT COSTS				
¢	$	$$	$$$	$$$$
Restaurants	under $10	$10–$14	$15–$22	$23–$30	over $30
Hotels	under $200	$200–$250	$251–$300	$301–$400	over $400

Restaurant prices are per person for a main course at dinner, or for a prix fixe if a set menu is the only option. Hotel prices are for two people in a standard double room in high season.

THE NAPA VALLEY

When it comes to wine production in the United States, Napa Valley rules the roost, with more than 275 wineries and many of the biggest brands in the business. Vastly diverse soils and microclimates give Napa winemakers the chance to make a tremendous variety of wines. But what's the area like beyond the glossy advertising and boldface names?

Wine and contemporary art find a home at di Rosa.

Napa—the valley's largest town—has a few cultural attractions and accommodations that are (relatively) reasonably priced. A few miles farther north, compact Yountville is a culinary boomtown, densely packed with top-notch restaurants and luxury hotels. Continuing north, St. Helena teems with elegant boutiques and restaurants; mellow Calistoga, known for spas and hot springs, feels a bit like an Old West frontier town and has a more casual attitude than many Wine Country towns.

ESSENTIALS

Contacts Napa Valley Destination Council (☎ *707/226–7459* ⊕ *www. legendarynapavalley.com*).

NAPA

46 mi from San Francisco via I–80 east and north, Rte. 37 west, and Rte. 29 north.

The town of Napa is the valley's largest, and visitors who get a glimpse of the strip malls and big-box stores from Highway 29 often speed right past on the way to the smaller and more seductive Yountville or St. Helena. But Napa doesn't entirely deserve its dowdy reputation. After many years as a blue-collar town that more or less turned its back on the Wine Country scene, Napa has spent the last few years attempting to increase its appeal to visitors, with somewhat mixed results. A walkway that follows the river through town, completed in 2008, makes the city more pedestrian-friendly, and new restaurants and hotels are continually popping up, but you'll still find a handful of empty storefronts among the wine bars, bookstores, and restaurants.

★   The majestic château of **Domaine Carneros** looks for all the world like it belongs in France, and in fact it does: It's modeled after the Château de la Marquetterie, an 18th-century mansion owned by the Taittinger family near Epernay, France. Carved into the hillside beneath the winery, Domaine Carneros's cellars produce delicate sparkling wines and a handful of still wines, like pinot and a merlot. They're served with cheese plates or caviar to those seated in the Louis XV–inspired salon or on the terrace overlooking the vineyards. Though this makes a visit here a tad more expensive than some stops on a winery tour, it's also one of the most opulent ways to enjoy the Carneros District. ⊠ *1240 Duhig Rd., Napa* ☎ *707/257–0101* ⊕ *www.domainecarneros.com* ⊠ *Tasting $6.75–$25, tour $25* ⊗ *Daily 10–6; tour daily at 11, 1, and 3.*

Fodor'sChoice ★   Metal sculptures of sheep grazing in the grass mark the entrance to **di Rosa**, a sprawling, art-filled property off the Carneros Highway. Thousands of 20th-century artworks by hundreds of Northern California artists crop up everywhere—in galleries, in the former di Rosa residence, on every lawn, in every courtyard, and even on the lake. If you stop by without a reservation, you'll only gain access to the Gatehouse Gallery, where there's a small collection of riotously colorful figurative and abstract sculpture and painting. ■TIP➔ **To see the rest of the property and artwork, you'll have to sign up for one of the various tours of the grounds (from 1 to 2½ hours).** Reservations for the tours are recommended. ⊠ *5200 Sonoma Hwy. (Carneros Hwy.), Napa* ☎ *707/226–5991* ⊕ *www.dirosaart.org* ⊠ *Free, tour $10–$15* ⊗ *Wed.–Fri. 9:30–3; Sat. by reservation; call for tour times.*

Fodor'sChoice ★   The **Hess Collection Winery** is a delightful discovery on Mt. Veeder, a winding 9 mi northwest of the city of Napa. The simple limestone structure contains Swiss owner Donald Hess's personal art collection, including mostly large-scale works by such contemporary European and American artists as Robert Motherwell and Frank Stella. Cabernet sauvignon is the real strength here, though Hess also produces some fine chardonnays. Self-guided tours of the art collection and guided tours of the winery's production facilities are both free. ⊠ *4411 Redwood Rd., west of Rte. 29, Napa* ☎ *707/255–1144* ⊕ *www.hesscollection. com* ⊠ *Tasting $10–$30* ⊗ *Daily 10–5:30; guided tours daily, usually hourly 10:30–3:30.*

WHERE TO EAT AND STAY

$$$ ITALIAN ★   ✗ **Bistro Don Giovanni.** At this lively bistro, the Cal-Italian food is simultaneously inventive and comforting: an excellent fritto misto of onions, fennel, calamari, and plump rock shrimp; risotto with scallops and wild mushrooms; pizza with caramelized onions and Gorgonzola; and tender braised lamb on a bed on fried polenta. Dishes roasted in the wood-burning oven are a specialty. Children are unusually welcome here, catered to with menu items like pizza topped with cheese, french fries, and "no green stuff." ⊠ *4110 Howard La./Rte. 29* ☎ *707/224–3300* ⊕ *www.bistrodongiovanni.com* ▤ *AE, D, DC, MC, V.*

$$$$ Fodor'sChoice ★   ▦ **Carneros Inn.** Freestanding board-and-batten cottages with rocking chairs on each porch are simultaneously rustic and chic at this luxurious property. **Pros:** cottages have lots of privacy; beautiful views from the hilltop pool; heaters on each private patio encourage lounging outside

in the evening. **Cons:** a long drive from destinations up-valley; smallish rooms with limited seating options. ⊠ *4048 Sonoma Hwy.* ☎ *707/299–4900* ⊕ *www.thecarnerosinn.com* ⇨ *76 cottages, 10 suites* ⌂ *In-room: a/c, safe, refrigerator, DVD, Internet. In-hotel: 3 restaurants, room service, bar, pool, gym, spa, laundry service, Wi-Fi hotspot, some pets allowed* ▭ *AE, D, DC, MC, V.*

YOUNTVILLE

13 mi north of the town of Napa on Rte. 29.

These days Yountville is something like Disneyland for food-lovers. It all started with Thomas Keller's French Laundry, one of the best restaurants in the United States. Now Keller is also behind two more casual restaurants a few blocks from his mother ship—and that's only the tip of the iceberg. You could stay here for a week and not exhaust all the options in this tiny town with a big culinary reputation. It's also well located for excursions to many big-name Napa wineries, especially those in the Stags Leap District, where big, bold cabernet sauvignons helped put the Napa Valley on the wine-making map.

It was the 1973 cabernet sauvignon produced by **Stag's Leap Wine Cellars** that put the winery—and the California wine industry—on the map by placing first in the famous Paris tasting of 1976. A visit to the winery is a no-frills affair; visitors in the tasting room are clearly serious about wine. It costs $30 to taste the top-of-the-line wines, including their limited-production estate-grown cabernets, a few of which sell for well over $100. If you're interested in more modestly priced wines, try the $15 tasting, which usually includes a sauvignon blanc, chardonnay, merlot, and cabernet. ⊠ *5766 Silverado Trail, Napa* ☎ *707/265–2441* ⊕ *www.cask23.com* ▱ *Tasting $15–$30, tour $40* ☉ *Daily 10–4:30; tour by appointment.*

28

WHERE TO EAT

$$$
ITALIAN
Fodor's Choice
★

✕ **Bottega.** At this lively trattoria, the menu is simultaneously soulful and inventive, transforming local ingredients into regional Italian dishes with a twist. The antipasti in particular shine: you can order olives grown on chef Michael Chiarello's own property in St. Helena or house-made charcuterie. Potato gnocchi might be served with duck and a chestnut ragù, and hearty main courses like braised short ribs may come on a bed of spinach prepared with preserved lemons. The vibe is more festival than formal, with exposed brick walls, an open kitchen, and paper-topped tables, but service is spot on. ⊠ *6525 Washington St.* ☎ *707/945–1050* ⊕ *www.botteganapavalley.com* ▭ *AE, MC, V* ☉ *No lunch Mon.*

$$$$
AMERICAN
Fodor's Choice
★

✕ **French Laundry.** An old stone building laced with ivy houses the most acclaimed restaurant in Napa Valley—and, indeed, one of the most highly regarded in the country. The restaurant's two prix-fixe menus (both $250), one of which is vegetarian, vary, but "oysters and pearls," a silky dish of pearl tapioca with oysters and white sturgeon caviar, is a signature starter. Some courses rely on luxe ingredients like foie gras, while others take humble foods like fava beans and elevate them to art. Reservations at French Laundry are hard-won, and not accepted more than two months in advance. ■**TIP**→ **Call two months ahead to the day at 10 am on the dot.** ✉ *6640 Washington St.* ☎ *707/944–2380* ⚖ *Reservations essential, jacket required* ⊕ *www.frenchlaundry.com* ⊟ *AE, MC, V* ⊗ *Closed 1st 2 or 3 wks in Jan. No lunch Mon.–Thurs.*

WHERE TO STAY

$-$$ 🏠 **Maison Fleurie.** If you'd like to be within easy walking distance of most
★   of Yountville's best restaurants, and possibly score a great bargain, look into this casual, comfortable inn. **Pros:** smallest rooms are some of the most affordable in town; free loaner bikes; refrigerator stocked with free soda. **Cons:** breakfast room can be crowded at peak times; bedding could be nicer. ✉ *6529 Yount St.* ☎ *707/944–2056 or 800/788–0369* ⊕ *www.maisonfleurienapa.com* ⟿ *13 rooms* ⚖ *In-room: a/c, refrigerator (some), DVD (some), no TV (some), Wi-Fi. In-hotel: pool, bicycles, Wi-Fi hotspot* ⊟ *AE, D, MC, V* ⧒❘ *CP.*

OAKVILLE

2 mi west of Yountville on Rte. 29.

There are two main reasons to visit the town of Oakville: its gourmet grocery store and its magnificent, highly exclusive wineries.

The **Oakville Grocery** (✉ *7856 St. Helena Hwy./Rte. 29* ☎ *707/944–8802*), built in 1881 as a general store, now carries a surprisingly wide range of unusual and chichi groceries and prepared foods. Unbearable crowds pack the narrow aisles on weekends, but it's still a fine place to sit on a bench out front and sip an espresso between winery visits.

Fodor's Choice   Though the fee for the combined tour and tasting is at the high end, **Far**
★   **Niente** is especially worth visiting if you're tired of elbowing your way through crowded tasting rooms and are looking for a more personal experience. Small groups are shepherded through the historic 1885 stone winery, including some of the 40,000 square feet of caves, for a lesson on the labor-intensive method for making Far Niente's two wines, a cabernet blend and a chardonnay. The next stop is the Carriage House, where you can see the founder's gleaming collection of classic cars. The tour ends with a seated tasting of wines and cheeses. ✉ *1350 Acacia Dr.* ☎ *707/944–2861* ⊕ *www.farniente.com* ⚖ *$50* ⊗ *Tasting and tour by appointment.*

RUTHERFORD

2 mi northwest of Oakville on Rte. 29.

From a fast-moving car, Rutherford is a quick blur of vineyards and a rustic barn or two, but don't speed by this tiny hamlet. With its singular microclimate and soil, this is an important viticultural center, with more big-name wineries than you can shake a corkscrew at. Cabernet sauvignon is king here. The well-drained, loamy soil is ideal for those vines, and since this part of the valley gets plenty of sun, the grapes develop exceptionally intense flavors.

Frog Leap's picturesque country charm extends all the way to the white picket fence.

Frog's Leap is the perfect place for wine novices to begin their education. The owner, John Williams, maintains a goofy sense of humor about wine that translates into an entertaining yet informative experience. You'll also find some fine zinfandel, cabernet sauvignon, merlot, chardonnay, sauvignon blanc, and rosé. The winery includes a red barn built in 1884, 5 acres of organic gardens, an eco-friendly visitor center, and, naturally, a frog pond topped with lily pads. The fun tour is highly recommended, but you can also just do a seated tasting of their wines, which takes place on a porch overlooking the garden, weather permitting. ⊠ *8815 Conn Creek Rd.* ☎ *707/963–4704* ⊕ *www.frogsleap.com* 🖿 *Tasting $20, tour $20.* ☉ *Mon.–Sat. 10–4; tour by appointment.*

Fodor's Choice ★

WHERE TO STAY

$$$$ ★ 🏨 **Auberge du Soleil.** Taking a cue from the olive-tree-studded landscape, this renowned hotel cultivates a Mediterranean look. It's luxury as simplicity: earth-tone tile floors, heavy wood furniture, and terra-cotta colors. **Pros:** stunning views; spectacular pool and spa areas; the most expensive suites are fit for a superstar. **Cons:** stratospheric prices; the two rooms in the main house get some noise from the bar and restaurant. ⊠ *180 Rutherford Hill Rd., off Silverado Trail north of Rte. 128* ☎ *707/963–1211 or 800/348–5406* ⊕ *www.aubergedusoleil.com* 🛏 *31 rooms, 21 suites* 🖒 *In-room: a/c, safe, refrigerator, DVD, Internet, Wi-Fi. In-hotel: 2 restaurants, room service, bar, tennis court, pool, gym, spa, laundry service, Wi-Fi hotspot* ⊟ *AE, D, DC, MC, V* ⧗ *BP.*

ST. HELENA

2 mi northwest of Oakville on Rte. 29.

Downtown St. Helena is a symbol of how well life can be lived in the Wine Country. Sycamore trees arch over Main Street (Route 29), a funnel of outstanding restaurants and tempting boutiques. At the north end of town looms the hulking stone building of the Culinary Institute of America. Weathered stone and brick buildings from the late 1800s give off that gratifying whiff of history.

Fodor'sChoice
★

Although an appointment is required to taste at **Joseph Phelps Vineyards,** it's worth the trouble. In fair weather the casual, self-paced wine tastings are held on the terrace of a huge, modern barnlike building with stunning views down the slopes over oak trees and orderly vines. Though the sauvignon blanc and viognier are good, the blockbuster wines are reds, like their flagship wine, a Bordeaux-style blend called Insignia. ⊠ *200 Taplin Rd.* ☎ *707/963–2745* ⊕ *www.jpvwines.com* ᵀ *Tasting $25* ☉ *Weekdays 10–3:30, weekends 10–2:30; tasting by appointment.*

WHERE TO EAT

¢–$
AMERICAN
★

✕ **Gott's Roadside.** A slick 1950s-style outdoor hamburger stand goes upscale at this hugely popular spot, where locals are willing to brave long lines to order juicy burgers, root-beer floats, and garlic fries. There are also plenty of choices you wouldn't have found 50 years ago, such as the ahi tuna burger and chicken club with pesto mayo. Try to get here early or late for lunch, or all the shaded picnic tables on the lawn might be filled with happy throngs. ⊠ *933 Main St.* ☎ *707/963–3486* ⊕ *www.gottsroadside.com* ▭ *AE, MC, V.*

$$$$
AMERICAN
Fodor'sChoice
★

✕ **The Restaurant at Meadowood.** Chef Christopher Kostow has garnered rave reviews (and three Michelin stars) for transforming seasonal local products (some grown right on the property) into elaborate, elegant fare. The chef's menu ($175), composed of eight or so courses, is the best way to appreciate the experience, but the gracious and well-trained servers provide some of the best service in the valley even if you're ordering a less extravagant meal. ⊠ *900 Meadowood La.* ☎ *707/967–1205* ⊕ *www.meadowood.com* ▭ *AE, D, DC, MC, V* ☉ *Closed Sun. No lunch.*

WHERE TO STAY

$$$$
Fodor'sChoice
★

▥ **Meadowood Resort.** A rambling lodge and several gray clapboard bungalows are scattered across this sprawling property, giving it the air of an exclusive New England retreat. **Pros:** site of one of Napa's best restaurants; lovely hiking trail on the property; the most gracious service in all of Napa. **Cons:** very expensive; most bathrooms are not as extravagant as at other similarly priced resorts. ⊠ *900 Meadowood La.* ☎ *707/963–3646 or 800/458–8080* ⊕ *www.meadowood.com* ⤳ *40 rooms, 45 suites* ⌂ *In-room: a/c, refrigerator, DVD, Internet, Wi-Fi. In-hotel: 2 restaurants, room service, bar, golf course, tennis courts, pools, gym, children's programs (ages 6–12, summer only), Wi-Fi hotspot* ▭ *AE, D, DC, MC, V.*

CALISTOGA

3 mi northwest of St. Helena on Rte. 29.

With false-fronted/Old West–style shops, 19th-century hotels, and unpretentious cafés lining Lincoln Avenue, the town's main drag, Calistoga has a slightly rough-and-tumble feel that's unique in the Napa Valley. It comes across as more down-to-earth than some of the polished towns to the south.

Ironically, Calistoga was developed as a tourist getaway. In 1859, maverick entrepreneur Sam Brannan snapped up 2,000 acres of prime property and laid out a resort, intending to use the area's natural hot springs as the main attraction. Brannan's gamble didn't pay off as he'd hoped, but the hotels and bathhouses won a local following. Many of them are still going, and you can come for an old-school experience of a mud bath or a dip in a warm spring-fed pool.

Fodor's Choice ★ **Schramsberg,** hidden on the hillside near Route 29, is one of Napa's oldest wineries. Founded in the 1860s, it now produces a variety of bubblies made using the traditional *méthode champenoise* process. If you want to taste, you must tour first, but what a tour: in addition to getting a glimpse of the winery's historic architecture, you get to tour the cellars dug in the late 19th century by Chinese laborers, where a mind-boggling 2 million bottles are stacked in gravity-defying configurations. The tour fee includes generous pours of several very different sparkling wines. ⊠ *1400 Schramsberg Rd.* ☎ *707/942–4558* ⊕ *www.schramsberg.com* 🖃 *Tasting and tour $40* ☉ *Tasting and tour by appointment.*

★ Possibly the most astounding sight in Napa Valley is your first glimpse of the **Castello di Amorosa,** which looks for all the world like a medieval castle, complete with drawbridge and moat, chapel, stables, and secret passageways. Some of the 107 rooms contain replicas of 13th-century frescoes, and the dungeon has an actual iron maiden from Nuremberg, Germany. You must pay for the tour to see the most of the extensive eight-level property, though paying for a tasting of their excellent Italian-style wines allows you access to a small portion of the astounding complex. ⊠ *4045 N. Saint Helena Hwy.* ☎ *707/967–6272* ⊕ *www. castellodiamorosa.com* 🖃 *Tasting $16–$26, tour $31–$41* ☉ *Mar.–Oct., daily 9:30–6; Nov.–Feb., daily 9:30–5; tour by appointment.*

WHERE TO STAY

$–$$ Fodor's Choice ★ 🏠 **Meadowlark Country House.** Twenty hillside acres just north of downtown Calistoga surround this decidedly laid-back but sophisticated inn. **Pros:** sauna next to the pool and hot tub; welcoming vibe attracts diverse guests; some of the most gracious innkeepers in Napa. **Cons:** clothing-optional pool policy isn't for everyone. ⊠ *601 Petrified Forest Rd.* ☎ *707/942–5651 or 800/942–5651* ⊕ *www.meadowlarkinn.com* 🛏 *5 rooms, 5 suites* ☖ *In-room: no phone, a/c, kitchen (some), refrigerator (some), DVD (some), Wi-Fi. In-hotel: pool, Internet terminal, Wi-Fi hotspot, some pets allowed* ▭ *AE, MC, V* ⦿⦿*BP.*

28

THE SONOMA VALLEY

Although the Sonoma Valley may not have quite the cachet of the neighboring Napa Valley, wineries here entice with their unpretentious attitude and smaller crowds. The Napa-style glitzy tasting rooms with enormous gift shops and $25 tasting fees are the exception here. Sonoma's landscape seduces, too, its roads gently climbing and descending on their way to wineries hidden from the road by trees.

The scenic valley, bounded by the Mayacamas Mountains on the east and Sonoma Mountain on the west, extends north from San Pablo Bay nearly 20 mi to the eastern outskirts of Santa Rosa. The varied terrain, soils, and climate allow grape growers to raise cool-weather varietals such as chardonnay and pinot noir as well as merlot, cabernet sauvignon, and other heat-seeking vines.

ESSENTIALS

Contacts Sonoma County Tourism Bureau (✉ *3637 Westwind Blvd., Santa Rosa* ☎ *707/522–5800 or 800/576–6662* ⊕ *www.sonomacounty.com*). **Sonoma Valley Visitors Bureau** (✉ *453 1st St. E, Sonoma* ☎ *707/996–1090 or 866/996–1090* ⊕ *www.sonomavalley.com*).

SONOMA

14 mi west of Napa on Rte. 12; 45 mi from San Francisco, north on U.S. 101, east on Rte. 37, and north on Rte. 121/12.

Founded in the early 1800s, Sonoma is the oldest town in the Wine Country, and one of the few where you can find some attractions not related to food and wine. The central **Sonoma Plaza** dates from the Mission era; surrounding it are 19th-century adobes, atmospheric hotels, and the swooping marquee of the 1930s Sebastiani Theatre. On summer days the plaza is a hive of activity, with children blowing off steam in the playground while their folks stock up on picnic supplies and browse the boutiques surrounding the square.

Fodor'sChoice ★ Although **Bartholomew Park Winery** was founded only in 1994, grapes were grown in some of its vineyards as early as the 1830s. The emphasis here is on handcrafted, single-varietal wines—cabernet, merlot, zinfandel, syrah, and sauvignon blanc. The wines themselves, available only at the winery, make a stop worth it, but another reason to visit is its small museum, with vivid exhibits about the history of the winery and the Sonoma region. Another plus is the beautiful, slightly off-the-beaten-path location in a 375-acre private park about 2 mi from downtown Sonoma. Pack a picnic to enjoy on the woodsy grounds. ✉ *1000 Vineyard La.* ☎ *707/939–3026* ⊕ *www.bartpark.com* 🗗 *Tasting $10, tour $20* ☉ *Daily 11–4:30, tour Fri. and Sat. at 11:30 by reservation.*

WHERE TO EAT

$$
AMERICAN
★
✕ **Harvest Moon Cafe.** It's easy to feel like one of the family at this little restaurant with an odd, zigzagging layout. Diners seated at one of the two tiny bars chat with the servers like old friends, but the husband-and-wife team in the kitchen is serious about the homey food, like half a grilled chicken served with polenta and tapenade and a

marinated-beet-and-frisee salad. Everything is so perfectly executed and the vibe so genuinely warm that a visit here is deeply satisfying. In fair weather, a spacious back patio, with seats arranged around a fountain, more than doubles the number of seats. ✉ *487 W. 1st St.* ☎ *707/933–8160* ⊕ *www.harvestmooncafesonoma.com* ⊟ *AE, D, MC, V* ☉ *Closed Tues.; no lunch Mon.–Sat.*

GLEN ELLEN

7 mi north of Sonoma on Rte. 12.

Craggy Glen Ellen embodies the difference between the Napa and Sonoma valleys. In small Napa towns such as St. Helena well-groomed sidewalks are lined with upscale boutiques and restaurants, but in Glen Ellen the crooked streets are shaded with stands of old oak trees and occasionally bisected by the Sonoma and Calabasas creeks.

Jack London, who represents Glen Ellen's rugged spirit, lived in the area for many years; the town commemorates him with place-names and nostalgic establishments.

★ One of the best-known local wineries is **Benziger Family Winery,** on a sprawling estate in a bowl with 360-degree sun exposure. Benziger is noted for its merlot, pinot noir, cabernet sauvignon, chardonnay, and sauvignon blanc. The tram tours here are especially interesting. On a ride through the vineyards, guides explain the regional microclimates and geography and give you a glimpse of the extensive cave system. Tours depart several times a day, weather permitting. Reservations are needed for smaller tours that conclude with a seated tasting ($40). ■TIP➔ Arrive before lunch for the best shot at joining a tour—and bring a picnic, since the grounds here are lovely. ✉ *1883 London Ranch Rd.* ☎ *707/935–3000* ⊕ *www.benziger.com* 🏷 *Tasting $10–$20, tour $15–$40* ☉ *Daily 10–5.*

WHERE TO EAT AND STAY

$$ ✕ **The Fig Cafe.** Pale sage walls, a high, sloping ceiling, and casual but

FRENCH very warm service set a sunny mood in this little bistro that's run by the

Fodor's Choice same team behind Sonoma's The Girl & the Fig. The restaurant's epony-

★ mous fruit shows up in all sorts of places, from salads to an apple and fig bread pudding. The small menu focuses on California and French comfort food, like steamed mussels served with terrific crispy fries, and a braised pot roast served with seasonal vegetables. ■TIP➔ The unusual no-corkage-fee policy makes it a great place to drink the wine you just discovered down the road. ✉ *13690 Arnold Dr.* ☎ *707/938–2130* ⊕ *www.thegirlandthefig.com* 🏷 *Reservations not accepted* ⊟ *D, MC, V* ☉ *No lunch weekdays.*

¢–$ 🏠 **Beltane Ranch.** On a slope of the Mayacamas range a few miles from

★ Glen Ellen, this 1892 ranch house stands in the shade of magnificent oak trees. **Pros:** casual, friendly atmosphere; reasonably priced; beautiful grounds with ancient oak trees. **Cons:** downstairs rooms get some noise from upstairs rooms; cooled with ceiling fans instead of air-conditioning. ✉ *11775 Sonoma Hwy./Rte. 12* ☎ *707/996–6501* ⊕ *www.beltaneranch.com* 🛏 *3 rooms, 3 suites* 🍴 *In-room: no phone, a/c, no TV, Wi-Fi. In-hotel: tennis court, Wi-Fi hotspot* ⊟ *MC, V* ⫿⊙⫿ *BP.*

28

KENWOOD

3 mi north of Glen Ellen on Rte. 12.

Blink and you might miss tiny Kenwood, which consists of little more than a few restaurants and shops and a historic train depot, now used for private events. But hidden in this pretty landscape of meadows and woods at the north end of Sonoma Valley are several good wineries, most just off the Sonoma Highway.

★   Named for St. Francis of Assisi, founder of the Franciscan order, which established missions and vineyards throughout California, **St. Francis Winery** has one of the most scenic locations in Sonoma, nestled at the foot of Mt. Hood. The visitor center beautifully replicates the California Mission style, with its red-tile roof and dramatic bell tower. Out back, a slate patio overlooks vineyards, lavender gardens, and hummingbirds flitting about the flower beds. The charm of the surroundings is matched by the wines, most of them red. In addition to the usual wine tastings, there are a variety of food and wine pairings available ($20 to $35); call or check their Website for times and details. ⊠ *100 Pythian Rd.* ☎ *800/543–7713* ⊕ *www.stfranciswinery.com* ⊠ *Tasting $10, tour $25* ☺ *Daily 10–5, tour weekdays at 11 and 2.*

ELSEWHERE IN SONOMA COUNTY

At nearly 1,598 square mi, there's much more to Sonoma County than the day-tripper favorites of Sonoma, Glen Ellen, and Kenwood. To the north is Healdsburg, a lovely small town with a rapidly rising buzz. The national media have latched onto it for its swank hotels and fine restaurants, and many Fodors.com readers recommend it as an ideal home base for wine tasting.

Within easy striking distance of Healdsburg are some of the Wine Country's most scenic vineyards, in the Alexander, Dry Creek, and Russian River valleys. And these lookers also happen to produce some of the country's best pinot noir, cabernet sauvignon, zinfandel, and sauvignon blanc. Though these regions are hardly unknown names, their quiet, narrow roads feel a world away from Highway 29 in Napa.

RUSSIAN RIVER VALLEY

10 mi northwest of Santa Rosa.

The Russian River flows all the way from Mendocino to the Pacific Ocean, but in terms of wine making, the Russian River Valley is centered on a triangle with points at Healdsburg, Guerneville, and Sebastopol. Tall redwoods shade many of the two-lane roads that access this scenic area, where, thanks to the cooling marine influence, pinot noir and chardonnay are the king and queen of grapes.

ESSENTIALS

Contacts Russian River Wine Road (⊠ *Box 46, Healdsburg* ☎ *707/433–4335 or 800/723–6336* ⊕ *www.wineroad.com).*

Fodor'sChoice **Iron Horse Vineyards** makes a wide variety of sparkling wines, from the
★ bright and austere to the rich and toasty, as well as estate chardonnays and pinot noirs. Three hundred acres of rolling, vine-covered hills, barn-like winery buildings, and a beautifully rustic outdoor tasting area with a view of Mt. St. Helena set it apart from stuffier spots. (Instead of providing buckets for you to dump out the wine you don't want to finish, they ask you to toss it into the grass behind you.) Tours are available by appointment on weekdays at 10 am. ⊠ *9786 Ross Station Rd., Sebastopol* 🕾 *707/887–1507* ⊕ *www.ironhorsevineyards.com* 🏮 *Tasting $10, tour $20* ☽ *Daily 10–4:30; tour weekdays at 10 by appointment.*

WHERE TO STAY

$$$–$$$$ ▦ **The Farmhouse Inn.** This pale yellow 1873 farmhouse and adjacent
Fodor'sChoice cottages offer individually decorated rooms with comfortable touches
★ such as down comforters and whirlpool tubs. **Pros:** one of Sonoma's best restaurants is on-site; free snacks, games, and movies available; extremely comfortable beds. **Cons:** rooms closest to the street get a bit of road noise. ⊠ *7871 River Rd., Forestville* 🕾 *707/887–3300 or 800/464–6642* ⊕ *www.farmhouseinn.com* 🛏 *12 rooms, 6 suites* ♿ *In-room: a/c, refrigerator, DVD, Wi-Fi. In-hotel: restaurant, pool, spa* 🖃 *AE, D, DC, MC, V* ⊙| *BP.*

HEALDSBURG

17 mi north of Santa Rosa on U.S. 101.

Just when it seems that the buzz about Healdsburg couldn't get any bigger, there's another article published in a glossy food or wine magazine about posh properties like the restaurant Cyrus. But you don't have to be a tycoon to stay here and enjoy the town. For every ritzy restaurant there's a great bakery or relatively modest B&B. A bandstand on Healdsburg's plaza hosts free summer concerts, where you might hear anything from bluegrass to Sousa marches. Add to that the fragrant magnolia trees shading the square and the bright flower beds, and the whole thing is as quaint as a Norman Rockwell painting.

The countryside around Healdsburg is the sort you dream about when you're planning a Wine Country vacation. Alongside the relatively untrafficked roads, many of the wineries here are barely visible, since they're tucked behind groves of eucalyptus or hidden high on fog-shrouded hills.

WHERE TO EAT AND STAY

$$$$ ✕ **Cyrus.** Hailed as the best thing to hit the Wine Country since French
AMERICAN Laundry, Cyrus has collected lots of awards and many raves from
Fodor'sChoice guests. The formal dining room, with its vaulted Venetian-plaster ceil-
★ ing, is a suitably plush setting for chef Douglas Keane's creative, subtle cuisine. Each night, diners have their choice of four set menus: five- and eight-course extravaganzas ($102 and $130), for both omnivores and vegetarians. Set aside three hours to work your way from savory starters like the terrine of foie gras with curried apple compote, to desserts such as the hazelnut *dacquoise* (layers of hazelnut and buttercream). If you've failed to make reservations, you can order à la carte at the

28

bar, which also has the best collection of cocktails and spirits in all of the Wine Country. ✉ *29 North St., Healdsburg* ☎ *707/433–3311* ⊕ *www.cyrusrestaurant.com* ♨ *Reservations essential* ▤ *AE, DC, MC, V* ⊘ *Closed Tues. and Wed. in winter. No lunch.*

$$$

★

⛉ **The Honor Mansion.** Each room is unique at this photogenic 1883 Italianate Victorian. **Pros:** spacious grounds with boccie and tennis courts, a putting green, and half-court for basketball; homemade sweets available at all hours; attentive staff. **Cons:** almost a mile from Healdsburg's plaza; on a moderately busy street. ✉ *14891 Grove St.* ☎ *707/433–4277 or 800/554–4667* ⊕ *www.honormansion.com* ⇝ *5 rooms, 8 suites* △ *In-room: a/c, safe (some), refrigerator (some), DVD (some), Wi-Fi. In-hotel: tennis court, pool, Internet terminal, Wi-Fi hotspot* ▤ *AE, MC, V* ⊘ *Closed 2 wks around Christmas* ⦿ *BP.*

DRY CREEK AND ALEXANDER VALLEYS

On the west side of U.S. 101, Dry Creek Valley remains one of the least-developed appellations in Sonoma. Zinfandel grapes flourish on the benchlands, whereas the gravelly, well-drained soil of the valley floor is better known for chardonnay and, in the north, sauvignon blanc. The wineries in this region tend to be smaller, which makes them a good bet on summer weekends, when larger spots and those along the main thoroughfares fill up with tourists.

The Alexander Valley, which lies northeast of Healdsburg, is similarly rustic, and you can see as many folks cycling along Highway 128 here as you can behind the wheel of a car. The largely family-owned wineries often produce zinfandel and chardonnay.

Fodor's Choice

★

Once you wind your way down **Preston Vineyards'** long driveway, flanked by vineyards and punctuated by the occasional olive tree, you'll be welcomed by the sight of a few farmhouses encircling a shady yard prowled by several friendly cats. In summer a small selection of organic produce grown in their gardens is sold from an impromptu stand on the front porch, and house-made bread and olive oil are available year-round. Owners Lou and Susan Preston are committed to organic growing techniques, and use only estate-grown grapes in their wines. ✉ *9282 W. Dry Creek Rd., Healdsburg* ☎ *707/433–3372* ⊕ *www.prestonvineyards.com* ⛉ *$5* ⊘ *Daily 11–4:30.*

Portland

WORD OF MOUTH

"I like to walk the bridges. There is a great walking path along
the waterfront, so you can walk up one side of the river, cross the
bridge and do the other side, and cross back on another bridge.
You can also rent bikes and do this."

—sunbum1944

WELCOME TO PORTLAND

TOP REASONS TO GO

★ **Unleash your inner foodie.** Don't miss an amazingly textured range of global delights, created with fresh, locally harvested ingredients.

★ **Beer "hop."** (Pun intended.) Thirty-five local microbrews and offbeat varieties with such names as Hallucinator, Doggie Claws, and Sock Knocker await.

★ **Experience McMenamins.** Visit one of the local chain's beautifully restored properties, such as a renovated 1915 elementary school turned hotel.

★ **Take a stroll through Washington Park.** The International Rose Test Garden, Japanese Garden, Oregon Zoo, World Forestry Center, and Children's Museum are all here.

★ **Peruse pages at Powell's City of Books.** The aisles of this city block–sized shop are filled with more than a million new and used books. Top off hours of literary wanderlust with a mocha or ginseng tea downstairs at World Cup Coffee and Tea House.

1 Downtown. At the center of it all, Portland's Downtown has museums, clubs, restaurants, parks, and unique shops. To get around downtown quickly, take the TriMet MAX light rail for free.

2 Pearl District and Old Town/Chinatown. The Pearl District, Portland's trendy and posh neighborhood, is teaming with upscale restaurants, bars, and shopping, along with pricey condos and artists' lofts. A visit here is rewarded with tantalizing bakeries and chocolatiers. Old Town/Chinatown offers variety, from cutting-edge to old-fashioned. This is the area for Asian-inspired public art, the LanSu Chinese Garden, and tours of the city's Shanghai Tunnels.

3 Nob Hill and Vicinity. From funky to fabulous, this neighborhood is also referred to as "Northwest 23rd" or "Northwest District." The exciting shopping, restaurants, and bars draw a younger but still sophisticated crowd.

4 Washington Park. Keep busy at the Oregon Zoo, Children's Museum, World Forestry Center, Hoyt Arboretum, Japanese Garden, International Rose Test Garden, Vietnam Veterans Memorial, and Oregon Holocaust Memorial. Nearby Forest Park is the largest forested area within city limits in the nation.

5 East of Willamette River. Ten bridges span the Willamette over to Portland's east side. It offers much of what downtown does: restaurants, attractions, architecture, history, and entertainment—but with

Map labels: N.W. Overton St., N.W. Marshall St., N.W. Lovejoy St., N.W. Kearney St., N.W. Johnson St., N.W. Irving St., N.W. Hoyt St., N.W. Glisan St., N.W. Flanders St., N.W. Couch St., W. Burnside St., 405, NOB HILL, PEARL DISTRICT, CENTRAL CITY STREETCAR, Civic Stadium, WASHINGTON PARK, Portland Art Museum, Portland State University, Mill St., 26, S.W. Broadway

0 — 1/4 mile
0 — 1/4 kilometer

GETTING ORIENTED

Geographically speaking, Portland is relatively easy to navigate. The city's 200-foot-long blocks are highly walkable, and mapped out into quadrants. The Willamette River divides east and west and Burnside Street separates north from south. "Northwest" refers to the area north of Burnside and west of the river; "Southwest" refers to the area south of Burnside and west of the river; "Northeast" refers to the area north of Burnside and east of the river; "Southeast" refers to the area south of Burnside and east of the river. As you travel around the Portland metropolitan area, keep in mind that named east and west streets intersect numbered avenues, run north–south, and begin at each side of the river. For instance, Southwest 12th Avenue is 12 blocks west of the Willamette. Most of downtown's streets are one-way.

29

fewer tourists. If you visit, you'll be rewarded with under-the-radar neighborhoods such as Belmont, Eastmoreland, Hawthorne, Laurelhurst, and Sellwood in the southeast and Alameda, Alberta Arts, Irvington, and the Lloyd District in the northeast.

6 **West of Downtown.** The lush hills at the west end of downtown hold stately

homes and excellent parks, and mark the starting point for much of the greater Portland metro area. Chain hotels and restaurants, ample parking, larger roads, and attractive settings help to make the area family- and budget-friendly.

What distinguishes Portland from the rest of America's cityscapes? Or from the rest of the world's urban destinations for that matter? In a Northwest nutshell: everything. For some, it's the wealth of cultural offerings and never-ending culinary choices; for others, it's Portland's proximity to the ocean and mountains, or simply the beauty of having all these attributes in one place.

Strolling through downtown or in one of Portland's numerous neighborhoods, you discover an unmistakable vibrancy to this city—one that is created by the clean air, the wealth of trees, and a blend of historic and modern architecture. Portland's various nicknames—Rose City, Bridgetown, Beervana, Brewtopia—tell its story in a nutshell as well.

Portland has a thriving cultural community, with ballet, opera, symphonies, theater, and art exhibitions both minor and major in scope. Portland also has long been considered a hub for indie music. Hundreds of bands flock to become part of the creative flow of alternative, jazz, blues, and rock that dominate the nightclub scene seven nights a week. Factor in an outrageous number of independent brewpubs and coffee shops—with snowboarding, windsurfing, or camping within an hour's drive—and it's easy to see why so many young people take advantage of Portland's eclectic indoor and outdoor offerings.

For people on a slower pace, there are strolls through never-ending parks, dimmed dining rooms for savoring innovative regional cuisine, and gorgeous cruises along the Willamette River aboard the *Portland Spirit*. Families can explore first-rate museums and parks, including the Children's Museum, the Oregon Museum of Science and Industry, and Oaks Park. At most libraries, parks, and recreational facilities, expect to find hands-on activities, music, story times, plays, and special performances for children. Many restaurants in and around Portland are family-friendly, and with immediate access to the MAX light rail and streetcars, toting kids around is easy.

PLANNING

WHEN TO GO

Portland's mild climate is best from June through September. Hotels are often filled in July and August, so it's important to book reservations in advance. Spring and fall are also excellent times to visit. The weather usually remains quite good, and the prices for accommodations, transportation, and tours can be lower (and the crowds much smaller) in the most popular destinations. In winter, snow is uncommon in the city but abundant in the nearby mountains, making the region a skier's dream. Average daytime summer highs are in the 70s; winter temperatures are generally in the 40s. Portland has an average of only 36 inches of rainfall a year—less than New York, Chicago, or Miami. In winter, however, the rain may never seem to end. More than 75% of Portland's annual precipitation occurs from October through March.

GETTING HERE

Air Travel. It takes about 5 hours to fly nonstop to Portland from New York, 4 hours from Chicago, and 2½ hours from Los Angeles. Flying from Seattle to Portland takes just under an hour; flying from Portland to Vancouver takes an hour and 15 minutes. **Portland International Airport** (PDX) (☎ 877/739–4636 ⊕ *www.flypdx.com*) is a sleek, modern airport with service to many national and international destinations. **TriMet's Red Line MAX light rail** (☎ 503/238–7433 ⊕ *www.trimet.org*) leaves the airport for downtown about every 15 minutes. Trains arrive at and depart from just outside the passenger terminal near the south baggage claim. The trip takes about 35 minutes, and the fare is $2.30. By taxi, the trip downtown takes about 30 minutes and costs about $35.

GETTING AROUND

Bike Travel. It's tough to find a more bike-friendly city in America. Visitors are impressed by the facilities available for bicyclists—more than 300 miles of bike lanes, paths, and boulevards. ⇨ *See Bicycling in Sports and Outdoors.*

Car Travel. I–5 enters Portland from the north and south. I–84, the city's major eastern approach, terminates in Portland. U.S. 26 and U.S. 30 are primary east–west thoroughfares. Bypass routes are I–205, which links I–5 and I–84 before crossing the Columbia River into Washington, and I–405, which arcs around western downtown.

From the airport to downtown, take I–205 south to westbound I–84. Drive west over the Willamette River and take the City Center exit. If going to the airport, take I–84 east to I–205 north; follow I–205 to the airport exit.

Traffic on I–5 north and south of downtown and on I–84 and I–205 east of downtown is heavy between 6 am and 9 am and between 4 and 8 pm. Four-lane U.S. 26 west of downtown can be bumper-to-bumper any time of day going to or from downtown.

Most city-center streets are one-way only, and Southwest 5th and 6th avenues between Burnside and Southwest Madison are limited to bus traffic.

29

CAR-RENTAL   Rates begin at $30 a day and $138 a week, not including the 17% Multnomah County tax if you rent in this county, which includes the airport. All major agencies are represented.

PARKING   Though there are several options, parking in downtown Portland can be tricky and expensive. If you require more than several hours, your most affordable and accessible option is to park in one of seven city-owned "Smart Park" lots.

Street parking is metered only, and requires you to visibly display a sticker on the inside of your curbside window. The meters that dispense the stickers take coins or credit cards. Metered spaces are mostly available for 90 minutes to three hours; parking tickets for exceeding the limit are

regularly issued. Once you get out of downtown and into residential areas, there's plenty of nonmetered street parking available.

Taxi Travel. Taxi fare is $2.50 at flag drop plus $2.30 per mi for one person. Each additional passenger pays $1. Cabs cruise the city streets, or you can phone for one.

Contacts Broadway Cab (☎ 503/227–1234). **New Rose City Cab** (☎ 503/282–7707). **Portland Taxi Company** (☎ 503/256–5400). **Radio Cab** (☎ 503/227–1212).

TriMet/MAX Travel. TriMet operates an extensive system of buses, street-cars, and light rail trains. The Central City streetcar line runs between Legacy Good Samaritan Hospital in Nob Hill, the Pearl District, downtown, and Portland State University. To Nob Hill it travels along 10th Avenue and then on Northwest Northrup; from Nob Hill it runs along Northwest Lovejoy and then on 11th Avenue. Trains stop every few blocks. Buses can operate as frequently as every five minutes or only once an hour.

Metropolitan Area Express, or MAX light rail, links the eastern and western Portland suburbs with downtown, Washington Park and the Oregon Zoo, the Lloyd Center district, the Convention Center, and the Rose Quarter. From downtown, trains operate daily 5:30 am–1 am and run about every 10 minutes Monday–Saturday and every 15 minutes on Sunday and holidays.

Bus, MAX, and streetcar fare is $2 for one or two zones, which covers most places you'll go, and $2.30 for three zones, which includes all of the city's outlying areas. A "Fareless Square" extends through downtown from I–405 to the Willamette River, and from Northwest Irving to the South Waterfront area, and includes the Lloyd Center stop across the river. The free area applies to MAX light rail and Portland Streetcar only. To qualify, your entire trip must stop and start in the fareless area. Maps are posted at all downtown train and streetcar stops.

Day passes for unlimited system-wide travel cost $4.75. Three-day, weekly, and monthly passes are available. As you board the bus, the driver will hand you a transfer ticket good for one to two hours on all buses and MAX trains. Be sure to hold on to it whether you're transferring or not; it also serves as proof that you have paid for your ride.

Contacts TriMet/MAX (☎ 503/238–7433 ⊕ www.trimet.org).

EXPLORING PORTLAND

DOWNTOWN

Portland has one of the most attractive, inviting downtown centers in the United States. It's clean, compact, and filled with parks, plazas, and fountains. Architecture fans find plenty to admire in its mix of old and new. Hotels, shops, museums, restaurants, and entertainment can all be found here, and much of the downtown area is part of the TriMet transit system's Fareless Square, within which you can ride the light rail or the Portland Streetcar for free.

WHAT TO SEE

Pioneer Courthouse Square. In many ways the living room, public heart, and commercial soul of downtown, Pioneer Square is not entirely square, rather an amphitheater-like brick piazza. Special seasonal, charitable, and festival-oriented events often take place in this premier people-watching venue. On Sunday **vintage trolley cars** (☎ *503/323–7363*) run from the MAX station here to Lloyd Center, with free service every half hour between noon and 6 pm. Call to check on the current schedule. You can pick up maps and literature about the city and the state here at the **Portland/Oregon Information Center** (☎ *503/275–8355* ⊕ *www.travelportland.com* ☉ *Weekdays 8:30–5:30, Sat. 10–4*). Directly across the street is one of downtown Portland's most familiar landmarks, the classically sedate **Pioneer Courthouse**. Built in 1869, it's the oldest public building in the Pacific Northwest. ⊠ *701 S.W. 6th Ave., Downtown.*

Fodor's Choice ★ **Portland Art Museum.** The treasures at the Pacific Northwest's oldest arts facility span 35 centuries of Asian, European, and American art. A high point is the Center for Native American Art, with regional and contemporary art from more than 200 tribes. The **Jubitz Center for Modern and Contemporary Art** contains six floors devoted entirely to modern art, with the changing selection chosen from more than 400 pieces in the Museum's permanent collection. The film center presents the annual Portland International Film Festival in February and the Northwest Film Festival in early November. Also, take a moment to linger in the peaceful outdoor sculpture garden. Kids under 18 are admitted free. ⊠ *1219 S.W. Park Ave., Downtown* ☎ *503/226–2811, 503/221–1156 film schedule* ⊕ *www.portlandartmuseum.org* ☒ *$12* ☉ *Tues., Wed., and Sat. 10–5, Thurs. and Fri. 10–8, Sun. noon–5.*

Portland Building. *Portlandia*, the second-largest hammered-copper statue in the world, surpassed only by the Statue of Liberty, kneels on the second-story balcony of one of the first postmodern buildings in the United States. Built in 1982, and architect Michael Graves's first major design commission, this 15-story office building is buff-color, with brown-and-blue trim and exterior decorative touches. A huge fiberglass mold of *Portlandia*'s face is exhibited in the second-floor Public Art Gallery, which provides a good overview of Portland's 1% for Art Program, and the hundreds of works on display throughout the city. ⊠ *1120 S.W. 5th Ave., Downtown* ☉ *Weekdays 8–6.*

29

PEARL DISTRICT AND OLD TOWN/CHINATOWN

The Old Town National Historic District, commonly called Old Town/Chinatown, is where Portland was born. The 20-square-block section, bounded by Oak Street to the south and Everett Street to the north, includes buildings of varying ages and architectural styles. Before it was renovated, this was skid row. Vestiges of it remain in parts of Chinatown; older buildings are slowly being remodeled, and over the last several years the immediate area has experienced a surge in development. MAX serves the area with a stop at the Old Town/Chinatown station.

Bordering Old Town to the northwest is the Pearl District. Formerly a warehouse area along the railroad yards, the Pearl District is the fastest-growing part of Portland. Mid-rise residential lofts have sprouted on almost every block, and boutiques, outdoor retailers, galleries, and trendy restaurants border the streets. The Portland Streetcar passes through here on its way from Nob Hill to downtown and Portland State University, with stops at two new, ecologically themed city parks.

WHAT TO SEE

Fodor's Choice ★ **Lan Su Chinese Garden.** In a twist on the Joni Mitchell song, the city of Portland and private donors took down a parking lot and unpaved paradise when they created this wonderland near the Pearl District and Old Town/Chinatown. It's the largest Suzhou-style garden outside China, with a large lake, bridged and covered walkways, koi- and water lily–filled ponds, rocks, bamboo, statues, waterfalls, and courtyards. A team of 60 artisans and designers from China literally left no stone unturned—500 tons of stone were brought here from Suzhou—in their efforts to give the windows, roof tiles, gateways, including a "moon-gate," and other architectural aspects of the garden some specific meaning or purpose. Also on the premises are a gift shop and a two-story teahouse overlooking the lake and garden. ⊠ *239 N.W. Everett, Old Town/Chinatown* ☎ *503/228–8131* ⊕ *www.lansugarden.org* ☜ *$8.50* ☾ *Nov.–Mar., daily 10–5; Apr.–Oct., daily 10–6.*

☺ Fodor's Choice ★ **Portland Saturday Market.** On weekends from March to Christmas, the west side of the Burnside Bridge and the Skidmore Fountain area has North America's largest open-air handicraft market. If you're looking for jewelry, yard art, housewares, and decorative goods made from every material under the sun, then there's an amazing collection of talented works on display here. Entertainers and food and produce booths add to the festive feel. If taking the MAX train to the market, get off at the Skidmore Fountain stop. ⊠ *Waterfront Park and Ankeny Park, both at S.W. Naito Pkwy. and S.W. Ankeny, Old Town/Chinatown* ☎ *503/222–6072* ⊕ *www.saturdaymarket.org* ☾ *Mar.–Dec., Sat. 10–5, Sun. 11–4:30.*

NOB HILL AND VICINITY

The showiest example of Portland's urban chic is Northwest 23rd Avenue—sometimes referred to with varying degrees of affection as "trendy-third"—a 20-block thoroughfare that cuts north–south through the neighborhood known as Nob Hill. Fashionable since the 1880s and still

Portland's Japanese Garden is said to be the most authentic Japanese garden outside Japan.

filled with Victorian houses, the neighborhood is a mixed-use cornucopia of Old Portland charm and New Portland hip. With its cafés, restaurants, galleries, and boutiques, it's a great place to stroll, shop, and people-watch. More restaurants, shops, and nightspots can be found on Northwest 21st Avenue, a few blocks away. The Portland Streetcar runs from Legacy Good Samaritan Hospital in Nob Hill, through the Pearl District on 10th and 11th avenues, connects with MAX light rail near Pioneer Courthouse Square downtown, and then continues on to Portland State University and RiverPlace on the Willamette River.

WASHINGTON PARK

The best way to get to Washington Park is via MAX light rail, which travels through a tunnel deep beneath the city's West Hills. Be sure to check out the Washington Park station, the deepest (260 feet) transit station in North America. Graphics on the walls depict life in the Portland area during the past 16.5 million years. There's also a core sample of the bedrock taken from the mountain displayed along the walls. Elevators to the surface put visitors in the parking lot for the Oregon Zoo, the World Forestry Center Discovery Museum, and the Children's Museum.

WHAT TO SEE

Fodor's Choice ★ **International Rose Test Garden.** Despite the name, these grounds are not an experimental greenhouse laboratory, but rather three terraced gardens, set on 4 acres, where 10,000 bushes and 400 varieties of roses grow. The flowers, many of them new varieties, are at their peak in June, July, September, and October. From the gardens you can see highly photogenic views of the downtown skyline and, on fine days, the Fuji-shaped slopes of Mt. Hood, 50 mi to the east. Summer concerts take place in the garden's amphitheater. Take MAX light rail to Washington Park station, and transfer to Bus No. 63 or Washington Park Shuttle. ⊠ *400 S.W. Kingston Ave., Washington Park* ☎ *503/823–3636* ⊕ *www.rosegardenstore.org* 🗐 *Free* ☉ *Daily dawn–dusk.*

Fodor's Choice
★
Japanese Garden. The most authentic Japanese garden outside Japan takes up 5½ acres of Washington Park above the International Rose Test Garden. This serene spot, designed by a Japanese landscape master, represents five separate garden styles: Strolling Pond Garden, Tea Garden, Natural Garden, Sand and Stone Garden, and Flat Garden. The Tea House was built in Japan and reconstructed here. The west side of the Pavilion has a majestic view of Portland and Mt. Hood. Take MAX light rail to Washington Park station, and transfer to Bus No. 63 or the Washington Park Shuttle. ⊠ *611 S.W. Kingston Ave., Washington Park* ☎ *503/223–1321* ⊕ *www.japanesegarden.com* 🗐 *$9.50* ☉ *Oct.–Mar., Mon. noon–4, Tues.–Sun. 10–4; Apr.–Sept., Mon. noon–7, Tues.–Sun. 10–7.*

EAST OF THE WILLAMETTE RIVER

Portland is known as the City of Roses, but the 10 distinctive bridges spanning the Willamette River have also earned it the name Bridgetown. The older drawbridges, near downtown, open several times a day to allow passage of large cargo ships and freighters. You can easily spend a couple of days exploring the attractions and areas on the east side of the river.

WHAT TO SEE

Fodor's Choice
★
Hawthorne District. This neighborhood stretching from the foot of Mt. Tabor to 30th Avenue attracts a more college-age, bohemian crowd than downtown or Nob Hill. With many bookstores, coffeehouses, taverns, restaurants, antiques stores, and boutiques filling the streets, it's easy to spend a few hours wandering here. ⊠ *S.E. Hawthorne Blvd. between 30th and 42nd Aves., Hawthorne District.*

29

Northeast Alberta Street. Quirky handicrafts by local artists are for sale inside the galleries, studios, coffeehouses, restaurants, and boutiques lining this street in the northeast Portland neighborhood. It's a fascinating place to witness the intersection of cultures and lifestyles in a growing city. Shops unveil new exhibits during an evening event called the Last Thursday Art Walk. The Alberta Street Fair in September showcases the area with arts-and-crafts displays and street performances. ⊠ *Between Martin Luther King Jr. Blvd. and 30th Ave., Alberta Arts District.*

North Mississippi Avenue. Four blocks of old storefronts reinvented as cafés, collectives, shops, and music venues along this north Portland street showcase the indie spirit of the city's do-it-yourselfers and creative types. Bioswale planter boxes, found-object fences, and café tables built from old doors are some of the innovations you'll see around this hip new district. At the hub of it all is the ReBuilding Center, an outlet for recycled building supplies that has cob (clay-and-straw) trees and benches built into the facade. Take MAX light rail to the

Albina/Mississippi station. ⊠ *Between N. Fremont and Shaver Sts., off N. Interstate Ave.*

Fodor'sChoice **Vera Katz Eastbank Esplanade.** A stroll along this 1½-mi pedestrian and
★ cycling path across from downtown is one of the best ways to experience the Willamette River and Portland's bridges close-up. Built in 2001, the esplanade runs along the east bank of the Willamette River between the Hawthorne and Steel bridges, and features a 1,200-foot walkway that floats atop the river, a boat dock, and public art. Pedestrian crossings on both bridges link the esplanade to Waterfront Park, making a 3-mi loop. Take MAX light rail to the Rose Quarter station. ⊠ *Parking at east end of Hawthorne Bridge, between Madison and Salmon Sts.*

WHERE TO EAT

Lovers of ethnic foods have their pick of Chinese, French, Indian, Peruvian, Italian, Japanese, Polish, Middle Eastern, Tex-Mex, Thai, and Vietnamese specialties. Most of the city's trendier restaurants and reliable classics are concentrated in Nob Hill, the Pearl District, and downtown. A smattering of cuisines can also be found on the east side of town as well, near Fremont, Hawthorne Boulevard, Sandy Boulevard, and Alberta Street.

Compared to other major cities, Portland restaurants aren't open quite as late, and it's unusual to see many diners after 11 pm even on weekends, though there are a handful of restaurants and popular bars that do serve late. Many diners dress casually for even higher-end establishments; jeans are acceptable almost everywhere.

WHAT IT COSTS				
	¢	$	$$	$$$	$$$$
Restaurants	under $10	$10–$16	$17–$23	$24–$30	over $30

Prices are per person, for a main course at dinner.

DOWNTOWN

$ ✕**Dan & Louis's Oyster Bar.** Oysters at this Portland landmark near the
SEAFOOD river come fried, stewed, or on the half shell. The clam chowder is tasty, but the crab stew is a rare treat. Combination dinners let you mix your fried favorites. The collection of steins, plates, and marine art has grown since the restaurant opened in 1907 to fill beams, nooks, crannies, and nearly every inch of wall. ⊠ *208 S.W. Ankeny St., Downtown* ☎ *503/227–5906* ⊕ *www.danandlouis.com* ☐ *AE, D, DC, MC, V.*

$$$$ ✕**El Gaucho.** Three dimly lit dining rooms with blue walls and striped
STEAK upholstery are an inviting place for those with healthy wallets. The spe-
Fodor'sChoice cialty here is 28-day, dry-aged, certified Angus beef, but chops, ribs, and
★ chicken entrées are also cooked in the open kitchen. The chateaubriand for two is carved tableside. Seafood lovers might want to try the tomato fennel bouillabaisse. Service is impeccable at this Seattle transplant in the elegant Benson Hotel. Each night live Latin guitar music serenades

the dinner guests. ✉ *319 S.W. Broadway, Downtown* ☎ *503/227–8794* ⊕ *www.elgaucho.com* ▭ *AE, DC, MC, V* ⊘ *No lunch.*

$$$ ✕ **Gracie's.** Stepping into this dining room is like stepping into a pres-
AMERICAN tigious 1940s supper club. Dazzling chandeliers, beautifully rich floor-
Fodor's Choice to-ceiling draperies, velvet couches, and marble-topped tables exude
★ class. Dishes like grilled swordfish and stuffed pork loin are perfectly
seasoned and served with seasonal vegetables. On weekends there's a
brunch menu that includes fresh fruit, waffles, and omelets. ✉ *Hotel
DeLuxe, 729 S.W. 15th Ave., Downtown* ☎ *503/222–2171* ⊕ *www.
graciesdining.com* ▭ *AE, D, MC, V.*

$$ ✕ **Higgins.** Chef Greg Higgins, former executive chef at the Heathman
FRENCH Hotel, focuses on ingredients from the Pacific Northwest and on organi-
Fodor's Choice cally grown herbs and produce while incorporating traditional French
★ cooking styles and other international influences into his menu. Start
with a salad of warm beets, asparagus, and artichokes, or the country-
style terrine of venison, chicken, and pork with dried sour cherries and
a roasted-garlic mustard. Main courses, which change seasonally, might
include dishes made with Alaskan spot prawns, halibut, duck, or pork
loin. Vegetarian options are available. A bistro menu is available in the
adjoining bar, where comfortable leather booths and tables provide an
alternative to the main dining room. ✉ *1239 S.W. Broadway, Downtown* ☎ *503/222–9070* ▭ *AE, D, DC, MC, V* ⊘ *No lunch weekends.*

$$ ✕ **Jake's Famous Crawfish.** Diners have been enjoying fresh Pacific North-
SEAFOOD west seafood in Jake's warren of wood-paneled dining rooms for more
than a century. The back bar came around Cape Horn during the 1880s,
and the chandeliers hanging from the high ceilings date from 1881.
The restaurant gained a national reputation in 1920, when crawfish
was added to the menu. White-coat waiters take your order from an
almost endless sheet of daily seafood specials year-round, but try to
come during crawfish season (May–September), when you can sample
the tasty crustacean in pie, cooked Creole style, or in a Cajun-style stew
over rice. ✉ *401 S.W. 12th Ave., Downtown* ☎ *503/226–1419* ⊕ *www.
mccormickandschmicks.com* ▭ *AE, D, DC, MC, V* ⊘ *No lunch Sun.*

PEARL DISTRICT

$$ ✕ **50 Plates.** You wish you had more room to try everything here, where
AMERICAN everything seems designed to put mom's tried-and-true favorites to the
Fodor's Choice test. Evoking regional cuisine from all 50 states, the restaurant creates
★ fresh culinary interpretations. The delightful "silver dollar sammies"
include sweet and spicy Carolina pulled pork on a sweet-potato roll and
a smoked portobello rendition with butter lettuce, fried green tomatoes,
and herbed goat cheese. There's also a crowd-pleasing succotash whose
components vary depending upon the availability of locally harvested
ingredients. The rich desserts include dark-chocolate fudge cake served
with homemade brown-sugar ice cream, and bananas Foster. ✉ *333
N.W. 13th Ave., Pearl District* ☎ *503/228–5050* ⊕ *www.50plates.com*
▭ *AE, MC, V.*

29

NOB HILL

$$$
AMERICAN

✕ **The Ringside.** This Portland institution has been famous for its beef for more than 50 years. Dine in cozy booths on rib eye, prime rib, and New York strip, which come in regular- or king-size cuts. Seafood lovers will find plenty of choices: a chilled seafood platter with an 8-ounce lobster tail, Dungeness crab, oysters, jumbo prawns, and Oregon bay shrimp. The onion rings, made with the local Walla Walla sweets variety, are equally renowned. ⊠ *2165 N.W. Burnside St., close to Nob Hill* ☎ *503/223–1513* ⊕ *www.ringsidesteakhouse.com* ⊟ *AE, D, MC, V* ⊘ *No lunch.*

BUCKMAN

$$
CONTINENTAL

✕ **clarklewis.** This cutting-edge restaurant, aka "darklewis" for its murky lighting, is making big waves for inventive farm-fresh meals served inside a former warehouse loading dock. Regional vegetables, seafood, and meat from local suppliers appear on a daily changing menu of pastas, entrées, and sides. Diners can order small, large, and family-style sizes, or let the chef decide with the fixed-price meal. Although the food is great, the lack of signage or a reception area can make your first visit feel a little like arriving at a party uninvited. ⊠ *1001 S.E. Water Ave., Buckman* ☎ *503/235–2294* ⊕ *www.clarklewispdx.com* ⊟ *AE, MC, V* ⊘ *Closed Sun. No lunch weekends.*

HAWTHORNE DISTRICT

$$$$
ITALIAN
Fodor's Choice
★

✕ **Genoa.** Widely regarded as the finest restaurant in Portland, Genoa serves a five-course prix-fixe Italian menu that changes with the availability of ingredients and the season. Diners can chose from several entrées; the portions are hearty, thoughtfully crafted, and paired with some vibrant accompaniments such as sautéed brussels-sprout leaves or roasted root vegetables. As for the dining room, its dark antique furnishings, long curtains, and dangling light fixtures all help make it feel sophisticated. Seating is limited to a few dozen diners, so service is excellent. ⊠ *2822 S.E. Belmont St., near Hawthorne District* ☎ *503/238–1464* ⌕ *Reservations essential* ⊕ *www.genoarestaurant. com* ⊟ *AE, D, DC, MC, V* ⊘ *No lunch.*

KERNS

$
THAI
Fodor's Choice
★

✕ **Lemongrass.** Set in an old house, this lovely, intimate establishment consistently serves tantalizing pad Thai and a garlic basil chicken with sauce so delicious you wish you had a straw. Fresh flowers adorn the white-linen tables. Dishes are cooked to order, and just about everything is delectable, including the chicken chili paste and peanut curry. ⊠ *1705 N.E. Couch St., Kerns* ☎ *503/231–5780* ⌕ *Reservations not accepted* ⊟ *No credit cards.*

RICHMOND

¢
ASIAN

✕ **Pok Pok.** There's no shortage of culinary adventure here. The food resembles what street vendors in Thailand would make: charcoal-grilled game hen stuffed with lemongrass or shredded chicken and coconut milk (made in-house). Diners have options of sitting outside by heated lamps under tents, or down below in the dark, funky cave. Foods are unique blends of flavors and spices, such as the coconut and jackfruit ice cream served on a sweet bun with sticky rice, condensed milk, chocolate syrup, and peanuts. ✉ *3226 S.E. Division St., Richmond* ☎ *503/232–1387* 🌐 *www.pokpokpdx.com* ▭ *MC, V.*

WHERE TO STAY

The hotels near the city center and on the riverfront are appealing for their proximity to Portland's attractions. MAX light rail is within easy walking distance of most properties. Additional accommodations clustered near the Convention Center and the airport are almost all chain hotels that tend to be less expensive than those found downtown. Several beautiful B&Bs are the northwest and northeast residential neighborhoods.

Most of Portland's luxurious hotels can be booked for under $250 per night. If you are willing to stay outside of the downtown area, you can easily find a room in a suburban chain hotel for well under $100 per night. Before booking your stay, visit 🌐 *www.travelportland.com* to check out "Portland Perks" packages.

Hotel reviews have been condensed for this book. Please go to Fodors.com for full reviews of each property.

WHAT IT COSTS

	¢	$	$$	$$$	$$$$
Hotels	under $100	$100–$150	$151–$200	$201–$250	over $250

Prices are for two people in a standard double room in high season, excluding tax.

DOWNTOWN

$$ **Benson Hotel.** The hand-carved Circassian walnut paneling from Russia and the Italian white-marble staircase are among the noteworthy design touches in Portland's grandest hotel.**Pros:** beautiful lobby; excellent location. **Cons:** hallways could use updating. ✉ *309 S.W. Broadway, Downtown* ☎ *503/228–2000 or 888/523–6766* 🌐 *www.bensonhotel.com* *287 rooms* *In-room: refrigerator (some), dial-up, Wi-Fi. In-hotel: 2 restaurants, room service, bar, gym, concierge, laundry service, Wi-Fi hotspot, parking (paid)* ▭ *AE, D, DC, MC, V.*

$$$ Fodor's Choice ★ **Heathman Hotel.** From the teak-paneled lobby to the rosewood elevators (with Warhol prints hung at each landing) and marble fireplaces, this hotel exudes refinement. **Pros:** superior service; central location adjoining the Performing Arts Center; renowned on-site restaurant. **Cons:** small rooms; expensive parking. ✉ *1001 S.W. Broadway, Downtown* ☎ *503/241–4100 or 800/551–0011* 🌐 *www.heathmanportland.com* *117 rooms, 33 suites* *In-room: refrigerator, Internet, Wi-Fi. In-hotel: restaurant, 24 hour room service, bar, fitness suite, concierge, laundry service, Wi-Fi hotspot, parking (paid), pets allowed* ▭ *AE, D, DC, MC, V.*

$$ Fodor's Choice ★ **Hotel deLuxe.** If you long to be transported back to the Hollywood glamour of the 1940s, this place is perfect. **Pros:** "pillow menu" and other extra touches lend an air of luxury; artistic vibe. **Cons:** older

windows in building can be drafty at night; cold bathroom floors. ⊠ *729 S.W. 15th Ave., Downtown* 🕾 *503/219–2094 or 866/895–2094* ⊕ *www.hoteldeluxeportland.com* 🖙 *130 rooms* ⚐ *In-room: refrigerator, Wi-Fi. In-hotel: restaurant, room service, bar, Wi-Fi hotspot, parking (paid), some pets allowed* ⊟ *AE, D, DC, MC, V* ⦿| *CP.*

$$$$ 🛏 **RiverPlace Hotel.** All the guest rooms here have muted color schemes, Craftsman-style desks, and ergonomic chairs, and over a quarter of them have amazing views of the river, marina, and skyline, as well as a landscaped courtyard. **Pros:** great location; wide selection of room options; great beds. **Cons:** no pool. ⊠ *1510 S.W. Harbor Way, Downtown* 🕾 *503/228–3233 or 800/227–1333* ⊕ *www.riverplacehotel.com* 🖙 *39 rooms, 45 suites* ⚐ *In-room: DVD, Wi-Fi. In-hotel: restaurant, room service, concierge, parking (paid)* ⊟ *AE, D, DC, MC, V.*

Fodor's Choice
★

IRVINGTON

$$ 🛏 **Lion and the Rose.** Oak and mahogany floors, original light fixtures, antique silver, and a coffered dining-room ceiling set a tone of formal elegance here, while the wonderfully friendly, accommodating, and knowledgeable innkeepers make sure that you feel perfectly at home. **Pros:** gorgeous house; top-notch service; afternoon tea available upon request. **Cons:** no elevator; fills up quickly (particularly in summer). ⊠ *1810 N.E. 15th Ave., Irvington* 🕾 *503/287–9245 or 800/955–1647* ⊕ *www.lionrose.com* 🖙 *8 rooms* ⚐ *In-room: Wi-Fi. In-hotel: no kids under 10* ⊟ *AE, D, DC, MC, V.*

Fodor's Choice
★

NORTHEAST PORTLAND

$ 🛏 **McMenamins Kennedy School.** In a renovated elementary school in northeast Portland, the Kennedy School may well be one of the most unusual hotels you'll ever encounter. **Pros:** funky and authentic Portland experience; room rates include movie admission and use of the year-round outdoor soaking pool. **Cons:** no bathtubs (shower stalls only) in bathrooms; no TVs in rooms; no elevator. ⊠ *5736 N.E. 33rd Ave., near Alberta District* 🕾 *503/249–3983* ⊕ *www.kennedyschool.com* 🖙 *35 rooms* ⚐ *In-room: no TV, Wi-Fi. In-hotel: restaurant, bars, Wi-Fi hotspot, parking (free)* ⊟ *AE, D, DC, MC, V* ⦿| *BP.*

Fodor's Choice
★

NIGHTLIFE

Every night performances from top-ranked dance, theater, and musical talent take the stage somewhere in Portland. You can take in true independent films, great performance art and plays and check out some of the Northwest's (and the country's) hottest bands at one of the city's many nightclubs.

BARS AND LOUNGES

From chic to cheap, cool to cultish, Portland's diverse bars and lounges blanket the town. The best way to experience some of the city's hottest spots is to check out the happy-hour menus found at almost all of Portland's bars; they offer excellent deals on both food and drinks. Many of the best bars and lounges in Portland are found in its restaurants.

DOWNTOWN

At the elegant **Heathman Hotel** (✉*1001 S.W. Broadway* ☎*503/241–4100*) you can sit in the marble bar or the wood-paneled Tea Court.

Huber's Cafe (✉*411 S.W. 3rd Ave.* ☎*503/228–5686*), the city's oldest restaurant, is notable for its Spanish coffee and old-fashioned feel.

The **Rialto** (✉ *529 S.W. 4th Ave.* ☎*503/228–7605*) is a large, dark bar with several pool tables and enthusiastic players as well as some of the best Bloody Marys in town.

With more than 120 choices, **Southpark** (✉*901 S.W. Salmon St.* ☎*503/326–1300*) is a perfect spot for a post-symphony glass of wine.

At **Veritable Quandary** (✉*1220 S.W. 1st Ave.* ☎*503/227–7342*), next to the river, you can sit on the cozy, tree-filled outdoor patio or in the glass atrium.

PEARL DISTRICT AND OLD TOWN/CHINATOWN

The modern bar at **Bluehour** (✉*250 N.W. 13th Ave., Pearl District* ☎*503/226–3394*) draws a chic crowd for specialty cocktails such as the Bluehour Breeze (house-infused grapefruit vodka with a splash of cranberry).

Henry's 12th Street Tavern (✉ *10 N.W. 12th Ave., Pearl District* ☎*503/227–5320*) has more than 100 beers on draft, plasma-screen TVs, and a billiards room in a building that was once Henry Weinhard's brewery.

At **Oba!** (✉*555 N.W. 12th Ave., Pearl District* ☎*503/228–6161*), plush tans and reds with lime-green backlit walls create a backdrop for South American salsa.

EAST OF WILLAMETTE RIVER

Artsy, hip east-siders, not to be mistaken for the jet-setters downtown, hang and drink martinis and wine at the minimalist **Aalto Lounge** (✉*3356 S.E. Belmont St.* ☎*503/235–6041*).

A laid-back beer-drinking crowd fills the **Horse Brass Pub** (✉*4534 S.E. Belmont St.* ☎*503/232–2202*), as good an English-style pub as you will find this side of the Atlantic, with more than 50 beers on tap.

The open, airy **Imbibe** (✉*2229 S.E. Hawthorne Blvd.* ☎*503/239–4002*) serves up creative cocktails, such as its namesake, the Imbibe Infusion— a thyme-and-ginger-infused vodka and strawberry martini with a touch of lemon.

29

BREWPUBS, MICROBREWERIES, AND PUB THEATERS

Portland is the proclaimed beer capital of the world, affectionately deemed "Beervana" and "Munich on the Willamette," boasting 35 craft breweriesoperating within the city limits. Some have attached pub operations, where you can sample a foaming pint of house ale. "Pub theaters," former neighborhood movie houses where patrons enjoy food, suds, and recent theatrical releases, are part of the microbrewery phenomenon. Many are branches of McMenamins, a locally owned chain of bars, restaurants, nightclubs, and hotels, and some of these pubs can be found in restored historic buildings.

The first McMenamins brewpub, the **Barley Mill Pub** (✉ *1629 S.E. Hawthorne Blvd., Hawthorne District* ☎ *503/231–1492*), is filled with Grateful Dead memorabilia and concert posters. It's a fun place for families.

BridgePort Brewpub + Bakery (✉ *1313 N.W. Marshall St.* ☎ *503/241–3612* ⊕ *www.bridgeportbrew. com*). Visit the oldest microbrewery in Portland, a beautiful brick-and-ivy building that is listed on the National Register of Historic Places. Their heritage beer, Blue Heron, was first brewed in 1987, and honors Portland's official city bird. Brewery tours are free and take place on Saturday at, 1, 3, and 5 pm.

Hopworks Urban Brewery "HUB" (✉ *2944 S.E. Powell Blvd.* ☎ *503/232–4677* ⊕ *www.hopworksbeer.com*). In addition to brewing only organic beer, the brewery is powered with 100% renewable energy. Pint picks include the Organic Survival "Seven-Grain" Stout, finished with the iconic Stumptown Hairbender espresso and their namesake Organic Hopworks IPA, a Northwest classic. Brewery tours, which cost $5, take place on Saturday at 11 am and 3 pm.

First opened in 1987, the **Mission Theatre** (✉ *1624 N.W. Glisan St., Nob Hill* ☎ *503/223–4527*) was the first McMenamins brew theater. It shows recent Hollywood offerings.

Ringlers (✉ *1332 W. Burnside St., Downtown* ☎ *503/225–0627*) occupies the first floor of the building that houses the famous Crystal Ballroom.

Ringlers Annex (✉ *1223 S.W. Stark St., Downtown* ☎ *503/525–0520*), one block east of Ringlers, is a pie-shaped corner pub where you can puff a cigar while drinking beer, port, or a single-malt scotch.

Widmer Brothers Brewing Company (✉ *929 N. Russell St.* ☎ *503/281–2437* ⊕ *www.widmer.com*). Founded in 1984, this is Oregon's largest brewery, and their Hefeweizen is still the top-selling craft beer in the state. Brewery tours take place on Friday at 3 pm, and Saturday at 11 am and noon.

> ### PUB THEATERS
>
> Sipping a pint of local brew is one of Oregon's favorite pastimes, but Portlanders have taken this a step further with so-called pub theaters—movie theaters showing second-run, classic, or cult films for $3 or so that let you buy a pitcher of good locally brewed beer and a slice of pizza to enjoy while watching.

COFFEEHOUSES AND TEAHOUSES

Coffee is to Portland as tea is to England. For Portlanders, sipping a cup of coffee is a right, a ritual, and a pastime that occurs no matter the time of day or night. There's no shortage of cafés in which to park and read, reflect, or rejuvenate for the long day or night of exploration ahead.

DOWNTOWN

Fodor's Choice ★ Serving quite possibly the best coffee around, **Stumptown Coffee Roasters** (⊠ 128 S.W. 3rd Ave., Downtown ☎ 503/295–6144) has three local cafés, where its beans are roasted daily on vintage cast-iron equipment for a consistent, fresh flavor.

NOB HILL AND VICINITY

One of the more highly trafficked locales in the Portland coffee scene, **World Cup Coffee and Tea** (⊠ 1740 N.W. Glisan St., Nob Hill ☎ 503/228–4152) sells excellent organic coffee and espresso in Nob Hill, as well as at its store in the Pearl District at the Ecotrust building and at Powell's City of Books on Burnside.

EAST OF WILLAMETTE RIVER

Rimsky Korsakoffee House (⊠ 707 S.E. 12th Ave., East of Willamette River ☎ 503/232–2640), one of the city's first coffeehouses, is still one of the best, especially when it comes to desserts.

Stumptown Coffee Roasters (⊠ 4525 S.E. Division St. ☎ 503/230–7702 ⊠ 3356 S.E. Belmont St. ☎ 503/232–8889) has two cafés on the east side. At the original site (S.E. Division), organic beans are still roasted daily. At the Stumptown Annex, the newer branch next door, patrons can participate in "cuppings" (tastings) daily at 3 pm.

With soft music and the sound of running water in the background, the **Tao of Tea** (⊠ 3430 S.E. Belmont St., East of Willamette River ☎ 503/736–0119) serves vegetarian snacks and sweets as well as more than 80 loose-leaf teas.

LIVE MUSIC

It's not simply the number of outstanding musicians that makes Portland unique, but their eclecticism. It's a city where stray-far-from-the-crowd individualism and a highly cooperative sense of community are prized in equal measure, and the local scene reflects that: talented, idiosyncratic musicians making all genres of music together. Whether you're interested in listening to a singer-songwriter tell it like it is as you sip Stumptown Coffee, getting down and dirty in a rocking dive bar, or simply dancing the night away to electronic trance beats, Portland's got you covered.

BLUES, FOLK, AND ROCK The **Aladdin Theater** (⊠ 3017 S.E. Milwaukie Ave., East of Willamette River ☎ 503/234–9694), in an old movie theater, is one of the best music venues in town. It serves microbrews and pizza.

Berbati's Pan (⊠ 10 S.W. 3rd Ave., Old Town ☎ 503/226–2122), on the edge of Old Town, has dancing and live music, everything from big band and swing to acid jazz, rock, and R&B.

The **Candlelight Room** (⊠ 2032 S.W. 5th Ave., Downtown ☎ 503/222–3378) presents blues nightly.

Crystal Ballroom. Restored by the McMenamin brothers, this ballroom transformed into one of Portland's most interesting music venues. Home to shows by nationally touring acts as well as locals, the spring-loaded ballroom floor makes dancing extra fun. ⊠ 1332 W. Burnside St., Downtown ☎ 503/225–0047.

29

Portland's vibrant music scene features a wealth of home-grown talent.

Dublin Pub (✉ *6821 S.W. Beaverton–Hillsdale Hwy., West of Downtown* ☎ *503/297–2889*), on the West Side, pours more than 50 beers on tap and hosts Irish bands and rock groups.

JAZZ Dubbed one of the world's "top 100 places to hear jazz" by *DownBeat*, **Jimmy Mak's** (✉ *300 S.W. 10th, Pearl District* ☎ *503/295–6542*) also serves Greek and Middle Eastern dishes and has a basement lounge outfitted with two pool tables and an Internet jukebox.

SHOPPING

One of Portland's greatest attributes is its neighborhoods' dynamic spectrum of retail and specialty shops. The Pearl District is known for chic interior design and high-end clothing boutiques. Trek over to the Hawthorne area and you'll discover wonderful stores for handmade jewelry, clothing, and books. The Northwest has some funky shops for housewares, clothing, and jewelry, while in the Northeast there are fabulous galleries and crafts. Downtown has a blend of it all, as well as bigger options, including the Pioneer Place Mall and department stores such as Nordstrom and Macy's.

No Portland shopping experience would be complete without a visit to the nation's largest open-air market, Saturday Market (⇨ *Exploring above*), where an array of talented artists converge to peddle handcrafted wares beyond your wildest do-it-yourself dreams. It's also open Sunday.

SHOPPING AREAS

Portland's main shopping area is **downtown,** between Southwest 2nd and 10th avenues and between Southwest Stark and Morrison streets. The major department stores are scattered over several blocks near Pioneer Courthouse Square. Northeast **Broadway** between 10th and 21st avenues is lined with boutiques and specialty shops. **Nob Hill,** north of downtown along Northwest 21st and 23rd avenues, has eclectic clothing, gift, book, and food shops. Most of the city's fine-art galleries are concentrated in the booming **Pearl District,** north from Burnside Street to Marshall Street between Northwest 8th and 15th avenues, along with furniture and design stores. **Sellwood,** 5 mi from the city center, south on Naito Parkway and east across the Sellwood Bridge, has more than 50 antiques and collectibles shops along southeast 13th Avenue, plus specialty shops and outlet stores for sporting goods. You can find the larger antiques stores near the intersection of Milwaukie Avenue and Bybee. **Hawthorne Boulevard** between 30th and 42nd avenues has a selection of alternative bookstores, coffeehouses, antiques stores, and boutiques.

SPECIALTY STORES

BOOKS

Fodor's Choice **Powell's City of Books** (✉ *1005 W. Burnside St., Downtown* ☎ *503/228–* ★ *4651* ⊕ *www.powells.com*), the largest retail store of used and new books in the world (with more than 1.5 million volumes), covers an entire city block on the edge of the Pearl District. It also carries rare and collectible books. There are also three branches in the Portland International Airport.

CLOTHING

Portland's best store for fine men's and women's clothing, **Mario's** (✉ *833 S.W. Morrison St., Downtown* ☎ *503/227–3477*) carries designer lines by Prada, Dolce & Gabbana, Etro, and Loro Piana—among others.

Niketown (✉ *930 S.W. 6th Ave., Downtown* ☎ *503/221–6453*), Nike's flagship retail store, has the latest and greatest in "swoosh"-adorned products. The high-tech setting has athlete profiles, photos, and interactive displays.

Portland Nike Factory Store (✉ *2650 N.E. Martin Luther King Jr. Blvd., East of Willamette River* ☎ *503/281–5901*) sells products that have been on the market six months or more.

Portland Outdoor Store (✉ *304 S.W. 3rd Ave., Downtown* ☎ *503/222– 1051*) stubbornly resists all that is trendy, both in clothes and decor, but if you want authentic Western gear—saddles, Stetsons, boots, or cowboy shirts—head here.

GIFTS

Made in Oregon (☎ *866/257–0938*), which sells books, smoked salmon, local wines, Pendleton woolen goods, carvings made of myrtle wood, and other products made in the state, has shops at Portland International Airport, the Lloyd Center, Washington Square, and Clackamas Town Center.

29

Even without getting a nod from Oprah in her magazine, **Moonstruck** (⊠ *526 N.W. 23rd Ave., Nob Hill* ☎ *503/542–3400*) would still be known as a chocolatier extraordinaire. Just a couple of the rich confections might sustain you if you're nibbling—water is available for palate cleansing in between treats—but whether you're just grazing or boxing some up for the road, try the Ocumarian Truffle, chocolate laced with chili pepper; the unusual kick of sweetness and warmth is worth experiencing.

OUTDOOR SUPPLIES

Columbia Sportswear (⊠ *911 S.W. Broadway, Downtown* ☎ *503/226–6800* ⊕ *www.columbia.com*), a local legend and global force in recreational outdoor wear, is especially strong in fashionable jackets, pants, and durable shoes.

OUTDOOR ACTIVITIES

Portlanders definitely gravitate to the outdoors, and they're well acclimated to the elements year-round—including winter's wind, rain, and cold. Once the sun starts to shine in spring and into summer, the city fills with hikers, joggers, and mountain bikers, who flock to Portland's hundreds of miles of parks, paths, and trails. The Willamette and Columbia rivers are used for boating and water sports—though it's not easy to rent any kind of boat for casual use. Locals also have access to a playground for fishing, camping, skiing, and snowboarding all the way through June, thanks to the proximity of Mt. Hood.

BICYCLING

Fodor's Choice ★ Bicycling is a cultural phenomenon in Portland—possibly the most beloved mode of transportation in the city. Besides the sheer numbers of cyclists you see on roads and pathways, you'll find well-marked bike lanes and signs reminding motorists to yield to cyclists.

BIKE RENTALS

Bikes can be rented at several places in the city. Rentals typically run from $20 to $50 per day with cheaper weekly rates from $75 to $150. Bike helmets are generally included in the cost of rental.

CityBikes Workers Cooperative (⊠ *734 S.E. Ankeny St., East of Willamette River* ☎ *503/239–6951*) rents hybrid bikes good for casual city riding.

Fat Tire Farm (⊠ *2714 N.W. Thurman St., West of Downtown* ☎ *503/222–3276*) rents mountain bikes, great for treks in Forest Park.

Waterfront Bicycle Rentals (⊠ *315 S.W. Montgomery St., Suite 3, Downtown* ☎ *503/227–1719*) is convenient for jaunts along the Willamette.

BIKING ROUTES

There are more than 300 mi of bicycle boulevards, lanes, and off-street paths in Portland. Accessible maps, specialized tours, parking capacity (including lockers and sheltered racks downtown), and bicycle-only traffic signals at confusing intersections make biking in the city easy. Cyclists can find the best routes by following green direction-and-distance signs that point the way around town, and the corresponding white dots on the street surface.

For more information on bike routes and resources in and around Portland, visit the **Department of Transportation** (⊕ *www.portlandonline. com/transportation*). You can download maps, or order "Bike There," a glossy detailed bicycle map of the metropolitan area.

PARKS

Portland is a city of parks with more than 12,000 acres of open spaces in more than 250 locations. There are 6 public gardens, 204 parks, 5 golf courses, and thousands of acres of urban forest.

Council Crest Park. The second-highest point in Portland, at 1,073 feet, is a superb spot to watch sunsets and sunrises. Along with great views of the Portland metro area, a clear day also affords views of the surrounding peaks—Mt. Hood, Mt. St. Helens, Mt. Adams, Mt. Jefferson, and Mt. Rainier. ⊠ *3400 Council Crest Dr., West of Downtown* ⊗ *5 am–midnight, closed to cars after 9 pm*

Forest Park. One of the nation's largest urban wildernesses (5,000 acres), this city-owned, car-free park has more than 50 species of birds and mammals and more than 70 mi of trails. Running the length of the park is the 24½-mi Wildwood Trail, which extends into Washington Park. The 11-mi Leif Erikson Drive, which picks up from the end of Northwest Thurman Street, is a popular place to jog or ride a mountain bike. The **Portland Audubon Society** (⊠ *5151 N.W. Cornell Rd.* ☎ *503/292–6855* ⊕ *www.audobonportland.org*) supplies free maps and sponsors a flock of bird-related activities, including guided bird-watching events. There's a hospital for injured and orphaned birds as well as a gift shop stocked with books and feeders. ⊠ *Past Nob Hill in Northwest District* ☎ *503/823–7529* ⊕ *www.forestparkconservancy. org* ⊗ *Daily dawn–dusk.*

Fodor'sChoice ★ **Governor Tom McCall Waterfront Park.** Named for a former governor revered for his statewide land-use planning initiatives, this park stretches north along the Willamette River for about a mile to Burnside Street. Broad and grassy, Waterfront Park's got a fine ground-level view of downtown Portland's bridges and skyline. The arching jets of water at the **Salmon Street Fountain** change configuration every few hours, and are a favorite cooling-off spot during summer. ⊠ *S.W. Naito Pkwy. (Front Ave.), from south of Hawthorne Bridge to Burnside Bridge, Downtown.*

Fodor'sChoice ★ **Laurelhurst Park.** Completed in 1914, resplendent Laurelhurst Park is evocative of another time, and gives you the urge to don a parasol. It's

29

ROSE CITY

True to the city's nicknames, Rose City or City of Roses, the fragrant favorite is found at many of the area's parks. There is no one official reason for the city's moniker, but many suggested ones. The first known reference was in 1888 at an Episcopal Church convention. And though the first Rose Festival was held in 1907, the city did not officially take the nickname until 2003.

no wonder that it was the first park to be put on the National Register of Historic Places. Take a stroll around the large spring-fed pond (granted a bit murky with algae) and keep an eye out for blue heron, the city's official bird. On the south side of this 26-acre park is one of the busiest basketball courts in town. Though the park is always beautiful, it is especially so in fall. ⊠ *S.E. 39th Ave. and Stark St., East of Willamette River* ⊗ *5 am–10:30 pm.*

Marquam Nature Park. Just minutes from downtown Marquam has 176 acres of greenery and 5 mi of trails to explore. No playgrounds or dog parks here, just peace and quiet. Maps of trails are available at the shelter at the base of the trails or on the Friends of Marquam Park Web site. ⊠ *S.W. Marquam St. and Sam Jackson Park Rd., West of Downtown* ⊕ *www.fnmp.org* ⊗ *5 am–midnight* ⚒ *Good for: nature lovers, hikers, solitude seekers.*

Mt. Tabor Park. A playground on top of a volcano cinder cone? Yup, that's here. The cinders, or glassy rock fragments, unearthed in the park's construction, were used to surface the respite's roads; the ones leading to the top are closed to cars, but popular with cyclists. They're also popular with cruisers—each August there's an old-fashioned soapbox derby. Picnic tables and tennis, basketball, and volleyball courts make Mt. Tabor Park perfection. ⊠ *S.E. 60th and Salmon Sts., East of Willamette River* ⊗ *5 am–midnight.*

Fodor's Choice
★

Oaks Bottom Wild Refuge. Bring your binoculars, because birds are plentiful here; more than 400 species have been spotted, including hawks, quail, pintails, mallards, coots, woodpeckers, kestrels, widgeons, hummingbirds, and the sedately beautiful blue heron. The 140-acre refuge is a flood-plain wetland—rare because it is in the heart of the city. The hiking isn't too strenuous, but wear sturdy shoes, as it can get muddy; part of the park is on top of a landfill layered with soil. ⊠ *S.E. 7th and Sellwood Ave., East of the Willamette* ⊗ *5 am–midnight.*

Fodor's Choice
★

Peninsula Park & Rose Garden. The "City of Roses" moniker started here, at this park that harks back to another time. The city's oldest (1909) public rose garden (and the only sunken one), houses almost 9,000 plantings and 65 varieties of roses. The daunting task of deadheading all these flowers is covered in classes taught to volunteers twice a season. The bandstand is a historic landmark, and the last of its kind in the city. There's also a 100-year-old fountain, playground, wading pool, tennis and volleyball courts, and picnic tables. ⊠ *700 N. Rosa Parks Way, East of the Willamette* ⊗ *5 am–midnight.*

Tryon Creek State Natural Area. Portland is chock-full of parks, but this is the only state park within city limits. And at 670 acres, there's plenty of room for all its admirers. The area was logged starting in the 1880s, and the natural regrowth has produced red alder, Douglas fir, big leaf maple, and western red cedar, giving home to more than 50 bird species. The eastern edge has a paved trail, in addition to 14 mi of trails for bikes, hikers, and horses. Before heading to the trails, stop by the nature center to check out the exhibits and topographical relief map. ⊠ *S.W. Boones Ferry Rd. and Terwilliger Blvd., West of Downtown* ☎ *503/636–4398* ⊕ *www.tryonfriends.org* ⊗ *Daily 7 am–8 pm, Nature Center 9–4.*

Seattle

WORD OF MOUTH

"Our daytime activities were: Coffee Walk with Seattle by Foot. That was fairly pleasant but if I had wanted to spend a few dollars more I probably would have liked a gourmet tour better. We took the watertaxi to West Seattle and rented bikes. That was a great day. We stopped by the Klondike Gold Rush museum one morning—FREE—that was well worth the hour or so spent there."

—suec1

WELCOME TO SEATTLE

TOP REASONS TO GO

★ **The World of SAM.** The Seattle Art Museum (SAM) features modern and Native American art; Olympic Sculpture Park showcases works by Calder and Serra amidst green space; and on Capitol Hill the Seattle Asian Art Museum, inside Volunteer Park, houses a fascinating collection.

★ **Discovery Park.** Densely forested trails spill out onto beaches with jaw-dropping vistas of Puget Sound at one of the city's best green spaces.

★ **Seattle Center.** Something for everyone: Pacific Science Center and Children's Museum; Experience Music Project/ Science Fiction Museum; the Seattle Center Skatepark; and the SIFF Film Center. Catch opera or ballet at McCaw Hall and theater performances at Intiman Theatre.

★ **Local Farmers' Markets.** Start at glorious Pike Place Market. Then visit smaller neighborhood markets in the University District, West Seattle, Columbia City, and along historic Ballard Avenue and Broadway on Capitol Hill.

1 Downtown. The only part of Seattle with sky-scrapers, along with most of the city's hotels and most popular tourist spots

2 Seattle Center, South Lake Union, and Queen Anne. Queen Anne rises up from Denny Way to the Ship Canal. At the bottom are the Space Needle, the Seattle Center, and the Experience Music Project. South Lake Union has the REI super-store, lakefront, and some eateries and hotels.

3 Pioneer Square. Seattle's oldest neighbor-hood has lovely redbrick and sandstone buildings, plus numerous galleries and antiques shops.

4 International District. The I.D. is a fun place to shop and eat. The stunning Wing Luke Asian Museum and Uwajimaya shop-ping center anchor the neighborhood.

5 Capitol Hill. The Hill has two faces: young and sassy and elegant and upscale. It has fantastic restaurants and nightlife.

6 West Seattle. On a peninsula west of the city proper, West Seattle has gorgeous Alki Beach and Lincoln Park.

GETTING ORIENTED

Hemmed in by mountains, hills, and multiple bodies of water, Seattle is anything but a linear, grid-lined city. The city can be baffling to navigate, especially if you delve into its residential neighborhoods. Water makes the best landmark. Both Elliott Bay and Lake Union are pretty hard to miss. When you are trying to get your bearings Downtown, Elliott Bay is a much more reliable landmark than the Space Needle. Remember that I–5 bisects the city (north–south). The major routes connecting the southern part of the city to the northern part are I–5, Aurora Avenue/ Highway 99, 15th Avenue NW (Ballard Bridge), and Westlake (Fremont Bridge) and Eastlake avenues. Streets in the Seattle area generally travel east to west, whereas avenues travel north to south.

30

Seattle isn't just a city—it's a feat of environmental engineering. When the Denny party arrived on its shores, "Seattle" was a series of densely forested valleys covered by Douglas fir, western hemlock, and red cedar; ridges that were far steeper than its current leg-burning hills surrounded it.

Present-day SoDo (the stadium district south of Downtown) was nothing but mudflats. Pioneer Square was actually an island of sorts, where Duwamish tribespeople crossed to the mainland over sandbars.

Once Seattle started to grow, its residents literally changed the city's geography. Massive Denny Hill once occupied the Belltown neighborhood—it simply had to go. The multistage "regrade" started in 1899 and was completed 32 years later. Dirt from the project helped fill in the tidelands, creating new land that supports what is now the entire waterfront district. The Denny Hill regrade was just one of dozens of projects; other equally ambitious earth-moving missions created the city you see today. One of the largest was the digging of the canal that links Lake Washington to Puget Sound, which required, in addition to the carving of the canal itself, the construction of large fixed bridges with drawbridges. Today construction of a new light rail line plus a replacement of the viaduct are examples of how the city is once again moving a lot of earth around.

It's hard to think of Seattle as anything but natural, though. After all, the city owes much of its appeal to its natural features—the myriad hills that did survive settlement offer views of mountain ranges and water, water, water. Outside of Downtown and other smaller commercial cores, Seattle's neighborhoods fan out in tangles of tree-lined streets. Massive parks like Discovery, Magnuson, and Washington Park Arboretum make Seattle one of the greenest and most livable cities in the nation. From the peaks of the Olympics or Cascades to an artistically landscaped garden in front of a classic Northwest bungalow, nature is in full effect every time you turn your head.

PLANNING

WHEN TO GO

Seattle is most enjoyable May through October. July through September is mostly dry, with warm days reaching into the mid-70s and 80s, with cooler nights. Although the weather can be dodgy, spring and fall are also excellent times to visit, as lodging and tour costs are usually much lower (and the crowds much smaller). In winter the weather can be dreary, but temperatures rarely dip below the low 40s; days are short, as well, because of Seattle's far-north location.

PLAN AHEAD

Ferries. Whale-watching/ferry ride vacation packages like those offered by the *Victoria Clipper* can be booked in advance. Washington State Ferries rarely accept reservations (only on international sailings to Sidney, B.C., for example), so be sure to plan island travel thoughtfully: Leave enough time in your schedule to arrive at the piers early—and to wait for the next ferry if you're last in line.

Hotel reservations. If you're arriving during high season or around major festivals and events, book as far in advance as possible. This extends past city limits—accommodations go fast (including campsites) on the San Juan Islands and the Olympic Peninsula. Waterfront or water-view hotels, like the Edgewater and the Inn at the Market, see their best rooms booked six months in advance.

Train tickets. Amtrak tickets to Portland and Vancouver, B.C., sell out on summer weekends, and last-minute fares can be quite expensive.

GETTING HERE

The major gateway is **Seattle–Tacoma International Airport** (SEA ☎ 206/ 787–5388 ⊕ *www.portseattle.org/seatac*), known locally as Sea-Tac. The airport is south of the city and reasonably close to it—non-rush-hours trips to Downtown sometimes take less than a half hour.

Charter flights and small carriers like Kenmore Air that operate shuttle flights between the cities of the Pacific Northwest land at **Boeing Field** (☎ 206/296–7380 ⊕ *www.kingcounty.gov/transportation/kcdot/ Airport.aspx*), which is between Sea-Tac and Seattle.

AIRPORT EASE

You can take Sound Transit's **Central Link Light Rail** (⊕ *www. soundtransit.org*) from Sea-Tac to Downtown. The train runs every 10 to 15 minutes from 5 am to 1 am weekdays and Saturday, and every 15 minutes from 6 am to midnight on Sunday. The Downtown terminus is Westlake Station, which is convenient to many hotels. The Sound Transit Central Link fare is $2.50 one-way.

GETTING AROUND

By Bus: The bus system will get you anywhere you need to go, although some routes require a time commitment and several transfers. Within the downtown core, however, the bus is efficient—and, most of the time it won't cost you a dime, thanks to the Ride-Free Area. The Trip Planner (⊕ *tripplanner.kingcounty.gov*) is a useful resource. (Fare: $2.25)

30

By Car: If you aren't staying in a central location, you may find Seattle's transit system frustrating. Access to a car is *almost* a necessity if you want to explore the residential neighborhoods beyond their commercial centers. If you want to do side trips to the Eastside (besides downtown Bellevue, which is easily reached by bus), Mt. Rainier, or pretty much any sight or city outside the Seattle limits (with the exception of Portland, Oregon, which is easily reached by train), you will definitely need a car. Before you book a car for city-only driving, ask your hotel if they offer car service. Many high-end hotels offer complimentary town-car service around Downtown and the immediate areas.

Car-rental rates in Seattle vary wildly, from $15 a day (if you snag your deal from an Internet discounter like Hotwire.com or Priceline.com) up to $70 a day. This does not include the car-rental tax of 18.5%. Try to avoid renting a car at the airport, where rental fees, surcharges, and taxes are higher. Most major rental agencies have offices Downtown or along the waterfront, within easy reach of the main hotel area.

In Washington State you must be 21 and hold a major credit card (many agencies accept debit cards with the MasterCard or Visa logo) to rent a car. Rates may be higher if you're under 25. You'll pay about $12 per day per child seat for children under age 4 or 40 pounds, or per booster seat for children ages 4 to 6 or under 60 pounds, both of which are compulsory in Washington State. You can also rent car seats and baby equipment from local services, such as Tiny Tots Travel (⊕ *www. tinytotstravel.com*).

By Monorail: Built for the 1962 World's Fair, the monorail (⊕ *www. seattlemonorail.com*) is the shortest transportation system in the city. It runs from Westlake Center (on 5th and Pine) to Seattle Center. But this is great for visitors who plan to spend a day at the Space Needle and the Seattle Center's museums. (Fare: $2)

By Seattle Streetcar: The second-shortest system in the city (⊕ *www. seattlestreetcar.org*) was built to connect Downtown to South Lake Union (directly east of Seattle Center). It runs from Westlake and Olive to the southern shore of Lake Union. (Fare: $2.25)

By Taxi: Seattle's taxi fleet is small, but you can sometimes hail a cab, especially Downtown. Most of the time you must call for one. Except on Friday and Saturday nights, you rarely have to wait more than a few minutes. Cabs can be pricey but useful, especially late at night when buses run infrequently. Two major cab companies are **Yellow Cab** (☎ *206/622–6500*) and **Farwest** (☎ *206/622–1717*).

VISITOR INFORMATION

Contact the **Seattle Visitors Bureau and Convention Center** (⊕ *www. visitseattle.org* ☎ *206/461–5800*) for help with everything from sightseeing to booking spa services. You can also follow their Twitter feed (⊕ *twitter.com/seattlemaven*). The main visitor information center is Downtown, at the Washington State Convention and Trade Center on 8th Avenue and Pike Street; it has a full-service concierge desk open daily 9 to 5 (in summer; weekdays only in winter). There's also an info booth at Pike Place Market.

A steel sculpture by Richard Serra at the Olympic Sculpture Park

EXPLORING SEATTLE

Each of Seattle's neighborhoods is distinctive in personality, and taking a stroll, browsing a bookstore, or enjoying a cup of coffee can feel different in every one. It's the adventure of exploring these vibrant neighborhoods that will really introduce you to the character of Seattle.

DOWNTOWN AND BELLTOWN

Downtown Seattle may not be the soul of the city, but it's certainly the heart. There's big-city skyline, as well as plenty of marvelous things to see and do in the Downtown area: the city's premier art museum, the eye-popping Rem Koolhaus–designed Central Library, lively Pike Place Market, and a major shopping corridor along 5th Avenue and down Pine Street. And, of course, there's the water: Elliott Bay beckons from every crested hill.

WHAT TO SEE

Belltown is Downtown's younger sibling, just north of Virginia Street (up to Denny Way) and stretching from Elliott Bay to 6th Avenue. Not too long ago Belltown was home to some of the most unwanted real estate in the city; the only scenesters around were starving artists. Today Belltown is increasingly hip, with luxury condos, trendy restaurants, and swanky bars and boutiques. (Most of the action happens between 1st and 4th avenues and between Bell and Virginia streets.)

Fodor's Choice ★ **Olympic Sculpture Park.** This 9-acre open-air park is the spectacular outdoor branch of the Seattle Art Museum. Nestled between Belltown and Elliott Bay, this gently sloping green space is planted with native shrubs

With more than 250 businesses, including 70 eateries and the very first Starbucks, Pike Place Market is a beloved Seattle icon.

and plants and crisscrossed with walking paths. On sunny days the park flaunts an astounding panorama of the Olympic Mountains, but even the grayest afternoon casts a favorable light on the site's sculptures. The grounds are home to works by such artists as Richard Serra, Roy McMakin, Louise Bourgeois, Mark di Suvero, and Alexander Calder, whose bright-red steel Eagle is a local favorite—indeed, you may even see a real bald eagle passing by overhead. The PACCAR Pavilion has a gift shop, café, and more information about the park. ⊠ *2901 Western Ave., between Broad and Bay Sts., Belltown* ☎ *206/654–3100* ⊕ *www. seattleartmuseum.org/visit/osp* ☒ *Free* ☉ *Park open daily sunrise–sunset. PACCAR Pavilion open May–Labor Day, Tues.–Sun. 10–5; Sept.–Apr., Tues.–Sun. 10–4.*

☉ **Pike Place Market.** Pike Place Market, one of the nation's largest and
Fodor'sChoice oldest public markets, plays host to happy, hungry crowds all year
★ round, but summer is when things really start to heat up. Strap on some walking shoes and enjoy its many corridors: shops and stalls provide a pleasant sensory overload—stroll among the colorful flower, produce, and fish displays, plus bustling shops and lunch counters. Specialty-food items, tea, honey, jams, comic books, beads, and cookware—you'll find it all here. Some favorite shops include DiLaurenti (for Italian snacks, meats, wine, and grocery items), World Spice, Market Spice Tea, and the Spanish Table. ⊠ *Pike Pl. at Pike St., west of 1st Ave., Downtown* ☎ *206/682–7453* ⊕ *www.pikeplacemarket.org* ☉ *Stall hrs vary: 1st-level shops Mon.–Sat. 10–6, Sun. 11–5; underground shops daily 11–5.*

☉ **Seattle Aquarium.** The city's renovated aquarium is more popular than
Fodor'sChoice ever. Among its most engaging residents are the sea otters—kids,
★

especially, seem able to spend hours watching the delightful antics of these creatures and their river cousins. In the Puget Sound Great Hall's "Window on Washington Waters" a slice of Neah Bay life is presented in a 20-foot-tall tank. The aquarium's darkened rooms and large, lighted tanks brilliantly display Pacific Northwest marine life. The "Life on the Edge" tide pools re-create Washington's rocky coast and sandy beaches. Huge glass windows provide underwater views of seals and sea otters; go up top to watch them play in their pools. Kids love the Discovery Lab, where they can touch starfish, sea urchins, and sponges, then examine baby barnacles and jellyfish. ✉ *1483 Alaskan Way, at Pier 59, Downtown* ☎ *206/386–4300* ⊕ *www.seattleaquarium. org* ✐ *$17* ⊙ *Daily 9:30–6 (last entry at 5).*

Fodor's Choice
★
Seattle Art Museum. Long the pride of the city's art scene, SAM is now better than ever after a massive expansion that connects the iconic old building on University Street (where sculptor Jonathan Borofsky's several-stories-high *Hammering Man* still pounds away) to a sleek, light-filled high-rise adjacent space on 1st Avenue and Union Street. The first floor includes the museum's fantastic shop and a café that focuses on local ingredients. The second floor features free exhibitions, including awesome large-scale installations. Recent exhibitions include a jaw-dropping collection of Picasso masterpieces. ✉ *1300 1st Ave., Downtown* ☎ *206/654–3100* ⊕ *www.seattleartmuseum.org* ✐ *$15, free 1st Thurs. of month* ⊙ *Wed. and weekends 10–5, Thurs. and Fri. 10–9, 1st Thurs. until midnight.*

Fodor's Choice
★
Seattle Central Library. The hub of Seattle's 25-branch library system, the Central Library's bold construction brings to mind a futuristic, multifaceted gemstone covered in steel webbing. Designed by renowned Dutch architect Rem Koolhaas and Joshua Ramus, this 11-story structure houses 1.45 million books—plus hundreds of computers with Internet access, an auditorium, and a café. Tours focusing on the building's architecture are offered several times a week on a first-come, first-served basis; call for a current schedule. ✉ *1000 4th Ave., Downtown* ☎ *206/386–4636* ⊕ *www.spl.org* ⊙ *Mon.–Thurs. 10–8, Fri. and Sat. 10–6, Sun. noon–6.*

30

SEATTLE CENTER, SOUTH LAKE UNION, AND QUEEN ANNE

Seattle Center is home to Seattle's version of the Eiffel Tower—the Space Needle—and is anchored by Frank Gehry's wild Experience Music Project building. The neighborhoods that bookend Seattle Center couldn't be more different: Queen Anne is all residential elegance (especially on top of the hill), while South Lake Union, once completely industrial, is becoming Seattle's next hot neighborhood.

WHAT TO SEE

Experience Music Project/Science Fiction Museum. Seattle's most controversial architectural statement is the 140,000-square-foot complex designed by architect Frank Gehry, who drew inspiration from electric guitars to achieve the building's curvy metallic design. The building stands out among the city's cookie-cutter high-rises, and therefore it's a fitting backdrop for rock memorabilia from the likes of Bob Dylan and the grunge-scene heavies. The Science Fiction Museum (SFM) has its own wing, and tackles the major themes of the genre in a way that's both smart and fun. ⊠ *325 5th Ave. N, between Broad and Thomas Sts., Seattle Center* ☎ *206/770–2700* ⊕ *www.empsfm.org* ⌲ *$15* ⊙ *Sept.– May, daily 10–5; rest of yr, daily 10–8.*

☺ **Space Needle.** The distinctive, towering structure of the 605-foot-high Space Needle is visible throughout much of Seattle—but the view from the inside out is even better. A less-than-one-minute ride up to the observation deck provides 360-degree vistas of Downtown Seattle, the Olympic Mountains, Elliott Bay, Queen Anne Hill, Lake Union, and the Cascade Range. The Needle was built just in time for the World's Fair in 1962, but has since been refurbished with kiosks, trivia-game stations for kids, and the glass-enclosed SpaceBase store. The top-floor SkyCity restaurant is better known for its revolving floor than its cuisine, but the menu has improved markedly in the last few years. ■ **TIP→ Don't bother doing the trip to the top of the Needle on rainy days—the view just isn't the same.** If you can't decide whether you want the daytime or nighttime view, for $24 you can buy a ticket that allows you to visit twice in one day. ⊠ *5th Ave. and Broad St., Seattle Center* ☎ *206/905–2100* ⊕ *www. spaceneedle.com* ⌲ *$18* ⊙ *Mon.–Thurs. 10 am–11 pm, Fri. and Sat. 9:30 am–11:30 pm, Sun. 9:30 am–11 pm.*

■ OFF THE
BEATEN
PATH

Fodor's Choice
★

Discovery Park. Discovery Park is Seattle's largest park, and it has an amazing variety of terrain: shaded, secluded forest trails lead to meadows, saltwater beaches, sand dunes, a lighthouse, and views that include Puget Sound, the Cascades, and the Olympics. There are 2.8 mi of trails through this urban wilderness, but the North Beach Trail, which takes you along the shore to the lighthouse, is a must-see. Head to the South Bluff Trail to get a view of Mt. Rainier. ⊠ *3801 W. Government Way, Magnolia* ✢ *From Downtown, take Elliot Ave. W (which turns into 15th Ave. W), and get off at Emerson St. exit and turn left onto W. Emerson. Make a right onto Gilman Ave. W (which eventually becomes W. Government Way). As you enter park, the road becomes Washington Ave.; turn left on Utah Ave.* ☎ *206/386–4236* ⊕ *www. cityofseattle.net/parks* ⌲ *Free* ⊙ *Park daily 6 am–11 pm, visitor center Tues.–Sun. 8:30–5.*

PIONEER SQUARE

Pioneer Square, directly south of Downtown, is Seattle's oldest neighborhood. It attracts visitors for its elegantly renovated (or in some cases replica) turn-of-the-20th-century redbrick buildings and its art galleries. It's undeniably the center of Seattle's arts scene—there are more galleries in this small neighborhood than we have room to list, and they make up the majority of its sights.

WHAT TO SEE

Bill Speidel's Underground Tour. Present-day Pioneer Square is actually one story higher than it used to be. After the Great Seattle Fire of 1889, Seattle's planners regraded the neighborhood's streets one level higher. The result: There is now an intricate and expansive array of subterranean passageways beneath Pioneer Square, and Bill Speidel's Underground

The Pioneer Square skyline is dominated by historic Smith Tower.

Tour is the only way to explore them. ■ **TIP→** Comfortable shoes, a love for quirky historical anecdotes, and an appreciation of bad puns are musts. Several tours are offered daily, and schedules change month to month: call or visit the Web site for a full list of tour times. ✉ *608 1st Ave., Pioneer Square* ☎ *206/682–4646* ⊕ *www.undergroundtour.com* 💲 *$15* ⊙ *Tours daily; call for schedules.*

Smith Tower. When it opened on July 4, 1914, Smith Tower was the tallest office building outside New York City and the fourth-tallest building in the world. The Smith Tower Observation Deck on the 35th floor is an open-air, wrap-around deck providing panoramic views of the surrounding historic neighborhood, the city skyline, and the mountains on clear days. ✉ *506 2nd Ave. S, Pioneer Square* ☎ *206/622–4004* ⊕ *www. smithtower.com/Observation.html* 💲 *$7.50* ⊙ *May–Sept., daily 10– sunset; Apr. and Oct., daily 10–5; Nov.–Mar., weekends only 10–4.*

GALLERIES

Fodor's Choice
★ **G. Gibson Gallery.** Vintage and contemporary photography is on exhibit in this elegant corner space, including shows by the likes of Michael Kenna as well as retrospectives of the works of Walker Evans and Berenice Abbott. The savvy gallery owner also shows contemporary paintings, sculpture, and mixed-media pieces. ✉ *300 S. Washington St., Pioneer Square* ☎ *206/587–4033* ⊕ *www.ggibsongallery.com* 💲 *Free* ⊙ *Tues.–Sat. 11–5.*

Fodor's Choice
★ **Greg Kucera Gallery.** One of the most important destinations on the First Thursday gallery walk, this gorgeous space is a top venue for national and regional artists. Be sure to check out the outdoor sculpture deck on the second level. If you have time for only one gallery visit, this is

the place to go. ⊠ *212 3rd Ave. S,
Pioneer Square* ☎ *206/624–0770*
⊕ *www.gregkucera.com* ✉ *Free*
☉ *Tues.–Sat. 10:30–5:30.*

★ **Stonington Gallery.** You'll see plenty
of cheesy tribal art knockoffs in
tourist-trap shops, but this elegant
gallery will give you a real look
at the best contemporary work of
Northwest Coast and Alaska tribal

GALLERY WALKS

It's fun to simply walk around
Pioneer Square and pop into gal-
leries. South Jackson Street to
Yesler between Western and 4th
Avenue South is a good area. Visit
⊕ www.artguidenw.com.

members. Three floors exhibit carvings, paintings, sculpture, and
mixed-media pieces. ⊠ *119 S. Jackson St., Pioneer Square* ☎ *206/405–
4040* ⊕ *www.stoningtongallery.com* ✉ *Free* ☉ *Weekdays 10–6, Sat.
10–5:30, Sun. noon–5.*

INTERNATIONAL DISTRICT

The I.D., as it's locally known, is synonymous with delectable dining—it
has many cheap Chinese restaurants (this is the neighborhood for barbecued duck), but the best eateries reflect its Pan-Asian spirit: Vietnamese,
Japanese, Malay, Cambodian. With the endlessly fun Uwajimaya shopping center and the gorgeously redesigned Wing Luke Asian Museum,
you now have something to do in between bites.

WHAT TO SEE

Fodor'sChoice **Uwajimaya.** This huge, fascinating Japanese supermarket is a feast for
★ the senses. A 30-foot-long red Chinese dragon stretches above colorful mounds of fresh produce and aisles of delicious packaged goods—
including spicy peas, sweet crackers, gummy candies, nut mixes, rice
snacks, and colorful sweets—from countries throughout Asia. A busy
food court serves sushi, Japanese bento-box meals, Chinese stir-fry com-
bos, and more. The housewares section is well stocked with dishes,
cookware, appliances, textiles, and gifts. There's also a small branch
of the famous Kinokuniya bookstore chain, selling paper goods, pens,
stickers, gift items, and many Asian-language books. The large parking lot is free for one hour with a minimum $5 purchase (which will be
no problem) or two hours with a minimum $10 purchase. ⊠ *600 5th
Ave. S, International District* ☎ *206/624–6248* ⊕ *www.uwajimaya.com*
☉ *Mon.–Sat. 7 am–10 pm, Sun. 9–9.*

Fodor'sChoice **Wing Luke Asian Museum.** Named for the Northwest's first Asian-Ameri-
★ can elected official, this gorgeous museum is in a renovated 1910 hotel
and commercial building that once was the first home for many new
immigrants. The museum surveys the history and cultures of people
from Asia and the Pacific islands who settled in the Pacific Northwest.
It provides a sophisticated and often somber look at how immigrants
and their descendants have transformed (and been transformed by)
American culture. The evolution of the museum has been driven by
community participation—the museum's library has an oral history lab
and many rotating exhibits. ⊠ *719 S. King St., International District*
☎ *206/623–5124* ⊕ *www.wingluke.org* ✉ *$12.95, free 1st Thurs. and
3rd Sat. of month* ☉ *Tues.–Sun. 10–5.*

CAPITOL HILL

With its mix of theaters and churches, quiet parks and nightclubs, stately homes and student apartments, Capitol Hill still deserves its reputation as Seattle's most eclectic neighborhood. Old brick buildings, modern apartment high-rises, colorfully painted two-story homes, and old-school mansions all occupy the same area. There are plenty of cute, quirky shops to browse in and quite a few fantastic coffee shops.

WHAT TO SEE

Volunteer Park and the Seattle Asian Art Museum. High above the mansions of North Capitol Hill sits 45-acre Volunteer Park, a grassy expanse perfect for picnicking, reading, and strolling. You can tell this is one of the city's older parks by the size of the trees and the rhododendrons, many of which were planted more than a hundred years ago. The Olmsted Brothers, the premier landscape architects of the day, helped with the final design in 1904; the park has changed surprisingly little since then. The manicured look of the park is a sharp contrast to the wilds of Discovery Park. In the center of the park is the **Seattle Asian Art Museum** (SAAM, a branch of the Seattle Art Museum), housed in a 1933 art moderne–style edifice. The museum's collections include thousands of paintings, sculptures, pottery, and textiles from China, Japan, India, Korea, and several Southeast Asian countries. ⊠ *Park entrance: 14th Ave. E at Prospect St., Capitol Hill* ⊕ *www.seattleartmuseum.org* ☎ *Museum 206/654–3100, conservatory 206/684–4743* ☜ *Park free; museum $7, free 1st Thurs. (all day) and 2nd Thurs. (5–9)* ☾ *Park daily sunrise–sunset; museum Wed.–Sun. 10–5, Thurs. until 9; conservatory Tues.–Sun. 10–4.*

ⵊ **Washington Park Arboretum.** As far as Seattle's green spaces go, this 230-
Fodor's Choice acre arboretum is arguably the most beautiful. On calm weekdays the
★ place feels really secluded; though there are trails, you feel like you're freer to roam here than at Discovery Park. The seasons are always on full display: In warm winters flowering cherries and plums bloom in its protected valleys as early as late February, while the flowering shrubs are in full bloom March through June. In autumn, trees and shrubs glow in glorious hues; in winter, plantings chosen specially for their stark and colorful branches dominate the landscape. From mid-February through mid-November, visit the peaceful **Japanese Garden**, a compressed world of mountains, forests, rivers, lakes, and tablelands. The pond, lined with blooming water irises in spring, has turtles and brightly colored koi. The Graham Visitors Center at the park's north end has brochures and walking-tour maps. ⊠ *2300 Arboretum Dr. E, Capitol Hill* ☎ *206/543–8800 arboretum, 206/684–4725 Japanese garden* ⊕ *depts.washington. edu/uwbg/index.php* ☜ *Free, Japanese garden $5* ☾ *Park open daily 7 am–sunset, visitor center daily 10–4. Japanese garden mid-Feb.–mid-Nov., daily 10–5, hrs vary seasonally, call to confirm.*

OFF THE BEATEN PATH

■ TIP➔ We may not have enough space here to wax poetic on all of Seattle's charms—or to even cover the amazing neighborhoods north of the ship canal, including the University District, Fremont, Wallingford, and Ballard—but that doesn't mean you shouldn't venture north. Two can't-miss spots are the Ballard Locks and Gas Works Park.

30

A tugboat passes through the Ballard Locks.

Hiram M. Chittenden Locks ("Ballard Locks"). The locks are an important passage in the 8-mi Lake Washington Ship Canal that connects Puget Sound to freshwater Lake Washington and Lake Union—and, on a sunny day this is a great place to visit. In addition to boat traffic, the Locks see an estimated half-million salmon and trout make the journey from saltwater to fresh each summer, with the help of a fish ladder. ⊠ *3015 N.W. 54th St., Ballard* ✢ *From Fremont, head north on Leary Way NW, west on N.W. Market St., and south on 54th St.* ☎ *206/783–7059* ☑ *Free* ⊗ *Locks daily 7 am–9 pm; visitor center Thurs.–Mon. 10–4; call for tour information and reservations.*

Gas Works Park. The park gets its name from the hulking remains of an old 1907 gas plant, which, far from being an eyesore, actually lends quirky character to the otherwise open, hilly, 20-acre park. Get a great view of Downtown Seattle while seaplanes rise up from the far shore of the lake; the best vantage point is from the zodiac sculpture at the top of the hill. ⊠ *2101 N. Northlake Way, at Meridian Ave. N (the north end of Lake Union) Wallingford* ⊗ *Daily 4 am–11:30 pm.*

WEST SEATTLE

Cross the bridge to West Seattle and it's another world altogether. Jutting out into Elliott Bay and Puget Sound, separated from the city by the Duwamish waterway, this out-of-the-way neighborhood covers most of the city's western peninsula—and, indeed, it has an identity of its own. In summer throngs of people hang out at Alki Beach—Seattle's taste of California.

WHAT TO SEE

Fodor's Choice ★ **Alki Point and Beach.** In summer, West Seattle's Alki Beach is as close to California as Seattle gets—and some hardy residents even swim in the cold, salty waters of Puget Sound here. This 2½-mi stretch of sand has views of the Seattle skyline and the Olympic Mountains, and the beach-front promenade is especially popular with skaters, joggers, and cyclists. Year-round, Seattleites come to build sand castles, beachcomb, and fly kites. Facilities include drinking water, grills, picnic tables, phones, and restrooms; restaurants line the street across from the beach. ■ TIP→ To get here from Downtown, take either I–5 south or Highway 99 south to the West Seattle Bridge (keep an eye out, as this exit is easy to miss) and exit onto Harbor Avenue SW, turning right at the stoplight. One of 195 Lady Liberty replicas found around the country lives near the 2700 block of Alki Avenue SW; it was erected by Boy Scouts in 1952.

WHERE TO EAT

Thanks to inventive chefs, first-rate local produce, adventurous diners, and a bold entrepreneurial spirit, Seattle has become one of the culinary capitals of the nation. Fearless young chefs have stepped in and raised the bar. Nowadays, fresh and often foraged produce, local seafood, and imaginative techniques make the quality of local cuisine even higher.

Chefs continuously fine-tune what can best be called Pacific Northwest cuisine, which features fresh, local ingredients, including anything from nettles and mushrooms foraged in nearby forests; colorful berries, apples, and cherries grown by Washington State farmers; and outstanding seafood from the cold northern waters of the Pacific Ocean, including wild salmon, halibut, oysters, and Dungeness crab.

WHAT IT COSTS AT DINNER					
	¢	$	$$	$$$	$$$$
Restaurants	under $8	$8–$16	$17–$24	$25–$32	over $32

Price per person for a median main course or equivalent combination of smaller dishes. Note: If a restaurant offers only prix-fixe (set-price) meals, it has been given the price category that reflects the full prix-fixe price.

DOWNTOWN AND BELLTOWN

$$$
NEW AMERICAN
Fodor's Choice ★

✕ **Boat Street Café & Kitchen.** Two rooms decorated in a French bistro–meets–Nantucket decor have a scattering of casual tables with fresh flowers and candles. Tables often fill up with couples at night, but the lunchtime scene runs the gamut from Downtown office workers to tourists. Food is understated, fresh, and divine: start with raw oysters and a crisp glass of white wine. Next up, sautéed Medjool dates sprinkled with *fleur de sel* and olive oil, a radish salad with pine nuts, or a plate of the famous house-made pickles. Entrées, too, take advantage of whatever is in season, so expect anything from Oregon hanger steak with olive tapenade to spring-onion flan and Alaskan halibut with cauliflower. Save room for desserts, such as wild blackberry clafouti, honey ice cream, and vanilla-bean *pot de crème*. Monday through Sunday,

30

brunch and lunch are served from 10:30 to 2:30. ⊠ *3131 Western Ave., Belltown* ☎ *206/632–4602* ⊕ *www.boatstreetcafe.com* ▤ *D, MC, V* ☾ *No dinner Sun. and Mon.*

$$$
FRENCH
Fodor'sChoice
★

✕ **Café Campagne/Campagne.** The white walls, picture windows, pressed linens, fresh flowers, and candles at charming French restaurant Campagne—which overlooks Pike Place Market and Elliott Bay—evoke Provence. So does the robust French country fare, with starters such as grilled house-made merguez sausage, pork rillettes, and gnocchi with artichokes and black-truffle butter. Main plates include pork short ribs with onion, raisin, and tomato compote and steamed mussels with expertly prepared *pommes frites.* ■ TIP→ Campagne is open only for dinner, but downstairs the equally charming (some would say even more authentic) Café Campagne serves breakfast, lunch, and dinner daily. The café is an exceptional place for a satisfying weekend brunch before hitting Pike Place Market on foot. Try the impeccable quiche du jour or brioche French toast with a big bowl of *café au lait.* ⊠ *Inn at the Market, 86 Pine St., Downtown* ☎ *206/728–2800* ⊕ *www.campagnerestaurant. com* ▤ *AE, DC, MC, V.*

$$$
MEDITERRANEAN
Fodor'sChoice
★

✕ **Lola.** Tom Douglas dishes out his signature Northwest style spiked with Greek and Mediterranean touches here—another huge success for the local celebrity chef, if not his best. Try a glorious tagine of goat meat with mustard and rosemary; grape leaf–wrapped trout; lamb burgers with chickpea fries; and scrumptious spreads including hummus and tzatziki. Booths are usually full at this bustling restaurant, which anchors the Hotel Ändra. The fabulous weekend brunches are deliciously inventive. ⊠ *2000 4th Ave., Belltown* ☎ *206/441–1430* ⊕ *www. tomdouglas.com* ▤ *D, MC, V.*

¢–$
BAKERY

✕ **Macrina Bakery.** One of Seattle's favorite bakeries is also popular for breakfast and brunch. With its perfectly executed breads and pastries—from Nutella brioche and ginger cookies to almond croissants and dark-chocolate sugar-dusted brownies—it has become a true Belltown institution, even if this small spot is usually too frenzied to invite the hours of idleness that other coffee shops may inspire. ■ TIP→ Macrina is an excellent place to take a delicious break on your way to or from the Olympic Sculpture Park. ⊠ *2408 1st Ave., Belltown* ☎ *206/448–4032* ⊕ *www.macrinabakery.com.*

$$$$
PACIFIC
NORTHWEST
Fodor'sChoice
★

✕ **Matt's in the Market.** One of the most beloved of Pike Place Market's restaurants, Matt's values intimate dining, fresh ingredients, and superb service. Perch at the bar for pints and a delicious pulled-pork or hot grilled-tuna sandwich or cup of gumbo, or be seated at a table for a seasonal menu that synthesizes the best picks from the restaurant's produce vendors and an excellent wine list. At dinner, starters might include such delectable items as Manila clams steamed in beer with herbs and chilies; entrées always include at least one catch of the day—such as whole fish in saffron broth or Alaskan halibut with pea vines—as well as such entrées as seafood stew or braised lamb shank with ancho chili. ⊠ *94 Pike St., Suite 32, Downtown* ☎ *206/467–7909* ⊕ *www. mattsinthemarket.com* ⌂ *Reservations essential* ▤ *MC, V* ☾ *Closed Sun.*

QUEEN ANNE

$$$$ ✕ **Canlis.** Canlis has been setting the standard for opulent dining in

PACIFIC Seattle since the 1950s. Executive chef Jason Franey (formerly of Man-

NORTHWEST hattan's acclaimed Eleven Madison Park) has retained the restaurant's signature insistence on the finest cuts of meat and the freshest produce. To start, try fresh braised veal cheek with lemon confit, fresh carrot soup, foie-gras terrine, or a Dungeness crab cake with Granny Smith apple. The famous Canlis salad is always a crowd-pleaser. But the entrées are the stars here: king salmon with lentils, Muscovy duck with hedgehog mushrooms, and Wagyu tenderloin served atop shallots. ■TIP➔ The only way to wash this divine food down is with a bottle from one of the finest—if not the finest—wine cellars in town. A banana-spiked *mille-feuille* or a "chocolate covered chocolate" molten creation should send you on your way happily. Canlis never fails to feel like a special-occasion splurge—make reservations well in advance, and request a table with a view. ✉ *2576 Aurora Ave. N, Queen Anne* ☎ *206/283–3313* ⊕ *www.canlis.com* ⌕ *Reservations essential; jacket required* ▭ *AE, DC, MC, V* ☾ *Closed Sun. No lunch.*

PIONEER SQUARE

$ ✕ **Salumi.** The chef-owner Armandino Batali (father of famed New

ITALIAN York chef Mario Batali) makes superior cured meats for this miniature

Fodor's Choice lunch spot run by his daughter, who serves up hearty, unforgettable

★ sandwiches filled with all sorts of goodies. Order a salami, bresaola, porchetta, meatball, oxtail, sausage, or lamb prosciutto sandwich with onions, peppers, cheese, and olive oil. Most people do opt for takeout, though; be prepared for a long line, which most likely will be stretching well beyond the front door. ■TIP➔ Note that Salumi is open only Tuesday–Friday from 11 am to 4 pm. ✉ *309 3rd Ave. S, Pioneer Square* ☎ *206/621–8772* ⊕ *www.salumicuredmeats.com* ▭ *AE, D, DC, MC, V* ☾ *Closed Sat.–Mon.*

THE INTERNATIONAL DISTRICT

$ ✕ **Tamarind Tree.** Wildly popular with savvy diners from across the city,

VIETNAMESE this Vietnamese haunt on the eastern side of the I.D. *really* doesn't look like much from the outside: You'll enter through a grungy parking lot (which it shares with a hair salon and an equally awesome Sichuanese restaurant). But once you're inside, a simple, large, and warm space welcomes you. The food is the real draw—try the tamarind tree spring rolls, which are stuffed with fresh herbs, fried tofu, peanuts, coconut, jicama, and carrots; authentic *bánh xèo*; spicy, authentic pho; various satisfying rice-and-chicken dishes; spicy-beef noodle soup; and, to finish, grilled banana cake with warm coconut milk. Service is attentive, but the waits can be long, even with reservations. ✉ *1036 S. Jackson St., International District* ☎ *206/860–1404* ⊕ *www.tamarindtreerestaurant.com* ⌕ *Reservations essential* ▭ *MC, V.*

30

CAPITOL HILL

$$$ ✕ **Anchovies & Olives.** A sleek, sophisticated space serves an equally posh

SEAFOOD clientele. An utterly exposed, simple kitchen set-up anchors this spot

Fodor's Choice in the ground floor of a residential high-rise at the eastern end of the

★ Pike–Pine Corridor. The food at this Ethan Stowell eatery is downright tantalizing, and the young line chefs and waitstaff are charming. Modern bent-wood wall coverings, artful lighting, a well-edited Italian wine list, and a lively small bar create the backdrop for some of the best, and most elegant, seafood dishes in the city, including mackerel with cauliflower and radicchio; skate wing with asparagus and saffron leeks; and clams with pine nuts and hot pepper. A small *crudo* selection and salads such as golden beets with almonds and endive will get the meal started. Plates are smaller and are easily shared. A tiny selection of desserts is equally sublime. Reservations are highly recommended. ⊠ *1550 15th Ave., at Pine St., Capitol Hill* ☎ *206/838–8080* ⊕ *www.anchoviesandolives.com* ⊟ *AE, MC, V.*

$$$–$$$$
NEW AMERICAN
Fodor's Choice
★

✕ **Lark.** Just off the Pike–Pine Corridor, in a converted garage with exposed beams and gauzy curtain dividers, Lark was one of the first restaurants to kick-start the small-plate trend in Seattle. And small plates often don't feel like enough, as the food is so mouthwateringly delicious—the idea is to order several and enjoy to your heart's content. You can always order more, and the expert servers can help you choose from an impressive wine list, and will happily offer up their opinions of the long menu, which is divided into cheese; vegetables and grains; charcuterie; fish; meat; and, of course, dessert. Seasonally inspired dishes include chicken-liver parfait with grilled ramps; pork rillettes with bright radishes; and carpaccio of yellowtail with preserved lemons. For dessert, try the Theo-chocolate madeleines (lots of them!). ◼TIP→ Reservations are recommended; if you do have to wait for a table, hop next door to Licorous (which also serves an abbreviated menu) for a distinctly cool libation. ⊠ *926 12th Ave., Capitol Hill* ☎ *206/323–5275* ⊕ *www.larkseattle.com* ⊟ *AE, MC, V.*

$$$
NEW AMERICAN
Fodor's Choice
★

✕ **Poppy.** Jerry Traunfeld's bright, airy restaurant on the northern end of Broadway is a feast for the senses. Deep-red walls, high-design lighting, friendly staff, and a happening bar area welcome you to this hip eatery with floor-to-ceiling windows. Start with one of the many interesting cocktails and eggplant fries with sea salt and honey; then you can peruse the interesting menu, which offers thali (and cleverly named "smalli")—inspired by an Indian meal of the same name in which a selection of different dishes is served in small compartments on a large platter. The inspired New American cuisine is completely dependent on seasonal bounty—you'll enjoy anything from stinging-nettle soup, braised Wagyu beef cheek with ginger; rhubarb pickles; onion-poppy naan; and roasted halibut with saffron leeks. ◼TIP→ Fantastic thali-style menus change regularly to reflect whatever is in season. It's a fun way to dine—make reservations, and come hungry and ready to be delighted. ⊠ *622 Broadway E, Capitol Hill* ☎ *206/324–1108* ⊕ *www.poppyseattle.com* ⊟ *AE, MC, V* ☺ *No lunch.*

¢
COFFEEHOUSE

✕ **Vivace Espresso Bar at Brix.** Vivace is considered by many (including us) to be the home of Seattle's finest espresso. A long, curving bar and a colorful mural add some character to a space that might otherwise feel ho-hum in Vivace's home on the ground floor of the upscale Brix condo complex on Broadway. The place has great energy—lively and bustling, where Hill residents tippity-tap on laptops and students hold study groups—but it's not necessarily a good spot for a quiet read. Pastries are a bit lackluster, but the espresso beverages more than make up for it. There's another branch right across the way from REI in South Lake Union, at 227 Yale Avenue North (☎ 206/388–5164). ✉ 532 Broadway Ave. E, Capitol Hill ☎ 206/860–2722 ⊕ www.espressovivace.com ▤ AE, MC, V.

WEST SEATTLE

$$$
NEW AMERICAN
Fodor's Choice
★

✕ **Spring Hill.** West Seattle's most exciting culinary beacon, Spring Hill takes quality and freshness seriously. A quietly hip vibe pervades this large eatery on California Avenue, with polished wood floors, simple seating, a huge bar surrounding an open kitchen, and gently mod wall treatments. Diners of all stripes relish the Pacific Northwest bounty, which is the star here, with raw oysters served atop a bundle of fresh seaweed; Dungeness crab with melted butter; house-made tagliatelle with crispy pork shoulder and fried parsley; Painted Hills hanger steak with beef-fat fries; Manila clams with razor-clam sausage and herbed mayo; and fresh halibut prepared to perfection. Weekend brunches are hoppin', and also more than worth the trek. ✉ 4437 California Ave. SW, West Seattle ☎ 206/935–1075 ⊕ www.springhillnorthwest.com ▤ AE, MC, V ☺ No dinner Sun.

WHERE TO STAY

Much like its culture, food, and fashion, Seattle's lodging offers something for everyone. There are grand, awe-inspiring vintage hotels; sleek, elegant, modern properties; green hotels with yoga studios and enough bamboo for an army of pandas; and wee B&Bs with sweet bedspreads and home-cooked breakfasts. Travelers who appreciate the anonymity of high-rise chains can comfortably stay here, while guests who want to feel like family can find the perfect boutique inn in which to lay their heads.

Hotel reviews have been condensed for this book. Please go to Fodors. com for full reviews of each property.

30

WHAT IT COSTS				
¢	$	$$	$$$	$$$$
Hotels	under $100	$100–$180	$181–$265	$266–$350	over $350

Prices reflect the rack rate of a standard double room for two people in high season, excluding the 12% (for hotels with fewer than 60 rooms) or 15.6% (for hotels with more than 60 rooms) city and state taxes.

DOWNTOWN AND BELLTOWN

$–$$
Fodor's Choice
★

🛏 **Ace Hotel.** The Ace is a dream come true for both penny-pinching hipsters and creative folks who appreciate unique minimalist decor. **Pros:** ultratrendy *and* affordable; cool art; free Wi-Fi. **Cons:** most rooms have shared bathrooms; not good for people who want pampering; lots of stairs to walk up to get to lobby. ✉ 2423 1st Ave., Belltown ☎ 206/448–4721 ⊕ www.acehotel.com 🛏 14 standard rooms, 14 deluxe rooms ☖ In-room: no a/c (some), refrigerator (some), Wi-Fi. In-hotel: laundry *facilities, Wi-Fi hotspot, parking (paid), some pets allowed* ▤ *AE, D, DC, MC, V.*

$$$$

☺

Fodor's Choice

★

🛏 **The Fairmont Olympic Hotel.** With marble floors, silk wallpaper, massive chandeliers, and sweeping staircases, this Old World hotel exudes elegance. **Pros:** elegant and spacious lobby; great location; excellent service; fabulous on-site dining. **Cons:** rooms are a bit small for the price; may be a little too old school for trendy travelers. ✉ *411 University St., Downtown* ☎ *206/621–1700 or 800/441–1414* ⊕ *www.fairmont. com/seattle* ⟿ *232 rooms, 218 suites* ⟐ *In-room: safe, DVD (some), Wi-Fi. In-hotel: 2 restaurants, room service, bar, pool, gym, children's programs, laundry service, Wi-Fi hotspot, parking (paid), some pets allowed* ▤ *AE, D, DC, MC, V.*

$$$$

☺

Fodor's Choice

★

🛏 **Four Seasons Hotel Seattle.** Just south of the Pike Place Market and steps from Benaroya Hall and the Seattle Art Museum, the Four Seasons is polished and elegant, with Eastern accents and plush furnishings set against a definite modern Northwest backdrop. **Cons:** Four Seasons regulars might not click with this modern take on the brand; some guests say service kinks need to be ironed out. ✉ *99 Union St., Downtown* ☎ *206/749–7000* ⊕ *www.fourseasons.com* ⟿ *134 rooms, 13 suites* ⟐ *In-room: safe, refrigerator (some), DVD, Wi-Fi. In-hotel: restaurant, room service, bar, pool, gym, spa, children's programs, laundry service, parking (paid), some pets allowed* ▤ *AE, D, DC, MC, V.*

$$$

Fodor's Choice

★

🛏 **Hotel 1000.** Chic and cosmopolitan, Hotel 1000 is luxe and decidedly modern—the centerpiece of the small lobby is a dramatically lighted glass staircase and original artwork by Pacific Northwest artist J.P. Canlis. **Pros:** lots of high-tech perks; guests feel pampered; hotel is hip without being alienating. **Cons:** rooms can be dark; rooms without views look out on a cement wall; restaurant can be overpriced. ✉ *1000 1st Ave., Downtown* ☎ *206/957–1000* ⊕ *www.hotel1000seattle.com* ⟿ *101 rooms, 19 suites* ⟐ *In-room: safe, refrigerator, DVD, Wi-Fi. In-hotel: restaurant, room service, bar, gym, spa, laundry service, Wi-Fi hotspot, parking (paid), some pets allowed* ▤ *AE, MC, V.*

$$–$$$

Fodor's Choice

★

🛏 **Hyatt at Olive 8.** Maybe it's the floor-to-ceiling windows flooding the place with light or the extensive Elaia Spa, but the guests always seem remarkably relaxed here.**Pros:** central location; superb amenities; environmental responsibility; wonderful spa. **Cons:** standard rooms have showers only; fee for Wi-Fi use. ✉ *1635 8th Ave., Downtown* ☎ *206/695–1234* ⊕ *www.olive8.hyatt.com* ⟿ *333 rooms, 13 suites* ⟐ *In-room: safe, refrigerator, Wi-Fi. In-hotel: restaurant, room service, bar, pool, gym, spa, laundry service, Internet terminal, Wi-Fi hotspot, parking (paid)* ▤ *AE, D, DC, MC, V.*

$$–$$$$

Fodor's Choice

★

🛏 **Inn at the Market.** From its heart-stopping views and comfortable rooms to its fabulous location and amazing fifth-floor deck perched above Puget Sound, the Inn at the Market is a place you'll want to visit again and again. **ros:** outstanding views from many rooms and roof deck; steps from Pike Place Market; complimentary town-car service for Downtown locations. **Cons:** little common space; not much in the way of amenities; a full renovation should take place in early 2011, so some rooms may be unavailable. ✉ *86 Pine St., Downtown* ☎ *206/443–3600 or 800/446–4484* ⊕ *www.innatthemarket.com* ⟿ *63*

*rooms, 7 suites ☐ In-room: safe, refrigerator, Wi-Fi. In-hotel: 3 res-
taurants, room service, laundry service, Wi-Fi hotspot, parking (paid)
☐ AE, D, DC, MC, V.*

CAPITOL HILL

¢–$ **11th Avenue Inn Bed & Breakfast.** The closest B&B to Downtown, the

Fodor'sChoice   11th Avenue Inn offers all the charm of a classic bed-and-breakfast

★   with the convenience of being near the action. **ros:** unpretentious take
on classic B&B; friendly staff. **Cons:** no a/c; although most guests are
courteous, sound does carry in old houses. ☐ *121 11th Ave. E, Capitol
Hill* ☎ *206/720–7161 or 800/720–7161* ⊕ *www.11thavenueinn.com*
☐ *8 rooms, 6 with bath ☐ In-room: no phones, Wi-Fi. In-hotel: Wi-Fi
hotspot, parking (paid), no kids under 12* ☐ *AE, D, MC, V* ☐ *BP.*

NIGHTLIFE

Seattle's amazing musical legacy is well known, but there's more to
nightlife scene than live music. In fact, these days there are far more
swanky bars and inventive pubs than music venues in the city. Seattle
is, bluntly put, a great place to drink. You can sip overly ambitious and
ridiculously named specialty cocktails in trendy lounges, get a lesson
from an enthusiastic sommelier in a wine bar or restaurant, or swill
cheap beer on the patio of a dive bar. The music scene is still kicking—
there's something going on every night of the week in nearly every
genre of music.

DOWNTOWN AND BELLTOWN

BARS AND LOUNGES

★   **Oliver's** (☐ *405 Olive Way, Downtown* ☎ *206/382–6995*), in the Mayflower Park Hotel, is famous for martinis. In fact, having a cocktail here
is like having afternoon tea in some parts of the world. Wing chairs,
low tables, and lots of natural light make it easy to relax after a hectic
day. Expect an unfussy crowd of regulars, hotel guests, and mature
Manhattan-sippers who appreciate old-school elegance.

Fodor'sChoice   **Zig Zag Café** (☐ *1501 Western Ave., Downtown* ☎ *206/625–1146*

★   ⊕ *zigzagseattle.com*) gives Oliver's at the Mayflower Hotel a run for
its money when it comes to pouring perfect martinis—plus, it's much
more eclectic and laid-back here. A mixed crowd of mostly locals hunts
out this unique spot at Pike Place Market's Hillclimb (a nearly hidden stairwell leading down to the piers). Several memorable cocktails
include the Don't Give Up the Ship (gin, Dubonnet, Grand Marnier,
and Fernet Branca) and Satan's Soulpatch (bourbon, sweet and dry
vermouth, Grand Marnier, orange, and orange bitters). A very simple
food menu includes cheese and meat plates, bruschetta, soup, salad,
olives, and nuts.

LIVE MUSIC

Fodor'sChoice   **The Crocodile** (☐ *2200 2nd Ave., Belltown* ☎ *206/441–7416* ⊕ *www.*

★   *thecrocodile.com*) is one of the few places that can call itself "the heart
and soul of Seattle" without raising many eyebrows. Indeed, it is—and

30

The Seattle music scene continues to be a flash point for indie bands.

has been since 1991—the heart and soul of Seattle's music scene. Nirvana, Pearl Jam, Mudhoney, and REM have all taken the stage here. Nightly shows are complemented by cheap beer on tap and pizza right next door at Via Tribunali. All hail the Croc!

CAPITOL HILL

BARS AND LOUNGES

Fodor's Choice ★ **Licorous** (✉ *928 12th Ave., Capitol Hill* ☎ *206/325–6947* ⊕ *www. licorous.com*) is Lark restaurant's attractive next-door bar, complete with a striking molded-tin ceiling, well-poured cocktails, and a dynamite whisky list. This well-designed space attracts an eclectic clientele, from young couples to larger groups and local regulars—all of whom enjoy a low-key evening sipping tasty specialty cocktails and munching tasty small dishes from an abbreviated Lark menu.

Fodor's Choice ★ **Quinn's** (✉ *1001 E. Pike St., Capitol Hill* ☎ *206/325–7711* ⊕ *www. quinnspubseattle.com*) is our favorite go-to place for a dynamite beer at a laid-back but very cool bar. A friendly, knowledgeable staff tends the bar and the tables at the gastropub serving yummy food (especially the burgers) and even better beers. It can be very busy on weekends, but if you arrive in early evening on a weekday you can sidle up to the bar, order some nibbles, and chat up the bartender about the numerous (rotating) brews on tap, including Belgian favorites, local IPAs, Russian River winners, and more.

★ **Smith** (✉ *332 15th Ave. E, Capitol Hill* ☎ *206/709–1099* ⊕ *www. smithpub.com*), a bit outside the Pike–Pine heart, on 15th Avenue East, is a large, dark space with portraits of ex-presidents and taxidermied birds all over the walls, plus a mixture of booth seating and large communal tables. Filled to brimming with tattooed hipsters on weekends, this is actually a super-friendly and inviting space, with a very solid menu of food (including a top-notch burger and sweet-potato fries) and a full bar. The beer selection is small but good, and the cocktail list is decent. It's great people-watching and very Capitol Hill.

SHOPPING

Shopping in Seattle is something best done gradually. Don't expect to find it all in one or two days' worth of blitz shopping tours. Downtown is the only area that allows for easy daylong shopping excursions. Belltown and Pioneer Square are also easy areas to patrol—most stores of note are within a few blocks. To find many of the stores that are truly special to Seattle, you'll have to branch out to Capitol Hill, Queen Anne, and northern neighborhoods like Ballard.

DOWNTOWN

Best shopping: 4th, 5th, and 6th avenues between Pine and Spring streets, and 1st Avenue between Virginia and Madison streets.

BOOKS AND PRINTED MATERIAL

Fodor's Choice ★ **Peter Miller Architectural & Design Books and Supplies.** Aesthetes and architects regularly haunt this floor-to-ceiling-stocked shop for all things design. Rare international architecture, art, and design books mingle with high-end products from Alessi and Iittala, while sleek notebooks, bags, portfolios, and drawing tools round out the collection. This is a great shop for quirky, unforgettable gifts, like a Black Dot sketchbook, an Arne Jacobsen wall clock, or an aerodynamic umbrella. ⊠ *1930 1st Ave., Downtown* ☎ *206/441–4114* ⊕ *www.petermiller.com.*

CHOCOLATE

Fodor's Choice ★ **Fran's Chocolates.** A Seattle institution, Fran's Chocolates has been making quality chocolates for decades. Their world-famous salted caramels are transcendent, as are delectable truffles, which are spiked with oolong tea, single-malt whisky, or raspberry, among other flavors. This shop is housed in the Four Seasons on 1st Avenue. ⊠ *1325 1st Ave., Downtown* ☎ *206/682–0168* ⊕ *www.franschocolates.com.*

GIFTS AND HOME DECOR

☾ Fodor's Choice ★ **Schmancy.** Weird and wonderful, this toy store is more surreal art funhouse than F.A.O. Schwarz. Pick up a crocheted zombie, a felted Ishmael's whale, your very own Hugh Hefner figurine—or how about a pork-chop pillow? Kids of all ages will flip over this quirky shop. Warning: Sense of humor required. ⊠ *1932 2nd Ave., Downtown* ☎ *206/728–8008* ⊕ *www.schmancytoys.com.*

★ **Sur La Table.** Culinary artists and foodies have flocked to this popular Pike Place Market destination since 1972. Sur La Table's flagship shop is packed to the rafters with many thousands of kitchen items, including an exclusive line of copper cookware, endless shelves of baking

30

equipment, tabletop accessories, cookbooks, and a formidable display of knives. ⊠ *84 Pine St., Downtown* ☎ *206/448–2244* ⊕ *www. surlatable.com.*

MALL

★ **Pacific Place Shopping Center.** Shopping, dining, and an excellent movie multiplex are wrapped around a four-story, light-filled atrium, making this a cheerful destination even on a stormy day. The mostly high-end shops include Tiffany & Co., MaxMara, Coach, and True Religion, though there's also L'Occitane, Ann Taylor, and J.Crew. A third-floor sky bridge provides a rainproof route to neighboring Nordstrom. One of the best things about the mall is its parking garage, which is surprisingly affordable, given its location, and has valet parking for just a few bucks more. ⊠ *600 Pine St., Downtown* ☎ *206/405–2655* ⊕ *www. pacificplaceseattle.com.*

WINE AND SPECIALTY FOODS

Fodor's Choice **DeLaurenti Specialty Food and Wine.** Attention foodies: Clear out your
★ hotel minibars and make room for delectable treats from DeLaurenti. And, if you're planning any picnics, swing by here first. Imported meats and cheeses crowd the deli cases, and packaged delicacies pack the aisles. Stock up on hard-to-find items like truffle-infused olive oil or excellent Italian vintages from the wine shop upstairs. ⊠ *1435 1st Ave., Downtown* ☎ *206/622–0141* ⊕ *www.delaurenti.com.*

BELLTOWN

Best shopping: Along 1st Avenue between Cedar and Virginia streets.

MUSIC

Singles Going Steady. If punk rock is more to you than anarchy symbols sewn on Target sweatshirts, you must stop at Singles Going Steady. Punk and its myriad subgenres on CD and vinyl are specialties, though they also stock rockabilly, indie rock, and hip-hop. It's a nice foil to the city's indie-rock-dominated record shops and a good reminder that Belltown is still more eclectic than its rising rents may indicate. ⊠ *2219 2nd Ave., Belltown* ☎ *206/441–7396* ⊕ *www.singlesgoingsteady.com.*

SOUTH LAKE UNION

OUTDOOR CLOTHING AND EQUIPMENT

Fodor's Choice **REI.** Recreational Equipment, Inc. (REI) is Seattle's sports-equipment
★ mega-mecca. The enormous store in South Lake Union has an incredible selection of outdoor gear—from polar-fleece jackets and wool socks to down vests, hiking boots, raingear, and much more—as well as its own 65-foot climbing wall. The staff is extremely knowledgeable; there always seems to be enough help on hand, even when the store is busy. You can test things out on the mountain-bike test trail or in the simulated rain booth. REI also rents gear such as tents, sleeping bags, skis, snowshoes, and backpacks. ⊠ *222 Yale Ave. N, South Lake Union* ☎ *206/223–1944* ⊕ *www.rei.com.*

PIONEER SQUARE

Best shopping: 1st Avenue S between Yesler Way and S. Jackson Street, and Occidental Avenue S between S. Main and Jackson streets.

ANTIQUES AND COLLECTIBLES

★ **Kagedo Japanese Art and Antiques.** Museum-quality works from the early 20th century and Japanese art in a variety of mediums are on display in this influential gallery. Among the treasures are intricately carved *okimono* sculptures, stone garden ornaments, and studio basketry. The gallery itself is worth a look—it's beautifully laid out, and includes a small rock garden and rice-paper screens that cover the storefront's picture windows. ✉ *520 1st Ave. S, Pioneer Square* ☎ *206/467–9077* ⊕ *www.kagedo.com.*

ART AND GIFTS

★ **Glass House Studio.** Seattle's oldest glassblowing studio and gallery lets you watch fearless artisans at work in the "hot shop." Some of the best glass artists in the country work out of this shop, and many of their impressive studio pieces are for sale, along with around 40 other Northwest artists represented by the shop. ✉ *311 Occidental Ave. S, Pioneer Square* ☎ *206/682–9939* ⊕ *www.glasshouse-studio.com.*

CAPITOL HILL

Best shopping: E. Pike and E. Pine streets between Bellevue Avenue and Madison Avenue E, E. Olive Way between Bellevue Avenue E and Broadway E, and Broadway E between E. Denny Way and E. Roy Street.

BOOKS AND MUSIC

Fodor's Choice
★ **Elliott Bay Book Company.** With infinitely browsable, welcoming shelves of books, underground parking, lovely skylights, and a café run by restaurateur Tamara Murphy, most argue that this is the best book store in the city. Elliott Bay hosts hundreds of author events every year, so nearly every day is an exciting one to visit the store, and the staff is knowledgeable and clever. As you enter, check out the great selection of Pacific Northwest history books and fiction titles by local authors, complete with handwritten recommendation cards from staff members. ✉ *1521 10th Ave., Capitol Hill* ☎ *206/624–6600* ⊕ *www.elliottbaybook.com.*

30

Sonic Boom Records. Sonic Boom carries a little bit of everything, but the emphasis is definitely on indie releases. Handwritten recommendation cards from the staff help you find local artists and the best new releases from independent Northwest labels. Discover new bands in the handy listening stations and check out the small but fantastic collection of books, gifts, and other rockin' paraphernalia. ✉ *1525 Melrose Ave., Capitol Hill* ☎ *206/568–2666* ⊕ *www.sonicboomrecords.com.*

GIFTS AND HOME DECOR

★ **Area 51.** Wander through this 10,000-square-foot temple of design and gape at the mix of retro-inspired new items and vintage, mid-century finds. Anything might materialize in this industrial space, from Eames replicas to clever coffee mugs, but it will all look like it's straight out of a handbook of the design trends from the middle of the last century. ✉ *401 E. Pine St., Capitol Hill* ☎ *206/568–4782* ⊕ *www.area51seattle.com.*

★ **NuBe Green.** An emphasis on recycled goods and sustainability is the mission of this well-presented store anchoring a corner of the Oddfellows Building. All items are sourced and made in the United States, including linens, candles, glass art, and even dog beds made from old jeans. Our favorite items are by local **Alchemy Goods** (⊕ *www.alchemygoods. com*), which recycles bicycle tubes, reclaimed vinyl mesh, and seatbelts into distinctively cool wallets and messenger bags. ✉ *912 E. Pine St., Capitol Hill* ☎ *206/402–4515* ⊕ *www.nubegreen.com.*

SPORTS AND ACTIVITIES

To the west of the city is Puget Sound, where sailors, kayakers, and anglers practice their sports. Lake Union and Lake Washington also provide residents with plenty of boating, kayaking, fishing, and swimming opportunities. Spectator sports are also appreciated here, as evidenced by raucous fans of the Mariners (⊕ *seattle.mariners.mlb.com*), Sounders (⊕ *www.soundersfc.com*), Huskies (⊕ *www.gohuskies.com*), and Seahawks (⊕ *www.seahawks.com*).

PARKS INFORMATION

King County Parks and Recreation (☎ *206/296–4232 for information and reservations* ⊕ *www.metrokc.gov/parks*) manages many of the parks outside city limits. To find out whether an in-town park baseball diamond or tennis court is available, contact the **Seattle Parks and Recreation Department** (☎ *206/684–4075* ⊕ *www.seattle.gov/parks*), which is responsible for most of the parks, piers, beaches, playgrounds, and courts within city limits. The department issues permits for events, arranges reservations for facilities, and staffs visitor centers and naturalist programs. The state manages several parks and campgrounds in greater Seattle. For more information contact **Washington State Parks** (☎ *360/902–8844 for general information, 888/226–7688 for campsite reservations* ⊕ *www.parks.wa.gov/parkpage.asp*).

BOATING AND KAYAKING

Fodor'sChoice **Agua Verde Paddle Club and Café.** Start out by renting a kayak and pad-
★ dling along either the Lake Union shoreline, with its hodgepodge of funky-to-fabulous houseboats and dramatic Downtown vistas, or Union Bay on Lake Washington, with its marshes and cattails. Afterward, take in the lakefront as you wash down some Mexican food (halibut tacos, anyone?) with a margarita. Kayaks are available March through October and are rented by the hour—$15 for singles, $18 for doubles. It pays to paddle midweek: The third hour is free on weekdays. ✉ *1303 N.E. Boat St., University District* ☎ *206/545–8570* ⊕ *www. aguaverde.com.*

SIDE TRIPS FROM SEATTLE

Fodor's Choice
★

Mt. Rainier National Park. Often veiled in mysterious clouds even when the surrounding forests and fields are bathed in sunlight, Mt. Rainier is the centerpiece of its namesake park. The impressive volcanic peak stands at an elevation of 14,411 feet, making it the fifth-highest peak in the lower 48 states. More than 2 million visitors a year enjoy spectacular views of the mountain and return home with a lifelong memory of its image.

GETTING THERE

Drive south on Interstate 5 to State Route 512 (Exit 127). Take SR 512 east to SR 7. Then drive south on SR 7 to SR 706 in Elbe. Finally, head east on SR 706 through Ashford to the Nisqually Entrance.

Fodor's Choice
★

San Juan Islands. There are 176 named islands in the San Juan archipelago, although these and large rocks around them amount to 743 at low tide and 428 at high tide. Sixty are populated (though most have only a house or two), and 10 are state marine parks, some of which are accessible only to kayakers navigating the Cascadia Marine Trail. The three largest islands, Lopez, Orcas, and San Juan, are served regularly by ferries and seaplanes, and get packed with visitors in summer. These islands support a little fishing and farming, but tourism generates by far the largest revenues.

Since the 1990s, gray whales have begun to summer here, instead of going north to their arctic breeding grounds; an occasional minke or humpback whale can also be seen frolicking in the kelp.

GETTING THERE

By Boat and Ferry: Ferries stop at the four largest islands: Lopez, Shaw, Orcas, and San Juan. Washington State Ferries depart from Anacortes, about 76 mi north of Seattle, to the San Juan Islands. For walk-on passengers, it's $13.45 from Anacortes to any point in the San Juan Islands. From Anacortes, vehicle and driver fares to the San Juans are $32–$36 to Lopez Island, $40–$44 to Orcas and Shaw islands, $48–$52 to Friday Harbor.

Clipper Navigation operates the passenger-only *Victoria Clipper* jet catamaran service between Pier 69 in Seattle and Friday Harbor. Boats leave daily in season at 7:45 am; reservations are strongly recommended. The journey costs $47–$52 one way. The *San Juan Island Commuter* has daily scheduled service in season to Orcas Island and Friday Harbor, as well as Lopez Island and a few other smaller islands. Ferries depart at 9:30 am from the Bellingham Cruise Terminal (about 1½ hours by car from Seattle). One-way fares start at $49.50.

■TIP→ Orcas, Lopez, and San Juan islands are extremely popular in high season; securing hotel reservations in advance is essential. Ferry lines are also far more common than in the winter months; contact Washington State Ferries before you travel.

Boat and Ferry Contacts **Clipper Navigation** (☎ *250/382–8100 in Victoria, 206/448–5000 in Seattle, 800/888–2535 in U.S.* ⊕ *www.clippervacations.com*).
San Juan Island Commuter (✉ *Bellingham Cruise Terminal, 355 Harris Ave., No. 104, Bellingham* ☎ *360/738–8099 or 888/443–4552* ⊕ *www.whales.com*).
Washington State Ferries (☎ *206/464–6400 or 888/808–7977, 800/843–3779 automated line in WA and BC* ⊕ *www.wsdot.wa.gov/ferries*).

30

INDEX

Coast: 41, SuperStock/age fotostock. 42 (bottom), Paul Tessier/iStockphoto. 42 (top), Denis Jr. Tangney/iStockphoto. 43, Andrea Pelletier/iStockphoto. 44, Aimin Tang/iStockphoto. 50, SuperStock/age fotostock. 57, Kindra Clineff. 59, Paul D. Lemke/iStockphoto. **Chapter 2: Boston:** 61-67, Kindra Clineff. 68, Jorge Salcedo/iStockphoto. 73, revjim5000/Flickr. 77, Israel Pabon/Shutterstock. 84, Kindra Clineff. **Chapter 3: Cape Cod:** 87, Kindra Clineff. 89-95, Denis Jr. Tangney/iStockphoto. 97, Kindra Clineff. 98, Guido Caroti. **Chapter 4: New York City:** 109, Kord.com/age fotostock. 110 (top), Martha Cooper/viestiphoto.com. 110 (bottom), Photodisc (Own). 111, Liberty Helicopters, Inc. 112, Corbis. 116, Heeb Christian/age fotostock. 118-19, kropic1/Shutterstock. 122, Ambient Images Inc. / Alamy. 125, Renaud Visage/age fotostock. 127, Rudy Sulgan/age fotostock. 130, Dina Litovsky/Stregoica Photography. 139, SIME s.a.s / eStock Photo. **Chapter 5: Philadelphia:** 141, drbueller/iStockphoto. 142 (bottom), sepavo/Shutterstock. 142 (top), Xiaoping Liang/iStockphoto. 143, K.L. Kohn/Shutterstock. 144, PdaMai/Shutterstock. 148, trekandshoot/Shutterstock. 155, Dave Newman/Shutterstock. 156, Aimin Tang/iStockphoto. 160, Photo by B. Krist for GPTMC. **Chapter 6: Washington, D.C.:** 165, Hemis / Alamy. 167 (top), Destination DC. 167 (bottom), Jeremy R. Smith Sr./Shutterstock. 168, PHC C.M. Fitzpatrick/Wikimedia Commons. 172, JTB Photo/Japan Travel. Bureau/photolibrary.com. 175, Visions of America, LLC / Alamy. 178, Wiskerke / Alamy. 188, Krista Rossow / age fotostock. 191, Alex Segre / Alamy. **The South:** 192-93, Steven Widoff / Alamy. 194, Busch Entertainment Corporation. 195 (left), Colin D. Young/Shutterstock. 195 (right), Orlando CVB. 196 (left), versageek/Flickr. 196 (right), Visit Florida. 197 (top left), NC Division of Tourism - Bill Russ. 197 (bottom left), Colin D. Young/Shutterstock. 197 (top center), Michael G Smith/Shutterstock. 197 (right), Brent Hilliard/Shutterstock. 198, SeaWorld Parks & Entertainment. 199 (left), Noam Wind/Shutterstock. 199 (right), NC Tourism - Bill Russ. 200, Visit Florida. 201 (left), The School House/Flickr. 201 (right), PrincessAshley/Flickr. 202, NC Tourism - Bill Russ. 203 (left), Library of Congress Prints and Photographs Division. 203 (right), Dana Ward/Shutterstock. 204, GlyndaK, Fodors. com member. **Chapter 7: North Carolina's Outer Banks:** 205, Jim West / age fotostock. 206-07, NC Tourism - Bill Russ. 208, Brian Leon/Flickr. 212, NC Tourism - Bill Russ. 215, Robb Helfrick . 217, Marvin Newman / age fotostock. **Chapter 8: Charleston, South Carolina:** 221, Dennis Hallinan / Alamy. 223 (top), William Struhs. 223 (middle), Charleston Area CVB. 223 (bottom), Charleston Area CVB for / www.Explorecharleston.com. 224, Charleston Area CVB. 227, Robb Helfrick . 228, Gabrielle Hovey/Shutterstock. 233, Jeff Greenberg / age fotostock. **Chapter 9: Orlando, Disney, and Theme Parks:** 235, VISIT FLORIDA. 236, SeaWorld Orlando. 237 (top), Nick Hotel. 237 (bottom), Universal Orlando. 238 and 241, Orlando CVB. 242, Universal Orlando. 248, ©Disney. 251, Universal Orlando. 253, SeaWorld Parks & Entertainment. **Chapter 10: Miami and Miami Beach:** 265, iStockphoto. 266, Stuart Westmorland/age fotostock. 267 (top), Jeff Greenberg/age fotostock. 267 (bottom), VISUM Foto GmbH / Alamy. 268, Ivan Cholakov Gostock-dot-net/Shutterstock. 271, Robert Harding Picture Library Ltd / Alamy. 273, Chuck Mason / Alamy. 283, iStockphoto. **Chapter 11: The Florida Keys:** 287, Stephen Frink / Aurora Photos. 288, Pawel Lipiec/iStockphoto. 289 (top left), Pacific Stock / SuperStock. 289 (top right), David L Amsler/iStockphoto. 289 (bottom), Visit Florida. 290, iStockphoto. 294, PBorowka/Shutterstock. 301, Starwood Hotels & Resorts. **Chapter 12: Nashville:** 303, niseag03/Denise Mattox/Flickr. 304 (bottom), grovesa16/Alison Groves/Flickr. 304 (top), David Liu/iStockphoto. 305, Cheekwood Botanical Garden & Museum of Art. 306, marc neppl/iStockphoto. 307, GRANT SMITH / age fotostock. 308, Frist Center for the Visual Arts. 311, dawnhops/Dawn Hopkins/Flickr. 315, niseag03/Denise Mattox/Flickr. **Chapter 13: New Orleans:** 317, howieluvzus/Howie Luvzus/Flickr. 318 (bottom), Carl Purcell/New Orleans Metropolitan Convention & Visitors Bureau. 318 (top), Harry Costner/New Orleans CVB. 319, Sara Essex Bradley/New Orleans Metropolitan Convention & Visitors Bureau. 320, Jose Gil/Shutterstock. 324-25, Toby Adamson / age fotostock. 330, Otokimus/Shutterstock. 336, Ray Devlin/Flickr. **The Midwest and the Rockies:** 340-41, Kipp Schoen/iStockphoto. 342, hikerboy, Fodors.com member. 343 (left), Eric Wunrow/CTO. 343 (right), nikitsin/Shutterstock. 344 (top left), Chad Coppess/SD Tourism. 344 (bottom left), Jim Bowen/Flickr. 344 (top center), Chad Coppess/SD Tourism. 344 (bottom center), Kirsten Coffman, Fodors.com member. 344 (right), Dave Jordano Photography, Inc. 345 (left), Pawel Gaul/iStockphoto. 345 (top center), Eric Wunrow/CTO. 345 (bottom right), Lee Prince/Shutterstock. 345 (top right), Jeffrey Beall/Wikimedia Commons. 346, Jeff Griffin/iStockphoto. 347 (left), Gene Vaught/Shutterstock. 347 (right), Laurin Rinder/Shutterstock. 348, Nelson Sirlin/Shutterstock. 349 (left), Janet Koelilng & Kerry Koepping/iStockphoto. 349 (right), EastVillage Images/Shutterstock. 352, iofoto/Shutterstock. 353 (left), The Art Institute of Chicago: Helen Birch Bartlett Memorial Collection, 1926.224. 353 (right), Curious-Carm, Fodors.com member. 354, TC, Fodors.com member. **Chapter 14: Chicago:** 355, Alan Copson / age fotostock. 356, City of Chicago/GRC. 357, Marina S, Fodors.com member. 358, amdeda/Flickr. 361, Kord.com / age fotostock.362, City of Chicago/GRC. 376, patrick frilet / age fotostock. **Chapter 15: Minneapolis and St. Paul:** 379-80, Meet Minneapolis. 381 (top), Meet Minneapolis. 381 (bottom), Geoffrey Kuchera/Shutterstock. 382, Meet Minneapolis. 383, CarbonSilver Photography (Greg Benz)/Shutterstock. 388, Near and Far Photography/Shutterstock. **Chapter 16: Denver, Boulder, and the Colorado Rockies:**

ABOUT OUR WRITERS

Fodor's aims to give you the best local insights by using writers who live in the destinations they cover. *Essential USA* is the work of the following team:

The Maine Coast: Laura Scheel

Boston: Bethany Cassin Beckerlegge, Amanda Knorr, Lisa Oppenheimer

Cape Cod: Sandy MacDonald, Janice Randall Rohlf, Laura Scheel

New York City: Alexander Basek, Lynne Arany, Joanna G. Cantor, Nicole Crane, Gary Lippman, Meryl D. Pearlstein, Adeena Sussman, Jacqueline Terrebonne

Philadelphia: Caroline Tiger, Robert DiGiacomo, Piers Marchant, Bernard Vaughan,

Washington, D.C.: Mark Sullivan, Beth Kanter, Cathy Sharpe, Elana Schor

North Carolina's Outer Banks: Liz Biro

Charleston, South Carolina: Melissa Bigner, Eileen Robinson Smith, Rob Young

Orlando, Disney, and Theme Parks: Jennie Hess

Miami and Miami Beach: Ana Maria Lima, Michael de Zayas, Teri Evans

The Florida Keys: Chelle Koster Walton

Nashville: Trisha Ping, Michael Ream

New Orleans: Michelle Delio, Kandace Power Graves, Paul A. Greenberg, Molly Jahncke, David Parker Jr., Sue Strachan, Jacqueline Terrebonne

Chicago: Kelly Aiglon, Heidi Moore, Roberta Sotonoff, Wendy Wollenberg

Minneapolis and St. Paul: Emily Peterson

Denver, Boulder, and the Colorado Rockies: Martha Conners, Kyle Wagner

Mount Rushmore and the Black Hills: Nyla Griffith, T. D. Griffith

Yellowstone National Park: Brian Kevin, Steve Pastorino

San Antonio, Austin, and the Texas Hill Country: Paris Permenter, John Bigley

Santa Fe and Taos: Andrew Collins, Georgia de Katona

Grand Canyon National Park: Carrie Frasure, Nyla Griffith, T. D. Griffith

Las Vegas: Xasmine Garza, Alexis C. Kelly, Matt Villano, Mike Weatherford

Southern Utah: John Blodgett, Swain Scheps

San Diego: Claire Deeks van der Lee, Maren Dougherty, Maria Hunt, Amanda Knoles, Christine Pae, AnnaMaria Stephens, Bobbi Zane

Los Angeles: Laura Randall, Cindy Arora, Tanvi Chheda, Arlene Dawson, Elline Lipkin, Lea Lion, Susan MacCallum-Whitcomb

Yosemite National Park: Sura Wood, Reed Parsell

San Francisco: Denise M. Leto, Fiona G. Parrott, Natasha Sarkisian, Sharon Silva, Sharron Wood, Sura Wood

Napa and Sonoma: Sharron Wood, Lisa M. Hamilton, Fiona G. Parrott

Portland: Janna Mock Lopez, Crystal Wood

Seattle: Carissa Bluestone, Cedar Burnett, Nick Horton, Heidi Leigh Johansen